MW00513660

PATTERNS ACROSS THE DISCIPLINES

Stuart Hirschberg

RUTGERS UNIVERSITY, NEWARK

MACMILLAN PUBLISHING COMPANY

NEW YORK

Credit acknowledgments appear at the back of the book on pages 753–758, which constitute an extension of the copyright page.

Copyright © 1988, Macmillan Publishing Company,
a division of Macmillan, Inc.

PRINTED IN THE UNITED STATES OF AMERICA

Macmillan Publishing Company
866 Third Avenue, New York, New York 10022

Collier Macmillan Canada, Inc.

LIBRARY OF CONGRESS CATALOGING-IN-PUBLICATION DATA

Hirschberg, Stuart.
    Patterns across the disciplines / Stuart Hirschberg.
        p.   cm.
    Includes index.
    ISBN 0–02–354771–5
    1. College readers.   2. English language—Rhetoric.
    3. Interdisciplinary approach in education.   I. Title.
    PE1417.H54 1988   87–27361
    808'.0427—dc 19   CIP

Printing: 1 2 3 4 5 6 7   Year: 8 9 0 1 2 3 4

For my nephews,
Michael and Mark

FOR THE INSTRUCTOR

Patterns Across the Disciplines is an interdisciplinary reader organized according to traditional rhetorical patterns. This text has two general aims: (1) to provide a complete range of informative, engaging, and enlightening readings, reflecting major academic and professional fields of study, to be used as materials for the teaching of discursive writing; while (2) giving students an extensive and varied acquaintance with significant information that is part of their cultural heritage.

Patterns Across the Disciplines provides classic, modern, and contemporary readings by major writers, scholars, and scientists in the liberal arts, political and social sciences, and sciences. It offers a variety of perspectives from the newer disciplines of Asian studies, criminal justice, bioethics, ethology, holocaust studies, urban studies, communications, and oceanography, in addition to readings from the traditional fields of history, philosophy, biology, literature, psychology, sociology, and mathematics.

Writing across the curriculum is based on the important concept that writing is an integral part of the ongoing intellectual process of learning in all disciplines. This text is designed to provide clear, accurate, and effective examples of the kinds of writing that professionals do in order to communicate with their colleagues and with audiences outside their specialized fields of study.

The ninety-three selections have been chosen for their interest, reading level, and length, and include a broad range of topics, authors, and disciplines, as well as a number of readings that offer students cross-cultural perspectives.

Besides the number and diversity of the selections, and the wide range of topics and styles represented, quite a few of the longer readings are included because of the value that more extensive readings have in allowing students to observe the development of ideas. For those who persevere, these selections may be among the most rewarding. The development of skills in reading and comprehension, and the concomitant improvement of writing skills, are clearly related to the length of time spent reading and studying significant content.

The ninety-three selections shed light on a myriad number of subjects—from Tutankhamen's tomb to space stations, concentration camps to kibbutz culture, the question of animal intelligence to the Turing test, solving the mystery of salmon migration to the moral dilemmas produced by new biotechnologies, Beethoven to the Beatles, the Russian revolution to Vietnam, the Pueblo Indians to contemporary Chinese culture, slavery to the historic 1954 *Brown* v. *Board of Education of Topeka* decision, the Socratic method to subliminal techniques, Einstein's formulation that $E = mc^2$ to Hiroshima, and other significant topics that are an indispensable part of a college education.

This text is the only interdisciplinary reader to introduce students to the problem-solving techniques that writers, scholars, and scientists use to generate new knowledge and solve problems within their particular disciplines. Each of the readings illustrates a specific rhetorical mode and accurately represents some of the best work done in particular fields of study. This twofold organization—by traditional writing strategies and curricular area—clearly shows how specialists in different disciplines narrate, describe, illustrate, compare and contrast, analyze processes, classify, invent analogies, explain causation, define, solve problems, and use strategies of argument to explore and explain important issues, clarify research procedures and methodologies, and argue for the acceptance of specific theories, interpretations, and results.

Some of the most stimulating writing in specific disciplines is represented through the work of such acclaimed writers, thinkers, and scholars as Mark Twain and D. H. Lawrence in literature, Arnold J. Toynbee and Barbara W. Tuchman in history, John Hersey and Tom Wolfe in journalism, Aristotle and Plato in philosophy, Sir James George Frazer and Ruth Benedict in anthropology, Earl Warren and Christopher D. Stone in law, Fred Hoyle and Carl Sagan in physics, Jean Henri Fabre and Charles Darwin in the biological sciences, Jane van Lawick-Goodall and Konrad Lorenz in the study of animal behavior, Thor Heyerdahl and Rachel Carson in ecology, Douglas R. Hofstadter and Christopher Evans in computer science, and Carl Jung and Sigmund Freud in psychology.

Patterns Across the Disciplines presents examples of the different kinds of formats and methodologies that professionals use to communicate with each other and with the general public. Students can see how specialists interpret facts and artifacts (such as photographs, art works, pottery, and fossils), define key terms, generate hypotheses, and construct coherent essays for their particular audiences. The liberal arts are represented through literary analyses, biographical sketches, belles-lettres, diary entries, and critiques of the visual and performing arts. Writing in the political and social sciences is illustrated by means of interviews, case studies, on-site reports, and court decisions. The physical and natural sciences are represented by examples of technical writing, scientific abstracts, research reports, and articles written by scientists for the general public.

The eleven chapters of *Patterns Across the Disciplines* are arranged to follow the sequence of traditional rhetorical patterns and to highlight common rhetorical features in the written products that have resulted from discipline-specific forms of inquiry and presentation of findings. Thus, the readings are intended to illustrate, clearly and logically, the various rhetorical modes and patterns of discourse as they enable writers in different disciplines to define a field of study, ask questions, assess evidence, make judgments, and draw conclusions as to what counts as knowledge.

"Narration" is the first chapter because most students can easily grasp a first-person account of a personal experience in the form of a diary, anecdote, or memoir, and understand how narratives are used as evidence by historians. "Description" follows, based on the idea that subjective and objective observations of people, places, and things serve a wide variety of purposes for writers in the liberal arts, political and social sciences, and sciences.

The methods of exposition whose purpose is to clarify, explain, and interpret are presented next: these writing strategies are arranged from exemplification (perhaps the most essential and widely used rhetorical form) through causal analysis and definition. Definition appears as the last expository technique because writers across the disciplines frequently draw from the entire spectrum of writing strategies (narration, description, exemplification, comparison and contrast, process analysis, classification, analogy, and cause and effect) to define technical terms, concepts, and processes. Definition also serves a vital role in establishing a field of study by setting its boundary with respect to other disciplines.

Although not one of the traditional rhetorical modes, "Problem Solving" is placed next in order to introduce students to the important, discipline-specific issues of (1) how problem-solving techniques are used within specific fields of study, and (2) how the assumptions, hypotheses, and theoretical models underlying disciplines change and evolve in response to contradictions or anomalies that challenge accepted paradigms. These strategies are so important that this text devotes a full chapter to exploring and illustrating the range of problem-solving techniques that writers in diverse areas— including ethics (Philip Wheelwright), bioethics (Leon R. Kass), archeology (Sir Leonard Woolley), law (Joel Seligman), business (Robert F. Hartley), computer science (Douglas R. Hofstadter), physics (Lincoln Barnett), oceanography (Thor Heyerdahl), and ecology (Rachel Carson)—use in their respective disciplines. By examining how researchers use certain strategies to identify problems, apply theoretical models, define constraints, use various search techniques, and check solutions against relevant criteria, students get a first-hand view of the kinds of strategies that specialists use to solve the problems they encounter within their specific academic areas.

New interpretations of known facts, solutions generated by the techniques of problem solving, and new theoretical models through which the disciplines themselves evolve must gain acceptance and be seen as valid by knowledgeable colleagues. The last chapter, "Argumentation and Persuasion," then takes up the question of how writers in the liberal arts, political and social sciences, and sciences rely on strategies of argument to convince specific audiences of the accuracy of their investigations and the validity of their conclusions.

Each chapter is introduced by a discussion of its rhetorical mode, explaining its function and illustrating, with relevant examples drawn from the selections that follow, how that particular pattern is used as a writing strategy in the liberal arts, political and social sciences, and sciences. A biographical sketch precedes each selection, gives background information on the author's life, and identifies the intended audience or the context in which the selection was written.

The Annotated Contents identifies the subject, purpose, and central idea of each selection. Additional contents arranged by theme, subject, and discipline are designed to allow the text to accommodate a variety of approaches to the teaching of writing. The individual instructor can use the alternate contents to reorganize the readings and ideas suggested by them in different ways for different purposes, while students— in whatever order they may read the selections—will find themselves caught up in the exhilarating experience of ongoing intellectual inquiry.

In the Thematic Contents, for example, the readings are organized to encourage the perception of multiple perspectives according to themes and topics that differentiate important areas in human experience. First, the individual experience of the quest for identity, the value of relationships, and the ultimate challenge of impending death; next, the collective experience of the human condition, the social fabric, crime and punishment, what we can learn about our collective nature from the study of other cultures, history, and social and technological visions of the future; and, finally, some of the dimensions of knowledge by which we seek to understand ourselves, through discoveries about man and living things, the environment, microcosms and macrocosms, the order of the mind, and the role played by art in creatively transforming how we perceive ourselves and the world.

Each of the selections is followed by a generous set of analytical questions that explores the substance of the piece and its rhetorical strategies. These class-tested questions are intended to engage students' interest in the key issues in the text and to direct their attention to the ways that authors adapt their presentations for specific audiences.

The writing suggestions are designed to elicit imaginative and thoughtful essays by encouraging students to draw on and respond to the issues, ideas, and problems encountered across the disciplines. The exercises vary in length and purpose, from the single-sentence summary to full-length essays, and have sufficient range to be useful for students at any level of freshman writing. Many writing assignments ask students to compare how writers in various disciplines bring different perspectives to the same subject for different audiences. For example, students might be asked to compare the views of Richard Selzer and Marya Mannes on abortion, Arthur Koestler and Edmund Wilson on communism, Jane van Lawick-Goodall and Donald Griffin on the unsuspected capabilities of primates, David Ricks and Robert Hartley on marketing mistakes, Melford Spiro and Studs Terkel on the work ethic in different cultures, Carl Jung and Sigmund Freud on the nature of the unconscious, Kenneth Stampp and Frederick Douglass on slavery, Christopher Stone and Rachel Carson on protection of the environment, or Thomas Robert Malthus and Charles Darwin on adaptive mechanisms for survival. By examining how different disciplines look at what appears to be the same thing, students can see how the same phenomenon becomes, in effect, a different object of inquiry according to the conceptual framework within which it is investigated.

A comprehensive *Instructor's Manual* provides (1) suggested answers to each of the end-of-selection questions on meaning and strategy; (2) sample outlines suggesting the coordination of reading and writing assignments for a full semester; (3) supplemental bibliographies of books and periodicals for students who wish to do further research on particular topics in various disciplines; and (4) suggested methods of developing the writing assignments, including specific guidance in critical reading of sources, preparation of summaries, and development of full-length essays designed to connect two or more selections for the purpose of comparative analysis.

ACKNOWLEDGMENTS

Special thanks for their friendship, intellectual stimulation, and camaraderie are due to the extraordinary group of teachers who were gathered under the auspices of the Woodrow Wilson Foundation, especially Peter G. Montague, Mary Ellen Capek, and Carolyn Q. Wilson. I am most grateful to John DeBenedetto and Mary Ann Materia for their assistance, and to Ronnie and Stuart Reichman for their innumerable contributions and support. A particular debt of gratitude is owed to all those teachers of composition who offered thoughtful comments and have given this book the benefit of their collective scholarship, judgment, and teaching experience. I would very much like to thank all the instructors who reviewed the various stages of the manuscript, including James Kinney, Virginia Commonwealth University; Peter J. McGuine, Georgia Institute of Technology; Christopher Thaiss, George Mason University; and John Trimbur, Boston University. I owe much to the able staff at Macmillan, especially to Laura Moore, Vicky Horbovetz, Wendy Polhemus-Annibell, Aliza Greenblatt, and John Sollami for their dedication, skill, and tireless efforts. No expression of thanks can adequately convey my appreciation for the sound editorial advice, wisdom, and forbearance of Eben W. Ludlow at Macmillan. To my wife, Terry, I am especially indebted for her good humor, good sense, and sound judgment.

S. H.

FOR THE STUDENT

Patterns Across the Disciplines provides clear, interesting, and engaging models of writing by major scholars, researchers, and scientists to show that writing is essential to learning in all academic fields of study. The selections are drawn equally from the liberal arts, the political and social sciences, and the sciences in order to reflect the traditional areas of study usually found in most undergraduate programs.

The book includes selections by classic, modern, and contemporary authors whose work, in many cases, provides the foundation of the broader intellectual heritage of a college education. The readings can help you acquire some of the essential skills you will need to develop in college. You will get a first-hand view of the kinds of strategies that writers use to draw inferences from data and evidence, to form clear thesis statements, and to master research procedures as they solve problems encountered in their specific academic areas.

In addition to readings from traditional disciplines such as history, philosophy, biology, literature, psychology, sociology, and mathematics, *Patterns Across the Disciplines* offers many thought-provoking and intriguing selections from a whole range of newer disciplines including Asian studies, aerospace engineering, computer science, oceanography, criminal justice, bioethics, holocaust studies, ethology (the study of animal behavior), urban studies, communications, and ecology.

To achieve clear, accurate, and effective communication, many authors, scholars, and scientists have adapted a variety of traditional writing strategies to meet the demands of style, format, and methodology within their particular fields of study. The ninety-three selections in *Patterns Across the Disciplines* (thirty from the liberal arts, thirty-three from the political and social sciences, and thirty from the sciences) were chosen because they illustrate how writers across the disciplines use traditional rhetorical patterns as an integral part of the reasoning methods and writing processes characteristic of academic inquiry. These rhetorical strategies are used by writers as a means to assemble evidence, support generalizations, convey meaning, give coherence to their writing, and most importantly, communicate what they have discovered to different audiences. Professional writers use different strategies to clarify and interpret their findings for fellow specialists than they use to communicate their discoveries to the general public.

Each of the eleven chapters in *Patterns Across the Disciplines* clearly shows how specialists in different academic fields of study (for example, historians, journalists, archeologists, sociologists, computer scientists, zoologists, astronomers, psychologists) narrate, describe, illustrate, compare and contrast, analyze processes, classify, invent analogies, explain causation, define, solve problems, and use strategies of argument and persuasion to explore and explain important issues, clarify research procedures and methodologies, and argue for the acceptance of specific theories, interpretations, and results. Thus, each chapter illustrates a specific rhetorical strategy and presents some of the best work done in particular disciplines.

Within each of the eleven chapters readings are grouped according to the different kinds of writing characteristic of the liberal arts, the political and social sciences, and the sciences.

THE LIBERAL ARTS

In the liberal arts, critiques of art, music, dance, drama, and film are a form of writing that presents an evaluation and interpretation of a work of art for the purpose of enhancing the audience's understanding. Critical essays can appear in a variety of forms, from quickly composed newspaper reviews to carefully formulated studies. The essays by Agnes de Mille, John Simon, D. H. Lawrence, Alan Wallach, Mark Twain, Phyllis McGinley, Jeff Greenfield, Stendhal, Gilbert Highet, Tom Wolfe, Ernest Hemingway, Ursula K. LeGuin, Edward Rothstein, and Susan Sontag will enable you to more fully appreciate the distinctive contributions of great composers, writers, playwrights, photographers, painters, and dancers. Journalism, as exemplified by the works of Jack London, John Hersey, and Marya Mannes, lets you see the writing skills necessary to carefully observe and faithfully record newsworthy occurrences.

By contrast, biographical writing is intended to bring personalities to life within the context of history. Here, James Boswell's description of Dr. Samuel Johnson gives you a brilliant and captivating account of a complex and distinguished personality.

Philosophy offers a means of discovering what it is possible to know. Essays by Aristotle, Plato, Philip Wheelwright, and David Hoekema exemplify the manner in which philosophers have probed the moral and ethical implications of people's actions and decisions. The new field of bioethics, illustrated with an essay by Leon R. Kass, raises basic ethical questions about choices precipitated by new biomedical technologies.

History explains how the present has been affected by the past by providing a clear account of the conditions in which societies have lived. Historical research by Barbara W. Tuchman, Arnold J. Toynbee, Kenneth Stampp, and Edmund Wilson, along with the memoirs of Frederick Douglass and diaries of Robert Falcon Scott, bring to life important military, social, economic, and political events from the past.

THE POLITICAL AND SOCIAL SCIENCES

In the social sciences, political science addresses itself to the study of how governments manage their affairs. Selections by Arthur Koestler, Aldous Huxley, Erwin Wickert, and Martin Luther King, Jr. inquire into the purpose of political states, the qualification and policy of rulers, the propriety of governmental control over the rights of individuals, and the efficacy of government management of social change. The application of these basic questions of equity and justice to actual legal and constitutional issues are covered in essays by Christopher D. Stone, Joel Seligman, Freda Adler, Sidney Hook, and Earl Warren.

In business, selections by Thomas Robert Malthus, Richard Rhodes, Robert F.

Hartley, and Jane Jacobs raise questions about what constitutes good management, how natural resources should be used, and consider significant issues of unemployment, the distribution of income within and between societies, and the changes wrought by technology.

Anthropology studies individual cultures using methods drawn from archeology, ethnographic observation, comparative analysis of physical and cultural features, and comparative linguistics. Selections by Ruth Benedict, Sir James George Frazer, Jessica Mitford, Howard Carter, Melford E. Spiro, and Sir Leonard Woolley inquire into why particular cultures have different and distinctive customs, habitations, folklore, mythologies, family structures, and cultural development.

Sociology is concerned with the observation, description, and explanation of the behavior of human beings in groups. Studies by John M. Darley and Bibb Latane, Oscar Handlin, J. Michael Polich and Bruce R. Orvis, Studs Terkel, Richard Rodriguez, Alison Lurie, Simone de Beauvoir, Leonard I. Stein, Henry Allen, Tadeusz Borowski, and John McMurtry investigate institutions within society, their origins, their capacity for accommodating social change, and the relationships and mechanisms within them that influence the behavior of individuals.

Communications is a newer discipline that uses methodologies drawn from the fields of psychology, journalism, film, advertising, and broadcasting. Essays by Herbert J. Gans and Wilson Bryan Key explore the effects of new technologies, the ways by which the media influence public opinion, and the manner in which news is reported.

The Sciences

In the sciences, psychology (which also can be classified with the social sciences) is the study of human behavior that encompasses physiological, experimental, social and clinical spheres of research. Important essays by Sigmund Freud, Carl G. Jung, Hans Selye, Elisabeth Kubler-Ross, and Thomas S. Szasz explore the fundamental areas of perception, memory, personality, and motivation.

The biological sciences, represented in works by Charles Darwin, Loren Eiseley, Jean Henri Fabre, Arthur D. Hasler and James A. Larsen, Constance Holden, Jane van Lawick-Goodall, Konrad Lorenz, Donald R. Griffin, and Hans Zinsser, include many subdisciplines that focus their attention on the anatomy, genetics, or physiology of animals and plants. In the professional areas, essays by John A. Parrish, Richard Selzer, and James Herriot, shed light on the practice of medicine and veterinary medicine. The biological sciences also encompass discoveries made by chemists, physicists, geologists, and meteorologists, in addition to the traditional findings of botanists and zoologists. The related disciplines of ecology and environmental studies, represented in the readings by Rachel Carson, Thor Heyerdahl, and Carl Sagan, document the intimate and precarious interrelationship between all living things and their environment.

The physical sciences and mathematics take as their objective the explanation of all manifestations of the physical world, from the microscopic to the cosmic. Physics and mathematics, represented in essays by Lincoln Barnett, Douglas R. Hofstadter, George A. Harter, Fred Hoyle, IBM, Charles H. Townes, Edward A. Feigenbaum and Pamela McCorduck, and Christopher Evans, are more important than ever because of developments in the space program, advances in computer theory and applications, the investigation of subatomic particles, and the challenge posed by nuclear power.

Stylistically, the readings include lively essays on childhood, clothes, and greeting cards, as well as absorbing and illuminating studies of bioethics, currency fluctuations, and artificial intelligence. You can see how professionals interpret facts and artifacts (such as photographs, art works, pottery, and fossils), define key terms, generate hypotheses, and construct coherent essays for their particular audiences. Because you will need to write frequently for a variety of purposes throughout your college education and professional life, good models of writing by scholars, researchers, and scientists from a wide range of disciplines can help you master the techniques of critical reading and effective writing.

The range and diversity of the selections in *Patterns Across the Disciplines* will enable you to see how each discipline brings to bear its own methods, theoretical models, and assumptions, and how writers in different academic areas adapt their presentations for particular audiences by choosing a suitable point of view, effective organization, and appropriate tone and style. You can see this most clearly when writers use different conceptual frameworks to view the same event or phenomenon. For example, you can view the same event, a Pueblo Indian corn dance, through the eyes of D. H. Lawrence, a great novelist and poet (in "The Dance of the Sprouting Corn"), and through the perspective of Ruth Benedict, a noted anthropologist (in "The Pueblos of New Mexico").

You will be able to compare the different perspectives brought to bear in:

- John Hersey's journalistic account of Hiroshima in "A Noiseless Flash from Hiroshima," and Carl Sagan's compelling analysis of the environmental consequences of nuclear war in "The Nuclear Winter."
- Erwin Wickert's analysis of the concept of *chi,* or public opinion, in "The Chinese and the Sense of Shame," and Sigmund Freud's theory of the "superego" as an internalized parental image in "Typical Dreams."
- Henry Allen's report on the techniques used to shape recruits into Marines in "The Corps," and John McMurtry's analysis of the methods used by football coaches to promote aggressiveness in the players in "Kill 'Em! Crush 'Em! Eat 'Em Raw!"

After reading George A. Harter's article, "Earth Applications," you should be able to see exactly which capabilities of a space station would be extremely useful in identifying oceanographic pollution problems of the kind discussed by Thor Heyerdahl in "How to Kill an Ocean."

So, too, Joel Seligman's analysis of the methods used to teach first-year law students in "Learning to Think Like a Lawyer" will enable you to more fully appreciate the legal reasoning of the 1954 Supreme Court decision *"Brown* v. *Board of Education of Topeka"* banning segregation in the public schools, written by former Chief Justice Earl Warren.

In these and many other cases, the purpose of this reader is to encourage you to become aware of the importance of the context in which a piece of writing is produced, and to see how the rhetorical patterns arise from the author's purposes, in specific contexts, for particular audiences. To assist you, each chapter is introduced by a discussion of the specific rhetorical pattern that the represented writers use to clarify ideas, analyze and interpret data, and communicate what they have discovered for their particular audiences.

Biographical sketches preceding each essay give background information on the writer's life and identify the context in which the selection was written. Each selection is followed by a set of questions for discussion and writing. As in the above examples, the "writing suggestions" often ask you to pull together several readings in order to respond to important ideas, issues, and problems encountered across the disciplines.

Aristotle said that human beings are capable of two intense pleasures: sex and thinking. While the first is clearly outside the scope of *Patterns Across the Disciplines*, this text can help you with the second.

S. H.

ANNOTATED CONTENTS

NARRATION

DESCRIPTION

Political and Social Sciences

Sciences

EXEMPLIFICATION

COMPARISON AND CONTRAST

Liberal Arts

Political and Social Sciences

PROCESS ANALYSIS

Political and Social Sciences

Sciences

CLASSIFICATION

Liberal Arts

Political and Social Sciences

Sciences

ANALOGY

Liberal Arts

Political and Social Sciences

Sciences

CAUSE AND EFFECT

Liberal Arts

Political and Social Sciences

ARGUMENTATION AND PERSUASION

Liberal Arts

THEMATIC CONTENTS

THE INDIVIDUAL EXPERIENCE

THE COLLECTIVE EXPERIENCE

The Human Condition

The Social Fabric

Crime and Punishment

Other Cultures

What We Learn from the Past

Visions of the Future

THE DIMENSIONS OF KNOWLEDGE

Discoveries About Man and Living Things

Discoveries About the Environment

Discoveries About Microcosms and Macrocosms

The Order of the Mind

The Transforming Power of Art

NARRATION

Narration is an essential technique used by writers across a wide range of disciplines. A historian recreating an account of a memorable incident from records and eyewitness reports, a doctor writing to share his experiences, an explorer recording his most private thoughts in a diary, a journalist reporting on the harrowing experiences in Marine boot camp, and a mathematician who invents an amusing dialogue to explain number theory, are all using narration, albeit for different purposes. The events related through narrative can entertain, inform, and dramatize an important moment, or clarify a complex idea, as we shall see in the selections that follow.

For example, in "Rumenotomy of a Cow" James Herriot relates an experience when his skill as a veterinarian was put to the test in treating a mysterious ailment of the cow owned by one of the "no-nonsense" Yorkshire farmers. Because of his successful diagnosis he was accepted as the local veterinarian. By telling when the story happened, who was involved, and how the events appeared from his own first-person point of view, Herriot provides his readers with a coherent framework in which to interpret the events of the story.

Effective narration focuses on a single significant action that dramatically changes the relationship of the writer (or main character) to his family, friends, or environment. A significant experience may be defined as a situation in which something important to the writer, or to the people he is writing about, is at stake.

Narratives can entertain or amuse, as Herriot's does, or be written to dramatize an idea or event important to the writer. Frederick Douglass' "The Narrative of the Life of Frederick Douglass, an American Slave" recounts the crucial incident that made him realize he was willing to risk his life to escape from slavery:

> In the early part of the year 1838, I became restless. I could see no reason why I should, at the end of each week, pour the reward of my toil into the purse of my master. When I carried to him my weekly wages, he would, after counting the money, look me in the face with a robber-like fierceness, and ask, "Is this all?" He was satisfied with nothing less than the last cent. He would, however, when I made

him six dollars, sometimes give me six cents, to encourage me. It had the opposite effect. I regarded it as a sort of admission of my right to the whole. . . .

Douglass begins his story just before the key episode and relates the details ("six dollars" for his master compared with "six cents" for himself) that permit his readers to understand what being a slave means, and to share Douglass' emerging resolve to escape from an intolerable situation. His story has the elements of a good narrative—the high drama of an event that permanently changes Douglass' life, combined with invaluable insights into a turbulent period of America's past.

Narration can appear in the form of public accounts, such as Herriot's anecdotes or Douglass' historical recollections, or as private diaries or personal journals. The diaries of Robert Falcon Scott were written as a record of the experiences that Scott and his men faced in their 1910 expedition into the Antarctic. Scott's diary entries are especially poignant because they were written with the knowledge that he and his men would soon perish and that the diary itself might never be found. One of Scott's last diary entries, from "Scott's Last March," recounts the fate of one of his fellow explorers:

> He [Oates] was a brave soul. This was the end. He slept through the night before last, hoping not to wake; but he woke in the morning—yesterday. It was blowing a blizzard. He said, "I am just going outside and may be some time." He went out in the blizzard and we have not seen him since. . . . We knew that poor Oates was walking to his death, but though we tried to dissuade him, we knew it was the act of a brave man and an English gentleman. We all hope to meet the end with a similar spirit, and assuredly the end is not far.

Scott's diaries, discovered almost one year later, shed light on the unforeseen circumstances that doomed his expedition. Scott recounts, without self-pity, the heroic manner in which his men faced the desperate situation.

Whereas each of the narratives described above was written using the first-person point-of-view, events can also be related through the more intimate second-person ("you") or objective "third-person" ("he," "she," "they") point-of-view. Henry Allen, a former Marine who is now a journalist for *The Washington Post*, tells of the harrowing experiences undergone by recruits during the last phase of their training at the Parris Island Boot Camp in "The Corps." Allen centers his account around the crucial role played by the "Ditch" in transforming raw recruits into Marines. The reader is immediately drawn into the scene when Allen shifts from an objective third-person viewpoint to a more immediate second-person perspective—in effect, subjecting the reader to the same commands ("YOU WILL JUMP . . . YOU WILL THEN CRAWL ON YOUR KNEES") that the recruits receive from their tyrannical drill instructor.

The use of dialogue is invaluable in creating a sense of dramatic immediacy through its ability to provide insight into the speaker's state of mind. The mathematician, Douglas R. Hofstadter, was so inspired by Lewis Carroll's story, "What the Tortoise Said to Achilles," that he borrowed the two main characters in "Aria with Diverse Variations" and created a narrative in which they converse amusingly on a variety of topics including number theory:

ACHILLES: There's no doubt in my mind. I wonder . . . Could it be that ALL even numbers (except 4) can be written as a sum of two odd primes?

TORTOISE: Hmm . . . That question rings a bell . . . Ah, I know why! You're

not the first person to ask that question. Why, as a matter of fact, in the year
1742, a mathematical amateur put forth this very question in a—
ACHILLES: Did you say 1742? Excuse me for interrupting, but I just noticed that
    1742 happens to be a rather interesting number, being a difference of two odd
    primes: 1747 and 5.
TORTOISE: By thunder! What a curious fact! I wonder how often one runs across
    an even number with that property.

The dialogue in this scene is important in creating the impression of two personalities,
each anxious to get their respective points across, interrupting each other in their
exchange of ideas. Hofstadter uses ironic give-and-take to create and sustain the
readers' sense that Achilles and the Tortoise are real characters, in order to convey
important mathematical ideas to his audience.

   Invariably, narration is often presented in the past tense, whereas dialogue is set
in the present (as if the dialogue is spoken at the moment it is read). This alternation
between background narrative (past tense) and foreground dialogue (present tense)
allows writers to summarize, explain, or interpret events using narration and to dramatize
important moments through dialogue. In "Welcome to Vietnam," John A. Parrish's
recollection of his initial experiences as a doctor in Vietnam alternates between past
and present tenses to heighten the ironic nature of his first briefing by Captain
Street:

> Street did not even slow down as we passed. "This is Graves," he said, as we
> walked by the front of the building. "This is the only part of the hospital company
> completely staffed by marines. From the field, the dead come directly here where
> they are washed down, identified, and put in the freezer until the next flight south.
> . . . On a hot, busy day this place smells terrible." Street seemed disgusted not
> only with the marines who worked in Graves, but also with anybody who would be
> stupid or inconsiderate enough to get killed on a hot and busy day.

The contrast between what Captain Street says, on the one hand, and how Parrish
reacts, on the other, is underscored by the movement between background narration
and foreground dialogue. Parrish is plainly dismayed by Captain street's lack of concern,
as a doctor, for his fellow soldiers.

   Narratives offer writers means by which they can discover the truth of their experiences
through the process of writing about them. When the writer is torn by conflicting
desires and only learns the truth about himself by telling his story, the resulting
account can be intensely dramatic. In "This Way for the Gas, Ladies and Gentlemen,"
Tadeusz Borowski, a Polish writer who survived Auschwitz by working as a hospital
orderly, relates his experiences from the viewpoint of a prisoner, also named Tadeusz,
who survived by working in a labor battalion:

> Only from this distance does one have a full view of the inferno on the teeming
> ramp. I see a pair of human beings who have fallen to the ground locked in a last
> desperate embrace. The man has dug his fingers into the woman's flesh and has
> caught her clothing with his teeth. She screams hysterically, swears, cries, until at
> last a large boot comes down over her throat and she is silent. They are pulled
> apart and dragged like cattle to the truck. . . .

Borowski recounts the scene as an eyewitness. The arrival and unloading of prisoners
is conveyed through a multitude of searing details. Most terrible of all, Borowski

ultimately realizes that he has become dehumanized and passive in the face of this atrocity.

Autobiographical narratives offer a way to gain insight into the meaning of our experiences. Arthur Koestler, a journalist and novelist, writes about how an improverished childhood predisposed him to become a communist in "Conversion":

> As an only child, I continued to be pampered by my parents; but, well aware of the family crisis, and torn by pity for my father, who was of a generous and somewhat childlike disposition, I suffered a pang of guilt whenever they bought me books or toys. This continued later on, when every suit I bought for myself meant so much less to send home. Simultaneously, I developed a strong dislike of the obviously rich; not because they could afford to buy things (envy plays a much smaller part in social conflict than is generally assumed) but because they were able to do so without a guilty conscience. Thus I projected a personal predicament onto the structure of society at large.

Koestler's narrative is shaped to reveal the connection between his childhood experiences and his later political activism. Most importantly, the process of writing itself allows Koestler to move toward a deeper understanding of his relationship to his own past.

Just as individuals can discover the meaning of past experiences through the process of writing about them, so historians use narration to focus on important moments of collective self-revelation. Edmund Wilson, a distinguished historian, employs a full spectrum of narrative techniques in "Lenin at the Finland Station" to recreate the moment at the railway station in Petrograd when Lenin's return from exile served as a signal for the Bolsheviks' seizure of power:

> The crowd carried Lenin on their shoulders to one of the armored cars that had been drawn up outside. . . . The square in front of the station was jammed: there they were, the textile workers, the metal workers, the peasant soldiers and sailors. There was no electric light in the square, but the searchlights showed red banners with gold lettering.

Wilson draws on records and eyewitness accounts from 1917 for specific details important in recreating the scene for his readers, summarizing the necessary background information in order to set the stage for this dramatic historic moment. Wilson is faithful to the actual facts, yet his account is compelling and memorable because of his extraordinary skill as a writer.

Narratives, in the works of Herriot, Douglass, Scott, Allen, and Parrish, are effective ways of sharing experiences. In the work of Hofstadter, narration is used to clarify important, abstract ideas. Narration is also a writing strategy that Koestler and Borowski use in their autobiographies to gain insight into their own lives. Historians, such as Wilson, rely on this pattern as well to investigate and preserve important historical events.

LIBERAL ARTS

Robert Falcon Scott

Scott's Last March

Robert Falcon Scott (1868–1912), British explorer and Naval Officer, led two expeditions into Antarctica. The first expedition (1901–1904) opened up previously unexplored southern latitudes. The second, begun in June 1910, with the objective of reaching the as-yet unattained South Pole, ended disastrously when, after travelling 1,842 miles by pony, sledge, and foot, Scott and his men discovered that they had been beaten to the Pole by the Norwegian, Roald Amundsen, and his party. Eight-hundred miles into the return trip, Scott and his men died from the effects of exhaustion, frost-bite, and the lack of food. At the time, they were only eleven miles from food and shelter. The final stages of the eight hundred mile sledge-haul back to the Base Camp are recorded here from Scott's diary, found when the frozen bodies of Scott and two of his men (Wilson and Bowers) were discovered by a relief party eight months later. The original diaries, now in the British Museum, are among the most moving documents in the English language.

Monday, February 19[*] —R. 33. Temp. −17°. We have struggled out 4.6 miles in a short day over a really terrible surface—it has been like pulling over desert sand, without the least glide in the world. If this goes on we shall have a bad time, but I sincerely trust it is only the result of the windless area close to the coast and that, as we are making steadily outwards, we shall shortly escape it. It is perhaps premature to be anxious about covering distance. In all other respects things are improving. We have our sleeping-bags spread on the sledge and they are drying, but, above all, we have our full measure of food again. To-night we had a sort of stew fry of pemmican and horseflesh, and voted it the best hoosh we had ever had on a sledge journey. The absence of poor Evans is a help to the commissariat, but if he had been here in a fit state we might have got along faster. I wonder what is in store for us, with some little alarm at the lateness of the season.

[*] At Shambles Camp on February 18 they had picked up a supply of horsemeat.

Friday, March 2.—Lunch. Misfortunes rarely come singly. We marched to the [Middle Barrier] depôt fairly easily yesterday afternoon, and since that have suffered three distinct blows which have placed us in a bad position. First we found a shortage of oil; with most rigid economy it can scarce carry us to the next depôt on this surface [71 miles away]. Second, Titus Oates disclosed his feet, the toes showing very bad indeed, evidently bitten by the late temperatures. The third blow came in the night, when the wind, which we had hailed with some joy, brought dark overcast weather. It fell below −40° in the night, and this morning it took 1½ hours to get our foot-gear on, but we got away before eight. We lost cairn and tracks together and made as steady as we could N. by W., but have seen nothing. Worse was to come—the surface is simply awful. In spite of strong wind and full sail we have only done 5½ miles. We are in a *very* queer street, since there is no doubt we cannot do the extra marches and feel the cold horribly.

Sunday, March 4.—Lunch. Things looking *very* black indeed. As usual we forgot our trouble last night, got into our bags, slept splendidly on good hoosh, woke and had another, and started marching. Sun shining brightly, tracks clear, but surface covered with sandy frost-rime. All the morning we had to pull with all our strength, and in 4½ hours we covered 3½ miles. Last night it was overcast and thick, surface bad; this morning sun shining and surface as bad as ever. Under the immediate surface crystals is a hard sastrugi surface, which must have been excellent for pulling a week or two ago. We are about 42 miles from the next depôt and have a week's food, but only about 3 to 4 days' fuel—we are as economical of the latter as one can possibly be, and we cannot afford to save food and pull as we are pulling. We are in a very tight place indeed, but none of us despondent *yet*, or at least we preserve every semblance of good cheer, but one's heart sinks as the sledge stops dead at some sastrugi behind which the surface sand lies thickly heaped. For the moment the temperature is in the −20°—an improvement which makes us much more comfortable, but a colder snap is bound to come again soon. I fear that Oates at least will weather such an event very poorly. Providence to our aid! We can expect little from man now except the possibility of extra food at the next depôt. It will be real bad if we get there and find the same shortage of oil. Shall we get there? Such a short distance it would have appeared to us on the summit! I don't know what I should do if Wilson and Bowers weren't so determinedly cheerful over things.

Monday, March 5.—Lunch. Regret to say going from bad to worse. We got a slant of wind yesterday afternoon, and going on 5 hours we converted our wretched morning run of 3½ miles into something over 9. We went to bed on a cup of cocoa and pemmican solid with the chill off. (R. 47.) The result is telling on all, but mainly on Oates, whose feet are in a wretched condition. One swelled up tremendously last night and he is very lame this morning. We started march on tea and pemmican as last night—we pretend to prefer the pemmican this way. Marched for 5 hours this morning over a slightly better surface covered with high moundy sastrugi. Sledge capsized twice; we pulled on foot, covering about 5½ miles. We are two pony marches and 4 miles about from our depôt. Our fuel dreadfully low and the poor Soldier nearly done. It is pathetic enough because we can do nothing for him; more hot food might do a little, but only a little, I fear. We none of us expected these terribly low temperatures, and of the rest of us Wilson is feeling them most; mainly, I fear, from his self-sacrificing devotion in doctoring Oates' feet. We cannot help each other, each has enough to do to take care of himself. We get cold on the march when the trudging is heavy, and the wind pierces our worn garments. The others, all of them, are unendingly cheerful when in the tent. We mean to see the game through with a proper spirit, but it's tough work to be pulling harder than we ever pulled in our lives for long hours, and to feel that the progress is so slow. One can only say "God help us!" and plod on our weary way, cold and very miserable, though outwardly cheerful. We talk of all sorts of subjects in the tent, not much of food now, since we decided to take the risk of running a full ration. We simply couldn't go hungry at this time.

Wednesday, March 7.—A little worse, I fear. One of Oates' feet *very* bad this morning; he is wonderfully brave. We still talk of what we will do together at home.

We only made 6½ miles yesterday. This morning in 4½ hours we did just over 4 miles. We are 16 from our depôt. If we only find the correct proportion of food there and this surface continues, we may get to the next depôt [Mt. Hooper, 72 miles farther] but not to One Ton Camp. We hope against hope that the dogs have been to Mt. Hooper; then we might pull through. If there is a shortage of oil again we can have little hope. One feels that for poor Oates the crisis is near, but none of us are improving, though we are wonderfully fit considering the really excessive work we are doing. We are only kept going by good food. No wind this morning till a chill northerly air came ahead. Sun bright and cairns showing up well. I should like to keep the track to the end.

Thursday, March 8.—Lunch. Worse and worse in morning; poor Oates' left foot can never last out, and time over foot-gear something awful. Have to wait in night foot-gear for nearly an hour before I start changing, and then am generally first to be ready. Wilson's feet giving trouble now. We did 4½ miles this morning and are now 8½ miles from the depôt— a ridiculously small distance to feel in difficulties, yet on this surface we know we cannot equal half our old marches, and that for that effort we expend nearly double the energy. The great question is, What shall we find at the depôt? If the dogs have visited it we may get along a good distance, but if there is another short allowance of fuel, God help us indeed. We are in a very bad way, I fear, in any case.

Saturday, March 10.—Things steadily downhill. Oates' foot worse. He has rare pluck and must know that he can never get through. He asked Wilson if he had a chance this morning, and of course Bill had to say he didn't know. In point of fact he has none. Apart from him, if he went under now, I doubt whether we could get through. With great care we might have a dog's chance, but no more. The weather conditions are awful, and our gear gets steadily more icy and difficult to manage. At the same time, of course, poor Titus is the greatest handicap. He keeps us waiting in the morning until we have partly lost the warming effect of our good breakfast, when the only wise policy is to be up and away at once; again at lunch. Poor chap! it is too pathetic to watch him; one cannot but try to cheer him up.

Yesterday we marched up the depôt, Mt. Hooper. Cold comfort. Shortage on our allowance all round.

This morning it was calm when we breakfasted, but the wind came from the W.N.W. as we broke camp. It rapidly grew in strength. After travelling for half an hour I saw that none of us could go on facing such conditions. We were forced to camp and are spending the rest of the day in a comfortless blizzard camp, wind quite foul. [R. 52.]

Sunday, March 11.—Titus Oates is very near the end, one feels. What we or he will do, God only knows. We discussed the matter after breakfast; he is a brave fine fellow and understands the situation, but he practically asked for advice. Nothing could be said but to urge him to march as long as he could. One satisfactory result to the discussion; I practically ordered Wilson to hand over the means of ending our troubles to us, so that any one of us may know how to do so. Wilson had no choice between doing so and our ransacking the medicine case. We have 30 opium tabloids apiece and he is left with a tube of morphine. So far the tragical side of our story.

The sky was completely overcast when we started this morning. We could see nothing, lost the tracks, and doubtless have been swaying a good deal since—3.1 miles for the forenoon—terribly heavy dragging—expected it. Know that 6 miles is about the limit of our endurance now, if we get no help from wind or surfaces. We have 7 days' food and should be about 55 miles from One Ton Camp to-night, 6 × 7 = 42, leaving us 13 miles short of our distance, even if things get no worse. Meanwhile the season rapidly advances.

Monday, March 12.—We did 6.9 miles yesterday, under our necessary average. Things are left much the same, Oates not pulling much, and now with hands as well as feet pretty well useless. We did 4 miles this morning in 4 hours 20 min.— we may hope for 3 this afternoon, 7 × 6 = 42. We shall be 47 miles from the depôt. I doubt if we can possibly do it. The surface remains awful, the cold intense, and our physical condition running down. God help us! Not a breath of favourable wind for more than a week, and apparently [we are] liable to head winds at any moment.

Wednesday, March 14.—No doubt about the going downhill, but everything going wrong for us. Yesterday we woke to a strong northerly wind with temp. −37°. Couldn't face it, so remained in camp till 2, then did 5¼ miles. Wanted to march later, but party feeling the cold badly as the breeze (N.) never took off entirely, and as the sun sank the temp. fell. Long time getting supper in dark.

This morning started with southerly breeze, set sail and passed another cairn at good speed; half-way, however, the wind shifted to W. by S. or W.S.W., blew through our wind clothes and into our mits. Poor Wilson horribly cold, could [not] get off ski for some time. Bowers and I practically made camp, and when we got into the tent at last we were all deadly cold. Then temp. now midday down −43° and the wind strong. We *must* go on, but now the making of every camp must be more difficult and dangerous. It must be near the end, but a pretty merciful end. Poor Oates got it again in the foot. I shudder to think what it will be like to-morrow. It is only with greatest pains rest of us keep off frostbites. No idea there could be temperatures like this at this time of year with such winds. Truly awful outside the tent. Must fight it out to the last biscuit, but can't reduce rations.

Friday, March 16, or Saturday 17.—Lost track of dates, but think the last correct. Tragedy all along the line. At lunch, the day before yesterday, poor Titus Oates said he couldn't go on; he proposed we should leave him in his sleeping-bag. That we could not do, and we induced him to come on, on the afternoon march. In spite of its awful nature for him he struggled on and we made a few miles. At night he was worse and we knew the end had come.

Should this be found I want these facts recorded. Oates' last thoughts were of his Mother, but immediately before he took pride in thinking that his regiment would be pleased with the bold way in which he met his death. We can testify to his bravery. He has borne intense suffering for weeks without complaint, and to the very last was able and willing to discuss outside subjects. He did not—would not—give up hope till the very end. He was a brave soul. This was the end. He slept through the night before last, hoping not to wake; but he woke in the morning—yesterday. It was blowing a blizzard. He said, "I am just going outside and may be some time," He went out into the blizzard and we have not seen him since.

I take this opportunity of saying that we have stuck to our sick companions to the last. In case of Edgar Evans, when absolutely out of food and he lay insensible, the safety of the remainder seemed to demand his abandonment, but Providence mercifully removed him at this critical moment. He died a natural death, and we did not leave him till two hours after his death. We knew that poor Oates was walking to his death, but though we tried to dissuade him, we knew it was the act of a brave man and an English gentlemen. We all hope to meet the end with a similar spirit, and assuredly the end is not far.

I can only write at lunch and then only occasionally. The cold is intense, $-40°$ at midday. My companions are unendingly cheerful, but we are all on the verge of serious frostbites, and though we constantly talk of fetching through, I don't think any one of us believes it in his heart.

We are cold on the march now, and at all times except meals. Yesterday we had to lie up for a blizzard and to-day we move dreadfully slowly. We are at No. 14 pony camp, only two pony marches from One Ton Depôt. We leave here our theodolite, a camera, and Oates' sleeping-bags. Diaries, etc., and geological specimens carried at Wilson's special request, will be found with us or on our sledge.

Sunday, March 18.—To-day, lunch, we are 21 miles from the depôt. Ill fortune presses, but better may come. We have had more wind and drift from ahead yesterday; had to stop marching; wind N.W., force 4, temp. $-35°$. No human being could face it, and we are worn out *nearly*.

My right foot has gone, nearly all the toes—two days ago I was proud possessor of best feet. These are the steps of my downfall. Like an ass I mixed a small spoonful of curry powder with my melted pemmican—it gave me violent indigestion. I lay awake and in pain all night; woke and felt done on the march; foot went and I didn't know it. A very small measure of neglect and I have a foot which is not pleasant to contemplate. Bowers takes first place in condition, but there is not much to choose after all. The others are still confident of getting through—or pretend to be—I don't know! We have the last *half* fill of oil in our primus and a very small quantity of spirit—this alone between us and thirst. The wind is fair for the moment, and that is perhaps a fact to help. The mileage would have seemed rediculously small on our outward journey.

Monday, March 19.—Lunch. We camped with difficulty last night and were dreadfully cold till after our supper of cold pemmican and biscuit and a half a pannikin of cocoa cooked over the spirit. Then, contrary to expectation, we got warm and all slept well. To-day we started in the usual dragging manner. Sledge dreadfully heavy. We are 15½ miles from the depôt and ought to get there in three days. What progress! We have two days' food, but barely a day's fuel. All our feet are getting bad—Wilson's best, my right foot worse, left all right. There is no chance to nurse one's feet till we can get hot food into us. Amputation is the least I can hope for now, but will the trouble spread? That is the serious question. The weather doesn't give us a chance—the wind from N. to N.W. and −40° temp. to-day.

Wednesday, March 21.—Got within 11 miles of depôt Monday night;* had to lie up all yesterday in severe blizzard. To-day forlorn hope, Wilson and Bowers going to depôt for fuel.

22 and 23.—Blizzard bad as ever—Wilson and Bowers unable to start—to-morrow last chance—no fuel and only one or two† of food left—must be near the end. Have decided it shall be natural—we shall march for the depôt with or without our effects and die in our tracks.

[*Thursday*] *March 29.*—Since the 21st we have had a continuous gale from W.S.W. and S.W. We had fuel to make two cups of tea apiece and bare food for two days on the 20th. Every day we have been ready to start for our depôt 11 *miles* away, but outside the door of the tent it remains a scene of whirling drift. I do not think we can hope for any better things now. We shall stick it out to the end, but we are getting weaker, of course, and the end cannot be far.

It seems a pity, but I do not think I can write more.

R. SCOTT.

Last entry. For God's sake look after our people.

[*During the Antarctic summer, eight months later, a relief party discovered the frozen bodies of Scott and two of his men, Wilson and Bowers. Wilson and Bowers were in their sleeping bags, while Scott had thrown back the flaps of his sleeping bag and opened his coat. Three notebooks were found. With the diaries in the tent were found the following letters:*]

To Mrs. E. A. Wilson

My Dear Mrs. Wilson,

If this letter reaches you, Bill [Dr. Wilson] and I will have gone out together. We are very near it now and I should like you to know how splendid he was at the end—everlastingly cheerful and ready to sacrifice himself for others, never a word of blame to me for leading him into this mess. He is not suffering, luckily, at least only minor discomforts.

His eyes have a comfortable blue look of hope and his mind is peaceful with the satisfaction of his faith in regarding himself as part of the great scheme of the

---

* The sixtieth camp from the Pole.
† Word missing: evidently "rations."

Almighty. I can do no more to comfort you than to tell you that he died as he lived, a brave, true man—the best of comrades and staunchest of friends.

My whole heart goes out to you in pity. . . .

Yours,
R. Scott

To Mrs. Bowers

My Dear Mrs. Bowers,

I am afraid this will reach you after one of the heaviest blows of your life.

I write when we are very near the end of our journey, and I am finishing it in company with two gallant, noble gentlemen. One of these is your son [Lt. Bowers]. He had come to be one of my closest and soundest friends, and I appreciate his wonderful upright nature, his ability and energy. As the troubles have thickened his dauntless spirit ever shone brighter and he has remained cheerful, hopeful, and indomitable to the end.

The ways of Providence are inscrutable, but there must be some reason why such a young, vigorous, and promising life is taken.

To the end he has talked of you and his sisters. One sees what a happy home he must have had, and perhaps it is well to look back on nothing but happiness.

He remains unselfish, self-reliant and splendidly hopeful to the end, believing in God's mercy to you. . . .

Yours,
R. Scott

To Sir J. M. Barrie

My Dear Barrie,

We are showing that Englishmen can still die with a bold spirit, fighting it out to the end. It will be known that we have accomplished our object in reaching the Pole, and that we have done everything possible, even to sacrificing ourselves in order to save sick companions. I think this makes an example for Englishmen of the future, and that the country ought to help those who are left behind to mourn us. I leave my poor girl and your godson, Wilson leaves a widow, and Edgar Evans also a widow in humble circumstances. Do what you can to get their claims recognized. Good-bye. I am not at all afraid of the end, but sad to miss many a humble pleasure which I had planned for the future on our long marches. I may not have proved a great explorer, but we have done the greatest march ever made and come very near to great success. . . . We are in a desperate state, feet frozen, etc. No fuel and a long way from food, but it would do your heart good to be in our tent, to hear our songs and the cheery conversation as to what we will do when we get to Hut Point.

Later.—We are very near the end, but have not and will not lose our good cheer. We have had four days of storm in our tent and nowhere's food or fuel. We did intend to finish ourselves when things proved like this, but we have decided to die naturally in the track.

As a dying man, my dear friend, be good to my wife and child. Give the boy a chance in life if the State won't do it. He ought to have good stuff in him. . . . I never met a man in my life whom I admired and loved more than you [Sir J. M. Barrie], but I could never show you how much your friendship meant to me, for you had much to give and I nothing.

Yours ever,
R. Scott

Message to the Public

The causes of the disaster are not due to faulty organisation, but to misfortune in all risks which had to be undertaken.

1. The loss of pony transport in March 1911 obliged me to start later than I had intended, and obliged the limits of stuff transported to be narrowed.
2. The weather throughout the outward journey, and especially the long gale in 83° S., stopped us.
3. The soft snow in lower reaches of glacier again reduced pace.

We fought these untoward events with a will and conquered, but it cut into our provision reserve.

Every detail of our food supplies, clothing and depôts made on the interior ice-sheet and over that long stretch of 700 miles to the Pole and back, worked out to perfection. The advance party would have returned to the glacier in fine form and with surplus of food, but for the astonishing failure of the man whom we had least expected to fail. Edgar Evans was thought the strongest man of the party.

The Beardmore Glacier is not difficult in fine weather, but on our return we did not get a single completely fine day; this with a sick companion enormously increased our anxieties.

As I have said elsewhere, we got into frightfully rough ice and Edgar Evans received a concussion of the brain—he died a natural death, but left us a shaken party with the season unduly advanced.

But all the facts above enumerated were as nothing to the surprise which awaited us on the Barrier. I maintain that our arrangements for returning were quite adequate, and that no one in the world would have expected the temperatures and surfaces which we encountered at this time of the year. On the summit in lat 85°, 86° we had −20°, −30°. On the Barrier in lat 82°, 10,000 feet lower, we had −30° in the day, −47° at night pretty regularly, with continuous head wind during our day marches. It is clear that these circumstances came on very suddenly, and our wreck is certainly due to this sudden advent of severe weather, which does not seem to have any satisfactory cause. I do not think human beings ever came through such a month as we have come through, and we should have got through in spite of the weather but for the sickening of a second companion, Captain Oates, and a shortage of fuel in our depôts for which I cannot account.* and finally, but for the storm which has fallen on us within 11 miles of the depôt at which we hoped to secure our final supplies. Surely misfortune could scarcely have exceeded this last blow. We arrived within 11 miles of our old One Ton Camp with fuel for one last meal and food for two days. For four† days we have been unable to leave the tent—the gale howling about us. We are weak, writing is difficult, but for my own sake I do not regret this journey, which has shown that Englishmen can endure hardships, help one another, and meet death with as great a fortitude as ever in the past. We took risks, we knew we took them; things have come out against us, and therefore we have no cause for complaint, but bow to the will of Providence, determined still to do our best to the last. But if we have been willing to give our lives to this enterprise, which is for the honour of our country, I appeal to our countrymen to see that those who depend on us are properly cared for.

Had we lived, I should have had a tale to tell of the hardihood, endurance, and courage of my companions which would have stirred the heart of every Englishman. These rough notes and our dead bodies must tell the tale, but surely, surely, a great rich country like ours will see that those who are dependent on us are properly provided for.

R. SCOTT

MEANING

1. Why was it important for Scott to continue keeping his diary when he knew that he and his men would perish and the diary might never be found?
2. What qualities of leadership would you say Scott possessed?
3. How did Scott wish himself and his men to be remembered by his countrymen in England?
4. What did the episode involving Titus Oates tell about both Oates' heroism and Scott's sense of responsibility toward his men?
5. Summarize the main reasons, according to Scott, why the expedition failed.

USING NARRATION TO CONVEY MEANING

1. What specific details convey the fact that the situation Scott and his men were in got progressively worse?
2. What in the narrative reveals why Scott wanted to lead his men on an expedition into the Antarctic?
3. What specific examples from the diary show that Scott wished it to provide an objective account of the expedition?

* *The fuel had evaporated.*
† *They lasted for six more days after this.*

4. What do the letters that Scott wrote to the families of his men reveal about Scott himself?

Writing Suggestions

1. As a research project, compare Scott's account of his expedition to the Antarctic with accounts by other explorers such as Roald Amundsen's *The South Pole* or Richard E. Byrd's *Little America*.
2. Try keeping a detailed diary for a two-week period. At the end of two weeks, determine whether or not something that you first thought a minor incident became an important one, or vice versa.

FREDERICK DOUGLASS

From The Narrative of the Life of Frederick Douglass, an American Slave

Frederick Douglass (1817–1895) was born into slavery in Maryland, where he worked as a field hand and servant. In 1838, after previous failed attempts to escape, for which he was beaten and tortured, he successfully made his way to New York using the identity papers of a freed black sailor. There he adopted the last name of Douglass and subsequently settled in New Bedford, Massachusetts. Douglass was the first black American to rise to prominence as a national figure. He gained renown as a speaker for the Massachusetts Anti-Slavery League and was an editor for the North Star, an abolitionist paper, from 1847–1860. He was a friend to John Brown, helped convince President Lincoln to issue the Emancipation Proclamation, and became ambassador to several foreign countries. The Narrative of the Life of Frederick Douglass, an American Slave *(1845) is one of the most illuminating of the many slave narratives written during the nineteenth century.*

I now come to that part of my life during which I planned, and finally succeeded in making my escape from slavery. But before narrating any of the peculiar circumstances, I deem it proper to make known my intention not to state all the facts connected with the transaction. My reasons for pursuing this course may be understood from the following: First, were I to give a minute statement of all the facts, it is not only possible, but quite probable, that others would thereby be involved in the most embarrassing difficulties. Secondly, such a statement would most undoubtedly induce greater vigilance on the part of slaveholders than has existed heretofore among them; which would, of course be the means of guarding a door whereby some dear brother bondman might escape his galling chains. I deeply regret the necessity that impels me to suppress any thing of importance connected with my experience in slavery. It would afford me great pleasure indeed, as well as materially add to the interest of my narrative, were I at liberty to gratify a curiosity, which I know exists in the minds of many, by an accurate statement of all the facts pertaining to my most fortunate escape. But I must deprive myself of this pleasure, and the curious of the gratification which such a statement would afford. I would allow myself to suffer under the greatest imputations which evil-minded men might suggest, rather than exculpate myself, and thereby run the hazard of closing the slightest avenue by which a brother slave might clear himself of the chains and fetters of slavery.

I have never approved of the very public manner in which some of our western friends have conducted what they call the *underground railroad*[1] but which, I think,

[1] Places of safety where escaping slaves could stay enroute to Canada.

by their open declarations, has been made most emphatically the *upperground railroad*. I honor those good men and women for their noble daring, and applaud them for willingly subjecting themselves to bloody persecution, by openly avowing their participation in the escape of slaves. I, however, can see very little good resulting from such a course, either to themselves or the slaves escaping, while, upon the other hand, I see and feel assured that those open declarations are a positive evil to the slaves remaining, who are seeking to escape. They do nothing towards enlightening the slave, whilst they do much towards enlightening the master. They stimulate him to greater watchfulness, and enhance his power to capture his slave. We owe something to the slaves south of the line as well as to those north of it; and in aiding the latter on their way to freedom, we should be careful to do nothing which would be likely to hinder the former from escaping from slavery. I would keep the merciless slave holder profoundly ignorant of the means of flight adopted by the slave. I would leave him to imagine himself surrounded by myriads of invisible tormentors, ever ready to snatch from his infernal grasp his trembling prey. Let him be left to feel his way in the dark; let darkness commensurate with his crime hover over him; and let him feel that at every step he takes, in pursuit of the flying bondman, he is running the frightful risk of having his hot brains dashed out by an invisible agency. Let us render the tyrant no aid; let us not hold the light by which he can trace the footprints of our flying brother. But enough of this. I will now proceed to the statement of those facts, connected with my escape, for which I am alone responsible, and for which no one can be made to suffer but myself.

In the early part of the year 1838, I became quite restless. I could see no reason why I should, at the end of each week, pour the reward of my toil into the purse of my master. When I carried to him my weekly wages, he would, after counting the money, look me in the face with a robber-like fierceness, and ask, "Is this all?" He was satisfied with nothing less than the last cent. He would, however, when I made him six dollars, sometimes give me six cents, to encourage me. It had the opposite effect. I regarded it as a sort of admission of my right to the whole. The fact that he gave me any part of my wages was proof, to my mind, that he believed me entitled to the whole of them. I always felt worse for having received any thing; for I feared that the giving me a few cents would ease his conscience, and make him feel himself to be a pretty honorable sort of robber. My discontent grew upon me. I was ever on the look-out for means of escape; and, finding no direct means, I determined to try to hire my time, with a view of getting money with which to make my escape. In the spring of 1838, when Master Thomas[2] came to Baltimore to purchase his spring goods, I got an opportunity, and applied to him to allow me to hire my time. He unhesitatingly refused my request, and told me this was another strategem by which to escape. He told me I could go nowhere but that he could get me; and that, in the event of my running away, he should spare no pains in his efforts to catch me. He exhorted me to content myself, and be obedient. He told me, if I would be happy, I must lay out no plans for the future. He said, if I behaved myself properly, he would take care of me. Indeed, he advised me to complete thoughtlessness of the future, and taught me to depend solely upon him for happiness. He seemed to see fully the pressing necessity of setting aside my intellectual nature, in order to contentment in slavery. But in spite of him, and even in spite of myself, I continued to think, and to think about the injustice of my enslavement, and the means of escape.

---

[2] Douglass's owner, Thomas Lloyd.

About two months after this, I applied to Master Hugh for the privilege of hiring my time. He was not acquainted with the fact that I had applied to Master Thomas, and had been refused. He too, at first, seemed disposed to refuse; but, after some reflection, he granted me the privilege, and proposed the following term: I was to be allowed all my time, make all contracts with those for whom I worked, and find my own employment; and, in return for this liberty, I was to pay him three dollars at the end of each week; find myself in calking tools, and in board and clothing. My board was two dollars and a half per week. This, with the wear and tear of clothing and calking tools, made my regular expenses about six dollars per week. This amount I was compelled to make up, or relinquish the privilege of hiring my time. Rain or shine, work or no work, at the end of each week the money must be forthcoming, or I must give up my privilege. This arrangement, it will be perceived, was decidedly in my master's favor. It relieved him of all need of looking after me. His money was sure. H received all the benefits of slaveholding without its evils; while I endured all the evils of a slave, and suffered all the care and anxiety of a freeman. I found it a hard bargain. But, hard as it was, I thought it better than the old mode of getting along. It was a step towards freedom to be allowed to bear the responsibilities of a freeman, and I was determined to hold on upon it. I bent myself to the work of making money. I was ready to work at night as well as day, and by the most untiring perseverance and industry, I made enough to meet my expenses, and lay up a little money every week. I went on thus from May till August. Master Hugh then refused to allow me to hire my time longer. The ground for his refusal was a failure on my part, one Saturday night, to pay him for my week's time. This failure was occasioned by my attending a camp meeting about ten miles from Baltimore. During the week, I had entered into an engagement with a number of young friends to start from Baltimore to the camp ground early Saturday evening; and being detained by my employer, I was unable to get down to Master Hugh's without disappointing the company. I knew that Master Hugh was in no special need of the money that night. I therefore decided to go to camp meeting and upon my return pay him the three dollars. I staid at the camp meeting one day longer than I intended when I left. But as soon as I returned, I called upon him to pay him what he considered his due. I found him very angry; he could scarce restrain his wrath. He said he had a great mind to give me a severe whipping. He wished to know how I dared go out of the city without asking his permission. I told him I hired my time, and while I paid him the price which he asked for it, I did not know that I was bound to ask him when and where I should go. This reply troubled him; and, after reflecting a few moments, he turned to me, and said I should hire my time no longer; that the next thing he should know of, I would be running away. Upon the same plea, he told me to bring my tools and clothing home forthwith. I did so, but instead of seeking work, as I had been accustomed to do previously to hiring my time, I spent the whole week without the performance of a single stroke of work. I did this in retaliation. Saturday night, he called upon me as usual for my week's wages. I told him I had no wages; I had done no work that week. Here we were upon the point of coming to blows. He raved, and swore his determination to get hold of me. I did not allow myself a single word; but was resolved, if he laid the weight of his hand upon me, it should be blow for blow. He did not strike me, but told me that he would find me in constant employment in future. I thought the matter over during the next day, Sunday, and finally resolved upon the third day of September, as the day upon which I would make a second attempt to secure my freedom. I now had three weeks during which to prepare for my journey. Early on Monday morning, before Master Hugh had time to make any engagement for me, I went out and got employment of Mr. Butler, as his ship-yard near the drawbridge, upon what is called the City Block, thus making it unnecessary for him to seek employment for me. At the end of the week, I brought him between eight and nine dollars. He seemed very well pleased, and asked me why I did not do the same the week before. He little knew what my plans were. My object in working steadily was to remove any suspicion he might entertain of my intent to run away; and in this I succeeded admirably. I suppose he thought I was never better satisfied with my condition than at the very time during which I was planning my escape. The second week passed, and again I carried him my full wages; and so well pleased was he, that he gave me twenty-five cents (quite a large sum for a slaveholder to give a slave) and bade me to make a good use of it. I told him I would.

Things went on without very smoothly indeed, but within there was trouble. It is impossible for me to describe my feelings as the time of my contemplated start drew near. I had a number of warm-hearted friends in Baltimore—friends that I loved almost as I did my life—and the thought of being separated from them forever was painful beyond expression. It is my opinion that thousands would escape from slavery, who now remain, but for the strong cords of affection that bind them to their friends. The thought of leaving my friends was decidedly the most painful thought with which I had to contend. The love of them was my tender point, and shook my decision more than all things else. Besides the pain of separation, the dread and apprehension of a failure exceeded what I had experienced at my first attempt. The appalling defeat I then sustained returned to torment me. I felt assured that, if I failed in this attempt, my case would be a hopeless one—it would seal my fate as a slave forever. I could not hope to get off with any thing less than the severest punishment, and being placed beyond the means of escape. It required no very vivid imagination to depict the most frightful scenes through which I should have to pass, in case I failed. The wretchedness of slavery, and the blessedness of freedom, were perpetually before me. It was life and death with me. But I remained firm, and, according to my resolution, on the third day of September, 1838, I left my chains, and succeeded in reaching New York without the slightest interruption of any kind. How I did so—what means I adopted—what direction I travelled, and by what mode of conveyance—I must leave unexplained, for the reasons before mentioned.

I have been frequently asked how I felt when I found myself in a free State. I have never been able to answer the question with any satisfaction to myself. It was a moment of the highest excitement I ever experienced. I suppose I felt as one may imagine the unarmed mariner to feel when he is rescued by a friendly man-of-war from the pursuit of a pirate. In writing to a dear friend, immediately after my arrival at New York, I said I felt like one who had escaped a den of hungry lions. This state of mind, however, very soon subsided; and I was again seized with a feeling of great insecurity and loneliness. I was yet liable to be taken back, and subjected to all the tortures of slavery. This in itself was enough to damp the ardor of my enthusiasm. But the loneliness overcame me. There I was in the midst of thousands, and yet a perfect stranger; without home and without friends, in the midst of thousands of my own brethren—children of a common Father, and yet I dared not to unfold to any one of them my sad condition. I was afraid to speak to any one for fear of speaking to the wrong one, and thereby falling into the hands of money-loving kidnappers, whose business it was to lie in wait for the panting fugitive, as the ferocious beasts of the forest lie in wait for their prey. The motto which I adopted when I started from slavery was this—"Trust no man!" I saw in every white man an enemy, and in almost every colored man cause for distrust. It was a most painful situation; and, to understand it, one must needs experience it, or imagine himself in similar circumstances. Let him be a fugitive slave in a strange land—a land given up to be the hunting-ground for slaveholders—whose inhabitants are legalized kidnappers—where he is every moment subjected to the terrible liability of being seized upon by his fellow-men, as the hideous crocodile seizes upon his prey!—I say, let him place himself in my situation—without home or friends—without money or credit—wanting shelter, and no one to give it—wanting bread, and no money to buy it—and at the same time let him feel that he is pursued by merciless men-hunters, and in total darkness as to what to do, where to go, or where to stay—perfectly helpless both as to the means of defense and means of escape—in the midst of plenty, yet suffering the terrible gnawings of hunger—in the midst of houses, yet having no home—among fellow-men, yet feeling as if in the midst of wild beasts, whose greediness to swallow up the trembling and half-famished fugitive is only equalled by that with which the monsters of the deep swallow up the helpless fish upon which they subsist—I say, let him be placed in this most trying situation—the situation in which I was placed—then, and not till then, will he fully appreciate the hardships of, and know how to sympathize with, the toil-worn and whip-scarred fugitive slave.

Thank Heaven, I remained but a short time in this distressed situation. I was relieved from it by the humane hand of Mr. David Ruggles, whose vigilance, kindness, and perseverance, I shall never forget. I am glad of an opportunity to express, as far as words can, the love and gratitude I bear him. Mr. Ruggles is now afflicted with blindness, and is himself in need of the same kind offices which he was once so forward in the performance of toward others. I had been in New York but a few days, when Mr. Ruggles sought me out, and very kindly took me to his boarding-house at the corner of Church and Lespenard Streets. Mr. Ruggles was then very deeply engaged in the memorable *Darg* case,[3] as well as attending to a number of other fugitive slaves, devising ways and means for their successful escape; and, though watched and hemmed in on almost every side, he seemed to be more than a match for his enemies.

Very soon after I went to Mr. Ruggles, he wished to know of me where I wanted to go; as he deemed it unsafe for me to remain in New York. I told him I was a calker, and should like to go where I could get work. I thought of going to Canada; but he decided against it, and in favor of my going to New Bedford, thinking I should be able to get work there at my trade. At this time, Anna,[4] my intended wife, came on; for I wrote to her immediately after my arrival at New York (notwithstanding my homeless, houseless, and helpless condition) informing her of my successful flight, and wishing her to come on forthwith. In a few days after her arrival, Mr. Ruggles called in the Rev. J. W. C. Pennington, who, in the presence of Mr. Ruggles, Mrs. Michaels, and two or three others, performed the marriage ceremony, and gave us a certificate, of which the following is an exact copy:

[3] Mr. Ruggles unsuccessfully tried to prevent the forced return of an escaped slave named Darg.
[4] She was free. [Douglass' note.]

This may certify, that I joined together in holy matrimony Frederick Johnson[5] and Anna Murray, as man and wife, in the presence of Mr. David Ruggles and Mrs. Michaels.

JAMES W. C. PENNINGTON
New York, Sept. 15, 1838.

Upon receiving this certificate, and a five-dollar bill from Mr. Ruggles, I shouldered one part of our baggage, and Anna took up the other, and we set out forthwith to take passage on board of the steamboat John W. Richmond for Newport, on our way to New Bedford. Mr. Ruggles gave me a letter to a Mr. Shaw in Newport, and told me, in case my money did not serve me to New Bedford, to stop in Newport and obtain further assistance; but upon our arrival at Newport, we were so anxious to get to a place of safety, that, notwithstanding we lacked the necessary money to pay our fare, we decided to take seats in the stage, and promise to pay when we got to New Bedford. We were encouraged to do this by two excellent gentlemen, residents of New Bedford, whose names I afterward ascertained to be Joseph Ricketson and William C. Taber. They seemed at once to understand our circumstances, and gave us such assurance of their friendliness as put us fully at ease in their presence. It was good indeed to meet with such friends, at such a time. Upon reaching New Bedford, we were directed to the house of Mr. Nathan Johnson, by whom we were kindly received, and hospitably provided for. Both Mr. and Mrs. Johnson took a deep and lively interest in our welfare. They proved themselves quite worthy of the name of abolitionists. When the stage-driver found us unable to pay our fare, he held on upon our baggage as security for the debt. I had but to mention the fact to Mr. Johnson, and he forthwith advanced the money.

We now began to feel a degree of safety, and to prepare ourselves for the duties and responsibilities of a life of freedom. On the morning after our arrival at New Bedford, while at the breakfast-table, the question arose as to what name I should be called by. The names given me by my mother was, "Frederick Augustus Washington Bailey." I, however, had dispensed with the two middle names long before I left Maryland so that I was generally known by the name of "Frederick Bailey." I started from Baltimore bearing the name of "Stanley." When I got to New York, I again changed my name to "Frederick Johnson," and thought that would be the last change. But when I got to New Bedford, I found it necessary again to change my name. The reason of this necessity was, that there were so many Johnsons in New Bedford, it was already quite difficult to distinguish between them. I gave Mr. Johnson the privilege of choosing me a name, but told him he must not take from me the name of "Frederick." I must hold on to that, to preserve a sense of my identity. Mr. Johnson had just been reading the "Lady of the Lake," [6] and at once suggested that my name be "Douglass." From that time until now I have been called "Frederick Douglass"; and as I am more widely known by that name than by either of the others, I shall continue to use it as my own.

I was quite disappointed at the general appearance of things in New Bedford. The impression which I had received respecting the character and condition of the people of the north, I found to be singularly erroneous. I had very strangely supposed,

[5] I had changed my name from *Frederick Bailey* to that of *Johnson* [Douglass' note]
[6] A poem by Sir Walter Scott (1771–1832), which centers around the exploits of Lord James Douglas, himself a fugitive.

while in slavery, that few of the comforts, and scarcely any of the luxuries, of life were enjoyed at the north, compared with what were enjoyed by the slaveholders of the south. I probably came to this conclusion from the fact that northern people owned no slaves. I supposed that they were about upon a level with the non-slaveholding population of the south. I knew *they* were exceedingly poor, and I had been accustomed to regard their poverty as the necessary consequence of their being non-slaveholders. I had somehow imbibed the opinion that, in the absence of slaves, there could be no wealth, and very little refinement. And upon coming to the north, I expected to meet with a rough, hard-handed, and uncultivated population, living in the most Spartan-like simplicity, knowing nothing of the ease, luxury, pomp, and grandeur of southern slaveholders. Such being my conjectures, any one acquainted with the appearance of New Bedford may very readily infer how palpably I must have seen my mistake.

In the afternoon of the day when I reached New Bedford, I visited the wharves, to take a view of the shipping. Here I found myself surrounded with the strongest proofs of wealth. Lying at the wharves, and riding in the stream, I saw many ships of the finest model, in the best order, and of the largest size. Upon the right and left, I was walled in by granite warehouses of the widest dimensions, stowed to their utmost capacity with the necessaries and comforts of life. Added to this, almost every body seemed to be at work, but noiselessly so, compared with what I had been accustomed to in Baltimore. There were no loud songs heard from those engaged in loading and unloading ships. I heard no deep oaths or horrid curses on the laborer. I saw no whipping of men; but all seemed to go smoothly on. Every man appeared to understand his work, and went at it with a sober, yet cheerful earnestness, which betokened the deep interest which he felt in what he was doing, as well as a sense of his own dignity as a man. To me this looked exceedingly strange. From the wharves I strolled around and over the town, gazing with wonder and admiration at the splendid churches, beautiful dwellings, and finely-cultivated gardens; evincing an amount of wealth, comfort, taste, and refinement, such as I had never seen in any part of slaveholding Maryland.

Every thing looked clean, new and beautiful. I saw few or no dilapidated houses, with poverty-stricken inmates; no half-naked children and barefooted women, such as I had been accustomed to see in Hillsborough, Easton, St. Michael's, and Baltimore. The people looked more able, stronger, healthier, and happier, than those of Maryland. I was for once made glad by a view of extreme wealth, without being saddened by seeing extreme poverty. But the most astonishing as well as the most interesting thing to me was the condition of the colored people, a great many of whom, like myself, had escaped thither as a refuge from the hunters of men. I found many, who had not been seven years out of their chains, living in finer houses, and evidently enjoying more of the comforts of life, than the average of slaveholders in Maryland. I will venture to assert that my friend Mr. Nathan Johnson (of whom I can say with a grateful heart, "I was hungry, and he gave me meat; I was thirsty, and he gave me drink; I was a stranger, and he took me in") lived in a neater house; dined at a better table; took, paid for, and read, more newspapers; better understood the moral, religious, and political character of the nation—than nine tenths of the slaveholders in Talbot county, Maryland. Yet Mr. Johnson was a working man. His hands were hardened by toil, and not his alone, but those also of Mrs. Johnson. I found the colored people much more spirited than I had supposed they would be. I found among them a determination to protect each other from the blood-thirsty kidnapper, at all hazards. Soon after my arrival, I was told of a circumstance which illustrated their spirit. A colored man and a fugitive slave were on unfriendly terms. The former was heard to threaten the latter with informing his master of his whereabouts. Straightway a meeting was called among the colored people, under the stereotyped[7] notice, "Business of importance!" The betrayer was invited to attend. The people came at the appointed hour, and organized the meeting by appointing a very religious old gentleman as president, who, I believe, made a prayer, after which he addressed the meeting as follows: *"Friends, we have got him here, and I would recommend that you young men just take him outside the door, and kill him!"* With this, a number of them bolted at him; but they were intercepted by some more timid than themselves, and the betrayer escaped their vengeance, and has not been seen in New Bedford since. I believe there have been no more such threats, and should there be hereafter, I doubt not that death would be the consequence.

I found employment, the third day after my arrival, in stowing a sloop with a load of oil. It was new, dirty, and hard work for me; but I went at it with a glad heart and a willing hand. I was now my own master. It was a happy moment, the rapture of which can be understood only by those who have been slaves. It was the first work, the reward of which was to be entirely my own. There was no Master Hugh standing ready, the moment I earned the money, to rob me of it. I worked that day with a pleasure I had never before experienced. I was at work for myself and newly-married wife. It was to me the startingpoint of a new existence. When I got through with that job, I went in pursuit of a job of calking; but such was the strength of prejudice against color, among the white calkers, that they refused to work with me, and of course I could get no employment.[8] Finding my trade of no immediate benefit, I threw off my calking habiliments, and prepared myself to do any kind of work I could get to do. Mr. Johnson kindly let me have his wood-horse and saw, and I very soon found myself a plenty of work. There was no work too hard—none too dirty. I was ready to saw wood, shovel coal, carry the hod, sweep the chimney, or roll oil casks—all of which I did for nearly three years in New Bedford, before I became known to the anti-slavery world.

In about four months after I went to New Bedford, there came a young man to me, and inquired if I did not wish to take the "Liberator."[9] I told him I did; but, just having made my escape from slavery, I remarked that I was unable to pay for it then. I, however, finally became a subscriber to it. The paper came, and I read it from week to week with such feelings as it would be quite idle for me to attempt to describe. The paper became my meat and my drink. My soul was set all on fire. Its sympathy for my brethren in bonds—its scathing denunciations of slaveholders—its faithful exposures of slavery—and its powerful attacks upon the upholders of the institution—sent a thrill of joy through my soul, such as I had never felt before!

I had not long been a reader of the "Liberator," before I got a pretty correct idea of the principles, measures and spirit of the anti-slavery reform. I took right hold of the cause. I could do but little; but what I could, I did with a joyful heart, and never felt happier than when in an anti-slavery meeting. I seldom had much to say at the meetings, because what I wanted to say was said so much better by others.

[7] A method of printing.
[8] I am told that colored persons can now get employment at calking in New Bedford—a result of antislavery effort. [Douglass' note.]
[9] The abolitionist newspaper edited by William Lloyd Garrison (1805–1879).

But, while attending an anti-slavery convention at Nantucket, on the 11th of August, 1841, I felt strongly moved to speak, and was at the same time much urged to do so by Mr. William C. Coffin, a gentleman who had heard me speak in the colored people's meeting at New Bedford. It was a severe cross, and I took it up reluctantly. The truth was, I felt myself a slave, and the idea of speaking to white people weighed me down. I spoke but a few moments, when I felt a degree of freedom, and said what I desired with considerable ease. From that time until now, I have been engaged in pleading the cause of my brethren—with what success, and with what devotion, I leave those acquainted with my labors to decide.

MEANING

1. What specific episode made Douglass realize that he wanted to escape?
2. Why did Douglass' experiences in the North make him question the assumptions about slavery producing wealth that he had accepted as true?
3. What strategies did Douglass employ to escape from slavery?
4. How did Douglass' view of himself as a human being change after he escaped to the North?
5. What convinced Douglass that New Bedford was indeed a land of opportunity for escaped slaves like himself?

USING NARRATION TO CONVEY MEANING

1. What details of appearance, action, and conversation does Douglass use to characterize people he mentions in his narrative such as the ever-helpful Mr. Ruggles?
2. How does Douglass arrange his narration to lead up to the central episode of "six cents for six dollars"?
3. What details make you realize the real dangers Douglass would have faced had he failed in his attempt to escape?

WRITING SUGGESTIONS

1. Discuss Douglass' experiences in light of the historical information provided by Kenneth Stampp (see the Process Analysis chapter, page 281).
2. What incident in your life would you identify as a significant turning point, as the "six cents for six dollars" episode was for Douglass? Begin your story just before the significant moment and use specific details to dramatize the importance of the event in making you want to change your life.

EDMUND WILSON

Lenin at the Finland Station

Edmund Wilson (1895–1972) was born in New Jersey and was educated at Princeton (where he began a lifelong friendship with F. Scott Fitzgerald). His definitive works of literary and social criticism, reviews, short stories, memoirs, and fiction have established him as a pre-eminent man of letters in the twentieth century. His principal works include Axel's Castle *(1931), a study of symbolist literature;* To the Finland Station *(1940), an examination of the historical and philosophical backgrounds of the Russian Revolution;* The Wound and the Bow *(1941), a seminal work using a Freudian approach; and* Patriotic Gore *(1962), a study of American writers during the Civil War. "Lenin at the Finland Station" appeared as the final chapter of the 1940 work and recreates the moment when Lenin's return from exile to Petrograd on a train from Finland served as a signal for the Bolsheviks' seizure of power.*

On January 22, 1917, Lenin said to an audience of young people in a lecture on the 1905 Revolution: "We of the older generation may not live to see the decisive battles of this coming revolution." On the 15th of February, he wrote his sister María, asking about certain sums of money which had been sent him without explanation from Russia, "Nádya," he told her, "is teasing me, says I'm beginning to draw my pension. Ha! ha! that's a good joke because living is infernally expensive, and my capacity for work is desperately low on account of my bad nerves."

They had been living on a small legacy which had been inherited by Krúpskaya's[1] mother. A broker in Vienna had taken half of it for transferring it to them in wartime, and there had not been very much more than the equivalent of a thousand dollars left. Their funds were so low in 1917 that Lenin tried to get his brother-in-law in Russia to arrange for the publication of a "pedagogical encyclopaedia," which he proposed to have Krúpskaya write.

They had lodged at first in Zürich at a boarding-house where "Ilyích[2] liked the simplicity of the service, the fact that the coffee was served in a cup with a broken handle, that we ate in the kitchen, that the conversation was simple." But it turned out to be an underworld hangout. There was a prostitute who "spoke quite openly of her profession," and a man who, though he "did not talk much," revealed "by the casual phrases he uttered that he was of an almost criminal type." They were interested in these people, but Krúpskaya insisted they should move, for fear they should get into trouble. So they transferred to a shoemaker's family, where they occupied a single room in an old and gloomy house that went back almost to the

[1] Lenin's wife, Nadézhda Konstantínova Krúpskaya.
[2] Lenin's full name was Vladímir Ilyích Ulyanov.

24

sixteenth century. They could have got a better room for the money: there was a sausage factory opposite their windows, and the stench was so overwhelming that they opened them only late at night and spent most of their time in the library. But Vladímir Ilyích would never consent to leave after he had heard his landlady declare that "the soldiers ought to turn their weapons against their governments." They often had only oatmeal for lunch, and when it got scorched, Lenin would say to the landlady: "We live in grand style, you see. We have roasts every day."

The years, as Valdímir had written his sister, had told pretty severely on their nerves. It had been hard, after 1905, to settle down to exile again, and that had been twelve years ago. Their comrades[3] had been cracking up even worse than after the arrests of the nineties. One of them went to pieces in Lenin's house and had delusions about seeing his sister, who had been hanged. Another had caught tuberculosis during a sentence in a penal regiment; they sent him to Davos, but he died. Another, a survivor of the Moscow insurrection, came to see them one day and "began talking excitedly and incoherently about chariots filled with sheaves of corn and beautiful girls standing in the chariots." Vladímir stayed with him while Nádya got a psychiatrist, who said the man was going crazy from starvation. Later, he tied stones to his feet and neck and drowned himself in the Seine. Another, a factory worker in Russia, who, due to his political activities, found it difficult to keep a job and was unable to support his wife and children, broke down and became an *agent provocateur*.[4] He took to drink, and one evening drove his family out of the house, stuffed up the chimney, lit the stove, and in the morning was found dead. Now they were plagued by a new kind of spies: not the old race of obvious dicks[5] who used to stand on the street-corners and wait for them and whom they could easily dodge, but plausible and exalted young men, who talked themselves into posts in the party.

They had gone to see the Lafargues in Paris, and Krúpskaya, a little excited at meeting the daughter of Marx, had babbled something rather inarticulately about the part that women were playing in the revolutionary movement; the conversation had lagged. Lenin had talked to Lafargue about the book, *Materialism and Empirio-Criticism*, that he was writing against the Marxist mystics, and Lafargue agreed about the hollowness of religion. Laura had glanced at her husband and said: "He will soon prove the sincerity of his convictions." Lenin had been deeply moved when he had heard of their double suicide. "If one cannot work for the Party any longer," he had said to Krúpskaya at the time, "one must be able to look truth in the face and die the way the Lafargues did."

Elizavéta Vasílevna, his mother-in-law, used to say to people: "He'll kill both Nadyú-sha and himself with that life." She herself died in 1915. She had wanted that last year to go to Russia, but there was no one to look after her there, and just before her death she said to Nádya, "I'll wait till I can go with you two." She had worked hard for the comrades as they came and went, had sewed "armor" into skirts and waistcoats in which illegal literature was to be carried and composed endless bogus letters that were to have messages written between the lines. Vladímir used to buy her presents in order to make her life a little more cheerful; once when she had failed to lay in cigarettes for a holiday, had ransacked the town to find her some. She had always regarded herself as a believer, and would not talk to them about

---

[3] Bolsheviks.

[4] A secret agent who acts to provoke suspected persons to acts that will make them liable to prosecution.

[5] Detectives.

sacred subjects; but had said suddenly, just before her death: "I used to be religious when I was young, but as I lived on and learned about life, I saw that it was all nonsense." And she asked to be cremated after her death. She died after an outing on a warm day of March, when she and Nádya had sat out for half an hour on a bench in the Berne forest.

Krúpskaya herself became ill after her mother's death. It was a recrudescence of an ailment that had first appeared in 1913. Something had gone wrong with her heart then; her hands had begun to tremble. The doctor had said that she had a weak heart and that her nerves were giving way. The cobbler's wife, who did their shopping—they were in Cracow now—was indignant: "Who said you were nervous—big ladies are nervous and throw the dishes around!" But she found that she couldn't work, and Vladímir took her to the mountains. It turned out that she had exophthalmic goiter. It had been always a slightly sore point with Nádya that people thought she looked like a fish. She complains in one of her early letters that Vladímir's sister Anna had said she had the look of a herring, and her conspiratorial names had been "Lamprey" and "Fish"; I once heard her described as "an old codfish" by a lady who had visited her in the Kremlin. Now the goiter, by swelling her neck and causing her eyes to protrude, intensified this effect. Vladímir had her operated on in Berne: the operation turned out to be difficult: they were working over her three hours without giving her an anesthetic—to the usual effect on Lenin that was produced by the presence of suffering. Lenin's letters through all this period show the strain of Nádya's illness.

One day in the middle of March when they had just finished eating dinner and Nádya had done the dishes and Ilyích was about to go to the library, a Polish comrade came bursting in, saying: "Haven't you heard the news? There's been a revolution in Russia!"

This time the defeats of the World War were carrying the tide across the barriers that had curbed it in 1905. The coal mines and factories of Poland had been lost with the Russian defeats; and half the production of the country was being expended on the fighting forces. On January 22, the anniversary of Father Gapón's demonstration, there had been a strike of a hundred and fifty thousand in Petrograd; and on March 8 a new general strike had begun: the workers poured into the streets. Now the army, full of peasant conscripts, could no longer be mobilized against them. Even the Cossacks, even the Semyónovsky Regiment, which had put down the Moscow insurrection, came over to the side of the rebels. The people were disgusted with the war, and they had completely lost confidence in the Tsar; the royal family, under the dominion of Raspútin[6] were secretly trying to make peace with the Germans: the big landlords and the bourgeoisie, who had an interest in continuing the war, were also eager to get rid of the autocracy. The Tsar himself had gone to General Headquarters in order to get away from the trouble; and when he attempted to return to Petrograd, the railroad workers held up his train. The whole machinery of the monarchy had stopped: the Tsar was forced to send his abdication by telegram, and a few days later was put under arrest. He had tried to dissolve the Fourth Duma,[7] as he had done with its predecessors, but this time they refused to disband,

[6] Grigori Efimovich (1871–1916), a peasant monk who exercised an extraordinary power over the court of Czar Nicholas II and Czarina Alexandra.
[7] Russian Parliament.

and formed a Provisional Committee, which appointed a Provisional Government. A Workers' Soviet, with an Executive Committee that included both Mensheviks and Bolsheviks, sprang to life from its paralyzation of 1905, like one of the victims of Koshchéy, the deathless enchanter of the Russian folk-tale, who was finally slain by the breaking of an egg: and the Committee decided to bring in the army and make it a Soviet of Workers' and Soldiers' Deputies.

Lenin had to depend on foreign newspapers; but through their blurred and biased despatches he managed to grasp the fundamental factors. In the few articles he wrote for *Právda,* which was now being published again, before he was able to return to Russia, he laid down the general assumptions on which he was afterwards to act. The power hung between the two bodies, Provisional Government and Petrograd Soviet—which represented two groupings of interests, irreconcilable with one another. The Soviet was the spokesman of the people, who wanted peace, bread, liberty, land. The Provisional Government, whatever it might say, was recruited from a bourgeoisie whose tendencies toward liberalism were limited to the desire to get rid of the Romanovs:[8] the Minister of War and Marine was Guchkóv, a big Moscow industrialist and real-estate owner; the Minister of Foreign Affairs was Milyukóv, a former professor of History and the founder of the Kadet Party—the principal leader of the Russian bourgeoisie; and the Minister of Justice was a young lawyer only a shade further to the left than the Kadets. This last was the son of old Kerénsky, the director of the *gimnáziya* at Simbírsk, who had given Vladímir Ulyánov a good character after the execution of his brother and had guaranteed that his mother would keep him out of trouble. Kerénsky[9] the younger had grown up to be a highly successful orator of the emotional and ornamental kind, badly spoiled by the ladies of Petrograd and cherishing an almost mystical conviction that he had been chosen for some illustrious role.

This government, Lenin said, could never give the people what they wanted. It could not give them peace, because it depended on the subsidy of France and England and was committed to carrying on their war; it had never yet said a word about repudiating the imperialistic policy of annexing Armenia, Galicia and Turkey and capturing Constantinople. It could not give them bread, because the only way to give them bread would be by violating the sanctities of both capital and landlordship, and the bourgeoisie by definition were bound to protect the principle of property. It would not give them freedom, because it was the government of those landlords and capitalists who had always shown themselves afraid of the people. The only potential allies of the Soviet were, first, the small peasants and the other impoverished groups in Russia, and second, the proletariat of the other warring nations.

The revolution was only as yet in its first and transitory phase, and it would still have to wrest the power away from the bourgeoisie. The workers, the peasants and the soldiers must organize all over Russia under the leadership of the Petrograd Soviet. They must do away with the old police and establish a "people's militia"; and this militia must take upon itself to distribute such food as there was, seeing to it "that every child should have a bottle of good milk and that no adult of a rich family should dare to take extra milk till the children had all been supplied," and "that the palaces and luxurious homes left by the Tsar and the aristocracy should not stand idle but should provide shelter for the homeless and destitute." The Soviet,

---

[8] Russian royal family.

[9] A moderate leader of the Socialist party who became head of the Provisional Government.

once it was dominant, must declare itself not responsible for treaties concluded by the monarchy or by any bourgeois government, and it must publish all secret treaties; it must propose an immediate armistice to all the nations; it must insist on the liberation of all colonies and dependent peoples; it must propose to the workers of all countries that they overthrow their bourgeois governments and transfer power to workers' Soviet; it must declare that the billion-dollar debts contracted by the bourgeois governments for the purpose of carrying on the war should be paid by the capitalists themselves: for the workers and peasants to pay interest on these debts "would mean paying tribute to the capitalists over a period of many, many years for having generously permitted the workers to kill one another over the division of spoils by the capitalists."— And now we must answer the objections of Kautsky, who writing on the Russian situation, warns us that "two things are absolutely necessary to the proletariat: democracy and socialism." But precisely what does this mean? Milyukóv would say he wanted democracy; Kerénsky would say he wanted socialism—

But here the fifth letter breaks off. Lenin is on his way to Russia and will not now be obliged to finish it.—The first days he had lain awake nights trying to work out ways to get back. The French and British would not give him a passport for the same reason that the British were to take Trotsky[10] off his ship at Halifax—though Plekhánov and other nationalist socialists were to be sent home in a British ironclad with a guard of torpedo-boats. The truth was that Milyukóv himself had telegraphed the Russian consuls not to repatriate the internationalist socialists. Lenin thought seriously about going in an airplane, but in the morning he knew he couldn't manage it. Then he decided he would have to get a false passport—if possible, a Swedish one, because a Swede would be least suspect. Unfortunately he knew no Swedish, and he wondered whether he could get enough up to pass himself off at the frontier; then concluded he ought not to take chances, ought not to try to speak at all; and wrote to a comrade in Sweden asking him to find two Swedish deaf mutes who looked like Zinóvyev and him. "You'll fall asleep," Krúpskaya told him," and see Mensheviks in your dreams, and you'll start swearing and shouting 'Scoundrels, scoundrels!' and give the whole plot away."

On March 19 there was a meeting of exiles to discuss getting back to Russia. Mártov had worked up a plan for persuading the German government to let them return through Germany in exchange for German and Austrian prisoners. Lenin leaped at the idea, which hadn't occurred to him; but nobody else wanted to risk it. Mártov himself got cold feet, and it was Lenin who put the scheme through. Appeals to the Swiss government came to nothing, and telegrams to Russia got no answers: the patriots of the Provisional Government did not want the internationalists back, and the socialist themselves were in doubt. "What torture it is for us all," Lenin wrote to the comrade in Stockholm, "to be sitting here at such a time!" He was sitting himself in his low-ceilinged room writing his *Letters from Afar*. At last Lenin wired the comrade in Sweden to send somebody to Chkheídze, the Menshevik who was President of the Petrograd Soviet, to appeal to him on the ground that it was his duty to get the stranded Mensheviks back. Other pressure was brought to bear, and permission was finally wired in the form, "Ulyánov must come immediately." It was arranged with the German ambassador in Switzerland that a party was to be sent through Germany: the Germans were hoping that Lenin would further disorganize

---

[10] Leon Trotsky (1877–1940) was, along with Lenin, one of the leading figures of the Russian Revolution.

the Russian government. It was agreed that while they were passing through Germany, nobody should leave the train or communicate with anyone outside, and that nobody should be allowed to enter without the permission of the Swiss socialist who accompanied them. The German government insisted that Lenin should receive a representative of the trade unions. Lenin told them that if any boarded the train, he would refuse to have anything to do with him.

When Lenin got the news that they could go, he insisted on their taking the next train, which left in a couple of hours. Krúpskaya didn't think she could get packed, settle her accounts with the landlady and take the books back to the library in time, and suggested that she might follow later. But Vladímir insisted she must come with him. They left a lot of their things in a box in the event that they might have to return. Their landlord, who has written an account of their tenancy, had never paid any special attention to them. When Frau Lenin had first come about the room, his wife had not wanted to take her: "You could see that she was the Russian type," and "she wore a dress that was a little bit short"; but when Lenin appeared himself, he made a better impression. They could see that he had strength in his chest: "My God," their son used to say, "he's got a neck like a bull!" For the rest, they were punctual about paying, and Herr Lenin got along well with his wife. "I think the two of them never quarreled. With Frau Lenin it was easy to get along. She was allowed to cook in our kitchen with my wife. We had agreed to let her do that. The two women always got along well together, which is something at wonder at, if one considers that the kitchen was a narrow intestine of a room, and that they had to squeeze by each other to pass. Frau Lenin would have made a good Hausfrau,[11] but she always had her mind on other work." When Frau Lenin mentioned to Frau Kammerer that she wanted to get to Russia, Frau Kammerer exexpressed concern about her going into "that insecure country at such an uncertain time." "You see, Frau Kammerer," Frau Lenin said, "that's where I have work to do. Here I have nothing to do." Her husband said to Herr Kammerer just before he left: "So, Herr Kammerer, now there's going to be peace."

In the train that left the morning of April 8 there were thirty Russian exiles, including not a single Menshevik. They were accompanied by the Swiss socialist Platten, who made himself responsible for the trip, and the Polish socialist Radek. Some of the best of the comrades had been horrified by the indiscretion of Lenin in resorting to the aid of the Germans and making the trip through an enemy country. They came to the station and besieged the travelers, begging them not to go. Lenin got into the train without replying a word. In the carriage he found a comrade, who had been suspected of being a stool-pigeon. "The man had made a little too sure of his seat. Suddenly we saw Lenin seize him by the collar and in an incomparably matter-of-fact manner pitch him out on to the platform."

The Germans overpowered them with meals of a size to which they were far from accustomed, in order to demonstrate to the Russians the abundance of food in Germany. Lenin and Krúpskaya, who had never up to now been in any of the belligerent countries during this later period of the War, were surprised, as they passed through Germany, at the absence of adult men: at the stations, in the fields and the city streets, there were only a few women and children, and boys and girls in their teens. Lenin believed they would be arrested as soon as they arrived in Russia, and

[11] Housewife.

he discussed with his comrades a speech of defense which he was preparing on the way. But on the whole he kept much to himself. At Stuttgart, the trade union man got on with a cavalry captain and sat down in a special compartment. He sent his compliments to the Russians through Platten, in the name of the liberation of peoples, and requested an interview. Platten answered that they did not want to talk to him and could not return his greeting. The only person who spoke to the Germans was the four-year-old son of one of the Russians, who stuck his head into the compartment and said in French: "What does the conductor do?"

On the way to Stockholm, Lenin declared that the Central Committee of the Party must positively have an office in Sweden. When they got in, they were met and feted by the Swedish socialist deputies. There was a red flag hung up in the waiting-room and a gigantic Swedish repast. Radek took Lenin to a shop and bought him a new pair of shoes, insisting that he was now a public man and must give some thought to the decency of his appearance; but Lenin drew the line at a new overcoat or extra underwear, declaring that he was not going to Russia to open a tailor's shop.

They crossed from Sweden to Finland in little Finnish sleighs. Platten and Radek were stopped at the Russian frontier. Lenin sent a telegram to his sisters, announcing that he was arriving Monday night at eleven. In Russianized Finland, Krúpskaya says, "everything was already familiar and dear to us: the wretched third-class cars, the Russian soldiers. It was terribly good." Here the soldiers were back in the streets again. The station platforms were crowded with soldiers. An elderly man picked the little boy up and fed him some Easter cheese. A comrade leaned out the window and shouted, "Long live the world revolution"; but the soldiers looked around at him puzzled. Lenin got hold of some copies of *Právda,* which Kámenev and Stalin were editing, and discovered that they were talking mildly of bringing pressure on the Provisional Government to make it open negotiations for peace, and loyally proclaiming that so long as the German army obeyed the Emperor, so long must the Russian soldier "firmly stand at his post, and answer bullet with bullet and shell with shell."

He was expressing himself on the subject when the train whistle blew and some soldiers came in. A lieutenant with a pale face walked back and forth past Lenin and Krúpskaya, and when they had gone to sit in a car that was almost empty, he came and sat down beside them. It turned out that he, too, believed in a war for defense. Lenin told him that they should stop the war altogether, and he, too, grew very pale. Other soldiers came into the car and they crowded around Lenin, some standing up on the benches. They were jammed so tight you could hardly move. "And as the minutes passed," says Krúpskaya, "they became more attentive, and their faces became more tense." He cross-examined them about their lives and about the general state of mind in the army: "How? what? why? what proportion?" reports a non-commissioned officer who was there.—Who were their commanders?—Mostly officers with revolutionary views.—Didn't they have a junior staff? didn't these take any part in the command? . . . Why was there so little promotion?—They didn't have the knowledge of operations, so they stuck to their old staff.—It would be better to promote the non-commissioned officers. The rank and file can trust its own people more than it can the white-handed ones.—He suggested that they ask the conductor to let them into a car with more space so that they could hold something in the nature of a meeting, and he talked to them about his "theses" all night.

Early in the morning, at Beloóstrov, a delegation of Bolsheviks got in, Kámenev and Stalin among them. The moment Lenin laid eyes on Kámenev, whom he had not seen in several years, he burst out: "What's this you're writing in *Právda?* We've just seen some numbers, and we gave it to you good and proper!" Lenin's younger sister María was also there, and a delegation of women workers. The women wanted Krúpskaya to say something, but she found that words had left her. There was a demand for Lenin to speak, and the train-crew, who knew nothing about their passenger except that he was somebody special, picked him up and carried him into the buffet and stood him on a table. A crowd slowly gathered around; then the conductor came up and told the trainmen that it was time to start on. Lenin cut short his speech. The train pulled out of the station. Lenin asked the comrades whether they thought that the group would be arrested as soon as they arrived in Petrograd. The Bolsheviks only smiled.

Two hundred years before, Giambattista Vico, at his books in a far corner of Europe the whole width of the continent away, in asserting that "the social world" was "certainly the work of man," had refrained from going further and declaring, as Grotius had done, that the social institutions of men could be explained in terms of man alone. Grotius, though one of Vico's masters, had been a Protestant and a heretic, and his great book had been put on the *Index,* so that Vico was afraid even to edit it. In the Catholic city of Naples, in the shadow of the Inquisition, Vico had to keep God in his system.[12]

At the end of the eighteenth century, Babeuf, who not only believed that human society had been made by man but who wanted to remake that society, had said in explaining his failure: "We have but to reflect for a moment on the multitude of passions in the ascendancy in this period of corruption we have come to, to convince ourselves that the chances against the possibility of realizing such a project are in the proportion of more than a hundred to one."

Lenin in 1917, with a remnant of Vico's God still disguised in the Dialectic, but with no fear of Roman Pope or Protestant Synod, not so sure of the controls of society as the engineer was of the engine that was taking him to Petrograd, yet in a position to calculate the chances with closer accuracy than a hundred to one, stood on the eve of the moment when for the first time in the human exploit the key of a philosophy of history was to fit an historical lock.

If the door that Lenin was to open did not give quite on the prospect he hoped, we must remember that of all the great Marxists he was least in love with prophetic visions, most readily readjusted his prospects. "Theoretical classification doesn't matter now," he had just written in *Letters from Afar,* apropos of whether the immediate measures he contemplated for feeding the Russian people should be regarded as constituting a "dictatorship of the proletariat" or a "revolutionary-democratic dictatorship of the proletariat and the poorest peasantry." . . . "It would be indeed a grave error if we tried now to fit the complex, urgent, rapidly-unfolding practical tasks of the revolution into the Procrustean bed of a narrowly conceived 'theory,' instead of regarding theory first of all and above all as a *guide to action.*"

We have watched the attempts of Michelet[13] to relive the recorded events of the past as a coherent artistic creation, and we have seen how the material of history always broke out of the pattern of art. Lenin is now to attempt to impose on the

---

[12] Vico (1668–1744) was an Italian historian who proposed the theory that history moves in cycles. Hugo Grotius (1583–1645), a Dutch jurist, began the study of international law. The *Index* is a list of prohibited books compiled by the Roman Catholic Church.

[13] Nineteenth-century French historian.

events of the present a pattern of actual direction which will determine the history of the future. We must not wonder if later events are not always amendable to this pattern. The point is that western man at this moment can be seen to have made some definite progress in mastering the greeds and the fears, the bewilderments, in which he has lived.

The terminal where the trains get in from Finland is today a little shabby stucco station, rubber-gray and tarnished pink, with a long trainshed held up by slim columns that branch where they meet the roof. On one side the trains come in; on the other are the doors to the waiting-rooms, the buffet and the baggage-room. It is a building of a size and design which in any more modern country of Europe would be considered appropriate to a provincial town rather than to the splendors of a capital; but, with its benches rubbed dull with waiting, its ticketed cakes and rolls in glass cases, it is the typical small station of Europe, the same with that sameness of all the useful institutions that have spread everywhere with middle-class enterprise. Today the peasant women with bundles and baskets and big handkerchiefs around their heads sit quietly on the benches.

But at the time of which I am writing there was a rest-room reserved for the Tsar, and there the comrades who met him took Lenin, when the train got in very late the night of April 16. On the platform he had been confronted by men come back from prison or exile, who greeted him with tears on their cheeks.

There is an account of Lenin's reception by N. Shukhánov, a nonparty socialist, who was present. He came walking into the Tsar's room at a speed that was almost running. His coat was unbuttoned; his face looked chilled; he was carrying a great bouquet of roses, with which he had just been presented. When he ran into the Menshevik, Chkeídze, the President of the Petrograd Soviet, he suddenly stopped in his tracks, as if he had come up against an unexpected obstacle. Chkheídze, without dropping the morose expression which he had been wearing while waiting for Lenin, addressed him in the sententious accents of the conventional welcoming speech. "Comrade Lenin," he said, "in the name of the Petrograd Soviet and of the whole revolution, we welcome you to Russia . . . *but* we consider that at the present time the principal task of the revolutionary democracy is to defend our revolution against every kind of attack, both from within and from without. . . . We hope that you will join us in striving toward this goal." Lenin stood there, says Sukhánov, "looking as if all this that was happening only a few feet away did not concern him in the least; he glanced from one side to the other; looked the surrounding public over, and even examined the ceiling of the 'Tsar's Room,' while rearranging his bouquet (which harmonized rather badly with his whole figure)." At last, turning away from the committee and not replying directly to the speech, he addressed the crowd beyond them: "Dear comrades, soldiers, sailors and workers, I am happy to greet in you the victorious Russian revolution, to greet you as the advance guard of the international proletarian army. . . . The war of imperialist brigandage is the beginning of civil war in Europe. . . . The hour is not far when, at the summons of our Comrade Karl Liebknecht, the people will turn their weapons against their capitalist exploiters. . . . In Germany, everything is already in ferment! Not today, but tomorrow, any day, may see the general collapse of European capitalism. The Russian revolution you have accomplished has dealt it the first blow and has opened a new epoch. . . . Long live the International Social Revolution!"

He left the room. On the platform outside, an officer came up and saluted. Lenin, surprised, returned the salute. The officer gave a command: a detachment of sailors with bayonets stood at attention. The place was being spotted by searchlights and bands were playing the *Marseillaise*. A great roar of a cheer went up from a crowd that was pressing all around. "What's this?" Lenin said, stepping back. They told him it was a welcome to Petrograd by the revolutionary workers and sailors: they had been roaring one word—"Lenin." The sailors presented arms, and their commander reported to Lenin for duty. It was whispered that they wanted him to speak. He walked a few paces and took off his bowler hat. "Comrade sailors," he said, "I greet you without knowing yet whether or not you have been believing in all the promises of the Provisional Government. But I am convinced that when they talk to you sweetly, when they promise you a lot, they are deceiving you and the whole Russian people. The people needs peace; the people needs bread; the people needs land. And they give you war, hunger, no bread—leave the landlords still on the land. . . . We must fight for the social revolution, fight to the end, till the complete victory of the proletariat. Long live the world social revolution!"

"How extraordinary it was!" says Sukhánov. "To us, who had been ceaselessly busy, who had been completely sunk in the ordinary vulgar work of the revolution, the current needs, the immediately urgent things that are inconspicuous 'in history,' " a sudden dazzling light seemed to flash. "Lenin's voice, issuing straight from the railway carriage, was a 'voice from the outside.' Upon us, in the midst of the revolution, broke—the truth, by no means dissonant, by no means violating its context, but a *new* and *brusque*, a somewhat stunning note." They were pulled up by the realization "that Lenin was undeniably right, not only in announcing to us that the world socialist revolution had begun, not only in pointing out the indissoluble connection between the world war and the collapse of the imperialist system, but in emphasizing and bringing to the fore the 'world revolution' itself, insisting that we must hold our course by it and evaluate in its light all the events of contemporary history." All this, they could now see, was unquestionable; but did he really understand, they wondered, how these ideas could be made practical use of in the politics of their own revolution? Did he really know the situation in Russia? Never mind for the present. The whole thing was very extraordinary!

The crowd carried Lenin on their shoulders to one of the armored cars that had been drawn up outside. The Provisional Government, who had done their best to bar the streets against the gathering throngs, had forbidden bringing out their cars, which could become formidable factors in a mass demonstration; but this had had no effect on the Bolsheviks. He had to make another speech, standing above the crowd on top of the car. The square in front of the station was jammed: there they were, the textile workers, the metal workers, the peasant soldiers and sailors. There was no electric light in the square, but the searchlights showed red banners with gold lettering.

The armored car started on, leading a procession from the station. The other cars dimmed their lights to bring out the brightness of Lenin's. In this light he could see the workers' guard stretching all along both sides of the road. "Those," says Krúpskaya, "who have not lived through the revolution cannot imagine its grand solemn beauty." The sailors had been the Kronstadt garrison; the searchlights were from the Peter-Paul Fortress. They were going to the Kshesíanskaya Palace, the house of the prima ballerina who had been the Tsar's mistress, which the Bolsheviks, in a gesture deliberately symbolic and much to the indignation of its inmate, had taken over for Party headquarters.

Inside it was all big mirrors, crystal candelabra, frescoed ceilings, satin upholstery, wide staircases and broad white cupboards. A good many of the bronze statues and marble cupids had been broken by the invaders; but the furniture of the ballerina had been carefully put away and replaced by plain chairs, tables and benches, set about, rather sparsely, where they were needed. Only a few Chinese vases, left stranded among the newspapers and manifestoes, were still getting in people's way. They wanted to give Lenin tea and to treat him to speeches of welcome, but he made them talk about tactics. The palace was surrounded by a crowd who were shouting for him to speak. He went out on a balcony to meet them. It was if all the stifled rebellion on which the great flat and heavy city had pressed with its pompous facades since the time of those artisans whom Peter the Great had sent to perish in building it in the swamp, had boiled up in a single night. And Lenin, who had talked only at party meetings, before audiences of Marxist students, who had hardly appeared in public in 1905, now spoke to them with a voice of authority that was to pick up all their undirected energy, to command their uncertain confidence, and to swell suddenly to a world-wide resonance.

Yet at first, as they heard him that night—says Sukhánov, who was standing outside—there were signs that they were shocked and frightened. As Lenin's hoarse accents crackled out over them, with his phrases about the "robber-capitalists . . . the destruction of the peoples of Europe for the profits of a gang of exploiters . . . what the defense of the fatherland means is the defense of the capitalists against everybody else"—as these phases broke over them like shells, the soldiers of the guard of honor itself muttered: "What's that? What's he saying? If he'd come down here, we'd show him!" They had, however, Sukhánov says, made no attempt to "show him" when he was talking to them face to face, and Sukhánov never heard of their doing so later.

He went in again, but had to return and make a second speech. When he came back, a meeting was called. In the great ballroom, the long speeches of welcome began to gush afresh. Trotsky says that Lenin endured their flood "like an impatient pedestrian in a doorway, waiting for the rain to stop." From time to time he glanced at his watch. When he spoke, he talked for two hours and filled his audience with turmoil and terror.

"On the journey here with my comrades," he said, "I was expecting that they would take us straight from the station to Peter and Paul.[14] We are far from that, it seems. But let us not give up the hope that we shall still not escape that experience." He swept aside agrarian reform and other legal measures proposed by the Soviet, and declared that the peasants themselves should organize and seize the land without the aid of governmental intervention. In the cities, the armed workers must take over the direction of the factories. He threw overboard the Soviet majority, and hauled the Bolsheviks themselves over the coals. The proletarian revolution was imminent: they must give no countenance to the Provisional Government. "We don't need any parliamentary republic. We don't need any bourgeois democracy. We don't need any government except the Soviet of Workers', Soldiers', and Peasants' Deputies!"

The speech, says Sukhánov, for all its "staggering content and its lucid and brilliant eloquence," conspicuously lacked "one thing: an analysis of the 'objective premises,'

---

[14] The name of a fortress, which was used as a prison.

of the social-economic foundations for socialism in Russia." But he goes on to say that he "came out on the street feeling as if I had been flogged over the head with a flail. Only one thing was clear: there was no way for me, a non-party man, to go along with Lenin. In delight I drank in the air, freshening now with spring. The morning had all but dawned, the day was already there." A young Bolshevik naval officer who took part in the meeting writes: "The words of Ilyích laid down a Rubicon[15] between the tactics of yesterday and today."

But most of the leaders were stunned. There was no discussion of the speech that night; but indignation was to break out the next day when Lenin discharged another broadside at a general meeting of the Social Democrats. "Lenin," declared one of the Bolsheviks, "has just now presented his candidacy for one throne in Europe which has been vacant thirty years: I mean, the throne of Bakúnin.[16] Lenin in new words is telling the same old story: it is the old discarded notions of primitive anarchism all over again. Lenin the Social Democrat, Lenin the Marxist, Lenin the leader of our militant Social Democracy—this Lenin is no more!" And the Left-Wing Bogdánov, who sat just under the platform, furiously scolded the audience: "You ought to be ashamed to applaud this nonsense—you cover yourselves with shame! And you call yourselves Marxists!"

The purpose of Lenin's speech had been to prevent a proposed amalgamation of Bolsheviks and Mensheviks; but at that moment it looked as if he was to have the effect of driving the Bolsheviks in the other direction. To many of the Bolsheviks themselves, it seemed, as it had done to his opponents after the rupture of 1903, that Lenin had simply succeeded in getting himself out on a limb.

The night of their arrival, Krúpskaya records, after the reception in the Kshesínsykaya Palace, she and Lenin "went home to our people, to Anna Ilyínishna and Mark Timoféyevich." María Ilyínishna was living with her brother-in-law and sister. Vladímir Ilyích and Nádya were given a separate room; and there they found that Anna's foster son had hung up over their beds the last words of the *Communist Manifesto:* "Workers of the World, Unite!"

Krúpskaya says she hardly spoke to Ilyích. "Everything was understood without words."

MEANING

1. What historical event is the subject of Wilson's narrative?
2. Why does Wilson show Lenin both as a private ordinary person and as an extraordinary historical figure? What is the effect of seeing Lenin first as a poor man with a sick wife and then as a leader cheered by the crowd?
3. To what extent does Wilson rely on records and eyewitness accounts for the actual facts of what happened?
4. What did you learn from Wilson's account about the procedures that historians use to report and interpret facts?

---

[15] The river Caesar crossed when entering Gaul; symbolically, a momentous step.
[16] A nineteenth-century Russian anarchist.

Using Narration to Convey Meaning

1. How does Wilson summarize background information to set the stage for the dramatic episode centering around Lenin?
2. To what extent does Wilson use parallelism to coordinate paragraphs that contain extensive summaries of complex information (e.g., articles Lenin wrote for *Právda*)?
3. How does Wilson use techniques normally used by writers of fiction—dialogue, anecdotes, dramatic contrast—to recreate the drama implicit in the historical event?

Writing Suggestions

1. Determine in what significant ways Wilson's account of this period in history resembles or differs from accounts given by either N. K. Krúpskaya (Lenin's wife) in *Memories of Lenin* or Boris Pasternak in *Doctor Zhivago*.
2. In your opinion, does Wilson believe that Lenin himself was the catalyst for the Russian Revolution or that the nature of the events themselves created the need for someone like Lenin to play a certain role? In short, does Wilson think that history makes men or that men make history?
3. People often remember where they were and what they were doing when a news story of national importance occurred. Tell about a time when you heard of such a significant event—assassination, hurricane, fire, political upheaval, war, and so on. Be sure to describe in detail your first reaction to the event and the discussions that you and your friends or family may have had about its significance.

POLITICAL AND SOCIAL SCIENCES

Arthur Koestler

Conversion

Arthur Koestler (1905–1983) was born in Budapest, Hungary, and attended the University of Vienna. Koestler was an editor of a Cairo weekly, a journalist covering the Mid-East and Paris, and a science editor for a German paper. He became a member of the Communist party in 1931. While serving as a war correspondent in Spain, he was captured by the Fascists, sentenced to death, and only released through the efforts of the British government. At the time of the Moscow "purge" trials in 1938, when many Bolshevik revolutionaries were tried and executed by the Soviet government, Koestler left the Communist party. These events were fictionalized in his novel, Darkness at Noon *(1940), which won him world recognition and was translated into more than thirty languages and produced as a Broadway play in 1951. "Conversion," from* The God That Failed *(1949), is Koestler's account of how the experiences of his childhood influenced him to accept the theories of Marx, Engels, and Lenin.*

A faith is not acquired by reasoning. One does not fall in love with a woman, or enter the womb of a church, as a result of logical persuasion. Reason may defend an act of faith—but only after the act has been committed, and the man committed to the act. Persuasion may play a part in a man's conversion; but only the part of bringing to its full and conscious climax a process which has been maturing in regions where no persuasion can penetrate. A faith is not acquired; it grows like a tree. Its crown points to the sky; its roots grow downward into the past and are nourished by the dark sap of the ancestral humus.

From the psychologist's point of view, there is little difference between a revolutionary and a traditionalist faith. All true faith is uncompromising, radical, purist; hence the true traditionalist is always a revolutionary zealot in conflict with pharisaian society, with the lukewarm corrupters of the creed. And vice versa: the revolutionary's Utopia, which in appearance represents a complete break with the past, is always modeled on some image of the lost Paradise, of a legendary Golden Age. The classless Communist society, according to Marx and Engels, was to be a revival, at the end of the dialectical spiral, of the primitive Communist society which stood at its beginning. Thus all true faith involves a revolt against the believer's social environment, and the projection into the future of an ideal derived from the remote past. All Utopias are fed from the sources of mythology; the social engineer's blueprints are merely revised editions of the ancient text.

Devotion to pure Utopia, and revolt against a polluted society, are thus the two poles which provide the tension of all militant creeds. To ask which of the two makes the current flow—attraction by the ideal or repulsion by the social environment—is to ask the old question about the hen and the egg. To the psychiatrist, both the craving for Utopia and the rebellion against the status quo are symptoms of social maladjustment. To the social reformer, both are symptoms of a healthy rational attitude. The psychiatrist is apt to forget that smooth adjustment to a deformed society creates deformed individuals. The reformer is equally apt to forget that hatred, even of the objectively hateful, does not produce that charity and justice on which a utopian society must be based.

Thus each of the two attitudes, the sociologist's and the psychologist's, reflects a half-truth. It is true that the case-history of most revolutionaries and reformers reveals a neurotic conflict with family or society. But this only proves, to paraphrase Marx, that a moribund society creates its own morbid gravediggers.

It is also true that in the face of revolting injustice the only honorable attitude is to revolt, and to leave introspection for better times. But if we survey history and compare the lofty aims, in the name of which revolutions were started, and the sorry end to which they came, we see again and again how a polluted civilization pollutes its own revolutionary offspring.

Fitting the two half-truths—the sociologist's and the psychologist's—together, we conclude that if on the one hand oversensitivity to social injustice and obsessional craving for Utopia are signs of neurotic maladjustment, society may, on the other hand, reach a state of decay where the neurotic rebel causes more joy in heaven than the sane executive who orders pigs to be drowned under the eyes of starving men. This in fact was the state of our civilization when, in December, 1931, at the age of twenty-six, I joined the Communist Party of Germany.

I became converted because I was ripe for it and lived in a disintegrating society thirsting for faith. But the day when I was given my Party card was merely the climax of a development which had started long before I had read about the drowned pigs or heard the names of Marx and Lenin. Its roots reach back into childhood; and though each of us, comrades of the Pink Decade, had individual roots with different twists in them, we are products of, by and large, the same generation and cultural climate. It is this unity underlying diversity which makes me hope that my story is worth telling.

I was born in 1905 in Budapest; we lived there till 1919, when we moved to Vienna. Until the First World War we were comfortably off, a typical Continental middle-middle-class family: my father was the Hungarian representative of some old-established British and German textile manufacturers. In September, 1914, this form of existence, like so many others, came to an abrupt end; my father never found his feet again. He embarked on a number of ventures which became the more fantastic the more he lost self-confidence in a changed world. He opened a factory for radioactive soap; he backed several crank-inventions (everlasting electric bulbs, self-heating bed bricks and the like); and finally lost the remains of his capital in the Austrian inflation of the early 'twenties. I left home at twenty-one, and from that day became the only financial support of my parents.

At the age of nine, when our middle-class idyl collapsed, I had suddenly become conscious of the economic Facts of Life. As an only child, I continued to be pampered by my parents; but, well aware of the family crisis, and torn by pity for my father, who was of a generous and somewhat childlike disposition, I suffered a pang of guilt whenever they bought me books or toys. This continued later on, when every suit I bought for myself meant so much less to send home. Simultaneously, I developed a strong dislike of the obviously rich; not because they could afford to buy things (envy plays a much smaller part in social conflict than is generally assumed) but because they were able to do so without a guilty conscience. Thus I projected a personal predicament onto the structure of society at large.

It was certainly a tortuous way of acquiring a social conscience. But precisely because of the intimate nature of the conflict, the faith which grew out of it became an equally intimate part of my self. It did not, for some years, crystallize into a political creed; at first it took the form of a mawkishly sentimental attitude. Every contact with people poorer than myself was unbearable—the boy at school who had no gloves and red chilblains on his fingers, the former traveling salesman of my father's reduced to cadging occasional meals—all of them were additions to the load of guilt on my back. The analyst would have no difficulty in showing that the roots of this guilt-complex go deeper than the crisis in our household budget; but if he were to dig even deeper, piercing through the individual layers of the case, he would strike the archetypal pattern which has produced millions of particular variations on the same theme—"Woe, for they chant to the sound of harps and anoint themselves, but are not grieved for the affliction of the people."

Thus sensitized by a personal conflict, I was ripe for the shock of learning that wheat was burned, fruit artificially spoiled and pigs were drowned in the depression years to keep prices up and enable fat capitalists to chant to the sound of harps, while Europe trembled under the torn boots of hunger-marchers and my father hid his frayed cuffs under the table. The frayed cuffs and drowned pigs blended into one emotional explosion, as the fuse of the archetype was touched off. We sang the "Internationale," but the words might as well have been the older ones: "Woe to the shepherds who feed themselves, but feed not their flocks."

In other respects, too, the story is more typical than it seems. A considerable proportion of the middle classes in central Europe was, like ourselves, ruined by the inflation of the 'twenties. It was the beginning of Europe's decline. This disintegration of the middle strata of society started the fatal process of polarization which continues to this day. The pauperized bourgeois became rebels of the Right or Left: Schickelgrüber and Djugashwili shared about equally the benefits of the social migration. Those who refused to admit that they had become déclassé, who clung to the empty shell of gentility, joined the Nazis and found comfort in blaming their fate on Versailles and the Jews. Many did not even have that consolation; they lived on pointlessly, like a great black swarm of tired winterflies crawling over the dim windows of Europe, members of a class displaced by history.

The other half turned Left, thus confirming the prophecy of the "Communist Manifesto":

> Entire sections of the ruling classes are . . . precipitated into the proletariat, or are at least threatened in their conditions of existence. They . . . supply the proletariat with fresh elements of enlightenment and progress.

That "fresh element of enlightenment," I discovered to my delight, was I. As long as I had been nearly starving, I had regarded myself as a temporarily displaced offspring of the bourgeoisie. In 1931, when at last I had achieved a comfortable income, I found that it was time to join the ranks of the proletariat. But the irony of this sequence only occurred to me in retrospect.

> The bourgeois family will vanish as a matter of course with the vanishing of Capital. . . . The bourgeois claptrap about the family and education, about the haloed correlation of parent and child, becomes all the more disgusting the more, by the action of modern industry, all family ties among the proletarians are torn asunder. . . .

Thus the "Communist Manifesto." Every page of Marx, and even more of Engels, brought a new revelation, and an intellectual delight which I had only experienced once before, at my first contact with Freud. Torn from its context, the above passage sounds ridiculous; as part of a closed system which made social philosophy fall into a lucid and comprehensive pattern, the demonstration of the historical relativity of institutions and ideals—of family, class, patriotism, bourgeois morality, sexual taboos— had the intoxicating effect of a sudden liberation from the rusty chains with which a pre-1914 middle-class childhood had cluttered one's mind. Today, when Marxist philosophy has degenerated into a Byzantine cult and virtually every single tenet of the Marxist program has become twisted round into its opposite, it is difficult to recapture that mood of emotional fervor and intellectual bliss.

I was ripe to be converted, as a result of my personal case-history; thousands of other members of the intelligentsia and the middle classes of my generation were ripe for it, by virtue of other personal case-histories; but, however much these differed from case to case, they had a common denominator: the rapid disintegration of moral values, of the pre-1914 pattern of life in postwar Europe, and the simultaneous lure of the new revelation which had come from the East.

I joined the Party (which to this day remains "the" Party for all of us who once belonged to it) in 1931, at the beginning of that short-lived period of optimism, of that abortive spiritual renaissance, later known as the Pink Decade. The stars of that treacherous dawn were Barbusse, Romain Rolland, Gide and Malraux in France; Piscator, Becher, Renn, Brecht, Eisler, Säghers in Germany; Auden, Isherwood, Spender in England; Dos Passos, Upton Sinclair, Steinbeck in the United States. (Of course, not all of them were members of the Communist Party.) The cultural atmosphere was saturated with Progressive Writers' congresses, experimental theaters, committees for peace and against Fascism, societies for cultural relations with the USSR, Russian films and avant-garde magazines. It looked indeed as if the Western world, convulsed by the aftermath of war, scourged by inflation, depression, unemployment and the absence of a faith to live for, was at last going to

> Clear from the head the masses of impressive rubbish;
> Rally the lost and trembling forces of the will.
> Gather them up and let them loose upon the earth.
> Till they construct at last a human justice.
>
> Auden

The new star of Bethlehem had risen in the East; and for a modest sum, Intourist was prepared to allow you a short and well-focused glimpse of the Promised Land.

I lived at that time in Berlin. For the last five years, I had been working for the Ullstein chain of newspapers—first as a foreign correspondent in Palestine and the Middle East, then in Paris. Finally, in 1930, I joined the editorial staff in the Berlin "House." For a better understanding of what follows, a few words have to be said about the House of Ullstein, symbol of the Weimar Republic.

Ullstein's was a kind of super-trust; the largest organization of its kind in Europe, and probably in the world. They published four daily papers in Berlin alone, among these the venerable *Vossische Zeitung,* founded in the eighteenth century, and the *B. Z. am Mittag,* an evening paper with a record circulation and a record speed in getting the news out. Apart from these, Ullstein's published more than a dozen weekly and monthly periodicals, ran their own news service, their own travel agency, etc., and were one of the leading book publishers. The firm was owned by the brothers Ullstein—they were five, like the original Rothschild brothers, and like them also, they were Jews. Their policy was liberal and democratic, and in cultural matters progressive to the point of avant-gardism. They were antimilitaristic, antichauvinistic, and it was largely due to their influence on public opinion that the policy of Franco-German rapprochement of the Briand-Stresemann era became a vogue among the progressive part of the German people. The firm of Ullstein was not only a political power in Germany; it was at the same time the embodiment of everything progressive and cosmopolitan in the Weimar Republic. The atmosphere in the "House" in the Kochstrasse was more that of a Ministry than of an editorial office.

My transfer from the Paris office to the Berlin house was due to an article I wrote on the occasion of the award of the Nobel Prize for Physics to the Prince de Broglie. My bosses decided that I had a knack for popularizing science (I had been a student of science in Vienna) and offered me the job of Science Editor of the *Vossische* and adviser on matters scientific to the rest of the Ullstein publications. I arrived in Berlin on the fateful day of September 14, 1930—the day of the Reichstag Election in which the National Socialist Party, in one mighty leap, increased the number of its deputies from 4 to 107. The Communists had also registered important gains; the democratic parties of the Center were crushed. It was the beginning of the end of Weimar; the situation was epitomized in the title of Knickerbocker's best-seller: *Germany,—Fascist or Soviet?* Obviously there was no "third alternative."

I did my job, writing about electrons, chromosomes, rocket-ships, Neanderthal men, spiral nebulae and the universe at large; but the pressure of events increased rapidly. With one-third of its wage-earners unemployed, Germany lived in a state of latent civil war, and if one wasn't prepared to be swept along as a passive victim by the approaching hurricane it became imperative to take sides. Stresemann's party was dead. The Socialists pursued a policy of opportunist compromise. Even by a process of pure elimination, the Communists, with the mighty Soviet Union behind them, seemed the only force capable of resisting the onrush of the primitive horde with its swastika totem. But it was not by a process of elimination that I became a communist. Tired of electrons and wave-mechanics, I began for the first time to read Marx, Engels, and Lenin in earnest. By the time I had finished with *Feuerbach* and *State and Revolution,* something had clicked in my brain which shook me like a mental explosion. To say that one had "seen the light" is a poor description of the mental rapture which only the convert knows (regardless of what faith he has been converted to). The new light seems to pour from all directions across the skull; the whole universe falls into pattern like the stray pieces of a jigsaw puzzle assembled by magic at one stroke. There is now an answer to every question, doubts and conflicts are a matter of the tortured past—a past already remote, when one had lived in dismal ignorance in the tasteless, colorless world of those who *don't know*. Nothing henceforth can disturb the convert's inner peace and serenity—except the occasional fear of losing faith again, losing thereby what alone makes life worth living, and falling back into the outer darkness, where there is wailing and gnashing of teeth. This may explain how Communists, with eyes to see and brains to think with, can still act in subjective *bona fides,* anno Domini 1949. At all times and in all creeds only a minority has been capable of courting excommunication and committing emotional harakiri in the name of an abstract truth.

MEANING

1. How did Koestler's impoverished childhood set the stage for his later conversion to communism?
2. What situation described by Koestler would be conducive to totally different interpretations by a psychiatrist and a social reformer?
3. How does Koestler's own experiences illustrate his belief that social reformers project "a personal predicament onto the structure of society at large"?
4. What connection does Koestler draw between his early efforts to salvage his family's fortune and his later convictions about saving the proletarians?
5. How does "Conversion" illustrate how writers discover their real motivations through the process of writing about earlier events in their lives?

USING NARRATION TO CONVEY MEANING

1. What clues does Koestler provide that foreshadow his eventual renunciation of communism?
2. How does Koestler let the reader share his feelings and reactions to a period in his life that changed him in a significant way?

WRITING SUGGESTIONS

1. As a research project, investigate and discuss the historical antagonism that existed between the Nazis and the communists during the period about which Koestler is writing.
2. Write a short essay based on your interpretation of Koestler's observation that the "reformer is equally apt to forget that hatred, even of the objectively hateful, does not produce that charity and justice on which a utopian society must be based."
3. Write about an experience in your own background that has remained mysterious to you and attempt to gain insight into your motivations through the process of autobiographical narrative.

HENRY ALLEN

The Corps

Henry Allen, born in 1941, served in the Marine Corp and is currently a reporter and writer for The Washington Post. *He is the author of the novel* Fool's Mercy (1982). *"The Corps," originally written in 1971, recounts the grueling experiences of Marine boot camp and sketches in vivid detail the drill instructors who invoke and exploit "primal dread." Allen's report emerged as the distilled core of his experiences as a reporter and a former Marine from over two hundred pages written over seventeen days.*

PARRIS ISLAND, S.C.—He is seething, he is rabid, he is wound up tight as a golf ball, with more adrenalin surging through his hypothalamus than a cornered slum rat, he is everything these Marine recruits with their heads shaved to dirty nubs have ever feared or even hoped a drill instructor might be.

He is Staff Sgt. Douglas Berry and he is rushing down the squad bay of Receiving Barracks to leap onto a table and brace at parade rest in which none of the recruits, daring glances from the position of attention, can see any more of him under the rake of his campaign hat than his lipless mouth chopping at them like a disaster teletype: WHEN I GIVE YOU THE WORD YOU WILL WALK YOU WILL NOT RUN DOWN THESE STEPS WHERE YOU WILL RUN YOU WILL NOT WALK TO THE YELLOW FOOTMARKS. . . .

Outside, Berry's two junior drill instructors, in raincoats over dress greens, sweat in a muggy February drizzle which shrinks the view down to this wooden World War II barracks, to the galvanized Butler hut across the company street, the overground steam pipes, a couple of palmetto trees, the raindrops beading on spitshined black shoes.

Sgt. Hudson mans the steps, Sgt. Burley the footmarks. They pace with a mannered strut, like men wearing white tie and tails, their hands folded behind their backs, their jaw muscles flexing. One senses there's none of the wisecracking "See Here, Private Hargrove," or "Sgt. Bilko" Army routine here, no hotshot recruits outsmarting dumb sarge for passes to town.

In fact, during his 63 days of training at Parris Island, unless a member of his immediate family dies, a recruit will get no liberty at all. He will also get no talking, no phone calls, no books or magazines, no television, radio or record players, no candy or gum, one movie, one newspaper a week, and three cigarettes a day. Unless he fouls up, gets sent to the brig or to motivation platoon, and loses the cigarettes.

WHEN I GIVE YOU THE WORD TO MOVE OUT YOU WILL MOVE OUT DO YOU UNDERSTAND ME?

Hudson meets the first one at the steps like a rotary mower ripping into a toad, so psyched he's actually dancing on tiptoe, with his face a choleric three-quarters of an inch from the private FASTER PRIVATE FASTER JUST TAKE YOUR DUMB TIME SWEETHEART MOVE! MOVE! as this hog, as recruits are colloquially known, piles out of the barracks in a stumble of new boots, poncho, laundry bag and the worst trouble his young ass has ever been in, no doubt about it when Burley meets him just like Hudson, in an astonishment of rage that roars him all the way down to the right front set of yellow footprints YOU LOCK YOUR BODY AT ATTENTION YOU LOCK YOUR BODY. . . .

Or maybe Burley writhes up around this private to hiss in his ear—and Burley is very good at this—*you hate me, don't you, you hate me, private, you'd better hate me because I hate you,* or any of the other litanies drill instructors have been barking and hissing at their charges ever since the first of more than one million Parris Island graduates arrived on this flea-ridden sand barren in 1911.

Until there are 60 of them out there in the drizzle with the drill instructors shouting themselves hoarse, 60 volunteers who had heard from countless older brothers and street corner buddies and roommates that it would be exactly like this but they volunteered anyhow, to be Marines.

Right now, with lips trembling, eyes shuttling YOU BETTER STOP THAT EYE-BALLING, PRIVATE! fat and forlorn, they look like 60 sex perverts trapped by a lynch mob. They are scared. They are scared as fraternity pledges during a cleverly staged hell week, shaking like boys about to abandon their virginity.

It's a primal dread that drill instructors invoke and exploit in eight weeks (soon to revert to the pre-Vietnam 11 weeks) of folk theater, a spectacle staged on the scale of the Passion Play at Oberammergau, an initiation that may be the only true rite of passage to manhood that America hasn't yet scoured away as an anthropological anachronism.

Fifteen minutes after that first recruit panicked out of receiving barracks, Berry, Burley and Hudson have stampeded all of them into their new squad bay. While 1st Lt. Roger McElrath lectures them on the vast variety of crimes and punishments on display in the Uniform Code of Military Justice, the D.I.s are hidden in a room called the drill instructor's house, changing their uniforms. Squared-away drill instructors change uniforms up to six times a day. It is no more possible for a drill instructor to appear sweatstained, soiled or wrinkled than a Vatican priest.

"Goddam, goddam, goddam," Hudson is saying, over and over. Fresh sweat blisters his brow. All of them are flushed and breathing hard, swearing and fumbling for cigarettes like a roller derby team at half time.

"They look good," Berry says. He's baby-faced, actually, earnest with a flair of cynicism, like a professional athlete. "We got 15 brothers (blacks). They'll pick up drill right away. The others can get the rhythm off them. Not too many fatbodies, not too many belligerents. This'll be a good platoon."

The problem for D.I.s picking up platoons isn't exhaustion, though, or even getting psyched to that glitter of madness, but "getting too psyched up, so psyched up you might grab a kid to straighten him out and BAM, that's it, it's your stripes," says Gunnery Sgt. Ronald Burns, a drill field veteran who now meets the late night buses hauling recruits in from the Charleston and Savannah airports.

Brutality to the Marines is like usury to Jews—a nightmare that threatens their very existence. It is also the leading figment of the Marine mystique and the stock brag of any Parris Island graduate. It is a legend like that of the "Old Corps," which always seems to have ended about three years ago. In the Old Corps, Marines tell each other, there was none of this Standard Operating Procedure (SOP) for recruit training, none of these maltreatment questionnaires and "swoop teams" of inspectors to hamstring the drill instructors.

Nothing to keep a D.I. from working over recruits during nightly "thump call," from slamming the whole platoon into "Chinese thinking position," an excruciating calisthenic in which you prop yourself solely on elbows and toes, and not to be confused with other outlawed old favorites such as six-point kneeling, steam engines, dry shaving, blanket parties, smoking under a blanket, the game of Flood and Air Raid, ethnic taunts, profanity, and allowing a recruit to eat all two pounds of the divinity fudge his girlfriend mailed him, eat it in three minutes flat, lover boy, every goddam crumb.

All outlawed now and outlawed too back in 1956, when rumors of Trumans' plans to merge the Corps into the Army still haunted Marines, and Staff Sgt. Matthew McKeon made every front page in America by leading an unauthorized night march into Ribbon Creek, out behind the rifle range, and six recruits drowned in a mass panic.

Since then, enforcement of the SOP has been screwed down tighter every year at both Parris Island and San Diego, a more recent recruit training base that trains enlistees from the western half of the country.

The SOP orders drill instructors to instill "instant obedience to orders." It also forbids them on pain of court-martial from touching a recruit, except to adjust a military position.

It prescribes 63 days of training which will include: 89 hours on firing the M-14 rifle, 60 hours of drill, 57 hours of physical training (PT), 23 hours of inspections and testing, 12 hours on clothing and equipment, 10 hours on history of the Marine Corps, and 114 hours of "commander's time," to include one hour each night of "free time" for writing and reading letters and doing anything else that does not involve talking, smoking, eating or leaving the squad bay. There are also endless hours of rifle cleaning, shoe shining, and singing of the Marine Corps hymn:

From the halls of Montezuma
To the shores of Tripoli . . .

"Parris Island is a game. If you can play by the rules, you do very well," says Lt. Scott Shaffer, a Navy psychologist (the Marines get medical and religious services from the Navy) who interviews a daily parade of bedwetters, attempted suicides, weepers, catatonics and others suspected mentally unfit for the Marine Corps.

"It's very behaviorally oriented, like a big Skinner box. You do well, you get rewarded. You do badly and you're punished. Positive and negative reinforcement. Personally, I'd like to see more positive reinforcement (reward)."

This doesn't explain, though, why anybody joins in the first place, especially in an age of beer machines in Navy barracks, and Army boot camps that promise you don't have to lose your dignity to get your training.

"They join because they want their girl to be proud of them, or their parents, or the gang on the block. Or they want to be proud of themselves. They want to be somebody, want to be able to go home a big, bad-ass Marine," says Gunnery Sgt. Mike "Big Mac" McCormick, who is all of that at 6-feet-4½ and 212 pounds, with five years on Parris Island drilling recruits and training drill instructors. "That's the best lever you've got on that recruit—pride. Next comes fear."

But neither pride, fear nor game theory can explain to anyone who has been through Parris Island why he endured those long, dusty, staggering exhaustions of runs, or the standing at attention in chow lines, thumbs locked to trouser seams while sand fleas put on a flying circus in his ears.

Or the incessant, insane, "Catch-22" paradoxes—a recruit pumping out jumping jacks, sweating his T-shirt translucent while his D.I. yells "DO YOU WANT TO DO MORE?" and the private, of course, answers "NO, SIR," until he realizes the correct answer is "YES, SIR," and the drill instructor tells him to stop doing any more, of course.

Given the fact that there are choices, such as the Air Force, which at least offers job-skill training, it would seem the only reason any human being puts up with Marine boot camp is that he wants to—a horrendous thought, if you're an enlightened believer in the basic rationality and pleasure drives of modern, educated man.

Think about it: drill instructors might as well be Pueblo shamans scaring candidates for tribal membership and manhood with nothing but masks and chants. (That wry ferocity drill instructors cultivate, the squinted eyes and the mouth about as generous as a snapping turtle's, and the jutjawed arrogance of their back-of-the-throat voices.)

And recruits, swaddled in their new uniforms and shorn of hair, are no more civilized, perhaps, than Australian aborigine boys who are circumcised and wrapped in blankets to be purified and symbolically reborn.

In *Man and His Symbols,* Joseph Henderson, a disciple of Carl Jung, states that the archetypal initiation that has pervaded all primitive cultures involves submission (enlistment), symbolic death by ordeal (degradation and physical demands far beyond what the recruit believes possible), and symbolic rebirth as a member of the collective consciousness (the Marine Corps).

It all fits, even the fact that the lessons taught at Parris Island involve stress or ceremony but few combat skills, except "instant obedience." The Marines leave the grenade throwing and small unit tactics and camouflage to Camp Lejeune, in North Carolina, where, for the first time, recruits are greeted as "Marine." Rifle firing is strictly on a formal bull's-eye target range, in the official National Rifle Association positions.

In fact, drill instructors may gain their extraordinary power from invoking all the archetypal terrors of initiation while never actually threatening the life of the recruit— a threat that would break the bond of trust between recruit and D.I., a bond so strong after only a few weeks that some drill instructors have been able to thump hell out of recruits with no fear they'll turn him in.

Like a score of fellow recruits Pvt. John Hedrick, 19, of Lynchburg, Va., answers only "Yessir my drill instructors treat me well, Nossir, there's no maltreatment, Yessir, I'd enlist again if I had it to do over."

Of course, there is bound to be some falling away from the faith, apostasies that drill instructors watch for with those quick glares, stalking up and down a row of recruits in a mess hall, say, making sure the hogs or ladies or maggots are popping those heels and squaring those corners.

The drill instructors watch because once a recruit sees the whole ritual is just a magic show, he loses both his fear of the D.I., and his motivation. And motivation is what Parris Island is all about. It not only makes you a Marine, not only makes you like it, but also makes you believe in it.

("The worst thumping I ever got was when the D.I. called the retreat from the Chosin reservoir an 'advance to the rear,' and I snickered," says Mike Jerace, who went through Parris Island in 1963.)

So secret doubters who stop shouting those yessirs at peak bellow, who stop trembling and panting like a dog in a thunderstorm to crank out one more pull-up, are apt to spend one to 10 days at motivation platoon: Last year, 3,384 of 28,153 Parris Island initiates did time at motivation platoon, and 557 were later discharged from the Marines "for reasons of defective attitude," said Capt. John Woggon, who directs Special Training Branch. (Which, besides motivating recruits who aren't putting out 100 percent, also takes a pound a day off "fatbodies," reconditions hospital discharges, and punishes legal offenders in its Correctional Custody Platoon.)

Motivation platoon is a ferocious speed-up of the carrot-and-stick routine, starting with eight to 20 maddening, grueling miles of speed march broken only by patriotic lectures and movies about epic Marine heroisms at Tarawa, Iwo Jima, Khe Sanh . . . Then fighting with padded "pugil sticks" between recruits who may never have been in a fight in their lives. And finally, lining up sweating and gritty, muscles shrill with fatigue, for The Ditch.

What happens to most recruits in eight weeks happens to most of motivation platoon in 30 minutes in The Ditch. The Ditch is Parris Island's last-chance purgatory, 480 meters of sand, mud, barbed wire and corrugated storm pipe all half-flooded with tidewater that these recruits will crawl through on their knees and bellies with metal rifle frames YOU WILL JUMP INTO THIS FIRST WATER OBSTACLE YOU WILL COMPLETELY IMMERSE YOURSELF YOU WILL THEN CRAWL ON YOUR KNEES DOWN THAT DITCH YELLING MARINE CORPS WITH EVERY BREATH YOU BREATHE. . . .

Baptism in a waist-deep mud puddle and the crawl begins. Shaved heads stream mud and water, mouths yaw wide as anatomy displays gasping MARINE CORPS, MARINE CORPS as they grind their way down that ditch like nothing so much as Mexican *penitentes* struggling on their knees for miles to win salvation at the Shrine of Our Lady, the ultimate prostration, the last plea . . .

Under the frantic frustration of the barbed wire, through the drainpipes that deliver them into a mock-up of an Indochinese village where they form up shivering and chanting MARINE CORPS while Staff Sgt. Sam Michaux pounds time with his boot. Then Michaux delivers the last speech before the penitents are sent back filthy and exhausted to their platoons.

"This is the world, sweeties, and your drill instructor wants to help you BUT BY GOD YOU BETTER HELP YOURSELVES because when the going gets rough, you can't say anymore I'M GONNA TAKE MY LITTLE RED WAGON AND GO HOME. The next time you think you can slack off you'd best remember that a HARD HEAD MAKES A SOFT ASS and yours is GONNA GET KICKED."

Meanwhile, Platoon 220, like another platoon yesterday, and another tomorrow, is just beginning its long initiation back in its barracks, or "barn," as the drill instructors call it, with its paint-flaked bunks lined up like stanchions, its bathroom of cement floors and naked squads of gleaming seatless toilets.

Cardboard placards advertise the Eleven General Orders like religious mottoes in the bare-bulb glare of this drizzly afternoon indoors. Decades of sweat and pivoting boots have worn the floors to a shine. Platoon 220's home is shabby but immaculate, like the tin-roof shack of a "good nigger," like Parris Island itself, in fact, a grim, mundane 3,300 habitable acres on which neatness and thrift are the only aesthetics, instant obedience the only ethic.

In the next eight weeks, Berry, Burley and Hudson will whipsaw these 60 recruits with reward and punishment. As former Marine commandant Gen. David M. Shoup once said, they will "receive, degrade, sanitize, immunize, clothe, equip, train, pain, scold, mold, sand and polish."

They will condition this stampede of adolescence until it understands a great paradox called military fear, a first law of survival that states the only thing you have to fear is not being scared enough to put up with the insult and hassle that are any military existence, with the chronic disaster of war.

Platoon 220 will discover the ease and convenience of this tautology just as they will discover that this fear, bleakness and degradation can yield a beauty they'll never be able to explain to anyone who hasn't gone through it and made it.

Eight weeks later, for instance, in the lambency of a Southern twilight in spring, Platoon 220 may fall out on the grinder for close order drill, which they'll be very good at by then, and they'll feel the cool flutter of their new tropical uniforms against their legs, and their rifles will flip from shoulder arms to port arms with one, crisp crash, and they'll lean back in a limber strut to the singsong of the D.I.'s cadence— a voice burnished by years of too much fatigue, coffee and cigarettes—the whole platoon floating across the quiet parade field like a ship at sea.

—March 5, 1972

MEANING

1. What changes in the recruits is Marine boot camp designed to produce?
2. What is the point of depriving the recruits of common items such as candy, gum, radios, and records?
3. Why does the fact that D.I.s can't be seen sweating widen the gap between recruits and D.I.s and make the recruits feel even worse?
4. What is the purpose of the Ditch? When do recruits encounter it and why is it so effective in changing their behavior?

USING NARRATION TO CONVEY MEANING

1. How is "The Corps" organized to answer the traditional questions in journalism of "who, what, where, when, and why"?
2. Evaluate the effectiveness of how Allen brings the reader into the story as someone who is being yelled at by the drill instructor.
3. How does Allen use dialogue to gain a sense of immediacy and realism?
4. What time markers such as "first" and "then" does Allen use to separate different stages of the recruits' training?
5. Locate and discuss effective figurative comparisons such as "fat and forlorn, they look like 60 sex perverts trapped by a lynch mob."

Writing Suggestions

1. How is the recruits' relationship to the drill instructors the same as the football players' relationship to their coaches as described by John McMurtry (see the "Analogy" chapter, page 427)?

2. What connections does this experience have with rituals of tribal initiation into manhood described by Benedict (see the "Comparison and Contrast" chapter, page 246)?

3. What features of "operant conditioning" described by B. F. Skinner are at work in molding the recruits into Marines? What might Thomas Szasz say about the success of this method (see the "Argument and Persuasion" chapter, page 726)?

4. Describe a situation where you were tested to your limits both physically and mentally. What character traits enabled you to meet the challenge?

TADEUSZ BOROWSKI

This Way for the Gas, Ladies and Gentlemen

Tadeusz Borowski (1922–1951) was born in the Soviet Ukraine of Polish parents and was educated by attending secret lectures at Warsaw University during the Nazi occupation of Poland. He published his first volume of verse, Whenever the Earth, *in 1942. The following year he was arrested by the Gestapo and ultimately sent to Auschwitz, where he survived by working as a hospital orderly. After the war, Borowski returned to Warsaw, where he lectured at the University. In 1946, the first of three collections based on his concentration camp experiences were published in Munich.* Farewell to Maria *and* A World of Stone *were published in Poland in 1948. The experience of his own dehumanization in the brutalizing conditions of Auschwitz formed the basis for his most significant work on the Holocaust, ironically titled, "This Way for the Gas, Ladies and Gentlemen (1967)." Borowski's searing, unsentimental portrayal of life in the concentration camps is told from the viewpoint of Vorabeiter ("foreman") Tadeusz, a narrator with whom Borowski himself is identified. Tragically, Borowski, who had survived the gas chambers and was seen as the bright hope of Polish literature, took his own life in July of 1951 at the age of 29 by turning on the gas.*

All of us walk around naked. The delousing is finally over, and our striped suits are back from the tanks of Cyclone B solution, an efficient killer of lice in clothing and of men in gas chambers. Only the inmates in the blocks cut off from ours by the "Spanish goats[1]" still have nothing to wear. But all the same, all of us walk around naked: the heat is unbearable. The camp has been sealed off tight. Not a single prisoner, not one solitary louse, can sneak through the gate. The labour Kommandos have stopped working. All day, thousands of naked men shuffle up and down the roads, cluster around the squares, or lie against the walls and on top of the roofs. We have been sleeping on plain boards, since our mattresses and blankets are still being disinfected. From the rear blockhouses we have a view of the F.K.L.—*Frauen Konzentration Lager;* there too the delousing is in full swing. Twenty-eight thousand women have been stripped naked and driven out of the barracks. Now they swarm around the large yard between the blockhouses.

The heat rises, the hours are endless. We are without even our usual diversion: the wide roads leading to the crematoria are empty. For several days now, no new transports have come in. Part of "Canada"[2] has been liquidated and detailed to a

---

[1] Crossed wooden beams wrapped in barbed wire.

[2] "Canada" designated wealth and well-being in the camp. More specifically, it referred to the members of the labour gang, or Kommando, who helped to unload the incoming transports of people destined for the gas chambers.

labour Kommando—one of the very toughest—at Harmenz. For there exists in the camp a special brand of justice based on envy: when the rich and mighty fall, their friends see to it that they fall to the very bottom. And Canada, our Canada, which smells not of maple forests but of French perfume, has amassed great fortunes in diamonds and currency from all over Europe.

Several of us sit on the top bunk, our legs dangling over the edge. We slice the neat loaves of crisp, crunchy bread. It is a bit coarse to the taste, the kind that stays fresh for days. Sent all the way from Warsaw—only a week ago my mother held this white loaf in her hands . . . dear Lord, dear Lord . . .

We unwrap the bacon, the onion, we open a can of evaporated milk. Henri, the fat Frenchman dreams aloud of the French wine brought by the transports from Strasbourg, Paris, Marseille . . . Sweat streams down his body.

"Listen, *mon ami,* next time we go up on the loading ramp, I'll bring you real champagne. You haven't tried it before, eh?"

"No. But you'll never be able to smuggle it through the gate, so stop teasing. Why not try and 'organize' some shoes for me instead—you know, the perforated kind, with a double sole, and what about that shirt you promised me long ago?"

"*Patience, patience.* When the new transports come, I'll bring all you want. We'll be going on the ramp again!"

"And what if there aren't any more 'cremo' transports?" I say spitefully. "Can't you see how much easier life is becoming around here: no limit on packages, no more beatings? You even write letters home . . . One hears all kind of talk, and, dammit, they'll run out of people!"

"Stop talking nonsense." Henri's serious fat face moves rhythmically, his mouth full of sardines. We have been friends for a long time, but I do not even know his last name. "Stop talking nonsense," he repeats, swallowing with effort. "They can't run out of people, or we'll starve to death in this blasted camp. All of us live on what they bring."

"All? We have our packages . . ."

"Sure, you and your friend, and ten other friends of yours. Some of you Poles get packages. But what about us, and the Jews, and the Russkis? And what if we had no food, no 'organization' from the transports, do you think you'd be eating those packages of yours in peace? We wouldn't let you!"

"You would, you'd starve to death like the Greeks. Around here, whoever has grub, has power."

"Anyway, you have enough, we have enough, so why argue?"

Right, why argue? They have enough. I have enough, we eat together and we sleep on the same bunks. Henri slices the bread, he makes a tomato salad. It tastes good with the commissary mustard.

Below us, naked, sweat-drenched men crowd the narrow barracks aisles or lie packed in eights and tens in the lower bunks. Their nude, withered bodies stink of sweat and excrement; their cheeks are hollow. Directly beneath me, in the bottom bunk, lies a rabbi. He has covered his head with a piece of rag torn off a blanket and reads from a Hebrew prayer book (there is no shortage of this type of literature at the camp), wailing loudly, monotonously.

"Can't somebody shut him up? He's been raving as if he'd caught God himself by the feet."

"I don't feel like moving. Let him rave. They'll take him to the oven that much sooner."

"Religion is the opium of the people," Henri, who is a Communist and a *rentier*, says sententiously. "If they didn't believe in God and eternal life, they'd have smashed the crematoria long ago."

"Why haven't you done it then?"

The question is rhetorical: the Frenchman ignores it.

"Idiot," he says simply, and stuffs a tomato in his mouth.

Just as we finish our snack, there is a sudden commotion at the door. The Muslims[3] scurry in fright to the safety of their bunks, a messenger runs into the Block Elder's shack. The Elder, his face solemn, steps out at once.

"Canada! *Antreten!* But fast! There's a transport coming!"

"Great God!" yells Henri, jumping off the bunk. He swallows the rest of his tomato, snatches his coat, screams *"Raus"* at the men below, and in a flash is at the door. We can hear a scramble in the other bunks. Canada is leaving for the ramp.

"Henri, the shoes!" I call after him.

"Keine Angst!" he shouts back already outside.

I proceeded to put away the food. I tie a piece of rope around the suitcase where the onions and the tomatoes from my father's garden in Warsaw mingle with Portuguese sardines, bacon from Lublin (that's from my brother), and authentic sweetmeats from Salonica. I tie it all up, pull on my trousers, and slide off the bunk.

"Platz!" I yell, pushing my way through the Greeks. They step aside. At the door I bump into Henri.

"Was ist los?"

"Want to come with us on the ramp?"

"Sure, why not?"

"Come along then, grab your coat! We're short of a few men. I've already told the Kapo," and he shoves me out of the barracks door.

We line up. Someone has marked down our numbers, someone up ahead yells, "March, march," and now we are running towards the gate, accompanied by the shouts of a multilingual throng that is already being pushed back to the barracks. Not everybody is lucky enough to be going on the ramp . . . We have almost reached the gate. *Links, zwei, drei, vier! Mutzen ab!* Erect, arms stretched stiffly along our hips, we march past the gate briskly, smartly, almost gracefully. A sleepy S.S. man with a large pad in his hand checks us off, waving us ahead in groups of five.

"Hundert!" he calls after we have all passed.

"Stimmt!" comes a hoarse answer from out front.

We march fast, almost as a run. There are guards all around, young men with automatics. We pass camp 11 B, then some deserted barracks and a clump of unfamiliar green—apple and pear trees. We cross the circle of watchtowers and, running, burst on to the highway. We have arrived. Just a few more yards. There, surrounded by trees, is the ramp.

A cheerful little station, very much like any other provincial railway stop: a small square framed by tall chestnuts and paved with yellow gravel. Not far off, beside the road, squats a tiny wooden shed, uglier and more flimsy than the ugliest and flimsiest railway shack; farther along lie stacks of old rails, heaps of wooden beams, barracks parts, bricks, paving stones. This is where they load freight for Birkenau: supplies

---

[3] "Muslim" was the camp name for a prisoner who had been destroyed physically and spiritually, and who had neither the strength nor the will to go on living—a man ripe for the gas chamber.

for the construction of the camp, and people for the gas chambers. Trucks drive around, load up lumber, cement, people—a regular daily routine.

And now the guards are being posted along the rails, across the beams, in the green shade of the Silesian chestnuts, to form a tight circle around the ramp. They wipe the sweat from their faces and sip out of their canteens. It is unbearably hot; the sun stands motionless at its zenith.

"Fall out!"

We sit down in the narrow streaks of shade along the stacked rails. The hungry Greeks (several of them managed to come along, God only knows how) rummage underneath the rails. One of them finds some pieces of mildewed bread, another a few half-rotten sardines. They eat.

"*Schweinedreck*," spits a young, tall guard with corn-coloured hair and dreamy blue eyes. "For God's sake, any minute you'll have so much food to stuff down your guts, you'll bust!" He adjusts his gun, wipes his face with a handkerchief.

"Hey you, fatso!" His boot lightly touches Henri's shoulder. "*Pass mal auf*, want a drink?"

"Sure, but I haven't got any marks," replies the Frenchman with a professional air.

"*Schade*, too bad."

"Come, come, Herr Posten, isn't my word good enough any more? Haven't we done business before? How much?"

"One hundred. *Gemacht?*"

"*Gemacht.*"

We drink the water, lukewarm and tasteless. It will be paid for by the people who have not yet arrived.

"Now you be careful." says Henri, turning to me. He tosses away the empty bottle. It strikes the rails and bursts into tiny fragments. "Don't take any money, they might be checking. Anyway, who the hell needs money? You've got enough to eat. Don't take suits either, or they'll think you're planning to escape. Just get a shirt, silk only, with a collar. And a vest. And if you find something to drink, don't bother calling me. I know how to shift for myself, but you watch your step or they'll let you have it."

"Do they beat you up here?"

"Naturally. You've got to have eyes in your ass. *Arschaugen.*"

Around us sit the Greeks, their jaws working greedily, like huge human insects. They munch on stale lumps of bread. They are restless, wondering what will happen next. The sight of the large beams and the stacks of rails has them worried. They dislike carrying heavy loads.

"*Was wir arbeiten?*" they ask.

"*Niks. Transport kommen, alles Krematorium. compris?*"

"*Alles verstehen,*" they answer in crematorium Esperanto. All is well—they will not have to move the heavy rails or carry the beams.

In the meantime, the ramp has become increasingly alive with activity, increasingly noisy. The crews are being divided into those who will open and unload the arriving cattle cars and those who will be posted by the wooden steps. They receive instructions on how to proceed most efficiently. Motor cycles drive up, delivering S.S. officers, bemedalled, glittering with brass, beefy men with highly polished boots and shiny, brutal faces. Some have brought their briefcases, others hold thin, flexible whips. This gives them an air of military readiness and agility. They walk in and out of the commissary—for the miserable little shack by the road serves as their commissary, where in the summertime they drink mineral water, *Studentenquelle*, and where in winter they can warm up with a glass of hot wine. They greet each other in the state-approved way, raising an arm Roman fashion, then shake hands cordially, exchanging warm smiles, discuss mail from home, their children, their families. Some stroll majestically on the ramp. The silver squares on their collars glitter, the gravel crunches under their boots, their bamboo whips snap impatiently.

We lie against the rails in the narrow streaks of shade, breathe unevenly, occasionally exchange a few words in our various tongues, and gaze listlessly at the majestic men in green uniforms, at the green trees, and at the church steeple of a distant village.

"The transport is coming," somebody says. We spring to our feet, all eyes turn in one direction. Around the bend, one after another, the cattle cars begin rolling in. The train backs into the station, a conductor leans out, waves his hand, blows a whistle. The locomotive whistles back with a shrieking noise, puffs, the train rolls slowly alongside the ramp. In the tiny barred windows appear pale, wilted, exhausted human faces, terror-stricken women with tangled hair, unshaven men. They gaze at the station in silence. And then, suddenly, there is a stir inside the cars and a pounding against the wooden boards.

"Water! Air!"—weary, desperate cries.

Heads push through the windows, mouths gasp frantically for air. They draw a few breaths, then disappear; others come in their place, then also disappear. The cries and moans grow louder.

A man in a green uniform covered with more glitter than any of the others jerks his head impatiently, his lips twist in annoyance. He inhales deeply, then with a rapid gesture throws his cigarette away and signals to the guard. The guard removes the automatic from his shoulder, aims, sends a series of shots along the train. All is quiet now. Meanwhile, the trucks have arrived, steps are being drawn up, and the Canada men stand ready at their posts by the train doors. The S.S. officer with the briefcase raises his hand.

"Whoever takes gold, or anything at all besides food, will be shot for stealing Reich property. Understand? *Verstanden?*"

"*Jawohl!*" we answer eagerly.

"*Also los!* Begin!"

The bolts crack, the doors fall open. A wave of fresh air rushes inside the train. People . . . inhumanly crammed, buried under incredible heaps of luggage, suitcases, trunks, packages, crates, bundles of every description (everything that had been their past and was to start their future). Monstrously squeezed together, they have fainted from heat, suffocated, crushed one another. Now they push towards the opened doors, breathing like fish cast out on the sand.

"Attention! Out, and take your luggage with you! Take out everything. Pile all your stuff near the exits. Yes, your coats too. It is summer. March to the left. Understand?"

"Sir, what's going to happen to us?" They jump from the train on to the gravel, anxious, worn-out.

"Where are you people from?"

"Sosnowiec-Bedzin. Sir, what's going to happen to us?" They repeat the question stubbornly, gazing into our tired eyes.

"I don't know, I don't understand Polish."

It is the camp law: people going to their death must be deceived to the very end. This is the only permissible form of charity. The heat is tremendous. The sun hangs directly over our heads, the white, hot sky quivers, the air vibrates, an occasional breeze feels like a sizzling blast from a furnace. Our lips are parched, the mouth fills with the salty taste of blood, the body is weak and heavy from lying in the sun. Water!

A huge, multicoloured wave of people loaded down with luggage pours from the train like a blind, mad river trying to find a new bed. But before they have a chance to recover, before they can draw a breath of fresh air and look at the sky, bundles are snatched from their hands, coats ripped off their backs, their purses and umbrellas taken away.

"But please sir, it's for the sun. I cannot . . ."

"*Verboten!*" one of us barks through clenched teeth. There is an S.S. man standing behind your back, calm, efficient, watchful.

"*Meine herrschaften,* this way, ladies and gentlemen, try not to throw your things around, please. Show some goodwill," he says courteously, his restless hands playing with the slender whip.

"Of course, of course," they answer as they pass, and now they walk alongside the train somewhat more cheerfully. A woman reaches down quickly to pick up her handbag. The whip flies, the woman screams, stumbles, and falls under the feet of the surging crowd. Behind her, a child cries in a thin little voice "Mamele!"—a very small girl with tangled black curls.

The heaps grow. Suitcases, bundles, blankets, coats, handbags that open as they fall, spilling coins, gold, watches; mountains of bread pile up at the exits, heaps of marmalade, jams, masses of meat, sausages; sugar spills on the gravel. Trucks, loaded with people, start up with a deafening roar and drive off amidst the wailing and screaming of the women separated from their children, and the stupefied silence of the men left behind. They are the ones who had been ordered to step to the right— the healthy and the young who will go to the camp. In the end, they too will not escape death, but first they must work.

Trucks leave and return, without interruption, as on a monstrous conveyor belt. A Red Cross van drives back and forth, back and forth, incessantly: it transports the gas that will kill these people. The enormous cross on the hood, red as blood, seems to dissolve in the sun.

The Canada men at the trucks cannot stop for a single moment, even to catch their breath. They shove the people up the steps, pack them in tightly, sixty per truck, more or less. Near by stands a young, clean-shaven "gentleman," an S.S. officer with a notebook in his hand. For each departing truck he enters a mark; sixteen gone means one thousand people, more or less. The gentleman is calm, precise. No truck can leave without a signal from him, or a mark in his notebook: *Ordnung muss sein.* The marks swell into thousands, the thousands into whole transports, which afterwards we shall simply call "from Salonica," "from Strasbourg." "from Rotterdam." This one will be called "Sosnowiec-Bedzin." The new prisoners from Sosnowiec-Bedzin will receive serial numbers 131–2—thousand, of course, though afterwards we shall simply say 131–2, for short.

The transports swell into weeks, months, years. When the war is over, they will count up the marks in their notebooks—all four and a half million of them. The bloodiest battle of the war, the greatest victory of the strong, united Germany. *Ein Reich, ein Volk, ein Führer*—and four crematoria.

The train has been emptied. A thin, pock-marked S.S. man peers inside, shakes his head in disgust and motions to our group, pointing his finger at the door.

"*Rein.* Clean it up!"

We climb inside. In the corners amid human excrement and abandoned wrist-watches lie squashed, trampled infants, naked little monsters with enormous heads and bloated bellies. We carry them out like chickens, holding several in each hand.

"Don't take them to the trucks, pass them on to the women," says the S.S. man, lighting a cigarette. His cigarette lighter is not working properly; he examines it carefully.

"Take them, for God's sake!" I explode as the women run from me in horror, covering their eyes.

The name of God sound strangely pointless, since the women and the infants will go on the trucks, every one of them, without exception. We all know what this means, and we look at each other with hate and horror.

"What, you don't want to take them?" asks the pock-marked S.S. man with a note of surprise and reproach in his voice, and reaches for his revolver.

"You mustn't shoot, I'll carry them." A tall grey-haired woman takes the little corpses out of my hands and for an instant gazes straight into my eyes.

"My poor boy," she whispers and smiles at me. Then she walks away, staggering along the path. I lean against the side of the train. I am terribly tired. Someone pulls at my sleeve.

"*En avant,* to the rails, come on!"

I look up, but the face swims before my eyes, dissolves, huge and transparent, melts into the motionless trees and the sea of people . . . I blink rapidly: Henri.

"Listen, Henri, are we good people?"

"That's stupid. Why do you ask?"

"You see, my friend, you see, I don't know why, but I am furious, simply furious with these people—furious because I must be here because of them. I feel no pity. I am not sorry they're going to the gas chamber. Damn them all! I could throw myself at them, beat them with my fists. It must be pathological, I just can't understand . . ."

"Ah, on the contrary, it is natural, predictable, calculated. The ramp exhausts you, you rebel—and the easiest way to relieve your hate is to turn against someone weaker. Why, I'd even call it healthy. It's simple logic, *compris?*" He props himself up comfortably against the heap of rails. "Look at the Greeks, they know how to make the best of it! They stuff their bellies with anything they find. One of them has just devoured a full jar of marmalade."

"Pigs! Tomorrow half of them will die of the shits."

"Pigs! You've been hungry."

"Pigs! I repeat furiously. I close my eyes. The air is filled with ghastly cries, the earth trembles beneath me, I can feel sticky moisture on my eyelids. My throat is completely dry.

The morbid procession streams on and on—trucks growl like mad dogs. I shut my eyes tight, but I can still see corpses dragged from the train, trampled infants, cripples piled on top of the dead, wave after wave . . . freight cars roll in, the heaps of clothing, suitcases and bundles grow, people climb out, look at the sun, take a few breaths, beg for water, get into the trucks, drive away. And again freight cars roll in, again people . . . The scenes become confused in my mind—I am not sure if all of this is actually happening, or if I am dreaming. There is a humming inside my head. I feel that I must vomit.

Henri tugs at my arm.

"Don't sleep, we're off to load up the loot."

All the people are gone. In the distance, the last few trucks roll along the road in clouds of dust, the train has left, several S.S. officers promenade up and down the ramp. The silver glitters on their collars. Their boots shine, their red, beefy faces shine. Among them there is a woman—only now I realize she has been here all along—withered, flat-chested, bony, her thin, colourless hair pulled back and tied in a "Nordic" knot; her hands are in the pockets of her wide skirt. With a rat-like resolute smile glued on her thin lips she sniffs around the corners of the ramp. She detests feminine beauty with the hatred of a woman who is herself repulsive, and knows it. Yes, I have seen her many times before and I know her well: she is the commandant of the F.K.L. She has come to look over the new crop of women, for some of them, instead of going on the trucks, will go on foot—to the concentration camp. There our boys, the barbers from Zauna, will shave their heads and will have a good laugh at their "outside world" modesty.

We proceed to load the loot. We lift huge trunks, heave them on to the trucks. There they are arranged in stacks, packed tightly. Occasionally somebody slashes one open with a knife, for pleasure or in search of vodka and perfume. One of the crates falls open; suits, shirts, books drop out on the ground . . . I pick up a small, heavy package. I unwrap it—gold, about two handfuls, bracelets, rings, brooches, diamonds . . .

"*Gib hier,*" an S.S. man says calmly, holding up his briefcases already full of gold and colourful foreign currency. He locks the case, hands it to an officer, takes another, an empty one, and stands by the next truck, waiting. The gold will go to the Reich.

It is hot, terribly hot. Our throats are dry, each word hurts. Anything for a sip of water! Faster, faster, so that it is over, so that we may rest. At last we are done, all the trucks have gone. Now we swiftly clean up the remaining dirt: there must be "no trace left of the *Schweinerei.*" But just as the last truck disappears behind the trees and we walk, finally, to rest in the shade, a shrill whistle sounds around the bend. Slowly, terribly slowly, a train rolls in, the engine whistles back with a deafening shriek. Again weary, pale faces at the windows, flat as though cut out of paper, with huge, feverishly burning eyes. Already trucks are pulling up, already the composed gentleman with the notebook is at his post, and the S.S. men emerge from the commissary carrying briefcases for the gold and money. We unseal the train doors.

It is impossible to control oneself any longer. Brutally we tear suitcases from their hands, impatiently pull off their coats. Go on, go on, vanish! They go, they vanish. Men, women, children. Some of them know.

Here is a woman—she walks quickly, but tries to appear calm. A small child with a pink cherub's face runs after her and, unable to keep up, stretched out his little arms and cries: "Mama! Mama!"

"Pick up your child, woman!"

"It's not mine, sir, not mine!" she shouts hysterically and runs on, covering her face with her hands. She wants to hide, she wants to reach those who will not ride the trucks, those who will go on foot, those who will stay alive. She is young, healthy, good-looking, she wants to live.

But the child runs after her, wailing loudly: "Mama, mama, don't leave me."

"It's not mine, not mine, no!"

Andrei, a sailor from Sevastopol, grabs hold of her. His eyes are glassy from vodka and the heat. With one powerful blow he knocks her off her feet, then, as she falls, takes her by the hair and pulls her up again. His face twitches with rage.

"Ah, you bloody Jewess! So you're running from your own child! I'll show you, you whore." His huge hand chokes her, he lifts her in the air and heaves her on to the truck like a heavy sack of grain.

"Here! And take this with you, bitch!" and he throws the child at her feet.

"*Gut gemacht,* good work. That's the way to deal with degenerate mothers." says the S.S. man standing at the foot of the truck "*Gut, gut, Russki.*"

"Shut your mouth," growls Andrei through clenched teeth, and walks away. From under a pile of rags he pulls out a canteen, unscrews the cork, takes a few deep swallows, passes it to me. The strong vodka burns the throat. My head swims, my legs are shaky, again I feel like throwing up.

And suddenly, above the teeming crowd pushing forward like a river driven by an unseen power, a girl appears. She descends lightly from the train, hops on to the gravel, looks around inquiringly, as if somewhere surprised. Her soft, blonde hair has fallen on her shoulders in a torrent, she throws it back impatiently. With a natural gesture she runs her hands down her blouse, casually straightens her skirt. She stands like this for an instant, gazing at the crowd, then turns and with a gliding look examines our faces, as though searching for someone. Unknowingly, I continue to stare at her, until our eyes meet.

"Listen, tell me, where are they taking us?"

I look at her without saying a word. Here, standing before me, is a girl, a girl with enchanting blonde hair, with beautiful breasts, wearing a little cotton blouse, a girl with a wise, mature look in her eyes. Here she stands, gazing straight into my face, waiting. And over there is the gas chamber; communal death, disgusting and ugly. And over in the other direction is the concentration camp, the shaved head, the heavy Soviet trousers in sweltering heat, the sickening, stale odour of dirty, damp female bodies, the animal hunger, the inhuman labour, and later the same gas chamber, only an even more hideous, more terrible death . . .

Why did she bring it? I think to myself, noticing a lovely gold watch on her delicate wrist. They'll take it away from her anyway.

"Listen, tell me," she repeats.

I remain silent. Her lips tighten.

"I know," she says with a shade of proud contempt in her voice, tossing her head. She walks off resolutely in the direction of the trucks. Someone tries to stop her; she boldly pushes him aside and runs up the steps. In the distance I can only catch a glimpse of her blonde hair flying in the breeze.

I go back inside the train; I carry out dead infants; I unload luggage. I touch corpses, but I cannot overcome the mounting, uncontrollable terror. I try to escape from the corpses, but they are everywhere: lined up on the gravel on the cement edge of the ramp, inside the cattle cars. Babies, hideous naked women, men twisted by convulsions. I run off as far as I can go, but immediately a whip slashes across my back. Out of the corner of my eye I see an S.S. man, swearing profusely. I stagger forward and run, lose myself in the Canada group. Now, at last, I can once more rest against the stack of rails. The sun has leaned low over the horizon and illuminates the ramp with a reddish glow; the shadows of the trees have become elongated, ghostlike. In silence that settles over nature at this time of day, the human cries seem to rise all the way to the sky.

Only from this distance does one have a full view of the inferno on the teeming ramp. I see a pair of human beings who have fallen to the ground locked in a last desperate embrace. The man has dug his fingers into the woman's flesh and has caught her clothing with his teeth. She screams hysterically, swears, cries, until at last a large boot comes down over her throat and she is silent. They are pulled apart and dragged like cattle to the truck. I see four Canada men lugging a corpse: a huge, swollen female corpse. Cursing, dripping wet from the strain, they kick out of their way some stray children who have been running all over the ramp, howling like dogs. The men pick them up by the collars, heads, arms, and toss them inside the trucks, on top of the heaps. The four men have trouble lifting the fat corpse on to the car, they call others for help, and all together they hoist up the mound of meat. Big, swollen, puffed-up corpses are being collected from all over the ramp: on top of them are piled the invalids, the smothered, the sick, the unconscious. The heap seethes, howls, groans. The driver starts the motor, the truck begins rolling.

"Halt! Halt!" an S.S. man yells after them. "Stop, damn you!"

They are dragging to the truck an old man wearing tails and a band around his arm. His head knocks against the gravel and pavement; he moans and wails in an uninterrupted monotone: "*ich will mit dem Herrn Kommandanten sprechen*—I wish to speak with the commandant . . ." With senile stubbornness he keeps repeating these words all the way. Thrown on the truck, trampled by others, choked, he still wails: "*Ich will mit dem* . . ."

"Look here, old man!" a young S.S. man calls, laughing jovially. "In half an hour you'll be talking to the top commandant! Only don't forget to greet him with a *Heil Hitler!*"

Several other men are carrying a small girl with only one leg. They hold her by the arms and the one leg. Tears are running down her face and she whispers faintly: "Sir, it hurts, it hurts . . ." They throw her on the truck on top of the corpses. She will burn alive along with them.

The evening has come, cool and clear. The stars are out. We lie against the rails. It is incredibly quiet. Anaemic bulbs hang from the top of the high lamp-posts; beyond the circle of light stretches an impenetrable darkness. Just one step, and a man could vanish for ever. But the guards are watching, their automatics ready.

"Did you get the shoes?" asks Henri.

"No."

"Why?"

"My God, man, I am finished, absolutely finished!"

"So soon? After only two transports? Just look at me, I . . . since Christmas, at least a million people have passed through my hands. The worst of all are the transports from around Paris—one is always bumping into friends."

"And what do you say to them?"

"That first they will have a bath, and later we'll meet at the camp. What would you say?"

I do not answer. We drink coffee with vodka; somebody opens a tin of cocoa and mixes it with sugar. We scoop it up by the handful, the cocoa sticks to the lips. Again coffee, again vodka.

"Henri, what are we waiting for?"

"There'll be another transport."

"I'm not going to unload it! I can't take any more."

"So, it's got you down? Canada is nice, eh?" Henri grins indulgently and disappears into the darkness. In a moment he is back again.

"All right. Just sit quietly and don't let an S.S. man see you. I'll try to find you your shoes."

"Just leave me alone. Never mind the shoes." I want to sleep. It is very late.

Another whistle, another transport. Freight cars emerge out of the darkness, pass under the lamp-posts, and again vanish in the night. The ramp is small, but the circle of lights is smaller. The unloading will have to be done gradually. Somewhere the trucks are growling. They back up against the steps, black, ghostlike, their search-lights flash across the trees. *Wasser! Luft!* The same all over again, like a late showing of the same film: a volley of shots, the train falls silent. Only this time a little girl pushes herself halfway through the small windows and losing her balance, falls out on to the gravel. Stunned, she lies still for a moment, then stands up and begins walking around in a circle, faster and faster, waving her rigid arms in the air, breathing loudly and spasmodically, whining in a faint voice. Her mind has given way in the inferno inside the train. The whining is hard on the nerves: an S.S. man approaches calmly, his heavy book strikes between her shoulders. She falls. Holding her down with his foot, he draws his revolver, fires once, then again. She remains face down, kicking the gravel with her feet, until she stiffens. They proceed to unseal the train.

I am back on the ramp, standing by the doors. A warm, sickening smell gushes from inside. The mountain of people filling the car almost halfway up to the ceiling is motionless, horribly tangled, but still steaming.

"Ausladen" comes the command. An S.S. man steps out from the darkness. Across his chest hangs a portable searchlight. He throws a stream of light inside.

"Why are you standing about like sheep? Start unloading!" His whip flies and falls across our backs. I seize a corpse by the hand; the fingers close tightly around mine. I pull back with a shriek and stagger away. My heart pounds, jumps up to my throat. I can no longer control the nausea. Hunched under the train I begin to vomit. Then, like a drunk, I weave over to the stack of rails.

I lie against the cool, kind metal and dream about returning to the camp, about my bunk, on which there is no mattress, about sleep among comrades who are not going to the gas tonight. Suddenly I see the camp as a haven of peace. It is true, others may be dying, but one is somehow still alive, one has enough food, enough strength to work . . .

The lights on the ramp flicker with a spectral glow, the wave of people—feverish, agitated, stupefied people—flows on and on, endlessly. They think that now they will have to face a new life in the camp, and they prepare themselves emotionally for the hard struggle ahead. They do not know that in just a few moments they will die, that the gold, money, and diamonds which they have so prudently hidden in their clothing and on their bodies are now useless to them. Experienced professionals will probe into every recess of their flesh, will pull the gold from under the tongue and the diamonds from the uterus and the colon. They will rip out gold teeth. In lightly sealed crates they will ship them to Berlin.

The S.S. men's black figures move about, dignified, businesslike. The gentleman with the notebook puts down his final marks, rounds out the figures: fifteen thousand.

Many, very many, trucks have been driven to the crematoria today.

It is almost over. The dead are being cleared off the ramp and piled into the last truck. The Canada men weighed down under a load of bread, marmalade and sugar, and smelling of perfume and fresh linen, line up to go. For several days the entire camp will live off this transport. For several days the entire camp will talk about "Sosnowiec-Bedzin." "Sosnowiec-Bedzin" was a good, rich transport.

The stars are already beginning to pale as we walk back to the camp. The sky grows translucent and opens high above our heads—it is getting light.

Great columns of smoke rise from the crematoria and merge up above into a huge black river which very slowly floats across the sky over Birkenau and disappears beyond the forests in the direction of Trzebinia. The "Sosnowiec-Bedzin" transport is already burning.

We pass a heavily armed S.S. detachment on its way to change guard. The men march briskly, in step, shoulder to shoulder, one mass, one will. "*Und morgen die ganze Welt . . .*" they sing at the top of their lungs. "*Rechts ran!* To the right march!" snaps a command from up front. We move out of their way.

Meaning

1. What task is performed by Tadeusz's labor battalion within the camp? For their work, what rewards and privileges does Tadeusz's group receive?
2. Explain how the lack of concern regarding fellow prisoners was a way of shielding oneself from a terrible reality. For example, why was there so much joking in a situation where it would seem humor could not exist?
3. What does Tadeusz reveal about his inner torment regarding the kind of person he has become in order to survive?

Using Narration to Convey Meaning

1. What is the effect of Borowski maintaining a first-person point of view throughout his narrative?
2. How does Borowski use irony in his account of the SS officers conversing while prisoners are being unloaded from the trains?
3. How does the equation of humans and insects symbolize the reduced value of human beings in the camp?
4. How does the episode centering on the young girl with one leg dramatize the indifference of the labor battalion toward the masses of people who have been and will be killed?
5. How does Borowski through his account of the arrival and unloading of prisoners control the pacing of his narrative?

Writing Suggestions

1. Discuss what you learned about the phenomena of dehumanization from Borowski's narrative.

2. Describe other environments that degrade people psychologically and/or physically and produce an attitude of "every man for himself."
3. In light of this account, what might explain why Borowski, many years after he was released from the camp and on the verge of becoming Poland's greatest writer, committed suicide?

SCIENCES

John A. Parrish

Welcome to Vietnam

John A. Parrish was born in 1939, in Louisville, Kentucky, graduated from Yale University Medical School in 1965, and served in Vietnam, where he received the Vietnamese Cross of Gallantry with Gold. Parrish currently teaches at Harvard Medical School and practices on the staff of Massachusetts General Hospital. He has written several medical textbooks and has contributed poetry to Harper's, *as well as editorials and reviews for the* Boston Globe. *In "Welcome to Vietnam," drawn from* 12, 20 and 5: A Doctor's Year in Vietnam *(1972), Parrish tells of his initial experiences upon his arrival in Vietnam.*

We introduced ourselves and stated our home states and places of training. Any special training beyond internship was listed beneath our names on the blackboard. There were four doctors straight from internship, one anesthesiologist, one general surgeon, and two partially trained internists. The four without specialty training were immediately assigned to infantry battalions, three of which were out in the field on maneuvers. The remaining four of us were assigned to the hospital company in Phu Bai.

Captain Street walked with us to the hospital compound to show us our new place of work. He was in no hurry. He had spent his entire tour of duty in Phu Bai except when in Da Nang on business. He was going home in eighty more days, and anything that would take up a few hours, or even minutes, was welcome. We were his most recent time passers.

The hospital company was on the edge of the compound situated next to the airstrip. The location not only made it easy to receive casualties, but also placed the hospital directly adjacent to the prime target for enemy mortars or rockets. The airstrip was always an early target during any kind of enemy attack.

The building farthest from the airstrip was a single, wooden "hooch" with a large, mobile refrigeration unit attached to the rear of the building. Three layers of sandbags protected each side. The sign on the front read, "Graves Registration."

63

Street did not even slow down as we passed. "This is Graves," he said, as we walked by the front of the building. "This is the only part of the hospital company completely staffed by marines. From the field, the dead come directly here where they are washed down, identified, and put in the freezer until the next flight south. They are embalmed in Da Nang or Saigon before shipment back to the States. The marines who staff this place are 'grunts' (foot soldiers) who volunteer for this duty, usually because they are cowards. Some are being punished. Others may be mentally ill or may want to be embalmers someday. One a hot, busy day this place smells terrible." Street seemed disgusted not only with the marines who worked in Graves, but also with anybody who would be stupid or inconsiderate enough to get killed on a hot and busy day.

We passed two large portable units that looked like large inflated tubes. "These are the MUST (Medical Unit Self-Contained Transportable) units; one is used as a medical ward, and the other as a surgery ward. The smaller units are attached to the main building. They house our operating rooms. We have six O.R.'s and an X-ray unit. Helicopters land here on the edge of the airstrip, and the casualties go directly to the main casualty sorting area called triage."

As Captain Street was talking, a helicopter settled down beyond us. Several marines ran out from the main building to meet the craft. They were handed a stretcher with a wounded marine, and the helicopter was gone. The stretcher bearers ran past us carrying a big Negro kid. He was completely nude. His M16 hung over the stretcher handle, and his boots rode between his legs. He was so black that the mud on his skin was light by comparison. He was long and muscular, and his spidery fingers curled tightly around the sides of the bouncing litter. His whole body was glistening with sweat that reflected highlights of the bright morning sun. The sweat on his forehead did not drip. It remained like tiny drops of oil and glue fastened tightly to his skin.

His eyelids were forced widely apart, and his stare was straight ahead into nowhere, seeing nothing, having seen too much. He threw back his head, and his white teeth parted as if he were trying to speak, to curse, to cry. A spasm of intolerable pain wrenched the muscles of his face into a mask that hid a grinning skeleton beneath. His chest heaved rapidly. The muscles of his steel arms bulged as he grasped the muddy stretcher. A small hole in his rigid abdomen permitted a steady snake of red and brown to spill onto the litter. The fluids created red blacks and brown purples on the green canvas. His left knee was flexed, and his long, uncircumsized penis lay over on his right upper thigh. His left foot arched as his toes grasped for the litter.

As he passed by, he raised his head almost involuntarily. It seemed as if the contracting straps of his neck muscles would tear off his jaw should his head not rise. His neck veins swelled in protest. His mouth began to open, at first for air, but then as a silent plea for help. He extended his dirty hand directly toward me, and I turned to follow him into triage.

Captain Street had not noticed him go by. He was still talking about the compound— something about the marines putting the retaining wall in the wrong place. He was ready to show us triage.

It was a large, open room measuring fifteen by twenty meters. Reinforced on the outside with sandbags, the walls protected floor-to-ceiling shelves filled with bandages, first-aid gear, and bottles of intravenous fluids. An unprotected tin roof was supported by four-by-fours. At the time, there were six men lined up on stretchers supported at either end by two lightweight metal sawhorses. Several doctors and corpsmen were quickly, but unexcitedly, working over the wounded. Captain Street was still talking, but I couldn't listen any longer.

On the first stretcher lay a boy whom, earlier in the day, any coach would have wanted as a tackle or a defensive end. But now, as he lay on his back, his left thigh pointed skyward and ended in a red brown, meaty mass of twisted ligaments, jellylike muscle, blood clots, and long bony splinters. There was no knee, and parts of the lower leg hung loosely by skin strips and fascial strings. A tourniquet had been placed around his thigh, and a corpsman was cutting through the strips of tissue with shears to remove the unviable dangling calf. Lying separately on the stretcher was a boot from which the lower leg still protruded.

In the second position a sweating doctor was administering closed cardiac massage on a flaccid, pale, thin boy with multiple wounds. A second doctor was bag breathing the boy. The vigorous chest compression seemed to be producing only the audible cracking of ribs.

In position three was the boy who minutes earlier had been carried past us. He already had intravenous fluids running into his arm, and a bandage was in place over his abdomen. He was vigorously protesting efforts to turn him over in order to examine his back. Positions four and five were occupied by two nude bodies quietly awaiting treatment. Their wounds were not serious. The next few positions for litters were empty. Off in the corner (position ten) lay a young man with his head wrapped tightly in blood-soaked, white bandages. No part of his body moved except for the slow, unsteady respiratory efforts of his chest. He had an endotracheal tube emerging from his nose, and each respiration made a grunting snort. No one was paying any attention to this man—a hopelessly damaged brain was awaiting death.

Captain Street never looked directly at any of the casualties. He showed us the rest of the hospital compound and left us with the hospital commander, a general surgeon who proved to be an intolerable, immature, egotistical, Napoleonic SOB, and an excellent surgeon. I liked him from the very first.

"Welcome to Vietnam," he said.

MEANING

1. How does Parrish's narrative demonstrate that the meaning of an event often depends on point of view? What event is distressing to Parrish and only "business as usual" to Captain Street?
2. Who works in the Graves Registration? What does Captain Street's characterization of these soldiers reveal about Street himself?
3. Why did Parrish like the hospital commander and dislike Captain Street?
4. What specific factors made practicing medicine under these conditions so difficult?

USING NARRATION TO CONVEY MEANING

1. Why does Parrish describe the physical layout of the compound before telling us about the wounded soldier?

2. What episodes and events can you point to in this seemingly objective account that would explain why Parrish might not like Captain Street?
3. How does every conversation reported by Parrish tell us something significant about the speaker?

Writing Suggestions

1. What similarities can you find between Street's attitude—anything that makes his job easier is good and anything that interferes with it is bad—and the "survive-at-any-price" mentality of the labor battalion in Borowski's account (see page 52)?
2. How does this real-life account differ from other portrayals of field hospitals such as the one in the television program "M.A.S.H."?

JAMES HERRIOT

Rumenotomy on a Cow

James Herriot, the renowned Scottish veterinarian (1916–   ) whose books and television series have made his experiences known and appreciated by millions, was born James Alfred Wight. His engaging autobiographical depictions of his life as a country veterinarian in the Yorkshire farmlands include All Creatures Great and Small *(1972),* All Things Bright and Beautiful *(1974),* All Things Wise and Wonderful *(1977), and* The Lord God Made Them All *(1981). These stories affirm, with compassion and humor, the ups and downs of veterinary life and the relationships of the country people and their animals. "Rumenotomy on a Cow," from* All Creatures Great and Small, *offers an ironic and amusing portrait of a country lad's first experience with animal surgery.*

I have a vivid recollection of a summer evening when I had to carry out a rumenotomy on a cow. As a rule I was inclined to play for time when I suspected a foreign body—there were so many other conditions with similar symptoms that I was never in a hurry to make a hole in the animal's side. But this time diagnosis was easy; the sudden fall in milk yield, loss of cudding; grunting, and the rigid, sunken-eyed appearance of the cow. And to clinch it the farmer told me he had been repairing a hen house in the cow pasture—nailing up loose boards. I knew where one of the nails had gone.

The farm, right on the main street of the village, was a favourite meeting place for the local lads. As I laid out my instruments on a clean towel draped over a straw bale a row of grinning faces watched from above the half door of the box; not only watched but encourged me with ribald shouts. When I was about ready to start it occurred to me that an extra pair of hands would be helpful, and I turned to the door. "How would one of you lads like to be my assistant?" There was even more shouting for a minute or two, then the door was opened and a huge young man with a shock of red hair ambled into the box; he was a magnificent sight with his vast shoulders and the column of sunburned neck rising from the open shirt. It needed only the bright blue eyes and the ruddy, high-cheekboned face to remind me that the Norsemen had been around the Dales a thousand years ago. This was a Viking.

I had him roll up his sleeves and scrub his hands in a bucket of warm water and antiseptic while I infiltrated the cow's flank with local anaesthetic. When I gave him artery forceps and scissors to hold he pranced around, making stabbing motions at the cow and roaring with laughter.

"Maybe you'd like to do the job yourself?" I asked. The Viking squared his great shoulders. "Aye, I'll 'ave a go," and the heads above the door cheered lustily.

As I finally poised my Bard Parker scalpel with its new razor-sharp blade over the cow, the air was thick with earthy witticisms. I had decided that this time I really would make the bold incision recommended in the surgery books; it was about time I advanced beyond the stage of pecking nervously at the skin. "A veritable blow," was how one learned author had described it. Well, that was how it was going to be.

I touched the blade down on the clipped area of the flank and with a quick motion of the wrist laid open a ten-inch wound. I stood back for a few second admiring the clean-cut edges of the skin with only a few capillaries spurting on to the glistening, twitching abdominal muscles. At the same time I noticed that the laughter and shouting from the heads had been switched off and was replaced by an eerie silence broken only by a heavy, thudding sound from behind me.

"Forceps please," I said, extending my hand back. But nothing happened. I looked round; the top of the half door was bare—not a head in sight. There was only the Viking spreadeagled in the middle of the floor, arms and legs flung wide, chin pointing to the roof. The attitude was so theatrical that I thought he was still acting the fool, but a closer examination erased all doubts: the Viking was out cold. He must have gone straight over backwards like a stricken oak.

The farmer, a bent little man who couldn't have scaled much more than eight stones, had been steadying the cow's head. He looked at me with the faintest flicker of amusement in his eyes. "Looks like you and me for it, then, guvnor." He tied the halter to a ring on the wall, washing his hands methodically and took up his place at my side. Throughout the operation, he passed me my instruments, swabbed away the seeping blood and clipped the sutures, whistling tunelessly through his teeth in a bored manner; the only time he showed any real emotion was when I produced the offending nail from the depths of the reticulum. He raised his eyebrows slightly, said " 'ello, 'ello," then started whistling again.

We were too busy to do anything for the Viking. Halfway through, he sat up, shook himself a few times then got to his feet and strolled with elaborate nonchalance out of the box. The poor fellow seemed to be hoping that perhaps we had noticed nothing unusual.

Meaning

1. How does this episode illustrate Herriot's desire to be perceived as a skillful veterinarian by the local farmers?
2. What diagnostic clues made Herriot believe that the cow needed an operation called a *rumenotomy*?
3. Why does Herriot decide to perform the operation in the most dramatic way possible?
4. How does the appearance and manner of the "Viking" make his reaction to the rumenotomy all the more ironic?

Using Narration to Convey Meaning

1. How does Herriot's use of local dialect enhance his anecdote?
2. How does Herriot create suspense by his assistant's reaction to the rumenotomy?

3. How does Herriot shape the story to reveal his feelings and to give the reader insight into his experiences as a young veterinarian?

WRITING SUGGESTIONS

1. Tell about an experience you may have had bringing a pet to a veterinarian. What was the diagnosis that was made and what treatment was recommended?
2. Rewrite Herriot's narrative from the "Viking's" point of view emphasizing the contrast between what he expected to see and what he actually saw.

Douglas R. Hofstadter

Aria with Diverse Variations

Douglas R. Hofstadter was born in New York City in 1945. He received his Ph.D. from the University of Oregon in 1975, taught Computer Science at Indiana University until 1984, and currently holds the Walgreen Chair in Human Understanding at the University of Michigan. Professor Hofstadter's books include Godel, Escher, Bach: An Eternal Golden Braid (1979), *for which he was awarded the Pulitzer Prize and the American Book Award; and* Metamagical Themas: Questing for the Essence of Mind and Pattern (1985), *which evolved from columns he wrote for* Scientific American. *"Aria with Diverse Variations," a chapter from* Godel, Escher, Bach, *reflects Hofstadter's love of mathematical paradox and illuminates the important idea that all sufficiently complicated systems (whether in mathematics, the art of Escher, or the music of Bach) contain true, but unprovable statements. Each chapter in* Godel, Escher, Bach *begins with a lively dialogue (as in the following exchange between Achilles and the Tortoise as to whether "every even number can be represented as a sum of two odd primes"), which plays metaphorically with the ideas that the chapter explores.*

Achilles has been unable to sleep these past few nights. His friend the Tortoise has come over tonight, to keep him company during these annoying hours.

TORTOISE: I am so sorry to hear of the troubles that have been plaguing you, my dear Achilles. I hope my company will provide a welcome relief from all the unbearable stimulation which has kept you awake. Perhaps I will bore you sufficiently that you will at long last go to sleep. In that way, I will be of some service. *1*

ACHILLES: Oh, no, I am afraid that I have already had some of the world's finest bores try their hand at boring me to sleep—and all, sad to say, to no avail. So you will be no match for them. No, Mr. T, I invited you over hoping that perhaps you could entertain me with a little this or that, taken from number theory, so that I could at least while away these long hours in an agreeable fashion. You see, I have found that a little number theory does wonders for my troubled psyche. *2*

TORTOISE: How quaint an idea! You know, it reminds me, just a wee bit, of the story of poor Count Kaiserling. *3*

ACHILLES: Who was he? *4*

TORTOISE: Oh, he was a Count in Saxony in the eighteenth century—a Count of *5* no account, to tell the truth—but because of him—well, shall I tell you the story? It is quite entertaining.

ACHILLES: In that case, by all means, do!   6

TORTOISE: There was a time when the good Count was suffering from sleeplessness,   7
and it just so happened that a competent musician lived in the same town, and
so Count Kaiserling commissioned this musician to compose a set of variations
to be played by the Count's court harpsichordist for him during his sleepless
nights, to make the hours pass by more pleasantly.

ACHILLES: Was the local composer up to the challenge?   8

TORTOISE: I suppose so, for after they were done, the Count rewarded him most   9
lucratively—he presented him with a gold goblet containing one hundred Louis
d'or.

ACHILLES: You don't say! I wonder where he came upon such a goblet and all   10
those Louis d'or, in the first place.

TORTOISE: Perhaps he saw it in a museum, and took a fancy to it.   11

ACHILLES: Are you suggesting he absconded with it?   12

TORTOISE: Now, now. I wouldn't put it exactly that way, but . . . Those days,   13
Counts could get away with most anything. Anyway, it is clear that the Count
was most pleased with the music, for he was constantly entreating his harpsichordist—a mere lad of a fellow, name of Goldberg—to play one or another of
these thirty variations. Consequently (and somewhat ironically) the variations
became attached to the name of young Goldberg, rather than to the distinguished
Count's name.

ACHILLES: You mean, the composer was Bach, and these were the so-called "Goldberg   14
Variations"?

TORTOISE: Do I ever! Actually, the work was entitled *Aria with Diverse Variations*,   15
of which there are thirty. Do you know how Bach structured these thirty magnificent
variations?

ACHILLES: Do tell.   16

TORTOISE: All the pieces—except the final one—are based on a single theme, which   17
he called an "aria." Actually, what binds them all together is not a common
melody, but a common harmonic ground. The melodies may vary, but underneath,
there is a constant theme. Only in the last variation did Bach take liberties. It
is a sort of "post-ending ending." It contains extraneous musical ideas having
little to do with the original Theme—in fact, two German folk tunes. That
variation is called a "quodlibet."

ACHILLES: What else is unusual about the Goldberg Variations?   18

TORTOISE: Well, every third variation is a canon. First a canon in which the two   19
canonizing voices enter on the SAME note. Second, a canon in which one of the
canonizing voices enters ONE NOTE HIGHER than the first. Third, one voice enters
TWO notes higher than the other. And so on, until the final canon has entries
just exactly one ninth apart. Ten canons, all told. And—

ACHILLES: Wait a minute. Don't I recall reading somewhere or other about fourteen   20
recently discovered Goldberg canons . . ."

TORTOISE: Didn't that appear in the same journal where they recently reported the   21
discovery of fourteen previously unknown days in November?

ACHILLES: No, it's true. A fellow named Wolff—a musicologist—heard about a special   22
copy of the Goldberg Variations in Strasbourg. He went there to examine it,
and to his surprise, on the back page, as a sort of "post-ending ending," he

found these fourteen new canons, all based on the first eight notes of the theme of the Goldberg Variations. So now it is known that there are in reality forty-four Goldberg Variations, not thirty.

TORTOISE: That is, there are forty-four of them, unless some other musicologist discovers yet another batch of them in some unlikely spot. And although it seems improbable, it is still possible, even if unlikely, that still another batch will be discovered, and then another one, and on and on and on . . . Why, it might never stop! We may never know if or when we have the full complement of Goldberg Variations.

ACHILLES: That is a peculiar idea. Presumably, everybody thinks that this latest discovery was just a fluke, and that we now really do have all the Goldberg Variations. But just supposing that you are right, and some more turn up sometime, we shall start to expect this kind of thing. At that point, the name "Goldberg Variations" will start to shift slightly in meaning, to include not only the known ones, but also any others which might eventually turn up. Their number—call it 'g'—is certain to be finite, wouldn't you agree?—but merely knowing that g is finite isn't the same as knowing how big g is. Consequently, this information won't tell us when the last Goldberg Variation has been located.

TORTOISE: That is certainly true.

ACHILLES: Tell me—when was it that Bach wrote these celebrated variations?

TORTOISE: It all happened in the year 1742, when he was Cantor in Leipzig.

ACHILLES: 1742: Hmm . . . That number rings a bell.

TORTOISE: It ought to, for it happens to be a rather interesting number, being a sum of two odd primes: 1729 and 13.

ACHILLES: By thunder! What a curious fact! I wonder how often one runs across an even number with that property. Let's see . . .

$$
\begin{aligned}
6 &= 3 + 3 \\
8 &= 3 + 5 \\
10 &= 3 + 7 = 5 + 5 \\
12 &= 5 + 7 \\
14 &= 3 + 11 = 7 + 7 \\
16 &= 3 + 13 = 5 + 11 \\
18 &= 5 + 13 = 7 + 11 \\
20 &= 3 + 17 = 7 + 13 \\
22 &= 3 + 19 = 5 + 17 = 11 + 11 \\
24 &= 5 + 19 = 7 + 17 = 11 + 13 \\
26 &= 3 + 23 = 7 + 19 = 13 + 13 \\
28 &= 5 + 23 = 11 + 17 \\
30 &= 7 + 23 = 11 + 19 = 13 + 17
\end{aligned}
$$

Now what do you know—according to my little table here, it seems to be quite a common occurrence. Yet I don't discern any simple regularity in the table so far.

TORTOISE: Perhaps there is no regularity to be discerned.

ACHILLES: But of course there is! I am just not clever enough to spot it right off the bat.

TORTOISE: You seem quite convinced of it.

ACHILLES: There's no doubt in my mind. I wonder . . . Could it be that ALL even numbers (except 4) can be written as a sum of two odd primes?

TORTOISE: Hmm . . . That question rings a bell . . . Ah, I know why! You're not the first person to ask that question. Why, as a matter of fact, in the year 1742, a mathematical amateur put forth this very question in a—

ACHILLES: Did you say 1742? Excuse me for interrupting, but I just noticed that 1742 happens to be a rather interesting number, being a difference of two odd primes: 1747 and 5.

TORTOISE: By thunder! What a curious fact! I wonder how often one runs across an even number with that property.

ACHILLES: But please don't let me distract you from your story.

TORTOISE: Oh, yes—as I was saying, in 1742, a certain mathematical amateur, whose name escapes me momentarily, sent a letter to Euler, who at the time was at the court of King Frederick the Great in Potsdam, and—well, shall I tell you the story? It is not without charm.

ACHILLES: In that case, by all means do!

TORTOISE: Very well. In his letter, this dabbler in number theory propounded an unproved conjecture to the great Euler: "Every even number can be represented as a sum of two odd primes." Now what was that fellow's name?

ACHILLES: I vaguely recollect the story, from some number theory book or other. Wasn't the fellow named "Kupfergödel"?

TORTOISE: Hmm . . . No, that sounds too long.

ACHILLES: Could it have been "Silberescher"?

TORTOISE: No, that's not it, either. There's a name on the tip of my tongue— ah—ah—oh yes! It was "Goldbach"! Goldbach was the fellow.

ACHILLES: I knew it was something like that.

TORTOISE: Yes—your guesses helped jog my memory. It's quite odd, how one occasionally has to hunt around in one's memory as if for a book in a library without call numbers . . . But let us get back to 1742.

ACHILLES: Indeed, let's. I wanted to ask you; did Euler ever prove that this guess by Goldbach was right?

TORTOISE: Curiously enough, he never even considered it worthwhile working on. However, his disdain was not shared by all mathematicians. In fact, it caught the fancy of many, and became known as the "Goldbach Conjecture."

ACHILLES: Has it ever been proven correct?

TORTOISE: No, it hasn't. But there have been some remarkable near misses. For instance, in 1931 the Russian number theorist Schnirelmann proved that any number—even or odd—can be represented as the sum of not more than 300,000 primes.

ACHILLES: What a strange result. Of what good is it?

TORTOISE: It has brought the problem into the domain of the finite. Previous to Schnirelmann's proof, it was conceivable that as you took larger and larger even numbers, they would require more and more primes to represent them. Some even number might take a trillion primes to represent it! Now it is known that that is not so—a sum of 300,000 primes (or fewer) will always suffice.

ACHILLES: I see.

TORTOISE: Then in 1937, a sly fellow named Vinogradov—a Russian too—managed to establish something far closer to the desired result: namely, every sufficiently large ODD number can be represented as a sum of no more than THREE odd primes. For example, $1937 = 641 + 643 + 653$. We could say that an odd number which is representable as a sum of three odd primes has "the Vinogradov property." Thus, all sufficiently large odd numbers have the Vinogradov property.

ACHILLES: Very well—but what does "sufficiently large" mean?

TORTOISE: It means that some finite number of odd numbers may fail to have the Vinogradov property, but there is a number—call it 'v'—beyond which all odd numbers have the Vinogradov property. But Vinogradov was unable to say how big v is. So in a way, v is like g, the finite but unknown number of Goldberg Variations. Merely knowing that v is finite isn't the same as knowing how big v is. Consequently, this information won't tell us when the last odd number which needs more than three primes to represent it has been located.

ACHILLES: I see. And so any sufficiently large even number $2N$ can be represented as a sum of FOUR primes, by first representing $2N - 3$ as a sum of three primes, and then adding back the prime number 3.

TORTOISE: Precisely. Another close approach is contained in the Theorem which says, "All even numbers can be represented as a sum of one prime and one number which is a product of at most two primes."

ACHILLES: This question about sums of two primes certainly leads you into strange territory. I wonder where you would be led if you looked at DIFFERENCES of two odd primes. I'll bet I could glean some insight into this teaser by making a little table of even numbers, and their representations as differences of two odd primes, just as I did for sums. Let's see . . .

$$2 = 5 - 3, \quad 7 - 5, \quad 13 - 11, \quad 19 - 17, \quad \text{etc.}$$
$$4 = 7 - 3, \quad 11 - 7, \quad 17 - 13, \quad 23 - 19, \quad \text{etc.}$$
$$6 = 11 - 5, \quad 13 - 7, \quad 17 - 11, \quad 19 - 13, \quad \text{etc.}$$
$$8 = 11 - 3, \quad 13 - 5, \quad 19 - 11, \quad 31 - 23, \quad \text{etc.}$$
$$10 = 13 - 3, \quad 17 - 7, \quad 23 - 13, \quad 29 - 19, \quad \text{etc.}$$

My gracious! There seems to be no end to the number of different representations I can find for these even numbers. Yet I don't discern any simple regularity in the table so far.

TORTOISE: Perhaps there is no regularity to be discerned.

ACHILLES: Oh, you and your constant rumblings about chaos! I'll hear none of that, thank you.

TORTOISE: Do you suppose that EVERY even number can be represented somehow as the difference of two odd primes?

ACHILLES: The answer certainly would appear to be yes, from my table. But then again, I suppose it could also be no. That doesn't really get us very far, does it?

TORTOISE: With all due respect, I would say there are deeper insights to be had on the matter.

ACHILLES: Curious how similar this problem is to Goldbach's original one. Perhaps it should be called a "Goldbach Variation."

TORTOISE: Indeed. But you know, there is a rather striking difference between the Goldbach Conjecture, and this Goldbach Variation, which I would like to tell you about. Let us say that an even number $2N$ has the "Goldbach property" if it is the SUM of two odd primes, and it has the "Tortoise property" if it is the DIFFERENCE of two odd primes.

ACHILLES: I think you should call it the "Achilles property." After all, I suggested the problem.

TORTOISE: I was just about to propose that we should say that a number which LACKS the Tortoise property has the "Achilles property."

ACHILLES: Well, all right . . .

TORTOISE: Now consider, for instance, whether 1 trillion has the Goldbach property or the Tortoise property. Of course, it may have both.

ACHILLES: I can consider it, but I doubt whether I can give you an answer to either question.

TORTOISE: Don't give up so soon. Suppose I asked you to answer one or the other question. Which one would you pick to work on?

ACHILLES: I suppose I would flip a coin. I don't see much difference between them.

TORTOISE: Aha! But there's a world of difference! If you pick the Goldbach property, involving SUMS of primes, then you are limited to using primes which are bounded between 2 and 1 trillion, right?

ACHILLES: Of course.

TORTOISE: So your search for a representation for 1 trillion as a sum of two primes IS GUARANTEED TO TERMINATE.

ACHILLES: Ahhh! I see your point. Whereas if I chose to work on representing 1 trillion as the DIFFERENCE of two primes, I would not have any bound on the size of the primes involved. They might be so big that it would take me a trillion years to find them.

TORTOISE: Or then again, they might not even EXIST! After all, that's what the question was asking—do such primes exist? It wasn't of much concern how big they might turn out to be.

ACHILLES: You're right. If they didn't exist, then a search process would lead on forever, never answering yes, and never answering no. And nevertheless, the answer would be no.

TORTOISE: So if you have some number, and you wish to test whether it has the Goldbach property or the Tortoise property, the difference between the two tests will be this: in the former, the search involved is GUARANTEED TO TERMINATE: in the latter, it is POTENTIALLY ENDLESS—there are no guarantees of any type. It might just go merrily on forever, without yielding an answer. And yet, on the other hand, in some cases, it might stop on the first step.

ACHILLES: I see there is a rather vast difference between the Goldbach and Tortoise properties.

TORTOISE: Yes, the two similar problems concern these vastly different properties. The Goldbach Conjecture is to the effect that all even numbers have the Goldbach property: the Goldbach Variation suggests that all even numbers have the Tortoise property. Both problems are unsolved, but what is interesting is that although they sound very much alike, they involve properties of whole numbers which are quite different.

ACHILLES: I see what you mean. The Goldbach property is a detectable, or recognizable property of any even number, since I know how to test for its presence—just embark on a search. It will automatically come to an end with a yes or no answer. The Tortoise property, however, is more elusive, since a brute force search just may never give an answer.

TORTOISE: Well, there may be cleverer ways of searching in the case of the Tortoise property, and maybe following one of them would always come to an end, and yield an answer.

ACHILLES: Couldn't the search only end if the answer were yes?

TORTOISE: Not necessarily. There might be some way of proving that whenever the search lasts longer than a certain length of time, then the answer must be no. There might even be some OTHER way of searching for the primes, not such a brute force way, which is guaranteed to find them if they exist, and to tell if they don't. In either case, a finite search would be able to yield the answer no. But I don't know if such a thing can be proven or not. Searching through infinite spaces is always a tricky matter, you know.

ACHILLES: So as things stand now, you know of no test for the Tortoise property which is guaranteed to terminate—and yet there MIGHT exist such a search.

TORTOISE: Right. I suppose one could embark on a search for such a search, but I can give no guarantee that that "meta-search" would terminate, either.

MEANING

1. How does the title "Aria with Diverse Variations" aptly express the technique that Hofstadter uses to develop his narrative essay?
2. What unusual mathematical properties are the subject of discussion in the dialogue between the Tortoise and Achilles?
3. What unusual mathematical properties do prime numbers possess?
4. What interesting mathematical property characterizes the number 1742?
5. How does this dialogue revolve around the idea of "limits"; that is, how does mathematics provide ways of knowing what limits there are and when they have been reached?
6. What is the connection between Bach's "Goldberg Variations" and the recursive method by which the dialogue between Achilles and the Tortoise develops?

USING NARRATION TO CONVEY MEANING

1. What technique of characterization does Hofstadter use to make Achilles and the Tortoise fully developed characters?
2. What part do puns, irony, whimsy, and humor play in portraying the mathematical points to the reader?
3. How is the dialogue itself structured as a "variation on a theme"; that is, how is the dialogue organized so that it actually embodies the ideas being presented?

Writing Suggestions

1. What is the paradox of Zeno and how is it related to the characters and ideas in Hofstadter's narrative?
2. Invent your own dialogue, complete with characters, to explain a mathematical principle or geometrical theorem you understand.
3. Compare this dialogue with the original work by Lewis Carroll, "What the Tortoise Said to Achilles," and discuss how each author used them for different purposes.

DESCRIPTION

Writers in different disciplines use description for a variety of purposes related to the goals of their particular fields of study. In the sciences, objective descriptions recreate the appearance of objects, events, or scenes. In the liberal arts, subjective description permits readers to empathize with the writer's feelings and reactions toward scenes, objects, or events. In both the liberal arts and the social and political sciences, we often encounter combinations of objective and subjective description.

D. H. Lawrence's evocation of a traditional Indian tribal dance in "The Dance of the Sprouting Corn" illustrates how powerfully description can work, in the hands of an artist, to recreate the sensory nature of an event through images of sight, sound, taste, smell, and touch. Lawrence's mastery of descriptive techniques enables him to mirror the motion, rhythm, and direction of the dancers through the language, rhythm, and pacing of his prose:

> Mindless, without effort, under the hot sun, unceasing, yet never perspiring nor even breathing heavily, they dance on and on. Mindless, yet still listening, observing. They hear the deep surging singing of the bunch of old men, like a great wind soughing. They hear the cries and yells of the man waving his bough by the drum. They catch the word of the song, and at a moment, shudder the black rattles, wheel, and the line breaks, women from men, they thread across to a new formation. And as the men wheel round, their black hair gleams and shakes, and the long fox-skin sways, like a tail.

Lawrence skillfully recreates the insistent rhythm and motion of the dance through techniques that lift this passage to the level of poetry. The dancers have no identity as individuals but only exist through the ceremony of the tribal dance. We can see, feel, and hear the dancers as if we are actually there, witnessing the traditional dance of the sprouting corn.

Subjective description is useful for communicating a writer's personal feelings and reactions to the idea, event, or person being described. As such, it is well-suited to portray a person so that the reader not only knows how the subject looked but gains insight into the person's unique qualities, character traits, and nature. James Boswell accomplishes this in his description of his lifelong friend, the renowned Dr. Samuel Johnson, a famous lexicographer who embodied a curious mixture of contradictions. The Dr. Johnson that Boswell knew could be fair and judicious despite his intimidating demeanor:

> Exulting in his intellectual strength and dexterity, he could, when he pleased, be the greatest sophist that ever contended in the lists of declamation; and, from a spirit of contradiction and a delight in showing his powers, he would often maintain the wrong side with equal warmth and ingenuity; so that when there was an audience, his real opinions could seldom be gathered from his talk . . . but he was too conscientious to make error permanent and pernicious by deliberately writing it. . . .

We learn that Dr. Johnson expected more of himself precisely because of his great intellectual gifts and held himself to a higher standard in writing than he did during public discourse, where he would delight in playing the devil's advocate for positions he did not espouse.

The ability of description to accurately convey physical characteristics (height, shape, dimensions, appearance) makes it an especially effective writing strategy for anthropologists, social scientists, and historians. Writing in these disciplines requires close observation and documentation of social, political, and cultural phenomena. In "The Myth and Ritual of Adonis," Sir James George Frazer, an eminent anthropologist, describes the commanding vistas and dramatic setting of an ancient temple used for the worship of Adonis in such telling detail that a long-forgotten monument comes to life for his readers:

> The temple, of which some massive hewn blocks and a fine column of Syenite granite still mark the site, occupied a terrace facing the source of the river and commanding a magnificent prospect. Across the foam and the roar of the waterfalls you look up to the cavern and away to the top of the sublime precipices above. So lofty is the cliff that the goats which creep along its ledges to browse on the bushes appear like ants to the spectator hundreds of feet below. . . .

Frazer appeals to the sense of sight when describing the goats that seem "like ants" on the top-most mountain ledges, the sense of touch in the rough surface of hewn granite, and the sense of sound in the torrential roar of waterfalls. The awesome grandeur of this scene documents how important the temple must have been as a focal point for ceremonies and rituals connected with the worship of Adonis.

Perhaps the most useful method of arranging details within a description is the technique of focusing on an impression that dominates the entire scene. This main impression can center around a prominent physical feature, a tower or church steeple, or a significant psychological trait, such as Dr. Johnson's judiciousness. A skillful writer will often arrange his or her description around this central impression, much the same way a good photographer will locate a focal point for pictures. Jack London, a novelist, uses this technique in his description of how San Francisco residents reacted to the devastating earthquake of 1906 in "The San Francisco Earthquake":

> Before the flames, throughout the night, fled tens of thousands of homeless ones. Some were wrapped in blankets. Others carried bundles of bedding and dear household treasures. Sometimes a whole family was harnessed to a carriage or delivery wagon that was weighted down with their possessions. Baby buggies, toy wagons, and go-carts were used as trucks, while every other person was dragging a trunk. Yet everybody

was gracious. The most perfect courtesy obtained. Never, in all San Francisco's history, were her people so kind and courteous as on this night of terror.

A wealth of specific descriptive details recreates the sights and sounds of the conflagration. Yet, the primary impression London communicates is that the citizens of San Francisco displayed forebearance and rare courtesy toward each other in the most trying of circumstances.

In "First Observations," Jane van Lawick-Goodall, a zoologist, finds description indispensable in order to document the "toolmaking" and "meat-eating" behavior of the chimpanzees she had observed over many months. What first strikes the reader is that van Lawick-Goodall uses details of appearance and behavior to assign descriptive names rather than numbers to individual chimpanzees. More importantly, her observations served as scientific evidence of phenomena contrary to what zoologists had previously believed. Chimpanzees were not solely vegetarians but hunted and killed other animals for food.

Whereas van Lawick-Goodall uses description for the purpose of documenting scientific observations, Agnes De Mille, a renowned choreographer, uses description for an entirely different purpose. She describes the great Russian ballerina, Pavlova, so that her readers can share the moment when De Mille decided to become a dancer herself. De Mille's description draws the reader's attention to Pavlova's physical appearance, gestures, style of performance, and the response she produced in her audiences. Through a multitude of evocative details we can literally "see" Pavlova's slight figure, miniscule slipper size, graceful long arms, legs, and neck, and accelerated hummingbird-like movements. De Mille carefully structures her description to present Pavlova first at rest, a diminuative figure who seems insignificant, then depicts her in motion when Pavlova magically becomes larger than life through her dancing.

Description is more effective when the writer arranges details so as to produce a certain effect on the audience. For example, in "Steerage" Oscar Handlin organizes the details of his description to give his readers insight into the cramped quarters and conditions of hardship that hundreds of thousands had to endure in order to immigrate to the United States on ships in the last century:

> Below decks is the place, its usual dimensions seventy-five feet long, twenty-five wide, five and a half high. Descend. In the fitful light your eye will discover a middle aisle five feet wide. It will be a while before you can make out the separate shapes within it, the water closets at either end (for the women; the men must go above deck), one or several cooking stoves, the tables. The aisle itself, you will see, is formed by two rows of bunks that run to the side of the ship.

Observe how Handlin arranges his description so that his readers "follow him" below decks and gradually discover what it must have been like to be an immigrant, living in cramped darkness, without enough food and water, on a forty-day journey. What is remarkable is that Handlin creates his compelling account from dry statistics that record the amount of food and water allocated, the physical dimensions of space below decks, and the length of the average voyage. Whatever principle of order a writer chooses (from top to bottom, left to right, far to near, or any variations of these), the presentation of details must seem natural. Handlin organizes his description in order to lead his readers through the scene in a way that evokes the experiences of the immigrants.

Another effective way of organizing a description is to select and present details in order to create a feeling of suspense. The archeologist, Howard Carter, uses this technique in "Finding the Tomb" to recreate the tension he and his crew felt at the actual moment when, after many years of research and excavations, the long sought-after tomb of Tutankhamen was finally unearthed:

> At first I could see nothing, the hot air escaping from the chamber causing the candle flame to flicker, but presently, as my eyes grew accustomed to the light, details of the room within emerged slowly from the mist, strange animals, statues, and gold—everywhere the glint of gold. For the moment—an eternity it must have seemed to the others standing by—I was struck dumb with amazement, and when Lord Carnarvon, unable to stand the suspense any longer, inquired anxiously, "Can you see anything?" it was all I could do to get out the words. "Yes, wonderful things.". . .

Carter introduces one detail after another to heighten suspense as to whether the tomb was still intact or had been previously ransacked by robbers. The description is arranged to transport the readers into the scene so that they see what Carter saw on that day—concealed treasures gradually emerging out of the darkness.

Realizing something new can be as dramatic as seeing something new. Richard Selzer, a medical doctor, describes his unexpected reaction to witnessing an abortion in "What I Saw at the Abortion":

> *I see something!* . . . And now I see that it is the hub of the needle in the woman's belly that has jerked. First to one side. Then to the other side. . . . Again! And I *know!* . . . It is the fetus struggling against the needle. Struggling? How can that be? I think: *that cannot be.* I think: the fetus feels no pain, cannot feel fear, has *no motivation.* It is merely reflex.
>
> I point to the needle.
>
> It is a reflex, says the doctor.

Although Selzer had been taught during his medical education that the fetus is unable to experience fear or pain, his senses tell him something quite different. The drama of this account arises from Selzer's emotional struggle against the evidence of his senses and the implications of what he saw.

Thus, description, as it is used by writers across many disciplines, is an indispensable tool for conveying the external appearance of persons, places, and things, and a means by which writers can relate their emotional reaction toward the subjects they describe.

LIBERAL ARTS

AGNES DE MILLE

Pavlova

Agnes De Mille, a principal figure in American dance, was born in New York City in 1908. She created distinctive American ballets, such as Rodeo *(1942) and* Tally-Ho *(1944), and brought her talents as an innovative choreographer to* Oklahoma! *(1943 and 1980),* Carousel *(1945),* Brigadoon *(1947),* Paint Your Wagon *(1951),* Gentlemen Prefer Blondes *(1949), and other musicals. De Mille's entertaining autobiographies,* Dance to the Piper *(1952) and* Reprieve: A Memoir *(1981) describe many exciting moments in her life. "Pavlova," from* Dance to the Piper, *contains De Mille's recollection of what she felt when she saw Anna Pavlova, the famed Russian ballerina, for the first time.*

Anna Pavlova! My life stops as I write that name. Across the daily preoccupation of lessons, lunch boxes, tooth brushings and quarrelings with Margaret flashed this bright, unworldly experience and burned in a single afternoon a path over which I could never retrace my steps. I had witnessed the power of beauty, and in some chamber of my heart I lost forever my irresponsibility. I was as clearly marked as though she had looked me in the face and called my name. For generations my father's family had loved and served the theater. All my life I had seen actors and actresses and had heard theater jargon at the dinner table and business talk of box-office grosses. I had thrilled at Father's projects and watched fascinated his picturesque occupations. I took a proprietary pride in the profitable and hasty growth of "The Industry." But nothing in his world or my uncle's prepared me for theater as I saw it that Saturday afternoon.

Since that day I have gained some knowledge in my trade and I recognize that her technique was limited; that her arabesques were not as pure or classically correct as Markova's, that her jumps and batterie were paltry, her turns not to be compared in strength and number with the strenuous durability of Baronova or Toumanova. I know that her scenery was designed by second-rate artists, her music was on a level with restaurant orchestrations, her company definitely inferior to all the standards we insist on today, and her choreography mostly hack. And yet I say that she was in her person the quintessence of theatrical excitement.

As her little bird body revealed itself on the scene, either immobile in trembling mystery or tense in the incredible arc which was her lift, her instep stretched ahead in an arch never before seen, the tiny bones of her hands in ceaseless vibration, her face radiant, diamonds glittering under her dark hair, her little waist encased in silk, the great tutu balancing, quickening and flashing over her beating, flashing, quivering legs, every man and woman sat forward, every pulse quickened. She never appeared to rest static, some part of her trembled, vibrated, beat like a heart. Before our dazzled eyes, she flashed with the sudden sweetness of a hummingbird in action too quick for understanding by our gross utilitarian standards, in action sensed rather than seen. The movie cameras of her day could not record her allegro. Her feet and hands photographed as a blur.

Bright little bird bones, delicate bird sinews! She was all fire and steel wire. There was not an ounce of spare flesh on her skeleton, and the life force used and used her body until she died of the fever of moving, gasping for breath, much too young.

She was small, about five feet. She wore a size one and a half slipper, but her feet and hands were large in proportion to her height. Her hand could cover her whole face. Her trunk was small and stripped of all anatomy but the ciphers of adolescence, her arms and legs relatively long, the neck extraordinarily long and mobile. All her gestures were liquid and possessed of an inner rhythm that flowed to inevitable completion with the finality of architecture or music. Her arms seemed to lift not from the elbow or the arm socket, but from the base of the spine. Her legs seemed to function from the waist. When she bent her head her whole spine moved and the motion was completed the length of the arm through the elongation of her slender hand and the quivering reaching fingers. I believe there has never been a foot like hers, slender, delicate and of such an astonishing aggressiveness when arched as to suggest the ultimate in human vitality. Without in any way being sensual, being, in fact, almost sexless, she suggested all exhilaration, gaiety and delight. She jumped, and we broke bonds with reality. We flew. We hung over the earth, spread in the air as we do in dreams, our hands turning in the air as in water—the strong forthright taut plunging leg balanced on the poised arc of the foot, the other leg stretched to the horizon like the wing of a bird. We lay balancing, quivering, turning, and all things were possible, even to us, the ordinary people.

I have seen two dancers as great or greater since, Alicia Markova and Margot Fonteyn, and many other women who have kicked higher, balanced longer or turned faster. These are poor substitutes for passion. In spite of her flimsy dances, the bald and blatant virtuosity, there was an intoxicated rapture, a focus of energy, Dionysian in its physical intensity, that I have never seen equaled by a performer in any theater of the world. Also she was the *first* of the truly great in our experience.

I sat with the blood beating in my throat. As I walked into the bright glare of the afternoon, my head ached and I could scarcely swallow. I didn't wish to cry. I certainly couldn't speak. I sat in a daze in the car oblivious to the grownups' ceaseless prattle. At home I climbed the stairs slowly to my bedroom and, shutting myself in, placed both hands on the brass rail at the foot of my bed, then rising laboriously to the tips of my white buttoned shoes I stumped the width of the bed and back again. My toes throbbed with pain, my knees shook, my legs quivered with weakness. I repeated the exercise. The blessed, relieving tears stuck at last on my lashes. Only by hurting my feet could I ease the pain in my throat.

Standing on Ninth Avenue under the El, I saw the headlines on the front page of the *New York Times*. It did not seem possible. She was in essence the denial of death. My own life was rooted to her in a deep spiritual sense and had been during the whole of my growing up. It mattered not that I had only spoken to her once and that my work lay in a different direction. She was the vision and the impulse and the goal.

MEANING

1. How did seeing Pavlova's performance change Agnes De Mille's life?
2. What features of Pavlova's appearance and dancing does De Mille find so enthralling?
3. What impression of Pavlova does the reader gain from De Mille's description?

USING DESCRIPTION TO CONVEY MEANING

1. What details does De Mille include to draw the reader's attention to Pavlova's diminuative size and ability to express emotion through gestures?
2. What qualities distinguish Pavlova from other famous dancers?
3. What words and phrases make the reader aware that De Mille has been inspired by Pavlova's performance?

WRITING SUGGESTIONS

1. Describe a performance you have seen that you would call inspiring. Organize your description around your main impression and use specific details of sight and sound to allow readers to share the moment.
2. Describe a person who might be as exciting a role model for you as Pavlova was for De Mille.
3. If you could appear on the cover of any magazine, which one would you choose— *Sports Illustrated, Time's* "Man of the Year," *Rolling Stone, Business Week, Ms., Psychology Today*—and for what achievement or quality would you be celebrated?
4. Pick any rock, country, or classical performer and describe this person, paying special attention to his or her style of performance, gestures, physical appearance, and voice quality, as well as the mood he or she creates, the instruments that are used, and the responses that are produced in the audience.

JACK LONDON

The San Francisco Earthquake

Jack London (1876–1916) was born John Griffith Chaney in San Francisco and took the name of his stepfather, John London. His impoverished childhood bred self-reliance: he worked in a canning factory and jute mill, as a longshoreman, robbed oyster beds as the self-styled "Prince of the Oyster Pirates," went to sea at seventeen, and took part in the Klondike gold-rush of 1897. He drew on these experiences and was profoundly influenced by the works of Marx, Kipling, and Nietzsche when he began writing his distinctive stories, often set in the Yukon, of the survival of men and animals in harsh environments. In The Call of the Wild *(1903),* The Sea Wolf *(1904),* White Fang *(1906),* The Iron Heel *(1908), and in short stories such as "Love of Life" (1906) and "To Build a Fire" (1910), London powerfully dramatizes the conflict between barbarism and civilization. During London's short turbulent life, his prolific output as a writer also included his work as a journalist. Among other assignments, he covered the Russo-Japanese War of 1904–1905 as a syndicated correspondent. "The San Francisco Earthquake" (1906) was the first in a series of reports that London wrote for* Collier's *Magazine on the April 18, 1906 catastrophe. His straightforward descriptive style influenced later writers such as Ernest Hemingway and Sherwood Anderson.*

The earthquake shook down in San Francisco hundreds of thousands of dollars' worth of walls and chimneys. But the conflagration that followed burned up hundreds of millions of dollars' worth of property. There is no estimating within hundreds of millions the actual damage wrought. Not in history has a modern imperial city been so completely destroyed. San Francisco is gone. Nothing remains of it but memories and a fringe of dwelling-houses on its outskirts. Its industrial section is wiped out. Its business section is wiped out. The factories and warehouses, the great stores and newspaper buildings, the hotels and the palaces of the nabobs, are all gone. Remains only the fringe of dwelling-houses on the outskirts of what was once San Francisco.

Within an hour after the earthquake shock the smoke of San Francisco's burning was a lurid tower visible a hundred miles away. And for three days and nights this lurid tower swayed in the sky, reddening the sun, darkening the day, and filling the land with smoke.

On Wednesday morning at a quarter past five came the earthquake. A minute later the flames were leaping upward. In a dozen different quarters south of Market Street, in the working-class ghetto, and in the factories, fires started. There was no opposing the flames. There was no organization, no communication. All the cunning adjustments of a twentieth century city had been smashed by the earthquake. The streets were humped into ridges and depressions, and piled with the debris of fallen walls. The steel rails were twisted into perpendicular and horizontal angles. The telephone and telegraph systems were disrupted. And the great water-mains had burst. All the shrewd contrivances and safe-guards of man had been thrown out of gear by thirty seconds' twitching of the earth-crust.

THE FIRE MADE ITS OWN DRAFT

By Wednesday afternoon, inside of twelve hours, half the heart of the city was gone. At that time I watched the vast conflagration from out on the bay. It was dead calm. Not a flicker of wind stirred. Yet from every side wind was pouring in upon the city. East, west, north, and south, strong winds were blowing upon the doomed city. The heated air rising made an enormous suck. Thus did the fire of itself build its own colossal chimney through the atmosphere. Day and night this dead calm continued, and yet, near to the flames, the wind was often half a gale, so mighty was the suck.

Wednesday night saw the destruction of the very heart of the city. Dynamite was lavishly used, and many of San Francisco's proudest structures were crumbled by man himself into ruins, but there was no withstanding the onrush of the flames. Time and again successful stands were made by the fire-fighters, and every time the flames flanked around on either side, or came up from the rear, and turned to defeat the hard-won victory.

An enumeration of the buildings destroyed would be a directory of San Francisco. An enumeration of the buildings undestroyed would be a line and several addresses. An enumeration of the deeds of heroism would stock a library and bankrupt the Carnegie Medal fund. An enumeration of the dead will never be made. All vestiges of them were destroyed by the flames. The number of victims of the earthquake will never be known. South of Market Street, where the loss of life was particularly heavy, was the first to catch fire.

Remarkable as it may seem, Wednesday night, while the whole city crashed and roared into ruin, was a quiet night. There were no crowds. There was no shouting and yelling. There was no hysteria, no disorder. I passed Wednesday night in the path of the advancing flames, and in all those terrible hours I saw not one woman who wept, not one man who was excited, not one person who was in the slightest degree panic-stricken.

Before the flames, throughout the night, fled tens of thousands of homeless ones. Some were wrapped in blankets. Others carried bundles of bedding and dear household treasures. Sometimes a whole family was harnessed to a carriage or delivery wagon that was weighted down with their possessions. Baby buggies, toy wagons, and go-carts were used as trucks, while every other person was dragging a trunk. Yet everybody was gracious. The most perfect courtesy obtained. Never, in all San Francisco's history, were her people so kind and courteous as on this night of terror.

A CARAVAN OF TRUNKS

All night these tens of thousands fled before the flames. Many of them, the poor people from the labor ghetto, had fled all day as well. They had left their homes burdened with possessions. Now and again they lightened up, flinging out upon the street clothing and treasures they had dragged for miles.

They held on longest to their trunks, and over these trunks many a strong man broke his heart that night. The hills of San Francisco are steep, and up these hills, mile after mile, were the trunks dragged. Everywhere were trunks, with across them lying their exhausted owners, men and women. Before the march of the flames were flung picket lines of soldiers. And a block at a time, as the flames advanced, these pickets retreated. One of their tasks was to keep the trunk-pullers moving. The exhausted creatures, stirred on by the menace of bayonets, would arise and struggle up the steep pavements, pausing from weakness every five or ten feet.

Often, after surmounting a heart-breaking hill, they would find another wall of flame advancing upon them at right angles and be compelled to change anew the line of their retreat. In the end, completely played out, after toiling for a dozen hours like giants, thousands of them were compelled to abandon their trunks. Here the shopkeepers and soft members of the middle class were at a disadvantage. But the working men dug holes in vacant lots and backyards and buried their trunks.

THE DOOMED CITY

At nine o'clock Wednesday evening I walked down through the very heart of the city. I walked through miles and miles of magnificent buildings and towering sky-scrapers. Here was no fire. All was in perfect order. The police patrolled the streets. Every building had its watchman at the door. And yet it was doomed, all of it. There was no water. The dynamite was giving out. And at right angles two different conflagrations were sweeping down upon it.

At one o'clock in the morning I walked down through the same section. Everything still stood intact. There was no fire. And yet there was a change. A rain of ashes was falling. The watchmen at the doors were gone. The police had been withdrawn. There were no firemen, no fire engines, no men fighting with dynamite. The district had been absolutely abandoned. I stood at the corner of Kearney and Market, in the very innermost heart of San Francisco. Kearney Street was deserted. Half a dozen blocks away it was burning on both sides. The street was a wall of flame, and against this wall of flame, silhouetted sharply, were two United States cavalrymen sitting their horses, calmly watching. That was all. Not another person was in sight. In the intact heart of the city two troopers sat their horses and watched.

SPREAD OF THE CONFLAGRATION

Surrender was complete. There was no water. The sewers had long since been pumped dry. There was no dynamite. Another fire had broken out further uptown, and now from three sides conflagrations were sweeping down. The fourth side had been burned earlier in the day. In that direction stood the tottering walls of the Examiner building, the burned-out Call building, the smoldering ruins of the Grand Hotel, and the gutted, devastated, dynamited Palace Hotel.

The following will illustrate the sweep of the flames and the inability of men to calculate their spread. At eight o'clock Wednesday evening I passed through Union Square. It was packed with refugees. Thousands of them had gone to bed on the grass. Government tents had been set up, supper was being cooked, and the refugees were lining up for free meals.

At half-past one in the morning three sides of Union Square were in flames. The fourth side, where stood the great St. Francis Hotel, was still holding out. An hour later, ignited from top and sides, the St. Francis was flaming heavenward. Union Square, heaped high with mountains of trunks, was deserted. Troops, refugees, and all had retreated.

A Fortune for a Horse!

It was at Union Square that I saw a man offering a thousand dollars for a team of horses. He was in charge of a truck piled high with trunks for some hotel. It had been hauled here into what was considered safety, and the horses had been taken out. The flames were on three sides of the Square, and there were no horses.

Also, at this time, standing beside the truck, I urged a man to seek safety in flight. He was all but hemmed in by several conflagrations. He was an old man and he was on crutches. Said he, "Today is my birthday. Last night I was worth thirty thousand dollars. I bought five bottles of wine, some delicate fish, and other things for my birthday dinner. I have had no dinner, and all I own are these crutches."

I convinced him of his danger and started him limping on his way. An hour later, from a distance, I saw the truckload of trunks burning merrily in the middle of the street.

On Thursday morning, at a quarter past five, just twenty-four hours after the earthquake, I sat on the steps of a small residence on Nob Hill. With me sat Japanese, Italians, Chinese, and Negroes—a bit of the cosmopolitan flotsam of the wreck of the city. All about were the palaces of the nabob pioneers of Forty-nine. To the east and south, at right angles, were advancing two mighty walls of flame.

I went inside with the owner of the house on the steps of which I sat. He was cool and cheerful and hospitable. "Yesterday morning," he said, "I was worth six hundred thousand dollars. This morning this house is all I have left. It will go in fifteen minutes." He pointed to a large cabinet. "That is my wife's collection of china. This rug upon which we stand is a present. It cost fifteen hundred dollars. Try that piano. Listen to its tone. There are few like it. There are no horses. The flames will be here in fifteen minutes."

Outside, the old Mark Hopkins residence, a palace, was just catching fire. The troops were falling back and driving the refugees before them. From every side came the roaring of flames, the crashing of walls, and the detonations of dynamite.

The Dawn of the Second Day

I passed out of the house. Day was trying to dawn through the smoke-pall. A sickly light was creeping over the face of things. Once only the sun broke through the smoke-pall, blood-red, and showing quarter its usual size. The smoke-pall itself, viewed from beneath, was a rose color that pulsed and fluttered with lavender shades. Then it turned to mauve and yellow and dun. There was no sun. And so dawned the second day on stricken San Francisco.

An hour later I was creeping past the shattered dome of the City Hall. Than it there was no better exhibit of the destructive forces of the earthquake. Most of the stone had been shaken from the great dome, leaving standing the naked frame-work of steel. Market Street was piled high with wreckage, and across the wreckage lay the overthrown pillars of the City Hall shattered into short crosswise sections.

This section of the city, with the exception of the Mint and the Post-Office, was already a waste of smoking ruins. Here and there through the smoke, creeping warily under the shadows of tottering walls, emerged occasional men and women. It was like the meeting of the handful of survivors after the day of the end of the world.

BEEVES SLAUGHTERED AND ROASTED

On Mission Street lay a dozen steers, in a neat row stretching across the street, just as they had been struck down by the flying ruins of the earthquake. The fire had passed through afterward and roasted them. The human dead had been carried away before the fire came. At another place on Mission Street I saw a milk wagon. A steel telegraph pole had smashed down sheer through the driver's seat and crushed the front wheels. The milkcans lay scattered around.

All day Thursday and all Thursday night, all day Friday and Friday night, the flames still raged.

Friday night saw the flames finally conquered, though not until Russian Hill and Telegraph Hill had been swept and three-quarters of a mile of wharves and docks had been licked up.

THE LAST STAND

The great stand of the fire-fighters was made Thursday night on Van Ness Avenue. Had they failed here, the comparatively few remaining houses of the city would have been swept. Here were the magnificent residences of the second generation of San Francisco nabobs, and these, in a solid zone, were dynamited down across the path of the fire. Here and there the flames leaped the zone, but these fires were beaten out, principally by the use of wet blankets and rugs.

San Francisco, at the present time, is like the crater of a volcano, around which are camped tens of thousand of refugees. At the Presidio alone are at least twenty thousand. All the surrounding cities and towns are jammed with the homeless ones, where they are being cared for by the relief committees. The refugees were carried free by the railroads to any point they wished to go, and it is estimated that over one hundred thousand people have left the peninsula on which San Francisco stood. The Government has the situation in hand, and, thanks to the immediate relief given by the whole United States, there is not the slightest possibility of a famine. The bankers and business men have already set about making preparations to rebuild San Francisco.

MEANING

1. Why was the behavior of the citizens during the earthquake and subsequent fire so commendable?

2. How much of San Francisco was destroyed by the subsequent fires in comparison to the damage done by the earthquake itself?
3. How does the reader know that London risked his own life several times to report accurately the extent of the destruction?
4. Why does the phrase "[my] fortune for a horse" (with its echo of Richard III's famous line "my kingdom for a horse") aptly express the desperate desire of the citizens to save what little they could?

Using Description to Convey Meaning

1. How is London's description enhanced by his use of figurative language and the imagery of warfare? What metaphors evoke the sights, sounds, tastes, and smells of the conflagration?
2. How does the shift from war imagery to the metaphor of a shipwreck reflect the new predicament faced by the citizens as survivors of the devastation?
3. What examples of courteous behavior does London cite that support the impression of civility under great stress?
4. What effect does London produce by reporting the event from many different vantage points within the city? Where, in his account, do these changes in location occur?
5. Which parts of this report are enhanced by London's skill as a novelist, using fictional techniques to dramatize real events? Where does London use specific facts and figures to provide an objective journalistic account?

Writing Suggestions

1. Describe the one inanimate object you would choose to save if there was a fire. Describe its physical characteristics and discuss why you would choose to save this particular item.
2. Write an account of a widely reported catastrophe. Provide accurate and objective information about what happened and describe the people involved, significant sights, sounds, and actions of the event, any actual conversations, and useful facts and figures that would help place the event in perspective.
3. Imagine yourself as an invisible, all-seeing witness in any of the following places: in the Garden of Eden; at the Salem witch trials; with the Beatles on their first American concert tour; where a new record has just been set for the Guinness Book of Records. Choose one of these situations or one of your own and describe the scene, using sensory details that recreate the event for your audience. Include any significant background information the reader may need.

JAMES BOSWELL

The Character of Samuel Johnson

James Boswell (1740–1795) was born in Edinburgh, Scotland, educated at Edinburgh University, and while studying civil law at Glasgow, began his lifelong pursuit of literary and political fame by publishing numerous pamphlets and verses. At the age of twenty, he went to London, befriended the Duke of York, took the first of many mistresses, and, on May 16, 1763, at Tom Davie's Bookshop in Russell Street, met the famous Dr. Samuel Johnson for the first of 276 occasions they would see each other. Boswell raised "social climbing" to an art form, introducing himself to such literary notables as Voltaire and Rousseau (whose advocacy of Corsican liberty inspired Boswell's first full-fledged work, in 1768, An Account of Corsica). *During 1773, he toured Scotland and the Hebrides with Dr. Johnson, was elected to Johnson's famous literary club, and began his* Journal of a Tour of the Hebrides, *which appeared in 1785 after Johnson's death. The perplexing contradictions within his illustrious friend's personality are described in "The Character of Samuel Johnson," an excerpt that concludes Boswell's major work,* The Life of Samuel Johnson (1891), *one of the greatest biographies ever written.*

The character of SAMUEL JOHNSON has, I trust, been so developed in the course of this work, that they who have honored it with a perusal, may be considered as well acquainted with him. As, however, it may be expected that I should collect into one view the capital and distinguishing features of this extraordinary man, I shall endeavor to acquit myself of that part of my biographical undertaking,[1] however difficult it may be to do that which many of my readers will do better for themselves.

His figure was large and well formed, and his countenance of the cast of an ancient statue; yet his appearance was rendered strange and somewhat uncouth by convulsive cramps, by the scars of that distemper which it was once imagined the royal touch could cure, and by a slovenly mode of dress. He had the use only of one eye; yet so much does mind govern and even supply the deficiency of organs, that his visual perceptions, as far as they extended, were uncommonly quick and accurate. So morbid was his temperament that he never knew the natural joy of a free and vigorous use of his limbs: when he walked, it was like the struggling gait of one in fetters; when he rode, he had no command or direction of his horse, but was carried as if in a balloon. That with his constitution and habits of life he should

---

[1] As I do not see any reason to give a different character of my illustrious friend now, from what I formerly gave, the greatest part of the sketch of him in my "Journal of a Tour to the Hebrides" is here adopted.—B.

have lived seventy-five years, is a proof that an inherent *vivida vis*[2] is a powerful preservative of the human frame.

Man is, in general, made up of contradictory qualities; and these will ever show themselves in strange succession, where a consistency in appearance at least, if not reality, has not been attained by long habits of philosophical discipline. In proportion to the native vigor of the mind, the contradictory qualities will be the more prominent, and more difficult to be adjusted; and, therefore, we are not to wonder that Johnson exhibited an eminent example of this remark which I have made upon human nature. At different times he seemed a different man, in some respects; not, however, in any great or essential article, upon which he had fully employed his mind, and settled certain principles of duty, but only in his manners, and in the display of argument and fancy in his talk. He was prone to superstition, but not to credulity. Though his imagination might incline him to a belief of the marvelous and the mysterious, his vigorous reason examined the evidence with jealousy. He was a sincere and zealous Christian, of high Church-of-England and monarchial principles, which he would not tamely suffer to be questioned; and had, perhaps, at an early period, narrowed his mind somewhat too much, both as to religion and politics. His being impressed with the danger of extreme latitude in either, though he was of a very independent spirit, occasioned his appearing somewhat unfavorable to the prevalence of that noble freedom of sentiment which is the best possession of man. Nor can it be denied, that he had many prejudices; which, however, frequently suggested many of his pointed sayings, that rather show a playfulness of fancy than any settled malignity. He was steady and inflexible in maintaining the obligations of religion and morality; both from a regard for the order of society, and from a veneration for the GREAT SOURCE of all order; correct, nay, stern in his taste; hard to please, and easily offended, impetuous and irritable in his temper, but of a most humane and benevolent heart,[3] which showed itself not only in a most liberal charity, as far as his circumstances would allow, but in a thousand instances of active benevolence. He was afflicted with a bodily disease which made him often restless and fretful; and with a constitutional melancholy, the clouds which darkened the brightness of his fancy, and gave a gloomy cast to his whole course of thinking: we, therefore, ought not to wonder at his sallies of impatience and passion at any time; especially when provoked by obtrusive ignorance, or presuming petulance; and allowance must be made for his uttering hasty and satirical sallies even against his best friends. And, surely, when it is considered, that, "amidst sickness and sorrow," he exerted his faculties in so many works for the benefit of mankind, and particularly that he achieved the great and admirable DICTIONARY of our language, we must be astonished at his resolution. The solemn text, "of him to whom much is given, much will be required," seems to have been ever present to his mind, in a rigorous sense, and to have made him dissatisfied with his labors and acts of goodness, however comparatively great; so that the unavoidable consciousness of his superiority was, in that respect, a cause of disquiet. He suffered so much from this, and from the gloom which perpetually haunted him and made solitude frightful, that it may be said of him, "If in this life only he had

---

[2] Lucretius, i. 72.

[3] In the *Olla Podrida*, a collection of essays published at Oxford, there is an admirable paper upon the character of Johnson, written by the Reverend Dr. Horne, the last excellent Bishop of Norwich. The following passage is eminently happy: "To reject wisdom, because the person of him who communicates it is uncouth, and his manners are inelegant; what is it but to throw away a pine-apple, and assign for a person the roughness of its coat?"—B.

hope, he was of all men most miserable." He loved praise, when it was brought to him; but was too proud to seek for it. He was somewhat susceptible of flattery. As he was general and unconfined in his studies, he cannot be considered as master of any one particular science; but he had accumulated a vast and various collection of learning and knowledge, which was so arranged in his mind, as to be ever in readiness to be brought forth. But his superiority over other learned men consisted chiefly in what may be called the art of thinking, the art of using his mind: a certain continual power of seizing the useful substance of all that he knew, and exhibiting it in a clear and forcible manner; so that knowledge, which we often see to be no better than lumber in men of dull understanding, was in him true, evident, and actual wisdom. His moral precepts are practical; for they are drawn from an initimate acquaintance with human nature. His maxims carry conviction; for they are founded on the basis of common sense, and a very attentive and minute survey of real life. His mind was so full of imagery, that he might have been perpetually a poet; yet it is remarkable, that, however rich his prose is in this respect, his poetical pieces, in general, have not much of that splendor, but are rather distinguished by strong sentiment, and acute observation, conveyed in harmonious and energetic verse, particularly in heroic couplets. Though usually grave, and even awful in his deportment, he possessed uncommon and peculiar powers of wit and humor; he frequently indulged himself in colloquial pleasantry; and the heartiest merriment was often enjoyed in his company; with this great advantage, that as it was entirely free from any poisonous tincture of vice or impiety, it was salutary to those who shared in it. He had accustomed himself to such accuracy in his common conversation,[4] that he at all times expressed

---

[4] Though a perfect resemblance of Johnson is not to be found in any age, parts of his character are admirably expressed by Clarendon in drawing that of Lord Falkland, whom the noble and masterly historian describes at his seat near Oxford: "Such an immenseness of wit, such a solidity of judgment, so infinite a fancy bound in by a most logical ratiocination. His acquaintance was cultivated by the most polite and accurate men, so that his house was a University in less volume, whither they came, not so much for repose as study, and to examine and refine those grosser propositions, which laziness and consent made current in conversation." Bayle's account of *Menage* may also be quoted as exceedingly applicable to the great subject of this work. "His illustrious friends erected a very glorious monument to him in the collection entitled "Menagiana." Those who judge of things aright, will confess that this collection is very proper to show the extent of genius and learning which was the character of Menage. And I may be bold to say, that *the excellent works he published will not distinguish him from other learned men so advantageously as this*. To publish books of great learning, to make Greek and Latin verses exceedingly well turned, is not a common talent, I own; neither is it extremely rare. It is incomparably more difficult to find men who can furnish discourse about an infinite number of things, and who can diversify them an hundred ways. How many authors are there who are admired for their works, on account of the vast learning that is displayed in them, who are not able to sustain a conversation. Those who know Menage only by his books, might think he resembled those learned men; but if you show the MENAGIANA, you distinguish him from them, and make him known by a talent which is given to very few learned men. There it appears that he was a man who spoke offhand a thousand good things. His memory extended to what was ancient and modern; to the court and to the city; to the dead and to the living languages; to things serious and things jocose; in a word, to a thousand sorts of subjects. That which appeared a trifle to some readers of the "Menagiana," who did not consider circumstances, caused admiration in other readers, who minded the difference between what a man speaks without preparation, and that which he prepares for the press. And, therefore, we cannot sufficiently commend the care which his illustrious friends took to erect a monument so capable of giving him immortal glory. They were not obliged to rectify what they had heard him say; for, in so doing, they had not been faithful historians of his conversation."—B.

his thoughts with great force, and an elegant choice of language, the effect of which was aided by his having a loud voice and a slow deliberate utterance. In him were united a most logical head with a most fertile imagination, which gave him an extraordinary advantage in arguing: for he could reason close or wide, as he saw best for the moment. Exulting in his intellectual strength and dexterity, he could, when he pleased, be the greatest sophist that ever contended in the lists of declamation; and, from a spirit of contradiction and a delight in showing his powers, he would often maintain the wrong side with equal warmth and ingenuity; so that when there was an audience, his real opinions could seldom be gathered from his talk; though when he was in company with a single friend, he would discuss a subject with genuine fairness; but he was too conscientious to make error permanent and pernicious by deliberately writing it; and, in all his numerous works he earnestly inculcated what appeared to him to be the truth; his piety being constant, and the ruling principle of all his conduct.

Such was SAMUEL JOHNSON, a man whose talents, acquirements, and virtues, were so extraordinary, that the more his character is considered, the more he will be regarded by the present age, and by posterity, with admiration and reverence.

MEANING

1. What new insight does Boswell give into the character of this famous figure?
2. What aspects of Dr. Johnson's character does Boswell find commendable?
3. What evidence does Boswell present to support his contention that Johnson lived his life according to the principle that "of him to whom much is given, much will be required"?
4. What character trait does Boswell emphasize by telling his readers that, although Dr. Johnson could argue equally well on both sides of an issue, he would never set down in writing an opinion to which he did not subscribe?

USING DESCRIPTION TO CONVEY MEANING

1. How does Boswell arrange his description to let the reader know that he respected Dr. Johnson for holding himself to a higher standard in writing than he did in public discourse?
2. How does Boswell organize his character sketch, within each paragraph, from sentence to sentence, to convey the extreme contradictions operating in Johnson's personality?

WRITING SUGGESTIONS

1. Describe a person from a photograph so that someone who has not seen the photograph would be able to recognize him or her from your description.

2. After examining Dr. Johnson's famous "dictionary," discuss how the definitions Johnson provides reflect those intellectual abilities and character traits described by Boswell.

3. Describe a person whose character seems made up of many contradictions. Organize your character sketch to emphasize each side of the person's nature.

D. H. LAWRENCE

The Dance of the Sprouting Corn

David Herbert Lawrence (1885–1930) was born in Eastwood (which became "Bestwood" in Sons and Lovers*), Nottinghamshire, England, one of five children of a coal miner and a teacher. Encouraged by his mother, Lawrence became a schoolmaster and began writing poetry and short stories. His first novels,* The White Peacock *(1911) and* The Trespasser *(1912), were followed by* Sons and Lovers *(1913), a superbly developed autobiographical account of Lawrence's early years, and* The Rainbow *(1915), a book that initiated a lifelong battle against obscenity charges. His enduring reputation rests on these works and* Women in Love *(1921),* Aaron's Rod *(1922),* Kangaroo *(1923), and the remarkable* Studies in Classic American Literature *and* The Plumed Serpent *(both 1926), along with many collections of short stories, travel books, and poetry. In poor health for most of his life, Lawrence ultimately died of the tuberculosis which claimed many lives of those born into the coal-mining towns of England. "The Dance of the Sprouting Corn" (1927) embodies Lawrence's great descriptive abilities in evoking the rhythms, sights, sounds, and magic of the ritual dance of Indians in the Southwest as they celebrate the resurgence of the sprouting corn.*

Pale, dry, baked earth, that blows into dust of fine sand. Low hills of baked pale earth, sinking heavily, and speckled sparsely with dark dots of cedar bushes. A river on the plain of drought, just a cleft of dark, reddish-brown water, almost a flood. And over all, the blue, uneasy, alkaline sky.

A pale, uneven, parched world, where a motor-car rocks and lurches and churns in sand. A world pallid with dryness, inhuman with a faint taste of alkali. Like driving in the bed of a great sea that dried up unthinkable ages ago, and now is drier than any other dryness, yet still reminiscent of the bottom of the sea, sand-hills sinking, and straight, cracked mesas, like cracks in the dry-mud bottom of the sea.

So, the mud church standing discreetly outside, just outside the pueblo, not to see too much. And on its façade of mud, under the timbered mud-eaves, two speckled horses rampant, painted by the Indians, a red piebald and a black one.

Swish! Over the logs of the ditch-bridge, where brown water is flowing full. There below is the pueblo, dried mud like mud-pie houses, all squatting in a jumble, prepared to crumble into dust and be invisible, dust to dust returning, earth to earth.

That they don't crumble is the mystery. That these little squarish mud-heaps endure for centuries after centuries, while Greek marble tumbles asunder, and cathedrals totter, is the wonder. But then, the naked human hand with a bit of new soft mud is quicker than time, and defies the centuries.

Roughly the low, square, mud-pie houses make a wide street where all is naked earth save a doorway or a window with a pale-blue sash. At the end of the street, turn again into a parallel wide, dry street. And there, in the dry, oblong aridity, there tosses a small forest that is alive; and thud—thud—thud goes the drum, and the deep sound of men singing is like the deep soughing of the wind, in the depths of a wood.

You realize that you had heard the drum from the distance, also the deep, distant roar and boom of the singing, but that you had not heeded, as you don't heed the wind.

It all tosses like young, agile trees in a wind. This is the dance of the sprouting corn, and evrybody holds a little, beating branch of green pine. Thud—thud—thud—thud—thud! goes the drum, heavily the men hop and hop and hop, sway, sway, sway, sway go the little branches of green pine. It tosses like a little forest, and the deep sound of men's singing is like the booming and tearing of a wind deep inside a forest. They are dancing the spring corn dance.

This is the Wednesday after Easter, after Christ Risen and the corn germinated. They danced on Monday and on Tuesday. Wednesday is the third and last dance of this green resurrection.

You realize the long lines of dancers, and a solid cluster of men singing near the drum. You realize the intermittent black-and-white fantasy of the hopping Koshare, the jesters, the Delight-Makers. You become aware of the ripple of bells on the knee-garters of the dancers, a continual pulsing ripple of little bells; and of the sudden wild, whooping yells from near the drum. Then you become aware of the seed-like shudder of the gourd rattles, as the dance changes, and the swaying of the tufts of green pine-twigs stuck behind the arms of all the dancing men, in the broad green arm-bands.

Gradually comes through to you the black, stable solidity of the dancing women, who poise like solid shadow, one woman behind each rippling, leaping male. The long, silky black hair of the women, streaming down their backs, and the equally long, streaming, gleaming hair of the males, loose over broad, naked, orange-brown shoulders.

Then the faces, the impassive, rather fat, golden-brown faces of the women, with eyes cast down, crowned above with the green tableta, like a flat tiara. Something strange and noble about the impassive, barefoot women in the short black cassocks, as they subtly tread the dance, scarcely moving, and yet edging rhythmically along, swaying from each hand the green spray of pine-twig out—out—out—out, to the thud of the drum, immediately behind the leaping fox-skin of the men dancers. And all the emerald-green, painted tabletas, the flat wooden tiaras shaped like a castle gateway, rise steady and noble from the soft, slightly bowed heads of the women, held by a band under the chin. All the tabletas down the line, emerald green, almost steady, while the bright black heads of the men leap softly up and down, between.

Bit by bit you take it in. You cannot get a whole impression, save of some sort of wood tossing, a little forest of trees in motion, with gleaming black hair and gold-ruddy breasts that somehow do not destroy the illusion of forest.

When you look at the women, you forget the men. The bare-armed, bare-legged, barefoot women with streaming hair and lofty green tiaras, impassive, downward-looking faces, twigs swaying outwards from subtle, rhythmic wrists; women clad in the black, prehistoric short gown fastened over one shoulder, leaving the other shoulder bare, and showing at the arm-place a bit of pink or white undershirt; belted also round the waist with a woven woollen sash, scarlet and green on the handwoven black cassock. The noble, slightly submissive bending of the tiara-ed head. The subtle measure of the bare, breathing, bird-like feet, that are flat, and seem to cleave to earth softly, and softly lift away. The continuous outward swaying of the pine-sprays.

But when you look at the men, you forget the women. The men are naked to the waist, and ruddy-golden, and in the rhythmic, hopping leap of the dance their breasts shake downwards, as the strong, heavy body comes down, down, down, down, in the downward plunge of the dance. The black hair streams loose and living down their backs, the black brows are level, the black eyes look out unchanging from under the silky lashes. They are handsome, and absorbed with a deep rhythmic absorption, which still leaves them awake and aware. Down, down, down they drop, on the heavy, ceaseless leap of the dance, and the great necklaces of shell-cores spring on the naked breasts, the neck-shell flaps up and down, the short white kilt of woven stuff, with the heavy woollen embroidery, green and red and black, opens and shuts slightly to the strong lifting of the knees: the heavy whitish cords that hang from the kilt-band at the side sway and coil forever down the side of the right leg, down to the ankle, the bells on the red-woven garters under the knees ripple without end, and the feet, in buckskin boots furred round the ankle with a beautiful band of skunk fur, black with a white tip, come down with a lovely, heavy, soft precision, first one, then the other, dropping always plumb to earth. Slightly bending forward, a black gourd rattle in the right hand, a small green bough in the left, the dancer dances the eternal drooping leap, that brings his life down, down, down, down from the mind, down from the broad, beautiful, shaking breast, down to the powerful pivot of the knees, then to the ankles, and plunges deep from the ball of the foot into the earth, towards the earth's red centre, where these men belong, as is signified by the red earth with which they are smeared.

And meanwhile, the shell-cores from the Pacific sway up and down, ceaselessly, on their breasts.

Mindless, without effort, under the hot sun, unceasing, yet never perspiring nor even breathing heavily, they dance on and on. Mindless, yet still listening, observing. They hear the deep, surging singing of the bunch of old men, like a great wind soughing. They hear the cries and yells of the man waving his bough by the drum. They catch the word of the song, and at a moment, shudder the black rattles, wheel, and the line breaks, women from men, they thread across to a new formation. And as the men wheel round, their black hair gleams and shakes, and the long fox-skin sways, like a tail.

And always, when they form into line again, it is a beautiful long straight line, flexible as life, but straight as rain.

The men round the drum are old, or elderly. They are all in a bunch, and they wear day dress, loose cotton drawers, pink or white cotton shirt, hair tied up behind with the red cords, and banded round the head with a strip of pink rag, or white rag, or blue. There they are, solid like a cluster of bees, their black heads with the pink rag circles all close together, swaying their pine-twigs with rhythmic, wind-swept hands, dancing slightly, mostly on the right foot, ceaselessly, and singing, their black bright eyes absorbed, their dark lips pushed out, while the deep strong sound rushes like wind, and the unknown words form themselves in the dark.

Suddenly the solitary man pounding the drum swings his drum round, and begins to pound on the other end, on a higher note, pang—pang—pang! instead of the previous brumm! brumm! brumm! of the bass note. The watchful man next the drummer yells and waves lightly, dancing on birdfeet. The Koshare make strange, eloquent gestures to the sky.

And again the gleaming bronze-and-dark men dancing in the rows shudder their rattles, break the rhythm, change into a queer, beautiful two-step, the long lines suddenly curl into rings, four rings of dancers, the leaping, gleaming-seeming men between the solid, subtle, submissive blackness of the women who are crowned with emerald-green tiaras, all going subtly round in rings. Then slowly they change again, and form a star. Then again, unmingling, they come back into rows.

And all the while, all the while the naked Koshare are threading about. Of bronze-and-dark men dancers there are some forty-two, each with a dark, crowned woman attending him like a shadow. The old men, the bunch of singers in shirts and tied-up black hair, are about sixty in number, or sixty-four. The Koshare are about twenty-four.

They are slim and naked, daubed with black-and-white earth, their hair daubed white and gathered upwards to a great knot on top of the head, whence springs a tuft of cornhusks, dry corn leaves. Though they wear nothing but a little black square cloth, front and back, at their middle, they do not seem naked, for some are white with black spots, like a leopard, and some have broad black lines or zigzags on their smeared bodies, and all their faces are blackened with triangles or lines till they look like weird masks. Meanwhile their hair, gathered straight up and daubed white and sticking up from the top of the head with corn-husks, completes the fantasy. They are anything but natural. Like blackened ghosts of a dead corn-cob, tufted at the top.

And all the time, running like queer spotted dogs, they weave nakedly through the unheeding dance, comical, weird, dancing the dance-step naked and fine, prancing through the lines, up and down the lines, and making fine gestures with their flexible hands, calling something down from the sky, calling something up from the earth, and dancing forward all the time. Suddenly as they catch a word from the singers, name of a star, of a wind, a name for the sun, for a cloud, their hands soar up and gather in the air, soar down with a slow motion. And again, as they catch a word that means earth, earth deeps, water within the earth, or red-earth-quickening, the hands flutter softly down, and draw up the water, draw up the earth-quickening, earth to sky, sky to earth, influences above to influences below, to meet in the germ-quick of corn, where life is.

And as they dance, the Koshare watch the dancing men. And if a fox-skin is coming loose at the belt, they fasten it as the man dances, or they stoop and tie another man's shoe. For the dancer must not hesitate to the end.

And then, after some forty minutes, the drum stops. Slowly the dancers file into one line, woman behind man, and move away, threading towards their kiva,[1] with no sound but the tinkle of knee-bells in the silence.

But at the same moment the thud of an unseen drum, from beyond, the soughing

---

[1] Ceremonial chamber of the Pueblo Indians.

of deep song approaching from the unseen. It is the other half, the other half of the tribe coming to continue the dance. They appear round the kiva—one Koshare and one dancer leading the rows, the old men all abreast, singing already in a great strong burst.

So, from ten o'clock in the morning till about four in the afternoon, first one-half then the other. Till at last, as the day wanes, the two halves meet, and the two singings like two great winds surge one past the other, and the thicket of the dance becomes a real forest. It is the close of the third day.

Afterwards, the men and women crowd on the roofs of the two low round towers, the kivas, while the Koshare run round jesting and miming, and taking big offerings from the women, loaves of bread and cakes of blue-maize meal. Women come carrying big baskets of bread and guayaba, on two hands, an offering.

And the mystery of germination, not procreation, but *putting forth,* resurrection, life springing within the seed, is accomplished. The sky has its fire, its waters, its stars, its wandering electricity, its winds, its fingers of cold. The earth has its reddened body, its invisible hot heart, its inner waters and many juices and unaccountable stuffs. Between them all, the little seed: and also man, like a seed that is busy and aware. And from the heights and from the depths man, the caller, calls: a man, the knower, brings down the influences and brings up the influences, with his knowledge: man, so vulnerable, so subject, and yet even in his vulnerability and subjection, a master, commands the invisible influences and is obeyed. Commands in that song, in that rhythmic energy of dance, in that still-submissive mockery of the Koshare. And he accomplishes his end, as master. He partakes in the springing of the corn, in the rising and budding and earing of the corn. And when he eats his bread, at last, he recovers all he once sent forth, and partakes again of the energies he called to the corn, from out of the wide universe.

MEANING

1. What result is the ritual of the "dance of the sprouting corn" designed to achieve?
2. What significance does Lawrence find in the fact that the "dance" is performed in the three days after Easter?
3. Why is it important that the dancers submerge their individual identities and perform the "dance" as a tribal unit?
4. What different roles are performed by separate groups of dancers during this ritual?

USING DESCRIPTION TO CONVEY MEANING

1. Which descriptive phrases recreate the insistent beat of the dancers as they move and chant?
2. How does Lawrence create a mood of expectancy by first describing the desert background, adobe houses, and distant sounds of drums, before focusing on the dancers?

3. What images of sight, sound, taste, touch, and smell does Lawrence use to recreate the scene for his readers?

4. Where does Lawrence use techniques found in poetry, such as alliteration and rhythmic phrasing, to express the rhythm and motion of the dance?

Writing Suggestions

1. What connections can you discover between the reasons for the performance of the "dance of the sprouting corn" (as an invocation to reawaken the corn) and Frazer's (see page 114) research into the myths and rituals surrounding the primitive corn gods?

2. How does Pavlova's dancing (see page 83) differ in purpose and technique from the ceremonial dance that Lawrence describes? Discuss the implications of these differences as they reveal cultural values.

POLITICAL AND SOCIAL SCIENCES

Oscar Handlin

Steerage

Oscar Handlin, born in 1915 in New York City, received his Ph.D. from Harvard in 1935. A distinguished social historian, Handlin is the author of many definitive works, including The Uprooted *(1951), which received the Pulitzer Prize,* Immigration as a Factor in American History *(1959),* Truth in History *(1979), and* The Distortion of America *(1981). He has also served as the editor of important works that interpret the immigrant experience in America, which include* Children of the Uprooted *(1966) and the* Harvard Encyclopedia of American Ethnic Groups *(1980). "Steerage," drawn from the second chapter of* The Uprooted, *conveys Handlin's mastery in compressing a wealth of detail on the immigrant experience into a few telling paragraphs.*

The difficulty of residence in the ports complicated the problems of securing passage. The overpowering desire to get away as soon as possible took precedence over every other consideration. The temptation was to regard the ship quickest found, the best. Haste often led to unexpected and tragic consequences.

Until after the middle of the nineteenth century, the emigrants were carried in sailing vessels, few in number, irregular in the routes they followed, and uncertain as to their destination. Often the masters of these craft did not know for which port they would head until the sails were set; generally the cargo dictated the course. But there was no assurance, even after the ship was under way, that wind or weather would not induce a change. Only rarely could the passengers protest or, as on the *Mary Ann* in 1817, actually revolt. The generality did not expect to be able to choose a precise place of landing in the New World; if they reached shore somewhere in America that was enough.

Nor could they be overly fastidious about the character of their conveyance. Reckoning up the sum of guarded coins, the emigrants knew how little power they had to

103

command favorable terms. The fare could, of course, be haggled over; there were no established rates and those who shared the same steerage would later discover that the charge varied from two to five pounds, depending upon the bargaining power of the various parties. But in the long run the shipmasters held the more favorable situation and could push the rate nearer the higher than the lower limit.

Indeed, as the volume of traffic mounted, the captains no longer had to trouble with these negotiations themselves. The business fell into the hands of middlemen. Enterprising brokers contracted for the steerage space of whole ships and then resold accommodations to prospective travelers. As might be expected, avarice magnified the fancied capacity of the vessels to an unbearable degree, in fact, to a degree that provoked government intervention. But even when the American and British governments began to regulate the number of passengers and, after 1850, even began to enforce those regulations, the emigrant was but poorly protected. The brokers continued to sell as many tickets as they could; and the purchasers above the legal limit, denied permission to board, could only hope to hunt up the swindler who had misled them and seek the return of their funds.

In time, at last, the day approached. On the morning the fortunate ones whose turn it was worriedly gathered their possessions, hastened from lodginghouse to ship's side. The children dragged along the trusses of straw on which they would sleep while the men wrestled onward with the cumbrous barrels that would hold their water, with the battered chests crammed with belongings. Not into the ship yet, but into a thronging expectant crowd they pushed their way, shoving to keep sight of each other, deafened by their own impatient noises and by the cries of peddlers who thrust at them now nuts and taffy for the moment, now pots and provisions for the way.

Some, having waited so long, would wait no more and tried to clamber up the dangling ropes. The most stayed anxiously still and when the moment came jostled along until they stood then upon the ship. And when they stood then upon the ship, when the Old Land was no longer beneath them, they sensed the sea in uneasy motion and knew they were committed to a new destiny. As they lined up for the roll call, their curious gaze sought out the features of this their unfamiliar home—the rising masts, the great folds of sail, the web of rigging, and the bold, pointing bowsprit. Silenced and as if immobilized by the decisiveness of the moment, they remained for a while on deck; and some, raising their eyes from examination of the ship itself, noticed the shores of the Mersey or Weser move slowly by. There was time, before they passed through the estuary to the empty ocean, to reflect on the long way they had come, to mingle with the hope and gratitude of escape the sadness and resentment of flight.

In the early days there was leisure enough for reflection on these matters. The journey was long, the average from Liverpool to New York about forty days. Favorable weather might lower the figure to a month, unfavorable raise it to two or three. The span was uncertain, for the ship was at the mercy of the winds and tides, of the primitive navigation of its masters, and of the ignorance of its barely skilled sailors.

These unsubstantial craft sailed always at the edge of danger from the elements. Wrecks were disastrous and frequent. A single year in the 1830's saw seventeen vessels founder on the run from Liverpool to Quebec alone. Occasional mutinies put the fate of all in dubious hands. Fire, caused by the carelessness of passengers or crew, added another hazard to the trials of the journey. At a blow, such catastrophes swept away scores of lives, ended without further ado many minor histories in the peopling of the new continent.

Other perils too, less dramatic but more pervasive, insidiously made shipwreck of hopes. In the slow-elapsing crossing, the boat became a circumscribed universe of its own, with its own harsh little way of life determined by the absence of space. Down to midcentury the vessels were pitifully small; three hundred tons was a good size. Yet into these tiny craft were crammed anywhere from four hundred to a thousand passengers.

These numbers set the terms of shipboard life. If they talked of it later, the emigrants almost forgot that there had also been cabins for the other sort of men who could pay out twenty to forty pounds for passage. Their own world was the steerage.

Below decks is the place, its usual dimensions seventy-five feet long, twenty-five wide, five and a half high. Descend. In the fitful light your eye will discover a middle aisle five feet wide. It will be a while before you can make out the separate shapes within it, the water closets at either end (for the women; the men must go above deck), one or several cooking stoves, the tables. The aisle itself, you will see, is formed by two rows of bunks that run to the side of the ship.

Examine a bunk. One wooden partition reaches from floor to ceiling to divide it from the aisle, another stretches horizontally from wall to aisle to create two decks. Within the partitions are the boxlike spaces, ten feet wide, five long, less than three high. For the months of the voyage, each is home for six to ten beings.

This was the steerage setting. Here the emigrants lived their lives, day and night. The more generous masters gave them access to a portion of the deck at certain hours. But bad weather often deprived the passengers of that privilege, kept them below for days on end.

Life was hard here. Each family received its daily ration of water, adding to it larger and larger doses of vinegar to conceal the odor. From the limited hoard of provisions brought along, the mother struggled to eke out food for the whole journey. She knew that if the potatoes ran out there would be only the captain to turn to, who could be counted on mercilessly to extort every last possession in return; some masters, in fact, deliberately deceived the emigrants as to the length of the journey, to be able to profit from the sale of food and grog. Later, at midcentury, the government would specify the supplies that had to be taken for each passenger. But there remained ways of avoiding such regulations; tenders followed the ships out of the harbor and carried back the casks checked on for the inspector.

It was no surprise that disease should be a familiar visitor. The only ventilation was through the hatches battened down in rough weather. When the close air was not stifling hot, it was bitter cold in the absence of fire. Rats were at home in the dirt and disorder. The result: cholera, dysentery, yellow fever, smallpox, measles, and the generic "ship fever" that might be anything. It was not always as bad as on the *April*, on which five hundred of eleven hundred Germans perished in the crossing; the normal mortality was about 10 per cent, although in the great year, 1847, it was closer to 20.

It was perhaps no consolation to these emigrants, but they were not the worst off. Among the Irish before 1850 there were some who had not the paltry price of a steerage passage, yet for whom there was no return from Liverpool. They had to find the means of a still cheaper crossing.

From Canada came awkward ships built expressly to bring eastward the tall timbers of American forests, lumbering vessels with great open holds not suited for the carriage of any west-bound cargo. From Nova Scotia and Newfoundland came fishing boats laden with the catch of the Grand Bank; these craft also could be entrusted with no cargo of value on their return. Formerly both types went back in ballast. Now they would bring the New World to Irishmen. The pittance these poor creatures could pay—ten to twenty shillings—was pure gain. As for the passengers, they would camp out in the empty stinking space below decks, spend an uneasy purgatory preparatory to the redemption by America.

From the harshness, the monotony, the misery of the journey, there was no effective relief. Government protection came late, was minimal, and lacked effective means of enforcement. After all, as the shipping agents argued, the emigrant had never known what it was to sleep in a bed. Give him pork and flour and you make the man sick. Let him lie on a good firm deck, eat salt herring, and he'll be hale and hearty.

Against the open brutalities, against the seamen who reckoned the women fair game, against the danger from within of petty theft and quarrels, the passengers formed spontaneous organizations of their own. The voluntary little associations were governed by codes of agreement, enforced by watchmen appointed from among themselves. But there was no power in these groups, on major matters, to resist the all-powerful captain and crew.

So they'd lie there, seafaring adventures out to discover new continents, amidst the retching, noisome stench, the stomach-turning filth of hundreds of bodies confined to close quarters. Many nights, and many days that were indistinguishable from nights, they could see, by the sickly light of swinging lanterns, the creaking ugly timbers crowding in about them; they could hear the sounds of men in uneasy silence, of children in fitful rest; everywhere they could sense the menace of hostile winds and waves, of indifferent companions, of repressed passions.

There are times when a man can take no more. Incidents occur: ugly noises of childbirth; sopping disorder when the sea seeps in in a storm; unsuccessful rat-hunts; the splash of burials under a dark sky and without the consolation of a priest. *Ah, we thought we couldn't be worse off than we war; but now to our sorrow we know the differ; for supposin we war dyin of starvation, it would still not be dyin like rotten sheep thrown into a pit, and the minit the breath is out of our bodies, flung into the sea to be eaten up by them horrid sharks.* And a red rage takes hold of the sufferers, of their survivors. They pace about in the warm sticky passage. They clench fists. But against whom shall they raise them? Indeed they are helpless, and they fall into meaningless arguments among themselves. Furious blows are given by the wrestling mass of men in the narrow spaces; until, exhausted, they stand back, angry, ashamed, pick up the pitiful belongings kicked loose, broken, wet from the bilge water oozing up through the spaces of the floor boards. They laugh only at the greater misery of others.

Substantial improvements in the conditions of the crossing came only as indirect results of changes in the techniques of ocean travel. The introduction of steam in the transatlantic service in the 1840s was the first step. The Cunard Line and its imitators pre-empted the high-class passenger business and drove the sailing ships back upon the immigrant trade. Competition for that trade lowered the costs and improved the accommodations. By 1860 it was possible to buy reasonably priced prepaid tickets and to travel on a reliable schedule.

After 1870 the situation was even better. The new era in international relations emphasized navalism and drew the major European nations into a warship building race. Great merchant fleets seemed the necessary complements. England, France, Germany, and Italy hurried to build up their tonnage. Toward that end they were willing to grant heavy subsidies to the operators of the lines bearing their flags. Under those circumstances the price of steerage passage on a steamship fell to as little as twelve dollars, and included food. By the end of that decade, steam had displaced sail in the emigrant-carrying business.

Now the duration of the journey fell until it took ten days or less. Comfort and safety increased also. By 1900, the traveler could count on a crossing of little more than a week in vessels of ten to twenty thousand tons. 24

MEANING

1. What circumstances made the forty-day journey, in steerage, from Liverpool to New York such a hardship for the immigrants?
2. What statistics does Handlin provide about the number of ships going to America, length of the voyage, amount of food and water rations, and exact physical dimensions of space below decks, to recreate an accurate and realistic description of what steerage was like for the immigrants?
3. What picture does Handlin present of the relationship between the people in steerage and the captain and crew of the ships?

USING DESCRIPTION TO CONVEY MEANING

1. What details allow the reader to feel what it must have been like to be an immigrant on this forty-day journey, living in cramped darkness below decks, without enough water and food?
2. How does Handlin organize his description so that the reader can enter the mind of the steerage passengers and share what they must have felt?
3. Discuss Handlin's use of the images of light and darkness to lead his readers below decks into the world of steerage.
4. How does Handlin's discussion of ineffective governmental agencies emphasize how self-reliant the immigrants had to be to survive?

WRITING SUGGESTIONS

1. Describe the experiences of a family member or friend who came to America as an immigrant.
2. Contrast the behavior of the immigrants in Handlin's account, who endured hardship because of their hope for a better life, with Borowski's re-enactment (see the "Narration" chapter, page 50) of the dehumanizing effect of being forcibly imprisoned, without hope, in a labor camp. What conclusions can you draw about the importance of "hope" to human beings?
3. Describe a physically and/or psychologically demanding period of time in your life. Use specific details to graphically recreate your experience.

HOWARD CARTER

Finding the Tomb

Howard Carter (1873–1939), the English archeologist whose work resulted in the discovery of the tomb of Tutankhamen, the boy king of the eighteenth dynasty (fourteenth century B.C.), was born in London and first went to Egypt as a draughtsman with the Archaeological Survey Department. Although his first excavations in the Valley of the Tomb of the Kings began in 1902, it was not until November 1922 that he made his greatest discovery at Thebes, along with his benefactor, Lord Carnarvon (who died in 1923, during the excavation of Tutankhamen's tomb, under mysterious circumstances). "Finding the Tomb," from Carter's three-volume account of the excavation, The Tomb of Tutankhamen (1933), describes the exciting story of one of the greatest archeological discoveries of all time.

The history of the Valley, as I have endeavoured to show in former chapters, has never lacked the dramatic element, and in this, the latest episode, it has held to its traditions. For consider the circumstances. This was to be our final season in the Valley. Six full seasons we had excavated there, and season after season had drawn a blank; we had worked for months at a stretch and found nothing, and only an excavator knows how desperately depressing that can be; we had almost made up our minds that we were beaten, and were preparing to leave the Valley and try our luck elsewhere; and then—hardly had we sat hoe to ground in our last despairing effort than we made a discovery that far exceeded our wildest dreams. Surely, never before in the whole history of excavation has a full digging season been compressed within the space of five days.

Let me try and tell the story of it all. It will not be easy, for the dramatic suddenness of the initial discovery left me in a dazed condition, and the months that have followed have been so crowded with incident that I have hardly had time to think. Setting it down on paper will perhaps give me a chance to realize what has happened and all that it means.

I arrived in Luxor on 28 October, and by 1 November I had enrolled my workmen and was ready to begin. Our former excavations had stopped short at the north-east corner of the tomb of Rameses VI, and from this point I started trenching southwards. It will be remembered that in this area there were a number of roughly constructed workmen's huts, used probably by the labourers in the tomb of Rameses. These huts, built about three feet above bed-rock, covered the whole area in front of the Ramesside tomb, and continued in a southerly direction to join up with a similar group of huts on the opposite side of the Valley, discovered by Davis in connexion with his work on the Akhenaten cache. By the evening of 3 November we had laid bare a sufficient number of these huts for experimental purposes, so, after we had planned and noted them, they were removed, and we were ready to clear away the three feet of soil that lay beneath them.

Hardly had I arrived on the work next morning (4 November) than the unusual silence, due to the stoppage of the work, made me realize that something out of the ordinary had happened, and I was greeted by the announcement that a step cut in the rock had been discovered underneath the very first hut to be attacked. This seemed too good to be true, but a short amount of extra clearing revealed the fact that we were actually in the entrance of a steep cut in the rock, some thirteen feet below the entrance to the tomb of Rameses VI, and a similar depth from the present bed level of the Valley. The manner of cutting was that of the sunken stairway entrance so common in the Valley, and I almost dared to hope that we had found our tomb at last. Work continued feverishly throughout the whole of that day and the morning of the next, but it was not until the afternoon of 5 November that we succeeded in clearing away the masses of rubbish that overlay the cut, and were able to demarcate the upper edges of the stairway on all its four sides.

It was clear by now beyond any question that we actually had before us the entrance to a tomb, but doubts, born of previous disappointments, persisted in creeping in. There was always the horrible possibility, suggested by our experience in the Thothmes III Valley, that the tomb was an unfinished one, never completed and never used: if it had been finished there was the depressing probability that it had been completely plundered in ancient times. On the other hand, there was just the chance of an untouched or only partially plundered tomb, and it was with ill-suppressed excitement that I watched the descending steps of the staircase, as one by one they came to light. The cutting was excavated in the side of a small hillock, and, as the work progressed, its western edge receded under the slope of the rock until it was, first partially, and then completely, roofed in, and became a passage, ten feet high by six feet wide. Work progressed more rapidly now; step succeeded step, and at the level of the twelfth, towards sunset, there was disclosed the upper part of a doorway, blocked, plastered, and sealed.

A sealed doorway—it was actually true, then! Our years of patient labour were to be rewarded after all, and I think my first feeling was one of congratulation that my faith in the Valley had not been unjustified. With excitement growing to fever heat I searched the seal impressions on the door for evidence of the identity of the owner, but could find no name: the only decipherable ones were those of the well-known royal necropolis seal, the jackal and nine captives. Two facts, however, were clear: first, the employment of this royal seal was certain evidence that the tomb had been constructed for a person of very high standing; and second, that the sealed door was entirely screened from above by workmen's huts of the Twentieth Dynasty was sufficiently clear proof that at least from that date it had never been entered. With that for the moment I had to be content.

While examining the seals I noticed, at the top of the doorway, where some of the plaster had fallen away, a heavy wooden lintel. Under this, to assure myself of the method by which the doorway had been blocked, I made a small peephole, just large enough to insert an electric torch, and discovered that the passage beyond the door was filled completely from floor to ceiling with stones and rubble—additional proof this of the care with which the tomb had been protected.

It was a thrilling moment for an excavator. Alone, save for my native workmen, I found myself, after years of comparatively unproductive labour, on the threshold of what might prove to be a magnificent discovery. Anything, literally anything, might lie beyond that passage, and it needed all my self-control to keep from breaking down the doorway, and investigating then and there.

One thing puzzled me, and that was the smallness of the opening in comparison with the ordinary Valley tombs. The design was certainly of the Eighteenth Dynasty. Could it be the tomb of a noble buried here by royal consent? Was it a royal cache, a hiding-place to which a mummy and its equipment had been removed for safety? Or was it actually the tomb of the king for whom I had spent so many years in search.

Once more I examined the seal impressions for a clue, but on the part of the door so far laid bare only those of the royal necropolis seal already mentioned were clear enough to read. Had I but known that a few inches lower down there was a perfectly clear and distinct impression of the seal of Tutankhamen, the king I most desired to find, I would have cleared on, had a much better night's rest in consequence, and saved myself nearly three weeks of uncertainty. It was late, however, and darkness was already upon us. With some reluctance I re-closed the small hole that I had made, filled in our excavation for protection during the night, selected the most trustworthy of my workmen—themselves almost as excited as I was—to watch all night above the tomb, and so home by moonlight, riding down the Valley.

Naturally my wish was to go straight ahead with our clearing to find out the full extent of the discovery, but Lord Carnarvon was in England, and in fairness to him I had to delay matters until he could come. Accordingly, on the morning of 6 November I sent him the following cable: "At last have made wonderful discovery in Valley; a magnificent tomb with seals intact; re-covered same for your arrival; congratulations."

My next task was to secure the doorway against interference until such time as it could finally be reopened. This we did by filling our excavation up again to surface level, and rolling on top of it the large flint boulders of which the workmen's huts had been composed. By the evening of the same day, exactly forty-eight hours after we had discovered the first step of the staircase, this was accomplished. The tomb had vanished. So far as the appearance of the ground was concerned there never had been any tomb, and I found it hard to persuade myself at times that the whole episode had not been a dream.

I was soon to be reassured on this point. News travels fast in Egypt, and within two days of the discovery congratulations, inquiries, and offers of help descended upon me in a steady stream from all directions. It became clear, even at this early stage, that I was in for a job that could not be tackled single-handed, so I wired to Callender, who had helped me on various previous occasions, asking him if possible to join me without delay, and to my relief he arrived on the very next day. On the 8th I had received two messages from Lord Carnarvon in answer to my cable, the first of which read, "Possibly come soon," and the second, received a little later, "Propose arrive Alexandria 20th."

We had thus nearly a fortnight's grace, and we devoted it to making preparations of various kinds, so that when the time of reopening came, we should be able, with the least possible delay, to handle any situation that might arise. On the night of the 18th I went to Cairo for three days, to meet Lord Carnarvon and make a number of necessary purchases, returning to Luxor on the 21st. On the 23rd Lord Carnarvon arrived in Luxor with his daughter, Lady Evelyn Herbert, his devoted companion in all his Egyptian work, and everything was in hand for the beginning of the second chapter of the discovery of the tomb. Callender had been busy all day clearing away the upper layer of rubbish, so that by morning we should be able to get into the staircase without any delay.

By the afternoon of the 24th the whole staircase was clear, sixteen steps in all, and we were able to make a proper examination of the sealed doorway. On the lower part the seal impressions were much clearer, and we were able without any difficulty to make out on several of them the name of Tutankhamen. This added enormously to the interest of the discovery. If we had found, as seemed almost certain, the tomb of that shadowy monarch, whose tenure of the throne coincided with one of the most interesting periods in the whole of Egyptian history, we should indeed have reason to congratulate ourselves.

With heightened interest, if that were possible, we renewed our investigation of the doorway. Here for the first time a disquieting element made its appearance. Now that the whole door was exposed to light it was possible to discern a fact that had hitherto escaped notice—that there had been two successive openings and reclosings of a part of its surface: furthermore, that the sealing originally discovered, the jackal and nine captives, had been applied to the re-closed portions, whereas the sealings of Tutankhamen covered the untouched part of the doorway, and were therefore those with which the tomb had been originally secured. The tomb then was not absolutely intact, as we had hoped. Plunderers had entered it, and entered it more than once—from the evidence of the huts above, plunderers of a date not later than the reign of Rameses VI—but that they had not rifled it completely was evident from the fact that it had been re-sealed.

Then came another puzzle. In the lower strata of rubbish that filled the staircase we found masses of broken potsherds and boxes, the latter bearing the names of Akhenaten, Smenkhkare and Tutankhamen, and, what was much more upsetting, a scarab of Thothmes III and a fragment with the name of Amenhetep III. Why this mixture of names? The balance of evidence so far would seem to indicate a cache rather than a tomb, and at this stage in the proceedings we inclined more and more to the opinion that we were about to find a miscellaneous collection of objects of the Eighteenth Dynasty kings, brought from Tell el Amarna by Tutankhamen and deposited here for safety.

So matters stood on the evening of the 24th. On the following day the sealed doorway was to be removed, so Callender set carpenters to work making a heavy wooden grille to be set up in its place. Mr. Engelbach, Chief Inspector of the Antiquities Department, paid us a visit during the afternoon, and witnessed part of the final clearing of rubbish from the doorway.

On the morning of the 25th the seal impressions on the doorway were carefully noted and photographed, and then we removed the actual blocking of the door, consisting of rough stones carefully built from floor to lintel, and heavily plastered on their outer faces to take the seal impressions.

This disclosed the beginning of a descending passage (not a staircase), the same width as the entrance stairway, and nearly seven feet high. As I had already discovered from my hole in the doorway, it was filled completely with stone and rubbble, probably the chip from its own excavation. This filling, like the doorway, showed distinct signs of more than one opening and re-closing of the tomb, the untouched part consisting of clean white chip, mingled with dust, whereas the disturbed part was composed mainly of dark flint. It was clear that an irregular tunnel had been cut through the original filling at the upper corner on the left side, a tunnel corresponding in position with that of the hole in the doorway.

As we cleared the passage we found, mixed with the rubble of the lower levels, broken potsherds, jar sealings, alabaster jars, whole and broken, vases of painted pottery, numerous fragments of smaller articles, and water skins, these last having obviously been used to bring up the water needed for the plastering of the doorways. These were clear evidence of plundering, and we eyed them askance. By night we had cleared a considerable distance down the passage, but as yet saw no sign of second doorway or of chamber.

The day following (26 November) was the day of days, the most wonderful that I have ever lived through, and certainly one whose like I can never hope to see again. Throughout the morning the work of clearing continued, slowly perforce, on account of the delicate objects that were mixed with the filling. Then, in the middle of the afternoon, thirty feet down from the outer door, we came upon a second sealed doorway, almost an exact replica of the first. The seal impressions in this case were less distinct, but still recognizable as those of Tutankhamen and of the royal necropolis. Here again the signs of opening and re-closing were clearly marked upon the plaster. We were firmly convinced by this time that it was a cache that we were about to open, and not a tomb. The arrangement of stairway, entrance passage and doors reminded us very forcibly of the cache of Akhenaten and Tyi material found in the very near vicinity of the present excavation by Davis, and the fact that Tutankhamen's seals occurred there likewise seemed almost certain proof that we were right in our conjecture. We were soon to know. There lay the sealed doorway, and behind it was the answer to the question.

Slowly, desperately slowly it seemed to us as we watched, the remains of passage debris that encumbered the lower part of the doorway were removed, until at last we had the whole door clear before us. The decisive moment had arrived. With trembling hands I made a tiny breach in the upper left-hand corner. Darkness and blank space, as far as an iron testing-rod could reach, showed that whatever lay beyond was empty, and not filled like the passage we had just cleared. Candle tests were applied as a precaution against foul gases, and then, widening the hole a little, I inserted the candle and peered in, Lord Carnarvon, Lady Evelyn and Callender standing anxiously beside me to hear the verdict. At first I could see nothing, the hot air escaping from the chamber causing the candle flame to flicker, but presently, as my eyes grew accustomed to the light, details of the room within emerged slowly from the midst, strange animals, statutes, and gold—everywhere the glint of gold. For the moment—an eternity it must have seemed to the others standing by—I was struck dumb with amazement, and when Lord Carnarvon, unable to stand the suspense any longer, inquired anxiously, "Can you see anything?" it was all I could do to get out the words. "Yes, wonderful things." Then, widening the hole a little further, so that we both could see, we inserted an electric torch.

MEANING

1. What is the significance of the archeological discovery that Carter made?
2. Why was it reasonable for Carter to assume that the tomb might have been already ransacked?
3. What obstacles did Carter have to overcome in continuing his search for the tomb for so many years?

4. Why was Carter encouraged by the condition of the royal seal on the door to the tomb?
5. Why did Carter fear that the tomb he discovered was only of minor importance rather than the long sought-after royal chamber?
6. Why did Carter delay opening the royal tomb until his patron, Lord Carnarvon, arrived from England?

USING DESCRIPTION TO CONVEY MEANING

1. How does Carter organize his essay to heighten suspense as to whether the tomb had been previously ransacked by grave-robbers, or was still intact?
2. How does Carter's detailed description help us to visualize the layout of the excavation?
3. What significant details does Carter include that communicate the exacting, methodical nature of archeological work?

WRITING SUGGESTIONS

1. Using Carter's description, try your hand at drawing a map of the site, including an interior view of Tutankhamen's tomb.
2. As a research project, investigate what archeologists have concluded about the reign of Tutankhamen or the significance of any of the individual items found in the tomb.
3. In a short essay, describe the circumstances of the discovery of the "Rosetta Stone" by one of Napoleon's soldiers on August 2, 1799, and its role in allowing archeologists to decipher and understand the previously hidden history of Egyptian culture revealed in hieroglyphs.
4. Nearly everyone has had the experience of entering a deserted house or building at night and discovering that it seemed quite different than it appeared in daylight. Write two short descriptions of the same building or house. In the first, tell how it looked in daylight. In the second, describe the same building at night, using words and phrases to create a mood of suspense.
5. What would an archeologist conclude about the culture that produced the various objects in your most cluttered desk drawer? What are some likely hypotheses about the functional or ritualistic purposes of two of these items?

SIR JAMES GEORGE FRAZER

The Myth and Ritual of Adonis

Sir James George Frazer (1854–1941) was born in Glasgow, Scotland, received a classical education at Trinity College in Cambridge, and published in 1890 the first edition of The Golden Bough, *one of the most important intellectual achievements of the twentieth century. The title is drawn from Book VI of the* Aeneid *and reflects Frazer's early investigations of the rites surrounding the worship of Diana. Ultimately,* The Golden Bough *became a work of twelve volumes (1911–1915) and an appendix (1936), documenting how rites and practices in European countries resembled the customs and beliefs of primitive societies. Although Frazer's work served as a catalyst for anthropologists such as Bronislaw Malinowski, the greatest influence of* The Golden Bough *was in fields outside of anthropology. The noted historian, Arnold Toynbee, and literary figures such as T. S. Eliot, Ezra Pound, D. H. Lawrence, and, most recently, Ted Hughes, are but a few of those in his debt. Freud, too, in* Totem and Taboo *(1913), cites Frazer's research. "The Myth and Ritual of Adonis," from* The Golden Bough, *describes rites and ceremonies that form a link between belief in the gods and seasonal vegetational cycles, and points out striking similarities between ancient myths and Christian beliefs.*

THE MYTH OF ADONIS

The spectacle of the great changes which annually pass over the face of the earth has powerfully impressed the minds of men in all ages, and stirred them to meditate on the causes of transformations so vast and wonderful. Their curiosity has not been purely disinterested; for even the savage cannot fail to perceive how intimately his own life is bound up with the life of nature, and how the same processes which freeze the stream and strip the earth of vegetation menace him with extinction. At a certain stage of development men seem to have imagined that the means of averting the threatened calamity were in their own hands, and that they could hasten or retard the flight of the seasons by magic art. Accordingly they performed ceremonies and recited spells to make the rain to fall, the sun to shine, animals to multiply, and the fruits of the earth to grow. In course of time the slow advance of knowledge, which has dispelled so many cherished illusions, convinced at least the more thoughtful portion of mankind that the alternations of summer and winter, of spring and autumn, were not merely the result of their own magical rites, but that some deeper cause, some mightier power, was at work behind the shifting scenes of nature. They now pictured to themselves the growth and decay of vegetation, the birth and death of living creatures, as effects of the waxing or waning strength of divine beings, of gods and goddesses, who were born and died, who married and begot children, on the pattern of human life.

Thus the old magical theory of the seasons was displaced, or rather supplemented, by a religious theory. For although men now attributed the annual cycle of change primarily to corresponding changes in their deities, they still thought that by performing certain magical rites they could aid the god who was the principle of life, in his struggle with the opposing principle of death. They imagined that they could recruit his failing energies and even raise him from the dead. The ceremonies which they observed for this purpose were in substance a dramatic representation of the natural processes which they wished to facilitate; for it is a familiar tenet of magic that you can produce any desired effect by merely imitating it. And as they now explained the fluctuations of growth and decay, of reproduction and dissolution by the marriage, the death, and the rebirth or revival of the gods, their religious or rather magical dramas turned in great measure on these themes. They set forth the fruitful union of the powers of fertility, the sad death of one at least of the divine partners, and his joyful resurrection. Thus a religious theory was blended with a magical practice. . . .

Of the changes which the seasons bring with them, the most striking within the temperate zone are those which affect vegetation. The influence of the seasons on animals, though great, is not nearly so manifest. Hence it is natural that in the magical dramas designed to dispel winter and bring back spring the emphasis should be laid on vegetation, and that trees and plants should figure in them more prominently than beasts and birds. Yet the two sides of life, the vegetable and the animal, were not dissociated in the minds of those who observed the ceremonies. Indeed they commonly believed that the tie between the animal and the vegetable world was even closer than it really is; hence they often combined the dramatic representation of reviving plants with a real or a dramatic union of the sexes for the purpose of furthering at the same time and by the same act the multiplication of fruits, of animals, and of men. To them the principle of life and fertility, whether animal or vegetable, was one and indivisible. To live and to cause to live, to eat food and to beget children, these were the primary wants of men in the past, and they will be the primary wants of men in the future so long as the world lasts. Other things may be added to enrich and beautify human life, but unless these wants are first satisfied, humanity itself must cease to exist. These two things, therefore, food and children, were what men chiefly sought to procure by the performance of magical rites for the regulation of the seasons.

Nowhere, apparently, have these rites been more widely and solemnly celebrated than in the lands which border the Eastern Mediterranean. Under the names of Osiris, Tammuz, Adonis, and Attis, the peoples of Egypt and Western Asia represented the yearly decay and revival of life, especially of vegetable life, which they personified as a god who annually died and rose again from the dead. In name and detail the rites varied from place to place: in substance they were the same. The supposed death and resurrection of this oriental deity, a god of many names but of essentially one nature, is now to be examined. We begin with Tammuz or Adonis.

The worship of Adonis was practised by the Semitic peoples of Babylonia and Syria, and the Greeks borrowed it from them as early as the seventh century before Christ. The true name of the deity was Tammuz: the appellation of Adonis is merely the Semitic *Adon*, "lord," a title of honour by which his worshippers addressed him. But the Greeks through a misunderstanding converted the title of honour into a proper name. In the religious literature of Babylonia Tammuz appears as the youthful spouse or lover of Ishtar, the great mother goddess, the embodiment of the reproductive energies of nature. The references to their connexion with each other in myth and ritual are both fragmentary and obscure, but we gather from them that every year Tammuz was believed to die, passing away from the cheerful earth to the gloomy subterranean world, and that every year his divine mistress journeyed in quest of him "to the land from which there is no returning, to the house or darkness, where dust lies on door and bolt." During her absence the passion of love ceased to operate: men and beasts alike forgot to reproduce their kinds: all life was threatened with extinction. So intimately bound up with the goddess were the sexual functions of the whole animal kingdom that without her presence they could not be discharged. . . .

Laments for the departed Tammuz are contained in several Babylonian hymns, which liken him to plants that quickly fade. He is

> A tamarisk that in the garden has drunk no water,
>   Whose crown in the field has brought forth no blossom.
> A willow that rejoiced not by the watercourse,
>   A willow whose roots were torn up. . . .

His death appears to have been annually mourned, to the shrill music of flutes, by men and women about midsummer in the month named after him, the month of Tammuz. The dirges were seemingly chanted over an effigy of the dead god, which was washed with pure water, anointed with oil, and clad in a red robe, while the fumes of incense rose into the air, as if to stir his dormant senses by their pungent fragrance and wake him from the sleep of death. . . .

The tragical story and the melancholy rites of Adonis are better known to us from the descriptions of Greek writers than from the fragments of Babylonian literature or the brief reference of the prophet Ezekiel, who saw the women of Jerusalem weeping for Tammuz at the north gate of the temple. Mirrored in the glass of Greek mythology, the oriental deity appears as a comely youth beloved by Aphrodite. In his infancy the goddess hid him in a chest, which she gave in charge to Persephone, queen of the nether world. But when Persephone opened the chest and beheld the beauty of the babe, she refused to give him back to Aphrodite, though the goddess of love went down herself to hell to ransom her dear one from the power of the grave. The dispute between the two goddesses of love and death was settled by Zeus, who decreed that Adonis should abide with Persephone in the under world for one part of the year, and with Aphrodite in the upper world for another part. At last the fair youth was killed in hunting by a wild boar, or by the jealous Ares, who turned himself into the likeness of a boar in order to compass the death of his rival. Bitterly did Aphrodite lament her loved and lost Adonis. . . .

Adonis in Syria

The myth of Adonis was localised and his rites celebrated with much solemnity at two places in Western Asia. One of these was Byblus on the coast of Syria, the other was Paphos in Cyprus. Both were great seats of the worship of Aphrodite, or rather of her Semitic counterpart, Astarte. . . . In historical times it [Byblus] ranked as a holy place, the religious capital of the country, the Mecca or Jerusalem of the Phoenicians. The city stood on a height beside the sea, and contained a great sanctuary of Astarte, where in the midst of a spacious open court, surrounded by cloisters and approached from below by staircases, rose a tall cone or obelisk, the holy image of the goddess. In this sanctuary the rites of Adonis were celebrated. Indeed the whole city was sacred to him, and the river Nahr Ibrahim, which falls into the sea a little to the south of Byblus, bore in antiquity the name of Adonis. . . .

The temple, of which some massive hewn blocks and a fine column of Syenite granite still mark the site, occupied a terrace facing the source of the river and commanding a magnificent prospect. Across the foam and the roar of the waterfalls you look up to the cavern and away to the top of the sublime precipices above. So lofty is the cliff that the goats which creep along its ledges to browse on the bushes appear like ants to the spectator hundreds of feet below. Seaward the view is especially impressive when the sun floods the profound gorge with golden light, revealing all the fantastic buttresses and rounded towers of its mountain rampart, and falling softly on the varied green of the woods which clothe its depths. It was here that, according to the legend, Adonis met Aphrodite for the first or the last time, and here his mangled body was buried. A fairer scene could hardly be imagined for a story of tragic love and death. . . .

In antiquity the whole of the lovely vale appears to have been dedicated to Adonis, and to this day it is haunted by his memory; for the heights which shut it in are crested at various points by ruined monuments of his worship, some of them over-hanging dreadful abysses, down which it turns the head dizzy to look and see the eagles wheeling about their nests far below. One such monument exists at Ghineh. The face of a great rock, above a roughly hewn recess, is here carved with figures of Adonis and Aphrodite. He is portrayed with spear in rest, awaiting the attack of a bear, while she is seated in an attitude of sorrow. . . . Every year, in the belief of his worshippers, Adonis was wounded to death on the mountains, and every year the face of nature itself was dyed with his sacred blood. So year by year the Syrian damsels lamented his untimely fate, while the red anemone, his flower, bloomed among the cedars of Lebanon, and the river ran red to the sea, fringing the winding shores of the blue Mediterranean, whenever the wind set inshore, with a sinuous band of crimson.

Adonis in Cyprus

The island of Cyprus lies but one day's sail from the coast of Syria. Indeed, on fine summer evenings its mountains may be descried looming low and dark against the red fires of sunset. With its rich mines of copper and its forest of firs and stately cedars, the island naturally attracted a commercial and maritime people like the Phoenicians; while the abundance of its corn, its wine, and its oil must have rendered it in their eyes a Land of Promise by comparison with the niggardly nature of their own rugged coast, hemmed in between the mountains and the sea. Accordingly they settled in Cyprus at a very early date and remained there long after the Greeks had also established themselves on its shores. . . .

The sanctuary of Aphrodite at Old Paphos (the modern Kuklia) was one of the most celebrated shrines in the ancient world. According to Herodotus, it was founded by Phoenician colonists from Ascalon; but it is possible that a native goddess of fertility was worshipped on the spot before the arrival of the Phoenicians, and that the newcomers identified her with their own Baalath or Astarte, whom she may have closely resembled. If two deities were thus fused in one, we may suppose that they were both varieties of that great goddess of motherhood and fertility whose worship appears to have been spread all over Western Asia from a very early time. The supposition is confirmed as well by the archaic shape of her image as by the licentious character of her rites; for both that shape and those rites were shared by her with other Asiatic deities. Her image was simply a white cone or pyramid. . . .

In Cyprus it appears that before marriage all women were formerly obliged by custom to prostitute themselves to strangers at the sanctuary of the goddess, whether she went by the name of Aphrodite, Astarte, or what not. Similar customs prevailed in many parts of Western Asia. Whatever its motive, the practice was clearly regarded, not as an orgy of lust, but as a solemn religious duty performed in the service of that great Mother Goddess of Western Asia whose name varied, while her type remained constant, from place to place. Thus at Babylon every woman, whether rich or poor, had once in her life to submit to the embraces of a stranger at the temple of Mylitta, that is, of Ishtar or Astarte, and to dedicate to the goddess the wages earned by this sanctified harlotry. The sacred precinct was crowded with women waiting to observe the custom. Some of them had to wait there for years. At Heliopolis or Baalbec in Syria, famous for the imposing grandeur of its ruined temples, the custom of the country required that every maiden should prostitute herself to a stranger at the temple of Astarte, and matrons as well as maids testified their devotion to the goddess in the same manner. The emperor Constantine abolished the custom, destroyed the temple, and built a church in its stead. In Phoenician temples women prostituted themselves for hire in the service of religion, believing that by this conduct they propitiated the goddess and won her favour. "It was a law of the Amorites, that she who was about to marry should sit in fornication seven days by the gate." At Byblus the people shaved their heads in the annual mourning for Adonis. Women who refused to sacrifice their hair had to give themselves up to strangers on a certain day of the festival, and the money which they thus earned was devoted to the goddess. A Greek inscription found at Tralles in Lydia proves that the practice of religious prostitution survived in that country as late as the second century of our era. . . .

We may conclude that a great Mother Goddess, the personification of all the reproductive energies of nature, was worshipped under different names but with a substantial similarity of myth and ritual by many peoples of Western Asia; that associated with her was a lover, or rather series of lovers, divine yet mortal, with whom she mated year by year, their commerce being deemed essential to the propagation of animals and plants, each in their several kind; and further, that the fabulous union of the divine pair was simulated and, as it were, multiplied on earth by the real, though temporary, union of the human sexes at the sanctuary of the goddess for the sake of thereby ensuring the fruitfulness of the ground and the increase of man and beast. . . .

THE RITUAL OF ADONIS

At the festivals of Adonis, which were held in Western Asia and in Greek lands, the death of the god was annually mourned, with a bitter wailing, chiefly by women; images of him, dressed to resemble corpses, were carried out as to burial and then thrown into the sea or into springs; and in some places his revival was celebrated on the following day. But at different places the ceremonies varied somewhat in the manner and apparently also in the season of their celebration. At Alexandria images of Aphrodite and Adonis were displayed on two couches; beside them were set ripe fruits of all kinds, cakes, plants growing in flower-pots, and green bowers twined with anise. The marriage of the lovers was celebrated one day, and on the morrow women attired as mourners, with streaming hair and bared breasts, bore the image of the dead Adonis to the sea-shore and committed it to the waves. Yet they sorrowed not without hope, for they sang that the lost one would come back again. The date at which this Alexandrian ceremony was observed is not expressly stated; but from the mention of the ripe fruits it has been inferred that it took place in late summer. In the great Phoenician sanctuary of Astarte at Byblus the death of Adonis was annually mourned, to the shrill wailing notes of the flute, with weeping, lamentation, and beating of the breast; but next day he was believed to come to life again and ascend up to heaven in the presence of his worshippers. The disconsolate believers, left behind on earth, shaved their heads as the Egyptians did on the death of the divine bull Apis; women who could not bring themselves to sacrifice their beautiful tresses had to give themselves up to strangers on a certain day of the festival, and to dedicate to Astarte the wages of their shame.

This Phoenician festival appears to have been a vernal one, for its date was determined by the discoloration of the river Adonis, and this has been observed by modern travellers to occur in spring. At that season the red earth washed down from the mountains by the rain tinges the water of the river, and even the sea, for a great way with a blood-red hue, and the crimson stain was believed to be the blood of Adonis, annually wounded to death by the boar on Mount Lebanon. Again, the scarlet anemone is said to have sprung from the blood of Adonis, or to have been stained by it; and as the anemone blooms in Syria about Easter, this may be thought to show that the festival of Adonis, or at least one of his festivals, was held in spring. The name of the flower is probably derived from Naaman ("darling"), which seems to have been an epithet of Adonis. The Arabs still call the anemone "wounds of the Naaman.". . .

In Attica, certainly, the festival fell at the height of summer. For the fleet which Athens fitted out against Syracuse, and by the destruction of which her power was permanently crippled, sailed at midsummer, and by an ominous coincidence the sombre rites of Adonis were being celebrated at the very time. As the troops marched down to the harbour to embark, the streets through which they passed were lined with coffins and corpse-like effigies, and the air was rent with the noise of women wailing for the dead Adonis. The circumstance cast a gloom over the sailing of the most splendid armament that Athens ever sent to sea. Many ages afterwards, when the Emperor Julian made his first entry into Antioch, he found in like manner the gay, the luxurious capital of the East plunged in mimic grief for the annual death of Adonis; and if he had any presentiment of coming evil, the voices of lamentation which struck upon his ear must have seemed to sound his knell.

The resemblance of these ceremonies to the Indian and European ceremonies which I have described elsewhere is obvious. In particular, apart from the somewhat doubtful date of its celebration, the Alexandrian ceremony is almost identical with the Indian. In both of them the marriage of two divine beings, whose affinity with vegetation seems indicated by the fresh plants with which they are surrounded, is celebrated in effigy, and the effigies are afterwards mourned over and thrown into the water. From the similarity of these customs to each other and to the spring and midsummer customs of modern Europe we should naturally expect that they all admit of a common explanation. Hence, if the explanation which I have adopted of the latter is correct, the ceremony of the death and resurrection of Adonis must also have been a dramatic representation of the decay and revival of plant life. The inference thus based on the resemblance of the customs is confined by the following features in the legend and ritual of Adonis. His affinity with vegetation comes out at once in the common story of his birth. He was said to have been born from a myrrh-tree, the bark of which bursting, after ten months' gestation, allowed the lovely infant to come forth. According to some, a boar rent the bark with his tusk and so opened a passage for the babe. A faint rationalistic colour was given to the legend by saying that his mother was a woman named Myrrh, who had been turned into a myrrh-tree soon after she had conceived the child. The use of myrrh as incense at the festival of Adonis may have given rise to the fable. We have seen that incense was burnt at the corresponding Babylonian rites, just as it was burnt by the idolatrous Hebrews in honour of the Queen of Heaven, who was no other than Astarte. Again, the story that Adonis spent half, or according to others a third, of the year in the lower world and the rest of it in the upper world, is explained most simply and naturally by supposing that he represented vegetation, especially the corn, which lies buried in the earth half the year and reappears above ground the other half. Certainly of the annual phenomena of nature there is none which suggests so obviously the idea of death and resurrection as the disappearance and reappearance of vegetation in autumn and spring. . . .

The annual death and revival of vegetation is a conception which readily presents itself to men in evey stage of savagery and civilisation; and the vastness of the scale on which this ever-recurring decay and regeneration takes place, together with man's initmate dependence on it for subsistence, combine to render it the most impressive annual occurrence in nature, at least within the temperate zones. It is no wonder that a phenomenon so important, so striking, and so universal should, by suggesting similar ideas, have given rise to similar rites in many lands. We may, therefore, accept as probable an explanation of the Adonis worship which accords so well with the facts of nature and with the analogy of similar rites in other lands. Moreover, the explanation is countenanced by a considerable body of opinion amongst the ancients themselves, who again and again interpreted the dying and reviving god as the reaped and sprouting grain.

The character of Tammuz or Adonis as a corn-spirit comes out plainly in an account of his festival given by an Arabic writer of the tenth century. In describing the rites and sacrifices observed at the different seasons of the year by the heathen Syrians of Harran, he says: "Tammuz (July). In the middle of this month is the festival of el-Bûgàt, that is, of the weeping women, and this is the Tâ-uz festival, which is celebrated in honour of the god Tâ-uz. The women bewail him, because his lord slew him so cruelly, ground his bones in a mill, and then scattered them to the wind. The women (during this festival) eat nothing which has been ground in a mill, but limit their diet to steeped wheat, sweet vetches, dates, raisins, and the like." Tâ-uz, who is no other than Tammuz, is here like Burn's John Barleycorn:

> They wasted o'er a scorching flame
> The marrow of his bones;
> But a miller us'd him worst of all—
> For he crush'd him between two stones.

This concentration, so to say, of the nature of Adonis upon the cereal crops is characteristic of the stage of culture reached by his worshippers in historical times.

They had left the nomadic life of the wandering hunter and herdsman far behind them; for ages they had been settled on the land, and had depended for their subsistence mainly on the products of tillage. The berries and roots of the wilderness, the grass of the pastures, which had been matters of vital importance to their ruder forefathers, were now of little moment to them: more and more their thoughts and energies were engrossed by the staple of their life, the corn; more and more accordingly the propitiation of the deities of fertility in general and of the corn-spirit in particular tended to become the central feature of their religion. The aim they set before themselves in celebrating the rites was thoroughly practical. It was no vague poetical sentiment which prompted them to hail with joy the rebirth of vegetation and to mourn its decline. Hunger, felt or feared, was the mainspring of the worship of Adonis. . . .

THE GARDENS OF ADONIS

Perhaps the best proof that Adonis was a deity of vegetation, and especially of the corn, is furnished by the gardens of Adonis, as they were called. These were baskets or pots filled with earth, in which wheat, barley, lettuces, fennel, and various kinds of flowers were sown and tended for eight days, chiefly or exclusively by women. Fostered by the sun's heat, the plants shot up rapidly, but having no root they withered as rapidly away, and at the end of eight days were carried out with the images of the dead Adonis, and flung with them into the sea or into springs.

These gardens of Adonis are most naturally interpreted as representatives of Adonis or manifestations of his power; they represented him, true to his original nature, in vegetable form, while the images of him, with which they were carried out and cast into the water, portrayed him in his later human shape. All these Adonis ceremonies, if I am right, were originally intended as charms to promote the growth or revival of vegetation; and the principle by which they were supposed to produce this effect was homoeopathic or imitative magic. For ignorant people suppose that by mimicking the effect which they desire to produce they actually help to produce it; thus by sprinkling water they make rain, by lighting a fire they make sunshine, and so on. Similarly, by mimicking the growth of the crops they hope to ensure a good harvest. The rapid growth of the wheat and barley in the gardens of Adonis was intended to make the corn shoot up; and the throwing of the gardens and of the images into the water was a charm to secure a due supply of fertilising rain. The same, I take it, was the object of throwing the effigies of Death and the Carnival into water in the corresponding ceremonies of modern Europe. Certainly the custom of drenching with water a leaf-clad person, who undoubtedly personifies vegetation, is still resorted to in Europe for the express purpose of producing rain. Similarly the custom of throwing water on the last corn cut at harvest, or on the person who brings it home (a custom observed in Germany and France, and till lately in England and Scotland), is in some places practised with the avowed intent to procure rain for the next year's crops. Thus in Wallachia and amongst the Roumanians in Transylvania, when a girl is bringing home a crown made of the last ears of corn cut at harvest, all who meet her hasten to throw water on her, and two farm-servants are placed at the door for the purpose; for they believe that if this were not done, the crops next year would perish from drought. At the spring ploughing in Prussia, when the ploughmen and sowers returned in the evening from their work in the fields, the farmer's wife and the servants used to splash water over them. The ploughmen and sowers retorted by seizing evey one, throwing them into the pond, and ducking them under the water. The farmer's wife might claim exemption on payment of a forfeit, but every one else had to be ducked. By observing this custom they hoped to ensure a due supply of rain for the seed. . . .

In Sardinia the gardens of Adonis are still planted in connexion with the great midsummer festival which bears the name of St. John. At the end of March or on the first of April a young man of the village presents himself to a girl, and asks her to be his *comare* (gossip or sweetheart), offering to be her *compare*. The invitation is considered as an honour by the girl's family, and is gladly accepted. At the end of May the girl makes a pot of the bark of the cork-tree, fills it with earth, and sows a handful of wheat and barley in it. The pot being placed in the sun and often watered, the corn sprouts rapidly and has a good head by Midsummer Eve (St. John's Eve, the twenty-third of June). The pot is then called *Erme* or *Nenneri*. On St. John's Day the young man and the girl, dressed in their best, accompanied by a long retinue and preceded by children gambolling and frolicking, move in procession to a church outside the village. Here they break the pot by throwing it against the door of the church. Then they sit down in a ring on the grass and eat eggs and herbs to the music of flutes. Wine is mixed in a cup and passed round, each one drinking as it passes. Then they join hands and sing "Sweethearts of St. John" (*Compare e comare di San Giovanni*) over and over again, the flutes playing the while. When they tire of singing they stand up and dance gaily in a ring till evening. This is the general Sardinian custom. As practised at Ozieri it has some special features. In May the pots are made of cork-bark and planted with corn, as already described. Then on the Eve of St. John the windowsills are draped with rich cloths, on which the pots are placed, adorned with crimson and blue silk and ribbons of various colours. On each of the pots they used formerly to place a statuette or cloth doll dressed as a woman, or a Priapus-like figure made of paste; but this custom, rigorously forbidden by the Church, has fallen into disuse. The village swains go about in a troop to look at the pots and their decorations and to wait for the girls, who assemble on the public square to celebrate the festival. Here a great bonfire is kindled, round which they dance and make merry. Those who wish to be "Sweethearts of St. John" act as follows. The young man stands on one side of the bonfire and the girl on the other, and they, in a manner, join hands by each grasping one end of a long stick, which they pass three times backwards and forwards across the fire, thus thrusting their hands thrice rapidly into the flames. This seals their relationship to each other. Dancing and music go on till late at night. The correspondence of these Sardinian pots of grain to the gardens of Adonis seems complete, and the images formerly placed in them answer to the images of Adonis which accompanied his gardens. . . .

In some parts of Sicily the gossips[1] of St. John present each other with plates of sprouting corn, lentils, and canary seed, which have been planted forty days before the festival. The one who receives the plate pulls a stalk of the young plants, binds it with a ribbon, and preserves it among his or her greatest treasures, restoring the platter to the giver. At Catania the gossips exchange pots of basil and great cucumbers; the girls tend the basil, and the thicker it grows the more it is prized.

In these midsummer customs of Sardinia and Sicily it is possible that St. John has replaced Adonis. . . .

---

[1] From the Anglo-Saxon word *godsibb*, which here means "companions" and has a positive connotation.

At the approach of Easter, Sicilian women sow wheat, lentils, and canary-seed in plates, which they keep in the dark and water every two days. The plants soon shoot up; the stalks are tied together with red ribbons, and the plates containing them are placed on the sepulchres which, with the effigies of the dead Christ, are made up in Catholic and Greek churches on Good Friday, just as the gardens of Adonis were placed on the grave of the dead Adonis. The practice is not confined to Sicily, for it is observed also at Cosenza in Calabria, and perhaps in other places. The whole custom—sepulchres as well as plates of sprouting grain—may be nothing but a continuation, under a different name, of the worship of Adonis.

Nor are these Sicilian and Calabrian customs the only Easter ceremonies which resemble the rites of Adonis. "During the whole of Good Friday a waxen effigy of the dead Christ is exposed to view in the middle of the Greek churches and is covered with fervent kisses by the thronging crowd, while the whole church rings with melancholy, monotonous dirges. Late in the evening, when it has grown quite dark, this waxen image is carried by the priests into the street on a bier adorned with lemons, roses, jessamine, and other flowers, and there begins a grand procession of the multitude, who move in serried ranks, with slow and solemn step, through the whole town. Every man carries his taper and breaks out into doleful lamentation. At all the houses which the procession passes there are seated women with censers to fumigate the marching host. Thus the community solemnly buries its Christ as if he had just died. At last the waxen image is again deposited in the church, and the same lugubrious chants echo anew. These lamentations, accompanied by a strict fast, continue till midnight on Saturday. As the clock strikes twelve, the bishop appears and announces the glad tidings that 'Christ is risen,' to which the crowd replies, 'He is risen indeed,' and at once the whole city bursts into an uproar of joy, which finds vent in shrieks and shouts, in the endless discharge of carronades and muskets, and the explosion of fire-works of every sort. In the very same hour people plunge from the extremity of the fast into the enjoyment of the Easter lamb and neat wine. . . .

When we reflect how often the Church has skilfully contrived to plant the seeds of the new faith on the old stock of paganism, we may surmise that the Easter celebration of the dead and risen Christ was grafted upon a similar celebration of the dead and risen Adonis, which, as we have seen reason to believe, was celebrated in Syria at the same season. The type, created by Greek artists, of the sorrowful goddess with her dying lover in her arms, resembles and may have been the model of the *Pietà* of Christian art, the Virgin with the dead body of her divine Son in her lap, of which the most celebrated example is the one by Michael Angelo in St. Peters. That noble group, in which the living sorrow of the mother contrasts so wonderfully with the languor of death in the son, is one of the finest compositions in marble. Ancient Greek art has bequeathed to us few works so beautiful, and more so pathetic.

In this connexion a well-known statement of Jerome[2] may not be without significance. He tells us that Bethelehem, the traditionary birthplace of the Lord, was shaded by a grove of that still older Syrian Lord, Adonis, and that where the infant Jesus had wept, the lover of Venus was bewailed. Though he does not expressly say so, Jerome seems to have thought that the grove of Adonis had been planted by the heathen

---

[2] Saint Jerome (340–420 A.D.), an early Christian scholar, one of the fathers of the church who was principally responsible for the Vulgate version of the Bible.

after the birth of Christ for the purpose of defiling the sacred spot. In this he may have been mistaken. If Adonis was indeed, as I have argued, the spirit of the corn, a more suitable name for his dwelling-place could hardly be found than Bethlehem, "the House of Bread," and he may well have been worshipped there at his House of Bread long ages before the birth of Him who said, "I am the bread of life."

Meaning

1. How were primitive magical rites designed to assure that children would be born and the crops would flourish?
2. Who is Adonis and what is the significance of his yearly demise and resurrection?
3. What ceremonies were performed during the rituals designed to worship Adonis?
4. What is the significance of the fact that Adonis often appears as the consort of Aphrodite, a goddess of fertility?
5. What evidence does Frazer provide that belief in fertility goddesses is far older than belief in male gods?
6. How does the story of Aphrodite's and Persephone's dispute over Adonis serve as an explanation of the yearly appearance and disappearance of vegetation?
7. What features from ancient rituals linking the dying and reviving Adonis with the "reaped and sprouted" grain does Frazer believe reappeared in Christianity?

Using Description to Convey Meaning

1. How does Frazer's description of the temple in Syria dedicated to Adonis use details of sight and sound to communicate the grandeur and importance of this ancient religious site?
2. What evidence does Frazer provide to document his discovery that prostitution played an important part in ceremonies performed in temples dedicated to goddesses linked with Adonis? What effect do you think Frazer's description of the customs of ritual prostitution had on his late-Victorian readers?
3. What specific customs does Frazer describe that show a possible relationship between ancient fertility and harvesting rituals and later rituals connected with Christianity?

Writing Suggestions

1. What elements in current marriage ceremonies seem to represent a continuation of rituals designed to ensure fertility and procreation?
2. What contemporary magical "rituals" in our society are designed to ensure a favorable outcome of events? For example, a baseball player's refusal to wash his lucky shirt while he's on a hitting streak and the elaborate rituals of grooming that precede an important date are designed to enhance the probability of a successful outcome.
3. As a research project, explore Shakespeare's incorporation of the legends surrounding Adonis in his long poem, "Venus and Adonis." Specifically, how does Shakespeare handle the episode of the "wounding of Adonis" that Frazer describes?

SCIENCES

Jane van Lawick-Goodall

First Observations

Jane van Lawick-Goodall, born in London, England in 1934, first worked as an assistant to the late Louis Leakey, curator of the National Museum of Natural History in Nairobi, Kenya. Through his efforts, van Lawick-Goodall was able to obtain financial backing for what became the Gombe Stream Research Center, for studies of chimpanzees and other primates in Gombe, Tanzania. Her unique research into chimpanzee behavior relied on first-hand observations of individual primates over long periods to study relationships, communication, hunting, feeding, dominance, sexuality, and territoriality in chimpanzee society. Van Lawick-Goodall discovered that chimpanzees were not exclusively vegetarians and, surprisingly, were capable of modifying and using tools to procure food. In addition to many scientific papers, van Lawick-Goodall is the author of In the Shadow of Man *(1971) and* The Chimpanzees of Gombe *(1986). In "First Observations," from* In the Shadow of Man, *van Lawick-Goodall describes the first time she actually observed David Graybeard (one of the chimpanzees she had named) engaged in meat-eating and tool-using behavior.*

For about a month I spent most of each day either on the Peak or overlooking Mlinda Valley where the chimps, before or after stuffing themselves with figs, ate large quantities of small purple fruits that tasted, like so many of their foods, as bitter and astringent as sloes or crab apples. Piece by piece, I began to form my first somewhat crude picture of chimpanzee life.

The impression that I had gained when I watched the chimps at the msulula tree of temporary, constantly changing associations of individuals within the community was substantiated. Most often I saw small groups of four to eight moving about together. Sometimes I saw one or two chimpanzees leave such a group and wander off on their own or join up with a different association. On other occasions I watched two or three small groups joining to form a larger one.

Often, as one group crossed the grassy ridge separating the Kasekela Valley from the fig trees in the home valley, the male chimpanzee, or chimpanzees, of the party

125

would break into a run, sometimes moving in an upright position, sometimes dragging a fallen branch, sometimes stamping or slapping the hard earth. These charging displays were always accompanied by loud pant-hoots and afterward the chimpanzee frequently would swing up into a tree overlooking the valley he was about to enter and sit quietly, peering down and obviously listening for a response from below. If there were chimps feeding in the fig trees they nearly always hooted back, as though in answer. Then the new arrivals would hurry down the steep slope and, with more calling and screaming, the two groups would meet in the fig trees. When groups of females and youngsters with no males present joined other feeding chimpanzees, usually there was none of this excitement; the newcomers merely climbed up into the trees, greeted some of those already there, and began to stuff themselves with figs.

While many details of their social behavior were hidden from me by the foliage, I did get occasional fascinating glimpses. I saw one female, newly arrived in a group, hurry up to a big male and hold her hand toward him. Almost regally he reached out, clasped her hand in his, drew it toward him, and kissed it with his lips. I saw two adult males embrace each other in greeting. I saw youngsters having wild games through the treetops, chasing around after each other or jumping again and again, one after the other, from a branch to a springy bough below. I watched small infants dangling happily by themselves for minutes on end, patting at their toes with one hand, rotating gently from side to side. Once two tiny infants pulled on opposite ends of a twig in a gentle tug-of-war. Often, during the heat of midday or after a long spell of feeding, I saw two or more adults grooming each other, carefully looking through the hair of their companions.

At that time of year the chimps usually went to bed late, making their nests when it was too dark to see properly through binoculars, but sometimes they nested earlier and I could watch them from the peak. I found that every individual, except for infants who slept with their mothers, made his own nest each night. Generally this took about three minutes: the chimp chose a firm foundation such as an upright fork or crotch, or two horizontal branches. Then he reached out and bent over smaller branches onto this foundation, keeping each one in place with his feet. Finally he tucked in the small leafy twigs growing around the rim of his nest and lay down. Quite often a chimp sat up after a few minutes and picked a handful of leafy twigs, which he put under his head or some other part of his body before settling down again for the night. One young female I watched went on and on bending down branches until she had constructed a huge mound of greenery on which she finally curled up.

I climbed up into some of the nests after the chimpanzees had left them. Most of them were built in trees that for me were almost impossible to climb. I found that there was quite complicated interweaving of the branches in some of them. I found, too, that the nests were never fouled with dung; and later, when I was able to get closer to the chimps, I saw how they were always careful to defecate and urinate over the edge of their nests, even in the middle of the night.

During that month I really came to know the country well, for I often went on expeditions from the Peak, sometimes to examine nests, more frequently to collect specimens of the chimpanzees' food plants, which Bernard Verdcourt had kindly offered to identify for me. Soon I could find my way around the sheer ravines and up and down the steep slopes of three valleys—the home valley, the Pocket, and

Mlinda Valley—as well as a taxi driver finds his way about in the main streets and byways of London. It is a period I remember vividly, not only because I was beginning to accomplish something at last, but also because of the delight I felt in being completely by myself. For those who love to be alone with nature I need add nothing further; for those who do not, no words of mine could ever convey, even in part, the almost mystical awareness of beauty and eternity that accompanies certain treasured moments. And, though the beauty was always there, those moments came upon me unaware: when I was watching the pale flush preceding dawn; or looking up through the rustling leaves of some giant forest tree into the greens and browns and black shadows that occasionally ensnared a bright fleck of the blue sky; or when I stood, as darkness fell, with one hand on the still-warm trunk of a tree and looked at the sparkling of an early moon on the never still, sighing water of the lake.

One day, when I was sitting by the trickle of water in Buffalo Wood, pausing for a moment in the coolness before returning from a scramble in Mlinda Valley, I saw a female bushbuck moving slowly along the nearly dry streambed. Occasionally she paused to pick off some plant and crunch it. I kept absolutely still, and she was not aware of my presence until she was little more than ten yards away. Suddenly she tensed and stood staring at me, one small forefoot raised. Because I did not move, she did not know what I was—only that my outline was somehow strange. I saw her velvet nostrils dilate as she sniffed the air, but I was downwind and her nose gave her no answer. Slowly she came closer, and closer—one step at a time, her neck craned forward—always poised for instant flight. I can still scarcely believe that her nose actually touched my knee; yet if I close my eyes I can feel again, in imagination, the warmth of her breath and the silken impact of her skin. Unexpectedly I blinked and she was gone in a flash, bounding away with loud barks of alarm until the vegetation hid her completely from my view.

It was rather different when, as I was sitting on the Peak, I saw a leopard coming toward me, his tail held up straight. He was at a slightly lower level than I, and obviously had no idea I was there. Ever since arrival in Africa I had had an ingrained, illogical fear of leopards. Already, while working at the Gombe, I had several times nearly turned back when, crawling through some thick undergrowth, I had suddenly smelled the rank smell of cat. I had forced myself on, telling myself that my fear was foolish, that only wounded leopards charged humans with savage ferocity.

On this occasion, though, the leopard went out of sight as it started to climb up the hill—the hill on the peak of which I sat. I quickly hastened to climb a tree, but halfway there I realized that leopards can climb trees. So I uttered a sort of halfhearted squawk. The leopard, my logical mind told me, would be just as frightened of me if he knew I was there. Sure enough, there was a thudding of startled feet and then silence. I returned to the Peak, but the feeling of unseen eyes watching me was too much. I decided to watch for the chimps in Mlinda Valley. And, when I returned to the Peak several hours later, there, on the very rock which had been my seat, was a neat pile of leopard dung. He must have watched me go and then, very carefully, examined the place where such a frightening creature had been and tried to exterminate my alien scent with his own.

As the weeks went by the chimpanzees became less and less afraid. Quite often when I was on one of my food-collecting expeditions I came across chimpanzees unexpectedly, and after a time I found that some of them would tolerate my presence provided they were in fairly thick forest and I sat still and did not try to move closer than sixty to eighty yards. And so, during my second month of watching from the Peak, when I saw a group settle down to feed I sometimes moved closer and was thus able to make more detailed observations.

It was at this time that I began to recognize a number of different individuals. As soon as I was sure of knowing a chimpanzee if I saw it again, I named it. Some scientists feel that animals should be labeled by numbers—that to name them is anthropomorphic—but I have always been interested in the *differences* between individuals, and a name is not only more individual than a number but also far easier to remember. Most names were simply those which, for some reason or other, seemed to suit the individuals to whom I attached them. A few chimps were named because some facial expression or mannerism reminded me of human acquaintances.

The easiest individual to recognize was old Mr. McGregor. The crown of his head, his neck, and his shoulders were almost entirely devoid of hair, but a slight frill remained around his head rather like a monk's tonsure. He was an old male—perhaps between thirty and forty years of age (the longevity record for a captive chimp is forty-seven years). During the early months of my acquaintance with him, Mr. McGregor was somewhat belligerent. If I accidentally came across him at close quarters he would threaten me with an upward and backward jerk of his head and a shaking of branches before climbing down and vanishing from my sight. He reminded me, for some reason, of Beatrix Potter's old gardener in *The Tale of Peter Rabbit*.

Ancient Flo with her deformed, bulbous nose and ragged ears was equally easy to recognize. Her youngest offspring at that time were two-year-old Fifi, who still rode everywhere on her mother's back, and her juvenile son, Figan, who was always to be seen wandering around with his mother and little sister. He was then about six years old; it was approximately a year before he would attain puberty. Flo often traveled with another old mother, Olly. Olly's long face was also distinctive; the fluff of hair on the back of her head—though no other feature—reminded me of my aunt, Olwen. Olly, like Flo, was accompanied by two children, a daughter younger than Fifi, and an adolescent son about a year older than Figan.

Then there was William, who, I am certain, must have been Olly's blood brother. I never saw any special signs of friendship between them, but their faces were amazingly alike. They both had long upper lips that wobbled when they suddenly turned their heads. William had the added distinction of several thin, deeply etched scar marks running down his upper lip from his nose.

Two of the other chimpanzees I knew well by sight at that time were David Graybeard and Goliath. Like David and Goliath in the Bible, these two individuals were closely associated in my mind because they were very often together. Goliath, even in those days of his prime, was not a giant, but he had a splendid physique and the springy movements of an athlete. He probably weighed about one hundred pounds. David Graybeard was less afraid of me from the start than were any of the other chimps. I was always pleased when I picked out his handsome face and well-marked silvery beard in a chimpanzee group, for with David to calm the others, I had a better chance of approaching to observe them more closely.

Before the end of my trial period in the field I made two really exciting discoveries— discoveries that made the previous months of frustration well worth while. And for both of them I had David Graybeard to thank.

One day I arrived on the Peak and found a small group of chimps just below me in the upper branches of a thick tree. As I watched I saw that one of them was holding a pink-looking object from which he was from time to time pulling pieces with his teeth. There was a female and a youngster and they were both reaching out toward the male, their hands actually touching his mouth. Presently the female picked up a piece of the pink thing and put it to her mouth: it was at this moment that I realized the chimps were eating meat.

After each bite of meat the male picked off some leaves with his lips and chewed them with the flesh. Often, when he had chewed for several minutes on this leafy wad, he spat out the remains into the waiting hands of the female. Suddenly he dropped a small piece of meat, and like a flash the youngster swung after it to the ground. Even as he reached to pick it up the undergrowth exploded and an adult bushpig charged toward him. Screaming, the juvenile leaped back into the tree. The pig remained in the open, snorting and moving backward and forward. Soon I made out the shapes of three small striped piglets. Obviously the chimps were eating a baby pig. The size was right and later, when I realized that the male was David Graybeard, I moved closer and saw that he was indeed eating piglet.

For three hours I watched the chimps feeding. David occasionally let the female bite pieces from the carcass and once he actually detached a small piece of flesh and placed it in her outstretched hand. When he finally climbed down there was still meat left on the carcass: he carried it away in one hand, followed by the others.

Of course I was not sure, then, that David Graybeard had caught the pig for himself, but even so, it was tremendously exciting to know that these chimpanzees actually ate meat. Previously scientists had believed that although these apes might occasionally supplement their diet with a few insects or small rodents and the like they were primarily vegetarians and fruit eaters. No one had suspected that they might hunt larger mammals.

It was within two weeks of this observation that I saw something that excited me even more. By then it was October and the short rains had begun. The blackened slopes were softened by feathery new grass shoots and in some places the ground was carpeted by a variety of flowers. The Chimpanzees' Spring, I called it. I had had a frustrating morning, trampling up and down three valleys with never a sign or sound of a chimpanzee. Hauling myself up the steep slope of Mlinda Valley I headed for the Peak, not only weary but soaking wet from crawling through dense undergrowth. Suddenly I stopped, for I saw a slight movement in the long grass about sixty yards away. Quickly focusing my binoculars I saw that it was a single chimpanzee, and just then he turned in my direction. I recognized David Graybeard.

Cautiously I moved around so that I could see what he was doing. He was squatting beside the red earth mound of a termite nest, and as I watched I saw him carefully push a long grass stem down into a hole in the mound. After a moment he withdrew it and picked something from the end with his mouth. I was too far away to make out what he was eating, but it was obvious that he was actually using a grass stem as a tool.

I knew that on two occasions casual observers in West Africa had seen chimpanzees using objects as tools: one had broken open palm-nut kernels by using a rock as a hammer, and a group of chimps had been observed pushing sticks into an underground bees' nest and licking off the honey. Somehow I had never dreamed of seeing anything so exciting myself.

For an hour David feasted at the termite mound and then he wandered slowly away. When I was sure he had gone I went over to examine the mound. I found a few crushed insects strewn about, and a swarm of worker termites sealing the entrances of the nest passages into which David had obviously been poking his stems. I picked up one of his discarded tools and carefully pushed it into a hole myself. Immediately I felt the pull of several termites as they seized the grass, and when I pulled it out there were a number of worker termites and a few soldiers, with big red heads, clinging on with their mandibles. There they remained, sticking out at right angles to the stem with their legs waving in the air.

Before I left I trampled down some of the tall dry grass and constructed a rough hide—just a few palm fronds leaned up against the low branch of a tree and tied together at the top. I planned to wait there the next day. But it was another week before I was able to watch a chimpanzee "fishing" for termites again. Twice chimps arrived, but each time they saw me and moved off immediately. Once a swarm of fertile winged termites—the princes and princesses, as they are called—flew off on their nuptial flight, their huge white wings fluttering frantically as they carried the insects higher and higher. Later I realized that it is at this time of year, during the short rains, when the worker termites extend the passages of the nest to the surface, preparing for these emigrations. Several such swarms emerge between October and January. It is principally during these months that the chimpanzees feed on termites.

On the eighth day of my watch David Graybeard arrived again, together with Goliath, and the pair worked for two hours. I could see much better: I observed how they scratched open the sealed-over passage entrances with a thumb or forefinger. I watched how they bit the ends off their tools when they became bent, or used the other end, or discarded them in favor of new ones. Goliath once moved at least fifteen yards from the heap to select a firm-looking piece of vine, and both males often picked three or four stems while they were collecting tools, and put the spares beside them on the ground until they wanted them.

Most exciting of all, on several occasions they picked small leafy twigs and prepared them for use by stripping off the leaves. This was the first recorded example of a wild animal not merely *using* an object as a tool, but actually modifying an object and thus showing the crude beginnings of tool*making*.

Previously man had been regarded as the only tool-making animal. Indeed, one of the clauses commonly accepted in the definition of man was that he was a creature who "made tools to a regular and set pattern." The chimpanzees, obviously, had not made tools to any set pattern. Nevertheless, my early observations of their primitive toolmaking abilities convinced a number of scientists that it was necessary to redefine man in a more complex manner than before. Or else, as Louis Leaky put it, we should by definition have to accept the chimpanzee as Man.

I sent telegrams to Louis about both of my new observations—the meat-eating and the toolmaking—and he was of course wildly enthusiastic. In fact, I believe that the news was helpful to him in his efforts to find further financial support for my work. It was not long afterward when he wrote to tell me that the National Geographic Society in the United States had agreed to grant funds for another year's research.

MEANING

1. Why would van Lawick-Goodall's discovery that chimpanzees modify and use grass straws to gather up termites necessitate a redefinition of "man."
2. Why did van Lawick-Goodall's observations of David Graybeard lead her to conclude

that chimpanzees, contrary to what was previously thought, were not solely vegetarians but hunted and killed other animals for food?

3. What previously unsuspected social interactions did van Lawick-Goodall observe among chimpanzees?

4. Why would van Lawick-Goodall's research have been much more difficult to conduct without David Graybeard's acceptance of her?

USING DESCRIPTION TO CONVEY MEANING

1. What observations does van Lawick-Goodall cite as evidence of toolmaking and meat-eating behavior in chimpanzees?

2. What details of appearance and behavior led van Lawick-Goodall to assign descriptive names to individual chimps?

3. What evidence does van Lawick-Goodall cite to support her belief that chimpanzees are surprisingly fastidious about the nests in which they sleep?

WRITING SUGGESTIONS

1. What were the advantages of giving descriptive names to the individual chimpanzees as opposed to the more traditional assignment of numbers?

2. Discuss how van Lawick-Goodall's research changed the previously held scientific view of both chimpanzees and man.

3. What surprising or unusual behavior have you ever observed in a pet? How did your observations change your previously held ideas about the capabilities and nature of the animal?

RICHARD SELZER

What I Saw at the Abortion

Richard Selzer was born in 1928 in Troy, New York. After receiving his M.D. from Albany Medical College in 1953, Selzer completed postdoctoral study at Yale (1957–1960) and is now a professor of surgery at the Yale University School of Medicine. Selzer's skill as a surgeon is matched by his skill as a writer; in 1975 he received the National Magazine Award from Columbia's School of Journalism for essays published in Esquire. *In his many books, including* Mortal Lessons *(1977),* Confessions of a Knife *(1979), and* Letters to a Young Doctor *(1982), Selzer draws on his experiences as a surgeon to take a hard look at the realities of illness, death, and disease that doctors must confront daily. "What I Saw at the Abortion," from* Mortal Lessons, *is characteristic of the way Selzer grapples with the actual conditions surgeons encounter; here, he describes the unexpected result and emotional impact of witnessing his first abortion.*

I am a surgeon. Particularities of sick flesh is everyday news. Escaping blood, all the outpourings of disease—phlegm, pus, vomitus, even those occult meaty tumors that terrify—I see as blood, disease, phlegm, and so on. I touch them to destroy them. But I do not make symbols of them.

What I am saying is that I have seen and I am used to seeing. We are talking about a man who has a trade, who has practiced it long enough to see no news in any of it. Picture this man, then. A professional. In his forties. Three children. Lives in a university town—so, necessarily, well—enlightened? Enough, anyhow. Successful in his work, yes. No overriding religious posture. Nothing special, then, your routine fellow, trying to do his work and doing it well enough. Picture him, this professional, a sort of scientist, if you please, in possession of the standard admirable opinions, positions, convictions, and so on—on this and that matter—on *abortion,* for example.

All right.
Now listen.

It is the western wing of the fourth floor of a great university hospital. I am present because I asked to be present. I wanted to see what I had never seen. An abortion.

The patient is Jamaican. She lies on the table in that state of notable submissiveness I have always seen in patients. Now and then she smiles at one of the nurses as though acknowledging a secret.

132

A nurse draws down the sheet, lays bare the abdomen. The belly mounds gently in the twenty-fourth week of pregnancy. The chief surgeon paints it with a sponge soaked in red antiseptic. He does this three times, each time a fresh sponge. He covers the area with a sterile sheet, an aperture in its center. He is a kindly man who teaches as he works, who pauses to reassure the woman.

He begins.

A little pinprick, he says to the woman.

He inserts the point of a tiny needle at the midline of the lower portion of her abdomen, on the downslope. He infiltrates local anesthetic into the skin, where it forms a small white bubble.

The woman grimaces.

That is all you will feel the doctor says. Except for a little pressure. But no more pain.

She smiles again. She seems to relax. She settles comfortably on the table. The worst is over.

The doctor selects a three-and-one-half-inch needle bearing a central stylet. He places the point at the site of the previous injection. He aims it straight up and down, perpendicular. Next he takes hold of her abdomen with his left hand, palming the womb, steadying it. He thrusts with his right hand. The needle sinks into the abdominal wall.

Oh, says the woman quietly.

But I guess it is not pain that she feels. It is more a recognition that the deed is being done.

Another thrust and he has speared the uterus.

We are in, he says.

He has felt the muscular wall of the organ gripping the shaft of his needle. A further slight pressure on the needle advances it a bit more. He takes his left hand from the woman's abdomen. He retracts the filament of the stylet from the barrel of the needle. A small geyser of pale yellow fluid erupts.

We are in the right place, says the doctor. Are you feeling any pain? he says.

She smiles, shakes her head. She gazes at the ceiling.

In the room we are six: two physicians, two nurses, the patient, and me.

The participants are busy, very attentive. I am not at all busy—but I am no less attentive. I want to see.

I see something!

It is unexpected, utterly unexpected, like a disturbance in the earth, a tumultuous jarring. I see something other than what I expected here. I see a movement—a small one. But I have seen it.

And then I see it again. And now I see that it is the hub of the needle in the woman's belly that has jerked. First to one side. Then to the other side. Once more it wobbles, is *tugged*, like a fishing line nibbled by a sunfish.

Again! And I *know!*

It is the *fetus* that worries thus. It is the fetus struggling against the needle. Struggling? How can that be? I think: *that cannot be*. I think: the fetus feels no pain, cannot feel fear, has no *motivation*. It is merely reflex.

I point to the needle.

It is a reflex, says the doctor.

By the end of the fifth month, the fetus weighs about one pound, is about twelve inches long. Hair is on the head. There are eyebrows, eyelashes. Pale pink nipples show on the chest. Nails are present, at the fingertips, at the toes.

At the beginning of the sixth month, the fetus can cry, can suck, can make a fist. He kicks, he punches. The mother can feel this, can *see* this. His eyelids, until now closed, can open. He may look up, down, sideways. His grip is very strong. He could support his weight by holding with one hand.

A reflex, the doctor says.

I hear him. But I saw something. I saw *something* in that mass of cells *understand* that it must bob and butt. And I see it again! I have an impulse to shove to the table—it is just a step—seize that needle, pull it out.

We are not six, I think. I think we are *seven*.

Something strangles *there*. An effort, its effort, binds me to it.

I do not shove to the table. I take no little step. It would be . . . well, madness. Everyone here wants the needle where it is. Six do. No, *five* do.

I close my eyes. I see the inside of the uterus. It is bathed in ruby gloom. I see the creature curled upon itself. Its knees are flexed. Its head is bent upon its chest. It is in fluid and gently rocks to the rhythm of the distant heartbeat.

It resembles . . . a sleeping infant.

Its place is entered by something. It is sudden. A point coming. A needle!

A spike of *daylight* pierces the chamber. Now the light is extinguished. The needle comes closer in the pool. The point grazes the thigh, and I stir. Perhaps I wake from dozing. The light is there again. I twist and straighten. My arms and legs *push*. My hand finds the shaft—grabs! I *grab*. I bend the needle this way and that. The point probes, touches on my belly. My mouth opens. Could I cry out? All is a commotion and a churning. There is a presence in the pool. An activity! The pool colors, reddens, darkens.

I open my eyes to see the doctor feeding a small plastic tube through the barrel of the needle into the uterus. Drops of pink fluid overrun the rim and spill onto the sheet. He withdraws the needle from around the plastic tubing. Now only the little tube protrudes from the woman's body. A nurse hands the physician a syringe loaded with a colorless liquid. He attaches it to the end of the tubing and injects it.

Prostaglandin, he says.

Ah, well, prostaglandin—a substance found normally in the body. When given in concentrated dosage, it throws the uterus into vigorous contraction. In eight to twelve hours, the woman will expel the fetus.

The doctor detaches the syringe but does not remove the tubing.

In case we must do it over, he says.

He takes away the sheet. He places gauze pads over the tubing. Over all this he applies adhesive tape.

I know. We cannot feed the great numbers. There is no more room. I know, I know. It is woman's right to refuse the risk, to decline the pain of childbirth. And an unwanted child is a very great burden. An unwanted child is a burden to himself. I know.

And yet . . . there is the flick of that needle. I *saw* it. I saw . . . I *felt*—in that room, a pace away, life prodded, life fending off, I saw life avulsed—swept by flood, blackening—then *out*.

There says the doctor, It's all over. It wasn't too bad, was it? he says to the woman.

She smiles. It is all over. Oh, yes.

And who would care to imagine that from a moist and dark commencement six months before there would ripen the cluster and globule, the sprout and pouch of man?

And who would care to imagine that trapped within the laked pearl and a dowry of yolk would lie the earliest stuff of dream and memory?

It is a persona carried here as well as person, I think. I think it is a signed piece, engraved with a hieroglyph of human genes.

I did not think this until I saw. The flick. The fending off.

We leave the room, the three of us, the doctors.

"Routine procedure," the chief surgeon says.

"All right," I say.

"Scrub nurse says first time you've seen one, Dick. First look at a purge," the surgeon says.

"That's right," I say. "First look."

"Oh, well," he says, "I guess you've seen everything else."

"Pretty much," I say.

"I'm not prying, Doctor," he says, "but was there something on your mind? I'd be delighted to field any questions . . ."

"No," I say. "No, thanks. Just simple curiosity."

"Okay," he says, and we all shake hands, scrub, change, and go to our calls.

I know, I know. The thing is normally done at sixteen weeks. Well, I've seen it performed at that stage, too. And seen . . . the flick. But I also know that in the sovereign state of my residence it is hospital policy to warrant the procedure at twenty-four weeks. And that in the great state that is adjacent, policy is enlarged to twenty-eight weeks.

Does this sound like argument? I hope not. I am not trying to argue. I am only saying I've *seen*. The flick. Whatever else may be said in abortion's defense, the vision of that other defense will not vanish from my eyes.

What I saw I saw as that: a *defense*, a motion *from*, an effort *away*. And it has happened that you cannot reason with me now. For what can language do against the truth of what I saw?

MEANING

1. How did this experience change Selzer's attitude toward abortion?
2. What does Selzer witness that seems to refute what he was taught about abortion in medical school regarding the inability of the fetus to experience pain or fear?
3. How does the reader know that Selzer is surprised that the surgeon, whom he describes as a "kindly" man, can remain emotionally uninvolved throughout the operation?

Using Description to Convey Meaning

1. Why does Selzer begin objectively, with a description of the operating room and surgical procedures, and then shift to a subjective viewpoint of the operation as perceived by the fetus?
2. What details establish Selzer's credibility as a trustworthy observer, who is not usually affected by what he sees in the operating room?
3. How does Selzer arrange the details in his account to emphasize his own delayed recognition of the nature of the event?
4. What medical terminology reported by Selzer suggests that removal of the fetus is equated with getting rid of a diseased part of the body?

Writing Suggestions

1. How is Selzer's perspective on the issue of abortion very different from Mannes' viewpoint on the same issue (see the "Argument and Persuasion" chapter, page 691).
2. How would the surgeon who performed the abortion have described it? What important differences would exist between his and Selzer's accounts of the same operation?

EXEMPLIFICATION

Good examples are an essential part of effective writing. A single well-chosen example or range of illustrations, introduced by "for example" or "for instance," can provide clear cases that document, substantiate, or illustrate the writer's ideas.

David A. Ricks, a business writer and marketing consultant, cites a number of classic examples in "What's In a Name?" to illustrate how company and product names can acquire unintended meanings when multinational corporations fail to take into account important differences in culture and language:

> For example, when the Coca-Cola Company was planning its strategy for marketing in China in the 1920s, it wanted to introduce its product with the English pronunciation of "Coca-Cola." A translator developed a group of Chinese characters which, when pronounced, sounded like the product name. These characters were placed on the cola bottles and marketed. Was it any wonder that sales levels were low? The characters actually translated to mean "a wax-flattened mare" or "bite the wax tadpole." Since the product was new, sound was unimportant to the consumers; meaning was vital. Today Coca-Cola is again marketing its cola in China. The new characters used on the bottle translate to "happiness in the mouth." . . .

Well-chosen examples are useful when writers wish to show the nature and character of a whole group through individual cases. In "Packaged Sentiment," Richard Rhodes uses examples of different types of greeting cards to illustrate how successful greeting-card manufacturers are in producing a range of cards that will be seen as uniquely personal by millions of people:

> For any given social occasion, depending on how well you know someone and what you want him to think of you, you may select a card for him that is Formal, Traditional, Humorous, Floral, Cute, Contemporary, or some other among Hallmark's many categories of mood. Two cards for a friend who is hospitalized give the flavor. One, an embossed vase of flowers, says "Glad your Operation's Over" on the cover. . . . The other card, a photograph of a cotton bunny in a flower-bedecked four-poster, opens with, "Hope you'll soon be out of the *blooming* bed!". . .

The messages quoted here represent thousands of other cards in the same category that communicate a similar message. Throughout "Packaged Sentiment," Rhodes illustrates important points by using examples that clearly show how greeting-card companies have designed and marketed specific types of cards to express a range of sentiments.

Journalists and social scientists often use typical case histories to represent classes or groups of people. John Hersey uses this technique in his historic account of six survivors of Hiroshima, "A Noiseless Flash from Hiroshima." The experiences of these six people stand for the experiences of untold thousands who were in Hiroshima the day the bomb was dropped. In each case, Hersey begins by identifying the person and then tells us about the events that occurred in his or her life a few minutes before the bomb exploded:

> At exactly fifteen minutes past eight in the morning, on August 6, 1945, Japanese time, at the moment when the atomic bomb flashed above Hiroshima, Miss Toshiko Sasaki, a clerk in the personnel department of the East Asia Tin Works, had just sat down at her place in the plant office and was turning her head to speak to the girl at the next desk. At that same moment, Dr. Masakazu Fujii was settling down cross-legged to read the Osaka *Asahi* on the porch of his private hospital . . . Mrs. Hatsuyo Nakamura, a tailor's widow, stood by the window of her kitchen. . . . Father Wilhelm Kleinsorge, a German priest of the Society of Jesus, reclined in his underwear on a cot . . . Dr. Terufumi Sasaki, a young member of the surgical staff . . . walked along one of the hospital corridors . . . and the Reverend Mr. Kiyoshi Tanimoto . . . paused at the door of a rich man's house in Koi. . . . A hundred thousand people were killed by the atomic bomb, and these six were among the survivors. . . .

By selecting six people to represent the thousands who survived Hiroshima, Hersey brings into human terms an event that otherwise would be beyond the reader's comprehension. Exemplification is extremely effective in allowing Hersey's readers to generalize from what these six individuals experienced to what all the people in Hiroshima suffered that day.

Studs Terkel, a reporter, frequently uses in-depth interviews as examples of contemporary attitudes toward various aspects of American life. In "Working," his extensive survey of American attitudes toward work, Terkel elicited responses from Terry Mason, a stewardess, which typify the challenges and rewards common to the lives of all stewardesses:

> "We have a union. It's a division of the pilots union. It helps us out on duty time and working privileges. It makes sure that if we're in Cleveland and stuck because of weather and thirteen hours have gone by, we can go to bed. Before we had a union the stew office would call and say, 'You're working another seven.' I worked one time thirty-six hours straight."

We learn that before stewardesses' had a union, they could be made to work for many more hours than was wise or safe. In the longer interview from which this excerpt is taken, we also discover how thoroughly a stewardess life and behavior must be regulated to produce an acceptable public image. Terkel shows us—through a wealth of details and insights into what a stewardess life is like—that the public does not have an accurate picture of the problems that stewardesses must confront.

In-depth interviews are a useful technique for social scientists because results gained from one interview can be accepted as typical of most members in the group being studied.

Exemplification is especially useful as a technique for bringing abstract concepts into a form that can be clearly understood. Although the idea of a data base might be difficult to grasp at first, the writers of the IBM technical manual, "Processing Information in a Data Base," use an extended example to illustrate why a data base is so well adapted for storing and retrieving information about individual patients:

> In the medical data base, the data that you're keeping is information about a particular patient. Information that is not associated with a particular patient is meaningless. For example, keeping information about a treatment given for a particular illness is meaningless if the illness isn't associated with a patient. ILLNESS, TREATMNT, BILLING, PAYMENT, and HOUSHOLD must always be associated with one of the clinic's patients to be meaningful information.

The basic idea is that many different kinds of information that hospitals keep on their patients can be stored in a data base in a way that facilitates easy access. This extended example of the various ways that a hospital might store and retrieve information reveals the basic capabilities that all data-base systems possess. Thus, the technical writers of the IBM manual make it possible for users with limited computer expertise to understand and appreciate the advantages of storing information in a data base.

In the related field of artificial intelligence (AI), computers can be programmed by experts in various fields to make logical inferences from specific "knowledge-bases." Edward A. Feigenbaum and Pamela McCorduck present a number of thought-provoking examples in "Speculations in Knowledge Futures" that clarify the possible future applications of systems of artificial intelligence:

> If the idea of a machine doctor repels you, consider that not everyone feels that way. Studies in England showed that many humans were much more comfortable (and candid) with an examination by a computer terminal than with a human physician, whom they perceived as somehow disapproving of them. "Mechanical" doctors are in fact systems that move methodically through possibilities making inferences and drawing conclusions. They often outperform the very experts who have programmed them because of their methodical ways; they don't skip or forget things, get tired or rushed, or fall subject to some of our other human failings. They will be on call at the patient's convenience, not just the physician's. And they can bring medicine to places where none now exists.

The key feature of such an "expert system" is that it accurately mimics the kind of interaction a patient might expect to have with a human doctor. The intriguing capabilities of artificial intelligence can thus be appreciated through down-to-earth examples that give readers an idea of what the future applications might be.

Illustrations may take a variety of forms, including case histories (as we shall see in Terkel's interview), single, multiple, or extended examples (as used by Rhodes, Hersey, IBM's technical writers, and Feigenbaum and McCorduck), as well as interesting anecdotes that make a point.

A former Ambassador to China, Erwin Wickert, relates an anecdote that exemplifies how important "shame" is in controlling behavior among the Chinese. In "The Chinese and the Sense of Shame," Wickert reports a story that illustrates the puritanical attitudes of the Communist Party officials toward a young girl suspected of being sexually intimate with a married coworker:

> The following story was told to me by a Chinese acquaintance who had been sent to work in a factory during the Cultural Revolution. It appears that one of his fellow workers, a young woman, had an affair with a married colleague whose family lived far away in the country, and who saw his wife for a few days a year at most. Accused by their workmates of sleeping together, the couple denied it. Nobody believed them, and a mood of hysteria developed, particularly among their female workmates. They were watched and spied on. Eventually, after keeping them under surveillance, members of the People's Militia succeeded in catching them in bed together. They were promptly arrested and marched off to the factory, whose Security Bureau personnel interrogated them with relish and broadcast the results of their inquisition to the rest of the workforce. Neither of them was permitted to go home throughout this time. They were held in isolation at the factory and compelled to sleep there until the board of inquiry ended by reprimanding them both. . . . but suicide is the usual outcome in such cases. Where shame is a living force, social sanctions against those who commit some disgraceful act are harsher than in societies ruled by laws alone.

Wickert's account reveals just how pervasive "shame" is as a force in the communal life of the Chinese people. Ironically, "shame" is just as powerful a force in controlling people's behavior in today's communist Chinese culture as it was in the traditional China of the past.

Personal observations, especially those made by trained scientists, can help substantiate a hypothesis, although a single example is rarely sufficient to support a generalization. In "The Dove and the Wolf," Konrad Lorenz's observations of various animal species led him to conclude that many supposedly meek species such as doves, deer, and hares were merciless, whereas several supposedly vicious species such as ravens and timber wolves were restrained by innate inhibitions against killing their own kind. To illustrate this surprising discovery, Lorenz gives a brief account of the last stages of combat between rival timber wolves:

> A dog or wolf that offers its neck to its adversary in this way will never be bitten seriously. The other growls and rumbles, snaps with his teeth in the empty air and even carries out, without delivering so much as a bite, the movement of shaking something to death in the empty air. However, this strange inhibition from biting persists only so long as the defeated dog or wolf maintains his attitude of humility. . . .

Lorenz relates this episode to illustrate his discovery that in some species "submission gestures" trigger an innate inhibition against killing a defeated rival. What astonishes Lorenz is that popular legends and folklore incorrectly portray the gentleness of doves, deer, and hares, and the supposed viciousness of wolves.

LIBERAL ARTS

David A. Ricks

What's In a Name?

David A. Ricks was born in 1942 in Washington, D.C. and earned his Ph.D. in business administration from Indiana University in 1970. Ricks has taught at Ohio State University (1975–1981), and is currently a professor of international business and director of the Ph.D. program in international business at the University of South Carolina. He is also editor-in-chief of the Journal of International Business Studies, and authored or coauthored six books and more than thirty articles on various aspects of international business strategies, including International Dimensions of Corporate Finance *(1978) and* Big Business Blunders: Mistakes in Multinational Marketing *(1983). He has appeared on the "Today Show," testified before Congress, and has been recognized as an authority in this area by publications such as the* Wall Street Journal, Business Week, *and* Forbes. *"What's In a Name?," originally published as Chapter Three of* Big Business Blunders, *underscores the importance of test marketing product or company names to avoid unintended humorous, offensive, or even obscene connotations when these names are translated into other languages.*

Shakespeare once queried, "What's in a name?" A number of business people, after a bit of international marketing, might appropriately respond, "More than you might think." Many companies have discovered that even something as seemingly innocuous as a name can prove insulting and embarrassing. Both product and company names can fall prey to such troubles.

Product Names

Product names often take on various unintended and hidden meanings. The experience of a major soapmaker serves as a classic example. When this company was considering a name for a new soap powder to be marketed internationally, it wisely ran a translation test of the proposed soap name in 50 major languages. In English and most of the major European languages, the name meant "dainty." In other tongues, however, the soap name did not translate so appropriately. In Gaelic, it became "song," in Flemish it meant "aloof," and it said "horse" in the language of one African tribe. In Persia, the name was translated as "hazy" or "dimwitted," and to the Koreans, the name sounded like a person out of his mind. Finally, in all of the Slavic languages, the name was considered obscene and offensive. Naturally, the proposed name was hastily abandoned. This experience, though, demonstrates the importance of a name and how carefully it should be considered prior to the introduction of the product.

Unusual Problems

Today, more and more firms are seeking assistance in hopes of avoiding costly and embarrasssing mistakes. Even the largest and most sophisticated firms are not immune to the difficulties of product-name interpretation. For example, when the Coca-Cola Company was planning its strategy for marketing in China in the 1920s, it wanted to introduce its product with the English pronunciation of "Coca-Cola." A translator developed a group of Chinese characters which, when pronounced, sounded like the product name. These characters were placed on the cola bottles and marketed. Was it any wonder that sales levels were low? The characters actually translated to mean "a wax-flattened mare" or "bite the wax tadpole." Since the product was new, sound was unimportant to the consumers; meaning was vital.[1] Today Coca-Cola is again marketing its cola in China. The new characters used on the bottle translate to "happiness in the mouth." From its first marketing attempts, Coca-Cola learned a valuable lesson in international marketing.

General Motors was faced with a similar problem. It was troubled by the lack of enthusiasm among the Puerto Rican auto dealers for its recently introduced Chevrolet "Nova." The name "Nova" meant "star" when literally translated. However, when spoken, it sounded like "no va" which, in Spanish, means "it doesn't go." This obviously did little to increase consumer confidence in the new vehicle. To remedy the situation, General Motors changed the automobile name "Caribe" and sales increased.

Other car manufacturers have also experienced comparable situations. In fact, problems with the names used in international automobile promotions seem to be frequent events. For example, difficulties arose during the translation of the name of the American car "Randan." Apparently this name was interpreted by the Japanese to mean "idiot." The American Motors Corporation's "Matador" name usually conjures up images of virility and strength, but in Puerto Rico it means "killer"—not a favorable connotation in a place with a high traffic fatality rate.

Ford encountered translation problems with some of its cars as well. It introduced a low cost truck, the "Fiera," into some of the less-developed countries. Unfortunately the name meant "ugly old woman" in Spanish. Needless to say, this name did not encourage sales. Ford also experienced slow sales when it introduced a top-of-the-line automobile, the "Comet," in Mexico under the name "Caliente." The puzzlingly low sales levels were finally understood when Ford discovered that "caliente" is slang for a streetwalker. Additional headaches were reportedly experienced when Ford's

---

[1] By reporting this incident in some of its annual reports, Coca-Cola has even laughed at itself.

"Pinto" was briefly introduced in Brazil under its English name. The name was speedily changed to "Corcel" (which means "horse" in Portuguese) after Ford discovered that the Portuguese slang translation of "pinto" is "a small male appendage."

The naming of a new automobile model to be marketed in Germany by Rolls Royce was a difficult undertaking. The company felt that the English name "Silver Mist" was very appealing but discovered that the name would undoubtedly not capture the German market as hoped. In German, the translated meaning of "mist" is actually "excrement," and the Germans could not possibly have found such a name appealing. Unfortunately, the Sunbeam Corporation did not learn of this particular translation problem in time and attempted to enter the German market advertising its new mist-producing hair curling iron, the "Mist-Stick." As should have been expected, the Germans had no interest in a "dung" or "manure" wand.

Firms occasionally try to enter the foreign market promoting a product bearing an untranslated name. Sometimes this tactic works, but other times it does not work as well as expected. At least one global firm can attest to this. The company consistently marketed one of its pieces of equipment under the name "Grab Bucket." To its chagrin, the firm learned that in Germany it was actually advertising the sale of cemetery plot flowers. In German, the word *grab* is interpreted as *grave*, and *bucket* is pronounced like *bouquet*. So because of these linguistic anomalies, the company did not appear to be selling what it thought at all.

Many companies have suffered similar pitfalls. A U.S. company was taken by surprise when it introduced its product in Latin America and learned that the name of the product meant "jackass oil" in Spanish. Another well-intentioned firm sold shampoo in Brazil under the name "Evitol." Little did it realize that it was claiming to be selling a "dandruff contraceptive." A manufacturing company sold its machines in the Soviet Union under the name "Bardak"—a word which signifies a brothel in Russian. An American product failed to capture the Swedish market; the product name translated to "enema," which the product was not. A Finnish brewery introduced two new beverages in the United States—"Koff" beer and "Siff" beer. Is it any wonder that sales were sluggish? Another name, unappealing to Americans, can be found on the package of a delicious chocolate and fruit product sold in German or European deli. The chocolate concoction has the undesirable English name "Zit!"

The reported troubles of an American company that markets Pet milk serves as one more example. This firm reportedly experienced difficulties introducing its product in French-speaking areas. It seems that the word *Pet* in French means, among other things, "to break wind." And had Colgate-Palmolive attempted to gain market entry with its Cue toothpaste in French-speaking regions, it too would have encountered comparable problems. *Cue* is a pornographic word in French.[2] An American woman will long remember her international experience with Coca-Cola. She was dispensing sample tasters of Fresca soda pop when she unintentionally elicited a great deal of laughter from passersby. She only later realized the cause when she discovered that in Mexican slang the word *Fresca* means *lesbian*.

Close examination of foreign markets and language differences are necessary and should be required before a product's domestically successful name is introduced abroad. Unfortunately, this simple warning is sometimes neglected in a company's enthusiasm to plunge into overseas marketing operations.

---

[2] It should be noted, however, that reports citing problems with the name "Cue" have been denied by the company.

Manufacturers often assume that products which have enjoyed domestic success   *12*
will naturally receive the same reception overseas. However, this is not always the
case as the following examples demonstrate. Princess Housewares, Inc., a large U.S.
appliance manufacturer, introduced a line of electric housewares in the German market.
The company's brand name, well known and highly regarded in the United States,
was relatively unknown in Germany. Its name, though, which had a definite American
sound, turned out to be a real drawback as the German consumers disliked the
American association.[3] Similarly, in the early 1960s General Mills spent over $1.4
million advertising its Betty Crocker cake mixes in an effort to gain entry into the
British market. The costly promotion, though, did not achieve the expected positive
results either. Although research revealed that the product itself was quite acceptable,
the British just could not identify with the exotic names given to the cake mixes.[4]

Name adaptations sometimes prove to be winners; other times they do not. The   *13*
Johnson Wax Company successfully introduced its product "Pledge" in Germany
under the name of "Pronto," but problems arose when the product entered the
market in the Netherlands as "Pliz." In Dutch, the pronunciation of "Pliz" sounds
like "Piss." Understandably, it was rather difficult for the customer of the conventional
Dutch grocery store to ask for the product.

Sometimes the required change in the product name is a rather simple one. Wrigley,   *14*
for example, merely altered the spelling of its "Spearmint" chewing gum to "Speermint"
to aid in the German pronunciation of the flavor. "Maxwell House" proved slightly
more difficult. The name was changed to "Maxwell Kaffee" in Germany, "Legal" in
France, and "Monky" in Spain.

As evidenced, firms have blundered by changing product names and by failing to   *15*
alter names. This is not to say, however, that one is "damned if you do and damned
if you don't." Adequate name assessments prior to market introduction can reduce
potential name blunders.

More Obscene Meanings

Inappropriate product names sometimes prove to be quite humorous, but in a   *16*
number of cases, the names have actually borne fairly obscene implications and connotations. A few illustrations of this type of blunder are cited below.

Bird's Eye considered itself quite fortunate when it discovered that a proposed   *17*
name for one of its fishfood products was inappropriate. Wisely, the company decided
against the name when it uncovered that the name translated to "genitals." Not all
firms have been so lucky. A well-known oil company was caught in an embarrassing
situation when it learned of the "indecent" name it had chosen for its products.
The company established operations in Indonesia and manufactured machinery displaying the name "Nonox." One can imagine the firm's discomfort when it was informed
that "Nonox" sounded similar to the Javanese slang word *Nonok* which is comparable
to the American idiom for female "private parts."

Obviously the employees who proposed the name "Joni" for a new facial cream   *18*
which was to be marketed in India had never read the erotic Indian classic *Kama*

[3] For a more complete discussion of this problem, see Robert D. Buzzell, "Can You Standardize Multinational,
Marketing?" *Harvard Business Review*, November–December 1968, pp. 102–13.
[4] Although the October 1, 1963 issue of *Forbes* reported this case in the article "General Mills: the General
and Betty Crocker," pp. 20–24, General Mills now denies the report.

Sutra. If they had, they would surely have known that the Hindu word *joni* represents the most intimate areas of the female body.

The example of a vitamin product introduced in South America serves as a final illustration of how product names can unintentionally become obscenities. In this case, a company introduced its vitamins as "Fundavit" and boasted that they satisfied the fundamental vitamin requirements. The name had to be modified when the firm learned that "fundola" in Spanish stands for the rear end of an attractive young female.

Other Offensive Names

As illustrated, certain product name choices can create embarrassing situations for companies when the names are interpreted as indecencies. On occasion, a company chooses a name which, although not obscene, turns out to be in poor taste and offensive to certain groups of people. One example is the name "Black Nikka" chosen for a brand of Japanese whiskey sold in the United States and found to be demeaning by some black Americans. Also consider the bold experiment in international marketing that brought together the state-controlled tobacco monopolies of five countries (France, Italy, Portugal, Austria, and Japan) to launch a major promotion of a new brand of cigarettes, "Champagne." This venture proved to be an embarrassment to the French government, and the case wound up in the international law courts with the French champagne producers in a fury. These producers claimed that the use of "Champagne" as a brand name "is deplorable, and the connection with health hazards may permanently damage our image."[5]

Yves St. Laurent drew some unwanted criticism when it named a new fragrance "Opium." Even though the advertising campaign was voted the best for 1978 by the Fragrance Foundation, it created a storm of protest. In general, it was simply viewed as poor judgment to name a fragrance after an illegal drug. The original French slogan "Pour celles qui s'adonnet á Yves St. Laurent" ("For those who are addicted to Yves St. Laurent") only tended to reinforce the resented "connections" and connotations. The Chinese also considered the use of the name "Opium" to be a racial slur. Public pressure eventually forced the company to discontinue the sales promotion in some places.[6] Therefore, it can not be stressed too strongly: Names must be chosen carefully.

COMPANY NAMES

Product names are not the only ones which can generate company blunders. If a firm name is misinterpreted or incorrectly translated, it too can cause the same types of humorous, obscene, offensive, or unexpected situations. A number of examples are described in the following paragraphs.

A private Egyptian airline, Misair, proved to be rather unpopular with the French nationals. Could the fact that the name, when pronounced, meant "misery" in French

---

[5] For further details, see Carolyn Pfaff, "Champagne Cigs Cause Headache," *Advertising Age,* March 30, 1981, p. 2.

[6] Background information is provided by Pat Sloan in "Fragrance under Fire: Opium Ads Go Up in Smoke," *Advertising Age,* June 4, 1979, p. 1.

have contributed to the airline's plight? Another airline trying to gain acceptance in Australia only complicated matters when it chose the firm name "EMU." The emu is an Australian bird which is incapable of flying. But EMU was not the only company to run into snags while conducting business in Australia. The AMF Corporation was forced to change its name. Why? Because AMF is the official designation for the Australian military forces. Similarly, Sears was forbidden to use its unchanged name in Spain. The company commanded respect and had developed a good reputation there, but since the Castillian Spanish pronunciation of Sears sounded much like "Seat" (the name of Spain's largest car manufacturer), Seat forced Sears to incorporate the name "Roebuck" on all of its products.

When Esso realized that its name phonetically meant "stalled car," it understood why it had had difficulties in the Japanese market. And was it any wonder that Ford ran into unexpected low sales levels in Spain? Apparently its cars were not popular with certain groups; some of the locals were interpreting the name "Ford" to mean "*F*abrica *O*rdinaria *R*eparaciones *D*iaviamente" (translation: "ordinarily, make repairs daily"). The Vicks Company, however, was more fortunate. It discovered that in German "Vicks" sounds like the most crude slang equivalent of intercourse and was able to change its name to an acceptable "Wicks."

As a final illustration, consider the trade magazine which promoted giftware and launched a worldwide circulation effort. The magazine used the word *gift* in its title and as part of its name. When it was later revealed that *gift* is the German word for *poison*, a red-faced publishing executive supposedly retorted that the Germans should simply find a new word for poison!

Of course not all companies have been forced to change names. In fact, some of them have traveled quite well. Kodak may be the most famous example. A research team deliberately "developed" this name after carefully searching for a word which was pronounceable everywhere but had no specific meaning anywhere. Exxon is another such name which was reportedly accepted only after a lengthy and expensive computer-assisted search.

SUMMARY

Multinational corporations have experienced many unexpected troubles concerning company or product names, and even attempts to alter names have led to blunders. It should be evident that careful planning and study of the potential market are necessary as name adaptation can be every bit as important as product or package modification.

MEANING

1. What are the most striking examples of company or product names that acquired unintended meanings and inadvertent connotations—ranging from the harmless and amusing to the insulting and obscene—because of the failure to understand important linguistic and cultural differences?
2. Why should a close examination of language differences be required before a product's domestically successful name is introduced abroad?

3. Why are examples of spectacular failures more valuable than success stories in teaching principles of international marketing and intercultural communication?
4. What are the advantages of computer-created names that have no specific meaning but are pronounceable everywhere throughout the world?

Using Exemplification to Convey Meaning

1. How do the examples that Ricks presents illustrate a broad range of unanticipated effects (harmless, amusing, insulting, embarrassing, costly) when product names are introduced without advance research into foreign markets?
2. What different kinds of examples does the author provide? Which are anecdotes, advertising slogans, acronyms, or attempts at idiomatic translation?
3. How do the author's examples illustrate the important concept that communications of any kind must be adapted for a specific audience to be effective?

Writing Suggestions

1. Consider the following list of brand names used by car manufacturers:
    a. Animal names that put the car owner in touch with nature, freedom, and excitement: Sky Hawk, Mustang, Cougar, Colt, Lynx, AMC Eagle.
    b. Names that imply power: Charger, Triumph, Fury, Firebird, Thunderbird.
    c. Names that carry status: Regal, Le Baron, Celebrity, Grand Am, Diplomat, Grand Marquis, Regency.
    d. Names of places that convey prestige and wealth: New Yorker, Parisienne, Riviera, Capri, Monte Carlo, Seville, El Dorado, Fifth Avenue.
    What additional categories of car names might be added to this list? (For example, what car names are sharp-edged weapons or the names of famous race courses?) How do these brand names invest cars (which in many cases are mechanically and structurally identical to each other) with symbolic associations chosen because of their persuasive qualities? Which names would lose the connotations they possess in our culture when marketed in other countries? Which names would gain additional connotations in different cultural contexts?
2. What idioms appearing on greeting cards in other languages would be misunderstood if translated literally, word for word, from the original language? What unintended meanings might be produced?

JOHN HERSEY

A Noiseless Flash from Hiroshima

John Hersey was born in 1914 in Tientsin, China. After graduating from Yale in 1936, Hersey's varied career included being a driver for Sinclair Lewis and a war correspondent in China and Japan. During World War II, he covered the war in the South Pacific, the Mediterranean, and Moscow for Time *magazine. He then became editor and correspondent for* Life *magazine, and made a trip to China and Japan for* Life, *and the* New Yorker *in 1945–1946. The* New Yorker *devoted its August 31, 1946 issue to the publication of Hersey's momentous work,* Hiroshima, *which reported the effects of the atomic bomb on the lives of six people. In 1985, Hersey did a follow-up report on what the lives of these six people had been like during the intervening forty years. Hersey's other books include* A Bell for Adano (1944), *which won the Pulitzer Prize,* The Wall (1950), The War Lover (1959), The Child Buyer (1960), White Lotus (1965), *and* The Conspiracy (1972). *Hersey's approach to journalism is always through the specific individuals who are caught up in historical events. In "A Noiseless Flash from Hiroshima," from* Hiroshima, *Hersey communicates the incalculable horror of the atomic bomb at Hiroshima through the images, emotions, and experiences of six people who survived.*

At exactly fifteen minutes past eight in the morning, on August 6, 1945, Japanese time, at the moment when the atomic bomb flashed above Hiroshima, Miss Toshiko Sasaki, a clerk in the personnel department of the East Asia Tin Works, had just sat down at her place in the plant office and was turning her head to speak to the girl at the next desk. At that same moment, Dr. Masakazu Fujii was settling down cross-legged to read the Osaka *Asahi* on the porch of his private hospital, overhanging one of the seven deltaic rivers which divide Hiroshima; Mrs. Hatsuyo Nakamura, a tailor's widow, stood by the window of her kitchen, watching a neighbor tearing down his house because it lay in the path of an air-raid-defense fire lane; Father Wilhelm Kleinsorge, a German priest of the Society of Jesus, reclined in his underwear on a cot on the top floor of his order's three-story mission house, reading a Jesuit magazine, *Stimmen der Zeit;* Dr. Terufumi Sasaki, a young member of the surgical staff of the city's large, modern Red Cross Hospital, walked along one of the hospital corridors with a blood specimen for a Wassermann test in his hand; and the Reverend Mr. Kiyoshi Tanimoto, pastor of the Hiroshima Methodist Church, paused at the door of a rich man's house in Koi, the city's western suburb, and prepared to unlaod a handcart full of things he had evacuated from town in fear of the massive B–29 raid which everyone expected Hiroshima to suffer. A hundred thousand people were killed by the atomic bomb, and these six were among the survivors. They still wonder why they lived when so many others died. Each of them counts many small items of chance or volition—a step taken in time, a decision to go indoors, catching one streetcar instead of the next—that spared him. And now each knows that in the act of survival he lived a dozen lives and saw more death than he ever thought he would see. At the time, none of them knew anything.

The Reverend Mr. Tanimoto got up at five o'clock that morning. He was alone in the parsonage, because for some time his wife had been commuting with their year-old baby to spend nights with a friend in Ushida, a suburb to the north. Of all the important cities of Japan, only two, Kyoto and Hiroshima, had not been visited in strength by *B-san*, or Mr. B, as the Japanese, with a mixture of respect and unhappy familiarity, called the B–29; and Mr. Tanimoto, like all his neighbors and friends, was almost sick with anxiety. He had heard uncomfortably detailed accounts of mass raids on Kure, Iwakuni, Tokuyama, and other nearby towns; he was sure Hiroshima's turn would come soon. He had slept badly the night before, because there had been several air-raid warnings. Hiroshima had been getting such warnings almost every night for weeks, for at that time the B–29s were using Lake Biwa, northeast of Hiroshima, as a rendezvous point, and no matter what city the Americans planned to hit, the Superfortresses streamed in over the coast near Hiroshima. The frequency of the warnings and the continued abstinence of Mr. B with respect to Hiroshima had made its citizens jittery; a rumor was going around that the Americans were saving something special for the city.

Mr. Tanimoto is a small man, quick to talk, laugh, and cry. He wears his black hair parted in the middle and rather long; the prominence of the frontal bones just above his eyebrows and the smallness of his mustache, mouth, and chin give him a strange, old-young look, boyish and yet wise, weak and yet fiery. He moves nervously and fast, but with a restraint which suggests that he is a cautious, thoughtful man. He showed, indeed, just those qualities in the uneasy days before the bomb fell. Besides having his wife spend the nights in Ushida, Mr. Tanimoto had been carrying all the portable things from his church, in the close-packed residential district called Nagaragawa, to a house that belonged to a rayon manufacturer in Koi, two miles from the center of town. The rayon man, a Mr. Matsui, had opened his then unoccupied estate to a large number of his friends and acquaintances, so that they might evacuate whatever they wished to a safe distance from the probable target area. Mr. Tanimoto had had no difficulty in moving chairs, hymnals, Bibles, altar gear, and church records by pushcart himself, but the organ console and an upright piano required some aid. A friend of his named Matsuo had, the day before, helped him get the piano out to Koi; in return, he had promised this day to assist Mr. Matsuo in hauling out a daughter's belongings. That is why he had risen so early.

Mr. Tanimoto cooked his own breakfast. He felt awfully tired. The effort of moving the piano the day before, a sleepless night, weeks of worry and unbalanced diet, the cares of his parish—all combined to make him feel hardly adequate to the new day's work. There was another thing, too: Mr. Tanimoto had studied theology at Emory College, in Atlanta, Georgia; he had graduated in 1940; he spoke excellent English; he dressed in American clothes; he had corresponded with many American friends right up to the time the war began; and among a people obsessed with a fear of being spied upon—perhaps almost obsessed himself—he found himself growing increasingly uneasy. The police had questioned him several times, and just a few days before, he had heard that an influential acquaintance, a Mr. Tanaka, a retired officer of the Toyo Kisen Kaisha steamship line, an anti-Christian, a man famous in Hiroshima for his showy philanthropies and notorious for his personal tyrannies, had been telling people that Tanimoto should not be trusted. In compensation, to show himself publicly a good Japanese, Mr. Tanimoto had taken on the chairmanship of his local *tonarigumi*, or Neighborhood Association, and to his other duties and concerns this position had added the business of organizing air-raid defense for about twenty families.

Before six o'clock that morning, Mr. Tanimoto started for Mr. Matsuo's house. There he found that their burden was to be a *tansu*, a large Japanese cabinet, full of clothing and household goods. The two men set out. The morning was perfectly clear and so warm that the day promised to be uncomfortable. A few minutes after they started, the air-raid siren went off—a minute-long blast that warned of approaching planes but indicated to the people of Hiroshima only a slight degree of danger, since it sounded every morning at this time, when an American weather plane came over. The two men pulled and pushed the handcart through the city streets. Hiroshima was a fan-shaped city, lying mostly on the six islands formed by the seven estuarial rivers that branch out from the Ota River; its main commercial and residential districts, covering about four square miles in the center of the city, contained three-quarters of its population, which had been reduced by several evacuation programs from a wartime peak of 380,000 to about 245,000. Factories and other residential districts, or suburbs, lay compactly around the edges of the city. To the south were the docks, an airport, and the island-studded Inland Sea. A rim of mountains runs around the other three sides of the delta. Mr. Tanimoto and Mr. Matsuo took their way through the shopping center, already full of people, and across two of the rivers to the sloping streets of Koi, and up them to the outskirts and foothills. As they started up a valley away from the tight-ranked houses, the all-clear sounded. (The Japanese radar operators, detecting only three planes, supposed that they comprised a reconnaissance.) Pushing the handcart up to the rayon man's house was tiring, and the men, after they had maneuvered their load into the driveway and to the front steps, paused to rest awhile. They stood with a wing of the house between them and the city. Like most homes in this part of Japan, the house consisted of a wooden frame and wooden walls supporting a heavy tile roof. Its front hall, packed with rolls of bedding and clothing, looked like a cool cave full of fat cushions. Opposite the house, to the right of the front door, there was a large, finicky rock garden. There was no sound of planes. The morning was still; the place was cool and pleasant.

Then a tremendous flash of light cut across the sky. Mr. Tanimoto has a distinct recollection that it travelled from east to west, from the city toward the hills. It seemed a sheet of sun. Both he and Mr. Matsuo reacted in terror—and both had time to react (for they were 3,500 yards, or two miles, from the center of the explosion). Mr. Matsuo dashed up the front steps into the house and dived among the bedrolls and buried himself there. Mr. Tanimoto took four or five steps and threw himself between two big rocks in the garden. He bellied up very hard against one of them. As his face was against the stone, he did not see what happened. He felt a sudden pressure, and then splinters and pieces of board and fragments of tile fell on him. He heard no roar. (Almost no one in Hiroshima recalls hearing any noise of the bomb. But a fisherman in his sampan on the Inland Sea near Tsuzu, the man with whom Mr. Tanimoto's mother-in-law and sister-in-law were living, saw the flash and heard a tremendous explosion; he was nearly twenty miles from Hiroshima, but the thunder was greater than when the B–29s hit Iwakuni, only five miles away.)

When he dared, Mr. Tanimoto raised his head and saw that the rayon man's house had collapsed. He thought a bomb had fallen directly on it. Such clouds of dust had risen that there was a sort of twilight around. In panic, not thinking for the moment of Mr. Matsuo under the ruins, he dashed out into the street. He noticed as he ran that the concrete wall of the estate had fallen over—toward the house rather than away from it. In the street, the first thing he saw was a squad of soldiers who had been burrowing into the hillside opposite, making one of the thousands of dugouts in which the Japanese apparently intended to resist invasion, hill by hill, life for life; the soldiers were coming out of the hole, where they should have been safe, and blood was running from their heads, chests, and backs. They were silent and dazed.

Under what seemed to be a local dust cloud, the day grew darker and darker.

At nearly midnight, the night before the bomb was dropped, an announcer on the city's radio station said that about two hundred B–29s were approaching southern Honshu and advised the population of Hiroshima to evacuate to their designated "safe areas." Mrs. Hatsuyo Nakamura, the tailor's widow, who lived in the section called Noboricho and who had long had a habit of doing as she was told, got her three children—a ten-year-old boy, Toshio, an eight-year-old girl, Yaeko, and a five-year-old girl, Myeko—out of bed and dressed them and walked with them to the military area known as the East Parade Ground, on the northeast edge of the city. There she unrolled some mats and the children lay down on them. They slept until about two, when they were awakened by the roar of the planes going over Hiroshima.

As soon as the planes had passed, Mrs. Nakamura started back with her children. They reached home a little after two-thirty and she immediately turned on the radio, which, to her distress, was just then broadcasting a fresh warning. When she looked at the children and saw how tired they were, and when she thought of the number of trips they had made in past weeks, all to no purpose, to the East Parade Ground, she decided that in spite of the instructions on the radio, she simply could not face starting out all over again. She put the children in their bedrolls on the floor, lay down herself at three o'clock, and fell asleep at once, so soundly that when planes passed over later, she did not waken to their sound.

The siren jarred her awake at about seven. She arose, dressed quickly, and hurried to the hosue of Mr. Nakamoto, the head of her Neighborhood Association, and asked him what she should do. He said that she should remain at home unless an urgent warning—a series of intermittent blasts of the siren—was sounded. She returned home, lit the stove in the kitchen, set some rice to cook, and sat down to read the morning's Hiroshima *Chugoku*. To her relief, the all-clear sounded at eight o'clock. She heard the children stirring, so she went and gave each of them a handful of peanuts and told them to stay on their bedrolls, because they were tired from the night's walk. She had hoped that they would go back to sleep, but the man in the house directly to the south began to make a terrible hullabaloo of hammering, wedging, ripping, and splitting. The prefectural government, convinced, as everyone in Hiroshima was, that the city would be attacked soon, had begun to press with threats and warnings for the completion of wide fire lanes, which, it was hoped, might act in conjunction with the rivers to localize any fires started by an incendiary raid; and the neighbor was reluctantly sacrificing his home to the city's safety. Just the day before, the prefecture had ordered all able-bodied girls from the secondary schools to spend a few days helping to clear these lanes, and they started work soon after the all-clear sounded.

Mrs. Nakamura went back to the kitchen, looked at the rice, and begn watching the man next door. At first, she was annoyed with him for making so much noise, but then she was moved almost to tears by pity. Her emotion was specifically directed toward her neighbor, tearing down his home, board by board, at a time when there was so much unavoidable destruction, but undoubtedly she also felt a generalized, community pity, to say nothing of self-pity. She had not had a easy time. Her husband, Isawa, had gone into the Army just after Myeko was born, and she had heard nothing from or of him for a long time, until, on March 5, 1942, she received a seven-word telegram: "Isawa died an honorable death at Singapore." She learned later that he had died on February 15th, the day Singapore fell, and that he had been a corporal. Isawa had been a not particularly propsperous tailor, and his only capital was a Sankoku sewing machine. After his death, when his allotments stopped coming, Mrs. Nakamura got out the machine and began to take in piecework herself, and since then had supported the children, but poorly, by sewing.

As Mrs. Nakamura stood watching her neighbor, everything flashed whiter than any white she had ever seen. She did not notice what happened to the man next door; the reflex of a mother set her in motion toward her children. She had taken a single step (the house was 1,350 yards, or three-quarters of a mile, from the center of the explosion) when something picked her up and she seemed to fly into the next room over the raised sleeping platform, pursued by parts of her house.

Timbers fell around her as she landed, and a shower of tiles pommelled her; everything became dark, for she was buried. The debris did not cover her deeply. She rose up and freed herself. She heard a child cry, "Mother, help me!" and saw her youngest—Myeko, the five-year-old—buried up to her breast and unable to move. As Mrs. Nakamura started frantically to claw her way toward the baby, she could see or hear nothing of her other children.

In the days right before the bombing, Dr. Masakazu Fujii, being propsperous, hedonistic, and at the time not too busy, had been allowing himself the luxury of sleeping until nine or nine-thirty, but fortunately he had to get up early the morning the bomb was dropped to see a house guest off on a train. He rose at six, and half an hour later walked with his friend to the station, not far away, across two of the rivers. He was back home by seven, just as the siren sounded its sustained warning. He ate breakfast and then, because the morning was already hot, undressed down to his underwear and went out on the porch to read the paper. This porch—in fact, the whole building—was curiously constructed. Dr. Fujii was the proprietor of a peculiarly Japanese institution: a private, single-doctor hospital. This building, perched beside and over the water of the Kyo River, and next to the bridge of the same name, contained thirty rooms for thirty patients and their kinfolk—for, according to Japanese custom, when a person falls sick and goes to a hospital, one or more members of his family go and live there with him, to cook for him, bathe, massage, and read to him, and to offer incesssant familial sympathy, without which a Japanese patient would be miserable indeed. Dr. Fujii had no beds—only straw mats—for his patients. He did, however, have all sorts of modern equipment: an X-ray machine, diathermy apparatus, and a fine tiled laboratory. The structure rested two-thirds on the land, one-third on piles over the tidal waters of the Kyo. This overhang, the part of the building where Dr. Fujii lived, was queer-looking, but it was cool in summer and from the porch, which faced away from the center of the city, the prospect of the river, with pleasure boats drifting up and down it, was always refreshing. Dr. Fujii had occasionally had anxious moments when the Ota and it mouth branches rose to flood, but the piling was apparently firm enough and the house had always held.

Dr. Fujii had been relatively idle for about a month because in July, as the number of untouched cities in Japan dwindled and as Hiroshima seemed more and more inevitably a target, he began turning patients away, on the ground that in case of a fire raid he would not be able to evacuate them. Now he had only two patients left—a woman from Yano, injured in the shoulder, and a young man of twenty-five recovering from burns he had suffered when the steel factory near Hiroshima in which he worked had been hit. Dr. Fujii had six nurses to tend his patients. His wife and children were safe; his wife and one son were living outside Osaka, and another son and two daughters were in the country on Kyushu. A niece was living with him, and a maid and a man-servant. He had little to do and did not mind, for he had saved some money. At fifty, he was healthy, convivial, and calm, and he was pleased to pass the evenings drinking whiskey with friends, always sensibly and for the sake of conversation. Before the war, he had affected brands imported from Scotland and America; now he was perfectly satisfied with the best Japanese brand, Suntory.

Dr. Fujii sat down cross-legged in his underwear on the spotless matting of the porch, put on his glasses, and started reading the Osaka *Asahi*. He liked to read the Osaka news because his wife was there. He saw the flash. To him—faced away from the center and looking at his paper—it seemed a brilliant yellow. Startled, he began to rise to his feet. In that moment (he was 1,550 yards from the center), the hospital leaned behind him rising and, with a terrible ripping noise, toppled into the river. The Doctor, still in the act of getting to his feet, was thrown forward and around and over; he was buffeted and gripped; he lost track of everything, because things were so speeded up; he felt the water.

Dr. Fujii hardly had time to think that he was dying before he realized that he was alive, squeezed tightly by two long timbers in a V across his chest, like a morsel suspended between two huge chopsticks—held upright, so that he could not move, with his head miraculously above water and his torso and legs in it. The remains of his hospital were all around him in a mad assortment of splintered lumber and materials for the relief of pain. His left shoulder hurt terribly. His glasses were gone.

Father Wilhelm Kleinsorge, of the Society of Jesus, was, on the morning of the explosion, in rather frail condition. The Japanese wartime diet had not sustained him, and he felt the strain of being a foreigner in an increasingly xenophobic Japan; even a German, since the defeat of the Fatherland, was unpopular. Father Kleinsorge had, at thirty-eight, the look of a boy growing too fast—thin in the face, with a prominent Adam's apple, a hollow chest, dangling hands, big feet. He walked clumsily, leaning forward a little. He was tired all the time. To make matters worse, he had suffered for two days, along with Father Cieslik, a fellow-priest, from a rather painful and urgent diarrhea, which they blamed on the beans and black ration bread they were obliged to eat. Two other priests then living in the mission compound, which was in the Nobori-cho section—Father Superior LaSalle and Father Schiffer—had happily escaped this affliction.

Father Kleinsorge woke up about six the morning the bomb was dropped, and half an hour later—he was a bit tardy because of his sickness—he began to read Mass in the mission chapel, a small Japanese-style wooden building which was without pews, since its worshippers knelt on the usual Japanese matted floor, facing an altar graced with splendid silks, brass, silver, and heavy embroideries. This morning, a Monday, the only worshippers were Mr. Takemoto, a theological student living in the mission house; Mr. Fukai, the secretary of the diocese; Mrs. Murata, the mission's devoutly Christian housekeeper; and his fellow-priests. After Mass, while Father Kleinsorge was reading the Prayers of Thanksgiving, the siren sounded. He stopped the service and the missionaries retired across the compound to the bigger building. There, in his room on the ground floor, to the right of the front door, Father Kleinsorge changed into a military uniform which he had acquired when he was teaching at the Rokko Middle School in Kobe and which he wore during air-raid alerts.

After an alarm, Father Kleinsorge always went out and scanned the sky, and in this instance, when he stepped outside, he was glad to see only the single weather plane that flew over Hiroshima each day about this time. Satisfied that nothing would happen, he went in and breakfasted with the other Fathers on substitute coffee and ration bread, which, under the circumstances, was especially repugnant to him. The Fathers sat and talked awhile, until, at eight, they heard the all-clear. They went then to various parts of the building. Father Schiffer retired to his room to do some writing. Father Cieslik sat in his room in a straight chair with a pillow over his stomach to ease his pain, and read. Father Superior LaSalle stood at the window of his room, thinking. Father Kleinsorge went up to a room on the third floor, took off all his clothes except his underwear, and stretched out on his right side on a cot and began reading his *Stimmen der Zeit*.

After the terrible flash—which, Father Kleinsorge later realized, reminded him of something he had read as a boy about a large meteor colliding with the earth—he had time (since he was 1,400 yards from the center) for one thought: A bomb has fallen directly on us. Then, for a few seconds or minutes, he went out of his mind.

Father Kleinsorge never knew how he got out of the house. The next things he was conscious of were that he was wandering around in the mission's vegetable garden in his underwear, bleeding slightly from small cuts along his left flank; that all the buildings round about had fallen down except the Jesuits' mission house, which had long before been braced and double-braced by a priest named Gropper, who was terrified of earthquakes; that the day had turned dark; and that Muratasan, the housekeeper, was nearby, crying over and over, "*Shu Jesusu, awaremi tamai!* Our Lord Jesus, have pity on us!"

On the train on the way into Hiroshima from the country, where he lived with his mother, Dr. Terufumi Sasaki, the Red Cross Hospital surgeon, thought over an unpleasant nightmare he had had the night before. His mother's home was in Mukaihara, thirty miles from the city, and it took him two hours by train and tram to reach the hospital. He had slept uneasily all night and had wakened an hour earlier than usual, and, feeling sluggish and slightly feverish, had debated whether to go to the hospital at all; his sense of duty finally forced him to go, and he had started out on the earlier train than he took most mornings. The dream had particularly frightened him because it was so closely associated, on the surface at least, with a disturbing actuality. He was only twenty-five years old and had just completed his training at the Eastern Medical University, in Tsingtao, China. He was something of an idealist and was much distressed by the inadequacy of medical facilities in the country town where his mother lived. Quite on his own, and without a permit, he had begun visiting a few sick people out there in the evenings, after his eight hours at the hopsital and four hours' commuting. He had recently learned that the penalty for practicing without a permit was severe; a fellow-doctor whom he had asked about it had given him a serious scolding. Nevertheless, he had continued to practice. In his dream, he had been at the bedside of a country patient when the police and the doctor he had consulted burst into the room, seized him, dragged him outside, and beat him up cruelly. On the train, he just about decided to give up the work in Mukaihara, since he felt it would be impossible to get a permit, because the authorities would hold that it would conflict with his duties at the Red Cross Hospital.

At the terminus, he caught a streetcar at once. (He later calculated that if he had taken his customary train that morning, and if he had had to wait a few minutes for the streetcar, as often happened, he would have been close to the center at the time of the explosion and would surely have perished.) He arrived at the hopsital at seven-forty and reported to the chief surgeon. A few minutes later, he went to a room on the first floor and drew blood from the arm of a man in order to perform a Wassermann test. The laboratory containing the incubators for the test was on the third floor. With the blood specimen in his left hand, walking in a kind of distraction he had felt all morning, probably because of the dream and his restless night, he started along the main corridor on his way toward the stairs. He was one step beyond an open window when the light of the bomb was reflected, like a gigantic photographic flash, in the corridor. He ducked down on one knee and said to himself, as only a Japanese would, "Sasaki, *gambare!* Be brave!" Just then (the building was 1,650 yards from the center), the blast ripped through the hospital. The glasses he was wearing flew off his face; the bottle of blood crashed against one wall; his Japanese slippers zipped out from under his feet—but otherwise, thanks to where he stood, he was untouched.

Dr. Sasaki shouted the name of the chief surgeon and rushed around to the man's office and found him terribly cut by glass. The hospital was in horrible confusion: heavy partitions and ceilings had fallen on patients, beds had overturned, windows had blown in and cut people, blood was spattered on the walls and floors, instruments were everywhere, many of the patients were running about screaming, many more lay dead. (A colleague working in the laboratory to which Dr. Sasaki had been walking was dead; Dr. Sasaki's patient, whom he had just left and who a few moments before had been dreadfully afraid of syphilis, was also dead.) Dr. Sasaki found himself the only doctor in the hospital who was unhurt.

Dr. Sasaki, who believed that the enemy had hit only the building he was in, got bandages and began to bind the wounds of those inside the hospital; while outside, all over Hiroshima, maimed and dying citizens turned their unsteady steps toward the Red Cross Hospital to begin an invasion that was to make Dr. Sasaki forget his private nightmare for a long, long time.

Miss Toshiko Sasaki, the East Asia Tin Works clerk, who is not related to Dr. Sasaki, got up at three o'clock in the morning on the day the bomb fell. There was extra housework to do. Her eleven-month-old brother, Akio, had come down the day before with a serious stomach upset; her mother had taken him to the Tamura Pediatric Hospital and was staying there with him. Miss Sasaki, who was about twenty, had to cook breakfast for her father, a brother, a sister, and herself, and—since the hospital, because of the war, was unable to provide food—to prepare a whole day's meals for her mother and the baby, in time for her father, who worked in a factory making rubber earplugs for artillery crews, to take the food by on his way to the plant. When she had finished and had cleaned and put away the cooking things, it was nearly seven. The family lived in Koi, and she had a forty-five-minute trip to the tin works, in the section of town called Kannonmachi. She was in charge of the personnel records in the factory. She left Koi at seven, and as soon as she reached the plant, she went with some of the other girls from the personnel department to the factory auditorium. A prominent local Navy man, a former employee, had committed suicide the day before by throwing himself under a train—a death considered honorable enough to warrant a memorial service, which was to be held at the tin works at ten o'clock that morning. In the large hall, Miss Sasaki and the others made suitable preparations for the meeting. This work took about twenty minutes.

Miss Sasaki went back to her office and sat down at her desk. She was quite far from the windows, which were off to her left, and behind her were a couple of tall bookcases containing all the books of the factory library, which the personnel department had organized. She settled herself at her desk, put some things in a drawer, and shifted papers. She thought that before she began to make entries in her lists of new employees, discharges, and departures for the Army, she would chat for a moment with the girl at her right. Just as she turned her head away from the windows, the room was filled with a blinding light. She was paralyzed by fear, fixed still in her chair for a long moment (the plant was 1,600 yards from the center).

Everything fell, and Miss Sasaki lost consciousness. The ceiling dropped suddenly and the wooden floor above collapsed in splinters and the people up there came down and the roof above them gave way; but principally and first of all, the bookcases right behind her swooped forward and the contents threw her down, with her left leg horribly twisted and breaking underneath her. There, in the tin factory, in the first moment of the atomic age, a human being was crushed by books.

MEANING

1. How do the experiences of the six people Hersey wrote about represent the experiences of untold thousands who were in Hiroshima the day the bomb exploded?
2. What is the significance of the title, "A Noiseless Flash from Hiroshima?"
3. What point does Hersey emphasize by contrasting the everyday preoccupations of the six people one second before the blast with the monumental problems of survival they faced immediately after the explosion?

USING EXEMPLIFICATION TO CONVEY MEANING

1. Why is exemplification a useful technique that permits Hersey's readers to generalize from what these six individuals saw, heard, touched, smelled, or tasted to what all the people in Hiroshima suffered that day?
2. In how many different places can you find Hersey referring to the exact time on the clock and why is this significant?

3. In what way is Hersey's journalistic technique an attempt to simulate what the eye of a camera might see and record?

4. How does Hersey's skill in reporting realistic details (for example, medical facilities overwhelmed by the great numbers of injured people) convey the true horror of the event?

WRITING SUGGESTIONS

1. Which of the six people seems the most real to you. Create a dialogue between yourself as interviewer and this person; what questions would you ask?

2. Discuss how the reactions of survivors in Hersey's account differ from the kinds of concerns that occupied the survivors of the San Francisco earthquake (see Jack London, page 86).

3. Using Hersey's article as a model, conduct several interviews with people who were present at an important event and build up a composite view of the meaning of the event through their reactions.

4. What physical effect produced by this single bomb, reported by Hersey, seems to support what Carl Sagan and his group predicted would be the environmental result of nuclear war (see the "Cause and Effect" chapter, page 506)?

POLITICAL AND SOCIAL SCIENCES

Studs Terkel

Working

Studs (Louis) Terkel was born in 1912 in New York City. He changed his name to "Studs," after Studs Lonigan, the central character in James T. Farrell's novels about the Chicago working-class Irish. After receiving his law degree from the University of Chicago in 1932, he worked as a civil service employee in Washington, D.C., as an actor, and as a movie-house manager, and then began a career in radio and television broadcasting. He served as moderator of several radio programs and "Studs' Place," a television show broadcast from Chicago (1950–1953). His interviews with ordinary people in everyday settings are extraordinarily revealing of the deep, rarely expressed or recorded concerns that people have about themselves, their work, and society. In "interview books" such as Division Street: America *(1967),* Hard Times: An Oral History of the Great Depression *(1970), and* Working: People Talk About What They Do All Day and How They Feel About What They Do *(1974), Terkel typically records ten times more material than appears in print. In these extensively revised, edited, and condensed oral histories, Terkel sometimes changes names to allow interviewees to speak freely. The following excerpt from* Working, *one of 133 tape-recorded interviews, is a revealing conversation with a stewardess that exemplifies one aspect of contemporary American attitudes toward work.*

Terry Mason—Airline Stewardess

She has been an airline stewardess for six years. She is twenty-six-years old, recently married. "The majority of airline stewardesses are from small towns. I myself am from Nebraska. It's supposed to be one of the nicest professions for a woman—if she can't be a model or in the movies. All the great benefits: flying around the world, meeting all those people. It is a nice status symbol."

"I have five older sisters and they were all married before they were twenty. The minute they got out of high school, they would end up getting married. That was the thing everybody did, was get married. When I told my parents I was going to the airlines, they got excited. They were so happy that one of the girls could go out and see the world and spend some time being single. I didn't get married until I was almost twenty-five. My mother especially thought it would be great that I could have the ambition, the nerve to go to the big city on my own and try to accomplish being a stewardess."

When people ask you what you're doing and you say stewardess, you're really proud, you think it's great. It's like a stepping stone. The first two months I started flying I had already been to London, Paris, and Rome. And me from Broken Bow, Nebraska. But after you start working, it's not as glamorous as you thought it was going to be.

They like girls that have a nice personality and that are pleasant to look at. If a woman has a problem with blemishes, they take her off. Until the appearance counselor thinks she's ready to go back on. One day this girl showed up, she had a very slight black eye. They took her off. Little things like that.

We had to go to stew school for five weeks. We'd go through a whole week of make-up and poise. I didn't like this. They make you feel like you've never been out in public. They showed you how to smoke a cigarette, when to smoke a cigarette, how to look at a man's eyes. Our teacher, she had this idea we had to be sexy. One day in class she was showing us how to accept a light for a cigarette from a man and never blow it out. When he lights it, just look in his eyes. It was really funny, all the girls laughed.

It's never proper for a woman to light her own cigarette. You hold it up and of course you're out with a guy who knows the right way to light the cigarette. You look into their eyes as they're lighting your cigarette and you're cupping his hand, but holding it just very light, so that he can feel your touch and your warmth. (Laughs.) You do not blow the match out. It used to be really great for a woman to blow the match out when she looked in his eyes, but she said now the man blows the match out.

The idea is not to be too obvious about it. They don't want you to look too forward. That's the whole thing, being a lady but still giving out that womanly appeal, like the body movement and the lips and the eyes. The guy's supposed to look in your eyes. You could be a real mean woman. You're a lady and doing all these evil things with your eyes.

She did try to promote people smoking. She said smoking can be part of your conversation. If you don't know what to say, you can always pull out a cigarette. She says it makes you more comfortable. I started smoking when I was on the airlines.

Our airline picks the girl-next-door type. At one time they wouldn't let us wear false eyelashes and false fingernails. Now it's required that you wear false eyelashes, and if you do not have the right length nails, you wear false nails. Everything is supposed to be becoming to the passenger.

That's the whole thing: meeting all these great men that either have great business backgrounds or good looking or different. You do meet a lot of movie stars and a lot of political people, but you don't get to really visit with them that much. You never really get to go out with these men. Stewardesses are impressed only by name people. But a normal millionaire that you don't know you're not impressed about.

The only thing that really thrills a stewardesses is a passenger like Kennedy or movie stars or somebody political. Celebrities.

I think our average age is twenty-six. But our supervisors tell us what kind of make-up to wear, what kind of lipstick to wear, if our hair is not the right style for us, if we're not smiling enough. They even tell us how to act when you're on a pass. Like last night I met my husband. I was in plain clothes. I wanted to kiss him. But I'm not supposed to kiss anybody at the terminal. You're not supposed to walk off with a passenger, hand in hand. After you get out of the terminal, that's all yours.

The majority of passengers do make passes. The ones that do make passes are married and are business people. When I tell them I'm married, they say, "I'm married and you're married and you're away from home and so am I and nobody's gonna find out." The majority of those who make passes at you, you wouldn't accept a date if they were friends of yours at home.

After I was a stewardess for a year, and I was single, I came down to the near North Side of Chicago, which is the swinging place for singles. Stewardess, that was a dirty name. In a big city, it's an easy woman. I didn't like this at all. All these books—*Coffee, Tea and Me.*

I lived in an apartment complex where the majority there were stewardesses.[1] The other women were secretaries and teachers. They would go to our parties and they would end up being among the worst. They never had stories about these secretaries and nurses, but they sure had good ones about stewardesses.

I meet a lot of other wives or single women. The first minute they start talking to me, they're really cold. They think the majority of stewardesses are snobs or they may be jealous. These women think we have a great time, that we are playgirls, that we have the advantage to go out with every type of man we want. So when they first meet us, they really turn off on us.

When you first start flying, the majority of girls do live in apartment complexes by the airport. The men they meet are airport employees: ramp rats, cleaning airplanes and things like that, mechanics, and young pilots, not married, ones just coming in fresh.

After a year we get tired of that, so we move into the city to get involved with men that are usually young executives, like at Xerox or something. Young businessmen in the early thirties and late twenties, they really think stewardesses are the gals to go out with if they want to get so far. They wear their hats and their suits and in the winter their black gloves. The women are getting older, they're getting twenty-four, twenty-five. They get involved with bartenders too. Stewardesses and bartenders are a pair. (Laughs.)

One time I went down into the area of swinging bars with two other girls. We just didn't want anybody to know that we were stewardesses, so we had this story made up that we were going to a women's college in Colorado. That went over. We had people that were talking to us, being nice to us, being polite. Down there, they wouldn't even be polite. They'd buy you drinks but then they'd steal your stool if you got up to go the restroom. But when they knew you weren't stewardesses, just young ladies that were going to a women's college, they were really nice to us.

---

[1] "In New York, stewardesses live five or six girls to one apartment. They think they can get by because they're in and out so much. But there's gonna be a few nights they're all gonna be home at once and a couple of 'em will have to sleep on the floor."

They say you can spot a stewardess by the way she wears her make-up. At that time we all had short hair and everybody had it cut in stew school exactly alike. If there's two blondes that have their hair cut very short, wearing the same shade of make-up, and they get into uniform, people say, "Oh, you look like sisters." Wonder why? (Laughs.)

The majority of us were against it because they wouldn't let you say how *you'd* like your hair cut, they wouldn't let you have your own personality, *your* makeup, *your* clothes. They'd tell you what length skirts to wear. At one time they told us we couldn't wear anything one inch above the knees. And no pants at that time. It's different now.

Wigs used to be forbidden. Now it's the style. Now it's permissible for nice women to wear wigs, eyelashes, and false fingernails. Before it was the harder looking women that wore them. Women showing up in pants, it wasn't ladylike. Hot pants are in now. Most airlines change style every year.

> She describes stewardess schools in the past as being like college dorms: it was forbidden to go out during the week; signing in and out on Friday and Saturday nights. "They've cut down stewardess school quite a bit. Cut down on how to serve meal classes and paperwork. A lot of girls get on aircraft these days and don't know where a magazine is, where the tray tables are for passengers . . . Every day we used to have an examination. If you missed over two questions, that was a failure. They'd ask us ten questions. If you failed two tests out of the whole five weeks, you would have to leave. Now they don't have any exams at all. Usually we get a raise every year. We haven't been getting that lately."

We have long duty hours. We can be on duty for thirteen hours. But we're not supposed to fly over eight hours. This is in a twenty-four-hour period. During the eight hours, you could be flying from Chicago to Flint, to Moline, short runs. You stop twenty minutes. So you get to New York finally, after five stops, let's say. You have an hour on your own. But you have to be on the plane thirty minutes before departure time. How many restaurants can serve you food in thirty minutes? So you've gone thirteen hours, off and on duty, having half-hours and no time to eat. This is the normal thing. If we have only thirty minutes and we don't have time to eat, it's our hard luck.

Pilots have the same thing too. They end up grabbing a sandwich and eating in the cockpit. When I first started flying we were not supposed to eat at all on the aircraft, even though there was an extra meal left over. Now we can eat in the buffet. We have to stand there with all those dirty dishes and eat our meals—if there's one left over. We cannot eat in the public eye. We cannot bring it out if there's an extra seat. You can smoke in the cockpit, in the restrooms, but not in the public's eye.

> "We have a union. It's a division of the pilots union. It helps us out on duty time and working privileges. It makes sure that if we're in Cleveland and stuck because of weather and thirteen hours have gone by, we can go to bed. Before we had a union the stew office would call and say, 'You're working another seven.' I worked one time thirty-six hours straight."

The other day I had fifty-five minutes to serve 101 coach passengers, a cocktail and full-meal service. You do it fast and terrible. You're very rude. You don't mean to be rude, you just don't have time to answer questions. You smile and you just ignore it. You get three drink orders in a hurry. There's been many times when you miss the glass, pouring, and you pour it in the man's lap. You just don't say I'm sorry. You give him a cloth and you keep going. That's the bad part of the job.

Sometimes I get tired of working first class. These people think they're great, paying for more, and want more. Also I get tired of coach passengers asking for something that he thinks he's a first-class passenger. We get this attitude of difference from our airlines. They're just dividing the class of people. If we're on a first-class pass, the women are to wear a dress or a nice pants suit that has a matching jacket, and the men are to dress with suit jacket and tie and white shirt. And yet so many types of first class passengers: some have grubby clothes, jeans and moccasins and everything. They can afford to dress the way they feel . . .

If I want to fly first class, I pay the five dollars difference. I like the idea of getting free drinks, free champagne, free wine. In a coach, you don't. A coach passenger might say, "Could I have a pillow?" So you give him a pillow. Then he'll say, "Could you bring me a glass of water?" A step behind him there's the water fountain. In first class, if the guy says, "I want a glass of water," even if the water fountain is right by his arm, you'd bring it for him. We give him all this extra because he's first class. Which isn't fair . . .

When you're in a coach, you feel like there's just head and head and head of people. That's all you can see. In first class, being less people, you're more relaxed, you have more time. When you get on a 727, we have one coatroom. Our airline tells us you hang up first-class coats only. When a coach passenger says, "Could you hang up my coat?" most of the time I'll hang it up. Why should I hang up first class and not coach?

One girl is for first class only and there's two girls for coach. The senior girl will be first class. That first-class girl gets used to working first class. If she happens to walk through the coach, if someone asks her for something, she'll make the other girls do it. The first stew always stays at the door and welcomes everybody aboard and says good-by to everybody when they leave. That's why a lot of girls don't like to be first class.

There's an old story on the airline. The stewardess asks if he'd like something to drink, him and his wife. He says, "I'd like a martini." The stewardess asks the wife, "Would you like a drink?" She doesn't say anything, and the husband says, "I'm sorry, she's not used to talking to the help." (Laughs.) When I started flying, that was the first story I heard.

I've never had the nerve to speak up to anybody that's pinched me or said something dirty. Because I've always been afraid of these onion letters. These are bad letters. If you get a certain amount of bad letters, you're fired. When you get a bad letter you have to go in and talk to the supervisor. Other girls now, there are many of 'em that are coming around and telling them what they feel. The passenger reacts: She's telling me off! He doesn't believe it. Sometimes the passenger needs it.

One guy got his steak and he said, "This is too medium. I want mine rarer." The girl said, "I'm sorry, I don't cook the food, it's precooked." He picked up the meal and threw it on the floor. She says, "If you don't pick the meal up right now, I'll make sure the crew members come back here and make you pick it up." (With awe) She's talking right back at him and loud, right in front of everybody. He really didn't think she would yell at him. Man, he picked up the meal . . . The younger girls don't take that guff any more, like we used to. When the passenger is giving you a bad time, you talk back to him.

It's always: the passenger is right. When a passenger says something mean, we're supposed to smile and say, "I understand." We're supposed to *really* smile because stewardesses' supervisors have been getting reports that the girls have been back-talking passengers. Even when they pinch us or say dirty things, we're supposed to smile at them. That's one thing they taught us at stew school. Like he's rubbing your body somewhere, you're supposed to just put his hand down and not say anything and smile at him. That's the main thing, smile.

When I first went to class, they told me I had a crooked smile. She showed me how to smile. She said, "Kinda press a little smile on"—which I did. "Oh, that's great," she said, "that's a *good* smile." But I couldn't do it. I didn't feel like I was doing it on my own. Even if we're sad, we're supposed to have a smile on our face.

I came in after a flight one day, my grandfather had died. Usually they call you up or meet you at the flight and say, "We have some bad news for you." I picked up this piece of paper in my mailbox and it says, "Mother called in. Your grandfather died today." It was written like, say, two cups of sugar. Was I mad! They wouldn't give me time off for the funeral. You can only have time off for your parents or somebody you have lived with. I had never lived with my grandparents. I went anyway.

A lot of our girls are teachers, nurses, everything. They do this part-time, 'cause you have enough time off for another kind of job. I personally work for conventions. I work electronic and auto shows. Companies hire me to stay in their booth and talk about products. I have this speech to tell. At others, all I do is pass out matches or candy. Nowadays every booth has a young girl in it.

People just love to drink on airplanes. They feel adventurous. So you're serving drinks and meals and there's very few times that you can sit down. If she does sit down, she's forgotten how to sit down and talk to passengers. I used to play bridge with passengers. But that doesn't happen any more. We're not supposed to be sitting down, or have a magazine or read a newspaper. If it's a flight from Boston to Los Angeles, you're supposed to have a half an hour talking to passengers. But the only time we can sit down is when we go to the cockpit. You're not supposed to spend any more than five minutes up there for a cigarette.

We could be sitting down on our jump seat and if you had a supervisor on board, she would write you up—for not mixing with the crowd. We're supposed to be told when she walks on board. Many times you don't know. They do have personnel that ride the flights that don't give their names—checking, and they don't tell you about it. Sometimes a girl gets caught smoking in the cabin. Say it's a long flight, maybe a night flight. You're playing cards with a passenger and you say, "Would it bother you if I smoke?" And he says no. She would write you up and get you fired for smoking in the airplane.

They have a limit on how far you can mix. They want you to be sociable, but if he offers you a cigarette, not to take it. When you're outside, they encourage you to take cigarettes.

You give your time to everybody, you share it, not too much with one passenger. Everybody else may be snoring away and there's three guys, maybe military, and they're wide awake 'cause they're going home and excited. So you're playing cards with 'em. If you have a supervisor on, that would be a no-no. They call a lot of things no-no's.

They call us professional people but they talk to us as very young, childishly. They check us all the time on appearance. They check our weight every month. Even though you've been flying twenty years, they check you and say that's a no-no. If you're not spreading yourself around passengers enough, that's a no-no. Not hanging up first-class passengers' coats, that's a no-no, even though there's no room in the coatroom. You're supposed to somehow make room. If you're a pound over, they can take you off flight until you get under.

Accidents? I've never yet been so scared that I didn't want to get in the airplane. But there've been times at take-offs, there's been something funny. Here I am thinking, What if I die today? I've got too much to do. I can't die today. I use it as a joke.

I've had emergencies where I've had to evacuate the aircraft. I was coming back from Las Vegas and being a lively stewardess I stayed up all night, gambled. We had a load full of passengers. The captain tells me we're going to have an emergency landing in Chicago because we lost a pin out of the nose gear. When we land, the nose gear is gonna collapse. He wants me to prepare the whole cabin for the landing, but not for two more hours. And not to tell the other stewardesses, because they were new girls and would get all excited. So I had to keep this in me for two more hours, wondering, Am I gonna die today? And this is Easter Sunday. And I was serving the passengers drinks and food and this guy got mad at me because his omelet was too cold. And I was gonna say, "You just wait buddy, you're not gonna worry about that omelet." But I was nice about it, because I didn't want to have trouble with a passenger, especially when I have to prepare him for an emergency.

I told the passengers over the intercom: "The captain says it's just a precaution, there's nothing to worry about." I'm just gonna explain how to get out of the airplane fast, how to be in a braced position. They can't wear glasses or high heels, purses, things out of aisles, under the seats. And make sure everybody's pretty quiet. We had a blind woman on with a dog. We had to get people to help her off and all this stuff.

They were fantastic. Nobody screamed, cried, or hollered. When we got on the ground, everything was fine. The captain landed perfect. But there was a little jolt, and the passengers started screaming and hollering. They held it all back and all of a sudden we got on the ground, blah.

I was great. (Laughs.) That's what was funny. I thought, I have a husband now. I don't know how he would take it, my dying on an airplane. So I thought, I can't die. When I got on the intercom, I was so calm. Also we're supposed to keep a smile on our face. Even during an emergency, you're supposed to walk through the cabin and make everybody feel comfortable with a smile. When you're on the jump seat everybody's looking at you. You're supposed to sit there, holding your ankles, in a position to get out of that airplane fast with a big fat smile on your face.

Doctors tell stewardesses two bad things about them. They're gonna get wrinkles all over their face because they smile with their mouth and their eyes. And also with the pressurization on the airplane, we're not supposed to get up while we're climbing because it causes varicose veins in our legs. So they say being a stewardess ruins your looks.

A lot of stewardesses wanted to be models. The Tanya girl used to be a stewardess on our airline. A stewardess is what they could get and a model is what they couldn't get. They weren't the type of person, they weren't that beautiful, they weren't that thin. So their second choice would be stewardess.

What did you want to be?

I wanted to get out of Broken Bow, Nebraska. (Laughs.)

POSTSCRIPT: "Every time I go home, they all meet me at the airplane. Not one of my sisters has been on an airplane. All their children think that Terry is just fantastic, because their mom and dad—my sisters and their husbands—feel so stupid. 'Look at us. I wish I could have done that.' I know they feel bad, that they never had the chance. But they're happy I can come home and tell them about things. I send them things from Europe. They get to tell all their friends that their sister's a stewardess. They get real excited about that. The first thing they come out and say. 'One of my sisters is a stewardess.'

"My father got a promotion with his company and they wrote in their business news that he had a family of seven, six girls and a boy, and one girl is a stewardess in Chicago. And went on to say what I did, and didn't say a word about anything else."

MEANING

1. What evidence can you find within this interview to show that Terry Mason had the approval of her family in becoming a stewardess?
2. In what particular ways does stewardess "school" attempt to mold the lives and behavior of the future stewardesses?
3. Explain the importance of the concept of the "public eye" in determining where and when stewardesses can eat or smoke.
4. Why does Terry treat passengers in first class differently from those traveling in coach?
5. What did Terry's performance during the emergency landing make you realize about her real capabilities compared to the duties she is usually called upon to perform?

USING EXEMPLIFICATION TO CONVEY MEANING

1. How does Terkel's interview with Terry Mason elicit responses that provide insight into what a stewardess' life is actually like?
2. How does Terkel prepare the reader to "meet" Terry Mason in the context of her working life?
3. Where do specific, lively, and appropriate illustrations help the reader to "see" the qualities of regimentation and paternalism that are such major parts of a stewardess' life?
4. What are some examples of the kinds of personal satisfactions that Terry has derived from her job as a stewardess?

Writing Suggestions

1. Discuss how Terry had to change herself, in terms of physical appearance and psychological attitude, in order to become a stewardess.
2. Using Terkel's interview as a model, conduct and report the results of interviews with people working in different kinds of jobs. In each case, try to provide exact quotes to reveal both the positive and negative feelings people have toward their work situations.
3. Compare the satisfactions, compromises, accommodations, sense of identity, and commitment experienced by Terry to Simone de Beauvoir's "married woman" (see the "Definition" chapter, page 547).

Richard Rhodes

Packaged Sentiment

Richard Rhodes was born in 1937 in Kansas City, Kansas. After graduating with honors from Yale in 1959, he worked as a book-editing manager for Hallmark Cards, Inc. (1962–1970) and as a contributing editor for Harper's *and* Playboy. *Rhodes has received various awards including a Guggenheim Fellowship (1974–1975) and a National Endowment for the Arts grant in writing (1978). He speaks as a voice from the Midwestern heartland—vigorous, sure, and unsentimental—in such works as* The Inland Ground: An Evocation of the American Middle West *(1970),* Looking for America: A Writer's Odyssey *(1979), and more than fifty articles in* Harper's, Red Book, Esquire, Playboy, *and* Reader's Digest. *His most recent work is the highly acclaimed* The Making of the Atomic Bomb *(1987), a probing analysis of the design, fabrication, testing, and use of thermonuclear devices. "Packaged Sentiment" (1971), an essay he wrote as an independent journalist, is a fascinating and comprehensive account of the greeting-card industry based on his own first-hand experiences.*

Christmas is come, the holiday season, and with it our annual deluge of cards, whose successful dispersal across the land the Postal Service heralds to justify failing us for the rest of the year. "By God, we moved the Christmas cards!" Well, half of all the personal mail moved annually in the United States is greeting cards. Cards for Christmas but also cards for New Year's, Valentine's Day, Easter, Mother's Day, Father's Day, Independence Day and Thanksgiving and Halloween, the official holidays of the American year. And for the occasions greeting-card people call "Everyday," though they are not, births and birthdays, graduations, weddings, anniversaries, showers, vacations, friendship, promotion, hello, love, thanks, goodbye, illness and bereavement, and even to have Thought O' You and for a Secret Pal. We are a nation not of letter writers but of card signers. If the personal letter is long dead, maimed by the penny post and murdered by the telephone, the mass-produced card thrives, picturing what we haven't skill to picture, saying what we haven't words to say. Cards knot the ties that bind in a land where a fourth of us change residence with every change of calendar and where grown children no longer live at home. They show us at our best, if in borrowed finery. You may buy a card made of pansies and doggerel or you may buy a card made of da Vinci and the Sermon on the Mount. Whoever receives it will understand what you meant, and that you meant well.

The Christmas card was an English invention, but the greeting card an American one. One hundred twenty-eight years ago this season, an Englishman distracted by business matters failed to get his Christmas cards written. Boldly he turned an embarrassment into an opportunity, commissioned a paper tableau of Pickwickians, their glasses raised in toast, and inside each engraved and colored folio he printed a verse. His friends' reactions were not recorded. No doubt some found the idea distastefully impersonal and lamented the decline of manners in a declining age. Others, alert for new twists, thought it charming. The sensible saw its efficiency. It met the first requirement of all mechanical inventions: it saved time.

We have taken the idea and made it ours. The English send few cards today, and Europeans fewer still. We send cards for everything, mechanizing and standardizing the complex relationships we maintain with one another, to give us time to breathe. We needn't be ashamed of our custom. Elegant mechanizing is what we do best. It is the form our national character has taken. Look at our office buildings raised on narrow pillars ten feet off the ground as if someone had dared us to float a fifty-story building in the air. Compare our white and graceful moon rockets to the Soviet Union's drab boiler plate. Look at our cards, little shuttles of sentiment weaving across the land.

Some of the old cards, the nineteenth-century cards that borrowed the Englishman's invention, were masterpieces of reproduction, printed in as many as twelve colors with verses selected in national contests with cash prizes, verses no better than they should be for all the fanfare. The Victorian Age produced German cards that opened up into three-dimensional sleighing scenes of marvelous intricacy, cards with moving parts, cards fringed like a love-seat pillow with gaudy silks, cards as ornate as any gingerbread house. Cards, one presumes, for the wealthy, because the rest of us hadn't begun sending them in today's incredible numbers, today's fifteen or twenty *billion* cards a year. Now that we do, the special effects that delicate handwork once supplied have had to be scaled down, though the cards we send today carry their weight of handwork too, and with it their weight of amusing stories, cautionary tales of American ingenuity gone berserk. I remember a humorous card that required for its gag a small plastic sack of what it called "belly-button fuzz" stapled below its punch line. No supplier could thumb out enough of the authentic material to meet the demand, so the manufacturer turned to the clothes dryers of a nearby college town, bought up the lint franchise, sterilized the lint to meet health regulations, and bagged it and stapled it on, by hand, and got the effect it was seeking and probably, college towns being college towns, got some belly-button fuzz too. "Attachments," such devices are called—plastic tears, toy scissors, miniature boxes of crayons, feathers, spring-and-paper jumping jacks, pencils, beans, the detritus of industrial civilization shrunk to card size. An attachment will sell a humorous card all by itself if it isn't stolen first, a problem for greeting-card manufacturers as surely as it is a problem for the sellers of screws and beads and hair ribbons in dime stores. Like children we lust to get our hands on little things, finding magic in tiny representations of the lumbering world.

NUGGETS OF EMOTION

The business of greeting cards began in the ambitions of hungry men, and they improvised as they went. There are schools of nursing and schools of nuclear physics, but there are no schools for the makers of greeting cards, only apprenticeships. When Joyce Hall of country Nebraska began his enterprise in Kansas City, Missouri, more than sixty years ago, there weren't even many kinds of cards. Christmas, Easter, birthdays, and weddings were about the only occasions we announced. Hall, Fred Rust of Rust Craft, and a few people like them had to teach us to send cards by making cards we wanted to send. In that work, Hall's career strikingly parallels the career of another Midwesterner, Walt Disney, for both men learned to parse our emotions and recast them in visual and verbal form. Disney, for example, took some shadowy figures from a fairy tale, clothed them in universals, and gave us the Seven Dwarfs. Hall and his people took our need to signal our degrees of social familiarity and our various notions of good taste and gave us a choice among greeting cards.

For any given social occasion, depending on how well you know someone and what you want him to think of you, you may select a card for him that is Formal, Traditional, Humorous, Floral, Cute, Contemporary, or some other among Hallmark's many categories of mood. Two cards for a friend who is hospitalized give the flavor. One, an embossed vase of flowers, says, "Glad your Operation's Over" on the cover, and inside:

> You're thought of so often
> As days come and go
> That this card comes to tell you,
> And then let you know
> How much you are wished
> A recovery that's quick—
> For someone like you
> Is too nice to be sick!

The other card, a photograph of a cotton bunny in a flower-bedecked four-poster, opens with, "Hope you'll soon be out of the *blooming bed!*" and carries the flower pun through:

> Sure like to see you back in the *pink,*
> So just take it easy, 'cause then
> You'll soon be in *clover,*
> Feeling just *rosy,*
> And fresh as a *daisy* again!

Moods and tones and levels, you see. You are not likely to send a Contemporary card to your maiden aunt nor a Formal card to your spouse. The greeting-card people give you a range of choices. It may be a narrower range than you would prefer, but if you are a sender of cards at all, the choices will not be so narrow that you turn away in disgust and write a letter. You may choose frank sentiment; humor ranging from the modestly ethnic (hillbillies, Indians, Dead End Kids—blacks, Italians, and Eastern Europeans are out today, though they used to be a staple) to the heavily punned to the backward compliment to the gentle slap; simple statement, favored for Christmas and sympathy cards, both occasions being to some people matters serious enough for prose; and a number of alternatives between. Visually, you may choose flowers, cartoons, arabesque gilding, photographs, even reproductions of fine art, though few enough of those because few people buy them. Or stylized little children with ink-drop eyes, or encrustations of plastic jewels, or velvet flocking, or metallic glitter. Variations in texture and surface are legion—and the pride of the older generation of greeting-card men, who believed in making a quality product, who learned what would sell by selling, and who relied for their judgment in such matters on what Joyce Hall once called "the vapors of past experience."

Even if you have never given thought to such matters as categories of emotion and levels of taste, greeting-card people know you operate by them, and know how many cards to make to meet your needs. Such is the variety, of cards and of needs, that the largest of the manufacturers, Hallmark Cards, would have collapsed a decade ago if the computer hadn't come along to speed their sorting. The company claims 12,000 products, counting each separate design a product, and the figure is certainly conservative. Twelve thousand different products in quantities of six to perhaps 20,000 different stores: you can do the multiplication yourself, but count in the envelopes; count in as many as ten or twenty different manufacturing operations on every card; count in all the designs being prepared for future publication, designs that pass through hundreds of hands at drawing boards and typewriters and approval committees and lithographic cameras and printing plants; count in all these different bits of information and many more besides, and you arrive at a total that demands the kinds of machines that track astronauts to the moon.

And count in one thing more: every display in every store is a modest computer of its own, each of its pockets filled with designs that favor the social and cultural biases of the neighborhood around the store, and among those favored designs the best sellers of the day. "Tailoring," Hallmark calls it—loading the display to favor the preferences of the young or old or black or white or Catholic or Jewish or rich or poor who regularly shop there. The salesman sets up the display with the help of the owner; after that the computer in Kansas City keeps track. The point, of course, is to give you a maximum range of choice among the choices available. Tucked away in the stock drawer below the display, quietly humming, an IBM card meters every design.

Despite appearances, then, greeting-card manufacture is no work of hand coloring performed by elderly ladies in lace. The Hallmark plant in Kansas City occupies two city blocks, and the company doesn't even do its own printing. Times Square would fit nicely inside the new distribution center Hallmark is building on a railroad spur outside of town. More than one printing firm in the United States owes its giant color presses to Hallmark orders, which is why the company gets the kind of quality it is known for—because it has the heft to stop the presses and pull a proof. It claims 400 artists in residence, the largest art department in the world, and if you include the girls who separate out the colors of a design by hand, a procedure that still costs less for certain designs than separating the colors by machine, the claim is fair.

So many different operations go into the production of greeting cards that even a glimpse of them boggles the mind, serene and simple as the cards look when they finally reach the store. Hallmark buys paper by the boxcar, paper of every imaginable texture and weight, parchment, deckle, bond, pebble-grained, leather-grained, cloth-grained, board, brown wrapping, hard-finished, soft-finished, smooth. Special committees earnestly debate the future popularity of roses or ragamuffins. An artist conceives a group of cards that feature cartoon mice, and the cards sell and the artist is rewarded with a trip to San Francisco. Down in the bowels of the building, behind a secret door, a master photographer labors as he has labored for most of a decade to perfect flat three-dimensional photography using a camera on which Hallmark owns the license, a camera that rolls around in a semicircle on model railroad tracks, its prisms awhirl. In California a contract artist makes dolls of old socks and ships them to Kansas City to be photographed for children's cards. Market-research girls carry cards mounted on black panels to meetings of women's clubs, where the ladies, at a charitable fifty cents a head, choose among different designs with the same verses, or different verses with the same design, helping Hallmark determine the very best that you might care to send. An engineer, a stack of handmade designs before him on his desk, struggles to arrange them on a lithography sheet to get the maximum number of designs per sheet so that they can be printed all at once with minimum waste of paper—"nesting," the process is called. Artists roam the streets of major cities at Christmastime, studying shop windows and the offerings of art galleries to discover new trends in visual design. A deputation of sales managers retreats to an Ozark resort for a multimedia presentation of next year's line. A mechanical genius grown old in the service of the firm remembers the tricks he has taught mere paper cards to do: walking, talking, sticking out their tongues, growling, snoring, squeaking, issuing forth perfume at the scratch of a fingernail across microscopic beads. An engineer sits down at a handwork table and conducts a motion study and designs a system and lines and lines of young girls in gray smocks follow the system to assemble a complicated card by hand, their hands making the memorized motions while they dream of boyfriends or listen to the rhythm of the gluing machines interweaving fugally along the line. A master engraver puts the finishing touches on a die that will punch a dotted line around a paper puppet on a get-well card. A committee of executives meets and decides that the pink of a card isn't cheerful enough and the cartoon figure on another card not sufficiently neuter to appeal both to men and to women. A shipment of paper for a line of children's books is frozen into a harbor in Finland when it should be steaming its way to a printing plant in Singapore. A baby leopard runs loose in the photography department while an editor upstairs sorts through another shipment of amateur verse mailed in by the card lovers of America. He has not found a writer worth encouraging in three years. Greeting cards aren't simply manufactured, like soap or breakfast cereal. They are rescued from the confusing crosscurrents of American life, every one of them a difficult recovery. John Donne found the King's likeness on a coin: greeting-card manufacturers must discover Everyman's likeness and somehow fix it on paper with all its idiosyncrasies smoothed away.

Hallmark employs far fewer writers than artists, about fifteen or twenty. Unlike designs, verses enjoy a long half-life if they are adjusted for minor changes in the language along the way. These days they are often selected—selected entire, not written—by computer from a stock of the most popular verses of the past. The writers try to think up new words, and from time to time they do. Greeting-card verse has come in for its share of ridicule, which perhaps it deserves, but before it is ridiculed its distinction ought to be explained. Most song lyrics look equally ridiculous when printed bald, because the rhetoric of a song lyric, the source of its emotional impact, is the music that accompanies it. The rhetoric of greeting-card verse is the card, the physical and visual accompaniment of the verse. A few greeting-card makers have caught on to the similarity between song lyrics and greeting-card verse and have begun to borrow effects they can use, as in this verse from one of American Greetings' new "Soft Touch" cards, cards for young people that feature soft-focus photography:

> untold the times i've kissed you
> in the moments i have missed you
> and our love goes on forever . . .
> with you softly on my mind

If that doesn't quite make sense, well, neither do most lyrics away from their music, or greeting-card verses away from their cards. A poem, a real poem, the thing itself, works no better on a greeting card or in a song, because it contains its own orchestration and goes dissonant when larded with the scrapings of Mantovani strings.

Modern young people don't like eight-line rhymed verses, preferring song words or evocative sentences. One card on my desk is captioned merely "Peace," which makes it appropriate to almost every occasion except Halloween. Finding the right words for a card is harder today than it used to be because a generation trained on the film expects the words and images to subtly interlock. Getting new words approved by management is harder still. Like most American corporations of healthy middle age, Hallmark has discovered the benefits of redundant personnel and of a certain resistance to fad. Good ideas don't come along every morning, and they must always be weighed against the success of the old: there are only so many pockets in a greeting-card display. Joyce Hall, a tall, spare man with a W. C. Fields nose and a lifetime of practical experience, used to approve every card Hallmark made, words, music, and all; and his son, Donald Hall, who is now president of the firm, still approves every Contemporary card that gets past his secretary, or did when I worked there. A friend of mine who free-lanced for Hallmark once earned that secretary's enmity with a design she thought in questionable taste. "It's nice, Bill," she told him, "but it's not Hallmark." You cannot be too careful, and who is to say she wasn't right?

If the process of selection was once a matter of subjective judgment, it is today at least outwardly scientific. For reasons that only statisticians understand, Kansas City is a superb test market. If products sell in Kansas City, they will sell to the nation, a fact that city sophisticates might soberly consider the next time they buy a card. The formula doesn't always work—the East Coast prefers the word "Pop" to the word "Dad" on its Father cards, for example—but it works often enough to keep Hallmark researchers close to home. Yet market research is often discounted at Hallmark. The vapors of past experiences still blow through the halls, and men whose only business experience has been with greeting cards still ignore the information of market tests if it conflicts with the information of the gut.

Daring subjectivity was Joyce Hall's genius, and remains a legacy of sorts in the hands of less remarkable men now that he has reluctantly relinquished command. Like every successful self-made man he has found retirement difficult. He is a man of quirks and crotchets and always was, but the enterprise he began out of a suitcase stashed under his bed at the Kansas City YMCA now ranks high on *Fortune* magazine's list of the 500 leading privately owned American corporations. The Hall family still owns the place lock, stock, and barrel. It is one of the few privately owned companies of any size left in Kansas City, where wealthy sons of fathers who sweated their way up from poverty tend to sell out to national conglomerations and pass their time at Martha's Vineyard or Harbor Point or Cannes. "You can teach your children everything but poverty," Hall once said, but he taught his son to care about the family firm; and today Hallmark thrives, branching out into gift books, stationery, party goods, calendars and albums, puzzles, candy, pens, urban redevelopment, retail stores on the Neiman-Marcus model, and whatever other enterprises it can find that fit its broad conception of its business, which it calls, modestly enough, "social expression."

GREEN CARDS DON'T SELL

I could complain against greeting cards. It isn't difficult to do in a world where more people feel pain than feel pleasure. There is even the risk that if I don't complain you will take me for a patsy. The greeting card's contribution to literacy will not be decisive, but I don't believe it does us that much harm. By definition, popular art can only be defended numerically, and to those who equate numbers with mediocrity, to the antipopulists, a numerical defense amounts to a certain conviction. Television is mediocre because it caters to popular taste, and greeting cards too. No. If either of them has a glaring weakness, it is that among their plethora of choices they do not give us all the choices we might want, or need. That is the effect of the marketplace, lopping off the ends of the bell curve, but the marketplace pays our bills. And if you would like to consider an opposing view, consider Joyce Hall's, who remembers this nation when it was largely rural and uneducated, and who believed that one of Hallmark's responsibilities was the elevation of American taste, a view that might seem didactic of him, but I was a country boy too, and the first play I ever saw, chills running down my back, was *Macbeth*, on television's *Hallmark Hall of Fame*.

Hallmark established its considerable reputation with thought and care, spending far less on advertising than most companies that make consumer products do. It sponsors television specials and between the acts simply shows its cards. Can you remember a year when the *Hall of Fame* didn't come in for at least one Emmy? Do you know how many Americans traipsed through art galleries they had never visited before to see the collection of paintings by Winston Churchill that Hallmark shipped around the land? No breath of public scandal has ever blown through the organization. It does not make napalm and until very recently was old-fashioned enough to pay its bills in cash. One of its best men, now retired, a German Jew named Hans Archenhold whose printing plant was seized by the Nazis, came to Kansas City in its gangster years and found the printing industry there a sty of kickbacks and corruption. With the leverage of Hallmark printing orders he helped to clean it up. Hall himself switched his employees from coffee to milk breaks during the Depression; reasoning, in memory of his own hungry years, that they probably ate no breakfast and might not be sure of lunch, and I doubt that many complained of paternalism. By all means rail against the size and impersonality of American corporations—your arguments will be well taken—but remember also that most are little Swedens now, dispensing profits and medical care and life insurance and retirement funds with a cheerful hand.

Today Hallmark's brand identity, an elusive commodity in a competitive society, approaches 100 per cent. Schoolchildren, asked to make cards in class, often draw a crown on the back of their productions or attempt the famous slogan, "When you care enough to send the very best," in sturdy Big Chief print. There are other greeting-card companies, American, Buzza-Cardozo, Rust Craft, and Hallmark's own poor cousin, Ambassador Cards, to name only the biggest, but the one giant has come to stand for them all.

Strangely, 80 per cent of the buyers of greeting cards are women. That is why cards are tested at women's clubs. Even cards for men are designed with a woman buyer in mind, featuring scenes so romantically masculine that only the coldest feminine heart would not be touched: pipes and slippers, a red-capped hunter knocking down a brace of ducks, a fleet of galleons in harbor unaccountably full-sailed, knightly shields and lordly crests, racy automobiles, workshop tools, or smiling Dad (Pop) himself. Why do women buy most of the cards? The answer may be simpler than it seems. Men think themselves too busy running the nation to find time for the smaller amenities, but they rationalize. The truth is that they are locked into an office or on a production line all day. Running an office, doing a job, no more takes all day than housework—few of us have brains that run so uniformly by the clock—but when the housework is done the woman who does it is free to go visiting or wander through the shops, while the man must shuffle papers and watch the clock. The woman may feel uncomfortable with her freedom, may feel she buys it at too high a price. It is her nonetheless, and she uses it, among other good works, to buy cards. The new cards, by the way, the cards for young people, don't draw such sharp distinctions between masculine and feminine roles. They are androgynous. We all are, underneath: the kids have found us out.

I suspect we send each other cards partly from guilt, believing we haven't kept our friendships in good repair. If we are gregarious, we are also shy, uneasy as only a people raised in a society straining toward egalitarianism can be. Most of us were never rich and never desperately poor. We never learned our place: we started this country so we wouldn't have to, but our mobility leaves us unsure of where our elbows belong. We are known for our humor, but not for our wit; for our ability, but not for our style; for our strength, but not for our grace. We find ourselves harried and we fumble, or think we do.

Our guilt is misplaced. Thoreau's three chairs for company and two for friendship nicely defines our human limits. They are no longer limits to which we can comfortably adhere. We would hurt too many feelings if we did, the feelings of the people we work with, of our relatives and our neighbors and the neighbors we left behind. Anyone who has moved recently knows how much sheer matter we accumulate in our houses, but imagine also the long list of acquaintances we have accumulated, back to our earliest years. If we are fond of people at all, we have met thousands in our lives. Perhaps that is why so few of us read. Perhaps our culture is really oral, despite the science fiction of our media, satellites above and wires and presses below and the air itself in fervent vibration. One recalls the theory that ghetto children have difficulty in school not because of deprivation but because of excess, of overstimulation by the teeming world in which they live. It is true to some degree of us all. With China and the Soviet Union, and for much of the same reasons of origin and purpose, we are a national people far more than we are local. Our traditions and our associations extend from ocean to ocean, and our burden of communication too. The Communist nations, not having finished their first industrial revolution, turn to party meetings and rallies to stay in touch; with a more ritualized social structure, we send cards.

Making greeting cards to suit us isn't easy. Try to imagine a card that would please both your grandmother and your revolutionary son—and yet your Christmas card probably did. For reasons no one knows, green cards don't sell. Writers of greeting cards must search their verses for unintentional double entendres, and because of that danger, the word "it" used as a direct object is taboo. "Today's your day to get *it!*" It won't do. St. Patrick's Day cards that kid Irish drinking habits elicit indignant letters from Hibernian Societies, a sign that the Irish are ready to melt the rest of the way into the pot. A card is two years in the making: what if hemlines change? Superman cards reached the stores the day the Superman fad collapsed. And what do you say, in a card, in mere words, to a widow whose world has emptied of the life she loved? (You say, in rhymed verse, that words can't express your sympathy.)

When I worked at Hallmark I sometimes thought of cards as pretty packages with nothing inside, but I am a year older now and I wonder. Perhaps, ephemeral though they are, they carry a greater weight of emotion to a greater number of people than we can bear to carry ourselves. They are tactful, discreet; they strike the right tone. Their designers sweat blood, believe me, to make them so. Even when they fail we forgive the sender and blame the card, as we forgive a caller a bad connection on the phone. Greeting cards have inertia. Like Santa's bag they hang a little behind. They are innately conservative because the occasions of our lives are too important for fads, of style or of spirit. Hallmark has discovered that the young people who buy its breezily pessimistic Contemporary cards return to more traditional forms when they acquire families and careers. Pessimism becomes a luxury they can no longer afford.

We grow older; the cards for our stops along the way await us in the store. They are not dangerous or subversive or mean; they espouse no causes except the old mute causes of life itself, birth and marriage and begetting and death, and these gently. I celebrate them as E. M. Forster celebrated democracy, with a hearty two cheers Merry Christmas.

MEANING

1. What aspects of our culture encourage the sending of mass-produced greeting cards in place of unique and personal messages?
2. What range of sentiments and emotional needs have greeting-card companies tried to fulfill through various types of cards?
3. How does the manufacturer use individual card-display setups to gather more accurate market research information about each community?
4. What explains the fact that, statistically, eighty percent of all greeting cards are purchased by women?

USING EXEMPLIFICATION TO CONVEY MEANING

1. How do the messages quoted by Rhodes represent similar messages on thousands of other cards designed to express the same sentiments?
2. What does Rhodes' description of nineteenth-century cards tell us about both the cards and the culture that produced them?
3. What background information does Rhodes give about the range of skills and different kinds of expertise required to produce greeting cards?
4. What features of Hallmark's design and manufacture of greeting cards does Rhodes discuss to illustrate techniques characteristic of an entire industry?

WRITING SUGGESTIONS

1. Discuss the informal "game" rules that govern the giving and receiving of greeting cards on various occasions. You might investigate the elements of reciprocity, keeping score, closeness of relationship, and society's expectations.
2. Describe the greeting cards that could be designed in the twenty-first century taking into account technological, social, and political, developments that you think might occur by then. For example, *"So happy to hear about your clone's graduation," "Congratulations on your new heart, liver, kidneys, lungs and head," "Good luck in your new home on the space station."*
3. Discuss your reactions to Rhodes' criticism that greeting cards mechanize and standardize complex relationships by limiting how emotions can be expressed on specific occasions.

ERWIN WICKERT

The Chinese and the Sense of Shame

Erwin Wickert was born in Brandenberg, Germany in 1915 and first visited China in 1936 when he was a student. He received his B.A. from Dickinson College, Pennsylvania in 1936 and his Ph.D. from the University of Heidelberg in 1939. From 1939 to 1945, Wickert was stationed in China and Japan as a member of the Diplomatic Corp. He has also served as German Ambassador in Bucharest, and from 1976 to 1980 was Ambassador to China from the German Federal Republic. Wickert has written several novels, memoirs, and is most noted in Germany as a writer of radio plays. "The Chinese and the Sense of Shame" is drawn from The Middle Kingdom: Inside China Today *(1981) and contains a wealth of observations and anecdotes that illuminate how strongly contemporary Chinese culture is still affected by the ancient fear of "shame" and "losing face."*

Chinese women were absurdly prudish, Herr M. complained bitterly—far more so than their sisters in any other socialist country. Herr M., who was making a television documentary about the women of China, cited an example.

While on location in Kaifeng, he had auditioned a delightful young engine driver and outlined the questions he proposed to ask her in front of the camera. She was quite prepared to answer all his questions save one, namely, whether she'd ever been in love. That would embarrass her, she said. She'd be bound to blush, and everyone would see because the film was being shot in colour. So saying, she turned crimson.

"And we hadn't started shooting!" sighed Herr M. "What a shame—what a picture she'd have made! Back home you can ask folks anything you like and they don't turn a hair. Nobody blushes these days except in romantic novels."

Yes indeed, what a shame!

Many people call *Jinpingmei* or *Kin Ping Meh* an erotic novel. Lin Yutang himself puts it in that category, like all Chinese, although it is one of the greatest novels in Chinese or any other language and defies such narrow classification.

Written four hundred years ago, *Kin Ping Meh* depicts every facet of contemporary life in a provincial Chinese city: wealth and poverty, corruption and integrity, crime and lubricity. The amatory exploits of its hero, Ximen Qing, though far from being its only theme, figure prominently. The erotic scenes are described with such gusto and love of detail that the English translator of the four-volume, unabridged edition (*The Golden Lotus*, London, 1959), was sometimes reduced to the same condition as the pretty young engine driver in Kaifeng. To spare his blushes, he reproduced the more daring passages in dry and pedantic Latin.

The book has been widely read in China, Emperor Kangxi, whose own brother had translated it into Manchurian, banned it as pornography in the seventeenth century. His edict seems to have been ineffective, for at least fourteen different editions appeared in that century alone. Emperor Qianlong, who reimposed the ban in the eighteenth century, was just as unsuccessful.

Once, when I was sitting in the embassy library with Günter Grass and half a dozen well-known Chinese authors, male and female, Grass inquired if our guests had read the novel. Not only had they read it, but they admitted as much without turning pink. Xie Bingxin, who was eighty, actually laughed.

Could it be obtained at any bookstore? asked Grass. This time the laughter was general. Of course not! Even if it were published in an edition of half a million copies, it would be sold out at once. Any new book sold out within hours, as we were well aware, but *Kin Ping Meh* . . . No, most of them had borrowed it from libraries.

Libraries open to all and sundry?

Oh, no, only members of the Writers' Association.

Now that the Gang of Four were no longer at the helm and far greater freedom was in prospect, said Grass, might the novel not be republished?

Here the going got harder and the replies more hesitant. No one cared to pronounce on the theme of greater intellectual freedom. Although Bai Hua, the young soldier-writer, had delivered a courageous address on the subject at the Writers' Congress only a few days earlier, he now said nothing.

Opinions were divided on whether or not it might be feasible to produce a new edition of the novel. Someone—I think it was the poetess Ke Yan—mooted the possibility of an expurgated version. There was general agreement that the book should only be made available to adults. Didn't such restrictions exist in Germany too?

Yes, I replied. "Morally injurious" literature could not be sold to minors in Germany either.

Someone else suggested that the novel might be published *neibu,* meaning "for internal use only." Even in imperial China, it had to a certain extent been sold *neibu,* or under the counter, and no one had ever discovered the author's identity. In the old days, educated people who wished to be taken seriously thought it better to disclaim having read such a notorious piece of fiction. They would have been ashamed to admit it.

Really? I said. Well, their prejudices seemed to have lived on. Whenever I passed some favourable comment on *Kin Ping Meh,* my Chinese friends would sigh and draw attention to the far more sophisticated *Dream of the Red Chamber. Kin Ping Meh* was cruder, admittedly, and I thoroughly appreciated the subtle characterization of *The Dream of the Red Chamber,* a novel of which I was also fond. On the other hand, I often became bored with the effeminate ways of its principal character, Bao Yü; with the ivory-tower effusions of the poetry club; with Bao Yü's problems in regard to maidservants and their delicate sensibilities; with the burial of flower petals in gardens; with people's habit of bursting into tears at the drop of a hat or going into a decline and lapsing into weeks of melancholia—in short, with the affectations and artificial problems of a great feudal household remote from real life. It had always puzzled me that, even in a communist country, literary critics found it possible to accept the parasitical existence of the Chia clan with only mild reprobation. It was Chinese prudery, then as now, that seemed to me to have denied *Kin Ping Meh* due recognition for its robust but often humorous social criticism, its all-embracing social compass.

Günter Grass wanted to know if our guests would dare to write a realistic description, either now or in the near future, of what two people did in bed together.

"For me the question doesn't arise," said Wang Meng. "I've no desire to, with so many other burning issues on my mind."

Wang Meng and all the other writers present had suffered persecution for many years. Most of them had been rusticated and compelled to work in people's communes. Wang Meng himself had spent seventeen years living in Uighur territory on the Sino-Soviet border. I still recall what he said when he visited me in Germany some time ago:

"Many things in the West escape my comprehension. Literature, films, the visual arts, life in general—they all impress me as over-sexualized and boring. I'm disappointed, not because I'm a prude, but because I ask myself: Are *these* your concerns in a world on the brink of an abyss?"

Yet Wang Meng must have been aware that in China, and Chinese universities in particular, underground literature of a purely pornographic and wholly unpolitical kind now flourishes alongside the political variety. They are copied by hand, but a change is already under way. The growth of tourism and of China's contacts with the West is bringing about a rapid increase in the smuggling of pornographic books and pictures. Western magazines of the *Playboy* genre fetch high prices on the black market. Shanghai already maintains a thriving trade in "dirty pictures," which are surreptitiously offered for sale on Nanking Road as they used to be in times gone by. Although some of this merchandise is said to be indigenous, imports from Hong Kong, Japan, Germany, and America are in greater demand, reputedly because they "offer" more.

We are sometimes told that prudishness and sexual inhibitions, which provide psychologists with such welcome scope for their many conflicting theories, are simply a product of Christian moral concepts. Although it is probably true that Christian moral inhibitions have done a great deal of mischief on this side of the world, non-Christian China is far more prudish and her sexual modesty far more effective, even today, than in our Western, Christian world. Thomas Meadows, a pioneer sinologist of the last century, found much to criticize in the classical philosophers of China because they had still to see the Gospel light. On the other hand, he commended them highly for the fact that none of their sacred books or annotations contained a single sentence "that may not be read aloud in any family circle in England." One suspects that the Holy Writ presented him with greater problems in this respect.

No dictatorship, that of the proletariat included, can tolerate permissiveness, hence the brief duration of the Soviet Union's "free love" phase. The strict tabooing of love in China cannot, however, be ascribed to socialism alone, still less to the sole influence of Chinese tradition.

Western opinion-makers often urge the public to cast off taboos because they are restrictive of freedom. As a corollary, they proclaim it heroic to destroy taboos and play with fire. Neither course of action is truly meaningful or truly heroic because closer scrutiny reveals that the taboos have long been dismantled and the fire has cooled.

It cannot be denied that freedom is restricted by the taboo of sexual shame, but is a "shameless" society worth striving for? Do its assets exceed its liabilities?

"And they were both naked, the man and his wife, and were not ashamed." That, according to the only report we possess, is how it was in the beginning. The picture did not change until the two inhabitants of Paradise had sampled the fateful apple. "And the eyes of them both were opened, and they knew they were naked; and they sewed fig leaves together, and made themselves aprons."

Since then, shame has been one of mankind's fundamental characteristics, a potent force in all societies that attach a high value to mores and morality, responsibility and good order. Shame sets bounds on what is permitted in social life. A force productive of tension, it can destroy human beings as well as limit their behaviour. History is littered with the names of those who preferred death to disgrace. Western examples are relatively few, Chinese innumerable.

Although it is undoubtedly true that freedom reigns in a "shameless" society, every passing day confirms that passion is being replaced by tedium, superficiality, aimlessness, loneliness, emptiness, and despair.

Early Chinese literature contains some ardent poems addressed by young girls to their lovers. Their outspoken invitations and thinly-veiled allusions to the pleasures of love are far from shameless, but neither are they coy.

Confucian commentators of later date were gravely perplexed by this. Like the interpreters of the Song of Solomon, they eventually decided to place an allegorical construction on such verses, though many of their exegeses were so factitious and far-fetched as to be almost unintelligible.

Although the Confucian interpreters are no more, some of these lyrics would cause problems in China's modern, communistically puritanical society. It would, for instance, be hard to imagine the following words, which were composed long before Confucius' day, being sung by a choir of women soldiers arrayed on stage or in front of a television camera. They occur in the *Shijing*, an anthology of popular songs:

> I implore you, young Zhung,
> leap not into our yard,
> burst not through our sandalwood!
> Not that I should be sorry if you did,
> but I fear people's wagging tongues.
> How I love you, young Zhung!
> But I so much fear
> what people say.

The author of this veiled invitation to Zhung, her lover, was not ashamed of herself for making it. Her action was not a sin in the eyes of Heaven, nor was her song a denial of erotic passion. It merely camouflaged what would, if openly displayed, have been an infringement of custom. Even in earliest times, love was *neibu*.

The girl's only fear was of wagging tongues—of what the neighbors would say if they saw young Zhung making his way to her through the hedge. She was afraid of being disgraced.

Just as "shame" possesses a dual significance in English, so the Chinese word *chi* can mean both disgrace and the sense of shame—and *chi* is an important concept in Confucian ethics:

"The Master said: 'If the people be guided by laws, and if it be endeavoured to keep order through punishment, they will seek to avoid punishment but will have no sense of shame. If they be guided by virtue, and if it be endeavoured to keep order through the rules of propriety, they will have a sense of shame and will, moreover, become good.' "

Laws can govern people's outward behaviour only, whereas the reasons for their behaviour repose within them. The refined and educated or "superior" person does not eschew crime for fear of punishment. He does so because he is deterred by shame, or fear of disgrace.

The missionary Richard Wilhelm translates *chi* as "conscience," but the Chinese have never associated it with obedience to divine commandments, nor can it be equated with Socrates' *daimonion*, the inner voice that admonished him whenever he threatened to offend against what was mentally discernible as good.

Chi, or shame, was what a person felt when he had offended against *li*, meaning decency, convention, good form, and much else besides. But the person who did so—who was guilty of unseemly and irresponsible conduct—was committing no sin and violating no divine commandment. Although he had transgressed the cosmic order of things, that and the earthly social system were congruent.

It is strange that the Chinese should have devoted so little discussion to the concept of shame, almost as if they considered it such a natural disciplinary power that no words need be wasted on it.

Education, says Confucius, renders a person capable of perceiving and adopting the norms of ethical conduct. The basis of ethical conduct is the categorical imperative embodied in this negative version of our own popular dictum: "Do not unto others that which you do not wish done unto yourself." Sense of shame, it is further stated, will deter a person from transgressing this rule.

Thus the courts of ancient times did not so much punish a crime definable in terms of evidence as penalize the state of mind that led to its perpetration. Judicial verdicts and sentences are still coloured by this attitude. In the penal code of the Qing dynasty, which remained valid until the beginning of the twentieth century, forty lashes were prescribed as the punishment for "shameless conduct." Shameless conduct itself remained undefined because everyone knew what it was. We, on the other hand, live in a shameless society, where it would be difficult to reach a consensus about what is shameless and what is not.

In China, whenever an offense against the rules of society became common knowledge, social retribution was swift and severe. The "shameless" person lost face and reputation, but only if his disgrace became known, if the story leaked out—if people started talking. So it was, at least, among the common folk or Old Hundred Families. This may be one reason for what strikes non-Chinese as an inordinate love of secrecy: the fear that, whether in the family, the village, or the government, matters may come to light which outsiders would regard as disgraceful, an occasion for gossip or even ridicule.

Those guilty of grave offences—gross shamelessness, so to speak—were naturally brought to trial. Penalties for the *xiao ren*, or Little People, tended to be harsher than those meted out to educated persons, who were (or were held to be) far more sensitive to punishment and keenly aware of their disgrace even before it had been advertised. They suffered not only from gossip but from a personal awareness that they had violated the code in which they had been reared. They internalized their shame, which could in certain circumstances affect them like the sense of guilt and sin from which it differed so greatly. Shame could not be mitigated by atonement. There was no authority, earthly or celestial, that could acquit them of shame by way of the confessional or by the direct exercise of divine clemency. All that could blur the memory of disgrace was future good behaviour and active remorse.

Because shame and disgrace can wound so deeply, the "superior" person takes care not to make his neighbour lose face or give him grounds for shame. He refrains from casting suspicion on him and rebuking him in another's presence. The least gesture, the mildest reproach, can be profoundly hurtful.

I recall an occasion when Jiang Nanxiang, China's Minister of Education, was a guest at the Press Club in Bonn. The walls were lined with humorous caricatures of German politicians in animal guise. The Chinese visitor made no comment, but his surprise and bewilderment were all too plain. How could anyone degrade a person, especially a politician in office, by depicting him as a fox or a squirrel? In the case of someone expelled from decent society, someone with a "black" past—a non-person or member of the Gang of Four, for example—anything goes. Where such people are concerned, the Chinese have no qualms about calumny and character assassination.

The sanctions applied by society to those who have transgressed its code are harsh and cruel, as Chinese children learn at a very tender age. They are reared, not in abhorrence of guilt and sin, but in fear of disgrace.

Although the legal penalties imposed on an educated person may once have been milder than those meted out to common folk, he was often harder hit by the moral condemnation of his peers. "It isn't done" was a punishment in itself, a rebuke that might lead to the ostracism of him who had violated the code of honour of the educated class—and that, in a society where no one could seek refuge in anonymity, constituted a severe penalty.

Censure as a form of punishment is not unique to the Chinese world. Among the patricians of ancient Rome, the censor's enunciation of a *nota censoria* sufficed to bring a person *infamia* and destroy his good name. This rebuke was administered not only when a law had been broken but in the case of acts within the law but considered unjust.

Shame is stronger than any law. In one of the earliest Chinese novellas, the tale of Prince Tan of Yan, a knight at the Crown Prince's table sings a satirical song about a guest whom he considers to have been unduly privileged. The guest, however, declares himself willing to risk death to avenge an old insult inflicted on the Crown Prince by killing its author, Qin Shihuang, China's First Emperor. At this, the author of the lampoon is overcome with shame. When the guest passes him, bound for an attempt on the Emperor's life, he cuts his throat 'in token of farewell.'

We meet similar incidents in Japanese literature and history. The *samurai*'s honour carried more weight with him than laws with the mass of the people. It compelled him, if disgraced, to commit *seppuku,*[1] or disembowel himself. In the old days, European officers who had violated their code of honour were under a similar compulsion. In extreme cases of dishonourable conduct, which far from always constituted a penal offence and might simply mean that they had incurred excessive gambling debts, they either resigned or shot themselves.

Just as the Chinese ruling class was expected to display a superior sense of responsibility, so it based its claim to rulership on a superior moral sense and an adherence to a stricter code of behaviour.

---

[1] The word *harakiri* "belly-slitting" is not commonly used in Japanese because of its crudity. *Seppuku,* the sinicized rendering of the same character, is considered less extreme.

Where statutory penalities are concerned, said Confucious, a man will try to evade them by subterfuge, lies, and legal quibbles. This he will do without the least embarrassment, whereas the person answerable to a code of honour will achieve nothing by splitting hairs.

Confucianism aspired to extend the strict code of the educated élite, insofar as this was possible, to the people as a whole. It wanted to render laws redundant by raising moral standards, and to use upbringing and education to transform Little People into Superior Persons who had no need of laws because a sense of shame would deter them from unseemly conduct.

The Gang of Four and their supporters, too, believed that people's awareness of a code was more effective than laws and edicts, and that education would remould the human being, transforming him into the different and superior creature known as the New Man. Daily political indoctrination was designed to enhance comrades' revolutionary consciousness, however, not their moral sense. The ultra-leftists held that, once the entire nation was imbued with revolutionary consciousness, production would rise to a level adequate for subsistence, and universal justice would prevail.

But they failed to create the New Man. The demands made on people's revolutionary consciousness changed so often that the one remaining constant was absolute obedience.

The Chinese Communist Party of today is less at pains to cultivate revolutionary consciousness. Instead, it falls back on old-established injunctions of the kind that also occur in the Confucian moral code—as, for instance, when it urges people to learn and heed "the Five Virtues" (decorum, courtesy, cleanliness, discipline, and morality) and "the Four Decencies" (decency of mental outlook, language, behaviour, and environment). Modern Chinese films ask: What is true love? What is nobility of mind? What does sacrifice entail? What constitutes true happiness? And, just as the Confucians drew their examples from anthologies of edifying tales full of dutiful sons, virtuous daughters, and righteous officials and judges, so the people—and young people in particular—are once more enjoined to follow the example of Lei Feng (1939–62), a model soldier and hero of labour who spent his short life doing good deeds.

But, just as the Confucians failed to educate the masses into paragons of virtue, so the Communist Party's efforts in the same direction are bound to miscarry. Life in a society of sanctimonious and superior people would bore the Chinese to distraction, especially as one of their favourite pasttimes is to note and comment on their neighbours' moral conduct. Tongue-wagging—malicious gossip of the sort dreaded by young Zhung's admirer three thousand years ago—is still a constant and ubiquitous threat.

The following story was told to me by a Chinese acquaintance who had been sent to work in a factory during the Cultural Revolution. It appears that one of his fellow workers, a young woman, had an affair with a married colleague whose family lived far away in the country, and who saw his wife for a few days a year at most. Accused by their workmates of sleeping together, the couple denied it. Nobody believed them, and a mood of hysteria developed, particularly among their female workmates. They were watched and spied on. Eventually, after keeping them under surveillance, members of the People's Militia succeeded in catching them in bed together. They were promptly arrested and marched off to the factory, whose Security Bureau personnel interrogated them with relish and broadcast the results of their inquisition to the rest of the workforce. Neither of them was permitted to go home throughout this time. They were held in isolation at the factory and compelled to sleep there until the board of inquiry ended by reprimanding them both.

But that was not the end of the affair. The young man had lost face and incurred ridicule. To be an object of derision and a target for detractors whom one cannot escape is hurtful beyond endurance. Icelandic sagas record that strong men could be so humiliated by satirical poems that their sole recourse was to flee the country. The Chinese worker had no such alternative.

The girl fared still worse. Her father beat her when she came home—she was in her mid-twenties—and then turned her out. Her family wanted nothing more to do with someone whose reputation bore a stain that could never be expunged, so she had to live with her disgrace. She was assigned to a labour unit which refused to release her for employment in another part of the country, where no one knew her story. Now that her family had disowned her, she too was deprived of human society and a means of escape.

I never heard how the story ended, but suicide is the usual outcome in such cases. Where shame is a living force, social sanctions against those who commit some disgraceful act are harsher than in societies ruled by laws alone.

Many Chinese emperors subjected their ministers and court officials to ungentle treatment, as we already know. They castrated, bisected, quartered, or simply beheaded them. Emperors of a milder disposition abstained from such unrefined methods. If need arose, the Son of Heaven sent an unwanted official the *bailing,* or white silken cord (actually a ribbon), which the unfortunate man proceeded to use in keeping with custom and propriety.

Although he had served the empire well and was loyal to the Emperor, General Nian Gengyao fell prey to slanderous intrigue. Emperor Yongzheng (1723–35), who resolved to get rid of him, sent the General a long, polished letter of farewell enclosing the silken cord. The Son of Heaven concluded his missive as follows.

> As I peruse this State Paper, I shed bitter tears. As Lord of the Universe, however, I am bound to exhibit unswerving justice in the matter of rewards and punishments. I remit the penalty of decapitation and grant you the privilege of suicide. With lavish generosity and merciful forbearance I have spared the lives of your entire family, with one exception. You would have to be stock or stone, if, even in the face of death, you failed to shed tears of joy and gratitude for the benefits bestowed on you by the Imperial Master whom you have so foully betrayed.

Although physical violence was often employed against officials during the Cultural Revolution, Red Guards and people with a high degree of revolutionary consciousness preferred to humiliate their opponents and make them look ridiculous. The widow of Marshal He Long, whom the Gang of Four abducted and murdered, records that his jailer, instead of giving him rice in a bowl, tipped it on to the floor of his cell so that he had to lap it up on all fours, like a dog.

Educated persons—dignitaries and public servants—were seldom chained or tortured in the old days. If convicted of some grave misdemeanour, they were sentenced to wear a white hat that would advertise their crime and keep its memory alive. The same disgrace was visited on many politicians, scholars, and public servants, both senior and junior, during the Cultural Revolution. To this day, refractory prisoners in penal establishments are made to wear "the cap of a bad element," so that disgrace will dog them even in the company of convicts like themselves.

Thousands of people jumped to their deaths during the Cultural Revolution, merely to avoid humiliation, sometimes after Red Guards had thrust them into an upper room with the window obligingly opened in advance. These victims of persecution, most of whom were intellectuals, acted as etiquette and education prescribed. "The spirit can be killed but not humiliated . . ." They, too, preferred death to dishonour.

Some days before leaving Peking we received a visit from Mrs Yü, who had brought us a farewell gift. It turned out to be a magnificent old court robe, richly embroidered from collar to hem. We were in two minds about accepting it.

Mrs Yü told us that the robe had belonged to her husband's grandfather, a mandarin of senior rank, who had worn it on ceremonial occasions. Red Guards had burst into her home during the Cultural Revolution, bent on subjecting her husband to "struggle." They searched the whole house and purloined several articles of value, notably a watch and a camera. When they came across the ceremonial robe, they forced her husband to put it on. Then they gummed a piece of wrapping paper to the back, scrawled the characters for "royalist" on it, stuck a dunce's hat on his head, and paraded him through the streets. Mrs Yü begged us to accept the robe as a gift. She and her husband no longer wished to keep it in their home, she said, but we ourselves might appreciate its handsome embroidery.

So the Red Guards had dressed her husband in this ludicrous costume and led him through the streets to roars of laughter from their comrades. Although they had humiliated him, not us, we experienced a vicarious pang of shame. In China, where shame and *li* count for more than they do with us, this treatment must have been almost too much for him to bear. Arrest and imprisonment or exile to the provinces he might have forgotten, but not the disgrace of that day.

Our reluctance evaporated. When Mrs Yü had gone, we took a closer look at her gift. A scrap of brown paper still adhered to the back. We have never removed it.

MEANING

1. How does Wickert use the censorship of an erotic novel, *Kin Ping Meh*, to illustrate his belief that "non-Christian China is far more prudish and her sexual modesty far more effective, even today, than in our western Christian world"?
2. Explain the importance of the concept of *chi* as a controlling force in the lives of the Chinese people.
3. What is the significance of the surprise shown by Chinese politicians to the animal caricatures of western politicians?
4. How was "shame" employed for political purposes, by the Red Guards, during the days of the Cultural Revolution?

USING EXEMPLIFICATION TO CONVEY MEANING

1. What illustrations do you find particularly effective in clarifying why the fear of "losing face" operates so strongly in China?
2. What examples drawn from his personal experiences does Wickert provide to show that "shame" operates with equal force in the new China as it did in previous times?
3. How does the story of the young girl caught in an illicit relationship illustrate the unexpected puritanical attitudes of the Communist Party in China?

4. Evaluate Wickert's strategy of using an unusually wide range of representative examples drawn from history, law, literature, and personal observations to explain and clarify what he means by the Chinese "sense of shame."

WRITING SUGGESTIONS

1. To what degree does the press play the role of accuser in identifying "shameful" conduct in our society?
2. As a research project, investigate whether there are cultures (e.g., Samoa) where "shame" exists but is not linked to sexuality, as it is in China.
3. What connections can you discover between the Chinese concept of *chi* and Freud's concept of the superego?
4. How is the "code of silence," or the silent treatment, a Western version of using "shame" to control behavior?

SCIENCES

IBM

Processing Information in a Data Base

IBM's staff of technical writers provide a helpful discussion in this essay on how information is stored and retrieved in a data base. They explain this concept using an extended example of how a hospital stores all necessary facts on patients so that specific data (name, address, illness, dates and types of treatment, attending physician, charges, and so on) can be easily retrieved.

This section describes what makes storing data in a data base different from other ways of storing data.

COMPARING WAYS TO STORE DATA

The advantage of storing and processing data in a data base is that all of the data appears only once, and that each program has to process only the data that it needs. One way to understand this is to compare three ways of storing data: in separate files, in a combined file, and in a data base.

Storing Data in Separate Files

If you keep separate files of data for each part of your organization, you can make sure that each program uses only the data it needs, but you have to store a lot of the data in several places at once. The problem with this is that redundant data takes up space that could be used for something else.

For example, suppose that a medical clinic keeps separate files for each of its departments, such as the clinic department, the accounting department, and the ophthalmology department.

- The clinic department keeps data about each patient that visits the clinic. For each patient, the clinic department needs to keep this information:

189

- The patient's identification number
- The patient's name
- The patient's address
- The patient's illnesses
- The date of each illness
- The date that the patient came to the clinic for treatment
- The treatment that was given for each illness
- The doctor that prescribed the treatment
- The charge for the treatment

● The accounting department also keeps information about each patient.
● The information that the accounting department might keep for each patient is:

- The patient's identification number
- The patient's name
- The patient's address
- The charge for the treatment
- The amount of the patient's payments

● The information that the ophthalmology department might keep for each of its patients is:

- The patient's identification number
- The patient's name
- The patients address
- The patient's illnesses that relate to ophthalmology
- The date of each illness
- The names of the members in the patient's household
- The relationship between the patient and each household member

If each of these departments keeps separate files, each department uses only the data that it needs, but a lot of data is redundant. For example, every department in the clinic uses at least the patient's number, name, and address. Updating the data is also a problem because if several departments change the same piece of data, you have to update the data in several places. Because of this, it's difficult to keep the data in each department's files current. There's a danger of having current data in one department and "old" data in another.

Storing Data in a Combined File

Another way to store data is to combine all of the files into one file for all of the departments at the clinic to use. In the medical example, the patient record that would be used by each department would contain these fields:

- The patient's identification number
- The patient's name
- The patient's address
- The patient's illnesses
- The date of each illness
- The date that the patient came to the clinic for treatment

- The treatment that was given for each illness
- The doctor that prescribed the treatment
- The charge for the treatment
- The amount of the patient's payments
- The names of the members in the patient's household
- The relationship between the patient and each household member

Using a combined file solves the updating problem because all of the data is in one place, but it creates a new problem: the programs that process this data have to access the entire data base record to get to the part that they need. For example, to process only the patient's number, charges, and payments, an accounting program has to access all of the other fields as well. In addition, changing the format of any of the fields within the patient's record affects all of the application programs, not just the programs that use that field. Using combined files can also involve security risks, since all of the programs have access to all of the fields in a record.

Storing Data in a Data Base

Storing data in a data base gives you the advantages of separate files and combined files: all of the data appears only once, and each program accesses only the data that it needs. This means that:

- When you update a field, you only have to update it in one place.
- Since you store each piece of information only in one place, you can't have an updated version of the information in one place and an out-of-date version of the information in another place.
- Each program accesses only the data it needs.
- You can keep programs from accessing private information.

In addition, storing data in a data base has two advantages that neither of the other ways has:

- If you change the format of part of a data base record, the change doesn't affect the programs that don't use the changed information.
- Programs aren't affected by how the data is stored.

Because the program is independent of the physical data, a data base can store all of the data only once and yet make it possible for each program to use only the data that it needs. In a data base, what the data looks like when it's stored, and what it looks like to an application program are two different things.

FIGURE 1

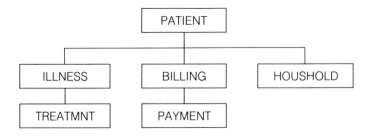

What the Data Looks Like When It's Stored

In IMS/VS, a record is stored and accessed in a hierarchy. A hierarchy shows how each piece of data in a record relates to other pieces of data in the record. Figure 1 shows the hierarchy you could use to store the patient information described earlier in this chapter.

IMS/VS connects the pieces of information in a data base record by defining the relationships between the pieces of information that relate to the same subject. The result of this is a data base hierarchy. The hierarchy shows how each piece of information is related to other pieces of information in the record. The relationship between two pieces of information in the hierarchy means that one piece of information is either dependent on or equal to another piece of information.

In the medical data base, the data that you're keeping is information about a particular patient. Information that is not associated with a particular patient is meaningless. For example, keeping information about a treatment given for a particular illness is meaningless if the illness isn't associated with a patient. ILLNESS, TREATMNT, BILLING, PAYMENT, and HOUSHOLD must always be associated with one of the clinic's patients to be meaningful information.

There are five kinds of information you're keeping about each patient. The information about the patient's illnesses, billings, and household depends directly on the patient. The information about the patient's treatments and the patient's payments depends respectively on the patient's illnesses, and the patient's payments as well.

Each of the pieces of data represented in Figure 1 is called a segment in the hierarchy. A segment is the smallest unit of data that an application program can retrieve from the data base. Each segment contains one or more fields of information. The PATIENT segment, for example, contains all of the information that relates strictly to the patient: the patient's identification number, the patient's name, and the patient's address.

What the Data Looks Like to Your Program

IMS/VS uses two kinds of control blocks to make it possible for application programs to be independent of the way in which you store the data in the data base. One control block defines the physical structure of the data base; another defines an application program's view of the data base:

• A data base description, or DBD, is a control block that describes the physical structure of the data base. The DBD also defines the appearance and contents, or fields, that make up each of the segment types in the data base.

For example, the DBD for the medical data base hierarchy shown in Figure 1 would describe to IMS/VS the physical structure of the hierarchy, and it would describe each of the six segment types in the hierarchy: PATIENT, ILLNESS, TREATMNT, BILLING, PAYMENT, and HOUSHOLD.

• A data base program communication block, or DB PCB, in turn, defines an application program's view of the data base. An application program often needs to process only some of the segments in a data base. A PCB defines which of the segments in the data base the program is allowed to access. The program is "sensitive" to the segments that it's allowed to access. The data structures that are available to the program contain only segments that the program is sensitive to.

For example, an accounting program that calculates and prints bills for the clinic's patients would need only the PATIENT, BILLING, and PAYMENT segments. You could define the data structure shown in Figure 2 in a DB PCB for this program.

FIGURE 2

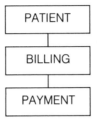

A program that updates the data base with information on patients' illnesses and treatments, on the other hand, would need to process the PATIENT, ILLNESS, and TREATMNT segments. You could define the data structure shown in Figure 3 for this program.

FIGURE 3

Sometimes a program needs to process all of the segments in the data base. When this is true, the program's view of the data base as defined in the DB PCB is the same as the DL/I hierarchy that's defined in the DBD.

Each DB PCB defines a way in which the application program views and processes the data base. The DB PCB also tells IMS/VS how the program is allowed to process the segments in the data structure—whether the program can only read them, or whether it can update segments as well.

A program specification block, or PSB, contains the DB PCBs for a particular application program. A program may use only one DB PCB—which means it processes only one data structure—or it may use several DB PCBs, one for each data structure. There is one PSB for each application program.

Since an application program processes only the segments in a data base that it requires, if you change the format of a segment that a program doesn't process, you don't have to change the program. A program is affected only by the segments that it accesses. In addition to being sensitive to only certain segments in a data base, a program can also be sensitive to only certain fields within a segment. This is called field level sensitivity. If you change a segment that the program isn't sensitive to, it doesn't affect the program. In the same way, if you change a field that the program isn't sensitive to, it doesn't affect the program.

How You Process a Data Base Record

A data base record is a root segment occurrence and all of its dependents. In the medical example, a data base record is all of the information about one patient. The PATIENT segment in the medical data base is called the root segment. The segments below the root segment are called dependents, or children, of the root. For example, ILLNESS, BILLING, and HOUSHOLD are all children of PATIENT. ILLNESS, BILLING, and HOUSHOLD are called direct dependents of PATIENT; TREATMNT and PAYMENT are also dependents of PATIENT, but they are not direct because they are at a lower level in the hierarchy.

Each data base record has only one root segment occurrence, but it may have several occurrences at lower levels. For example, the data base record for a patient contains only one occurrence of the PATIENT segment type, but it may contain several ILLNESS and TREATMNT segment occurrences for that patient.

To process the information in the data base, your application program communicates with IMS/VS in three ways:

- Passing control: IMS/VS passes control to your application program through an entry statement in your program. Your program returns control to IMS/VS when it has finished its processing.
- Communicating processing requests: Your program communicates processing requests to IMS/VS by issuing calls to Data Language I, or DL/I. DL/I is an access method that handles the data in the data base.
- Exchanging information with DL/I: Your program exchanges information with DL/I through two areas in your program. First, DL/I reports the results of your calls in the DB PCB. Your program builds a mask of the DB PCB and uses this mask to check the results of the calls. Second, when you request a segment from the data base, DL/I returns the segment to your I/O area. When you want to update a segment in the data base, you place the new value of the segment in the I/O area.

An application program can read and update a data base. When you update a data base, you can replace segments, delete segments, or add segments. You indicate to DL/I the segment you want to process, and whether you want to read or update it, in a DL/I call.

Meaning

1. How does this example of a medical data base illustrate the enormous flexibility of all data-base systems for storing and retrieving information?
2. What advantage is offered by organizing a hospital's data base so that all information

(regarding illness, treatment, billing, payment, and household) is stored in relationship to a particular patient?

3. How is information in a data base structured to match the different kinds of inquiries that might be made about it?
4. How is the way in which information is stored in a data base analogous to how information appears in a book (e.g., in number of pages, number of lines per page, number of characters per line)?

USING EXEMPLIFICATION TO CONVEY MEANING

1. How does IBM's example of the way a hospital might store and retrieve information illustrate and clarify basic capabilities possessed by all data base systems?
2. What steps do the technical writers of this IBM manual take to ensure that even readers with limited computer expertise can understand and appreciate the advantages of storing information in the form of a data base?
3. Why is exemplification especially useful as a strategy in technical writing for translating abstract ideas and concepts into specific cases that can be clearly understood?

WRITING SUGGESTIONS

1. How would you use the capabilities for organizing information in a data base described by IBM to organize a greeting-card data base using information provided by Richard Rhodes (see page 168).
2. Discuss any current business application of a data base.

Edward A. Feigenbaum
Pamela McCorduck

Speculations in Knowledge Futures

Edward A. Feigenbaum was born in New Jersey in 1936. He received his Doctorate from the Carnegie Institute of Technology in 1960 and has been a professor of computer science at Stanford University since 1969. Feigenbaum is noted for developing the concept of "knowledge-based" systems, which use artificial intelligence to make decisions normally made by human experts. He is coauthor of The Handbook of Artificial Intelligence *(1981) and a founder of TeKnowledge, Inc., the first knowledge engineering company.*

Pamela McCorduck, born in Liverpool, England in 1940, received an M.F.A. from Columbia University in 1970. She wrote two novels before beginning Machines Who Think: A Personal Inquiry Into the History and Prospects of Artificial Intelligence *(1979), a work now considered a standard reference in the field.*

Both Feigenbaum and McCorduck have collaborated on The Fifth Generation: Artificial Intelligence and Japan's Computer Challenge to the World *(1983). "Speculations in Knowledge Futures," drawn from this work, presents an engrossing account of practical applications for artificial intelligence (AI) in the fields of medicine, education, journalism, and even the neighborhood library.*

If the creation of artificial intelligence is among the most challenging and controversial tasks the human mind has ever put itself to, if the difficulties often seem overwhelming, that has never prevented the field from being surrounded by fantastic predictions for the future. But the truth is that no one knows exactly what surprises are in store for us all. We can only speculate.

The "Mechanical" Doctor

Many kinds of expertise are unevenly distributed in the world. Medicine is a perfect example. That is one reason the U.S. National Institutes of Health have been at the forefront of supporting expert systems research. It isn't just that the natives of Ulan Bator don't have the same access to medical care as the natives of Los Angeles; it's that the natives of Fresno don't have it either, and poor people in Los Angeles aren't as fortunate in their medical attention as well-off people.

If the idea of a machine doctor repels you, consider that not everyone feels that way. Studies in England showed that many humans were much more comfortable (and candid) with an examination by a computer terminal than with a human physician,

196

whom they perceived as somehow disapproving of them. "Mechanical" doctors are in fact systems that move methodically through possibilities, making inferences and drawing conclusions. They often outperform the very experts who have programmed them because of their methodical ways; they don't skip or forget things, get tired or rushed, or fall subject to some of our other human failings. They will be on call at the patient's convenience, not just the physician's. And they can bring medicine to places where none now exists.

The Intelligent Library

One application anybody interested in knowledge will welcome is the intelligent library. Nowadays, a library has information, even knowledge, but you must supply the intelligence. You pick among topics in the card catalog; you browse in the stacks, sorting and choosing; you go to the reference librarian in despair.

The intelligent library, based on knowledge information processing systems, will supply intelligence along with knowledge and information. It will be active, not passive. It will conduct a dialogue with you, inferring from what you tell it what it is you really want. You can ask a question, state a goal, and by asking you questions in turn, it will infer your desires and try to meet them. It will even prompt you with connected topics you hadn't, at that moment, thought of. It will test your hypotheses, verify your hunches, and explain until you really understand.

All this is done by inference: sometimes the library doesn't have the direct answer, but it can reason its way through the information glut and present you with plausible scenarios, explaining at your request its reasons for arriving at those scenarios.

Does the end of libraries as we know them mean the end of books? Probably not for a long time, if ever. We still write (some) letters, even though we have telephones, Telexes, and other forms of sending messages to each other. Books may very well become pieces of art in the distant future; meanwhile, their great advantages of high resolution, portability, and random access (you can riffle through the pages so easily) will have to be met by any system that wants to replace them. One can imagine such solutions: a personal book-size "reading machine" that allows you to slip chips in and go with them where you will, spring hillside or pleasure cruise; that even allows you to flip from written word to spoken word if you'd rather hear than see.

The Intelligent Tutor

A leading Western intellectual, realizing that he knew nothing about science, recently cried out that the universe had gone silent on him. That reaction seemed a bit perfervid, but if he can hold out, help is on the way.

There are many topics we know nothing about, but would like to know something about, if it weren't so painful to learn. As it happens, the pain is inflicted in two ways: first, it is difficult to make your mind grasp concepts that are quite alien from those you're used to dealing with; and second, it is a terrible embarrassment for a grownup to keep on admitting that he just doesn't understand. Thus most of us simply close off whole areas of human intellectual achievement because the difficulties overwhelm us. If, however, we had an infinitely patient, intelligent, and nonjudgmental tutor, we might feel different.

"What can you tell me about physics?" you ask your intelligent tutor in a discreet aside. SHALL WE BEGIN WITH THE UNIFIED THEORY? it asks. "Sure," you say, "why not?" Your intelligent tutor may be talking to you; words may be appearing in print on some sort of receiver, but soon pictures will start to appear. Even today, with the help of computer graphics, phenomena that could not be pictured any other way can be realized pictorially: theorems become breathtakingly beautiful visual designs, their regularity and elegance presented in a visual—and visceral—way that rewrites the old Chinese adage to say that a picture is worth ten thousand terms.

With the intelligent tutor, the experience of knowledge will be available at any level you want, from general undetailed introduction for the novice to detailed instruction in specialities only an expert might want. When the first explanation of a concept fails to penetrate, the intelligent tutor (either because you have told it so explicitly, or because it has determined that fact for itself by testing you slyly) will try rephrasing the concept, using analogies, pictures, mathematical terms—whatever is necessary to make you understand. If you don't understand even then, it will tactfully tell you what you can indeed absorb, and neither of you need worry about what you cannot.

KNOWLEDGE SIMULATORS: "GAMES" FOR TEACHING

If such tutors are available for adults—and the Japanese count on them to continue the process of lifelong learning for their ever more elderly population—what might education for children look like?

One answer came from a recent symposium devoted to video games. That might seem like an odd forum in which to ponder the educational possibilities of the intelligent computer, but learning was the main theme of nearly all the speakers.

Several speakers who are working on the frontiers, well beyond the relatively simple shoot-em-ups in present-day arcades, reminded their scholarly audience that video games are in their infancy in every sense of the term. But even at this primitive stage, it is easy to imagine the kinds of games that are possible in the future, once much higher degrees of computer speed and memory are available, coupled with highly sophisticated graphics capabilities and reasoning power. Perhaps the most important property these future games will have is that although they'll be fun, for that's in the nature of games, they'll teach—painlessly and naturally.

Already certain special groups have such "games" specially designed for them. Pilots learning to fly the latest commercial jet do not take one out for a spin the first time at the controls. Instead, they have $10 million toys called simulators that give them as precisely as possible the feeling of flying the craft they will eventually fly for real.

We have peculiar and mainly pejorative associations with the idea of games—surely they can't be serious, and they have little to do with the business of functioning in an adult world. But of course games have everything to do with that. Scientists often describe what they do as a glorious game, and so do securities analysts (the phrase is "to play the stock market," after all). Some games designers argue persuasively that even today, at the admittedly primitive level where video games have arrived, they can stimulate the intellect and teach various skills and facts as well as anything yet devised. A current game called "Time Zone" pushes the player backward into history, allowing him to participate in the assassination of Julius Caesar (but not to prevent it), to persuade Benjamin Franklin face to face to sign the Declaration of

Independence (but not to succeed at that), and so forth. Present-day games even have time constraints—in "Detective," evidence will disappear if the player doesn't reason his way to it quickly enough, and once gone, it's gone for the duration of the game. The player must use his wits to compensate. Does such a game teach reasoning skills, or is it simply fun?

If all this is how children might someday learn, what is to become of classrooms? In the very long run, they may meet the same fate as other precomputing organizations, which is to say, having outlived their usefulness, they will simply wither away and die. But for the foreseeable future, classrooms of some sort will surely exist, if only because the most exuberant games, or simulations, or fantasies, or whatever name we have for those activities by then, will require installations of a size and expense that most families won't want to undertake for themselves. Moreover, children need the company of other children, and the new classrooms will be one place where they'll get it.

Will human teachers disappear? Probably not. But children will learn in a much more independent fashion than they do now, having control over what they learn and when they learn it. Will children be equipped to make those decisions wisely? Only if the learning games they are presented with are designed to impart wisdom. AI researchers have long hoped that by discovering how to design an intelligent computer program, they will shed some light on the human learning process—at the moment, after all, we do nothing but spray words at our pupils and hope some of them stick. One of the great challenges educators and cognitive psychologists face in the next few years is to design games that teach the skills necessary for participation in a new world. Perhaps their first task is to identify those skills.

THE INTELLIGENT NEWSPAPER

Some people think current events are fascinating. Some people think they are so ephemeral that any time spent on them is time squandered. Your intelligent newspaper will know the way you feel and behave accordingly.

It will know because you will have trained it yourself. In a none-too-arduous process, you will have informed your intelligent newsgathering system about the topics that are of special interest to you. Editorial decisions will be made by you, and your system will be able to act upon them thereafter. It will have hundreds, perhaps thousands, of competing news sources to choose from, and it will understand (because you have told it) which news sources you trust most, which dissenting opinions you wish to be exposed to, and when not to bother you at all.

You could let your intelligent system infer your interests indirectly by watching you as you browse. What makes you laugh? It will remember and gather bits of fantasia to amuse you. What makes you steam? It may gather information about that, too, and then give you names of groups that are organized for or against that particular outrage. What's going on in the neighborhood? You'll be happy to know the crime rate is down over this time last year (or unhappy to know it's up); that Mr. and Mrs. Morton in the next block have just had a baby girl named Joanna and thank everybody for their interest. You can even program in some randomness: surprise me every now and then, you can say to your intelligent newsgatherer, and your trivia file will grow apace.

KIPS AT HOME

Although expert systems will probably be developed for businesses first, home applications will probably not be far behind. Home video games and computers are simply precursors of much more sophisticated systems that might offer advice on everything from nutrition and tax computation to exercise and legal questions. An electronic, interactive Dr. Spock might assist parents even more effectively than the printed Dr. Spock has for decades.

Expert systems might advise on any number of other tasks: talking you through the job of fixing a leaky toilet—not the model toilet that appears in the fix-it books but is always just different enough from yours to be almost useless, but your toilet—step by step. Or your automobile, or your home computer. How about the gardening coach you can carry through the vegetable patch, discussing proper fertilizers, weather patterns, pest control, and the pleasures of dirt under your fingernails? How about an intelligent dictionary or, better, an intelligent encyclopedia? All yours, all solving problems you want to solve at the moment, and not some abstract, generalized problem that might or might not have bearing on your situation.

All very unexceptional, McCorduck thinks, just the sort of predictions that have been floating around the field for years, firmly grounded in what certainly, in principle, can be done and probably will be. She has other desires and is therefore gratified to read that one purpose of the Japanese Fifth Generation is to alleviate the problems of aging. She exults. For years she's been nagging for, promoting, advocating the geriatric robot. She'd all but lost hope, watching her friends in AI create intelligent physician-machines, intelligent geologist-machines, even intelligent military-spy-machines, but never anything down-home useful. Time is getting on. The geriatric robot might soon be a matter of immediate personal concern.

The geriatric robot is wonderful. It isn't hanging about in the hopes of inheriting your money—nor of course will it slip you a little something to speed the inevitable. It isn't hanging about because it can't find work elsewhere. It's there because it's yours. It doesn't just bathe you and feed you and wheel you out into the sun when you crave fresh air and a change of scene, though of course it does all those things. The very best thing about the geriatric robot is that it *listens*. "Tell me again," it says, "about how wonderful/dreadful your children are to you. Tell me again that fascinating tale of the coup of '63. Tell me again . . ." And it means it. It never gets tired of hearing those stories, just as you never get tired of telling them. It knows your favorites, and those are its favorites too. Never mind that this all ought to be done by human caretakers; humans grow bored, get greedy, want variety. It's part of our charm.

MEANING

1. What is the value of an expert system, programmed to make logical inferences from a specific knowledge base, which could provide the same kind of skilled advice one might get from a professional?
2. Why is the ability to make inferences the most important feature of expert systems or artificial-intelligence (AI) programs?
3. How do the examples offered by Feigenbaum and McCorduck clarify possible future applications of AI systems?

Using Exemplification to Convey Meaning

1. Which examples dramatize most effectively the capabilities of AI systems in providing helpful information and advice?
2. Which examples illustrate the importance of an expert system's ability to continue asking questions until it identifies what the questioner really wants to know?
3. Taken together, how well do the authors' examples reveal, in a clear and unambiguous way, the nature of artificial intelligence?

Writing Suggestions

1. How do data bases (see page 189) differ significantly from the various knowledge bases and AI systems described by Feigenbaum and McCorduck?
2. Discuss other applications where an expert system might be of potential value (e.g., medical diagnostic programs might substitute in situations where doctors are not available).
3. Discuss the advantages and disadvantages of having a computer "teacher" rather than a human one for a specific field of interest such as biology, accounting, or American literature.

Konrad Lorenz

The Dove and the Wolf

Konrad Lorenz, born in 1903 in Vienna, Austria, was a joint recipient of the 1973 Nobel Prize for Physiology. He is considered an outstanding naturalist and zoologist and the father of the science of ethology, which he founded along with Niko Tinbergen in the late 1930s to study animal behavior under natural conditions. Lorenz's pioneering investigation of instinctive behavior of animals in the wild has disclosed profound connections between animal instincts and behavior patterns, with wide-ranging implications for man. The results of Lorenz's research have appeared in King Solomon's Ring *(1949),* Man Meets Dog *(1950),* Evolution and the Modification of Behavior *(1961), and his most widely known work,* King Solomon's Ring *(1952) a far-reaching investigation of the instinct of aggression in a range of species. "The Dove and the Wolf," from* On Aggression, *presents startling examples of aggressive instincts that discredit the traditional views of two species, doves and wolves.*

It is early one Sunday morning at the beginning of March, when Easter is already in the air, and we are taking a walk in the Vienna forest whose wooded slopes of tall beeches can be equalled in beauty by few and surpassed by none. We approach a forest glade. The tall smooth trunks of the beeches soon give place to the Hornbeam which are clothed from top to bottom with pale green foliage. We now tread slowly and more carefully. Before we break through the last bushes and out of cover on to the free expanse of the meadow, we do what all wild animals and all good naturalists, wild boars, leopards, hunters and zoologists would do under similar circumstances: we reconnoitre, seeking, before we leave our cover, to gain from it the advantage which it can offer alike to hunter and hunted, namely, to see without being seen.

Here, too, this age-old strategy proves beneficial. We do actually see someone who is not yet aware of our presence, as the wind is blowing away from him in our direction: in the middle of the clearing sits a large fat hare. He is sitting with his back to us, making a big V with his ears, and is watching intently something on the opposite edge of the meadow. From this point, a second and equally large hare emerges and with slow dignified hops, makes his way towards the first one. There follows a measured encounter, not unlike the meeting of two strange dogs. This cautious mutual taking stock soon develops into sparring. The two hares chase each other round, head to tail, in minute circles. This giddy rotating continues for quite a long time. Then suddenly, their pent-up energies burst forth into a battle royal. It is just like the outbreak of war, and happens at the very moment when the long mutual threatening of the hostile parties has forced one to the conclusion that neither dares to make a definite move. Facing each other, the hares rear up on their hind legs and, straining to their full height, drum furiously at each other with their fore pads. Now they clash in flying leaps and, at last, to the accompaniment of squeals and grunts, they discharge a volley of lightning kicks, so rapidly that only a slow motion camera could help us to discern the mechanism of these hostilities. Now, for the time being, they have had enough, and they recommence their circling, this time much faster than before; then follows a fresh, more embittered bout. So engrossed are the two champions, that there is nothing to prevent myself and my little daughter from tiptoeing nearer, although that venture cannot be accomplished in silence. Any normal and sensible hare would have heard us long ago, but this is March and March Hares are mad! The whole boxing match looks so comical that my little daughter, in spite of her iron upbringing in the matter of silence when watching animals, cannot restrain a chuckle. That is too much even for March Hares—two flashes in two different directions and the meadow is empty, while over the battlefield floats a fistful of fluff, light as a thistledown.

It is not only funny, it is almost touching, this duel of the unarmed, this raging fury of the meek in heart. But are these creatures really so meek? Have they really got softer hearts than those of the fierce beasts of prey? If, in a zoo, you ever watched two lions, wolves or eagles in conflict, then, in all probability, you did not feel like laughing. And yet, these sovereigns come off no worse than the harmless hares. Most people have the habit of judging carnivorous and herbivorous animals by quite inapplicable moral criteria. Even in fairy-tales, animals are portrayed as being a community comparable to that of mankind, as though all species of animals were beings of one and the same family, as human beings are. For this reason, the average person tends to regard the animal that kills animals in the same light as he would the man that kills his own kind. He does not judge the fox that kills a hare by the same standard as the hunter who shoots one for precisely the same reason, but with that severe censure that he would apply to the gamekeeper who made a practice of shooting farmers and frying them for supper! The "wicked" beast of prey is branded as a murderer, although the fox's hunting is quite as legitimate and a great deal more necessary to his existence than is that of the gamekeeper, yet nobody regards the latter's "bag" as his prey, and only one author, whose own standards were indicted by the severest moral criticism, has dared to dub the fox-hunter "the unspeakable in pursuit of the uneatable"! In their dealing with members of their own species, the beasts and birds of prey are far more restrained than many of the "harmless" vegetarians.

Still more harmless than a battle of hares appears the fight between turtle- or ring-doves. The gentle pecking of the frail bill, the light flick of the fragile wing seems, to the uninitiated, more like a caress than an attack. Some time ago I decided to breed a cross between the African blond ring-dove and our own indigenous somewhat frailer turtle-dove, and, with this object, I put a tame, home-reared male turtle-dove and a female ring-dove together in a roomy cage. I did not take their original scrapping seriously. How could these paragons of love and virtue dream of harming one another? I left them in their cage and went to Vienna. When I returned, the next day, a horrible sight met my eyes. The turtle-dove lay on the floor of the cage; the top of his head and neck, as also the whole length of his back, were not only plucked bare of feathers, but so frayed as to form a single wound dripping with blood. In the middle of this gory surface, like an eagle on his prey, stood the second harbinger of peace. Wearing that dreamy facial expression that so appeals to our sentimental observer, this charming lady pecked mercilessly with her silver bill in the wounds of her prostrated mate. When the latter gathered his last resources in a final effort to escape, she set on him again, struck him to the floor with a light clap of her wing and continued with her slow pitiless work of destruction. Without my interference she would undoubtedly have finished him off, in spite of the fact that she was already so tired that she could hardly keep her eyes open. Only in two other instances have I seen similar horrible lacerations inflicted on their own kind by vertebrates: once, as an observer of the embittered fights of cichlid fishes who sometimes actually skin each other, and again as a field surgeon, in the late war, where the highest of all vertebrates perpetrated mass mutilations on members of his own species. But to return to our "harmless" vegetarians. The battle of the hares which we witnessed in the forest clearing would have ended in quite as horrible a carnage as that of the doves, had it taken place in the confines of a cage where the vanquished could not flee the victor.

If this is the extent of the injuries meted out to their own kind by our gentle doves and hares, how much greater must be the havoc wrought amongst themselves by those beasts to whom nature has relegated the strongest weapons with which to kill their prey? One would certainly think so, were it not that a good naturalist should always check by observation even the most obvious-seeming inferences before he accepts them as truth. Let us examine that symbol of cruelty and voraciousness, the wolf. How do these creatures conduct themselves in their dealings with members of their own species? At Whipsnade, that zoological country paradise, there lives a pack of timber wolves. From the fence of a pine-wood of enviable dimensions we can watch their daily round in an environment not so very far removed from conditions of real freedom. To begin with, we wonder why the antics of the many woolly, fat-pawed whelps have not led them to destruction long ago. The efforts of one ungainly little chap to break into a gallop have landed him in a very different situation from that which he intended. He stumbles and bumps heavily into a wicked-looking old sinner. Strangely enough, the latter does not seem to notice it, he does not even growl. But now we hear the rumble of battle sounds! They are low, but more ominous than those of a dog-fight. We are watching the whelps and have therefore only become aware of this adult fight now that it is already in full swing.

An enormous old timber wolf and a rather weaker, obviously younger one are the opposing champions and they are moving in circles round each other, exhibiting admirable "footwork." At the same time, the bared fangs flash in such a rapid exchange of snaps that the eye can scarcely follow them. So far, nothing has really happened. The jaws of one wolf close on the gleaming white teeth of the other who is on the alert and wards off the attack. Only the lips have received one or two minor injuries. The younger wolf is gradually being forced backwards. It dawns upon us that the older one is purposely manouvering him towards the fence. We wait with breathless anticipation what will happen when he "goes to the wall." Now he strikes the wire netting, stumbles . . . and the old one is upon him. And now the incredible happens, just the opposite of what you would expect. The furious whirling of the grey bodies has come to a sudden standstill. Shoulder to shoulder they stand, pressed against each other in a stiff and strained attitude, both heads now facing in the same direction. Both wolves are growling angrily, the elder in a deep bass, the younger in higher tones, suggestive of the fear that underlies his threat. But notice carefully the position of the two opponents; the older wolf has his muzzle close, very close against the neck of the younger, and the latter holds away his head, offering unprotected to his enemy the bend of his neck, the most vulnerable part of his whole body! Less than an inch from the tensed neck-muscles, where the jugular vein lies immediately beneath the skin, gleam the fangs of his antagonist from beneath the wickedly retracted lips. Whereas, during the thick of the fight, both wolves were intent on keeping only their teeth, the one invulnerable part of the body, in opposition to each other, it now appears that the discomfited fighter proffers intentionally that part of his anatomy to which a bite must assuredly prove fatal. Appearances are notoriously deceptive, but in his case, surprisingly, they are not!

This same scene can be watched any time wherever street-mongrels are to be found. I cited wolves as my first example because they illustrate my point more impressively than the all-too familiar domestic dog. Two adult male dogs meet in the street. Stiff-legged, with tails erect and hair on end, they pace towards each other. The nearer they approach, the stiffer, higher and more ruffled they appear, their advance becomes slower and slower. Unlike fighting cocks they do not make their encounter head to head, front against front, but make as though to pass each other, only stopping when they stand at last flank to flank, head to tail, in close juxtaposition. Then a strict ceremonial demands that each should sniff the hind regions of the other. Should one of the dogs be overcome with fear at this juncture, down goes his tail between his legs and he jumps with a quick, flexible twist, wheeling at an angle of 180 degrees thus modestly retracting his former offer to be smelt. Should the two dogs remain in an attitude of self-display, carrying their tails as rigid as standards, then the sniffing process may be of a long protracted nature. All may be solved amicably and there is still the chance that first one tail and then the other may begin to wag with small but rapidly increasing beats and then this nerve-racking situation may develop into nothing worse than a cheerful canine romp. Failing this solution the situation becomes more and more tense, noses begin to wrinkle and to turn up with a vile, brutal expression, lips begin to curl, exposing the fangs on the side nearer the opponent. Then the animals scratch the earth angrily with their hind feet, deep growls rise from their chests, and, in the next moment, they fall upon each other with loud piercing yells.

But to return to our wolves, whom we left in a situation of acute tension. This was not a piece of inartistic narrative on my part, since the strained situation may continue for a great length of time which is minutes to the observer, but very probably seems hours to the losing wolf. Every second you expect violence and await with bated breath the moment when the winner's teeth will rip the jugular vein of the loser. But your fears are groundless, for it will not happen. In this particular situation, the victor will definitely not close on his less fortunate rival. You can see that he would like to, but he just cannot! A dog or wolf that offers its neck to its adversary in this way will never be bitten seriously. The other growls and grumbles, snaps with his teeth in the empty air and even carries out, without delivering so much as a bite, the movement of shaking something to death in the empty air. However, this strange inhibition from biting persists only so long as the defeated dog or wolf maintains his attitude of humility. Since the fight is stopped so suddenly by this action, the victor frequently finds himself straddling his vanquished foe in anything but a comfortable position. So to remain, with his muzzle applied to the neck of the "under-dog" soon becomes tedious for the champion, and, seeing that he cannot bite anyway, he soon withdraws. Upon this, the under-dog may hastily attempt to put distance between himself and his superior. But he is not usually successful in this, for, as soon as he abandons his rigid attitude of submission, the other again falls upon him like a thunderbolt and the victim must again freeze into his former posture. It seems as if the victor is only waiting for the moment when the other will relinquish his submissive attitude, thereby enabling him to give vent to his urgent desire to bite. But, luckily for the "under-dog," the top-dog at the close of the fight is overcome by the pressing need to leave his trade-mark on the battlefield, to designate it as his personal property—in other words, he must lift his leg against the nearest upright object. This right-of-possession ceremony is usually taken advantage of by the under-dog to make himself scarce.

By this commonplace observation, we are here, as so often, made conscious of a problem which is actual in our daily life and which confronts us on all sides in the most various forms. Social inhibitions of this kind are not rare, but so frequent that we take them for granted and do not stop to think about them. An old German proverb says that one crow will not peck out the eye of another and for once the proverb is right. A tame crow or raven will no more think of pecking at your eye than he will at that of one of his own kind. Often when Roah, my tame raven, was sitting on my arm, I purposely put my face so near to his bill that my open eye came close to its wickedly curved point. Then Roah did something positively touching. With a nervous, worried movement he withdrew his beak from my eye, just as a father who is shaving will hold back his razor blade from the inquisitive fingers of his tiny daughter. Only in one particular connection did Roah ever approach my eye with his bill during this facial grooming. Many of the higher, social birds and mammals, above all monkeys, will groom the skin of a fellow-member of their species in those parts of his body to which he himself cannot obtain access. In birds, it is particularly the head and the region of the eyes which are dependent on the attentions of a fellow. In my description of the jackdaw, I have already spoken of the gestures with which these birds invite one another to preen their head feathers. When, with half-shut eyes, I held my head sideways towards Roah, just as corvine birds do to each other, he understood this movement in spite of the fact that I have no head feathers to ruffle, and at once began to groom me. While doing so, he never pinched my skin, for the epidermis of birds is delicate and would not stand such rough treatment. With wonderful precision, he submitted every attainable hair to a dry-cleaning process by drawing it separately through his bill. He worked with the same intensive concentration that distinguishes the "lousing" monkey and the operating surgeon. This is not meant as a joke: the social grooming of monkeys, and particularly of anthropoid apes has not the object of catching vermin—these animals usually have none—and is not limited to the cleaning of the skin, but serves also more remarkable operations, for instance the dexterous removal of thorns and even the squeezing-out of small carbuncles.

The manipulations of the dangerous-looking corvine beak round the open eye of a man naturally appear ominous and, of course, I was always receiving warnings from onlookers at this procedure. "You never know—a raven is a raven—" and similar words of wisdom. I used to respond with the paradoxical observation that the warner was for me potentially more dangerous than the raven. It has often happened that people have been shot dead by madmen who have masked their condition with the cunning and pretence typical of such cases. There was always a possibility, though admittedly a very small one, that our kind adviser might be afflicted with such a disease. But a sudden and unpredictable loss of the eye-pecking inhibition in a healthy, mature raven is more unlikely by far than an attack by a well-meaning friend.

Why has the dog the inhibition against biting his fellow's neck? Why has the raven an inhibition against pecking the eye of his friend? Why has the ring-dove no such "insurance" against murder? A really comprehensive answer to these questions is almost impossible. It would certainly involve a *historical* explanation of the process by which these inhibitions have been developed in the course of evolution. There is no doubt that they have arisen side by side with the development of the dangerous weapons of the beast of prey. However, it is perfectly obvious why these inhibitions are necessary to all weapon-bearing animals. Should the raven peck, without compunction, at the eye of his nest-mate, his wife or his young, in the same way as he pecks at any other moving and glittering object, there would, by now, be no more ravens in the world. Should a dog or wolf unrestrainedly and unaccountably bite the neck of his packmates and actually execute the movement of shaking them to death, then his species also would certainly be exterminated within a short space of time.

The ring-dove does not require such an inhibition since it can only inflict injury to a much lesser degree, while its ability to flee is so well developed that it suffices to protect the bird even against enemies equipped with vastly better weapons. Only under the unnatural conditions of close confinement which deprive the losing dove of the possibility of flight does it become apparent that the ring-dove has no inhibitions which prevent it from injuring or even torturing its own kind. Many other "harmless" herbivores prove themselves just as unscrupulous when they are kept in narrow captivity. One of the most disgusting, ruthless and blood-thirsty murderers is an animal which is generally considered as being second only to the dove in the proverbial gentleness of its nature, namely the roe-deer. The roe-buck is about the most malevolent beast I know and is possessed, into the bargain, of a weapon, its antlers, which it shows mighty little restraint in putting into use. The species can "afford" this lack of control since the fleeing capacity even of the weakest doe is enough to deliver it from the strongest buck. Only in very large paddocks can the roe-buck be kept with females of his own kind. In smaller enclosures, sooner or later he will drive his fellows, females and young ones included, into a corner and gore them to death. The only "insurance against murder" which the roe-deer possesses, is based on the fact that the onslaught of the attacking buck proceeds relatively slowly. He does not rush with lowered head at his adversary as, for example, a ram would do, but he approaches quite slowly, cautiously feeling with his antlers for those of his opponent. Only when the antlers are interlocked and the buck feels firm resistance does he thrust with deadly earnest. According to the statistics given by W. T. Hornaday, the former director of the New York Zoo, tame deer cause yearly more serious accidents than captive lions and tigers, chiefly because an uninitiated person does not recognize the slow approach of the buck as an earnest attack, even when the animal's antlers have come dangerously near. Suddenly there follows, thrust upon thrust, the amazingly strong stabbing movement of the sharp weapon, and you will be lucky if you have time enough to get a good grip on the aggressor's antlers. Now there follows a wrestling-match in which the sweat pours and the hands drip blood, and in which even a very strong man can hardly obtain mastery over the roe-buck unless he succeeds in getting to the side of the beast and bending his neck backwards. Of course, one is ashamed to call for help—until one has the point of an antler in one's body! So take my advice and if a charming, tame roe-buck comes playfully towards you, with a characteristic prancing step and flourishing his antlers gracefully, hit him, with your walking stick, a stone or the bare fist, as hard as you can, on the side of his nose, before he can apply his antlers to your person.

And now, honestly judged: who is really a "good" animal, my friend Roah to whose social inhibitions I could trust the light of my eyes, or the gentle ring-dove that in hours of hard work nearly succeeded in torturing its mate to death? Who is

a "wicked" animal, the roe-buck who will slit the bellies even of females and young
of his own kind if they are unable to escape him, or the wolf who cannot bite his
hated enemy if the latter appeals to his mercy?

Now let us turn our mind to another question. Wherein consists the essence of
all the gestures of submission by which a bird or animal of a social species can
appeal to the inhibitions of its superior? We have just seen, in the wolf, that the
defeated animal actually facilitates his own destruction by offering to the victor those
very parts of his body which he was most anxious to shield as long as the battle was
raging. All submissive attitudes with which we are so far familiar, in social animals,
are based on the same principle: The supplicant always offers to his adversary the
most vulnerable part of his body, or, to be more exact, that part *against which every
killing attack is inevitably directed!* In most birds, this area is the base of the skull.
If one jackdaw wants to show submission to another, he squats back on his hocks,
turns away his head, at the same time drawing in his bill to make the nape of his
neck bulge, and, leaning towards his superior, seems to invite him to peck at the
fatal spot. Seagulls and herons present to their superior the top of their head, stretching
their neck forward horizontally, low over the ground, also a position which makes
the supplicant particularly defenceless.

With many gallinaceous birds, the fights of the males commonly end by one of
the combatants being thrown to the ground, held down and then scalped as in the
manner described in the ring-dove. Only one species shows mercy in this case, namely
the turkey: and this one only does so in response to a specific submissive gesture
which serves to forestall the intent of the attack. If a turkey-cock has had more than
his share of the wild and grotesque wrestling-match in which these birds indulge,
he lays himself with outstretched neck upon the ground. Whereupon the victor behaves
exactly as a wolf or dog in the same situation, that is to say, he evidently *wants* to
peck and kick at the prostrated enemy, but simply cannot: he would if he could but
he can't! So, still in threatening attitude, he walks around and around his prostrated
rival, making tentative passes at him, but leaving him untouched.

This reaction—though certainly propitious for the turkey species—can cause a
tragedy if a turkey comes to blows with a peacock, a thing which not infrequently
happens in captivity, since these species are closely enough related to "appreciate"
respectively their mutual manifestations of virility. In spite of greater strength and
weight the turkey nearly always loses the match, for the peacock flies better and has
a different fighting technique. While the red-brown American is muscling himself
up for the wrestling-match, the blue East-Indian has already flown above him and
struck at him with his sharply pointed spurs. The turkey justifiably considers this
infringement of his fighting code as unfair and, although he is still in possession of
his full strength, he throws in the sponge and lays himself down in the above depicted
manner now. And a ghastly thing happens: the peacock does not "understand" this
submissive gesture of the turkey, that is to say, it elicits no inhibition of his fighting
drives. He pecks and kicks further at the helpless turkey, who, if nobody comes to
his rescue, is doomed, for the more pecks and blows he receives, the more certainly
are his escape reactions blocked by the psycho-physiological mechanism of the submissive attitude. It does not and cannot occur to him to jump up and run away.

The fact that many birds have developed special "signal organs" for eliciting this
type of social inhibition, shows convincingly the blind instinctive nature and the
great evolutionary age of these submissive gestures. The young of the water-rail, for
example, have a bare red patch at the back of their head which, as they present it

meaningly to an older and stronger fellow, takes on a deep red colour. Whether, in higher animals and man, social inhibitions of this kind are equally mechanical, need not for the moment enter into our consideration. Whatever may be the reasons that prevent the dominant individual from injuring the submissive one, whether he is prevented from doing so by a simple and purely mechanical reflex process or by a highly philosophical moral standard, is immaterial to the practical issue. The essential behaviour of the submissive as well as of the dominant partner remains the same: the humbled creature suddenly seems to lose his objections to being injured and removes all obstacles from the path of the killer, and it would seem that the very removal of these outer obstacles raises an insurmountable inner obstruction in the central nervous system of the aggressor.

And what is a human appeal for mercy after all? Is it so very different from what we have just described? The Homeric warrior who wishes to yield and plead mercy, discards helmet and shield, falls on his knees and inclines his head, a set of actions which should make it easier for the enemy to kill, but, in reality, hinders him from doing so. As Shakespeare makes Nestor say to Hector:

> "Thou hast hung thy advanced sword i' the air,
> Not letting it decline on the declined."

Even to-day, we have retained many symbols of such submissive attitudes in a number of our gestures of courtesy: bowing, removal of the hat, and presenting arms in military ceremonial. If we are to believe the ancient epics, an appeal to mercy does not seem to have raised an "inner obstruction" which was entirely insurmountable. Homer's heroes were certainly not as soft-hearted as the wolves of Whipsnade! In any case, the poet cites numerous instances where the supplicant was slaughtered with or without compunction. The Norse heroic sagas bring us many examples of similar failures of the submissive gesture and it was not till the era of knight-errantry that it was no longer considered "sporting" to kill a man who begged for mercy. The Christian knight is the first who, for reasons of traditional and religious morals, is as chivalrous as is the wolf from the depth of his natural impulses and inhibitions. What a strange paradox!

Of course, the innate, instinctive, fixed inhibitions that prevent an animal from using his weapons indiscriminately against his own kind are only a functional analogy, at the most a slight foreshadowing, a genealogical predecessor of the social morals of man. The worker in comparative ethology does well to be very careful in applying moral criteria to animal behaviour. But here, I must myself own to harbouring sentimental feelings: I think it a truly magnificent thing that one wolf finds himself unable to bite the proffered neck of the other, but still more so that the other relies upon him for his amazing restraint. Mankind can learn a lesson from this, from the animal that Dante calls "la bestia senza pace."[1] I at least have extracted from it a new and deeper understanding of a wonderful and often misunderstood saying from the Gospel which hitherto had only awakened in me feelings of strong opposition: "And unto him that smiteth thee on the one cheek offer also the other" (St. Luke VI, 26). A wolf has enlightened me: not so that your enemy may strike you again do you turn the other cheek toward him, but to make him unable to do it.

When, in the course of its evolution, a species of animals develops a weapon which may destroy a fellow-member at one blow, then, in order to survive, it must

[1] The first Canto of Dante's *Inferno* represents a she-wolf, "the beast who cannot be placated."

develop, along with the weapon, a social inhibition to prevent a usage which could endanger the existence of the species. Among the predatory animals, there are only a few which lead so solitary a life that they can, in general, forego such restraint. They come together only at the mating season when the sexual impulse outweighs all others, including that of aggression. Such unsociable hermits are the polar bear and the jaguar and, owing to the absence of these social inhibitions, animals of these species, when kept together in Zoos, hold a sorry record for murdering their own kind. The system of special inherited impulses and inhibitions, together with the weapons with which a social species is provided by nature, form a complex which is carefully computed and self-regulating. All living beings have received their weapons through the same process of evolution that moulded their impulses and inhibitions; for the structural plan of the body and the system of behavior of a species are parts of the same whole.

> "If such a Nature's holy plan,
> Have I not reason to lament
> What man has made of man?"

Wordsworth is right: there is only one being in possession of weapons which do not grow on his body and of whose working plan, therefore, the instincts of his species know nothing and in the usage of which he has no correspondingly adequate inhibition. That being is man. With unarrested growth his weapons increase in monstrousness, multiplying horribly within a few decades. But innate impulses and inhibitions, like bodily structures, need time for their development, time on a scale in which geologists and astronomers are accustomed to calculate, and not historians. We did not receive our weapons from nature. We made them ourselves, of our own free will. Which is going to be easier for us in the future, the production of the weapons or the engendering of the feeling of responsibility that should go along with them, the inhibitions without which our race must perish by virtue of its own creations? We must build up these inhibitions purposefully for we cannot rely upon our instincts. Fourteen years ago, in November 1935, I concluded an article on "Morals and Weapons of Animals" which appeared in a Viennese journal, with the words, "The day will come when two warring factions will be faced with the possibility of each wiping the other out completely. The day may come when the whole of mankind is divided into two such opposing camps. Shall we then behave like doves or like wolves? The fate of mankind will be settled by the answer to this question." We may well be apprehensive.

Meaning

1. What discoveries did Lorenz make that refute popular misconceptions regarding the supposed meekness of doves, deer, and hares and the seeming viciousness of wolves?
2. What innate inhibitions did Lorenz discover in his pet raven?
3. Why are some species restrained by innate inhibitions against killing a defeated rival within their own species?
4. In battles between timber wolves, what role do "gestures of submission" play in triggering inhibitions against their killing each other?

5. Why are encounters between a turkey-cock and peacock so often fatal for the turkey?
6. To what degree does Lorenz believe that law, religion, and moral codes are adaptive replacements meant to serve the same purpose in man as innate inhibitions do in other species?

Using Exemplification to Convey Meaning

1. What specific features of wolves does Lorenz describe to illustrate an innate inhibition against killing that is generic to many species?
2. How does the episode of the "dueling hares" make the point that popular legends and folklore can often be wrong?
3. How does Lorenz organize his essay to place his discussion of the domestic dogs' behavior in the context of his research on timber wolves?

Writing Suggestions

1. Investigate which commonplace gestures—for example, bowing and hand-shaking— have their origin in "submission gestures" designed to protect the potential combatants.
2. What existing legal, moral, or religious codes are adequate in a nuclear age to protect man from himself in the same way that innate inhibitions against killing defeated rivals protect other species?

COMPARISON AND CONTRAST

While the poet might extol the virtues of his lady love as being "beyond compare" and an enthusiastic football fan might say the same of her team, most things can be compared. Two fishermen trying to decide whether a fish they have caught is a "small-mouth" or a "largemouth" bass, or the same fishermen arguing over which kind of fish is tastier, are using the intellectual strategy of comparison and contrast.

Physiologists compare heart functions in individuals of different ages, musicologists study Mozart's use of the same melody in different compositions, biochemists contrast molecular structures of compounds before and after gene splicing, meteorologists compare and contrast barometric pressures in different regions to spot hurricanes, and political scientists use this basic method to explain similarities and differences between the popular vote and the electoral vote.

In "William L. Haney and Jan van Eyck," Alan Wallach, an art historian, discloses surprising points of coincidence, in both subjects and methods, in the work of William L. Haney, a twentieth-century painter, and Jan van Eyck, a fifteenth-century artist. The comparison is illuminating because it shows how both Haney and van Eyck portrayed the newly emerging materialism in their respective cultures. Wallach identifies the features that both Haney and van Eyck share as artists and then uses these points of comparison to organize his essay:

> There are several other points at which Haney and van Eyck intersect. Both produce densely packed images that demand close study. Both employ "submerged symbolism." Both claim painting's superiority to other contemporary art forms. (Van Eyck made this point by featuring architecture and trompel 'oeil sculpture in his compositions. Haney is similarly fascinated with television. . .) . Finally, Haney, who allies himself with the surrealist strain in early modernism, paints with something of van Eyck's fervor and hallucinatory intensity.

Here the comparative method works to reveal far more about the distinctive nature of each artist than could have been shown by separate analyses. Wallach uses a point-by-point comparison to create a continual contrast—from paragraph to paragraph and from sentence to sentence—between the subject matters and techniques of two painters separated by five hundred years.

Another way of arranging a discussion of similarities and differences relies on a subject-by-subject comparison. Using this method, the writer balances a list of relevant points on one side with those on the other. Aristotle uses this subject-by-subject method in "Youth and Old Age" to present a philosophical analysis of the differences between the young and the old. He first discusses the motives and behavior of the young:

> Their lives are mainly spent not in memory but in expectation; for expectation refers to the future, memory to the past, and youth has a long future before it and a short past behind it: on the first day of one's life one has nothing at all to remember, and can only look forward. . . .

Following his discussion of the young, Aristotle retraces the same points as they apply to the old:

> They live by memory rather than by hope; for what is left to them of life is but little as compared with the long past; and hope is of the future, memory of the past. This, again, is the cause of their loquacity; they are continally talking of the past, because they enjoy remembering it. . . .

The comparative method serves Aristotle well as a way of getting his audience to perceive the basic differences between the young and the old, and to understand why people of different ages perceive the world in such diverse ways. However, we should keep in mind that the same phenomenon will become a different object of inquiry according to the framework within which it is studied. For example, a medical researcher might compare the old and the young according to physiological differences of muscle tone, reaction time, hormonal balances, or other physical criteria.

Comparisons, whether arranged point-by-point or subject-by-subject, may be employed to (1) provide insight into the subjects being compared (as we shall see in the selections by Wallach and Aristotle) or (2) evaluate two subjects in order to decide which one is better. In an evaluative comparison, the writer lists the positive and negative qualities of each side, and then decides between the two based on some stipulated criteria. Richard Rodriguez does this in "On Becoming a Chicano" when he compares the Mexican-American culture of his childhood with the cloistered atmosphere of academic studies:

> So much of what my work in the British Museum lacked, my parents' culture possessed. They were people not afraid to generalize or to find insights in their generalities. Most important, they had the capacity to make passionate statements, something I was beginning to doubt my dissertation would ever allow me to do. I needed to learn how to trust the use of "I" in my writing the way they trusted its use in their speech. Thus developed a persistent yearning for the very Chicano culture that I had abandoned as useless.

Based on a comparison of the qualities of each "world," Rodriguez decides that he has indeed lost a sense of self-confidence by moving from the open Mexican-American culture of his childhood into the self-critical atmosphere of the academic world.

Dramatic contrast is a favorite device of satirists who expose hypocrisy by reminding people of what they really do, as opposed to what they profess. In "The Lowest Animal," Mark Twain contrasts the behavior of humans with that of animals in comparable situations in order to deflate the high opinion the human species has of itself. Each of Twain's "experiments" is meant to show the preponderance in man of such traits as greed and cruelty, and to parody Darwin's theory (then currently popular) that man was the apex of all living species.

Although Twain's "experiments" are hypothetical and meant to underscore ironic insights, the comparative technique is indispensable as a way of structuring real scientific experiments. Such is the case in a fascinating study, reported by Constance Holden in "Identical Twins Reared Apart" which followed nine sets of identical twins who were separated at birth, raised in different environments, and then reunited. Holden reports that when one of the sets of twins, Oskar and Jack, first saw each other:

> Similarities started cropping up as soon as Oskar arrived at the airport. Both were wearing wire-rimmed glasses and mustaches, both sported two-pocket shirts with epaulets. They shared idiosyncrasies galore: they like spicy foods and sweet liqueurs, are absentminded, have a habit of falling asleep in front of the television, think it's funny to sneeze in a crowd of strangers, flush the toilet before using it, store rubber bands on their wrists, read magazines from back to front, dip buttered toast in their coffee. Oskar is domineering toward women and yells at his wife, which Jack did before he was separated. . . . Although the two were raised in different cultures and speak different languages . . . the two supply "devastating" evidence against the feminist contention that children's personalities are shaped differently according to the sex of those who rear them, since Oskar was raised by women and Jack by men.

Holden's analysis of different characteristics and traits is developed through a point-by-point comparison of striking similarities in behavior between each of the nine sets of twins. For Holden, the number and range of similarities shared by each set of twins argues for the overwhelming importance of heredity, rather than environment, in shaping human behavior.

The scientific experiment reported by Holden is based on an equal comparison of both sides. Yet, writers frequently develop one side of a comparison more completely than the other, particularly when their audience is already familiar with one of the subjects. Phyllis McGinley, for example, is mainly interested in how children differ from adults in their attitudes toward material goods, discovering new things, and reading habits in "Are Children People?" McGinley knows her readers are chiefly interested in the unique traits that make children a species unto themselves and arranges her essay proportionately to fulfill her audience's expectations.

So too, Ruth Benedict, in her classic study comparing the Zuñi, a Pueblo tribe, with the Plains Indians, provides a fuller treatment of the unusual, unegotistical cultural values of the Zuñi than she does of the more familiar, power-seeking rituals of the Plains Indians:

> His [the Plains Indian warrior's] deeds of prowess were counted for him personally, and it was his prerogative to boast of them on ritual occasions, and to use them in every way to further his personal ambitions.
>
> The ideal man of the Pueblos is another order of being. Personal authority is

perhaps the most vigorously disparaged trait in Zuñi. "A man who thirsts for power or knowledge, who wishes to be as they scornfully phrase it 'a leader of his people,' receives nothing but censure and will very likely be persecuted for sorcery," and he often has been. . . .

Benedict's comparison effectively discloses significant differences between these two tribes not only in their respective attitudes toward power but in the way they view the use of drugs, sex, torture, visions, and ritual dancing. Just as the strategy of comparing one culture to another is essential to anthropology, other social sciences use comparisons to explain and evaluate different groups and subgroups within a society. In "The Rights of Victims," Sidney Hook compares and contrasts the rights that criminals receive under the law with the corresponding rights of victims:

> No matter how we seek to escape from acknowledging it, there is a direct conflict between the rights of their past and potential victims. In some classes of cases it is clear that the greater the right of the person accused of crime, the less the right of his future victim. For example, the right of a person out on bail for a crime of violence, to receive bail when he is charged with committing the same type of violent offence, and to be granted bail even when he is charged with committing the offence a third time—a right which he legitimately claims since he has not yet been found guilty of the first offence—conflicts head-on with the rights of his victims who can legitimately claim that they suffered this violence because the person at bar enjoyed his constitutional right to be free on bail. . . .

Hook's comparison leads him to conclude that potential victims receive far fewer rights than criminals do under existing law. Hook's evaluation, based on balancing the relative merits of both sides, leads him to conclude that potential victims should be accorded greater rights than they currently receive.

Scientists, too, sometimes move beyond purely neutral comparisons of two subjects to express personal opinions. In "Rats and Men," Hans Zinsser, a bacteriologist, sees many disturbing similarities between rats and men as they complete with each other in the centuries-old struggle for food and space:

> In the first place, like man, the rat has become practically omnivorous. It eats anything that lets it and—like man—devours its own kind, under stress. It breeds at all seasons and—again like man—it is most amorous in the springtime. It hybridizes easily and, judging by the strained relationship between the black and the brown rat, develops social or racial prejudices against this practice. The sex proportions are like those among us. Inbreeding takes place readily. The males are larger, the females fatter. It adapts itself to all kinds of climates. It makes ferocious war upon its own kind, but has not, as yet, become nationalized. So far, it still has stuck to tribal wars—like man before nations were invented. . . .

Since the differences between the two species are so obvious, Zinsser focuses instead on unsuspected specific attributes that both men and rats share. Thought-provoking comparisons can work both ways—to make us aware of dramatic differences between people, ideas, or situations we had casually assumed were quite similar, or to surprise us with hidden resemblances between things that looked quite different.

LIBERAL ARTS

Alan Wallach

William L. Haney and Jan van Eyck

Alan Wallach was born in Brooklyn, New York in 1942 and received his Ph.D. from Columbia in 1973. Wallach has taught at both the University of California at Los Angeles and Stanford University. He is currently a professor of art history at Kean College of New Jersey, and has written many articles on the history of museums and nineteenth- and twentieth-century American art. His writings have appeared in Art Bulletin, Marxist Perspectives, Art History, Art Criticism, *and* ARTS *magazine. These include "The Voyage of Life as Popular Art" (1977), "The Avant-Garde of the Eighties" (1981), and "Thomas Cole and the Aristocracy" (1981). He has coauthored "The Museum of Modern Art as Late Capitalist Ritual" (1978) and "The Universal Survey Museum" (1980). In 1987, Wallach was the recipient of a Smithsonian Senior Post-Doctoral Research Fellowship for work on a book on Thomas Cole's patronage of the Hudson River School of Painting. "William L. Haney and Jan van Eyck," which appeared in* ARTS *(1984), compares the subjects, artistic methods, and underlying philosophy in paintings by William L. Haney, a twentieth-century realist, with the work of Jan van Eyck, a fifteenth-century artist who is credited with beginning the depiction of middle-class materialism in painting.*

The paintings in William L. Haney's recent exhibition treat the following subjects: the New York Stock Exchange, an NBC sound stage, the videotaping of Michael Jackson's "Thriller," women body builders, a C.A.T. scan machine in operation, punks and preppies, a TV commercial being shot at Lincoln Center, President Reagan and his "Star Wars" laser. Haney's style along with his subject matter links him to the tradition of critical realism going back to Courbet. Yet if I were asked what painter Haney most reminded me of, I would not immediately think of a recent realist artist. Instead, I would choose a painter with no direct historical connection to Haney: Jan van Eyck.

At first my choice might seem far-fetched. More than five centuries separate the two artists. They belong to different worlds, different social circumstances. Moreover, their painting methods have little in common. Although a realist, Haney has none of the obsession with textures and minute detail that distinguishes van Eyck's compositions. What then could be the point of comparing the two painters?

Van Eyck marked the beginnings of middle-class materialism in painting. Exploiting the new medium of oil paint, he depicted a world of objects, an objectified world in which the spiritual was for the first time ruthlessly subordinated to the material. Before a van Eyck painting was a Madonna or an Annunciation, it was a catalogue, an inventory of possessions: furs, silks, embroidery, jewelry, vases, carved chairs, canopied beds, tiled floors, Persian rugs, etc.

Van Eyck's paintings epitomized the contradiction the medium of oil paint has imposed on artists ever since the 15th century: the contradiction between the materialism that is inseparable from the oil paint medium and the immaterial ideas and beliefs that motivate artistic creation. For van Eyck the problem was to depict somehow the spirituality that materialism had relegated to the realm of the invisible. As a 20th-century realist, Haney wrestles with a similar difficulty: how to portray the social and political reality that lies below the surface of contemporary life.

In attempting to find a way to picture the invisible, Haney has arrived at a solution comparable to van Eyck's. This is not to say that the terms of the solution are identical. For van Eyck, the invisible could be described by theology; for Haney, the description would probably come from social and economic theory. But in both cases, a similar artistic method is used to achieve insight into an underlying metaphysic.

Erwin Panofsky observed that van Eyck painted "reconstructions of the visible world." This is also true for Haney. In neither case is there any question of the artist representing an actual scene. Both painters create the illusion of a unified composition, but under close inspection the unity almost immediately breaks down and the painting becomes a composite of scenes and details.

In a work like *The Madonna of Canon van der Paele,* van Eyck painted his figures in different perspectives and his composition was pulled together by the architecture surrounding the figures. In Haney's paintings, several different scenes are often brought together with little or no concern for the plausibility of the juxtaposition and, as in van Eyck's painting, it is the architecture which holds the elements of the composition in place. In *C.A.T. Scanner,* the control room in the foreground contains two adjacent windows, one revealing a patient in the C.A.T. scan chamber, the other showing a patient in an emergency unit.

Or consider Haney's *The Root of It All* in which the Gold Ring of the American Stock Exchange, drastically foreshortened and made to resemble a casino gambling table, occupies the foreground of the composition while the view of the New York Stock Exchange interior behind the table is painted in a different perspective. Haney further complicates things by placing near the front of the Gold Ring an anamorphic image of a black man's severed head.

This composite method allows the artist to juxtapose different aspects of his subject, thus demonstrating their relatedness. For example, the severed head in *The Root of It All* makes visible the connections between the abstract and seemingly neutral activity of stock trading and the merciless oppression and exploitation of black (South African?) labor.

Another composite technique Haney shares with van Eyck is the picture-within-a-picture. Van Eyck's *Giovanni Arnolfini and his Bride* contains a convex mirror at the rear of the marriage chamber which reflects in extraordinary detail the couple and the otherwise invisible witnesses to the scene. In *A Present Tense of Extinct Too,*

Haney's painting of a CBS sound stage, five television monitors play a similar role, commenting on the picture and augmenting its meaning with images of the Vietnam war, a 19th-century buffalo hunt, a mushroom cloud, etc.

There are several other points at which Haney and van Eyck intersect. Both produce densely packed images that demand close study. Both employ "submerged symbolism." Both claim painting's superiority to other contemporary art forms. (Van Eyck made this point by featuring architecture and trompel'oeil sculpture in his compositions. Haney is similarly fascinated with television; four of the eight large paintings in his exhibition show videotaping, TV studios, TV cameramen, etc.) Finally, Haney, who allies himself with the surrealist strain in early modernism, paints with something of van Eyck's fervor and hallucinatory intensity.

Yet in the end no comparison can be drawn between Haney's vision and van Eyck's. Van Eyck's paintings take religious faith as their premise: to the problems of this world they bring the solutions of the next. Haney possesses no comparable system of belief. He sets out to grasp the essence of comtemporary reality using contemporary means. Thus his paintings promise no redemption, no resolution to the conflicts they portray. They offer only their insights. The rest, as they say, is up to us.

MEANING

1. What surprisingly similar points of comparison does the art critic, Alan Wallach, disclose between the work of William L. Haney, a twentieth-century painter, and Jan van Eyck, a fifteenth-century artist?
2. How do the subjects and methods in van Eyck's and Haney's paintings reveal their attitudes toward the materialism of their respective societies?
3. How does Haney use unusual associative techniques in his paintings to reveal unsuspected relationships and to comment on the values of modern society?
4. How do multiple composites of individual images create an associative chain in Haney's painting *The Root of It All;* that is, what connections does the "severed head" have with gold, segregation, apartheid, fear, greed, the "Gold Ring" of the American Stock Exchange, and South Africa? What is the significance of the name of this painting?

USING COMPARISON AND CONTRAST TO CONVEY MEANING

1. How does this kind of a comparison differ from one whose purpose is to evaluate which artist's work is better?
2. Why does the comparative method work to reveal far more about the distinctive nature of each artist than might have been disclosed by separate analyses?
3. In what circumstances does Wallach use a point-by-point comparison, rather than a first-one-then-the-other method to compare the subjects and techniques of these two painters who lived five hundred years apart?
4. Why does Wallach devote more of his essay to exploring the similarities rather than the differences between Haney and van Eyck?

WRITING SUGGESTIONS

1. How do multiple composites of individual images create an associative chain in Haney's painting, *A Present Tense of Extinct Too*? How do the composite images of the mushroom cloud, buffalo hunt, and Vietnam express his concerns about modern society? What is the relationship between the subject matter of this painting and its title?

2. Describe the images that Haney might use in a painting of Madonna singing "Material Girl" or of Marilyn Monroe singing "Diamonds Are a Girl's Best Friend."

3. Discuss your favorite painting and compare and contrast it to Haney's work in terms of the subject matter, method, and feelings expressed.

MARK TWAIN

The Lowest Animal

Mark Twain (1835–1910), the pseudonym of Samuel Langhorn Clemens, was brought up in Hannibal, Missouri. After serving as a printer's apprentice, Twain became a steamboat pilot on the Mississippi (1857–1861), adopting his pen name from the leadsman's call ("mark twain" means "by the mark two fathoms") sounding the river in shallow places. After an unsuccessful attempt to mine gold in Nevada, Twain edited the Virginia City Enterprise. *In 1865 in the New York* Saturday Press, *Twain published "Jim Smiley and His Jumping Frog," which then became the title story of* The Celebrated Jumping Frog of Calvaleras County and Other Sketches *(1867). His reputation as a humorist was enhanced by* Innocents Abroad *(1869), a comic account of his travels through France, Italy, and Palestine, and* Roughing It *(1872), a delightful spoof of his mining misadventures. His acknowledged masterpieces are* The Adventures of Tom Sawyer *(1876) and its sequel* The Adventures of Huckleberry Finn *(1885), works of great comic power and social insight. Twain's later works, including* The Man that Corrupted Hadleyburg *(1900), a fable about greed, and* The Mysterious Stranger *(1916), published six years after Twain's death, assail hypocrisy as endemic to the human condition. "The Lowest Animal" (1906) shows Twain at his most iconoclastic, formulating a scathing comparison between man and the so-called lower animals.*

I have been studying the traits and dispositions of the "lower animals" (so-called), and contrasting them with the traits and dispositions of man. I find the result humiliating to me. For it obliges me to renounce my allegiance to the Darwinian theory of the Ascent of Man from the Lower Animals; since it now seems plain to me that that theory ought to be vacated in favor of a new and truer one, this new and truer one to be named the Descent of Man from the Higher Animals.

In proceeding toward this unpleasant conclusion I have not guessed or speculated or conjectured, but have used what is commonly called the scientific method. That is to say, I have subjected every postulate that presented itself to the crucial test of actual experiment, and have adopted it or rejected it according to the result. Thus I verified and established each step of my course in its turn before advancing to the next. These experiments were made in the London Zoological Gardens, and covered many months of painstaking and fatiguing work.

Before particularizing any of the experiments, I wish to state one or two things which seem to more properly belong in this place than further along. This in the interest of clearness. The massed experiments established to my satisfaction certain generalizations, to wit:

1. That the human race is of one distinct species. It exhibits slight variations—in color, stature, mental caliber, and so on—due to climate, environment, and so forth; but it is a species by itself, and not to be confounded with any other.
2. That the quadrupeds are a distinct family, also. This family exhibits variations—in color, size, food preferences and so on; but it is a family by itself.
3. That the other families—the birds, the fishes, the insects, the reptiles, etc.—are more or less distinct, also. They are in the procession. They are links in the chain which stretches down from the higher animals to man at the bottom.

Some of my experiments were quite curious. In the course of my reading I had come across a case where, many years ago, some hunters on our Great Plains organized a buffalo hunt for the entertainment of an English earl—that, and to provide some fresh meat for his larder. They had charming sport. They killed seventy-two of those great animals; and ate part of one of them and left the seventy-one to rot. In order to determine the difference between an anaconda and an earl—if any—I caused seven young calves to be turned into the anaconda's cage. The grateful reptile immediately crushed one of them and swallowed it, then lay back satisfied. It showed no further interest in the calves, and no disposition to harm them. I tried this experiment with other anacondas; always with the same result. The fact stood proven that the difference between an earl and an anaconda is that the earl is cruel and the anaconda isn't; and that the earl wantonly destroys what he has no use for, but the anaconda doesn't. This seemed to suggest that the anaconda was not descended from the earl. It also seemed to suggest that the earl was descended from the anaconda, and had lost a good deal in the transition.

I was aware that many men who have accumulated more millions of money then they can ever use have shown a rabid hunger for more, and have not scrupled to cheat the ignorant and the helpless out of their poor servings in order to partially appease that appetite. I furnished a hundred different kinds of wild and tame animals the opportunity to accumulate vast stores of food, but none of them would do it. The squirrels and bees and certain birds made accumulations, but stopped when they had gathered a winter's supply, and could not be persuaded to add to it either honestly or by chicane. In order to bolster up a tottering reputation the ant pretended to store up supplies, but I was not deceived. I know the ant. These experiments convinced me that there is this difference between man and the higher animals: he is avaricious and miserly, they are not.

In the course of my experiments I convinced myself that among the animals man is the only one that harbors insults and injuries, broods over them, waits till a chance offers, then takes revenge. The passion of revenge is unknown to the higher animals.

Roosters keep harems, but it is by consent of their concubines; therefore no wrong is done. Men keep harems, but it is by brute force, privileged by atrocious laws which the other sex is allowed no hand in making. In this matter man occupies a far lower place than the rooster.

Cats are loose in their morals, but not consciously so. Man, in his descent from the cat, has brought the cat's looseness with him but has left the unconsciousness behind—the saving grace which excuses the cat. The cat is innocent, man is not.

Indecency, vulgarity, obscenity—these are strictly confined to man; he invented them. Among the higher animals there is no trace of them. They hide nothing; they are not ashamed. Man, with his soiled mind, covers himself. He will not even enter a drawing room with his breast and back naked, so alive are he and his mates to indecent suggestion. Man is "The Animal that Laughs." But so does the monkey, as Mr. Darwin pointed out; and so does the Australian bird that is called the laughing jackass. No—Man is the Animal that Blushes. He is the only one that does it—or has occasion to.

At the head of this article we see how "three monks were burnt to death" a few days ago, and a prior "put to death with atrocious cruelty." Do we inquire into the details? No; or we should find out that the prior was subjected to unprintable multilations. Man—when he is a North American Indian—gouges out his prisoner's eyes; when he is King John, with a nephew to render untroublesome, he uses a red-hot iron; when he is religious zealot dealing with heretics in the Middle Ages, he skins his captive alive and scatters salt on his back; in the first Richard's time he shuts up a multitude of Jew families in a tower and sets fire to it; in Columbus's time he captures a family of Spanish Jews and—but *that* is not printable; in our day in England a man is fined ten shillings for beating his mother nearly to death with a chair, and another man is fined forty shillings for having four pheasant eggs in his possession without being able to satisfactorily explain how he got them. Of all the animals, man is the only one that is cruel. He is the only one that inflicts pain for the pleasure of doing it. It is a trait that is not known to the higher animals. The cat plays with the frightened mouse; but she has this excuse, that she does not know that the mouse is suffering. The cat is moderate—unhumanly moderate: she only scares the mouse, she does not hurt it; she doesn't dig out its eyes, or tear off its skin, or drive splinters under its nails—man-fashion; when she is done playing with it she makes a sudden meal of it and puts it out of its trouble. Man is the Cruel Animal. He is alone in that distinction.

The higher animals engage in individual fights, but never in organized masses. Man is the only animal that deals in that atrocity of atrocities, War. He is the only one that gathers his brethren about him and goes forth in cold blood and with calm pulse to exterminate his kind. He is the only animal that for sordid wages will march out, as the Hessians did in our Revolution, and as the boyish Prince Napoleon did in the Zulu war, and help to slaughter strangers of his own species who have done him no harm and with whom he has no quarrel.

Man is the only animal that robs his helpless fellow of his country—takes possession of it and drives him out of it or destroys him. Man has done this in all the ages. There is not an acre of ground on the globe that is in possession of its rightful owner, or that has not been taken away from owner after owner, cycle after cycle, by force and bloodshed.

Man is the only Slave. And he is the only animal who enslaves. He has always been a slave in one form or another, and has always held other slaves in bondage under him in one way or another. In our day he is always some man's slave for wages, and does that man's work; and this slave has other slaves under him for minor wages, and they do *his* work. The higher animals are the only ones who exclusively do their own work and provide their own living.

Man is the only Patriot. He sets himself apart in his own country, under his own flag, and sneers at the other nations, and keeps multitudinous uniformed assassins on hand at heavy expense to grab slices of other people's countries, and keep *them* from grabbing slices of *his*. And in the intervals between campaigns he washes the blood off his hands and works for "the universal brotherhood of man"—with his mouth.

Man is the Religious Animal. He is the only Religious Animal. He is the only animal that has the True Religion—several of them. He is the only animal that loves his neighbor as himself, and cuts his throat if his theology isn't straight. He has made a graveyard of the globe in trying his honest best to smooth his brother's path to happiness and heaven. He was at it in the time of the Caesars, he was at it in Mahomet's time, he was at it in the time of the Inquisition, he was at it in France a couple of centuries, he was at it in England in Mary's day, he has been at it ever since he first saw the light, he is at it today in Crete—as per the telegrams quoted above—he will be at it somewhere else tomorrow. The higher animals have no religion. And we are told that they are going to be left out, in the Hereafter. I wonder why? It seems questionable taste.

Man is the Reasoning Animal. Such is the claim. I think it is open to dispute. Indeed, my experiments have proven to me that he is the Unreasoning Animal. Note his history, as sketched above. It seems plain to me that whatever he is he is *not* a reasoning animal. His record is the fantastic record of a maniac. I consider that the strongest count against his intelligence is the fact that with that record back of him he blandly sets himself up as the head animal of the lot: whereas by his own standards he is the bottom one.

In truth, man is incurably foolish. Simple things which the other animals easily learn, he is incapable of learning. Among my experiments was this. In an hour I taught a cat and a dog to be friends. I put them in a cage. In another hour I taught them to be friends with a rabbit. In the course of two days I was able to add a fox, a goose, a squirrel and some doves. Finally a monkey. They lived together in peace; even affectionately.

Next, in another cage I confined an Irish Catholic from Tipperary, and as soon as he seemed tame I added a Scotch Presbyterian from Aberdeen. Next a Turk from Constantinople; a Greek Christian from Crete; an Armenian; a Methodist from the wilds of Arkansas; a Buddhist from China; a Brahman from Benares. Finally, a Salvation Army Colonel from Wapping. Then I stayed away two whole days. When I came back to note results, the cage of Higher Animals was all right, but in the other there was but a chaos of gory odds and ends of turbans and fezzes and plaids and bones and flesh—not a specimen left alive. These Reasoning Animals had disagreed on a theological detail and carried the matter to a Higher Court.

One is obliged to concede that in true loftiness of character, Man cannot claim to approach even the meanest of the Higher Animals. It is plain that he is constitutionally incapable of approaching that altitude; that he is constitutionally afflicted with a Defect which must make such approach forever impossible, for it is manifest that this defect is permanent in him, indestructible, ineradicable.

I find this Defect to be *the Moral Sense.* He is the only animal that has it. It is the secret of his degradation. It is the quality *which enables him to do wrong.* It has no other office. It is incapable of performing any other function. It could never have been intended to perform any other. Without it, man could do no wrong. He would rise at once to the level of the Higher Animals.

Since the Moral Sense has but the one office, the one capacity—to enable man to do wrong—it is plainly without value to him. It is as valueless to him as is disease. In fact, it manifestly is a disease. *Rabies* is bad, but it is not so bad as this disease. Rabies enables a man to do a thing which he could not do when in a healthy state: kill his neighbor with a poisonous bite. No one is the better man for having rabies. The Moral Sense enables a man to do wrong. It enables him to do wrong in a thousand ways. Rabies is an innocent disease, compared to the Moral Sense. No one, then, can be the better man for having the Moral Sense. What, now, do we find the Primal Curse to have been? Plainly what it was in the beginning: the infliction upon man of the Moral Sense; the ability to distinguish good from evil; and with it, necessarily, the ability to *do* evil; for there can be no evil act without the presence of consciousness of it in the doer of it.

And so I find that we have descended and degenerated, from some far ancestor—some microscopic atom wandering at its pleasure between the mighty horizons of a drop of water perchance—insect by insect, animal by animal, reptile by reptile, down the long highway of smirchless innocence, till we have reached the bottom stage of development—namable as the Human Being. Below us—nothing. Nothing but the Frenchman.

MEANING

1. How are Twain's experiments—comparing human behavior to that of animals in various situations—intended to puncture some illusions the human species has about itself?
2. In what way do each of Twain's experiments reveal that animals are superior to man?
3. How do Twain's experiments provide an ironic commentary to Darwin's thesis that humans are at the apex of all other species?
4. How does Twain's sarcastic reference to the French show that he applies all foregoing criticisms to himself?

USING COMPARISON AND CONTRAST TO CONVEY MEANING

1. Why does Twain choose a point-by-point rather than a subject-by-subject method of organization for his essay?
2. How does this type of evaluative comparison differ from one designed to provide equal information about the two subjects being compared?
3. What specific words and phrases clearly express Twain's attitude toward his subjects? For example, what is the significance of the title?

WRITING SUGGESTIONS

1. What altruistic aspects of human behavior would have weakened Twain's evaluations had he taken them into account?
2. Analyze the work of any contemporary social satirist (Gary Trudeau, Mark Russell, Art Buchwald), working in any medium, to discover how artists and writers use their art to express criticism of modern culture.
3. Compare and contrast the works of two satirists from different eras or cultures to discover what techniques are characteristic of all satire. For example, do Twain, Voltaire, Swift, Huxley, and Orwell emphasize the role of evil in order to arouse moral indignation about social abuses?

PHYLLIS McGINLEY

Are Children People?

Phyllis McGinley (1905–1978) was born in Ontario, Oregon. After graduating from the University of Utah, McGinley held a variety of jobs including English teacher in New Rochelle, New York, copywriter for an advertising agency, and poetry editor for Town and Country. *Her poetry and essays speak with warmth and wit of the satisfactions of being a suburban housewife and mother. She won the Pulitzer Prize in 1961 for her volume of collected poetry,* Times Three, *with a preface by W. H. Auden. Over the four decades of her writing career she wrote eighteen books, among which* A Wreath of Christmas Legends *(1967) and* Saint-Watching *(1969) show her deepening religious convictions and compassionate intelligence. As the author of many children's books, McGinley was well aware of the differences in outlook that create misunderstandings between adults and children. Her lighthearted treatment of this theme forms the basis of her essay "Are Children People?," taken from her second volume of essays* Sixpence in Her Shoe *(1964).*

The problem of how to live with children isn't as new as you might think. Centuries before the advent of Dr. Spock or the PTA, philosophers debated the juvenile question, not always with compassion. There's a quotation from one of the antique sages floating around in what passes for my mind which, for pure cynicism, could set a Montaigne or a Mort Sahl back on his heels.

"Why," asks a disciple, "are we so devoted to our grandchildren?"

And the graybeard answers, "Because it is easy to love the enemies of one's enemies."

Philosopher he may have been but I doubt his parental certification. Any parent with a spark of natural feeling knows that children aren't our enemies. On the other hand, if we're sensible we are aware that they aren't really our friends, either. How can they be, when they belong to a totally different race?

Children admittedly are human beings, equipped with such human paraphernalia as appetites, whims, intelligence, and even hearts, but any resemblance between them and people is purely coincidental. The two nations, child and grown-up, don't behave alike or think alike or even see with the same eyes.

Take that matter of seeing, for example. An adult looks in the mirror and notices what? A familiar face, a figure currently overweight, maybe, but well-known and resignedly accepted; two arms, two legs, an entity. A child can stare into the looking glass for minutes at a time and see only the bone buttons on a snowsuit or a pair of red shoes.

Shoes, in fact, are the first personal belongings a child really looks at in an objective sense. There they are to adore—visible, shiny, round-toed ornamental extensions of himself. He can observe them in that mirror or he can look down from his small height to admire them. They are real to him, unlike his eyes or his elbows. That is why, for a child, getting a pair of new shoes is like having a birthday. When my daughters were little they invariably took just-acquired slippers to bed with them for a few nights, the way they'd take a cuddle toy or smuggle in a puppy.

Do people sleep with their shoes? Of course not. Nor do they lift them up reverently to be fondled, a gesture children offer even to perfect strangers in department stores. I used to think that a child's life was lived from new shoe to new shoe, as an adult lives for love or payday or a vacation.

Children, though, aren't consistent about their fetish. By the time they have learned to tie their own laces, they have lapsed into an opposite phase. They start to discard shoes entirely. Boys, being natural reactionaries, cling longer than girls to their first loves, but girls begin the discalced stage at twelve or thirteen—and it goes on interminably. Their closets may bulge with footwear, with everything from dubious sneakers to wisps of silver kid, while most of the time the girls themselves go unshod. I am in error, too, when I speak of shoes as reposing in closets. They don't. They lie abandoned under sofas, upside down beside the television set, rain-drenched on verandas. Guests in formal drawing rooms are confronted by them and climbers on stairways imperiled. When the phase ends, I can't tell you, but I think only with premature senescence.

My younger daughter, then a withered crone of almost twenty, once held the odd distinction of being the only girl on record to get her foot stabbed by a rusty nail at a Yale prom. She was, of course, doing the Twist barefoot, but even so the accident seems unlikely. You can't convince me it could happen to an adult.

No, children don't look at things in the same light as people. Nor do they hear with our ears, either. Ask a child a question and he has an invariable answer: "What?" (Though now and then he alters it to "Why?")

Or send one on a household errand and you will know that he—or she—is incapable of taking in a simple adult remark. I once asked an otherwise normal little girl to bring me the scissors from the kitchen drawer, and she returned, after a mysterious absence of fifteen minutes, lugging the extension hose out of the garage. Yet the young can hear brownies baking in the oven two blocks away from home or the faintest whisper of parents attempting to tell each other secrets behind closed doors.

They can also understand the language of babies, the most esoteric on earth. Our younger child babbled steadily from the age of nine months on, although not for a long while in an intelligible tongue. Yet her sister, two years older, could translate for us every time.

"That lady's bracelet—Patsy wishes she could have it," the interpreter would tell me; and I had the wit hastily to lift my visitor's arm out of danger.

Or I would be instructed, "She'd like to pat the kitten now."

"We used occasionally to regret their sibling fluency of communication. Once we entertained at Sunday dinner a portrait painter known rather widely for his frequent and publicized love affairs. He quite looked the part, too, being so tall and lean and rakish, with such a predatory moustache and so formidable a smile, that my husband suggested it was a case of art imitating nature.

The two small girls had never met him, and when the baby saw him for the first time she turned tail and fled upstairs.

The older, a gracious four, came back into the living room after a short consultation, to apologize for her sister's behavior. "You see," she told him winningly, "Patsy thinks you're a wolf."

It was impossible to explain that they had somehow confused the moustache and the smile with a description of Little Red Riding Hood's arch foe and were not referring to his private life. We let it pass. I often thought, however, that it was a pity the older girl's pentecostal gifts did not outlast kindergarten. She would have been a great help to the United Nations.

Young mothers have to study such talents and revise their methods of child rearing accordingly. To attempt to treat the young like grown-ups is always a mistake.

Do people, at least those outside of institutions, drop lighted matches into wastebaskets just to see what will happen? Do they tramp through puddles on purpose? Or prefer hot dogs or jelly-and-mashed-banana sandwiches to lobster Thermidor? Or, far from gagging on the abysmal inanities of *Raggedy Ann,* beg to have it read to them every evening for three months?

Indeed, the reading habits alone of the younger generation mark them off from their betters. What does an adult do when he feels like having a go at a detective story or the evening paper? Why, he picks out a convenient chair or props himself up on his pillows, arranges the light correctly for good vision, turns down the radio, and reaches for a cigarette or a piece of chocolate fudge.

Children, however, when the literary urge seizes them, take their comic books to the darkest corner of the room or else put their heads under the bedcovers. Nor do they sit *down* to read. They wander. They lie on the floor with their legs draped over the coffee table, or, alternatively, they sit on the coffee table and put the book on the floor. Or else they lean against the refrigerator, usually with the refrigerator door wide open. Sometimes I have seen them retire to closets.

Children in comfortable positions are uncomfortable—just as they are miserable if they can't also have the phonograph, the radio, the television and sometimes the telephone awake and lively while they pore on *The Monster of Kalliwan* or *The Jungle Book.*

But then, children don't walk like people, either—sensibly, staidly, in a definite direction. I am not sure they ever acquire our grown-up gaits. They canter, they bounce, they slither, slide, crawl, leap into the air, saunter, stand on their heads, swing from branch to branch, limp like cripples, or trot like ostriches. But I seldom recall seeing a child just plain walk. They can, however, dawdle. The longest period of recorded time is that interval between telling children to undress for bed and the ultimate moment when they have brushed their teeth, said their prayers, eaten a piece of bread and catsup, brushed their teeth all over again, asked four times for another glass of milk, checked the safety of their water pistols or their tropical fish, remembered there was something vital they had to confide to you, which they have forgotten by the time you reach their side, switched from a panda to a giraffe and back to the panda for the night's sleeping companion, begged to have the light left on in the hall, and finally, being satisfied that your screaming voice is in working order, fallen angelically into slumber.

Apprentice parents are warned to disregard at least nine-tenths of all such requests as pure subterfuge but to remember that maybe one of the ten is right and reasonable, like the night-light or the value of a panda when one is in a panda mood.

Not that reason weighs much with children. It is the great mistake we make with a child, to think progeny operate by our logic. The reasoning of children, although it is often subtle, differs from an adult's. At base there is usually a core of sanity, but one must disentangle what the lispers mean from what they say.

"I believe in Santa Claus," a daughter told me years ago, when she was five or six. "And I believe in the Easter Rabbit, too. But I just can't believe in Shirley Temple."

Until I worked out a solution for this enigmatic statement, I feared for the girl's mind. Then I realized that she had been watching the twenty-one-inch screen. After all, if you are six years old and see a grown-up Shirley Temple acting as mistress of ceremonies for a TV special one evening and the next day observe her, dimpled and brief-skirted, in an old movie, you are apt to find the transformation hard to credit.

I managed to unravel that utterance, but I never did pierce through to the heart of a gnomic pronouncement made by a young friend of hers. He meandered into the backyard one summer day when the whole family was preparing for a funeral. Our garden is thickly clustered with memorials to defunct wildlife, and on this particular afternoon we were intent on burying another robin.

John looked at the hole.

"What are you doing?" he asked, as if it weren't perfectly apparent to the most uninformed.

"Why, John," said my husband, "I'm digging a grave."

John considered the matter a while. Then he inquired again, with all the solemnity of David Susskind querying a senator, "Why don't you make it a double-decker?"

Not even Echo answered that one, but I kept my sense of proportion and went on with the ceremonies. You need a sense of proportion when dealing with children, as you also need a sense of humor. Yet you must never expect the very young to have a sense of humor of their own. Children are acutely risible, stirred to laughter by dozens of human mishaps, preferably fatal. They can understand the points of jokes, too, so long as the joke is not on them. Their egos are too new, they have not existed long enough in the world to have learned to laugh at themselves. What they love most in the way of humor are riddles, elementary puns, nonsense, and catastrophe. An elderly fat lady slipping on the ice in real life or a man in a movie falling from a fifteen-foot ladder equally transports them. They laugh at fistfights, clowns, people kissing each other, and buildings blowing up. They don't, however, enjoy seeing their parents in difficulties. Parents, they feel, were put on earth solely for their protection, and they cannot bear to have the fortress endangered.

Their peace of mind, their safety, rests on grown-up authority; and it is that childish reliance which invalidates the worth of reasoning too much with them. The longer I lived in a house with children, the less importance I put on cooperatively threshing out matters of conduct or explaining to them our theories of discipline. If I had it to do over again I wouldn't reason with them at all until they arrived at an *age* of reason—approximately twenty-one. I would give them rules to follow. I would try to be just, and I would try even harder to be strict. I would do no arguing. Children, in their hearts, like laws. Authority implies an ordered world, which is what they—and, in the long run, most of the human race—yearn to inhabit. In law there is freedom. But too permissive and they feel lost and alone. Children are forced to live very rapidly in order to live at all. They are given only a few years in which to learn hundreds of thousands of things about life and the planet and themselves. They haven't time to spend analyzing the logic behind every command or taboo, and they resent being pulled away by it from their proper business of discovery.

When our younger and more conversational daughter turned twelve, we found she was monopolizing the family telephone. She would reach home after school at 3:14 and at 3:15 the instrument would begin to shrill, its peal endless till bedtime. For once we had the good sense neither to scold nor to expostulate. We merely told her she could make and receive calls only between five and six o'clock in the afternoon. For the rest of the day, the telephone was ours. We expected tears. We were braced for hysterics. What we got was a calm acceptance of a Rule. Indeed, we found out later, she boasted about the prohibition—it made her feel both sheltered and popular.

But, then, children are seldom resentful, which is another difference between them and people. They hold grudges no better than a lapdog. They are too inexperienced to expect favors from the world. What happens to them happens to them, like an illness; and if it is too extravagantly unfair, they forget about it. Parents learn that a child's angry glare or floods of tears after a punishment or a scolding may send the grown-up away feeling like a despotic brute; but that half an hour later, with adult feelings still in tatters, the child is likely as not to come flying into the room, fling both carefree arms about the beastly grown-up's neck, and shout, "I love you," into her ear.

The ability to forget a sorrow is childhood's most enchanting feature. It can also be exasperating to the pitch of frenzy. Little girls return from school with their hearts broken in two by a friend's treachery or a teacher's injustice. They sob through the afternoon, refuse dinner, and go to sleep on tear-soaked pillows. Novice mothers do not sleep at all, only lie awake with the shared burden for a nightlong companion. Experienced ones know better. They realize that if you come down in the morning to renew your solacing, you will meet—what? Refreshed, whole-hearted offspring who can't under*stand* what you're talking about. Beware of making childhood's griefs your own. They are no more lasting than soap bubbles.

I find myself hoaxed to this day by the recuperative powers of the young, even when they top me by an inch and know all about modern art. More than once I have been called long distance from a college in New England to hear news of impending disaster.

"It's exam time and I'm down with this horrible cold," croaks the sufferer, coughing dramatically. "Can you rush me that prescription of Dr. Murphy's? I don't trust our infirmary."

Envisioning flu, pneumonia, wasting fever, and a lily maid dead before her time, I harry the doctor into scribbling his famous remedy and send it by wire. Then after worrying myself into dyspepsia, I call two days later to find out the worst. An unfogged voice answers me blithely.

"What cold?" it inquires.

Ephemeral tragedies, crises that evaporate overnight are almost certain to coincide with adolescence. Gird yourselves for them. Adolescence is a disease more virulent than measles and difficult to outgrow as an allergy. At its onset parents are bewildered like the victim. They can only stand by with patience, flexibility, and plenty of food in the larder. It's amazing how consoling is a batch of cookies in an emergency. If it doesn't comfort the child, at least it helps the baker. I stopped in at a neighbor's house the other day and found her busily putting the frosting on a coconut cake.

"It's for Steven," she told me. "His pet skunk just died, and I didn't know what else to do for him."

Food helps more than understanding. Adolescence doesn't really want to be understood. It prefers to live privately in some stone tower of its own building, lonely and unassailable. To understand is to violate. This is the age—at least for girls—of hidden diaries, locked drawers, unshared secrets. It's a trying time for all concerned. The only solace is that they do outgrow it. But the flaw there is that eventually they outgrow being children too, becoming expatriates of their own tribe.

For, impossible as it seems when one first contemplates diapers and croup, then tantrums, homework, scouting, dancing class, and finally the terrible dilemmas of the teens, childhood does come inexorably to an end. Children turn into people. They speak rationally if aloofly, lecture you on manners, condescend to teach you about eclectic criticism, and incline to get married. And there you are, left with all that learning you have so painfully accumulated in twenty-odd years and with no more progeny on whom to lavish it.

Small wonder we love our grandchildren. The old sage recognized the effect but not the cause. Enemies of our enemies indeed! They are our immortality. It is they who will inherit our wisdom, our experience, our ingenuity.

Except, of course, that the grandchildren's parents will listen benevolently (are they not courteous adults?) and not profit by a word we tell them. They must learn for themselves how to speak in another language and with an alien race.

MEANING

1. What are some of the specific points of behavior in which children and adults differ. For example, how do children differ from adults in their attitude toward material goods, attention span, and desire to discover things for themselves?
2. Why does a child's sense of freedom depend on the existence of an ongoing framework of adult protection?
3. What examples does McGinley provide to illustrate that the "proper business" of children is "discovery"?

USING COMPARISON AND CONTRAST TO CONVEY MEANING

1. Since McGinley knows that her readers are already familiar with how adults behave, how does she proportion her essay to concentrate on those traits that make children so unique?
2. What words or phrases serve as transitions in McGinley's discussion when she moves from children to adults?
3. What principle of organization governs the order in which McGinley presents children's character traits?
4. Is McGinley's comparison designed to provide insight into the subjects being compared or does she compare two subjects in order to decide which one is better?

WRITING SUGGESTIONS

1. If you have ever returned to a place where you lived as a child, compare and contrast the differences between how it appeared to you then with your present-day impressions.
2. How have your reactions to horror movies changed from the way you reacted to movies of the same type as a child?

ARISTOTLE

Youth and Old Age

Aristotle (384–323 B.C.) was born at Stagira in Macedon and was sent by his family in 367 B.C. to be educated in Athens, where he studied under Plato for twenty years. Although a Platonist initially, Aristotle later became convinced of the need for empirical observation, rejected the Platonic doctrine of ideal forms, and developed his own views in his extensive writings on philosophical, political, and scientific issues. He tutored the future Alexander the Great in 342 B.C. after which he returned to Athens to establish his school, the Lyceum. Aristotle's existing works, covering logic, ethics, metaphysics, physics, zoology, politics, rhetoric and poetics, were transcribed from notes he used for his lectures. His writings were crucial in shaping the thought of many cultures and were regarded as the basis of all knowledge for over fourteen hundred years. In "Youth and Old Age," Aristotle perceptively balances the strengths and weaknesses of youth against those of old age. These empirically based observations were made by Aristotle in the context of his discussion as to how arguments should be adapted for various audiences.

Young men have strong passions, and tend to gratify them indiscriminately. Of the bodily desires, it is the sexual by which they are most swayed and in which they show absence of self-control. They are changeable and fickle in their desires, which are violent while they last, but quickly over: their impulses are keen but not deep-rooted, and are like sick people's attacks of hunger and thirst. They are hot-tempered and quick-tempered, and apt to give way to their anger; bad temper often gets the better of them, for owing to their love of honor they cannot bear being slighted, and are indignant if they imagine themselves unfairly treated. While they love honour, they love victory still more; for youth is eager for superiority over others, and victory is one form of this. They love both more than they love money, which indeed they love very little, not having yet learnt what it means to be without it—this is the point of Pittacus' remark about Amphiaraus. They look at the good side rather than the bad, not having yet witnessed many instances of wickedness. They trust others readily, because they have not yet often been cheated. They are sanguine; nature warms their blood as though with excess of wine; and besides that, they have as yet met with few disappointments. Their lives are mainly spent not in memory but in expectation; for expectation refers to the future, memory to the past, and youth has a long future before it and a short past behind it: on the first day of one's life one has nothing at all to remember, and can only look forward. They are easily cheated, owing to the sanguine disposition just mentioned. Their hot tempers and hopeful dispositions make them more courageous than older men are; the hot temper prevents

232

fear, and the hopeful disposition creates confidence; we cannot feel fear so long as we are feeling angry, and any expectation of good makes us confident. They are shy, accepting the rules of society in which they have been trained, and not yet believing in any other standard of honour. They have exalted notions, because they have not yet been humbled by life or learnt its necessary limitations; moreover, their hopeful disposition makes them think themselves equal to great things—and that means having exalted notions. They would always rather do noble deeds than useful ones: their lives are regulated more by moral feeling than by reasoning; and whereas reasoning leads us to choose what is useful, moral goodness leads us to choose what is noble. They are fonder of their friends, intimates, and companions than older men are, because they like spending their days in the company of others, and have not yet come to value either their friends or anything else by their usefulness to themselves. All their mistakes are in the direction of doing things excessively and vehemently. They disobey Chilon's precept[1] by overdoing everything; they love too much and hate too much, and the same with everything else. They think they know everything, and are always quite sure about it; this, in fact, is why they overdo everything. If they do wrong to others, it is because they mean to insult them, not to do them actual harm. They are ready to pity others, because they think every one an honest man, or anyhow better than he is: they judge their neighbour by their own harmless natures, and so cannot think he deserves to be treated in that way. They are fond of fun and therefore witty, wit being well-bred insolence.

Such, then, is the character of the Young. The character of Elderly Men—men who are past their prime—may be said to be formed for the most part of elements that are the contrary of all these. They have lived many years; they have often been taken in, and often made mistakes; and life on the whole is a bad business. The result is that they are sure about nothing and under-do everything. They 'think', but they never 'know'; and because of their hesitation they always add a 'possibly' or a 'perhaps,' putting everything this way and nothing positively. They are cynical; that is, they tend to put the worse construction on everything. Further, their experience makes them distrustful and therefore suspicious of evil. Consequently they neither love warmly nor hate bitterly, but following the hint of Bias they love as though they will some day hate and hate as though they will some day love. They are small-minded, because they have been humbled by life: their desires are set upon nothing more exalted or unusual than what will help them to keep alive. They are not generous, because money is one of the things they must have, and at the same time their experience has taught them how hard it is to get and how easy to lose. They are cowardly, and are always anticipating danger; unlike that of the young, who are warm-blooded, their temperament is chilly; old age has paved the way for cowardice; fear is, in fact, a form of chill. They love life; and all the more when their last day has come, because the object of all desire is something we have not got, and also because we desire more strongly that which we need most urgently. They are too fond of themselves; this is one form that small-mindedness takes. Because of this, they guide their lives too much by considerations of what is useful and too little by what is noble—for the useful is what is good for oneself, and the noble what is good absolutely. They are not shy, but shameless rather; caring less for what is noble than for what is useful, they feel contempt for what people may think of them. They lack confidence in the future; partly through experience—for most things

---

[1] This precept states "(do) nothing to excess."

go wrong, or anyhow turn out worse than one expects; and partly because of their cowardice. They live by memory rather than by hope; for what is left to them of life is but little as compared with the long past; and hope is of the future, memory of the past. This, again, is the cause of their loquacity; they are continually talking of the past, because they enjoy remembering it. Their fits of anger are sudden but feeble. Their sensual passions have either altogether gone or have lost their vigour: consequently they do not feel their passions much, and their actions are inspired less by what they do feel than by the love of gain. Hence men at this time of life are often supposed to have a self-controlled character; the fact is that their passions have slackened, and they are slaves to the love of gain. They guide their lives by reasoning more than by moral feeling; reasoning being directed to utility and moral feeling to moral goodness. If they wrong others, they mean to injure them, not to insult them. Old men may feel pity, as well as young men, but not for the same reason. Young men feel it out of kindness; old men out of weakness, imagining that anything that befalls any one else might easily happen to them, which, as we saw, is a thought that excites pity. Hence they are querulous, and not disposed to jesting or laughter—the love of laughter being the very opposite of querulousness.

Such are the characters of Young Men and Elderly Men. People always think well of speeches adapted to, and reflecting, their own character; and we can now see how to compose our speeches so as to adapt both them and ourselves to our audiences.

MEANING

1. What important basic differences in motives and behavior does Aristotle identify as distinguishing the "young" from the "old"?
2. What reasons does Aristotle give for his belief that old men act from self-serving interests while young men act from altruistic motives?
3. What part does memory play in explaining why the young and the old perceive the world so differently?

USING COMPARISON AND CONTRAST TO CONVEY MEANING

1. Why does Aristotle choose to first describe the young and then the old rather than interweaving the points of comparison between the two?
2. What examples provide the clearest support for Aristotle's comparative analysis of the differences separating the young and the old?

WRITING SUGGESTIONS

1. If you feel Aristotle's evaluative comparison is unfair, what corrections would you make based on your own observations?
2. Discuss how the differences Aristotle describes would be altered in extended families where the old and young live together.

POLITICAL AND SOCIAL SCIENCES

Richard Rodriguez

On Becoming a Chicano

Richard Rodriguez was born in 1944 in San Francisco. After receiving his Master's degree from Columbia in 1969, Rodriguez pursued his graduate studies at both the University of California at Berkeley and the Warburg Institute in London (1972–1973). Rodriguez was on a Fulbright fellowship in London, studying English Renaissance Literature, when he decided to leave the world of academic studies. His autobiography, Hunger of Memory: The Education of Richard Rodriguez *(1982), received the Christopher award. This work analyzes the predicament often encountered by those who acquire a new language and culture at the expense of the traditional culture in which they were raised. "On Becoming a Chicano" is Rodriguez's uncommonly sensitive account of how he found himself between two worlds, at home in neither.*

Today I am only technically the person I once felt myself to be—a Mexican-American, a Chicano. Partly because I had no way of comprehending my racial identity except in this technical sense, I gave up long ago the cultural consequences of being a Chicano.

The change came gradually but early. When I was beginning grade school, I noted to myself the fact that the classroom environment was so different in its styles and assumptions from my own family environment that survival would essentially entail a choice between both worlds. When I became a student, I was literally "remade"; neither I nor my teachers considered anything I had known before as relevant. I had to forget most of what my culture had provided, because to remember it was a disadvantage. The past and its cultural values became detachable, like a piece of clothing grown heavy on a warm day and finally put away.

Strangely, the discovery that I have been inattentive to my cultural past has arisen because others—student colleagues and faculty members—have started to assume that I am a Chicano. The ease with which the assumption is made forces me to suspect that the label is not meant to suggest cultural, but racial, identity. Nonetheless, as a graduate student and a prospective university faculty member, I am routinely expected to assume intellectual leadership *as a member of a racial minority*. Recently, for example, I heard the moderator of a panel discussion introduce me as "Richard Rodriguez, a Chicano intellectual." I wanted to correct the speaker—because I felt guilty representing a non-academic cultural tradition that I had willingly abandoned. So I can only guess what it would have meant to have retained my culture as I entered the classroom, what it would mean for me to be today a "Chicano intellectual." (The two words juxtaposed excite me; for years I thought a Chicano had to decide between being one or the other.)

Does the fact that I barely spoke any English until I was nine, or that as a child I felt a surge of self-hatred whenever a passing teenager would yell a racial slur, or that I saw my skin darken each summer—do any of these facts shape the ideas which I have or am capable of having? Today, I suspect they do—in ways I doubt the moderator who referred to me as a "Chicano intellectual" intended. The peculiar status of being a "Chicano intellectual" makes me grow restless at the thought that I have lost at least as much as I have gained through education.

I remember when, 20 years ago, two grammar-school nuns visited my childhood home. They had come to suggest—with more tact than was necessary, because my parents accepted without question the church's authority—that we make a greater effort to speak as much English around the house as possible. The nuns realized that my brothers and I led solitary lives largely because we were barely able to comprehend English in a school where we were the only Spanish-speaking students. My mother and father complied as best they could. Heroically, they gave up speaking to us in Spanish—the language that formed so much of the family's sense of intimacy in an alien world—and began to speak a broken English. Instead of Spanish sounds, I began hearing sounds that were new, harder, less friendly. More important, I was encouraged to respond in English.

The change in language was the most dramatic and obvious indication that I would become very much like the "gringo"—a term which was used descriptively rather than pejoratively in my home—and unlike the Spanish-speaking relatives who largely constituted my preschool world. Gradually, Spanish became a sound freighted with only a kind of sentimental significance, like the sound of the bedroom clock I listened to in my aunt's house when I spent the night. Just as gradually, English became the language I came not to *hear* because it was the language I used every day, as I gained access to a new, larger society. But the memory of Spanish persisted as a reminder of the society I had left. I can remember occasions when I entered a room and my parents were speaking to one another in Spanish; seeing me, they shifted into their more formalized English. Hearing them speak to me in English troubled me. The bonds their voices once secured were loosened by the new tongue.

This is not to suggest that I was being *forced* to give up my Chicano past. After the initial awkwardness of transition, I committed myself, fully and freely, to the culture of the classroom. Soon what I was learning in school was so antithetical to what my parents knew and did that I was careful about the way I talked about myself at the evening dinner table. Occasionally, there were moments of childish cruelty: a son's condescending to instruct either one of his parents about a "simple" point of English pronunciation or grammar.

Social scientists often remark, about situations such as mine, that children feel a sense of loss as they move away from their working-class identifications and models. Certainly, what I experienced, others have also—whatever their race. Like other generations of, say, Polish-American or Irish-American children coming home from college, I was to know the silence that ensues so quickly after the quick exchange of news and the dwindling of common interests.

In addition, however, education seemed to mean not only a gradual dissolving of familial and class ties but also a change of racial identity. The new language I spoke was only the most obvious reason for my associating the classroom with "gringo" society. The society I knew as Chicano was barely literate—in English *or* Spanish— and so impatient with either prolonged reflection or abstraction that I found the academic environment a sharp contrast. Sharpening the contrast was the stereotype of the Mexican as a mental inferior. (The fear of this stereotype has been so deep that only recently have I been willing to listen to those, like D. H. Lawrence, who celebrate the "non-cerebral" Mexican as an alternative to the rational and scientific European man.) Because I did not know how to distinguish the healthy non-rationality of Chicano culture from the mental incompetency of which Chicanos were unjustly accused, I was willing to abandon my non-mental skills in order to disprove the racist's stereotype.

I was wise enough not to feel proud of the person education had helped me to become. I knew that education had led me to repudiate my race. I was frequently labeled a *pocho*, a Mexican with gringo pretentions, not only because I could not speak Spanish but also because I would respond in English with precise and careful sentences. Uncles would laugh good-naturedly, but I detected scorn in their voices. For my grandmother, the least assimilated of my relations, the changes in her grandson since entering school were expecially troubling. She remains today a dark and silently critical figure in my memory, a reminder of the Mexican-Indian ancestry that somehow my educational success has violated.

Nonetheless, I became more comfortable reading or writing careful prose than talking to a kitchen filled with listeners, withdrawing from situations to reflect on their significance rather than grasping for meaning at the scene. I remember, one August evening, slipping away from a gathering of aunts and uncles in the backyard, going into a bedroom tenderly lighted by a late sun, and opening a novel about life in nineteenth-century England. There, by an open window, reading, I was barely conscious of the sounds of laughter outside.

With so few fellow Chicanos in the university, I had no chance to develop an alternative consciousness. When I spent occasional weekends tutoring lower-class Chicano teenagers or when I talked with Mexican-American janitors and maids around the campus, there was a kind of sympathy—a sense, however privately held—that we knew something about one another. But I regarded them all primarily as people from my past. The maids reminded me of my aunts (similarly employed); the students I tutored reminded me of my cousins (who also spoke English with barrio accents).

When I was young, I was taught to refer to my ancestry as Mexican-American. *Chicano* was a word used among friends or relatives. It implied a familiarity based on shared experience. Spoken casually, the term easily became an insult. In 1968 the word *Chicano* was about to become a political term. I heard it shouted into microphones as Third World groups agitated for increased student and faculty representation in higher education. It was not long before I *became* a Chicano in the eyes of students and faculty members. My racial identity was assumed for only the simplest reasons: my skin color and last name.

On occasion I was asked to account for my interests in Renaissance English literature. When I explained them, declaring a need for cultural assimilation, on the campus, my listener would disagree. I sensed suspicion on the part of a number of my fellow minority students. When I could not imitate Spanish pronunciations or the dialect of the barrio, when I was plainly uninterested in wearing ethnic costumes and could not master a special handshake that minority students often used with one another, they knew I was different. And I was. I was assimilated into the culture of a graduate department of English. As a result, I watched how in less than five years nearly every minority graduate student I knew dropped out of school, largely for cultural reasons. Often they didn't understand the value of analyzing literature in professional jargon, which others around them readily adopted. Nor did they move as readily to lofty heights of abstraction. They became easily depressed by the seeming uselessness of the talk they heard around them. "It's not for real," I still hear a minority student murmur to herself and perhaps to me, shaking her head slowly, as we sat together in a class listening to a discussion on punctuation in a Renaissance epic.

I survived—thanks to the accommodation I had made long before. In fact, I prospered, partly as a result of the political movement designed to increase the enrollment of minority students less assimilated than I in higher education. Suddenly grants, fellowships, and teaching offers became abundant.

In 1972 I went to England on a Fulbright scholarship. I hoped the months of brooding about racial identity were behind me. I wanted to concentrate on my dissertation, which the distractions of an American campus had not permitted. But the freedom I anticipated did not last for long. Barely a month after I had begun working regularly in the reading room of the British Museum, I was surprised, and even frightened, to have to acknowledge that I was not at ease living the rarefied life of the academic. With my pile of research file cards growing taller, the mass of secondary materials and opinions was making it harder for me to say anything original about my subject. Every sentence I wrote, every thought I had, became so loaded with qualifications and footnotes that it said very little. My scholarship became little more than an exercise in caution. I had an accompanying suspicion that whatever I did manage to write and call my dissertation would be of little use. Opening books so dusty that they must not have been used in decades, I began to doubt the value of writing what only a few people would read.

Obviously, I was going through the fairly typical crisis of the American graduate student. But with one difference: After four years of involvement with questions of racial identity, I now saw my problems as a scholar in the context of the cultural issues that had been raised by my racial situation. So much of what my work in the British Museum lacked, my parents' culture possessed. They were people not afraid to generalize or to find insights in their generalities. More important, they had the capacity to make passionate statements, something I was beginning to doubt my dissertation would ever allow me to do. I needed to learn how to trust the use of "I" in my writing the way they trusted its use in their speech. Thus developed a persistent yearning for the very Chicano culture that I had abandoned as useless.

Feelings of depression came occasionally but forcefully. Some days I found my work so oppressive that I had to leave the reading room and stroll through the museum. One afternoon, appropriately enough, I found myself in an upstairs gallery containing Mayan and Aztec sculptures. Even there the sudden yearning for a Chicano past seemed available to me only as nostalgia. One morning, as I was reading a book about Puritan autobiography, I overheard two Spaniards whispering to one another. I did not hear what they said, but I did hear the sound of their Spanish—and it embraced me, filling my mind with swirling images of a past long abandoned.

I returned from England, disheartened, a few months later. My dissertation was coming along well, but I did not know whether I wanted to submit it. Worse, I did not know whether I wanted a career in higher education. I detested the prospect of spending the rest of my life in libraries and classrooms, in touch with my past only through the binoculars nostalgia makes available. I knew that I could not simply re-create a version of what I would have been like had I not become an academic. There was no possibility of going back. But if the culture of my birth was to survive, it would have to animate my academic work. That was the lesson of the British Museum.

I frankly do not know how my academic autobiography will end. Sometimes I think I will have to leave the campus, in order to reconcile my past and present. Other times, more optimistically, I think that a kind of negative reconciliation is already in progress, that I can make creative use of my sense of loss. For instance, with my sense of the cleavage between past and present, I can, as a literary critic, identify issues in Renaissance pastoral—a literature which records the feelings of the courtly when confronted by the alternatives of rural and rustic life. And perhaps I can speak with unusual feeling about the price we must pay, or have paid, as a rational society for confessing seventeenth-century Cartesian faiths. Likewise, because of my sense of cultural loss, I may be able to identify more readily than another the ways in which language has meaning simply as sound and what the printed word can and cannot give us. At the very least, I can point up the academy's tendency to ignore the cultures beyond its own horizons.

February 1974

On my job interview the department chairman has been listening to an oral version of what I have just written. I tell him he should be very clear about the fact that I am not, at the moment, confident enough to call myself a Chicano. Perhaps I never will be. But as I say all this, I look at the interviewer. He smiles softly. Has he heard what I have been trying to say? I wonder. I repeat: I have lost the ability to bring my past into my present; I do not know how to be a Chicano reader of Spenser or Shakespeare. All that remains is a desire for the past. He sighs, preoccupied, looking at my records. Would I be interested in teaching a course on the Mexican novel in translation? Do I understand that part of my duties would require that I become a counselor of minority students? What was the subject of that dissertation I did in England? Have I read the book on the same subject that was just published this month?

Behind the questioner, a figure forms in my imagination: my grandmother, her face solemn and still.

MEANING

1. What qualities did Rodriguez feel he lost by moving from the open and confident Mexican-American culture of his childhood into the cloistered, self-critical atmosphere of the academic world?

2. How did Rodriguez discover what leaving the past behind had cost him, in personal terms, while working on his dissertation in England?
3. How does the title, "On Becoming a Chicano," aptly express the point that Rodriguez had to consciously recover values he had discarded?

USING COMPARISON AND CONTRAST TO CONVEY MEANING

1. Why are the episodes concerning Rodriguez's grandmother central to understanding his sense of guilt over losing the values he learned in childhood?
2. What words or phrases express Rodriguez's sense of regret over losing the Chicano culture of his childhood?
3. Does Rodriguez organize his essay on a point-by-point or subject-by-subject basis, or does he use a mixture of the two strategies?

WRITING SUGGESTIONS

1. Are any of Rodriguez's observations appropriate to describe your own experiences in attending college?
2. Write an essay discussing the advantages and disadvantages of bilingualism using either a point-by-point or subject-by-subject method of organization.

SIDNEY HOOK

The Rights of the Victims

Sidney Hook was born in 1902 in New York City and received his Ph.D. from Columbia University in 1927. An eminent philosopher and legal scholar, he is Professor Emeritus at New York University, a senior research fellow of the Hoover Institution on War, Revolution, and Peace in Stanford, California, an organizer of Americans for Intellectual Freedom, and an active member of many other organizations, including the Committee Against Academic Discrimination and for Academic Integrity. Hook is the author of innumerable volumes, from The Metaphysics of Pragmatism *(1927), with an introduction by John Dewey, to* Pragmatism and the Tragic Sense of Life *(1974),* Revolution, Reform and Social Justice *(1975), and* Philosophy and Public Policy *(1980). Hook is an engaged social philosopher in the pragmatic mold of John Dewey, taking unpopular positions and defending them with eloquence and intellectual fervor. Not surprisingly, the one quality he values most is "moral courage," a trait fully evident in his essay, "The Rights of the Victims" (1972), which identifies points of conflict between the rights of criminals and the rights of potential victims.*

. . . American judicial opinions as well as academic treatises on criminology reveal a growing and thoughtful sensitivity to the possibility that the procedures by which defendants in criminal cases are booked and tried, and the evidence against them evaluated, may lead to miscarriages of justice. Legal practices that were once accepted without any qualms and doubts at a time when the U.S. Bill of Rights was adopted as a safeguard of the basic liberties of the people against the possible tyranny of the state, 18th-century practices that endured far into the 20th century, have been discarded in recent years in consequence of new, more enlightened readings or interpretations of our constitutional rights.

There are those who maintain that the alarming increase in crimes of violence is a direct consequence of the liberal modifications of our arrest and indictment procedures, of U.S. Supreme Court decisions that allegedly have shackled the law enforcement authorities and resulted in an ever larger number of recidivists or repeaters among criminal defendants. However, such an inference may be a case of the fallacy of *post hoc ergo propter hoc.* Causal questions in human affairs are notoriously difficult to resolve because of the number of variables involved. Striking correlations are not always evidence of causal connections. For the purpose of my analysis, it is not necessary either to reject or accept the view—asserted by some with great confidence—concerning the influence of court decisions on criminal behaviour. I suspend judgment about the *causes* of the current increase in crimes of violence, and take my point of departure only from the indisputable fact that the marked and alarming increase in domestic violence has indeed occurred. . . .

Why should we as citizens be concerned with the human and legal rights of persons accused of breaking the law? Why should we seek to liberalise the processes of law enforcement by raising protective hedges around such persons, thus making their conviction more difficult?

The answers summarise a library of literature. First, over and above any considerations of humanitarianism, we wish to avoid the danger of convicting the accused on the basis of plausible evidence, when he in ultimate fact may be innocent. The conviction of an innocent man comes closest in the intuitive judgment of mankind to being an absolute wrong. Second, even if we do not make the presumption of innocence, there is a good reason why we should want to defend and extend the rights of those accused of crime. For hard as it may be for us to imagine, someday we ourselves may be in the dock facing criminal charges of one kind or another. The quirks of fate or hazard of fortune or the hidden purpose of providence—call it what you will—have caught up even the most straitlaced and chokered individuals in tragic and violent situations, as bizarre as they were unexpected. And not all of them have been crimes of passion. There is a perennial and humbling wisdom in the Puritan's admonition to his son as they witnessed a wretch being dragged to the gallows: "There but for the Grace of God go I. . . . ." Both Boethe and Tolstoy, who understood the human heart because they saw deeply into their own, have acknowledged that there is no crime in the calendar of human folly and bestiality which in some situations they could not conceive themselves committing. And if we pride ourselves on our own immunity from temptation, it may testify not so much to our incorruptibility as to our lack of imaginative power.

This is the case for the rights of the criminal or the person accused of crime—and a powerful case it is. But before we bring in judgment we must perform another act of imaginative identification, much simpler and more natural, and that is with ourselves as victims of crimes of violence.

Granted that I am a potential criminal, I am also a potential victim of crime. The U.S. statistics of mounting violence show that cases of murder, non-negligent man-slaughter, and forcible rape have skyrocketed. It has been estimated that in America's large metropolitan centres the risk of becoming the victim of a serious crime has more than doubled in the last decade. Since many crimes of violence are committed by repeaters, the likelihood of my becoming a victim of crime is much greater than the likelihood of my becoming a criminal. Therefore, the protection of my right not to be mugged, assaulted, or murdered looms much larger in my mind than my rights as a criminal defendant.

. . . The potential victim has at least just as much a human right not to be violently molested, interfered with, and outraged as the person accused of such crimes has to have a fair trial and a skillful defence. As a citizen, most of the rights guaranteed me under the Bill of Rights become nugatory if I am hopelessly crippled by violence, and all of them become extinguished if I am killed. The rights of victims' are recognised in some legal jurisdictions which compensate them for disasters in which they become involved through no fault of their own. In England, it has been suggested that the assets of apprehended criminals who have committed capital crimes be distributed to the dependants of their victims. But my point here is that this emerging legal right of the victim is dependent upon the prior recognition of his moral right not to be victimised by the lawbreaker.

No matter how we seek to escape from acknowledging it, there is a direct conflict between the rights of their past and potential victims. In some classes of cases it is clear that the greater the right of the person accused of crime, the less the right of his future victim. For example, the right of a person out on bail for a crime of violence, to receive bail when he is charged with committing the same type of violent offence, and to be granted bail even when he is charged with committing the offence a third time—a right which he legitimately claims since he has not yet been found guilty of the first offence—conflicts head-on with the rights of his victims who can legitimately claim that they suffered this violence because the person at bar enjoyed his constitutional right to be free on bail. Those who fail to see this do not understand the nature of moral decision. It is not a choice between good and bad, right or wrong—this represents no moral choice but merely summarises the completed moral judgment. It is a choice between good and good, right and right, and, sometimes, between the good and the right. They also fail to see that this conflict of rights is expressed in the U.S. Constitution's Bill of Rights in which the free exercise of religion conflicts with the principle of separation of state and church, and in which the right to a free press may conflict with the right to a fair trial. In consequence, they ignore or underestimate the law-making powers of the U.S. Supreme Court, some of whose Justices in the past deceived themselves with the absurd view that the rights of the Bill of Rights are *absolute* and cannot be abridged under any circumstances. If rights conflict, they obviously cannot *all* be absolute.

Why has this conflict between the rights of the potential criminals and the rights of the potential victims not been previously recognised?

Among the reasons undoubtedly has been the fact that in all periods, except the present, when the rights of criminals and those accused of crime were being recognised, the incidence of violent crime was, relative to preceding periods, declining. Where crime was rife, the human rights of those accused of crime were hardly recognised or ruthlessly sacrificed on the altar of law and order. . . .

. . . I submit that at the present juncture of events, because of our American cities have become more dangerous to life and limb than the darkest jungle, we must give priority to the rights of potential victims. I am prepared to weaken the guarantees and privileges to which I am entitled as a potential criminal, or as a defendant, in order to strengthen my rights and safeguards as a potential victim. Purely on the basis of probabilities, I am convinced that I run a greater danger of suffering disaster as a potential victim than as a potential criminal or defendant. It is these probabilities that shift from one historical period to another that must be the guide of wise, prudent, and just administration of the law. . . .

When we read that preventive detention at the discretion of the judge (by denial of bail to repeated offenders charged with extremely violent crimes) is denounced by some judicial figures as a "betrayal of elementary justice," as "smacking of the concentration camps of Hitler and Stalin"; when we read that a person jailed for the death of 12 persons is freed from jail and the case against him dismissed because the prosecution's only evidence against him was a voluntary confession to the police who had failed to inform him of his rights; when we read that a man who murdered one of three hostages he had taken had a record of 25 arrests ranging from armed robbery to aggravated assault and battery, and that at the time of his arrest, he was free on bail awaiting grand jury action on charges in five separate cases in a two-month period preceding the murder; when we read that a man whose speeding car had been stopped by a motor-cycle policeman who, without a search warrant, forced him to open his trunk that contained the corpses of a woman and two children, walks out of court scot-free because the evidence is ruled inadmissible—we can only conclude with Mr. Bumble that the law is an ass.

The true wisdom of the law consists in recognising the conflict of rights and adjudicating the conflict by a decision that strengthens the whole structure of rights in the community. At a time when crime is rife, if the proof of a grave crime like murder is incontestable on the basis of evidence that may be "tainted" because the law-enforcement officer disregarded the niceties of procedure, then legal action should be taken against these officers by the state or by the defendant rather than giving, in effect, a grant of immunity to a murderer.

We wish to reduce the role of violence in human affairs without sacrificing the principles of justice. The extension of the privileges against self-incrimination to absurd lengths by American judges who abandoned common sense in a desire to establish a reputation for liberalism has, to my knowledge, no parallel in any other national legal jurisdiction. To elicit relevant testimony it has required legislation that has enabled some criminal defendants to purchase an undeserved immunity from punishment for very serious crimes. The statistics of violent crimes show that our situation is much too serious to indulge in sentimentalism at the expense of our fellow-citizens. . . .

MEANING

1. What three areas does Hook identify where potential victims have far fewer rights than criminals do under existing laws?
2. Why does Hook believe that any rights that criminals enjoy under the law automatically infringe on the corresponding rights of victims?

USING COMPARISON AND CONTRAST TO CONVEY MEANING

1. Does Hook give greater emphasis proportionately to one side, and if so, why?
2. What examples does Hook use to support his contention that there is a clear relationship between the number of crimes committed in a society and the way rights are allocated to citizens in that society?
3. Why does Hook ask the reader to imagine himself or herself as the victim rather than as the criminal?
4. How does Hook use the comparative method to support his recommendation that potential victims should be granted greater rights?

Writing Suggestions

1. How adequately does recent legislation mandating restitution for victims of crime address Hook's concerns? What further reforms are still needed?
2. Drawing on your own experiences, give examples of when your rights as an individual came into conflict with the rights of others. For example, what might a smoker say about laws prohibiting smoking in all public places?

Ruth Benedict

The Pueblos of New Mexico

*Ruth Benedict (1887–1948) was born in New York City and received her Ph.D.
in anthropology from Columbia University in 1923, studying under the renowned
Franz Boas. Her dissertation,* The Concept of the Guardian Spirit in North
America, *investigated American Indian religion after extensive field work among
the Serrano Indians of Southern California. Her best known work,* Patterns of
Culture (1934), *has been translated into fourteen languages and documents
her belief that all cultures are ruled by dominant patterns, akin to strongly
developed individual personality traits. Benedict found that each of the three
cultures she studied were dominated by a single psychological profile. She psychoan-
alyzed cultures as if they were individuals, finding the Zuñi of New Mexico to
be "Apollonian" in their sobriety, the Kwakiutl of Vancouver Island "Dionysian"
in their desire for intoxication, and the Dobu of Melanesia "schizophrenic" in
their morbid fear of each other. With her two-volume study,* Zuñi Mythology
(1935), *Benedict clearly established herself as the first American woman to become
a leading figure in anthropological research. "The Pueblos of New Mexico,"
taken from her pioneering work,* Patterns of Culture, *is the classic comparative
study of the Zuñi and Plains Indians.*

The Pueblo Indians of the Southwest are one of the most widely known primitive
peoples in Western civilization. They live in the midst of America, within easy reach
of any transcontinental traveller. And they are living after the old native fashion.
Their culture has not disintegrated like that of all the Indian communities outside
of Arizona and New Mexico. Month by month and year by year, the old dances of
the gods are danced in their stone villages, life follows essentially the old routines,
and what they have taken from our civilization they have remodelled and subordinated
to their own attitudes.

They have a romantic history. All through that part of America which they still
inhabit are found the homes of their cultural ancestors, the cliff-dwellings and great
planned valley cities of the golden age of the Pueblos. Their unbelievably numerous
cities were built in the twelfth and thirteenth centuries, but we can follow their
history much further back to its simple beginnings in one-room stone houses to
each of which an underground ceremonial chamber was attached. These early Pueblo
people, however, were not the first who had taken this Southwest desert for their
home. An earlier people, the Basketmakers, had lived there so long before that we
cannot calculate the period of their occupancy, and they were supplanted, and perhaps
largely exterminated, by the early Pueblo people.

The Pueblo culture flourished greatly after it had settled upon its arid plateau. It had brought with it the bow and arrow, a knowledge of stone architecture, and a diversified agriculture. Why it chose for the site of its greatest development the inhospitable, almost waterless valley of the San Juan, which flows into the Colorado River from the north, no one ventures to explain. It seems one of the most forbidding regions in the whole of what is now the United States, yet it was here that there grew up the greatest Indian cities north of Mexico. These were of two kinds, and they seem to have been built by the same civilization at the same period: the cliff-dwellings, and the semicircular valley citadels. The cliff-dwellings dug into the sheer face of the precipice, or built on a ledge hundreds of feet from the valley floor, are some of the most romantic habitations of mankind. We cannot guess what the circumstances were that led to the construction of these homes, far from the cornfields and far from any water-supply, which must have been serious if they were planned as fortifications, but some of the ruins enduringly challenge our admiration of ingenuity and beauty. One thing is never omitted in them, no matter how solid the rock ledge upon which the pueblo is built: the underground ceremonial chamber, the kiva, is hewed out to accommodate a man upright, and is large enough to serve as a gathering-room. It is entered by a ladder through a hatchway.

The other type of dwelling was a prototype of the modern planned city: a semicircular sweep of wall that rose three stories at the fortified exterior and was terraced inward as it approached the underground kivas that clustered in the embrace of the great masonry arms. Some of these great valley cities of this type have not only the small kivas, but one great additional temple similarly sunk into the earth and of the most finished and perfect masonry.

The peak of Pueblo civilization had been reached and passed before the Spanish adventurers came searching for cities of gold. It seems likely that the Navajo-Apache tribes from the north cut off the supplies of water from the cities of these ancient peoples and overcame them. When the Spanish came, they had already abandoned their cliff-dwellings and great semicircular cities and had settled along the Rio Grande in villages they still occupy. Toward the west there were also Acoma, Zuñi, and Hopi, the great western Pueblos.

Pueblo culture, therefore, has a long homogeneous history behind it, and we have special need of this knowledge of it because the cultural life of these peoples is so at variance with that of the rest of North America. Unfortunately archaeology cannot go further and tell us how it came about that here in this small region of America a culture gradually differentiated itself from all those that surrounded it and came always more and more drastically to express a consistent and particular attitude toward existence. . . .

The Zuñi are a ceremonious people, a people who value sobriety and inoffensiveness above all other virtues. Their interest is centered upon their rich and complex ceremonial life. Their cults of the masked gods, of healing, of the sun, of the sacred fetishes, of war, of the dead, are formal and established bodies of ritual with priestly officials and calendric observances. No field of activity competes with ritual for foremost place in their attention. Probably most grown men among the western Pueblos give to it the greater part of their waking life. It requires the memorizing of an amount of word-perfect ritual that our less trained minds find staggering, and the performance of neatly dovetailed ceremonies that are charted by the calendar and complexly interlock all the different cults and the governing body in endless formal procedure.

The ceremonial life not only demands their time; it preoccupies their attention. Not only those who are responsible for the ritual and those who take part in it, but all the people of the Pueblo, women and families who 'have nothing,' that is, that have no ritual possessions, centre their daily conversation about it. While it is in progress, they stand all day as spectators. If a priest is ill, or if no rain comes during his retreat, village gossip runs over and over his ceremonial missteps and the implications of his failure. Did the priest of the masked gods give offence to some supernatural being? Did he break his retreat by going home to his wife before the days were up? These are the subjects of talk in the village for a fortnight. If an impersonator wears a new feather on his mask, it eclipses all talk of sheep or gardens or marriage or divorce. . . .

If they are asked the purpose of any religious observance, they have a ready answer. It is for rain. This is of course a more or less conventional answer. But it reflects a deep-seated Zuñi attitude. Fertility is above all else the blessing within the bestowal of the gods, and in the desert country of the Zuñi plateau, rain is the prime requisite for the growth of crops. The retreats of the priests, the dances of the masked gods, even many of the activities of the medicine societies are judged by whether or not there has been rain. To "bless with water" is the synonym of all blessing. Thus, in the prayers, the fixed epithet the gods apply in blessing to the rooms in Zuñi to which they come, is "water-filled," their ladders are "water-ladders," and the scalp taken in warfare is "the water-filled covering." The dead, too, come back in the rain clouds, bringing the universal blessing. People say to the children when the summer afternoon rain clouds come up the sky, "Your grandfathers are coming," and the reference is not to individual dead relatives, but applies impersonally to all for-bears. The masked gods also are the rain and when they dance they constrain their own being—rain—to descend upon the people. The priests, again, in their retreat before their altars sit motionless and withdrawn for eight days, summoning the rain.

> From wherever you abide permanently
> You will make your roads come forth.
> Your little wind blown clouds,
> Your thin wisp of clouds
> Replete with living waters,
> You will send forth to stay with us.
> Your fine rain caressing the earth,
> Here at Itiwana[1]
> The abiding place of our fathers,
> Our mothers,
> The ones who first had being,
> With your great pile of waters
> You will come together.

Rain, however, is only one of the aspects of fertility for which prayers are constantly made in Zuñi. Increase in the gardens and increase in the tribe are thought of together. They desire to be blessed with happy women:

---

[1] "The Middle," the ceremonial name of Zuñi, the centre of the world. [Author's note.]

> Even those who are with child,
> Carrying one child on the back,
> Holding another on a cradle board,
> Leading one by the hand,
> With yet another going before. . . .

Like all the Pueblos, and perhaps in greater degree than the rest, Zuñi is rich. It has gardens and peach orchards and sheep and silver and turquoise. These are important to a man when they make it possible for him to have a mask made for himself, or to pay for the learning of ritual, or to entertain the tribal masked gods at the Shalako. For this last he must build a new house for the gods to bless at housewarming. All that year he must feed the cult members who build for him, he must provide the great beams for the rafters, he must entertain the whole tribe at the final ceremony. There are endless responsibilities he must assume. For this purpose he will plant heavily the year before and increase his herd. He will receive help from his clan group, all of which he must return in kind. Riches used in this way are of course indispensable to a man of prestige, but neither he nor anyone else is concerned with the reckoning of possessions, but with the ceremonial rôle which he has taken. A "valuable" family, in native parlance, is always a family which owns permanent fetishes, and a man of importance is one who has undertaken many ceremonial rôles.

All the traditional arrangements tend to make wealth play as small a part as possible in the performance of ritual prerogatives. Ceremonial objects, even though they are recognized personal property and attained by the expenditure of money and effort, are free to the use of anyone who can employ them. There are many sacred things too dangerous to be handled except by those who have qualified, but the tabus are not property tabus. Hunting fetishes are owned in the hunters' society, but anyone who is going hunting may take them for his use. He will have to assume the usual responsibilities for using holy things; he will have to plant prayer-sticks and be continent and benevolent for four days. But he pays nothing, and those who possess the fetishes as private property have no monopoly of their supernatural powers. Similarly a man who has no mask borrows one freely and is not thought of as a beggar or a suppliant. . . .

The basic contrast between the Pueblos and the other cultures of North America is the contrast that is named and described by Nietzsche in his studies of Greek tragedy. He discusses two diametrically opposed ways of arriving at the values of existence. The Dionysian pursues them through "the annihilation of the ordinary bounds and limits of existence"; he seeks to attain in his most valued moments escape from the boundaries imposed upon him by his five senses, to break through into another order of experience. The desire of the Dionysian, in personal experience or in ritual, is to press through it toward a certain psychological state, to achieve excess. The closest analogy to the emotions he seeks is drunkenness, and he values the illuminations of frenzy. With Blake, he believes "the path of excess leads to the palace of wisdom." The Apollonian distrusts all this, and has often little idea of the nature of such experiences. He finds means to outlaw them from his conscious life. He "knows but one law, measure in the Hellenic sense." He keeps the middle of the road, stays within the known map, does not meddle with disruptive psychological states. In Nietzsche's fine phrase, even in the exaltation of the dance he "remains what he is, and retains his civic name." . . .

The American Indians as a whole, and including those of Mexico, were passionately Dionysian. They valued all violent experience, all means by which human beings may break through the usual sensory routine, and to all such experiences they attributed the highest value.

The Indians of North America outside the Pueblos have, of course, anything but a uniform culture. They contrast violently at almost every point, and there are eight of them that it is convenient to differentiate as separate culture areas. But throughout them all, in one or another guise, there run certain fundamental Dionysian practices. The most conspicuous of these is probably their practice of obtaining supernatural power in a dream or vision. . . . On the western plains men sought these visions with hideous tortures. They cut strips from the skin of their arms, they struck off fingers, they swung themselves from tall poles by straps inserted under the muscles of their shoulders. They went without food and water for extreme periods. They sought in every way to achieve an order of experience set apart from daily living. . . .

On the western plains they believed that when the vision came it determined their life and the success they might expect. If no vision came, they were doomed to failure. "I was going to be poor; that is why I had no vision." If the experience was of curing, one had curing powers, if of warfare, one had warrior's powers. If one encountered Double Woman, one was a transvestite and took woman's occupations and habits. If one was blessed by the mythical Water Serpent, one had supernatural power for evil and sacrificed the lives of one's wife and children in payment for becoming a sorcerer. Any man who desired general strengthening or success in particular venture sought visions often. They were necessary for warpaths and for curings and for all kinds of miscellaneous occasions: calling the buffalo, naming chidren, mourning, revenge, finding lost articles. . . .

It might be from a dream that the supernatural power came to them. Some of the accounts of visions are unmistakable dream experiences, whether they occurred in sleep or under less normal conditions. Some tribes valued the dreams of sleep more highly than any other experiences. Lewis and Clark complained when they crossed the western plains in the early days that no night was fit for sleeping; some old man was always rousing to beat on his drum and ceremonially rehearse the dream he had just had. It was a valuable source of power.

In any case the criterion of whether or not the experience had power was necessarily a matter for the individual to decide. It was recognized as subjective, no matter what other social curbs were imposed upon its subsequent practice. Some experiences had power and some had not, and they distinguished by the flash of significance that singled out those that were valuable. . . .

This belief in the power of a vision experience on the western plains is a cultural mechanism which gives a theoretically unlimited freedom to the individual. He might go out and get this supremely coveted power, no matter to what family he belonged. Besides this, he might claim his vision as authority for any innovation, any personal advantage which he might imagine, and this authority he invoked was an experience in solitude which in the nature of the case could not be judged by another person. It was, moreover, probably the experience of greatest instability that he could achieve. It gave individual initiative a scope which is not easily equalled. . . .

Everywhere among the North American Indians, therefore, except in the Southwest Pueblos, we encounter this Dionysian dogma and practice of the vision-dream from which comes supernatural power. The Southwest is surrounded by peoples who seek the vision by fasting, by torture, by drugs and alcohol. But the Pueblos do not accept disruptive experiences and they do not derive supernatural power from them. If a Zuñi Indian has by chance a visual or auditory hallucination it is regarded as a sign of death. It is an experience to avoid, not one to seek by fasting. . . . The Pueblos are close to the Mexican plateau where the peyote button is obtained, and the Apache and the tribes of the plains with which they came most in contact were peyote-eaters. But the practice gained no foothold in the pueblos. A small anti-government group in Taos, the most atypical and Plains-like of the Pueblos, has recently taken it up. But elsewhere it has never been accepted. In their strict Apollonian *ethos,* the Pueblos distrust and reject those experiences which take the individual in any way out of bounds and forfeit his sobriety.

This repugnance is so strong that it has even been sufficient to keep American alcohol from becoming an administrative problem. Everywhere else on Indian reservations in the United States alcohol is an inescapable issue. There are no government regulations that can cope with the Indian's passion for whiskey. But in the pueblos the problem has never been important. They did not brew any native intoxicant in the old days, nor do they now. Nor is it a matter of course, as it is for instance with the near-by Apaches, that every trip to town, for old men or young, is a debauch. It is not that the Pueblos have a religious tabu against drinking. It is deeper than that. Drunkenness is repulsive to them. In Zuñi after the early introduction of liquor, the old men voluntarily outlawed it, and the rule was congenial enough to be honoured.

Torture was even more consistently rejected. The Pueblos, especially the eastern Pueblos, were in contact with two very different cultures in which self-torture was of the greatest importance, the Plains Indians and the Mexican Penitentes. Pueblo culture also shares many traits with the now extinct torture-using civilization of ancient Mexico, where on all occasions one drew blood from parts of one's own body, especially from the tongue, as an offering to the gods. On the plains, self-torture was specialized as a technique for obtaining states of self-oblivion during which one obtained a vision. . . .

The Pueblos do not understand self-torture. Every man's hand has its five fingers, and unless they have been tortured to secure a sorcery confession they are unscarred. There are no cicatrices upon their backs, no marks where strips of skin have been taken off. They have no rites in which they sacrifice their own blood, or use it for fertility. They used to hurt themselves to a certain extent in a few initiations at the moments of greatest excitement, but in such cases the whole matter was almost an affair of collegiate exuberance. In the Cactus Society, a warrior cult, they dashed about striking themselves and each other with cactus-blade whips; in the Fire Society they tossed fire about like confetti. Neither psychic danger nor abnormal experience is sought in either case. Certainly in the observed fire tricks of the Pueblos—as also in the fire tricks of the Plains—it is not self-torture that is sought. In the Fire Walk, whatever the means employed, feet are not burned, and when the fire is taken into the mouth the tongue is not blistered. . . .

If ecstasy is not sought by fasting, by torture, or by drugs or alcohol, or under the guise of the vision, neither is it induced in the dance. Perhaps no people in North America spend more time in the dance than the Southwest Pueblos. But their object in it never is to attain self-oblivion. It is by the frenzy of the dance that the Greek cult of Dionysus was best known, and it recurs over and over in North America. The Ghost Dance of the Indians that swept the country in the 1870's was a round dance danced monotonously till the dancers, one after the other, fell rigid, prostrate on the ground. During their seizure they had visions of deliverance from the whites, and meanwhile the dance continued and others fell. It was the custom in most of the dozens of tribes to which it penetrated to hold the dance every Sunday. There were other and older dances also that were thoroughly Dionysian. The tribes of northern Mexico danced, frothing at the mouth, upon the altar. The shamans' dances of California required a cataleptic seizure. . . .

Of all this there is no suggestion in all the dance occasions of Zuñi. The dance, like their ritual poetry, is a monotonous, compulsion of natural forces by reiteration. The tireless pounding of their feet draws together the mist in the sky and heaps it into the piled rain clouds. It forces out the rain upon the earth. They are bent not at all upon an ecstatic experience, but upon so thorough-going an identification with nature that the forces of nature will swing to their purposes. This intent dictates the form and spirit of Pueblo dances. There is nothing wild about them. It is the cumulative force of the rhythm, the perfection of forty men moving as one, that makes them effective.

No one has conveyed this quality of Pueblo dancing more precisely than D. H. Lawrence. "All the men sing in unison, as they move with the soft, yet heavy bird tread which is the whole of the dance, with bodies bent a little forward, shoulders and heads loose and heavy, feet powerful but soft, the men tread the rhythm into the centre of the earth. The drums keep up the pulsating heart beat and for hours, hours, it goes on." Sometimes they are dancing the sprouting corn up out of the earth, sometimes they are calling the game animals by the tramp of their feet, sometimes they are constraining the white cumulus clouds that are slowly piling up the sky on a desert afternoon. Even the presence of these in the sky, whether or not they vouchsafe rain, is a blessing from the supernaturals upon the dance, a sign that their rite is accepted. If rain comes, that is the sign and seal of the power of their dance. It is the answer. They dance on through the swift Southwest downpour, their feathers wet and heavy, their embroidered kilts and mantles drenched. But they have been favoured by the gods. The clowns make merry in the deep adobe mud, sliding at full length in the puddles and paddling in the half-liquid earth. It is their recognition that their feet in the dance have the compulsion of natural forces upon the storm clouds and have been powerful to bring the rain. . . .

Without initiative and the ability to act alone, an Indian of the plains was not recognized in his society. The testimony of early explorers, the rise of outstanding individuals in their conflicts with the whites, the contrast with the Pueblos, all go to show how their institutions fostered personality, almost in the Nietzschean sense of the superman. They saw life as the drama of the individual progressing upward through grades of men's societies, through acquisition of supernatural power, through feasts and victories. The initiative rested always with him. His deeds of prowess were counted for him personally, and it was his prerogative to boast of them on ritual occasions, and to use them in every way to further his personal ambitions.

The ideal man of the Pueblos is another order of being. Personal authority is perhaps the most vigorously disparaged trait in Zuñi. "A man who thirsts for power or knowledge, who wishes to be as they scornfully phrase it 'a leader of his people,' receives nothing but censure and will very likely be persecuted for sorcery," and he often has been. Native authority of manner is a liability in Zuñi, and witchcraft is the ready charge against a person who possesses it. He is hung by the thumbs until he "confesses." It is all Zuñi can do with a man of strong personality. The ideal man in Zuñi is a person of dignity and affability who has never tried to lead, and who has never called forth comment from his neighbours. Any conflict, even though all right is on his side, is held against him. Even in contests of skill like their foot-races, if a man wins habitually he is debarred from running. They are interested in a game that a number can play with even chances, and an outstanding runner spoils the game: they will have none of him.

A good man has, in Dr. Bunzel's words, "a pleasing address, a yielding disposition, and a generous heart." The highest praise, describing an impeccable townsman, runs: "He is a nice polite man. No one ever hears anything from him. He never gets into trouble. He's Badger clan and Muhekwe kiva, and he always dances in the summer dances." He should "talk lots," as they say—that is, he should always set people at their ease—and he should without fail co-operate easily with others either in the field or in ritual, never betraying a suspicion of arrogance or a strong emotion.

He avoids office. He may have it thrust upon him, but he does not seek it. When the kiva offices must be filled, the hatchway of the kiva is fastened and all the men are imprisoned until someone's excuses have been battered down. The folktales always relate of good men their unwillingness to take office—though they always take it. A man must avoid the appearance of leadership. When the chosen person has been prevailed upon and has been initiated in the office, he has not been given authority in our sense. His post carries with it no sanction for important action. The council of Zuñi is made up of the highest priests, and priests have no jurisdiction in cases of conflict or violence. They are holy men and must not have a quarrel put before them. Only the war chiefs have some measure of executive authority, not in war so much as in peace-time policing powers. They make proclamation of a coming rabbit hunt, or coming dances, they summon priests and co-operate with the medicine societies. The crime that they traditionally have to deal with is witchcraft. Another crime, that of betraying to the uninitiated boys the secret of the kachinas, is punished by the masked gods themselves, summoned by the head of the kachina cult. There are no other crimes. Theft rarely occurs and is a private matter. Adultery is no crime and the strain that arises from such an act is easily taken care of under their marriage arrangements. Homicide, in the one case that is remembered, was settled quickly by payments between the two families. . . .

This same lack of personal exercise of authority is as characteristic of domestic situations as it is of religious. The matrilineal and matrilocal household of course makes necessary a different allocation of authority from that with which we are familiar. But matrilineal societies do not usually dispense with a male person of authority in the household even though the father does not qualify. The mother's brother as the male head of the matrilineal household is arbiter and responsible head. But Zuñi does not recognize any authority as vested in the mother's brother, and certainly not in the father. Neither of them disciplines the children of his household. Babies are much fondled by the men folk. They carry them when they are ailing and hold them in their laps evenings. But they do not discipline them. The virtue of co-operation holds domestic life true to form just as it holds religious life, and no situations arise that need to be drastically handled. What would they be? Marriage is in other cultures the almost universal occasion where some authority is exercised. But among the Pueblos it is arranged with little formality. Marriage elsewhere in the world involves property rights and economic exchange, and on all such occasions the elders have prerogatives. But in Zuñi marriage there are no stakes in which the elders are interested. The slight emphasis upon possessions among the Pueblos makes a casual affair not only of the elsewhere difficult situation of marriage but of a dozen others, àll those which according to other cultural forms involve investment of group property for the young man. Zuñi simply eliminates the occasions.

Every arrangement militates against the possibility of the child's suffering from an Oedipus complex. Malinowski[2] has pointed out for the Trobriands that the structure of society gives to the uncle authority that is associated in our culture with the father. In Zuñi, not even the uncles exercise authority. Occasions are not tolerated which would demand its exercise. The child grows up without either the resentments or the compensatory day-dreams of ambition that have their roots in this familiar situation. When the child himself becomes an adult, he has not the motivations that lead him to imagine situations in which authority will be relevant. . . .

Just as according to the Zuñi ideal a man sinks his activities in those of the group and claims no personal authority, so also he is never violent. Their Apollonian commitment to the mean in the Greek sense is never clearer than in their cultural handling of the emotions. Whether it is anger or love or jealousy or grief, moderation is the first virtue. The fundamental tabu upon their holy men during their periods of office is against any suspicion of anger. Controversies, whether they are ceremonial or economic or domestic, are carried out with an unparalleled lack of vehemence.

Every day in Zuñi there are fresh instances of their mildness. One summer a family I knew well had given me a house to live in, and because of some complicated circumstances another family claimed the right to dispose of the dwelling. When feeling was at its height, Quatsia, the owner of the house, and her husband were with me in the livingroom when a man I did not know began cutting down the flowering weeds that had not yet been hoed out of the yard. Keeping the yard free of growth is a chief prerogative of a house-owner, and therefore the man who claimed the right to dispose of the house was taking this occasion to put his claim publicly upon record. He did not enter the house or challenge Quatsia and Leo, who were inside, but he hacked slowly at the weeds. Inside, Leo sat immobile on his heels against the wall, peaceably chewing a leaf. Quatsia, however, allowed herself to flush. "It is an insult," she said to me. "The man out there knows that Leo is serving as priest this year and he can't be angry. He shames us before the whole village by taking care of our yard." The interloper finally raked up his wilted weeds, looked proudly at the neat yard, and went home. No words were ever spoken between them. For Zuñi it was an insult of sorts, and by his morning's work on the yard the rival claimant sufficiently expressed his protest. He pressed the matter no further.

Marital jealously is similarly soft-pedalled. They do not meet adultery with violence. A usual response on the plains to the wife's adultery was to cut off the fleshy part of her nose. This was done even in the Southwest by non-Pueblo tribes like the Apache. But in Zuñi the unfaithfulness of the wife is no excuse for violence. The husband does not regard it as a violation of his rights. If she is unfaithful, it is normally a first step in changing husbands, and their institutions make this sufficiently easy so that it is a really tolerable procedure. They do not contemplate violence.

Wives are often equally moderate when their husbands are known to be unfaithful. As long as the situation is not unpleasant enough for relations to be broken off, it is ignored. The season before one of Dr. Bunzel's visits in Zuñi one of the young husbands of the household in which she lived had been carrying on an extra-marital

---

[2] Bronislaw Malinowski (1884–1942), the eminent Polish anthropologist who did extensive field work among the Trobriand Islanders.

affair that became bruited about all over the pueblo. The family ignored the matter completely. At last the white trader, a guardian of morals, expostulated with the wife. The couple had been married a dozen years and had three children; the wife belonged to an important family. The trader set forth with great earnestness the need of making a show of authority and putting an end to her husband's outrageous conduct. "So," his wife said, "I didn't wash his clothes. Then he knew that I knew that everybody knew, and he stopped going with that girl." It was effective, but not a word was passed. There were no outbursts, no recriminations, not even an open recognition of the crisis.

Wives, however, are allowed another course of action which is not sanctioned in the case of deserted husbands. A wife may fall upon her rival and beat her up publicly. They call each other names and give each other a black eye. It never settles anything, and even in the rare cases when it occurs, it dies down as quickly as it has flared. It is the only recognized fist-fight in Zuñi. If on the other hand a woman remains peacefully with her husband while he conducts amour after amour, her family are angry and bring pressure to bear upon her to separate from him. "Everybody says she must love him," they say, and all her relatives are ashamed. She is disobeying the rules that are laid down for her.

For the traditional course is that of divorce. If a man finds his wife's female relatives uncongenial, he is free to return to his mother's household. It provides a means of avoiding domestic intimacy with individuals he dislikes, and he merely dissolves the relationships which he has found difficult to handle amicably. . . .

The attitude toward sex in Zuñi parallels certain standards we know in our civilization as Puritanical, but the contrasts are quite as striking as the parallels. The Puritan attitude toward sex flows from its identification as sin, and the Zuñi have no sense of sin. Sin is unfamiliar to them, not only in sex but in any experience. They do not suffer from guilt complexes, and they do not consider sex as a series of temptations to be resisted with painful efforts of the will. Chastity as a way of life is regarded with great disfavour, and no one in their folktales is criticized more harshly than the proud girls who resist marriage in their youth. They stay in and work, ignoring the occasions when they should legitimately be admired by the young men. But the gods do not take the steps they were supposed to take in Puritan ethics. They come down and contrive in spite of obstacles to sleep with them, and teach them delight and humility. By these "amiable disciplinary means" they bring it about that the girl shall embrace in marriage the proper happiness of mortals.

Pleasant relations between the sexes are merely one aspect of pleasant relations with human beings. Where we make a fundamental distinction, their phrase of commendation is, "Everybody likes him. He is always having affairs with women." Or, "Nobody likes him. He never has trouble over women." Sex is an incident in the happy life.

Their cosmological ideas are another form in which they have given expression to their extraordinarily consistent spirit. The same lack of intensity, of conflict, and of danger which they have institutionalized in this world, they project also upon the other world. The supernaturals, as Dr. Bunzel says, "have no animus against man. Inasmuch as they may withhold their gifts, their assistance must be secured by offerings, prayers and magical practices." But it is no placation of evil forces. The idea is foreign to them. They reckon, rather, that the supernaturals like what men like, and if men like dancing so will the supernaturals. Therefore they bring the supernaturals back to dance in Zuñi by donning their masks, they take out the medicine bundles and 'dance' them. It gives them pleasure. Even the corn in the storeroom must be danced. "During the winter solstice, when all ritual groups are holding their ceremonies, the heads of households take six perfect ears of corn and hold them in a basket while they sing to them. This is called 'dancing the corn' and is performed that the corn may not feel neglected during the ceremonial season." So too the great Dance of the Corn, now no longer performed, culminated in this enjoyment they had the means of sharing with the corn ears. . . .

It is difficult for us to lay aside our picture of the universe as a struggle between good and evil and see it as the Pueblos see it. They do not see the seasons, nor man's life, as a race run by life and death. Life is always present, death is always present. Death is no denial of life. The seasons unroll themselves before us, and man's life also. Their attitude involves "no resignation, no subordination of desire to a stronger force, but the sense of man's oneness with the universe." When they pray they say to their gods,

> We shall be one person.

They exchange intimate relationship terms with them:

> Holding your country,
> Holding your people,
> You will sit down quietly for us.
> As children to one another
> We shall always remain.
> My child,
> My mother,
> According to my words
> Even so may it be.

They speak of exchanging breath with their gods:

> . . .Do not despise the breath of your fathers,
> But draw it into your body. . . .
> That we may finish our roads together.
> May my father bless you with life;
> May your road be fulfilled.

The breath of the gods is their breath, and by their common sharing all things are accomplished.

MEANING

1. What significant differences does Benedict discover between the Zuñi and Plains Indians in their use of drugs and alcohol and their attitudes toward power, sex, torture, visions, and ritual dancing?
2. How do visions serve as a form of guidance for the Plains Indians?
3. What significant difference in attitude separates the Zuñi from the Plains Indians in the value they attach to the individual; for which tribe is the community more important?

4. How does Benedict use Nietzsche's distinction between Apollonian and Dionysian qualities to compare the unegotistical cultural values of the Zuñi to the power-seeking behavior of the Plains Indians?

Using Comparison and Contrast to Convey Meaning

1. Why does Benedict proportion her essay to provide a fuller discussion of the customs and habits of the Zuñi rather than those of the Plains Indians?
2. What examples does Benedict provide that illustrate the importance of religious rituals for the Zuñi?
3. What specific cases does Benedict cite to illustrate contrasting attitudes of the Plains Indians and the Zuñi in their ritual use of the dance?
4. Why is the comparative method displayed in this classic essay so essential to the discipline of anthropology?

Writing Suggestions

1. What broad differences in emphasis and outlook can you observe between D. H. Lawrence's literary treatment of the dance of the sprouting corn (see the "Description" chapter, page 97) and Benedict's anthropological study of the same ceremony? How are these differences attributable to the different methods and purposes of each author's discipline?
2. Draw the underground ceremonial chamber, the kiva, based on details found in Benedict's article.
3. In what ways are the Zuñi like the American Puritans?
4. Draw on Benedict's distinction between Apollonian and Dionysian qualities to compare baseball with football, classical music with rock, or any two items in the same class such as clothes or automobiles, which manifest these kinds of differences.
5. How effectively did the movie, "A Man Called Horse," recreate the customs, described by Benedict, of the Plains Indians' use of torture to confirm manhood?

SCIENCES

HANS ZINSSER

Rats and Men

Hans Zinsser (1878–1940) was born in New York City and raised in a household where he learned to speak German and French. He received his M.D. from the Columbia College of Physicians and Surgeons in 1903 and was Professor of Bacteriology and Immunology at both Stanford and Columbia University. From 1923 onwards Zinsser held the Charles Wilder Professorship at Harvard Medical School. After visits to Serbia in 1915 as a member of the American Red Cross Commission, Zinsser turned his attention to research into epidemic typhus and did further field investigations in the Soviet Union (1923), Mexico (1931), and China (1938). He wrote about these experiences in Rats, Lice, and History *(1935) and* As I Remember Him *(1940). Because of Zinsser's vivid writing style, these two books achieved wide popularity far beyond the medical community. In addition to his research in the production of an effective vaccine against typhus, Zinsser did important work on the immunological aspects of tuberculosis. He coauthored a standard reference work,* A Textbook of Bacteriology *(1910), which went through eight editions and was translated into many foreign languages, including Chinese. "Rats and Men," a provocative chapter from* Rats, Lice, and History, *discusses the relationship between the spread of typhus and unsuspected similarities between the species of rat and man.*

It is quite impossible to make a case for the presence of true rats in Europe proper during classical times, much as this would clarify the epidemiological situation. It is conceivable that the manner of transmission of plague and typhus may have undergone modification since the Peloponnesian Wars[1] by changed adaptations to hosts, both insect and rodent. But it would seem much more likely that the zoölogical differentiations between rodents so similar and closely related as mice and rats were inaccurate in ancient records, and that rats may have existed—though undomesticated. This would give us a wider latitude for speculation regarding the nature of epidemics, which, to

---

[1] A series of wars fought between the city-states of Athens and Sparta, 431–404 B.C.

259

be sure, were rarely, under the circumstances of ancient life, as widespread or deadly as they became with the later concentrations of population and or urban habits. At any rate, if rats had been present in those times in anything like the numbers in which they are found to-day, we should probably have reliable records. It may well be that the frugality of well-run households, like that of Penelope,[2] gave little encouragement to house rats to become parasitic on man to the extent to which they have since.

All this is conjecture. According to the wisest students of the subject, there is no certain knowledge of rats in Europe, within historic periods, until shortly after the Crusades. In prehistoric days they certainly existed there—but later disappeared. Fossil remains of rats have been found in the Pliocene period of Lombardy (the Mastodon period of Europe) and in the later Pleistocene of Crete. They were present during the glacial period with the lake dwellers, whom they pestered in Mecklenburg and Western Germany. From that time on, there were either few or no rats until thousands of years later.

In regard to the reappearance of rats in Europe, our industrious colleagues, the zoölogists, have gathered an immense amount of information, much of which has been interestingly summarized by Barrett-Hamilton and Hinton in their *History of British Mammals,* and by Donaldson in his *Memoir on the Rat.* Before we proceed to this subject, however, it will be profitable to consider the striking analogy between rats and men. More than any other species of animal, the rat and mouse have become dependent on man, and in so doing they have developed characteristics which are amazingly human.

In the first place, like man, the rat has become practically omnivourous. It eats anything that lets it and—like man—devours its own kind, under stress. It breeds at all seasons and—again like man—it is most amorous in the springtime.[3] It hybridizes easily and, judging by the strained relationship between the black and the brown rat, develops social or racial prejudices against this practice. The sex proportions are like those among us. Inbreeding takes place readily. The males are larger, the females fatter. It adapts itself to all kinds of climates. It makes ferocious war upon its own kind, but has not, as yet, become nationalized. So far, it has still stuck to tribal wars—like man before nations were invented. If it continues to ape man as heretofore, we may, in a few centuries, have French rats eating German ones, or Nazi rats attacking Communist or Jewish rats; however, such a degree of civilization is probably not within the capacities of any mere animal. Also—like man—the rat is individualistic

---

[2] The long-suffering wife of Odysseus in Homer's epic, *The Odyssey.* [Zinsser's note.]

[3] On first sight, the fertility of rats would seem far to outstrip that of man; for rats reach adolescence when a little more than half grown, and produce one or two litters a year, averaging from five to ten in number. The difference from man, however, is not so striking if one remembers Donaldson's calculation that one rat year equals thirty years for man, and makes the comparison with human society of former years—in savage communities, or before the humane and sane practice of birth control had begun to weaken the inhibitions of religion in such matters. Many examples not too unlike conditions among rats could be cited—such as, for instance, the story of Samuel Wesley, father of John, which we take from a review by J. C. Minot of Laver's biography of Wesley. Samuel had fourteen children with his good Sukey before 1701, when he left her because she refused to pray for William III as the lawful King of England. On the accession of Queen Anne, he was reconciled and bestowed five more children upon the fortunate woman. The oldest of these pledges of reconciliation was the immortal John Wesley. [Zinsser's note.]

until it needs help. That is, it fights bravely alone against weaker rivals, for food or for love; but it knows how to organize armies and fight in hordes when necessary.

Donaldson, basing his calculations mainly on stages in the development of the nervous system, reckons three years of a rat life as ninety years for man. By this scale, the rat reaches puberty at about sixteen, and arrives at the menopause at the equivalent of forty-five. In following man about all over the earth, the rat has—more than any other living creature except man—been able to adapt itself to any conditions of seasonal changes or climate.

The first rat to arrive in Europe was *Mus rattus*—the black rat, house rat, or ship rat. It may have wandered in between 400 and 1100 A.D., with the hordes that swept into Europe from the East in that period of great unrest—the *Völkerwanderung*.[4] It may not have arrived until somewhat later, when the first Crusaders returned. It is not mentioned in the Epinal Glossary of 700 A.D., but may have been meant by the word "raet" in the English Archbishop Ælfric's Vocabulary of 1000 A.D. But the authorities from whom we cite this call attention to the fact that the word "rata" was the Provençal for the domestic mouse of that time, and the word may have been introduced into England.[5] Hamilton and Hinton say that the first clear differentiation between rats and mice is found in the writings of Giraldus Cambrensis (1147–1223). After that date, it is referred to frequently.

As to the Eastern origin of the black rat, there seems to be no difference of opinion among authorities, though there is much uncertainty about the exact part of the Orient from which it came. De L'Isle believes that the *Mus alexandrinus* represents the source stock of the European *Mus rattus*. This—the Alexandrine rat—did not, according to him, become parasitic on human society until the seventh century—living before this time a wild existence, possibly in the Arabian deserts, a fact which would account for its failure to migrate into classical Europe with trade, and, in the early Middle Ages, with Saracen invasions. By the time of the Crusaders, it had begun to domesticate and consequently to follow human travel. Being a climber and therefore a ship rat, it spread rapidly to Mediterranean ports, where, according to Hamilton and Hinton, its arrival by sea is witnessed to by the name πυότιχος[6] applied to it by the modern Greeks; "pantagena" by the Venetians. The Genoese mistook it for a mole, calling it "Salpa," another point of evidence that it may have been new to them.

From the time of its arrival, the rat spread across Europe with a speed superior even to that of the white man in the Americas. Before the end of the thirteenth century, it had become a pest. The legend of the *Rattenfänger von Hameln*[7] who piped the children into the hollow Koppenberg because the town refused his pay for piping the rats into the Weser, is placed at or about 1284. By this time, the rat

[4] The great migrations. [Zinsser's note.]

[5] Rats and mice belong to the same genus, and the closeness of the relationship is attested by the experiment of Ivanoff, who artifically inseminated a white mouse with the sperm of a white rat, and obtained two hybrids after a pregnancy of twenty-seven days. Mice may have developed out of rats under circumstances which made it less desirable to be large and ferocious than to be able to get into a smaller hole—the advantages of which may be appreciated by those of us who have lived in the world during the postwar years. [Zinsser's note.]

[6] "Of the sea." [Zinsser's note.]

[7] The Pied Piper of Hamelin. [Zinsser's note.]

had penetrated into England. It had reached Ireland some time before this, where it was the "foreign" or "French" mouse,"ean francach." Our authorites tell us that in Ireland, even until very recent times, everything foreign was called "francach," or French. A little later, the rat was in Denmark, Norway, and the adjacent islands. By Shakespeare's time, the black rat was so formidable a nuisance that days of prayer for protection against its ravages were set aside, and rat catchers (see *Romeo and Juliet*, Act III) were important officials, probably calling themselves, as they would to-day, scientists or artists (or "rattors"—*cf.* "realtors" and "morticians").

For twice as long as the Vandals had their day in North Africa, or the Saracens in Spain, or the Normans in Italy, the black rats had their own way in Europe. Their reign covered the periods of the devastating epidemics of plague that swept through the battle areas of the Thirty Years' War and the later ones of the seventeenth century. And during the centuries of its supremacy there occurred the most destructive typhus epidemics, accompanying wars and famines, that have occurred up to our own time. Whether the black rats of mediaeval Europe played a rôle in these remains uncertain. That they played the leading part in the plague epidemics of this time seems beyond question.

But just as the established civilizations of Northern Europe were swept aside by the mass invasions of barbarians from the East, so the established hegemony of the black rat was eventually wiped out with the incursion of the hordes of the brown rat, or *Mus decumanus*—the ferocious, shortnosed, and short-tailed Asiatic that swept across the Continent in the early eighteenth century; until at the present time, the slender-nosed, long-tailed, climbing *Mus rattus* has been all but exterminated in its former strongholds, and continues to thrive only in relatively small groups along the littoral, in seaports, on islands, or in countries like South American and other tropical regions where it is not confined to parasitic life in competition with its larger and more barbaric rival, or where the brown *conquistadores* have not yet arrived. It maintains its former superiority only on ships where, because of its greater ability in climbing, it can still hold its own.[8]

The brown rat, too, came from the East. It is now known as the "common" rat and, because of a mistaken notion of its origin, as *Mus norvegicus*. Its true origin, according to Hamilton and Hinton, is probably Chinese Mongolia or the region east of Lake Baikal, in both of which places forms resembling it have been found indigenous. The same writers quote Blasius, who believes that the ancients about the Caspian Sea may have known this rat. Claudius Ælianus, a Roman rhetorician of the second century, in his *De Animalium Natura*, speaks of "little less than Ichneumons, making periodical raids in infinite numbers" in the countries along the Caspian, "swimming over rivers holding each other's tails." This may or may not be so; but it seems certain that this rat was not known in Western Europe until the eighteenth century.

Pallas (1831), in his *Zoögraphica Rooso-Asiatica*, records that in 1727—a mouse year—great masses of these rats swam across the Volga after an earthquake. They invaded Astrakhan, and thence rapidly spread westward. They reached England, probably by ship, in 1728, and were unjustly called the "Hanoverian rat" because of the unpopularity of the House of Hanover, though probably they had not arrived in Germany at that time. They were seen in Prussia in 1750, and were common by 1780. This rat was unknown to Buffon in 1753 and to Linnæus in 1758—but both

---

[8] In a recent rat survey of Boston, black rats were found in only a single small and circumscribed area, close to the docks. [Zinsser's note.]

of these gentlemen were already "famous" scientists at this time, and most likely occupied in attending committee meetings. The brown rat arrived in Norway in 1762, a little later in Spain, and in Scotland about 1770. By 1775 it had come to America from England. It apears to have had a hard time only in countries where the population is what is spoken as of "thrifty." In Scotland, it took from 1776 to 1834 to get from Selkirk to Morayshire; it did not dare enter Switzerland until 1869, and has never done very well among the Switzers. It spread slowly across our continent, owing to deserts, rivers, and long distances between "hand-outs." Consequently, it did not arrive in California until shortly after 1851. Now that it is there, it thrives in that wonderful climate as hardly elsewhere. At the present time the rat has spread across the North American Continent from Panama to Alaska, has penetrated to all the less tropical parts of South America, to the South Sea Islands, to New Zealand, and to Australia. In fact, it has conquered the world. Only the extreme cold of Greenland does not seem to attract it. Unlike the Eskimo, it has had the good sense, whenever introduced to the arctic regions, to wander southward at the first opportunity.

Wherever it has gone, it has driven out the black rat and all rival rodents that compete with it. From the point of view of all other living creatures, the rat is an unmitigated nuisance and pest. There is nothing that can be said in its favor.[9] It can live anywhere and eat anything. It burrows for itself when it has to, but, when it can, it takes over the habitations of other animals, such as rabbits, and kills them and their young. It climbs and it swims.

It carries diseases of man and animals—plague, typhus, trichinella spiralis, rat-bite fever, infectious jaundice, possibly Trench fever, probably foot-and-mouth disease and a form of equine "influenza." Its destructiveness is almost unlimited. Lantz, of the United States Department of Agriculture, has made some approximate estimates of this, as follows (we abbreviate):—

Rats destroy cultivated grain as seeds, sprouts, or after ripening.

They eat Indian corn, both during growth and in the cribs, and have been known to get away with half of the crop. A single rat can eat from forty to fifty pounds a year.

They destroy merchandise, both stored and in transit, books, leather, harness, gloves, cloth, fruit, vegetables, peanuts, and so forth.

The rat is the greatest enemy of poultry, killing chicks, young turkeys, ducks, pigeons; also eating enormous numbers of eggs.

Rats destroy wild birds, ducks, woodcocks, and song birds.

They attack bulbs, seeds, and young plants or flowers.

They cause enormous damage to buildings, by gnawing wood, pipes, walls, and foundations.

[9] Of course, rats might form a cheap source of food. They have been eaten without harm under stress—at the siege of Paris in 1871, and before that by the French garrison at Malta in 1798, where, according to Lantz, food was so scarce that a rat carcass brought a high price. The same writer states that Dr. Kane of the arctic ship *Advance* ate rats through the winter, and avoided scurvy—from which his more fastidious companions all suffered. For the following story we cannot vouch. It is related to us that a learned specialist on rodents was lecturing, some years ago, in one of the more distinguished university centres in the United States. After the lecture, he was taken to a restaurant famous for its terrapin. He enjoyed his meal and praised the quality of the *pièce de résistance*, but recognized the bones on his plate as those of rats. He is said later to have visited the albino rattery where the "terrapin" was bred. The matter might be looked into as a commercial possibility. Robert Southey once suggested that the first requisite to successful rat eradication was to make them a table delicacy. [Zinsser's note.]

Hagenbeck had to kill three elephants because the rats had gnawed their feet. Rats have killed young lambs and gnawed holes in the bellies of fat swine.

They have gnawed holes in dams and started floods; they have started fires by gnawing matches; they have bitten holes in mail sacks and eaten the mail; they have actually caused famines in India by wholesale crop destruction in scant years.

They have nibbled at the ears and noses of infants in their cribs; starving rats once devoured a man who entered a disused coal mine.

A rat census is obviously impossible. It is quite certain, however, that they breed more rapidly than they are destroyed in many places in the world. We can appraise the rat population only by the numbers that are killed in organized rat campaigns and by the amount of destruction they cause. In about 1860, Shipley tells us, there was a slaughterhouse for horses on Montfaucon, which it was planned to remove farther away from Paris. The carcasses of horses amounted to sometimes thirty-five a day, and were regularly cleaned up completely by rats in the following night. Dusaussois had the idea of trying to find out how many rats were engaged in this gruesome traffic. He set horse-meat bait in enclosures from which the exit of rats could be prevented, and in the course of the first night killed 2650. By the end of a month, he had killed over 16,000. Shipley estimates that there are about forty million rats in England at one time. In 1881 there was a rat plague in certain districts of India. The crops of the preceding two years were below average and a large part of them had been destroyed by rats. Rewards offered for rat destruction led to a killing of over 12,000,000 rats. Shipley estimtes that a single rat does about 7s. 6d. worth of damage in a year, which makes a charge of £15,000,000 upon Great Britain and Ireland. It costs about sixty cents to two dollars a year to feed a rat on grain. Every rat on a farm costs about fifty cents a year. Lantz adds to this that hotel managers estimate five dollars a year as a low estimate of the loss inflicted by a rat. He thinks that in the thickly populated parts of the country an estimate of one rat per acre is not excessive, and that in most of our cities there are as many rats as people. He investigated, in 1909, the approximate total damage by rats in the cities of Washington and Baltimore. From the data he obtained, he calculated the annual damage in the two cities as amounting to $400,000 and $700,000 respectively—which, considering the populations, amounted to an average loss of $1.27 a year per person. On the same basis, the urban population of the United States, at that time 28,000,000 people, sustained an annual direct injury of $35,000,000 a year. In Denmark, the estimated rat cost is about $1.20 a person; in Germany, eighty-five cents a person; in France, a little over a dollar. Add to this the inestimable depreciation of property and the costs of protection.

All this has nothing to do with our main subject, but we were started on rats, and it is just as well to give thought to the problem of what rat extermination for sanitary purposes is likely to mean in other respects.

The tremendous speed with which rats swarmed over the continents of the world can be readily understood if one reads the observations of actual rat migrations made in modern times. The seasonal migration of rats from buildings to the open fields takes place with the coming of the warm weather and the growth of vegetation; and a return to shelter follows with the cold weather. Dr. Lantz tells us that in 1903 hordes of rats migrated over several counties in Western Illinois, suddenly appearing when for several years no abnormal numbers had been seen. An eyewitness stated to Lantz that, as he was returning to his home on a moonlight night, he heard a rustling in a near-by field, and saw a great army of rats cross the road in front of him. The army of rats stretched away as far as he could see in the moonlight. This, to be sure, was before the Eighteenth Amendment,[10] but there must have been some fact behind it, since heavy damage was caused by rats in the entire surrounding country of farms and villages in the ensuing winter and summer. On one farm, in the month of April, about 3500 rats were caught in traps. Lantz himself saw a similar migration in the valley of the Kansas River, in 1904; and Lantz, being at that time an officer and gentleman of the United States Agricultural Service, cannot be under the suspicion that is aroused by accounts of armies of rats seen by moonshine. In England a general movement of rats inland from the coast occurs every October, and this migration is connected with the closing of the herring season. During the herring catch, rats swarm all over the coast, attracted by the food supply of herring cleaning; when it is over, they go back to their regular haunts. In South America, Lantz advises us, rat plagues are periodic in Paraná, in Brazil, and occur at intervals of about thirty years. In Chile, the same thing has been observed, at intervals of fifteen to twenty-five years. Studies of these migrations have shown that the rat plagues are associated with the ripening and decay of a dominant species of bamboo in each country. For a year or two, the ripening seed in the forests supplies a favorite food for the rats. They multiply enormously, and eventually, this food supply failing, they go back to the cultivated areas. A famine was caused in 1878 in the state of Paraná by the wholesale destruction of the corn, rice, and mandioca crops by rats. The invasion of Bermuda by rats in 1615, and their sudden disappearance, are as dramatic as the rise and fall of some of the short-lived Indian empires of Central and South America. Black rats appeared in that year, and within the two following ones increased with alarming rapidity. They devoured fruits, plants, and trees to such an extent that a famine resulted, and a law required every man in the islands to keep twelve traps set. Nothing, however, was of any use, until finally the rats disappeared with a suddenness that makes it almost necessary to assume that they died of a pestilence.

As we have indicated in a preceding paragraph, the natural history of the rat is tragically similar to that of man. Offspring of widely divergent evolutionary directions, men and rats reached present stages of physical development within a few hundred thousand years of each other—since remnants of both are found in the fossils of the glacial period.

Some of the more obvious qualities in which rats resemble men—ferocity, omnivorousness, and adaptability to all climates—have been mentioned above. We have also alluded to the irresponsible fecundity with which both species breed at all seasons of the year with a heedlessness of consequences which subjects them to a wholesale disaster on the inevitable, occasional failure of the food supply. In this regard, it is only fair to state—in justice to man—that, as far as we can tell, the rat does this of its own free and stupid gluttony, while man has tradition, piety, and the duty of furnishing cannon fodder to contend with, in addition to his lower instincts. But these are, after all, phenomena of human biology, and man cannot be absolved of responsibility for his stupidities because they are the results of wrong-headedness rather than the consequences of pure instinct—certainly not if they result in identical disasters.

Neither rat nor man has achieved social, commercial, or economic stability. This has been, either perfectly or to some extent, achieved by ants and by bees, by some

[10] An ironic reference to prohibition.

birds, and by some of the fishes in the sea. Man and the rat are merely, so far, the most successful animals of prey. They are utterly destructive of other forms of life. Neither of them is of the slightest earthly use to any other species of living things. Bacteria nourish plants; plants nourish man and beast. Insects, in their well-organized societies, are destructive of one form of living creature, but helpful to another. Most other animals are content to lead peaceful and adjusted lives, rejoicing in vigor, grateful for this gift of living, and doing the minimum of injury to obtain the things they require. Man and the rat are utterly destructive. All that nature offers is taken for their own purposes, plant or beast.

Gradually these two have spread across the earth, keeping pace with each other and unable to destroy each other, though continually hostile. They have wandered from East to West, driven by their physical needs, and—unlike any other species of living things—have made war upon their own kind. The gradual, relentless, progressive extermination of the black rat by the brown has no parallel in nature so close as that of the similar extermination of one race of man by another. Did the Danes conquer England; or the Normans the Saxon-Danes; or the Normans the Sicilian-Mohammedans; or the Moors the Latin-Iberians; or the Franks the Moors; or the Spanish the Aztecs and the Incas; or the Europeans in general the simple aborigines of the world by qualities other than those by which *Mus decumanus* has driven out *Mus rattus?* In both species the battle has been pitilessly to the strong. And the strong have been pitiless. The physically weak have been driven before the strong—annihilated, or constrained to the slavery of doing without the bounties which were provided for all equally. Isolated colonies of black rats survive, as weaker nations survive until the stronger ones desire the little they still possess.

The rat has an excuse. As far as we know, it does not appear to have developed a soul, or that intangible quality of justice, mercy, and reason that psychic evolution has bestowed upon man. We must not expect too much. It takes a hundred thousand years to alter the protuberances on a bone, the direction of a muscle; much longer than this to develop a lung from a gill, or to atrophy a tail. It is only about twenty-five hundred years since Plato, Buddha, and Confucius; only two thousand years since Christ. In the meantime, we have had Homer and Saint Francis, Copernicus and Galileo; Shakespeare, Pascal, Newton, Goethe, Bach, and Beethoven, and a great number of lesser men and women of genius who have demonstrated the evolutionary possibilities of the human spirit. If such minds have been rare, and spread thinly over three thousand years, after all, they still represent the spots that indicate the high possibilities of fortunate genetic combinations. And these must inevitably increase if the environment remains at all favorable. If no upward progress in spirit or intelligence seems apparent let us say, between the best modern minds and that of Aristotle, we must remember that, in terms of evolutionary change, three thousand years are negligible. If, as in the last war and its subsequent imbecilities, mankind returns completely to the rat stage of civilization, this surely shows how very rudimentary an emergence from the Neanderthal our present civilization represents—how easily the thin, spiritual veneer is cracked under any strain that awakens the neolithic beast within. Nevertheless, for perhaps three or five thousand years, the beast has begun to ponder and grope. Isolated achievements have demonstrated of what the mind and spirit are capable when a happy combination of genes occurs under circumstances that permit the favored individual to mature. And the most incomprehensible but hopeful aspect of the matter is the fact that successive generations have always bred an adequate number of individuals sufficiently superior to the brutal mass to keep alive a reverence for these supreme achievements and make them a cumulative heritage. It is more than likely—biologically considered—that by reason of this progressive accumulation of the best that superior specimens of our species have produced, the evolution toward higher things may gain velocity with time, and that in another hundred thousand years the comparison of the race of men with that of rats may be less humiliatingly obvious.

Man and the rat will always be pitted against each other as implacable enemies. And the rat's most potent weapons against mankind have been its perpetual maintenance of the infectious agents of plague and of typhus fever.

MEANING

1. Why will "man and the rat always be pitted against each other as implacable enemies," as Zinsser says, in their centuries-old competition?
2. What significant information has Zinsser's research on rats revealed?
3. What is the current result of the antagonism that has been observed throughout history between the two main species of rats?

USING COMPARISON AND CONTRAST TO CONVEY MEANING

1. What scientific data, fossil sources, and zoological records does Zinsser cite to document the incredible story of the rats "worldwide migration"?
2. How does Zinsser organize his essay to transfer the results of his research on rats to human beings?
3. Does Zinsser's method of comparison raise rats to the level of man or lower man to the level of rats?

WRITING SUGGESTIONS

1. How have fictional treatments of rats (e.g., the depiction of the rat named "Ben" in the movie *Willard*) drawn on characteristics identified by Zinsser?
2. Using Zinsser's essay as a guide, explore another species that competes with man for food and space.

CONSTANCE HOLDEN

Identical Twins Reared Apart

Constance Holden, born in 1941, is a writer for Science *magazine, whose col-*
umn, "News and Comment," discusses the implications of issues on the forefront
of scientific research. Holden is particularly interested in questions of the rela-
tionship between mind and body. "Identical Twins Reared Apart," from
Science *(1980), reports on a comparative study conducted by Thomas J.*
Bouchard at the University of Minnesota, which pointed to the importance of
heredity rather than environment in shaping human behavior. Holden
develops a point-by-point comparison of the striking similarities in behavior
between nine sets of identical twins, who were separated at birth, raised in
different environments, and then brought together. Holden is currently doing
research for a series of articles on the behavioral mechanisms underlying ad-
dictions.

Bridget and Dorothy are 39-year-old British housewives, identical twins raised apart who first met each other a little over a year ago. When they met, to take part in Thomas Bouchard's twin study at the University of Minnesota, the manicured hands of each bore seven rings. Each also wore two bracelets on one wrist and a watch and a bracelet on the other. Investigators in Bouchard's study, the most extensive investigation ever made of identical twins reared apart, are still bewitched by the seven rings. Was it coincidence, the result of similar influences, or is this small sign of affinity a true, even inevitable, manifestation of the mysterious and infinitely complex interaction of the genes the two women have in common?

Investigators have been bemused and occasionally astonished at similarities between long-separated twins, similarities that prevailing dogma about human behavior would ordinarily attribute to common environmental influences. How is it, for example, that two men with significantly different upbringings came to have the same authoritarian personality? Or another pair to have similar histories of endogenous depression? Or still another pair to have virtually identical patterns of headaches?

These are only bits and pieces from a vast amount of data, none of it yet analyzed, being collected by the University of Minnesota twin study that began last March. So provocative have been some of the cases that the study has already received much attention in the press, and it is bound to get a lot more. The investigation is extremely controversial, aimed, as it is, directly at the heart of the age-old debate about heredity versus environment. Identical twins reared apart have been objects of scrutiny in the past, notably in three studies conducted in England, Denmark, and the United States. An indication of the sensitivity of this subject is the fact that the last one in this country was completed more than 40 years ago,[1] although the rarity of cases has also made this type of research rather exotic. The Minnesota investigators, however, have been able to locate more twin pairs than they expected. So far they have processed nine pairs of identical or monozygotic twins (as well as several pairs of fraternal or dizygotic twins used as controls) and, owing to the publicity given the project, have managed to locate 11 additional pairs to take part in the study.

The Minnesota study is unprecedented in its scope, using a team of psychologists, psychiatrists, and medical doctors to probe and analyze every conceivable aspect of the twins' life histories, medical histories and physiology, tastes, psychological inclinations, abilities, and intelligence. It began when Bouchard, a psychologist who specializes in investigating individual differences, heard of a pair of twins separated from birth, both coincidentally named Jim by their adoptive families, who were reunited at the age of 39. Bouchard did not have to look far to set up his study team, as Minnesota is a hotbed of twin research. There, ready to go to work, were Irving Gottesman, a behavioral geneticist who has spent his career studying twins and whose particular interest is the etiology of schizophrenia; psychologist David Lykken, who has been looking at the brain waves of twins for 10 years, psychologist Auke Tellegen, who recently completed a new personality questionnaire that is being used on the twins; and psychiatrist Leonard Heston, who has studied heritability of mental disorders with adopted children.

Bouchard has taken an eclectic approach in developing the battery of exercises through which the twins are run. Each pair goes through 6 days of intensive testing. In addition to detailed medical histories including diet, smoking, and exercise, the twins are given electrocardiograms, chest x-rays, heart stress tests, and pulmonary exams. They are injected with a variety of substances to determine allergies. They are wired to electroencephalographs to measure their brain wave responses to stimuli in the form of tones of varying intensity, and given other psychophysiological tests to measure such responses as reaction times. Several handedness tests are given to ascertain laterality.

The physiological probes are interspersed with several dozen pencil-and-paper tests, which over the week add up to about 15,000 questions; these cover family and childhood environment, fears and phobias, personal interests, vocational interests, values, reading and TV viewing habits, musical interests, aesthetic judgement tests, and color preferences. They are put through three comprehensive psychological inventories. Then there is a slew of ability tests: the Wechsler Adult Intelligence Scale (the main adult IQ test) and numerous others that reveal skills in information processing, vocabulary, spatial abilities, numerical processing, mechanical ability, memory, and so forth. Throughout the 6 days there is much overlap and repetition in the content of questions, the intent being to "measure the same underlying factor at different times," says Bouchard. Mindful of charges of investigator bias in the administration of IQ tests in past twin studies, Bouchard has contracted with outside professionals to come in just for the purpose of administering and scoring the Wechsler intelligence test.

And the upshot of all this probing? Although the data have not yet been interpreted, there have already been some real surprises. Bouchard told *Science:* "I frankly expected far more differences [between twins] than we have found so far. I'm a psychologist,

---

[1] A. H. Newman, F. N. Freeman, and K. J. Holzinger wrote up their study of 19 twin pairs in a 1937 book, *Twins: A Study of Heredity and Environment.*

not a geneticist. I want to find out how the environment works to shape psychological traits." But the most provocative morsels that have so far become available are those that seem to reveal genetic influences at work.

Take the "Jim twins," as they have come to be known. Jim Springer and Jim Lewis were adopted as infants into working-class Ohio families. Both liked math and did not like spelling in school. Both had law enforcement training and worked part-time as deputy sheriffs. Both vacationed in Florida, both drove Chevrolets. Much has been made of the fact that their lives are marked by a trail of similar names. Both had dogs named Toy. Both married and divorced women named Linda and had second marriages with women named Betty. They named their sons James Allan and James Alan, respectively. Both like mechanical drawing and carpentry. They have almost identical drinking and smoking patterns. Both chew their fingernails down to the nubs.

But what investigators thought "astounding" was their similar medical histories. In addition to having hemorrhoids and identical pulse and blood pressure and sleep patterns, both had inexplicably put on 10 pounds at the same time in their lives. What really gets the researchers is that both suffer from "mixed headache syndrome"— a combination tension headache and migraine. The onset occurred in both at the age of 18. They have these late-afternoon headaches with the same frequency and same degree of disability, and the two used the same terms to describe the pain.

The twins also have their differences. One wears his hair over his forehead, the other has it slicked back with sideburns. One expresses himself better orally, the other in writing. But although the emotional environments in which they were brought up were different, the profiles on their psychological inventories were much alike.

Another much-publicized pair are 47-year-old Oskar Stöhr and Jack Yufe. These two have the most dramatically different backgrounds of all the twins studied. Born in Trinidad of a Jewish father and a German mother, they were separated shortly after birth. The mother took Oskar back to Germany, where he was raised as a Catholic and a Nazi youth by his grandmother. Jack was raised in the Caribbean, as a Jew, by his father, and spent part of his youth on an Israeli kibbutz. The two men now lead markedly different lives. Oskar is an industrial supervisor in Germany, married, a devoted union man, a skier. Jack runs a retail clothing store in San Diego, is separated, and describes himself as a workaholic.

But similarities started cropping up as soon as Oskar arrived at the airport. Both were wearing wire-rimmed glasses and mustaches, both sported two-pocket shirts with epaulets. They share idiosyncrasies galore: they like spicy foods and sweet liqueurs, are absentminded, have a habit of falling asleep in front of the television, think it's funny to sneeze in a crowd of strangers, flush the toilet before using it, store rubber bands on their wrists, read magazines from back to front, dip buttered toast in their coffee. Oskar is domineering toward women and yells at his wife, which Jack did before he was separated. Oskar did not take all the tests because he speaks only German (some are scheduled to be administered to him in German), but the two had very similar profiles on the Minnesota Multiphastic Personality Inventory (the MMPI was already available in German). Although the two were raised in different cultures and speak different languages, investigator Bouchard professed himself struck by the similarities in their mannerisms, the questions they asked, their "temperament, tempo, the way they do things"—which are, granted, relatively intangible when it comes to measuring them. Bouchard also thinks the two supply "devastating" evidence against the feminist contention that children's personalities are shaped differently according to the sex of those who rear them, since Oskar was raised by women and Jack by men.

Other well-publicized twin pairs are Bridget and Dorothy, the British housewives with the seven rings, and Barbara and Daphne, another pair of British housewives. Both sets are now in their late 30's and were separated during World War II. Bridget and Dorothy are of considerable interest because they were raised in quite different socioeconomic settings—the class difference turns out mainly to be reflected in the fact that the one raised in modest circumstances has bad teeth. Otherwise, say the investigators, they share "striking similarities in all areas," including another case of coincidence in naming children. They named their sons Richard Andrew and Andrew Richard, respectively, and their daughters Catherine Louise and Karen Louise. (Bouchard is struck by this, as the likelihood of such a coincidence would seem to be lessened by the fact that names are a joint decision by husband and wife.) On ability and IQ tests the scores of the sisters were similar, although the one raised in the lower class setting had a slightly higher score.

The other British twins, Daphne and Barbara, are fondly remembered by the investigators as the "giggle sisters." Both were great gigglers, particularly together, when they were always setting each other off. Asked if there were any gigglers in their adoptive families, both replied in the negative. The sisters also shared identical coping mechanisms in the face of stress: they ignored it, managed to "read out" such stimuli. In keeping with this, both flatly avoided conflict and controversy—neither, for example, had any interest in politics. Such avoidance of conflict is "classically regarded as learned behavior," says Bouchard. Although the adoptive families of the two women were not terribly different, "we see more differences within families than between these two."

Only fragmentary information is available so far from the rest of the nine sets of twins, but it supplies abundant food for new lines of inquiry. Two 57-year-old women, for example, developed adult-onset diabetes at the same time in their lives. One of a pair of twins suffers from a rare neurological disease that has always been thought to be genetic in origin. Another area where identical twins differ is in their allergies.

Psychiatrically, according to Heston, who conducts personal interviews with all the twins, there has been remarkable agreement. "Twins brought up together have very high concordance in pschiatric histories," he says. (For example, if one identical twin has schizophrenia, the other one stands a 45 percent chance of developing it.) But what is surprising is that "what we see [with the twins in the study] is pretty much the same as in twins brought up together." By and large, he says, they share very similar phobias, and he has noted more than one case where both twins had histories of endogenous depression. In one case, twins who had been brought up in different emotional environments—one was raised in a strict disciplinarian household, the other had a warm, tolerant, loving mother—showed very similar neurotic and hypochondriacal traits. Says Heston, "things that I would never have thought of—mild depressions, phobias—as being in particular genetically mediated . . . now, at least, there are grounds for a very live hypothesis" on the role of genes not only in major mental illnesses, where chemistry clearly plays a part, but in lesser emotional disturbances.

Other odds and ends:

Two men brought up in radically different environments—one an uneducated manual laborer, the other highly educated and cosmopolitan—turned out to be great raconteurs. (They did, however, have very different IQ scores. The numbers are confidential but the difference was close to the largest difference on record for identical twins, 24 points.)

One of the greatest areas of discordance for twins was smoking. Of the nine pairs, there were four in which one twin smoked and the other did not. No one has an explanation for this. But, surprisingly, in at least one case a lifelong heavy smoker came out just as well on the pulmonary exam and heart stress test as did the nonsmoker.

In a couple of cases, one of a twin pair wore glasses and the other did not. But when their eyes were checked, it was found that both members of each pair required the same correction.

In the fascinating tidbit category: One pair of female twins was brought together briefly as children. Each wore her favorite dress for the occasion. The dresses were identical.

What is to be made of all this? As Tellegen warns, any conclusions at this point are "just gossip." The similarities are somehow more fascinating than the differences, and it could well be that the subjective impression they make on the investigators is heavier than is justified. Nonetheless, even the subjective impressions offer fertile grounds for speculation. Bouchard, for example, thinks that the team may discover that identical twins have a built-in penchant for a certain level of physical exertion. The latest pair to visit the laboratory, for example—23-year-old males—both eschew exercise (although both are thin as rails).

Lykken, who does the tests on the twins' central nervous systems, uses the case of the seven rings as an example for one of his tentative ideas. Fondness for rings is obviously not hereditary, but groups of unrelated genes on different chromosomes, producing pretty hands and other characteristics, may combine to result in beringedness. These traits, called idiographic—meaning particular to an individual rather than shared across a population—may not be as much a result of chance as has been thought. "There are probably other traits that are idiographic that may be almost inevitable given the [gene] combination. . . . More of these unique characteristics than we previously thought may be determined by a particular combination of genes." Lykken adds, "people get so upset when you suggest that the wiring diagram can influence the mind." But to believe otherwise "requires a naïve dualism . . . an assumption that mental events occur independent of the physical substrate."

Such talk begins to sound pretty deterministic, but Lykken insists that when the mass of data has been ordered "there will be material that will make environmentalists very happy and material that will make hereditarians very happy." One thing that will not make the environmentalists happy is the fact that IQ seems to have a high degree of heritability, as indicated by the fact that of all the tests administered to identical twins separately reared, IQ shows the highest concordance. It is even higher than the introversion-extroversion personality trait, a venerable measure in psychological testing that shows higher concordance than other conventional categories such as sense of well-being, responsibility, dominance, and ego strength.

As several investigators mentioned to *Science*, the scores of identical twins on many psychological and ability tests are closer than would be expected for the same person taking the same test twice. Lykken also found this to be true of brain wave tracings, which is probably the most direct evidence that identical twins are almost identically wired. Several researchers also felt that there is something to the idea that identical twins reared apart may be even more similar in some respects than those reared together. The explanation is simple: competition between the two is inevitable; hence if the stronger or taller of the two excels at sports, the other twin, even if equal in inclination and ability, will avoid sports altogether in order not to be overshadowed. Or one twin will choose to be a retiring type in order not to compete with his extroverted sibling. In short, many twins, in the interest of establishing their individuality, tend to exaggerate their differences.

Although the tentativeness of the findings so far must be repeatedly emphasized, at least one of the Minnesota researchers believes it may be safe to hypothesize that only extreme differences in environment result in significant differences between identical twins. Lykken says, after observing so many similarities, that it is tempting to conclude that "native ability will show itself over a broad range" of backgrounds. So either a seriously impoverished or a greatly enriched environment is required "to significantly alter its expression."

Such an idea, if it gained broad acceptance, would have major impacts on social policies. But Bouchard wants to keep his study separate from politics, emphasizing instead that the research is "very much exploratory."

The data, once assembled and analyzed, should provide a gold mine of new hypotheses. If a great many pairs of twins are collected, says Bouchard, they may be able to present the findings quantitatively, otherwise, the findings will be in the form of case histories. Tellegen, however, whose main interest is the methodology, says "we want to invent methods for analyzing traits in an objective manner, so we can get statistically cogent conclusions from a single case." He points out that psychoanalytic theory was developed from intensive study of small numbers of people and that behavioral psychologist B. F. Skinner similarly was able to develop his theories by studying small numbers of animals. Take the twins with the identical headache syndromes: with just one pair of twins the door is opened to a new field of research.

The twin study may also make it clear that estimating the relative contribution of heredity and environment to mental and psychological traits can never be boiled down to percentages. Some people, for example, may have authoritarian personalities no matter what their upbringing; the authoritarianism of others may be directly traceable to their environment. Similarly, with intelligence, some people may be smart or dumb regardless of outside influences, whereas the intelligence of others may be extremely malleable. Theoretically, variations from individual to individual in malleability and susceptibility may be so great that any attempt to make a generalization about the relative contribution of "innate" characteristics to a certain trait across a population would have no meaning.

Twin studies have been regarded with suspicion in some quarters because, according to Gottesman, the behavioral geneticist who worked with James Shields in England, they were "originally used to prove a genetic point of view." The most notorious of these were the studies of Cyril Burt on intelligence of twins reared separately, which were subsequently discredited. But, says Gottesman, "this study is a continuation of the efforts of Shields and Nielson [Niels Juel-Nielsen, a psychiatrist at the University of Odense in Denmark] to challenge received wisdom about the roles of genes and environment." Everyone, observes Gottesman, "seems to have made up their minds one way or the other." With such a dearth of data of the kind that can only be obtained by studying persons with identical genes raised in different environments, people have been free to be as dogmatic as they please.

Bouchard had a devil of a time getting funding for his study. Various probes at the National Institutes of Health were discouraged on the grounds that the study was too multidisciplinary for any institute to embrace it. He finally got some money from the National Science Foundation.

Although the ultimate conclusions of the study may well be susceptible to sensationalizing, Gordon Allen of the National Institute of Mental Health, head of the International Twin Society, does not believe it will find any "new and unique answers." The sample will not be large enough for that, and besides, too few of the twin pairs were reared in environments so radically different as to bring genetically based behavioral similarities into stark relief.

The most solid and unequivocal evidence will be that supplied by the physiological findings. Although the similarities are the most titillating to most observers, it is the discordances that will be the most informative. For any difference between a pair of identical twins is "absolute proof that that is not completely controlled by heredity."

At this point, no one can make any generalizations beyond that made by James Shields, who died last year. Shields wrote that the evidence so far showed that "MZ [monozygotic] twins do not have to be brought up in the same subtly similar family environment for them to be alike." He concluded, "I doubt if MZ's will ever be numerous and representative enough to provide the main evidence about environment, or about genetics, but . . . they can give unique real-life illustrations of some of the many possible pathways from genes to human behavior—and so will always be of human and scientific interest."

MEANING

1. How did Holden's article influence your thinking as to whether heredity or environment is more important in shaping human behavior?
2. What types of similarities were discovered by researchers who studied the nine sets of identical twins who were reunited after having been separated at birth and raised in different environments?
3. Why, for the purposes of this study, were the amazing similarities shared by each set of twins more important than any apparent differences?

USING COMPARISON AND CONTRAST TO CONVEY MEANING

1. What steps does Holden take to immediately engage the reader's interest while placing the Minnesota study in its scientific context?
2. Using any one set of twins (the Jims, Oskar and Jack, Bridget and Dorothy, or Daphne and Barbara), discuss how Holden's report of point-by-point similarities in behavior underscores the overriding importance of heredity, rather than environment, in shaping human behavior.
3. Why would this be considered multidisciplinary research? Discuss the contributions that other disciplines made to this study.

WRITING SUGGESTIONS

1. Which set of twins did you find the most fascinating—the Jims, Oskar and Jack, Bridget and Dorothy, or Daphne and Barbara—and why?

2. In a study of this type, are physiological similarities (such as a predisposition to migraine headaches) more significant than psychological similarities (such as matters of taste in clothes, food, colors)?

3. Do the results of this study mean that disciplines that study social change as a key determinant of human behavior will have to rethink their basic assumptions?

4. As an exercise in imagination, describe a meeting between yourself and an identical twin brother or sister you have never met before. Your twin has, however, grown up in an entirely different environment, perhaps even a different part of the world. Compare and contrast the similarities and differences between you and your newly found twin.

PROCESS
ANALYSIS

One of the most effective ways to clarify the nature of something is to explain how it works. Process analysis divides a complex procedure into separate and easy-to-understand steps in order to explain how something works, how something happened, or how an action should be performed.

Process analysis is ideally suited to explain how a product is manufactured and should include data on the equipment used, operations performed, standards used to measure success, and other pertinent technical information. A writer explaining how paper is produced might divide the process into different phases, beginning with (1) trees being stripped of bark and put into a revolving drum, (2) chemical treatment applied under steam pressure to produce woodpulp; (3) the screening, washing, bleaching, drying, and compression of the woodpulp; (4) pressing the paper between cold metal rollers to produce a smooth finish; (5) the winding of paper onto large spools; and (6) cutting the paper into individual sheets. In technical writing, graphs, charts, diagrams, and flowcharts are also useful in helping the reader to visualize the individual phases or steps in a complex procedure.

Process analysis requires the writer to include all necessary steps in the procedure and to demonstrate how each step is related to preceding and subsequent steps in the overall sequence. Writers in fields as diverse as psychology, business, manufacturing, history, cultural anthropology, journalism, and zoology all use process analysis to develop, organize, and present information.

Kenneth Stampp, a noted historian, investigates a past era in our country's history when blacks were brought to America as slaves in "To Make Them Stand in Fear." Stampp analyzes the instructions given by manuals that told slaveowners, step by step, how to break the spirits of newly transported blacks in order to change them into "proper" slaves:

> Here, then, was the way to produce the perfect slave: accustom him to rigid discipline, demand from him unconditional submission, impress upon him his innate inferiority, develop in him a paralyzing fear of white men, train him to adopt the master's code of good behavior, and instill in him a sense of complete dependence. This, at least, was the goal.

Stampp's analysis of source documents reveals that slaveowners used behavior-modification techniques to produce "respectful" and "docile" slaves. The process began with a series of measures designed to enforce external discipline. Later on, attention shifted to measures designed to encourage psychological conditioning, so that, in theory at least, the slave would control himself through the perceptions of inferiority he had internalized.

Jessica Mitford studied cultural customs from an anthropological perspective. What interests her, especially, is why our culture attaches such importance to the manner of preparation, arrangement, positioning, and display of the bodies of those who have died. To answer this question, she has done extensive research into the procedures used by undertakers and describes the sequence of techniques they use to create, insofar as it is possible, the illusion of life in "Mortuary Solaces":

> Jones is now ready for casketing (this is the present participle of the verb "to casket"). In this operation his right shoulder should be depressed slightly "to turn the body a bit to the right and soften the appearance of lying flat on the back." Positioning the hands is a matter of importance, and special rubber positioning blocks may be used. The hands should be cupped slightly for a more lifelike, relaxed appearance. Proper placement of the body requires a delicate sense of balance. It should lie as high as possible in the casket, yet not so high that the lid, when lowered, will hit the nose. On the other hand, we are cautioned, placing the body too low "creates the impression that the body is in a box."

Mitford's ironic analysis of this process is drawn from undertakers' manuals that give explicit instructions as to the steps that should be taken in the preparing and displaying of the body. The fastidious concern for how the body will look to the viewing public reveals, for Mitford, a deep cultural need to deny death, which the funeral profession answers with their own macabre form of "make-believe."

Whereas writers like Stampp and Mitford quote from instructional manuals to show the inner workings of a historical or cultural process, many social and political commentators use process analysis to provide a first-hand account of changes as they occur. Tom Wolfe analyzes the process by which an entirely new form of popular literature developed in "The New Journalism." The emergence of this new genre, which Wolfe termed the "New Journalism," whose practitioners include Hunter Thompson, Truman Capote, Norman Mailer, Joan Didion, and Wolfe himself, resulted from journalists' aspirations to move into the elevated literary circles of novelists:

> The similarity between the early days of the novel and the early days of the New Journalism is not merely coincidental. In both cases we are watching the same process. We are watching a group of writers coming along, working in a genre regarded as Lower Class (the novel before the 1850's, slick-magazine journalism before the 1960's), who discover the joys of detailed realism and its strange powers. . . .

Journalists who were once content to simply report the facts now aspired to make their stories more interesting, lifelike, and dramatic. They now began, according to Wolfe, to reshape their reports using a variety of techniques, such as characterization, dialogue, and scene-setting, adapted from novel writers (who, ironically, were viewed with the same low regard before the 1850s as journalists were seen before the 1960s).

To be effective, process analysis should emphasize the significance of each step in the overall sequence and help the reader understand how each step emerges from the preceding stage and flows into the next. In "Bull Fighting," Ernest Hemingway divides the action of a bullfight into three separate stages that follow each other in a set pattern, corresponding to the three acts of a tragedy. Hemingway's analysis reveals that the ritualized confrontation, violence, and death in a bullfight are meant to lead the audience through an experience as carefully constructed as a Greek tragedy. Hemingway divides the action of the bullfight into clearly demarcated stages. The entrance of the bull into the arena, the role of the picadors on horseback, the planting of darts into the bull to enrage him, and the torero's skill in letting the bull pass as closely as possible, before finally killing him—all work together to produce an effect of pity and terror identical to that produced by Greek tragedy.

Process analysis is especially useful in taking an abstract concept or idea and describing how it works by breaking it into a number of distinct and easily understandable phases. Carl Jung uses this technique in "The Personal and the Collective Unconscious" to explain how dreams act as a safety valve to maintain the balance between different levels of the psyche. Jung's research disclosed that one part of the mind we are not aware of—the "unconscious"—corrects the excesses and limitations of the conscious mind—the "ego"—through "archetypal" images expressed in dreams. Jung correlated the kinds of dreams his patients had with their particular psychological maladies, and found, for example, that patients who consciously thought of themselves as always being right, were corrected by their dreams in which they appeared at fault.

From evidence provided by his patients and his analysis of the images, dreams, myths, and fantasies in art and folklore, Jung hypothesized that dreams act as a regulator to maintain a balance within the psyche as a whole. Jung's theory of the existence of a "collective unconscious" illustrates how the way in which a phenomena is described is itself a theoretical construct developed for the specific purpose of defining and advancing a particular discipline. That is, the processes that disciplines choose to use in their investigations are as dependent on theoretical models within the discipline as they are on objective phenomena.

Often the phenomena scientists study are objective and yet appear mysterious. In "The Homing Salmon" biologists Arthur D. Hasler and James A. Larsen seek to explain the mystery of how salmon are able to return over nine-hundred miles to the exact stream in which they were born. To understand the mechanism involved, Hasler and Larsen conducted experiments designed to discover whether salmon had the ability to perceive, recognize, and even be conditioned by the particular odors in the stream where the salmon were spawned:

> All this suggested a clear-cut working hypothesis for investigating the mystery of the homing of salmon. We can suppose that every little stream has its own characteristic odor, which stays the same year after year; that young salmon become conditioned to this odor before they go to sea; that they remember the odor as they grow to maturity, and that they are able to find it and follow it to its source when they come back upstream to spawn.

Hasler and Larsen subdivided the process of the salmon's migration into a number of distinct and identifiable stages, and demonstrated how each stage could be explained in terms of olfactory conditioning. The biological basis of the salmon's incredible homing instinct is due to the fact that salmon are conditioned to recognize the odor of the streams in which they were spawned. Hasler and Larsen's description of their research is a classic illustration of how scientists can use process analysis in order to formulate, test, and confirm scientific hypotheses.

Richard Rhodes, a writer adept in describing manufacturing processes, uses this form of analysis in "Watching the Animals" to take his readers behind the scenes at a meat-processing plant to observe first-hand the many steps and different skills necessary to produce packaged meat products. Rhodes's article illustrates how food (in this case, pork products) goes through many stages before it reaches us in the neatly packaged form we take for granted in the supermarket. In one of the last stages:

> We pass to the other side of the chamber and find two workers with wide knives scraping off the few patches of hair that remain. The carcasses then pass through great hellish jets of yellowish-blue gas flame to singe the skin and harden it. The last step is polishing: more brushes. Our pig has turned pink and clean as a baby.

In the article from which this excerpt is taken, Rhodes breaks the overall process into a number of distinct and easily understandable stages, and describes, step by step, what happens at each stage in the meat-processing plant, from the arrival of the live pig to the package of bacon ready for our tables.

LIBERAL ARTS

Kenneth M. Stampp

To Make Them Stand in Fear

Kenneth M. Stampp was born in 1912 in Milwaukee, Wisconsin and earned his Ph.D. from the University of Wisconsin in 1942. Stampp is the Morrison Professor of American History at the University of California at Berkeley and has served as president of the Organization of American Historians. He has been Harmsworth Professor of American History at Oxford University, a Fulbright lecturer at the University of Munich, and has received two Guggenheim fellowships. In addition to editing The Causes of the Civil War *(1974), Stampp is the author of many distinguished studies including* And the War Came *(1950) and* The Peculiar Institution: Slavery in the Ante-Bellum South *(1956). In "To Make Them Stand in Fear," taken from this latter work, Stampp lets the facts of brutal exploitation speak for themselves as he describes the step-by-step process by which slavemasters in the South sought to break the spirits of newly arrived blacks.*

A wise master did not take seriously the belief that Negroes were natural-born slaves. He knew better. He knew that Negroes freshly imported from Africa had to be broken to bondage; that each succeeding generation had to be carefully trained. This was no easy task, for the bondsman rarely submitted willingly. Moreover, he rarely submitted completely. In most cases there was no end to the need for control—at least not until old age reduced the slave to a condition of helplessness.

Masters revealed the qualities they sought to develop in slaves when they singled out certain ones for special commendation. A small Mississippi planter mourned the death of his "faithful and dearly beloved servant" Jack: "Since I have owned him he has been true to me in all respects. He was an obedient trusty servant. . . . I never knew him to steal nor lie and he ever set a moral and industrious example to those around him. . . . I shall ever cherish his memory." A Louisiana sugar planter lost a "very valuable Boy" through an accident: "His life was a very great one. I have always found him willing and obedient and never knew him to fail to do anything he was put to do." These were "ideal" slaves, the models slaveholders had in mind as they trained and governed their workers.

How might this ideal be approached? The first step, advised those who wrote discourses on the management of slaves, was to establish and maintain strict discipline. An Arkansas master suggested the adoption of the "Army Regulations as to the discipline in Forts." "They must obey at all times, and under all circumstances, cheerfully and with alacrity," affirmed a Virginia slaveholder. "It greatly impairs the happiness of a negro, to be allowed to cultivate an insubordinate temper. Unconditional submission is the only footing upon which slavery should be placed. It is precisely similar to the attitude of a minor to his parent, or a soldier to his general." A South Carolinian limned a perfect relationship between a slave and his master: "that the slave should know that his master is to govern absolutely, and he is to obey implicitly. That he is never for a moment to exercise either his will or judgment in opposition to a positive order."

The second step was to implant in the bondsmen themselves a consciousness of personal inferiority. They had "to know and keep their places," to "feel the difference between master and slave," to understand that bondage was their natural status. They had to feel that African ancestry tainted them, that their color was a badge of degradation. In the country they were to show respect for even their master's nonslave-holding neighbors; in the towns they were to give way on the streets to the most wretched white man. The line between the races must never be crossed, for familiarity caused slaves to forget their lowly station and to become "impudent."

Frederick Douglass explained that a slave might commit the offense of impudence in various ways: "in the tone of an answer; in answering at all; in not answering; in the expression of countenance; in the motion of the head; in the gait, manner and bearing of the slave." Any of these acts, in some subtle way, might indicate the absence of proper subordination. "In a well regulated community," wrote a Texan, "a negro takes off his hat in addressing a white man. . . . Where this is not enforced, we may always look for impudent and rebellious negroes."

The third step in the training of slaves was to awe them with a sense of their master's enormous power. The only principle upon which slavery could be maintained, reported a group of Charlestonians, was the "principle of fear." In his defense of slavery James H. Hammond admitted that this, unfortunately, was true but put the responsibility upon the abolitionists. Antislavery agitation had forced masters to strengthen their authority: "We have to rely more and more on the power of fear. . . . We are determined to continue masters, and to do so we have to draw the reign tighter and tighter day by day to be assured that we hold them in complete check." A North Carolina mistress, after subduing a troublesome domestic, realized that it was essential "to make them stand in fear"!

In this the slaveholders had considerable success. Frederick Douglass believed that most slaves stood "in awe" of white men; few could free themselves altogether from the notion that their masters were "invested with a sort of sacredness." Olmsted saw a small white girl stop a slave on the road and boldly order him to return to his plantation. The slave fearfully obeyed her command. A visitor in Mississippi claimed that a master, armed only with a whip or cane, could throw himself among a score of bondsmen and cause them to "flee with terror." He accomplished this by the "peculiar tone of authority" with which he spoke. "Fear, awe, and obedience . . . are interwoven into the very nature of the slave."

The fourth step was to persuade the bondsmen to take an interest in the master's enterprise and to accept his standards of good conduct. A South Carolina planter explained: "The master should make it his business to show his slaves, that the advancement of his individual interest, is at the same time an advancement of theirs. Once they feel this, it will require but little compulsion to make them act as it becomes them." Though slaveholders induced only a few chattels to respond to this appeal, these few were useful examples for others.

The final step was to impress Negroes with their helplessness, to create in them "a habit of perfect dependence" upon their masters. Many believed it dangerous to train slaves to be skilled artisans in the towns, because they tended to become self-reliant. Some thought it equally dangerous to hire them to factory owners. In the Richmond tobacco factories they were alarmingly independent and "insolent." A Virginian was dismayed to find that his bondsmen, while working at an iron furnace, "got a habit of roaming about and *taking care of themselves.*" Permitting them to hire their own time produced even worse results. "No higher evidence can be furnished of its baneful effects," wrote a Charlestonian, "than the unwillingness it produces in the slave, to return to the regular life and domestic control of the master."

A spirit of independence was less likely to develop among slaves kept on the land, where most of them became accustomed to having their master provide their basic needs, and where they might be taught that they were unfit to look out for themselves. Slaves then directed their energies to the attainment of mere "temporary ease and enjoyment." "Their masters," Olmsted believed, "calculated on it in them—do not wish to cure it—and by constant practice encourage it."

Here, then, was the way to produce the perfect slave: accustom him to rigid discipline, demand from him unconditional submission, impress upon him his innate inferiority, develop in him a paralyzing fear of white men, train him to adopt the master's code of good behavior, and instill in him a sense of complete dependence. This, at least, was the goal.

But the goal was seldom reached. Every master knew that the average slave was only an imperfect copy of the model. He knew that some bondsmen yielded only to superior power—and yielded reluctantly. This complicated his problem of control.

Meaning

1. How was the process that Stampp investigated designed to transform newly arrived blacks into docile slaves who believed that what was good for the slaveowners was good for them as well?
2. What kind of instruction was provided in the source manuals from which Stampp quotes?
3. Why was the psychological conditioning that produced helplessness and dependency ultimately more important to the process than physical constraints?
4. Why was a spirit of independence least likely to develop amongst slaves kept on the land and most likely to develop amongst those who could hire themselves out independently?

Using Process Analysis to Convey Meaning

1. How is Stampp's analysis arranged to emphasize that the conditioning process moved through separate stages from external control of behavior to a state where the slave controlled his own behavior?
2. How did Stampp's use of source documents, including extensive quotations from discourses on the management of slaves, typify the methods that historians use to reconstruct and interpret past events?

Writing Suggestions

1. How does the historian's analysis of past events resemble, yet differ from, the analysis of current political or social events by news commentators?
2. Reread Frederick Douglass' account of his flight to freedom (see page 15) and identify those episodes that illustrate the conditioning process that Stampp describes.
3. What connections can you discern between the techniques used to program slaves and the methods described by Henry Allen (see page 43) used to shape the behavior of recruits? How, for example, do both processes begin with external discipline and conclude with psychological self-conditioning?
4. What other "brainwashing" processes are you aware of that could be divided into stages and analyzed using the technique of process analysis. For example, how do some religious cults use a process of "love bombing" to condition the behavior of new members?

ERNEST HEMINGWAY

Bull Fighting

Ernest Hemingway (1899–1961), an American novelist and writer of short stories, was born in Oak Park, Illinois. After working as a reporter on the Kansas City Star, *Hemingway served as a volunteer in 1918 with an ambulance unit on the Italian front and was gravely wounded. These wartime experiences formed the basis for his 1929 novel,* A Farewell to Arms. *After the war, Hemingway was a correspondent for the Toronto* Star, *settling in Paris, and living there as an expatriate, along with other literary figures, including Ezra Pound, Gertrude Stein, and Ford Maddox Ford. Hemingway's unique style of understated narration and clipped dialogue propelled English literature in a new direction. The extraordinary quality of his short stories, in the collections* Three Stories and Ten Poems *(1923),* In Our Time *(1925),* Men Without Women *(1927), and* Winner Take Nothing *(1933), have been to a great extent eclipsed by his more famous novels. These celebrated works include* The Sun Also Rises *(1926), on the so-called "lost generation";* Death in the Afternoon *(1932), celebrating bull-fighting;* For Whom the Bell Tolls *(1940), on the Spanish Civil War; and his masterful novella,* The Old Man and the Sea *(1952), for which he won the Pulitzer Prize. In 1954, Hemingway was awarded the Nobel Prize for Literature. After a long illness, Hemingway shot himself in July 1961. "Bull Fighting" (1932) is Hemingway's skillful portrayal of the underlying sequence of choreographed actions that comprise a bullfight.*

The bull ring or Plaza de Toros was a big, tawny brick amphitheatre standing at the end of a street in an open field. The yellow and red Spanish flag was floating over it. Carriages were driving up and people getting out of buses. There was a great crowd of beggars around the entrance. Men were selling water out of big terra cotta water bottles. Kids sold fans, canes, roasted salted almonds in paper spills, fruit, and slabs of ice cream. The crowd was gay and cheerful but all intent on pushing toward the entrance. Mounted civil guards with patent leather cocked hats and carbines slung over their backs sat their horses like statues, and the crowd flowed through.

Inside they all stood around in the bull ring, talking and looking up in the grandstand at the girls in the boxes. Some of the men had field glasses in order to look better. We found our seats and the crowd began to leave the ring and get into the rows of concrete seats. The ring was circular—that sounds foolish, but a boxing ring is square—with a sand floor. Around it was a red board fence—just high enough for a man to be able to vault over it. Between the board fence, which is called the barrera, and the first row of seats ran a narrow alley way. Then came the seats which were just like a football stadium except that around the top ran a double circle of boxes.

Every seat in the amphitheatre was full. The arena was cleared. Then on the far side of the arena out of the crowd, four heralds in medieval costume stood up and blew a blast on their trumpets. The band crashed out, and from the entrance on the far side of the ring four horsemen in black velvet with ruffs around their necks rode out into the white glare of the arena. The people on the sunny side were baking in the heat and fanning themselves. The whole sol side was a flicker of fans.

Behind the four horsemen came the procession of the bull fighters. They had been all formed in ranks in the entrance way ready to march out, and as the music started they came. In the front rank walked the three espadas or toreros, who would have charge of the killing of the six bulls of the afternoon.

They came walking out in heavily brocaded yellow and black costumes, the familiar "toreador" suit, heavy with gold embroidery, cape, jacket, shirt and collar, knee breeches, pink stockings, and low pumps. Always at bull fights afterwards the incongruity of those pink stockings used to strike me. Just behind the three principals—and after your first bull fight you do not look at their costumes but their faces—marched the teams or cuadrillas. They are dressed in the same way but not as gorgeously as the matadors.

Back of the teams ride the picadors. Big, heavy, brown-faced men in wide flat hats, carrying lances like long window poles. They are astride horses that make Spark Plug look as trim and sleek as a King's Plate winner. Back of the pics come the gaily harnessed mule teams and the red-shirted monos or bull ring servants.

The bull fighters march in across the sand to the president's box. They march with easy professional stride, swinging along, not in the least theatrical except for their clothes. They all have the easy grace and slight slouch of the professional athlete. From their faces they might be major league ball players. They salute the president's box and then spread out along the barrera, exchanging their heavy brocaded capes for the fighting capes that have been laid along the red fence by the attendants.

We leaned forward over the barrera. Just below us the three matadors of the afternoon were leaning against the fence talking. One lighted a cigaret. He was a short, clear-skinned gypsy, Gitanillo, in a wonderful gold brocaded jacket, his short pigtail sticking out under his black cocked hat.

"He's not very fancy," a young man in a straw hat, with obviously American shoes, who sat on my left, said.

"But he sure knows bulls, that boy. He's a great killer."

"You're an American, aren't you?" asked Mike.

"Sure," the boy grinned. "But I know this gang. That's Gitanillo. You want to watch him. The kid with the chubby face is Chicuelo. They say he doesn't really like bull fighting, but the town's crazy about him. The next to him is Villalta. He's the great one."

I had noticed Villalta. He was straight as a lance and walked like a young wolf. He was talking and smiling at a friend who leaned over the barrera. Upon his tanned cheekbone was a big patch of gauze held on with adhesive tape.

"He got gored last week at Malaga," said the American.

The American, whom later we were to learn to know and love as the Gin Bottle King, because of a great feat of arms performed at an early hour of the morning with a container of Mr. Gordon's celebrated product as his sole weapon in one of the four most dangerous situations I have ever seen, said: "The show's going to begin."

Out in the arena the picadors had galloped their decrepit horses around the ring, sitting straight and stiff in their rocking chair saddles. Now all but three had ridden out of the ring. These three were huddled against the red painted fence of the barrera. Their horses backed against the fence, one eye bandaged, their lances at rest.

In rode two of the marshals in the velvet jackets and white ruffs. They galloped up to the president's box, swerved and saluted, doffing their hats and bowing low. From the box an object came hurtling down. One of the marshals caught it in his plumed hat.

"The key to the bull pen," said the Gin Bottle King.

The two horsemen whirled and rode across the area. One of them tossed the key to a man in torero costume, they both saluted with a wave of their plumed hats, and had gone from the ring. The big gate was shut and bolted. There was no more entrance. The ring was complete.

The crowd had been shouting and yelling. Now it was dead silent. The man with the key stepped toward an iron barred, low, red door and unlocked the great sliding bar. He lifted it and stepped back. The door swung open. The man hid behind it. Inside it was dark.

Then, ducking his head as he came up out of the dark pen, a bull came into the arena. He came out all in a rush, big, black and white, weighing over a ton and moving with a soft gallop. Just as he came out the sun seemed to dazzle him for an instant. He stood as though he were frozen, his great crest of muscle up, firmly planted, his eyes looking around, his horns pointed forward, black and white and sharp as porcupine quills. Then he charged. And as he charged I suddenly saw what bull fighting is all about.

For the bull was absolutely unbelievable. He seemed like some great prehistoric animal, absolutely deadly and absolutely vicious. And he was silent. He charged silently and with a soft galloping rush. When he turned he turned on his four feet like a cat. When he charged the first thing that caught his eyes was a picador on one of the wretched horses. The picador dug his spurs into the horse and they galloped away. The bull came on in his rush, refused to be shaken off, and in full gallop crashed into the animal from the side, ignored the horse, drove one of his horns high into the thigh of the picador, and tore him, saddle and all, off the horse's back.

The bull went on without pausing to worry the picador lying on the ground. The next picador was sitting on his horse braced to receive the shock of the charge, his lance ready. The bull hit him sideways on, and horse and rider went high up in the air in a kicking mass and fell across the bull's back. As they came down the bull charged into them. The dough-faced kid, Chicuelo, vaulted over the fence, ran toward the bull and flopped his cape into the bull's face. The bull charged the cape and Chicuelo dodged backwards and had the bull clear in the arena.

Without an instant's hesitation the bull charged Chicuelo. The kid stood his ground, simply swung back on his heels and floated his cape like a ballet dancer's skirt into the bull's face as he passed.

"Olé!"—pronounced Oh-Lay!—roared the crowd.

The bull whirled and charged again. Without moving Chicuelo repeated the performance. His legs rigid, just withdrawing his body from the rush of the bull's horns and floating the cape out with that beautiful swing.

Again the crowd roared. The Kid did this seven times. Each time the bull missed him by inches. Each time he gave the bull a free shot at him. Each time the crowd roared. Then he flopped the cape once at the bull at the finish of a pass, swung it around behind him and walked away from the bull to the barrera.

"He's the boy with the cape all right," said the Gin Bottle King. "That swing he did with the cape's called a Veronica."

The chubby faced Kid who did not like bull fighting and had just done the seven wonderful Veronicas was standing against the fence just below us. His face glistened with sweat in the sun but was almost expressionless. His eyes were looking out across the arena where the bull was standing making up his mind to charge a picador. He was studying the bull because a few minutes later it would be his duty to kill him, and once he went out with his thin, red-hilted sword and his piece of red cloth to kill the bull in the final set it would be him or the bull. There are no drawn battles in bull fighting.

I am not going to describe the rest of that afternoon in detail. It was the first bull fight I ever saw, but it was not the best. The best was in the little town of Pamplona high up in the hills of Navarre, and came weeks later. Up in Pamplona, where they have held six days of bull fighting each year since 1126 A.D., and where the bulls race through the streets of the town each morning at six o'clock with half the town running ahead of them. Pamplona, where every man and boy in town is an amateur bull fighter and where there is an amateur fight each morning that is attended by 20,000 people in which the amateur fighters are all unarmed and there is a casualty list at least equal to a Dublin election. But Pamplona, with the best bull fight and the wild tale of the amateur fights, comes in the second chapter.

I am not going to apologize for bull fighting. It is a survival of the days of the Roman Coliseum. But it does need some explanation. Bull fighting is not a sport. It was never supposed to be. It is a tragedy. A very great tragedy. The tragedy is the death of the bull. It is played in three definite acts.

The Gin Bottle King—who, by the way, does not drink gin—told us a lot of this that first night as we sat in the upstairs room of the little restaurant that made a specialty of roast young suckling pig, roasted on an oak plank and served with a mushroom tortilla and vino rojo. The rest we learned later at the bull fighters' pensione in the Via San Jeronimo, where one of the bull fighters had eyes exactly like a rattlesnake.

Much of it we learned in the sixteen fights we saw in different parts of Spain from San Sebastian to Granada.

At any rate bull fighting is not a sport. It is a tragedy, and it symbolizes the struggle between man and the beasts. There are usually six bulls to a fight. A fight is called a corrida de toros. Fighting bulls are bred like race horses, some of the oldest breeding establishments being several hundred years old. A good bull is worth about $2,000. They are bred for speed, strength and viciousness. In other words a good fighting bull is an absolutely incorrigible bad bull.

Bull fighting is an exceedingly dangerous occupation. In sixteen fights I saw there were only two in which there was no one badly hurt. On the other hand it is very remunerative. A popular espada gets $5,000 for his afternoon's work. An unpopular espada though may not get $500. Both run the same risks. It is a good deal like Grand Opera for the really great matadors except they run the chance of being killed every time they cannot hit high C.

No one at any time in the fight can approach the bull at any time except directly from the front. That is where the danger comes. There are also all sorts of complicated passes that must be done with the cape, each requiring as much technique as a champion billiard player. And underneath it all is the necessity for playing the old tragedy in the absolutely custom bound, law-laid-down way. It must all be done gracefully, seemingly effortlessly and always with dignity. The worst criticism the Spaniards ever make of a bull fighter is that his work is "vulgar."

The three absolute acts of the tragedy are first the entry of the bull when the picadors receive the shock of his attacks and attempt to protect their horses with their lances. Then the horses go out and the second act is the planting of the banderillos. This is one of the most interesting and difficult parts but among the easiest for a new bull fight fan to appreciate in technique. The banderillos are three-foot, gaily colored darts with a small fish hook prong in the end. The man who is going to plant them walks out into the arena alone with the bull. He lifts the banderillos at arm's length and points them toward the bull. Then he calls "Toro! Toro!" The bull charges and the banderillero rises to his toes, bends in a curve forward and just as the bull is about to hit him drops the darts into the bull's lump just back of his horns.

They must go in evenly, one on each side. They must not be shoved, or thrown or stuck in from the side. This is the first time the bull has been completely baffled, there is the prick of the darts that he cannot escape and there are no horses for him to charge into. But he charges the man again and again and each time he gets a pair of the long banderillos that hang from his hump by their tiny barbs and flop like porcupine quills.

Last is the death of the bull, which is in the hands of the matador who has had charge of the bull since his first attack. Each matador has two bulls in the afternoon. The death of the bull is most formal and can only be brought about in one way, directly from the front by the matador who must receive the bull in full charge and kill him with a sword thrust between the shoulders just back of the neck and between the horns. Before killing the bull he must first do a series of passes with the muleta, a piece of red cloth he carries about the size of a large napkin. With the muleta the torero must show his complete mastery of the bull, must make the bull miss him again and again by inches, before he is allowed to kill him. It is in this phase that most of the fatal accidents occur.

The word "toreador" is obsolete Spanish and is never used. The torero is usually called an espada or swordsman. He must be proficient in all three acts in the fight. In the first he uses the cape and does veronicas and protects the picadors by taking the bull out and away from them when they are spilled to the ground. In the second act he plants the banderillos. In the third act he masters the bull with the muleta and kills him.

Few toreros excel in all three departments. Some, like young Chicuelo, are unapproachable in their cape work. Others like the late Joselito are wonderful banderilleros. Only a few are great killers. Most of the greatest killers are gypsies.

Meaning

1. What are the three separate stages of the bullfight that Hemingway characterizes as the "three absolute acts of the tragedy"?

2. According to Hemingway, how does the ritualized violence of the bullfight serve an important and traditional purpose?
3. How are the traditional characteristics of tragedy, requiring conflict between a protagonist and an antagonist, replayed during the bullfight?

USING PROCESS ANALYSIS TO CONVEY MEANING

1. How does Hemingway's style—understated, terse, unemotional, restrained—convey respect for the very same qualities shown by "toreros," who let the bull pass as closely as possible, while remaining unemotional and restrained in their movements?
2. How does Hemingway's initial description supply important information that his readers will need to fully understand his subsequent analysis?
3. What time markers and other guide words does Hemingway make use of to carefully divide the action of the bullfight into separate stages?

WRITING SUGGESTIONS

1. Analyze other sports (e.g., auto-racing, boxing) where elements of violence and potential tragedy are at least as important as they are in a bullfight.
2. Analyze deer-hunting, big game-fishing, or any other sport that has its own rituals, meanings, special clothing, and equipment.
3. Discuss the relationship between this essay and any of Hemingway's short stories or novels where the confrontation between man and animal is an integral part of the story (e.g., *The Old Man and the Sea*).

Tom Wolfe

The New Journalism

Tom Wolfe was born in 1931 in Richmond, Virginia. Wolfe received a Doctorate in American Studies from Yale in 1957, and worked as a reporter for the Springfield Union (1956–1959), The Washington Post (1959–1962), and became feature writer for the New York Herald Tribune's Sunday supplement (now New York Magazine). Wolfe's dissatisfaction with traditional techniques led to the birth of the "New Journalism." This unique form of journalistic writing incorporates slang, eccentric punctuation, vernaculars of different subcultures, and subjective perceptions, using narrative techniques—scene-by-scene construction, personal viewpoint, details on furnishings, clothes, and social status— usually associated with fiction. Wolfe's article on custom cars for Esquire (1963), and definitive portraits of alternate life-styles in The Kandy-Kolored Tangerine Flake Streamline Baby (1965), The Pump House Gang (1968), and The Electric Kool-Aid Acid Test (1968), are written in styles that echo their subjects. Wolfe's intensively researched study of the astronauts, in The Right Stuff (1979), won an American National Book Award, Critic's Circle Award, and became a popular film. In "The New Journalism," an excerpt from "Why They Aren't Writing the Great American Novel Anymore (1972), Wolfe tells the behind-the-scenes story of how the New Journalism came into being.

All of a sudden, in the mid-Sixties, here comes a bunch of slick-magazine and Sunday-supplement writers with no literary credentials whatsoever in most cases—only they're using all the techniques of the novelists, even the most sophisticated ones—and on top of that they're helping themselves to the insights of the men of letters while they're at it—and at the same time they're still doing their low-life legwork, their "digging," their hustling, their damnable Locker Room Genre reporting—they're taking on *all* of these roles at the same time—in other words, they're ignoring literary class lines that have been almost a century in the making.

The panic hit the men of letters first. If the lumpenproles[1] won their point, if their new form achieved any sort of literary respectability, if it were somehow accepted as "creative," the men of letters stood to lose even their positions as the reigning practitioners of nonfiction. They would get bumped down to Lower Middle Class. This was already beginning to happen. The first indication I had came in an article in the June, 1956, *Atlantic* by Dan Wakefield, entitled "The Personal Voice and the Impersonal Eye." The gist of the piece was that this was the first period in anybody's memory when people in the literary world were beginning to talk about nonfiction as a serious artistic form. Norman Podhoretz had written a piece in *Harper's* in

---

[1] The disenfranchised or those who have lost status.

1958 claiming a similar status for the "discursive prose" of the late Fifties, essays by people like James Baldwin and Isaac Rosenfeld. But the excitement Wakefield was talking about had nothing to do with essays or any other traditional nonfiction. Quite the contrary; Wakefield attributed the new prestige of nonfiction to two books of an entirely different sort: *In Cold Blood*, by Truman Capote, and a collection of magazine articles with a title in alliterative trochaic pentameter that I am sure would come to me if I dwelled upon it.[2]

Capote's story of the life and death of two drifters who blew the heads off a wealthy farm family in Kansas ran as a serial in *The New Yorker* in the Fall of 1965 and came out in book form in February of 1966. It was a sensation—and a terrible jolt to all who expected the accursed New Journalism or Parajournalism to spin itself out like a fad. Here, after all, was not some obscure journalist, some free-lance writer, but a novelist of long standing . . . whose career had been in the doldrums . . . and who suddenly, with this one stroke, with this turn to the damnable new form of journalism, not only resuscitated his reputation but elevated it higher than ever before . . . and became a celebrity of the most amazing magnitude in the bargain. People of all sorts read *In Cold Blood*, people at every level of taste. Everybody was absorbed in it. Capote himself didn't call it journalism; far from it; he said he had invented a new literary genre, "the nonfiction novel." Nevertheless, his success gave the New Journalism, as it would soon be called, an overwhelming momentum.

Capote had spent five years researching his story and interviewing the killers in prison, and so on, a very meticulous and impressive job. But in 1966 you started seeing feats of reporting that were extraordinary, spectacular. Here came a breed of journalists who somehow had the moxie to talk their way inside of any milieu, even closed societies, and hang on for dear life. A marvelous maniac named John Sack talked the Army into letting him join an infantry company at Fort Dix, M Company, 1st Advanced Infantry Training Brigade—not as a recruit but as a reporter—and go through training with them and then to Vietnam and into battle. The result was a book called *M* (appearing first in *Esquire*), a nonfiction *Catch-22* and, for my money, still the finest book in any genre published about the war. George Plimpton went into training with a professional football team, the Detroit Lions, in the role of reporter playing rookie quarterback, rooming with the players going through their workouts and finally playing quarterback for them in a preseason game—in order to write *Paper Lion*. Like Capote's book, *Paper Lion* was read by people at every level of taste and had perhaps the greatest literary impact of any writing about sports since Ring Lardner's short stories. But the all-time free-lance writer's Brass Stud Award went that year to an obscure California journalist named Hunter Thompson who "ran" with the Hell's Angels for eighteen months—as a reporter and not a member, which might have been safer—in order to write *Hell's Angels: The Strange and Terrible Saga of the Outlaw Motorcycle Gang*. The Angels wrote his last chapter for him by stomping him half to death in a roadhouse fifty miles from Santa Rosa. All through the book Thompson had been searching for the single psychological or sociological insight that would sum up all he had seen, the single golden *aperçu*; and as he lay sprawled there on the floor coughing up blood and teeth, the line he had been looking for came to him in a brilliant flash from out of the heart of darkness: "Exterminate all the brutes!"

[2] Wolfe's book, *Kandy-Kolored, Tangerine-Flake Streamlined Baby* (1965).

At the same time, 1966 and 1967, Joan Didion was writing those strange Gothic articles of hers about California that were eventually collected in *Slouching Towards Bethlehem*. Rex Reed was writing his celebrity interviews—this was an old journalistic exercise, of course, but no one had ever quite so diligently addressed himself to the question of, "What is So-and-so *really* like?" (Simone Signoret, as I recall, turned out to have the neck, shoulders and upper back of a middle linebacker.) James Mills was pulling off some amazing reporting feats of his own for *Life* in pieces such as "The Panic in Needle Park," "The Detective," and "The Prosecutor." The writer-reporter team of Garry Wills and Ovid Demaris was doing a series of brilliant pieces for *Esquire*, culminating in "You All Know Me—I'm Jack Ruby!"

And then, early in 1968, another novelist turned to nonfiction, and with a success that in its own way was as spectacular as Capote's two years before. This was Norman Mailer writing a memoir about an antiwar demonstration he had become involved in, "The Steps of the Pentagon." The memoir, or autobiography (Appendix III), is an old genre of nonfiction, of course, but this piece was written soon enough after the event to have a journalistic impact. It took up an entire issue of *Harper's Magazine* and came out a few months later under the title of *The Armies Of The Night*. Unlike Capote's book, Mailer's was not a popular success; but within the literary community and among intellectuals generally it couldn't have been a more tremendous *succès d'estime*.[3] At the time Mailer's reputation had been deteriorating in the wake of two inept novels called *An American Dream* (1968) and *Why Are We In Vietnam?* (1967). He was being categorized somewhat condescendingly as a journalist, because his nonfiction, chiefly in *Esquire*, was obviously better work. *The Armies Of The Night* changed all that in a flash. Like Capote, Mailer had a dread of the tag that had been put on him—"journalist"—and had subtitled his book "The Novel as History; History as The Novel." But the lesson was one that nobody in the literary world could miss. Here was another novelist who had turned to some form of accursed journalism no matter what name you gave it, and had not only revived his reputation but raised it to a point higher than it had ever been in his life.

By 1969 no one in the literary world could simply dismiss this new journalism as an inferior genre. The situation was somewhat similar to the situation of the novel in England in the 1850's. It was yet to be canonized, sanctified and given a theology, but writers themselves could already feel the new Power flowing.

The similarity between the early days of the novel and the early days of the New Journalism is not merely coincidental. In both cases we are watching the same process. We are watching a group of writers coming along, working in a genre regarded as Lower Class (the novel before the 1850's, slick-magazine journalism before the 1960's), who discover the joys of detailed realism and its strange powers. Many of them seem to be in love with realism for its own sake; and never mind the "sacred callings" of literature. They seem to be saying: "Hey! Come here! This is the way people are living now—just the way I'm going to show you! It may astound you, disgust you, delight you or arouse your contempt or make you laugh. . . . Nevertheless, this is what it's like! It's *all* right here! You won't be bored! Take a look!"

If you follow the progress of the New Journalism closely through the 1960s, you see an interesting thing happening. You see journalists learning the techniques of realism—particularly of the sort found in Fielding, Smollett, Balzac, Dickens and

[3] Critical rather than popular success.

Gogol—from scratch. By trial and error, by "instinct" rather than theory, journalists began to discover the devices that gave the realistic novel its unique power, variously known as its "immediacy," its "concrete reality," its "emotional involvement," its "gripping" or "absorbing" quality.

This extraordinary power was derived mainly from just four devices, they discovered. The basic one was scene-by-scene construction, telling the story by moving from scene to scene and resorting as little as possible to sheer historical narrative. Hence the sometimes extraordinary feats of reporting that the new journalists undertook: so that they could actually witness the scenes in other people's lives as they took place— and record the dialogue in full, which was device No. 2. Magazine writers, like the early novelists, learned by trial and error something that has since been demonstrated in academic studies: namely, that realistic dialogue involves the reader more completely than any other single device. It also establishes and defines character more quickly and effectively than any other single device. (Dickens has a way of fixing a character in your mind so that you have the feeling he has described every inch of his appearance— only to go back and discover that he actually took care of the physical description in two or three sentences; the rest he had accomplished with dialogue.) Journalists were working on dialogue of the fullest, most completely revealing sort in the very moment when novelists were cutting back, using dialogue in more and more cryptic, fey and curiously abstract ways.

The third device was the so-called "third-person point of view," the technique of presenting every scene to the reader through the eyes of a particular character, giving the reader the feeling of being inside the character's mind and experiencing the emotional reality of the scene as he experiences it. Journalists had often used the first-person point of view—"I was there"—just as autobiographers, memoirists and novelists had. This is very limiting for the journalist, however, since he can bring the reader inside the mind of only one character—himself—a point of view that often proves irrelevant to the story and irritating to the reader. Yet how could a journalist, writing nonfiction, accurately penetrate the thoughts of another person?

The answer proved to be marvelously simple: interview him about his thoughts and emotions, along with everything else. This was what Gay Talese did in order to write *Honor Thy Father*, in *M*, John Sack had gone a step further and used both third-person point of view and the interior monologue to a limited extent.

The fourth device has always been the least understood. This is the recording of everyday gestures, habits, manners, customs, styles of furniture, clothing, decoration, styles of traveling, eating, keeping house, modes of behaving toward children, servants, superiors, inferiors, peers, plus the various looks, glances, poses, styles of walking and other symbolic details that might exist within a scene. Symbolic of what? Symbolic, generally, of people's *status life* using that term in the broad sense of the entire pattern of behavior and possessions through which people express their position in the world or what they think it is or what they hope it to be. The recording of such details is not mere embroidery in prose. It lies as close to the center of the power of realism as any other device in literature.

When we talk about the "rise" or "death" of literary genres, we are talking about status, mainly. The novel no longer has the supreme status it enjoyed for ninety years (1875–1965), but neither has the New Journalism won it for itself. The status of the New Journalism is not secure by any means. In some quarters the contempt for it is boundless . . . even breathtaking. . . . With any luck at all the new genre will never be sanctified, never be exalted, never given a theology. I probably shouldn't even go around talking it up the way I have in this piece. All I meant to say when I started out was that the New Journalism can no longer be ignored in an artistic sense. The rest I take back. . . . The hell with it. . . . Let chaos reign . . . louder music, more wine. . . . The hell with the standings. . . . The top rung is up for grabs. All the old traditions are exhausted, and no new one is yet established. All bets are off! the odds are canceled! it's anybody's ball game! . . . the horses are all drugged! the track is glass! . . . and out of such glorious chaos may come, from the most unexpected source, in the most unexpected form, some nice new fat Star Streamer Rockets that will light up the sky.

MEANING

1. In what way does the "New Journalism" diverge from traditional journalism? What qualities does it emphasize that traditional journalism did not?
2. What reasons does Wolfe give to support his belief that the "New Journalism" will produce a new popular form of literature that will be as important as the traditional novel?
3. What specific stages does Wolfe identify in his account of the process by which the "New Journalism" developed?
4. What devices, adapted from techniques used in fiction, does the "New Journalism" use to draw the reader into the scene?
5. Who are the writers Wolfe cites whose work typifies the "New Journalism"?

USING PROCESS ANALYSIS TO CONVEY MEANING

1. Why was Truman Capote's novel *In Cold Blood* a milestone along the way in the development of the "New Journalism"?
2. What examples does Wolfe provide to show that the techniques of the "New Journalism" were adaptable to a broad range of subjects?
3. How did the successes of Hunter Thompson, Joan Didion, Norman Mailer, George Plimpton, and Wolfe himself mark key stages in the recognition of nonfiction as a serious artistic form?

WRITING SUGGESTIONS

1. Using any news story that you consider to be an example of the "New Journalism," evaluate how different elements from fiction—realistic dialogue, scene-by-scene construction, third-person point of view, exact recording of gestures and facial expressions—contribute to the effectiveness of the news story.
2. Discuss any nonfiction novel—other than those mentioned by Wolfe—that had an obvious journalistic inception.
3. Do you agree with Wolfe that the "New Journalism" has produced a new popular form of literature at least as important as the traditional novel?

POLITICAL AND SOCIAL SCIENCES

JESSICA MITFORD

Mortuary Solaces

Jessica Mitford was born in 1917 in Gloucestershire, England. After emigrating to the United States in 1939, Mitford worked as the executive secretary for the Civil Rights Congress in Oakland, California. Mitford's crusading investigative studies include the much-acclaimed The American Way of Death. *(1963), a book violently denounced by the funeral industry;* The Trial of Dr. Spock, William Sloane Coffin, Jr., Michael Ferber, Mitchell Goodman, and Marcus Raskin *(1969), an examination of conspiracy laws; and* Kind and Usual Punishment: The Prison Business *(1973), an expose of the widespread use of prisoners as subjects in psychological and physiological research. In 1973, Mitford was named Distinguished Visiting Professor in Sociology at San Jose State College, conducting seminars in "muckraking," a subject she covers thoroughly in* Poison Penmanship: The Gentle Art of Muckraking *(1979). In "Mortuary Solaces,' from* The American Way of Death, *Mitford provides an acerbic account, buttressed by extensive research and quotations from the funeral industry's handbooks, of the processes used to prepare dead bodies for public display.*

Embalming is indeed a most extraordinary procedure, and one must wonder at the docility of Americans who each year pay hundreds of millions of dollars for its perpetuation, blissfully ignorant of what it is all about, what is done, how it is done. Not one in ten thousand has any idea of what actually takes place. Books on the subject are extremely hard to come by. They are not to be found in most libraries or bookshops.

In an era when huge television audiences watch surgical operations in the comfort of their living rooms, when, thanks to the animated cartoon, the geography of the digestive system has become familiar territory even to the nursery school set, in a land where the satisfaction of curiosity about almost all matters is a national pastime, the secrecy surrounding embalming can, surely, hardly be attributed to the inherent gruesomeness of the subject. Custom in this regard has within this century suffered a complete reversal. In the early days of American embalming, when it was performed in the home of the deceased, it was almost mandatory for some relative to stay by the embalmer's side and witness the procedure. Today, family members who might wish to be in attendance would certainly be dissuaded by the funeral director. All others, except apprentices, are excluded by law from the preparation room.

A close look at what does actually take place may explain in large measure the undertaker's intractable reticence concerning a procedure that has become his major *raison d'être*. Is it possible he fears that public information about embalming might lead patrons to wonder if they really want this service? If the funeral men are loath to discuss the subject outside the trade, the reader may, understandably, be equally loath to go on reading at this point. For those who have the stomach for it, let us part the formaldehyde curtain. . . .

The body is first laid out in the undertaker's morgue—or rather, Mr. Jones is reposing in the preparation room—to be readied to bid the world farewell.

The preparation room in any of the better funeral establishments has the tiled and sterile look of a surgery, and indeed the embalmer-restorative artist who does his chores there is beginning to adopt the term "dermasurgeon" (appropriately corrupted by some mortician-writers as "demisurgeon") to describe his calling. His equipment, consisting of scalpels, scissors, augurs, forceps, clamps, needles, pumps, tubes, bowls and basins, is crudely imitative of the surgeon's as is his technique, acquired in a nine- or twelve-month post-high-school course in an embalming school. He is supplied by an advanced chemical industry with a bewildering array of fluids, sprays, pastes, oils, powders, creams, to fix or soften tissue, shrink or distend it as needed, dry it here, restore the moisture there. There are cosmetics, waxes and paints to fill and cover features, even plaster of Paris to replace entire limbs. There are ingenious aids to prop and stabilize the cadaver: a Vari-Pose Head Rest, the Edwards Arm and Hand Positioner, the Repose Block (to support the shoulders during the embalming), and the Throop Foot Positioner, which resembles an old-fashioned stocks.

Mr. John H. Eckels, president of the Eckels College of Mortuary Science, thus describes the first part of the embalming procedure: "In the hands of a skilled practitioner, this work may be done in a comparatively short time and without mutilating the body other than by slight incision—so slight that it scarcely would cause serious inconvenience if made upon a living person. It is necessary to remove the blood, and doing this not only helps in the disinfecting, but removes the principal cause of disfigurements due to discoloration."

Another textbook discusses the all-important time element: "The earlier this is done, the better, for every hour that elapses between death and embalming will add to the problems and complications encountered. . . ." Just how soon should one get going on the embalming? The author tells us, "On the basis of such scanty information made available to this profession through its rudimentary and haphazard system of technical research, we must conclude that the best results are to be obtained if the subject is embalmed before life is completely extinct—that is, before cellular death has occurred. In the average case, this would mean within an hour after somatic death." For those who feel that there is something a little rudimentary, not to say haphazard, about this advice, a comforting thought is offered by another writer. Speaking of fears entertained in early days of premature burial, he points out, "One of the effects of embalming by chemical injection, however, has been to dispel fears of live burial." How true, once the blood is removed, chances of live burial are indeed remote.

To return to Mr. Jones, the blood is drained out through the veins and replaced by embalming fluid pumped in through the arteries. As noted in *The Principles and Practices of Embalming*, "every operator has a favorite injection and drainage point—a fact which becomes a handicap only if he fails or refuses to forsake his favorites when conditions demand it." Typical favorites are the carotid artery, femoral artery, jugular vein, subclavian vein. There are various choices of embalming fluid. If Flextone is used, it will produce a "mild, flexible rigidity. The skin retains a velvety softness, the tissues are rubbery and pliable. Ideal for women and children." It may be blended with B. and G. Products Company's Lyf-Lyk tint, which is guaranteed to reproduce "nature's own skin texture . . . the velvety appearance of living tissue." Suntone comes in three separate tints: Suntan; Special Cosmetic Tint, a pink shade "especially indicated for young female subjects"; and Regular Cosmetic Tint, moderately pink.

About three to six gallons of a dyed and perfumed solution of formaldehyde, glycerin, borax, phenol, alcohol and water is soon circulating through Mr. Jones, whose mouth has been sewn together with a "needle directed upward between the upper lip and gum and brought out through the left nostril," with the corners raised slightly "for a more pleasant expression." If he should be bucktoothed, his teeth are cleaned with Bon Ami and coated with colorless nail polish. His eyes, meanwhile, are closed with flesh-tinted eye caps and eye cement.

The next step is to have at Mr. Jones with a thing called a trocar. This is a long, hollow needle attached to a tube. It is jabbed into the abdomen, poked around the entrails and chest cavity, the contents of which are pumped out and replaced with "cavity fluid." This done, and the hole in the abdomen sewn up, Mr. Jones's face is heavily creamed (to protect the skin from burns which may be caused by leakage of the chemicals), and he is covered with a sheet and left unmolested for a while. But not for long—there is more, much more, in store for him. He has been embalmed, but not yet restored, and the best time to start the restorative work is eight to ten hours after embalming, when the tissues have become firm and dry.

The object of all this attention to the corpse, it must be remembered, is to make it presentable for viewing in an attitude of healthy repose. "Our customs require the presentation of our dead in the semblance of normality . . . unmarred by the ravages of illness, disease or mutilation," says Mr. J. Sheridan Mayer in his *Restorative Art*. This is rather a large order since few people die in the full bloom of health, unravaged by illness and unmarked by some disfigurement. The funeral industry is equal to the challenge: "In some cases the gruesome appearance of a mutilated or disease-ridden subject may be quite discouraging. The task of restoration may seem impossible and shake the confidence of the embalmer. This is the time for intestinal fortitude and determination. Once the formative work is begun and affected tissues are cleaned or removed, all doubts of success vanish. It is surprising and gratifying to discover the results which may be obtained."

The embalmer, having allowed an appropriate interval to elapse, returns to the attack, but now he brings into play the skill and equipment of sculptor and cosmetician. Is a hand missing? Casting one in plaster of Paris is a simple matter. "For replacement purposes, only a cast of the back of the hand is necessary; this is within the ability of the average operator and is quite adequate." If a lip or two, a nose or an ear should be missing, the embalmer has at hand a variety of restorative waxes with which to model replacements. Pores and skin texture are simulated by stippling with a little brush, and over this cosmetics are laid on. Head off? Decapitation cases are rather routinely handled. Ragged edges are trimmed, and head joined to torso with a series of splints, wires and sutures. It is a good idea to have a little something at the neck—a scarf or high collar—when time for viewing comes. Swollen mouth? Cut out tissue as needed from inside the lips. If too much is removed, the surface contour can easily be restored by padding with cotton. Swollen necks and cheeks are reduced by removing tissue through vertical incisions made down each side of the neck. "When the deceased is casketed, the pillow will hide the suture incisions . . . as an extra precaution against leakage, the suture may be painted with liquid sealer."

The opposite condition is more likely to present itself—that of emaciation. His hypodermic syringe now loaded with massage cream, the embalmer seeks out and fills the hollowed and sunken areas by injection. In this procedure the backs of the hands and fingers and the under-chin area should not be neglected.

Positioning the lips is a problem that recurrently challenges the ingenuity of the embalmer. Closed too tightly, they tend to give a stern, even disapproving expression. Ideally, embalmers feel, the lips should give the impression of being ever so slightly parted, the upper lip protruding slightly for a more youthful appearance. This takes some engineering, however, as the lips tend to drift apart. Lip drift can sometimes be remedied by pushing one or two straight pins through the inner margin of the lower lip and then inserting them between the two front upper teeth. If Mr. Jones happens to have no teeth, the pins can just as easily be anchored in his Armstrong Face Former and Denture Replacer. Another method to maintain lip closure is to dislocate the lower jaw, which is then held in its new position by a wire run through holes which have been drilled through the upper and lower jaws at the midline. As the French are fond of saying, *if faut souffrir pour être belle.*[1]

If Mr. Jones has died of jaundice, the embalming fluid will very likely turn him green. Does this deter the embalmer? Not if he has intestinal fortitude. Masking pastes and cosmetics are heavily laid on, burial garments and casket interiors are color-correlated with particular care, and Jones is displayed beneath rose-colored lights. Friends will say, "How *well* he looks." Death by carbon monoxide, on the other hand, can be rather a good thing from the embalmer's viewpoint: "One advantage is the fact that this type of discoloration is an exaggerated form of a natural pink coloration." This is nice because the healthy glow is already present and needs but little attention.

The patching and filling completed, Mr. Jones is now shaved, washed and dressed. Cream-based cosmetic, available in pink, flesh, suntan, brunette and blond, is applied to his hands and face, his hair is shampooed and combed (and, in the case of Mrs. Jones, set), his hands manicured. For the horny-handed son of toil special care must be taken; cream should be applied to remove ingrained grime, and the nails cleaned. "If he were not in the habit of having them manicured in life, trimming and shaping is advised for better appearance—never questioned by kin."

Jones is now ready for casketing (this is the present participle of the verb "to casket"). In this operation his right shoulder should be depressed slightly "to turn the body a bit to the right and soften the appearance of lying flat on the back." Positioning the hands is a matter of importance, and special rubber positioning blocks

---

[1] "One must suffer to be beautiful."

may be used. The hands should be cupped slightly for a more lifelike, relaxed appearance. Proper placement of the body requires a delicate sense of balance. It should lie as high as possible in the casket, yet not so high that the lid, when lowered, will hit the nose. On the other hand, we are cautioned, placing the body too low "creates the impression that the body is in a box."

Jones is next wheeled into the appointed slumber room where a few last touches may be added—his favorite pipe placed in his hand or, if he was a great reader, a book propped into position. (In the case of little Master Jones a Teddy bear may be clutched.) Here he will hold open house for a few days, visiting hours 10 A.M. to 9 P.M.

MEANING

1. How do undertakers use a whole range of cosmetic techniques to create, as much as possible, an illusion of life and make the shock of death more manageable?
2. Why, in Mitford's opinion, does our culture surround mortuary practices with such a cloak of secrecy?
3. Into what stages does Mitford divide the process of "casketing"?
4. Why was this article considered to be an exposé of the funeral industry when it was first published in 1963?
5. From a mortician's point of view, why are deaths from certain causes preferable?

USING PROCESS ANALYSIS TO CONVEY MEANING

1. How does Mitford's avoidance of traditional euphemisms and use of irony reveal her attitude toward an industry that she feels exploits the public?
2. What use does Mitford make of various "how to" undertaker's manuals to satirize a profession that prefers the public to view it as dignified.
3. How does the final reference to the injunction against "placing the body too low" lest it create "'the impression that the body is in a box'" capture the essential quality that characterizes the whole process?

WRITING SUGGESTIONS

1. To what extent do you feel that Mitford overlooks the positive side of creating the illusion, through cosmetic means, that the dead person is just asleep? Might not mortuary practices serve a valuable psychological purpose in getting people through the difficult period just after the death of a family member or friend?
2. Discuss the use of embalming as it relates to the fear of being buried alive. You might wish to read works by Edgar Allen Poe ("A Cask of Amontillado" or "Premature Burial") where this fear is a source of horror.
3. What connections can you discover between the practices Mitford discusses and

the cosmetic industry's use of "scare tactics" to promote products that supposedly preserve youth and beauty?

4. As a research project, contrast the "cosmetic" procedures described by Mitford with the religious purposes of the ancient Egyptian practice of embalming. What might an anthropologist say could be learned about these two cultures from the way they bury their dead?

RICHARD RHODES

Watching the Animals

Richard Rhodes was born in Kansas City, Kansas in 1937. Rhodes graduated with honors from Yale University in 1959, worked for Hallmark Cards, Inc. (1962–1970), and was a contributing editor for both Harper's *and* Playboy. *Rhodes received a Guggenheim Fellowship (1974–1975) and a National Endowment for the Arts grant in writing (1978). In addition to more than fifty articles in* Harper's, Red Book, Esquire, Playboy, *and* Reader's Digest, *Rhodes has written* Inland Ground: An Evocation of the American Middle West *(1970),* Looking for America: A Writer's Odyssey *(1979), and the critically-acclaimed* The Making of the Atomic Bomb *(1987). Rhodes's ability to cut through to th essentials and follow an action from its onset to its completion is clearly seen in "Watching the Animals" (1970), an absorbing and realistic account of the processing of pigs into foodstuffs by the I-D Packing Company of Des Moines, Iowa.*

The loves of flint and iron are naturally a little rougher than those of the nightingale and the rose.

—Ralph Waldo Emerson

I remembered today about this country lake in Kansas where I live: that it is artificial, built at the turn of the century, when Upton Sinclair was writing *The Jungle*, as an ice lake. The trains with their loads of meat from the Kansas City stockyards would stop by the Kaw River, across the road, and ice the cars. "You have just dined," Emerson once told what must have been a shocked Victorian audience, "and however scrupulously the slaughterhouse is concealed in the graceful distance of miles, there is complicity, expensive races—race living at the expense of race. . . ."

The I-D Packing Company of Des Moines, Iowa: a small outfit which subcontracts from Armour the production of fresh pork. It can handle about 450 pigs an hour on its lines. No beef or mutton. No smoked hams or hot dogs. Plain fresh pork. A well-run outfit, with federal inspectors alert on all the lines.

The kind of slaughterhouse Upton Sinclair was talking about doesn't exist around here any more. The vast buildings still stand in Des Moines and Omaha and Kansas City, but the operations are gone. The big outfits used to operate on a profit margin of 1.5 per cent, which didn't give them much leeway, did it. Now they are defunct, and their buildings, which look like monolithic enlargements of concentration-camp barracks, sit empty, the hundreds of windows broken, dusty, jagged pieces of glass sticking out of the frames as if the animals heard the good news one day and leaped out the nearest exit. Even the stockyards, miles and miles of rotting, weathered board pens, floors paved fifty years ago by hand with brick, look empty, though I am told cattle receipts are up compared to what they were a few years back. The new thing is small, specialized, efficient houses out where the cattle are, in Denver, in Phoenix, in Des Moines, especially in Texas, where the weather is more favorable to fattening cattle. In Iowa the cattle waste half their feed just keeping warm in the wintertime. But in Iowa or in Texas, the point of meat-packing today is refrigeration. It's cheaper to ship cold meat than live animals. So the packing plants have gone out to the farms and ranches. They are even beginning to buy up the ranches themselves so that they won't have to depend on the irregularities of farmers and cattlemen who bring their animals in only when the price is up or the ground too wet for plowing. Farmhouses stand empty all over America. Did you know that? The city has already won, never mind how many of our television shows still depict the hardy bucolic rural. I may regret the victory, but that's my lookout. We are an urban race now, and meat is something you buy shrink-wrapped at the supermarket.

There are no stockyards inside the I-D Packing Company. The pigs arrive by trailer truck from Sioux City and other places. Sometimes a farmer brings in two or three in the back of his pickup. He unloads them into the holding pens, where they are weighed and inspected, goes into the office and picks up his check. The men, except on the killing floor, are working on the cooled carcasses of yesterday's kill anyway, so there is time to even out the line. Almost everything in a packinghouse operates on a chain line, and for maximum profit that line must be full, 450 carcasses an hour at the I-D Packing Company, perhaps 300 heavies if today is heavies day— sows, overgrown hogs. Boars presumably escape the general fate. Their flesh is flavored with rut and tastes like an unventilated gymnasium locker room.

Down goes the tail gate and out come the pigs, enthusiastic after their drive. Pigs are the most intelligent of all farm animals, by actual laboratory test. Learn the fastest, for example, to push a plunger with their foot to earn a reward of pelletized feed. And not as reliable in their instincts. You don't have to call cattle to dinner. They are waiting outside the fence at 4:30 sharp, having arrived as silently as the Vietcong. But perhaps that is pig intelligence too: let you do the work, laze around until the last minute, and then charge over and knock you down before you can slop the garbage into the trough. Cattle will stroll one by one into a row of stalls and usually fill them in serial order. Not pigs. They squeal and nip and shove. Each one wants the entire meal for himself. They won't stick together in a herd, either. Shoot out all over the place, and you'd damned better have every gate closed or they'll be in your garden and on your lawn and even in your living room, nodding by the fire.

They talk a lot, to each other, to you if you care to listen. I am not romanticizing pigs. They always scared me a little on the farm, which is probably why I watched them more closely than the other animals. They do talk: low grunts, quick squeals, a kind of hum sometimes, angry shrieks, high screams of fear.

I have great respect for the I-D Packing Company. They do a dirty job and do it as cleanly and humanely as possible, and do it well. They were nice enough to let me in the door, which is more than I can say for the Wilson people in Omaha, where I first tried to arrange a tour. What are you hiding, Wilson people?

Once into the holding pen, the pigs mill around getting to know each other. The I-D holding pens are among the most modern in the nation, my spokesman told me. Tubular steel painted tinner's red to keep it from rusting. Smooth concrete floors with drains so that the floors can be washed down hygienically after each lot of pigs is run through.

The pigs come out of the first holding pen through a gate that allows only one to pass at a time. Just beside the gate is a wooden door, and behind the door is the first worker the pigs encounter. He has a wooden box beside him filled with metal numbers, the shape of each number picked out with sharp needles. For each lot of pigs he selects a new set of numbers—2473, say—and slots them into a device like a hammer and dips it in nontoxic purple dye. As a pig shoots out of the gate he hits the pig in the side with the numbers, making a tattoo. The pig gives a grunt—it doesn't especially hurt, pigskin is thick, as you know—and moves on to one of several smaller pens where each lot is held until curtain time. The tattoo, my spokesman told me, will stay on the animal through all the killing and cleaning and cutting operations, to the very end. Its purpose is to identify any animal or lot of animals which might be diseased, so that the seller can be informed and the carcasses destroyed. Rather too proud of his tattooing process, I thought, but then, you know the tattoos I am thinking about.

It would be more dramatic, make a better story, if the killing came last, but it comes first. We crossed a driveway with more red steel fencing. Lined up behind it, pressing into it because they sensed by now that all was not well with them, were perhaps a hundred pigs. But still curious, watching us go by in our long white canvas coats. Everyone wore those, and hard plastic helmets, white helmets for the workers, yellow helmets for the foremen. I got to be a foreman.

Before they reach their end, the pigs get a shower, a real one. Water sprays from every angle to wash the farm off of them. Then they begin to feel crowded. The pen narrows like a funnel; the drivers behind urge the pigs forward, until one at a time they climb onto a moving ramp. The ramp's sides move as well as its floor. The floor is created to give the pigs footing. The sides are made of blocks of wood so that they will not bruise, and they slant inward to wedge the pigs along. Now they scream, never having been on such a ramp, smelling the smells they smell ahead. I do not want to overdramatize, because you have read all this before. But it was a frightening experience, seeing their fear, seeing so many of them go by. It had to remind me of things no one wants to be reminded of anymore, all mobs, all death marches, all mass murders and extinctions, the slaughter of the buffalo, the slaughter of the Indian, the Inferno, Judgment Day, complicity, expensive races, race living at the expense of race. That so gentle a religion as Christianity could end up in Judgment Day. That we are the most expensive of races, able in our affluence to hire others of our kind to do this terrible necessary work of killing another race of creatures so that we may feed our oxygen-rich brains. Feed our children, for that matter.

At the top of the ramp, one man. With rubber gloves on, holding two electrodes that looked like enlarged curling irons except that they sported more of those needles. As a pig reached the top, this man jabbed the electrodes into the pig's butt and shoulder, and that was it. No more pain, no more fear, no more mudholes, no more sun in the lazy afternoon. Knocked instantly unconscious, the pig shuddered in a long spasm and fell onto a stainless steel table a foot below the end of the ramp. Up came another pig, and the same result. And another, and another, 450 an hour, 3,600 a day, the belts returning below to coax another ride.

The pigs are not dead, merely unconscious. The electrodes are humane, my spokesman said, and relatively speaking, that is true. They used to gas the pigs—put them on a conveyor belt that ran through a room filled with anesthetic gas. That was humane too. The electrodes are more efficient. Anesthesia relaxes the body and loosens the bowels. The gassed pigs must have been a mess. More efficient, then, to put their bodies in spasm.

They drop to the table, and here the endless chain begins. A worker takes the nearest dangling chain by its handle as it passes. The chain is attached at the top to a belt of links, like a large bicycle chain. At the bottom the dangling chain has a metal handle like the handle on a bike. The chain runs through the handle and then attaches to the end of the handle, so that by sliding the handle the worker forms a loop. Into the loop he hooks one of the pig's hind feet. Another worker does the same with the other foot. Each has his own special foot to grab, or the pig would go down the line backwards, which would not be convenient. Once hooked into the line, the pig will stay in place by the force of its own weight.

Now the line ascends, lifting the unconscious animal into the air. The pig proceeds a distance of ten feet, where a worker standing on a platform deftly inserts a butcher knife into its throat. They call it "sticking," which it is. Then all hell breaks loose, if blood merely is hell. It gushes out, at about a 45-degree angle downward, thick as a ship's hawser, pouring directly onto the floor. Nothing is so red as blood, an incandescent red and most beautiful. It is the brightest color we drab creatures possess. Down on the floor below, with a wide squeegee on a long handle, a worker spends his eight hours a day squeegeeing that blood, some of it clotted, jellied, now, into an open drain. It is cycled through a series of pipes into a dryer, later to be made into blood meal for animal feed.

The line swings around a corner, high above the man with the squeegee, around the drain floor, turns left at the next corner, and begins to ascend to the floor above. This interval—thirteen seconds, I think my spokesman said, or was it thirty?—so that the carcass may drain completely before further processing. Below the carcass on the ascent is a trough like those lowered from the rear of cement trucks, there to catch the last drainings of blood.

Pigs are not skinned, as cattle are, unless you are after the leather, and we are after the meat. But the hair must be taken off, and it must first be scalded loose. Courteously, the line lowers the carcass into a long trough filled with water heated to 180 degrees. The carcass will float if given a chance, fat being lighter than water, so wooden pushers on crankshafts spaced equally along the scalding tank immerse and roll the carcasses. Near the end of the trough, my spokesman easily pulls out a tuft of hair. The line ascends again, up and away, and the carcass goes into a chamber where revolving brushes as tall as a man whisk away the hair. We pass to the other side of the chamber and find two workers with wide knives scraping off the few patches of hair that remain. The carcasses then pass through great hellish jets of yellowish-blue gas flame to singe the skin and harden it. The last step is polishing: more brushes. Our pig has turned pink and clean as a baby.

One of the small mercies of a slaughterhouse: what begins as a live animal loses all similarity as the processing goes on, until you can actually face the packaged meat at the exit door and admire its obvious flavor.

The polished carcasses swing through a door closed with rubber flaps, and there, dear friends, the action begins. Saws. Long knives. Butcher knives. Drawknives. Boning knives. Wails from the saws, large and small, that are driven by air like a dentist's drill. Shouts back and forth from the men, jokes, announcements, challenges. The temperature down to 50 degrees, everyone keen. Men start slicing off little pieces of the head right inside the door, each man his special slice, throwing them onto one of several lines that will depart for special bins. A carcass passes me and I see a bare eyeball staring, stripped of its lids. Deft knives drop the head from the neck leaving it dangling by a two-inch strip of skin. Around a corner, up to a platform, and three men gut the carcasses, great tubs of guts, each man taking the third carcass as it goes by. One of them sees me with my tape recorder and begins shouting at us something like "I am the greatest!" A crazy man, grinning and roaring at us, turning around and slipping in the knife, and out comes everything in one great load flopped onto a stainless-steel trough. And here things divide, and so must our attention.

My spokesman is proud of his chitterling machine. "I call them chitlins, but they're really chitterlings." It is the newest addition to his line. A worker separates the intestines from the other internal organs and shoves them down a slide, gray and shiny. Another worker finds one end and feeds it onto a steel tube flushed with water. Others trim off connective tissue, webbings, fat. The intestines shimmer along the tube into a washing vat, skinny up to the top of the machine where they are cooled, skinny back down where they are cooled further, and come out the other side ready for the supermarket. A worker drops them into wax buckets, pops on a lid, and packs them into shipping boxes. That is today's chitlin machine. They used to have to cool the chitlins overnight before they could be packaged. Now five men do the work of sixteen, in less time.

The remaining organs proceed down a waist-high conveyor; on the other side of the same walkway, the emptied carcasses pass; on a line next to the organ line the heads pass. By now all the meat has been trimmed off each head. A worker sockets them one at a time into a support like a footrest in a shoeshine parlor and a wedge neatly splits them in half. Out come the tongues, out come the brains, and at the end of the line, out come the pituitaries, each tiny gland being passed to a government inspector in white pants, white shirt, and a yellow hard hat, who looks it over and drops it into a wax bucket. All these pieces, the brain, the tongue, the oddments of sidemeat off the head and carcass, will become "by-products": hot dogs, baloney, sausage. You are what you eat.

The loudest noise in the room comes from the big air-saw used to split the carcass in half down the backbone, leaving, again, connections at the butt end and between the shoulders. Other workers trim away interior fat, and then the carcasses proceed down their chain at 50 miles an hour to the blast freezer, 25 below zero and no place for mere mortals, to be chilled overnight.

Coming out of the freezer in another part of the room is yesterday's kill, cold and solid and smooth. A worker splits apart the two sides; the hams come off and go onto their own line; the shoulders come off and go onto theirs, to be made into picnics, shoulder roasts, trotters. Away goes the valuable loin, trimmed out deftly by a worker with a drawknife. Away goes the bacon. Chunks and strips of fat go off from everywhere in buckets carried on overhead hooks to a grinder that spins out worms of fat and blows them through a tube directly to the lard-rendering vats. Who uses lard anymore, I ask my spokesman. I don't know, he says, I think we export most of it.

At the end of all these lines men package the component parts of pig into wax-paper-lined cartons, load the cartons onto pallets, forklift the pallets into spotless aluminum trailers socketed right into the walls of the building so that I do not even realize I am inside a truck until my spokesman tells me, and off they go to Armour.

Processing an animal is exactly the opposite of processing a machine: the machine starts out with components and ends up put together; the animal starts out put together and ends up components. No clearer illustration of the law of entropy has ever been devised.

And that is a tour of a slaughterhouse, as cheerful as I could make it.

But the men there. Half of them blacks, some Mexicans, the rest whites. It gets harder and harder to hire men for this work, even though the pay is good. The production line keeps them hopping; they take their breaks when there is a break in the line, so that the killing floor breaks first, and their break leaves an empty space ten minutes long in the endless chain, which, arriving at the gutting operation, allows the men there to break, and so on. Monday morning absenteeism is a problem, I was told. Keeping the men under control can be a problem, too, I sensed: when the line broke down briefly during my tour, the men cheered as convicts might at a state license-plate factory when the stamping machine breaks down. It cannot be heartening to kill animals all day.

There is a difference, too, between the men who work with the live animals and hot carcasses and those who cut up the cold meat, a difference I remember from my days of butchering on the farm: the killing unsettles, while the cold cutting is a craft like carpentry or plumbing and offers the satisfactions of craftsmanship. The worker with the electrodes jammed them into the animal with anger and perverse satisfaction, as if he were knocking off the enemy. The worker at the guts acted as if he were wrestling bears. The hot workers talked to themselves, yelled at each other, or else lapsed into that strained silence you meet in deeply angry men; the cold workers said little but worked with deftness and something like pride. They knew they were good, and they showed off a little, zip zip, as we toured by. They used their hands as if they knew how to handle tools, and they did.

The technology at the I-D Packing Company is humane by present standards, at least so far as the animals are concerned. Where the workers are concerned, I'm not so sure. They looked to be in need of lulling.

Beyond technology is the larger question of attitude. Butchering on the farm when I was a boy had the quality of a ceremony. We would select, say, a steer, and pen it separately overnight. The next morning several of us boys—this was a boys' home as well as a farm—would walk the steer to a large compound and leave it standing, trusting as hell, near the concrete-floored area where we did the skinning and gutting. Then the farm manager, a man of great kindness and reserve, would take aim with a .22 rifle at the crosspoint of two imaginary lines drawn from the horns to the opposite eyes. And hold his bead until the steer was entirely calm, looking at him, a certain shot, because this man did not want to miss, did not want to hurt the animal he was about to kill. And we would stand in a spread-out circle, at a respectful distance, tense with the drama of it, because we didn't want him to miss either.

The shot cracked out, the bullet entered the brain, and the animal instantly collapsed. Then the farm manager handed back the rifle, took a knife, ran forward, and cut into the throat. Then we dragged the steer onto the concrete, hooked its back legs through the Achilles tendons to a cross tree, and laboriously winched it into the air with a differential pulley. Four boys usually did the work, two older, two younger. The younger boys were supposed to be learning this skill, and you held your stomach together as best you could at first while the older boys played little tricks like, when they got there in the skinning, cutting off the pizzle and whipping it around your neck, but even these crudities had their place: they accustomed you to contact with flesh and blood.

And while the older boys did their work of splitting the halves with a hacksaw, you got to take the guts, which on the farm we did not save except for the liver, the heart, and the sweetbreads, in a wheelbarrow down to the back lane where you built with wood you had probably cut yourself, a most funereal pyre. Then we doused the guts with gasoline, tossed in a match, and Whoosh! off they went. And back on the concrete, the sawing done, the older boys left the sides hanging overnight in the winter cold to firm the meat for cutting.

By now it was noon, time for lunch, and you went in with a sort of pride that you had done this important work, and there on the table was meat some other boys had killed on some other ceremonial day. It was bloody work, of course, and sometimes I have wondered how adults could ask children to do such work, but it was part of a coherent way of life, as important as plowing or seeding or mowing or baling hay. It had a context, and I was literary enough even then to understand that burning the guts had a sacrificial significance. We could always have limed them and dumped them into a ditch. Lord knows they didn't burn easily.

I never saw our farm manager more upset than the day we were getting ready to butcher five pigs. He shot one through the nose rather than through the brain. It ran screaming around the pen, and he almost cried. It took two more bullets to finish the animal off, and this good man was shaking when he had finished. "I hate that," he said to me. "I hate to have them in pain. Pigs are so damned hard to kill clean."

But we don't farm anymore. The coherence is gone. Our loves are no longer the loves of flint and iron, but of the nightingale and the rose, and so we delegate our killing. Our farm manager used to sleep in the sheep barn for nights on end to be sure he was there to help the ewes deliver their lambs, ewes being so absentminded they sometimes stop labor with the lamb only halfway out. You saw the beginning and the end on the farm, not merely the prepackaged middle. Flint and iron, friends, flint and iron. And humility, and sorrow that this act of killing must be done, which is why in those days good men bowed their heads before they picked up their forks.

Meaning

1. Outline the stages described by Rhodes by which pork products appear in our supermarkets neatly packaged and ready for consumption.
2. What different kinds of skills must workers have to transform live animals into packaged meat products?
3. How does the title—"Watching the Animals"—raise expectations in the reader's mind that contrast ironically with the true subject of Rhodes' essay?
4. Why is the concept of "race living at the expense of race" (in Emerson's phrase) so important to the development of Rhodes' essay?

USING PROCESS ANALYSIS TO CONVEY MEANING

1. What measures does Rhodes take to let the reader know that he is being shown an activity that normally is hidden from public view?
2. How does Rhodes organize his essay to follow the predetermined sequence that must take place in order for meat to be processed?
3. What does Rhodes' characterization of the pigs awaiting slaughter (their intelligence, the different sounds they make, their seeming awareness of what awaits them) make you realize about the stressful circumstances the workers in this stage must endure?
4. How does Rhodes use a flashback at the end of his article to focus on what has been lost and gained through the increased use of technology in meat processing?

WRITING SUGGESTIONS

1. Using the essays by Rhodes and Mitford, discuss the increasing tendency in modern life to conceal natural processes that in the past were routinely encountered by people as part of their everyday lives.
2. Can you explain, in light of this article, why someone would prefer to be a vegetarian?
3. Comment on the reasons why animals with ritualistic significance, such as the bull in Hemingway's essay, are treated very differently from animals without symbolic or ceremonial meaning, like the pig in Rhodes' article.

SCIENCES

Arthur D. Hasler
James A. Larsen

The Homing Salmon

Arthur D. Hasler, born in 1908 in Lehi, Utah, earned a Ph.D. in zoology from the University of Wisconsin in 1937 and is currently emeritus professor of zoology at the University of Wisconsin, Madison. Hasler has served as the President of many scientific associations, including the American Society of Zoologists, Ecology Society of America, International Association of Ecologists, and American Society of Limnology and Oceanography. Hasler's pioneering studies into the migration of fishes and limnology (the study of fresh-water habitats) successfully illuminated the crucial role played by the sense of smell in orienting fishes to parent streams.

James A. Larsen, born in 1921 in Rhinelander, Wisconsin, earned a Ph.D. in ecology in 1968 and has distinguished himself both as a botanist, studying bioclimatology in the Arctic, and as a science writer.

"The Homing Salmon" joins the respective talents of these two researchers and describes an ingenious experiment designed to investigate the mysterious riddle of how the adult Chinook salmon finds its way back to the stream where it was born, nearly nine hundred miles away.

A learned naturalist once remarked that among the many riddles of nature, not the least mysterious is the migration of fishes. The homing of salmon is a particularly dramatic example. The Chinook salmon of the U.S. Northwest is born in a small stream, migrates downriver to the Pacific Ocean as a young smolt and, after living in the sea for as long as five years, swims back unerringly to the stream of its birth to spawn. Its determination to return to its birthplace is legendary. No one who has seen a 100-pound Chinook salmon fling itself into the air again and again until it is exhausted in a vain effort to surmount a waterfall can fail to marvel at the strength of the instinct that draws the salmon upriver to the stream where it was born.

How do salmon remember their birthplace, and how do they find their way back, sometimes from 800 or 900 miles away? This enigma, which has fascinated naturalists for many years, is the subject of the research to be reported here. The question has an economic as well as a scientific interest, because new dams which stand in the salmon's way have cut heavily into salmon fishing along the Pacific Coast. Before long nearly every stream of any appreciable size in the West will be blocked by dams. It is true that the dams have fish lifts and ladders designed to help salmon to hurdle them. Unfortunately, and for reasons which are different for nearly every dam so far designed, salmon are lost in tremendous numbers.

There are six common species of salmon. One, called the Atlantic salmon, is of the same genus as the steelhead trout. These two fish go to sea and come back upstream to spawn year after year. The other five salmon species, all on the Pacific Coast, are the Chinook (also called the king salmon), the sockeye, the silver, the humpback and the chum. The Pacific salmon home only once: after spawning they die.

A young salmon first sees the light of day when it hatches and wriggles up through the pebbles of the stream where the egg was laid and fertilized. For a few weeks the fingerling feeds on insects and small aquatic animals. Then it answers its first migratory call and swims downstream to the sea. It must survive many hazards to mature: an estimated 15 percent of the young salmon are lost at every large dam, such as Bonneville, on the downstream strip; others die in polluted streams; many are swallowed up by bigger fish in the ocean. When, after several years in the sea, the salmon is ready to spawn, it responds to the second great migratory call. It finds the mouth of the river by which it entered the ocean and then swims steadily upstream, unerringly choosing the correct turn at each tributary fork, until it arrives at the stream, where it was hatched. Generation after generation, families of salmon return to the same rivulet so consistently that populations in streams not far apart follow distinctly separate lines of evolution.

The homing behavior of the salmon has been convincingly documented by many studies since the turn of the century. One of the most elaborate was made by Andrew L. Pritchard, Wilbert A. Clemens and Russell E. Foerster in Canada. They marked 469,326 young sockeye salmon born in a tributary of the Fraser River, and they recovered nearly 11,000 of these in the same parent stream after the fishes' migration to the ocean and back. What is more, not one of the marked fish was ever found to have strayed to another stream. This remarkable demonstration of the salmon's precision in homing has presented an exciting challenge to investigators.

At the Wisconsin Lake Laboratory during the past decade we have been studying the sense of smell in fish, beginning with minnows and going on to salmon. Our findings suggest that the salmon identifies the stream of its birth by odor and literally smells its way home from the sea.

Fish have an extremely sensitive sense of smell. This has often been observed by students of fish behavior. Karl von Frisch showed that odors from the injured skin of a fish produce a fright reaction among its schoolmates. He once noticed that when a bird dropped an injured fish in the water, the school of fish from which it had been seized quickly dispersed and later avoided the area. It is well known that sharks and tuna are drawn to a vessel by the odor of bait in the water. Indeed, the time-honored custom of spitting on bait may be founded on something more than superstition; laboratory studies have proved that human saliva is quite stimulating to the taste buds of a bullhead. The sense of taste of course is closely allied to the sense of smell. The bullhead has taste buds all over the surface of its body; they are especially numerous on its whiskers. It will quickly grab a piece of meat that touches any part of its skin. But it becomes insensitive to taste and will not respond in this way if a nerve serving the skin buds is cut.

The smelling organs of fish have evolved in a great variety of forms. In the bony fishes the nose pits have two separate openings. The fish takes water into the front opening as it swims or breathes (sometimes assisting the intake with cilia), and then the water passes out through the second opening, which may be opened and closed rhythmically by the fish's breathing. Any odorous substances in the water stimulate the nasal receptors chemically, perhaps by an effect on enzyme reactions, and the resulting electrical impulses are relayed to the central nervous system by the olfactory nerve.

The human nose, and that of other land vertebrates, can smell a substance only if it is volatile and soluble in fat solvents. But in the final analysis smell is always aquatic, for a substance is not smelled until it passes into solution in the mucous film of the nasal passages. For fishes, of course, the odors are already in solution in their watery environment. Like any other animal, they can follow an odor to its source, as a hunting dog follows the scent of an animal. The quality or effect of a scent changes as the concentration changes; everyone knows that an odor may be pleasant at one concentration and unpleasant at another.

When we began our experiments, we first undertook to find out whether fish could distinguish the odors of different water plants. We used a special aquarium with jets which could inject odors into the water. For responding to one odor (by moving toward the jet), the fish were rewarded with food; for responding to another odor, they were punished with a mild electric shock. After the fish were trained to make choices between odors, they were tested on dilute rinses from 14 different aquatic plants. They proved able to distinguish the odors of all these plants from one another.

Plants must play an important role in the life of many freshwater fish. Their odors may guide fish to feeding grounds when visibility is poor, as in muddy water or at night, and they may hold young fish from straying from protective cover. Odors may also warn fish away from poisons. In fact, we discovered that fish could be put to use to assay industrial pollutants: our trained minnows were able to detect phenol, a common pollutant, at concentrations far below those detectable by man.

All this suggested a clear-cut working hypothesis for investigating the mystery of the homing of salmon. We can suppose that every little stream has its own characteristic odor, which stays the same year after year; that young salmon become conditioned to this odor before they go to sea; that they remember the odor as they grow to maturity, and that they are able to find it and follow it to its source when they come back upstream to spawn.

Plainly there are quite a few ifs in this theory. The first one we tested was the question: Does each stream have its own odor? We took water from two creeks in Wisconsin and investigated whether fish could learn to discriminate between them. Our subjects, first minnows and then salmon, were indeed able to detect a difference. If, however, we destroyed a fish's nose tissue, it was no longer able to distinguish between the two water samples.

Chemical analysis indicated that the only major difference between the two waters lay in the organic material. By testing the fish with various fractions of the water separated by distillation, we confirmed that the identifying material was some volatile organic substance.

The idea that fish are guided by odors in their migrations was further supported by a field test. From each of two different branches of the Issaquah River in the State of Washington we took a number of sexually ripe silver salmon which had come home to spawn. We then plugged with cotton the noses of half the fish in each group and placed all the salmon in the river below the fork to make the upstream run again. Most of the fish with unplugged noses swam back to the stream they had selected the first time. But the "odor-blinded" fish migrated back in random fashion, picking the wrong stream as often as the right one.

In 1949 eggs from salmon of the Horsefly River in British Columbia were hatched and reared in a hatchery in a tributary called the Little Horsefly. Then they were flown a considerable distance and released in the main Horsefly River, from which they migrated to the sea. Three years later 13 of them had returned to their rearing place in the Little Horsefly, according to the report of the Canadian experimenters.

In our own laboratory experiments we tested the memory of fish for odors and found that they retained the ability to differentiate between odors for a long period after their training. Young fish remembered odors better than the old. That animals "remember" conditioning to which they have been exposed in their youth, and act accordingly, has been demonstrated in other fields. For instance, there is a fly which normally lays its eggs on the larvae of the flour moth, where the fly larvae then hatch and develop. But if larvae of this fly are raised on another host, the beeswax moth, when the flies mature they will seek out beeswax moth larvae on which to lay their eggs, in preference to the traditional host.

With respect to the homing of salmon we have shown, then, that different streams have different odors, that salmon respond to these odors and that they remember odors to which they have been conditioned. The next question is: Is a salmon's homeward migration guided solely by its sense of smell? If we could decoy homing salmon to a stream other than their birthplace, by means of an odor to which they were conditioned artificially, we might have not only a solution to the riddle that has puzzled scientists but also a practical means of saving the salmon—guiding them to breeding streams not obstructed by dams.

We set out to find a suitable substance to which salmon could be conditioned. A student, W. J. Wisby, and I [Arthur Hasler] designed an apparatus to test the reactions of salmon to various organic odors. It consists of a compartment from which radiate four runways, each with several steps which the fish must jump to climb the runway. Water cascades down each of the arms. An odorous substance is introduced into one of the arms, and its effect on the fish is judged by whether the odor appears to attract fish into that arm, to repel them or to be indifferent to them.

We needed a substance which initially would not be either attractive or repellent to salmon but to which they could be conditioned so that it would attract them. After testing several score organic odors, we found that dilute solutions of morpholine neither attracted nor repelled salmon but were detectable by them in extremely low concentrations—as low as one part per million. It appears that morpholine fits the requirements for the substance needed: it is soluble in water; it is detectable in extremely low concentrations; it is chemically stable under stream conditions. It is neither an attractant nor a repellent to unconditioned salmon, and would have meaning only to those conditioned to it.

Federal collaborators of ours are now conducting field tests on the Pacific Coast to learn whether salmon fry and fingerlings which have been conditioned to morpholine can be decoyed to a stream other than that of their birth when they return from the sea to spawn. Unfortunately this type of experiment may not be decisive. If the salmon are not decoyed to the new stream, it may simply mean that they cannot be drawn by a single substance but will react only to a combination of subtle odors in their parent stream. Perhaps adding morpholine to the water is like adding the whistle of a freight train to the quiet strains of a violin, cello and flute. The salmon may still seek out the subtle harmonies of an odor combination to which they have been reacting by instinct for centuries. But there is still hope that they may respond to the call of the whistle.

MEANING

1. Why is the process by which salmon are able to return over nine hundred miles to the exact stream in which they were born the subject of scientific investigation?
2. What assumptions about the salmon's homing mechanism was Hasler's experiment designed to test?
3. How did Hasler's experiment show that each phase in the salmon's migration could be explained in terms of subsequent stages of conditioning?

USING PROCESS ANALYSIS TO CONVEY MEANING

1. What technical terms do the authors define to help their audience understand the processs they are investigating?
2. Discuss how Hasler's experiments were designed to test the hypothesis that salmon can recognize the particular odor of the streams in which they are spawned.
3. In what way does this article illustrate how process analysis enables scientists to formulate and test explanations of how things works?
4. How might the organization of Hasler and Larsen's article serve as a model for other science writers in presenting their research results?

WRITING SUGGESTIONS

1. Since a salmon reproduces only once in its lifetime, why would the results of Hasler and Larsen's research play a key role in decisions as to where to place dams in the tributaries of streams?
2. What experience can you relate concerning a pet that found its way home over a long distance? Did this phenomena convince you of the existence of a homing instinct akin to that demonstrated by the salmon?
3. As a research project, discover what other mechanisms scientists have identified as being responsible for migratory behavior in other species. For example, what has been discovered to explain the seasonal migration of wildebeest herds in East Africa or the yearly return of swallows to Capistrano?

Carl Gustav Jung

The Personal and the Collective Unconscious

Carl G. Jung (1875–1961), the father of analytical psychology, was born in Kesswil, Switzerland, into a deeply religious family where Jung's father, his maternal grandfather, and eight of his uncles were pastors. At the age of thirteen, Jung entered the Gymnasium in Basal, studied religion and philosophy, and read the works of Goethe, Meister Eckhart, Hegel, and Schopenhauer. After receiving an M.D. from the University of Basal, Jung earned a Doctorate from the University of Zurich in 1902. Jung's interest in psychiatry led to a correspondence and friendship with Freud, although Jung gradually came to doubt the importance that Freud attached to sexual conflicts in childhood. In 1914, Jung formally severed all connections with Freudian psychoanalysis to develop his own school of analyticial psychology. Jung believed that, underlying the personal unconscious that Freud had identified, lay a substratum, which Jung termed the "collective unconscious." This deeper level expressed itself through archaic myths and archetypes, a concept he developed in The Psychology of the Unconscious *(1913). Jung's further research, published in* Psychological Types *(1921), explained personality as a series of oppositions and introduced the terms "extrovert" and "introvert" into our language. In "The Personal and the Collective Unconscious," drawn from* Two Essays on Analytical Psychology, *(1953) Jung explains his view of the compensatory relationship between the unconscious and conscious minds within the self.*

In Freud's view, as most people know, the contents of the unconscious are limited to infantile tendencies which are repressed because of their incompatible character. Repression is a process that begins in early childhood under the moral influence of the environment and lasts throughout life. Through analysis the repressions are removed and the repressed wishes made conscious.

According to this theory, the unconscious contains only those parts of the personality which could just as well be conscious and are in fact suppressed only through upbringing. Although from one point of view the infantile tendencies of the unconscious are the most conspicuous, it would nonetheless be incorrect to define or evaluate the unconscious entirely in these terms. The unconscious has still another side to it: it includes not only repressed contents, but also all psychic material that lies below the threshold of consciousness. It is impossible to explain the subliminal[1] nature of all this material on the principle of repression; otherwise, through the removal of repressions, a man would acquire a phenomenal memory which would thenceforth forget nothing.

[1] Below the threshold of conscious awareness.

316

We therefore emphatically say that in addition to the repressed material the unconscious contains all those psychic components that have fallen below the threshold, including subliminal sense-perceptions. Moreover we know, from abundant experience as well as for theoretical reasons, that the unconscious also contains components that have *not yet* reached the threshold of consciousness. These are the seeds of future conscious contents. Equally we have reason to suppose that the unconscious is never at rest in the sense of being inactive, but is continually engaged in grouping and regrouping its contents. Only in pathological cases can this activity be regarded as completely autonomous; normally it is co-ordinated with the conscious mind in a compensatory relationship.

It is to be assumed that all these contents are personal in so far as they are acquired during the individual's life. Since this life is limited, the number of acquired contents in the unconscious must also be limited. This being so, it might be thought possible to empty the unconscious either by analysis or by making a complete inventory of unconscious contents, on the ground that the unconscious cannot produce anything more than is already known and accepted in the conscious mind. We should also have to infer, as already indicated, that if one could stop the descent of conscious contents into the unconscious by doing away with repression, unconscious productivity would be paralysed. This is possible only to a very limited extent, as we know from experience. We urge our patients to hold fast to repressed contents that have been reassociated with consciousness, and to assimilate them into their plan of life. But this procedure, as we may daily convince ourselves, makes no impression on the unconscious, since it calmly continues to produce dreams and fantasies which, according to Freud's original theory, must arise from personal repressions. If in such cases we pursue our observations systematically and without prejudice, we shall find material which, although similar in form to the previous personal contents, yet seems to contain allusions that go far beyond the personal sphere. . . .

There are present in every individual, besides his personal memories, the great "primordial" images, as Jacob Burckhardt once aptly called them, the inherited powers of human imagination as it was from time immemorial. The fact of this inheritance explains the truly amazing phenomenon that certain motifs from myths and legends repeat themselves the world over in identical forms. It also explains why it is that our mental patients can reproduce exactly the same images and associations that are known to us from the old texts. I give some examples of this in my book *Symbols of Transformations*. In so doing I do not by any means assert the inheritance of ideas, but only of the possibility of such ideas, which is something very different.

In this further stage of treatment, then, when fantasies are produced which no longer rest on personal memories, we have to do with the manifestations of a deeper layer of the unconscious where the primordial images common to humanity lie sleeping. I have called these images or motifs "archetypes," also "dominants" of the unconscious. For a further elucidaton of the idea I must refer the reader to the relevant literature.

This discovery means another step forward in our understanding: the recognition, that is, of two layers in the unconscious. We have to distinguish between a personal unconscious and an impersonal or transpersonal unconscious. We speak of the latter also as the collective unconscious, because it is detached from anything personal and is entirely universal, and because its contents can be found everywhere, which is naturally not the case with the personal contents. The personal unconscious contains lost memories, painful ideas that are repressed (i.e., forgotten on purpose), subliminal perceptions, by which are meant sense-perceptions that were not strong enough to reach consciousness, and finally, contents that are not yet ripe for consciousness. It corresponds to the figure of the shadow so frequently met with in dreams.

The primordial images are the most ancient and the most universal "thought-forms" of humanity. They are as much feelings as thoughts; indeed, they lead their own independent life rather in the manner of part-souls, as can easily be seen in those philosophical or Gnostic systems which rely on awareness of the unconscious as the source of knowledge. The idea of angels, archangels, "principalities and powers" in St. Paul, the archons of the Gnostics, the heavenly hierarchy of Dionysius the Areopagite, all come from the perception of the relative autonomy of the archetypes. . . .

The greatest and best thoughts of man shape themselves upon these primordial images as upon a blueprint. I have often been asked where the archetypes or primordial images come from. It seems to me that their origin can only be explained by assuming them to be deposits of the constantly repeated experiences of humanity. One of the commonest and at the same time most impressive experiences is the apparent movement of the sun every day. We certainly cannot discover anything of the kind in the unconscious, so far as the known physical process is concerned. What we do find, on the other hand, is the myth of the sun-hero in all its countless modifications. It is this myth, and not the physical process, that forms the sun archetype. The same can be said of the phases of the moon. The archetype is a kind of readiness to produce over and over again the same or similar mythical ideas. Hence it seems as though what is impressed upon the unconscious were exclusively the subjective fantasy-ideas aroused by the physical process. Therefore we may take it that archetypes are recurrent impressions made by subjective reactions. Naturally this assumption only pushes the problem further back without solving it. There is nothing to prevent us from assuming that certain archetypes exist even in animals, that they are grounded in the peculiarities of the living organism itself and are therefore direct expressions of life whose nature cannot be further explained. Not only are the archetypes, apparently, impressions of ever-repeated typical experiences, but, at the same time, they behave empirically like agents that tend towards the repetition of these same experiences. For when an archetype appears in a dream, in a fantasy, or in life, it always brings with it a certain influence or power by virtue of which it either exercises a numinous or a fascinating effect, or impels to action.

"No mortal mind can plumb the depths of nature"—nor even the depths of the unconscious. We do know, however, that the unconscious never rests. It seems to be always at work, for even when asleep we dream. There are many people who declare that they never dream, but the probability is that they simply do not remember their dreams. It is significant that people who talk in their sleep mostly have no recollection either of the dream which started them talking, or even of the fact that they dreamed at all. Not a day passes but we make some slip of the tongue, or something slips our memory which at other times we know perfectly well, or we are seized by a mood whose cause we cannot trace, etc: These things are all symptoms of some consistent unconscious activity which becomes directly visible at night in dreams, but only occasionally breaks though the inhibitions imposed by our daytime consciousness.

So far as our present experience goes, we can lay it down that the unconscious processes stand in a compensatory relation to the conscious mind. I expressly use the word "compensatory" and not the word "opposed," because conscious and unconscious are not necessarily in opposition to one another, but complement one another to form a totality, which is the *self*. According to this definition the self is a quantity that is superordinate to the conscious ego. It embraces not only the conscious but also the unconscious psyche, and is therefore, so to speak, a personality which we *also* are. It is easy enough to think of ourselves as possessing part-souls. Thus we can, for instance, see ourselves as a persona without too much difficulty. But it transcends our powers of imagination to form a clear picture of what we are as a self, for in this operation the part would have to comprehend the whole. There is little hope of our ever being able to reach even approximate consciousness of the self, since however much we may make conscious there will always exist an indeterminate and indeterminable amount of unconscious material which belongs to the totality of the self. Hence the self will always remain a superordinate quantity.

The unconscious processes that compensate the conscious ego contain all those elements that are necessary for the self-regulation of the psyche as a whole. On the personal level, these are the not consciously recognized personal motives which appear in dreams, or the meanings of daily situations which we have overlooked, or conclusions we have failed to draw, or affects we have not permitted, or criticisms we have spared ourselves. But the more we become conscious of ourselves through self knowledge, and act accordingly, the more the layer of the personal unconscious that is superimposed on the collective unconscious will be diminished. In this way there arises a consciousness which is no longer imprisoned in the petty, oversensitive, personal world of the ego, but participates freely in the wider world of objective interests. This widened consciousness is no longer that touchy, egotistical bundle of personal wishes, fears, hopes, and ambitions which always has to be compensated or corrected by unconscious counter-tendencies; instead, it is a function of relationship to the world of objects, bringing the individual into absolute, binding, and indissoluble communion with the world at large. The complications arising at this stage are no longer egotistic wish-conflicts, but difficulties that concern others as much as oneself. At this stage it is fundamentally a question of collective problems, which have activated the collective unconscious because they require collective rather than personal compensation. We can now see that the unconscious produces contents which are valid not only for the person concerned, but for others as well, in fact for a great many people and possibly for all.

The Elgonyi, natives of the Elgon forests, of central Africa, explained to me that there are two kinds of dreams: the ordinary dream of the little man, and the "big vision" that only the great man has, e.g., the medicine-man or chief. Little dreams are of no account, but if a man has a "big dream" he summons the whole tribe in order to tell it to everybody.

How is a man to know whether his dream is a "big" or a "little" one? He knows it by an instinctive feeling of significance. He feels so overwhelmed by the impression it makes that he would never think of keeping the dream to himself. He *has* to tell it, on the psychologically correct assumption that it is of general significance. Even with us the collective dream has a feeling of importance about it that impels communication. It springs from a conflict of relationship and must therefore be built into our conscious relations, because it compensates these and not just some inner personal quirk.

The processes of the collective unconscious are concerned not only with the more or less personal relations of an individual to his family or to a wider social group, but with his relations to society and to the human community in general. The more general and impersonal the condition that releases the unconscious reaction, the more significant, bizarre, and overwhelming will be the compensatory manifestation. It impels not just private communication, but drives people to revelations and confessions, and even to a dramatic representation of their fantasies.

I will explain by an example how the unconscious manages to compensate relationships. A somewhat arrogant gentleman once came to me for treatment. He ran a business in partnership with his younger brother. Relations between the two brothers were very strained, and this was one of the essential causes of my patient's neurosis. From the information he gave me, the real reason for the tension was not altogether clear. He had all kinds of criticisms to make of his brother, whose gifts he certainly did not show in a very favorable light. The brother frequently came into his dreams, always in the role of a Bismarck, Napoleon, or Julius Caesar. His house looked like the Vatican or Yildiz Kiosk. My patient's unconscious evidently had the need to exalt the rank of the younger brother. From this I concluded that he was setting himself too high and his brother too low. The further course of analysis entirely justified this inference.

Another patient, a young woman who clung to her mother in an extremely sentimental way, always had very sinister dreams about her. She appeared in the dreams as a witch, as a ghost, as a pursuing demon. The mother had spoilt her beyond all reason and had so blinded her by tenderness that the daughter had no conscious idea of her mother's harmful influence. Hence the compensatory criticism exercised by the unconscious.

I myself once happened to put too low a value on a patient, both intellectually and morally. In a dream I saw a castle perched on a high cliff, and on the topmost tower was a balcony, and there sat my patient. I did not hesitate to tell her this dream at once, naturally with the best results.

We all know how apt we are to make fools of ourselves in front of the very people we have unjustly underrated. Naturally the case can also be reversed, as once happened to a friend of mine. While still a callow student he had written to Virchow, the pathologist, craving an audience with "His Excellency." When, quaking with fear, he presented himself and tried to give his name, he blurted out, "My name is Virchow." Whereupon His Excellency, smiling mischievously, said, "Ah! So your name is Virchow too?" The feeling of his own nullity was evidently too much for the unconscious of my friend, and in consequence it instantly prompted him to present himself as equal to Virchow in grandeur.

In these more personal relations there is of course no need for any very collective compensations. One the other hand, the figures employed by the unconscious in our first case are of a definitely collective nature: they are universally recognized heroes. Here there are two possible interpretations: either my patient's younger brother is a man of acknowledged and far-reaching collective importance, or my patient is overestimating his own importance not merely in relation to his brother but in relation to everybody else as well. For the first assumption there was no support at all, while for the second there was the evidence of one's own eyes. Since the man's extreme arrogance affected not only himself, but a far wider social group, the compensation availed itself of a collective image.

The same is true of the second case. The "witch" is a collective image; hence we must conclude that the blind dependence of the young woman applied as much to the wider social group as it did to her mother personally. This was indeed the case, in so far as she was still living in an exclusively infantile world, where the world was identical with her parents. These examples deal with relations within the personal orbit. There are, however, impersonal relations which occasionally need unconscious compensation. In such cases collective images appear with a more or less mythological character. Moral, philosophical, and religous problems are, on account of their universal validity, the most likely to call for mythological compensation. In the aforementioned novel by H. G. Wells we find a classical type of compensation: Mr. Preemby, a midget personality, discovers that he is really a reincarnation of Sargon, King of Kings. Happily, the genius of the author rescues poor old Sargon from pathological absurdity, and even gives the reader a chance to appreciate the tragic and eternal meaning in this lamentable affray. Mr. Preemby, a complete nonentity, recognizes himself as the point of intersection of all ages past and future. This knowledge is not too dearly bought at the cost of a little madness, provided that Preemby is not in the end devoured by that monster of a primordial image—which is in fact what nearly happens to him.

The universal problem of evil and sin is another aspect to our impersonal relations to the world. Almost more than any other, therefore, this problem produces collective compensations. One of my patients, aged sixteen, had as the initial symptom of a severe compulsion neurosis the following dream: *He is walking along an unfamiliar street. It is dark, and he hears steps coming behind him. With a feeling of fear he quickens his pace. The footsteps come nearer, and his fear increases. He begins to run. But the footsteps seem to be overtaking him. Finally he turns round, and there he sees the devil. In deathly terror he leaps into the air and hangs there suspended.* This dream was repeated twice, a sign of its special urgency.

It is a notorious fact that the compulsion neuroses, by reason of their meticulousness and ceremonial punctilio; not only have the surface appearance of a moral problem but are indeed brim-full of inhuman beastliness and ruthless evil, against whose integration[2] the otherwise very delicately organized personality puts up a desperate struggle. This explains why so many things have to be performed in ceremonially "correct" style, as though to counteract the evil hovering in the background. After this dream the neurosis started, and its essential feature was that the patient had, as he put it, to keep himself in a "provisional" or "uncontaminated" state of purity. For this purpose he either severed or made "invalid" all contact with the world and with everything that reminded him of the transitoriness of human existence, by means of lunatic formalities, scrupulous cleansing ceremonies, and the anxious observance of innumerable rules and regulations of an unbelievable complexity. Even before the patient had any suspicion of the hellish existence that lay before him, the dream showed him that if he wanted to come down to earth again there would have to be a pact with evil.

Elsewhere I have described a dream that illustrates the compensation of a religious problem in a young theological student. He was involved in all sorts of difficulties of belief, a not uncommon occurrence in the man of today. In his dream he was the pupil of the "white magician," who, however, was dressed in black. After having instructed him up to a certain point, the white magician told him that they now needed the "black magician." The black magician appeared, but clad in a white robe. He declared that he had found the keys of paradise, but needed the wisdom of the white magician in order to understand how to use them. This dream obviously contains the problem of opposites which, as we know, has found in Taoist philosophy

---

[2] Becoming aware of hidden aspects of one's own nature—which often presents a threatening aspect (here, "beastliness" and "evil").

a solution very different from the views prevailing in the West. The figures employed by the dream are impersonal collective images corresponding to the nature of the impersonal religious problem. In contrast to the Christian view, the dream stresses the relativity of good and evil in a way that immediately calls to mind the Taoist symbol of Yin and Yang.

We should certainly not conclude from these compensations that, as the conscious mind becomes more deeply engrossed in universal problems, the unconscious will bring forth correspondingly far-reaching compensations. There is what one might call a legitimate and an illegitimate interest in impersonal problems. Excursions of this kind are legitimate only when they arise from the deepest and truest needs of the individual; illegitimate when they are either mere intellectual curiosity or a flight from unpleasant reality. In the latter case the unconscious produces all too human and purely personal compensations, whose manifest aim is to bring the conscious mind back to ordinary reality. People who go illegitimately mooning after the infinite often have absurdly banal dreams which endeavour to damp down their ebullience. Thus, from the nature of the compensation, we can at once draw conclusions as to the seriousness and rightness of the conscious strivings.

There are certainly not a few people who are afraid to admit that the unconscious could ever have "big" ideas. They will object, "But do you really believe that the unconscious is capable of offering anything like a constructive criticism of our Western mentality?" Of course, if we take the problem intellectually and impute rational intentions to the unconscious, the thing becomes absurd. But it would never do to foist our conscious psychology upon the unconscious. Its mentality is an instinctive one; it has no differentiated functions, and it does not "think" as we understand "thinking." It simply creates an image that answers to the conscious situation. This image contains as much thought as feeling, and is anything rather than a product of rationalistic reflection. Such an image would be better described as an artistic vision. We tend to forget that a problem like the one which underlies the dream last mentioned cannot, even to the conscious mind of the dreamer, be an intellectual problem, but is profoundly emotional. For a moral man the ethical problem is a passionate question which has its roots in the deepest instinctual processes as well as in his most idealistic aspirations. The problem for him is devastatingly real. It is not surprising, therefore, that the answer likewise springs from the depths of his nature. The fact that everyone thinks his psychology is the measure of all things, and, if he also happens to be a fool, will inevitably think that such a problem is beneath his notice, should not trouble the psychologist in the least, for he has to take things objectively, as he finds them, without twisting them to fit his subjective suppositions. The richer and more capacious natures may legitimately be gripped by an impersonal problem, and to the extent that this is so, their unconscious can answer in the same style. And just as the conscious mind can put the question, "Why is there this frightful conflict between good and evil?," so the unconscious can reply, "Look closer! Each needs the other. The best, just because it is the best, holds the seed of evil, and there is nothing so bad but good can come of it."

It might then dawn on the dreamer that the apparently insoluble conflict is, perhaps, a prejudice, a frame of mind conditioned by time and place. The seemingly complex dream-image might easily reveal itself as plain, instinctive common sense, as the tiny germ of a rational idea, which a maturer mind could just as well have thought consciously. At all events Chinese philosophy thought of it ages ago. The singularly apt, plastic configuration of thought is the prerogative of that primitive, natural spirit which is alive in all of us and is only obscured by a onesided conscious development. If we consider the unconscious compensations from this angle, we might justifiably be accused of judging the unconscious too much from the conscious standpoint. And indeed, in pursuing these reflections, I have always started from the view that the unconscious simply reacts to the conscious contents, albeit in a very significant way, but that it lacks initiative. It is, however, far from my intention to give the impression that the unconscious is merely reactive in all cases. On the contrary there is a host of experiences which seem to prove that the unconscious is not only spontaneous but can actually take the lead. There are innumerable cases of people who lingered on in a pettifogging unconsciousness, only to become neurotic in the end. Thanks to the neurosis contrived by the unconscious, they are shaken out of their apathy, and this in spite of their own laziness and often desperate resistance.

Yet it would, in my view, be wrong to suppose that in such cases the unconscious is working to a deliberate and concerted plan and is striving to realize certain definite ends. I have found nothing to support this assumption. The driving force, so far as it is possible for us to grasp it, seems to be in essence only an urge towards self-realization. If it were a matter of some general teleological plan, then all individuals who enjoy a surplus of unconsciousness would necessarily be driven towards higher consciousness by an irresistible urge. That is plainly not the case. There are vast masses of the population who, despite their notorious unconsciousness, never get anywhere near a neurosis. The few who are smitten by such a fate are really persons of the "higher" type, who, for one reason or another, have remained too long on a primitive level. Their nature does not in the long run tolerate persistence in what is for them an unnatural torpor. As a result of their narrow conscious outlook and their cramped existence they save energy; bit by bit it accumulates in the unconscious and finally explodes in the form of a more or less acute neurosis. This simple mechanism does not necessarily conceal a "plan." A perfectly understandable urge towards self-realization would provide a quite satisfactory explanation. We could also speak of a retarded maturation of the personality.

Since it is highly probable that we are still a long way from the summit of absolute consciousness, presumably everyone is capable of wider consciousness, and we may assume accordingly that the unconscious processes are constantly supplying us with contents which, if consciously recognized, would extend the range of consciousness. Looked at in this way, the unconscious appears as a field of experience of unlimited extent. If it were merely reactive to the conscious mind, we might aptly call it a psychic mirror-world. In that case, the real source of all contents and activities would lie in the conscious mind, and there would be absolutely nothing in the unconscious except the distorted reflections of conscious contents. The creative process would be shut up in the conscious mind, and anything new would be nothing but conscious invention or cleverness. The empirical facts give the lie to this. Every creative man knows that spontaneity is the very essence of creative thought. Because the unconscious is not just a reactive mirror-reflection, but an independent, productive activity, its realm of experience is a self-contained world, having its own reality, of which we can only say that it affects us as we affect it—precisely what we say about our experience of the outer world. And just as material objects are the constituent elements of this world, so psychic factors constitute the objects of that other world.

The idea of psychic objectivity is by no means a new discovery. It is in fact one of the earliest and most universal achievements of humanity: it is nothing less than the conviction as to the concrete existence of a spirit-world. The spirit-world was certainly never an invention in the sense that fire-boring was an invention; it was far rather the experience, the conscious acceptance of a reality in no way inferior to that of the material world. I doubt whether primitives exist anywhere who are not acquainted with magical influence or a magical substance. ("Magical" is simply another word for "psychic.") It would also appear that practically all primitives are aware of the existence of spirits. "Spirit" is a psychic fact. Just as we distinguish our own bodiliness from bodies that are strange to us, so primitives—if they have any notion of "souls" at all—distinguish between their own souls and the spirits, which are felt as strange and as "not belonging." They are objects of outward perception, whereas their own soul (or one of several souls where a plurality is assumed), though believed to be essentially akin to the spirits, is not usually an object of so-called sensible perception. After death the soul (or one of the plurality of souls) becomes a spirit which survives the dead man, and often it shows a marked deterioration of character that partly contradicts the notion of personal immortality. The Bataks, of Sumatra, go so far as to assert that the people who were good in this life turn into malign and dangerous spirits. Nearly everything that the primitives say about the tricks which the spirits play on the living, and the general picture they give of the *revenants*,[3] corresponds down to the last detail with the phenomena established by spiritualistic experience. And just as the communications from the "Beyond" can be seen to be the activities of broken-off bits of the psyche, so these primitive spirits are manifestations of unconscious complexes. The importance that modern psychology attaches to the "parental complex" is a direct continuation of primitive man's experience of the dangerous power of the ancestral spirits. Even the error of judgment which leads him unthinkingly to assume that the spirits are realities of the external world is carried on in our assumption (which is only partially correct) that the real parents are responsible for the parental complex. In the old trauma theory of Freudian psychoanalysis, and in other quarters as well, this assumption even passed for a scientific explanation. (It was in order to avoid this confusion that I advocated the term "parental imago.")[4]

The simple soul is of course quite unaware of the fact that his nearest relations, who exercise immediate influence over him, create in him an image which is only partly a replica of themselves, while its other part is compounded of elements derived from himself. The imago is built up of parental influences plus the specific reactions of the child; it is therefore an image that reflects the object with very considerable qualifications. Naturally, the simple soul believes that his parents are as he sees them. The image is unconsciously projected, and when the parents die, the projected image goes on working as though it were a spirit existing on its own. The primitive then speaks of parental spirits who return by night (*revenants*), while the modern man calls it a father or mother complex.

The more limited a man's field of consciousness is, the more numerous the psychic contents (imagos) which meet him as quasi-external apparitions, either in the form of spirits, or as magical potencies projected upon living people (magicians, witches, etc.). At a rather higher stage of development, where the idea of the soul already exists, not all the imagos continue to be projected (where this happens, even trees and stones talk), but one or the other complex has come near enough to consciousness to be felt as no longer strange, but as somehow "belonging." Nevertheless, the feeling

---

[3]Ghosts that return, from the French verb *revenir*.
[4]The "parental image" is the representation of the parent created within the unconscious, which may or may not correspond to the actual parent.

that it "belongs" is not at first sufficiently strong for the complex to be sensed as a subjective content of consciousness. It remains in a sort of no man's land between conscious and unconscious, in the half-shadow, in part belonging or akin to the conscious subject, in part an autonomous being, and meeting consciousness as such. At all events it is not necessarily obedient to subjective intentions, it may even be of a higher order, more often than not a source of inspiration or warning, or of "supernatural" information. Psychologically such a content could be explained as a partly autonomous complex that is not yet fully integrated. The archaic souls, the *ba* and *ka* of the Egyptians, are complexes of this kind. At a still higher level, and particularly among the civilized peoples of the West, this complex is invariably of the feminine gender . . . a fact for which deeper and cogent reasons are not lacking.

MEANING

1. What did Jung discover about how dreams act as a "safety valve" to maintain the balance between the unconscious and conscious levels of the mind?
2. According to Jung, what means does the unconscious use to "look over your shoulder" and keep you from fooling yourself that you are either far better or far worse than you really are?
3. What connection did Jung find between the dreams of the theology student and the doubts this patient experienced about the depth of his religious faith?
4. What role is played by symbolic images in dreams, or "archetypes" from the "collective unconscious," in projecting answers to moral or ethical questions beyond the capacity of the conscious mind?

USING PROCESS ANALYSIS TO CONVEY MEANING

1. Why does Jung devote space to summarizing background information and spelling out the differences between his theories and those of Freud?
2. How does Jung use process analysis to organize his discussion of how the "unconscious" operates?
3. How does Jung use evidence from a wide range of sources, including the dreams of his patients and the legends of primitive tribes, art, and folklore, to demonstrate the existence of an all-pervasive "collective unconscious"?
4. How do the examples of (a) the "arrogant gentleman" who dreamt about his younger brother, (b) the dependent young woman who had sinister dreams about the mother she was so "devoted" to, and (c) Jung's own dreams about a patient he had undervalued illustrate how the unconscious provides a self-regulatory mechanism for the personality as a whole?

WRITING SUGGESTIONS

1. What connections can you discern between the manner in which instinct guides behavior in the salmon (see Hasler & Larsen, page 311) and the way in which

"archetypes" in the "collective unconscious" guide individuals toward what Jung called "self-realization"?

2. How does Freud's theory that the unconscious is limited solely to what has been repressed from childhood onward (a process, Freud says, that can be reversed by psychoanalysis) differ from Jung's theory of a "collective unconscious" that contains images, dreams, myths, and fantasies, which were not in the conscious mind originally?

3. What does Jung have to say about the reason for ancestor worship among Indian tribes? How is Jung's distinction between the "big" and "little" dreams of primitive peoples accurately illustrated by what Benedict found among the Pueblo Indians (see the "Comparison and Contrast" chapter, page 246)?

CLASSIFICATION

Writers use classification to sort, group, and collect things into categories or classes based on one or more criteria. Criteria are features that members of the group all possess or share in common. The purposes of the classifier determine which specific features are selected as the basis of the classification. Thus, classification is, first and foremost, an intellectual activity based on discovering generic characteristics shared by members of a group, according to the interests of the writer.

Effective classifications shed light on the nature of what is being classified by identifying significant features, using these features as criteria in a systematic way, dividing phenomena into at least two different classes on the basis of these criteria, and presenting the results in a logical and consistent manner.

Metallurgists, for instance, still classify a certain group of metallic elements, from amongst all the other metals found in nature, as being the so-called "noble metals." Metals in this group include platinum, gold, and silver, as well as the less well-known iridium, rhodium, osmium, ruthenium, and palladium. Each of these metallic elements possesses certain unique features that are also possessed by other metals in this group. They are all found alone, rather than in combination with other elements, are chemically unreactive, and hence, do not readily form compounds. The classification, "noble metals," is meant to designate the characteristics these metals share in common.

The specific categories into which items are grouped depends on what criteria are being applied. Applying different principles of classification based on designated features will yield different groupings. Most people might simply classify drugs according to the different forms (capsules, pills, liquids, gas, ointments, or powders) in which they appear. Pharmacologists, by contrast, classify drugs according to the different kinds of effects they have on the body. Thus, one category is comprised of drugs that combat bacteria, such as antibiotics and sulfa drugs. A second category is made up of drugs that prevent disease, such as vaccines and antiserums. A third group consists of drugs that affect the cardiovascular system, such as antiarrhythmics and vasodilators. A fourth group is made up of drugs that affect the body's nervous system, such as analgesics, opiates, anesthetics, stimulants, and depressants. Classifica-

327

tion is an invaluable method of imposing a pattern on material that otherwise would remain unorganized.

Equally as important, once a classification is established it becomes a framework into which new information can be placed. For example, in the area of film studies, critics have discovered that many popular films can be classified as belonging to specific film genres. Films within specific genres share common characteristics of similar subject matter, similar methods of characterization, dialogue, costume, setting, and formula plot. The western film (*High Noon, Silverado*), the horror film (*Frankenstein; Poltergeist*), the comedy film (*It Happened One Night; National Lampoon's Animal House; Splash*), the science-fiction film (*The Day the Earth Stood Still; Star Trek IV: The Voyage Home*), the gangster film (*Little Caesar; Godfather I* and *II*), the musical (*The Sound of Music; A Chorus Line*), and the adventure film (*Captain Blood; Raiders of the Lost Ark*)—are all some of the specific film genres that have been identified and classified. Indeed, the very existence of these established genres makes it possible for audiences to enjoy spoofs such as Mel Brook's parody of the muscial in *The Producers*, the western in *Blazing Saddles*, the horror film in *Young Frankenstein*, the suspense thriller à la Hitchcock in *High Anxiety*, and the science-fiction film in *Spaceballs*.

George A. Harter, a NASA scientist, uses classification to shed light on the different kinds of capabilities an earth-orbiting space station would possess in "Earth Applications." Because of its vantage point, an earth-orbiting space station would offer an unrivaled means for sensing changes in global weather systems, detecting the presence of fish in oceans, and identifying subsurface geological formations of potential value. Harter discusses a range of specific "earth applications"—including easier manufacture of pharmaceuticals, the fabrication of superior forms of metal alloys, and global weather forecasting—that one space station could perform more efficiently than could many satellites, each launched to perform separate functions.

Classification is equally well-suited to clarify complex, subjective psychological phenomena. The French novelist, Stendhal, classifies the mysterious phenomenon "love" into four different types (although he admits "one could easily adopt eight or ten shades") in "The Crystallization of Love." Stendhal says that love may, on the one hand, be entirely selfless, while on the other, it may be merely a projection meant to enhance the lover's own self-esteem:

On Love

I am trying to account for that passion all of whose developments are inherently beautiful.

There are four different kinds of love:

1. Passion-love, that of the Portuguese Nun, of Héloïse for Abélard. . . .

2. Sympathy-love, such as was prevalent in Paris in 1760, and is found in the memoirs and romances of that period. . . . It is true that if you strip this poor form of love of its vanity, very little remains. . . .

3. Sensual love.

Whilst out shooting, to meet a fresh, pretty country girl who darts away into a wood. Every one knows the love founded on pleasures of this kind; however unromantic and wretched one's character, it is there that one starts at the age of sixteen.

4. Vanity-love.

The great majority of men, especially in France, desire and possess a fashionable woman as they would possess a fine horse, as a necessary luxury for a young man.

Their vanity, more or less flattered and more or less stimulated, gives rise to rapture. . . .

Stendhal's purpose in classifying love into these four different kinds is to make it easier for his readers to recognize each type, to evaluate them against each other, and ultimately to avoid self-deception.

Gilbert Highet analyzes Lincoln's "Gettysburg Address" to discover how different types of rhetorical figures contributed to the eloquence and impact of this famous speech. Highet, a rhetorician and classicist, locates two types of rhetorical figures, antithesis and tricolon, and shows how Lincoln used them to organize the ideas and language of the "Gettysburg Address." Highet points out that the types of rhetorical figures that Lincoln used in creating the "Gettysburg Address" were precisely those first identified and taught by ancient Greek rhetoricians. Lincoln's care in drafting the speech for this particular occasion reveals a sophisticated knowledge of the principles of effective public discourse.

In "Sisters in Crime," Freda Adler uses classification as a means of correlating, organizing, and clarifying information gathered from statistics to demonstrate that a new class of criminal has emerged in society. This class is comprised of women who have turned from petty crimes, such as prostitution and shoplifting, to major crimes, such as bank robbery and murder:

> Like her sisters in legitimate fields, the female criminal is fighting for her niche in the hierarchy, for, curiously enough, the barriers of male chauvinsim in some areas of criminal activity are no less formidable than those which confront female newcomers in the world of business. There is, perhaps, no more macho group than the traditional "family" units of organized crime. "It was just a while ago that we got our first female loan shark here in the city," said a New York assistant district attorney. "That was something new. That was strictly an organized crime thing in the past. . . ."

Adler draws on in-depth interviews with prison inmates and a number of case studies to document the extent to which women now have entered the previously male-dominated sector of major and violent crimes. In the essay from which this excerpt is drawn, Adler speculates that this previously unrecognized sociological phenomena (dramatized in the 1985 movie *Prizzi's Honor*) might be an unanticipated result of the quest for "equal opportunity" encouraged by the Women's Liberation Movement.

In "Kibbutz: Venture in Utopia," Melford E. Spiro discovered, as an on-site observer, that kibbutz life was organized according to the relative status attached to different types of work. This hierarchy of value is the basis of Spiro's use of classification, as an anthropologist, to organize his discussion of all aspects of kibbutz life:

> Not all work, however, is equally valued. Physical labor enjoys the greatest prestige. The further removed it is from physical labor, the less prestige a job confers. This means, of course, that pure intellectual work does not confer great prestige, despite the fact that Kiryat Yedidim is a highly cultured community, one which is devoted to intellectual and artistic experience. Of the various categories of physical labor, agricultural labor is valued the most. Even among the agricultural branches, however, differential stereotypes have arisen. Those who work in the orchards and vineyards are thought to be intellectual, easygoing people, who are not particularly energetic. Shepherds are supposedly romantic, and inclined to be a bit lazy. On the other hand, the *falachim*, those who work in the grain fields, are presumably hard, energetic workers. . . .

Physically demanding forms of labor such as grain harvesting are valued more than work done in the orchards and vineyards, which, in turn, is seen as morally superior to nonphysical labor. Spiro uses classification as an analytical tool to reveal how the learned cultural values of kibbutz life are based on the "moral value of labor."

In "Stages of Dying," Elisabeth Kubler-Ross classifies the results gathered from interviewing over five hundred terminally ill patients. It is important, says Dr. Kubler-Ross, for a society that generally denies death to learn that people react to impending death with a whole range of responses. Kubler-Ross discovers that the typical reactions experienced by people who must come to terms with the fact that they are going to die falls into five categories: denial, anger, bargaining, repression, and acceptance:

> Most patients promise something in exchange for prolongation of life. Many a patient wants to live just long enough for the children to get out of school. The moment they have completed high school, he may ask to live until the son gets married. And the moment the wedding is over, he hopes to live until the grandchild arrives. These kinds of bargains are compromises, the patient's beginning acknowledgement that his time is limited, and an expression of finiteness, all necessary in reaching a stage of acceptance. . . .

Based on her research, Kubler-Ross believes that medical students, nurses, and the clergy have much to learn from terminally ill patients, as does a society that exhibits a cultural bias against the dying. Further, more effective counseling should be provided to the friends and relatives of these patients, and especially to the brothers and sisters of terminally ill children.

In "Values in the News," media expert Herbert J. Gans delves into the question of why there is so little "good news" reported by the news media. Gans believes that an important but generally unrecognized principle of selection determines what kinds of stories are considered worthy of being reported. He calls this principle "disorder" or the disturbance of the *status quo* in various contexts:

> Disorder stories fall into four major cateories: natural, technological, social, and moral. Natural disorder news deals with natural disasters, such as floods and earth-quakes, as well as industrial accidents which can be ascribed to natural forces, such as many but not all plane crashes or mine cave-ins. Technological disorder concerns accidents which cannot be ascribed to nature. Social disorder news deals with activities which disturb the public peace and may involve violence or the threat of violence against life or physical property; it also includes the deterioration of valued institutions, such as the nuclear two-parent family. Moral disorder news reports transgressions of laws and mores which do not necessarily endanger the social order. . . .

Gans says that almost all news stories can be classified according to the kind of "disorder" they report. The evening news is filled with stories that deal with disasters of nature (earthquakes, tornados), moral abuse (insider trading on Wall Street), techno-logical disorder (nuclear accidents, toxic waste spills), and social disorder (drug abuse). Gans is concerned that the media reports only those stories that conform to this principle of "disorder" and even goes so far as to reshape the reporting of events to fit this hidden agenda.

LIBERAL ARTS

STENDHAL

The Crystallization of Love

Stendhal (the pseudonym of Marie Henri Beyle, 1783–1842), a French novelist, essayist, and critic, was born and educated in Grenoble, France. In 1806, in the service of Napoleon, he saw Germany, Austria, and witnessed the climactic battle at Moscow. He left the army in 1813 and traveled to Italy, which became his second home and where he stayed for seven years, immersing himself in music, literature, art, and society. While in Italy, he wrote his first work under the name Stendhal, Rome, Naples, and Florence in 1817 *(1817). An unhappy love affair during this period awakened his interest in the psychology of love, the results of which appear in his well-known work* On Love *(1822), which Freud praised as "a manifestation of psychological genius." The novels on which Stendhal's fame rests,* The Red and the Black *(1831) and* The Charterhouse of Parma *(1839), display an intimate understanding of human nature, expressed with an irony that springs from Stendhal's awareness of his own capacity for self-deception, especially in matters of the heart. As Stendhal himself predicted, his work became appreciated only after his death. In "The Crystallization of Love," from* On Love, *Stendhal expresses his belief that behavior is governed by passions and self-interest, and presents a classification of four different types of love.*

CHAPTER I

ON LOVE

I AM trying to account for that passion all of whose developments are inherently beautiful.

There are four different kinds of love:

1. Passion-love, that of the Portuguese Nun, of Héloïse for Abélard, of Captain de Vésel, of the Cento man-at-arms.[1]

2. Sympathy-love, such as was prevalent in Paris in 1760, and is found in the memoirs and romances of that period, in Crébillon, Lauzun, Duclos, Marmontel, Chamfort, Madame d'Épinary, etc., etc.

It is a picture in which everything, even to the shadows, must be rose coloured, and into which nothing unpleasant must intrude under any pretext whatever, at the risk of infringing custom, fashion, refinement, etc. A well-bred man knows in advance everything that he must do and expect in the various stages of this kind of love; as there is nothing passionate or unexpected about it, it is often more refined than real love, for it is always sprightly; it is like a cold and pretty miniature compared with a picture by the Caracci; and, whereas passion-love carries us away against all our interests, sympathy-love always knows how to adjust itself to them. It is true that if you strip this poor form of love of its vanity, very little remains; without its vanity, it is like a feeble convalescent who is scarcely able to drag himself along.

3. Sensual love.

Whilst out shooting, to meet a fresh, pretty country girl who darts away into a wood. Every one knows the love founded on pleasures of this kind; however unromantic and wretched one's character, it is there that one starts at the age of sixteen.

4. Vanity-love.

The great majority of men, especially in France, desire and possess a fashionable woman as they would possess a fine horse, as a necessary luxury for a young man. Their vanity, more or less flattered and more or less stimulated, gives rise to rapture. Sometimes sensual love is present also, but not always; often there is not even sensual pleasure. The Duchesse de Chaulnes used to say that a duchess is never more than thirty years old to a snob; and people who frequented the Court of that upright man, King Louis of Holland, still recall with amusement a pretty woman at the Hague who could never bring herself to think a man anything but charming if he was a Duke or a Prince. But, faithful to the monarchic principle, as soon as a Prince arrived at Court she dropped the Duke. She was a kind of insignia of the Corps Diplomatique.

The most agreeable form of this rather insipid relationship is the one in which sensual pleasure is increased by habit. In that case past memories make it seem something like real love; there is piqued vanity and sadness on being abandoned; and, becoming seized by romantic ideas, you begin to think you are in love and melancholy, for your vanity always aspires to have a great passion to its credit. The one thing certain is that to whatever kind of love one owes one's pleasures, so long as they are accompanied by mental exhilaration, they are very keen and their memory is entrancing; and in this passion, contrary to most others, the memory of what we have lost always seems sweeter than anything that we can hope for in the future.

Sometimes, in vanity-love, habit and the despair of finding anything better produces a kind of friendship, the least agreeable of all its kinds; it prides itself on its *security*, etc.

---

[1] The *Letters of a Portuguese Nun*, a popular work in the seventeenth and eighteenth centuries, which told the story of a woman who was still in love even though she had been seduced and abandoned. Monsieur Beyle's friends often asked him who this captain and this man-at-arms were; he always replied that he had forgotten their story.

Sensual pleasure, being part of our nature, is within the grasp of every one, but it only holds a very low place in the eyes of tender and passionate beings. Although they may be ridiculous in drawing-rooms, although worldly people may often make them unhappy by their intrigues, on the other hand they taste pleasures utterly inaccessible to those hearts who only thrill to vanity or to gold.

Some virtuous and affectionate women have almost no idea at all of sensual pleasure; they have only very rarely laid themselves open to it, if I may put it so, and even then the raptures of passion-love have almost made them forget the pleasures of the body.

Some men are the victims and instruments of a satanic pride, a sort of Alfieri pride. These people, who are perhaps cruel because, like Nero, they live in constant fear, judging every one by their own heart, these people, I say, cannot obtain any sensual pleasure unless it is accompanied by circumstances which flatter their pride abnormally, that is to say, unless they can perpetrate some cruelty on the companion of their pleasures. . . . These men cannot feel the emotion of security with anything less.

However, instead of distinguishing four different kinds of love, one could easily adopt eight or ten shades. There are perhaps as many different ways of feeling as of seeing amongst men; but these differences in terms do not affect the reasoning that follows. Every kind of love that one meets here below is born, lives, dies or becomes immortal, according to the same laws.

CHAPTER II

The Birth of Love

THIS is what goes on in the mind:
1. Admiration.
2. One says to one's self: "How delightful to kiss her, to be kissed in return," etc.
3. Hope.
One studies her perfections. It is at this moment that a woman should surrender herself, to get the greatest possible sensual pleasure. The eyes of even the most modest women light up the moment hope is born; passion is so strong and pleasure is so acute that they betray themselves in the most obvious manner.
4. Love is born.
To love is to derive pleasure from seeing, touching and feeling through all one's senses and as closely as possible, a lovable person who loves us.
5. The first crystallization begins.
We take a joy in attributing a thousand perfections to a woman of whose love we are sure; we analyze all our happiness with intense satisfaction. This reduces itself to giving ourselves an exaggerated idea of a magnificent possession which has just fallen to us from Heaven in some way we do not understand, and the continued possession of which is assured to us.

This is what you will find if you let a lover turn things over in his mind for twenty-four hours.

In the salt mines of Salzburg a bough stripped of its leaves by winter is thrown into the depths of the disused workings; two or three months later it is pulled out again, covered with brilliant crystals: even the tiniest twigs, no bigger than a tomtit's claw, are spangled with a vast number of shimmering, glittering diamonds, so that the original bough is no longer recognizable.

I call crystallization that process of the mind which discovers fresh perfections in its beloved at every turn of events.[2]

For instance, should a traveller speak of the coolness of Genoese orange groves by the seashore on a scorching summer day, you immediately think how delightful it would be to enjoy this coolness in her company!

One of your friends breaks his arm out hunting: how sweet, you think, to be nursed by a woman you love! To be with her always and to revel in her constant love would almost make your pain blessed; and you leave your friend's broken arm still more firmly convinced of the angelic sweetness of your mistress. In short, it is sufficient to think of a perfection in order to see it in the person you love.

This phenomenon which I have allowed myself to call *crystallization*, arises from the promptings of Nature which urge us to enjoy ourselves and drive the blood to our brains, from the feeling that our delight increases with the perfections of the beloved, and from the thought: "She is mine." The savage has no time to get beyond the first step. He grasps his pleasures, but his brain is concentrated on following the buck fleeing from him through the forest, and with whose flesh he must repair his own strength as quickly as possible, at the risk of falling beneath the hatchet of his enemy.

At the other extreme of civilization, I have no doubt that a sensitive woman arrives at the point of experiencing no sensual pleasure except with the man she loves. This is in direct opposition to the savage. But, amongst civilized communities woman has plenty of leisure, whilst the savage lives so close to essentials that he is obliged to treat his female as a beast of burden. If the females of many animals have an easier lot, it is only because the subsistence of the males is more assured.

But let us leave the forests and return to Paris. A passionate man sees nothing but perfection in the woman he loves; and yet his affections may still wander, for the spirit wearies of monotony, even in the case of the most perfect happiness.

So what happens to rivet his attention is this:

6. Doubt is born.

When his hopes have first of all been raised and then confirmed by ten or a dozen glances, or a whole series of other actions which may be compressed into a moment or spread over several days, the lover, recovering from his first amazement and growing used to his happiness, or perhaps merely guided by theory which, based always on his most frequent experiences, is really only correct in the case of light women, the lover, I say, demands more positive proofs of love and wants to advance the moment of his happiness.

If he takes too much for granted he will be met with indifference, coldness or even anger: in France there will be a suggestion of irony which seems to say: "You think you have made more progress than you really have." A woman behaves in this way either because she is recovering from a moment of intoxication and obeys the behests of modesty, which she is alarmed at having transgressed, or merely from prudence or coquettishness.

The lover begins to be less sure of the happiness which he has promised himself; he begins to criticize the reasons he gave himself for hoping.

He tries to fall back on the other pleasures of life. *He finds they no longer exist.* He is seized with a dread of appalling misery, and his attention becomes concentrated.

---

[2] Stendhal uses the word *crystallization* to express "that act of folly that makes us attribute every beauty and every kind of perfection to the woman we are beginning to love."

7. Second crystallization.

Now begins the second crystallization, producing as its diamonds various confirmations of the following idea:

"She loves me."

Every quarter of an hour, during the night following the birth of doubt, after a moment of terrible misery, the lover says to himself: "Yes, she loves me"; and crystallization sets to work to discover fresh charms; then gaunt-eyed doubt grips him again and pulls him up with a jerk. His heart misses a beat; he says to himself: "But does she love me?" Through all these harrowing and delicious alternations the poor lover feels acutely: "With her I would experience joys which she alone in the world could give me."

It is the clearness of this truth and the path he treads between an appalling abyss and the most perfect happiness, that make the second crystallization appear to be so very much more important than the first.

The lover hovers incessantly amongst these three ideas:

1. She is perfect in every way.
2. She loves me.
3. How can I get the strongest possible proof of her love for me?

The most heart-rending moment in love that is still young is when it finds that it has been wrong in its chain of reasoning and must destroy a whole agglomeration of crystals.

Even the fact of crystallization itself begins to appear doubtful.

CHAPTER III

. . . The thing that ensures the duration of love is the second crystallization, during which at every moment one realizes that one must either be loved or perish. How, with this conviction ever present in one's mind, and grown into a habit by several months of love, can one bear even the thought of ceasing to love? The more determined a man's character, the less liable is he to be inconstant.

This second crystallization is practically non-existent in love inspired by women who surrender themselves too quickly.

As soon as the crystallizations have taken place, especially the second one, which is much the stronger, indifferent eyes no longer recognize the bough:

For, 1. It is adorned by perfections or diamonds which they do not see;

2. It is adorned by perfections which are not perfections in their sight. . . .

CHAPTER IV

In the mind of a completely unbiased person, that, for instance, of a young girl living in a country house in an isolated part of the country—the most insignificant unexpected event may lead to a little admiration, and if this is followed by the slightest ray of hope, it causes the birth of love and crystallization.

In a case of this kind, the first attraction of love is that it is a distraction.

Surprise and hope are powerfully assisted by the need of love and the melancholy which one has at the age of sixteen. It is fairly clear that the main anxiety of that age is a thirst for love, and it is characteristic of that thirst not to be unreasonably particular about the kind of draught that chance may offer to slake it. . . .

CHAPTER V

MAN is not free to refuse to do the thing which gives him more pleasure than any other conceivable action.

Love is like a fever; it comes and goes without the will having any part in the process. That is one of the principal differences between sympathy-love and passion-love, and one can only congratulate one's self on the fine qualities of the person one loves as on a lucky chance.

Love, indeed, belongs to every age: take, for instance, the passion of Madame du Deffand for the unattractive Horace Walpole. . . .

CHAPTER VI

The Salzburg Bough

DURING love, crystallization hardly ever stops. This is its history: so long as you are on a distant footing with the person you love, crystallization takes place from an *imaginary solution;* it is only in your imagination that you are certain of the existence of any particular perfection in the woman you love. After you have arrived at terms of intimacy, constantly renewed fears are calmed by more real solutions. In this way, happiness is never uniform except in its source. Every day has a different flower.

If the loved woman surrenders to the passion she feels and falls into the grievous error of killing fear by the ardour of her transports, crystallization stops for a moment; but, when love loses its ardour, that is to say, its fears, it acquires the charm of complete unconstraint, of boundless confidence, and a sweet familiarity comes to deaden all the sorrows of life and bring fresh interest into one's pleasures.

If you are deserted, crystallization starts again; and the thought of every act of admiration and each delight which she can bestow on you and of which you had ceased to think, ends in this harrowing reflection: "That rapturous joy will *never* be mine again! And it is through my own fault that I have lost it!" If you try to find happiness in emotions of a different kind your heart refuses to react to them. . . .

CHAPTER VII

Differences Between the Birth of Love in the Two Sexes

WOMEN attach themselves by their favours. As nineteen-twentieths of their ordinary day-dreams are connected with love, these day-dreams are all concentrated on one person after intimacy; they endeavour to justify such an extraordinary proceeding, so decisive and so contrary to all the habits of modesty. Men have no task of this kind to perform; later, a woman's imagination pictures minutely and at her leisure such moments of delight.

Since love makes one doubt even the most clearly proven things, the woman who before intimacy was so sure that her lover was a man above the common herd, is terrified lest he has only been trying to add another woman to his list of conquests, as soon as she thinks she has nothing more to refuse him.

That is the moment for the appearance of the second crystallization which, because of the fear that accompanies it, is much the stronger.

A woman thinks that from being a queen she has made herself a slave. This state of mind and soul is encouraged by the nervous intoxication which is the result of indulgence in pleasures which are all the more emotional in proportion to the rarity of their occurrence. Again, a woman seated before her embroidery frame, a dull form of work which only occupies her hands, dreams of her lover, whereas he, galloping across the plains with his squadron, is in a position where the slightest miscalculation may lead to his being placed under arrest.

I should imagine, therefore, that the second crystallization is much stronger in the case of women, because they have more to fear, their vanity and honour are at stake, and they have less to distract them from it. . . .

MEANING

1. How does Stendhal characterize each of the four kinds of love he identifies?
2. What part does crystallization play in determining whether love, at one extreme, is entirely selfless, or at the other extreme, an egotistical expression of self-flattery where qualities attributed to another person enhance the lover's own self-esteem?
3. How are the reactions of women in love different from those of men?

USING CLASSIFICATION TO CONVEY MEANING

1. How does Stendhal's categorization of love into four different kinds make this mysterious phenomena easier to understand?
2. How does Stendhal's arrangment of his essay into short chapters make it easier to evaluate the different kinds of love he describes?
3. Which examples and comparisons did you find particularly effective in revealing something previously hidden about the nature of love?

WRITING SUGGESTIONS

1. How do women's magazines exploit one or more of the four types of love in their stories, articles, or advertising?
2. How do modern romance novels focus on the stereotyped kinds of love classified by Stendhal?
3. What different kinds of friendship can you identify? How would you characterize each one? Are there any types of friendship in which self-flattery, or what Stendhal calls "crystallization," plays a major part? What important truth about friendship as a phenomena does your classification reveal?

GILBERT HIGHET

The Gettysburg Address

Gilbert Highet (1906–1978) was born in Glasgow, Scotland and educated at the University of Glasgow and Oxford University. From 1937–1972 Highet was professor of Greek, Latin, and comparative literature at Columbia University. His many distinguished books include The Classical Tradition: Greek and Roman Influences on Western Literature *(1949),* The Anatomy of Satire *(1962), and* The Immortal Profession: The Joy of Teaching and Learning *(1976). He was particularly successful in bridging the gap from classicism to popular culture as an editor for the Book of the Month Club, chairman of the editorial board of* Horizon *magazine, and literary critic for* Harper's. *"The Gettysburg Address," from* A Clerk of Oxenford *(1954), shows Highet at his most illuminating in his analysis of the structure, themes, and rhetoric of Lincoln's famous speech.*

Fourscore and seven years ago our fathers brought forth on this continent, a new nation, conceived in Liberty, and dedicated to the proposition that all men are created equal.

Now we are engaged in a great civil war, testing whether that nation or any nation so conceived and so dedicated, can long endure. We are met on a great battle-field of that war. We have come to dedicate a portion of that field, as a final resting place for those who here gave their lives that that nation might live. It is altogether fitting and proper that we should do this.

But, in a larger sense, we can not dedicate—we can not consecrate—we can not hallow—this ground. The brave men, living and dead, who struggled here, have consecrated it, far above our poor power to add or detract. The world will little note, nor long remember, what we say here, but it can never forget what they did here. It is for us the living, rather, to be dedicated here to the unfinished work which they who fought here have thus far so nobly advanced. It is rather for us to be here dedicated to the great task remaining before us—that from these honored dead we take increased devotion to that cause for which they gave the last full measure of devotion—that we here highly resolve that these dead shall not have died in vain—that this nation, under God, shall have a new birth of freedom—and that government of the people, by the people, for the people, shall not perish from the earth.

Fourscore and seven years ago . . .

These five words stand at the entrance to the best-known monument of American prose, one of the finest utterances in the entire language and surely one of the greatest

338

speeches in all history. Greatness is like granite: it is molded in fire, and it lasts for many centuries.

Fourscore and seven years ago. . . . It is strange to think that President Lincoln was looking back to the 4th of July 1776, and that he and his speech are now further removed from us than he himself was from George Washington and the Declaration of Independence. Fourscore and seven years before the Gettysburg Address, a small group of patriots signed the Declaration. Fourscore and seven years after the Gettysburg Address, it was the year 1950, and that date is already receding rapidly into our troubled, adventurous, and valiant past.

Inadequately prepared and at first scarcely realized in its full importance, the dedication of the graveyard at Gettysburg was one of the supreme moments of American history. The battle itself had been a turning point of the war. On the 4th of July 1863, General Meade repelled Lee's invasion of Pennsylvania. Although he did not follow up his victory, he had broken one of the most formidable aggressive enterprises of the Confederate armies. Losses were heavy on both sides. Thousands of dead were left on the field, and thousands of wounded died in the hot days following the battle. At first, their burial was more or less haphazard; but thoughtful men gradually came to feel that an adequate burying place and memorial were required. These were established by an interstate commission that autumn, and the finest speaker in the North was invited to dedicate them. This was the scholar and statesman Edward Everett of Harvard. He made a good speech—which is still extant: not at all academic, it is full of close strategic analysis and deep historical understanding.

Lincoln was not invited to speak, at first. Although people knew him as an effective debater, they were not sure whether he was capable of making a serious speech on such a solemn occasion. But one of the impressive things about Lincoln's career is that he constantly strove to *grow*. He was anxious to appear on that occasion and to say something worthy of it. (Also, it has been suggested, he was anxious to remove the impression that he did not know how to behave properly—an impression which had been strengthened by a shocking story about his clowning on the battlefield of Antietam the previous year). Therefore when he was invited he took considerable care with his speech. He drafted rather more than half of it in the White House before leaving, finished it in the hotel at Gettysburg the night before the ceremony (not in the train, as sometimes reported). and wrote out a fair copy next morning.

There are many accounts of the day itself, 19 November 1863. There are many descriptions of Lincoln, all showing the same curious blend of grandeur and awkwardness, or lack of dignity, or—it would be best to call it humility. In the procession he rode horseback: a tall lean man in a high plug hat, straddling a short horse, with his feet too near the ground. He arrived before the chief speaker, and had to wait patiently for half an hour or more. His own speech came right at the end of a long and exhausting ceremony, lasted less than three minutes, and made little impression on the audience. In part this was because they were tired, in part because (as eyewitnesses said) he ended almost before they knew he had begun, and in part because he did not speak the Address, but read it, very slowly, in a thin high voice, with a marked Kentucky accent, pronouncing "to" as "toe" and dropping his final R's.

Some people of course were alert enough to be impressed. Everett congratulated him at once. But most of the newspapers paid little attention to the speech, and some sneered at it. The *Patriot and Union* of Harrisburg wrote, "We pass over the silly remarks of the President; for the credit of the nation we are willing . . . that they shall no more be repeated or thought of"; and the London *Times* said, "The ceremony was rendered ludicrous by some of the sallies of that poor President Lincoln," calling his remarks "dull and commonplace." The first commendation of the Address came in a single sentence of the Chicago *Tribune,* and the first discriminating and detailed praise of it appeared in the Springfield *Republican,* the Providence *Journal,* and the Philadelphia *Bulletin.* However, three weeks after the ceremony and then again the following spring, the editor of *Harper's Weekly* published a sincere and thorough eulogy of the Address, and soon it was attaining recognition as a masterpiece.

At the time, Lincoln could not care much about the reception of his words. He was exhausted and ill. In the train back to Washington, he lay down with a wet towel on his head. He had caught smallpox. At that moment he was incubating it, and he was stricken down soon after he reentered the White House. Fortunately it was a mild attack, and it evoked one of his best jokes: he told his visitors, "At last I have something I can give to everybody."

He had more than that to give to everybody. He was a unique person, far greater than most people realize until they read his life with care. The wisdom of his policy, the sources of his statesmanship—these were things too complex to be discussed in a brief essay. But we can say something about the Gettysburg Address as a work of art.

A work of art. Yes: for Lincoln was a literary artist, trained both by others and by himself. The textbooks he used as a boy were full of difficult exercises and skillful devices in formal rhetoric, stressing the qualities he practiced in his own speaking: antithesis, parallelism, and verbal harmony. Then he read and reread many admirable models of thought and expression: the King James Bible, the essays of Bacon, the best plays of Shakespeare. His favorites were *Hamlet, Lear, Macbeth, Richard III,* and *Henry VIII,* which he had read dozens of times. He loved reading aloud, too, and spent hours reading poetry to his friends. (He told his partner Herndon that he preferred getting the sense of any document by reading it aloud.) Therefore his serious speeches are important parts of the long and noble classical tradition of oratory which begins in Greece, runs through Rome to the modern world, and is still capable (if we do not neglect it) of producing masterpieces.

The first proof of this is that the Gettysburg Address is full of quotations—or rather of adaptations—which give it strength. It is partly religious, partly (in the highest sense) political: therefore it is interwoven with memories of the Bible and memories of American history. The first and the last words are Biblical cadences. Normally Lincoln did not say "fourscore" when he meant eight; but on this solemn occasion he recalled the important dates in the Bible—such as the age of Abram when his first son was born to him, and he was "fourscore and six years old."[1] Similarly he did not say there was a chance that democracy might die out: he recalled the somber phrasing of the Book of Job—where Bildad speaks of the destruction of one who shall vanish without a trace, and says that "his branch shall be cut off; his remembrance shall perish from the earth."[2] Then again, the famous description of our State as "government of the people, by the people, for the people" was adumbrated by Daniel Webster in 1830 (he spoke of "the people's government, made for the

---

[1] Gen. 16.16.
[2] Job 18.16–17.

people, made by the people, and answerable to the people") and then elaborated in 1854 by the abolitionist Theodore Parker (as "government of all the people, by all the people, for all the people"). There is good reason to think that Lincoln took the important phrase "under God" (which he interpolated at the last moment) from Weems, the biographer of Washington; and we know that it had been used at least once by Washington himself.

Analyzing the Address further, we find that it is based on a highly imaginative theme, or group of themes. The subject is—how can we put it so as not to disfigure it?—the subject is the kinship of life and death, that mysterious linkage which we see sometimes as the physical succession of birth and death in our world, sometimes as the contrast, which is perhaps a unity, between death and immortality. The first sentence is concerned with birth:

> Our *fathers brought forth* a *new* nation, *conceived* in liberty.

The final phrase but one expresses the hope that

> this nation, under God, shall have a *new birth* of freedom.

And the last phrase of all speaks of continuing life as the triumph over death. Again and again throughout the speech, this mystical contrast and kinship reappear: "those who *gave their lives* that that nation might *live*," "the brave men *living* and *dead*," and so in the central assertion that the dead have already consecrated their own burial place, while "it is for us, the *living*, rather to be dedicated . . . to the great task remaining." The Gettysburg Address is a prose poem; it belongs to the same world as the great elegies, and the adagios of Beethoven.

Its structure, however, is that of a skillfully contrived speech. The oratorical pattern is perfectly clear. Lincoln describes the occasion, dedicates the ground, and then draws a larger conclusion by calling on his hearers to dedicate themselves to the preservation of the Union. But within that, we can trace his constant use of at least two important rhetorical devices.

The first of these is *antithesis*: opposition, contrast. The speech is full of it. Listen:

> The world will little *note*
>   nor long *remember*   what *we say* here
>   but   it can never *forget*   what *they did* here.

And so in nearly every sentence: "brave men, *living* and *dead*"; "to *add* or *detract*." There is the antithesis of the Founding Fathers and the men of Lincoln's own time:

> Our *fathers brought forth* a new nation . . .
> now *we* are testing whether that nation . . . can *long endure*.

And there is the more terrible antithesis of those who have already died and those who still live to do their duty. Now, antithesis is the figure of contrast and conflict. Lincoln was speaking in the midst of a great civil war.

The other important pattern is different. It is technically called *tricolon*—the division of an idea into three harmonious parts, usually of increasing power. The most famous phrase of the Address is a tricolon:

> government of the people
>   by the people
>   and   for the people.

The most solemn sentence is a tricolon:

> we cannot dedicate
> we cannot consecrate
> we cannot hallow this ground.

And above all, the last sentence (which has sometimes been criticized as too complex) is essentially two parallel phrases, with a tricolon growing out of the second and then producing another tricolon: a trunk, three branches, and a cluster of flowers. Lincoln says that it is for his hearers to be dedicated to the great task remaining before them. Then he goes on,

> that from these honored dead

—apparently he means "in such a way that from these honored dead"—

> we take increased devotion to that cause.

Next, he restates this more briefly:

> that we here highly resolve . . .

And now the actual resolution follows, in three parts of growing intensity:

> that these dead shall not have died in vain
> that this nation, under God, shall have a new birth of freedom

and that (one more tricolon)

> government of the people
>   by the people
>   and   for the people
> shall not perish from the earth.

Now, the tricolon is the figure which, through division, emphasizes basic harmony and unity. Lincoln used antithesis because he was speaking to a people at war. He used the tricolon because he was hoping, planning, praying for peace.

No one thinks that when he was drafting the Gettysburg Address, Lincoln deliberately looked up these quotations and consciously chose these particular patterns of thought. No, he chose the theme. From its development and from the emotional tone of the entire occasion, all the rest followed, or grew—by that marvelous process of choice and rejection which is essential to artistic creation. It does not spoil such a work of art to analyze it as closely as we have done; it is altogether fitting and proper that we should do this: for it helps us to penetrate more deeply into the rich meaning of the Gettysburg Address, and it allows us the very rare privilege of watching the workings of a great man's mind.

MEANING

1. Why was the Battle of Gettysburg important enough to warrant a presidential address?
2. What three principles of rhetorical organization did Lincoln utilize in creating the Gettysburg Address?
3. How do metaphors of "birth" and "death" contribute to the strength and eloquence of the Gettysburg Address?

USING CLASSIFICATION TO CONVEY MEANING

1. What evidence does Highet give of Lincoln's care in drafting the speech for this particular occasion?
2. How does the anecdote Highet quotes correct the popular impression that Lincoln lacked a sense of humor?
3. Where does Lincoln draw upon the language and rhythm of the Bible to give his speech a sense of solemnity and importance?
4. How does Lincoln's use of different types of rhetorical figures show that he was more sophisticated than previously thought?
5. What documentary evidence does Highet draw upon to illustrate his assertion that Lincoln became aware that he had given a great speech?

WRITING SUGGESTIONS

1. Pick out one sentence from the Gettysburg Address and diagram it to illustrate syntactical relationships or Lincoln's use of two types of rhetorical figures—antithesis and tricolon.
2. Analyze any other example of effective public discourse, such as John F. Kennedy's inaugural address or Martin Luther King, Jr.'s "I Have a Dream" (see the Argument and Persuasion" chapter, page 710), and classify the rhetorical strategies employed.

W. E. Barton, *Lincoln at Gettysburg* (Bobbs-Merrill, 1930).

R. P. Basler, "Abraham Lincoln's Rhetoric," *American Literature* 11 (1939–40), 167–82.

L. E. Robinson, *Abraham Lincoln as a Man of Letters* (Chicago, 1918).

POLITICAL AND SOCIAL SCIENCES

Herbert J. Gans

Values in the News

Herbert J. Gans was born in 1927 in Cologne, Germany. Gans became a U.S. citizen in 1945 and received his Ph.D. from the University of Pennsylvania in 1957. He has worked as a sociologist in the Departments of Psychiatry at Massachusetts General Hospital and Harvard Medical School (1957–1958), and has taught at the Institute of Urban Studies, University of Pennsylvania since 1958. Gans' most influential work, Deciding What's News: A Study of CBS Evening News, NBC Nightly News, Newsweek and Time *(1979), is based on his ten-year study of the values, pressures, and standards that shape editorial judgments in the news industry as to what events should or should not be reported as news. In "Values in the News," from* Deciding What's News, *Gans reveals how news is categorized according to the unwritten rules of American journalism.*

Social Order and National Leadership

If one looks at the actors and activities which have dominated the news over the years, it is possible to divide much of what appears on television and in the magazines, particularly as hard news, into two types of stories. One type can be called disorder news, which reports threats to various kinds of order, as well as measures taken to restore order. The second type deals with the routine activities of leading public officials: the day-to-day decisions, policy proposals, and recurring political arguments, as well as the periodic selection of new officials, both through election and appointment. These story types in turn suggest two additional values: the desirability of social order (but as will be seen, of a certain type) and the need for national leadership in maintaining that order.

Disorder and Order

Disorder stories fall into four major categories: natural, technological, social, and moral. Natural disorder news deals with natural disasters, such as floods and earthquakes, as well as industrial accidents which can be ascribed to natural forces, such as many but not all plane crashes or mine cave-ins. Technological disorder concerns accidents which cannot be ascribed to nature. Social disorder news deals with activities which disturb the public peace and may involve violence or the threat of violence against life or physical property; it also includes the deterioration of valued institutions, such as the nuclear two-parent family. Moral disorder news reports transgressions of laws and mores which do not necessarily endanger the social order. . . .

These categories are not used by journalists, nor are they hard and fast. A major fire may first be reported as a natural or technological disaster, but if there is evidence of human failure or arson, it soon becomes a moral disorder story. Similarly, once social disorder ends, the news looks for the responsible parties and identifies agents of moral disorder. Conversely, when high officials are guilty of moral disorder, the news may raise the possibility of resulting social disorder. If people lose faith in their leaders, there is fear that the social fabric may unravel.

Social Disorder News

American news media have always emphasized stories of social disorder, both at home and abroad. Foreign news is, as I suggested in Chapter 1, limited to violent political disorder, but domestic news also keeps track of nonviolent and nonpolitical demonstrations. (Conflict among public officials is reported so matter-of-factly that it is a routine activity story rather than disorder news; the conflict is expected; and because it involves officials rather than ordinary people, it is not treated as a threat to the public peace.)

During the 1960s, domestic social disorder news was dominated by the ghetto disturbances and by anti-war marches, demonstrations, and "trashings." Marches and demonstrations are, from one point of view, protest activities, but the news almost always treated them as potential or actual dangers to the social order. In the beginning, the television cameras focused mainly on bearded and other unusual-looking participants who were, in those days, assumed to threaten the social order by their very appearance. Later, when demonstrations became a conventional strategy, they became particularly newsworthy when reporters noticed trouble.

At first, "trouble" was defined as stone throwing and other physical or verbal violence against the police, or fights between demonstrators and hecklers, often from the American Nazi party. Marches, especially those involving large numbers, were deemed potential threats to the social order because so many people were involved; consequently, trouble was almost inevitable, and if it did not take place, that fact was also newsworthy. "Violence," as well as trouble, was perceived as action against constituted legal authority; and until the 1968 Chicago Democratic Convention, police violence against the demonstrators was viewed as action taken to restore order and was rarely called violence. What the demonstrators described as police brutality was at best shown in passing on television, while day-to-day police brutality in the ghettos was not normally news, perhaps because it was routine.

The turning point in the treatment of anti-war demonstrators came in Chicago when the behavior of the police was reported almost universally as a "police riot." Still, earlier events, and news about them, contributed to the change, for after the ghetto disturbances, police brutality against its residents began to be newsworthy. More important, perhaps, earlier in 1968, most national news media had been persuaded by the Tet offensive that the Vietnam War could or should not be continued. From then on, the news started to see the demonstrators more as protesters, and to pay closer attention to the middle-class, middle-aged, and conventionally dressed young marchers. Eventually, some demonstrations even began to be seen as responses to the moral disorder on the part of the president and his hawkish policy makers.

Disorder news could, of course, be analyzed as valuing disorder, and some critics of the news media have charged that overly liberal journalists have done so to justify the need for political change. Actually, however, domestic disorder stories are, except in unusual circumstances, as much concerned with the restoration of order by public officials as with the occurrence of disorder. For example, the Kerner Commission study of the network television coverage of the 1967 uprisings showed that only about 3 percent of the sequences were devoted to what it called riot actions, 2 percent more to injuries and deaths, and at least 34 percent to what I call order restoration. Although the emphasis on order restoration could be explained by the inability of television to gain immediate camera access to the disorder, the newsmagazines were not hampered by such considerations. Even so, *Newsweek*'s ghetto-disturbance stories, in my 1967 sample, devoted four times as much text to police and army attempts to restore order as to descriptions of the disturbances.

After the disturbances had ended, the concern with order restoration continued, for television documentaries and special sections of the newsmagazines suggested, without condoning participants in the disturbances, that racial segregation and, to a lesser extent, economic inequality, had helped to bring them about, the implication being that government and economic reforms were necessary to prevent their recurrence. On both practical and moral grounds, the news argued for a more altruistic democracy and a more responsible capitalism. By the start of the 1970s, however, the fear of ghetto disorders had disappeared, and so had the pleas for reform, although they returned briefly after the looting that accompanied the 1977 power failure in New York City. This time, the looters were criticized more harshly than in the 1960s because they had taken advantage of the city's disability, were thought to be employed, and were taking luxury goods rather than necessities. Even so, *Time* called once more for reform, in a cover story entitled "The Underclass," although the magazine treated that class more as a racial group than as an economic one.

Another illustration of the value placed on order restoration can be found in the news about events that do not, on the surface, deal with disorder. A television report covering a demonstration outside the White House moments after Richard Nixon made his resignation speech emphasized that the demonstration was quiet and that there were no signs of incipient panic or violence. Likewise, in the hours after John Kennedy's assassination, network anchorpersons and reporters frequently pointed out that the country was not panicking. Later, I learned that they were, in fact, worried about possible panics and immediately looked for stories which would indicate that none were taking place. They also sought to allay panic by reporting that the transition of Lyndon Johnson to the presidency was taking place quickly and in an orderly fashion. For the same reason, the anchorpersons also took pains to dispel a rumor that the Russians were about to take advantage of the president's death to launch a war.

I do not mean to suggest, however, that the fears of a Russian move originated with the journalists; in describing Richard Nixon's inability to govern during his last days in the White House, Woodward and Bernstein suggest that then Secretary of State Henry Kissinger was considering "the possibility that some foreign power would do something foolish." Still, the fears expressed in the news underline the generic concern with order and suggest the extent to which order is thought to depend upon the president, which reflects, among other things, the value placed on his leadership.

Moral Disorder News

The moral disorder story is a hallowed tradition in modern American journalism, prototypically taking the form of exposés based on investigative reporting. Such exposés reveal instances of legal or moral transgression, particularly by public officials and other prestigious individuals who, by reason or virtue of their power and prestige, are not expected to misbehave.

The prime exposé of the 1970s was Watergate. Although defenders of the Nixon Administration have accused the news media of exaggerating the transgressions involved in the events and of blowing up the story in order to drive a president disliked by many journalists out of office, the story was a prototypical exposé, which would have been dealt with in much the same manner had the scandals been committed by a more popular president. Later investigations of CIA and FBI scandals, which implicated Presidents Kennedy and Johnson, were carried out just as energetically. Some observers have also suggested that the news exaggerated Nixon's transgressions by combining individual and often unrelated activities into a single scandal; but exposés are, by their nature, structured to point the finger at a morally disorderly leader, and sometimes, investigative reporting efforts do not see the light of day until a villain is found. Traditionally, exposés have concentrated on politicians or other public officials resorting to nepotism, unethical campaign practices, bribery, and taking money out of the public till, although sometimes, exposés are more institutional, dealing with the failure of public agencies to serve their constituents or clients, or more frequently, with wasting the taxpayers' money.

Nevertheless, the vast majority of moral disorder stories do not involve investigative reporting; often they deal with routine phenomena, such as violent or nonviolent crime or political acts, which are treated as violations of altruistic democracy. Such common practices as logrolling, deals, patronage appointments, or the failure of election candidates to abide by campaign promises are reported in such a way as to indicate that these practices are immoral.

In most moral disorder stories, the values being violated are never made explicit, and that they are being violated is not discussed. Still, the participants in a moral disorder story know they are being identified as transgressors and react accordingly. After an election in New Jersey, supporters of the losing candidate, who was then on trial for bribery and had been accused of conducting a racist campaign, smashed television cameras and attacked reporters. The values in the news, against corruption and for racial integration, had led to campaign stories which the candidate and his supporters felt were responsible for his defeat.

News stories which are announced, or in Erving Goffman's terminology, "framed," as exposés make the search for moral disorder explicit, forcing those identified as transgressors into the difficult position of defending their practices, while at the same time reaffirming the moral values on which the exposé is based. Few people can do so without being defensive, particularly on television documentaries, which are television's primary genre for exposés. Among recent examples are "Migrant," in which fruit-company executives had to react against the documented exploitation of migrant workers; and "The Selling of the Pentagon," in which Defense Department officials had to respond to what the documentary makers considered deviant public-relations practices. If the transgressors refuse to be interviewed, their refusal is also reported and becomes a virtual admission of guilt.

In such instances, the news media become guardians of a moral order; as a result, reporters are generally viewed as representatives of that order, even if they are not looking for moral disorder news. Consequently, when they, and especially television camera crews, arrive on a scene, people begin to perform not only physically for the camera but also morally, denying or eliminating behavior that could be judged as moral disorder. Beatings or tortures of prisoners did not take place in South Vietnam or the American South when cameras were present. Public and private agencies spruce up their physical environment when reporters are expected, just as the Chinese authorities temporarily "opened" their society when American television crews arrived to film life in China during and after President Nixon's visit. Berelson's classic study of the 1945 New York City newspaper strike showed that when the newspapers were not publishing, politicians sometimes ignored the honesty values which are defended in and guarded by the news media.

The Nature of Order in the News

The frequent appearance of disorder stories suggests that order is an important value in the news, but order is a meaningless term unless one specifies what order and whose order is being valued. For one thing, there are different types of order; a society can have violence in the streets and a stable family life at home, or public peace and a high rate of family instability. Also, what order is will be judged differently by different people. To the affluent, the slums will appear orderly as long as there are no disturbances and crime does not spill over into wealthy districts; but for slum dwellers, order cannot exist until exploitation, as well as crime, is eliminated. For the parent generation, adolescent order exists when adolescents abide by parental rules; for the young people, order is also freedom of interference from adults.

What Order in the News? The conception of order in the news varies with each type of disorder. In news about natural disasters, order is defined as the preservation of life and property; despite the concern for nature, flood stories do not often worry about how the flood may harm the river. Among technological disasters, plane crashes are usually more newsworthy than the winter breakdowns of tenement furnaces, even if they result in the same number of deaths. Yet, here as elsewhere, disorder news is affected by whose order is being upset.

Social disorder is generally defined as disorder in the public areas of the society. A protest march in which three people die would be headline national news, whereas a family murder that claimed three victims would be a local story. Disorders in affluent areas of elite institutions are more likely to be reported than their occurrence elsewhere. In the 1960s, the looting of a handful of stores on New York's Fifth Avenue received as much attention as a much larger looting spree taking place in a ghetto that same day. Peaceful demonstrations on college campuses, especially elite ones, are usually more newsworthy than those in factories or prisons. But the major public area is the seat of government; thus, a trouble-free demonstration in front of a city hall or a police station is news, whereas that in front of a store is not.

Still, the most important criterion of worthiness is the target of the demonstration. Ultimately, social disorder is equated with political disorder; similarly, social order is viewed as the absence of violent or potentially violent threats to the authority of public officials, particularly the president. The anti-war demonstrations of the past decade were covered as disorder stories because they were aimed at presidents, and campus protests against government war policies were more often reported than protests against college-administration policies. Likewise, the 1978 coal strike did not become a magazine cover story until it involved the president. Just as low-level public officials and corporate leaders get into the news only when they quarrel with the president, the activities of ordinary people must also touch the Oval Office before they are newsworthy.

Even so, the conception of political order in the news transcends public officials and even the president. Now and then, such officials are themselves treated by the news as potential threats to order, either because they resort to "demagoguery," which may stir up the passions of their followers—as in the case of Governors George Wallace and Lester Maddox—or because they act in ways that may encourage ordinary people to question the legitimacy of authority, and subsequently to ignore the rules which underlie the political order. In the waning days of the Nixon Administration, the news frequently expressed concern about the possibility and consequences of widespread cynicism toward and lack of trust for the presidency (rather than toward the incumbent president); and when Richard Nixon was reported to have underpaid his taxes, there were stories which speculated whether ordinary taxpayers would follow his example.

Beneath the concern for political order lies another, perhaps even deeper concern for social cohesion, which reflects fears that not only the official rules of the political order but also the informal rules of the social order are in danger of being disobeyed. This is apparent in the nonpolitical stories that either become or do not become news. Hippies and college dropouts of the 1960s were newsworthy in part because they rejected the so-called Protestant work ethic; even now, drug use by the young, and its consequences, is in the news more than alcohol use because it signifies a rejection of traditional methods of seeking oblivion or mind expansion. Indeed, the news evaluates the young almost entirely in terms of what adult rules they are in the process of rejecting, be they of dress, decorum, or sexual behavior. Rising divorce rates, falling rates of marriage and fertility, and increasing cohabitation without benefit of clergy, all of which suggest a rejection of the conventional rules of family life, are therefore more frequently in the news than family conflict (other than wife beating and child abuse). Whatever its effect on family life, conflict is not viewed as indicative of the decline of the family. The romanticization of the past as an era in which formal and informal rules *were* obeyed betrays the same fear of contemporary disintegration, and the frequent celebration of past ways in the news may reflect an implicit ideal for the future. As Eric Sevareid put it during the live television coverage of the marriage of Princess Anne of England: "A people needs the past to hold them together."

Moral disorder stories are, in the end, cued to much the same concern for social cohesion, particularly those stories which report violations of the mores rather than the laws. Such stories are based on the premise that the activities of public officials, public agencies, and corporations should derive from the same moral and ethical values that are supposed to apply to personal, familial, and friendship relations. Even if every political reporter knows that politicians cannot operate with the same ideal of honesty as friends, the failure of politicians to do so continues to be news. In fact, insofar as the news conceives of nation and society anthropomorphically, as having a will and as being held together by moral fibers, the social order persists because it is based on moral values, and the violation of these values is thus an invitation to political and social disintegration. In the last analysis, the values underlying social and moral disorder news are the same, although the two types of news differ in subject and object: social disorder news monitors the respect of citizens for authority, while moral disorder stories evaluate whether authority figures respect the rules of the citizenry.

MEANING

1. What important but generally unrecognized principle determines why news reports focus on some kinds of stories and not on others?
2. What characterizes each of the four types of news stories that Gans identifies?
3. How does Gans' analysis answer the perennial question as to why there is so little "good" news reported?
4. What steps do news organizations take to balance stories that report "social disorder" with stories that emphasize the "restoration of order" by public officials.

USING CLASSIFICATION TO CONVEY MEANING

1. Evaluate the effectiveness of the examples Gans provides to illustrate how the media tends to reshape events to fit its own agenda.
2. Explain how the principle of disorder can manifest itself in so many apparently different contexts.
3. How does a story originally reported as one type (e.g., a natural disaster such as a mine explosion) become another type of story in a follow-up report (e.g., a mine explosion caused by lax safety standards)?

WRITING SUGGESTIONS

1. Analyze the news stories in a local or national newspaper, and classify news reports according to whether they deal with natural, technological, social, or moral, disorders.
2. Describe a news story that was first reported in one category (e.g., as a natural disaster) and the followed-up with reports that placed it in another category (e.g., a natural disaster that led to social disorder or a technological foul-up that was discovered to have been caused by political malfeasance).
3. Compare the reporting of the same story in different newspapers to see how the same news is reported differently.

Melford E. Spiro

Kibbutz: Venture in Utopia

Melford E. Spiro was born in 1920 in Cleveland, Ohio and received his Ph.D. from Northwestern University in 1950. After teaching anthropology at the University of Washington in Seattle and the University of Chicago, Spiro, since 1968, has been professor of anthropology at the University of California at San Diego, La Jolla. He was president of the American Ethnological Society (1967–1968). Spiro has done extensive anthropological field work in Burma and Israel, and among the Ojibwa Indians of Wisconsin. His writings include Kibbutz: Venture in Utopia *(1956; revised, 1971), the standard reference work on collective settlements in Israel,* Children of the Kibbutz *(1958),* Context and Meaning in Cultural Anthropology *(1965), and* Burmese Supernaturalism *(1967). "Kibbutz: Venture in Utopia," an excerpt from the 1971 revision of the 1956 work of the same name, contains Spiro's analysis, based on eleven months of field work, of the five principles of moral behavior upon which kibbutz culture is founded.*

The strength of the kibbutz lies in its essential social nature which strives for the complete harmony of the individual and the group in every sphere of life, for the maximum development of each individual . . . and for the constant deepening of human ethical relations.

From a kibbutz statement of principle[1]

To have begun this monograph in the usual fashion, with a description of the natural environment or of the subsistence economy of Kiryat Yedidim, would do violence to the inner meaning of its culture, as the above quotation indicates. Kiryat Yedidim, to be sure, is an agricultural village consisting of men and women who inhabit a common geographic area and who make their living by tilling the soil in a cooperative fashion. But Kiryat Yedidim is also—and primarily—a fellowship of those who share a common faith and who have banded together to implement that faith. To live *in* Kiryat Yedidim means to become a member *of a* kibbutz, and membership in a kibbutz entails more than voting at town meetings, or driving a tractor in the wheat fields, or living in a lovely village. It means, primarily, becoming a *chaver kibbutz* (a comrade of the kibbutz), that is, a person who is dedicated to the social, economic, and national ideals for which the kibbutz stands.[2] These ideals were formulated before Kiryat Yedidim came into being and, indeed, it was founded with the purpose

---

[1] All quotations from official kibbutz and Federation publications and speeches have been translated from their original Hebrew by the author.

[2] A chaver (pl., chaverim) is a kibbutz member. The term, literally, means "companion" or "comrade."

of bringing these ideals into being.[3] Hence, these ideals must be understood, if Kiryat Yedidim is to be understood.

Probably the single most important ideal upon which the entire kibbutz culture is based is what might be termed the moral value of labor. It is no accident, for example, that today, when the entire kibbutz movement is experiencing a profound crisis, it is this principle of *avodah atzmit*, or self-labor, which has become the measure of the devotion of a kibbutz to its original ideals. The founders of Kiryat Yedidim, in many instances, were intellectuals for whom labor was a "calling" rather than a habit. For them, labor was not merely a means for the satisfaction of human needs; rather, labor itself was viewed as a need—probably man's most important need— the satisfaction of which became an end in itself. *Ki ha-avodah hi chayenu* is the way the kibbutz expresses it. "For labor is (the essence of) our life"; and this phrase may be said to be the *leitmotif* of kibbutz living.

This attitude toward labor did not, of course, originate with the vattikim,[4] the founders, of Kiryat Yedidim. Emphasis on labor had long been integral to the *chalutz*, or pioneering, tradition in Zionism. As early as 1882, when one of the first contingents of Russian Jews migrated to Palestine, the ideal of labor on the land was already in process of formulation.[5] As one pioneer put it:

> Farmer! Be a free man among men, but a slave to the soil . . . Kneel and bow down to it every day. Nurse its furrows—and then even its stony clods will yield a blessing! And in this "slavery" remember that you are a tiller of the soil! A tiller of the soil in Palestine! This must become a badge of honor among our people.[6]

But the most important influence came from the pioneers of the Second Aliya (1904–1914) and, specifically, from the seer of the Palestinian labor movement, A. D. Gordon (1856–1922). It was Gordon who invented the term, *dat ha-avodah*, "the religion of labor." For him labor was a uniquely creative act, as well as an

---

[3] In *Cooperative Living in Palestine*, Infield writes that the kibbutz "unlike the utopian communities, did not originate in a deliberate attempt to mold a new form of social organization on the foundation of a preconceived theory. It came into being, rather, in much the same way as any other normal community. Basically, what shaped its character was the necessity for adaptation to the unusual conditions obtaining in Palestine. Hence, the peculiar social structure was necessary to ensure survival." (p. 25.) Although this statement may characterize the earliest kibbutzim, it does not apply to Kiryat Yedidim or to most of the other kibbutzim that were founded by members of the various European Zionist youth movements. In the case of Kiryat Yedidim, as we shall see, its ideals, and the social structure which was evolved to implement these ideals, took shape much before it was founded.

[4] A *vattik* (pl., vattikim), is, literally, a "veteran." This term is used in Israel to refer to the early pioneers and settlers. In the kibbutz it refers to the founders of the kibbutz in contrast to those who joined it at a later date.

[5] Palestinian immigration history, since the beginnings of the Zionist movement, is conventionally divided into a series of successive waves of immigration. The first wave, known as the "First Aliya" (1882–1904), consisted for the most part of gentlemen-farmers who settled in villages and managed their plantations which were worked by hired Arab labor. Only a small number professed the ideal of labor, but the germ of this ideal is to be found as early as this Aliya, as the quotation indicates. The ideal of labor and the various labor institutions were forged, however, by the "Second Aliya" (1904–1914) and by the "Third Aliya" (1919–1924). The founders of Kiryat Yedidim were early participants in the latter wave of immigration. See Lotta Levensohn, *Outline of Zionist History*.

[6] Kutland, p. 7.

ultimate value. Through labor, he taught, man became one with himself, society, and nature. But, he warned, it would not be easy:

> A people that has become accustomed to every mode of life save the natural one—the life of self-conscious and self-supporting labor—such a people will never become a living, natural laboring people unless it strain every fibre of its will to attain that goal. Labor is not merely the factor which establishes man's contact with the land and his claim to the land; it is also the principle force in the building of a national civilization. Labor is a great human ideal for the future, and a great ideal is like the healing sun. We need fanatics of labor in the most exalted sense of the word.[7]

Gordon's "religion of labor" not only influenced his own generation of Zionist pioneers, but it served to shape the subsequent history of Jewish labor enterprise in Palestine. Hence, the stress in Kiryat Yedidim on labor as a "calling" is an ideal which it shares, not only with other collective and cooperative settlements, but with the entire labor movement in Israel.

This attitude to labor is particularly significant and, in a profoundly psychological sense, explicable only in view of the *petit bourgeois* backgrounds of the vattikim. Before their immigration to Israel, they had not engaged in physical labor; moreover, they were reared in a culture that demeaned labor, as well as the laborer. The persons who were looked down upon in the *shtetl*, the Eastern European villages in which the vattikim were born, were the *proste*. *Prost* is the Yiddish equivalent of "crude" or "vulgar," and the attitude towards unskilled workers on the part of the shtetl is revealed most clearly in its appellation of these workers as the proste. In the shtetl:

> It is better . . . to be a salesman than to be an artisan. A salesman works with his brain, an artisan merely with his brawn.
>
> For a man who "comes from yikhus" (a respected family) to engage in manual labor, even under stress of economic necessity, is a calamity for manual labor has come to symbolize the antithesis of the social ideal—a life devoted entirely to study.[8]

Hence, the ideal of work as an ultimate value—the dat ha-avodah—represents, in the case of the vattikim, a cultural revolution; to achieve it they had to overcome the resistance of both their trained values and their untrained muscles. It is little wonder that one of their first goals was *kibbush ha-avodah*, "the conquest of labor."[9]

Kiryat Yedidim, then, is not a worker's community in the same sense that many of the utopian societies of nineteenth-century America were. This is a community which was founded, for the most part, by middle-class intellectuals who deliberately chose to be workers; by so choosing, they reversed both the traditional prestige hierarchy and the historical aspiration of upward mobility. Instead of aspiring to "rise" in the social ladder, they aspired to "descend." For the chaverim, then, it is not business (as in European bourgeois culture) or scholarship (as in the shtetl culture), but

---

[7] *Ibid.*, p. 9.

[8] Zhotowaski and Herzog, p. 247.

[9] Kibbush ha-avodah had another meaning, in addition to the one attributed to it here. In the early days of Second Aliya, when Jewish landowners preferred to employ cheap Arab labor, a major aim of the Jewish labor movement was to gain a foothold in those sectors of the economy which were closed to them. And this was another sense in which the "conquest of labor" was used.

labor which is the highest vocational goal. This goal, it must be stressed, is primarily a spiritual goal—it is a means to self-realization. As the chalutz folk-song has it: "To Palestine we have come, to build and to be built in it (the land)." This Tolstoyan attitude toward work could be evolved, it is not hazardous to say, only by romantic, urban intellectuals.

The "moral value of labor" stresses not only the latter aspect of the principle of avodah atzmit, self-*labor;* the former aspect, which emphasizes *self*-labor, is equally important. This general principle of the labor movement, when applied to the kibbutz, means that no one may be employed from the outside to work in the kibbutz, and that all work must be performed by the members of the kibbutz. Exceptions might be made in certain kinds of labor for which chaverim may have had no training, such as house construction or language instruction in the high school, but no exception may be made in the case of other kinds of labor, no matter how difficult or repulsive they might be. The opposition to hired labor is based on three ethical considerations. First, there is the *mystique* of labor—already hinted at—which stresses the dignity and creativeness of labor and the need to strike roots in the soil. Then, there is the fear, which first arose when the Arabs were the majority group in Palestine, that the introduction of hired labor would open the way to the employment of cheap Arab *fellah* labor. If this happened, it was thought, the kibbutz would eventually become a plantation, worked by Arab labor for the benefit of (what would then become) the leisure class kibbutz owners. The socialist ideology of Kiryat Yedidim, with its abhorrence of "surplus value" and its notion that all wage labor entails exploitation, is the third ethical opposition to hired labor and the insistence on self-labor.[10]

The chaverim, in short, constitute a class conscious proletariat, *par excellence;* and it is not surprising that one's prestige in Kiryat Yedidim is determined primarily by excellence in and devotion to one's work.

[10] The opposition to hired labor has created many tensions for Kiryat Yedidim, in both its intra- and extra-kibbutz relations. With the great movement of mass immigration into the country, the government of Israel has been hard pressed to find employment for the immigrants (the majority of whom do not wish to become members of kibbutzim), and has appealed to the kibbutzim to hire them. The refusal of many of the kibbutzim to comply with this request has created considerable resentment against them, and has led to charges of "anti-Zionism" and "irresponsibility." Nevertheless, the Federation has remained firm in its opposition to the use of hired labor, insisting that the entire structure of the kibbutz would change as a result of this innovation; for the members of the kibbutz would then become a "leisure class" of experts and managers, who would supervise the work of others. This prediction has been confirmed in the case of those kibbutzim—members of the other two federations—who have adopted the policy of hiring workers.

But the use of hired labor would solve not only a governmental problem; it would solve an equally pressing kibbutz problem. The most acute economic problem of Kiryat Yedidim, for example, is a shortage of manpower. As its services have expanded, women have been removed from the agricultural branches of the economy, resulting in a critical labor shortage. The obvious solution to this problem is the hiring of workers, and there are some chaverim who openly advocate this solution. Thus far, the economy has not suffered too much, because of temporary solutions to the problem: (1) the drafting of high school students for special assignments, such as a special grapefruit or potato harvest; (2) the suspension of a sabbath for some special task that must be done immediately, and the drafting of the entire kibbutz for the job; (3) the work performed by the youth groups living in the kibbutz, as well as that performed by various training groups which are sent to the kibbutzim to work. If this third source of labor were to dry up, the kibbutz would have little alternative but to hire labor or to devise some compromise solution.

Not all work, however, is equally valued. Physical labor enjoys the greatest prestige. The further removed it is from physical labor, the less prestige a job confers. This means, of course, that pure intellectual work does not confer great prestige, despite the fact that Kiryat Yedidim is a highly cultured community, one which is devoted to intellectual and artistic experience. Of the various categories of physical labor, agricultural labor is valued the most. Even among the agricultural branches, however, differential stereotypes have arisen. Those who work in the orchards and vineyards are thought to be intellectual, easygoing people, who are not particularly energetic. Shepherds are supposedly romantic, and inclined to be a bit lazy. On the other hand, the *falachim,* those who work in the grain fields, are presumably hard, energetic workers. They enjoy a national reputation, moreover, for the stereotype has it that the falachim of the past have become the country's leaders, and have built the important labor institutions. It is difficult to assess the relative physical difficulty of these various occupations. It is probably true that, in many respects, the falach has the hardest job, and there are certain periods—such as the harvest, when the combines work almost twenty-four hours a day—which demand almost superhuman effort. But there is another, and probably more cogent, reason for his prestige which has little to do with the difficulty of his work. The kibbutz, as will be noted in the discussion of economic organization, distinguishes between "productive" work and "services." The former enjoys the greater prestige, and (or, perhaps, because) it yields a cash income. Hence, *falcha*—cereal crops—is the most important agricultural branch in the kibbutz economy, for it normally yields the highest economic return. The economic importance of the branch has been generalized to the social importance of the person who works in that branch.

The importance attached to work is in constant evidence in Kiryat Yedidim and almost everyone responds to it. Work has become almost a compulsive habit, so that absence from work, even for good cause, elicits feelings of guilt. For three months, for example, the author had been working in the fields with a chavera whose work was characterized by drive and great energy, and who seldom took a break. He was amazed to discover somewhat later that this labor was tortuous to her; she could not tolerate the heat, and she suffered constant pains in her arms and hands. Again, a chavera of the kibbutz donated one day a week to work in an immigrants' camp. She became quite ill, and was ordered to bed by the doctor. She complained, however, that she must return to her work, and when she heard that there was no one to take her place in the camp, she insisted on rising from her sickbed and returning to the camp. It is interesting to note in this connection that, according to the kibbutz nurse, there are no cases of malingering or of "gold-bricking." How compelling this drive for work can become, even for an outsider, is illustrated by an experience of the author. It was mutually decided that he would pay for his expenses by working half a day and by paying the kibbutz for the other half-day. Toward the end of the study, it became apparent that it would be impossible to complete his projected research aims, unless he had more free time for his research. He obtained permission from the Secretariat to work only one-quarter time for two months and to make up the difference in cash payment. As soon as he started his quarter-time schedule, however, the author realized that he would accomplish little work. His own guilt feelings were too great. No one mentioned the fact that he was not working regular hours, and probably few knew of it; nevertheless, he felt that he was shirking his responsibility. He stayed away from public places during the day, trying to avoid the chaverim. The influence of this dominant attitude is so great, that a complete stranger becomes acculturated to it within a few months.[11]

Since labor is of such great importance, it follows that the individual who shirks his work responsibilities, or who is inefficient in his work, does not enjoy the respect of his fellows. Regardless of his other talents, the *batlan*, or the lazy person, occupies the position of lowest prestige in the prestige hierarchy of Kiryat Yedidim.

A second moral principle of kibbutz culture is that the property used and produced by the entire community rightfully belongs to the entire community. Hence, the economy rests on the public ownership of property. The land inhabited and worked by the kibbutz is not owned by any individual or by any family, nor even by the kibbutz itself. It is owned, rather, by the entire nation, having been acquired by a national agency, the *Keren Kayemet* (Jewish National Fund), by funds raised through voluntary contributions. The Keren Kayemet rents the land to the kibbutz on a ninety-nine year renewable lease, for which the latter pays an annual rent (starting only after its fifth year) of 2 percent of the original cost of the land, plus improvements. National ownership of land is an ethical imperative, it is believed, because it precludes such "evils" as land speculation, absentee ownership, and "unearned" income through rent. Moreover, it prevents the rise of a society composed of a landed gentry and a disinherited peasantry.

Although its land is owned by the nation, all other property in Kiryat Yedidim is owned collectively by the members of the kibbutz. Ideally, the individual owns nothing with the exception of small personal gifts and those personal effects which he may buy with his annual "vacation allowance" of nine Israeli pounds (approximately nine dollars). Hence, the house in which he lives, the trucks and tractors he operates, the cattle he cares for, the clothes he wears, and the food he eats are owned by the kibbutz. Since private property has been abolished, the individual receives no wages for his work; since he lives in a house owned by the kibbutz, he pays no rent; and since he eats in the kibbutz dining room, he has no food bills. Moreover, he receives his clothes, like everyone else, from the kibbutz clothing room; smaller articles, like combs, toothbrushes, etc., he obtains at the kibbutz "store." Should he be ill, his medical and hospital bills are taken care of by the kibbutz. In short, the individual has no money, nor does he need any, because his economic needs are satisfied by the kibbutz.

The principle of public ownership derives, of course, from the emphasis placed on the moral value of equality. Private property, it is felt, together with the profit motive and the competitiveness that accompany it, destroy the bonds of brotherhood. The kibbutz insists that only in the absence of private property is it possible to establish an economic system in which economic classes and economic inequalities are abolished and, consequently, in which greater brotherhood can be achieved.

Communal ownership, then, is related to another moral principle underlying kibbutz culture: the principle of social and economic *equality*. In the event that Kiryat Yedidim

---

[11] The author's personality must, of course, be taken into account here. But these reactions are particularly significant by contrast with his experience on another field trip. In a study of a Micronesian culture— also highly cooperative—the author spent full time at research, and though the people furnished him with food and other necessities, he did not pay them, nor did he work in the economy. It nevertheless did not occur to him to feel guilty, since leisure is important and labor is at a minimum in this society.

does not have enough goods or services to supply all its members equally, distribution is regulated according to seniority of arrival in the country. For example, the new housing development, consisting of two-room, instead of the usual one-room apartments, is open only to those persons who have been in the country for at least thirty years. Except for such special cases, however, economic distribution is formally equal. In the distribution of clothes, for example, all women receive one good dress every two years, and a plain dress on alternate years. Men receive three pairs of *shabbat* (sabbath) pants and four shirts every year.[12]

In the past the emphasis on formal economic equality was taken much more literally than it is today. Clothes, for example, were not marked in the laundry, on the principle that all clothes were publicly owned. Hence, a person did not receive from the laundry the same clean clothes that he had previously worn. Instead, he was given the first pair of pants, dress, or socks that happened to be on top of the laundry pile. This, of course, created highly ludicrous situations, such as tall persons having to wear short pants, or slender persons being forced to wear large dresses. This system, known as *kommuna alef* (first commune), was soon modified at the insistence of the women, who demanded that they be fitted for dresses. The sizes of the clothes were marked, so that a chaver, when he came for his weekly laundry, would not necessarily receive the same clothes he had worn the week before, but he would, at least, receive his own size.

In the middle 1930's *kommuna bet* (second commune) was instituted. It was becoming apparent that the chaverim were not entirely careful with the clothes they wore, and there was a high percentage of torn and soiled clothes. It was felt that if the clothes were marked, and if each chaver were to receive the same clothes from the laundry, he could then be held responsible for their care. This is the system that is still in operation. All clothing, like everything else, is technically owned by the kibbutz. But each chaver receives his clothing allowance for the year, and the clothes he receives are "his," in the sense that they are marked with his name, he wears them, and he is responsible for them.[13]

Despite this formal equality in the basic necessities, certain inequalities in luxuries have arisen due to conditions not provided for in the formal structure of the kibbutz. Some people receive presents of food, clothing, furniture, etc., from relatives who do not reside in Kiryat Yedidim, while others do not. Some individuals, moreover, work outside the kibbutz during their vacations, and purchase what they please with the money they earn. Some have relatives or friends outside the kibbutz with whom they can stay when they go to the cities, which enables them to save from their annual "vacation money" what others must pay in hotel and restaurant bills. This saving enables them to purchase small personal objects. As a result of all these factors, the complete economic equality that once characterized the kibbutz has been slightly qualified.

It may be stated as a general rule, however, that all individuals receive the same clothing allotment, eat the same food in the communal dining room, and enjoy the same (approximately) housing conditions, regardless of their economic skill, their economic importance to the kibbutz, their prestige, or their power. For, despite its awareness that persons differ greatly in ability or in skill—though it seems that it

---

[12] Dress clothes are called shabbat clothes, which, when they become worn, are used as work clothes.

[13] It is of interest to note that the negligence that was discovered in the care of clothing under kommuna *alef* was not discovered in the care of land, houses, or other capital goods.

denied it, or at least ignored it, in its early history—the kibbutz insists that such differences should not be used as a basis for differences in privileges. All individuals have an equal right to the good things of the community, although they do not contribute to it equally.

This observation serves to remind us that the equality principle of kibbutz culture is qualified by another ethical consideration—that of need. The kibbutz believes in the principle of "from each according to his ability, to each according to his need," a principle, which conflicts at times with its principle of equality. In resolving this conflict, it is usually the "need," rather than the equality, that prevails. A field hand, whose relative productivity is great, eats the common austerity fare of the dining room,[14] though he has worked strenuously in the hot Israeli sun; but an office worker (of low prestige in the kibbutz value hierarchy), whose productivity is low, may receive a special diet, comparatively sumptuous, because of some physical condition. A man with children works no harder than a man without children; but the kibbutz provides not only for his wants, but also for the care of his children. In effect, those with no children, or with few children, subsidize those who do have children.

Not so obvious upon first arrival in Kiryat Yedidim, but just as important for an understanding of kibbutz culture, is the social equality which exists, and of which one becomes acutely aware whenever he leaves the kibbutz for even a short time. There is no class structure in Kiryat Yedidim, and there is no differential reward system for different kinds of labor based on some ranking technique. Some kinds of work, as has already been observed, are valued more highly than others; but those who occupy the more highly valued jobs receive no greater reward than the others. The important psychological fact about kibbutz culture is that everyone, regardless of his work, is viewed as a worker, with the same privileges and responsibilities as anyone else. Menial work, which in capitalist society might mark one as a social inferior, does not carry that stigma in Kiryat Yedidim. The general manager—the highest elective officer in the kibbutz—is not the social superior of the cleaner of the latrines. Hence, there is no work which a person is ashamed to accept because it would demean him socially. There is, thus, little if any subordination of one group of individuals to another; there is no polarization of society into those who command and those who obey, those who are respected and those who respect. There is no need for some to be subservient before others, or to be "nice" to them, for fear of losing their jobs. In short, many of the social inequalities existing in a stratified society do not exist in Kiryat Yedidim.[15]

This achievement can be illustrated by two examples. The recently arrived European physician, not a member of the kibbutz, asked one of the women for the name of the "maid" in the clinic. She did not understand to whom he was referring until he explained that he meant the woman who regularly cleaned the clinic. The woman then explained to him that there were no "maids" in Kiryat Yedidim, that this woman would probably be sitting next to him at dinner that evening, and, moreover, that this "maid" was an important official in the kibbutz. While making a survey of the various types of kibbutzim, we arrived at a certain kibbutz in order to interview a

[14] Because of the mass immigration to Israel that accompanied the founding of the State, food was scarce before and during the period of this study. Hence the scarcity that characterized Kiryat Yedidim was a national, rather than a kibbutz, phenomenon. The author has been informed that the national, and presumably the kibbutz, situation has been considerably improved since that period.

[15] Those kibbutzim that have introduced industry into their economy have, thereby, made possible the rise of a class system. See Rosenfeld, pp. 766–774.

member of the Israeli Parliament. We were told, on our arrival, that he was to be found in the cemetery—for his job, when Parliament was not in session, consisted in caring for the graveyard. He came to greet us in his work clothes and kindly consented to grant us an interview in the meadow, for his wife, who worked nights in the dairy, was sleeping in their room.

It should be emphasized that the absence of social classes as conventionally conceived, does not imply the absence of either some type of ranking system in Kiryat Yedidim or of "horizontal" social groupings. The kibbutz is *not* a homogeneous concentration of persons, all of whom enjoy equal prestige and power, and each of whom interacts with all others with equal frequency. On the contrary, differential prestige and power as well as social cliques are to be found in Kiryat Yedidim; and it may be well to delineate their broad outlines at the very beginning.

Although the various kibbutz offices are held on a temporary and a rotation basis, those who happen to hold these offices do enjoy considerable power. Moreover, as is noted below, though the tenure of office is limited to two or three years, only a small number of chaverim possess the necessary skills required to cope with the complexities of such offices as general manager, secretary, treasurer, etc., so that in effect these offices rotate among a small core of twelve to fifteen persons.[16] Hence, power within the kibbutz is not equally distributed; it is, rather, concentrated within this small core. It should nevertheless be emphasized that those who occupy these offices enjoy no special privileges and receive no material rewards.[17] Their power, moreover, is limited by the fact that major decisions are made, not by them, but by the town meeting; and that they are under the constant surveillance of the town meeting, and subject to its power of recall. At the same time this core is not a united group, but is comprised of individuals and of sub-groups who disagree, and are often in conflict, with each other. Finally, this is neither a closed nor a self-appointed group. Rather, it is a group whose members are elected by the kibbutz on the basis of ability and demonstrated performance, and one which is always open to recruits chosen by the town meeting should it deem them capable of holding office.

Many of these same considerations apply to those who enjoy prestige. With one possible exception, prestige in Kiryat Yedidim is a function of achieved, rather than of ascribed, status; and the persons of prestige constitute a social category rather than a social group. Prestige is achieved by being a productive and devoted worker, by implementing kibbutz ideals in one's daily life, by being a "synthetic personality,"[18] and by being a vattik, a founder of the kibbutz. The first three qualifications are, of course, attained only through achievement and they are open to all. The fourth, though not open to present achievement, was attained through past achievement. Moreover, it is not sufficient merely to *be* a vattik; to merit prestige, the vattik must constantly validate his status by his daily behavior rather than by resting on the glories of his past. Nor, it should be noted, is the prestige of the vattikim inherited by their children. The latter must achieve their own prestige through the same avenues that are open to children of other chaverim, and the status of their parents confers upon them no competitive advantage.

[16] For a discussion of these offices and of the problem of tenure, see below pp. 78–83, 94–96.
[17] See below, pp. 96–97.
[18] See below, p. 153.

But Kiryat Yedidim is not only stratified by power and prestige. It may be subdivided into "horizontal" groups, as well; that is, into friendship groups or cliques, based on at least four factors: age, occupation, residential contiguity, and interests. Usually these criteria overlap, for friendship groups—as measured by social visiting in the evening—usually consist of individuals of the same generation; the latter, in turn, usually share the same interests; and, as a result of the kibbutz system of distributing housing,[19] they usually live in the same living area. The kibbutz itself recognizes what it calls, four age "layers," and it is rare that a clique consists of individuals from overlapping "layers." Not all members of the same layer, however, comprise a single clique. Within the layers cliques are formed on the basis of common interests—intellectual, political, discontent, etc.

This combination of age and residential contiguity does not account for all cliques, for it is sometimes overruled by occupational interests and by power position. Those who comprise the small core which holds power are not necessarily a friendship group, but they are, nevertheless, characterized by a high frequency of interaction, since it is they who must meet—frequently over a cup of tea in the evening—to solve the many problems that are constantly arising in the kibbutz; and they are not always of the same generation, nor do they live in spatial proximity.

Similarly, workers in some economic branches—the shepherds, for example—establish a strong *esprit de corps* which may carry over to their non-working hours. Hence, though not of the same generation and though they do not share a common living area, they constitute a clique based on personal friendship which had its origin in a common occupational interest. It should be noted, moreover, that to the extent that some economic branches are unisexual in character—as the shepherds—membership in the cliques is also unisexual, so that sex becomes a criterion for social grouping.

Another principle underlying the culture of Kiryat Yedidim is that of individual liberty; indeed, the kibbutz prides itself on being the freest society in the world. In the early history of Kiryat Yedidim, emphasis on freedom meant primarily freedom from the "artificial conventions" of an urban civilization. Once it was settled on its own land, however, and the necessity for some kind of social organization and authority arose, this earlier notion of freedom was expanded to include opposition to any system of authority. The kibbutz, it was assumed, was an "organic community," and its work would somehow get accomplished without the necessity of investing any individual or individuals with power over their fellows. Hence, Kiryat Yedidim had no officers, and all decisions were made in informal group discussions that included neither a chairman nor an agenda. As it grew larger, however, and as its economy expanded, it became evident that some kind of formal organization was required and that it was necessary to delegate power. But in order to prevent any individual from acquiring personal power and/or to prevent the rise of an entrenched bureaucracy, it was decided that all offices—from the most menial to that of the general manager—should be held for a maximum of two or three years. This tenure limitation, it was hoped, would lead to a rotation of individuals in the various power

[19] Housing in Kiryat Yedidim expands by the addition of whole new developments, rather than by the addition of single units. Since the new developments usually represent considerable improvements over their predecessors, they are allocated according to a priority system, usually based on seniority. The vattikim, for example, are now living in the newly constructed housing project while their married children are living—on the other side of the village—in the wooden houses which have been successively occupied by the vattikim, by a later group of settlers, and now by the adult children.

positions, and would, therefore, ensure the maximum liberty of the kibbutz members.

This emphasis on freedom, it should be noted, is manifested not only in its formal structure, but in its freedom of expression as well. Any curtailment of freedom of speech or of reading is abhorrent to its members, and no censorship of any kind exists.

Finally, a discussion of the moral postulates of this culture must include the principle which might be termed the moral value of the group. The group, in kibbutz culture, is not only a means to the happiness of the individual; the group and group processes are moral ends in their own right. This has three aspects. It means, first, that the interests of the individual must be subordinate to the interests of the group. When the needs of the individual and those of the group come into conflict, the individual is expected to abdicate his needs in favor of the group's. This applies to vocational interests, as well as ideological convictions. A person's vocational preferences are usually considered in deciding his work assignment; but if the kibbutz requires his labor or skill in some special branch, he is expected to recognize the paramount needs of the group. The same logic applies to ideological matters. An individual is permitted complete freedom in the process of arriving at political decisions and in attempting to convince others of his point of view. But once a formal decision is reached by the kibbutz, he is expected to acquiesce in its decision and to support it, however much it conflicts with his personal views.[20]

A second aspect of the emphasis on the ethical value of the group involves the assumption that the individual's motivations will always be directed to the promotion of the group's interests, as well as of his own. Behavior is expected to be characterized by *ezra hadadit*, or mutual aid. This means that every member of the kibbutz is responsible for the welfare of every other member and for the welfare of the kibbutz as a whole, just as the kibbutz is responsible for the welfare of each individual. The consequence of this principle is that no one is to suffer for lack of medical care, education for his children, food, shelter, clothing, or any other need, as long as the kibbutz can provide him with these requirements.

The emphasis on the moral value of the group means, finally, that group living and group experiences are valued more lightly than their individual counterparts. Indeed, so important is the value of group experience that those chaverim who seek a great degree of privacy are viewed as "queer." The kibbutz is interested in creating a *chevra*. The ultimate criterion of either a good kibbutz, a good high school, or a good kindergarten, is whether or not it has become a chevra. The term, chevra, literally, denotes a society; but its connotation—and its meaning for Kiryat Yedidim— is a group which is characterized by intimacy of interaction, and by mutual concern, if not by love. A chevra, in short, is a *gemeinschaft* or, to use their term, an "organic community." It is apparent, therefore, that the individualist, the person who cherishes his own privacy more than a group experience, constitutes a threat to the group. His desire for privacy either prevents the group from becoming a chevra, or symbolizes the fact that it is not a chevra, for if it were, he would prefer to be with the group than to be alone.[21]

---

[20] This entire paragraph serves to indicate that the individual's freedom is restricted in many ways, despite the kibbutz emphasis of liberty.

[21] The belief in the primacy of the group has many ramifications. In the realm of art, for example, a teacher criticized *Tobacco Road* because it is "pornographic," and because it represents the feeling of the author alone, and not of the group. A chaver criticized the novel, *Young Hearts*, because it is "not

In this respect, the kibbutz shows its kinship with the shtetl. The following description of the shtetl applies, without qualification, to Kiryat Yedidim.

> To insist on privacy if you are not sinning is a serious misdemeanor . . . One of the worst things you can say of a man is, "he keeps it for himself" or "he hides it from others" whether "it" is money or wisdom, clothes or news.
>
> Locked doors, isolation, avoidance of community control, arouse suspicion . . . "Home people," *heymisheh mentschen* . . . are free to come in whenever they like at any time of the day . . .
>
> Withdrawal is felt as attack, whether physical or psychological, and isolation is intolerable. "Life is with people". . .
>
> Everywhere people cluster to talk, at home, in the market place, on the street. Everyone wants to pick up the latest news, the newest gossip . . .
>
> The freedom to observe and to pass judgment on one's fellows, the need to communicate and share events and emotions is inseparable from a strong feeling that individuals are responsible to and for each other.[22]

These moral postulates constitute the social ethics of Kiryat Yedidim and represent, for them, the basic tenets of socialism. But socialism is only one of the twin principles on which kibbutz culture rests; the other principle is Zionism. For Kiryat Yedidim, the kibbutz is not only a means to social and personal liberation, it is a means to national liberation, as well. Socialism, as defined by the tenets described in this chapter, represents the universalistic principle of kibbutz culture; Zionism represents its particularistic, Jewish principle. It is no accident, therefore, that Kiryat Yedidim was founded in Palestine rather than in Eastern Europe, the birthplace of the founders.

The Zionist convictions of Kiryat Yedidim which, for the most part, they share with the entire Zionist movement, may be simply stated. The Jews constitute a Nation, however dispersed they may have been in the last 1900 years of their history, and however lacking they may have been in the external *accoutrement* of nationhood. Every Nation has not only a right, but a duty to survive and to perpetuate its national

---

true." When the writer protested that the author may have presented the "truth" as he saw it, he retorted, "Literature must express the feeling of the entire group, and not of one individual, or it is not literature." A kibbutz intellectual criticized Chagall as being "unrealistic," in the sense that he evades the important social problems and becomes absorbed in his *private* fantasies.

Moreover, this emphasis on the group explains why The Federation is entirely opposed to what it calls, "careerism." In speeches and articles attempting to encourage the city youth to join the kibbutz movement, opposition to the pursuit of a personal career is a constant theme. In the present world, with its oppressions and inequities, it is argued it is indecent to pursue a personal career, to seek one's personal pleasure, or to satisfy selfish ambition. The morally sensitive person eschews personal ambition and a desire for a better personal life in order to work for a better world.

This emphasis on the group and its welfare, moreover, probably accounts for the almost complete absence of concern with psychiatric values in the kibbutz. At no time during this study did the writer hear any conversation dealing with such topics as "peace of mind," "personality adjustment," "freedom from anxiety," and the host of other psychological concerns that are endemic in contemporary American culture. At times, one hears talk concerning an individual's lack of integration into the kibbutz, a problem which is of serious concern to the chaverim; but one seldom hears discussions of intra-personal adjustment. The elimination of *social* conflicts and of *international* tensions, and the achievement of *world* peace—these are the goals to be achieved, not their individual counterparts.

[22] Zhorowski and Herzog, pp. 225–227.

culture. The physical survival of the Jewish Nation is under a constant threat as long as the Jews remain a national minority living among other political Nations. Only in their own "historical homeland" is it possible for them to escape antisemitism and to escape their anomalous minority status. But this minority status has not only made the Jews an easy target for antisemitism, it has distorted their psychological and cultural complexion. Being deprived of numerous channels for economic activity, the Jews have been forced into a narrow range of economic outlets—they have become "middlemen." Middlemen are not only economic parasites, but they become distorted by the very nature of their work. They have no appreciation for nature and, hence, strike no roots in the soil; they have no understanding of the essential dignity and creativity of physical labor; they develop a sterile intellectualism, a scholasticism which has no basis in real life.

Zionism can change all these characteristics. By living in their own "homeland," Jews are no longer economic parasites, for they are not only middlemen, but they also work the land and run the factories. Having "normalized," that is, broadened, their economic base to include the entire range of economic activities, the cultural and intellectual life of the Jews will become "normalized" as well, since it will have its roots in the creative life of the people. And this economic and cultural normalization, in conjunction with its national normalization—escape from a minority status and, hence, from antisemitism—will enable the Jews to take their rightful and normal place among the nations of the world. In short, Zionism, for Kiryat Yedidim, although a particularistic movement, has as its ultimate aim a universalistic and humanistic goal. This goal is not the geographic segregation of Jews, with the intention of developing specific Jewish characteristics that will separate the Jews from the non-Jewish world. Its aim, rather, is the concentration of Jews in their homeland so that they may develop a "normal" national life which, in turn, will enable them to interact with the rest of the world as normal human beings, rather than as members of a dependent, parasitic, fearful minority. For Kiryat Yedidim, then, national liberation is not only as important as social and personal liberation, it is a necessary condition for their existence.

This is not to say, however, that its conception of Zionism does not contain much of the ethnocentrism that characterizes other nationalist philosophies. Like other Israelis, the chaverim polarize their world into *Aretz,* whose literal meaning is "country," but which is used to refer to *the* country, Israel; and *chutz la-aretz,* which refers to the rest of the world (literally, "outside the country"). So, too, they polarize the peoples of the world into *Yehudim,* a term which includes Israeli and non-Israeli Jews alike, and *Goyim* (literally, nations), the rest of mankind. This distinction is rhetorical, inherited from an epoch in which the world was polarized into friend (Jews) and foe (the rest of mankind). Nevertheless, it does not take long for one to realize that this rhetoric expresses an important contemporary psychological attitude. The ethnocentrism of the chaverim is expressed, moreover, in their insistence that all Jews ought to settle in Israel, and in their expressed amazement that any Jew who has visited Israel should want to return to his native country.

The Zionist philosophy of Kiryat Yedidim serves to explain some of its important characteristics and behavior. Its emphasis on physical labor and its choice of rural, rather than urban living, stems not only from its general social philosophy, but from its Zionist convictions: the "normalization" of Jewish national life requires that Jews return to physical labor and that they strike roots in the soil. Moreover, the very geographic location of the kibbutz was dictated by its Zionist conviction. Kiryat Yedidim was founded on what was then swampland, in an area which was remote from Jewish settlement. This was part of deliberate Zionist settlement policy, whose aim was to drain the Palestinian swampland so that more acreage could be brought under cultivation, and to continuously extend the frontiers of Jewish colonization so that all of mandated Palestine would be dotted with Jewish settlements.

It is this same Zionist philosophy that today motivates Kiryat Yedidim, together with other kibbutzim, to devote so much of its manpower and energies to non-kibbutz, nationalist goals. During, and immediately following, World War II kibbutz members were to be found in Europe in the vanguard of those who risked their lives in order to smuggle Jewish refugees out of Europe and into Palestine. Since the war, the kibbutzim have lent some of their members for work in the refugee camps that are scattered throughout Israel. Finally, since Kiryat Yedidim views itself as a Zionist agency, it has opened its doors for the settlement and rehabilitation of refugee youth. When children from Hitler's Europe and, more recently, from Moslem countries arrived in Israel, the country was faced with the problem of how to provide for their care. The kibbutzim, in an agreement with the Jewish Agency, agreed to accept groups of adolescents who would live and be educated in a kibbutz until they were prepared to take their place in the life of the country. And when one group leaves, another takes its place. The kibbutzim provide them with food, shelter, and their entire education. This is not to say that their motivations were entirely altruistic. Kiryat Yedidim, for example, derives some benefit from this arrangement in the stipend it receives from the Agency for each child it accepts and in the work performed by the youths in the kibbutz economy. The fact is, however, that the financial gain is small, and is more than offset by the great inconveniences which this arrangement causes the kibbutz, all of whose facilities are already strained.

These, then, are the moral postulates of Kiryat Yedidim and, indeed, of all kibbutzim. They are important, not only because they constitute the basis for the social structure of the kibbutz, but because they provide a clue to an important premise of its living: the premise that life is serious. It is serious because the realization of these values, rather than immediate pleasure or self-seeking, is taken to be the purpose of living.

MEANING

1. What are the five moral principles according to which kibbutz life is organized?
2. How does the value placed on physical labor determine the relative status of different types of work in the kibbutz?
3. According to this principle, why is grain harvesting valued more than work done in the orchards or vineyards?
4. How is kibbutz life set up to prevent people from becoming attached to their private material belongings?
5. What measures prevent any particular individual from keeping power for too long a period of time?

USING CLASSIFICATION TO CONVEY MEANING

1. How is Spiro's work as an on-site observer typical of the way anthropologists do research to discover how values are learned within cultures?
2. What examples does Spiro provide to illustrate the difference in the degree of freedom that individuals have before and after important decisions are made?
3. How does Spiro use classification to organize his discussion of all aspects of kibbutz life around the central feature of "the moral value of labor"?

WRITING SUGGESTIONS

1. What examples can you think of that dramatically illustrate the major differences between our culture and life on the kibbutz?
2. In what way is the Zuñi attitude toward group welfare and private property (see Ruth Benedict, page 246) similar to attitudes found on the kibbutz?
3. Compare differences in attitude toward work that Spiro found among the members of the kibbutz with what Studs Terkel discovered as a result of his interview with the stewardess (see Terkel, page 159).

Freda Adler

Sisters in Crime

Freda Adler was born in 1934 in Philadelphia, Pennsylvania and received a Ph.D. from the University of Pennsylvania in 1971. She is professor of criminal justice at Rutgers University, Newark, and has received the Herbert Bloch Award from the American Society of Criminology (1972). Adler served as a member of the editorial board of Criminology: An Interdisciplinary Journal *(1971–1973), and is the author of many works, including* The Treatment of Drug Abuse in Pennsylvania *(1973) and her widely acclaimed study* Sisters in Crime *(1975). Her research, based on a three-year study involving interviews with inmates, police officers, administrators, and judges, disclosed a surprising shift in the pattern of female crime—away from minor crimes such as shoplifting and prostitution, toward the major crimes of robbery and burglary. "Sisters in Crime," excerpted from Adler's 1975 work, presents an analysis of how the new "equal opportunity" for women in crime and the appearance of new classes of female criminals are connected to the women's emancipation movement.*

Characteristically, major social movements are spawned in obscurity at the periphery of public awareness, seem to burst suddenly and dramatically into public view, and eventually fade into the landscape not because they have diminished but because they have become a permanent part of our perceptions and experience. Thus it has been with the liberation of the female criminal, whose coming was foretold in song and foreshadowed in unisexual styles of dress and hair and attitude long before it appeared on police blotters. The portrait of the breathless, squeaky-voiced, empty-headed female professing awed admiration over some incredibly routine male accomplishment began to look less like a stereotype than a caricature. Even motherhood, in an era of zero-population goals and the diminishing status of homemaking, has been too closely linked with antiquated male domination to remain forever sacred. In spite of the cultural lag of white-male bias, the *Zeitgeist* of liberation has been moving irresistably across the land. A generation militantly young, black, and female has stirred to storm and controversy previously whispered plaints whose answer, as Bob Dylan so eloquently lyricized, "is blowing in the wind." The term "social movement" is a useful abstraction to describe the distillation of innumerable events which together form a trend. But in another sense there are no social movements, only individuals reacting to the immediacy of their own felt experience. Such an individual is Marge.

Marge is forty-three years old, with brown hair headed for gray and muscular legs somewhat the worse for wear. Soft-spoken and hovering just this side of being quite plump, Marge has spent a good many years on those legs earning a living. Since her husband disappeared one day eighteen years ago, she has worked a total of fifteen years either as a waitress or a barmaid. During those years, she supported and raised two sons, one of whom eventually worked his way through a small state college and is currently a teacher. The other one, younger, died four years ago as a result of a bad bag of heroin he pumped into his arm.

Deserted, with two small children, Marge was forced to get the first job she had ever had. It was as a barmaid, in a small restaurant-lounge. Not long afterward, she gave her first serious thought to being a prostitute—like a fellow barmaid who was developing a very lucrative following among the bar's male clientele.

But soon Marge gave up the idea of prostitution—partly because of her figure which she didn't feel was suited for the trade, and partly because of her "strong Catholic upbringing." She explained, "I just never felt right in that kind of thing. Now it didn't bother me that other girls I knew were turning tricks; I just couldn't bring myself to stay with it. I guess underneath it all, I was more strait-laced than I knew."

In place of prostitution, Marge found a more acceptable degree of reprehensibility in shoplifting. "Boosting" from department stores became a regular habit with her. At first she began by putting small items, like watches, into her pocket. Later, she progressed to more sophisticated methods. She wore large baggy coats which could conceal things like toasters and radios, then began to sew large bag-like pockets inside the coats to facilitate even larger load handling. She shoplifted for years, and was caught only once. On that occasion she was allowed to go free on her own recognizance and, although threatened with further prosecution, never heard of the incident again.

Five years ago Marge robbed her first bank. The planning took her some months. "It was something that came to me all of a sudden. . . . I had a couple of big debts and I was getting tired of working like I was. . . I wanted a bit of easy time. I mean, the kids were getting older and I was still working and, after all those years, I needed a break. I guess maybe I got the idea from watching TV or something, I don't remember. But it surprised me; like, I first thought of it seriously and thought. 'No, I couldn't do that . . . I'm a woman,' you know? But when I thought more about it, what the hell, it didn't seem so bad. The other girls I knew were boosting or [credit] carding. They said I must be crazy when we talked about it one day. We never really thought about a woman hitting a bank before . . . but then soon after that, I heard on the radio of a lady who hit a bank and got away and I figured, what the hell, if she can do it, why can't I?"

After many months of careful planning and observation, Marge attempted to rob one particular bank. That first attempt was a failure. She walked in and approached the teller's window, but was unable to go through with the robbery. "I just asked for change for a ten-dollar bill and felt like a real smacked-ass to myself." Two months later, though, she went through with it and went on to rob two more banks before she was finally caught. After the first one it seemed easy to her. "I just walked in, walked out, and went home to count the money. I always thought it would be a lot harder . . . a lot more dangerous. I did take a gun each time, but it was never loaded and I only really had to show it to one teller. The others just put the money in the bag when I asked them to. . . . I remember that first job. It was like a cheap high afterward. I went home and turned on the radio to see what they would say about me on the news."

To her disappointment, after that first heist, police described her to the news media as a "male dressed in women's clothing," That upset Marge a bit. "Well, I mean, I know I'm no beauty queen, but I didn't think I was that bad . . . and who the hell ever saw a man with plucked eyebrows?"

During her third try, Marge was stopped on her way out of the bank by policemen responding to a silent alarm. She gave up peacefully. ("What the hell else could I do, the gun wasn't loaded or anything.") She is currently serving an indefinite prison term for robbery.

In a number of ways, Marge is typical of a new breed of women criminals making their appearance across America. She, along with thousands of others, has stepped across the imaginary boundary line which once separated crimes into "masculine" and "feminine" categories. Marge is a member of the new "liberation movement" which is spreading through the ranks of the nation's female offenders, but Marge would be the last person in the world to accredit her actions to any sort of a "liberation." She, like the majority of incarcerated women throughout the country, comes from a lower socioeconomic level and tends to identify with a value code embracing the "traditional" image of women.

"Most of the women we've gotten in the past have had what you could call a 'traditional' view of themselves as women," explained one female counselor who has worked for nearly two decades in a major East Coast correctional institution for women. "They have very strong feelings about what a woman 'should be' and that image has to do with the woman mostly as a homebody who had babies, gratifies her man's sexual wishes and otherwise keeps her mouth shut. Despite the fact that they themselves may have been quite aggressive, they hold a view that 'good' women are passive.

"I don't mean that in a derogatory way, but they tend to be from lower socioeconomic backgrounds and, among other things, they are not particularly well read or educated. Their thinking about a woman's place is even more strongly stereotyped than other women in their same age bracket who have broader, more sophisticated backgrounds.

"Prisons are just a microcosm of larger society, so like everywhere else, there is a great deal of friction between the older women and the new 'lib' type we are currently getting. Perhaps that friction is a bit more intense here than on the outside."

Marge will not tolerate the mention of women's liberation; she considers it synonymous with lesbian. She feels that "women's lib" is an organization of "kooks," and scoffs at the mention of any connection between her latest criminal actions and the beliefs of the female emancipation movement. Ironically, her feelings are similar to those expressed by countless prison administrators, police officials, and other law-enforcement authorities who believe that the women's liberation movement is in no way connected to the sharply rising crime rate of women in America. Indeed, many of them won't admit that such a female crime wave even exists. The facts, however, show not only that it exists, but also that it is growing at an alarming rate. . . .

The question we should be asking is not why women are commiting male crimes, but what has taken them so long to start and why is the time now propitious. From this perspective, women are no more enigmatic than men. Like other oppressed classes they have always had the same aspirations as the dominant class but, lacking direct means, have utilized ploys, ruses, and indirection.[1] Their resort to petty social

---

[1] For a more explicit theoretical discussion of cultural goals and institutionalized means see, Robert K. Merton, *Social Theory and Social Structure* (New York: The Free Press, 1967 [originally published in 1949], p. 146.

gambits and petty crimes was a reflection more of their petty strengths than their petty drives.

"It was the radios that changed things for me: like I got a whole new look at what I was doing," said a female inmate at a California prison. Sentenced in connection with a number of drug and drug-related charges, she said that she had supported her drug addiction in part by working as a prostitute. And, according to her account, she had also moonlighted as a shoplifter . . . for a start.

"I needed more money, you know, and I was always taking these small transitor radios because there was this guy who would take all the radios I could give him for five or ten dollars each. So I needed more money for drugs, and the only thing I could think of at first was 'take more radios.' Then one day it hit me. Wow! It was weird. What the hell was I doing just taking radios all these months? I was knocking myself out for a bunch of five-buck radios. I don't know what it was at the time, but like, I couldn't see myself taking anything other than that. Like I had a block or something. Then it was like a flash. I got with a friend—she was strung out too—and we started taking color-TV sets. We got them from the loading docks of a couple of stores which left them sitting there for a while if you caught the trucks just right. We just picked one up and pushed it into the truck and drove off. I got about a dozen of them until I got busted, you know, on the drug thing.

"I can see it now . . . how dumb I was. I mean, if I was going to rip something off, why the hell didn't I take Cadillacs for all that time instead of some goddamned radios? It took me a long while to see that. A long while."

. . .

In the same way that women are demanding equal opportunity in fields of legitimate endeavor, a similar number of determined women are forcing their way into the world of major crimes.

• A Florida female parolee: "I don't think women are sitting down and saying, 'Oh, gee, I'll be liberated. I'll rob a bank.' Things are different today. I was living alone for years. It wasn't any real thought of 'liberation' that had to do with what I was doing. I wanted the money. If I was going to put myself out, I intended to aim as high as I could. I got caught, but a lot of others don't. Off the record I'll tell you, they'd never pinch me again because I've learned a lot now. I'd be a lot more careful."

• A Pennsylvania female inmate: "I'm not the only one, I know a lot of sisters who got tired of hanging with some dude who took all their money while they took all the heat that was coming down. I know one sister—she cut her pimp up over a five-dollar bill. It wasn't the money see. It just got to be too much for her. I get out of here and you better believe that no man's going to do a thing on me again. I don't need them. I got it together for myself now. I can handle my own action."

• A Chicago female inmate: "It's like what they say, you know, about mountains. You climb them because they're there. Well, that's the way it is with banks and department stores; that's where the money is. It's not a question of money. That's it. Money."

It is this segment of women who are pushing into—and succeeding at—crimes which were formerly committed by males only. Females like Marge are now being found not only robbing banks singlehandedly, but also committing assorted armed robberies, muggings, loan-sharking operations, extortion, murders, and a wide variety of other aggressive, violence-oriented crimes which previously involved only men.

Like her sisters in legitimate fields, the female criminal is fighting for her niche in the hierarchy, for, curiously enough, the barriers of male chauvinism in some areas of criminal activity are no less formidable than those which confront female newcomers in the world of business. There is, perhaps, no more macho group than the traditional "family" units of organized crime. "It was just a while ago that we got our first female loan shark here in the city," said a New York assistant district attorney. "That was something new. That was strictly an organized crime thing in the past. She was a free-lancer, though. Even today, you don't get women operating on that level with the mob. They wouldn't stand for it. In a lot of ways they are a very conservative bunch of guys."

In a book which probes the inner logistics of the Mafia, Nicholas Gage points out the strict roles which are currently allowed for women with syndicate families:

> In the Mafia a woman may be a means to a profitable alliance with another Mafia "family"; a showcase for displaying her husband's wealth, status, and power; a valuable piece of property; a loyal helpmate; a good cook; a showy and ego-boosting mistress. But what she may never be is a liberated woman.[2]

Given the status of women in the Mafia, the organization clearly has a long way to go before it can be considered an equal-opportunity employer. While it is not likely that we will see the ascension of a family "Godmother" in the near future, it does appear certain that the status of women in the Mafia may well change, if only for purely pragmatic reasons. The mob, like other successful organizations, reacts to competition and accomplishment. They are not likely to ignore the increasing numbers of women who are using guns, knives, and wits to establish themselves as full human beings, as capable of violence and aggression as any man.

By every indicator available, female criminals appear to be surpassing males in the rate of increase for almost every major crime. Although males continue to commit the greater absolute number of offenses, it is the women who are committing those same crimes at yearly rates of increase now running as high as six and seven times faster than males.[3]

Like her legitimate-based sister, the female criminal knows too much to pretend, or return to her former role as a second-rate criminal confined to "feminine" crimes such as shoplifting and prostitution. She has had a taste of financial victory. In some cases, she has had a taste of blood. Her appetite, however, appears to be only whetted:

> "Crime is like anything else; the people learn and explore wider areas as they go along and gain confidence," explained a Los Angeles police lieutenant, who was openly dismayed while speaking of the increasing numbers of women being brought into his station house. "You know how it is with a child . . . you can watch it grow and develop. It's like that with women we're getting. First it was a shock to be getting so many females. Now it's repeaters. You can see them grow in confidence. Like they opened a new door and realized all of a sudden that they can walk through

[2] Nicholas Gage: *The Mafia Is Not an Equal Opportunity Employer* (New York: McGraw-Hill, 1971), p. 95.

[3] Crime in the United States, Uniform Crime Reports, United States Department of Justice (Washington, D.C.: U.S. Government Printing Office, 1972), p. 124.

it. The second time, they don't hesitate; they barge right in. The only way I can think to describe it is that it's like a lion cub. O.K., it gets its first taste of red meat. It doesn't wait to be fed any longer. It goes out and begins to learn how to hunt. That is what I see with a lot of these women. They've had the taste. It's not as hard as they thought to hit a drugstore or whatever. They'll go into the slammer with others and they learn to be better as criminals. It's started now and you can't break the cycle. You can only wish it hadn't started."

The extent to which women have thrown themselves into criminal endeavors can be approximated from the FBI's yearly Uniform Crime Reports, the closest thing the United States has to a comprehensive national statistical overview of its crime situation. In spite of a number of methodological problems[4] —such as a variability in number and distribution of sources, erratic reporting, and inconsistencies in adhering to a universal code of crime definitions—these statistics nevertheless suggest broad trends of criminal behavior on a national scale. During the twelve years from 1960 through 1972, the FBI monitored 2430 law-enforcement agencies across the country, recording the number and causes for all arrests. While arrests are not synonymous with crimes, they are generally a reliable indication that a crime has been committed. As one might expect, the absolute number of males arrested exceeds that of females, but what is noteworthy is that the arrest rate among females is rising nearly three times faster than males. During the twelve-year period between 1960 and 1972 the number of women arrested for robbery rose by 277 per cent, while the male figure rose 169 per cent. Dramatic differences are found in embezzlement (up 280 per cent for women, 50 per cent for men), larceny (up 303 per cent for women, 82 per cent for men), and burglary (up 168 per cent for women, 63 per cent for men).[5] Except for parity in the categories of murder and aggravated assault, the picture of female arrest rates rising several times faster than male arrest rates is a consistent one for all offenses.

Murder and aggravated assault, curiously, remain the exceptions. In these categories, the rates of men are not significantly different from those of women, although both are rising. Since these are primarily crimes of passion in which well over half of the victim-offender relationships are interpersonal,[6] as opposed to the economically motivated offenses, it would appear that the liberated female criminals, like their male counterparts, are chiefly interested in improving their financial circumstances and only secondarily in committing violence.

A thirty-eight-year-old Miami, Florida, woman currently on parole explains: "I had a gun when I went into this one place . . . it was a motel. But I never would have used it. I wanted the cash. I didn't want to hurt anyone. Most places employees understand that. They give you the cash quietly. They understand what's going on . . . you're not out to get them, you just want the money. It's a transaction between you and a large institution. There is no reason why they should get hurt. I think most of the people in the joint [jail] work the same way. It's not like they get a gun

---

[4] For a critique of the Uniform Crime Reports, see Marvin E. Wolfgang, "Uniform crime Report: A Critical Appraisal," *University of Pennsylvania Law Review,* April 1963, III:708–738.

[5] Uniform Crime Reports, *op. cit.,* p. 124.

[6] Marvin E. Wolfgang, *Patterns in Criminal Homicide* (New York: John Wiley & Sons, 1958), Chapter 11. For a further discussion of the victim/offender relationship, see David Ward, Maurice Jackson, and Renee Ward, "Crimes of Violence by Women," in *Crimes of Violence,* eds. Donald Mulvihill, *et al.* (Washington, D.C.: U.S. Government Printing Office, 1969).

and decide to kill someone to get some money. Most are sorry that they even had a gun with them. It's harder that way when you get busted. There are some who are into the guns; who'll blast someone just for the hell of it, but they're a separate breed. Most of us are just in it for the bread. That's all. Guns, knives, and the rest are a sort of necessary window dressing . . . which at times can get out of hand."

. . .

If the adult arrest rates say anything about what is happening now, the crime rates for persons under eighteen say something perhaps even more about the woman of the future. The criminal behavior of the female juvenile closely parallels that of her adult sister,[7] portending a protracted association between females and crime. During the period between 1960 and 1972 the number of females under eighteen arrested for robbery jumped by 508 per cent, while the juvenile male figure rose 250 per cent. Likewise, other figures mounted: larceny (up 334 per cent for girls, 84 per cent for boys), burglary (up 177 percent for girls, 70 percent for boys), auto theft (up 110 per cent for girls, 38 per cent for boys). In this area, at least, there is no generation gap. Similar to their adult counterparts, there was no significant difference in the arrest increase for murder between males and females, suggesting that economic goals take precedence over violent ones for little sister also.

Aside from the victims, the people most directly and dangerously involved with criminals are the police. They work at the crossroads of the criminal world and society at large, and therefore give us a unique perspective, which has the advantage of being formed from direct contact with the events.

Lieutenant Peter Quinn has spent the last fifteen years with the New York City police force. Quinn's is a city notorious for having the worst happen first. What occurs criminally, as well as culturally, in New York City has an uncanny habit of being a harbinger of things to come in the rest of the country.

"Oh, it's been very obvious to me over these last years that something is happening out there," said the lieutenant, motioning toward the window in his office at the 77th Precinct Headquarters. Outside, the Bedford-Stuyvesant section was teeming in the noonday sun. "We're seeing more and more women all the time. I never really thought much about it . . . as a trend, I mean. I suppose it has to do with women's own image of themselves . . . you know, women know more about what they want, and they want more of the things that men used to have. Whatever the reasons, we see a lot more women purse snatchers, robbers, and a lot more mixed robbery teams, with men and women working as equal partners. Before, it would be only men.

"Even so," Quinn continued, "we're all still a bit less suspicious of women than we are of men. That may change, though, in the future. . . . Like I remember a few years ago, when you would have hesitated to ever put handcuffs on a woman. Not today . . . you *have* to put cuffs on them now. They'll get you just like any man will, if you don't. They've proved that to me."

A less official, perhaps, but no less authoritative view of what is happening to women can be heard from the taxi drivers who must drive in Quinn's area, as well as throughout the rest of the city. "Now I don't come here during the night," explained one driver headed out of Bedford-Stuyvesant. "I know the law says you

[7] Uniform Crime Reports, *op. cit.,* p. 124.

gotta take fares anywhere, but not me. I don't get killed to collect a salary for nobody. And it ain't just men. Twice I've had women trying to pull something on me in the last year. They had guns, the whole works. And that ain't just me talking. Go see the other drivers around town . . . see if they ain't been hit by women. It's gotten awful here lately. You can't trust nobody. Men, women, they're all the same. Don't trust none of them."

In midtown New York, at the police administration building on Broome Street, Lieutenant Lucy Acerra told a similar story. The lieutenant is coordinator of the eight precincts in the city which have female police officers. In her twenty years on the force she has come in contact with innumerable women offenders.

"Now today, the majority of women you see are narcotic addicts. But even they have changed . . . their attitude about themselves, the world. Years ago, you'd have a female addict, she'd be docile, almost embarrassed. Very quiet. Today . . . they come in the door screaming and never let up. They are much more demanding than ever before."

Not far away from Acerra's office, another lieutenant in the district attorney's office shook his head while telling how the city recently apprehended its first female loan shark. It is an indication that women are getting into the nitty-gritty, big-time underworld type of operation.

During the 1971–1972 period, 3742 cities across the country reported figures similar to those which troubled New York. Each had its regional peculiarities, but the basic theme was the same. In that year, arrests for index crimes (those crimes considered by the FBI to be serious and to have high reportability) of urban males under eighteen decreased by 1 per cent, while female juveniles increased by 6 per cent. For adults, the picture was similar—males dropping by 0.1 per cent and females rising by 6 per cent. Nor was this trend confined to the cities. Out past the suburbs into the traditionally conservative areas, female arrests for major crimes increased by 14 per cent, while males declined by 0.2 per cent. Clearly, the same drama was playing to different crowds, city by city and section by section, across the country-and the villain in each case was the female.

In 1968, the women of America passed something of a milestone in their criminal development: while their crime rate on all fronts was quietly increasing, the first of their number made her way into the FBI's infamous "ten most wanted" list. The list had been in existence since 1950 and had never included a woman before. So on December 28, 1968, it was a novelty to see Ruth Eisemann-Schier's name added for her part in a ransom-kidnaping. But the novelty soon wore off. Five months later the second woman, Marie Dean Arrington, appeared on the list. A convicted murderer, she was sought for escaping from a Florida prison farm—she had scaled two barbed-wire fences and disappeared. Since that time, the inclusion of women on the "ten most wanted" list has become normal procedure. During the past few years, women included on the list have been wanted for murder, bank robbery, kidnaping, and a variety of violent, revolutionary acts. . . .[8]

Women's unaccustomed involvement in crimes which require high levels of violence or potential violence is not limited to the sensational, but can be seen in other, less publicized areas. In the cities, for instance, young girls are now taking to the streets just as boys have traditionally done. It has now become quite common for adolescent girls to participate in muggings, burglaries, and extortion rings which prey on school-

[8] Among them: Bernardine Rae Dohrn, Katherine Ann Power, Susan Edith Saxe, Angela Yvonne Davis.

mates. Perhaps the most telling sign of change on this level can be found in a closer inspection of the gangs which have terrorized cities for years. Gang activity is no longer the all-male domain it once was. Girls can now be found participating in all gang activities with a greater degree of equality. Indeed, in New York City there are currently two all-girl gangs. In London, where British statistics reflect a similar female crime wave, female adolescents have become a problem of major proportions.[9]

In one Piccadilly Circus incident, several young women attacked and severely beat a business executive. After taking the man's wallet and watch, the females—described later as being "in their late teens or early twenties"—attacked another man who attempted to aid the victim. That man fled. Finally, the women were approached by a lone, uniformed law officer whom they also managed to knock unconscious before they made their successful escape from the scene. Scotland Yard and public officials have recently been voicing alarm and dismay about these gangs of young girls now numbering in the dozens, who roam the city streets.[10] Armed with switchblades, razors, clubs, and fists, their members are known to delight in "granny bashing," the attack of elderly ladies, usually at night.

Throughout the United States also, it appears that older ladies of the streets are assuming a more aggressive attitude toward the world. Prostitutes—formerly considered docile body-peddlers—are now taking a much harder line toward their work and clients. In New York City and other major urban areas, hookers who have taken to mugging people on the sidewalk have become a substantial police problem. Streetwalkers from coast to coast—a large percentage of whom are now narcotic addicts—are demonstrating a new willingness to moonlight on their primary occupation and supplement their income by "rolling" their "marks" or sticking up innocent passersby.

In recent years, the prostitutes of New York have been in the headlines for a number of sensational crimes: Pasquale Bottero, an Italian glass-company executive, was stabbed to death by prostitutes outside the New York Hilton; Charles Addams, the cartoonist, rebuffed two streetwalkers' advances and received a splash of acid in his face; Franz Josef Strauss, the former defense minister of West Germany, was severely beaten and robbed near the Plaza Hotel by hookers. And these are only the headline-worthy instances. . . .

The entrance of women into the major leagues of crime underscores the point that the incidence and kinds of crime are more closely associated with social than sexual factors. This is so for at least three reasons. First, while cupidity may be universal, ability and opportunity are less evenly distributed. Housewives might pilfer from the supermarket while doing the grocery shopping, but could not embezzle from a corporation unless they work out of the executive office. Secondly, since a crime is a transgression as socially defined by the group in power, authorities are prone to overlook upper-class practices and lean a bit too heavily on the lower class. "The law," declared Anatole France, "forbids the rich as well as the poor from sleeping under bridges and stealing bread in the marketplace." Arrests for prostitution are a pertinent example. If sex on the open market is an illegal commodity, then penalties should fall on the buyer as well as the seller, particularly if it can be established that the buyer understood the nature of the transaction and was a material

---

[9] *Girl Offenders Aged 17 to 20 Years*, a Home Office Research Unit Report (London: Her Majesty's Stationery Office, 1972), p. 3.

[10] *Time*, October 16, 1972. In London, girl gangs are known as "bovver" (cockney for "bother," which means "fight") birds.

participant. But such is not the case. While prostitution continues to be a crime for which a significant number of women are arrested every year, the number of males arrested for consorting with prostitutes is so small that it does not even merit a special category in the Uniform Crime Reports. The third reason why kinds of crimes are more closely linked with social roles than sex has to do with mental sets. According to the group-system hypothesis,[11] behavior is directed by a largely conscious desire to please one's own significant groups, and by a predominantly unconscious tendency to conform to an early ingrained set of attitudes. So decisive is this set for the way we think and feel and act that few people breach its boundaries, even in imagination, even in deviance. We go crazy and we go criminal along the wellworn paths that our "mazeway" has constructed for us. Running amuck is not something that Bostonians do, nor do sex-kittens rob banks—they peddle their bodies as untold generations of sex-kittens before them have done. How else can we understand the female (or, for that matter, male) offender except in the context of her social role? The mother becomes the child-beater, the shopper the shoplifter, and the sex-object the prostitute. Adolescent girls have a particularly difficult task because they are attempting to negotiate puberty with nowhere near the spatial and sexual freedom of males. That they often deviate outside their narrow confines is understandable.

In the emergence of women as a socially rising group, we are witnessing an interesting phenomenon which has implications for other upwardly mobile groups. As they become more visible in positions of prestige and power, they receive more attention from the media, and are thus further bolstered in their rising achievement. Old mental sets of devaluation and self-contempt gradually yield to new ones of pride, and sometimes on overcompensating arrogance. Black shifts from denigration to beautiful. Sexually active bachelor women are no longer "ruined" but "free" or, at the very least, "the ruined Maid," as Thomas Hardy described her, exacts no small tribute of envy from her raw country sister. How quaint seem the fallen women of literature—the Charlotte Temples and Hester Prynnes and Catherine Barkleys—who earned red letters or died in childbirth to mark well for generations of women the evils of extramarital sex. They are quaint because women are increasingly imitating men's attitude toward sex rather than submitting to one he designed for her, and they are quaint because sex is no longer the best road out of the female ghetto. In her education, in her jobs, and in her crimes she has found much faster routes to travel. The journey, relatively speaking, has just begun. While the rate of increase of major crimes for women is surpassing that for males, the data[12] still provide some justification for the epithet "fair sex" in that men continue to commit the majority of crimes, and that the highest proportion of females are still arrested for larceny, primarily shoplifting.[13]

However, even here a comparison of figures for 1960 and 1972 shows an unmistakable across-the-board trend. Females are cutting themselves in for a bigger piece of the pie in every category but murder and, in a few—like the subtotal for major crimes,

[11] Herbert M. Adler, M.D., and Van Buren O. Hammett, M.D., "Crisis, Conversion, and Cult formation: An Examation of a Common Psychosocial Sequence," *American Journal of Psychiatry*, August 1973, 138:861–64; and Herbert M. Adler, M.D., and Van Buren O. Hammett, M.D., "The Doctor-Patient Relationship Revisited," *Annals of Internal Medicine*, April 1973, 78:595–98.

[12] Figures calculated from data of Uniform Crime Reports, *op. cit.*, p. 124.

[13] For a comprehensive discussion of shoplifting, see Mary Owen Cameron, *The Booster and the Snitch* (New York: The Free Press, 1964). See also, T. C. N. Gibbens and Joyce Prince, *Shoplifting* (London: The Institute for the Study and Treatment of Delinquency), 1962.

forgery and counterfeiting, and fraud and embezzlement—that piece is 80 to 100 per cent bigger than it had been twelve years before.

In summary, what we have described is a gradual but accelerating social revolution in which women are closing many of the gaps, social and criminal, that have separated them from men. The closer they get, the more alike they look and act. This is not to suggest that there are no inherent differences. Differences do exist . . . but it seems clear that those differences are not of prime importance in understanding female criminality. The simplest and most accurate way to grasp the essence of women's changing patterns is to discard dated notions of femininity. That is a role that fewer and fewer women are willing to play. In the final analysis, women criminals are human beings who have basic needs and abilities and opportunities. Over the years these needs have not changed, nor will they. But women's abilities and opportunities have multiplied, resulting in a kaleidoscope of changing patterns whose final configuration will be fateful for all of us.

MEANING

1. Why have increasingly greater numbers of women chosen to enter the previously male-dominated sector of major and violent crime?
2. What correlation does Adler find between the new involvement of women in major crime and the aftermath of the Women's Liberation Movement?
3. How do the limitations put on women within organized-crime families promote the emergence of female criminal "free-lancers"?
4. How does Marge's case typify the experience of many women who have turned from petty crimes, such as prostitution, to major crimes, such as bank robbery?

USING CLASSIFICATION TO CONVEY MEANING

1. How does Adler use classification as a means of correlating statistical information from police records to recognize the existence of a new class of criminal comprised of women engaged in major and violent crimes?
2. How does Adler, a social scientist, use in-depth interviews with inmates in prison and case studies to document the extent and depth of female criminal activity?

WRITING SUGGESTIONS

1. Discuss your reaction to Adler's hypothesis that the rising rate of female crime is a manifestation of the desire for "equal opportunity" stimulated by the Women's Liberation Movement.
2. How did the 1985 movie, *Prizzi's Honor*, dramatize the previously unrecognized social phenomena that is the subject of Adler's article?

SCIENCES

Elisabeth Kubler-Ross

Stages of Dying

Elisabeth-Kubler-Ross was born in Zurich, Switzerland in 1926. After receiving her M.D. from the University of Zurich in 1957, Kubler-Ross took residencies in psychiatry at Manhattan State Hospital, Montefiore Hospital, and Colorado General Hospital. She has taught at both the University of Colorado School of Medicine and the University of Chicago. Her first and still most influential book, On Death and Dying *(1969), changed the way the medical profession viewed terminally ill patients so that medical education now routinely includes required courses on death and dying. Kubler-Ross' work, in volumes such as* Questions and Answers on Death and Dying *(1974),* Death: The Final Stage of Growth *(1975), and* To Live Until We Say Goodbye *(1978), has established her as the pre-eminent authority in this field, and she has been instrumental in starting the HOSPICE movement. "Stages of Dying" (1972) summarizes the results of her research with hundreds of terminally ill patients who, Kubler-Ross believes, have much to teach medical students, nurses, and members of the clergy.*

People used to be born at home and die at home. In the old days, children were familiar with birth and death as part of life. This is perhaps the first generation of American youngsters who have never been close by during the birth of a baby and have never experienced the death of a beloved family member.

Nowadays when people grow old, we often send them to nursing homes. When they get sick, we transfer them to a hospital, where children are usually unwelcome and are forbidden to visit terminally ill patients—even when those patients are their parents. This deprives the dying patient of significant family members during the last few days of his life and it deprives the children of an experience of death, which is an important learning experience.

At the University of Chicago's Billings Hospital, some of my colleagues and I interviewed and followed approximately 500 terminally ill patients in order to find out what they could teach us and how we could be of more benefit, not just to them but to the members of their families as well. We were most impressed by the fact that even those patients who were not told of their serious illness were quite aware of its potential outcome. They were not only able to say that they were close to dying, but many were able to predict the approximate time of their death.

It is important for next of kin and members of the helping professions to understand these patients' communications in order to truly understand their needs, fears, and fantasies. Most of our patients welcomed another human being with whom they could talk openly, honestly, and frankly about their predicament. Many of them shared with us their tremendous need to be informed, to be kept up-to-date on their medical condition, and to be told when the end was near. We found out that patients who had been dealt with openly and frankly were better able to cope with the imminence of death and finally to reach a true stage of acceptance prior to death.

Two things seem to determine the ultimate adjustment to a terminal illness. When patients were allowed hope at the beginning of a fatal illness and when they were informed that they would not be deserted "no matter what," they were able to drop their initial shock and denial rather quickly and could arrive at a peaceful acceptance of their finiteness.

Most patients respond to the awareness that they have a terminal illness with the statement, "Oh no, this can't happen to me." After the first shock, numbness, and need to deny the reality of the situation, the patient begins to send out cues that he is ready to "talk about it." If *we*, at that point, need to deny the reality of the situation, the patient will often feel deserted, isolated, and lonely and unable to communicate with another human being what he needs so desperately to share.

When, on the other hand, the patient has one person with whom he can talk freely, he will be able to talk (often for only a few minutes at a time) about his illness and about the consequences of his deteriorating health, and he will be able to ask for help. Sometimes, he'll need to talk about financial matters; and, toward the end of the life, he will frequently ask for some spiritual help.

Most patients who have passed the stage of denial will become angry as they ask the question, "Why me?" Many look at others in their environment and express envy, jealousy, anger, and rage toward those who are young, healthy, and full of life. These are the patients who make life difficult for nurses, physicians, social workers, clergymen, and members of their families. Without justification they criticize everyone.

What we have to learn is that the stage of anger in terminal illness is a blessing, not a curse. These patients are not angry at their families or at the members of the helping professions. Rather, they are angry at what these people represent: health, pep, energy.

Without being judgmental, we must allow these patients to express their anger and dismay. We must try to understand that the patients have to ask, "Why me?" and that there is no need on our part to answer this question concretely. Once a patient has ventilated his rage and his envy, then he can arrive at the bargaining stage. During this time, he's usually able to say. "Yes, it is happening to me—*but.*" The *but* usually includes a prayer to God: "If you give me one more year to live, I will be a good Christian (or I'll go to the synagogue every day)."

Most patients promise something in exchange for prolongation of life. Many a patient wants to live just long enough for the children to get out of school. The moment they have completed high school, he may ask to live until the son gets married. And the moment the wedding is over, he hopes to live until the grandchild arrives. These kinds of bargains are compromises, the patient's beginning acknowledgement that his time is limited, and an expression of finiteness, all necessary in reaching a stage of acceptance. When a patient drops the *but,* then he is able to say, "Yes, me." At this point, he usually becomes very depressed. And here again we have to allow him to express his grief and his mourning.

If we stop and think how much we would grieve if we lost a beloved spouse, it will make us realize what courage it takes for a man to face his own impending death, which involves the loss of everyone and everything he has ever loved. This is a thousand times more crushing than to become a widow or a widower.

To such patients, we should never say, "Come on now, cheer up." We should allow them to grieve, to cry. And we should even convey to them that "it takes a brave person to cry," meaning that it takes courage to face death. If the patient expresses his grief, he will feel more comfortable, and he will usually go through the stage of depression much more rapidly than he will if he has to suppress it or hide his tears.

Only through this kind of behavior on our part are our patients able to reach the stage of acceptance. Here, they begin to separate themselves from the interpersonal relationships in their environment. Here, they begin to ask for fewer and fewer visitors. Finally, they will require only one beloved person who can sit quietly and comfortably near.

This is the time when a touch becomes more important than words, the time when a patient may simply say one day. "My times is very close now, and it's all right." It is not necessarily a happy stage, but the patient now shows no more fear, bitterness, anguish, or concern over unfinished business. People who have been able to sit through this stage with patients and who have experienced the beautiful feeling of inner and outer peace that they show will soon appreciate that working with terminally ill patients is not a morbid, depressing job but can be an inspiring experience.

The tragedy is that in our death-denying society, people grow up uncomfortable in the presence of a dying patient, unable to talk to the terminally ill and lost for words when they face a grieving person.

We tried to use dying patients as teachers. We talked with these patients so they could teach our young medical students, social work students, nurses, and members of the clergy about one part of life that all of us eventually have to face. When we interviewed them, we had a screened window setup in which we were able to talk with them in privacy while our students observed and listened. Needless to say this observation was done with the knowledge and agreement of our patients.

This teaching by dying patients who volunteered this service to us enabled them to share some of their turmoil and some of their needs with us. But perhaps more important than that, they were able to help our own young students to face the reality of death, to identify at times with our dying patients, and to become aware of their own finiteness.

Many of our young students who originally were petrified at the thought of facing dying patients were eventually able to express to us their own concerns, their own fears, and their own fantasies about dying. Most of our students who have been able to attend one quarter or perhaps a semester of these weekly death-and-dying seminars have learned to come to grips with their own fears of death and have ultimately become good counselors to terminally ill patients.

One thing this teaches us is that it would be helpful if we could rear our children with the awareness of death and of their own finiteness. Even in a death-denying society, this can be and has been done.

In our hospital we saw a small child with acute leukemia. She made the rounds and asked the adults, "What is it going to be like when I die?" The grown-ups responded in a variety of ways, most of them unhelpful or even harmful for this little girl who was searching for an answer. The only message she really received through the grown-ups' response was that they had a lot of fear when it came to talking about dying.

When the child confronted the hospital chaplain with the same question, he turned to her and asked, "What do you think it's going to be like?" She looked at him and said, "One of these days I'm going to fall asleep and when I wake up I'm going to be with Jesus and my little sister." He then said something like "That should be very beautiful." The child nodded and happily returned to play. Perhaps this is an exaggerated example, but I think it conveys how children face the reality even of their own death if the adults in their environment don't make it a frightening, horrible experience to be avoided at all costs.

The most forgotten people in the environment of the dying patient are the brothers and sisters of dying children. We have seen rather tragic examples of siblings who were terribly neglected during the terminal illness of a brother or a sister. Very often those children are left alone with many unanswered questions while the mother attends the dying child in the hospital and the father doesn't come home from work because he wants to visit the hospital in the evening.

The tragedy is that these children at home not only are anxious, lonely, and frightened at the thought of their sibling's death, but they also feel that somehow their wish for a sibling to "drop dead" (which all children have at times) is being fulfilled. When such a sibling actually dies, they feel responsible for the death, just as they do when they lose a parent during the preschool years. If these children receive no help prior to, and especially immediately after, the death of a parent or a sibling, they are likely to grow up with abnormal fears of death and a lot of unresolved conflicts that often result in emotional illness later on in life.

We hope that teachers are aware of the needs of these children and can make themselves available to them in order to elicit expression of their fears, their fantasies, their needs. If they're allowed to express their anger for being neglected and their shame for having "committed a crime," then these children can be helped before they develop permanent emotional conflict.

A beautiful example of death education in an indirect way is expressed in a letter I received from a man who became aware of my work and felt the need to convey some of his life experiences to me. I will quote his letter verbatim because it shows what an early childhood memory can do for a man when he's faced with the imminent death of his own father.

> Dear Dr. Ross: May I commend you and your colleagues who took part in the Conference on "death. . . ."
>
> I am a production-line brewery worker here in Milwaukee who feels strongly on this subject. Because of your efforts, maybe one day we can all look death in the eye. . . . In reading and rereading the enclosed account of your meeting, I found myself with the urge to relate to you a personal experience of my own.
>
> About six years ago, my dad was a victim of terminal cancer. He was a tough, life-loving 73-year-old father of 10 with 10 grandchildren who kept him aglow and

always on the go. It just couldn't be that his time had come. The last time I saw him alive was the result of an urgent phone call from my sister. "You'd better come home as soon as possible; it's Pa."

The 500-mile drive to northern Minnesota wasn't the enjoyable trip that so many others had been. I learned after I arrived that he wasn't in the hospital, but at home. I also learned that "he didn't know." The doctor told the family that it was up to us to tell him or not tell him. My brother and sisters who live in the area thought it best "not to" and so advised me.

When I walked in on him, we embraced as we always did when we'd visit about twice or so each year. But this time it was different—sort of restrained and lacking the spirit of earlier get-togethers; and each of us, I know, sensed this difference.

Then, some hours later, after the usual kinds of questions and answers and talk, it was plain to me that he appeared so alone and withdrawn, almost moody or sulking. It was scary to see him just sitting there, head in hand, covering his eyes. I didn't know what to say or do. I asked if he'd care for a drink—no response. Something had to give. It all seemed so cruel. So I stepped into the kitchen and poured me a good one—and another. This was it, and if he didn't "know," he would now.

I went over and sat down beside and sort of facing him, and I was scared. I was always scared of my father, but it was a good kind of fear, the respectful kind. I put one hand on his shoulder and the other on his knee. I said, "Pa, you know why I came home, don't you? This is the last time we will be together." The dam burst. He threw his arms around me, and just hung on.

And here's the part I'll never forget and yet always cherish. I remember when our tears met, I recalled, in a sort of vivid flashback, a time 30 years before when I was five or six and he took me out into the woods to pick hazelnuts. My very first big adventure! I remembered being afraid of the woods. Afraid of bears or monsters or something that would eat me up. But even though I was afraid, I at the same time was brave, because my big strong daddy was with me.

Needless to say, thanks to that hazelnut hunt, I knew how my dad was feeling at that moment. And I could only hope that I gave him some small measure of courage; the kind he had given me. I do know he was grateful and appreciated my understanding. As I remember, he regained his composure and authority enough to scold *me* for crying. It was at the kitchen table, after a couple or three fingers of brandy, that we talked and reminisced and planned. I would even guess he was eager to start a long search for his wife, who also had known how to die. . . .

What I am trying to convey is that everything depends on the way we rear our children. If we help them to face fear and show them that through strength and sharing we can overcome even the fear of dying; then they will be better prepared to face any kind of crisis that might confront them, including the ultimate reality of death.

MEANING

1. Why is it important for a society that denies death and hides the dying to have accurate information about an experience everyone must undergo?

2. What characteristics distinguish the typical reactions Kubler-Ross discovered through her interviews of over five hundred terminally ill people of (a) denial, (b) anger, (c) bargaining, (d) depression, and (e) acceptance?
3. What can medical students, nurses, and the clergy learn from terminally ill patients?
4. Why is it especially important to provide counseling to the brothers and sisters of terminally ill children?

USING CLASSIFICATION TO CONVEY MEANING

1. How does Kubler-Ross use excerpts from the conversations, anecdotes, and letters of her patients to make her analysis less clinical and more human?
2. How do each of the four sections of Kubler-Ross' essay teach us something new that she herself has learned from interviewing over five hundred terminally ill patients?
3. How does Kubler-Ross draw upon her analysis to support her recommendations for more effective counseling of the relatives and friends of terminally ill patients.

WRITING SUGGESTIONS

1. Investigate the role that "HOSPICE" has played in addressing many of the problems that Kubler-Ross discovered in her research.
2. What common attitudes have Kubler-Ross and Jessica Mitford (see page 297) discovered in the way our society attempts to come to terms with death?

GEORGE A. HARTER

Earth Applications

George A. Harter, born in 1928, received M.S. degrees from both Purdue University and Ohio State University, and has held a variety of technical, management, and executive positions. He is currently a Vice President of the Electronics and Defense Section at TRW, Inc., and is serving as Chairman of the Space Applications Board of the National Research Council. "Earth Applications," drawn from Harter's 1985 report for NASA, The Space Station, *projects what a space station would look like and explores its potential capabilities as well as its scientific and commercial applications.*

"Earth applications" is a term that over the years has taken on different meanings and different emphasis. Currently, it means any space endeavor that benefits man's nonmilitary activities on earth. As shown in [the table] this includes (1) communications through the use of satellites; (2) remote sensing of the earth for the purposes of ocean surveillance and earth resources assessment; (3) weather observation and the atmospheric sciences associated with the understanding of weather prediction and climatology; and most recently, (4) materials science and biological processing, which have moved into space to aid in their research through the use of an environment that has little or no gravitational effects.

Earth applications has been a part of NASA's activities since the inception of NASA. In each of the areas now characterized under the term "earth applications," NASA has provided the initial proof of concept and has been responsible for the demonstration of most of the enabling technology.

Communications: Except for AT&T's low earth orbit satellite TELSTAR, flown in 1962, the basic research, development, and demonstration (RD&D) that established the practicality of satellite communications was done by NASA, with substantial industrial involvement. RD&D for direct broadcast satellites, including early attempts to develop market constituencies, was also done by NASA.

Communication by satellite is now a significant commercial enterprise with promising growth potential. Already, two thirds of all overseas telephone traffic is carried over satellite links. Domestic television service has become almost entirely dependent on satellite communications, and promises to expand its services in the future through the development of satellites that broadcast directly to the individual viewer.

Point-to-point satellite communications has been a commercial activity ever since the Communications Satellite Act of 1962 established COMSAT and designated it to represent U.S. interests in international, commercial satellite communications. The Federal Communications Commission's (FCC) "open skies" decision in 1970 opened domestic satellite communications services to competition among commercial entities. By 1982, there were four separate domestic systems in orbit, with a total of ten

Earth Applications

Communications	Remote Sensing	Manufacturing in Space
Telephone	Ocean	Materials
Television	Earth Resources	Biological Substances
Digital Data	Environment	

satellites providing voice, data, video, and networking distribution services to a variety of clients: (1) the Comstar system of COMSAT General, (2) RCA American Communications, (3) Western Union's Westar, and (4) Satellite Business Systems (SBS). In addition, several other firms, among them Fairchild Industries' American Satellite Co., Southern Pacific Communications, and Xerox Corporation's XTEN, supply specialized communications services through transponders leased from satellite-owning corporations. Other firms, not in the business of transmission, lease satellite data or voice channels directly from members of other sets of carriers. In addition, COMSAT General owns and operates the Marisat system, providing message and data transmission services to ships at sea.

In 1980, because of growing concern over the perceived loss of a technological lead in communications satellites, NASA reactivated its R&D program. This work is directed toward wide-band transponder capability intended to explore the allocated but unoccupied bands at 30/20 gigahertz. Technologies under development include on-board switching, solid-state transmitters, switched, multiple-beam antennas, and low-noise receivers for satellite use. NASA hopes to demonstrate these technologies in orbit on a new satellite, to be developed for launch in the late 1980's.

Satellite remote sensing: The use of satellites is an important component of the general field of detecting, recognizing, and evaluating objects from a distance by means of advanced electro-optical instruments with man/machine interpretation. Satellite remote sensing is used in conjunction with aerial photography and aerial radar scanning to assess and help to improve the productivity of the surface of the earth, to help locate subsurface resources, and to understand, forecast, and eventually help control the environment.

Satellite remote sensing is usually thought of in the following three categories: (1) ocean sensing, (2) earth resources sensing, and (3) environmental sensing. Listed in this order, they lead from an area with no current operational systems to an area that has had operational space systems for 25 years.

1. Ocean sensing: This is the newest, least-developed of the satellite remote sensing efforts. NASA, NOAA, DOD and the oceanographic science community all recognize the tremendous potential that satellites have for the study of the world's oceans. Gathering oceanic data from satellites may be the only reasonable way to observe oceanic processes routinely. Currently, there are no existing or planned U.S. civilian operational ocean-sensing satellite systems.

NASA's Seasat, which was flown in 1978 and failed prematurely after six months, was a satellite demonstration to show what an operational ocean-sensing system could do. Each of Seasat's complement of sensors had been flown before but never together on a civilian, ocean-oriented spacecraft.

Along with Seasat, data from the Nimbus and the Geodynamic Experimental Ocean Satellite (GEOS) has been used in ocean studies. Nimbus is classed as an experimental weather/climate spacecraft; GEOS was primarily used to study ocean waves. The data these satellites supply consists primarily of global wind fields, sea states, surface temperature, ice coverage, and ocean color.

Seasat data has demonstrated that scatterometer observations enable space mapping of the detailed structure of the ocean surface wind fields, including atmospheric fronts and typhoons. Altimeter observations enable mapping of surface waves and circulation features such as the Gulf Stream and mesoscale eddies. Microwave radiometer observations enable mapping of the characteristics of sea ice. Color scanner observations enable mapping of chlorophyll concentration. Taken collectively, these observations can help enable the determination of the general circulation of the ocean—both the wind-driven and geostrophic components.

2. Earth resources sensing: This U.S. program addresses the need for gathering the vital information required for managing the world's limited food, water, energy supplies, and mineral resources, and for identifying potential geodetic (primarily earthquake) hazards. Many Federal agencies use space data in the day-to-day conduct of their missions.

Numerous state and local governments, many in conjunction with academia, use satellite data for a whole range of projects, including land cover classification, wetland development, and water management. The universities are studying ways to manipulate the data and apply them to a variety of problems. Industry has made some use of space-generated data, especially in its search for nonrenewable resources. Several companies that are characterized as "value-added" firms take the raw satellite data, manipulate it, integrate it with other data, and sell the information products to a variety of users.

Currently, there are no plans for a Federal operational earth resources sensing satellite system. NOAA has assumed operation of NASA's experimental Landsat system, but there are no plans for the government to continue to operate a satellite land remote sensing system once the existing Landsat staellites fail. NASA's principal activities include pursuing the R&D necessary for developing and improving space remote sensing capabilities and the related information extraction techniques. Its goal is to establish the routine use of global data collection systems.

3. Environmental sensing: Understanding the dynamics and limitations of our environment is essential to our long-term survival and important in many day-to-day activities. The global interrelationships between the atmosphere, ocean, land, and space environments can be studied only from space. These programs are aided by data from the ocean and earth resources sensing systems.

The operational meteorological satellite systems of NOAA (GOES and Tiros) form the backbone of the environmental program. Prediction of the weather, monitoring and control of pollution, ship routing, storm warning, and modeling of long-term trends in the climate and stratosphere are all areas of study.

NOAA's operational responsibility regarding weather and climate is to monitor the weather and prepare weather forecasts for a myriad of users. NOAA, therefore, has the responsibility for the ground-based observation systems, the operational meteorological satellite system, and the related receiving, analyzing, and disseminating systems that turn the space and ground data into weather forecasts. For the space segment, NOAA coordinates with NASA for the improvement of the space-related systems and for the procurement of spacecraft and launch arrangements. NOAA is also charged with conducting R&D in the analysis and application of satellite data.

The primary and routine use of the satellite data from the NOAA system is, of course, weather prediction. NOAA transforms the data into a broad variety of weather projections and distributes it throughout the world. The data is widely used by meteorologists and environmental scientists in government and academia in routine operations throughout the world and is considered indispensible for conducting atmospheric analyses and preparing short-range weather forecasts.

NASA studies and flight missions are directed at all characteristics of the atmosphere, including upper atmospheric and tropospheric air quality, global weather, severe storms, oceanic processes, and general climate.

NASA launched three atmospheric research/demonstration satellites in the late 1970's: Nimbus–7, and the Stratospheric Aerosol and Gas Experiment (SAGE). As noted earlier, Seasat has ceased to function, but it did return significant oceanic data, which is being studied. SAGE primarily measures atmospheric concentrations of ozone and aerosols in an attempt to show how pollutants might be transported globally. NASA plans to launch the Earth Radiation Budget Experiments (ERBE) spacecraft in the mid-1980's. ERBE will measure the radiation balance over the globe to gain basic insights into the reasons for climatic fluctuations. NASA's advanced planning includes the use of satellites for the simultaneous global study of the radiative, chemical, and dynamic processes occurring in the upper atmosphere.

Severe storms, tornados, damaging downdrafts, and destructive lightning are being studied by NOAA and NASA to improve observation and forecasting of such events.

NASA is currently studying the requirements for a combined Earth Observing System (EOS). The concept is to fly all of the compatible earth observation sensors on a single large platform, with the platform in an orbit similar to the Landsat earth resources satellite so that the system can map the earth with an update frequency of one or two weeks. With all the sensors on a single platform, data will be gathered simultaneously from the different electromagnetic spectral bands as well as altimeters, scatterometers, etc. This will provide the potential for merging data which cannot be directly or easily correlated from separate systems with different viewing times and repeat cycles. NASA's study includes the requirements for a ground system for merging and distributing the data.

Materials processing in space (*MPS*): MPS is both a set of new technologies designed to exploit the unique environment of space and a developing program to implement these technologies. The unique properties that make space an enticing environment for processing certain kinds of materials are (1) the availability of unlimited, unfiltered solar radiation; (2) the existence of a near-perfect vacuum; (3) a range of temperatures, from -200 to $+200°F$; and most important (4) microgravity—an almost complete absence of gravitational force. With the exception of long-term microgravity, these properties can be approximated well enough on earth to allow their extended effects on materials processing to be investigated. The factor of microgravity, however, is what makes MPS so attractive.

Process variables such as temperature, composition, and fluid flow may be controlled far better in an environment of microgravity. As a result, some materials may be manufactured in space with greater precision and fewer defects; others, which cannot be made at all on earth, may become possible for the first time. MPS looks particularly promising for pharmaceuticals, electronic components, optical equipment, and metal alloys.

Already, a U.S. program to implement these technologies is taking shape. NASA has established an MPS program to pursue the basic science and the applied R&D of microgravity environments. Within NASA's MPS program, a Commerical Applications Office has been set up to encourage the private sector to participate.

During the years of the Apollo program, several unusual phenomena, peculiar to microgravity, were first observed. Initially considered only as posing problems in the engineering of space systems, these phenomena were later recognized as clues for inventing processes to manufacture products in space for use on earth. To broaden the discussion, NASA organized symposia in 1968 and 1969 for industry representatives to discuss the possibilities of MPS. NASA also established in 1969 a new program, "Materials Science and Manufacturing in Space."

Through the early 1970's, research in space was conducted on the Apollo, Skylab, and Apollo–Soyuz missions. Aboard Apollo 14, 16, and 17, several necessarily brief, but important, experiments were performed to investigate certain basic processes (i.e., heat flow and convection, electrophoresis, and composite casting). Skylab allowed much more extensive experimentation. Altogether, three teams of astronauts conducted 15 MPS experiments. Skylab's materials processing facilities, which included a multipurpose electric furnace, provided the means of studying more complex processes: crystal growth, metal alloying eutectics, welding and brazing, fluid effects, and combustion. Again, the 1975 flight of the Apollo–Soyuz Test Project continued the research conducted on the Apollo and Skylab missions. The processes investigated included: electrophoresis, crystal growth of semiconductors, processing of magnets, convection induced by surface tension, density separation during solidification of two alloys, and halide eutectic growth. Throughout these missions, the experiments performed in space were essentially repetitions of techniques used in terrestrial materials processing.

The future evolution of MPS experimentation lies in the direction of providing an extended microgravity environment along with more complex hardware. The first step in this evolution is taking place with the space shuttle and its associated Spacelab, which was developed by the European Space Agency in cooperation with NASA. Multiple experiments have already been flown and significant results achieved. The first commercial products to come out of this activity are uniform-sized latex microspheres. They were manufactured using a device known as the Latex Polymer Reactor. The microspheres are a critical element used in diagnostic medicine to determine human tissue porosity (e.g., in glaucoma analysis to determine the size of the eye drainage channel). Significant results have also been attained in the area of pharmaceuticals. McDonnell Douglas and Johnson and Johnson are experimenting with electrophoresis for separating biological material. To date, their shuttle mid-deck experiments have demonstrated a 700-fold improvement in the yield of pure material over similar earth-based tests. The planned commercialization of this process will produce pharmaceuticals which are important in the treatment of cancer and kidney disease.

Spacelab is the centerpiece of NASA's MPS system. It provides a habitable laboratory for scientists and engineers to work comfortably in space. Two MPS instruments have been developed for deployment on the third Spacelab mission. The fluid experiment systems use Schlieren photography and holography to study fluid behavior and the growth of crystals from fluids under microgravity. In the vapor crystal growth system, crystals are grown from vapors of impure solid materials; the results are recorded by video and photomicroscopy.

The next step toward routine production of materials in space will be an MPS laboratory aboard a permanent manned space station. This type of facility will permit more extensive experimentation and will not have the time constraints in experiment execution that result from the relatively short time Spacelab can stay in orbit.

MEANING

1. What different kinds of functions, both proven and potential, could a space station perform?
2. What different kinds of information would a space station, because of its vantage point, be able to receive about the oceans, geological formations, and global weather systems?
3. Why is it more advantageous to have one space station performing many different kinds of functions than launching separate satellites to perform separate functions?
4. Why does a gravity-free environment make it much easier to manufacture some kinds of pharmaceuticals and fabricate superior forms of metal alloys?
5. Why is it important for a satellite that converts the sun's light to electricity to always be in a near polar orbit?

USING CLASSIFICATION TO CONVEY MEANING

1. How is Harter's presentation of a space station's capabilities influenced by the fact that he is himself a NASA scientist involved in the design and construction of such systems?
2. Which kinds of "earth applications" are discussed as realistic ways of solving existing problems and which "applications" are still theoretical?
3. Harter does not discuss the potential military uses of space stations; how would his article have been altered if he had included them?

WRITING SUGGESTIONS

1. Which of the problems described by Thor Heyerdahl (see the "Problem Solving," chapter, page 645) or Carl Sagan (see the "Cause and Effect" chapter, page 506) could be investigated using the advanced capabilities of space stations presented by Harter?
2. Do you agree or disagree with the assertion that human beings are not really necessary to permanently man space stations? Explain your position.

ANALOGY

Analogy is an extraordinarily useful tool that researchers and writers in different disciplines use to clarify subjects that otherwise might prove difficult to understand, unfamiliar, or hard to visualize. An engineer might draw a down-to-earth comparison using the wearing of both belt and suspenders as a practical means of clarifying the concept that important components in an aircraft should be "fail-safe":

> In a more general sense the term *fail-safe* is used to describe components (particularly electrical) which fail in such a way that they do not endanger the whole system. As applied to structures, the term is used to mean redundancy or "belt-and-braces." In fear of losing his trousers, a gentleman may reassure himself by wearing either a belt or braces of great strength, but it would be more practical to wear both a normal pair of braces and a normal belt, each ensuring against failure of the other. In the event of either one failing, the other would serve until the failed component could be replaced or repaired. This practical alternative to high component reliability involves two features: redundancy (duplication or even triplication of components) and inspectability. Belt-and-braces provide no special security unless there is an indication when the braces or the belt fail. (J. E. D. Williams, *The Operation of Airliners,* reprinted in *English Studies Series 9,* eds. Vera Adamson and M. J. B. Lower, Oxford University Press, 1973, pp. 53–54.)

The analogy works here to explain the technical concept of "redundancy and inspectability" in terms of a much easier-to-visualize relationship. Relevant features from one class of objects (items used to hold up clothing) are used to suggest the value of comparable features in an engineering context. Analogies are especially useful to scientists and technicians in situations such as this where a difficult-to-understand term or process can be readily grasped through more familiar counterparts.

The greater the number of similarities that the writer is able to draw between what his audience finds familiar and the newer complex idea he is trying to clarify, the more successful the analogy. A scientist will often use analogies to explain concepts that by their nature involve immense distances or speeds or minute dimensions.

In "The Continuous Creation of the Universe," Fred Hoyle, scientist and astronomer, uses a surprisingly mundane object to convey the size and placement of galaxies in respect to each other amidst an expanding universe whose immense distances exceed the grasp of our senses:

> Galaxies are rushing away from each other at enormous speeds, which for the most distant galaxies that we can see with the biggest telescopes become comparable with the speed of light itself.
>
> My nonmathematical friends often tell me that they find it difficult to picture this expansion. Short of using a lot of mathematics I cannot do better than use the analogy of a balloon with a large number of dots marked on its surface. If the balloon is blown up the distances between the dots increase in the same way as the distances between the galaxies. . . .

The analogy is structured to bring out a number of convincing similarities between the principles governing an expanding universe and the appearance of increasing space between dots on an expanding balloon. Although Hoyle's analogical equation of an expanding universe to an expanding balloon is extremely useful, the analogy is incorrect in several literal respects, as Hoyle himself is quick to admit:

> For example, the dots on the surface of a balloon would themselves increase in size as the balloon was being blown up. This is not the case for the galaxies, for their internal gravitational fields are sufficiently strong to prevent any such expansion. A further weakness of our analogy is that the surface of an ordinary balloon is two dimensional—that is to say, the points of its surface can be described by two co-ordinates; for example, by latitude and longitude. In the case of the Universe we must think of the surface as possessing a third dimension. . . .

The passage shows that an important part of creating effective analogies is knowing just how far to extend them. Every analogy holds up until the differences (two-dimensional space instead of three dimensions; expanding dots instead of galaxies that remain constant in size) become more significant than the similarities. As long as analogies do not overstep logical boundaries or focus on similarities that are irrelevant, they are an unparalleled means of clarifying innovative but hard-to-visualize scientific theories. Analogies, however, can never substitute for proof.

Just as scientists will often use analogies to explain concepts that by their nature involve immense distances, we also find that the minute dimensions and fantastic speeds encountered in the field of computer science require researchers to explain complex processes through more familiar counterparts. For example, in "The Revolution Begins," Christopher Evans dramatizes the startling increase in processing speeds of modern integrated electronic circuits. To help his readers visualize what a switching speed of a billion times a second might mean, he suggests that we:

> Imagine a British billionaire who decides that he is going to hand out a pound note to everyone who comes up to him—just one pound each. A long line forms and the billionaire starts handing out his pounds. He moves quickly and manages to get rid of them at the rate of one every ten seconds, but being human he can only keep it up for eight hours a day, five days a week. How long will it take him to dispose of his billion? . . . Does it seem conceivable, for example, that the billionaire could have started as far back as the Battle of Waterloo? Well, in fact he would have had to start before that. The Great Fire of London? No, he would have been counting away while Old St Paul's blazed. The execution of Anne Boleyn?

No, he would have been counting then too. Agincourt? No. Battle of Hastings? No, further still. To cut a long story short, you would have to go back to the year 640 or thereabouts before you would see the billionaire handing over his first pound note. But that is just a taste of the cake. A billion times per second is no longer considered to be anything like the upper limit of computer processing speeds. . . .

Think how very difficult it would be to try to imagine this mind-boggling speed without Evans' clever and entertaining analogy. Enlivening scientific ideas and observations through interesting analogies sometimes leads scientists to see things in new ways. For example, in "The Praying Mantis," Henri Fabre, the father of entomology, reveals that the praying mantis was the subject of several misconceptions. Close observation of the remorseless efficiency with which the mantis killed locusts and grasshoppers led him to declare:

> Good people, with your childish simplicity, how great was your mistake! Those sanctimonious airs are a mask for Satanic habits; those arms folded in prayer are cut-throat weapons: they tell no beads, they slay whatever passes within range. Forming an exception which one would never have suspected in the herbivorous order of the Orthoptera, the Mantis feeds exclusively on living prey. . . .

Fabre draws analogies between pruning hooks, grapnels, needles, and saws, and parts of the mantis' anatomy to dispel popular illusions about the "praying" nature of the mantis:

> When at rest, the trap is folded and pressed back against the chest and looks quite harmless. There you have the insect praying. But, should a victim pass, the attitude of prayer is dropped abruptly. Suddenly unfolded, the three long sections of the machine throw to a distance their terminal grapnel, which harpoons the prey and, in returning, draws it back between the two saws. The vice closes with a movement like that of the fore-arm and the upper arm; and all is over: Locusts, Grasshoppers and others even more powerful, once caught in the mechanism with its four rows of teeth, are irretrievably lost. Neither their desperate fluttering nor their kicking will make the terrible engine release its hold.

But the mantis has still another even more terrible feature, which Fabre highlights through the shocking analogy between the mantis and a female, who dispatches her mate not merely after reproduction but during it:

> The male, absorbed in the performance of his vital functions, holds the female in a tight embrace. But the wretch has no head; he has no neck; he has hardly a body. . . . Love is stronger than death, men say. Taken literally, the aphorism has never received a more brilliant confirmation. . . .
>
> Eating the lover after consummation of marriage, making a meal of the exhausted dwarf, henceforth good for nothing, can be understood, to some extent, in the insect world, which has no great scruples in matters of sentiment; but gobbling him up during the act goes beyond the wildest dreams of the most horrible imagination. I have seen it done with my own eyes and have not yet recovered from my astonishment.

Writers who comment on social interactions often draw on analogies to reveal unsuspected resemblances between seemingly different types of human behavior. For example, in "The Language of Clothes," Alison Lurie draws on an analogy between clothes and language to document her belief that items of clothing act as individual words in a language of fashion that is just as expressive as speech. Lurie touches on similarities between ways of speaking and different kinds of dress. Certain kinds of clothes that appear to be archaic, conventional, or eccentric may correspond to the use of local dialect, foreign expressions, and even slang to make a personal statement.

So too, in "Kill 'Em! Crush 'Em! Eat 'Em Raw!," John McMurtry, a former linebacker who became a philosophy professor, formulates an intriguing analogy between football and war to persuade his audience to consider that violence in football might not be a result of the game but rather its main point:

> The family resemblance between football and war is, indeed, striking. Their languages are similar: "field general," "long bomb," "blitz," "take a shot," "front line," "pursuit," "good hit," "the draft" and so on. Their principles and practices are alike: mass hysteria, the art of intimidation, absolute command and total obedience, territorial aggression, censorship, inflated insignia and propaganda, blackboard manoeuvres and strategies, drills, uniforms, formations, marching bands and training camps. And the virtues they celebrate are almost identical: hyper-aggressiveness, coolness under fire and suicidal bravery. . . .

McMurtry's tactics here are based on getting his audience to agree, point by point, that because war and football are so similar in many known respects, they might well be similar in other less obvious ways as expressions of an aggressive and competitive society.

The game analogy has proved particularly useful for social psychologists and psychiatrists in providing a model through which to study group behavior. Leonard I. Stein studied the interactions between doctors and nurses and summarized the results for his colleagues in the medical community in "Male and Female: The Doctor-Nurse Game":

> The relationship between the doctor and the nurse is a very special one. . . . When, however, it is observed carefully in an interactional framework, the relationship takes on a new dimension and has a special quality which fits a game model. . . . The object of the game is as follows: the nurse is to be bold, have initiative, and be responsible for making significant recommendations, while at the same time she must appear passive. This must be done in such a manner so as to make her recommendations appear to be initiated by the physician. . . . The cardinal rule of the game is that open disagreement between the players must be avoided at all costs. Thus, the nurse must communicate her recommendations without appearing to be making a recommendation statement. The physician, in requesting a recommendation from a nurse, must do so without appearing to be asking for it. . . .

The game analogy makes it possible for Dr. Stein to demonstrate that correct game-playing by doctors and nurses is intended to reduce stress, bypass confrontation, and maintain the *status-quo*. At the same time, Stein can be critical of a "game" whose ground rules enforce rigid stereotyped gender responses.

In addition to scientific and social concepts, writers and researchers in a wide range of disciplines use analogies to express technical concepts that otherwise might be difficult to understand. In "Faulty Feedback to Cities," Jane Jacobs, the noted urbanologist, uses an easy-to-visualize biological image of the self-correcting nature of our breathing systems to explain how the relative strength or weakness of the national currency against foreign currencies can disrupt the economies of different cities within a country. Jacobs clarifies an abstract economic concept—"currencies are powerful carriers of feedback information"—by using a much easier-to-grasp biological image.

In "Challenge and Response," historian Arnold Toynbee employs an unusual analogy to illuminate the crucial differences he has discovered between societies, both those that remain static and those that respond creatively to challenge:

> Primitive societies, as we know them by direct observation, may be likened to people lying torpid upon a ledge on a mountain-side, with a precipice below and a precipice above; civilizations may be likened to companions of these sleepers who have just risen to their feet and have started to climb up the face of the cliff above. . . . We can observe that, for every single one now strenuously climbing, twice that number . . . have fallen back onto the ledge defeated. . . .

Toynbee's analogy of "cliff-climbers" and "ledge sitters" allows his audience to easily grasp the contrast between cultures that remain stagnant and those that are dynamic. The analogy captures the readiness of some societies to risk a possible fall in order to leave the relative safety of the ledge and climb the precipice in search of the ledge above.

In addition to clarifying abstract concepts and processes, analogies are ideally suited to transmit religious truths in the form of parables and metaphors. An aptly chosen metaphor can create a memorable image capable of conveying truth in a way that is permanent and vivid. For example, Maurice Nicoll, a psychologist who studied with Jung, interprets the psychological meaning of one of Christ's parables:

> Christ said: "And whosoever shall give to drink unto one of these little ones a cup of cold water only, in the name of a disciple, verily I say unto you, he shall in no wise lose his reward." (Matt. x, 42).

> Here a literal-minded person will think that all that is necessary is to give a cup of cold water to a child. But if the water means Truth, then the phrase refers to the handing on of Truth, however poorly. And "little one" here does not mean a child (in the Greek) but a person small in understanding. Let us also notice that, to receive Truth, the mind must be like a cup, which receives what is poured into it. That is, a man must be ready and willing to be taught, so that his mind is like a cup to receive water. So the phrase "giving a cup of water" refers both to receiving Truth and handing it on to others. (Maurice Nicoll, *The New Man* [Shambhala: Boulder, Colorado and London, 1984], p. 9.)

An effective analogy provides a way to shed new light on hidden, difficult, or complex ideas by relating them to everyday human experience. One of the most famous analogies ever conceived, Plato's "The Allegory of the Cave," uses a series of comparisons to explore how life-long conditioning deludes man into mistaking illusions for reality:

> Behold! Human beings living in an underground den, which has a mouth open towards the light and reaching all along the den; here they have been from their childhood, and have their legs and necks chained so that they cannot move, and can only see before them, being prevented by the chains from turing around their heads. Above and behind them is a fire blazing at a distance. . . .

Plato explains that in this den the prisoners, who have never seen anything outside the cave, mistake shadows cast on the wall by reflected fire light for realities. If they were free to leave the cave, they would be dazzled by the sunlight. It is ironic, says Plato, that once their eyes had adjusted to the light, they would be unable, if they then returned to the cave, to see as well as the others. Moreover, if they persisted in trying to lead their fellow prisoners out of the cave into the light, the others would find their claim of greater light outside the cave ridiculous. Thus, each element in the analogy—the fire, the prisoners, the shadows, the dazzling light—offers an unparalleled means for grasping the Platonic ideal of truth as a greater reality beyond the illusory shadows of what we mistake as the "real" world.

Besides linking things in new ways, the analogical method often stimulates creative solutions to experimental problems where logic has failed. The value of a fortuitous analogy was crucial to Alexander Graham Bell in his invention of the telephone. Faced with the apparently insurmountable problem of how to construct the physical apparatus of the telephone's receiver, Bell had a brilliant insight:

> It struck me that the bones of the human ear were very massive, indeed, as compared with the delicate thin membranes that operated them, and the thought occurred that if a membrane so delicate could move bones relatively so massive, why should not a thicker and stouter piece of membrane move my piece of steel . . . and the telephone was conceived. (As quoted in *Problem Solving and Comprehension*, eds. Arthur Whimbey and Jack Lockhead, 3rd ed. [Lawrence Erlbaum Associates, 1985], p. 142.

The problem was solved by creatively perceiving a new connection through the analogical equivalence of the receiver's internal mechanism and the bone structure of the human ear.

Analogies are extraordinarily useful to natural and social scientists, poets, philosophers, and inventors as an intellectual strategy and rhetorical technique for clarifying difficult subjects, explaining unfamiliar terms and processes, transmitting religious truths through parables, and spurring creativity in problem solving by opening the mind to new ways of looking at things.

LIBERAL ARTS

Arnold J. Toynbee

Challenge and Response

Arnold J. Toynbee (1889–1975), perhaps the greatest modern historian, was educated at Winchester and Balliol College, Oxford. He was professor of Byzantine and modern Greek language, literature, and history at King's College, London (1919–1924). From 1925 to 1955, when he retired, Toynbee held the Chair of research professor of international history at the University of London, and was also the director of studies at the Royal Institute of International Affairs. His monumental comparison of the historical patterns of twenty-six civilizations, in A Study of History, *was published in ten volumes between 1934 and 1954. Toynbee's research focused on questions of how civilizations were created and why some flourished while others failed. Toynbee discovered that challenges (such as those of climate and foreign invasion) great enough to cause extinction of culture if not met successfully, but not so severe that the culture could not respond creatively, was the ideal condition in which great civilizations developed. In "Challenge and Response," from* A Study of History, *Toynbee uses analogy as his main expository principle to synthesize conclusions he reached on the rise and decline of civilizations.*

The Problem Stated

What is the essential difference between the primitive and the higher societies? It does not consist in the presence or absence of institutions for institutions are the vehicles of the impersonal relations between individuals in which all societies have their existence, because even the smallest of primitive societies is built on a wider basis than the narrow circle of an individual's direct personal ties. Institutions are attributes of the whole genus "societies" and therefore common properties of both its species. Primitive societies have their institutions—the religion of the annual agricultural cycle; totemism and exogamy; tabus, initiations and age-classes; segregations of the sexes, at certain stages of life, in separate communal establishments—and some

397

of these institutions are certainly as elaborate and perhaps as subtle as those which are characteristic of civilizations.

Nor are civilizations distinguished from primitive societies by the division of labour, for we can discern at least the rudiments of the division of labour in the lives of primitive societies also. Kings, magicians, smiths and minstrels are all "specialists"— though the fact that Hephaestus,[1] the smith of Hellenic legend, is lame, and Homer, the poet of Hellenic legends, is blind, suggests that in primitive societies specialism is abnormal and apt to be confined to those who lack the capacity to be "all-round men" or "jacks of all trades."

An essential difference between civilizations and primitive societies *as we know them* (the *caveat*[2] will be found to be important) is the direction taken by mimesis or imitation. Mimesis is a generic feature of all social life. Its operation can be observed both in primitive societies and in civilizations, in every social activity from the imitation of the style of film-stars by their humbler sisters upwards. It operates, however, in different directions in the two species of society. In primitive societies, as we know them, mimesis is directed towards the older generation and towards dead ancestors who stand, unseen but not unfelt, at the back of the living elders, reinforcing their prestige. In a society where mimesis is thus directed backward towards the past, custom rules and society remains static. On the other hand, in societies in process of civilization, mimesis is directed towards creative personalities who commanded a following because they are pioneers. In such societies, "the cake of custom," as Walter Bagehot[3] called it in his *Physics and Politics,* is broken and society is in dynamic motion along a course of change and growth.

But if we ask ourselves whether this difference between primitive and higher societies is permanent and fundamental, we must answer in the negative; for, if we only know primitive societies in a static condition, that is because we know them from direct observation only in the last phases of their histories. Yet, though direct observation fails us, a train of reasoning informs us that there must have been earlier phases in the histories of primitive societies in which these were moving more dynamically than any 'civilized' society has moved yet. We have said that primitive societies are as old as the human race, but we should more properly have said that they are older. Social and institutional life of a kind is found among some of the higher mammals other than man, and it is clear that mankind could not have become human except in a social environment. This mutation of sub-man into man, which was accomplished, in circumstances of which we have no record, under the aegis of primitive societies, was a more profound change, a greater step in growth, than any progress which man has yet achieved under the aegis of civilization.

Primitive societies, as we know them by direct observation, may be likened to people lying torpid upon a ledge on a mountain-side, with a precipice below and a precipice above; civilizations may be likened to companions of these sleepers who have just risen to their feet and have started to climb up the face of the cliff above; while we for our part may liken ourselves to observers whose field of vision is limited to the ledge and to the lower slopes of the upper precipice and who have come upon the scene at the moment when the different members of the party happen to be in these respective postures and positions. At first sight we may be inclined to

---

[1] The Greek god of fire, metallurgy, and craftsmanship.

[2] Something important to remember, a significant reservation.

[3] Nineteenth-century economist.

draw an absolute distinction between the two groups, acclaiming the climbers as athletes and dismissing the recumbent figures as paralytics; but on second thoughts we shall find it more prudent to suspend judgement.

After all the recumbent figures cannot be paralytics in reality; for they cannot have been born on the ledge, and no human muscles except their own can have hoisted them to this halting-place up the face of the precipice below. On the other hand, their companions who are climbing at the moment have only just left this same ledge and started to climb the precipice above; and, since the next ledge is out of sight, we do not know how high or how arduous the next pitch may be. We only know that it is impossible to halt and rest before the next ledge, wherever that may lie, is reached. Thus, even if we could estimate each present climber's strength and skill and nerve, we could not judge whether any of them have any prospect of gaining the ledge above, which is the goal of their present endeavours. We can, however, be sure that some of them will never attain it. And we can observe that, for every single one now strenuously climbing, twice that number (our extinct civilization) have fallen back onto the ledge, defeated. . . .

This alternating rhythm of static and dynamic, of movement and pause and movement, has been regarded by many observers in many different ages as something fundamental in the nature of the Universe. In their pregnant imagery the sages of the Sinic[4] Society described these alternations in terms of Yin and Yang—Yin the static and Yang the dynamic. The nucleus of the Sinic character which stands for Yin seems to represent dark coiling clouds overshadowing the Sun, while the nucleus of the character which stands for Yang seems to represent the unclouded sun-disk emitting its rays. In the Chinese formula Yin is always mentioned first, and within our field of vision, we can see that our breed, having reached the "ledge" of primitive human nature 300,000 years ago, has reposed there for ninety-eight per cent of that period before entering on the Yang-activity of civilization. We have now to seek for the positive factor, whatever it may be, which has set human life in motion again by its impetus. . . .

THE MYTHOLOGICAL CLUE

An encounter between two superhuman personalities is the plot of some of the greatest dramas that the human imagination has conceived. An encounter between Yahweh[5] and the Serpent is the plot of the story of the Fall of Man in the Book of Genesis; a second encounter between the same antagonists, transfigured by a progressive enlightenment of Syriac souls, is the plot of the New Testament which tells the story of the Redemption; an encounter between the Lord and Satan is the plot of the Book of Job; an encounter between the Lord and Mephistopheles is the plot of Goethe's *Faust;* an encounter between Gods and Demons is the plot of the Scandinavian *Voluspa;*[6] an encounter between Artemis and Aphrodite[7] is the plot of Euripides' *Hippolytus.*

We find another version of the same plot in that ubiquitous and ever-recurring

[4] "Sinic" refers to the Chinese.

[5] Jehovah.

[6] An ancient epic poem in Old Norse.

[7] The play by Euripides focuses on Aphrodite's (the goddess of love) revenge against Hippolytus, who was vowed to chastity as a follower of Artemis (Diana).

myth—a "primordial image" if ever there was one—of the encounter between the Virgin and the Father of her Child. The characters in this myth have played their allotted parts on a thousand different stages under an infinite variety of names: Danae and the Shower of Gold; Europa and the Bull; Semele the Stricken Earth and Zeus the Sky that launches the thunderbolt; Creusa and Apollo in Euripides' *Ion;* Psyche and Cupid; Gretchen and Faust. The theme recurs, transfigured, in the Annuniciation. In our own day in the West this protean myth has re-expressed itself as the last word of our astronomers on the genesis of the planetary system, as witness the following *credo:*

> "We believe . . . that some two thousand million years ago . . . a second star, wandering blindly through space, happened to come within hailing distance of the Sun. Just as the Sun and Moon raise tides on the Earth, this second star must have raised tides on the surface of the Sun. But they would be very different from the puny tides which the small mass of the Moon raises in our oceans; a huge tidal wave must have travelled over the surface of the Sun, ultimately forming a mountain of prodigious height, which would rise ever higher and higher as the cause of the disturbance came nearer and nearer. And, before the second star began to recede, its tidal pull had become so powerful that this mountain was torn to pieces and threw off small fragments of itself, much as the crest of a wave throws off spray. These small fragments have been circulating round their parent sun ever since. They are the planets, great and small, of which our Earth is one."[8]

Thus out of the mouth of the mathematical astronomer, when all his complex calculations are done, there comes forth, once again, the myth of the encounter between the Sun Goddess and her ravisher that is so familiar a tale in the mouths of the untutored children of nature.

The presence and potency of this duality in the causation of the civilizations whose geneses we are studying is admitted by a Modern Western archaeologist whose studies begin with a concentration on environment and end with an intuition of the mystery of life:

> "Environment . . . is not the total causation in culture-shaping. . . . It is, beyond doubt, the most conspicuous single factor. . . . But there is still an indefinable factor which may best be designated quite frankly as x, the unknown quantity, apparently psychological in kind. . . . If x be not the most conspicuous factor in the matter, it certainly is the most important, the most fate-laden."[9]

In our present study of history this insistent theme of the superhuman encounter has asserted itself already. At an early stage we observed that "a society . . . is confronted in the course of its life by a succession of problems" and that "the presentation of each problem is a challenge to undergo an ordeal."

Let us try to analyse the plot of this story or drama which repeats itself in such different contexts and in such various forms.

We may begin with two general features: the encounter is conceived of as a rare and sometimes as a unique event; and it has consequences which are vast in proportion to the vastness of the breach which it makes in the customary course of nature.

---

[8] Sir James Jeans, *The Mysterious Universe* (Cambridge: Cambridge University Press, 1930), pp. 1–2.
[9] P. A. Means, *Ancient Civilizations of the Andes* (New York and London: Scribners, 1931), pp. 25–26.

Even in the easy-going world of Hellenic mythology, where the gods saw the daughters of men that they were fair, and had their way with so many of them that their victims could be marshalled and paraded in poetic catalogues, such incidents never ceased to be sensational affairs and invariably resulted in the births of heroes. In the versions of the plot in which both parties to the encounter are superhuman, the rarity and momentousness of the event are thrown into stronger relief. In the Book of Job, "the day when the Sons of God came to present themselves before the Lord, and Satan came also among them," is evidently conceived of as an unusual occasion; and so is the encounter between the Lord and Mephistopheles in the "Prologue in Heaven" (suggested, of course, by the opening of the Book of Job) which starts the action of Goethe's *Faust*. In both these dramas the consequences on Earth of the encounter in Heaven are tremendous. The personal ordeals of Job and Faust represent, in the intuitive language of fiction, the infinitely multiple ordeal of mankind; and, in the language of theology, the same vast consequence is represented as following from the superhuman encounters that are portrayed in the Book of Genesis and in the New Testament. The expulsion of Adam and Eve from the Garden of Eden, which follows the encounter between Yahweh and the Serpent, is nothing less than the Fall of Man; the passion of Christ in the New Testament is nothing less than Man's Redemption. Even the birth of our planetary system from the encounter of two suns, as pictured by our modern astronomer, is declared by the same authority to be "an event of almost unimaginable rarity."

In every case the story opens with a perfect state of Yin. Faust is perfect in knowledge; Job is perfect in goodness and prosperity; Adam and Eve are perfect in innocence and ease; the Virgins—Gretchen, Danae and the rest—are perfect in purity and beauty. In the astronomer's universe the Sun, a perfect orb, travels on its course intact and whole. When Yin is thus complete, it is ready to pass over into Yang. But what is to make it pass? A change in a state which, by definition, is perfect after its kind can only be started by an impulse or motive which comes from outside. If we think of the state as one of physical equilibrium, we must bring in another star. If we think of it as one of psychic beatitude or *nirvana*,[10] we must bring another actor on to the stage: a critic to set the mind thinking again by suggesting doubts; an adversary to set the heart feeling again by instilling distress or discontent or fear or antipathy. This is the role of the Serpent in Genesis, of Satan in the Book of Job, or Mephistopheles in *Faust*, of Loki in the Scandinavian mythology, of the Divine Lovers in the Virgin myths.

In the language of science we may say that the function of the intruding factor is to supply that on which it intrudes with a stimulus of the kind best calculated to evoke the most potently creative variations. In the language of mythology and theology, the impulse or motive which makes a perfect Yin-state pass over into new Yang-activity comes from an intrusion of the Devil into the universe of God. The event can best be described in these mythological images because they are not embarrassed by the contradiction that arises when the statement is translated into logical terms. In logic, if God's universe is perfect, there cannot be a Devil outside it, while, if the Devil exists, the perfection which he comes to spoil must have been incomplete already through the very fact of his existence. This logical contradiction, which cannot be logically resolved, is intuitively transcended in the imagery of the poet and prophet,

[10] In Buddhism, a state of enlightenment free from passion and illusion.

who give glory to an omnipotent God yet take it for granted that He is subject to two crucial limitations.

The first limitation is that, in the perfection of what He has created already, He cannot find an opportunity for further creative activity. If God is conceived of as transcendent, the works of creation are as glorious as ever they were but they cannot "be changed from glory into glory." The second limitation on God's power is that when the opportunity for fresh creation is offered to Him from outside He cannot but take it. When the Devil challenges Him He cannot refuse to take the challenge up. God is bound to accept the predicament because He can refuse only at the price of denying His own nature and ceasing to be God.

If God is thus not omnipotent in logical terms, is He still mythologically invincible? If He is bound to take up the Devil's challenge, is He also bound to win the ensuing battle? In Euripides' *Hippolytus*, where God's part is played by Artemis and the Devil's by Aphrodite, Artemis is not only unable to decline the combat but is foredoomed to defeat. The relations between the Olympians are anarchic and Artemis in the epilogue can console herself only by making up her mind that one day she will play the Devil's role herself at Aphrodite's expense. The result is not creation but destruction. In the Scandinavian version destruction is likewise the outcome in Ragnarök[11] — when "Gods and Demons slay and are slain"—though the unique genius of the author of *Voluspa* makes his Sibyl's vision pierce the gloom to behold the light of a new dawn beyond it. On the other hand, in another version of the plot, the combat which follows the compulsory acceptance of the challenge takes the form, not of an exchange of fire in which the Devil has the first shot and cannot fail to kill his man, but of a wager which the Devil is apparently bound to lose. The classic works in which this wager *motif* is worked out are the Book of Job and Goethe's *Faust*.

It is in Goethe's drama that the point is most clearly made. After the Lord has accepted the wager with Mephistopheles in Heaven, the terms are agreed on Earth, between Mephistopheles and Faust, as follows:

> *Faust.*   Comfort and quite—no, no! none of these
> For me—I ask them not—I seek them not.
> If ever I upon the bed of sloth
> Lie down and rest, then be the hour in which
> I so lie down and rest my last of life.
> Canst thou by falsehood or by flattery
> Delude me into self-complacent smiles,
> Cheat me into tranquillity? Come then,
> And welcome, life's last day—be this our wager.
> *Meph.*   Done.
> *Faust.*   Done, say I: clench we at once the bargain.
> If ever time should flow so calmly on,
> Soothing my spirits in such oblivion
> That in the pleasnt trance I would arrest
> And hail the happy moment in its course,

---

[11] In the *Volupsa*, a destructive battle between the gods and the powers of evil led by Loki, gives way to a vision (by the Sibyl, Voluspa) of a world resurrected through the efforts of the god Balder, where the sole surviving human beings, called "Life" and "Desiring Life" repopulate the earth.

> Bidding it linger with me. . . .
> Then willingly do I consent to perish.[12]

The bearing of this mythical compact upon our problem of the geneses of civilizations can be brought out by identifying Faust, at the moment when he makes his bet, with one of those "awakened sleepers" who have risen from the ledge on which they had been lying torpid and have started to climb on up the face of the cliff. In the language of our simile, Faust is saying: "I have made up my mind to leave this ledge and climb this precipice in search of the next ledge above. In attempting this I am aware that I am leaving safety behind me. Yet, for the sake of the possibility of achievement, I will take the risk of a fall and destruction."

In the story as told by Goethe the intrepid climber, after an ordeal of mortal dangers and desperate reverses, succeeds in the end in scaling the cliff triumphantly. In the New Testament the same ending is given, through the revelation of a second encounter between the same pair of antagonists, to the combat between Yahweh and the Serpent which, in the original version in Genesis, had ended rather in the manner of the combat between Artemis and Aphrodite in the *Hippolytus*.

In Job, *Faust* and the New Testament alike it is suggested, or even declared outright, that the wager cannot be won by the Devil; that the Devil, in meddling with God's work, cannot frustrate but can only serve the purpose of God, who remains master of the situation all the time and gives the Devil rope for the Devil to hang himself. Then has the Devil been created? Did God accept a wager which He knew He could not lose? That would be a hard saying; for if it were true the whole transaction would have been a sham. An encounter which was no encounter could not produce the consequences of an encounter—the vast cosmic consequence of causing Yin to pass over into Yang. Perhaps the explanation is that the wager which the Devil offers and which God accepts covers, and thereby puts in real jeopardy, a part of God's creation but not the whole of it. The part really is at stake; and, though the whole is not, the chances and changes to which the part is exposed cannot conceivably leave the whole unaffected. In the language of mythology, when one of God's creatures is tempted by the Devil, God Himself is thereby given the opportunity to re-create the World. The Devil's intervention, whether it succeeds or fails on the particular issue—and either result is possible—has accomplished that transition from Yin to Yang for which God has been yearning.

As for the human protagonist's part, suffering is the keynote of it in every presentation of the drama, whether the player of the part is Jesus or Job or Faust or Adam and Eve. The picture of Adam and Eve in the Garden of Eden is a reminiscence of the Yin-state to which primitive man attained in the food-gathering phase of economy, after he had established his ascendancy over the rest of the flora and fauna of the Earth. The Fall, in response to the temptation to eat of the Tree of the Knowledge of Good and Evil, symbolizes the acceptance of a challenge to abandon this achieved integration and to venture upon a fresh differentiation out of which a fresh integration may—or may not—arise. The expulsion from the Garden into an unfriendly world in which the Woman must bring forth children in sorrow and the Man must eat bread in the sweat of his face, is the ordeal which the acceptance of the Serpent's challenge has entailed. The sexual intercourse between Adam and Eve, which follows,

[12] *Faust*, ll. 1692–1706 (John Anster's translation).

is an act of social creation. It bears fruit in the birth of two sons who impersonate two nascent civilizations: Abel the keeper of sheep and Cain the tiller of the ground.

In our own generation, one of our most distinguished and original-minded students of the physical environment of human life tells the same story in his own way:

> "Ages ago a band of naked, houseless, fireless savages started from their warm home in the torrid zone and pushed steadily northward from the beginning of spring to the end of summer. They never guessed that they had left the land of constant warmth until in September they began to feel an uncomfortable chill at night. Day by day it grew worse. Not knowing its cause, they travelled this way or that to escape. Some went southward, but only a handful returned to their former home. There they resumed the old life, and their descendants are untutored savages to this day. Of those who wandered in other directions, all perished except one small band. Finding that they could not escape the nipping air, the members of this band used the loftiest of human faculties, the power of conscious invention. Some tried to find shelter by digging in the ground, some gathered branches and leaves to make huts and warm beds, and some wrapped themselves in the skins of the beasts that they had slain. Soon these savages had taken some of the greatest steps towards civilization. The naked were clothed; the houseless sheltered; the improvident learnt to dry meat and store it, with nuts, for the winter; and at last the art of preparing fire was discovered as a means of keeping warm. Thus they subsisted where at first they thought that they were doomed. And in the process of adjusting themselves to a hard environment they advanced by enormous strides, leaving the tropical part of mankind far in the rear."[13]

A classical scholar likewise translates the story into the scientific terminology of our age:

> "It is . . . a paradox of advancement that, if Necessity be the mother of Invention, the other parent is Obstinacy, the determination that you will go on living under adverse conditions rather than cut your losses and go where life is easier. It was no accident, that is, that civilization, as we know it, began in that ebb and flow of climate, flora and fauna which characterizes the fourfold Ice Age. Those primates who just 'got out' as arboreal conditions wilted retained their primacy among the servants of natural law, but they forewent the conquest of nature. Those others won through, and became men, who stood their ground when they were no more trees to sit in, who 'made do' with meat when fruit did not ripen, who made fires and clothes rather than follow the sunshine; who fortified their lairs and trained their young and vindicated the reasonableness of a world that seemed so reasonless."[14]

The first stage, then, of the human protagonist's ordeal is a transition from Yin to Yang through a dynamic act—performed by God's creature under temptation from the Adversary—which enables God Himself to resume His creative activity. But this progress has to be paid for; and it is not God but God's servant, the human sower, who pays the price. Finally, after many vicissitudes, the sufferer triumphant serves as the pioneer. The human protagonist in the divine drama not only serves

---

[13] Ellsworth Huntington, *Civilization and Climate*, 3rd edition (New Haven: Yale University Press, 1924), pp. 405–406.

[14] J. L. Myres, *Who Were the Greeks?* (Berkeley: University of California Press, 1930), pp. 277–278.

God by enabling Him to renew His creation but also serves his fellow men by pointing the way for others to follow. . . .

The Myth Applied to the Problem

The Unpredictable Factor

By the light of mythology we have gained some insight into the nature of challenges and responses. We have come to see that creation is the outcome of an encounter, that genesis is a product of interaction. . . . We shall no longer be surprised if, in the production of civilizations, the same race or the same environment appears to be fruitful in one instance and sterile in another. . . . We shall be prepared now to recognize that, even if we were exactly acquainted with all the racial, environmental, and other data that are capable of being formulated scientifically, we should not be able to predict the outcome of the interaction between the forces which these data represent, any more than a military expert can predict the outcome of a battle or campaign from an "inside knowledge" of the dispositions and resources of both the opposing general staffs, or a bridge expert the outcome of a game from a similar knowledge of all the cards in every hand.

In both these analogies "inside knowledge" is not sufficient to enable its possessor to predict results with any exactness or assurance because it is not the same thing as complete knowledge. There is one thing which must remain an unknown quantity to the best-informed onlooker because it is beyond the knowledge of the combatants, or players, themselves; and it is the most important term in the equation which the would-be calculator has to solve. This unknown quantity is the reaction of the actors to the ordeal when it actually comes. These psychological momenta, which are inherently impossible to weigh and measure and therefore to estimate scientifically in advance, are the very forces which actually decide the issue when the encounter takes place. And that is why the very greatest military geniuses have admitted an incalculable element in their successes. If religious, they have attributed their victories to God, like Cromwell; if merely superstitious, to the ascendancy of their "star," like Napoleon.

Meaning

1. In his comprehensive study of past human civilizations, what primary difference did Toynbee discover between primitive and higher cultures?
2. What relationship does Toynbee identify between the force that challenges some societies to become creative and the traditional concept of the "evil one"?
3. How do the Chinese symbols for opposite types of activity—Yin and Yang—illustrate Toynbee's analogy?
4. What effect did Toynbee's unusual, wide-ranging synthesis of many disciplines—including economics, philosophy, archeology, physics, literature, and religion—have on your understanding of what historians do?

Using Analogy to Convey Meaning

1. What did Toynbee's analogy of the "cliff-climbers" and "ledge-sitters" make you realize as to why some societies move forward while other societies remain where they are?
2. What purpose does myth serve in the context of Toynbee's article, in providing a prescientific explanation for the forces that shape human history?
3. Evaluate the effectiveness of Toynbee's use of analogy as an expository technique to organize observations garnered from a lifetime of research.

Writing Suggestions

1. Using Toynbee's analogy, explain why you would describe the Zuñis (see Ruth Benedict, page 246) as either "cliff-climbers" or "ledge-sitters."
2. Using Toynbee's schema, discuss why you would classify some countries in the world today as "cliff-climbers" and other countries as "ledge-sitters."
3. What evidence could you present that our society is different from those Toynbee discusses, which worship the past and look toward dead ancestors for guidance?
4. In what ways did mythology fulfill many of the same needs for clarifying man's relationship to natural phenomena as science does today?

PLATO

The Allegory of the Cave

Plato (428–347 B.C.), the philosopher who was a pupil of Socrates and the teacher of Aristotle, went into exile after the death of Socrates in 399 B.C. Plato returned to Athens in 380 B.C. to establish his school, known as the Academy, where he taught for the next forty years. Most of Plato's works are cast in the form of dialogues between Socrates and his students. The earliest of these, the Ion, Euthyphro, Protagoras, *and* Gorgias, *illustrate the so-called Socratic Method, in which questions are asked until contradictions in the answers given disclose the truth. Later in his life, Plato also wrote the* Crito, Apology, Phaedo, Symposium, *and* Timaeus, *among other dialogues, as well as his influential treatises,* The Republic *and* The Laws. *Plato's formative influence on Western thought can be traced to his belief that the soul and the body had distinct and separate existences, and that beyond the world of the senses existed an eternal order of ideal Forms. In "The Allegory of the Cave," from* The Republic, *Plato creates an extended analogy to dramatize the importance of recognizing that the "unreal" world of the senses and physical phenomena are merely shadows cast by the immortal light of the "real" world of ideal Forms.*

Socrates: And now, I said, let me show in a figure[1] how far our nature is enlightened or unenlightened:—Behold! human beings living in an underground den, which has a mouth open towards the light and reaching all along the den; here they have been from their childhood, and have their legs and necks chained so that they cannot move, and can only see before them, being prevented by the chains from turning round their heads. Above and behind them a fire is blazing at a distance, and between the fire and the prisoners there is a raised way; and you will see, if you look, a low wall built along the way, like the screen which marionette players have in front of them, over which they show the puppets.

Glaucon: I see.

And do you see, I said, men passing along the wall carrying all sorts of vessels, and statues and figures of animals made of wood and stone and various materials, which appear over the wall? Some of them are talking, others silent.

The den, the prisoners: the light at a distance;

[1] A picture of image.

You have shown me a strange image, and they are strange prisoners.

Like ourselves, I replied; and they see only their own shadows, or the shadows of one another, which the fire throws on the opposite wall of the cave?

the low wall, and the moving figures of which the shadows are seen on the opposite wall of the den.

True, he said; how could they see anything but the shadows if they were never allowed to move their heads?

And of the objects which are being carried in like manner they would only see the shadows?

Yes, he said.

And if they were able to converse with one another, would they not suppose that they were naming what was actually before them?

Very true.

And suppose further that the prison had an echo which came from the other side, would they not be sure to fancy when one of the passers-by spoke that the voice which they heard came from the passing shadow?

The prisoners would mistake the shadows for realities.

No question, he replied.

To them, I said, the truth would be literally nothing but the shadows of the images.

That is certain.

And now look again, and see what will naturally follow if the prisoners are released and disabused of their error. At first, when any of them is liberated and compelled suddenly to stand up and turn his neck round and walk and look towards the light, he will suffer sharp pains; the glare will distress him, and he will be unable to see the realities of which in his former state he had seen the shadows; and then conceive some one saying to him, that what he saw before was an illusion, but that now, when he is approaching nearer to being and his eye is turned towards more real existence, he has a clearer vision,— what will be his reply? And you may further imagine that his instructor is pointing to the objects as they pass and requiring him to name them,—will he not be perplexed? Will he not fancy that the shadows which he formerly saw are truer than the objects which are now shown to him?

And when released, they would still persist in maintaining the superior truth of the shadows.

Far truer.

And if he is compelled to look straight at the light, will he not have a pain in his eyes which will make him turn away to take refuge in the objects of vision which he can see, and which he will conceive to be in reality clearer than the things which are now being shown to him?

True, he said.

And suppose once more, that he is reluctantly dragged up a steep and rugged ascent, and held fast until he is forced into the presence of the sun himself, is he not likely to be pained and irritated. When he approaches the light his eyes will be dazzled, and he will not be able to see anything at all of what are now called realities.

Not all in a moment, he said.

He will require to grow accustomed to the sight of the upper world. And first he will see the shadows best, next the reflections of men and other objects in the water, and then the objects themselves; then he will gaze upon the light of the moon and the stars and the spangled heaven; and he will see the sky and the stars by night better than the sun or the light of the sun by day?

Certainly.

Last of all he will be able to see the sun, and not mere reflections of him in the water, but he will see him in his own proper place, and not in another; and he will contemplate him as he is.

Certainly.

He will then proceed to argue that this is he who gives the season and the years, and is the guardian of all that is in the visible world, and in a certain way the cause of all things which he and his fellows have been accustomed to behold?

Clearly, he said, he would first see the sun and then reason about him.

And when he remembered his old habitation, and the wisdom of the den and his fellow-prisoners, do you not suppose that he would felicitate himself on the change, and pity them?

Certainly, he would.

And if they were in the habit of conferring honours among themselves on those who were quickest to observe the passing shadows and to remark which of them went before, and which followed after, and which were together; and who were therefore best able to drawn conclusions as to the future, do you think that he would care for such honours and glories, or envy the possessors of them? Would he not say with Homer,

'Better to be the poor servant of a poor master",

and to endure anything, rather than think as they do and live after their manner?

Yes, he said, I think that he would rather suffer anything than entertain those false notions and live in this miserable manner.

When dragged upwards, they would be dazzled by excess of light.

At length they will see the sun and understand his nature.

They would then pity their old companions of the den,

Imagine once more, I said, such an one coming suddenly out of the sun to be replaced in his old situation; would he not be certain to have his eyes full of darkness?

To be sure, he said.

And if there were a contest, and he had to compete in measuring the shadows with the prisoners who had never moved out of the den, while his sight was still weak, and before his eyes had become steady (and the time which would be needed to acquire this new habit of sight might be very considerable), would he not be ridiculous? Men would say of him that up he went and down he came without his eyes; and that it was better not even to think of ascending; and if any one tried to loose another and lead him up to the light, let them only catch the offender, and they would put him to death.

But when they returned to the den they would see much worse than those who had never left it.

No question, he said.

This entire allegory, I said, you may now append, dear Glaucon, to the previous argument; the prison-house is the world of sight, the light of the fire is the sun, and you will not misapprehend me if you interpret the journey upwards to be the ascent of the soul into the intellectual world according to my poor belief, which, at your desire, I have expressed—whether rightly or wrongly God knows. But, whether true or false, my opinion is that in the world of knowledge the idea of good appears last of all, and is seen only with an effort; and when seen, is also inferred to be the universal author of all things beautiful and right, parent of light and of the lord of light in this visible world, and the immediate source of reason and truth in the intellectual; and that this is the power upon which he who would act rationally either in public or private life must have his eye fixed.

The prison is the world of sight, the light of the fire is the sun.

I agree, he said, as far as I am able to understand you.

MEANING

1. Why is an allegory more useful to express Plato's view of man's predicament then a simple analogy would be?
2. Explain in your own words why the prisoners in the cave believe the shadows on the wall are real.
3. Why would a prisoner who is released and allowed to leave the cave be unwilling to believe that what he was seeing was real?
4. After his eyes adjusted to the light, what would the released prisoner think about his former life inside the cave?
5. If the prisoner then returned to the cave and was unable to see in the dark as well as the others, how would people in the cave respond to his claim of greater

light outside? Why would they not be willing to let any of the other prisoners follow him into the light?

6. Plato used this allegory as a teaching tool. If you were one of his philosophy students, what would the allegorical equivalence or meaning of the cave, the prisoners, the fire, the sun, and the shadows make you realize about the human condition?

Using Analogy to Convey Meaning

1. How is Plato's allegory structured to reveal the meaning of the sun, which at first so dazzles the prisoner with light that he can see nothing at all?
2. Appraise the effectiveness of Plato's equivalence of the sun with the "idea of good" that "appears last of all, and is seen only with an effort."
3. What in Plato's allegory would make his audience feel a sense of surprise and discovery about their own perceptions of the world?
4. How does Plato's use of a situation that could have literally happened enhance the effectiveness of his allegory for you?

Writing Suggestions

1. Apply the "allegory of the cave" to one of the following situations and discuss where the analogy would hold true and where it would break down:
a. If one were permitted to leave the authoritarian state-controlled environment described by Aldous Huxley in his study of the manipulation of truth in Nazi Germany (see page 489), would the experience be similar to that of the prisoner who was allowed to leave the cave?
b. If a member of a religious cult were to be abducted by de-programmers, would the former cult member react in similar ways to the released prisoner in Plato's allegory?
2. What is the significance of Susan Sontag's use of the title, "In Plato's Cave," in her essay on photography (see page 526) now that you have read the original allegory. According to Sontag, in what sense can photography perpetuate a false view of the world?

POLITICAL AND SOCIAL SCIENCES

Alison Lurie

The Language of Clothes

Alison Lurie, born in 1926 in Chicago, Illinois, is associate professor of English at Cornell University. Lurie is the author of several novels including Love and Friendship *(1962),* Imaginary Friends, *(1967),* The War Between the Tates *(1974), later made into a movie for television, and* Foreign Affairs, *which won a Pulitzer Prize for Fiction in 1984. Her fiction is characterized by a sense of the fragility of social relationships and compassionate insight into fragmented lives. The following excerpts from* The Language of Clothes *(1982) show Lurie to be a shrewd observer of the contemporary scene as she explains how the kinds of clothes we chose to wear are a symbolic vocabulary intended to express diverse meanings.*

For thousands of years human beings have communicated with one another first in the language of dress. Long before I am near enough to talk to you on the street, in a meeting or at a party, you announce your sex, age and class to me through what you are wearing—and very possibly give me important information (or misinformation) as to your occupation, origin, personality, opinions, tastes, sexual desires and current mood. I may not be able to put what I observe into words, but I register the information unconsciously; and you simultaneously do the same for me. By the time we meet and converse we have already spoken to each other in an older and more universal tongue.

. . .

If clothing is a language, it must have a vocabulary and a grammar like other languages. Of course, as with human speech, there is not a single language of dress, but many: some (like Dutch and German) closely related and others (like Basque)

413

almost unique. And within every language of clothes there are many different dialects and accents, some almost unintelligible to members of the mainstream culture. Moreover, as with speech, each individual has his own stock of words and employs personal variations of tone and meaning.

THE VOCABULARY OF FASHION

The vocabulary of dress includes not only items of clothing but also hairstyles, accessories, jewelry, makeup and body decoration. Theoretically, at least, this vocabulary is as large as or larger than that of any spoken tongue, since it includes every garment, hairstyle and type of body decoration ever invented. In practice, of course, the sartorial resources of an individual may be very restricted. Those of a sharecropper, for instance, may be limited to five or ten "words" from which it is possible to create only a few "sentences" almost bare of decoration and expressing only the most basic concepts. A so-called fashion leader, on the other hand, may have several hundred "words" at his or her disposal, and thus be able to form thousands of different "sentences" that will express a wide range of meanings. Just as the average English-speaking person knows many more words than he or she will ever use in conversation, so all of us are able to understand the meaning of styles we will never wear.

To choose clothes, either in a store or at home, is to define and describe ourselves. Occasionally, of course, practical considerations enter into these choices: considerations of comfort, durability, availability and price. Especially in the case of persons of limited wardrobe, an article may be worn because it is warm or rainproof or handy to cover up a wet bathing suit—in the same way that persons of limited vocabulary use the phrase "you know" or adjectives such as "great" or "fantastic." Yet, just as with spoken language, such choices usually give us some information, even if it is only equivalent to the statement "I don't give a damn what I look like today."

ARCHAIC WORDS

Besides containing "words" that are taboo, the language of clothes, like speech, also includes modern and ancient words, words of native and foreign origin, dialect words, colloquialisms, slang and vulgarities. Genuine articles of clothing from the past (or skillful imitations) are used in the same way a writer or speaker might use archaisms: to give an air of culture, erudition or wit. Just as in educated discourse, such "words" are usually employed sparingly, most often one at a time—a single Victorian cameo or a pair of 1940s platform shoes or an Edwardian velvet waistcoat, never a complete costume. A whole outfit composed of archaic items from a single period, rather than projecting elegance and sophistication, will imply that one is on one's way to a masquerade, acting in a play or film or putting oneself on display for advertising purposes. Mixing garments from several different periods of the past, on the other hand, suggests a confused but intriguingly "original" theatrical personality. It is therefore often fashionable in those sections of the art and entertainment industry in which instant celebrities are manufactured and sold.

When using archaic words, it is essential to choose ones that are decently old. The sight of a white plastic Courrèges miniraincoat and boots (in 1963 the height of fashion) at a gallery opening or theater today would produce the same shiver of ridicule and revulsion as the use of words such as "groovy," "Negro" or "self-actualizing."

In *Taste and Fashion*, one of the best books ever written on costume, the late James Laver proposed a timetable to explain such reactions; this has come to be known as Laver's Law. According to him, the same costume will be:

Indecent	10 years before its time
Shameless	5 years before its time
Daring	1 year before its time
Smart	
Dowdy	1 year after its time
Hideous	10 years after its time
Ridiculous	20 years after its time
Amusing	30 years after its time
Quaint	50 years after its time
Charming	70 years after its time
Romantic	100 years after its time
Beautiful	150 years after its time

Laver possibly overemphasizes the shock value of incoming fashion, which today may be seen merely as weird or ugly. And, of course, he is speaking of the complete outfit, or "sentence." The speed with which a single "word" passes in and out of fashion can vary, just as in spoken and written languages.

FOREIGN WORDS

The appearance of foreign garments in an otherwise indigenous costume is similar in function to the use of foreign words or phrases in standard English speech. This phenomenon, which is common in certain circles, may have several different meanings.

First, of course, it can be a deliberate sign of national origin in someone who otherwise, sartorially or linguistically speaking, has no accent. Often this message is expressed through headgear. The Oxford-educated Arab who tops his Savile Row[1] suit with a turban is telling us graphically that he has not been psychologically assimilated, that his ideas and opinions remain those of an Asian. As a result, we tend to see the non-European in Western dress with native headgear or hairdo as dignified, even formidable, while the reverse outfit—the Oriental lady in a kimono and a plastic rain hat or the sheikh in native robes and a black bowler—appears comic. Such costumes seem to announce that their wearers, though not physically at east in our country, have their heads full of half-baked Western ideas.

More often the wearing of a single foreign garment, like the dropping of a foreign word or phrase in conversation, is meant not to advertise foreign origin or allegiance but to indicate sophistication. It can also be a means of advertising wealth. When we see a fancy Swiss watch, we know that its owner either bought it at home for three times the price of a good English or American watch or else he or she spent even more money traveling to Switzerland.

[1] A fashionable street in London where men's expensive, custom-made suits are tailored and sold.

SLANG AND VULGAR WORDS

Casual dress, like casual speech, tends to be loose, relaxed and colorful. It often contains what might be called "slang words": blue jeans, sneakers, baseball caps, aprons, flowered cotton housedresses and the like. These garments could not be worn on a form occasion without causing disapproval, but in ordinary circumstances they pass without remark. "Vulgar words" in dress, on the other hand, give emphasis and get immediate attention in almost any circumstances, just as they do in speech. Only the skillful can employ them without some loss of face, and even then they must be used in the right way. A torn, unbuttoned shirt, or wildly uncombed hair, can signify strong emotions: passion, grief, rage, despair. They are most effective if people already think of you as being neatly dressed, just as the curses of well-spoken persons count for more than those of the customarily foulmouthed.

Items of dress that are the sartorial equivalent of forbidden words have more impact when they appear seldom and as if by accident. The Edwardian lady, lifting her heavy floor-length skirt to board a tram, appeared unaware that she was revealing a froth of lacy petticoats and embroidered black stockings. Similarly, today's braless executive woman, leaning over her desk at a conference, may affect not to now that her nipples show through her silk blouse. Perhaps she does not know it consciously; we are here in the ambiguous region of intention versus interpretation which has given so much trouble to linguists.

PERSONAL FASHION: SITUATION AND SELF

As with speech, the meaning of any costume depends on circumstances. It is not "spoken" in a vacuum but at a specific place and time, any change in which may alter its meaning. Like the remark "Let's get on with this damn business," the two-piece tan business suit and boldly striped shirt and tie that signify energy and determination in the office will have quite another resonance at a funeral or picnic.

In language we distinguish between someone who speaks a sentence well—clearly, and with confidence and dignity—and someone who speaks it badly. In dress, too, manner is as important as matter, and in judging the meaning of any garment we will automatically consider whether it fits well or is too large or too small, whether it is old or new and especially whether it is in good condition, slightly rumpled and soiled or crushed and filthy. Cleanliness may not always be next to godliness, but it is usually regarded as a sign of respectability or at least self-respect. It is also a sign of status, since to be clean and neat involves the expense of time and money.

In a few circles, of course, disregard for cleanliness has been considered a virtue. Saint Jerome's remark that "the purity of the body and its garments means the impurity of the soul" inspired generations of unwashed and smelly hermits. In the '60s some hippies and mystics scorned overly clean and tidy dress as a sign of compromise with the establishment and too great an attachment to the things of this world. There is also a more widespread rural and small-town dislike of the person whose clothes are too clean, slick and smooth. He—or she—is suspected of being untrustworthy, a smoothy or a city slicker.

In general, however, to wear dirty, rumpled or torn clothing is to invite scorn and condescension. This reaction is ancient; indeed, it goes back beyond the dawn of humanity. In most species, a strange animal in poor condition—mangy, or with matted and muddy fur—is more likely to be attacked by other animals. In the same way, shabbily dressed people are more apt to be treated shabbily. A man in a clean, well-pressed suit who falls down in a central London or Manhattan street is likely to be helped up sooner than one in filthy tatters.

ECCENTRIC AND CONVENTIONAL SPEECH

In dress as in language, there is a possible range of expression from the most eccentric statement to the most conventional. At one end of the spectrum is the outfit of which the individual parts or "words" are highly incongruent, marking its wearer (if not on stage or involved in some natural disaster) as very peculiar or possibly deranged. Imagine, for instance, a transparent sequined evening blouse over a dirty Victorian cotton petticoat and black rubber galoshes. (I have observed this getup in real life; it was worn to a lunch party at a famous Irish country house.) If the same costume were worn by a man, or if the usual grammatical order of the sentence were altered—one of the galoshes placed upside down on the head, for example—the effect of insanity would be even greater.

At the opposite end of the spectrum is the costume that is the equivalent of a cliché; it follows some established style in every particular and instantly establishes its wearer as a doctor, a debutante, a hippie or a whore. Such outfits are not uncommon, for as two British sociologists have remarked, "Identification with and active participation in a social group always involves the human body and its adornment and clothing." The more significant any social role is for an individual, the more likely he or she is to dress for it. When two roles conflict, the costume will either reflect the more important one or it will combine them, sometimes with incongruous effects, as in the case of the secretary whose sober, efficient-looking dark suit only partly conceals a tight, bright low-cut blouse.

The cliché outfit may in some cases become so standardized that it is spoken of as a "uniform": the pin-striped suit, bowler and black umbrella of the London City man, for instance, or the blue jeans and T-shirts of high school students. Usually, however, these costumes only look like uniforms to outsiders; peers will be aware of significant differences. The London businessman's tie will tell his associates where he went to school; the cut and fabric of his suit will allow them to guess at his income. High school students, in a single glance, can distinguish new jeans from those that are fashionably worn, functionally or decoratively patched or carelessly ragged; they grasp the fine distinctions of meaning conveyed by straight-leg, flared, boot-cut and peg-top. When two pairs of jeans are identical to the naked eye, a label handily affixed to the back pocket gives useful information, identifying the garment as expensive (so-called designer jeans) or discount-department store. And even within the latter category there are distinctions: In our local junior high school according to a native informant, "freaks always wear. Lees, greasers wear Wranglers and everyone else wears Levis."

Of course, all these students are identical only below the waist; above it they may wear anything from a lumberjack shift to a lace blouse. Grammatically, this costume seems to be a sign that in their lower or physical natures these persons are alike, however dissimilar they may be socially, intellectually or esthetically. If this is so, the opposite statement can be imagined—and was actually made by my own college classmates 30 years ago. During the daytime we wore identical baggy sweaters over a wide variety of slacks, plaid kilts, full cotton or straight tweed or slinky jersey skirts, ski pants and Bermuda shorts. "We're all nice coeds from the waist up; we think and talk alike," this costume proclaimed, "but as women we are infinitely various."

DRESSING FOR "SUCCESS"

For over 100 years books and magazines have been busy translating the correct language of fashion, telling men and women what they should wear to seem genteel, rich, sophisticated and attractive to the other sex. Journals addressed to what used to be called "the career girl" advised her how to dress to attract "the right kind of man"—successful, marriage-minded. Regardless of the current fashion, a discreet femininity was always recommended: soft fabrics and colors, flowers and ruffles in modest profusion, hair slightly longer and curlier than that of the other girls in the office. The costume must be neither too stylish (suggesting expense to the future husband) nor dowdy (suggesting boredom). Above all, a delicate balance must be struck between the prim and the seductive, one tending not to attract men and the other to attract the wrong kind. Times have changed somewhat, and the fashion pages of magazines such as *Cosmopolitan* now seem to specialize in telling the career girl what to wear to charm the particular wrong type of man who reads *Playboy*, while the editorial pages tell her how to cope with the resulting psychic damage.

Two recent paperbacks, *Dress for Success* and *The Woman's Dress for Success Book*, by John T. Molloy, instruct businessmen and businesswomen how to select their clothes so that they will look efficient, authoritative and reliable even when they are incompetent, weak and shifty. Molloy, who is by no means unintelligent, claims that his "wardrobe engineering" is based on scientific research and opinion polls. Also, in a departure from tradition, he is interested in telling women how to get promoted, not how to get married. The secret, apparently, is to wear an expensive but conventional "skirted suit" in medium-gray or navy wool with a modestly cut blouse. No sweaters, no pants, no very bright colors, no cleavage, no long or excessively curly hair.

Anyone interested in scenic variety must hope that Molloy is mistaken; but my own opinion polling, unfortunately, backs him up. A fast-rising lady executive in a local bank reports to me—reluctantly—that "suits do help separate the women from the girls—provided the women can tolerate the separation, which is another question altogether."

MALEVOLENT CLOTHING

At the other extreme from clothing which brings good luck and success in the garment of ill-omen. The most common and harmless version of this is the dress, suit or shirt which (like some children) seems to attract or even to seek out dirt, grease, protruding nails, falling ketchup and other hazards. Enid Nemy, who has written perceptively about such clothes for *The New York Times*, suggests that they may be lazy: "They'd just as soon rest on a hanger, or in a box—and they revolt when they're hauled into action." Or, she adds, they may be snobs, unwilling to associate with ordinary people. Whatever the cause, such accident-prone garments rarely if ever reform, and once one has been identified it is best to break off relations with it immediately. Otherwise, like accident-prone persons, it is apt to involve you in much inconvenience and possibly actual disaster, turning some important interview or romantic tryst into a scene of farce or humiliation. More sinister, and fortunately more rare, is the garment which seems to attract disasters to you rather than to itself. Ms. Nemy mentions an orange linen dress that apparently took a dislike to its owner, Margaret Turner of Dover Publications. Orange clothes, as it happens, do occasionally arouse hostility in our culture, but this dress seems to have been a special case. "Women friends seemed cattier, men seemed more aloof and I'd get into bad situations with my boss," Ms. Turner reported. "And that wasn't all. I'd spill coffee, miss train connections and the car would break down."

For some people the daily task of choosing a costume is tedious, oppressive or even frightening. Occasionally, such people tell us that fashion is unnecessary; that in the ideal world of the future we will all wear some sort of identical jump suit— washable, waterproof, stretchable, temperature-controlled, timeless, ageless and sexless. What a convenience, what a relief it will be, they say, never to worry about how to dress for a job interview, a romantic tryst or a funeral!

Convenient, perhaps, but not exactly a relief. Such a utopia would give most of us the same kind of chill we feel when a stadium full of Communist-bloc athletes in identical sports outfits, shouting slogans in unison, appears on TV. Most people do not want to be told what to wear any more than they want to be told what to say. In Belfast recently, 400 Irish Republican prisoners "refused to wear any clothes at all, draping themselves day and night in blankets," rather than put on prison uniforms. Even the offer of civilian-style dress did not satisfy then; they insisted on wearing their own clothes brought from home or nothing. Fashion is free speech, and one of the privileges, if not always one of the pleasures, of a free world.

MEANING

1. What does Lurie's discussion of the "language" of clothes make you realize about this underestimated nonverbal means of expressing attitudes and feelings?
2. What connections does Lurie discover between the condition of someone's clothing and the willingness of bystanders to help that person?
3. What is Lurie's attitude toward recent "dress-for-success" books, which, she believes, "instruct businessmen and businesswomen how to select their clothes so that they will look efficient, authoritative and reliable even when they are incompetent, weak and shifty"?
4. At each point in drawing an analogy between clothes and language, Lurie touches on similarities between ways of speaking and different kinds of dress. Explain what Lurie means by clothes that appear to be "archaic," "foreign," "slang," "vulgar," "eccentric," or "conventional."
5. What does "Laver's Law" express?

USING ANALOGY TO CONVEY MEANING

1. What level of fashion sophistication does Lurie assume her audience possesses?
2. Which examples cited by Lurie to support her extended analogy between language and clothes seem especially convincing?

3. Since choosing a wardrobe provides a means for defining one's identity, how does Lurie's reference to the four hundred Irish prisoners who refused to wear any clothes at all rather than wear prison uniforms substantiate her central idea?

Writing Suggestions

1. Go through you own wardrobe and classify items of clothing you wear according to the "statement" you want to make in different contexts. Can you find examples of archaic and foreign dress, slang dress, vulgar dress, eccentric dress, and conventional dress?
2. Does the principle embodied in "Laver's Law" also seem to apply to the history of ideas; that is, could you find examples of ideas that are ahead of their time, chic at the moment, or antiquated?
3. Interpret the "language" and significance of costumes described by Ruth Benedict (see page 246) (e.g., "If an impersonator wears a new feather on his mask, it eclipses all talk of sheep or gardens or marriage or divorce. . . .").

JANE JACOBS

Faulty Feedback to Cities

Jane Jacobs was born in 1916 in Scranton, Pennsylvania. In 1952, she became an associate editor of Architectural Forum, *writing on the problems of New York, Chicago, Washington, D.C., Baltimore, and San Francisco. Jacobs has contributed articles on urban affairs to a wide variety of journals, including* Atlantic, Harper's, Saturday Review, Commentary, The New Republic, *and* Commonwealth *magazine. In her books,* The Death and Life of Great American Cities *(1961) and* The Economy of Cities *(1969), Jacobs takes a realistic and pragmatic approach to questions of urban planning, manufacturing, and trade. In contrast to most urbanologists, Jacobs believes that industry originated primarily in the cities rather than in rural areas. In "Faulty Feedback to Cities," taken from* Cities and the Wealth of Nations *(1969), Jacobs uses analogy as her chief rhetorical device to explain how national currencies are powerful carriers of feedback information.*

We must suppose that the very earliest proto-cities and cities, trading with one another in prehistoric times, bartered the obsidian, copper, shells, animals, horn, pigments, rushes or other goods of their territories they had to trade. Unmediated by currency, bartered goods would have fluctuated sensitively in value relative to one another. An item in high demand would command good volumes and varieties of imports for a settlement, but if demand fell off as additional sources of supply or substitutes were found, the superseded product would command diminishing imports, just as a falling currency does. Then the settlement exporting it would be in trouble unless it hustled up something else worth trading or else imitated on its own behalf some of the artifacts it had formerly imported, a process we call "economic borrowing" when we find evidence of it in prehistoric times.

Once cities invented currencies, at first each had its own: at any rate, the very early city-states of which we have knowledge in Mediterranean Europe, the Near East, China and India created their own currencies and circulated them in trade. Their coinages were typically based on metals with widely accepted intrinsic values. But even so, the coins, like much later paper currencies based on a gold or silver standard, necessarily fluctuated with respect to the goods or labor they could command in given cities at given times. Grain cost more in a city-state that had suffered bad crops than if it was gotten in one where the harvest had been good. Iron swords diminished the value set on bronze swords. Perhaps pottery had once upon a time diminished the value set on skulls.

After an ancient city-state had been conquered by a more powerful neighbor and thus converted to a provincial city, or after it had voluntarily surrendered much of its sovereignty to a federation, it seems typically to have continued, nevertheless, to mint and circulate a currency of its own. Even the Roman Empire only gradually eliminated the non-Roman currencies of its conquered provinces and dependencies; only later still, in an unsuccessful effort to combat inflation at the time of Diocletian did Rome decree standardized prices, which is to say really rigidly standardized currency values, throughout its realm.

In early medieval Europe, city currencies once again became the norm, not the exception. Venice welcomed and used imperial Byzantine coinage because of its trade with the Eastern Empire, but Venice circulated its own currency as well. The cities that rose in the wake of Venice and extended their own volatile trading networks also commonly created their own currencies. For example, the north German and Baltic cities of the Hanseatic League were united in many common purposes but they had no league currency. Member cities created their own, as well as devising instruments comparable to our letters of credit and certificates of deposit for use in their intercity, multicurrency trading.

Medieval city currencies of Europe persisted into Renaissance times, and indeed multiplied as European economic life itself developed with the multiplying of cities. Even currencies that did not originate in cities proper such as Florence, Genoa or Amsterdam must often have worked much as if they were the currencies of city-states because the principalities doing the minting were often so small themselves. For instance, the currency of Brandenburg was the currency of Berlin, that of Saxony the currency of Dresden, that of the Dukedom of Milan the currency of Milan, and so on. Many such currencies persisted even into recent times. German monetary union was not instituted until 1857, as a precursor to formation of the German Empire. Except during one brief and ill-fated experience with centralized government inspired by the French Revolution, Swiss cities, as cantons, retained the power to create their own currencies until after 1848.

Today we take it for granted that the elimination of multitudinous currencies in favor of fewer national or imperial currencies represents economic progress and pro-motes the stability of economic life. But this conventional belief is at least worth questioning in view of the function that currencies serve as economic feedback controls. I am going to argue that national or imperial currencies give faulty and destructive feedback to city economies and that this in turn leads to profound structural economic flaws, some of which cannot be overcome no matter how hard we try.

As we all know, when a nation's currency declines in value relative to currencies of other nations with which it trades, theoretically the very decline itself ought to help correct the nation's economy. Automatically its exports become cheaper to customer nations, hence its export sales should increase; and at the same time, its imports automatically become more expensive, and this should help its own manufacturers. Theoretically, then, a declining national currency ought to work automatically like both an export subsidy and a tariff, coming into play precisely when a nation begins to run a deficit in its international balance of payments because it is exporting too little and importing too much. Furthermore, this automatic export subsidy and tariff ought to remain in play precisely as long as it is needed, no longer. If that were indeed the effect that national-currency fluctuations had, they would be elegant examples of feedback control, registering that a correction is necessary and, at the same time, triggering the appropriate correction.

To understand why national currencies don't actually perform that constructive function, we need to understand how feedback controls work. First of all, it is of the essence that the feedback information governs a responding mechanism. For example, in our breathing, a momentary rise in the level of carbon dioxide in the bloodstream automatically triggers off the brain stem's breathing center to shoot a message to the diaphragm to contract and allow the lungs to fill again. In this case the triggering information is the amount of carbon dioxide in the blood, and the responding mechanism is the diaphragm. As organisms, we depend on vast arrays of feedback controls, each working so appropriately and automatically that we are unaware we have them until researchers tell us so. Unstable systems require continual corrections and adjustments, otherwise they would soon succumb to their own instabilities.

Without having called them feedback controls, I have already mentioned many in this book. For instance, when new enterprises in a city multiply and diversify rapidly, the information feeds back in the form of crowding, inconvenience and increasing competition for city space; it triggers off the appropriate correction: some enterprises move out of the city into the region, although still within reach of the city services and markets they require. Similarly, the information that city jobs and markets have simultaneously increased feeds back into the system in the form of rural labor shortages in a city's own hinterland. That triggers the appropriate correction: use of rural labor-saving equipment, or development of it if need be. City regions are the outcomes of many different corrections triggered by many different inputs of feedback information. To be sure, the corrections are not wholly automatic, but then, neither is our breathing. We can hold our breath—within limits.

Feedback controls always work on their own terms regardless of what we might prefer. For exmaple, when a government prints money exuberantly, the information feeds back into the system and triggers the appropriate correction: a given unit of money buys less. Wishes for a different correction, economic expansion, don't avail; expansion is a different response, under quite different controls. Analogically, the common thermostat works beautifully at its own corrective task of registering changes in temperature and triggering the appropriate corrections, but it is futile to wish that it would govern the speed of a rotary mill because that is the task we want done; however, a different feedback control does exactly that. In short, feedback controls are built right into the systems they correct, and the corrections they trigger are not discretionary. They are precisely to the point, and the point is always the specific correction of results of specific previous happenings.

The trouble with national currencies as constructive feedback controls is not that they are feeble at the job. They are anything but that. Those dreary little columns of international exchange-rate figures in the back pages of newspapers, creeping from day to day in this direction or that with their little fractions of percentage points, can represent power of life or death over entire industries. A gradually accruing 10 percent rise in the value of the English pound in 1979 and 1980 forced the major producers of English china and earthenware to lay off workers, and put several of the smaller producers out of business altogether, priced out of foreign markets which, until then, had remained strong for these wares. The rising pound was simultaneously pricing the wares out of their domestic markets too, as foreign imports became cheaper. The chairman of the largest producer, Wedgwood, blamed the rise of the pound on a combination of North Sea oil production off Scotland, which had improved Great Britain's balance of trade, and the government's policy of setting interest rates high in order to try to improve the economy by attracting foreign capital. He was probably right. For his own enterprise the consequences were massive layoffs and a decision on the part of the company that for its own survival it must transplant much of its production permanently out of Britain, into customer nations.

Currencies are powerful carriers of feedback information, then, and potent triggers of adjustments, but in their own terms. National currencies register, above all, consolidated information on a nation's international trade. When net international exports of goods or services rise, relative to those of other nations, the currency, being in demand, rises in value; when exports fall off, it declines in value. International imports and exports of capital work in just the opposite way. If a country has been importing more capital than it has exported (by borrowing abroad, for example), the value of its currency is automatically bolstered. Conversely, if it has exported more capital than it has been importing (by lending, making gifts, paying interest on prior foreign loans, exporting the profits of foreign-owned industries), the value of its currency is automatically depressed to that extent. This is why imports of foreign capital into Britain (stimulated by rising interest rates there) and the production of North Sea oil, improving Britain's balance of international trade, were acting in concert to raise the value of the pound.

The reverse effects of movements of capital do not long overrule a currency's feedback concerning international trade in goods and services. That factor dominates over the long term. For example, suppose a nation borrows heavily abroad to develop its economy. Its currency's value is automatically bolstered from the very fact of the borrowing itself. But then suppose that the development schemes do not pay off in expanded international exports of goods and services, or else in replaced foreign imports. The currency must then decline. The cost of interest on the loan, which seemed so feasible when the loan itself was bolstering the debtor nation's currency, becomes devastating as the currency declines. That is why heavy international borrowing that does not pay off in a heavily improved balance of trade for the debtor nation can abruptly bankrupt a country unless its lenders agree to keep lending to it and to ease up on repayments and interest. The threat then, of course, becomes bankruptcy for the lenders.

Because currency feedback information is so potent, and because so often the information is not what governments want to hear, nations commonly go to extravagant lengths to try to block off or resist the information. Furthermore, when the information does come through—as sooner or later it always does, no matter what the evasions—the effects can be inappropriate, to say the least, as they were in the English Midlands, where most of the nation's potteries are located. Unemployment was already high in England generally and very high in the Midlands; the country was already suffering from declining exports of its manufactures, and had been for decades. But those realities were overridden by the other realities of the North Sea oil and the imports of foreign capital being stimulated by the interest rates offered.

National currencies, then, are potent feedback but impotent at triggering appropriate corrections. To picture how such a thing can be, imagine a group of people who are all properly equipped with diaphragms and lungs but who share only one single brainstem breathing center. In this goofy arrangement, the breathing center would receive consolidated feedback on the carbon-dioxide level of the whole group without discriminating among the individuals producing it. Everybody's diaphragm would thus be triggered to contract at the same time. But suppose some of those people were sleeping, while others were playing tennis. Suppose some were reading about feedback controls, while others were chopping wood. Some would have to halt what they were doing and subside into a lower common denominator of activity. Worse yet, suppose some were swimming and diving, and for some reason, such as the breaking of the surf, had no control over the timing of their submersions. Imagine what would happen to them. In such an arrangement, feedback control would be working perfectly on its own terms but the results would be devastating because of a flaw designed right into the system.

I have had to propose a preposterous situation because systems as structurally flawed as this don't exist in nature; they wouldn't last. Nor do they exist in the machines we deliberately design to incorporate mechanical, chemical or electronic feedback controls; machines this badly conceived wouldn't work. Nations, from this point of view, don't work either, yet do exist.

Nations are flawed in this way because they are not discrete economic units, although intellectually we pretend that they are and compile statistics about them based on that goofy premise. Nations include, among other things in their economic grab bags, differing city economies that need different corrections at given times, and yet all share a currency that gives all of them the same information at a given time. The consolidated information is bad specific information for them even with respect to their foreign trade, and it is no information at all with respect to their trade with one another, as opposed to their international trade. Yet this wretched feedback is powerful stuff.

Because currency feedback, at bottom, all has to do with imports and exports and the balance or lack of balance between them, the appropriate responding mechanisms for such information are cities and their regions. Cities are the specific economic units that can replace imports with their own production, and the specific units that cast up streams of new kinds of exports. It is bootless to suppose that amorphous, undifferentiated statistical collections of a nation's economies perform those functions, because they don't.

Ideally, at a time when a city's exports are doing well, it needs to receive as wide a range and as great a volume of earned imports as it can, especially from other cities, because those funds of earned imports are the grist the city must have for its vital process of import-replacing. Conversely, at a time when its exports are in decline, imports should ideally become expensive because to escape decline from diminishing export work a city desperately needs to replace wide ranges of its imports with local production. It also needs maximum stimulation for tentative new types of export work it may soon be capable of casting up. In other words, with falling exports a city needs a declining currency working like an automatic tariff and an automatic export subsidy—but only for as long as they are necessary. Once its exports are doing well, it needs a rising currency to earn the maximum variety and quantity of imports it can. Individual city currencies indeed serve as elegant feedback controls because they trigger specifically appropriate corrections to specific responding mechanisms.

This is a built-in design advantage that many cities of the past had but which almost none have now. Singapore and Hong Kong, which are oddities today, have their own currencies and so they possess this built-in advantage. They have no need of tariffs or export subsidies. Their currencies serve those functions when needed. but only as long as needed. Detroit, on the other hand, has no such advantage. When its export work first began to decline it got no feedback, so Detroit merely declined, uncorrected.

MEANING

1. In paragraph (6), Jacobs says "today we take it for granted that the elimination of multitudinous currencies in favor of fewer national or imperial currencies represents economic progress and promotes the stability of economic life. But this conventional belief is at least worth questioning in view of the function that currencies serve as economic feedback controls." What does this make you realize about the reason why Jacobs uses an analogy that is so drastic and involves life or death?
2. What is the relationship between a city's imports and exports and its vulnerability to changes in national currency rates?
3. Why are cities or regions more important than countries, according to Jacobs, as a basic unit of economic reaction?

USING ANALOGY TO CONVEY MEANING

1. Evaluate the effectiveness of Jacobs' startling analogy to alert her audience of economists to an unsuspected problem?
2. Based on Jacobs' analogy, what would be a "worst case scenario" if her insights were ignored by government economists?
3. What are the specific point-by-point resemblances between Jacobs' analogy and the economic predicament she foresees?

WRITING SUGGESTIONS

1. Discuss to what degree the predicament Jacobs describes might prevail in very large, medium-size, and small corporations. What connections can you discover between lack of effective feedback control and size of the corporation?
2. Use Jacobs' concept of faulty feedback to analyze and discuss how the lack of communication between the design engineers, managers, and politicians played a part in the 1986 "Challenger" disaster.

John McMurtry

Kill 'Em! Crush 'Em! Eat 'Em Raw!

John McMurtry was born in Toronto, Canada, in 1939 and received his B.A. from the University of Toronto, where he played college football. McMurtry subsequently was a linebacker for the Calgary Stampeders in the Canadian Football League. After a brief career as a football player (which ended abruptly because of injuries), McMurtry earned a Ph.D. in philosophy at the University of London. Since 1970, McMurtry has been professor of social and political philosophy at the University of Guelph in Ontario. In addition to The Structure of Marx's World-View *(1978), McMurtry has written a number of intriguing essays, including "Kill 'Em! Crush 'Em! Eat 'Em Raw!," which originally appeared in* Macleans *magazine in 1971. In this essay McMurtry casts a critical eye on society's love of violent sports through a thought-provoking analogy between football and war.*

A few months ago my neck got a hard crick in it. I couldn't turn my head; to look left or right I'd have to turn my whole body. But I'd had cricks in my neck since I started playing grade-school football and hockey; so I just ignored it. Then I began to notice that when I reached for any sort of large book (which I do pretty often as a philosophy teacher at the University of Guelph) I had trouble lifting it with one hand. I was losing the strength in my left arm, and I had such a steady pain in my back I often had to stretch out on the floor of the room I was in to relieve the pressure.

A few weeks later I mentioned to my brother, an orthopedic surgeon, that I'd lost the power in my arm since my neck began to hurt. Twenty-four hours later I was in a Toronto hospital not sure whether I might end up with a wasted upper limb. Apparently the steady pounding I had received playing college and professional football in the late Fifties and early Sixties had driven my head into my backbone so that the discs had crumpled together at the neck—"acute herniation"—and had cut the nerves to my left arm like a pinched telephone wire (without nerve stimulation, of course, the muscles atrophy, leaving the arm crippled). So I spent my Christmas holidays in the hospital in heavy traction and much of the next three months with my neck in a brace. Today most of the pain has gone, and I've recovered most of the strength in my arm. But from time to time I still have to don the brace, and surgery remains a possibility.

Not much of this will surprise anyone who knows football. It is a sport in which body wreckage is one of the leading conventions. A few days after I went into hospital for that crick in my neck, another brother, an outstanding football player in college, was undergoing spinal surgery in the same hospital two floors above me. In his case

427

it was a lower, more massive herniation, which every now and again buckled him so that he was unable to lift himself off his back for days at a time. By the time he entered the hospital for surgery he had already spent several months in bed. The operation was successful, but, as in all such cases, it will take him a year to recover fully.

These aren't isolated experiences. Just about anybody who has ever played football for any length of time, in high school, college or one of the professional leagues, has suffered for it later physically.

Indeed, it is arguable that body shattering is the very *point* of football, as killing and maiming are of war. (In the United States, for example, the game results in 15 to 20 deaths a year and about 50,000 major operations on knees alone.) To grasp some of the more conspicuous similarities between football and war, it is instructive to listen to the imperatives most frequently issued to the players by their coaches, teammates and fans. "Hurt 'em!" "Level 'em!" "Kill 'em!" "Take 'em apart!" Or watch for the plays that are most enthusiastically applauded by the fans. Where someone is "smeared," "knocked silly," "creamed," "nailed," "broken in two," or even "crucified." (One of my coaches when I played corner linebacker with the Calgary Stampeders in 1961 elaborated, often very inventively, on this language of destruction: admonishing us to "unjoin" the opponent, "make 'im remember you" and "stomp 'im like a bug.") Just as in hockey, where a fight will bring fans to their feet more often than a skillful play, so in football the mouth waters most of all for the really crippling block or tackle. For the kill. Thus the good teams are "hungry," the best players are "mean," and "casualties" are as much a part of the game as they are of a war.

The family resemblance between football and war is, indeed, striking. Their languages are similar: "field general," "long bomb," "blitz," "take a shot," "front line," "pursuit," "good hit," "the draft" and so on. Their principles and practices are alike: mass hysteria, the art of intimidation, absolute command and total obedience, territorial aggression, censorship, inflated insignia and propaganda, blackboard manoeuvres and strategies, drills, uniforms, formations, marching bands and training camps. And the virtues they celebrate are almost identical: hyper-aggressiveness, coolness under fire and suicidal bravery. All this has been implicitly recognized by such jock-loving Americans as media stars General Patton and President Nixon, who have talked about war as a football game. Patton wanted to make his Second World War tank men look like football players. And Nixon, as we know, was fond of comparing attacks on Vietnam to football plays and drawing coachly diagrams on a blackboard for TV war fans.

One difference between war and football, though, is that there is little or no protest against football. Perhaps the most extraordinary thing about the game is that the systematic infliction of injuries excites in people not concern, as would be the case if they were sustained at, say, a rock festival, but a collective rejoicing and euphoria. Players and fans alike revel in the spectacle of a combatant felled into semiconsciousness, "blindsided," "clotheslined" or "decapitated." I can remember, in fact, being chided by a coach in pro ball for not "getting my hat" injuriously into a player who was already lying helpless on the ground. (On another occasion, after the Stampeders had traded the celebrated Joe Kapp to BC, we were playing the Lions in Vancouver and Kapp was forced on one play to run with the ball. He was coming "down the chute," his bad knee wobbling uncertainly, so I simply dropped on him like a blanket. After I returned to the bench I was reproved for not exploiting the opportunity to unhinge his bad knee.)

After every game, of course, the papers are full of reports on the day's injuries, a sort of post-battle "body count," and the respective teams go to work with doctors and trainers, tape, whirlpool baths, cortisone and morphine to patch and deaden the wounds before the next game. Then the whole drama is reenacted—injured athletes held together by adhesive, braces and drugs—and the days following it are filled with even more feverish activity to put on the show yet again at the end of the next week. (I remember being so taped up in college that I earned the nickname "mummy.") The team that survives this merry-go-round spectacle of skilled masochism with the fewest incapacitating injuries usually wins. It is a sort of victory by ordeal: "We hurt them more than they hurt us."

My own initiation into this brutal circus was typical. I loved the game from the moment I could run with a ball. Played shoeless on a green open field with no one keeping score and in a spirit of reckless abandon and laughter, it's a very different sport. Almost no one gets hurt and it's rugged, open and exciting (it still is for me). But then, like everything else, it starts to be regulated and institutionalized by adult authorities. And the fun is over.

So it was as I began the long march through organized football. Now there was a coach and elders to make it clear by their behavior that beating other people was the only thing to celebrate and that trying to shake someone up every play was the only thing to be really proud of. Now there were severe rule enforcers, audiences, formally recorded victors and losers, and heavy equipment to permit crippling bodily moves and collisions (according to one American survey, more than 80% of all football injuries occur to fully equipped players). And now there was the official "given" that the only way to keep playing was to wear suffocating armor, to play to defeat, to follow orders silently and to renounce spontaneity for joyless drill. The game had been, in short, ruined. But because I loved to play and play skillfully, I stayed. And progressively and inexorably, as I moved through high school, college and pro leagues, my body was dismantled. Piece by piece.

I started off with torn ligaments in my knee at 13. Then, as the organization and the competition increased, the injuries came faster and harder. Broken nose (three times), broken jaw (fractured in the first half and dismissed as a "bad wisdom tooth," so I played with it for the rest of the game), ripped knee ligaments again. Torn ligaments in one ankle and a fracture in the other (which I remember feeling relieved about because it meant I could honorably stop drill-blocking a 270-pound defensive end). Repeated rib fractures and cartilage tears (usually carried, again, through the remainder of the game). More dislocations of the left shoulder than I can remember (the last one I played with because, as the Calgary Stampeder doctor said, it "couldn't be damaged any more"). Occasional broken or dislocated fingers and toes. Chronically hurt lower back (I still can't lift with it or change a tire without worrying about folding). Separated right shoulder (as with many other injuries, like badly bruised hips and legs, needled with morphine for the games). And so on. The last pro game I played—against Winnipeg Blue Bombers in the Western finals in 1961—I had a recently dislocated left shoulder, a more recently wrenched right shoulder and a chronic pain centre in one leg. I was so tied up with soreness I couldn't drive my car to the airport. But it never occurred to me or anyone else that I miss a play as a corner linebacker.

By the end of my football career, I had learned that physical injury—giving it and taking it—is the real currency of the sport. And that in the final analysis the "winner" is the man who can hit to kill even if only half his limbs are working. In brief, a warrior game with a warrior ethos into which (like almost everyone else I played with) my original boyish enthusiasm had been relentlessly taunted and conditioned.

In thinking back on how all this happened, though, I can pick out no villians. As with the social system as a whole, the game has a life of its own. Everyone grows up inside it, accepts it and fulfills its dictates as obediently as zealots. Far from ever questioning the principles of the activity, people simply concentrate on executing these principles more aggressively than anybody around them. The result is a group of people who, as the leagues become of a higher and higher class, are progressively insensitive to the possibility that things could be otherwise. Thus, in football, anyone who might question the wisdom or enjoyment of putting on heavy equipment on a hot day and running full speed at someone else with the intention of knocking him senseless would be regarded simply as not really a devoted athlete and probably "chicken." The choice is made straightforward. Either you, too, do your very utmost to efficiently smash and be smashed, or you admit incompetence or cowardice and quit. Since neither of these admissions is very pleasant, people generally keep any doubts they have to themselves and carry on.

Of course, it would be a mistake to suppose that there is more blind acceptance of brutal practices in organized football than elsewhere. On the contrary, a recent Harvard study has approvingly argued that football's characteristics of "impersonal acceptance of inflicted injury," an overriding "organization goal," the "ability to turn oneself on and off" and being, above all, "out to win" are of "inestimable value" to big corporations. Clearly, our sort of football is no sicker than the rest of our society. Even its organized destruction of physical well-being is not anomalous. A very large part of our wealth, work and time is, after all, spent in systematically destroying and harming human life. Manufacturing, selling and using weapons that tear opponents to pieces. Making ever bigger and faster predator-named cars with which to kill and injure one another by the million every year. And devoting our very lives to outgunning one another for power in an ever more destructive rat race. Yet all these practices are accepted without question by most people, even zealously defended and honored. Competitive, organized injuring is integral to our way of life, and football is simply one of the more intelligible mirrors of the whole process: a sort of colorful morality play showing us how exciting and rewarding it is to Smash Thy Neighbor.

Now it is fashionable to rationalize our collaboration in all this by arguing that, well, man *likes* to fight and injure his fellows and such games as football should be encouraged to discharge this original-sin urge into less harmful channels than, say, war. Public-show football, this line goes, plays the same sort of cathartic role as Aristotle said stage tragedy does: without real blood (or not much), it releases players and audience from unhealthy feelings stored up inside them.

As an ex-player in this seasonal coast-to-coast drama, I see little to recommend such a view. What organized football did to me was make me *suppress* my natural urges and re-express them in an alienating, vicious form. Spontaneous desires for free bodily exuberance and fraternization with competitors were shamed and forced under ("If it ain't hurtin' it ain't helpin' ") and in their place were demanded armoured mechanical moves and cool hatred of all opposition. Endless authoritarian drill and dressing-room harangues (ever wonder why competing teams can't prepare for a game in the same dressing room?) were the kinds of mechanisms employed to reconstruct joyful energies into mean and alien shapes. I am quite certain that everyone else around me was being similarly forced into this heavily equipped military precision and angry antagonism, because there was always a mutinous attitude about full-dress practices, and everybody (the pros included) had to concentrate incredibly hard for days to whip themselves into just one hour's hostility a week against another club. The players never speak of these things, of course, because everyone is so anxious to appear tough.

The claim that men like seriously to battle one another to some sort of finish is a myth. It only endures because it wears one of the oldest and most propagandized of masks—the romantic combatant. I sometimes wonder whether the violence all around us doesn't depend for its survival on the existence and preservation of this tough-guy disguise.

As for the effect of organized football on the spectator, the fan is not released from supposed feelings of violent aggression by watching his athletic heroes perform it so much as encouraged in the view that people-smashing is an admirable mode of self-expression. The most savage attackers, after all, are, by general agreement, the most efficient and worthy players of all (the biggest applause I ever received as a football player occurred when I ran over people or slammed them so hard they couldn't get up). Such circumstances can hardly be said to lessen the spectators' martial tendencies. Indeed it seems likely that the whole show just further develops and titillates the North American addiction for violent self-assertion. Perhaps it is for this reason that Trudeau became a national hero when he imposed the "big play," the War Measures Act, to smash the other team, the FLQ and its supporters, at the height of the football season. Perhaps, as well, it helps explain why the greater the zeal of U.S. political leaders as football fans (Johnson, Nixon, Agnew), the more enthusiastic the commitment to hard-line politics. At any rate there seems to be a strong correlation between people who relish tough football and people who relish intimidating and beating the hell out of commies, hippies, protest marchers and other opposition groups.

Watching well-advertised strong men knock other people around, make them hurt, is in the end like other tastes. It does not weaken with feeding and variation in form. It grows.

I got out of football in 1962. I had asked to be traded after Calgary had offered me a $25-a-week-plus-commissions off-season job as a clothing-store salesman. ("Dear Mr. Finks:" I wrote. [Jim Finks was then the Stampeders' general manager.] "Somehow I do not think the dialectical subtleties of Hegel, Marx and Plato would be suitably oriented amidst the environmental stimuli of jockey shorts and herringbone suits. I hope you make a profitable sale or trade of my contract to the East.") So the Stampeders traded me to Montreal. In a preseason intersquad game with the Alouettes I ripped the cartilages in my ribs on the hardest block I'd ever thrown. I had trouble breathing and I had to shuffle-walk with my torso on a tilt. The doctor in the local hospital said three weeks rest, the coach said scrimmage in two days. Three days later I was back home reading philosophy.

MEANING

1. Why does McMurtry's analogy between football and war illustrate how latent human aggression can be magnified and channeled into war?
2. What are some of the specific points that McMurtry says relates football to war?

USING ANALOGY TO CONVEY MEANING

1. What effect does McMurtry's lengthy description of his own football injuries have on your reading of this piece?
2. What level of knowledge about football does McMurtry assume on the part of his audience?
3. To what degree is it realistic for McMurtry to assume that his equation of football and war would cause an audience who likes football to see that the same impulses exhibited in football can lead to war?

WRITING SUGGESTIONS

1. Discuss areas connecting war and football that McMurtry might have overlooked. For example, might the press serve the same function as the cheerleaders? Might the World Court or International Red Cross serve as referees who lack the power to stop the game? In war, what would be the "football"?
2. How do the uniforms worn by football players contribute to what Alison Lurie (see "The Language of Clothes," page 413) might call a vocabulary of aggression?
3. Discuss the connections between McMurtry's after-the-fact account of his football experiences and the gradual enlightenment of the prisoner in Plato's allegory (see "The Allegory of the Cave," page 407).
4. In light of Ruth Benedict's article, "The Pueblos of New Mexico," (see page 246), what characteristics might link the Plains Indians to football and the Zuñi to baseball?

Leonard I. Stein

Male and Female: The Doctor-Nurse Game

Leonard I. Stein was born in 1929, Hartford, Connecticut. After earning his M.D. from the University of Wisconsin, Stein interned at Los Angeles County General Hospital (1960–1961) and took his residency in psychiatry at University Hospital, Madison, Wisconsin (1961–1964). He is currently professor of medicine at the University of Wisconsin Medical School and the medical director of the Dane County Mental Health Center in Madison. Stein received the American Psychological Association's Gold Achievement Award in 1974, has been published extensively in journals such as Archives of General Psychiatry, Quarterly Journal of Studies on Alcoholism, American Journal of Psychiatry, *and has coedited* Alternatives to Mental Hospital Treatment *(1977). In "Male and Female: The Doctor-Nurse Game" (1967) this perceptive psychiatrist uses game theory to explain the role-playing behavior of doctors and nurses.*

The relationship between the doctor and the nurse is a very special one. There are few professions where the degree of mutual respect and cooperation between co-workers is as intense as that between the doctor and nurse. Superficially, the stereotype of this relationship has been dramatized in many novels and television serials. When, however, it is observed carefully in an interactional framework, the relationship takes on a new dimension and has a special quality which fits a game model. The underlying attitudes which demand that this game be played are unfortunate. These attitudes create serious obstacles in the path of meaningful communications between physicians and nonmedical professional groups.

The physician traditionally and appropriately has total responsibility for making the decisions regarding the management of his patients' treatment. To guide his decisions he considers data gleaned from several sources. He acquires a complete medical history, performs a thorough physical examination, interprets laboratory findings, and at times, obtains recommendations from physician-consultants. Another important factor in his decision-making are the recommendations he receives from the nurse. The interaction between doctor and nurse through which these recommendations are communicated and received is unique and interesting.

THE GAME

One rarely hears a nurse say, "Doctor I would recommend that you order a retention enema for Mrs. Brown." A physician, upon hearing a recommendation of that nature, would gape in amazement at the effrontery of the nurse. The nurse, upon hearing

433

the statement, would look over her shoulder to see who said it, hardly believing the words actually came from her own mouth. Nevertheless, if one observes closely, nurses make recommendations of more import every hour and physicians willingly and respectfully consider them. If the nurse is to make a suggestion without appearing insolent and the doctor is to seriously consider that suggestion, their interaction must not violate the rules of the game.

Object of the game. The object of the game is as follows: the nurse is to be bold, have initiative, and be responsible for making significant recommendations, while at the same time she must appear passive. This must be done in such a manner so as to make her recommendations appear to be initiated by the physician.

Both participants must be acutely sensitive to each other's nonverbal and cryptic verbal communications. A slight lowering of the head, a minor shifting of position in the chair, or a seemingly nonrelevant comment concerning an event which occurred eight months ago must be interpreted as a powerful message. The game requires the nimbleness of a high wire acrobat, and if either participant slips the game can be shattered; the penalties for frequent failure are apt to be severe.

Rules of the game. The cardinal rule of the game is that open disagreement between the players must be avoided at all costs. Thus, the nurse must communicate her recommendations without appearing to be making a recommendation statement. The physician, in requesting a recommendation from a nurse, must do so without appearing to be asking for it. Utilization of this technique keeps anyone from committing themselves to a position before a sub rosa agreement on that position has already been established. In that way open disagreement is avoided. The greater the significance of the recommendation, the more subtly the game must be played.

To convey a subtle example of the game with all its nuances would require the talents of a literary artist. Lacking these talents, let me give you the following example which is unsubtle, but happens frequently. The medical resident on hospital call is awakened by telephone at 1:00 A.M. because a patient on a ward, not his own, has not been able to fall asleep. Dr. Jones answers the telephone and the dialogue goes like this:

> This is Dr. Jones.
> (An open and direct communication.)
> Dr. Jones, this is Miss Smith on 2W—Mrs. Brown, who learned today of her father's death, is unable to fall asleep.
> (This message has two levels. Openly, it describes a set of circumstances, a woman who is unable to sleep and who that morning received word of her father's death. Less openly, but just as directly, it is a diagnostic and recommendation statement; i.e., Mrs. Brown is unable to sleep because of her grief, and she should be given a sedative. Dr. Jones, accepting the diagnostic statement and replying to the recommendation statement, answers.)
> What sleeping medication has been helpful to Mrs. Brown in the past?
> (Dr. Jones, not knowing the patient, is asking for a recommendation from the nurse, who does know the patient, about what sleeping medication should be prescribed. Note, however, his question does not appear to be asking her for a recommendation. Miss Smith replies.)
> Pentobarbital mg 100 was quite effective night before last.
> (A disguised recommendation statement. Dr. Jones replies with a note of authority in his voice.)

Pentobarbital mg 100 before bedtime as needed for sleep; got it?
(Miss Smith ends the conversation with the tone of a grateful supplicant.)
Yes, I have, and thank you very much doctor.

The above is an example of a successfully played doctor-nurse game. The nurse made appropriate recommendations which were accepted by the physician and were helpful to the patient. The game was successful because the cardinal rule was not violated. The nurse was able to make her recommendation without appearing to, and the physician was able to ask for recommendations without conspicuously asking for them.

The scoring system. Inherent in any game are penalties and rewards for the players. In game theory the doctor-nurse game fits the nonzero sum game model. It is not like chess, where the players compete with each other and whatever one player loses the other wins. Rather, it is the kind of game in which the rewards and punishments are shared by both players. If they play the game successfully they both win rewards, and if they are unskilled and the game is played badly, they both suffer the penalty.

The most obvious reward from the well-played game is a doctor-nurse team that operates efficiently. The physician is able to utilize the nurse as a valuable consultant, and the nurse gains self-esteem and professional satisfaction from her job. The less obvious rewards are no less important. A successful game creates a doctor-nurse alliance; through this alliance the physician gains the respect and admiration of the nursing service. He can be confident that his nursing staff will smooth the path for getting his work done. His charts will be organized and waiting for him when he arrives, the ruffled feathers of patients and relatives will have been smoothed down, and his pet routines will be happily followed, and he will be helped in a thousand and one other ways.

The doctor-nurse alliance sheds its light on the nurse as well. She gains a reputation for being a "damn good nurse." She is respected by everyone and appropriately enjoys her position. When physicians discuss the nursing staff it would not be unusual for her name to be mentioned with respect and admiration. Their esteem for a good nurse is no less than their esteem for a good doctor.

The penalties for a game failure, on the other hand, can be severe. The physician who is an unskilled gamesman and fails to recognize the nurses' subtle recommendation messages is tolerated as a "clod." If, however, he interprets these messages as insolence and strongly indicates he does not wish to tolerate suggestions from nurses, he creates a rocky path for his travels. The old truism "If the nurse is your ally you've got it made, and if she has it in for you, be prepared for misery" takes on lifesized proportions. He receives three times as many phone calls after midnight than his colleagues. Nurses will not accept his telephone orders because "telephone orders are against the rules." Somehow, this rule gets suspended for the skilled players. Soon he becomes like Joe Bfstplk in the "Li'l Abner" comic strip. No matter where he goes, a black cloud constantly hovers over his head.

The unskilled gamesman nurse also pays heavily. The nurse who does not view her role as that of consultant, and therefore does not attempt to communicate recommendations, is perceived as a dullard and is mercifully allowed to fade into the woodwork.

The nurse who does see herself as a consultant but refuses to follow the rules of the game in making her recommendations has hell to pay. The outspoken nurse is labeled a "bitch" by the surgeon. The psychiatrist describes her as unconsciously suffering from penis envy and her behavior is the acting out of her hostility towards men. Loosely translated, the psychiatrist is saying she is a bitch. The employment of the unbright outspoken nurse is soon terminated. The outspoken bright nurse whose recommendations are worthwhile remains employed. She is, however, constantly reminded in a hundred ways that she is not loved.

GENESIS OF THE GAME

To understand how the game evolved, we must comprehend the nature of the doctors' and nurses' training which shaped the attitudes necessary for the game.

Medical student training. The medical student in his freshman year studies as if possessed. In the anatomy class he learns every groove and prominence on the bones of the skeleton as if life depended on it. As a matter of fact, he literally believes just that. He not infrequently says, "I've got to learn it exactly; a life may depend on me knowing that." A consequence of this attitude, which is carefully nurtured throughout medical school, is the development of a phobia: the overdetermined fear of making a mistake. The development of this fear is quite understandable.The burden the physician must carry is at times almost unbearable. He feels responsible in a very personal way for the lives of his patients. When a man dies leaving young children and a widow, the doctor carries some of her grief and despair inside himself; and when a child dies, some of him dies too. He sees himself as a warrior against death and disease. When he loses a battle, through no fault of his own, he nevertheless feels pangs of guilt, and he relentlessly searches himself to see if there might have been a way to alter the outcome. For the physician a mistake leading to a serious consequence is intolerable, and any mistake reminds him of his vulnerability. There is little wonder that he becomes phobic. The classical way in which phobias are managed is to avoid the source of the fear. Since it is impossible to avoid making some mistakes in an active practice of medicine, a substitute defensive maneuver is employed. The physican develops the belief that he is omnipotent and omniscient, and therefore incapable of making mistakes. This belief allows the phobic physician to actively engage in his practice rather than avoid it. The fear of committing an error in a critical field like medicine is unavoidable and appropriately realistic. The physician, however, must learn to live with the fear rather than handle it defensively through a posture of omnipotence. This defense markedly interferes with his interpersonal professional relationships.

Physicians, of course, deny feelings of omnipotence. The evidence, however, renders their denials to whispers in the wind. The slightest mistake inflicts a large narcissistic wound. Depending on his underlying personality structure the physician may obsess for days about it, quickly rationalize it away, or deny it. The guilt produced is unusually exaggerated and the incident is handled defensively. The ways in which physicians enhance and support each other's defenses when an error is made could be the topic of another paper. The feeling of omnipotence becomes generalized to other areas of his life. A report of the Federal Aviation Agency (FAA), as quoted in *Time Magazine* (August 5, 1966), states that in 1964 and 1965 physicians had a fatal-accident rate four times as high as the average for all other private pilots. Major causes of the high death rate were risk-taking attitudes and judgments. Almost all of the accidents occurred on pleasure trips, and were therefore not necessary risks to get to a patient needing emergency care. The trouble, suggested an FAA official, is that too many doctors fly with "the feeling that they are omnipotent." Thus, the extremes to which the physician may go in preserving his self-concept of omnipotence may threaten his own life. This overdetermined preservation of omnipotence is indicative of its brittleness and its underlying foundation of fear or failure.

The physician finds himself trapped in a paradox. He fervently wants to give his patient the best possible medical care, and being open to the nurses' recommendations helps him accomplish this. On the other hand, accepting advice from nonphysicians is highly threatening to his omnipotence. The solution for the paradox is to receive sub rosa recommendations and make them appear to be initiated by himself. In short, he must learn to play the doctor-nurse game.

Some physicians never learn to play the game. Most learn in their internship, and a perceptive few learn during their clerkships in medical school. Medical students frequently complain that the nursing staff treats them as if they had just completed a junior Red Cross first-aid class instead of two years of intensive medical training. Interviewing nurses in a training hospital sheds considerable light on this phenomenon. In their words they said,

> A few students just seem to be with it, they are able to understand what you are trying to tell them, and they are a pleasure to work with; most, however, pretend to know everything and refused to listen to anything we have to say and I guess we do give them a rough time.

In essence, they are saying that those students who quickly learn the game are rewarded, and those that do not are punished.

Most physicians learn to play the game after they have weathered a few experiences like the one described below. On the first day of his internship, the physician and nurse were making rounds. They stopped at the bed of a fifty-two-year-old woman who, after complimenting the young doctor on his appearance, complained to him of her problem with constipation. After several minutes of listening to her detailed description of peculiar diets, family home remedies, and special exercises that had helped her constipation in the past, the nurse politely interrupted the patient. She told her the doctor would take care of the problem and that he had to move on because there were other patients waiting to see him. The young doctor gave the nurse a stern look, turned toward the patient, and kindly told her he would order an enema for her that very afternoon. As they left the bedside, the nurse told him the patient had had a normal bowel movement every day for the past week and that in the twenty-three days the patient had been in the hospital she had never once passed up an opportunity to complain of her constipation. She quickly added that *if* the doctor wanted to order an enema, the patient would certainly receive one. After hearing this report the intern's mouth fell open and the wheels began turning in his head. He remembered the nurse's comment to the patient that "the doctor had to move on," and it occurred to him that perhaps she was really giving him a message. This experience and a few more like it, and the young doctor learns to listen for the subtle recommendations the nurses make.

Nursing student training. Unlike the medical student who usually learns to play the game after he finishes medical school, the nursing student begins to learn it early in her training. Throughout her education she is trained to play the doctor-nurse game.

Student nurses are taught how to relate to physicians. They are told he has infinitely more knowledge than they, and thus he should be shown the utmost respect. In addition, it was not many years ago when nurses were instructed to stand whenever a physician entered a room. When he would come in for a conference the nurse was expected to offer him her chair, and when both entered a room the nurse would open the door for him and allow him to enter first. Although these practices are no longer rigidly adhered to, the premise upon which they were based is still promulgated. One nurse described that premise as, "He's God almighty and your job is to wait on him."

To inculcate subservience and inhibit deviancy, nursing schools, for the most part, are tightly run, disciplined institutions. Certainly there is great variation among nursing schools, and there is little question that the trend is toward giving students more autonomy. However, in too many schools this trend has not gone far enough, and the climate remains restrictive. The student's schedule is firmly controlled and there is very little free time. Classroom hours, study hours, mealtime, and bedtime with lights out are rigidly enforced. In some schools meaningless chores are assigned, such as cleaning bedsprings with cotton applicators. The relationship between student and instructor continues this military flavor. Often their relationship is more like that between recruit and drill sergeant than between student and teacher. Open dialogue is inhibited by attitudes of strict black and white, with few, if any, shades of gray. Straying from the rigidly outlined path is sure to result in disciplinary action.

The inevitable result of these practices is to instill in the student nurse a fear of independent action. This inhibition of independent action is most marked when relating to physicians. One of the students' greatest fears is making a blunder while assisting a physician and being publicly ridiculed by him. This is really more a reflection of the nature of their training than the prevalence of abusive physicians. The fear of being humiliated for a blunder while assisting in a procedure is generalized to the fear of humiliation for making any independent act in relating to a physician, especially the act of making a direct recommendation. Every nurse interviewed felt that making a suggestion to a physician was equivalent to insulting and belittling him. It was tantamount to questioning his medical knowledge and insinuating he did not know his business. In light of her image of the physician as an omniscient and punitive figure, the questioning of his knowledge would be unthinkable.

The student, however, is also given messages quite contrary to the ones described above. She is continually told that she is an invaluable aid to the physician in the treatment of the patient. She is told that she must help him in every way possible, and she is imbued with a strong sense of responsibility for the care of her patient. Thus she, like the physician, is caught in a paradox. The first set of messages implies that the physician is omniscient and that any recommendation she might make would be insulting to him and leave her open to ridicule. The second set of messages implies that she is an important asset to him, has much to contribute, and is duty-bound to make those contributions. Thus, when her good sense tells her a recommendation would be helpful to him she is not allowed to communicate it directly, nor is she allowed not to communicate it. The way out of the bind is to use the doctor-nurse game and communicate the recommendation without appearing to do so.

FORCES PRESERVING THE GAME

Upon observing the indirect interactional system which is the heart of the doctor-nurse game, one must ask the question, "Why does this inefficient mode of communication continue to exist?" The forces mitigating against change are powerful.

Rewards and punishments. The doctor-nurse game has a powerful innate self-perpetuating force—its system of rewards and punishments. One potent method of shaping behavior is to reward one set of behavioral patterns and to punish patterns which deviate from it. As described earlier, the rewards given for a well-played game and the punishments meted out to unskilled players are impressive. This sytem alone would be sufficient to keep the game flourishing. The game, however, has additional forces.

The strength of the set. It is well recognized that sets are hard to break. A powerful attitudinal set is the nurse's perception that making a suggestion to a physician is equivalent to insulting and belittling him. An example of where attempts are regularly made to break this set is seen on psychiatric treatment wards operating on a therapeutic community model. This model requires open and direct communication between members of the team. Psychiatrists working in these settings expend a great deal of energy in urging for and rewarding openness before direct patterns of communication become established. The rigidity of the resistance to break this set is impressive. If the physician himself is a prisoner of a set and therefore does not actively try to destroy it, change is near impossible.

The need for leadership. Lack of leadership and structure in any organization produces anxiety in its members. As the importance of the organization's mission increases, the demand by its members for leadership commensurately increases. In our culture human life is near the top of our hierarchy of values, and organizations which deal with human lives, such as law and medicine, are very rigidly structured. Certainly some of this is necessary for the systematic management of the task. The excessive degree of rigidity, however, is demanded by its members for their own psychic comfort rather than for its utility in efficiently carrying out its mission. The game lends support to this thesis. Indirect communication is an inefficient mode of transmitting information. However, it effectively supports and protects a rigid organizational structure with the physician in clear authority. Maintaining an omnipotent leader provides the other members with a great sense of security.

Sexual roles. Another influence perpetuating the doctor-nurse game is the sexual identity of the players. Doctors are predominately men and nurses are almost exclusively women. There are elements of the game which reinforce the stereotyped roles of male dominance and female passivity. Some nursing instructors explicitly tell their students that their femininity is an important asset to be used when relating to physicians.

THE COMMUNITY

The doctor and nurse have a shared history and thus have been able to work out their game so that it operates more efficiently than one would expect in an indirect system. Major difficulty arises, however, when the physician works closely with other disciplines which are not normally considered part of the medical sphere. With expanding medical horizons encompassing cooperation with sociologists, engineers, anthropologists, computer analysts, etc., continued expectation of a doctor-nurselike interaction by the physician is disastrous. The sociologist, for example, is not willing to play that kind of game. When his direct communications are rebuffed the relationship breaks down.

The major disadvantage of a doctor-nurselike game is its inhibitory effect on open dialogue which is stifling and anti-intellectual. The game is basically a transactional neurosis, and both professions would enhance themselves by taking steps to change the attitudes which breed the game. . . .

Meaning

1. What did Stein's analysis show you about the degree to which informal sets of rules govern the practice of medicine?
2. What aspects in the training of doctors and nurses make it almost inevitable that recommendations for patient treatment can only be exchanged through the indirect route described by Stein?
3. How does correct "game-playing" reward the participants by reducing stress, bypassing confrontation, obtaining approval, and maintaining the status quo?
4. Discuss whether you agree with Stein's assessment that ultimately this "game" is a self-destructive "transactional neurosis."

Using Analogy to Convey Meaning

1. In what way does the game analogy clarify what otherwise might be a difficult-to-understand social and psychological phenomena?
2. This article originally appeared in a professional journal for the medical community; what effect might Stein hope his game analysis would have on his audience?
3. Evaluate the effectiveness of Stein's use of a nonthreatening game analogy to get a hearing for a serious problem from a profession that is resistant to change.
4. Stein spells out some of the advantages in using a game model to analyze a real-life situation; what are some of the disadvantages?

Writing Suggestions

1. Use Stein's game model to investigate the "interactional framework" between English composition instructors and their students. How do the participants "avoid confrontation, reduce stress, and obtain approval" from each other?
2. How does the meaning of "game" as Stein uses it differ from the usual idea of what a game is?
3. What other professions also have their own "games"? How are the games played?

SCIENCES

Fred Hoyle

The Continuous Creation of the Universe

Sir Fred Hoyle, an astro-physicist, was born in 1915 in Yorkshire, England, and earned an M.A. in 1939 from Cambridge University. After 1945, Hoyle taught mathematics at Cambridge and, in 1966, he became the director of the Cambridge Institute of Theoretical Astronomy. Between 1945 and 1973, Hoyle published significant theoretical work suggesting modifications of the general theory of relativity. He served as president of the Royal Astronomical Society from 1971 through 1973, the year in which he was knighted. Hoyle's theories of "continuous creation," which he espoused along with astronomers Thomas Gold and Hermann Bondi, were later displaced in favor of the "big-bang" theory of creation. His book, The Nature of the Universe *(1950; revised 1960), achieved wide popularity because of Hoyle's talent for clearly explaining the complex ideas in astronomy and physics. He has also written a number of science-fiction novels, some in collaboration with his son, Geoffrey. In "The Continuous Creation of the Universe" (1950), Hoyle uses an analogy drawn from common experience to help his readers visualize the abstract concept of an expanding universe.*

At the risk of seeming a little repetitive I should like to begin this chapter by recalling some of our previous results. One of the things I have been trying to do is to break up our survey of the Universe into distinct parts. We started with the Sun and our system of planets. To get an idea of the size of this system we took a model with the Sun represented by a ball about six inches in diameter. In spite of this enormous reduction of scale we found that our model would still cover the area of a small town. On the same scale the Earth has to be represented by a speck of dust, and the nearest stars are 2,000 miles away. So it is quite unwieldy to use this model to describe the positions of even the closest stars.

Some other means had to be found to get to grips with the distances of the stars in the Milky Way. Choosing light as our measure of distance, we saw that light takes several years to travel to us from near-by stars, and that many of the stars in the Milky Way are at a distance of as much as 1,000 light years. But the Milky Way is only a small bit of a great disk-shaped system of gas and stars that is turning in space like a great wheel. The diameter of the disk is about 60,000 light years. This distance is so colossal that there has only been time for the disk to turn round about twenty times since the oldest stars were born—about 4,000,000,000 years ago. And this is in spite of the tremendous speed of nearly 1,000,000 miles an hour at which the outer parts of the disk are moving. We also saw that the Sun and our planets lie together near the edge of our Galaxy, as this huge disk is called.

Now we shall go out into the depths of space far beyond the confines of our own Galaxy. Look out at the heavens on a clear night; if you want a really impressive sight do so from a steep mountainside or from a ship at sea. As I have said before, by looking at any part of the sky that is distant from the Milky Way you can see right out of the disk that forms our Galaxy. What lies out there? Not just scattered stars by themselves, but in every direction space is strewn with whole galaxies, each one like our own. Most of these other galaxies—or extra-galactic nebulae as astronomers often call them—are too faint to be seen with the naked eye, but vast numbers of them can be observed with a powerful telescope. When I say that these other galaxies are similar to our Galaxy, I do not mean that they are exactly alike. Some are much smaller than ours, others are not disk-shaped but nearly spherical in form. The basic similarity is that they are all enormous clouds of gas and stars, each one with anything from 100,000,000 to 10,000,000,000 or so members.

Although most of the other galaxies are somewhat different from ours, it is important to realize that some of them are indeed very like our Galaxy even so far as details are concerned. By good fortune one of the nearest of them, only about 700,000 light years away, seems to be practically a twin of our Galaxy. You can see it for yourself by looking in the constellation of Andromeda. With the naked eye it appears as a vague blur, but with a powerful telescope it shows up as one of the most impressive of all astronomical objects. On a good photograph of it you can easily pick out places where there are great clouds of dust. These clouds are just the sort of thing that in our own Galaxy produces the troublesome fog I mentioned in earlier talks. It is this fog that stops us seeing more than a small bit of our own Galaxy. If you want to get an idea of what our Galaxy would look like if it were seen from outside, the best way is to study this other one in Andromeda. If the truth be known I expect that in many places there living creatures are looking out across space at our Galaxy. They must be seeing much the same spectacle as we see when we look at their galaxy.

It would be possible to say a great deal about all these other galaxies: how they are spinning round like our own; how their brightest stars are supergiants, just like those of our Galaxy; and how in those where supergiants are common, wonderful spiral patterns are found. . . . We can also find exploding stars in these other galaxies. In particular, supernovae[1] are so brilliant that they show up even though they are very far off. Now the existence of supernovae in other galaxies has implications for our cosmology. You will remember that in a previous chapter I described the way in which planetary systems like our own come into being; the basic requirement of the process was the supernova explosion. So we can conclude, since supernovae occur in the other galaxies, planetary systems must exist there just as in our own.

---

[1] An extraordinarily bright star that radiates between ten million and one hundred million times as much energy as does our sun.

Moreover, by observing the other galaxies we get a far better idea of the rate at which supernovae occur than we could ever get from our Galaxy alone. A general survey by the American observers Baade and Zwicky has shown that on the average there is a supernova explosion every four or five hundred years in each galaxy. So, remembering our previous argument, you will see that on the average each galaxy must contain more than 1,000,000 planetary systems.

How many of these gigantic galaxies are there? Well, they are strewn through space as far as we can see with the most powerful telescopes. Spaced apart at an average distance of rather more than 1,000,000 light years, they certainly continue out to the fantastic distance of 1,000,000,000 light years. Our telescopes fail to penetrate further than that, so we cannot be certain that the galaxies extend still deeper into space, but we feel pretty sure that they do. One of the questions we shall have to consider later is what lies beyond the range of our most powerful instruments. But even within the range of observation there are about 100,000,000 galaxies. With upward of 1,000,000 planetary systems per galaxy the combined total for the parts of the Universe that we can see comes out at more than a hundred million million. I find myself wondering whether somewhere among them there is a cricket team that could beat the Australians.

We now come to the important question of where this great swarm of galaxies has come from. Perhaps I should first remind you of what was said when we were discussing the origin of the stars. We saw that in the space between the stars of our Galaxy there is a tenuous gas, the interstellar gas. At one time our Galaxy was a whirling disk of gas with no stars in it. Out of the gas, clouds condensed, and then in each cloud further condensations were formed. This went on until finally stars were born. Stars were formed in the other galaxies in exactly the same way. But we can go further than this and extend the condensation idea to include the origin of the galaxies themselves. Just as the basic step in explaining the origin of the stars is the recognition that a tenuous gas pervades the space within a galaxy, so the basic step in explaining the origin of the galaxies is the recognition that a still more tenuous gas fills the whole of space. It is out of this general background material, as I shall call it, that the galaxies have condensed.

Here now is a question that is important for our cosmology. What is the present density of the background material? The average density is so low that a pint measure would contain only about one atom. But small as this is, the total amount of the background material exceeds about a thousandfold the combined quantity of material in all the galaxies put together. This may seem surprising but it is a consequence of the fact that the galaxies occupy only a very small fraction of the whole of space. You see here the characteristic signature of the New Cosmology. We have seen that inside our Galaxy the interstellar gas outweighs the material in all the stars put together. Now we see that the background material outweighs by a large margin all the galaxies put together. And just as it is the interstellar gas that controls the situation inside our Galaxy, so it is the background material that controls the Universe as a whole. This will become increasingly clear as we go on.

The degree to which the background material has to be compressed to form a galaxy is not at all comparable with the tremendous compression necessary to produce a star. This you can see by thinking of a model in which our Galaxy is represented by a fifty-cent piece. Then the blob of background material out of which our Galaxy condensed would be only about a foot in diameter. This incidentally is the right way to think about the Universe as a whole. If in your mind's eye you take the average galaxy to be about the size of a bee—a small bee, a honeybee, not a bumblebee—our Galaxy, which is a good deal larger than the average, would be roughly represented in shape and size by the fifty-cent piece, and the average spacing of the galaxies would be about three yards, and the range of telescopic vision about a mile. So sit back and imagine a swarm of bees spaced about three yards apart and stretching away from you in all directions for a distance of about a mile. Now for each honeybee substitute the vast bulk of a galaxy and you have an idea of the Universe that has been revealed by the large American telescopes.

Next I must introduce the idea that this colossal swarm is not static: it is expanding. There are some people who seem to think that it would be a good idea if it was static. I disagree with this idea, if only because a static universe would be very dull. To show you what I mean by this I should like to point out that the Universe is wound up in two ways—that is to say, energy can be got out of the background material in two ways. Whenever a new galaxy is formed, gravitation supplies energy. For instance, gravitation supplies the energy of the rotation that develops when a galaxy condenses out of the background material. And gravitation again supplies energy during every subsequent condensation of the interstellar gas inside a galaxy. It is because of this energy that a star becomes hot when it is born. The second source of energy lies in the atomic nature of the background material. It seems likely that this was originally pure hydrogen. This does not mean that the background material is now entirely pure hydrogen, because it gets slightly adulterated by some of the material expelled by the exploding supernovae. As a source of energy hydrogen does not come into operation until high temperatures develop—and this only arises when stars condense. It is this second source of energy that is more familiar and important to us on the Earth.

Now, why would a Universe that was static on a large scale, that was not expanding in fact, be uninteresting? Because of the following sequence of events. Even if the Universe were static on a large scale it would not be locally static: that is to say, the background material would condense into galaxies, and after a few thousand million years this process would be completed—no background would be left. Furthermore, the gas out of which the galaxies were initially composed would condense into stars. When this stage was reached hydrogen would be steadily converted into helium. After several hundreds of thousands of millions of years this process would be everywhere completed and all the stars would evolve toward the black dwarfs[2] I mentioned in a previous chapter. So finally the whole Universe would become entirely dead. This would be the running down of the Universe that was described so graphically by Jeans.[3]

One of my main aims will be to explain why we get a different answer to this when we take account of the dynamic nature of the Universe. You might like to know something about the observational evidence that the Universe is indeed in a dynamic state of expansion. Perhaps you've noticed that a whistle from an approaching train has a higher pitch, and from a receding train a lower pitch, than a similar whistle from a stationary train. Light emitted by a moving source has the same property. The pitch of the light is lowered, or as we usually say reddened, if the source is moving away from us. Now we observe that the light from the galaxies is reddened, and the degree of reddening increases proportionately with the distance

---

[2] Burned-out stars.
[3] Sir James Jeans (1877–1946), distinguished British astronomer and physicist.

of a galaxy. The natural explanation of this is that the galaxies are rushing away from each other at enormous speeds, which for the most distant galaxies that we can see with the biggest telescopes become comparable with the speed of light itself.

My nonmathematical friends often tell me that they find it difficult to picture this expansion. Short of using a lot of mathematics I cannot do better than use the analogy of a balloon with a large number of dots marked on its surface. If the balloon is blown up the distances between the dots increase in the same way as the distances between the galaxies. Here I should give a warning that this analogy must not be taken too strictly. There are several important respects in which it is definitely misleading. For example, the dots on the surface of a balloon would themselves increase in size as the balloon was being blown up. This is not the case for the galaxies, for their internal gravitational fields are sufficiently strong to prevent any such expansion. A further weakness of our analogy is that the surface of an ordinary balloon is two dimensional—that is to say, the points of its surface can be described by two co-ordinates; for example, by latitude and longitude. In the case of the Universe we must think of the surface as possessing a third dimension. This is not as difficult as it may sound. We are all familiar with pictures in perspective—pictures in which artists have represented three-dimensional scenes on two-dimensional canvases. So it is not really a difficult conception to imagine the three dimensions of space as being confined to the surface of a balloon. But then what does the radius of the balloon represent, and what does it mean to say that the balloon is being blown up? The answer to this is that the radius of the balloon is a measure of time, and the passage of time has the effect of blowing up the balloon. This will give you a very rough, but useful, idea of the sort of theory investigated by the mathematician.

The balloon analogy brings out a very important point. It shows we must not imagine that we are situated at the center of the Universe, just because we see all the galaxies to be moving away from us. For, whichever dot you care to choose on the surface of the balloon, you will find that the other dots all move away from it. In other words, whichever galaxy you happen to be in, the other galaxies will appear to be receding from you.

Now let us consider the recession of the galaxies in a little more detail. The greater the distance of a galaxy the faster it is receding. Every time you double the distance you double the speed of recession. The speeds come out as vast beyond all precedent. Near-by galaxies are moving outward at several million miles an hour, whereas the most distant ones that can be seen with our biggest telescopes are receding at over 200,000,000 miles an hour. This leads us to the obvious question: If we could see galaxies lying at even greater distances; would their speeds be still vaster? Nobody seriously doubts that this would be so, which gives rise to a very curious situation that I will now describe.

Galaxies lying at only about twice the distance of the furthest ones that actually can be observed with the new telescope at Mount Palomar would be moving away from us at a speed that equalled light itself. Those at still greater distances would have speeds of recession exceeding that of light. Many people find this extremely puzzling because they have learned from Einstein's special theory of relativity that no material body can have a speed greater than light. This is true enough in the special theory of relativity which refers to a particularly simple system of space and time. But it is not true in Einstein's general theory of relativity, and it is in terms of the general theory that the Universe has to be discussed. The point is rather difficult, but I can do something toward making it a little clearer. The further a galaxy is away from us the more its distance will increase during the time required by its light to reach us. Indeed, if it is far enough away the light never reaches us at all because its path stretches faster than the light can make progress. This is what is meant by saying that the speed of recession exceeds the velocity of light. Events occurring in a galaxy at such a distance can never be observed at all by anyone inside our Galaxy, no matter how patient the observer and no matter how powerful his telescope. All the galaxies that we actually see are ones that lie close enough for their light to reach us in spite of the expansion of space that's going on. But the struggle of the light against the expansion of space does show itself, as I said before, in the reddening of the light.

As you will easily guess, there must be intermediate cases where a galaxy is at such a distance that, so to speak, the light it emits neither gains ground nor loses it. In this case the path between us and the galaxy stretches at just such a rate as exactly compensates for the velocity of the light. The light gets lost on the way. It is a case, as the Red Queen remarked to Alice, of "taking all the running you can do to keep in the same place." We know fairly accurately how far away a galaxy has to be for this special case to occur. The answer is about 2,000,000,000 light years, which is only about twice as far as the distances that we expect the giant telescope at Mount Palomar to penetrate. This means that we are already observing about half as far into space as we can ever hope to do. If we built a telescope a million times as big as the one at Mount Palomar we could scarcely double our present range of vision. So what it amounts to is that owing to the expansion of the Universe we can never observe events that happen outside a certain quite definite finite region of space. We refer to this finite region as the observable Universe. The word "observable" here does not mean that we actually observe, but what we could observe if we were equipped with perfect telescopes.

MEANING

1. What does Hoyle's detailed description of the immensity of the known universe make you realize about the need scientists might have for using analogies to explain their theories?
2. Why does the degree of redness in the wave lengths of light emanating from the galaxies serve as evidence for Hoyle's contention that the universe is not static but expanding?
3. Why would a galaxy receding faster than the speed of light be invisible, even to observers looking through telescopes much more powerful than any we have now?

USING ANALOGY TO CONVEY MEANING

1. What advantage can you see in Hoyle's use of down-to-earth analogies to explain abstract mathematical concepts?
2. Why is Hoyle's use of the balloon analogy in his theory of an expanding universe so effective in communicating the increasing distances between galaxies?

3. What are the physical features in an expanding universe that cannot be expressed through the balloon analogy?
4. Hoyle uses other analogies besides the balloon to describe hard-to-visualize astrophysical phenomena. Choose and discuss the effectiveness of one of these.

WRITING SUGGESTIONS

1. Discuss why the red spectrum of light from a receding galaxy represents the same kind of phenomena as a whistle of lower pitch from a receding train.
2. Hoyle says that he does not accept the "big-bang" theory for the creation of the universe, which most scientists now favor, "since it puts the basic assumption out of sight where it can never be challenged by a direct appeal to observation." What is the "big-bang" theory and which do you favor as a better explanation for the phenomena Hoyle discusses?
3. Choose any other mysterious phenomena in the universe (e.g., "black holes" in space) and explain it using a down-to-earth analogy.

CHRISTOPHER EVANS

The Revolution Begins

Christopher Evans (1931–1979) was born in Aberdovey, Wales. Evans received his Ph.D. from Reading, England, and served as the head of the Man-Computer Interaction Section, computer science division of the National Physical Laboratory, England, from 1963 until his untimely death in 1979. He was acknowledged as one of the world's leading experts on computers, and Evans' unique background in psychology and computer science are reflected in his wide range of published writings. He coedited Brain Physiology and Psychology *(1966)*, Cybernetics *(1968), and* Attention in Neurophysiology *(1969). Evans wrote* Psychology: A Dictionary of the Mind, Brain, and Behavior *(1978)*, The Mighty Micro: The Impact of the Computer Revolution *(1979), which became a six-part television series, and* The Micro Millennium *(1980), published posthumously and from which our selection is taken. In "The Revolution Begins," Evans uses an ingenious analogy to explain the incredible processing speed of a computer.*

Miniaturization did not stop when it came to etching complete circuits on a chip. With the technique known as large-scale integration, first hundreds, then thousands, and even tens of thousands of individual units could be amassed on one slice of semi-conductor. And still the process of miniaturization continued, is continuing, and so far as one can see will continue into the foreseeable future. The units of which computers are made are getting smaller and smaller, shrinking beyond the range of ordinary microscopes into the infinities of the molecular world. So rapid is the rate of progress that advance seems to be following advance on almost a monthly basis. At the time of writing the very latest memories, effectively containing a hundred thousand switching units, are being squeezed onto a chip, and may well be on the market by the time this book is published. On the horizon, or to be more exact on the laboratory bench, and scheduled for operation within a year or so, are the first million-unit chips.

Now a million is a peculiar number which gets flung around more and more as inflation makes government budgets soar into the stratosphere. It is easy, therefore, to devalue the concept of a machine made up of a million individual components, and yet which would still nestle on a fingernail. To get a rough idea of what we're talking about, suppose one expanded these units up to the size of the tubes in the original ENIAC and laid them side by side on a flat surface so that they were two inches apart—what size would this turn out to be? The answer is that it would be as big as a football field.

But let us look at it another way. When the first big computers attracted the attention of the Press in the early '50s, they were given the not totally misleading name of "electronic brains." The human brain itself is made up of minute electronic binary switching units called neurones, and there are an awful lot of them—about ten thousand million in all. But even assuming that neurones and electronic switching units are functionally equivalent, it was ridiculous, scientists used to argue, to talk of computers as "brains" and even more ridiculous, scientists used to argue, to talk of computers as "brains" and even more ridiculous to imagine them doing brain-like things. Why, if you wanted to build a computer which contained the same number of functional elements as the brain, you would end up with something the size of New York City and drawing more power than the whole of the subway system!

This daunting example was generally used to silence the brain / computer parallelists in the all-tube days of the early '50s and it makes quaint reading when you come across it today. By the early '60s, with transistorization, the computer / brain had shrunk to the size of the Statue of Liberty, and a ten-kilowatt generator would have kept it ticking over nicely. By the early '70s, with integrated circuits, there had been a further compression: it was down to the size of a Greyhound bus, and you could ran it off a mains plug. By the mid '70s it was the size of a TV set, and at the time of writing is that of a typewriter. And such is the pace of development that, allowing a one-year lag between the time I write these words and the time you read them, the incredible shrinking brain will have continued to shrink—to what size? My guess is that it will be no bigger than a human brain, perhaps even smaller. And to power it, a portable radio battery will suffice.

These careering changes, which will shortly lead to computers paralleling the brain both in size and in the number of their individual components, do not allow one to draw other parallels. Assuming one makes such a brain model and it sits there, capable of calculating at computer-like speeds, it will still be unable to perform any of the functions of a human brain. To do so it would have to be programmed appropriately, and the programming problems would be colossal. But this does not imply that it could *never* be so programmed, a topic which we will be picking up later. It is also fair to say that the computer would have an enormous edge on switching speed. The human brain would be chugging along at a hundred cycles per second, while no computer could be satisfied with a switching speed of less than a million cycles! Here again we have to pause and contemplate just what we are talking about.

Most people reckon a second to be rather a short period. There is not much you can do with it—blink an eye, speak one short word or read about ten characters of text. The idea that an electromechanical relay can flick back and forth twenty times in a single second sets up an image of a blurring, clattering bit of metal, and when you get to tubes operating thousands of times a second you move into a scale of time with which you have no touch-points. But what about millions of times a second? Are we not in danger of losing contact with the concept altogether? But this is just the beginning, and if you have not thought much about these things you had better steel yourself for a shock when I tell you that computers already exist whose switching potential is in the nanosecond range—this is billions of times in each tick of the clock. Once again we need to at least try to get this in perspective and can perhaps manage it by spreading time out with a broader brush. Since we so frequently hear the word "billion" employed in terms of money (I am talking about the American billion—a thousand million), let us use a context which is both monetary and temporal.

Imagine a British billionaire who decides that he is going to hand out a pound note to everyone who comes up to him—just one pound each. A long line forms and the billionaire starts handing out his pounds. He moves quickly and manages to get rid of them at the rate of one every ten seconds, but being human he can only keep it up for eight hours a day, five days a week. How long will it take him to dispose of his billion? Suppose that he has just handed out his last note, how long ago would it have been since he handed over his first one? Ten years? Twenty? Most people, when asked this question, take a jump in the dark and come up with a figure between ten and fifty years in the past. Once in a while someone will give you a date in the nineteenth century. Does that seem plausible or might it be even earlier? Does it seem conceivable, for example, that the billionaire could have started as far back as the Battle of Waterloo? Well, in fact he would have had to start before that. The Great Fire of London? No, he would have been counting away while Old St Paul's blazed. The execution of Anne Boleyn? No, he would have been counting then too. Agincourt? No. Battle of Hastings? No, further still. To cut a long story short, you would have to go back to the year 640 or thereabouts before you would see the billionaire handing over his first pound note. But that is just a taste of the cake. A billion times per second is no longer considered to be anything like the upper limit of computer processing speeds. Some recent observations indicate that on the surfaces of some of the latest semi-conductor materials, tiny magnetic elements can be seen switching, admittedly in an uncontrolled way, at rates approaching a trillion a second.

Carry the analogy to a trillionaire who wants to get rid of his money and you dive back in time beyond Christ, beyond Rome, beyond Greece, Stonehenge, Egypt and the Pyramids, before architecture, literature and language, and back to the Pliocene Age when Europe was encrusted with ice and the mammoth and woolly rhinoceros were the kings. There is no other word for it—such switching speeds are fantastic. And yet they are real: computers can operate at such speeds, and Man will find a way of making use of them.

Which brings us to the question of just what possible use could be found for these extremely fast, extremely small computers and their even faster, even smaller progeny. Surely there must be an upper limit to the speed with which people would want to calculate? Is it really going to help a company whose total tax and wage structure is handled by its own computer in one hour, to have it dealt with by the next generation of machines in one second? Alternatively, supposing that, using current memory technologies, all personnel details could be recorded on a flat magnetic disc the size of a 45 rpm record, what possible advantage could there be in storing it all on something the size of a postage stamp? These may seem to be natural questions, as indeed they are, but they are not the most important ones and they miss one or two big points.

Firstly, while massive increases in processing speeds are helpful when it comes to number-crunching, they begin to have far more dramatic yield when the power of the computer is directed towards tasks of a non-numerical nature. The distinction between numerical and non-numerical needs to be made with care, but we are talking about tasks where the computer's intellectual potential, its capacity for problem-solving, for fact finding, for logical analysis rather than for purely routine calculation, come to the fore. The use of the word "intellectual" in connection with computers is also treading on dangerous ground, but once computers move from routine to analytical and integrative functions, the increases in processing speed will begin to pay off and they will be able to tackle more complex problems.

The second point concerns reductions in size. Why make computers so small that if you drop one on the floor you are in danger of walking off with it stuck to the heel of your shoe? There are three answers to this question and together they sum up one of the most important single factors about the pace of computer development over the next few years. Very small computers have enormous advantages: firstly, because they consume minute amounts of power; secondly, because they are very cheap, thirdly, because they are extremely portable and can therefore be put to use in all kinds of different places. Indeed, we are shortly moving into the phase where computers will become one of the cheapest pieces of technology on earth—cheaper than TV sets (they already are), cheaper than portable typewriters, cheaper even than transistor radios. They will also, for exactly the same reasons, become the most common pieces of technology in the world, and the most useful.

MEANING

1. What does Evans' discussion of important developments at the frontiers of computer science reveal about the speed and size of computer circuits?
2. How will increasing processing speeds enable computers to not merely process numbers faster than ever, but make it possible for intelligent computers to solve problems using human logic?

USING ANALOGY TO CONVEY MEANING

1. How does Evans' use of the billionaire analogy help translate the computer scientist's concept of the "nanosecond" into a framework that is easier to comprehend?
2. What does Evans wish to illustrate when he compares the size of present components with tubes used in the original "ENIAC"?
3. To what degree is Evans successful in using comparisons and analogies to convey his enthusiasm about continual new developments in computer science?

WRITING SUGGESTIONS

1. Describe what kinds of functions you would like to see computers be able to perform in the future.
2. Evans uses an analogy to make understandable fantastic speeds in a microscopic environment (just as Fred Hoyle used an analogy to put into concrete terms immense distances beyond the grasp of our senses). In what way could the analogy of the sun within the solar system be used to explain the role of the heart in the human body?
3. How have more powerful computers made privacy an important issue?

Jean Henri Fabre

The Praying Mantis

Jean Henri Fabre (1823–1915), considered the father of entomology, received a Doctorate in natural sciences in 1864, Paris. Fabre published the first of his many distinctive works on the biology and behavior of insects in 1855. In the following year, Fabre was awarded the Prix Montyon for experimental physiology by the Institute of France. Charles Darwin praised the value of Fabre's research, in 1859, in his On the Origin of Species. *Fabre disclosed the importance of instinct in the habits of many insects, including dung beetles, and discovered how wasps paralyze their prey in response to specific stimulating zones. Fabre's major scientific work, the ten-volume* Souvenirs Entomologiques *(1878–1907), was accomplished between his retirement from academic life and the time of his death at age ninety-two. In "The Praying Mantis," from* The Insect World *(1949), Fabre uses dramatic analogies to convey the cannibalistic mating habits of the praying mantis with his characteristic blend of meticulous observations and engaging style.*

Another creature of the south is at least as interesting as the Cicada, but much less famous, because it makes no noise. Had Heaven granted it a pair of cymbals, the one thing needed, its renown would eclipse the great musician's, for it is most unusual in both shape and habits. Folk hereabouts call it *lou Prègo-Diéu,* the animal that prays to God. Its official name is the Praying Mantis. . . .

The language of science and the peasant's artless vocabulary agree in this case and represent the queer creature as a pythoness[1] delivering her oracles or an ascetic rapt in pious ecstasy. The comparison dates a long way back. Even in the time of the Greeks the insect was called *Mántis,* the divine, the prophet. The tiller of the soil is not particular about analogies: where points of resemblance are not too clear, he will make up for their deficiencies. He saw on the sun-scorched herbage an insect of imposing appearance, drawn up majestically in a half-erect posture. He noticed its gossamer wings, broad and green, trailing like long veils of finest lawn; he saw its fore-legs, its arms so to speak, raised to the sky in a gesture of invocation. That was enough; popular imagination did the rest; and behold the bushes from ancient times stocked with Delphic priestesses, with nuns in orison.

Good people, with your childish simplicity, how great was your mistake! Those sanctimonious airs are a mask for Satanic habits; those arms folded in prayer are cut-throat weapons: they tell no beads, they slay whatever passes within range. Forming

---

[1] A reference to the priestess who served Apollo at Delphi and to the sacred serpent in the caves of Mount Parnassus from which the oracles were delivered.

452

an exception which one would never have suspected in the herbivorous order of the Orthoptera, the Mantis feeds exclusively on living prey. She is the tigress of the peaceable entomological tribes, the ogress in ambush who levies a tribute of fresh meat. Picture her with sufficient strength; and her carnivorous appetites, combined with her traps of horrible perfection, would make her the terror of the country-side. The *Prègo-Dièu* would become a devilish vampire.

Apart from her lethal implement, the Mantis has nothing to inspire dread. She is not without a certain beauty, in fact, with her slender figure, her elegant bust, her pale-green colouring and her long gauze wings. No ferocious mandibles, opening like shears; on the contrary, a dainty pointed muzzle that seems made for billing and cooing. Thanks to a flexible neck, quite independent of the thorax, the head is able to move freely, to turn to right or left, to bend, to lift itself. Alone among insects, the Mantis directs her gaze; she inspects and examines; she almost has a physiognomy.

Great indeed is the contrast between the body as a whole, with its very pacific aspect, and the murderous mechanism of the forelegs, which are correctly described as raptorial.[2] The haunch is uncommonly long and powerful. Its function is to throw forward the rat-trap, which does not await its victim but goes in search of it. The snare is decked out with some show of finery. The base of the haunch is adorned on the inner surface with a pretty, black mark, having a white spot in the middle; and a few rows of bead-like dots complete the ornamentation.

The thigh, longer still, a sort of flattened spindle, carries on the front half of its lower surface two rows of sharp spikes. In the inner row there are a dozen, alternately black and green, the green being shorter than the black. This alternation of unequal lengths increases the number of cogs and improves the effectiveness of the weapon. The outer row is simpler and has only four teeth. Lastly, three spurs, the longest of all, stand out behind the two rows. In short, the thigh is a saw with two parallel blades, separated by a groove in which the leg lies when folded back.

The leg, which moves very easily on its joint with the thigh, is likewise a double-edged saw. The teeth are smaller, more numerous and closer together than those on the thigh. It ends in a strong hook whose point vies with the finest needle for sharpness, a hook fluted underneath and having a double blade like a curved pruning-knife.

This hook, a most perfect instrument for piercing and tearing, has left me many a painful memory. How often, when Mantis-hunting, clawed by the insect which I had just caught and not having both hands at liberty, have I been obliged to ask somebody else to release me from my tenacious captive! To try to free yourself by force, without first disengaging the claws implanted in your flesh, would expose you to scratches similar to those produced by the thorns of a rose-tree. None of our insects is so troublesome to handle. The Mantis claws you with her pruning-hooks, pricks you with her spikes, seizes you in her vice and makes self-defence almost impossible if, wishing to keep your prize alive, you refrain from giving the pinch of the thumb that would put an end to the struggle by crushing the creature.

When at rest, the trap is folded and pressed back against the chest and looks quite harmless. There you have the insect praying. But, should a victim pass, the attitude of prayer is dropped abruptly. Suddenly unfolded, the three long sections of the machine throw to a distance their terminal grapnel, which harpoons the prey

[2] Able to readily grasp victims.

and, in returning, draws it back between the two saws. The vice closes with a movement like that of the fore-arm and the upper arm; and all is over: Locusts, Grasshoppers and others even more powerful, once caught in the mechanism with its four rows of teeth, are irretrievably lost. Neither their desperate fluttering nor their kicking will make the terrible engine release its hold.

An uninterrupted study of the Mantis' habits is not practicable in the open fields; we must rear her at home. There is no difficulty about this: she does not mind being interned under glass, on condition that she be well fed. Offer her choice viands, served up fresh daily, and she will hardly feel her absence from the bushes.

As cages for my captives I have some ten large wire-gauze dishcovers, the same that are used to protect meat from the Flies. Each stands in a pan filled with sand. A dry tuft of thyme and a flat stone on which the laying may be done later constitute all the furniture. These huts are placed in a row on the large table in my insect laboratory, where the sun shines on them for the best part of the day. I install my captives in them, some singly, some in groups.

It is in the second fortnight of August that I begin to come upon the adult Mantis in the withered grass and on the brambles by the roadside. The females, already notably corpulent, are more frequent from day to day. Their slender companions, on the other hand, are rather scarce; and I sometimes have a good deal of difficulty in making up my couples, for there is an appalling consumption of these dwarfs in the cages. Let us keep these atrocities for later and speak first of the females.

They are great eaters, whose maintenance, when it has to last for some months, is none too easy. The provisions, which are nibbled at disdainfully and nearly all wasted, have to be renewed almost every day. I trust that the Mantis is more economical on her native bushes. When game is not plentiful, no doubt she devours every atom of her catch; in my cages she is extravagant, often dropping and abandoning the rich morsel after a few mouthfuls, without deriving any further benefit from it. This appears to be her particular method of beguiling the tedium of captivity.

To cope with these extravagant ways I have to employ assistants. Two or three small local idlers, bribed by the promise of a slice of melon or bread-and-butter, go morning and evening to the grass-plots in the neighbourhood and fill their game-bags—cases made of reed-stumps—with live Locusts and Grasshoppers. I on my side, net in hand, make a daily circuit of my enclosure, in the hope of obtaining some choice morsel for my boarders.

These tit-bits are intended to show me to what lengths the Mantis' strength and daring can go. They include the big Grey Locust . . . , who is larger than the insect that will consume him; the White-faced Decticus, armed with a vigorous pair of mandibles whereof our fingers would do well to fight shy; the quaint Tryxalis, who wears a pyramid-shaped mitre on her head; the Vine Ephippiger, who clashes cymbals and sports a sword at the bottom of her pot-belly. To this assortment of game that is not any too easy to tackle, let us add two monsters, two of the largest Spiders of the district: the Silky Epeira, whose flat, festooned abdomen is the size of a franc piece; and the Cross Spider, or Diadem Epeira, who is hideously hairy and obese.

I cannot doubt that the Mantis attacks such adversaries in the open, when I see her, under my covers, boldly giving battle to whatever comes in sight. Lying in wait among the bushes, she must profit by the fat prizes offered by chance even as, in the wire cage, she profits by the treasures due to my generosity. Those big hunts, full of danger, are no new thing: they form part of her normal existence. Nevertheless they appear to be rare, for want of opportunity, perhaps to the Mantis' deep regret.

Locusts of all kinds, Butterflies, Dragon-flies, large Flies, Bees and other moderate-sized captures are what we usually find in the lethal limbs. Still the fact remains that, in my cages, the daring huntress recoils before nothing. Sooner or later, Grey Locust and Dectius, Epeira and Tryxalis are harpooned, held tight between the saws and crunched with gusto. The facts are worth describing.

At the sight of the Grey Locust who has heedlessly approached along the trelliswork of the cover, the Mantis gives a convulsive shiver and suddenly adopts a terrifying posture. An electric shock would not produce a more rapid effect. The transition is so abrupt, the attitude so threatening that the observer beholding it for the first time at once hesitates and draws back his fingers, apprehensive of some unknown danger. Old hand as I am, I cannot even now help being startled, should I happen to be thinking of something else.

You see before you, most unexpectedly, a sort of bogey-man or Jack-in-the-box. The wing-covers open and are turned back on either side, slantingly; the wings spread to their full extent and stand erect like parallel sails or like a huge heraldic crest towering over the back; the tip of the abdomen curls upwards like a crosier, rises and falls, relaxing with short jerks and a sort of sough, a "Whoof! Whoof!" like that of a Turkeycock spreading his tail. It reminds one of the puffing of a startled Adder.

Planted defiantly on its four hind-legs, the insect holds its long bust almost upright. The murderous legs, originally folded and pressed together upon the chest, open wide, forming a cross with the body and revealing the arm-pits decorated with rows of beads and a black spot with a white dot in the centre. These two faint imitations of the eyes in a Peacock's tail, together with the dainty ivory beads, are warlike ornaments kept hidden at ordinary times. They are taken from the jewel-case only at the moment when we have to make ourselves brave and terrible for battle.

Motionless in her strange posture, the Mantis watches the Locust, with her eyes fixed in his direction and her head turning as on a pivot whenever the other changes his place. The object of this attitudinizing is evident: the Mantis wants to strike terror into her dangerous quarry, to paralyze it with fright, for, unless demoralized by fear, it would prove too formidable.

Does she succeed in this? Under the shiny head of the Decticus, behind the long face of the Locust, who can tell what passes? No sign of excitement betrays itself to our eyes on those impassive masks. Nevertheless it is certain that the threatened one is aware of the danger. He sees standing before him a spectre, with uplifted claws, ready to fall upon him; he feels that he is face to face with death; and he fails to escape while there is yet time. He who excels in leaping and could so easily hop out of reach of those talons, he, the big-thighed jumper, remains stupidly where he is, or even draws nearer with a leisurely step.

They say that little birds, paralysed with terror before the open jaws of the Snake, spell-bound by the reptile's gaze, lose their power of flight and allow themselves to be snapped up. The Locust often behaves in much the same way. See him within reach of the enchantress. The two grapnels fall, the claws strike, the double saws close and clutch. In vain the poor wretch protests: he chews space with his mandibles and, kicking desperately, strikes nothing but the air. His fate is sealed. The Mantis furls her wings, her battle-standard; she resumes her normal posture; and the meal begins.

In attacking the Tryxalis and the Ephippiger, less dangerous game than the Grey Locust and the Decticus, the spectral attitude is less imposing and of shorter duration. Often the throw of the grapnels is sufficient. This is likewise so in the case of the Epeira, who is grasped round the body with not a thought of her poison-fangs. With the smaller Locusts, the usual fare in my cages as in the open fields, the mantis seldom employs her intimidation-methods and contents herself with seizing the reckless one that passes within her reach.

When the prey to be captured is able to offer serious resistance, the Mantis has at her service a pose that terrorizes and fascinates her quarry and gives her claws a means of hitting with certainty. Her rat-traps close on a demoralized victim incapable of defence. She frightens her victim into immobility by suddenly striking a spectral attitude.

The wings play a great part in this fantastic pose. They are very wide, green on the outer edge, colourless and transparent every elsewhere. They are crossed lengthwise by numerous veins, which spread in the shape of a fan. Other veins, transversal and finer, intersect the first at right angles and with them form a multitude of meshes. In the spectral attitude, the wings are displaced and stand upright in two parallel planes that almost touch each other, like the wings of a Butterfly at rest. Between them the curled tip of the abdomen moves with sudden starts. The sort of breath which I have compared with the puffing of an Adder in a posture of defence comes from this rubbing of the abdomen against the nerves of the wings. To imitate the strange sound, all that you need do is to pass your nail quickly over the upper surface of an unfurled wing.

Wings are essential to the male, a slender pigmy who has to wander from thicket to thicket at mating-time. He has a well-developed pair, more than sufficient for his flight, the greatest range of which hardly amounts to four or five of our paces. The little fellow is exceedingly sober in his appetites. On rare occasions, in my cages, I catch him eating a lean Locust, an insignificant, perfectly harmless creature. This means that he knows nothing of the spectral attitude which is of no use to an unambitious hunter of his kind.

On the other hand, the advantage of the wings to the female is not very obvious, for she is inordinately stout at the time when her eggs ripen. She climbs, she runs; but, weighed down by her corpulence, she never flies. Then what is the object of wings, of wings, too, which are seldom matched for breadth?

The question becomes more significant if we consider the Grey Mantis . . . ., who is closely akin to the Praying Mantis. The male is winged and is even pretty quick at flying. The female, who drags a great belly full of eggs, reduces her wings to stumps and, like the cheesemakers of Auvergne and Savory, wears a short-tailed jacket. For one who is not meant to leave the dry grass and the stones, this abbreviated costume is more suitable than superfluous gauze furbelows. The Grey Mantis is right to retain but a mere vestige of the cumbrous sails.

Is the other wrong to keep her wings, to exaggerate them, even though she never flies? Not at all. The Praying Mantis hunts big game. Sometimes a formidable prey appears in her hiding-place. A direct attack might be fatal. The thing to do is first to intimidate the new-comer, to conquer his resistance by terror. With this object she suddenly unfurls her wings into a ghost's winding-sheet. The huge sails incapable of flight are hunting-implements. This stratagem is not needed by the little Grey Mantis, who captures feeble prey, such as Gnats and newborn Locusts. The two huntresses, who have similar habits and, because of their stoutness, are neither of them able to fly, are dressed to suit the difficulties of the ambuscade. The first, an impetuous amazon, puffs her wings into a threatening standard; the second, a modest fowler, reduces them to a pair of scanty coat-tails.

In a fit of hunger, after a fast of some days' duration, the Praying Mantis will gobble up a Grey Locust whole, except for the wings, which are too dry; and yet the victim of her voracity is as big as herself, or even bigger. Two hours are enough for consuming this monstrous head of game. An orgy of the sort is rare. I have witnessed it once or twice and have always wondered how the gluttonous creature found room for so much food and how it reversed in its favour the axiom that the cask must be greater than its contents. I can but admire the lofty privileges of a stomach through which matter merely passes, being at once digested, dissolved and done away with.

The usual bill of fare in my cages consists of Locusts of greatly varied species and sizes. It is interesting to watch the Mantis nibbling her Acridian, firmly held in the grip of her two murderous fore-legs. Notwithstanding the fine, pointed muzzle, which seems scarcely made for this gorging, the whole dish disappears, with the exception of the wings, of which only the slightly fleshy base is consumed. The legs, the tough skin, everything goes down. Sometimes the Mantis seizes one of the big hinder thighs by the knuckle-end, lifts it to her mouth, tastes it and crunches it with a little air of satisfaction. The Locust's fat and juicy thigh may well be a choice morsel for her, even as a leg of mutton is for us.

The prey is first attacked in the neck. While one of the two lethal legs holds the victim transfixed through the middle of the body, the other presses the head and makes the neck open upwards. The Mantis' muzzle roots and nibbles at this weak point in the armour with some persistency. A large wound appears in the head. The Locust gradually ceases kicking and becomes a lifeless corpse; and, from this moment, freer in its movements, the carnivorous insect picks and chooses its morsel.

The Mantis naturally wants to devour the victuals in peace, without being troubled by the plunges of a victim who absolutely refuses to be devoured. A meal liable to interruptions lacks savour. Now the principal means of defence in this case are the hind-legs, those vigorous levers which can kick out so brutally and which moreover are armed with toothed saws that would rip open the Mantis' bulky paunch if by ill-luck they happen to graze it. What shall we do to reduce them to helplessness, together with the others, which are not dangerous but troublesome all the same, with their desperate gesticulations?

Strictly speaking, it would be practicable to cut them off one by one. But that is a long process and attended with a certain risk. The Mantis has hit upon something better. She has an intimate knowledge of the anatomy of the spine. By first attacking her prize at the back of the half-opened neck and munching the cervical ganglia, she destroys the muscular energy at its main seat; and inertia supervenes, not suddenly and completely, for the clumsily-constructed Locust has not the Bee's exquisite and frail vitality, but still sufficiently, after the first mouthfuls. Soon the kicking and the gesticulating die down, all movements ceases and the game, however big it be, is consumed in perfect quiet.

The little that we have seen of the Mantis' habits hardly tallies with what we might have expected from her popular name. To judge by the term *Prègo-Diéu*, we should look to see a placid insect, deep in pious contemplation; and we find ourselves in the presence of a cannibal, of a ferocious spectre munching the brain of a panic-stricken victim. Nor is even this the most tragic part. The Mantis has in store for us, in her relations with her own kith and kin, manners even more atrocious than those prevailing among the Spiders, who have an evil reputation in this respect.

To reduce the number of cages on my big table and give myself a little more space while still retaining a fair-sized menagerie, I install several females, sometimes as many as a dozen, under one cover. So far as accommodation is concerned, no fault can be found with the common lodging. There is room and to spare for the evolutions of my captives, who naturally do not want to move about much with their unwieldy bellies. Hanging to the trelliswork of the dome, motionless they digest their food or else await an unwary passer-by. Even so do they act when at liberty in the thickets.

Cohabitation has its dangers. I know that even Donkeys, those peace-loving animals, quarrel when hay is scarce in the manger. My boarders, who are less complaisant, might well, in a moment of dearth, become sour-tempered and fight among themselves. I guard against this by keeping the cages well supplied with Locusts, renewed twice a day. Should civil war break out, famine cannot be pleaded as the excuse.

At first, things go pretty well. The community lives in peace, each Mantis grabbing and eating whatever comes near her, without seeking strife with her neighbours. But this harmonious period does not last long. The bellies swell, the eggs are ripening in the ovaries, marriage and laying-time are at hand. Then a sort of jealous fury bursts out, though there is an entire absence of males who might be held responsible for feminine rivalry. The working of the ovaries seems to pervert the flock, inspiring its members with a mania for devouring one another. There are threats, personal encounters, cannibal feasts. Once more the spectral pose appears, the hissing of the wings, the fearsome gesture of the grapnels outstretched and uplifted in the air. No hostile demonstration in front of a Grey Locust or White-faced Decticus could be more menacing.

For no reason that I can gather, two neighbors suddenly assume their attitude of war. They turn their heads to right and left, provoking each other, exchanging insulting glances. The "Puff! Puff!" of the wings rubbed by the abdomen sounds the charge. When the duel is to be limited to the first scratch received, without more serious consequences, the lethal fore-arms, which are usually kept folded, open like the leaves of a book and fall back sideways, encircling the long bust. It is a superb pose, but less terrible than that adopted in a fight to the death.

Then one of the grapnels, with a sudden spring, shoots out to its full length and strikes the rival; it is no less abruptly withdrawn and resumes the defensive. The adversary hits back. The fencing is rather like that of two Cats boxing each other's ears. At the first blood drawn from her flabby paunch, or even before receiving the last wound, one of the duellists confesses herself beaten and retires. The other furls her battle-standard and goes off elsewhither to meditate the capture of a Locust, keeping apparently calm, but ever ready to repeat the quarrel.

Very often, events take a more tragic turn. At such times, the full posture of the duels to the death is assumed. The murderous fore-arms are unfolded and raised in the air. Woe to the vanquished! The other seizes her in her vice and then and there proceeds to eat her, beginning at the neck, of course. The loathsome feast takes place as calmly as though it were a matter of crunching up a Grasshopper. The diner enjoys her sister as she would a lawful dish; and those around do not protest, being quite willing to do as much on the first occasion.

Oh, what savagery! Why, even Wolves are said not to eat one another. The Mantis has no such scruples; she banquets off her fellows when there is plenty of her favorite game, the Locust, around her. She practises the equivalent of cannibalism, that hideous peculiarity of man.

These aberrations, these child-bed cravings can reach an even more revolting stage. Let us watch the pairing and, to avoid the disorder of a crowd, let us isolate the couples under different covers. Each pair shall have its own home, where none will come to disturb the wedding. And let us not forget the provisions, with which we will keep them well supplied, so that there may be no excuse of hunger.

It is near the end of August. The male, that slender swain, thinks the moment propitious. He makes eyes at his strapping companion; he turns his head in her direction; he bends his neck and throws out his chest. His little pointed face wears an almost impassioned expression. Motionless, in this posture, for a long time he contemplates the object of his desire. She does not stir, is as though indifferent. The lover, however, has caught a sign of acquiescence, a sign of which I do not know the secret. He goes nearer; suddenly he spreads his wings, which quiver with a convulsive tremor. This is his declaration. He rushes, small as he is, upon the back of his corpulent companion, clings on as best he can, steadies his hold. As a rule, the preliminaries last a long time. At last, coupling takes place and is also long drawn out, lasting for five or six hours.

Nothing worthy of attention happens between the two motionless partners. They end by separating, but only to unite again in a more intimate fashion. If the poor fellow is loved by his lady as the vivifier of her ovaries, he is also loved as a piece of highly-flavoured game. And, that same day, or at latest on the morrow, he is seized by his spouse, who first gnaws his neck, in accordance with precedent, and then eats him deliberately, by little mouthfuls, leaving only the wings. Here we have no longer a case of jealously in the harem, but simply a depraved appetite.

I was curious to know what sort of reception a second male might expect from a recently fertilized female. The result of my enquiry was shocking. The Mantis, in many cases, is never sated with conjugal raptures and banquets. After a rest that varies in length, whether the eggs be laid or not, a second male is accepted and then devoured like the first. A third succeeds him, performs his function in life, is eaten and disappears. A fourth undergoes a like fate. In the course of two weeks I thus see one and the same Mantis use up seven males. She takes them all to her bosom and makes them all pay for the nuptial ecstasy with their lives.

Orgies such as this are frequent, in varying degrees, though there are exceptions. On very hot days, highly charged with electricity, they are almost the general rule. At such times the Mantes are in a very irritable mood. In the cages containing a large colony, the females devour one another more than ever; in the cages containing separate pairs, the males, after coupling, are more than ever treated as an ordinary prey.

I should like to be able to say, in mitigation of these conjugal atrocities, that the Mantis does not behave like this in a state of liberty; that the male, after doing his duty, has time to get out of the way, to make off, to escape from his terrible mistress, for in my cages he is given a respite, lasting sometimes until next day. What really occurs in the thickets I do not know, chance, a poor resource, having never instructed me concerning the love-affairs of the Mantis when at large. I can only go by what happens in the cages, when the captives, enjoying plenty of sunshine and food and spacious quarters, do not seem to suffer from homesickness in any way. What they do here they must also do under normal conditions.

Well, what happens there utterly refutes the idea that the males are given time to escape. I find, by themselves, a horrible couple engaged as follows. The male, absorbed in the performance of his vital functions, holds the female in a tight embrace. But the wretch has no head; he has no neck; he has hardly a body. The other, with her muzzle turned over her shoulder continues very placidly to gnaw what remains of his gentle swain. And, all the time, that masculine stump, holding on firmly, goes on with the business!

Love is stronger than death, men say. Taken literally, the aphorism has never received a more brilliant confirmation. A headless creature, an insect amputated down to the middle of the chest, a very corpse persists in endeavouring to give life. It will not let go until the abdomen, the seat of the procreative organs, is attacked.

Eating the lover after consummation of marriage, making a meal of the exhausted dwarf, henceforth good for nothing, can be understood, to some extent, in the insect world, which has no great scruples in matters of sentiment; but gobbling him up during the act goes beyond the wildest dreams of the most horrible imagination. I have seen it done with my own eyes and have not yet recovered from my astonishment.

MEANING

1. Why, according to Fabre, has the name "praying" mantis led to misconceptions about its nature?
2. What natural features in the praying mantis' armory of weapons make it a terror in its own world?
3. What strategy does the mantis use to intimidate prey twice its size?
4. How does the female mantis treat her mate during and after reproduction?

USING ANALOGY TO CONVEY MEANING

1. Discuss the benefits of Fabre's dramatic methods of presenting the mantis according to the scale of its world, in which it appears huge and terrifying, as opposed to our own, where it appears tiny and delicate.
2. How does the indirect comparison or analogy between the mantis and a fashionable lady (paragraph 4) make "her" behavior all the more shocking?
3. How does Fabre's use of analogy in paragraphs 6–9 focus the reader's attention on the mantis' efficiency as a predator?
4. Evaluate the effectiveness of Fabre's methods in adding dramatic interest to what is usually a rather dry subject—entomology.
5. Discuss how Fabre's comparison between insect and human courtship rituals serve to make the reader aware of how the mantis actually behaves.

Writing Suggestions

1. After observing an insect or some other diminuitive creature, possibly including a micro-organism viewed through a microscope, apply Fabre's methods of analogy and detail to highlight important and unusual features.
2. Since a scientist with a literary sensibility is rare, do you feel that Fabre's ability to make the world of insects interesting and entertaining makes him less credible as a scientific observer? Does his lively style achieve its effects at the expense of substance and objectivity? Discuss your reactions.

CAUSE AND EFFECT

Whereas process analysis explains *how* something works, causal analysis seeks to discover *why* something happened, or why it will happen by dividing an ongoing stream of events into causes and effects. Writers may proceed from a given effect and seek to discover what cause or chain of causes could have produced the observed effect, or show how further effects will flow from a known cause.

For example, the method of casual analysis was crucial to Sir Isaac Newton in the formulation of his three important "laws of motion." When Newton observed that (1) all objects remain at rest or move with constant velocity unless acted upon by a force, (2) the acceleration of a body is proportional to the force acting upon it, and (3) to every action there is an equal and opposite reaction, he was identifying the causal relationships between mass, motion, and acceleration.

Causal analysis is an invaluable analytical technique used across the disciplines. Because of the complexity of causal relationships, researchers try to identify, as precisely as possible, the contributory factors in any causal sequence. The direct or immediate causes of the event are those most likely to have triggered the actual event. Yet, behind direct causes may lie indirect or remote causes that set the stage or create the framework in which the event could occur. By the same token, long-term future effects are much more difficult to identify than are immediate, short-term effects.

Determining with any degree of certainty that *x* caused *y* is more complicated in situations where one cause may have produced multiple effects or the same effect could have been produced by multiple causes. Causal analysis can get off the track when writers confuse sequence with causation. Simply because A preceded B does not necessarily mean that A caused B. Perhaps A and B might both have been caused by some as yet unknown event C. This confusion of antecedent or correlation with causation is called the *post hoc* fallacy, from the Latin *post hoc, ergo propter hoc* (literally, "after this, therefore because of this"). Darrell Huff, in *How to Lie with Statistics*

(New York: W. W. Norton, 1982), p. 90, gives an amusing example of the *post hoc* fallacy:

> As an instance of the nonsense or spurious correlation that is a real statistical fact, someone has gleefully pointed to this: There is a close relationship between the salaries of Presbyterian ministers in Massachusetts and the price of rum in Havana. Which is the cause and which is the effect? In other words, are the ministers benefiting from the rum trade or supporting it? All right. That's so farfetched that it is ridiculous at a glance. But watch out for other applications of *post hoc* logic that differ from this one only in being more subtle. In the case of the ministers and the rum it is easy to see that both figures are growing because of the influence of a third factor: the historic and world-wide rise in the price level of practically everything.

A common error takes place when a necessary condition is mistaken for the cause. Most college students will agree that taking a course is a necessary condition to receiving an A; it is equally obvious that taking the course, while necessary, does not of itself cause the student to receive the A.

These theoretical considerations become very important in any "real-world" causal analysis. For example, a specialist in forensic medicine, brought in to help investigate a murder, will use causal analysis to determine the time and method of death. The approximate time of death can be estimated from the temperature of the body, the amount of clothing worn, the temperature of the surroundings, and the rate at which a dead body normally loses heat. Forensic techniques can also determine the cause of death. Analysis of a stab wound can disclose the size and shape of the weapon used, while analysis of a gunshot wound can reveal the distance and angle from which the bullet was fired, the caliber of the bullet, and even the type of gun used. By the same token, forensic chemists can identify from bits of paint the year, make, and model of a car that struck a hit-and-run victim.

Causes and effects can occur in connecting sequences of "chains of causation." For instance, the chain of consequences resulting from the ever-increasing cost of college was the subject of a 1985 report by the Carnegie Foundation for the Advancement of Teaching. As found by the report: (1) the cost of college, as reflected in tuitions, is rising faster than the inflation rate. The high cost of college makes it necessary for students to depend increasingly on outside support. As a consequence, (2) students borrow about ten billion dollars a year from the federal Guaranteed Student Loan program. The Foundation also discovered that (3) colleges increasingly offer students loans rather than scholarships or grants.

The immediate results are that (a) the proportion of undergraduates borrowing money for college rose from eleven to thirty percent from 1975 to 1984 and (b) average student indebtedness rose from $2,100 in 1975 to $7,900 in 1984. Next, the Foundation investigated some probable long-term effects. A student graduating with $8,000 in federal loan debt repayable at eight percent interest would owe $1,192 a year over ten years or $11,920. That amount would be eleven percent of a beginning engineer's discretionary annual income, twenty-one percent of a beginning nurse's disposable income, twenty-six percent of a beginning social worker's income, and thirty-three percent of a beginning teacher's income.

These facts produced two disturbing effects. The most obvious was that (1) students who borrow money for education often study in fields that will lead to jobs with high starting salaries so that they can pay back their loans faster; and (2) undergraduates frequently do not pursue careers in their field of prime interest; instead, economics is often the deciding factor. For instance, the Foundation discovered that (a) only one-third of those whose expected major was engineering or computer science declared these as areas of prime interest, (b) while nineteen percent said they planned business careers, only forty-seven percent of these declared business to be their field of prime interest, and (c) while only two percent selected music as their career choice, eighty-three percent of these said music was their prime interest.

The Foundation did not look into the long-term consequences for our society when so many young people enter professions that do not hold much interest for them, influenced by the economics of having to repay sizeable debts originally incurred to attend college. This example illustrates a chain of causation, where each effect itself becomes the cause of a further effect.

In this chapter we offer a variety of illustrations of different types of causal analyses across a broad range of disciplines. In "Why People Don't Help in a Crisis," social psychologists John M. Darley and Bibb Latane designed experiments to identify what factors make people, when they are part of a group, unwilling to aid victims they would have helped on a one-to-one basis. Darley and Latane discovered a clear correlation between the numbers of people witnessing an emergency and the willingness of any one individual to come to the aid of the victim. Surprisingly, the more people in a group, the less likely any one person was to volunteer to help the victim:

> A person trying to interpret a situation often looks at those around him to see how he should react. If everyone else is calm and indifferent, he will tend to remain so; if everyone else is reacting strongly, he is likely to become aroused. This tendency is not merely slavish conformity; ordinarily we derive much valuable information about new situations from how others around us behave. It's a rare traveler, who, in picking a roadside restaurant, chooses to stop at one where no other cars appear in the parking lot.

Darley and Latane's experiment successfully disclosed a significant correlation between a measurable cause (number of bystanders) and an observable effect (willingness of any one individual to aid the victim). Causal analysis is an important tool used by researchers to discover the means by which social pressures control the behavior of people in groups. In this case, Darley and Latane's results challenged the traditional idea that apathy is the reason bystanders are unwilling to help victims of street crime.

Although causal analysis seeks to identify specific reasons why a particular event has happened or will happen, it is crucial for researchers to be able to distinguish remote causes from immediate ones. Whereas a remote cause may create the possibility for an event to occur, an immediate cause triggers the actual event. Wilson Bryan Key, a communications specialist, wanted to discover why so many viewers of William Friedkin's movie, *The Exorcist*, became fearful, angry, and even physically sick after seeing the film. In "*The Exorcist* Massage Parlor," Key reveals that Friedkin had predisposed audiences to be frightened by interweaving images on the screen with sounds of squealing pigs and infuriated bees, submerged into the soundtrack at a level below the audience's conscious awareness. This subliminal use of sound, while not perceived consciously, created an undertone of fear that amplified the frightening nature of the images on the screen. Although an audience seeing *The Exorcist* might think that their anxiety was caused mainly by the images on the screen, Key's research disclosed that the ultimate cause of the audience's anxiety was an instinctive fear that these "archetypal" sounds produce in human beings. Without these subliminal sounds the movie would have been less frightening. Moreover, interviews with theatre staff who heard the soundtrack before actually viewing the film, revealed that they often experienced the same reactions of hysteria and anxiety as did members of the audience.

This same technique of distinguishing between predisposing and triggering causes is used by Aldous Huxley, political essayist and author of *Brave New World* (1932) to answer the question of why one particular segment of the German population was so easily swayed by Hitler's rhetoric:

> Hitler made his strongest appeal to those members of the lower middle classes who had been ruined by the inflation of 1923, and then ruined all over again by the depression of 1929 and the following years. "The masses" of whom he speaks were these bewildered, frustrated and chronically anxious millions. To make them more masslike, more homogeneously subhuman, he assembled them, by the thousands and the tens of thousands, in vast halls and arenas, where individuals could lose their personal identity, even their elementary humanity, and be merged with the crowd. . . .

In this passage from "Propaganda Under a Dictatorship," Huxley uses causal analysis to emphasize that the people most likely to yield to propaganda were those whose security had been destroyed by previous financial disasters. That is, previous cycles of financial instability (the disastrous inflation of 1923 and the depression of 1929) played a crucial role in predisposing the lower-middle classes, those whose security was most affected by the financial turmoil, to become receptive to Hitler's propaganda. Hitler, says Huxley, used techniques of propaganda—mass marches, repetition of slogans, scapegoating—to manipulate the segment of the population who were the least secure and most fearful.

Sometimes causal analysis attempts to show how each cause produces an effect, which then acts as a cause of a further effect. This "chain of causation" is illustrated by Jeff Greenfield's analysis of how the Beatles' music started a chain of events that ultimately had a profound political impact on our society:

> The real political impact of the Beatles was not in any four-point program or in an attack on injustice or the war in Vietnam. It was instead in the counterculture they had helped to create. Somewhere in the nineteen-sixties, millions of people began to regard themselves as a class separate from mainstream society *by virtue of their youth and the sensibility that youth produced.*

In essence, the Beatles and their music served as catalysts in creating a "counterculture" of millions of people who were inspired by the Beatles' ideal of communality (as expressed in their lyrics, "a little help from your friends") as an answer to an increasingly alienated society. Although the Beatles' music was, as Greenfield believes, nonpolitical and nonviolent, the climate created (culminating in 1969 at Woodstock) resulted in vast numbers of people who felt they could make a political impact and change society. To express this concept, Greenfield titles his essay: "The Beatles: They Changed Rock, Which Changed the Culture, Which Changed Us."

Causal analysis is an indispensable analytical method in the physical and biological sciences. In "How Flowers Changed the World," a fascinating application of this technique can be seen in Loren Eiseley's analysis of the chain of cause and effect that began with the appearance of flowering plants, or angiosperms, and led to the eventual existence of warm-blooded mammals. Flowers and vegetation played an indispensable role in preparing the way for mammalian life by adding great quantities of oxygen (through photosynthesis) to the atmosphere. The importance of this can be appreciated when, says Eiseley, we realize that:

> A high metabolic rate and the maintenance of a constant body temperature are supreme achievements in the evolution of life. They enable an animal to escape, within broad limits, from the overheating or the chilling of its immediate surroundings, and at the same time to maintain a peak mental efficiency. Creatures without a high metabolic rate are slaves to weather. Insects in the first frosts of autumn all run down like little clocks. Yet if you pick one up and breathe warmly upon it, it will begin to move about once more.

Eiseley points out how the appearance of flowers and vegetation produced more oxygen which, in turn, made it possible for mammals with higher metabolic rates to exist. If flowers had not appeared, animals would have remained reptilian, slow-moving, and completely dependent on the temperatures of their world. By contrast, higher metabolic rates unchained animals from the climate. And, all this, says Eiseley, is due to the flower.

Historians use causal analysis to put events into perspective. Barbara W. Tuchman's investigation of the fall of Troy, the mismanagement of the American Revolution by the British, and the debacle in Vietnam in "Epilogue: 'A Lantern on the Stern,'" led her to believe that "folly" has always been a major cause of disastrous governmental policies. The leaders in bureaucracies are particularly prone to fall back on automatic ways of doing things precisely at those times when creative decision making is required to avoid disastrous consequences. Ironically, says Tuchman, this is often true just at those moments in history when leaders are under the greatest pressure to make wise policy decisions. Throughout history, time and time again, overburdened leaders fall back on traditional solutions that might have worked for past crises but are inappropriate in their circumstances. This phenomenon, which Tuchman calls "folly," is the most common cause of political disasters.

It is most important that causal analysis demonstrate the means (sometimes called the "agency") by which an effect could have been produced. Each of the writers represented in this chapter is obligated to show how specific causes they identify could have produced the effects in question. Tuchman must illustrate how the decision-making process of bureaucrats is flawed by "folly"; Eiseley must show how higher metabolic rates of mammals depend on more oxygen; Greenfield must demonstrate how the nonpolitical nature of the Beatles' music could have produced a political effect; Huxley must disclose how the German masses were manipulated by Hitler's propaganda; Key must establish how a subliminal soundtrack could affect movie audiences without their knowledge; and Darley and Latane must prove how the size of a crowd determines the willingness of bystanders to aid victims of street crime.

In each of these cases, the authors deal with effects that are both real and observable. Carl Sagan, on the other hand, in "The Nuclear Winter," must show how an effect that has never been observed could be produced. Most people would not be convinced that the most devastating effect of even a small-scale nuclear war would be mass starvation. Yet, Sagan's research leads him to conclude that this would be the ultimate consequence of any nuclear exchange:

> In the baseline case, land temperatures, except for narrow strips of coastline, dropped to minus 25° Celsius (minus 13° Fahrenheit) and stayed below freezing for months— even for a summer war. . . . because the temperatures would drop so catastrophically,

virtually all crops and farm animals, at least in the Northern Hemisphere, would be destroyed, as would most varieties of uncultivated or domesticated food supplies. Most of the human survivors would starve.

The fatal chain of consequences that even a small-scale nuclear war would produce begins with (1) dust lofted into the atmosphere, producing (2) a greater than expected drop in global temperatures, lasting (3) much longer than anticipated, and resulting in (4) the extinction of crops and animals and (5) mass starvation among human beings. In the article from which this passage is taken, Sagan draws on many different kinds of evidence, including the computer's ability to stimulate hypothetical scenarios, to support the "nuclear-winter" hypothesis. Because of the hypothetical nature of this thesis, Sagan is obligated to show how the ecosystem is much more vulnerable—and the consequences of even a small-scale nuclear war much more extreme—than scientists previously believed.

LIBERAL ARTS

Jeff Greenfield

The Beatles: They Changed Rock, Which Changed the Culture, Which Changed Us

Jeff Greenfield, born in 1943 in New York City, graduated from Yale University School of Law in 1967 and worked as a legislative aide to the late Senator Robert Kennedy. In addition to writing informative books on sports, the media, politics, and popular culture, Greenfield has worked as a commentator for major television networks and is currently news-media analyst for ABC television. His writings include A Populist Manifesto *(1972), coauthored with Jack Newfield,* Where Have You Gone, Joe Dimaggio? *(1973),* Television: The First Fifty Years *(1977), and* The Real Campaign: How the Media Missed the Story of the 1980 Campaign *(1982). "The Beatles: They Changed Rock, Which Changed the Culture, Which Changed Us" (1975) is Greenfield's insightful analysis of the far-reaching effects initiated by the Beatles' arrival on the American scene in 1964.*

They have not performed together on stage for more than eight years. They have not made a record together in five years. The formal dissolution of their partnership in a London courtroom last month was an echo of an ending that came long ago. Now each of them is seeking to overcome the shadow of a past in which they were bound together by wealth, fame and adulation of an intensity unequaled in our culture. George Harrison scorns talk of reunion, telling us to stop living in the past. John Lennon told us years ago that "the dream is over."

He was right: When the Beatles broke up in 1970 in a welter of lawsuits and recriminations, the sixties were ending as well—in spirit as well as by the calendar. Bloodshed and bombings on campus, the harsh realities beneath the facile hopes for a "Woodstock nation," the shabby refuse of counterculture communities, all helped kill the dream.

469

What remains remarkable now, almost 20 years after John Lennon started playing rock 'n' roll music, more than a decade after their first worldwide conquest, is how appealing this dream was; how its vision of the world gripped so much of a generation; how that dream reshaped our recent past and affects us still. What remains remarkable is how strongly this dream was triggered, nurtured and broadened by one rock 'n' roll band of four Englishmen whose entire history as a group occurred before any of them reached the age of 30.

Their very power guarantees that an excursion into analysis cannot fully succeed. Their songs, their films, their lives formed so great a part of what we listened to and watched and talked about that everyone affected by them still sees the Beatles and hears their songs through a personal prism. And the Beatles themselves never abandoned a sense of self-parody and put-on. They were, in Richard Goldstein's phrase, "the clown-gurus of the sixties." Lennon said more than once that the Beatles sometimes put elusive references into their songs just to confuse their more solemn interpreters. "I am the egg man," they sang, not "egghead."

Still, the impact of the Beatles cannot be waved away. If the Marx they emulated was Groucho, not Karl, if their world was a playground instead of a battleground, they still changed what we listened to and how we listened ot it; they helped make rock music a battering ram for the youth culture's assault on the mainstream, and that assault in turn changed our culture permanently. And if the "dream" the Beatles helped create could not sustain itself in the real world, that speaks more to our false hopes than to their promises. They wrote and sang songs. We turned it into politics and philosophy and a road map to another way of life. The Beatles grew up as children of the first generation of rock 'n' roll, listening to and imitating the music of Little Richard, Larry Williams, Chuck Berry, Elvis Presley, and the later, more sophisticated sounds of the Shirelles and the Miracles. It was the special genius of their first mentor, Brian Epstein, to package four Liverpool working-class "rockers" as "mods," replacing their greasy hair, leather jackets, and on-stage vulgarity with jackets, ties, smiles and carefully groomed, distinctive haircuts. Just as white artists filtered and softened the raw energy of black artists in the nineteen-fifties, the Beatles at first were softer, safer versions of energetic rock 'n roll musicians. The words promised they only wanted to hold hands; the rhythm was more insistent.

By coming into prominence early in 1964, the Beatles probably saved rock 'n' roll from extinction. Rock in the early nineteen-sixties existed in name only; apart from the soul artists, it was a time of "shlock rock," with talentless media hypes like Fabian and Frankie Avalon riding the crest of the American Bandstand wave. By contrast, the Beatles provided a sense of musical energy that made successful a brilliant public-relations effort. Of course, the $50,000 used to promote the Beatles' first American appearance in February, 1964, fueled some of the early hysteria; so did the timing of their arrival.

Coming as it did less than a hundred days after the murder of John Kennedy, the advent of the Beatles caught America aching for any diversion to replace the images of a flat-draped casket and a riderless horse in the streets of Washington.

I remember a Sunday evening in early February, standing with hundreds of curious collegians in a University of Wisconsin dormitory, watching these four longhaired (!) Englishmen trying to be heard over the screams of Ed Sullivan's audience. Their music seemed to me then derivative, pleasant and bland, a mixture of hard rock and the sounds of the black groups then popular. I was convinced it would last six months, no more.

The Beatles, however, had more than hype; they had talent. Even their first hits, "I Want to Hold Your Hand," "She Loves You," "Please Please Me," "I Saw Her Standing There," had a hint of harmonies and melodies more inventive than standard rock tunes. More important, it became immediately clear that the Beatles were hipper, more complicated, than the bovine rock stars who could not seem to put four coherent words together.

In the spring of 1964, John Lennon published a book, "In His Own Write," which, instead of a ghost-written string of "groovy guides for keen teens," offered word plays, puns and black-humor satirical sketches. A few months later came the film "A Hard Day's Night," and in place of the classic let's-put-on-a-prom-and-invite-the-TeenChords plot of rock movies, the Beatles and director Richard Lester created a funny movie parodying the Beatles's own image.

I vividly recall going to that film in the midst of a National Student Association congress; at that time, rock 'n' roll was regarded as high-school nonsense by this solemn band of student-body presidents and future C.I.A. operatives. But after the film, I sensed a feeling of goodwill and camaraderie among that handful of rock fans who had watched this movie: The Beatles were media heroes without illusion, young men glorying in their sense of play and fun, laughing at the conventions of the world. They were worth listening to and admiring.

The real surprise came at the end of 1965, with the release of the "Rubber Soul" album. Starting with that album, and continuing through "Revolver" and "Sgt. Pepper's Lonely Hearts Club Band," the Beatles began to throw away the rigid conventions of rock 'n' roll music and lyrics. The banal abstract, second-hand emotions were replaced with sharp, sometimes mordant portraits of first-hand people and experiences, linked to music that was more complicated and more compelling than rock had ever dared attempt. The Beatles were drawing on their memories and feelings, not those cut from Tin Pan Alley cloth.

"Norwegian Wood" was about an unhappy, inconclusive affair ("I once had a girl / or should I say / she once had me"). "Michelle" and "Yesterday" were haunting, sentimental ballads, and Paul McCartney dared sing part of "Michelle" in French—most rock singers regarded English as a foreign language. "Penny Lane" used cornets to evoke the suggestion of a faintly heard band concert on a long-ago summer day. Staccato strings lent urgency to the story of "Eleanor Rigby."

These songs were different from the rock music that our elders had scorned with impunity. Traditionally, rock 'n' roll was rigidly structured: 4 / 4 tempo, 32 bars, with a limited range of instruments. Before the Beatles, rock producer Phil Spector had revolutionized records by adding strings to the drums, bass, sax and guitar, but the chord structure was usually limited to a basic blues or ballad pattern. Now the Beatles, with the kind of visibility that made them impossible to ignore, were expanding the range of rock, musically and lyrically. A sitar—a harpsichord effect—a ragtime piano—everything was possible.

With the release of "Sgt. Pepper" in the spring of 1967, the era of rock as a strictly adolescent phenomenon was gone. One song, "A Day in the Life," with its recital of an ordinary day combined with a dreamlike sense of dread and anxiety, made it impossible to ignore the skills of Lennon and McCartney. A decade earlier, Steve Allen mocked the inanity of rock by reading "Hound Dog" or "Tutti-Frutti" as if they were serious attempts at poetry. Once "Sgt. Pepper" was recorded, Partisan Review was lauding the Beatles, Ned Rorem proclaimed that "She's Leaving Home" was "equal to any song Schubert ever wrote," and a Newsweek critic meant it when he wrote: " 'Strawberry Fields Forever' [is] a superb Beatleizing of hope and despair in which the four minstrels regretfully recommend a Keatsian lotus-land of withdrawal from the centrifugal stresses of the age."

"We're so well established," McCartney had said in 1966, "that we can bring fans along with us and stretch the limits of pop." By using their fame to help break through the boundaries of rock, the Beatles proved that they were not the puppets of backstage manipulation or payola or hysterical 14-year-olds. Instead, they helped make rock music *the* music of an entire international generation. Perhaps for the first time in history, it was possible to say that tens of millions of people, defined simply by age, were all doing the same thing: they were listening to rock 'n' roll. That fact changed the popular culture of the world.

Rock 'n' roll's popularity had never been accompanied by respectability, even among the young. For those of us with intellectual pretenses, rock 'n' roll was like masturbation: exciting, but shameful. The culturally alienated went in for cool jazz, and folk music was the vehicle for the politically active minority. (The growth of political interest at the start of the sixties sparked something of a folk revival.)

Along with the leap of Bob Dylan into rock music, the Beatles destroyed this division. Rock 'n' roll was now broad enough, free enough, to encompass every kind of feeling. Its strength had always been rooted in the sexual energy of its rhythms; in that sense, the outraged parents who had seen rock as a threat to their children's virtue were right. Rock 'n' roll made you want to move and shake and get physically excited. The Beatles proved that this energy could be fused with a sensibility more subtle than the "let's-go-down-to-the-gym-and-beat-up-the-Coke-machine" quality of rock music.

In 1965, Barry McGuire recorded the first "rock protest" song (excluding the teen complaints of the Coasters and Chuck Berry). In his "Eve of Destruction," we heard references to Red China, Selma, Alabama, nuclear war and middle-class hypocrisy pounded out to heavy rock rhythms. That same year came a flood of "good time" rock music, with sweet, haunting melodies by groups like the Lovin' Spoonful and the Mamas and the Papas. There *were* no limits to what could be done; and the market was continually expanding.

The teen-agers of the nineteen-fifties had become the young adults of the nineteen-sixties, entering the professions, bringing with them a cultural frame of reference shaped in good measure by rock 'n' roll. The "youth" market was enormous—the flood of babies born during and just after World War II made the under-25 population group abnormally large; their tastes were more influential than ever before. And because the music had won acceptability, rock 'n' roll was not judged indulgently as a "boys will be boys" fad. Rock music was expressing a sensibility about the tangible world—about sensuality, about colors and sensations, about the need to change consciousness. And this sensibility soon spilled over into other arenas.

Looking back on the last half of the last decade, it is hard to think of a cultural innovation that did not carry with it the influence of rock music, and of the Beatles in particular: the miniskirt, discothèques, the graphics of Peter Max, the birth of publications like Rolling Stone, the "mind-bending" effects of TV commercials, the success of "Laugh-In" on television and "Easy Rider" in the movies—all of these cultural milestones owe something to the emergence of rock music as the most compelling and pervasive force in our culture.

This is especially true of the incredible spread of drugs—marijuana and the hallucinogens most particularly—among the youth culture. From "Rubber Soul" through "Sgt. Pepper," Beatle music was suffused with a sense of mystery and mysticism: odd choral progressions, mysterious instruments, dreamlike effects, and images that did not seem to yield to "straight" interpretation. Whether specific songs ("Lucy in the Sky with Diamonds," "A Little Help From My Friends") were deliberately referring to drugs is beside the point. The Beatles were publicly recounting their LSD experiences, and their music was replete with antirational sensibility. Indeed, it was a commonplace among my contemporaries that Beatle albums could not be understood fully without the use of drugs. For "Rubber Soul," marijuana; for "Sgt. Pepper," acid. When the Beatles told us to turn off our minds and float downstream, uncounted youngsters assumed that the key to this kind of mind-expansion could be found in a plant or a pill. Together with "head" groups like Jefferson Airplane and the Grateful Dead, the Beatles were, consciously or not, a major influence behind the spread of drugs.

In this sense, the Beatles are part of a chain: (1) the Beatles opened up rock; (2) rock changed the culture; (3) the culture changed us. Even limited to their impact as musicians, however, the Beatles were as powerful an influence as any group or individual; only Bob Dylan stands as their equal. They never stayed with a successful formula; they were always moving. By virtue of their fame, the Beatles were a giant amplifier, spreading "the word" on virtually every trend and mood of the last decade.

They were never pure forerunners. The Yardbirds used the sitar before the Beatles; the Beach Boys were experimenting with studio enhancement first; the Four Seasons were using elaborate harmonies before the Beatles. They were never as contemptuously antimiddle-class or decadent as the Kinks or the Rolling Stones; never as lyrically compelling as Dylan; never as musically brilliant as the Band; never as hallucinogenic as the San Francisco groups. John Gabree, one of the most perceptive of the early rock writers, said that "their job, and they have done it well, has been to travel a few miles behind the avant-garde, consolidating gains and popularizing new ideas."

Yet this very willingness meant that new ideas did not struggle and die in obscurity; instead, they touched a hundred million minds. Their songs reflected the widest range of mood of any group of their time. Their openness created a kind of salon for a whole generation of people, an idea exchange into which the youth of the world was wired. It was almost inevitable that, even against their will, their listeners shaped a dream of politics and lifestyle from the substance of popular music. It is testament both to the power of rock music, and to the illusions which can be spun out of impulses.

The Beatles were not political animals. Whatever they have done since going their separate ways, their behavior as a group reflected cheerful anarchy more than political rebellion. Indeed, as editorialists, they were closer to The Wall Street Journal than to Ramparts. "Taxman" assaults the heavy progressive income tax ("one for you, 19 for me"), and "Revolution" warned that "if you go carrying pictures of Chairman Mao / you ain't gonna make it with anyone anyhow."

The real political impact of the Beatles was not in any four-point program or in an attack on injustice or the war in Vietnam. It was instead in the counterculture they had helped to create. Somewhere in the nineteen-sixties, millions of people began to regard themselves as a class separate from mainstream society *by virtue of their youth and the sensibility that youth produced.*

The nineteen-fifties had produced the faintest hint of such an attitude in the defensive love of rock 'n' roll; if our parents hated it, it had to be good. The sixties had expanded this vague idea into a battle cry. "Don't trust anyone over 30!"—shouted from a police car in the first massive student protest of the dacade at Berkeley—suggested an outlook in which the mere aging process was an act of betrayal, in which youth itself was a moral value. Time magazine made the "under-25 generation" its Man of the Year in 1967, and politicians saw in the steadily escalating rebellion among the middle-class young a constituency and a scapegoat.

The core value of this "class" was not peace or social justice; it was instead a more elusive value, reflected by much of the music and by the Beatles' own portrait of themselves. It is expressed best by a scene from their movie "Help!" in which John, Paul, George and Ringo enter four adjoining row houses. The doors open—and suddenly the scene shifts inside, and we see that these "houses" are in fact one huge house; the four Beatles instantly reunite.

It is this sense of communality that was at the heart of the youth culture. It is what we wished to believe about the Beatles, and about the possibilities in our own lives. If there is one sweeping statement that makes sense about the children of the last decade, it is that the generation born of World War II was saying "no" to the atomized lives their parents had so feverishly sought. The most cherished value of the counterculture—preached if not always practiced—was its insistence on sharing, communality, a rejection of the retreat into private satisfaction. Rock 'n' roll was the magnet, the driving force, of a shared celebration, from Alan Freed's first mammoth dance parties in Cleveland in 1951, to the Avalon Ballroom in San Francisco, to the be-ins in our big cities to Woodstock itself. Spontaneous gathering was the ethic: Don't plan it, don't think about it, *do* it—you'll get by with a little help from your friends.

In their music, their films, their sense of play, the Beatles reflected this dream of a ceaseless celebration. If there *was* any real "message" in their songs, it was the message of Charles Reich: that the world would be changed by changing the consciousness of the new generation. "All you need is love," they sang. "Say the word [love] and you'll be free." "Let it be." "Everything's gonna be all right."

As a state of mind, it was a pleasant fantasy. As a way of life, it was doomed to disaster. The thousands of young people who flocked to California or to New York's Lower East Side to join the love generation found the world filled with people who did not share the ethic of mutual trust. The politicization of youth as a class helped to divide natural political allies and make politics more vulnerable to demagogues. As the Beatles found in their own personal and professional lives, the practical outside world has a merciless habit of intruding into fantasies; somebody has to pay the bills and somebody has to do the dishes in the commune and somebody has to protect us from the worst instincts of other human beings. John Lennon was expressing some very painful lessons when he told Rolling Stone shortly after the group's breakup that "nothing happened except we all dressed up . . . the same bastards are in control, the same people are runnin' everything."

MEANING

1. How did the arrival of the Beatles start a chain of events that ultimately had a profound political impact on our society?
2. Why were the Beatles and their music so influential in creating a "counterculture" of millions of people?

3. In what way did the Beatles embody an ideal of communality—"a little help from your friends"—as an answer to an increasingly alienated society?
4. How did the Beatles' gift for not taking themselves seriously, through self-parody, contribute to their longevity?
5. Did the Beatles reshape political and social ideals with their music or did existing social trends cause them to adapt their music to the times?

Using Cause and Effect to Convey Meaning

1. How does Greenfield's article take into account traditional journalistic questions—"what?" "who?" "when?" "where?" and "how?"—to create a factual background for his causal analysis?
2. How does Greenfield show that each link in the chain is capable of producing the next step in the chain; that is, how is each cause also an effect of a previous cause?
3. How does Greenfield use the event of Woodstock to support his assertion in the title: "The Beatles: They Changed Rock, Which Changed the Culture, Which Changed Us"?

Writing Suggestions

1. How might a musician take an approach completely different from Greenfield's in discussing the Beatles' musical contributions? For example, what unusual changes did the Beatles make in instrumentation, recording techniques, or use of melodies from cultures other than their own?
2. What present-day groups, if any, are as influential in changing today's culture as the Beatles were in their time? Explain the reasons behind your choice.
3. Take any one of the Beatles' songs and analyze the story it tells and the message it communicates.
4. As a research project, read Tom Wolfe's "The Electric Kool-Aid Acid Test" about Ken Kesey's experiments with the Merry Pranksters and The Grateful Dead. Discuss how The Grateful Dead produced changes in American culture at least as important, yet different from, those produced by the Beatles.

Barbara W. Tuchman

Epilogue: "A Lantern on the Stern"

Barbara W. Tuchman was born in 1912 in New York City. After graduating from Radcliffe in 1933, she worked as an editorial assistant for The Nation, *and later, in 1937 and 1938, covered the Spanish Civil War. In 1939, Tuchman was a correspondent based in London for the* New Statesman and Nation. *She achieved prominence as a historian with* The Zimmerman Telegram *(1958), which disclosed efforts by a German foreign minister to create an alliance with Mexico (in return for promised territory) before World War I. Tuchman gained international recognition with* The Guns of Ausust *(1962), a Pulitzer Prize-winning account of the beginnings of World War I, and* Stilwell and the American Experience in China *(1971), for which she won her second Pulitzer Prize. Tuchman's recent works include* A Distant Mirror: The Calamitous 14th Century *(1978) and* The March of Folly: From Troy to Vietnam *(1984), a brilliant analysis of the causes of governmental folly in four decisive turning points in history. "Epilogue: 'A Lantern on the Stern'" is the concluding chapter from the latter work where Tuchman summarizes how large a part "folly" played in the Trojan war, in the Protestant Secession from the Papacy, in George III's loss of the American colonies, and in America's disastrous thirty-year involvement in Vietnam.*

If pursuing disadvantage after the disadvantage has become obvious is irrational, then rejection of reason is the prime characteristic of folly. According to the Stoics, reason was the "thinking fire" that directs the affairs of the world, and the emperor or ruler of the state was considered to be "the servant of divine reason [appointed] to maintain order on earth." The theory was comforting, but then as now "divine reason" was more often than not overpowered by non-rational human frailties—ambition, anxiety, status-seeking, face-saving, illusions, self-delusions, fixed prejudices. Although the structure of human thought is based on logical procedure from premise to conclusion, it is not proof against the frailties and the passions.

Rational thought clearly counseled the Trojans to suspect a trick when they woke to find the entire Greek army had vanished, leaving only a strange and monstrous prodigy beneath their walls. Rational procedure would have been, at the least, to test the Horse for concealed enemies as they were urgently advised to do by Capys the Elder, Laocoon and Cassandra. That alternative was present and available yet discarded in favor of self-destruction.

In the case of the Popes, reason was perhaps less accessible. They were so imbued by the rampant greed and grab and uninhibited self-gratification of their time that a rational response to the needs of their constituency was almost beyond their scope.

476

It would have required a culture of different values. One might suppose that an ordinary instinct of self-preservation would have taken notice of the rising dissatisfaction lapping like flood water at their feet, but their view of the Papacy was temporal and secular, and they were too immersed in princely wars and in private consumption and display to take alarm at the intangible of discontent. The Papacy's folly lay not so much in being irrational as in being totally estranged from its appointed task.

The successive measures taken with regard both to the American colonies and to Vietnam were so plainly grounded in preconceived fixed attitudes and so regularly contrary to common sense, rational inference and cogent advice that, as folly, they speak for themselves.

In the operations of government, the impotence of reason is serious because it affects everything within reach—citizens, society, civilization. It was a problem of deep concern to the Greek founders of Western thought. Euripides, in his last plays, conceded that the mystery of moral evil and of folly could no longer be explained by external cause, by the bite of Atē, as if by a spider, or by other intervention of the gods. Men and women had to confront it as part of their being. His Medea knows herself to be controlled by passion "stronger than my purposes." Plato, some fifty years later, desperately wanted man to grasp and never let go of the "sacred golden cord of reason," but ultimately he too had to acknowledge that his fellow-beings were anchored in the life of feelings, jerked like puppets by the strings of desires and fears that made them dance. When desire disagrees with the judgment of reason, he said, there is a disease of the soul, "And when the soul is opposed to knowledge, or opinion or reason which are her natural laws, that I call folly."

When it came to government, Plato assumed that a wise ruler would take most care of what he loved most, that is, what fitted best with his own interests, which would be equivalent to the best interests of the state. Since he was not confident that the rule always operated the way it should, Plato advised as a cautionary procedure that the future guardians of the state should be watched and tested during their period of maturing to ensure that they conducted themselves according to the rule.

With the advent of Christianity, personal responsibility was given back to the external and supernatural, at the command of God and the Devil. Reason returned for a brief brilliant reign in the 18th century, since when Freud has brought us back to Euripides and the controlling power of the dark, buried forces of the soul, which not being subject to the mind are incorrigible by good intentions or rational will.

Chief among the forces affecting political folly is lust for power, named by Tacitus as "the most flagrant of all the passions." Because it can only be satisfied by power over others, government is its favorite field of exercise. Business offers a kind of power, but only to the very successful at the very top, and without the dominion and titles and red carpets and motorcycle escorts of public office. Other occupations—sports, sciences, the professions and the creative and performing arts—offer various satisfactions but not the opportunity for power. They may appeal to status-seekers and, in the form of celebrity, offer crowd worship and limousines and prizes, but these are the trappings of power, not the essence. Government remains the paramount area of folly because it is there that men seek power over others—only to lose it over themselves.

Thomas Jefferson, who held more and higher offices than most men, took the sourest view of it. "Whenever a man has cast a longing eye on [office]," he wrote to a friend, "a rottenness begins in his conduct." His contemporary across the Atlantic, Adam Smith, was if anything more censorious. "And thus *Place* . . . is the end of half the labors of human life; and is the cause of all the tumult and bustle, all the rapine and injustice which avarice and ambition have introduced into this world." Both were speaking of moral failure, not of competence. When that comes into question, it gains no higher rating from other statesmen. In the 1930s, when a chairman was being sought for the Senate investigation of the munitions industry, a leader of the peace movement asked the advice of Senator George Norris. Ruling himself out as too old, Norris went down the list of his colleagues, crossing off one after the other as too lazy, too stupid, too close to the Army, as moral cowards or overworked or in poor health or having conflict of interest or facing re-election. When he had finished he had eliminated all but Senator Gerald Nye, the only one out of the 96 whom he deemed to have the competence, independence and stature for the task. Much the same opinion in different circumstances was pronounced by General Eisenhower in discussing the need for inspired leaders to create a United States of Europe as the only way to preserve Europe's security. He did not think it would happen, because "Everyone is too cautious, too fearful, too lazy, and too ambitious (personally)." Odd and notable is the appearance of lazy in both catalogues.

A greater inducement to folly is excess of power. After he had conceived his wonderful vision of philosopher-kings in the Republic, Plato began to have doubts and reached the conclusion that laws were the only safeguard. Too much power given to anything, like too large a sail on a vessel, he believed, is dangerous; moderation is overthrown. Excess leads on the one hand to disorder and on the other to injustice. No soul of man is able to resist the temptation of arbitrary power, and there is "No one who will not under such circumstances become filled with folly, the worst of diseases." His kingdom will be undermined and "all his power will vanish from him." Such indeed was the fate that overtook the Renaissance Papacy to the point of half, if not all, of its power; and Louis XIV, although not until after his death; and—if we consider the American Presidency to confer excess of power—Lyndon Johnson, who was given to speaking of "*my* air force" and thought his position entitled him to lie and deceive; and, most obviously, Richard Nixon.

Mental standstill or stagnation—the maintenance intact by rulers and policy-makers of the ideas they started with—is fertile ground for folly. Montezuma is a fatal and tragic example. Leaders in government, on the authority of Henry Kissinger, do not learn beyond the convictions they bring with them; these are "the intellectual capital they will consume as long as they are in office." Learning from experience is a faculty almost never practiced. Why did American experience of supporting the unpopular party in China supply no analogy to Vietnam? And the experience of Vietnam none for Iran? And why has none of the above conveyed any inference to preserve the present government of the United States from imbecility in El Salvador? "If men could learn from history, what lessons it might teach us!" lamented Samuel Coleridge. "But passion and party blind our eyes, and the light which experience gives us is a lantern on the stern which shines only on the waves behind us." The image is beautiful but the message misleading, for the light on the waves we have passed through should enable us to infer the nature of the waves ahead.

In its first stage, mental standstill fixes the principles and boundaries governing a political problem. In the second stage, when dissonances and failing function begin to appear, the initial principles rigidify. This is the period when, if wisdom were operative, re-examination and re-thinking and a change of course are possible, but they are rare as rubies in a backyard. Rigidifying leads to increase of investment and the need to protect egos; policy founded upon error multiples, never retreats. The greater the investment and the more involved in it the sponsor's ego, the more unaccept-able is disengagement. In the third stage, pursuit of failure enlarges the damages until it causes the fall of Troy, the defection from the Papacy, the loss of a trans-Atlantic empire, the classic humiliation in Vietnam.

Persistence in error is the problem. Practitioners of government continue down the wrong road as if in thrall to some Merlin with magic power to direct their steps. There are Merlins in early literature to explain human aberration, but freedom of choice does exist—unless we accept the Freudian unconscious as the new Merlin. Rulers will justify a bad or wrong decision on the ground, as a historian and partisan wrote of John F. Kennedy, that "He had no choice," but no matter how equal two alternatives may appear, there is always freedom of choice to change or desist from a counter-productive course if the policy-maker has the moral courage to exercise it. He is not a fated creature blown by the whims of Homeric gods. Yet to recognize error, to cut losses, to alter course, is the most repugnant option in government.

For a chief of state, admitting error is almost out of the question. The American misfortune during the Vietnam period was to have had Presidents who lacked the self-confidence for the grand withdrawal. We come back again to Burke: "Magnanimity in politics is not seldom the truest wisdom, and a great Empire and little minds go ill together." The test comes in recognizing when persistence in error has become self-damaging. A prince, says Machiavelli, ought always to be a great asker and a patient hearer of truth about those things of which he has inquired, and he should be angry if he finds that anyone has scruples about telling him the truth. What government needs is great askers.

Refusal to draw inference from negative signs, which under the rubric "wooden-headedness" has played so large a part in these pages, was recognized in the most pessimistic work of modern times, George Orwell's *1984*, as what the author called "Crimestop." "Crimestop means the faculty of stopping short, as though by instinct, at the threshold of any dangerous thought. It includes the power of not grasping analogies, of failing to perceive logical errors, of misunderstanding the simplest argu-ments . . . and of being bored and repelled by any train of thought which is capable of leading in a heretical direction. Crimestop, in short, means protective stupidity."

The question is whether or how a country can protect itself from protective stupidity in policy-making, which in turn raises the question whether it is possible to educate for government. Plato's scheme, which included breeding as well as educating, was never tried. A conspicuous attempt by another culture, the training of the mandarins of China for administrative function, produced no very superior result. The mandarins had to pass through years of study and apprenticeship and weeding out by a series of stiff examinations, but the successful ones did not prove immune to corruption and incompetence. In the end they petered out in decadence and ineffectiveness.

Another such scheme used aliens. The Turkish Janissaries were the better-known military arm of a larger body—the Kapi Kullari, or Slave Institution—which filled every civil post from palace cook to Grand Vizier. Made up of Christian children taken from their parents and brought up and exhaustively trained by the Ottoman Turks for official functions in what may have been the most complete educational system ever devised, they were legally slaves of the Sultan, converted to Islam, forbidden to have families or own property. Free of these distractions, it was supposed they would be able to devote themselves singlemindedly to the state and its sovereign, on whom they were entirely dependent for pay and the necessities of life. The Sultan thus acquired a body not only of first-class administrators, but of strong supporters of his absolutism. Although the system worked to excellent effect, it did not save the Ottoman Empire from slow degeneration; nor, in the end, could the system save itself. In the course of time, the military branch gained growing power, defied the marriage ban and assumed hereditary rights, perpetuated themselves as a permanent and dominant clan, and eventually, in inevitable challenge to the ruler, attempted to seize power in overt revolt. They were slaughtered and destroyed, bringing down the rest of the Slave Institution with them, while the Grand Turk dwindled into dotage.

In 17th-century Europe, after the devastation of the Thirty Years' War, Prussia, when it was still Brandenburg, determined to create a strong state by means of a disciplined army and a trained civil service. Applicants for the civil positions, drawn from commoners in order to offset the nobles' control of the military, had to complete a course of study covering political theory, law and legal philosophy, economics, history, penology and statutes. Only after passing through various stages of examination and probationary terms of office did they receive definitive appointments and tenure and opportunity for advancement. The higher civil service was a separate branch, not open to promotion from the middle and lower levels.

The Prussian system proved so effective that the state was able to survive both military defeat by Napoleon in 1807 and the revolutionary surge of 1848. But by then it had begun to congeal, like the mandarins, losing many of its most progressive citizens in emigration to America. Prussian energies, however, succeeded in 1871 in uniting the German states in an empire under Prussian hegemony. Its very success contained the seed of ruin, for it nourished the arrogance and power-hunger that from 1914 through 1918 was to bring it down.

Political shock moved the English to give attention to the problem. Neither the loss of America nor the storm waves of the French Revolution shook their system of government, but in the mid-19th century, when the rumble from below was growing louder, the revolutions of 1848 on the Continent had effect. Instead of taking refuge in reactionary panic, as might have been expected, the authorities, with commendable enterprise, ordered an investigation of their own government practices, which were then virtually the private preserve of the propertied class. The result was a report on the need for a permanent civil service to be based on training and specialized skills and designed to provide continuity and maintenance of the long view as against transient issues and political passions. Though strongly resisted, the system was adopted in 1870. It has produced distinguished civil servants, but also Burgess, MacLean, Philby and Blunt. The history of British government in the last hundred years suggests that factors other than the quality of its civil service determine a country's fate.

In the United States, the civil service was established chiefly as a barrier to patronage and the pork-barrel, rather than in search of excellence. By 1937, a presidential commission, finding the system inadequate, was urging the development of a "real career service . . . requiring personnel of the highest order, competent, highly trained, loyal, skilled in their duties by reason of long experience, and assured of continuity." After much effort and some progress, that goal is still not reached, but even if it had been, it would not affect elected officials and high appointments—that is, government at the top.

In America, where the electoral process is drowning in commercial techniques of fund-raising and image-making, we may have completed a circle back to a selection process as unconcerned with qualifications as that which made Darius King of Persia.

When he and six fellow conspirators, as recorded by Herodotus, overthrew the reigning despot, they discussed what kind of government—whether a monarchy of one or an oligarchy of the wisest men—they should establish. Darius argued that they should keep to the rule of one and obtain the best government by choosing "the very best man in the whole state." Being persuaded, the group agreed to ride out together next morning and he whose horse was the first to neigh at sunrise should be King. By ruse of a clever groom who tethered a favorite mare at the critical spot, Darius' horse performed on time and his fortunate master, thus singled out as the best man for the job, ascended the throne.

Factors other than random selection subdue the influence of the "thinking fire" on public affairs. For the chief of state under modern conditions, a limiting factor is too many subjects and problems in too many areas of government to allow solid understanding of any of them, and too little time to think between fifteen-minute appointments and thirty-page briefs. This leaves the field open to protective stupidity. Meanwhile bureaucracy, safely repeating today what it did yesterday, rolls on as ineluctably as some vast computer, which, once penetrated by error, duplicates it forever.

Above all, lure of office, known in our country as Potomac fever, stultifies a better performance of government. The bureaucrat dreams of promotion, higher officials want to extend their reach, legislators and the chief of state want re-election; and the guiding principle in these pursuits is to please as many and offend as few as possible. Intelligent government would require that the persons entrusted with high office should formulate and execute policy according to their best judgment, the best knowledge available and a judicious estimate of the lesser evil. But re-election is on their minds, and that becomes the criterion.

Aware of the controlling power of ambition, corruption and emotion, it may be that in the search for wiser government we should look for the test of character first. And the test should be moral courage. Montaigne adds, "Resolution and valor, not that which is sharpened by ambition but that which wisdom and reason may implant in a well-ordered soul." The Lilliputians in choosing persons for public employment had similar criteria. "They have more regard for good morals than for great abilities," reported Gulliver, "for, since government is necessary to mankind, they believe . . . that Providence never intended to make management of publick affairs a mystery, to be comprehended only by a few persons of sublime genius, of which there are seldom three born in an age. They suppose truth, justice, temperance and the like to be in every man's power: the practice of which virtues, assisted by experience and a good intention, would qualify any man for service of his country, except where a course of study is required."

While such virtues may in truth be in every man's power, they have less chance in our system than money and ruthless ambition to prevail at the ballot box. The problem may be not so much a matter of educating officials for government as educating the electorate to recognize and reward integrity of character and to reject the ersatz. Perhaps better men flourish in better times, and wiser government requires the nourishment of a dynamic rather than a troubled and bewildered society. If John Adams was right, and government is "little better practiced now than three or four thousand years ago," we cannot reasonably expect much improvement. We can only muddle on as we have done in those same three or four thousand years, through patches of brilliance and decline, great endeavor and shadow.

Meaning

1. What disastrous events throughout history does Tuchman cite as being the results of "folly" or "protective stupidity"?
2. Why are bureaucracies particularly prone to fall back on automatic ways of doing things precisely during those crucial moments when creative responses are necessary?
3. What role did "folly" or "protective stupidity" play in (a) in the fall of Troy, (b) in seventeenth-century Europe, and (c) in Vietnam?
4. What did Tuchman's analysis reveal about how often overburdened leaders retreat to the "protection" of past policies, which then prove tragically unsuited for the circumstances of the present?

Using Cause and Effect to Convey Meaning

1. Why is the title, "A Lantern on the Stern," an apt image to describe the process of historical hindsight?
2. How does Tuchman structure her analysis to demonstrate that "folly" in governmental affairs is produced by a tragic chain of cause and effect?
3. How does Tuchman's essay illustrate the process by which historians try to understand and interpret past events?

Writing Suggestions

1. Discuss the connection between Tuchman's concept of "folly" or "protective stupidity" in bureaucracies and Freud's concept of "self-censorship" or "denial" as a defense mechanism in individuals (see page 732).
2. Analyze any current international conflict in terms of Tuchman's ideas of "folly" or "protective stupidity." What potentially tragic, and inappropriate, policies are being relied on in these circumstances to solve problems that demand new responses?
3. Discuss Tuchman's essay in light of Marshall McLuhan's statement (Marshall McLuhan and Quentin Fiore, *The Medium Is the Message* [New York: Bantam Books, 1967], pp 74–75): "when faced with a totally new situation, we tend always to attach ourselves to the objects, to the flavor of the most recent past. We look at the present through a rear-view mirror. We march backwards into future."

POLITICAL AND SOCIAL SCIENCES

John M. Darley
Bibb Latané

Why People Don't Help in a Crisis

John M. Darley was born in 1938 in Minneapolis, Minnesota, and received his Ph.D. in 1965 from Harvard University. Since 1972, he has been professor of psychology at Princeton University. The focus of his research as a social psychologist concerns the principles of moral judgment in children and adults. With Bibb Latané, Darley has coauthored The Unresponsive Bystander: Why Doesn't He Help *(1970) and* Help in a Crisis: Bystander Response to an Emergency *(1976). Darley has also contributed over thirty articles and reviews to psychology journals.*

Bibb Latané was born in New York City in 1937 and received his Ph.D. from the University of Minnesota in 1963. For many years he was the director of the Behavioral Sciences Laboratory at Ohio State University. He is currently professor of psychology at the University of North Carolina, Chapel Hill. Latané is a recipient of a Guggenheim Fellowship (1974–1975).

Darley and Latané shared the socio-psychological essay prize from the American Association for the Advancement of Science in 1963 for their research on causes of bystander noninvolvment. "Why People Don't Help in a Crisis" (1968), an essay drawn from their prize-winning research, describes an ingenious experiment designed to identify the true causes of noninvolvment in bystanders who witness street crimes.

Kitty Genovese is set upon by a maniac as she returns home from work at 3 A.M. Thirty-eight of her neighbors in Kew Gardens, N.Y., come to their windows when she cries out in terror; not one comes to her assistance, even though her assailant takes half an hour to murder her. No one so much as calls the police. She dies.

Andrew Mormille is stabbed in the head and neck as he rides in a New York City subway train. Eleven other riders flee to another car as the 17-year-old boy bleeds to death; not one comes to his assistance, even though his attackers have left the car. He dies.

Eleanor Bradley trips and breaks her leg while shopping on New York City's Fifth Avenue. Dazed and in shock, she calls for help, but the hurrying stream of people simply parts and flows past. Finally, after 40 minutes, a taxi driver stops and helps her to a doctor.

How can so many people watch another human being in distress and do nothing? Why don't they help?

Since we started research on bystander responses to emergencies, we have heard many explanations for the lack of intervention in such cases. "The megalopolis in which we live makes closeness difficult and leads to the alienation of the individual from the group," says the psychoanalyst. "This sort of disaster," says the sociologist, "shakes the sense of safety and sureness of the individuals involved and causes psychological withdrawal." "Apathy," says others. "Indifference."

All of these analyses share one characteristic: they set the indifferent witness apart from the rest of us. Certainly not one of us who reads about these incidents in horror is apathetic, alienated or depersonalized. Certainly these terrifying cases have no personal implications for us. We needn't feel guilty, or re-examine ourselves, or anything like that. Or should we?

If we look closely at the behavior of witnesses to these incidents, the people involved begin to seem a little less inhuman and a lot more like the rest of us. They were not indifferent. The 38 witnesses of Kitty Genovese's murder, for example, did not merely look at the scene once and then ignore it. They continued to stare out of their windows, caught, fascinated, distressed, unwilling to act but unable to turn away.

Why, then, didn't they act?

There are three things the bystander must do if he is to intervene in an emergency: *notice* that something is happening; *interpret* that event as an emergency; and decide that he has *personal responsibility* for intervention. As we shall show, the presence of other bystanders may at each stage inhibit his action.

The Unseeing Eye

Suppose that a man has a heart attack. He clutches his chest, staggers to the nearest building and slumps sitting to the sidewalk. Will a passerby come to his assistance? First, the bystander has to notice that something is happening. He must tear himself away from his private thoughts and pay attention. But Americans consider it bad manners to look closely at other people in public. We are taught to respect the privacy of others, and when among strangers we close our ears and avoid staring. In a crowd, then, each person is less likely to notice a potential emergency than when alone.

Experimental evidence corroborates this. We asked college students to an interview about their reactions to urban living. As the students waited to see the interviewer, either by themselves or with two other students, they filled out a questionnaire. Solitary students often glanced idly about while filling out their questionnaires; those in groups kept their eyes on their own papers.

As part of the study, we staged an emergency: smoke was released into the waiting room through a vent. Two thirds of the subjects who were alone noticed the smoke immediately, but only 25 percent of those waiting in groups saw it as quickly. Although eventually all the subjects did become aware of the smoke—when the atmosphere grew so smoky as to make them cough and rub their eyes—this study indicates that the more people present, the slower an individual may be to perceive an emergency and the more likely he is not to see it at all.

SEEING IS NOT NECESSARILY BELIEVING

Once an event is noticed, an onlooker must decide if it is truly an emergency. Emergencies are not always clearly labeled as such; "smoke" pouring into a waiting room may be caused by fire, or it may merely indicate a leak in a steam pipe. Screams in the street may signal an assault or a family quarrel. A man lying in a doorway may be having a coronary—or he may simply be sleeping off a drunk.

A person trying to interpret a situation often looks at those around him to see how he should react. If everyone else is calm and indifferent, he will tend to remain so; if everyone else is reacting strongly, he is likely to become aroused. This tendency is not merely slavish conformity; ordinarily we derive much valuable information about new situations from how others around us behave. It's a rare traveler who, in picking a roadside restaurant, chooses to stop at one where no other cars appear in the parking lot.

But occasionally the reactions of others provide false information. The studied nonchalance of patients in a dentist's waiting room is a poor indication of their inner anxiety. It is considered embarrassing to "lose your cool" in public. In a potentially acute situation, then, everyone present will appear more unconcerned than he is in fact. A crowd can thus force inaction on its members by implying, through its passivity, that an event is not an emergency. Any individual in such a crowd fears that he may appear a fool if he behaves as though it were.

To determine how the presence of other people affects a person's interpretation of an emergency, Latané and Judith Rodin set up another experiment. Subjects were paid $2 to participate in a survey of game and puzzle preferences conducted at Columbia University by the Consumer Testing Bureau. An attractive young market researcher met them at the door and took them to the testing room, where they were given questionnaires to fill out. Before leaving, she told them that she would be working next door in her office, which was separated from the room by a folding room-divider. She then entered her office, where she shuffled papers, opened drawers and made enough noise to remind the subjects of her presence. After four minutes she turned on a high-fidelity tape recorder.

On it, the subjects heard the researcher climb up on a chair, perhaps to reach for a stack of papers on the bookcase. They heard a loud crash and a scream as the chair collapsed and she fell, and they heard her moan, "Oh, my foot . . . I . . . I . . . can't move it. Oh, I . . . can't get this . . . thing . . . off me." Her cries gradually got more subdued and controlled.

Twenty-six people were alone in the waiting room when the "accident" occurred. Seventy percent of them offered to help the victim. Many pushed back the divider to offer their assistance; others called out to offer their help.

Among those waiting in pairs, only 20 percent—8 out of 40—offered to help.

The other 32 remained unresponsive. In defining the situation as a nonemergency, they explained to themselves why the other member of the pair did not leave the room; they also removed any reason for action themselves. Whatever had happened, it was believed to be not serious. "A mild sprain," some said. "I didn't want to embarrass her." In a "real" emergency, they assured us, they would be among the first to help.

The Lonely Crowd

Even if a person defines an event as an emergency, the presence of other bystanders may still make him less likely to intervene. He feels that his responsibility is diffused and diluted. Thus, if your car breaks down on a busy highway, hundreds of drivers whiz by without anyone's stopping to help—but if you are stuck on a nearly deserted country road, whoever passes you first is likely to stop.

To test this diffusion-of-responsibility theory, we simulated an emergency in which people overheard a victim calling for help. Some thought they were the only person to hear the cries; the rest believed that others heard them, too. As with the witnesses to Kitty Genovese's murder, the subjects could not *see* one another or know what others were doing. The kind of direct group inhibition found in the other two studies could not operate.

For the simulation, we recruited 72 students at New York University to participate in what was referred to as a "group discussion" of personal problems in an urban university. Each student was put in an individual room equipped with a set of headphones and a microphone. It was explained that this precaution had been taken because participants might feel embarrassed about discussing their problems publicly. Also, the experimenter said that he would not listen to the initial discussion, but would only ask for reactions later. Each person was to talk in turn.

The first to talk reported that he found it difficult to adjust to New York and his studies. Then, hesitantly and with obvious embarrassment, he mentioned that he was prone to nervous seizures when he was under stress. Other students then talked about their own problems in turn. The number of people in the "discussion" varied. But whatever the apparent size of the group—two, three or six people—only the subject was actually present; the others, as well as the instructions and the speeches of the victim-to-be, were present only on a pre-recorded tape.

When it was the first person's turn to talk again, he launched into the following performance, becoming louder and having increasing speech difficulties: "I can see a lot of er of er how other people's problems are similar to mine because er I mean er they're not er e-easy to handle sometimes and er I er um I think I I need er if if could er er somebody er er er give me give me a little er give me a little help here because er I er *uh* I've got a a one of the er seiz-er er things coming *on* and and er uh uh (choking sounds) . . ."

Eighty-five percent of the people who believed themselves to be alone with the victim came out of their room to help. Sixty-two percent of the people who believed there was *one* other bystander did so. Of those who believed there were four other bystanders, only 31 percent reported the fit. The responsibility-diluting effect of other people was so strong that single individuals were more than twice as likely to report the emergency as those who thought other people also knew about it.

The Lesson Learned

People who failed to report the emergency showed few signs of the apathy and indifference thought to characterize "unresponsive bystanders." When the experimenter entered the room to end the situation, the subject often asked if the victim was "all right." Many of them showed physical signs of nervousness; they often had trembling hands and sweating palms. If anything, they seemed more emotionally aroused than did those who reported the emergency. Their emotional behavior was a sign of their continuing conflict concerning whether to respond or not.

Thus, the stereotype of the unconcerned, depersonalized *homo urbanus*,[1] blandly watching the misfortunes of others, proves inaccurate. Instead, we find that a bystander to an emergency is an anguished individual in genuine doubt, wanting to do the right thing but compelled to make complex decisions under pressure of stress and fear. His reactions are shaped by the actions of others—and all too frequently by their inaction.

And we are that bystander. Caught up by the apparent indifference of others, we may pass by an emergency without helping or even realizing that help is needed. Once we are aware of the influence of those around us, however, we can resist it. We can choose to see distress and step forward to relieve it.

Meaning

1. What experiment did Darley and Latané design to discover why bystanders were unwilling in some situations to help victims of street crime?
2. How did Darley and Latané's results challenge the usual concept of apathy and indifference as an explanation of why people do not come to the aid of victims?
3. What factors seem to determine if a bystander is willing to help a victim of street crime?

Using Cause and Effect to Convey Meaning

1. How do these psychologists use causal analysis to discover the means by which social pressures control the behavior of people in groups?
2. What evidence do Darley and Latané present to disprove the traditional view that bystanders who fail to help others are merely apathetic?
3. How would a criminologist or journalist have reported the same phenomena? By contrast, what features make this essay suitable for Darley and Latané's intended audience of colleagues?

Writing Suggestions

1. What ethical questions are involved when social scientists, like Darley and Latané, set up experiments that use deception to manipulate subjects in order to obtain

[1] City dweller.

data? For further research, compare this experiment to Stanley Milgram's classic investigation of "authoritarianism" (Stanley Milgram, "Some Conditions of Obedience and Disobedience to Authority," *Human Relations*, Vol. 18, No. 1, 1965, pp. 57–76).

2. Apply the discoveries made by Darley and Latané to Huxley's discussion (see page 466) of how crowds were made susceptible to manipulation by Hitler.

ALDOUS HUXLEY

Propaganda Under a Dictatorship

Aldous Huxley (1894–1963) was born in Surrey, England, and was educated at Eaton and Balliol College, Oxford. Despite a serious eye disease, Huxley read with the aid of a magnifying glass and graduated from Oxford in 1915 with honors in English literature. After joining the staff of Atheneum, a literary magazine, in 1919, he began writing the novels, essays, and short stories that would bring him international fame. His brilliant social satires and wide-ranging essays on architecture, science, music, history, philosophy, and religion explore the relationship between man and society. Brave New World (1932) is his best-known satire on how futuristic mass technology will achieve a sinister utopia of scientific breeding and conditioned happiness. In Ape and Essence (1948), he explores an alternate future where subhuman survivors of an atomic war scratch for existence. Huxley's other works, including Eyeless in Gaza (1936), After Many a Summer (1939), Time Must Have a Stop (1944), The Doors of Perception (1954), Heaven and Hell (1956), and Island (1962), can be seen as attempts to search in new spiritual directions—through mysticism, mescaline, and parapsychology—as a reaction to the grim future he so devastastingly portrayed. In "Propaganda Under a Dictatorship," from Brave New World Revisited (1958), Huxley reveals how the manipulation of language in the propaganda of Nazi Germany conditioned the thoughts and behavior of the masses.

At his trial after the Second World War, Hitler's Minister for Armaments, Albert Speer, delivered a long speech in which, with remarkable acuteness, he described the Nazi tyranny and analyzed its methods. "Hitler's dictatorship," he said, "differed in one fundamental point from all its predecessors in history. It was the first dictatorship in the present period of modern technical development, a dictatorship which made complete use of all technical means for the domination of its own country. Through technical devices like the radio and the loud-speaker, eighty million people were deprived of independent thought. It was thereby possible to subject them to the will of one man. . . . Earlier dictators needed highly qualified assistants even at the lowest level—men who could think and act independently. The totalitarian system in the period of modern technical development can dispense with such men; thanks to modern methods of communication, it is possible to mechanize the lower leadership. As a result of this there has arisen the new type of the uncritical recipient of orders."

In the Brave New World of my prophetic fable technology had advanced far beyond the point it had reached in Hitler's day; consequently the recipients of orders were far less critical than their Nazi counterparts, far more obedient to the order-giving elite. Moreover, they had been genetically standarized and postnatally conditioned to perform their subordinate functions, and could therefore be depended upon to behave almost as predictably as machines. As we shall see in a later chapter, this conditioning of "the lower leadership" is already going on under the Communist dictatorships. The Chinese and the Russians are not relying merely on the indirect effects of advancing technology; they are working directly on the psychophysical organisms of their lower leaders, subjecting minds and bodies to a system of ruthless and, from all accounts, highly effective conditioning. "Many a man," said Speer, "has been haunted by the nightmare that one day nations might be dominated by technical means. That nightmare was almost realized in Hitler's totalitarian system." Almost, but not quite. The Nazis did not have time—and perhaps did not have the intelligence and the necessary knowledge—to brainwash and condition their lower leadership. This, it may be, is one of the reasons why they failed.

Since Hitler's day the armory of technical devices at the disposal of the would-be dictator has been considerably enlarged. As well as the radio, the loud-speaker, the moving picture camera and the rotary press, the contemporary propagandist can make use of television to broadcast the image as well as the voice of his client, and can record both image and voice on spools of magnetic tape. Thanks to technological progress, Big Brother can now be almost as omnipresent as God. Nor is it only on the technical front that the hand of the would-be dictator has been strengthened. Since Hitler's day a great deal of work has been carried out in those fields of applied psychology and neurology which are the special province of the propagandist, the indoctrinator and the brainwasher. In the past these specialists in the art of changing people's minds were empiricists. By a method of trial and error they had worked out a number of techniques and procedures, which they used very effectively without, however, knowing precisely why they were effective. Today the art of mind-control is in process of becoming a science. The practitioners of this science know what they are doing and why. They are guided in their work by theories and hypotheses solidly established on a massive foundation of experimental evidence. Thanks to the new insights and the new techniques made possible by these insights, the nightmare that was "all but realized in Hitler's totalitarian system" may soon be completely realizable.

But before we discuss these new insights and techniques let us take a look at the nightmare that so nearly came true in Nazi Germany. What were the methods used by Hitler and Goebbels for "depriving eighty million people of independent thought and subjecting them to the will of one man"? And what was the theory of human nature upon which those terrifyingly successful methods were based? These questions can be answered, for the most part, in Hitler's own words. And what remarkably clear and astute words they are! When he writes about such vast abstractions as Race and History and Providence, Hitler is strictly unreadable. But when he writes about the German masses and the methods he used for dominating and directing them, his style changes. Nonsense gives place to sense, bombast to a hard-boiled and cynical lucidity. In his philosophical lucubrations Hitler was either cloudily day-dreaming or reproducing other people's half-baked notions. In his comments on crowds and propaganda he was writing of things he knew by firsthand experience. In the words of his ablest biographer, Mr. Alan Bullock, "Hitler was the greatest demagogue in history." Those who add, "only a demagogue," fail to appreciate the nature of political power in an age of mass politics. As he himself said, "To be a leader means to be able to move the masses." Hitler's aim was first to move the masses and then, having pried them loose from their traditional loyalties and moralities, to impose upon them (with the hypnotized consent of the majority) a new authoritarian order of his own devising. "Hitler," wrote Hermann Rauschning in 1939, "has a deep respect for the Catholic church and the Jesuit order; not because of their Christian doctrine, but because of the 'machinery' they have elaborated and controlled, their hierarchical system, their extremely clever tactics, their knowledge of human nature and their wise use of human weaknesses in ruling over believers." Ecclesiasticism without Christianity, the discipline of a monastic rule, not for God's sake or in order to achieve personal salvation, but for the sake of the State and for the greater glory and power of the demagogue turned Leader—this was the goal toward which the systematic moving of the masses was to lead.

Let us see what Hitler thought of the masses he moved and how he did the moving. The first principle from which he started was a value judgment: the masses are utterly contemptible. They are incapable of abstract thinking and uninterested in any fact outside the circle of their immediate experience. Their behavior is determined, not by knowledge and reason, but by feelings and unconscious drives. It is in these drives and feelings that "the roots of their positive as well as their negative attitudes are implanted." To be successful a propagandist must learn how to manipulate these instincts and emotions. "The driving force which has brought about the most tremendous revolutions on this earth has never been a body of scientific teaching which has gained power over the masses, but always a devotion which has inspired them, and often a kind of hysteria which has urged them into action. Whoever wishes to win over the masses must know the key that will open the door of their hearts." . . . In post-Freudian jargon, of their unconscious.

Hitler made his strongest appeal to those members of the lower middle classes who had been ruined by the inflation of 1923, and then ruined all over again by the depression of 1929 and the following years. "The masses" of whom he speaks were these bewildered, frustrated and chronically anxious millions. To make them more masslike, more homogeneously subhuman, he assembled them, by the thousands and the tens of thousands, in vast halls and arenas, where individuals could lose their personal identity, even their elementary humanity, and be merged with the crowd. A man or woman makes direct contact with society in two ways: as a member of some familial, professional or religious group, or as a member of a crowd. Groups are capable of being as moral and intelligent as the individuals who form them; a crowd is chaotic, has no purpose of its own and is capable of anything except intelligent action and realistic thinking. Assembled in a crowd, people lose their powers of reasoning and their capacity for moral choice. Their suggestibility is increased to the point where they cease to have any judgment or will of their own. They become very excitable, they lose all sense of individual or collective responsibility, they are subject to sudden accesses of rage, enthusiasm and panic. In a word, a man in a crowd behaves as though he had swallowed a large dose of some powerful intoxicant. He is a victim of what I have called "herd-poisoning." Like alcohol, herd-poison is an active, extraverted drug. The crowd-intoxicated individual escapes from responsibility, intelligence and morality into a kind of frantic, animal mindlessness.

During his long career as an agitator, Hitler had studied the effects of herd-poison and had learned how to exploit them for his own purposes. He had discovered that the orator can appeal to those "hidden forces" which motivate men's actions, much more effectively than can the writer. Reading is a private, not a collective activity. The writer speaks only to individuals, sitting by themselves in a state of normal sobriety. The orator speaks to masses of individuals, already well primed with herd-poison. They are at his mercy and, if he knows his business, he can do what he likes with them. As an orator, Hitler knew his business supremely well. He was able, in his own words, "to follow the lead of the great mass in such a way that from the living emotion to his hearers the apt word which he needed would be suggested to him and in its turn this would go straight to the heart of his hearers." Otto Strasser called him a "loud-speaker, proclaiming the most secret desires, the least admissible instincts, the sufferings and personal revolts of a whole nation." Twenty years before Madison Avenue embarked upon "Motivational Research," Hitler was systematically exploring and exploiting the secret fears and hopes, the cravings, anxieties and frustrations of the German masses. It is by manipulating "hidden forces" that the advertising experts induce us to buy their wares—a toothpaste, a brand of cigarettes, a political candidate. And it is by appealing to the same hidden forces— and to others too dangerous for Madison Avenue to meddle with—that Hitler induced the German masses to buy themselves a Fuehrer, an insane philosophy and the Second World War.

Unlike the masses, intellectuals have a taste for rationality and an interest in facts. Their critical habit of mind makes them resistant to the kind of propaganda that works so well on the majority. Among the masses "instinct is supreme, and from instinct comes faith. . . . While the healthy common folk instinctively close their ranks to form a community of the people" (under a Leader, it goes without saying) "intellectuals run this way and that, like hens in a poultry yard. With them one cannot make history; they cannot be used as elements composing a community." Intellectuals are the kind of people who demand evidence and are shocked by logical inconsistencies and fallacies. They regard over-simplification as the original sin of the mind and have no use for the slogans, the unqualified assertions and sweeping generalizations which are the propagandist's stock in trade. "All effective propaganda," Hitler wrote, "must be confined to a few bare necessities and then must be expressed in a few stereotyped formulas." These stereotyped formulas must be constantly repeated, for "only constant repetition will finally succeed in imprinting an idea upon the memory of a crowd." Philosophy teaches us to feel uncertain about the things that seem to us self-evident. Propaganda, on the other hand, teaches us to accept as self-evident matters about which it would be reasonable to suspend our judgment or to feel doubt. The aim of the demagogue is to create social coherence under his own leadership. But, as Bertrand Russell has pointed out, "systems of dogma without empirical foundations, such as scholasticism, Marxism and fascism, have the advantage of producing a great deal of social coherence among their disciples." The demagogic propagandist must therefore be consistently dogmatic. All his statements are made without qualification. There are no grays in his picture of the world; everything is either diabolically black or celestially white. In Hitler's words, the propagandist should adopt "a systematically one-sided attitude towards every problem that has to be dealt with." He must never admit that he might be wrong or that people with a different point of view might be even partially right. Opponents should not be argued with; they should be attacked, shouted down, or, if they become too much of a nuisance, liquidated. The morally squeamish intellectual may be shocked by this kind of thing. But the masses are always convinced that "right is on the side of the active aggressor."

Such, then, was Hitler's opinion of humanity in the mass. It was a very low opinion. Was it also an incorrect opinion? The tree is known by its fruits, and a theory of human nature which inspired the kind of techniques that proved so horribly effective must contain at least an element of truth. Virtue and intelligence belong to human beings as individuals freely associating with other individuals in small groups. So do sin and stupidity. But the subhuman mindlessness to which the demagogue makes his appeal, the moral imbecility on which he relies when he goads his victims into action, are characteristic not of men and women as individuals, but of men and women in masses. Mindlessness and moral idiocy are not characteristically human attributes; they are symptoms of herd-poisoning. In all the world's higher religions, salvation and enlightenment are for individuals. The kingdom of heaven is within the mind of a person, not within the collective mindlessness of a crowd. Christ promised to be present where two or three are gathered together. He did not say anything about being present where thousands are intoxicating one another with herd-poison. Under the Nazis enormous numbers of people were compelled to spend an enormous amount of time marching in serried ranks from point A to point B and back again to point A. "This keeping of the whole population on the march seemed to be a senseless waste of time and energy. Only much later," adds Hermann Rauschning, "was there revealed in it a subtle intention based on a well-judged adjustment of ends and means. Marching diverts men's thoughts. Marching kills thought. Marching makes an end of individuality. Marching is the indispensable magic stroke performed in order to accustom the people to a mechanical, quasi-ritualistic activity until it becomes second nature."

From his point of view and at the level where he had chosen to do his dreadful work, Hitler was perfectly correct in his estimate of human nature. To those of us who look at men and women as individuals rather than as members of crowds, or of regimented collectives, he seems hideously wrong. In an age of accelerating over-population, of accelerating over-organization and even more efficient means of mass communication, how can we preserve the integrity and reassert the value of the human individual? This is a question that can still be asked and perhaps effectively answered. A generation from now it may be too late to find an answer and perhaps impossible, in the stifling collective climate of that future time, even to ask the question.

MEANING

1. What role was played by the disastrous inflation of 1923 and the depression of 1929 in setting the stage for Hitler's rise to power?
2. How did Hitler act as an "amplifier" to project to the masses their own fears and frustrations?
3. What propaganda techniques did Hitler use to manipulate the masses whose security had been destroyed by previous financial disasters?
4. According to Huxley, what was Hitler's opinion of the masses whom he manipulated?

USING CAUSE AND EFFECT TO CONVEY MEANING

1. What reasons does Huxley present to explain why one segment of the German population was particularly vulnerable to Hitler's propaganda techniques?

2. How is Huxley's essay organized to explore both the immediate and distant causes of the triumph of propaganda under Hitler's dictatorship?
3. What examples does Huxley provide of more contemporary uses of propaganda techniques of stereotyped slogans, repetition, and guilt or virtue by association?

Writing Suggestions

1. What similarities can you discern between techniques described by Huxley and those used to shape the behavior of recruits in Marine boot camp (see Henry Allen, page 43)?
2. Analyze any contemporary example of political propaganda to determine whether the techniques of guilt or virtue by association, labeling, stereotyping, repetition, and manipulation by selective censorship are used?

WILSON BRYAN KEY

The Exorcist Massage Parlor

Wilson Bryan Key was born in 1925 in Richmond, California, and received his Ph.D in communication from the University of Denver in 1971. He has been professor of journalism at the University of Denver, University of Kansas, Boston University, and University of Western Ontario. Key has been the president of Mediaprobe: The Center for the Study of Media, Inc., since 1973. Key was the first to document the widespread use of subliminals in mass media in his books Subliminal Seduction: Ad Media's Manipulation of a Not-So-Innocent America (*1973*), Media Sexploitation (*1976*), *and* The Clam Plate Orgy: And Other Subliminals the Media Use to Manipulate Your Behavior (*1980*). Besides these pioneering works, Key is the author of more than three hundred research studies for private corporations and governments. In "The Exorcist Massage Parlor," from* Media Sexploitation, *Key offers a fascinating analysis of how William Friedkin, director of the movie* The Exorcist, *systematically wove various animal sounds into the film's soundtrack to manipulate the audience's reactions.*

AUDITORY ARCHETYPES

The Exorcist was remarkable in the way both audio and visual were integrated and mutually reinforced. The sound track, for which the movie won an Academy Award, was a brilliant example of creative subliminal sound engineering. Similar techniques have been used for years in other movies and by the popular music recording industry.

In several dozen interviews with theater employees—refreshment stand attendants, ushers, and ticket takers who had only heard the movie's sound track for several days before actually viewing the film, all reported extreme discomfort from the sound. The discomfort could not be verbally explained, but all agreed it was directly related to the sound track. Each of the theater staffs interviewed reported employees who became ill after finally seeing the film in its entirety—from mild to extreme nausea and hysteria.

Friedkin openly admitted he had used several natural sound effects in the movie's auditory background. One of these, he explained, was the sound of angry, agitated bees. After provoking a jar of bees into excited anger, he recorded their buzzing, then rerecorded the buzzing at sixteen different frequencies. He finally mixed the sixteen frequencies of buzzing together in what might be consciously heard as a single sound—a super buzzing of infuriated bees virtually unrecognizable at conscious levels. This sound of angry bees wove in and out of scenes throughout the film.

Virtually all humans (some much more strongly than others) respond with hysteria, fear, and intense anxiety to the sound of angry, buzzing bees, even if they have never in their lives experienced the actual sound. Many animals respond similarly. Perhaps the strongest verbally definable emotion triggered by the bee buzzing is fear

495

or fright—a near panic-filled desire to run, flee, and escape from the threat. Carl Jung's theory of archetypes suggests that this sound—as the emotional reaction appears to cross cultures—could qualify as an archetypal symbol.

In many cultures the bee has been symbolically associated with death and immortality. In several ancient civilizations, dead bodies were smeared with honey as food for the soul. Indeed, honey was often used as an embalming fluid. Over many centuries in Europe, bees were prohibited from use in barter for fear they might take offense and destroy crops and flocks in retribution. Bees appeared as symbols of death, fear, and power in ancient Egypt, Germany, China, Greece, Italy, and Japan, in early Christian art, in both Hebrew and Moslem traditions, and in Norse mythology. The Hindu god Krishna was often described as hovering in the form of a bee. Souls have often been thought to swarm as bees migrating from hives.

There is never any conscious awareness, of course, within *The Exorcist* audience of angry bees buzzing. However, there are easily observable levels of anxiety produced by the sound as it weaves in and out of various scenes. The bee sound appeared, for example, in the scene where Father Merrin first visits Regan's bedroom while he removed various objects from a pouch, symbolically letting the invisible bees out of the bag.

SYMBOLS OF EVIL

Another auditory archetype mixed subtly into the sound track was the terrified squealing of pigs while they were being slaughtered. Few sounds strike terror so deeply into the heart of man. This sound will affect virtually all humans even though they may never have experienced the squealing or sight of an actual pig. The expression "squealing like a stuck pig" has even gone into the language.

Pigs have been portrayed in various symbolic relationships with man for at least half a million years. Even today, the pig is considered one of the most intelligent of domestic animals—by human standards, of course. The pig, at least for modern man, was cursed by bad table manners that emphasize the pig's filth, greed, gluttony, and lethargy. Nevertheless, in many ancient cultures, pigs were often substituted for human victims during religious sacrifices. A black pig has often been symbolic in Christian art of the devil and Satan. In many civilizations the pig was thought to be a demon that injured fertility heroes in the groin, rendering them sterile. In Celtic mythology pigs were even portrayed as returning to life after being eaten. And, of course, in one of the New Testament's most celebrated exorcisms, Christ drove a legion of devils into a herd of swine which, maddened, threw themselves into a lake much as Father Karras flung his possessed body out the window.

In addition to the pigs' squealing hidden in *The Exorcist* sound track, Regan's grotesque, filthy face during the exorcism scene often resembled that of a pig. Further, subliminal reinforcement for the pig symbol is obtained by the word PIG written as graffiti on a ledge at the left side of the stairs looking down behind the house where the deaths occurred. This staircase, and the consciously unnoticed word PIG, appeared many times throughout the movie. Friedkin explained how the sound track often mixed the angry bee buzz with the pig squeals. The two sounds wove in and out of the film, coordinating with the visual.

Embedded in the sound, under the voices and surface sounds apparent in the exorcism scene, was what seemed to be the roaring of lions or large cats. A third of the audience surveyed described a feeling of being devoured or struggling against being devoured. There were also orgasmic sexual sounds in the exorcism scene that appeared to involve both males and females.

Sound is extremely important in the management and control of any group of individuals, certainly for those in a theater. Famed movie director Alfred Hitchcock ranked sound as more vital to the success of his famous suspense movies than his visual illusions.

In a recent Muzak Corporation advertisement, the company actually presented its services, background music for stores and offices, as an "environmental management" technique.

In Western society surprisingly little is publicly known about sound and its effect upon behavior. The consciously available portion of sound frequency ranges from 20 to 20,000 cycles per second—or so advertise the high-fidelity appliance manufacturers. Most theaters have sound equipment that will produce audible sound in this range. As a practical matter, however, few individuals can consciously hear over 17,000 cps or under 200 cps, especially young people whose hearing has been permanently dampened by high-volume electronic amplification.

Sound, nevertheless, can be perceived at each end of the spectrum beyond the consciously perceived frequencies. Resonance and other sound qualities also play parts in the subliminal perception of sound. To illustrate, some Moog synthesizers are capable of producing sound at 20,000 cps or higher and under 20 cps. You can consciously hear nothing at these high or low frequencies, but if volume or resonance is increased, most people become extermely agitated. If information is included in these subliminal frequencies, it will instantly be perceived at the unconscious level.

HYPNOTIC INDUCTIONS

When normal voice volume levels in *The Exorcist* were reduced, the audience was required to strain or increase attention or concentration upon the dialogue. This is almost a standard hypnotic induction technique, compelling the subject to concentrate upon one sensory data source. The audience uniformly leaned forward in their seats to hear, for example, the charming conversation between mother and daughter in the bedroom scene at the film's beginning. Similarly, many scenes throughout the movie were momentarily out of focus. Again, the audience—like puppets being manipulated with strings—leaned forward, concentrating on the visual images as they tried to correct for the blurred focus. Much of the dialogue between shock scenes was muted or whispered, so as to regain audience involvement.

When humans are led toward hypnosis, they become highly suggestible. Their emotions become more easily manipulated, managed, and controlled the further they proceed along the induction path.

Friedkin utilized little music in the sound track, though he credited works by Hans Werner Henzle, George Crumb, Anton Webern, and five other composers. Like all good background music, the themes were purposely designed for subliminal consumption. The consumption of music and sound generally followed two patterns. One pattern built slowly from plateau to plateau, always intensifying the audience's emotional response. Indeed, in a sample of roughly fifty women who had seen the movie, over half candidly admitted *The Exorcist* excited them sexually. Most cited the sound track as the apparent source of this excitement.

The other general sound pattern abruptly jarred the audience into a tension state. Loud, sharp noises—bells ringing, doors slamming, dogs barking—preceded and followed by extended periods of electronic silence. The sound would gradually increase to a crescendo, then abruptly trail off to nothingness, or cut off sharply. This technique is primarily an attention-holding-tension-building device. Physiological tension was also increased by silences. For example, the early scene in the attic—which was abruptly broken by a loud, sharp noise.

Jumping the sound from one scene to the next—as a continuity and tension-building device, quite similar to the pink roses used visually—was done throughout the film. An important sound jump occurred during Father Karras's first visit to the house. During the preceding scene, in the dream sequence where Karras's mother climbs the subway stairs, the street sound was unrecognizable as a rather high frequency, moderately loud-volume sound. In the next scene where Karras visited the house, the sound was the same except a truck gear shift was heard and the sound increased in frequency. The gear shift identified the background noise, reducing audience tension for the priest's first visit with Regan, where the tension again built toward a tense climax.

LOUD SILENCES

The Exorcist silences were not completely silent. They were electronic silences, with low-frequency background hums. The silences were only silent in contrast to high and increasing volume sequences. These silences also formed a series of plateaus which gradually increased in volume and decreased in time interval as the story moved toward various climactic situations. Silences, like the sounds, were used to produce within the audience a series of emotional plateaus. These silences became louder and louder and more and more rapid as each segment progressed. The tension and release, tension and release, tension and release, always building higher and higher and higher, induced—by itself—exhaustion and even nausea for many in the audience.

Another manifestation of tension management in the audience was coughing. The audience coughed heavily at predictable intervals throughout the movie. Audience coughing was recorded at several theaters and always appeared at roughly the same point in the story. This was compared with cough reactions in several other action-type films, *The Sting, Executive Decision,* and *Papillon. The Exorcist,* in comparison, produced notably stronger and more predictable cough patterns. There were, apparently, subliminal cues in the visual or auditory stimuli that motivated the coughing.

Coughing is a tension release and appeared to occur roughly within thirty seconds after the auditory tension peaks were released. The first sounds of the evil force in the attic sounded like coughing, followed by a rasping bronchial sound. Coughing, of course, can lead to an upset stomach.

The changes of Regan's voice—from that of a twelve-year-old girl to that of the devil—were carefully synthesized with the visual changes in her appearance. At some point during this transition, the girl's voice was replaced by the voice of Mercedes McCambridge, an actress with a deep husky voice. Friedkin admitted to putting the actress's voice through a filter to produce a voice unidentifiable as either male or female.

In other words, the devil's voice was consciously perceived as androgenous, or hermaphroditic. This voice quality would not be meaningful at the conscious level, but would be subliminally apparent. No matter how natural voices are disguised, hypnotized humans are able to identify male or female voice characteristics. It would not be an exaggeration to state that *The Exorcist* visual effects were only props for the sound. A large proportion of the audience recalled the sound with great discomfort weeks after leaving the theater.

MEANING

1. According to Key, why did so many viewers of *The Exorcist* become fearful, angry, and even physically sick or hysterical after seeing the movie?
2. What conclusions did Key draw from interviews with theatre staff who heard the movie soundtrack before actually viewing *The Exorcist?*
3. What different kinds of natural sounds did Friedkin admit to recording and interweaving subliminally into the soundtrack of the movie to produce instinctive reactions of fear from the audience?

USING CAUSE AND EFFECT TO CONVEY MEANING

1. How does Key organize his study to clearly show that audiences were manipulated as much by the subliminal soundtrack as they were by the images on the screen?
2. What examples does Key provide to support his assertion that Friedkin used "archetypal" sounds that produce instinctive fear?
3. What examples does Key provide of Friedkin's use of two general sound patterns to introduce music and sound into *The Exorcist?*

WRITING SUGGESTIONS

1. What connections can you discover between the audience's responses to subliminal cues in *The Exorcist* and Jung's discovery of the role played by "archetypes" in the "collective unconscious" projected in legends, myths, folklore, and dreams (see page 316)?
2. Describe other areas of society where you believe subliminal messages are embedded. For example, how does the frequent use of scenes containing water as a backdrop for cigarette ads (misty mornings, waterfalls, glaciers, snow-topped mountains) enhance the subconscious appeal of cigarettes and result in higher sales?
3. How does the conscious decision to use subliminal techniques for purposes of self-improvement—through prerecorded tapes that contain subliminal messages for stopping smoking, business success, or losing weight—differ from the phenomena analyzed by Key?

SCIENCES

Loren Eiseley

How Flowers Changed the World

Loren Eiseley (1907–1977) was born in Lincoln, Nebraska and received his Ph.D. from the University of Pennsylvania in 1937. His academic career encompassed the teaching of anthropology, sociology, and the history of science at the University of Kansas, Oberlin College, Columbia, Berkeley, Harvard, and the University of Pennsylvania. His abilities as a natural scientist were matched by an equal sensitivity to language: Darwin's Century *(1958) won the National Phi Beta Kappa Science Award and the Atheneum of Philadelphia Literature Award. Eiseley's writing displays imagination, a passionate concern for the environment, and scientific lucidity. His works include* The Immense Journey *(1957),* The Firmament of Time *(1960),* The Mind As Nature *(1962),* The Unexpected Universe *(1969),* The Invisible Pyramid *(1970), and* The Night Country *(1971). His last book,* All the Strange Hours: The Excavation of a Life *(1975), is an autobiographical account of his life as an educator, scientist, poet, and author. In "How Flowers Changed the World," which first appeared in* The Immense Journey, *Eiseley reveals the causal relationship between the evolution of flowers and the subsequent development of warm-blooded mammals and human life on earth.*

If it had been possible to observe the Earth from the far side of the solar system over the long course of geological epochs, the watchers might have been able to discern a subtle change in the light emanating from our planet. That world of long ago would, like the red deserts of Mars, have reflected light from vast drifts of stone and gravel, the sands of wandering wastes, the blackness of naked basalt, the yellow dust of endlessly moving storms. Only the ceaseless marching of the clouds and the intermittent flashes from the restless surface of the sea would have told a different story, but still essentially a barren one. Then, as the millennia rolled away and age followed age, a new and greener light would, by degrees, have come to twinkle across those endless miles.

This is the only difference those far watchers, by the use of subtle instruments, might have perceived in the whole history of the planet Earth, Yet that slowly growing green twinkle would have contained the epic march of life from the tidal oozes upward across the raw and unclothed continents. Out of the vast chemical bath of the sea—not from the deeps, but from the element-rich, light-exposed platforms of the continental shelves—wandering fingers of green had crept upward along the meanderings of river systems and fringed the gravels of forgotten lakes.

In those first ages plants clung of necessity to swamps and watercourses. Their reproductive processes demanded direct access to water. Beyond the primitive ferns and mosses that enclosed the borders of swamps and streams the rocks still lay vast and bare, the winds still swirled the dust of a naked planet. The grass cover that holds our world secure in place was still millions of years in the future. The green marchers had gained a soggy foothold upon the land but that was all. They did not reproduce by seeds but by microscopic swimming sperm that had to wriggle their way through water to fertilize the female cell. Such plants in their higher forms had clever adaptations for the use of rain water in their sexual phases, and survived with increasing success in a wet land environment. They now seem part of man's normal environment. The truth is, however, that there is nothing very "normal" about nature. Once upon a time there were no flowers at all.

A little while ago—about one hundred million years, as the geologist estimates time in the history of our four-billion-year-old planet—flowers were not to be found anywhere on the five continents. Wherever one might have looked, from the poles to the equator, one would have seen only the cold dark monotonous green of a world whose plant life possessed no other color.

Somewhere, just a short time before the close of the Age of Reptiles, there occurred a soundless, violent explosion. It lasted millions of years, but it was an explosion, nevertheless. It marked the emergence of the angiosperms—the flowering plants. Even the great evolutionist, Charles Darwin, called them "an abominable mystery," because they appeared so suddenly and spread so fast.

Flowers changed the face of the planet. Without them, the world we know—even man himself—would never have existed. Francis Thompson, the English poet, once wrote that one could not pluck a flower without troubling a star. Intuitively he had sensed like a naturalist the enormous interlinked complexity of life. Today we know that the appearance of the flowers contained also the equally mystifying emergence of man.

If we were to go back into the Age of Reptiles, its drowned swamps and birdless forest would reveal to us a warmer but, on the whole, a sleepier world than that of today. Here and there, it is true, the serpent heads of bottom-feeding dinosaurs might be upreared in suspicion of their huge flesh-eating compatriots. Tyrannosaurs, enormous bipedal caricatures of men, would stalk mindlessly across the sites of future cities and go their slow way down into the dark of geologic time.

In all that world of living things nothing saw save with the intense concentration of the hunt, nothing moved except with the grave sleepwalking intentness of the instinct-driven brain. Judged by modern standards, it was a world in slow motion, a cold-blooded world whose occupants were most active at noonday but torpid on chill nights, their brains damped by a slower metabolism than any known to even the most primitive of warm-blooded animals today.

A high metabolic rate and the maintenance of a constant body temperature are supreme achievements in the evolution of life. They enable an animal to escape, within broad limits, from the overheating or the chilling of its immediate surroundings, and at the same time to maintain a peak mental efficiency. Creatures without a high metabolic rate are slaves to weather. Insects in the first frosts of autumn all run down like little clocks. Yet if you pick one up and breathe warmly upon it, it will begin to move about once more.

In a sheltered spot such creatures may sleep away the winter, but they are hopelessly immobilized. Though a few warm-blooded mammals, such as the woodchuck of our day, have evolved a way of reducing their metabolic rate in order to undergo winter hibernation, it is a survival mechanism with drawbacks, for it leaves the animal helplessly exposed if enemies discover him during his period of suspended animation. Thus bear or woodchuck, big animal or small, must seek, in this time of descending sleep, a safe refuge in some hidden den or burrow. Hibernation is, therefore, primarily a winter refuge of small, easily concealed animals rather than of large ones.

A high metabolic rate, however, means a heavy intake of energy in order to sustain body warmth and efficiency. It is for this reason that even some of these later warm-blooded mammals existing in our day have learned to descend into a slower, unconscious rate of living during the winter months when food may be difficult to obtain. On a slightly higher plane they are following the procedure of the cold-blooded frog sleeping in the mud at the bottom of a frozen pond.

The agile brain of the warm-blooded birds and mammals demands a high oxygen consumption and food in concentrated forms, or the creatures cannot long sustain themselves. It was the rise of flowering plants that provided that energy and changed the nature of the living world. Their appearance parallels in a quite surprising manner the rise of the birds and mammals.

Slowly, toward the dawn of the Age of Reptiles, something over two hundred and fifty million years ago, the little naked sperm cells wriggling their way through dew and raindrops had given way to a kind of pollen carried by the wind. Our present-day pine forests represent plants of a pollen-disseminating variety. Once fertilization was no longer dependent on exterior water, the march over drier regions could be extended. Instead of spores simple primitive seeds carrying some nourishment for the young plant had developed, but true flowers were still scores of millions of years away. After a long period of hesitant evolutionary groping, they exploded upon the world with truly revolutionary violence.

The event occurred in Cretaceous times in the close of the Age of Reptiles. Before the coming of the flowering plants our own ancestral stock, the warm-blooded mammals, consisted of a few mousy little creatures hidden in trees and underbrush. A few lizard-like birds with carnivorous teeth flapped awkwardly on ill-aimed flights among archaic shrubbery. None of these insignificant creatures gave evidence of any remarkable talents. The mammals in particular had been around for some millions of years, but had remained well lost in the shadow of the mighty reptiles. Truth to tell, man was still, like the genie in the bottle, encased in the body of a creature about the size of a rat.

As for the birds, their reptilian cousins the Pterodactyls, flew farther and better. There was just one thing about the birds that paralleled the physiology of the mammals. They, too, had evolved warm blood and its accompanying temperature control. Nevertheless, if one had been seen stripped of his feathers, he would still have seemed a slightly uncanny and unsightly lizard.

Neither the birds nor the mammals, however, were quite what they seemed. They were waiting for the Age of Flowers. They were waiting for what flowers, and with them the true encased seed, would bring. Fish-eating, gigantic leather-winged reptiles, twenty-eight feet from wing tip to wing tip, hovered over the coasts that one day would be swarming with gulls.

Inland the monotonous green of the pine and spruce forests with their primitive wooden cone flowers stretched everywhere. No grass hindered the fall of the naked seeds to earth. Great sequoias towered to the skies. The world of that time has a certain appeal but it is a giant's world, a world moving slowly like the reptiles who stalked magnificently among the boles of its trees.

The trees themselves are ancient, slow-growing and immense, like the redwood groves that have survived to our day on the California coast. All is stiff, formal, upright and green, monotonously green. There is no grass as yet; there are no wide plains rolling in the sun, no tiny daisies dotting the meadows underfoot. There is little versatility about this scene; it is, in truth, a giant's world.

A few nights ago it was brought home vividly to me that the world has changed since that far epoch. I was awakened out of sleep by an unknown sound in my living room. Not a small sound—not a creaking timber or a mouse's scurry—but a sharp, rending explosion as though an unwary foot had been put down upon a wine glass. I had come instantly out of sleep and lay tense, unbreathing. I listened for another step. There was none.

Unable to stand the suspense any longer, I turned on the light and passed from room to room glancing uneasily behind chairs and into closets. Nothing seemed disturbed, and I stood puzzled in the center of the living room floor. Then a small button-shaped object upon the rug caught my eye. It was hard and polished and glistening. Scattered over the length of the room were several more shining up at me like wary little eyes. A pine cone that had been lying in a dish had been blown the length of the coffee table. The dish itself could hardly have been the source of the explosion. Beside it I found two ribbon-like strips of a velvety-green. I tried to place the two strips together to make a pod. They twisted resolutely away from each other and would no longer fit.

I relaxed in a chair, then, for I had reached a solution of the midnight disturbance. The twisted strips were wistaria pods that I had brought in a day or two previously and placed in the dish. They had chosen midnight to explode and distribute their multiplying fund of life down the length of the room. A plant, a fixed, rooted thing, immobilized in a single pod, had devised a way of propelling its offspring across open space. Immediately there passed before my eyes the million airy troopers of the milkweed pod and the clutching hooks of the sandburs. Seeds on the coyote's tail, seeds on the hunter's coat, thistledown mounting on the winds—all were somehow triumphing over life's limitations. Yet the ability to do this had not been with them at the beginning. It was the product of endless effort and experiment.

The seeds on my carpet were not going to lie stiffly where they had dropped like their antiquated cousins, the naked seeds on the pine-cone scales. They were travelers. Struck by the thought, I went out next day and collected several other varieties. I line them up now in a row on my desk—so many little capsules of life, winged, hooked or spiked. Every one is an angiosperm, a product of the true flowering plants. Contained in these little boxes is the secret of that far-off Cretaceous explosion of a hundred million years ago that changed the face of the planet. And somewhere in here, I think, as I spoke seriously at one particularly resistant seedcase of a wild grass, was once man himself.

Meaning

1. How did the appearance of flowers unchain creatures from their dependency on the climate and make possible the existence of mammalian life?
2. Why did the appearance of flowering plants make it possible for creatures to evolve with higher metabolic rates?
3. If flowering plants had not appeared, why would birds still be flying reptiles?

Using Cause and Effect to Convey Meaning

1. How does Eiseley use the illustration of the exploding seed pod to support his hypothesis about the crucial role played by flowering plants or angiosperms?
2. What words or phrases does Eiseley use as markers to separate the key stages in the chain of causation that eventually resulted in the evolution of warm-blooded mammals?
3. What measures does Eiseley take to adapt his knowledge of complex biological processes so that readers without a scientific background can understand his ideas?

Writing Suggestions

1. Explore the conflict between Charles Darwin's theory of gradual evolution over vast periods of time (see the Argument and Persuasion chapter, page 715) and what Eiseley terms the "abominable mystery" of the sudden and inexplicable appearance of flowering plants.
2. Discuss how any other seemingly innocuous plant, insect, or animal plays an indispensable role in nature.

CARL SAGAN

The Nuclear Winter

Carl Sagan, a modern-day Renaissance man of science, was born in 1934 in New York. After graduating with both a B.A. and a B.S. degree from the University of Chicago, Sagan completed his M.S. in physics and earned a Ph.D. in astronomy and astro-physics in 1960. Sagan was nominated to join the Smithsonian Astrophysical Observatory in 1962. At the same time, he also worked with the Nobel-prize winner Joshua Lederberg, investigating the origins of life on earth, and taught genetics at Stanford. Sagan then taught astronomy at Harvard until 1968, when he became professor of astronomy and space sciences at Cornell University. He is currently the director of the Laboratory for Planetary Studies. Sagan was awarded the NASA medal for exceptional scientific achievement in 1972, after his hypotheses about Mars were validated by data obtained from the 1971 Mars Mariner expedition. Since 1968, Sagan has been the editor of Icarus, *the international journal of astronomy, and has written many distinguished books. His works include* The Cosmic Connection (1973), *which received the Campbell Award for best science book; the Pulitzer-prize winning* Dragons of Eden (1977); Broca's Brain (1979), *on developments in neurophysiology; and* Cosmos (1980), *which accompanied his widely-acclaimed television series. In "The Nuclear Winter" (1983), Sagan explores the unforeseen and devastating physical and chemical effects of even a small-scale nuclear war on the earth's biosphere and life on earth.*

Except for fools and madmen, everyone knows that nuclear war would be an unprecedented human catastrophe. A more or less typical strategic warhead has a yield of 2 megatons, the explosive equivalent of 2 million tons of TNT. But 2 million tons of TNT is about the same as all the bombs exploded in World War II—a single bomb with the explosive power of the entire Second World War but compressed into a few seconds of time and an area 30 or 40 miles across . . .

In a 2-megaton explosion over a fairly large city, buildings would be vaporized, people reduced to atoms and shadows, outlying structures blown down like matchsticks and raging fires ignited. And if the bomb were exploded on the ground, an enormous crater, like those that can be seen through a telescope on the surface of the Moon, would be all that remained where midtown once had been. There are now more than 50,000 nuclear weapons, more than 13,000 megatons of yield, deployed in the arsenals of the United States and the Soviet Union—enough to obliterate a million Hiroshimas.

But there are fewer than 3000 cities on the Earth with populations of 100,000 or more. You cannot find anything like a million Hiroshimas to obliterate. Prime military and industrial targets that are far from cities are comparatively rare. Thus, there are vastly more nuclear weapons than are needed for any plausible deterrence of a potential adversary.

Nobody knows, of course, how many megatons would be exploded in a real nuclear war. There are some who think that a nuclear war can be "contained," bottled up before it runs away to involve much of the world's arsenals. But a number of detailed analyses, war games run by the U.S. Department of Defense, and official Soviet pronouncements all indicate that this containment may be too much to hope for: Once the bombs begin exploding, communications failures, disorganization, fear, the necessity of making in minutes decisions affecting the fates of millions, and the immense psychological burden of knowing that your own loved ones may already have been destroyed are likely to result in a nuclear paroxysm. Many investigations, including a number of studies for the U.S. government, envision the explosion of 5000 to 10,000 megatons—the detonation of tens of thousands of nuclear weapons that now sit quietly, inconspicuously, in missile silos, submarines and long-range bombers, faithful servants awaiting orders.

The World Health Organization, in a recent detailed study chaired by Sune K. Bergstrom (the 1982 Nobel laureate in physiology and medicine), concludes that 1.1 billion people would be killed outright in such a nuclear war, mainly in the United States, the Soviet Union, Europe, China and Japan. An additional 1.1 billion people would suffer serious injuries and radiation sickness, for which medical help would be unavailable. It thus seems possible that more than 2 billion people—almost half of all the humans on Earth—would be destroyed in the immediate aftermath of a global thermonuclear war. This would represent by far the greatest disaster in the history of the human species and, with no other adverse effects, would probably be enough to reduce at least the Northern Hemisphere to a state of prolonged agony and barbarism. Unfortunately, the real situation would be much worse.

In technical studies of the consequences of nuclear weapons explosions, there has been a dangerous tendency to underestimate the results. This is partly due to a tradition of conservatism which generally works well in science but which is of more dubious applicability when the lives of billions of people are at stake. In the Bravo test of March 1, 1954, a 15-megaton thermonuclear bomb was exploded on Bikini Atoll. It had about double the yield expected, and there was an unanticipated last-minute shift in the wind direction. As a result, deadly radioactive fallout came down on Rongelap in the Marshall Islands, more than 200 kilometers away. Almost all the children on Rongelap subsequently developed thyroid nodules and lesions, and other long-term medical problems, due to the radioactive fallout.

Likewise, in 1973, it was discovered that high-yield airbursts will chemically burn the nitrogen in the upper air, converting it into oxides of nitrogen; these, in turn, combine with and destroy the protective ozone in the Earth's stratosphere. The surface of the Earth is shielded from deadly solar ultraviolet radiation by a layer of ozone so tenuous that, were it brought down to sea level, it would be only 3 millimeters thick. Partial destruction of this ozone layer can have serious consequences for the biology of the entire planet.

These discoveries, and others like them, were made by chance. They were largely unexpected. And now another consequence—by far the most dire—has been uncovered, again more or less by accident.

The U.S. Mariner 9 spacecraft, the first vehicle to orbit another planet, arrived at Mars in late 1971. The planet was enveloped in a global dust storm. As the fine particles slowly fell out, we were able to measure temperature changes in the atmosphere and on the surface. Soon it became clear what had happened:

The dust, lofted by high winds off the desert into the upper Martian atmosphere, had absorbed the incoming sunlight and prevented much of it from reaching the ground. Heated by the sunlight, the dust warmed the adjacent air. But the surface, enveloped in partial darkness, became much chillier than usual. Months later, after the dust fell out of the atmosphere, the upper air cooled and the surface warmed, both returning to their normal conditions. We were able to calculate accurately, from how much dust there was in the atmosphere, how cool the Martian surface ought to have been.

Afterwards, I and my colleagues, James B. Pollack and Brian Toon of NASA's Ames Research Center, were eager to apply these insights to the Earth. In a volcanic explosion, dust aerosols are lofted into the high atmosphere. We calculated by how much the Earth's global temperature should decline after a major volcanic explosion and found that our results (generally a fraction of a degree) were in good accord with actual measurements. Joining forces with Richard Turco, who has studied the effects of nuclear weapons for many years, we then began to turn our attention to the climatic effects of nuclear war. [The scientific paper, "Global Atmospheric Consequences of Nuclear War," was written by R. P. Turco, O. B. Toon, T. P. Ackerman, J. B. Pollack and Carl Sagan. From the last names of the authors, this work is generally referred to as "TTAPS."]

We knew that nuclear explosions, particularly groundbursts, would lift an enormous quantity of fine soil particles into the atmosphere (more than 100,000 tons of fine dust for every megaton exploded in a surface burst). Our work was further spurred by Paul Crutzen of the Max Planck Institute for Chemistry in Mainz, West Germany, and by John Birks of the University of Colorado, who pointed out that huge quantities of smoke would be generated in the burning of cities and forests following a nuclear war.

Groundbursts—at hardened missile silos, for example—generate fine dust. Airbursts—over cities and unhardened military installations—make fires and therefore smoke. The amount of dust and soot generated depends on the conduct of the war, the yields of the weapons employed and the ratio of groundbursts to airbursts. So we ran computer models for several dozen different nuclear war scenarios. Our baseline case, as in many other studies, was a 5000-megaton war with only a modest fraction of the yield (20 percent) expended on urban or industrial targets. Our job, for each case, was to follow the dust and smoke generated, see how much sunlight was absorbed and by how much the temperatures changed, figure out how the particles spread in longitude and latitude, and calculate how long before it all fell out in the air back onto the surface. Since the radioactivity would be attached to these same fine particles, our calculations also revealed the extent and timing of the subsequent radioactive fallout.

Some of what I am about to describe is horrifying. I know, because it horrifies me. There is a tendency—psychiatrists call it "denial"—to put it out of our minds, not to think about it. But if we are to deal intelligently, wisely, with the nuclear arms race, then we must steel ourselves to contemplate the horrors of nuclear war.

The results of our calculations astonished us. In the baseline case, the amount of sunlight at the ground was reduced to a few percent of normal—much darker, in daylight, than in a heavy overcast and too dark for plants to make a living from photosynthesis. At least in the Northern Hemisphere, where the great preponderance of strategic targets lies, an unbroken and deadly gloom would persist for weeks.

Even more unexpected were the temperatures calculated. In the baseline case, land temperatures, except for narrow strips of coastline, dropped to minus 25° Celsius (minus 13° Fahrenheit) and stayed below freezing for months—even for a summer war. (Because the atmospheric structure becomes much more stable as the upper atmosphere is heated and the low air is cooled, we may have severely *under*estimated how long the cold and the dark would last.) The oceans, a significant heat reservoir, would not freeze, however, and a major ice age would probably not be triggered. But because the temperatures would drop so catastrophically, virtually all crops and farm animals, at least in the Northern Hemisphere, would be destroyed, as would most varieties of uncultivated or domesticated food supplies. Most of the human survivors would starve.

In addition, the amount of radioactive fallout is much more than expected. Many previous calculations simply ignored the intermediate time-scale fallout. That is, calculations were made for the prompt fallout—the plumes of radioactive debris blown downwind from each target—and for the long-term fallout, the fine radioactive particles lofted into the stratosphere that would descend about a year later, after most of the radioactivity had decayed. However, the radioactivity carried into the upper atmosphere (but not as high as the stratosphere) seems to have been largely forgotten. We found for the baseline case that roughly 30 percent of the land at northern midlatitudes could receive a radioactive dose greater than 250 rads, and that about 50 percent of northern midlatitudes could receive a dose greater than 100 rads. A 100-rad dose is the equivalent of about 1000 medical X-rays. A 400-rad dose will, more likely than not, kill you.

The cold, the dark and the intense radioactivity, together lasting for months, represent a severe assault on our civilization and our species. Civil and sanitary services would be wiped out. Medical facilities, drugs, the most rudimentary means for relieving the vast human suffering, would be unavailable. Any but the most elaborate shelters would be useless, quite apart from the question of what good it might be to emerge a few months later. Synthetics burned in the destruction of the cities would produce a wide variety of toxic gases, including carbon monoxide, cyanides, dioxins and furans. After the dust and soot settled out, the solar ultraviolet flux would be much larger than its present value. Immunity to disease would decline. Epidemics and pandemics would be rampant, especially after the billion or so unburied bodies began to thaw. Moreover, the combined influence of these severe and simultaneous stresses on life are likly to produce even more adverse consequences—biologists call them synergisms—that we are not yet wise enough to foresee.

So far, we have talked only of the Northern Hemisphere. But it now seems—unlike the case of a single nuclear weapons test—that in a real nuclear war, the heating of the vast quantities of atmospheric dust and soot in northern midlatitudes will transport these fine particles toward and across the Equator. We see just this happening in Martian dust storms. The Southern Hemisphere would experience effects that, while less severe than in the Northern Hemisphere, are nevertheless extremely ominous. The illusion with which some people in the Northern Hemisphere reassure themselves—catching an Air New Zealand flight in a time of serious international crisis, or the like—is now much less tenable, even on the narrow issue of personal survival for those with the price of a ticket.

But what if nuclear wars *can* be contained, and much less than 5000 megatons is detonated? Perhaps the greatest surprise in our work was that even small nuclear wars can have devastating climatic effects. We considered a war in which a mere 100 megatons were exploded, less than one percent of the world arsenals, and only in low-yield airbursts over cities. This scenario, we found, would ignite thousands of fires, and the smoke from these fires alone would be enough to generate an epoch of cold and dark almost as severe as in the 5000-megaton case. The threshold for what Richard Turco has called The Nuclear Winter is very low.

Could we have overlooked some important effect? The carrying of dust and soot from the Northern to the Southern Hemisphere (as well as more local atmospheric circulation) will certainly thin the clouds out over the Northern Hemisphere. But, in many cases, this thinning would be insufficient to render the climatic consequences tolerable—and every time it got better in the Northern Hemisphere, it would get worse in the Southern.

Our results have been carefully scrutinized by more than 100 scientists in the United States, Europe and the Soviet Union. There are still arguments on points of detail. But the overall conclusion seems to be agreed upon: There are severe and previously unanticipated global consequences of nuclear war—subfreezing temperatures in a twilit radioactive gloom lasting for months or longer.

Scientists initially underestimated the effects of fallout, were amazed that nuclear explosions in space disabled distant satellites, had no idea that the fireballs from high-yield thermonuclear explosions could deplete the ozone layer and missed altogether the possible climatic effects of nuclear dust and smoke. What else have we overlooked?

Nuclear war is a problem that can be treated only theoretically. It is not amenable to experimentation. Conceivably, we have left something important out of our analysis, and the effects are more modest than we calculate. On the other hand, it is also possible—and, from previous experience, even likely—that there are further adverse effects that no one has yet been wise enough to recognize. With billions of lives at stake, where does conservatism lie—in assuming that the results will be better than we calculate, or worse?

Many biologists, considering the nuclear winter that these calculations describe, believe they carry somber implications for life on Earth. Many species of plants and animals would become extinct. Vast numbers of surviving humans would starve to death. The delicate ecological relations that bind together organisms on Earth in a fabric of mutual dependency would be torn, perhaps irreparably. There is little question that our global civilization would be destroyed. The human population would be reduced to prehistoric levels, or less. Life for any survivors would be extremely hard. And there seems to be a real possibility of the extinction of the human species.

It is now almost 40 years since the invention of nuclear weapons. We have not yet experienced a global thermonuclear war—although on more than one occasion we have come tremulously close. I do not think our luck can hold forever. Men and machines are fallible, as recent events remind us. Fools and madmen do exist, and sometimes rise to power. Concentrating always on the near future, we have ignored the long-term consequences of our actions. We have placed our civilization and our species in jeopardy.

Fortunately, it is not yet too late. We can safeguard the planetary civilization and the human family if we so choose. There is no more important or more urgent issue.

MEANING

1. What previously unanticipated effect of thermonuclear explosions does Sagan describe in "The Nuclear Winter?"
2. What connection does Sagan draw between discoveries made by the Mariner 9 expedition to Mars and his own research into the global lowering of temperatures that would follow a nuclear war?
3. What medical problems were discovered to be due to radioactive fallout after the thermonuclear explosion on Bikini Atoll?
4. Why is even partial destruction of the ozone layer by thermonuclear explosions so deadly for the biology of the planet?
5. How was Sagan's research aided by the computer's ability to simulate hypothetical situations?

USING CAUSE AND EFFECT TO CONVEY MEANING

1. Why is the title, "The Nuclear Winter," an apt image to express the results of the causal sequence that would be produced by even a small-scale nuclear war?
2. How does Sagan emphasize the connections between dust lofted into the atmosphere, unexpected drops in global temperatures, duration of the cold, extinction of crops and animals, and starvation of human beings? That is, how does Sagan show that each effect also acts as a cause of a further effect?
3. What different kinds of evidence does Sagan draw on to support the nuclear-winter hypothesis?
4. Why does Sagan mention that one hundred scientists have checked the validity of his findings?

WRITING SUGGESTIONS

1. Sagan points out that scientists have been wrong before and could be wrong again in underestimating the true effects of a nuclear war. Discuss this in light of what Sagan calls "denial" or what Barbara Tuchman identifies as "protective stupidity" (see page 476).
2. In what way would the effects of nuclear war described by Sagan produce a world like that before the appearance of flowering plants (see Loren Eiseley, page 501)?

DEFINITION

Definition is a useful method for specifying the basic nature of any phenomenon, idea, or thing. Discussing whether Jack has a "sense of humor" or Jill has "charisma" depends on establishing a clearly defined, commonly agreed-upon meaning for the terms involved. Frequently, we arrive at the meaning of a concept, like a "sense of humor," by giving synonyms such as "waggish," "playful," "witty," or "droll" to clarify the meaning of the term or phrase in question.

By contrast, dictionaries use a more formal method for establishing exact meanings. Dictionaries place the subject to be defined in the context of the general class of things to which it belongs, and then give distinguishing features that differentiate the term from all other subjects in its class with which it might be confused.

We can see the same technique operating when zoologists specify the phylum, class, order, family, genus, and species for any creature. Just as the dictionary provides both the general class and distinguishing features for any term, zoologists normally refer to an animal by giving its generic and specific names together. Thus, a species of wild sheep, known as the "bighorn," found in western North America, would be called *bovidae: ovis canadensis*. At first glance, the bighorn sheep might easily be mistaken for the mountain goat, because both bighorn sheep and mountain goat have coarse coats of hair ranging in color from creamy white to brown and both are members of the family of hollow-horned ruminents called *bovidae*. A zoologist would notice important distinguishing features or *differentae* between the two species. Bighorn sheep, unlike goats, lack scent glands at the base of the tail, do not have beards, and have narrow noses with concave foreheads, whereas goats have narrow noses with convex foreheads. A zoological dictionary that defines the bighorn by putting it in a class and then telling how it could be distinguished from other members of that class would indeed be invaluable in separating the sheep from the goat.

Traditional methods of definition are useful as long as the meaning of the term being defined has already been established, is generally agreed upon, or does not change its meaning in a different context. Many disciplines need to define new terms or concepts, or redefine old ones as the results of new research become known. Thus, the term *node* is defined one way in anatomy (a concentrated swelling, such

513

as in "lymph node"), another in physics (as the point in a string where the least vibration occurs), still differently in botany (as the stem joint out of which a leaf grows), and, again, with a different meaning in astronomy (a point where a planet's orbit appears to cross the sun's apparent path across the heavens).

The range of methods available to writers for the definition of technical terms, concepts, and processes goes well beyond the abbreviated, formula type of definition found in dictionaries. Writers can draw on any or all of the writing strategies previously discussed—narration, description, exemplification, comparison and contrast, process analysis, classification, analogy, and cause and effect—to clarify and define the basic nature of any idea, term, condition, or phenomenon.

In "The Married Woman," for example, Simone de Beauvoir employs narration and description in a series of anecdotes that allow her readers to perceive how much of the married woman's life is defined by a fruitless struggle against dirt, dust, and disorder:

> The maniac housekeeper wages her furious war against dirt, blaming life itself for the rubbish all living growth entails. When any living being enters her house, her eye gleams with a wicked light: "Wipe your feet, don't tear the place apart, leave that alone!" She wishes those of her household would hardly breathe; everything means more thankless work for her. Severe, preoccupied, always on the watch, she loses *joie de vivre*, she becomes overprudent and avaricious. She shuts out the sunlight, for along with that comes insects, germs, and dust, and besides, the sun ruins silk hangings and fades upholstery; she scatters naphthalene, which scents the air. She becomes bitter and disagreeable and hostile to all that lives: the end is sometimes murder.

Simone de Beauvoir's descriptive anecdote allows her readers to immediately see the features and specific qualities she considers essential in defining her subject. Repetitive, never-ending household tasks are, for de Beauvoir, what defines the married woman's life. De Beauvoir's observations, first made in 1952, provided a conceptual focus for the Women's Liberation Movement, which arose concomitantly with the re-entry of women into the labor force.

Edward Rothstein, a music critic, offers a range of examples in "Why We Live in the Musical Past" to illustrate the extent to which music written in the nineteenth century has "come to *define* our ideas of what music should be:"

> Many of the scheduled works [of the New York Philharmonic]—including Schubert's "Unfinished" Symphony, Mussorgsky's "Pictures at an Exhibition," Tchaikovsky's Fifth Symphony—are the musical equivalents of "best-sellers." Each season they are repeatedly played, if not by the Philharmonic then by another local or visiting orchestra. Apart from such other 19th-century masters as Berlioz, Bruckner, Liszt, Wagner, Strauss and Dvorak, there are a few familiar "modern" works—Barber's Adagio for Strings, Debussy's "La Mer"—a few selections by other repeated moderns like Elgar, Walton, Sibelius and Bernstein, and a handful of novelties by Carter, Druckman and others.

Examples drawn from actual concert programs are especially useful in clarifying an abstract concept like nineteenth-century music, which would be difficult to define in a single phrase. Although much of Rothstein's essay identifies the features that distinguish nineteenth-century music (narrative style, elaborate orchestration, and strong melodic line), this passage illustrates the popularity of nineteenth-century music among twentieth-century audiences by citing examples of how frequently this music is performed.

Another useful method for defining concepts is comparison and contrast. This is how Hans Selye, in "What Is Stress?," demonstrates that stress has a specific discipline-related meaning that is quite different from what most people assume it to be:

> *"Stress is the nonspecific response of the body to any demand made upon it. . . .*
>
> Each drug or hormone has such specific actions: diuretic drugs increase the production of urine; the hormone adrenalin augments the pulse rate and blood pressure, simultaneously raising blood sugar, whereas the hormone insulin decreases blood sugar. Yet, no matter what kind of derangement is produced, all these agents have one thing in common; they also increase the demand for readjustment. This demand is nonspecific; it requires adaptation to a problem, irrespective of what that problem may be.

Selye identifies the essential characteristics of stress by citing evidence that stress is always an "adaptation to a problem" produced in response to different kinds of physiological stimuli. Here we can see how the process of defining key terms helps to establish a discipline or field of study (research into what stress is) as well as set its boundaries with respect to other disciplines (in this case, physiology and psychology).

Sometimes the best way of clarifying an unfamiliar technical process is to explain it in terms of what it can do. In "Harnessing Light," Charles E. Townes, whose Nobel Prize-winning research made possible the discovery of the laser, uses this type of operational definition to give his readers insight into the distinctive nature of his invention:

> As it turned out, I was much too conservative; the field has developed far beyond my imagination and along paths I could not have foreseen at the time. Surveyors use the laser to guarantee straight lines; surgeons to weld new corneas into place and burn away blood clots; industry to drill tiny, precise holes; communications engineers to send information in vast quantities through glass fiber pipes. It is even built into the supermarket checkout scanner that reads prices by bouncing a beam of laser light off a pattern imprinted on the item.

The broad range of applications that Townes describes gives the reader insight into the unique properties that make the laser such an incredible invention. Technical writing depends on clear functional definitions to clarify the distinctive nature of processes, whether as well-known as "lithography" or as specialized as the "Fretz-Moon process" for continuous pipe welding.

The need to have a clear grasp of the nature of the thing being defined can be readily seen in "Alcohol Problems," which represents J. Michael Polich and Bruce R. Orvis' research to develop a useful definition of "alcoholism." In the past, treatment of alcoholism has been hampered by lack of a commonly agreed-upon definition among psychologists, sociologists, physicians, and clergy. In creating their definition, Polich and Orvis use classification to systematically group alcohol-related problems together to show that alcoholism should be considered primarily a form of psychological dependence, and only secondarily a physiological disease. By classifying alcohol-related problems, Polich and Orvis are able to isolate the controlling characteristic that defines the disease. Polich and Orvis believe that a clearer conception of the principles that explain alcoholism will, in turn, make possible more efficient allocation of social resources for treatment. Again, we can see how the process of defining key concepts demarcates a particular field of study (in this case, the study of alcoholism).

Another useful strategy for defining a phenomenon, idea, or process is to identify the circumstances that brought it about or the principles and laws that control its operation. This type of definition seeks to establish causes or consequences. In "On Photography: 'In Plato's Cave,'" Susan Sontag wonders what causes camera owners to want to shoot, collect, and display photographs. She also is curious as to what effects or consequences the popularity of photography has had on society. By answering these questions, Sontag is, in effect, defining "photography:"

> Memorializing the achievements of individuals considered as members of families (as well as other groups) is the earliest popular use of photography. For at least a century, the wedding photograph has been as much a part of the ceremony as the prescribed verbal formulas. Cameras go with family life. According to a sociological study done in France, most households have a camera, but a household with children is twice as likely to have at least one camera as a household in which there are no children. . . .

Sontag distinguishes photography from other forms of social amusement by pointing out how frequently camera ownership goes along with family life. Elsewhere in her essay, Sontag uses a variety of methods (including narration, exemplification, and classification) in addition to causal analysis to reveal the basic nature of photography as a "social rite, a defense against anxiety, and a tool of power."

Another way of defining a term is based on looking at the etymology or history of the term itself as an important clue to illuminating its meaning. Frank Nuessel uses this approach in his analysis of how ageist language negatively stereotypes older people in "Old Age Needs a New Home":

> The overwhelming majority of words and phrases for elders are unfavorable and prejudicial. . . . In this regard, the extensive, pejorative, and ageist vocabulary of the English language constitutes a verbal record of this society's fear of getting old.

Nuessel is particularly concerned that the use of dehumanizing language facilitates abuse and mistreatment of older people. He points out that denigration of individuals through negative labeling is often the first step toward disenfranchisement. Nuessel documents this phenomenon by showing how the etymology and history of words used to describe the elderly have acquired negative connotations in direct proportion to society's fear of getting old. This approach has been successfully used by researchers in many disciplines to show how the meanings of words that we take for granted are, in fact, products of historical change.

Within this chapter, a music critic characterizes nineteenth-century music, sociologists unravel the meanings that alcoholism has acquired, a contemporary author provides insight into the larger role that photography plays in our culture, a feminist looks critically at the life of the married woman, a scientist defines the phenomenon of stress, a linguist looks at the perjorative associations of words used to describe older people, and a physicist whose research led to the discovery of the laser specifies the essential attributes of his invention.

It must also be said that while writers in a variety of disciplines are concerned with formulating new definitions of ideas, conditions, and phenomena, or redefining old terms or concepts in light of the results of current research, we must also keep in mind that words change meaning and take on different cultural weight over time as part of wider historical processes.

LIBERAL ARTS

Edward Rothstein

Why We Live in the Musical Past

Edward Rothstein, born in 1952, is music critic for The New Republic *and* Vanity Fair, *and senior editor for the Free Press, Macmillan, Inc. Rothstein's graduate studies included work in mathematics, literature, and philosophy at the University of Chicago, Brandeis, and Columbia. His essays on literature, science, culture, and all aspects of musical history and performance have appeared in the* New York Review of Books, Commentary, The American Scholar, Musical Quarterly, *and the* Washington Post. *His essay, "The Body of Bach," was chosen to appear in* The Best American Essays 1986. *Rothstein's knowledgeable discussions of how the quality of musical reproduction varies with different kinds of audio technology have also appeared in* The Absolute Sound. *"Why We Live in the Musical Past," which originally appeared in the* New York Times (1982), *analyzes the programmatic, narrative, and mythic qualities that define nineteenth-century music. In this article, Rothstein offers a provocative theory as to why the musical tastes of twentieth-century concert-goers remain fixated in nineteenth-century musical repertory.*

We are living in a most peculiar musical age. Musical life is booming, audiences are growing, seasons are expanding, conservatories are turning out virtuosos. In New York, well over a *hundred* concerts are given every week. There is an extraordinary bustle and whirl in the music world and its accompanying business. But in the midst of all that activity, there is a certain stillness, an immovable center. For our musical life is based upon repetition.

In recent weeks, for example, the New York Philharmonic and the Metropolitan Opera have announced their programs for the coming season. At the Philharmonic, there are, of course, some unusual offerings. A concert performance of Janacek's "From the House of the Dead" is planned as are programs devoted to Shostakovich and to the Polish modern, Witold Lutoslawski—all reflecting growing interest in Slavic and Eastern European composers. There is also a "retrospective" of six compositions by Schoenberg planned, concentrating on his earliest music.

But the repertory of the Philharmonic is actually dominated by familiarly repeated works of the 19th-century musical tradition—including Mozart on one end and a few moderns like Rachmaninoff on the other. Out of the more than 90 compositions the Philharmonic is performing in 125 concerts with more than 35 different programs, only *six* works will be new to New York; *three* of those will be world premieres. The most heavily represented composers are Mozart, with seven works, including four popular piano concertos, and Beethoven with six works, including three familiar symphonies. Brahms is among the next most often scheduled composers, represented by the First Piano Concerto, First Symphony, Violin Concerto and Tragic Overture. Schumann is also heavily represented.

Many of the scheduled works—including Schubert's "Unfinished" Symphony, Mussorgsky's "Pictures at an Exhibition," Tchaikovsky's Fifth Symphony—are the musical equivalents of "best-sellers." Each season they are repeatedly played, if not by the Philharmonic then by another local or visiting orchestra. Apart from such other 19th-century masters as Berlioz, Bruckner, Liszt, Wagner, Strauss and Dvorak, there are a few familiar "modern" works—Barber's Adagio for Strings, Debussy's "La Mer"— a few selections by other repeated moderns like Elgar, Walton, Sibelius and Bernstein, and a handful of novelties by Carter, Druckman and others.

At the Metropolitan Opera, programming is similar. There are new productions of Strauss's "Arabella," Verdi's "Macbeth" and Mozart's "Idomeneo." The acclaimed production of Mussorgsky's "Boris Godunov" will return as will Debussy's "Pelléas et Mélisande" and the "Parade" trilogy, with its ballet and two 20th-century operas. But 12 out of the 21 operatic productions being offered next season—over *half* the repertory—were premiered in the 55 years between 1830 and 1885, five of those are by Verdi. Only *three* works premiered after 1905, one is the familiar "Der Rosenkavalier."

"The seasons of both the Met and the Philharmonic, then, are intensely focussed on the 19th-century repertory. That policy is a resounding success: halls are filled to over 90 percent of capacity; at least 12,000 seats are filled at the four weekly Philharmonic concerts; more than 25,000 tickets are sold to the seven weekly Met performances. This programming speaks for the tastes of the musical mainstream.

Elsewhere, the same repertory is also repeated by popular demand. The Mostly Mozart Festival will soon return as well, with its repetitive festivities. The massive replays of Classical and Romantic music, occasionally interrupted by a new or recent work, have become an accepted part of the musical scene.

But as we know, in previous centuries new works were the rule and not the exception. Bach had a new cantata ready every Sunday, Mozart composed new concertos for his important appearances. 19th-century concert halls and opera houses thrived on premieres. Something changed in this century. The repertory congealed. Our institutions have become repetitive museums.

There is, of course, repetition in the other arts as well. But only in music is the new so sweepingly rejected and the old so worshipfully celebrated. New plays are at the heart of every theater season, new paintings appear on living room walls with insouciant ease, fiction is read hot off the presses. To get an idea of the peculiarity of our musical life, imagine most movie theaters as re-run houses; imagine if most publishers specialized in Dickens and Thackeray.

Still more peculiar is the restricted historical range of our musical life. The 19th-century supplies nearly all of our repertory. For most audiences, the Baroque era is worth only an occasional visit, the Renaissance is a novelty, the Middle Ages an eccentricity.

Of course, the 19th-century repertory is a great achievement of Western European culture; it is extraordinarily profound and exciting, worthy of living with, not just listening to. Given its immense riches many listeners hardly will risk an evening on a third-rate new composition. The repetitive musical culture has, in fact, been attributed to a failure of contemporary composition. Other explanations blame the lack of adventurous listeners, the stodgy institutions, the commercialization of classical music or the stagnation of the recording industry.

Each of these explanations has some validity. But they reduce an exceedingly complex cultural phenomenon to matters of taste and commerce. They do not explain why repetition has become so extensive in its own right, and why those repetitions should be so exclusively centered upon the 19th-century tradition.

We do not, for example, turn to this repertory simply because the "new" is unappreciated; in fact, for most audiences, the "new" is unnecessary. The 19th century satisfies our musical needs; it has a special meaning. This is not just because 19th-century music is "great" or has beautiful melodies—the melodies of the Renaissance are just as beautiful, largely unperformed early music just as "great." The point is that the 19th-century has actually come to *define* our ideas of what music should be. The Philharmonic and the Metropolitan Opera were founded in the 19th-century; the symphony orchestra, the concert hall and grand opera have their origins in the same period. We live in a 19th-century musical culture.

Why then, is this music so tirelessly repeated? There are the obvious reasons— because it is pleasurable, rewarding, beautiful. But our repetitions are also similar to the demands made in childhood, demands to hear a story told again and again; such demands are echoed in many of the repetitions of culture and religion.

As children we did not ask for retellings in order to learn more; we simply wanted to hear tales told again. Children ask to hear the stories they know the best, stories they know so well, they could easily tell them themselves.

Sigmund Freud referred to the "child's peculiar pleasure in constant repetition." In "Beyond the Pleasure Principle," he writes: "If a child has been told a nice story, he will insist on hearing it over and over again rather than a new one; and he will remorselessly stipulate that the repetition shall be an identical one and will correct any alterations of which the narrator may be guilty."

Of course, contemporary musical audiences are not merely children listening to papa composers tell stories. But the requests are similar; certain works are selected as "favorites"—Beethoven's Fifth Symphony, Chopin's Waltzes, Verdi's "La Traviata." These are known best, demanded most and varied least. Recordings also offer musical tales in precise, unaltered repetitions.

Freud linked compulsions to repeat to the nature of instinct—the effort "to restore an earlier state of things." Repetition of a story, in this view, involves an attempt to comprehend or restore a dramatic or psychological situation contained within the tale.

Both Bruno Bettelheim and Erich Fromm have continued this argument, demonstrating that stories contain conflicts and situations which the child is attempting to master or understand. In "Hansel and Gretel," for example, a struggle with parental figures is enacted in the children's exile from home and their overcoming of the witch. Particular moments are always psychologically significant to a child—when the prince rescues the sleeping beauty, when the wolf in grandma's clothing bares his teeth. "Tell it to me again," says the child, "the part where. . . ." Psychologists remind us: the child is never just listening to a story; he is dreaming of his own life.

The story involves not just fantasy, but the real world of parents, authority, conflict; that is why children prefer that stories be told by a parent instead of read in a book or recited by a friend. It may be that our repeated listening to music involves a similar state-of-mind. "Play it again," say our concert audiences, "the Beethoven 'Emperor'." We reflect on psychological or social situations embodied in the music, which take on additional power when told in their social setting, the concert hall.

What is special about our chosen repertory? First of all, 19th-century music really is written in the form of a story, with elaborate narrative programs. While programs in Baroque repertory centered on *images*, such as the warbling of a bird, Romantic and late Classical programs allude to narrative *journeys*, invoking Faust, Shakespeare, literary adventures.

These programs are supported by a narrative musical style. In a Baroque fugue, basic thematic material is an unchanged part of a complex musical architecture; but the dominant musical forms of our repertory treat a theme as if it were a character in a novel, subject to events which affect its character, until it is restored, transformed, all tensions resolved. Early sonatas by Haydn, for example, with their surprising wit and dramatic character can be compared to picaresque novels or opera buffa; later sonatas, by Lizst or Brahms, with their passionate mediations, can be compared to the Romantic confessional literature.

That is why we treat these works as stories and listen with rapt attention. If we also respond so strongly, it is because of their meanings. Music after early Classicism was not written for a patron, a court performance, church service or folk celebration; it was the first music written for "the public"—the new middle class—to be heard in concert halls. These musical narratives are similar to the novel which came to maturity in the same period. The novels of Austen, Dickens, or George Eliot were precisely observed tales about the social order and the willful individual, about the middle-class public and its ambitious, desirous and reflective citizens. Musical narratives by middle-class composers have the same spirit.

The symphonic repertory is suffused with psychological detail and epic tension, with encounters between public order (massive blocks of sound, regular harmonics, sturdy resolutions) and more unstable private passions (surprising dissonances, melancholy melodies, rhythmic disruption). These conflicts are the themes of grand opera as well. In "Don-Carlo," an individual's desires threaten the social and familial order; in "Macbeth," ambition does the same. The heroic Siegried is the savior and destroyer of the order of the gods. In grand opera, stable social hierarchies are threatened by the hero's yearning, or (as in "Carmen") by a woman outside the social order who inspires troubling desires and ambitions.

These were then, forms of bourgeois theater that spoke directly to the new public. The 19th-century concerto, with its heroic soloist pitted against a grand orchestral order, can be almost Dickensian in its melodramatic confrontations and coincidences. The charismatic conductor binding the orchestra into a single society, and the flamboyant virtuoso, victoriously braving instrumental dangers, embody the dreams of the middle-class.

Music has always been written for a specific audience. The music of the 19th-century was directed at the bourgeoisie. Even today, a century later, we treasure these tales; our audience is still the middle-class. As children do with resonant stories, we demand the repetition of this music, attempting to savor and master its situations and resolutions.

But this music is more than just social adventure. The anthropologist Claude Lévi-Strauss has suggested that this repertory has a *mythological* function in society. In "Myth and Meaning," Mr. Lévi Strauss asserts that after the 16th-century, myth receded in importance; the novel and music took its place. "The music that took over the traditional function of mythology," he argues, "reached its full development with Mozart, Beethoven, and Wagner in the 18th and 19th centuries."

One function of myth, in Mr. Lévi-Strauss's view, is to show how a culture's customs of marriage, government or economy are related to more universal natural forces. Prometheus brings fire from the gods; Moses brings down laws from Mt. Sinai; medicine, in many myths, is taught to man by animals. In his musical analogy the anthropologist suggests that our repertory serves this mythological function: it dramatizes how bourgeois society is connected to the primal forces which lie outside it.

In opera, this was, in fact a major theme, not just in Wagner's overtly mythic "Ring." Again and again, opera shows the social order both animated and threatened by primal passions. The bourgeois family, for example, is one arena for mythic tensions. Carmen—a gypsy on the outskirts of the social order—seduces the soldier away from familial responsibilities; in "Il Trovatore," another gypsy steals a child from an aristocratic father; in "La Traviata," the "fallen woman" is a threat to Germont, the bourgeois father; in "Robert le Diable" the father is the devil himself.

Similar concerns with irrational forces lying behind a rational order can be heard throughout the symphonic music of the 19th-century. The figure of the devil in 19th-century music is just one example of the music's mythic concerns—in Berlioz's "Symphonie Fantastique," in Liszt's "Faust" and "Mephisto." Even the "virtuoso"— a favorite 19th-century persona—was a figure with frightening powers from outside the musical and social order; Paganini was considered demonic.

So when we listen to this repertory with as much avidity and passion as we do, it is not merely because it is "great." The foundations of contemporary society lie in the 19th-century; we share its mythology. Even today, musical myths speak with authority about our rational bourgeois society, its fragility and its strengths.

The mythological nature of the repertory also provides insight into our musical repetitions. Mircea Eliade, a historian of religion, has explained that in ancient cultures, myths are connected with ritualist repetitions. Even in contemporary religion, for example, the ritual of Mass regularly enacts the myth of the Eucharist, Sabbath rituals regularly recall the myth of God's rest after the Creation. Through these repetitions, societies act "to regenerate themselves periodically."

This is precisely what happens in our secular musical world. If 19th-century music has the function of myth in our society, the concert hall is a cross between a theater and a temple. The concert has the airs of a repeated ritual, communally celebrated in our modern religion of high art. The musical myths, telling of our social origins and our connections with primal forces, are told and retold.

The "great" 19th-century composer himself becomes a mythic figure in these rituals. The heroes of myth, Mr. Eliade points out, are not just individuals who lived at a particular time and place; they are representative of primal forces. Moses and Jesus and Mohammed, in the mythologies of three religions, speak for the divine realm. So too with Mozart, Beethoven, Wagner; no matter how program notes describe their lives or surroundings, we treat the music as if it derived from a transcendental source. In Peter Shaffer's Broadway play "Amadeus," this split between music and the historical individual is taken as self-evident: Mozart is crude and awful; his music is magical, a revelation.

Musically, then, we have turned these "great" composers into a pantheon of gods who lived at the beginning of our musical age. They stand outside of history, delivering regenerative messages from the musical beyond. And we honor their messages with unstinting devotion at every concert. When we repeat these myths we invoke our gods and celebrate our mythological past, regenerating ourselves with the concert ritual.

Of course, nuances and qualifications have to be added to these speculations about myth and story in the 19th-century; Mozart, for example, needs slightly different treatment. Clearly, the art works of a century cannot be treated only with sweeping abstractions. But in repeating this repertory with such regularity, we have already acknowledged its shared meanings. The expansion of middle-class audiences in recent decades has solidified the repertory's secure position.

Meanwhile the 19th-century forms of grand opera and symphony orchestra remain alien to the mainstream of contemporary expression. Music has moved on to other things, alienated and private statements, complex illuminations, attempts to recreate ritual in the repetitions of Minimalism. The middle-class is no longer its subject or its audience.

So our repetitions of 19th-century repertory have a darker, more disturbing side. On a vast scale, we mythologize the 19th-century. We anxiously savor music at its most heroic moment, before it went awry with the beginnings of modernism. We attempt, perhaps, to "restore an earlier state of things." We define what music should be by repeating the works of a single European century. Like myths, these works give our origins; like fairy tales, they offer us promises. But there is something in the present that they miss; they do not show us the future.

MEANING

1. Why has the type of music written in the nineteenth century come to define modern ideas of what music should be?
2. What percentage of concert programs are made up of works that were composed in the nineteenth century?
3. What different kinds of theories does Rothstein offer to explain why concert-goers prefer to hear music written by composers of the last century?
4. How does the narrative style of nineteenth-century music make it more accessible to modern audiences than other kinds of music?

USING DEFINITION TO CONVEY MEANING

1. What examples does Rothstein provide to document the popularity of nineteenth-century music?
2. What features distinguish nineteenth-century music from the music of other eras?
3. How does Rothstein use theories from psychology and anthropology to explain the overwhelming preference shown by audiences for music of this type?

Writing Suggestions

1. Discuss how a piece written by any nineteenth-century composer illustrates the typical characteristics that define music from this era.
2. Do any nonclassical musical works exhibit any of the features that Rothstein identifies as being characteristic of nineteenth-century music? What mythic, dramatic, or narrative elements are present?

Susan Sontag

On Photography: "In Plato's Cave"

Susan Sontag, an influential critic and novelist, was born in 1933 in New York City. After graduating from the University of Chicago in 1951, Sontag received an M.A. and Ph.D. from Harvard. Sontag has taught English and philosophy at the University of Connecticut, Harvard, Sarah Lawrence, the City College of New York, and Columbia, and was a Writer in Residence in 1964 at Rutgers University. She has received numerous fellowships from the Rockefeller Foundation, the Ingram Merrill Foundation, and the Guggenheim Foundation, as well as the Arts and Letters Award from the American Academy of Arts and Letters (1976) and the National Book Critics Circle prize (1978). Sontag is most noted for her critical essays, including Against Interpretation and Other Essays *(1966), a collection of essays that defines "camp" sensibility and served as a guide to developments in avant-garde culture;* Styles of Radical Will *(1969), promoting a radical esthetic;* Illness As Metaphor *(1977), against the stereotyped use of cancer as social metaphor; and* On Photography *(1977), a penetrating account of the role photography occupies in our culture. She is the author of several novels,* The Benefactor *(1963) and* Death Kit *(1967), and has written and directed several movies,* Duet for Cannibals *(1969) and* Brother Carl *(1971), as well as a documentary about Israel,* Promised Land *(1974). "On Photography: 'In Plato's Cave'" shows Sontag at her most erudite and illuminating as she defines the many roles photography plays in contemporary life.*

Humankind lingers unregenerately in Plato's cave, still reveling, its ageold habit, in mere images of the truth. But being educated by photographs is not like being educated by older, more artisanal images. For one thing, there are a great many more images around, claiming our attention. The inventory started in 1839 and since then just about everything has been photographed, or so it seems. This very insatiability of the photographing eye changes the terms of confinement in the cave, our world. In teaching us a new visual code, photographs alter and enlarge our notions of what is worth looking at and what we have a right to observe. They are a grammar and, even more importantly, an ethics of seeing. Finally, the most grandiose result of the photographic enterprise is to give us the sense that we can hold the whole world in our heads—as an anthology of images.

To collect photographs is to collect the world. Movies and television programs light up walls, flicker, and go out; but with still photographs the image is also an object, lightweight, cheap to produce, easy to carry about, accumulate, store. In Godard's *Les Carabiniers* (1963), two sluggish lumpen-peasants are lured into joining the King's Army by the promise that they will be able to loot, rape, kill, or do whatever else they please to the enemy, and get rich. But the suitcase of booty that Michel-Ange and Ulysse triumphantly bring home, years later, to their wives turns out to contain only picture postcards, hundreds of them, of Monuments, Department Stores, Mammals, Wonders of Nature, Methods of Transport, Works of Art, and other classified treasures from around the globe. Godard's gag vividly parodies the equivocal magic of the photographic image. Photographs are perhaps the most mysterious of all the objects that make up, and thicken, the environment we recognize as modern. Photographs really are experience captured, and the camera is the ideal arm of consciousness in its acquisitive mood.

To photograph is to appropriate the thing photographed. It means putting oneself into a certain relation to the world that feels like knowledge—and, therefore, like power. A now notorious first fall into alienation, habituating people to abstract the world into printed words, is supposed to have engendered that surplus of Faustian energy and psychic damage needed to build modern, inorganic societies. But print seems a less treacherous form of leaching out the world, of turning it into a mental object, than photographic images, which now provide most of the knowledge people have about the look of the past and the reach of the present. What is written about a person or an event is frankly an interpretation, as are handmade visual statements, like paintings and drawings. Photographed images do not seem to be statements about the world so much as pieces of it, miniatures of reality that anyone can make or acquire.

Photographs, which fiddle with the scale of the world, themselves get reduced, blown up, cropped, retouched, doctored, tricked out. They age, plagued by the usual ills of paper objects; they disappear; they become valuable, and get bought and sold; they are reproduced. Photographs, which package the world, seem to invite packaging. They are stuck in albums, framed and set on tables, tacked on walls, projected as slides. Newspapers and magazines feature them; cops alphabetize them; museums exhibit them; publishers compile them.

For many decades the book has been the most influential way of arranging (and usually miniaturizing) photographs, thereby guaranteeing them longevity, if not immortality—photographs are fragile objects, easily torn or mislaid—and a wider public. The photograph in a book is, obviously, the image of an image. But since it is, to begin with, a printed, smooth object, a photograph loses much less of its essential quality when reproduced in a book than a painting does. Still, the book is not a wholly satisfactory scheme for putting groups of photographs into general circulation. The sequences in which the photographs are to be looked at is proposed by the order of pages, but nothing holds readers to the recommended order or indicates the amount of time to be spent on each photograph. Chris Marker's film, *Si j'avais quatre dromadaires* (1966), a brilliantly orchestrated meditation on photographs of all sorts and themes, suggests a subtler and more rigorous way of packaging (and enlarging) still photographs. Both the order and the exact time for looking at each photograph are imposed; and there is a gain in visual legibility and emotional impact. But photographs transcribed in a film cease to be collectable objects, as they still are when served up in books.

Photographs furnish evidence. Something we hear about, but doubt, seems proven when we're shown a photograph of it. In one version of its utility, the camera record incriminates. Starting with their use by the Paris police in the murderous roundup of Communards in June 1871, photographs became a useful tool of modern states in the surveillance and control of their increasingly mobile populations. In another version of its utility, the camera record justifies. A photograph passes for incontrovertible proof that a given thing happened. The picture may distort; but there is always a presumption that something exists, or did exist, which is like what's in the picture. Whatever the limitations (through amateurism) or pretensions (through artistry) of the individual photographer, a photograph—any photograph—seems to have a more innocent, and therefore more accurate, relation to visible reality than do other mimetic objects. Virtuosi of the noble image like Alfred Stieglitz and Paul Strand, composing mighty, unforgettable photographs decade after decade, still want, first of all, to show something "out there," just like the Polaroid owner for whom photographs are a handy, fast form of note-taking, or the shutterbug with a Brownie who takes snapshots as souvenirs of daily life.

While a painting or a prose description can never be other than a narrowly selective interpretation, a photograph can be treated as a narrowly selective transparency. But despite the presumption of veracity that gives all photographs authority, interest, seductiveness, the work that photographers do is no generic exception to the usually shady commerce between art and truth. Even when photographers are most concerned with mirroring reality, they are still haunted by tacit imperatives of taste and conscience. The immensely gifted members of the Farm Security Administration photographic project of the late 1930s (among them Walker Evans, Dorothea Lange, Ben Shahn, Russell Lee) would take dozens of frontal pictures of one of their sharecropper subjects until satisfied that they had gotten just the right look on film—the precise expression on the subject's face that supported their own notions about poverty, light, dignity, texture, exploitation, and geometry. In deciding how a picture should look, in preferring one exposure to another, photographers are always imposing standards on their subjects. Although there is a sense in which the camera does indeed capture reality, not just interpret it, photographs are as much an interpretation of the world as paintings and drawings are. Those occasions when the taking of photographs is relatively undiscriminating, promiscuous, or self-effacing do not lessen the didacticism of the whole enterprise. This very passivity—and ubiquity—of the photographic record is photography's "message," its aggression.

Images which idealize (like most fashion and animal photography) are no less aggressive than work which makes a virtue of plainness (like class pictures, still lifes of the bleaker sort, and mug shots). There is an aggression implicit in every use of the camera. This is as evident in the 1840s and 1850s, photography's glorious first two decades, as in all the succeeding decades, during which technology made possible an ever increasing spread of that mentality which looks at the world as a set of potential photographs. Even for such early masters as David Octavius Hill and Julia Margaret Cameron who used the camera as a means of getting painterly images, the point of taking photographs was a vast departure from the aims of painters. From its start, photography implied the capture of the largest possible number of subjects. Painting never had so imperial a scope. The subsequent industrialization of camera technology only carried out a promise inherent in photography from its very beginning: to democratize all experiences by translating them into images.

That age when taking photographs required a cumbersome and expensive contraption—the toy of the clever, the wealthy, and the obsessed—seems remote indeed from the era of sleek pocket cameras that invite anyone to take pictures. The first cameras, made in France and England in the early 1840s, had only inventors and buffs to operate them. Since they were then no professional photographers, there could not be amateurs either, and taking photographs had no clear social use; it was a gratuitous, that is, an artistic activity, though with few pretensions to being an art. It was only with its industrialization that photography came into its own as art. As industrialization provided social uses for the operations of the photographer, so the reaction against these uses reinforced the self-consciousness of photography-as-art.

Recently, photography has become almost as widely practiced amusement as sex   *10* and dancing—which means that, like every mass art form, photography is not practiced by most people as an art. It is mainly a social rite, a defense against anxiety, and a tool of power.

Memorializing the achievements of individuals considered as members of families   *11* (as well as of other groups) is the earliest popular use of photography. For at least a century, the wedding photograph has been as much a part of the ceremony as the prescribed verbal formulas. Cameras go with family life. According to a sociological study done in France, most households have a camera, but a household with children is twice as likely to have at least one camera as a household in which there are no children. Not to take pictures of one's children, particularly when they are small, is a sign of parental indifference, just as not turning up for one's graduation picture is a gesture of adolescent rebellion.

Through photographs, each family constructs a portrait-chronicle of itself—a portable   *12* kit of images that bears witness to its connectedness. It hardly matters what activities are photographed so long as photographs get taken and are cherished. Photography becomes a rite of family life just when, in the industrializing countries of Europe and America, the very institution of the family starts undergoing radical surgery. As that claustrophobic unit, the nuclear family, was being carved out of a much larger family aggregate, photography came along to memorialize, to restate symbolically, the imperiled continuity and vanishing extendedness of family life. Those ghostly traces, photographs, supply the token presence of the dispersed relatives. A family's photograph album is generally about the extended family—and, often, is all that remains of it.

As photographs give people an imaginary possession of a past that is unreal, they   *13* also help people to take possession of space in which they are insecure. Thus, photography develops in tandem with one of the most characteristic of modern activities: tourism. For the first time in history, large numbers of people regularly travel out of their habitual environments for short periods of time. It seems positively unnatural to travel for pleasure without taking a camera along. Photographs will offer indisputable evidence that the trip was made, that the program was carried out, that fun was had. Photographs document sequences of consumption carried on outside the view of family, friends, neighbors. But dependence on the camera, as the device that makes real what one is experiencing, doesn't fade when people travel more. Taking photographs fills the same need for the cosmopolitans accumulating photograph-trophies of their boat trip up the Albert Nile or their fourteen days in China as it does for lower-middle-class vacationers taking snapshots of the Eiffel Tower or Niagara Falls.

A way of certifying experience, taking photographs is also a way of refusing it—   *14* by limiting experience to a search for the photogenic, by converting experience into an image, a souvenir. Travel becomes a strategy for accumulating photographs. The very activity of taking pictures is soothing, and assuages general feelings of disorientation that are likely to be exacerbated by travel. Most tourists feel compelled to put the camera between themselves and whatever is remarkable that they encounter. Unsure of other responses, they take a picture. This gives shape to experience: stop, take a photograph, and move on. The method especially appeals to people handicapped by a ruthless work ethic—Germans, Japanese, and Americans. Using a camera appeases the anxiety which the work-driven feel about not working when they are on vacation and supposed to be having fun. They have someting to do that is like a friendly imitation of work: they can take pictures.

People robbed of their past seem to make the most fervent picture takers, at home and abroad. Everyone who lives in an industrialized society is obliged gradually to give up the past, but in certain countries, such as the United States and Japan, the break with the past has been particularly traumatic. In the early 1970s, the fable of the brash American tourist of the 1950s and 1960s, rich with dollars and Babbittry, was replaced by the mystery of the group-minded Japanese tourist, newly released from his island prison by the miracle of overvalued yen, who is generally armed with two cameras, one on each hip.

Photography has become one of the principal devices for experiencing something, for giving an appearance of participation. One full-page ad shows a small group of people standing pressed together, peering out of the photograph, all but one looking stunned, excited, upset. The one who wears a different expression holds a camera to his eye; he seems self-possessed, is almost smiling. While the others are passive, clearly alarmed spectators, having a camera has transformed one person into something active, a voyeur: only he has mastered the situation. What do these people see? We don't know. And it doesn't matter. It is an Event: something worth seeing—and therefore worth photographing. The ad copy, white letters across the dark lower third of the photograph like news coming over a teletype machine, consists of just six words: ". . . Prague . . . Woodstock . . . Vietnam . . . Sapporo . . . Londonderry . . . LEICA." Crushed hopes, youth antics, colonial wars, and winter sports are alike—are equalized by the camera. Taking photographs has set up a chronic voyeuristic relation to the world which levels the meaning of all events.

A photograph is not just the result of an encounter between an event and a photographer; picture-taking is an event in itself, and one with ever more peremptory rights—to interfere with, to invade, or to ignore whatever is going on. Our very sense of situation is now articulated by the camera's interventions. The omnipresence of cameras persuasively suggests that time consists of interesting events, events worth photographing. This, in turn, makes it easy to feel that any event, once underway, and whatever its moral character, should be allowed to complete itself—so that something else can be brought into the world, the photograph. After the event has ended, the picture will still exist, conferring on the event a kind of immortality (and importance) it would never otherwise have enjoyed. While real people are out there killing themselves or other real people, the photographer stays behind his or her camera, creating a tiny element of another world: the image-world that bids to outlast us all.

Photographing is essentially an act of non-intervention. Part of the horror of such memorable coups of contemporary photojournalism as the pictures of a Vietnamese bonze reaching for the gasoline can, of a Bengali guerrilla in the act of bayoneting a trussed-up collaborator, comes from the awareness of how plausible it has become, in situations where the photographer has the choice between a photograph and a life, to choose the photograph. The person who intervenes cannot record; the person who is recording cannot intervene. Dziga Vertov's great film, *Man with a Movie Camera* (1929), gives the ideal image of the photographer as someone in perpetual movement, someone moving through a panorama of disparate events with such agility and speed that any intervention is out of the question. Hitchcock's *Rear Window* (1954) gives the complementary image: the photographer played by James Stewart has an intensified relation to one event, through his camera, precisely because he has a broken leg and is confined to a wheelchair; being temporarily immobilized prevents him from acting on what he sees, and makes it even more important to take pictures. Even if incompatible with intervention in a physical sense, using a camera is still a form of participation. Although the camera is an observation station, the act of photographing is more than passive observing. Like sexual voyeurism, it is a way of at least tacitly, often explicitly, encouraging whatever is going on to keep on happening. To take a picture is to have an interest in things as they are, in the status quo remaining unchanged (at least for as long as it takes to get a "good" picture), to be in complicity with whatever makes a subject interesting, worth photographing—including, when that is the interest, another person's pain or misfortune.

"I always thought of photography as a naughty thing to do—that was one of my favorite things about it," Diane Arbus wrote," and when I first did it I felt very perverse." Being a professional photographer can be thought of as naughty, to use Arbus's pop word, if the photographer seeks out subjects considered to be disreputable, taboo, marginal. But naughty subjects are harder to find these days. And what exactly is the perverse aspect of picture-taking? If professional photographers often have sexual fantasies when they are behind the camera, perhaps the perversion lies in the fact that these fantasies are both plausible and so inappropriate. In *Blowup* (1966), Antonioni has the fashion photographer hovering convulsively over Verushka's body with his camera clicking. Naughtiness, indeed! In fact, using a camera is not a very good way of getting at someone sexually. Between photographer and subject, there has to be distance. The camera doesn't rape, or even possess, though it may presume, intrude, trespass, distort, exploit, and, at the farthest reach of metaphor, assassinate— all activities that, unlike the sexual push and shove, can be conducted from a distance, and with some detachment.

There is a much stronger sexual fantasy in Michael Powell's extraordinary movie *Peeping Tom* (1960), which is not about a Peeping Tom but about a psychopath who kills women with a weapon concealed in his camera, while photographing them. Not once does he touch his subjects. He doesn't desire their bodies; he wants their presence in the form of filmed image—showing them experiencing their own death— which he screens at home for his solitary pleasure. The movie assumes connections between impotence and aggression, professionalized looking and cruelty, which point to the central fantasy connected with the camera. The camera as phallus is, at most, a flimsy variant of the inescapable metaphor that everyone unselfconsciously employs. However hazy our awareness of this fantasy, it is named without subtlety whenever we talk about "loading" and "aiming" a camera, about "shooting" a film.

The old-fashioned camera was clumsier and harder to reload than a brown Bess musket. The modern camera is trying to be a ray gun. One ad reads:

> The Yashica Electro–35 GT is the spaceage camera your family will love. Take beautiful pictures day or night. Automatically. Without any nonsense. Just aim, focus and shoot. The GT's computer brain and electronic shutter will do the rest.

Like a car, a camera is sold as a predatory weapon—one that's as automated as possible, ready to spring. Popular taste expects an easy, an invisible technology.

Manufacturers reassure their customers that taking pictures demands no skill or expert knowledge, that the machine is all-knowing, and responds to the slightest pressure of the will. It's as simple as turning the ignition key or pulling the trigger.

Like guns and cars, cameras are fantasy-machines whose use is addictive. However, despite the extravagances of ordinary language and advertising, they are not lethal. In the hyperbole that markets cars like guns, there is at least this much truth: except in wartime, cars kill more people than guns do. The camera / gun does not kill, so the ominous metaphor seems to be all bluff—like a man's fantasy of having a gun, knife, or tool between his legs. Still, there is something predatory in the act of taking a picture. To photograph people is to violate them, by seeing them as they never see themselves, by having knowledge of them they can never have, it turns people into objects that can be symbolically possessed. Just as the camera is a sublimation of the gun, to photograph someone is a sublimated murder—a soft murder, appropriate to a sad, frightened time.

Eventually, people might learn to act out more of their aggressions with cameras and fewer with guns, with the price being an even more image-choked world. One situation where people are switching from bullets to film is the photographic safari that is replacing the gun safari in East Africa. The hunters have Hasselblads instead of Winchesters; instead of looking through a telescopic sight to aim a rifle, they look through a viewfinder to frame a picture. In end-of-the-century London, Samuel Butler complained that "there is a photographer in every bush, going about like a roaring lion seeking whom he may devour." The photographer is now charging real beasts, beleaguered and too rare to kill. Guns have metamorphosed into cameras in this earnest comedy, the ecology safari, because nature has ceased to be what it always had been—what people needed protection from. Now nature—tamed, endangered, mortal—needs to be protected from people. When we are afraid, we shoot. But when we are nostalgic, we take pictures.

It is a nostalgic time right now, and photographs actively promote nostalgia. Photography is an elegiac art, a twilight art. Most subjects photographed are, just by virtue of being photographed, touched with pathos. An ugly or grotesque subject may be moving because it has been dignified by the attention of the photographer. A beautiful subject can be the object of rueful feelings, because it has aged or decayed or no longer exists. All photographs are *memento mori*. To take a photograph is to participate in another person's (or thing's) mortality, vulnerability, mutability. Precisely by slicing out this moment and freezing it, all photographs testify to time's relentless melt.

Cameras began duplicating the world at that moment when the human landscape started to undergo a vertiginous rate of change: while an untold number of forms of biological and social life are being destroyed in a brief span of time, a device is available to record what is disappearing. The moody, intricately textured Paris of Atget and Brassaï is mostly gone. Like the dead relatives and friends preserved in the family album, whose presence in photographs exorcises some of the anxiety and remorse prompted by their disappearance, so the photographs of neighborhoods now torn down, rural places disfigured and made barren, supply our pocket relation to the past.

A photograph is both a pseudo-presence and a token of absence. Like a wood fire in a room, photographs—especially those of people, of distant landscapes and faraway cities, of the vanished past—are incitements to reverie. The sense of the unattainable that can be evoked by photographs feeds directly into the erotic feelings of those for whom desirability is enhanced by distance. The lover's photograph hidden in a married woman's wallet, the poster photograph of a rock star tacked up over an adolescent's bed, the campaign-button image of a politician's face pinned on a voter's coat, the snapshots of a cabdriver's children clipped to the visor—all such talismanic use of photographs express a feeling both sentimental and implicitly magical: they are attempts to contact or lay claim to another reality.

Photographs can abet desire in the most direct, utilitarian way—as when someone collects photographs of anonymous examples of the desirable as an aid to masturbation. The matter is more complex when photographs are used to stimulate the moral impulse. Desire has no history—at least, it is experienced in each instance as all foreground, immediacy. It is aroused by archetypes and is, in that sense, abstract. But moral feelings are embedded in history, whose personae are concrete, whose situations are always specific. Thus, almost opposite rules hold true for the use of the photograph to awaken desire and to awaken conscience. The images that mobilize conscience are always linked to a given historical situation. The more general they are, the less likely they are to be effective.

A photograph that brings news of some unsuspected zone of misery cannot make a dent in public opinion unless there is an appropriate context of feeling and attitude. The photographs Mathew Brady and his colleagues took of the horrors of the battlefields did not make people any less keen to go on with the Civil War. The photographs of ill-clad, skeletal prisoners held at Andersonville inflamed Northern public opinion—against the South. (The effect of the Andersonville photographs must have been partly due to the very novelty, at that time, of seeing photographs.) The political understanding that many Americans came to in the 1960s would allow them, looking at the photographs Dorothea Lange took of Nisei on the West Coast being transported to internment camps in 1942, to recognize their subject for what it was—a crime committed by the governments against a large group of American citizens. Few people who saw those photographs in the 1940s could have had so unequivocal a reaction; the grounds for such a judgment were covered over by the pro-war consensus. Photographs cannot create a moral position, but they can reinforce one—and can help build a nascent one.

Photographs may be more memorable than moving images, because they are a neat slice of time, not a flow. Television is a stream of underselected images, each of which cancels its predecessor. Each still photograph is a privileged moment, turned into a slim object that one can keep and look at again. Photographs like the one that made the front page of most newspapers in the world in 1972—a naked South Vietnamese child just sprayed by American napalm, running down a highway toward the camera, her arms open, screaming with pain—probably did more to increase the public revulsion against the war than a hundred hours of televised barbarities.

One would like to imagine that the American public would not have been so unanimous in its acquiescence to the Korean War if it had been confronted with photographic evidence of the devastation of Korea, an ecocide and genocide in some respects even more thorough than those inflicted on Vietnam a decade later. But the supposition is trivial. The public did not see such photographs because there was, ideologically, no space for them. No one brought back photographs of daily life in Pyongyang, to show that the enemy had a human face, as Felix Greene and Marc Riboud brought back photographs of Hanoi. Americans did have access to photographs of the suffering of the Vietnamese (many of which came from military sources and were taken with quite a different use in mind) because journalists felt backed in their efforts to obtain those photographs, the event having been defined by a significant number of people as a savage colonialist war. The Korean War was understood differently—as part of the just struggle of the Free World against the Soviet Union and China—and, given that characterization, photographs of the cruelty of unlimited American firepower would have been irrelevant.

Though an event has come to mean, precisely, something worth photographing, it is still ideology (in the broadest sense) that determines what constitutes an event. There can be no evidence, photographic or otherwise, of an event until the event itself has been named and characterized. And it is never photographic evidence which can construct—more properly, identify—events; the contribution of photography always follows the naming of the event. What determines the possibility of being affected morally by photographs is the existence of a relevant political consciousness. Without a politics, photographs of the slaughter-bench of history will most likely be experienced as, simply, unreal or as a demoralizing emotional blow.

The quality of feeling, including moral outrage, that people can muster in response to photographs of the oppressed, the exploited, the starving, and the massacred also depends on the degree of their familiarity with these images. Don McCullin's photographs of emaciated Biafrans in the early 1970s had less impact for some people than Werner Bischof's photographs of Indian famine victims in the early 1950s because those images had become banal, and the photographs of Tuareg families dying of starvation in the sub-Sahara that appeared in magazines everywhere in 1973 must have seemed to many like an unbearable replay of a now familiar atrocity exhibition.

Photographs shock insofar as they show something novel. Unfortunately, the ante keeps getting raised—partly through the very proliferation of such images of horror. One's first encounter with the photographic inventory of ultimate horror is a kind of revelation, the prototypically modern revelation: a negative epiphany. For me, it was photographs of Bergen-Belsen and Dachau which I came across by chance in a bookstore in Santa Monica in July 1945. Nothing I have seen—in photographs or in real life—ever cut me as sharply, deeply, instantaneously. Indeed, it seems plausible to me to divide my life into two parts, before I saw those photographs (I was twelve) and after, thought it was several years before I understood fully what they were about. What good was served by seeing them? They were only photographs—of an event I had scarcely heard of and could do nothing to affect, of suffering I could hardly imagine and could do nothing to relieve. When I looked at those photographs, something broke. Some limit had been reached, and not only that of horror; I felt irrevocably grieved, wounded, but a part of my feelings started to tighten; something went dead; something is still crying.

To suffer is one thing; another thing is living with the photographed images of suffering, which does not necessarily strengthen conscience and the ability to be compassionate. It can also corrupt them. Once one has seen such images, one has started down the road of seeing more—and more. Images transfix. Images anesthetize. An event known through photographs certainly becomes more real than it would have been if one had never seen the photographs—think of the Vietnam War. (For a counter-example, think of the Gulag Archipelago, of which we have no photographs.) But after repeated exposure to images it also becomes less real.

The same law holds for evil as for pornography. The shock of photographed atrocities wears off with repeated viewings, just as the surprise and bemusement felt the first time one sees a pornographic movie wear off after one sees a few more. The sense of taboo which makes us indignant and sorrowful is not much sturdier than the sense of taboo that regulates the definition of what is obscene. And both have been sorely tried in recent years. The vast photographic catalogue of misery and injustice throughout the world has given everyone a certain familiarity with atrocity, making the horrible seem more ordinary—making it appear familiar, remote ("it's only a photograph"), inevitable. At the time of the first photographs of the Nazi camps, there was nothing banal about these images. After thirty years, a saturation point may have been reached. In these last decades, "concerned" photography has done at least as much to deaden conscience as to arouse it.

The ethical content of photographs is fragile. With the possible exception of photographs of those horrors, like the Nazi camps, that have gained the status of ethical reference points, most photographs do not keep their emotional charge. A photograph of 1900 that was affecting then because of its subject would, today, be more likely to move us because it is a photograph taken in 1900. The particular qualities and intentions of photographs tend to be swallowed up in the generalized pathos of time past. Aesthetic distance seems built into the very experience of looking at photographs, if not right away, then certainly with the passage of time. Time eventually positions most photographs, even the most amateurish, at the level of art.

The industrialization of photography permitted its rapid absorption into rational—that is, bureaucratic—ways of running society. No longer toy images, photographs became part of the general furniture of the environment—touchstones and confirmations of that reductive approach to reality which is considered realistic. Photographs were enrolled in the service of important institutions of control, notably the family and the police, as symbolic objects and as pieces of information. Thus, in the bureaucratic cataloguing of the world, many important documents are not valid unless they have, affixed to them, a photograph-token of the citizen's face.

The "realistic" view of the world compatible with bureaucracy redefines knowledge—as techniques and information. Photographs are valued because they give information. They tell one what there is; they make an inventory. To spies, meteorologists, coroners, archaeologists, and other information professionals, their value is inestimable. But in the situations in which most people use photographs, their value as information is of the same order as fiction. The information that photographs can give starts to seem very important at that moment in cultural history when everyone is thought to have a right to something called news. Photographs were seen as a way of giving information to people who do not take easily to reading. The *Daily News* still calls itself "New York's Picture Newspaper," its bid for populist identity. At the opposite end of the scale, *Le Monde*, a newspaper designed for skilled, well-informed readers, runs no photographs at all. The presumption is that, for such readers, a photograph could only illustrate the analysis contained in an article.

A new sense of the notion of information has been constructed around the photographic image. The photograph is a thin slice of space as well as time. In a world ruled by photographic images, all borders ("framing") seem arbitrary. Anything can be separated, can be made discontinuous, from anything else: all that is necessary is to frame the subject differently. (Conversely, anything can be made adjacent to anything else.) Photography reinforces a nominalist view of social reality as consisting of small units of an apparently infinite number—as the number of photographs that could be taken of anything is unlimited. Through photographs, the world becomes a series of unrelated, freestanding particles; and history, past and present, a set of anecdotes and *faits divers*. The camera makes reality atomic, manageable, and opaque. It is a view of the world which denies interconnectedness, continuity, but which confers on each moment the character of a mystery. Any photograph has multiple meanings; indeed, to see something in the form of a photograph is to encounter a potential object of fascination. The ultimate wisdom of the photographic image is to say: "There is the surface. Now think—or rather feel, intuit—what is beyond it, what the reality must be like if it looks this way." Photographs, which cannot themselves explain anything, are inexhaustible invitations to deduction, speculation, and fantasy.

Photography implies that we know about the world if we accept it as the camera records it. But this is the opposite of understanding, which starts from *not* accepting the world as it looks. All possibility of understanding is rooted in the ability to say no. Strictly speaking, one never understands anything from a photograph. Of course, photographs fill in blanks in our mental pictures of the present and the past: for example, Jacob Riis's images of New York squalor in the 1880s are sharply instructive to those unaware that urban poverty in late-nineteenth-century America was really that Dickensian. Nevertheless, the camera's rendering of reality must always hide more than it discloses. As Brecht points out, a photograph of the Krupp works reveals virtually nothing about that organization. In contrast to the amorous relation, which is based on how something looks, understanding is based on how it functions. And functioning takes place in time, and must be explained in time. Only that which narrates can make us understand.

The limit of photographic knowledge of the world is that, while it can goad conscience, it can, finally, never be ethical or political knowledge. The knowledge gained through still photographs will always be some kind of sentimentalism, whether cynical or humanist. It will be a knowledge at bargain prices—a semblance of knowledge, a semblance of wisdom; as the act of taking pictures is a semblance of appropriation, a semblance of rape. They very muteness of what is, hypothetically, comprehensible in photographs is what constitutes their attraction and provocativeness. The omnipresence of photographs has an incalculable effect on our ethical sensibility. By furnishing this already crowded world with a duplicate one of images, photography makes us feel that the world is more available than it really is.

Needing to have reality confirmed and experience enhanced by photographs is an aesthetic consumerism to which everyone is now addicted. Industrial societies turn their citizens into image-junkies; it is the most irresistible form of mental pollution. Poignant longings for beauty, for an end to probing below the surface, for a redemption and celebration of the body of the world—all these elements of erotic feeling are affirmed in the pleasure we take in photographs. But other, less liberating feelings are expressed as well. It would not be wrong to speak of people having a *compulsion* to photograph: to turn experience itself into a way of seeing. Ultimately, having an experience becomes identical with taking a photograph of it, and participating in a public event comes more and more to be equivalent to looking at it in photographed form. That most logical of nineteenth-century aesthetes, Mallarmé, said that everything in the world exists in order to end in a book. Today everything exists to end in a photograph.

MEANING

1. Why does camera ownership frequently go along with having a family?
2. How do photographs help people preserve an illusion of the past and "take possession" of space in which they are insecure?
3. Why are photographs more acceptable as evidence than even the most descriptive prose? Why is "a picture worth a thousand words?"

USING DEFINITION TO CONVEY MEANING

1. What examples does Sontag present to document her view that photography is an amusement practiced as "a social rite, a defense against anxiety, and a tool of power?"
2. What use does Sontag make of other rhetorical patterns, such as narration, description, comparison, process analysis, classification, analogy, and causation, to reveal the basic nature of photography?
3. How does Sontag's reference to the "allegory of the cave" (see Plato, Page 407) emphasize the possibility of mistaking image for reality in photography?

WRITING SUGGESTIONS

1. What additional uses for photographs can you think of that Sontag did not mention? For example, how have the chances of finding missing children been increased by placing photos on billboards and milk cartons?
2. As a research project, visit an exhibition of photographs and analyze the factors that go into making such an exhibit successful. Were the photos placed at eye level, was there effective contrast between individual photos, was the exhibit thematically organized, and did the arrangement of the photos tell a story; consider these and other aspects.
3. Everyone has seen photographs of Hiroshima. After reading John Hersey's account (see page 148), evaluate which medium was more effective—the photographs or Hersey's report.
4. What part have photographs of war or famine conditions played in arousing the public's indignation or compassion? Would the public's response to these situations have been the same without pictures?

POLITICAL AND SOCIAL SCIENCES

J. Michael Polich
Bruce R. Orvis

Alcohol Problems

*J. Michael Polich and Bruce R. Orvis, behavioral scientists at the Rand Corpora-
tion, have done definitive research on alcoholism and drug dependency. Polich
was born in Moline, Illinois, in 1945, and received his B.A. from Dartmouth
and Ph.D. in sociology from Harvard. He is the author of several articles and
books on the prevalence and treatment of alcohol and drug abuse, including*
The Course of Alcoholism: Four Years After Treatment *(1981). In 1984,
Polich coauthored* Strategies for containing Adolescent Drug Use.
*Bruce R. Orvis was born in 1949 in New York City, and received his B.A.
from the University of Rochester and his M.A. and Ph.D. in psychology from
the University of California at Los Angeles. Besides studies into the prevalence
and treatment of alcohol abuse, Orvis is currently directing a longitudinal
study designed to evaluate how different kinds of incentives influence the productivity of nonmilitary federal employees. He is one of the authors of* Effectiveness
and Cost of Alcohol Rehabilitation in the United States Air Force *(1981).
"Alcohol Problems" is drawn from the 1979 study that Polich and Orvis conducted
into the prevalence of alcohol problems in the United States Air Force, based on
data gathered from a survey of 3,148 active-duty Air Force personnel. This
report broke new ground in formulating a clear definition of "alcoholism" and
showed that 13.9 percent of Air Force personnel are affected by alcohol problems.*

The scientific literature on alcohol problems contains a vast array of definitions,
measures, and methods for counting and classifying the behaviors that fit the term.
Virtually all definitions reflect a judgment that alcohol problems are "problems" because
they are injurious; that is, because they damage or disrupt the individual or his

associates. Apart from this, studies diverge on the question of what should be included under one heading.

A striking range of alcohol-related behaviors could be classified as injurious. At one extreme are behaviors that are clearly dangerous to health. In this class are such patterns as consuming alcohol at an extremely high rate over a long period, leading directly to liver disease. At the other extreme are behaviors that may have no determinate damaging consequences for the individual but are viewed as socially unacceptable by one's spouse, friends, or employers. Compounding this confusion is the fact that many kinds of alcohol-related behavior are viewed as injurious only in certain situations; for example, drinking any alcohol on the job is usually proscribed in the United States but not in many other countries.

These circumstances have led to a proliferation of definitions and doctrines on the subject of alcohol. No single interpretation is universally accepted. Indeed, there is intense debate over such basic definitional questions as whether the most serious manifestations of alcohol disorders should be treated as "diseases" (Keller, 1976; Robinson, 1972; Room, 1972). Some order may be brought into this confusion by distinguishing two main traditions in the prevalence literature: a tradition of studies of *clinical alcoholism*, and a sequence of more recent studies of *problem drinking*.

CLINICAL ALCOHOLISM

Central Components of Alcoholism Definitions

Alcoholism, treated as a clinically observed syndrome of problems associated with alcohol, has a multiplicity of definitions arising from its long history as a focus of humanitarian, social, and medical concern. In earlier periods, many accounts simply treated "drunkenness" as a moral problem without differentiating individual instances of intoxication from more chronic or severe manifestations of a continuing disorder (Keller, 1976). In this simple model, amount of alcohol consumption and intoxication were the subjects of interest. By the early 20th century, however, medically and psychologically oriented researchers were beginning to construct a series of different criteria for an "alcohol illness." These observers were impressed with the apparent compulsion of certain heavy drinkers to continue excessive consumption of alcohol despite serious consequences and even despite their expressed intention and desire to stop. Because of an apparent overwhelming need, or a "morbid insatiable craving" for alcohol (Paredes, 1976), such drinkers could be described as possessed of a psychiatric condition, variously described as "dipsomania," alcoholism, or (slightly later) alcohol addiction. Thus, the notion of *inability to control drinking* became a central part of the conception of alcoholism very early.

The other central component of most historical conceptions of alcoholism is the notion of *damage caused by alcohol*, especially physical damage leading to observable symptoms of functional impairment. Although clergymen, social workers, and psychologists have emphasized the social and behavioral damage excessive alcohol use can cause, medical doctors have exercised greater influence on definitional matters. Accordingly, many definitions of alcoholism concentrate on the physical sequelae of heavy alcohol consumption, such as liver disease and central nervous system disturbances. That this conception is still as powerful as ever may be seen from the "definition of alcoholism" recently offered in the *Annals of Internal Medicine,* which states succinctly that alcoholism "is characterized by tolerance and physical dependency or pathological organic changes, or both—all the direct or indirect consequences of the alcohol ingested" (National Council on Alcoholism, 1976). Obvious in this formulation is the primary role played by physical *consequences* of alcohol consumption. This emphasis on alcoholism's effects rather than on the behavior that constitutes alcoholism is frequently found in medically oriented research.

Addiction and Loss of Control

Elements of these primary components were interwoven into the theoretical formulation of the most influential author in the field, E. M. Jellinek. In proposing the "disease concept of alcoholism," Jellinek (1960) suggested that alcoholism might be treated as a disease with a biological basis in certain physiological alterations. Jellinek described these alterations as increased tolerance to the drug, adaptive cell metabolism, and the appearance of withdrawal symptoms when the drug is no longer taken. The crucial signal of the disorder was "loss of control"—the alcoholic's inability to moderate or stop drinking despite the most sincere desire to do so. In this view, the ingestion of any alcohol begins a reaction in which a physical demand or need for alcohol is felt ever more strongly.

These ideas, supplemented with informal data from Alcoholics Anonymous members, were the basis of Jellinek's elaborate theory, a notable aspect of which was the postulation of phases of alcoholism development. These were thought to begin with alcoholic blackouts and preoccupation with alcohol, to lead through the development of loss of control, and to end in a final stage characterized by physical deterioration, unemployment, loss of family and friends, and other adverse consequences associated with clinical alcoholism. Even though Jellinek proposed this theory as a working hypothesis, it immediately became the preeminent model for definition and diagnosis of alcohol problems.

Conceptions of Dependence

The notion of "alcohol dependence" was introduced partly as a euphemism for "addiction," as the criterion for the most severe alcohol syndrome. It achieved a new status when the World Health Organization (1952) adopted it in its definition of alcoholism. Partly at Jellinek's instigation, the WHO at that time declared:

> Alcoholics are those excessive drinkers whose dependence upon alcohol has attained such a degree that it shows a noticeable mental disturbance or an interference with their bodily and mental health, their interpersonal relations, and their smooth social and economic functioning, or who show the prodromal signs of such development.

In this view, then, alcoholics are a special subset of "excessive drinkers" (any drinkers whose drinking deviates from the community norms in quantity, frequency, or circumstance). The peculiar feature of alcoholics, setting them off from other excessive drinkers, is their dependence on alcohol. Although it has never been entirely clear, in this usage the term "alcoholics" would seem to include only those dependent people who actually experience adverse effects ("interference with bodily or mental health," etc.). Thus, this influential definition appears to require three elements for alcoholism: deviant drinking, dependence, and adverse effects of drinking.

The most nebulous concept in this formulation is the notion of dependence. Deviant drinking and adverse effects can be observed, however relative they may be in different social environments; but dependence lacks a clear measure. If the definition of dependence is not to rest almost exclusively on the subject's self-report that he desires alcohol, such a measure is essential. In recent years an increasingly popular measure has been that of *physical dependence*, characterized by the appearance of a withdrawal syndrome when alcohol use is reduced or terminated. The symptoms of alcohol withdrawal are gross tremor, hallucinations, seizures, and delirium tremens in acute cases; milder cases have many other less specific symptoms (e.g., nervousness and sleeplessness). Recent physiological research suggests that the attainment of high blood alcohol concentration is a crucial aspect in the process of developing physical dependence and withdrawal symptoms (Gross, 1977). Thus, the concept of physical dependence on alcohol is a useful criterion for alcoholism, and the occurrence of withdrawal symptoms is a serviceable indicator in empirical studies.

Dependence is closely linked to another physiological phenomenon, *tolerance*, which refers to the body's ability to function in an outwardly normal manner even in the presence of high concentrations of ethanol (absolute alcohol). The most widely distributed diagnostic scheme, that proposed by the National Council on Alcoholism (1972), treats as a "classical" and "definite" indication of alcoholism *either* the appearance of withdrawal symptoms *or* the evidence of tolerance. According to this scheme, tolerance is indicated by a blood alcohol concentration of .15 without obvious intoxication. The judgment of what constitutes intoxication, however, is so subjective that this criterion has not as yet received much use in the empirical literature.

Other Indications of Alcoholism

We have discussed only the indicators that are most important for conceptions of the nature of alcoholism and alcohol dependence. Other indicators are frequently used in practice because of their status as strong correlates of alcoholism. Most prominent among these are various disease complications linked to alcohol consumption (e.g., alcoholic hepatitis or cirrhosis) and "blackouts" (memory lapse about events occurring during drinking the day or night before). Filstead et al. (1976) reported the ratings of such indicators, in terms of their usefulness for diagnosis, given by a sample of 362 physicians belonging to a U.S. medical society concerned with alcoholism. Over two-thirds of the group endorsed both the disease complications and the occurrence of blackouts as definite indicators of alcoholism. In the same sample, a similar proportion recognized all of the other criteria of dependence mentioned above (tremors, tolerance, subjective loss of control, etc.).

Definitions Based on Consumption

In all of these recent conceptions the actual amount of alcohol consumed by the individual plays a fairly minor role. The narrow context of the Jellinek theory makes this apparent anomaly comprehensible, because Jellinek was at pains to distinguish addicted drinkers ("real" alcoholics) from other excessive drinkers. Not being addicted, other excessive drinkers could be controlled through normal social mechanisms of education, law enforcement, etc; but the addicted drinker, by definition, could not control his consumption and hence was unreachable by traditional sanctions. In this black-and-white world, amount of consumption made little difference. The addicted alcoholic taking just one drink was in much more danger than the "chronic habitual excessive drinker" taking ten drinks.

Partly because of the divergence between this conception and the empirical evidence on alcohol consumption patterns, a school of thought has emerged recently that seeks to reemphasize the importance of amount of consumption (Schmidt, 1976). Loosely known as the "single-distribution" model, the theory advanced by this group derives its force from the strong aggregate correlations between cirrhosis mortality rates and mean per capital alcohol consumption in many populations. Numerous studies treating both cross-sectional and longitudinal international comparisons have shown that the level of mortality due to cirrhosis in a population is strongly related to the mean per capita alcohol consumption in the same population. . . .

The "single-distribution" theory has been used primarily to argue that the rate of "chronic excessive consumption" can be reduced by controlling the mean per capita consumption rate in the whole population. However, its implications for the definition of alcohol problems are also very important. It implies that at certain levels of consumption, serious adverse consequences become quite likely. Whether people showing those levels should be termed "alcoholics" is a semantic question. Nevertheless, it is clearly important to distinguish such people because of the adverse effects they are likely to experience.

Dependence, Adverse Effects, and High Consumption

Given these diverse definitions and viewpoints, what can we conclude about the proper criteria for severe alcohol problems? First, we should emphasize that there are at least three important and conceptually independent factors in drinking behavior that have historically been confused or combined:

1. *Alcohol dependence*, recognized primarily by physical dependence (withdrawal symptoms and / or tolerance) and loss of control;
2. *The other adverse effects* of heavy alcohol consumption, such as physical diseases (cirrhosis, hepatitis, cerebellar degeneration, etc.) and psychological and social impairments (unemployment, loss of family and friends, trouble with police, etc.); and
3. *Alcohol consumption*, the total quantity of ethanol consumed per day.

We have tried to separate these in the discussion. The original Jellinek formulation emphasizes dependence, although adverse effects are also mentioned. The 1952 WHO definition requires all three—dependence, adverse effects, and heavy (or at least deviant) consumption. The NCA diagnostic criteria accept any manifestation of either dependence or serious adverse effects, especially medical effects. Finally, the single-distribution school emphasizes heavy consumption, but perhaps admits serious medical conditions as well.

Several recent writers have recognized the conceptual confusion of this area and have pleaded for a clear distinction between the *condition* of alcohol dependence and the *harm* caused by either heavy consumption or dependence. Davies (1976) suggests that alcoholism be defined as alcohol use that results in either dependence or substantial harm. Edwards (1976) also argues for defining dependence separately from the harmful consequences of alcohol use. Both commentaries avoid the term "alcoholism," which has been used in so many diverse ways that it has taken on excess meaning. Such a view finds increasing acceptance. The most recent evidence of the trend in this direction is the report of a new expert committee on definitions for the World Health Organization (Edwards et al., 1977). The committee explicitly avoided a definition of the term "alcoholism," preferring to talk instead about manifold "alcohol-related disabilities."

In this committee's view, the central disability related to alcohol is that of dependence—a chronic reliance on alcohol characterized by alterations of behavior away from normal patterns in consumption, subjective state, and physical state. Apart from dependence, the committee saw no particular commonality among all of the other disabilities that alcohol can cause. In particular, it emphasized that empirical evidence does not warrant an assumption that nondependent people with some "drinking problems" will necessarily progress into full-blown dependence (Edwards et al., 1977).

Our view is very much in sympathy with the conceptual distinctions advanced by this most recent WHO committee. The notions of alcohol dependence and the harmful consequences of alcohol are conceptually independent dimensions and should be addressed separately. Serious consequences can exist without any apparent dependence, and vice versa (Davies, 1976). This fact is obscured if a group of "alcoholics" is defined to be coterminous with one of the categories (or if the definition contains only their intersection). Scientific research is better served by an examination of the various phenomena and the interrelations among them.

All the definitions discussed above were developed through clinical experience, emphasizing alcohol dependence and its associated disabilities. Because these are the most serious manifestations of alcohol problems, this emphasis may be justified from a clinical point of view. In a study of prevalence rates, however, the sizes of various groups are of primary importance, and the alcohol-dependent group is very small. Many more people in any population are affected by alcohol problems of the nondependent kind than are affected by dependence. An assessment of the extent of alcohol problems in any population must therefore examine the other ways in which people get into trouble because of alcohol use.

CONCEPTUAL APPROACH OF THIS STUDY

The approach of this study has much in common with the literature just cited, but it also has a somewhat different emphasis. Our objective is not to isolate a particular clinical syndrome, nor is it to describe any and all types of alcohol problems that Air Force personnel may have encountered. Rather, we intend to isolate and identify groups of people who are *seriously affected by alcohol to the extent that official intervention may be appropriate*. The effect may be one that harms or seriously threatens to harm the indivdual, his immediate family, or the Air Force. Alcohol dependence, damage done to the person's health, accidents he may have, family problems, lowered productivity, or the necessity for increased law enforcement are instances of alcohol problems that fall under our purview, because all imply possible intervention.

Unlike many previous studies, this one attempts explicitly to distinguish two basic types of alcohol problems as follows:

• *Alcohol Dependence.* A chronic behavioral pattern indicating that the individual consumes high amounts of alcohol and relies on alcohol in everyday functioning.
• *Adverse Effects of Alcohol.* Any type of serious consequence of drinking not reflected under alcohol dependence if it results in concrete and serious damage or disruption to the individual's life or to the Air Force.

In general, we expect that people identified as "alcohol dependent" will show much higher levels of alcohol consumption, physical damage, work impairment, and chronicity of the condition. In contrast, those identified as having "adverse effects" should show lower rates of these problems and more intermittence in the condition. Alcohol-dependent people will be those for whom intensive treatment may be most appropriate.

In developing criteria to distinguish these two groups from the remainder of the Air Force population, we are guided by two considerations. First, we propose to use criteria that are concrete and minimally dependent on individual variations in attitudes and values. We do not, for example, wish to define as an "adverse effect" a behavior that does not cause serious trouble for the individual even though his spouse or his friends may object mildly to his drinking (or to any drinking). Our criteria are to be confined to *prima facie* evidence of damage (e.g., alcohol consumption at levels high enough to cause liver damage or that clearly interferes with work); or those that are so repugnant to the community that outsiders take drastic action (e.g., neighbors call police or spouses leave the subject because of drinking). Second, we propose to use policy-relevant criteria. At a minimum, the categories we distinguish should imply different intervention strategies to correct the problem. The criteria should not rest exclusively upon subjective or introspective judgments by the individual. Finally, the criteria should be generally useful in diagnosis, identification, or classification.

BIBLIOGRAPHY

DAVIES, DAVID L., "Definitional Issues in Alcoholism," in Tartar and Sugarman (eds.) (1976), pp. 53–73.

EDWARDS, GRIFFITH, "The Alcohol Dependence Syndrome: Usefulness of an Idea," in Edwards and Grant (eds.) (1976), pp. 135–156.

EDWARDS, GRIFFITH, ET AL., *Alcohol-Related Disabilities*, Offset Publication Number 32, World Health Organization, Geneva, 1977.

FILSTEAD, WILLIAM J., MARSHALL J. GOBY, AND NELSON J. BRADLEY, "Critical Elements in the Diagnosis of Alcoholism: A National Survey of Physicians," *Journal of the American Medical Association* 236: 2767–2769, 1976.

JELLINEK, E. M., *The Disease Concept of Alcoholism*, Hillhouse Press, New Brunswick, N.J., 1960.

KELLER, MARK, "The Disease Concept of Alcoholism Revisited," *Journal of Studies on Alcohol* 37: 1694–1717, 1976.

National Council on Alcoholism, "Criteria for the Diagnosis of Alcoholism," *Annals of Internal Medicine* 77: 249–258, 1972.

———, "Definition of Alcoholism," *Annals of Internal Medicine* 85: 764, 1976.

PAREDES, ALFONSO, "The History of the Concept of Alcoholism," in Tartar and Sugarman (eds.) (1976), pp. 9–52.

ROBINSON, DAVID, "The Alcohologist's Addiction: Some Implications of Losing Control over the Disease Concept of Alcoholism," *Quarterly Journal of Studies on Alcohol* 33: 1028–1042, 1972.

ROOM, ROBIN, "Comment on 'The Alcohologist's Addiction,'" *Quarterly Journal of Studies on Alcohol* 33: 1049–1059, 1972.

SCHMIDT, WOLFGANG, "Cirrhosis and Alcohol Consumption: An Epidemiological Perspective," in Edwards and Grant (1976), pp. 15–47.

World Health Organization, *Report of the Second Session of the Alcoholism Subcommittee, Expert*

Committee on Mental Health, Technical Report Series Number 48, World Health Organization, Geneva, 1952.

Meaning

1. What aspect of alcoholism do Polich and Orvis stipulate as the controlling characteristic that defines the disease and should guide its treatment?
2. How has treatment of alcoholism in the past been hampered by lack of a commonly agreed upon definition as to what it really is?
3. What different features of alcoholism have been emphasized by sociologists, psychologists, physicians, and the clergy, respectively?
4. Why would a clearer conception of the principles that explain alcoholism lead to more efficient allocation of social resources in the treatment of the disease?

Using Definition to Convey Meaning

1. How do Polich and Orvis use the method of formal definition, placing the subject in a class and distinguishing it from all other members of that class, to show that alcoholics differ from other excessive drinkers?
2. How do Polich and Orvis draw on the theory advanced by Jellinek, explaining how alcoholism develops, in creating their own definition?
3. How do Polich and Orvis use classification to systematically group alcohol-related problems to show that alcoholism should be primarily considered a form of psychological dependence?

Writing Suggestions

1. Using Polich and Orvis' article as a model, develop a useful definition for another kind of addiction that has both psychological and physiological components.
2. Discuss any of the different substance-abuse programs available that attempt to help people with addictions. What range of treatments do these programs offer?

Simone de Beauvoir

The Married Woman

Simone de Beauvoir (1908–1986), a prominent French novelist, essayist, and pioneer of the Womens Movement, was born in Paris and studied philosophy at the Sorbonne, where she later taught from 1941 through 1943. de Beauvoir's literary career is intertwined with that of Jean Paul Sartre's and the French Existentialist Movement. Her many illuminating works include All Men Are Mortal *(1946; trans. 1947);* The Second Sex *(1949; trans. 1956), her most influential book;* The Mandarins *(1954; trans. 1957), winner of the Prix Goncourt (1954);* A Very Easy Death *(trans. 1966), a touching account of the death of Francoise de Beauvoir, the author's mother; and* All Said and Done *(trans. 1974), one of several brilliant autobiographical memoirs. In "The Married Woman," from* The Second Sex, *de Beauvoir defines, with eloquence and profound insight, the life of servitude and frustration that is the fate of "the married woman."*

Few tasks are more like the torture of Sisyphus than housework, with its endless repetition: the clean becomes soiled, the soiled is made clean, over and over, day after day. The housewife wears herself out marking time, she makes nothing, simply perpetuates the present. She never senses conquest of a positive Good, but rather indefinite struggle against negative Evil. A young pupil writes in her essay: "I shall never have house-cleaning day"; she thinks of the future as constant progress toward some unknown summit; but one day, as her mother washes the dishes, it comes over her that both of them will be bound to such rites until death. Eating, sleeping, cleaning—the years no longer rise up toward heaven, they lie spread out ahead, gray and identical. The battle against dust and dirt is never won.

Washing, ironing, sweeping, ferreting out rolls of lint from under wardrobes—all this halting of decay is also the denial of life; for time simultaneously creates and destroys, and only its negative aspect concerns the housekeeper. Hers is the position of the Manichaeist, regarded philosophically. The essence of Manichaeism is not solely to recognize two principles, the one good, the other evil; it is also to hold that the good is attained through the abolition of evil and not by positive action. In this sense Christianity is hardly Manichaeist in spite of the existence of the devil, for one fights the demon best by devoting oneself to God and not by endeavoring to conquer the evil one directly. Any doctrine of transcendence and liberty subordinates the defeat of evil to progress toward the good. But woman is not called upon to build a better world: her domain is fixed and she has only to keep up the never ending struggle against the evil principles that creep into it; in her war against dust, stains, mud, and dirt she is fighting sin, wrestling with Satan.

But it is a sad fate to be required without respite to repel an enemy instead of working toward positive ends, and very often the housekeeper submits to it in a kind of madness that may verge on perversion, a kind of sado-masochism. The maniac housekeeper wages her furious war against dirt, blaming life itself for the rubbish all living growth entails. When any living being enters her house, her eye gleams with a wicked light: "Wipe your feet, don't tear the place apart, leave that alone!" She wishes those of her household would hardly breathe; everything means more thankless work for her. Severe, preoccupied, always on the watch, she loses *joie de vivre*, she becomes overprudent and avaricious. She shuts out the sunlight, for along with that come insects, germs, and dust, and besides, the sun ruins silk hangings and fades upholstery; she scatters naphthalene, which scents the air. She becomes bitter and disagreeable and hostile to all that lives: the end is sometimes murder.

The healthy young woman will hardly be attracted by so gloomy a vice. Such nervousness and spitefulness are more suited to frigid and frustrated women, old maids, deceived wives, and those whom surly and dictatorial husbands condemn to a solitary and empty existence. I knew an old beldame, once gay and coquettish, who got up at five each morning to go over her closets; married to a man who neglected her, and isolated on a lonely estate, with but one child, she took to orderly housekeeping as others take to drink. In this insanity the house becomes so neat and clean that one hardly dares live in it; the woman is so busy she forgets her own existence. A household, in fact, with its meticulous and limitless tasks, permits to woman a sado-masochistic flight from herself as she contends madly with the things around her and with herself in a state of distraction and mental vacancy. And this flight may often have a sexual tinge. It is noteworthy that the rage for cleanliness is highest in Holland, where the women are cold, and in puritanical civilizations, which oppose an ideal of neatness and purity to the joys of the flesh. If the Mediterranean Midi lives in a state of joyous filth, it is not only because water is scarce there: love of the flesh and its animality is conducive to toleration of human odor, dirt, and even vermin.

The preparation of food, getting meals, is work more positive in nature and often more agreeable than cleaning. First of all it means marketing, often the bright spot of the day. And gossip on doorsteps, while peeling vegetables, is a gay relief for solitude; to go for water is a great adventure for half-cloistered Mohammedan women; women in markets and stores talk about domestic affairs, with a common interest, feeling themselves members of a group that—for an instant—is opposed to the group of men as the essential to the inessential. Buying is a profound pleasure, a discovery, almost an invention. As Gide says in his *Journal*, the Mohammedans, not knowing gambling, have in its place the discovery of hidden treasure; that is the poetry and the adventure of mercantile civilizations. The housewife knows little of winning in games, but a solid cabbage, a ripe Camembert, are treasures that must be cleverly won from the unwilling storekeeper; the game is to get the best for the least money; economy means not so much helping the budget as winning the game. She is pleased with her passing triumph as she contemplates her well-filled larder.

Gas and electricity have killed the magic of fire, but in the country many women still know the joy of kindling live flames from inert wood. With her fire going, woman becomes a sorceress; by a simple movement, as in beating eggs, or through the magic of fire, she effects the transmutation of substances: matter becomes food. There is enchantment in these alchemies, there is poetry in making preserves; the housewife has caught duration in the snare of sugar, she has enclosed life in jars.

Cooking is revolution and creation; and a woman can find special satisfaction in a successful cake or a flaky pastry, for not everyone can do it: one must have the gift.

Here again the little girl is naturally fond of imitating her elders, making mud pies and the like, and helping roll real dough in the kitchen. But as with other housework, repetition soon spoils these pleasures. The magic of the oven can hardly appeal to Mexican Indian women who spend half their lives preparing tortillas, identical from day to day, from century to century. And it is impossible to go on day after day making a treasure-hunt of the marketing or ecstatically viewing one's highly polished faucets. The male and female writers who lyrically exalt such triumphs are persons who are seldom or never engaged in actual housework. It is tiresome, empty, monotonous, as a career. If, however, the individual who does such work is also a producer, a creative worker, it is as naturally integrated in life as are the organic functions; for this reason housework done by men seems much less dismal; it represents for them merely a negative and inconsequential moment from which they quickly escape. What makes the lot of the wife-servant ungrateful is the division of labor which dooms her completely to the general and the inessential. Dwelling-place and food are useful for life but give it no significance: the immediate goals of the housekeeper are only means, not true ends. She endeavors, naturally, to give some individuality to her work and to make it seem essential. No one else, she thinks, could do her work as well; she has her rites, superstitions, and ways of doing things. But too often her "personal note" is but a vague and meaningless rearrangement of disorder.

Woman wastes a great deal of time and effort in such striving for originality and unique perfection; this gives her task its meticulous, disorganized, and endless character and makes it difficult to estimate the true load of domestic work. Recent studies show that for married women housework averages about thirty hours per week, or three fourths of a working week in employment. This is enormous if done in addition to a paid occupation, little if the woman has nothing else to do. The care of several children will naturally add a good deal to woman's work: a poor mother is often working all the time. Middle-class women who employ help, on the other hand, are almost idle; and they pay for their leisure with ennui. If they lack outside interests, they often multiply and complicate their domestic duties to excess, just to have something to do.

The worst of it all is that this labor does not even tend toward the creation of anything durable. Woman is tempted—and the more so the greater pains she takes—to regard her work as an end in itself. She sighs as she contemplates the perfect cake just out of the oven: "it's a shame to eat it!" It is really too bad to have husband and children tramping with their muddy feet all over her waxed hardwood floors! When things are used they are soiled or destroyed—we have seen how she is tempted to save them from being used; she keeps preserves until they get moldy; she locks up the parlor. But times passes inexorably; provisions attract rats; they become wormy; moths attack blankets and clothing. The world is not a dream carved in stone, it is made of dubious stuff subject to rot; edible material is as equivocal as Dali's fleshy watches: it seems inert, inorganic, but hidden larvae may have changed it into a cadaver. The housewife who loses herself in things becomes dependent, like the things, upon the whole world: linen is scorched, the roast burns, chinaware gets broken; these are absolute disasters, for when things are destroyed, they are gone forever. Permanence and security cannot possibly be obtained through them. The pillage and bombs of war threaten one's wardrobes, one's house.

The products of domestic work, then, must necessarily be consumed; a continual renunciation is required of the woman whose operations are completed only in their destruction. For her to acquiesce without regret, these minor holocausts must at least be reflected in someone's joy or pleasure. But since the housekeeper's labor is expended to maintain the *status quo*, the husband, coming into the house, may notice disorder or negligence, but it seems to him that order and neatness come of their own accord. He has a more positive interest in a good meal. The cook's moment of triumph arrives when she puts a successful dish on the table: husband and children receive it with warm approval, not only in words, but by consuming it gleefully. The culinary alchemy then pursues its course, food becomes chyle and blood.

Thus, to maintain living bodies is of more concrete, vital interest than to keep a fine floor in proper condition; the cook's effort is evidently transcended toward the future. If, however, it is better to share in another's free transcendence than to lose oneself in things, it is not less dangerous. The validity of the cook's work is to be found only in the mouths of those around her table; she needs their approbation, demands that they appreciate her dishes and call for second helpings; she is upset if they are not hungry, to the point that one wonders whether the fried potatoes are for her husband or her husband for the fried potatoes. This ambiguity is evident in the general attitude of the housekeeping wife: she takes care of the house for her husband; but she also wants him to spend all he earns for furnishings and an electric refrigerator. She desires to make him happy; but she approves of his activities only in so far as they fall within the frame of happiness she has set up.

There have been times when these claims have in general found satisfaction: times when such felicity was also man's ideal, when he was attached above all to his home, to his family, and when even the children chose to be characterized by their parents, their traditions, and their past. At such times she who ruled the home, who presided at the dinner table, was recognized as supreme; and she still plays this resplendent role among certain landed proprietors and wealthy peasants who here and there perpetuate the patriachal civilization.

But on the whole marriage is today a surviving relic of dead ways of life, and the situation of the wife is more ungrateful than formerly, because she still has the same duties but they no longer confer the same rights, privileges, and honors. Man marries today to obtain an anchorage in immanence, but not to be himself confined therein; he wants to have hearth and home while being free to escape therefrom; he settles down but often remains a vagabond at heart; he is not contemptuous of domestic felicity, but he does not make of it an end in itself; repetition bores him; he seeks after novelty, risk, opposition to overcome, companions and friends who take him away from solitude *à deux*. The children, even more than their father, want to escape beyond family limits: life for them lies elsewhere, it is before them; the child always seeks what is different. Woman tries to set up a universe of permanence and continuity; husband and children wish to transcend the situation she creates, which for them is only a given environment. This is why, even if she is loath to admit the precarious nature of the activities to which her whole life is devoted, she is nevertheless led to impose her services by force: she changes from mother and housewife into harsh stepmother and shrew.

Thus woman's work within the home gives her no autonomy; it is not directly useful to society, it does not open out on the future, it produces nothing. It takes on meaning and dignity only as it is linked with existent beings who reach out beyond themselves, transcend themselves, toward society in production and action.

That is, far from freeing the matron, her occupation makes her dependent upon husband and children; she is justified through them; but in their lives she is only an inessential intermediary. That "obedience" is legally no longer one of her duties in no way changes her situation; for this depends not on the will of the couple but on the very structure of the conjugal group. Woman is not allowed to *do* something positive in her work and in consequence win recognition as a complete person. However respected she may be, she is subordinate, secondary, parasitic. The heavy curse that weighs upon her consists in this: the very meaning of her life is not in her hands. That is why the successes and the failures of her conjugal life are much more gravely important for her than for her husband; he is first a citizen, a producer, secondly a husband; she is before all, and often exclusively, a wife; her work does not take her out of her situation; it is from the latter, on the contrary, that her work takes its value, high or low. Loving, generously devoted, she will perform her tasks joyously; but they will seem to her mere dull drudgery if she performs them with resentment. In her destiny they will never play more than an inessential role; they will not be a help in the ups and downs of conjugal life. We must go on to see, then, how woman's condition is concretely experienced in life—this condition which is characterized essentially by the "service" of the bed and the "service" of the housekeeping and in which woman finds her place of dignity only in accepting her vassalage.

MEANING

1. What characteristics are encompassed within de Beauvoir's definition of the married woman?
2. Why does the "legend of Sisyphus" characterize the nature of the tasks housewives must perform?
3. What aspects of housework undermine independence and subordinate individuality to time-consuming repetitive daily tasks?
4. Why is preparing food a more desirable kind of task for the married woman than cleaning the house?

USING DEFINITION TO CONVEY MEANING

1. How does de Beauvoir use anecdotes to allow her readers to "see" the essential nature of the married woman's life?
2. What positive features, attributes, and qualities does de Beauvoir omit from her definition of the married woman?
3. How is de Beauvoir's definition strengthened by comparisons with tasks performed by Mexican Indian women, Mohammedan women, women in Holland, and women in the Mediterranean area?
4. How does de Beauvoir contrast the tasks of the married woman with work that men do outside of the home to emphasize the disadvantages of the married woman's life?

WRITING SUGGESTIONS

1. Analyze one of the short stories or novels written by Kate Chopin in light of de Beauvoir's observations.
2. Discuss your reaction to de Beauvoir's statement that a woman's work within the home "is not directly useful to society, it does not open out on the future, it produces nothing."
3. How do changes in society since de Beauvoir wrote "The Married Woman" in 1952—the Women's Liberation Movement, re-entry of women into the labor force, higher divorce rate—make her observations more or less relevant?

SCIENCES

FRANK NUESSEL

Old Age Needs a New Name: But Don't Look For it in Webster's

Frank Nuessel was born in 1943 and received his Ph.D. from the University of Illinois, Urbana-Champaign in 1973. Since 1982, Nuessel has been professor of Spanish and linguistics at the University of Louisville. He edited Linguistic Approaches to the Romance Lexicon (1978) *and is the author of a number of studies on general linguistics, phonology, and morphology, including "An Annotated, Critical Bibliography of Generative-based Grammatical Analyses of Spanish: Syntax and Semantics,"* Bilingual Review (1979). *In "Old Age Needs a New Name: But Don't Look For it in Webster's," which first appeared in* Aging (1984), *Nuessel discloses how society's current view of old people reveals a systematic pattern of discrimination as damaging as sexism or racism.*

The phenomenon of ageism has existed far longer than the term refers to this practice. This new word was first coined in 1967 by Robert N. Butler, former director of the National Institute on Aging. Butler (1975:12) specified that ageism "can be seen as a process of systematic stereotyping of and discrimination against people because they are old, just as racism and sexism accomplish this with skin color and gender. Old people are characterized as senile, rigid in thought and manner, old-fashioned in morality and skills. . . . Ageism allows the younger generations to see old people as different from themselves; thus they subtly cease to identify with their elders as human beings."

Evidence for the acceptance of this concept may be found in the fact that an entry for this term now exists in *The American Heritage Dictionary of the English Language* (1979:24) which defines ageism as "discrimination based on age, especially discrimination against middle-aged and elderly people."

Ageism is a doubly harmful form of prejudice. First, it lumps together and sets apart a significant and heterogeneous group of people within our society. Second, this misperception leads to a negative self-image on the part of the elderly. Brubaker and Powers (1976:442) have observed that "the character of the stereotype of old age . . . is at issue because it affects not only the manner in which younger persons perceive and interact with aged individuals but also influences the self-definitions and behavior of older persons."

EUPHEMISMS AND LOADED WORDS

There are a number of words commonly used to refer to older people, but the determination of an appropriate designation for this sector of our society continues to be problematic.

Louis Harris and Associates conducted a poll (Ward, 1979:165) for the National Council on the Aging in order to determine an acceptable label for elders. Disagreement, however, over the proper and correct designation continues. *Senior citizen*, preferred by one-third and liked by one-half of the respondents in the Harris survey, was proclaimed a euphemism by the Usage panel of *The American Heritage Dictionary of the English Language* and was acceptable to only 47 percent of that jury. In fact, Fischer (1978:94) has observed that ". . . praise words invented for old people . . . such as *senior citizen* are often laden with a heavy freight of sarcasm." One term which is seemingly devoid of the pejorative connotations that some of the Harris survey participants attached to other expressions (*senior citizen, retired person, mature American, older American, golden ager, old-timer, old man / old woman*) is the word *elder* which is rapidly emerging as the semantically neutral and preferred name for this group.

The dictionary offers few positive adjectives for alluding to elders. Examples of such favorable age-specific words are rare, e.g., *mature, mellow, sage, venerable*, and *veteran*. Even the adjective *mature* is quickly being transformed into a euphemism, i.e., a substitution of an agreeable or pleasant-sounding word for one which conjures up unpleasant and unappealing images. In addition, the descriptive adjectives *aged* and *old* normally only carry positive implications if these qualities refer to inanimate objects such as cheese, wood, brandy, or lace. The overwhelming majority of words and phrases for elders are unfavorable and prejudicial (Nuessel, 1982). In this regard, the extensive, pejorative, and ageist vocabulary of the English language constitutes a verbal record of this society's fear of getting old.

Ageist language belongs to two separate realms. One group of expressions specifically denotes elders. The other segment comprises words with connotations, or intensional significance, associated exclusively with elders.

Ageist language is often doubly pernicious because many of the words denigrate individuals on the basis of both age and gender (Matthews, 1979; Sontag, 1972). For example, *beldam* (e), *biddy, crone, granny, grimalkin, hag, harridan* and *witch* all denote elder females with undesirable physical features or objectionable behavior. In the same vein, another set of ageist expressions is marked for the male sex. Such nouns as *codger, coot*, and *geezer*, depict elder males in an unflattering way by ascribing aberrant behavior to them.

When appended to any of a number of terms that designate people with bad habits, personality quirks, and other displeasing traits (*crank, fogy, fool, fossil, fuddy-duddy, grump, miser*, and *reprobate*), the adjective *old* (a word encumbered with almost completely negative implications) creates a set of hybrid noun phrases that truly demean and defame our elders. In the future, it is conceivable that the word *old* may undergo a semantic shift to an entirely positive concept through public education and activities. Such a phenomenon occurred in the 1960's when the term *black* acquired the sense of cultural pride and awareness for another oppressed minority.

Many of the adjectives frequently assigned to elders are predominantly negative. In general, they assign unpleasant physical (*infirm, doddering, decrepit*), behavioral (*cantankerous, cranky*), and mental (*senile, foolish, rambling*) characteristics to a group of people who are as diverse in personality, intellect and health status as any other segment of our society.

Unfortunately, the childhood refrain, "sticks and stones may break my bones but words will never hurt me," is not true. In fact, language can be a very potent and harmful instrument, because stereotypic vocabulary has the power to shape people's concepts of reality. The public often comes to believe the preconceptions that are the basis of stereotypes and thus fails to differentiate individual uniqueness.

Dehumanization is the net effect of employing prejudicial language of any kind. Such depersonalization facilitates abuse and mistreatment of vulnerable minorities (especially elders) by a systematic devaluation of their dignity and worth. This form of disenfranchisement facilitates their subjugation because it enables elders to be segregated into urban ghettos, nursing homes, and other modern warehouses for presumed undesirables. In this regard Bosmajian (1974:6) has observed that ". . . names, words and language . . . can also be used to dehumanize human beings and to 'justify' their suppression and even their extermination." The use of euphemistic labels to describe nursing homes and retirement villages (*Tendercare, Crystal Pines, Forest Villa, Leisure World, Sunset Lodge* etc.) eases the public's guilt and remorse over accepting the isolation of elders. To ignore the awesome power of linguistic labeling is to contribute to the continued mistreatment of the elderly.

AGEISM IN DRAMATIC SCRIPTS

Written language (dramatic literature, film and television scripts, commercial advertising copy) is the common source of the portrayal of elders in movies, television, videocassettes, cartoons and radio. Scripts frequently include, in parentheses, stage directions and character descriptions, such as physical qualities and personality traits. Intonation, stress, rhythm of voices as well as gestures are generally designated by adverbial phrases (*feebly, weakly, in a deteriorated condition, in a senile state*) or by highly specific verbal expressions (*teeter, dodder, mumble, mutter, drool*). The selection of such stereotypic phraseology intensifies ageist images in a particularly malicious fashion. Often, however, the mere use of such adjectives as *old, elderly,* and *aged* is sufficient to cause actors and actresses to perform a role according to certain prevailing social preconceptions about elders—so powerful are the presuppositions entailed in these words.

ELIMINATING THE DISTORTIONS

We are beginning to see some efforts to correct ageism in films, radio and TV. The Gray Panthers, for example, have developed the Media Watch Observer's Report Form in response to the problem of misrepresentation of elders in mass communications.

The approach, a response to offenses already committed, has an important educational function if the distortions reported are properly publicized (letters to the editor, local news coverage, etc.)

More important, however, is the elimination of these distortions prior to their public dissemination. Two publications designed to prevent ageist portrayal of older people now exist. The first is *Truth About Aging: Guidelines for Accurate Communications*, by Mary E. Spencer, a 1984 publication of the American Association of Retired Persons. Copies of this pamphlet are available for AARP, 1909 K Street, Washington, D.C. 20049.

The second publication, *Media Guidelines for Sexuality and Aging*, by Carol Jean Wisnieski, Susan Leigh Star and Christiane Herrmann, is available free from Carol Jean Wisnieski, 348 Diamond Street, San Francisco, California 94114. This two-page set of guidlines has been reproduced in Richard H. Davis', *Television and The Aging Audience*, which was published by The University of Southern California Press, in 1980 (pp. 83 and 84).

Continual vigilance will be necessary if ageism is to be reduced significantly, if not eradicated, from our language and literature. One positive step has already begun in this regard. The newly established national intergenerational organization, Understanding Aging, Incorporated (Center for Understanding Aging, Conant Schools, Acton, MA 01720), has recently established an award for authors who portray elders in a realistic and nonstereotypic fashion.

As previously suggested in this article, the scarcity of positive words in the English language referring to old age is probably merely a reflection of society's fear of growing old. Perhaps Americans will have to come to better terms with the last stage of life before words will come into common usage that truly describe the attributes of our older population. But since it may take a while for Americans to get over their love affair with youth, there are steps we can take in the meantime to begin to eradicate ageism. One of these steps involves making the public more aware of the damaging effects of ageist language.

REFERENCES

BOSMAJIAN, HAIG. 1975. *The Languages of Oppression*. Washington, D.C.: Public Affairs Press.

BRUBAKER, TIMOTHY, AND EDWARD POWERS. 1976. "The Stereotypes of Old: A Review and Alternative Approach." *Journal of Gerontology* 31, 441–447.

BUTLER, ROBERT N. 1969. "Age-ism: Another Form of Bigotry." *The Gerontologist* 9, 243–246.

BUTLER, ROBERT N. 1975. *Why Survive? Being Old In America*. New York: Harper and Row.

FISCHER, DAVID HACKETT. 1978. *Growing Old in America*. Expanded ed. Oxford: Oxford University Press.

MATTHEWS, SARAH. 1979. *The Social World of Old Women: Management of Self-identity*. Sage Library of Social Research (Vol. 78). Beverly Hills, CA: Sage Publications.

MORRIS, WILLIAM (Ed.). 1979. *The American Heritage Dictionary of the English Language*. Boston, MA: Houghton Mifflin Company.

NUESSEL, FRANK. 1982. "The Language of Ageism." *The Gerontologist* 22, 273–276.

SONTAG, SUSAN. 1972. "The Double Standard of Aging." *The Saturday Review* (September 23), 29–38.

WARD, RUSSELL. 1979. *The Aging Experience: An Introduction to Social Gerontology*. New York: J. P. Lippincott Company.

MEANING

1. How does ageist language negatively stereotype older people?
2. How does society's fear of growing old reflect itself in the ageist language used to describe older people?
3. How does the use of dehumanizing langauge make it possible to justify discounting a particular group and ignoring their civil rights? That is, how does ageist language pave the way for abuse and mistreatment of older people?
4. What bias does Nuessel discover in the way older people are portrayed in films, on television, and in commercials?

USING DEFINITION TO CONVEY MEANING

1. How does Nuessel document the phenomenon of ageism by showing how the etymology of words used to describe the elderly have acquired negative connotations as society's fear of growing old increases?
2. What evidence does Nuessel offer to document the stereotyped way older people are portrayed in film, television, and commercials?
3. How does Nuessel's analysis of ageist language demonstrate that negative labeling, whether on the basis of age, sex, race, or religion, is frequently the first step toward disenfranchisement?

WRITING SUGGESTIONS

1. Design an informal experiment that would be useful in monitoring ageist stereotyping in different areas. For example, how are older people depicted in newspaper stories, on local television news, and on national television programs? What differences, if any, exist in the way older men and women are portrayed in these three areas?
2. Survey ads to determine how advertisers use scare tactics that suggest you will be treated badly if you do not buy a product that will keep you "young, productive, energetic, or sexy"?

HANS SELYE

What Is Stress?

Hans Selye (1907–1982) was born in Vienna, Austria, and earned both an M.D. and Ph.D. in Prague, 1931, as well as a D.Sc. from McGill University in 1942. He taught biochemistry and histology at McGill, and was the director of the Institute of Experimental Medicine and Surgery at the University of Montreal (1945–1976). Seyle's innovative research on the nature of stress brought him international recognition in the form of the medal of the Swedish Medical Society (1965), the Canadian Centennial medal (1967), the Rudolf Virchow Gold Medal (1970), and the Killam Prize (1974). Selye's prolific research into the nature of stress includes The Story of the Adaptation Syndrome *(1952)*, Stress Without Distress *(1974)*, and The Stress of Life *(2nd ed., 1976). In* "What Is Stress?," *(1974), Selye defines the nature of this often misunderstood term.*

Everybody has it, everybody talks about it, yet few people have taken the trouble to find out what stress really is. Many words have become fashionable when scientific research revealed a new concept likely to influence our way of thinking about major issues of life or to affect our everyday conduct. Such terms as "Darwinian evolution," "allergy," and "psychoanalysis" have all had their peaks of popularity in drawing-room or cocktail-party conversations; but rarely are the opinions about them based on a study of technical works written by the scientists who established these concepts.

Nowadays, we hear a great deal at social gatherings about the stress of executive life, retirement, exercise, family problems, pollution, air traffic control, or the death of a relative. But how many of those defending their strong convictions about these matters with heated arguments have bothered to learn the scientific meaning of stress and the mechanism of its workings? Most people have never even wondered whether there is a difference between stress and distress!

The word "stress," like "success," "failure," or "happiness," means different things to different people, so that defining it is extremely difficult although it has become part of our daily vocabulary. Is stress merely a synonym for distress? Is it effort, fatigue, pain, fear, the need for concentration, the humiliation of censure, the loss of blood, or even an unexpected great success which requires complete reformulation of one's entire life? The answer is yes and no. That is what makes the definition of stress so difficult. Every one of these conditions produces stress, but none of them can be singled out as being "it," since the word applies equally to all the others.

Yet, how are we to cope with the stress of life if we cannot even define it? The businessman who is under constant pressure from his clients and employees alike, the air-traffic controller who knows that a moment of distraction may mean death to hundreds of people, the athlete who desperately wants to win a race, and the husband who helplessly watches his wife slowly and painfully dying of cancer, all suffer from stress. The problems they face are totally different, but medical research has shown that in many respects the body responds in a stereotyped manner, with identical biochemical changes, essentially meant to cope with any type of increased demand upon the human machinery. The stress-producing factors—technically called *stressors*—are different, yet they all elicit essentially the same biological stress response. This distinction between stressor and stress was perhaps the first important step in the scientific analysis of that most common biological phenomenon that we all know only too well from personal experience.

But if we want to use what the laboratory has taught us about stress in formulating our own philosophy of life, if we want to avoid its bad effects and yet be able to enjoy the pleasures of accomplishment, we have to learn more about the nature and mechanism of stress. In order to succeed in this, in order to arrive at a basis for a scientific philosophy of conduct—a rational prophylactic and therapeutic science of human behavior—we must concentrate in this somewhat difficult first chapter on the fundamental technical data which the laboratory has given us.

In writing this book, it seemed logical to begin with what the physician means by the term *stress*, at the same time familiarizing the reader with the few technical expressions that are essential.

Stress is the nonspecific response of the body to any demand made upon it. To understand this definition we must first explain what we mean by *nonspecific*. Each demand made upon our body is in a sense unique, that is, *specific*. When exposed to cold, we shiver to produce more heat, and the blood vessels in our skin contract to diminish the loss of heat from the body surfaces. When exposed to heat, we sweat because the evaporation of perspiration from the surface of our skin has a cooling effect. When we eat too much sugar and the blood-sugar level rises above normal, we excrete some of it and burn up the rest so that the blood sugar returns to normal. A great muscular effort, such as running up many flights of stairs at full speed, makes increased demands upon our musculature and cardiovascular system. The muscles will need supplemental energy to perform this unusual work; hence, the heart will beat more rapidly and strongly, and the blood pressure will rise to dilate the vessels, thereby increasing the flow of blood to the muscles.

Each drug or hormone has such specific actions: diuretic drugs increase the production of urine; the hormone adrenalin augments the pulse rate and blood pressure, simultaneously raising blood sugar, whereas the hormone insulin decreases blood sugar. Yet, no matter what kind of derangement is produced, all these agents have one thing in common; they also increase the demand for readjustment. This demand is nonspecific; it requires adaptation to a problem, irrespective of what that problem may be.

In other words, in addition to their specific actions, all agents to which we are exposed also produce a nonspecific increase in the need to perform adaptive functions and thereby to re-establish normalcy. This is independent of the specific activity that caused the rise in requirements. The nonspecific demand for activity as such is the essence of stress.

From the point of view of its stress-producing or stressor activity, *it is immaterial whether the agent or situation we face is pleasant or unpleasant;* all that counts is the intensity of the demand for readjustment or adaptation. The mother who is suddenly told that her only son died in battle suffers a terrible mental shock; if years later it turns out that the news was false and the son unexpectedly walks into her room alive and well, she experiences extreme joy. The specific results of the two events, sorrow and joy, are completely different, in fact, opposite to each other, yet their stressor effect—the nonspecific demand to readjust herself to an entirely new situation—may be the same.

It is difficult to see how such essentially different things as cold, heat, drugs, hormones, sorrow, and joy could provoke an identical biochemical reaction in the body. Nevertheless, this is the case; it can now be demonstrated, by highly objective quantitative biochemical determinations, that certain reactions are totally nonspecific, and common to all types of exposure.

It has taken medicine a long time to accept the existence of such a stereotyped response. It did not seem logical that different tasks, in fact any task, should require the same response. Yet, if you come to think of it, there are many analogies in everyday life in which highly specific things or events share the same nonspecific feature. At first sight it is difficult to see what could be the common denominator between a man, a table, and a tree, yet they all have weight. There is no object completely devoid of weight; the pressure exerted on the scale balance does not depend upon such a specific feature as temperature, color, or shape, any more than the stressor effect of a demand upon the body depends on the kind of adaptive reaction that is required to meet it.

Or consider the appliances in a house that has heaters, refrigerators, bells, and light bulbs, which respectively produce heat, cold, sound, or light, in a most specific manner; yet to function they all depend upon one common factor—electricity. A member of a primitive tribe who never heard of electricity would find it very difficult to accept that all the manifold phenomena just mentioned depend upon the satisfaction of a common demand: the provision of electrical energy.

WHAT STRESS IS NOT

Since the term "stress" is often used quite loosely, many confusing and contradictory definitions of it have been formulated; hence, it will be useful to add a few remarks stating clearly what it is not.

Stress is not merely nervous tension. This fact must be especially emphasized, since most laymen and even many scientists tend to identify biological stress with nervous exhaustion or intense emotional arousal. Indeed, quite recently, Dr. John W. Mason, a former president of the American Psychosomatic Society and one of the most distinguished investigators of the psychologic and psychiatric aspects of biological stress, devoted an excellent essay to an analysis of my stress theory. He suggested that the common denominator of stressors may simply be activation of "the physiological apparatus involved in emotional or arousal reactions to threatening or unpleasant factors in the life situation as a whole." In man, with his highly developed nervous system, emotional stimuli are in fact the most common stressors—and, of course, these would be encountered most frequently in psychiatric patients.

It must not be forgotten, however, that stress reactions do occur in lower animals that have no nervous system, and even in plants. Furthermore, the so-called stress of anesthesia is a well-recognized phenomenon in surgery, and numerous investigators have tried to eliminate this undersirable complication of the loss of consciousness.

Stress is not always the nonspecific result of damage. We have seen that it is immaterial whether a stressor is pleasant or unpleasant; its stressor effect depends merely on the intensity of the demand made upon the adaptive capacity of the body. Any kind of normal activity—a game of chess or even a passionate embrace—can produce considerable stress without causing harmful effects. Damaging or unpleasant stress is "distress."

The word "stress" allegedly came into common English usage, via Old French and Middle English, as "distress." The first syllable eventually was lost through slurring, as children turn "because" into "cause." In the light of our investigations, the true meaning of the two words became totally different despite their common ancestry, just as in correct usage we distinguish between "because" (since) and "cause" (reason). Activity associated with stress may be pleasant or unpleasant; distress is always disagreeable.

Stress is not something to be avoided. In fact, it is evident from the definition given at the beginning of this chapter that it cannot be avoided.

In common parlance, when we say someone is "under stress," we actually mean under excessive stress or distress, just as the statement "he is running a temperature" refers to an abnormally high temperature, that is, fever. Some heat production is essential to life.

Similarly, no matter what you do or what happens to you, there arises a demand for the necessary energy required to maintain life, to resist aggression and to adapt to constantly changing external influences. Even while fully relaxed and asleep, you are under some stress. Your heart must continue to pump blood, your intestines to digest last night's dinner, and your muscles to move your chest for respiration. Even your brain is not at rest while you are dreaming. *Complete freedom from stress is death.*

MEANING

1. What popular misconceptions about stress does Selye's exact scientific definition correct?
2. What different kinds of physiological responses did Selye measure in order to identify the precise effects of stress on the human body?
3. Why is the fact that people under anesthesia show signs of stress so significant in supporting Selye's definition?

USING DEFINITION TO CONVEY MEANING

1. How does the elevation of blood sugar caused by adrenalin and the lowering of blood sugar caused by insulin both illustrate what Selye defines as "stress."
2. How does the wide range of examples Selye presents, including the businessman, the air-traffic controller, the athlete, and the husband, make his definition more accurate?

3. What analogies does Selye create to explain the role of stress as a common adaptation to many different physical and psychological situations?
4. How does Selye use comparison and contrast to define "stress" by specifying what it is not?

WRITING SUGGESTIONS

1. Look up the word *stress* in the unabridged Old English Dictionary and discuss the different contexts in which the word or its synonyms have appeared over the previous two centuries. What is the etymology of the term *stress?*
2. Describe your reactions to both a positive and a negative event that produced stress, as Selye defines it. Compare your reactions, psychological and physiological, to determine if your responses to the events were the same even though the situations that produced stress seemed to be quite different.

CHARLES H. TOWNES

Harnessing Light

Charles H. Townes, born in 1915, received a Ph.D. in physics from the California Institute of Technology in 1939. He has been chairman of the physics department at Columbia University (1952–1955), and professor of physics and provost at Massachusetts Institute of Technology. Since 1967, Townes has been University professor of physics at the University of California at Berkeley. His research into molecular and nuclear structure, masers, lasers, and quantum electronics resulted in his being awarded the Nobel Prize in Physics in 1964. Townes' current research interests are in microwave spectroscopy and radio and infrared astronomy. In "Harnessing Light" (1984), Townes tells about the research that led to the discovery of the laser and defines the distinctive qualities possessed by this new technological phenomenon.

The laser was born early one beautiful spring morning on a park bench in Washington, D.C. As I sat in Franklin Square, musing and admiring the azaleas, an idea came to me for a practical way to obtain a very pure form of electromagnetic waves from molecules. I had been doggedly searching for new ways to produce radio waves at very high frequencies, too high for the vacuum tubes of the day to generate. This short-wavelength radiation, I felt, would permit extremely accurate measurement and analysis, giving new insights into physics and chemistry.

As it turned out, I was much too conservative; the field has developed far beyond my imagination and along paths I could not have foreseen at the time. Surveyors use the laser to guarantee straight lines; surgeons to weld new corneas into place and burn away blood clots; industry to drill tiny, precise holes; communications engineers to send information in vast quantities through glass fiber pipes. It is even built into the supermarket checkout scanner that reads prices by bouncing a beam of laser light off a pattern imprinted on the item.

But in the spring of 1951, as I sat on my park bench, it was all yet to come. In the quest for short-wavelength radio waves, I built on the knowledge of the time. In general terms, it was this. Atoms and molecules can absorb radiation as light, as radio waves, or as heat. The radiation is absorbed in the form of a quantum, or tiny packet of energy, that pushes the atom from one energy level to a higher one by exactly the amount of absorbed energy. The atom excited in this way may spontaneously fall to a lower energy level. As it does, it gives up a quantum of radiant energy and releases a burst of electromagnetic radiation, usually in the form of light. This happens in the sun, where atoms are excited by heat agitation or radiation and then drop to a lower level of energy, releasing light. But I was focusing on another way of producing radiation, understood in theory since Einstein discussed it in 1917: the stimulated emission of radiation.

In this case, radiation such as light passing by stimulates an atom to give up its energy to the radiation, at exactly the same frequency and radiated in exactly the same direction, and then drop to a lower state. If this process happened naturally, light striking one side of a black piece of paper would emerge from the other side stronger than it went in—and that's what happens in a laser. But such extraordinary behavior requires an unusual condition: More atoms must be in an excited energy state than in a lower energy one.

That morning in the park, I realized that if man was to obtain wavelengths shorter than those that could be produced by vacuum tubes, he must use the ready-made small devices known as atoms and molecules. And I saw that by creating this effect in a chamber with certain critical dimensions, the stimulated radiation could be reinforced, becoming steady and intense.

Later discussions with my students at Columbia University over lunch produced a new vocabulary. We chose the name "maser," for microwave amplification by stimulated emission of radiation, for a device based on the fundamental principle. We also proposed, somewhat facetiously, the "iraser" (infrared amplification by stimulated emission of radiation), "laser" (light amplification), and 'xaser" (X-ray amplification). Maser and laser stuck.

The first device to use the new amplifying mechanism was a maser built around ammonia gas, since the ammonia molecule was known to interact more strongly than any other with microwaves. A three-year thesis project of graduate student James Gordon, with assistance from Herbert Zeiger, a young postdoctoral physicist, succeeded and immediately demonstrated the extreme purity of the frequency of radiation produced by the natural vibrations of ammonia molecules. A pure frequency can be translated into accurate timekeeping. Suppose we know that the power from a wall outlet has a frequency of exactly 60 cycles per second. It then takes exactly 1/60th of a second to complete one cycle, one second to complete 60 cycles, one minute for 3,600 of them, and so on. To build an accurate clock, we have only to count the cycles. In the mid-1950s, when the first ammonia maser was completed, the best clocks had a precision of about one part in a billion, about the same accuracy of the Earth's rotation about its axis. Today, a hydrogen maser is the heart of an atomic clock accurate to one part in 100 trillion, an improvement by a factor of at least 10,000. Such a clock, if kept running, would be off by no more than one second in every few million years.

The new process also immediately provided an amplifier for radio waves much more sensitive than the best then available. Later refinements provided very practical amplifiers, and masers now are typically used to communicate in space over long distances and to pick up radio waves from distant galaxies. Astrophysicists recently have discovered *natural* masers in interstellar space that generate enormous microwave intensity from excited molecules.

Although my main interest in stimulated emission of radiation had been to obtain wavelengths shorter than microwaves, the new possibilities for superaccurate clocks and supersensitive amplifiers, and their scientific uses, occupied everyone's attention for some time. By 1957 I felt it was time to get back on the track of shorter wavelengths. I decided that it would actually be easier to make a big step than a small one and jump immediately to light waves—wavelengths in the visible or short infrared, almost 10,000 times higher in frequency than microwaves. But there was a sticky problem: What kind of resonating chamber would function at a single and precisely correct frequency but could be built using ordinary engineering techniques? My friend Arthur

Schawlow, then at the Bell Telephone Laboratories, helped provide the answer: an elongated chamber with a mirror at each end.

In December of 1958 we published a paper that discussed this and other aspects of a practical laser and set off an intense wave of efforts to build one. In 1960 Theodore H. Maiman, a physicist with Hughes Aircraft Company, demonstrated the first operating laser, while Ali Javan, William R. Bennett Jr., and Donald R. Herriott at Bell Labs built a second, completely different type. Rather than using gas, Maiman's laser used a small cylinder of synthetic ruby, its ends polished into mirrored surfaces. The firing of a helical flashbulb surrounding the rod triggered the ruby to send out a brief, intense pulse of laser light. Soon there were many variations on the laser theme, using different atoms or molecules and different methods of providing them with energy, but all used a mirrored chamber.

The laser quickly gained great notoriety with the public as a "death ray"; it is a popular science fiction motif and one with undeniable dramatic appeal. Lasers certainly have the power to injure. Even a weak laser shone into the eye will be focused by the lens of the eye onto the retina and damage it. But laser beams are not very advantageous as military weapons. Guns are cheaper, easier to build and use, and, in most cases, much more effective. Science fiction's death ray is still mostly science fiction, and it is likely to remain so.

The laser is, however, extremely powerful. The reason is that stimulated amplification adds energy "coherently"—that is, in exactly the same direction as the initial beam. This coherence conveys surprising properties. A laser emitting one watt of light has only a hundredth the power of a 100-watt light bulb. Yet the beam of a one-watt laser directed at the moon was seen by television equipment on the lunar surface when all the lights of our greatest cities were undetectable—simply because the beam is so directional. A simple lens can focus the beam of light from an ordinary one-watt laser into a spot so small that it produces 100 million watts per square centimeter, enormously greater than the intensity from any other type of source.

But a one-watt laser is not even a particularly powerful one. Pulsed lasers can produce a *trillion* watts of power by delivering energy over a very short period but at enormous levels. This power may last only one ten-billionth of a second, but during that time a lens can concentrate it to a level of 100 million million million watts per square centimeter. The trillion watts that such a laser delivers is approximately equal to the average amount of electric power being used over the entire Earth at any one time. Focused by a lens, this concentration or power is 100 trillion times greater than the light at the surface of the sun. It will melt or tear apart any substance, including atoms themselves. Drilling through diamonds is easy for a laser beam and produces no wear. Lasers have been developed that can compact small pellets of material and then heat them in a sudden flash to reproduce conditions similar to those in the sun's interior, where nuclear fusion occurs.

The laser's directed intensity quickly made it an effective industrial tool. Lasers cut or weld delicate electronic circuits or heavy metal parts. They can melt or harden the surface of a piece of steel so quickly that under a very thin skin, the metal is still cool and undamaged. Industrial interest was especially high. By the end of the 1960s, most new lasers were being designed in industrial laboratories, though many are important tools in university laboratories.

How useful lasers and quantum electronics have been to scientists is indicated by the fact that besides Nobel Prizes for work leading to the devices themselves, they have played an important role in other Nobel awards—for example, the one to Dennis

Gabor of the University of London for the idea of holography (three-dimensional laser photography); the one to Schawlow of Stanford University for versatile new types of laser spectroscopy; to Nicolaas Bloembergen of Harvard University for discoveries in nonlinear optics made possible by high-intensity laser beams; and one to Arno Penzias and Robert W. Wilson of the Bell Telephone Laboratories for the discovery of microwave radiation from the Big Bang which initiated our universe. While the latter discovery might possible have been made by other techniques, it was facilitated by very sensitive maser amplification.

Because of the unswerving directionality of laser beams, probably more lasers have been sold for producing the straight lines needed in surveying than for any other single purpose. The laser is now a common surveying instrument that helps to lay out roads.

Laser beams also can measure distance conveniently. By bouncing the beam from a reflector, a surveyor can measure distances to high precision. Beams sent from Earth have been bounced off reflectors placed on the moon by astronauts. By generating a short light pulse and measuring the elapsed time before it returns, the distance to the moon can be measured within one inch. Such measurements have revealed effects of general relativity and thus refined our knowledge of the theory of gravitation.

In scientific equipment or simply in machine shops, the laser's pure frequency allows the beam to be reflected and the peaks and troughs of its wave matched with those of the first part of the beam, thus providing distance measurements to within a small fraction of one wavelength—40 millionths of an inch. In scientific experiments, changes of length as small as one hundredth of the diameter of an atom have been measured in this way. There are efforts to use such supersensitive measurements to detect the gravity waves due to motions of distant stars.

Because lasers can be so finely focused and their intensity adjusted to make controlled cuts, they are used as a surgeon's scalpel. Not only can they be very precisely directed, but a particular color can be chosen to destroy certain types of tissue while leaving others relatively intact, an especially valuable effect for some cancers. In cutting, the laser also seals off blood vessels so that there is relatively little bleeding. For the eye, laser light has the interesting ability to go harmlessly through the pupil and perform operations within.

Of all the ways our lives are likely to be affected by lasers, perhaps none will be so unobtrusive and yet more important than cheaper and more effective communications. Within many metropolitan areas, the number of radio or television stations must be limited because the number of available frequencies is limited. For the same reason, large numbers of conversations cannot simultaneously be carried on a single telephone wire. But light is a superhighway of frequencies; a single light beam can, in principle, carry all the radio and TV stations and all telephone calls in the world without interfering with one another. These light beams can be transmitted on glass fibers one-tenth the size of a human hair. In crowded cities where streets have been dug up for years and jammed beneath with all manner of pipes and wires, these tiny fibers can fit into the smallest spaces and provide enormous communication capacity. In long distance communication, they may replace most cables, and even satellites.

Even after the laser was invented and its importance recognized, it was by no means clear, even to those who worked on it, that it would see so many striking applications. And much undoubtedly lies ahead.

MEANING

1. Why is "the stimulated emission of radiation" a crucial concept in understanding how the laser became possible?
2. What unique properties does the laser possess that makes it such an incredible invention?
3. Why must all resonating chambers, whether they use ammonia gas, synthetic ruby, or other substances, have mirrored surfaces to generate laser light?
4. What other Nobel Prize-winning research did the discovery of the laser make possible?

USING DEFINITION TO CONVEY MEANING

1. How does the enormous range of applications cited by Townes affect your perception of the laser's importance?
2. How does Townes use an operational definition to give his readers insight into the distinctive nature of his invention? That is, how does he define the laser by describing what it does?
3. Which parts of the article did you find more intriguing—the stories about how the laser was invented, descriptions of how the laser works, or the many examples of the laser's uses?

WRITING SUGGESTIONS

1. Although Townes dismisses the credibility of the use of the laser as a "death ray," what developments have taken place that make the use of lasers in outer space for military purposes a distinct possibility?
2. How is one of the following dependent on the laser: holography, fiber optics, surveying instruments, or microsurgery?

PROBLEM SOLVING

Although not a rhetorical strategy as such, the range of problem-solving techniques that writers in diverse areas use to identify problems, apply theoretical models, define constraints, use various search techniques, and check solutions against relevant criteria are an important part of all academic and professional research.

Each of the three broad areas in the curriculum—liberal arts, political and social sciences, and sciences—seeks different kinds of knowledge and, therefore, has a different method of inquiry. That is to say, each area stipulates what kinds of problems or issues it considers worth addressing. The liberal arts aim at enriching our sense of human experiences to allow us to feel, as fully as possible, what the often inexpressible, qualitative sense of being human actually means. This primary concern with the re-creation and communication of inner-felt human experience defines the kinds of problems and methods used to address them in the liberal arts.

In essence, this is the kind of knowledge that the great writers, artists, and thinkers represented in this reader aim at communicating. Recall how effectively D. H. Lawrence recreates the world of the Pueblos and the kinds of imaginative insight into that experience that are preserved for all future readers. So, too, James Boswell's account conveys the multifaceted reality of Dr. Johnson's personality with such force that the audience feels they have actually met the distinguished lexicographer. Similarly, Agnes De Mille gives us the experience of watching Pavlova dance as De Mille herself saw her, while Ernest Hemingway conveys the drama, meaning, and significance of the bullfight. For the artist, the question is how well the techniques of the craft have been used to bring the audience into direct contact with the internal, real-life experiences that each artist strives to express. For the audience, the question is the same, but from a different viewpoint: How effectively does the artist's work convey insight into human nature?

Using different techniques, Aristotle helps his audience appreciate what it means to be young and what it means to be old, Plato creates a sublime allegory to express his view of the reality of the human condition, and Edmund Wilson recreates a moment in history through a richly detailed, perceptively arranged, and well-documented set of facts. Thus, the main issues and problems connected with the liberal arts are those of interpretation and meaning. One interpretation will be better than another if, like Gilbert Highet's analysis of the structure, themes, and rhetoric of the "Gettysburg Address," it helps the reader more fully appreciate the significance and depth of the work.

The broadest perspectives are brought to bear by academic disciplines in the liberal arts which interpret the meaning of an individual work as it relates to other works of that type and to the historical context in which it was produced. For example, recall how Alan Wallach uses the methodology of art historians when he views particular paintings by William L. Haney and Jan van Eyck as they relate to the larger social and cultural contexts in which they were produced. Although each of these interpretations are well-supported, effective accounts, they do not foreclose the possibility of new, different, and equally convincing interpretations. This open-endedness of the interpretive issues and problems is characteristic of the humanities and liberal arts.

The kinds of knowledge sought and the procedures used by the political and social sciences are quite different from those of the liberal arts. These disciplines have, to a large extent, adapted the techniques and objectives of the physical and natural sciences to study how human beings interact within the context of social, political, business, legal, psychological, and cultural relationships. The social sciences are often referred to as the "behavioral" sciences because they focus on what can be objectively observed about human beings—their actions or behavior. These disciplines seek to discover causal connections (sometimes expressed as statistical laws), which have both descriptive and predictive value, and which can be confirmed or refuted by data from subsequent research.

Questions to be answered or problems to be solved are expressed in the form of hypotheses whose validity can be measured by empirical means. For example, recall the classic experiment by John Darley and Bibb Latane, which used small groups of people to test their "diffusion-of-responsibility" theory to solve the problem of "why people don't help in a crisis." By varying the number of people who thought others also were aware of a crisis, Darley and Latane demonstrated, in a quantifiable form, a plausible mechanism to explain the real causes of seeming apathy in bystanders to victims of street crime. Presumably, other social scientists conducting comparable experiments would obtain similar results. To ensure an objectivity comparable to that of the sciences, social researchers rely on statistical surveys, questionnaires, and other data-gathering techniques. Using these methods, J. Michael Polich and Bruce R. Orvis studied a sample of 3,148 active-duty Air Force personnel and found that 13.9 percent were affected by "alcohol problems."

Social scientists draw on a whole range of theoretical models to explain human behavior, from the "game theory" applied by Leonard I. Stein to explain the interactions between doctors and nurses, to the "role theory," applied by Melford E. Spiro, in his on-site study of kibbutz life, to explore how individual behavior is conditioned by the expectations of the surrounding culture. The range of theories available often raises the question as to which theoretical model should be applied to explain the data in question.

A much more serious problem for the political and social sciences revolves around the question of whether objectivity on the part of the observer is possible or even desirable. Can the social scientist, as a human being, knowingly decide to suspend his or her own values when investigating groups of people or other cultures? Whereas it is not obvious how Leonard Spiro felt toward members of the kibbutz or how Ruth Benedict felt toward the Zuñi and Plains Indians, Jessica Mitford's sarcastic description of the processes used by the funeral industry clearly reveals her bias against them.

An even more telling criticism of the application of the objective methods of the sciences to the study of human behavior is made by the psychiatrist, Thomas S. Szasz, as we shall see later on in the "Argumentation and Persuasion" chapter. He and others argue that to study human beings as if they were objects ignores what is in reality the most important aspect of human nature—consciousness. We must keep in mind, however, that the social sciences only came into existence in the last century through the work of Sir James George Frazer and others. In one sense, social scientists are still struggling to find a theoretical model distinct from those of the liberal arts— which emphasize conscious meaning and perceived significance—and those of the sciences—which use purely objective methods of inquiry.

The types of information sought and the methods employed within the domain of the sciences aim at providing an accurate, systematic, and comprehensive account of the world around us, as well as a framework within which new hypotheses can be put forward and evaluated. The way science solves problems and generates new knowledge can be seen by carefully examining the procedures used by limnologists Arthur Hasler and James Larsen in their classic research. Recall how their experiments pinpointed the role played by the sense of smell in solving the mystery of how salmon could find their way back to the exact streams where they were born from distances as great as nine hundred miles. Well-documented observations, based on the recovery of individually marked salmon in the streams where they were born, established the "homing instinct" as a problem needing scientific investigation.

Once observations show the existence of a mysterious phenomenon, or an "anomaly," scientists formulate a hypothesis or tentative explanation to account for this otherwise inexplicable event. This hypothesis, if true, should have both descriptive and predictive value; that is, the hypothesis must state that in particular circumstances certain kinds of things will occur. These events, if observed and measured, will confirm the truth of the hypothesis. Scientists then must design specific experiments to measure in objective and quantifiable form whether the hypothesis provides an adequate explanation of the phenomenon. Hasler and Larsen's experiments were designed to test their hypothesis that the salmon identifies the stream of its birth by odor and "literally smells its way home from the sea." The essential feature of scientific research depends on the design of the experiment, which makes it possible to isolate, control, and measure the role played by one key variable. In this case, half of a group of salmon were marked and deprived of their olfactory sense, while the other half were used as a control group. After they were released, it was determined that the control group correctly returned as usual to the original stream, whereas the "odor-blinded" fish migrated in random fashion "picking the wrong stream as often as the right one." Subsequent experiments confirmed that Hasler and Larsen's hypothesis was indeed a satisfactory explanation of a previously inexplicable phenomenon.

The above example of how the scientific method is applied underscores the crucial role played by observation in identifying "anomalies," which run counter to commonly accepted assumptions. Recall Jean Henri Fabre's meticulous observations of the cannibalistic mating habits of the praying mantis, Jane van Lawick-Goodall's detailed reports of unexpected "tool-using" and "toolmaking" behavior by chimpanzees, and Konrad Lorenz's first-hand observations of a previously unsuspected innate inhibition in timber wolves against killing members of their own species—all of which led to critical re-evaluations of traditional scientific theories.

We must remember that theories and even scientific laws are always open to new observations of the kind presented by Donald Griffin (as we shall see in the chapter following this one), who suggests that primates may be capable of communicating with humans; Carl Sagan, who formulated the hypothesis of a "nuclear winter"; and Constance Holden, who describes an experiment that suggests the over-riding impor-tance of heredity over environment in shaping human behavior.

Sometimes the anomalies observed and the theories formulated to explain them are in such conflict with existing paradigms or agreed-upon scientific "laws" that they demand the establishment of new theoretical models to guide further research. Such was the case with Sigmund Freud's discovery that ideas unacceptable to the conscious mind were repressed and could manifest themselves in slips of the tongue, lapses of memory, hysteria, and as disguised wish-fulfillments in dreams. So, too, Charles Darwin's observations, in the Galapagos Islands, of adaptive mutations in finches, tortoises, and other species ultimately led him to formulate a "theory of evolution," which proposed that both humans and apes evolved from a common primate ancestor. By challenging existing theories and replacing them with new theoreti-cal models both Freud and Darwin created new fields of study and advanced all of science.

The preceding account should give you some idea of the extent to which problem-solving techniques are used within specific fields of study and how the assumptions, hypotheses, and theoretical models underlying disciplines change and evolve in response to contradictions or anomalies that challenge accepted paradigms.

The historian Edmund Wilson, trying to decide on how best to communicate his understanding of a world-transforming event; the social scientists, J. Michael Polich and Bruce R. Orvis, faced with the problem of clarifying the real nature of alcoholism; a researcher into animal behavior, Donald Griffin, searching for the exact experimental design necessary to measure primate intelligence—all use many of the same techniques in solving problems within their respective disciplines. That is, despite the fact that the liberal arts, political and social sciences, and sciences rely on their own distinctive theoretical models to generate new knowledge, researchers across the disciplines often rely on many of the same strategies to solve problems they encounter within the context of their particular fields of study.

The process by which problems are solved across the disciplines usually involves: recognizing and defining the problem, using various search techniques to discover a solution, verifying the solution, and communicating it to a particular audience, who might need to know the history of the problem, the success or failure of previous attempts to solve it, and other relevant information.

The nine problem solvers presented in this chapter—including Philip Wheelwright (philosophy), Leon R. Kass (bioethics), Sir Leonard Woolley (archeology), Joel Selig-man (law), Robert F. Hartley (business), Douglas R. Hofstader (computer science), Lincoln Barnett (physics), Thor Heyerdahl (oceanography), and Rachel Carson (ecol-ogy)—will give you a first-hand view of how problem-solving techniques are used in the liberal arts, political and social sciences, and sciences.

Recognizing the Existence and Nature of the Problem

The first step in solving a problem is recognizing that a problem exists. Often the magnitude of the problem is obvious from serious effects that the problem is causing. For Thor Heyerdahl, who originated the famous *Kon-Tiki* and *Ra* expeditions, the dramatic effects of midocean pollution were warning signals, as he describes in "How to Kill an Ocean":

> We treat the ocean as if we believed that it is not part of our own planet—as if the blue waters curved into space somewhere beyond the horizon where our pollutants would fall off the edge, as ships were believed to do before the days of Christopher Columbus. . . . What we consider too dangerous to be stored under technical control ashore we dump forever out of sight at sea, whether toxic chemicals or nuclear waste. Our only excuse is the still-surviving image of the ocean as a bottomless pit.

Rachel Carson, too, in her study of pesticides (*Silent Spring*), looked beyond the immediate short-term solutions to spotlight disastorous long-term effects most people never considered:

> The chemicals to which life is asked to make its adjustment are . . . the synthetic creations of man's inventive mind, brewed in his laboratories, and having no counterparts in nature.
>
> To adjust to these chemicals would require time on the scale that is nature's; it would require not merely the years of a man's life but the life of generations. And even this, were it by some miracle possible, would be futile, for the new chemicals come from our laboratories in an endless stream; almost five hundred annually find their way into actual use in the United States alone. The figure is staggering and its implications are not easily grasped—500 new chemicals to which the bodies of men and animals are required somehow to adapt each year, chemicals totally outside the limits of biologic experience.

Although DDT worked quickly and was inexpensive to use, Carson reveals in "The Obligation to Endure" that unforeseen side-effects included illness in those who used the pesticide, destruction of species of helpful insects, and the contamination of the entire food chain.

Defining the Problem

When the problem has been clearly perceived, it is often helpful to present it in a single, clearcut example. In "The Meaning of Ethics," Philip Wheelwright uses the following situation to define the nature of an ethical problem:

> Arthur Ames is a rising young district attorney engaged on his most important case. A prominent political boss has been murdered. Suspicion points at a certain exconvict, known to have borne the politician a grudge. Aided by the newspapers, which have reported the murder in such a way as to persuade the public of the suspect's guilt, Ames feels certain that he can secure a conviction on the circumstantial evidence in his possession. If he succeeds in sending the man to the chair he will become a strong candidate for governor at the next election.
>
> During the course of the trial, however, he accidentally stumbles on some fresh

evidence, known only to himself and capable of being destroyed if he chooses, which appears to establish the ex-convict's innocence. If this new evidence were to be introduced at the trial an acquittal would be practically certain. What ought the District Attorney to do? . . .

The way Wheelwright frames this example defines the actions that can be performed, the context in which the actions must take place, and the inner and outer constraints that make this example a good illustration of an ethical problem.

In all disciplines, definition of the problem must include a description of the initial state, the goal to be reached, the actions that can be performed, and the restrictions that limit what can and cannot be done. Recognizing constraints is crucial. Some limits can be clearly defined, whereas others are merely implied by the givens of the situation, and must be inferred if the problem is to be successfully attempted. Thus, Leon R. Kass, a bioethicist, looks beyond the immediate benefits that advances in biotechnology have brought in "The New Biology." He discovers a problem that will inevitably confront all those who must decide who should receive the benefits of this new technology:

> The introduction of any biomedical technology presents a new instance of an old problem—how to distribute scarce resources justly. We should assume that demand will usually exceed supply. Which people should receive a kidney transplant or an artificial heart? Who should get the benefits of genetic therapy or of brain stimulation? Is "first-come, first-served" the fairest principle? Or are certain people "more worthy," and if so, on what grounds?

Inevitably, the costly nature of these procedures will make choices necessary. How much is a human life worth and who should be given the power to decide whether, for example, a playwright or a NASA technician will receive a needed kidney transplant? Such constraints or limits on how problems can be solved make it necessary to identify which are the most important criteria—economic or moral, for instance— by which to make decisions.

Representing the Problem in Relevant Form

Often problems are so complex that it is useful to represent them in simplified form. Translating the problem into a sketch or other visual representation is valuable because it lets the problem solver perceive the overall shape of the problem without being overwhelmed by its details. Expert problem solvers find it useful to construct a mental picture of the problem or to put it on paper, whether in the form of a mathematical equation, displayed as a diagram, or represented conceptually in language. For example, in "Learning to Think Like a Lawyer," the case study reported by Joel Seligman is one that first-year law students at Harvard used to learn the principles of contract law:

> Like many cases in first-year law casebooks, the facts in *Hamer* v. *Sidway* seem slightly ridiculous. At a family gathering in 1869, an uncle promised his nephew that if he refrained from drinking, using tobacco, swearing, and playing cards or billiards for money until he turned twenty-one the uncle would pay him $5,000. The nephew agreed and six years later wrote to his uncle that he had lived up to his promise. "Dear Nephew," the uncle replied, "I have no doubt but you have, for which you shall have $5,000, as I promised you." But before the nephew collected

the money, the uncle died. The almost comic-opera question of the lawsuit was: Can the virtuous nephew collect the $5,000 from the recalcitrant executor of his uncle's estate? The case is included in virtually every modern American contracts casebook because it illustrates some of the most fundamental principles of contracts law.

Experts differ from inexperienced problem solvers in their ability to draw on a greater range of knowledge and recognize a variety of distinct problem "types" important in their particular disciplines. The better the problem solver, the greater the repertoire of "types," "models," "scripts" or "concepts" (as they have been variously termed) from which he or she can draw. Furthermore, experts use their greater understanding of problem "types" to run through mental "simulations" of different potential solutions.

An ingenious hypothetical scenario was designed by Alan Turing, as Douglas R. Hofstadter tells us in his essay, "The Turing Test." The central problem in the development of artificial intelligence still remains that of devising a way to know whether a machine can think. Turing's classic formulation of the problem placed a machine in a closed room to test whether people would be fooled into thinking it was a human being based on its responses, communicated by teletype into a nearby room:

> [The Turing Test] is played with three people: a man (A), a woman (B), and an interrogator (C), who may be of either sex. The interrogator stays in a room apart from the other two. The object of the game for the interrogator is to determine which of the other two is the man and which is the woman. He knows them by labels X and Y, and at the end of the game he says either "X is A and Y is B" or "X is B and Y is A." The interrogator is allowed to put questions to A and B thus:
>
> C: Will X please tell me the length of his or her hair?
>
> Now suppose X is actually A, then A must answer. It is A's object in the game to try to cause C to make the wrong identification. His answer might therefore be
>
> "My hair is shingled, and the longest strands are about nine inches long."
>
> In order that tones of voice may not help the interrogator the answers should be written, or better still, typewritten. The ideal arrangement is to have a teleprinter communicating between the two rooms. . . .
>
> We now ask the question, "What will happen when a machine takes the part of A in this game?" Will the interrogator decide wrongly as often when the game is played like this as he does when the game is played between a man and a woman? These questions replace our original, "Can machines think?"

Employing Search Techniques to Look for a Solution

Hofstadter's ingenious example makes it possible to evaluate different paths by which the solution can be reached. These paths reflect search techniques that problem solvers use to find their way through the maze of the problem. The most common search technique is the trial-and-error method, where new information gained along the way gradually leads to new, more productive approaches. However, in many situations it would be impractical to try every possible combination within the time available. Better methods of searching for a solution, called heuristics, include "working backwards," and means-ends analyses. "Working backwards" assumes that the goal has been reached and simply asks what is the step immediately before the goal, that would lead to it—then the step before that, and so on. Means-ends analysis is also a more systematic approach than trial-and-error; it asks what actions can be taken, step by step, to reduce the distance between the initial state of the problem and the goal.

Breaking the Problem into Easier-to-Solve Subproblems

Sometimes the most effective strategy consists of breaking the problem into subproblems that are easier to solve. A top–down approach to problem solving replaces a complex problem with several simpler, easier-to-handle individual problems. In his investigation of the background and causes that led to the demise of the 1958 Ford Edsel—"The Edsel: Marketing, Planning and Research Gone Awry"—Robert Hartley broke the overall problem into smaller individual problems pertaining to (1) market research, (2) sales techniques, (3) quality control, and (4) the state of the economy in 1958:

> #### What Went Wrong?
> So carefully planned. Such a major commitment of manpower and financial resources, supported by decades of experience in producing and marketing automobiles. How could this have happened? Where were the mistakes? Could they have been prevented? As with most problems there is no one simple answer. The marketplace is complex. Many things contributed to the demise of the Edsel: among them, poor judgment by people who should have known better (except that they were so confident because of the abundance of planning) and economic conditions outside the company's control. We will examine some of the factors that have been blamed for Edsel's failure. None of these alone would have been sufficient to destroy the Edsel; in combination, the car didn't have a chance.

By breaking the problem into parts, Hartley was able to identify the individual elements responsible for the Edsel's failure, including the switch from big cars to economy cars, underfinanced dealerships, poor workmanship, and the onset of a recession.

Using Analogies to Reformulate the Problem Through a Change in Perspective

Although restructuring may work with some types of problems, researchers frequently need to go outside the domain of the problem as it is presented. They do this in several ways, but one of the most useful and creative techniques requires researchers to consider analogous problems in order to transfer discoveries made in other contexts. Alexander Graham Bell's invention of the telephone was based on a direct analogy between the mechanical linkage of the membranes and bones of the human ear and the magnetic linkage in a receiver, between a metal diaphragm and an electromagnet. Using analogies to gain insights and to solve problems is common to all disciplines, from literature to physics.

So, too, in "Einstein's Relativity," Lincoln Barnett's account of Einstein's thought processes reveal, (1) if a problem cannot be solved by assuming there is a solution and then working backwards, or (2) by rearranging the elements of the problem in different ways, sometimes the problem can be reformulated through a change in perspective:

By further deduction from his principle of Relativity of mass, Einstein arrived at a conclusion of incalculable importance to the world. His train of reasoning ran somewhat as follows: since the mass of a moving body increases as its motion increases, and since motion is a form of energy (kinetic energy), then the increased mass of a moving body comes from its increased energy. In short, energy has mass! By a few comparatively simple mathematical steps, Einstein found the value of the equivalent mass m in any unit of energy E and expressed it by the equation $m = E/c^2$. Given this relation a high school freshman can take the remaining algebraic step necessary to write the most important and certainly the most famous equation in history: $E = mc^2$.

At one crucial point in his research, Einstein is said to have imagined what it would be like to ride on a beam of light travelling through the universe. From this new perspective, he felt intuitively much of what his later equations would bear out. This technique is called "analogous thinking" and has proved of immense value in problem solving where an experimenter has reached a dead-end. Einstein formed a personal analogy by putting himself directly in the problem situation, but there are other types of analogies as well, including direct, symbolic, and fantasy analogies.

Designing Experiments to Identify and Determine the Most Important Variable

Besides these search techniques, including trial-and-error, means-end analysis, working backwards, breaking problems into subproblems, and discovering useful analogies, another technique exists for efficiently allocating problem-solving resources. Experiments can be designed to isolate the single most important variable within a problem.

In the scores of notebooks that contain records of Edison's laboratory experiments, we can see that he directed his attention to working with one isolated variable in order to be able to correctly assess the contribution of that one factor to his overall experiment. The entry in his notebooks for October 22, 1879, the day when he invented the incandescent light bulb, demonstrates the success of this particular search technique. After hundreds of experiments, Edison took an ordinary piece of cotton thread and carbonized it into a filament to produce a high resistant element:

> October 22: We made some very interesting experiments on straight carbon from cotton threads, so. We took a piece of 6 cord thread, #24, which is about 13 thousandths of an inch thickness, and, after fastening to platinum (lead-in wire) we carbonized in a closed chamber. We put it in a bulb and *in vacuo*; it had resistance of 113 ohms start and afterward went up to 140 ohms. (Reprinted from Matthew Johnson's *Edison: A Biography* [McGraw-Hill, 1959], p. 55.

The use of experiments designed to isolate and measure a single important factor is common to researchers in a variety of disciplines. Social scientists and psychologists use control groups as the constant framework against which to measure results. The experimental group differs from the control group in one important feature that is manipulated. By holding all but one variable fixed, it becomes possible to control and measure what experimenters suspect to be the most important factor. Today, powerful computers make it possible to simulate the effects of different variables in a whole range of situations from automobile design to cell proliferation.

Although this overview of the problem-solving process has described various search techniques or heuristics, there is no set order that determines whether one strategy should be tried before another. Frequently, results will depend on using an entire range of search techniques, because the more alternatives generated the better the chances of finding a solution to the problem. Also, any search may uncover facts that require the problem to be redefined; this is typical of the process of scientific analysis whereby observation of facts leads to a hypothesis, which additional facts either support or refute.

Verifying the Solution

When at last a solution presents itself, it must meet all the tests specific to the problem and take into account all pertinent data uncovered during the search. For example, in "The Flood," Sir Leonard Woolley, the renowned archeologist who first excavated the city of Ur, describes the final phases of an archeological dig that shed new light on the nature of the flood described in Genesis.

> The level at which we started had been the ground surface about 2600 B.C. Almost immediately we came on the ruins of houses slightly older than that; we cleared them away and found more houses below them. In the first twenty feet we dug through no fewer than eight sets of houses, each of which had been built over the ruins of the age before. Then the house ruins stopped and we were digging through a solid mass of potsherds wherein, at different levels, were the kilns in which the pots had been fired. . . . And then came the clean, water-laid mud, eleven feet of it, mud which on analysis proved to be the silt brought down by the River Euphrates from its upper reaches hundreds of miles away; and under the silt, based on what really was virgin soil, the ruins of the houses that had been overwhelmed by the flood and buried deep beneath the mud carried by its waters.
>
> This was the evidence we needed; a flood of a magnitude unparalleled in any later phase of Mesopotamian history; and since, as the pottery proved, it had taken place some little while before the time of the Erech dynasty, this was the Flood of the Sumerian king-lists and that of the Sumerian legend and that of Genesis.

Woolley systematically moves (1) to analyze the nature of the problem, (2) to create a set of procedures to deal with it, (3) to allocate his resources for the most productive excavations, and (4) verifies his hypothesis in relationship to all pertinent data. Woolley's excavations can serve as a model of the progress that applied problem-solving techniques can yield.

Communicating the Solution to Others

New interpretations of known facts, solutions generated by the techniques of problem solving, and new theoretical models through which the disciplines themselves evolve must gain acceptance and be seen as valid by knowledgable colleagues. This chapter and the next, "Argumentation and Persuasion," will take up the question of how writers in the liberal arts, political and social sciences, and sciences rely on strategies of argument to convince specific audiences of the accuracy of their investigations and the validity of their conclusions.

LIBERAL ARTS

Philip Wheelwright

The Meaning of Ethics

Philip Wheelwright (1901–1970) was born in Elizabeth, New Jersey, and earned a Ph.D. from Princeton University in 1924. He was professor of philosophy at Princeton, Dartmouth, and the University of California at Riverside. His many influential studies of philosophy and ethics include A Critical Introduction To Ethics *(1935, 3rd ed., rev. 1959),* The Burning Fountain: A Study in the Language of Symbolism *(1954, rev. ed. 1968),* Philosophy As the Art of Living *(1956), first given as the Tully Cleon Knoles lectures,* Heraclitus *(1959), and* Valid Thinking *(1962). In "The Meaning of Ethics," from* A Critical Introduction to Ethics *(1959), Wheelwright discusses the essential elements involved in solving ethical problems.*

For you see, Callicles, our discussion is concerned with a matter in which even a man of slight intelligence must take the profoundest interest—namely, what course of life is best. —SOCRATES, in Plato's *Gorgias*

Man is the animal who can reflect. Like other animals, no doubt, he spends much of his time in merely reacting to the pressures and urgencies of his environment. But being a man he has moments also of conscious stock-taking, when he becomes aware not only of his world but of himself confronting his world, evaluating it, and making choices with regard to it. It is this ability to know himself and on the basis of self-knowledge to make evaluations and reflective choices that differentiates man from his subhuman cousins.

There are, as Aristotle has pointed out, two main ways in which man's power of reflection becomes active. They are called, in Aristotle's language, *theoretikos* and *praktikos* respectively; which is to say, thinking about what is actually the case and thinking about what had better be done. In English translation the words *contemplative* and *operative* probably come closest to Aristotle's intent. To think contemplatively is to ask oneself what *is;* to think operatively is to ask oneself what to *do.* These are the two modes of serious, one might even say of genuine thought—as distinguished from daydreams, emotional vaporizings, laryngeal chatter, and the repetition of clichés. To think seriously is to think either for the sake of knowing things as they are or for the sake of acting upon, and producing or helping to produce, things as they might be.

Although in practice the two types of thinking are much interrelated, it is operative thinking with which our present study is primarily concerned. Ethics, although it must be guided, limited, and qualified constantly by considerations of what is actually the case, is focused upon questions of what should be done. The converse, however, does not follow. Not all questions about what should be done are ethical questions. Much of our operative thinking is given to more immediate needs—to means whereby some given end can be achieved. A person who deliberates as to the most effective way of making money, or of passing a course, or of winning a battle, or of achieving popularity, is thinking operatively, but if that is as far as his planning goes it cannot be called ethical. Such deliberations about adapting means to an end would acquire an ethical character only if some thought were given to the nature and value of the end itself. Ethics cannot dispense with questions of means, but neither can it stop there.

Accordingly, ethics may be defined as that branch of philosophy which is the systematic study of reflective choice, of the standards of right and wrong by which it is to be guided, and of the goods toward which it may ultimately be directed. The relation between the parts of this definition, particularly between standards of right and wrong on the one hand and ultimately desirable goods on the other, will be an important part of the forthcoming study.

THE NATURE OF MORAL DELIBERATION

The soundest approach to ethical method is through reflection on our experience of moral situations which from time to time we have had occasion to face, or through an imagined confrontation of situations which others have faced and which we can thus make sympathetically real to ourselves. For instance:

> Arthur Ames is a rising young district attorney engaged on his most important case. A prominent political boss has been murdered. Suspicion points at a certain ex-convict, known to have borne the politician a grudge. Aided by the newspapers, which have reported the murder in such a way as to persuade the public of the suspect's guilt, Ames feels certain that he can secure a conviction on the circumstantial evidence in his possession. If he succeeds in sending the man to the chair he will become a strong candidate for governor at the next election.
>
> During the course of the trial, however, he accidentally stumbles on some fresh evidence, known only to himself and capable of being destroyed if he chooses, which appears to establish the ex-convict's innocence. If this new evidence were to be introduced at the trial an acquittal would be practically certain. What ought the District Attorney to do? Surrender the evidence to the defence, in order that, as a matter of fair play, the accused might be given every legitimate chance of establishing his innocence? But to do that will mean the loss of a case that has received enormous publicity; the District Attorney will lose the backing of the press; he will appear to have failed, and his political career may be blocked. In that event not only will he himself suffer disappointment, but his ample plans for bestowing comforts on his

family and for giving his children the benefits of a superior education may have to be curtailed. On the other hand, ought he to be instrumental in sending a man to the chair for a crime that in all probability he did not commit? And yet the ex-convict is a bad lot; even if innocent in the present case he has doubtless committed many other crimes in which he has escaped detection. Is a fellow like that worth the sacrifice of one's career? Still, there is no proof that he has ever committed a crime punishable by death. Until a man had been proved guilty he must be regarded, by a sound principle of American legal theory, as innocent. To conceal and destroy the new evidence, then, is not that tantamount to railroading an innocent man to the chair?

So District Attorney Ames reasons back and forth. He knows that it is a widespread custom for a district attorney to conceal evidence prejudicial to his side of a case. But is the custom, particularly when a human life is at stake, morally right? A district attorney is an agent of the government, and his chief aim in that capacity should be to present his accusations in such a way as to ensure for the accused not condemnation but justice. The question, then, cannot be answered by appealing simply to law or to legal practice. It is a moral one: *What is Arthur Ames' duty? What ought he to do?*

Benjamin Bates has a friend who lies in a hospital, slowly dying of a painful and incurable disease. Although there is no hope of recovery, the disease sometimes permits its victim to linger on for many months, in ever greater torment and with threatened loss of sanity. The dying man, apprised of the outcome and knowing that the hospital expenses are a severe drain on his family's limited financial resources, decides that death had better come at once. His physician, he knows, will not run the risk of providing him with the necessary drug. There is only his friend Bates to appeal to.

How shall Bates decide? Dare he be instrumental in hastening another's death? Has he a moral right to be accessory to the taking of a human life? Besides, suspicion would point his way, and his honorable motives would not avert a charge of murder. On the other hand, can he morally refuse to alleviate a friend's suffering and the financial distress of a family when the means of doing so are in his hands? And has he not an obligation to respect a friend's declared will in the matter? To acquiesce and to refuse seem both somehow in different ways wrong, yet one course or the other must be chosen. *What ought Bates to do? Which way does his duty lie?*

In the city occupied by Crampton College a strike is declared by the employees of all the public-transit lines. Their wages have not been increased to meet the rising cost of living, and the justice of their grievance is rather widely admitted by neutral observers. The strike ties up business and causes much general inconvenience; except for the people who have cars of their own or can afford taxi fare, there is no way of getting from one part of the city to another. Labor being at this period scarce, an appeal is made by the mayor to college students to serve the community by acting in their spare time as motormen and drivers. The appeal is backed by a promise of lucrative wages and by the college administration's agreement to cooperate by permitting necessary absences from classes.

What ought the students of Crampton College to do? If they act as strike-breakers, they aid in forcing the employees back to work on the corporation's own terms. Have they any right to interfere so drastically and one-sidedly in the lives and happiness of others? On the other hand, if they turn down the mayor's request the community will continue to suffer grave inconveniences until the fight is somehow settled. *What is the students' duty in the matter? What is the right course for them to follow?*

These three situations, although perhaps unusual in the severity of their challenge, offer examples of problems distinctively moral. When the act of moral deliberation implicit in each of them is fully carried out, certain characteristic phases can be discerned.

(i) *Examination and clarification of the alternatives.* What are the relevant possibilities of action in the situation confronting me? Am I clear about the nature of each? Have I clearly distinguished them from one another? And are they mutually exhaustive, or would a more attentive search reveal others? In the case of District Attorney Ames, for example, a third alternative might have been to make a private deal with the exconvict by which, in exchange for his acquittal, the District Attorney would receive the profits from some lucrative racket of which the ex-convict had control. No doubt to a reputable public servant this line of conduct would be too repugnant for consideration; it exemplifies, nevertheless, the everpresent logical possibility of going "between the horns"[1] of the original dilemma.

(ii) *Rational elaboration of consequences.* The next step is to think out the probable consequences of each of the alternatives in question. As this step involves predictions about a hypothetical future, the conclusions can have, at most, a high degree of probability, never certainty. The degree of probablity is heightened according as there is found some precedent in past experience for each of the proposed choices. Even if the present situation seems wholly new, analysis will always reveal *some* particulars for which analogies in past experience can be found or to which known laws of causal sequence are applicable. Such particulars will be dealt with partly by analogy (an act similar to the one now being deliberated about had on a previous occasion such and such consequences) and partly by the inductive-deductive method: appealing to general laws (deduction) which in turn have been built up as generalizations from observed particulars (induction). Mr. Ames, we may suppose, found the materials for this step in his professional knowledge of law and legal precedent, as well as in his more general knowledge of the policies of the press, the gullibility of its readers, and the high cost of domestic luxuries.

(iii) *Imaginative projection of the self into the predicted situation.* It is not enough to reason out the probable consequences of a choice. In a moral deliberation the chief interests involved are not scientific but human and practical. The only way to judge the comparative desirability of two possible futures is to live through them both in imagination. The third step, then, is to project oneself imaginatively into the future; i.e., establish a dramatic identification of the present self with that future self to which the now merely imagined experiences may become real. Few persons, unfortunately, are capable of an imaginative identification forceful enough to give the claims of the future self an even break. Present goods loom larger than future goods, and goods in the immediate future than goods that are remote. The trained ethical thinker must have a sound *temporal perspective,* the acquisition of which is to be sought by a frequent, orderly, and detailed exercise of the imagination with respect to not yet actual situations.

(iv) *Imaginative identification of the self with the points of view of those persons whom the proposed act will most seriously affect.* Whatever decision I make here and

---

[1] In essence, finding a viable third alternative.

now, if of any importance, is likely to have consequences, in varying degrees, for persons other than myself. An important part of a moral inquiry is to envisage the results of a proposed act as they will appear to those other persons affected by them. I must undertake, then, a dramatic identification of my own self with the selves of other persons. The possibility of doing this is evident from a consideration of how anyone's dramatic imagination works in the reading of a novel or the witnessing of a play. If the persons in the novel or play are dramatically convincing it is not because their characters and actions have been established by logical proof, but because they are presented so as to provoke in the reader an impulse to project himself into the world of the novel or play, to identify himself with this and that character in it, to share their feelings and moods, to get their slant on things.

In most persons, even very benevolent ones, the social consciousness works by fits and starts. To examine fairly the needs and claims of other selves is no less hard and is often harder than to perform a similar task with regard to one's future self. Accordingly the ethical thinker must develop *social perspective*—that balanced appreciation of others' needs and claims which is the basis of justice.

In this fourth, as in the third step, the imaginative projection is to be carried out for each of the alternatives, according as their consequences shall have been predicted by Step ii.

(v) *Estimation and comparison of the values involved.* Implicit in the third and fourth steps is a recognition that certain values both positive and negative are latent in each of the hypothetical situations to which moral choice may lead. The values must be made explicit in order that they may be justly compared, for it is as a result of their comparison that a choice is to be made. To make values explicit is to give them a relatively abstract formulation; they still, however, derive concrete significance from their imagined exemplifications. District Attorney Ames, for example, might have envisaged his dilemma as a choice between family happiness and worldly success on the one hand as against professional honor on the other. Each of these is undoubtedly good, that is to say a value, but the values cannot be reduced to a common denominator. Family happiness enters as a factor into Benjamin Bates' dilemma no less than into that of Arthur Ames, but it stands to be affected in a different way and therefore, in spite of the identical words by which our linguistic poverty forces us to describe it, it does not mean the same thing. Family happiness may mean any number of things; so may success, and honor—although these different meanings have, of course, an intelligible bond of unity. Arthur Ames' task is to compare not just any family happiness with any professional honor but the particular exemplifications of each that enter into his problem. The comparison is not a simple calculation but an imaginative deliberation, in which the abstract values that serve as the logical ground of the comparison are continuous with, and interactive with, the concrete particulars that serve as its starting-point.

(vi) *Decision.* Comparison of the alternative future situations and the values embodied in each must terminate in a decision. Which of the possible situations do I deem it better to bring into existence? There are no rules for the making of this decision. I must simply decide as wisely and as fairly and as relevantly to the total comparison as I can. Every moral decision is a risk, for the way in which a person decides is a factor in determining the kind of self he is going to become.

(vii) *Action.* The probable means of carrying out the decision have been established by Step ii. The wished-for object or situation is an end, certain specific means toward the fulfillment of which lie here and now within my power. These conditions supply the premises for an ethical syllogism. When a certain end, x, is recognized as the best of the available alternatives, and when the achievement of it is seen to be possible through a set of means a, b, c . . . which lie within my power, then whichever of the means a, b. c . . . is an action that can here and now be performed becomes at just this point my duty. If the deliberative process has been carried out forcefully and wisely it will have supplied a categorical answer to the question, What ought I to do?—even though the answer in some cases may be, Do nothing.

Naturally, not all experiences of moral deliberation and choice reveal these seven phases in a distinct, clear-cut way. Nor is the order here given always the actual order. Sometimes we may begin by deliberating about the relative merits of two ends, seeking the means simultaneously with this abstract inquiry, or after its completion. The foregoing analysis does, however, throw some light on the nature of a moral problem, and may be tested by applying it to the three cases described at the beginning of the chapter.

MEANING

1. How is Wheelwright's definition of ethics based on the human capacity to consider the "questions of what should be done"?
2. What kinds of ethical dilemmas do Wheelwright's three hypothetical situations illustrate?
3. Why does solving an ethical problem always involve an examination of alternatives and consideration of consequences?
4. What role does the imagination play in situations where two or more future outcomes are possible?
5. Why is the ability to create hypothetical situations so important in Stages iii and iv of the problem-solving process that Wheelwright describes?
6. How is Wheelwright's emphasis on a fair consideration of how any proposed action will affect others an essential component of ethical inquiry?

USING PROBLEM SOLVING TO CONVEY MEANING

1. How does Wheelwright organize his discussion to emphasize the strategies by which ethics identifies moral problems, explores possible courses of action, recognizes constraints, and evaluates possible solutions?
2. Discuss Wheelwright's use of logical connectives, subheadings, and transitions to guide the reader through each of the different stages in the process.
3. Evaluate the effectiveness of Wheelwright's use of examples to define different contexts in which moral problems can occur.

WRITING SUGGESTIONS

1. Choose one of Wheelwright's three hypothetical cases and using his outline of stages in the problem-solving process describe what you would do in the situation and why.

2. Identify, analyze, and discuss the ethical problems raised by any widely publicized business story that illustrates a conflict between profit making and social responsibility. For example, you might choose a product liability case (such as the one brought against the A. H. Robbins Co. for injury caused by the Dalkon Shield, or the case brought against Ford in 1980, charging that Ford was criminally reckless in selling Pintos with gas tanks that exploded in rear-end collisions) or an environmental case (such as the actions taken in 1979 against Metropolitan Edison Co., operators of the Three Mile Island nuclear power plant).

3. Read and analyze the ethical dilemmas inherent in any of the situations presented by any of the writers in this reader. For example, you might choose to explore the ethical problems in the works by Richard Selzer, Robert Falcon Scott, Tadeusz Borowski, Howard Carter, Jessica Mitford, Sidney Hook, John Darley and Bibb Latane, Marya Mannes, or Christopher Stone.

Leon R. Kass

The New Biology

Leon R. Kass was born in 1939 in Chicago, Illinois. After receiving his M.D. from the University of Chicago in 1962, Kass earned a Ph.D. in biochemistry and molecular biology from Harvard in 1967. Kass's intense concern over the ethical and social implications of advances in biomedical science and technology led him to become executive secretary of the Committee on the Life Sciences and Social Policy of the National Academy of Sciences (1970–1972). Kass served as senior research professor of bioethics at the Kennedy Institute, and associate professor of neurology and philosophy, Georgetown University, 1974–1976. Dr. Kass is Professor in the College and The Committee on Social Thought, The University of Chicago, and author of Toward a More Natural Science: Biology and Human Affairs *(1985). He is currently at work on a book exploring the relationship of metabolism to the dietary laws of the Old Testament. In "The New Biology" (1971), this eminent bioethicist identifies the issues and problems that will confront the next generation because of current advances in biomedical technology.*

Recent advances in biology and medicine suggest that we may be rapidly acquiring the power to modify and control the capacities and activities of men by direct intervention and manipulation of their bodies and minds. Certain means are already in use or at hand, others await the solution of relatively minor technical problems, while yet others, those offering perhaps the most precise kind of control, depend upon further basic research. Biologists who have considered these matters disagree on the question of how much how soon, but all agree that the power for "human engineering," to borrow from the jargon, is coming and that it will probably have profound social consequences.

These developments have been viewed both with enthusiasm and with alarm; they are only just beginning to receive serious attention. Several biologists have undertaken to inform the public about the technical possibilities, present and future. Practitioners of social science "futurology" are attempting to predict and describe the likely social consequences of and public responses to the new technologies. Lawyers and legislators are exploring institutional innovations for assessing new technologies. All of these activities are based upon the hope that we can harness the new technology of man for the betterment of mankind.

Yet this commendable aspiration points to another set of questions, which are, in my view, sorely neglected—questions that inquire into the meaning of phrases such as the "betterment of mankind." A *full* understanding of the new technology of man requires an exploration of ends, values, standards. What ends will or should the

586

new techniques serve? What values should guide society's adjustments? By what standards should the assessment agencies assess? Behind these questions lie others: what is a good man, what is a good life for man, what is a good community? This article is an attempt to provoke discussion of these neglected and important questions.

While these questions about ends and ultimate ends are never unimportant or irrelevant, they have rarely been more important or more relevant. That this is so can be seen once we recognize that we are dealing here with a group of technologies that are in a decisive respect unique: the object upon which they operate is man himself. The technologies of energy or food production, of communication, of manufacture, and of motion greatly alter the implements available to man and the conditions in which he uses them. In contrast, the biomedical technology works to change the user himself. To be sure, the printing press, the automobile, the television, and the jet airplane have greatly altered the conditions under which and the way in which men live; but men as biological beings have remained largely unchanged. They have been, and remain, able to accept or reject, to use and abuse these technologies; they choose, whether wisely or foolishly, the ends to which these technologies are means. Biomedical technology may make it possible to change the inherent capacity for choice itself. Indeed, both those who welcome and those who fear the advent of "human engineering" ground their hopes and fears in the same prospect: *that man can for the first time re-create himself.*

Engineering the engineer seems to differ in kind from engineering his engine. Some have argued, however, that biomedical engineering does not differ qualitatively from toilet training, education, and moral teachings—all of which are forms of so-called "social engineering," which has man as its object, and is used by one generation to mold the next. In reply, it must at least be said that the techniques which have hitherto been employed are feeble and inefficient when compared to those on the horizon. This quantitative difference rests in part on a qualitative difference in the means of intervention. The traditional influences operate by speech or by symbolic deeds. They pay tribute to man as the animal who lives by speech and who understands the meanings of actions. Also, their effects are, in general, reversible, or at least subject to attempts at reversal. Each person has greater or lesser power to accept or reject or abandon them. In contrast, biomedical engineering circumvents the human context of speech and meaning, bypasses choice, and goes directly to work to modify the human material itself. Moreover, the changes wrought may be irreversible.

In addition, there is an important practical reason for considering the biomedical technology apart from other technologies. The advances we shall examine are fruits of a large, humane project dedicated to the conquest of disease and the relief of human suffering. The biologist and physician, regardless of their private motives, are seen, with justification, to be the well-wishers and benefactors of mankind. Thus, in a time in which technological advance is more carefully scrutinized and increasingly criticized, biomedical developments are still viewed by most people as benefits largely without qualification. The price we pay for these developments is thus more likely to go unrecognized. For this reason, I shall consider only the dangers and costs of biomedical advance. As the benefits are well known, there is no need to dwell upon them here. My discussion is deliberately partial.

I begin with a survey of the pertinent technologies. Next, I will consider some of the basic ethical and social problems in the use of these technologies. Then, I will briefly raise some fundamental questions to which these problems point. Finally, I shall offer some very general reflections on what is to be done.

The Biomedical Technologies

The biomedical technologies can be usefully organized into three groups, according to their major purpose: (i) control of death and life, (ii) control of human potentialities, (iii) control of human achievement. The corresponding technologies are (i) medicine, especially the arts of prolonging life and of controlling reproduction, (ii) genetic engineering, and (iii) neurological and psychological manipulation. I shall briefly summarize each group of techniques.

(1) *Control of death and life.* Previous medical triumphs have greatly increased average life expectancy. Yet other developments, such as organ transplantation or replacement and research into aging, hold forth the promise of increasing not just the average, but also the maximum life expectancy. Indeed, medicine seems to be sharpening its tools to do battle with death itself, as if death were just one more disease.

More immediately and concretely available techniques of prolonging life—respirators, cardiac pacemakers, artificial kidneys—are already in the lists against death. Ironically, the success of these devices in forestalling death has introduced confusion in determining that death has, in fact, occurred. The traditional signs of life—heartbeat and respiration—can now be maintained entirely by machines. Some physicians are now busily trying to devise so-called "new definitions of death," while others maintain that the technical advances show that death is not a concrete event at all, but rather a gradual process, like twilight, incapable of precise temporal localization.

The real challenge to death will come from research into aging and senescence, a field just entering puberty. Recent studies suggest that aging is a genetically controlled process, distinct from disease, but one that can be manipulated and altered by diet or drugs. Extrapolating from animal studies, some scientists have suggested that a decrease in the rate of aging might also be achieved simply by effecting a very small decrease in human body temperature. According to some estimates, by the year 2000 it may be technically possible to add from 20 to 40 useful years to the period of middle life.

Medicine's success in extending life is already a major cause of excessive population growth: death control points to birth control. Although we are already technically competent, new techniques for lowering fertility and chemical agents for inducing abortion will greatly enhance our powers over conception and gestation. Problems of definition have been raised here as well. The need to determine when individuals acquire enforceable legal rights gives society an interest in the definition of human life and of the time when it begins. These matters are too familiar to need elaboration.

Technologies to conquer infertility proceed alongside those to promote it. The first successful laboratory fertilization of human egg by human sperm was reported in 1969.[1] In 1970, British scientists learned how to grow human embryos in the laboratory up to at least the blastocyst stage (that is, to the age of 1 week).[2] We may soon hear about the next stage, the successful reimplantation of such an embryo into a woman previously infertile because of oviduct disease. The development of an artificial placenta, now under investigation, will make possible full laboratory control of fertilization and gestation. In addition, sophisticated biochemical and cytological techniques of monitoring the "quality" of the fetus have been and are being developed

---

[1] R. G. Edwards, B. D. Bavister, P. C. Steptoe, *Nature* 221, 632 (1969).
[2] R. G. Edwards, P. C. Steptoe, J. M. Purdy, *ibid.* 227, 1307 (1970).

and used. These developments not only give us more power over the generation of human life, but make it possible to manipulate and to modify the quality of the human material.

(2) *Control of human potentialities.* Genetic engineering, when fully developed, will wield two powers not shared by ordinary medical practice. Medicine treats existing individuals and seeks to correct deviations from a norm of health. Genetic engineering, in contrast, will be able to make changes that can be transmitted to succeeding generations and will be able to create new capacities, and hence to establish new norms of health and fitness.

Nevertheless, one of the major interests in genetic manipulation is strictly medical: to develop treatments for individuals with inherited diseases. Genetic disease is prevalent and increasing, thanks partly to medical advances that enable those affected to survive and perpetuate their mutant genes. The hope is that normal copies of the appropriate gene, obtained biologically or synthesized chemically, can be introduced into defective individuals to correct their deficiencies. This *therapeutic* use of genetic technology appears to be far in the future. Moreover, there is some doubt that it will ever be practical, since the same end could be more easily achieved by transplanting cells or organs that could compensate for the missing or defective gene product.

Far less remote are technologies that could serve *eugenic* ends. Their development has been endorsed by those concerned about a general deterioration of the human gene pool and by others who believe that even an undeteriorated human gene pool needs upgrading. Artificial insemination with selected donors, the eugenic proposal of Herman Muller,[3] has been possible for several years because of the perfection of methods for long-term storage of human spermatozoa. The successful maturation of human oocytes in the laboratory and their subsequent fertilization now make it possible to select donors of ova as well. But a far more suitable technique for eugenic purposes will soon be upon us—namely, nuclear transplantation, or cloning. Bypassing the lottery of sexual recombination, nuclear transplantation permits the asexual reproduction or copying of an already developed individual. The nucleus of a mature but unfertilized egg is replaced by a nucleus obtained from a specialized cell of an adult organism or embryo (for example, a cell from the intestines or the skin). The egg with its transplanted nucleus develops as if it had been fertilized and, barring complications, will give rise to a normal adult organism. Since almost all the hereditary material (DNA) of a cell is contained within its nucleus, the renucleated egg and the individual into which it develops are genetically identical to the adult organism that was the source of the donor nucleus. Cloning could be used to produce sets of unlimited numbers of genetically identical individuals, each set derived from a single parent. Cloning has been successful in amphibians and is now being tried in mice; its extension to man merely requires the solution of certain technical problems.

Production of man-animal chimeras by the introduction of selected nonhuman material into developing human embryos is also expected. Fusion of human and nonhuman cells in tissue culture has already been achieved.

Other, less direct means for influencing the gene pool are already available, thanks to our increasing ability to identify and diagnose genetic diseases. Genetic counselors can now detect biochemically and cytologically a variety of severe genetic defects (for example, Mongolism, Tay-Sachs disease) while the fetus is still in utero. Since treatments are at present largely unavailable, diagnosis is often followed by abortion of the affected

---

[3] H. J. Miller, *Science* 134, 643 (1961).

fetus. In the future, more sensitive tests will also permit the detection of heterozygote carriers, the unaffected individuals who carry but a single dose of a given deleterious gene. The eradication of a given genetic disease might then be attempted by aborting all such carriers. In fact, it was recently suggested that the fairly common disease cystic fibrosis could be completely eliminated over the next 40 years by screening all pregnancies and aborting the 17,000,000 unaffected fetuses that will carry a single gene for this disease. Such zealots need to be reminded of the consequences should each geneticist be allowed an equal assault on his favorite genetic disorder, given that each human being is a carrier for some four to eight such recessive, lethal genetic diseases.

(3) *Control of human achievement.* Although human achievement depends at least in part upon genetic endowment, heredity determines only the material upon which experience and education impose the form. The limits of many capacities and powers of an individual are indeed genetically determined, but the nurturing and perfection of these capacities depend upon other influences. Neurological and psychological manipulation hold forth the promise of controlling the development of human capacities, particularly those long considered most distinctively human: speech, thought, choice, emotion, memory, and imagination.

These techniques are now in a rather primitive state because we understand so little about the brain and mind. Nevertheless, we have already seen the use of electrical stimulation of the human brain to produce sensations of intense pleasure and to control rage, the use of brain surgery (for example, frontal lobotomy) for the relief of severe anxiety, and the use of aversive conditioning with electric shock to treat sexual perversion. Operant-conditioning techniques are widely used, apparently with success, in schools and mental hospitals. The use of so-called consciousness-expanding and hallucinogenic drugs is widespread, to say nothing of tranquilizers and stimulants. We are promised drugs to modify memory, intelligence, libido, and aggressiveness.

The following passages from a recent book by Yale neurophysiologist José Delgado—a book instructively entitled *Physical Control of the Mind: Toward a Psychocivilized Society*—should serve to make this discussion more concrete. In the early 1950's, it was discovered that, with electrodes placed in certain discrete regions of their brains, animals would repeatedly and indefatigably press levers to stimulate their own brains, with obvious resultant enjoyment. Even starving animals preferred stimulating these so-called pleasure centers to eating. Delgado comments on the electrical stimulation of a similar center in a human subject.[4]

> The patient reported a pleasant tingling sensation in the left side of her body "from my face down to the bottom of my legs." She started giggling and making funny comments, stating that she enjoyed the sensation "very much." Repetition of these stimulations made the patient more communicative and flirtatious, and she ended by openly expressing her desire to marry the therapist.

And one further quotation from Delgado.[5]

> Leaving wires inside of a thinking brain may appear unpleasant or dangerous, but actually the many patients who have undergone this experience have not been concerned about the fact of being wired, nor have they felt any discomfort due to the presence

---

[4] J. M. R. Delgado, *Physical Control of the Mind: Toward a Psychocivilized Society* (Harper & Row, New York, 1969), p. 185.

[5] *Ibid.*, p. 88.

of conductors in their heads. Some women have shown their feminine adaptability to circumstances by wearing attractive hats or wigs to conceal their electrical headgear, and many people have been able to enjoy a normal life as outpatients, returning to the clinic periodically for examination and stimulation. In a few cases in which contacts were located in pleasurable areas, patients have had the opportunity to stimulate their own brains by pressing the button of a portable instrument, and this procedure is reported to have therapeutic benefits.

It bears repeating that the sciences of neurophysiology and psychopharmacology are in their infancy. The techniques that are now available are crude, imprecise, weak, and unpredictable, compared to those that may flow from a more mature neurobiology.

BASIC ETHICAL AND SOCIAL PROBLEMS IN THE USE OF BIOMEDICAL TECHNOLOGY

After this cursory review of the powers now and soon to be at our disposal, I turn to the questions concerning the use of these powers. First, we must recognize that questions of use of science and technology are always moral and political decisions to develop or to use biomedical technology—and decisions *not* to do so—inevitably contain judgments about value. This is true even if the values guiding those decisions are not articulated or made clear, as indeed they often are not. Secondly, the value judgments cannot be derived from biomedical science. This is true even if scientists themselves make the decisions.

These important points are often overlooked for at least three reasons.

1. They are obscured by those who like to speak of "the control of nature by science." It is men who control, not that abstraction "science." Science may provide the means, but men choose the ends; the choice of ends comes from beyond science.
2. Introduction of new technologies often appears to be the result of no decision whatsoever, or of the culmination of decisions too small or unconscious to be recognized as such. What can be done is done. However, someone is deciding on the basis of some notions of desirability, no matter how self-serving or altruistic.
3. Desires to gain or keep money and power no doubt influence much of what happens, but these desires can also be formulated as reasons and then discussed and debated.

Insofar as our society has tried to deliberate about questions of use, how has it done so? Pragmatists that we are, we prefer a utilitarian calculus: we weigh "benefits" against "risks," and we weigh them for both the individual and "society." We often ignore the fact that the very definitions of "a benefit" and "a risk" are themselves based upon judgments about value. In the biomedical areas just reviewed, the benefits are considered to be self-evident: prolongation of life, control of fertility and of population size, treatment and prevention of genetic disease, the reduction of anxiety and aggressiveness, and the enhancement of memory, intelligence, and pleasure. The assessment of risk is, in general, simply pragmatic—will the technique work effectively and reliably, how much will it cost, will it do detectable bodily harm, and who will complain if we proceed with development? As these questions are familiar and congenial, there is no need to belabor them.

The very pragmatism that makes us sensitive to considerations of economic cost often blinds us to the larger social costs exacted by biomedical advances. For one thing, we seem to be unaware that we may not be able to maximize all the benefits, that several of the goals we are promoting conflict with each other. On the one hand, we seek to control population growth by lowering fertility; on the other hand, we develop techniques to enable every infertile woman to bear a child. On the one hand, we try to extend the lives of individuals with genetic disease; on the other, we wish to eliminate deleterious genes from the human population. I am not urging that we resolve these conflicts in favor of one side or the other, but simply that we recognize that such conflicts exist. Once we do, we are more likely to appreciate that most "progress" is heavily paid for in terms not generally included in the simple utilitarian calculus.

To become sensitive to the larger costs of biomedical progress, we must attend to several serious ethical and social questions. I will briefly discuss three of them: (i) questions of distributive justice, (ii) questions of the use and abuse of power, and (iii) questions of self-degradation and dehumanization.

DISTRIBUTIVE JUSTICE

The introduction of any biomedical technology presents a new instance of an old problem—how to distribute scarce resources justly. We should assume that demand will usually exceed supply. Which people should receive a kidney transplant or an artificial heart? Who should get the benefits of genetic therapy or of brain stimulation? Is "first-come, first-served" the fairest principle? Or are certain people "more worthy," and if so, on what grounds?

It is unlikely that we will arrive at answers to these questions in the form of deliberate decisions. More likely, the problem of distribution will continue to be decided ad hoc and locally. If so, the consequence will probably be a sharp increase in the already far too great inequality of medical care. The extreme case will be longevity, which will probably be, at first, obtainable only at great expense. Who is likely to be able to buy it? Do conscience and prudence permit us to enlarge the gap between rich and poor, especially with respect to something as fundamental as life itself?

Questions of distributive justice also arise in the earlier decisions to acquire new knowledge and to develop new techniques. Personnel and facilities for medical research and treatment are scarce resources. Is the development of a new technology the best use of the limited resources, given current circumstances? How should we balance efforts aimed at prevention against those aimed at cure, or either of these against efforts to redesign the species? How should we balance the delivery of available levels of care against further basic research? More fundamentally, how should we balance efforts in biology and medicine against efforts to eliminate poverty, pollution, urban decay, discrimination, and poor education? This last question about distribution is perhaps the most profound. We should reflect upon the social consequences of seducing many of our brightest young people to spend their lives locating the biochemical defects in rare genetic diseases, while our more serious problems go begging. The current squeeze on money for research provides us with an opportunity to rethink and reorder our priorities.

Problems of distributive justice are frequently mentioned and discussed, but they are hard to resolve in a rational manner. We find them especially difficult because of the enormous range of conflicting values and interests that characterizes our pluralistic society. We cannot agree—unfortunately, we often do not even try to agree—on standards for just distribution. Rather, decisions tend to be made largely out of a clash of competing interests. Thus, regrettably, the question of how to distribute justly often gets reduced to who shall decide how to distribute. The question about justice has led us to the question about power.

USE AND ABUSE OF POWER

We have difficulty recognizing the problems of the exercise of power in the biomedical enterprise because of our delight with the wondrous fruits it has yielded. This is ironic because the notion of power is absolutely central to the modern conception of science. The ancients conceived of science as the *understanding* of nature, pursued for its own sake. We moderns view science as power, as *control* over nature; the conquest of nature "for the relief of man's estate" was the charge issued by Francis Bacon, one of the leading architects of the modern scientific project.[6]

Another source of difficulty is our fondness for speaking of the abstraction "Man." I suspect that we prefer to speak figuratively about "Man's power over Nature" because it obscures an unpleasant reality about human affairs. It is in fact particular men who wield power, not Man. What we really mean by "Man's power over Nature" is a power exercised by some men over other men, with a knowledge of nature as their instrument. Please note that I am not yet speaking about the problem of the misuse or abuse of power. The point is rather that the power which grows is unavoidably the power of only some men, and that the number of powerful men decreases as power increases.

Specific problems of abuse and misuse of specific powers must not, however, be overlooked. Some have voiced the fear that the technologies of genetic engineering and behavior control, though developed for good purposes, will be put to evil uses. These fears are perhaps somewhat exaggerated, if only because biomedical technologies would add very little to our highly developed arsenal for mischief, destruction, and stultification. Nevertheless, any proposal for large-scale human engineering should make us wary. Consider a program of positive eugenics based upon the widespread practice of asexual reproduction. Who shall decide what constitutes a superior individual worthy of replication? Who shall decide which individuals may or must reproduce, and by which method? These are questions easily answered only for a tyrannical regime.

Concern about the use of power is equally necessary in the selection of means for desirable or agreed-upon ends. Consider the desired end of limiting population growth. An effective program of fertility control is likely to be coercive. Who should decide the choice of means? Will the program penalize "conscientious objectors"?

Serious problems arise simply from obtaining and disseminating information, as in the mass screening programs now being proposed for detection of genetic disease. For what kinds of disorders is compulsory screening justified? Who shall have access to the data obtained, and for what purposes? To whom does information about a person's genotype belong? In ordinary medical practice, the patient's privacy is protected

---

[6] F. Bacon, *The Advancement of Learning, Book I,* H. G. Dick, Ed. (New York: Random House, 1955), p. 193.

by the doctor's adherence to the principle of confidentiality. What will protect his privacy under conditions of mass screening?

More than privacy is at stake if screening is undertaken to detect psychological or behavioral abnormalities. A recent proposal, tendered and supported high in government, called for the psychological testing of all 6-year-olds to detect future criminals and misfits. The proposal was rejected; current tests lack the requisite predictive powers. But will such a proposal be rejected if reliable tests become available? What if certain genetic disorders, diagnosable in childhood, can be shown to correlate with subsequent antisocial behavior? For what degree of correlation and for what kinds of behavior can mandatory screening be justified? What use should be made of the data? Might not the dissemination of the information itself undermine the individual's chance for a worthy life and contribute to his so-called antisocial tendencies?

Consider the seemingly harmless effort to redefine clinical death. If the need for organs for transplantation is the stimulus for redefining death, might not this concern influence the definition at the expense of the dying? One physician, in fact, refers in writing to the revised criteria for declaring a patient dead as a "new definition of heart donor eligibility."[7]

Problems of abuse of power arise even in the acquisition of basic knowledge. The securing of a voluntary and informed consent is an abiding problem in the use of human subjects in experimentation. Gross coercion and deception are now rarely a problem; the pressures are generally subtle, often related to an intrinsic power imbalance in favor of the experimentalist.

A special problem arises in experiments on or manipulations of the unborn. Here it is impossible to obtain the consent of the human subject. If the purpose of the intervention is therapeutic—to correct a known genetic abnormality, for example—consent can reasonably be implied. But can anyone ethically consent to nontherapeutic interventions in which parents or scientists work their wills or their eugenic visions on the child-to-be? Would not such manipulation represent in itself an abuse of power, independent of consequences?

There are many clinical situations which already permit, if not invite, the manipulative or arbitrary use of powers provided by biomedical technology: obtaining organs for transplantation, refusing to let a person die with dignity, giving genetic counselling to a frightened couple, recommending eugenic sterilization for a mental retardate, ordering electric shock for a homosexual. In each situation, there is an opportunity to violate the will of the patient or subject. Such opportunities have generally existed in medical practice, but the dangers are becoming increasingly serious. With the growing complexity of the technologies, the technician gains in authority, since he alone can understand what he is doing. The patient's lack of knowledge makes him deferential and often inhibits him from speaking up when he feels threatened. Physicians *are* sometimes troubled by their increasing power, yet they feel they cannot avoid its exercise. "Reluctantly," one commented to me, "we shall have to play God." With what guidance and to what ends I shall consider later. For the moment, I merely ask: "By whose authority?"

While these questions about power are pertinent and important, they are in one sense misleading. They imply an inherent conflict of purpose between physician and patient, between scientist and citizen. The discussion conjures up images of master and slave, of oppressor and oppressed. Yet it must be remembered that conflict

---

[7] D. D. Rutstein, *Daedalus* (Spring 1969), p. 523.

of purpose is largely absent, especially with regard to general goals. To be sure, the purposes of medical scientists are not always the same as those of the subjects experimented on. Nevertheless, basic sponsors and partisans of biomedical technology are precisely those upon whom the technology will operate. The will of the scientist and physician is happily married to (rather, is the offspring of) the desire of all of us for better health, longer life, and peace of mind.

Most future biomedical technologies will probably be welcomed, as have those of the past. Their use will require little or no coercion. Some developments, such as pills to improve memory, control mood, or induce pleasure, are likely to need no promotion. Thus, even if we should escape from the dangers of coercive manipulation, we shall still face large problems posed by the voluntary use of biomedical technology, problems to which I now turn.

VOLUNTARY SELF-DEGRADATION AND DEHUMANIZATION

Modern opinion is sensitive to problems of restriction of freedom and abuse of power. Indeed, many hold that a man can be injured only by violating his will. But this view is much too narrow. It fails to recognize the great dangers we shall face in the use of biomedical technology, dangers that stem from an excess of freedom, from the uninhibited exercises of will. In my view, our greatest problem will increasingly be one of voluntary self-degradation, or willing dehumanization.

Certain desired and perfected medical technologies have already had some dehumanizing consequences. Improved methods of resuscitation have made possible heroic efforts to "save" the severely ill and injured. Yet these efforts are sometimes only partly successful; they may succeed in salvaging individuals with severe brain damage, capable of only a less-than-human, vegetating existence. Such patients, increasingly found in the intensive care units of university hospitals, have been denied a death with dignity. Families are forced to suffer seeing their loved ones so reduced, and are made to bear the burdens of a protracted death watch.

Even the ordinary methods of treating disease and prolonging life have impoverished the context in which men die. Fewer and fewer peeople die in the familiar surroundings of home or in the company of family and friends. At that time of life when there is perhaps the greatest need for human warmth and comfort, the dying patient is kept company by cardiac pacemakers and defibrillators, respirators, aspirators, oxygenators, catheters, and his intravenous drip.

But the loneliness is not confined to the dying patients in the hospital bed. Consider the increasing number of old people who are still alive, thanks to medical progress. As a group, the elderly are the most alienated members of our society. Not yet ready for the world of the dead, not deemed fit for the world of the living, they are shunted aside. More and more of them spend the extra years medicine has given them in "homes for senior citizens," in chronic hospitals, in nursing homes—waiting for the end. We have learned how to increase their years, but we have not learned how to help them enjoy their days. And yet, we bravely and relentlessly push back the frontiers against death.

Paradoxically, even the young and vigorous may be suffering because of medicine's success in removing death from their personal experience. Those born since penicillin represent the first generation ever to grow up without the experience or fear of probable unexpected death at an early age. They look around and see that virtually all of their friends are alive. A thoughtful physician, Eric Cassell, has remarked on this in "Death and the Physician":[8]

> While the gift of time must surely be marked as a great blessing, the *perception* of time, as stretching out endlessly before us, is somewhat threatening. Many of us function best under deadlines, and tend to procrastinate when time limits are not set. . . . Thus, this unquestioned boon, the extension of life, and the removal of the threat of premature death, carries with it an unexpected anxiety: the anxiety of an unlimited future.
>
> In the young, the sense of limitless time has apparently imparted not a feeling of limitless opportunity, but increased stress and anxiety, in addition to the anxiety which results from other modern freedoms: personal mobility, a wide range of occupational choice, and independence from the limitations of class and familial patterns of work. . . . A certain aimlessness (often ringed around with great social consciousness) characterizes discussions about their own aspirations. The future is endless, and their inner demands seem minimal. Although it may appear uncharitable to say so, they seem to be acting in a way best described as "childish"—particularly in their lack of a time sense. They behave as though there were no tomorrow or as though the time limits imposed by the biological facts of life had become so vague for them as to be nonexistent.

Consider next the coming power over reproduction and genotype. We endorse the project that will enable us to control numbers and to treat individuals with genetic disease. But our desires outrun these defensible goals. Many would welcome the chance to become parents without the inconvenience of pregnancy; others would wish to know in advance the characteristics of their offspring (sex, height, eye color, intelligence); still others would wish to design these characteristics to suit their tastes. Some scientists have called for the use of the new technologies to assure the "quality" of all new babies.[9] As one obstetrician put it: "The business of obstetrics is to produce *optimum* babies." But the price to be paid for the "optimum baby" is the transfer of procreation from the home to the laboratory and its coincident transformation into manufacture. Increasing control over the product is purchased by the increasing depersonalization of the process. The complete depersonalization of procreation (possible with the development of an artificial placenta) shall be, in itself, seriously dehumanizing, no matter how optimum the product. It should not be forgotten that human procreation not only issues new human beings, but is itself a human activity.

Procreation is not simply an activity of the rational will. It is a more complete human activity precisely because it engages us bodily and spiritually, as well as rationally. Is there perhaps some wisdom in that mystery of nature which joins the pleasure of sex, the communication of love, and the desire for children in the very activity by which we continue the chain of human existence? Is not biological parenthood a built-in "mechanism," selected because it fosters and supports in parents an adequate concern for and commitment to their children? Would not the laboratory production of human beings no longer be *human* procreation? Could it keep human parenthood human?

The dehumanizing consequences of programmed reproduction extend beyond the mere acts and processes of life-giving. Transfer of procreation to the laboratory will

[8] E. J. Cassell, *Commentary* (June 1969), p. 73.
[9] B. Glass, *Science* 171, 23 (1971).

no doubt weaken what is presently for many people the best remaining justification and support for the existence of marriage and the family. Sex is now comfortably at home outside of marriage; child-rearing is progressively being given over to the state, the schools, the mass media, and the child-care centers. Some have argued that the family, long the nursery of humanity, has outlived its usefulness. To be sure, laboratory and governmental alternatives might be designed for procreation and child-rearing, but at what cost?

This is not the place to conduct a full evaluation of the biological family. Nevertheless, some of its important virtues are, nowadays, too often overlooked. The family is rapidly becoming the only institution in an increasingly impersonal world where each person is loved not for what he does or makes, but simply because he is. The family is also the institution where most of us, both as children and as parents, acquire a sense of continuity with the past and a sense of commitment to the future. Without the family, we would have little incentive to take an interest in anything after our own deaths. These observations suggest that the elimination of the family would weaken ties to past and future, and would throw us, even more than we are now, to the mercy of an impersonal, lonely present.

Neurobiology and psychobiology probe most directly into the distinctively human. The technological fruit of these sciences is likely to be both more tempting than Eve's apple and more "catastrophic" in its result. One need only consider contemporary drug use to see what people are willing to risk or sacrifice for novel experiences, heightened perceptions, or just "kicks." The possibility of drug-induced, instant, and effortless gratification will be welcomed. Recall the possibilities of voluntary self-stimulation of the brain to reduce anxiety, to heighten pleasure, or to create visual and auditory sensations unavailable through the peripheral sense organs. Once these techniques are perfected and safe, is there much doubt that they will be desired, demanded, and used?

What ends will these techniques serve? Most likely, only the most elemental, those most tied to the bodily pleasures. What will happen to thought, to love, to friendship, to art, to judgment, to public-spiritedness in a society with a perfected technology of pleasure? What kinds of creatures will we become if we obtain our pleasure by drug or electrical stimulation without the usual kind of human efforts and frustrations? What kind of society will we have?

We need only consult Aldous Huxley's prophetic novel *Brave New World* for a likely answer to these questions. There we encounter a society dedicated to homogeneity and stability, administered by means of instant gratifications and peopled by creatures of human shape but of stunted humanity. They consume, fornicate, take "soma," and operate the machinery that makes it all possible. They do not read, write, think, love, or govern themselves. Creativity and curiosity, reason and passion, exist only in a rudimentary and multilated form. In short, they are not men at all.

True, our techniques, like theirs, may in fact enable us to treat schizophrenia, to alleviate anxiety, to curb aggressiveness. We, like they, may indeed be able to save mankind from itself, but probably only at the cost of its humanness. In the end, the price of relieving man's estate might well be the abolition of man.

There are, of course, many other routes leading to the abolition of man. There are many other and better known causes of dehumanization. Disease, starvation, mental retardation, slavery, and brutality—to name just a few—have long prevented many, if not most, people from living a fully human life. We should work to reduce and eventually to eliminate these evils. But the existence of these evils should not prevent us from appreciating that the use of the technology of man, uninformed by wisdom concerning proper human ends, and untempered by an appropriate humility and awe, can unwittingly render us all irreversibly less than human. For, unlike the man reduced by disease or slavery, the people dehumanized á la *Brave New World* are not miserable, do not know that they are dehumanized, and, what is worse, would not care if they knew. They are, indeed, happy slaves, with a slavish happiness.

Some Fundamental Questions

The practical problems of distributing scarce resources, of curbing the abuses of power, and of preventing voluntary dehumanization point beyond themselves to some large, enduring, and most difficult questions: the nature of justice and the good community, the nature of man and the good for man. My appreciation of the profundity of these questions and my own ignorance before them makes me hesitant to say any more about them. Nevertheless, previous failures to find a shortcut around them have led me to believe that these questions must be faced if we are to have any hope of understanding where biology is taking us. Therefore, I shall try to show in outline how I think some of the larger questions arise from my discussion of dehumanization and self-degradation.

My remarks on dehumanization can hardly fail to arouse argument. It might be said, correctly, that to speak about dehumanization presupposes a concept of "the distinctively human." It might also be said, correctly, that to speak about wisdom concerning proper human ends presupposes that such ends do in fact exist and that they may be more or less accessible to human understanding, or at least to rational inquiry. It is true that neither presupposition is at home in modern thought.

The notion of the "distinctively human" has been seriously challenged by modern scientists. Darwinists hold that man is, at least in origin, tied to the subhuman; his seeming distinctiveness is an illusion or, at most, not very important. Biochemists and molecular biologists extend the challenge by blurring the distinction between the living and the nonliving. The laws of physics and chemistry are found to be valid and are held to be sufficient for explaining biological systems. Man is a collection of molecules, an accident on the stage of evolution, endowed by chance with the power to change himself, but only along determined lines.

Psychoanalysts have also debunked the "distinctly human." The essence of man is seen to be located in those drives he shares with other animals—pursuit of pleasure and avoidance of pain. The so-called "higher functions" are understood to be servants of the more elementary, the more base. Any distinctiveness of "dignity" that man has consists of his superior capacity for gratifying his animal needs.

The idea of "human good" fares no better. In the social sciences, historicists and existentialists have helped drive this question underground. The former hold all notions of human good to be culturally and historically bound, and hence mutable. The latter hold that values are subjective: each man makes his own, and ethics becomes simply the cataloging of personal tastes.

Such appear to be the prevailing opinions. Yet there is nothing novel about reductionism, hedonism, and relativism; these are doctrines with which Socrates contended. What is new is that these doctrines seem to be vindicated by scientific advance. Not only do the scientific notions of nature and of man flower into verifiable predictions, but they yield marvelous fruit. The technological triumphs are held to validate their scientific foundations. Here, perhaps, is the most pernicious result of technological progress—more dehumanizing than any actual manipulation of technique, present or future. We are witnessing the erosion, perhaps the final erosion of the idea of man as something splendid or divine, and its replacement with a view that sees man, no less than nature, as simply more raw material for manipulation and homogenization. Hence, our peculiar moral crisis. We are in turbulent seas without a landmark precisely because we adhere more and more to a view of nature and of man which both gives us enormous power and, at the same time, denies all possibility of standards to guide its use. Though well-equipped, we know not who we are nor where we are going. We are left to the accidents of our hasty, biased, and ephemeral judgments.

Let us not fail to note a painful irony: our conquest of nature has made us the slaves of blind chance. We triumph over nature's unpredictabilities only to subject ourselves to the still greater unpredictability of our capricious wills and our fickle opinions. That we have a method is no proof against our madness. Thus, engineering the engineer as well as the engine, we race our train we know not where.

While the disastrous consequences of ethical nihilism are insufficient to refute it, they invite and make urgent a reinvestigation of the ancient and enduring questions of what is proper life for a human being, what is a good community, and how are they achieved. We must not be deterred from these questions simply because the best minds in human history have failed to settle them. Should we not rather be encouraged by the fact that they considered them to be the most important questions?

As I have hinted before, our ethical dilemma is caused by the victory of modern natural science with its non-teleological view of man. We ought therefore to reexamine with great care the modern notions of nature and of man, which undermine those earlier notions that provide a basis for ethics. If we consult our common experience, we are likely to discover some grounds for believing that the questions about man and human good are far from closed. Our common experience suggests many difficulties for the modern "scientific view of man." For example, this view fails to account for the concern for justice and freedom that appears to be characteristic of all human societies. It also fails to account for or to explain the fact that men have speech and not merely voice, that men can choose and act and not merely move or react. It fails to explain why men engage in moral discourse, or, for that matter, why they speak at all. Finally, the "scientific view of man" cannot account for scientific inquiry itself, for why men seek to know. Might there not be something the matter with a knowledge of man that does not explain or take account of his most distinctive activities, aspirations, and concerns?

MEANING

1. What important point does Kass make about the degree to which new developments in biotechnology now make it possible for the first time for man to change himself?
2. Why do recent capabilities developed by biomedical technology necessitate a discussion of moral and ethical problems?
3. How is biotechnology qualitatively different from ordinary forms of "social engineering"?
4. Why have new biomedical developments made new definitions of death, birth, and motherhood necessary?

5. What specific ethical concerns does Kass mention in areas where biomedical progress may entail costs to society?

Using Problem Solving to Convey Meaning

1. Which examples presented by Kass dramatize the necessity of identifying what criteria should be used in deciding who should receive the benefits of the new technology?
2. What parts of Kass' discussion made you aware that new technologies have created a problem that had never existed before?
3. Evaluate Kass' success in defining the boundaries of what is essentially a new discipline—bioethics.
4. How does Kass organize his article to distinguish between the key areas of the "control of life and death" and the "control of human potentialities"?

Writing Suggestions

1. Discuss the social or religious implications of any one of the biomedical technologies that Kass explores.
2. Apply the criteria of solving ethical problems outlined by Philip Wheelwright (see page 579) to any one specific situation discussed by Kass (e.g., the possibilities of eradicating genetic diseases).

POLITICAL AND SOCIAL SCIENCES

Sir Leonard Woolley

The Flood

Sir Leonard Woolley (1880–1960) was born in London, England. He was educated at New College, Oxford, and was an assistant to Sir Arthur Evans at the Ashmolean Museum in 1905. After a period of field work in the Near East, Woolley was appointed director of the British Museum expedition to Carchemish in 1912. He was accompanied there by T. E. Lawrence (better known as "Lawrence of Arabia"), with whom he coauthored The Wilderness of Zin *(1915), an account of their discoveries. After directing a joint expedition of the British Museum and the Museum of the University of Pennsylvania, Woolley, in 1926, discovered and excavated the royal tombs at Ur, whose treasures invited comparisons with the discoveries by Schliemann (at Mycenae) and those of Carter and Lord Carnarvon (of Tutankhamen's Tomb). Woolley's excavations at Ur revealed the existence and importance of Sumerian culture in Mesopotamia. His remarkably clear and readable accounts of his archeological discoveries were published in* Ur of the Chaldees *(1929),* The Sumerians *(1930), and* Excavations at Ur: A Record of Twelve Years' Work *(1954). In "The Flood," from* Myth or Legend *(1968), Woolley describes the ingenious method he used to solve the age-old problem of proving the authenticity of the Biblical flood.*

There can be few stories more familiar to us than that of the Flood. The word "antediluvian" has passed into common speech, and Noah's Ark is still one of the favourite toys of the children's nursery.

The Book of Genesis tells us how the wickedness of man was such that God repented Him that He had made man upon the earth, and decided to destroy all flesh; but Noah, being the one righteous man, found grace in the eyes of the Lord. So Noah was bidden by God to build an ark, and in due time he and all his family went in, with all the beasts and the fowls of the air, going in two by two; and the doors of the ark were shut and the rain was upon the earth for forty days and forty nights, and the floods prevailed exceedingly and the earth was covered, and all flesh that moved upon the earth died, and Noah only remained alive and they that were with him in the ark. And then the floods abated. Noah sent out a raven and a dove, and at last the dove brought him back an olive leaf, proof that the dry land had appeared. And they all went forth out of the ark, and Noah built an altar and offered sacrifice, and the Lord smelt a sweet savour and promised that never again would He smite everything living, as He had done; and God set His bow in the clouds as a token of the covenant that there should not any more be a flood to destroy the earth.

For many centuries, indeed until only a few generations ago, the story of Noah was accepted as an historical fact; it was part of the Bible, it was the inspired Word of God, and therefore every word of it must be true. To deny the story was to deny the Christian faith.

Then two things happened. On the one hand scholars, examining the Hebrew text of Genesis, discovered that it was a composite narrative. There had been two versions of the Flood story which differed in certain small respects, and these two had been skillfully combined into one by the Jewish scribes four or five hundred years before the time of Christ, when they edited the sacred books of their people and gave to them the form which they have to-day. That discovery shook the faith of many old-fashioned believers, or was indignantly denied by them; they said that it was an attack on the Divine Word. Really, of course, it was nothing of the sort. Genesis is an historical book, and the writer of history does not weave the matter out of his imagination; he consults older authorities of every sort and quotes them as freely and as often as may be. The older the authorities are, and the more his account embodies theirs, the more reason we have to trust what he writes; if it be insisted that his writings are divinely inspired, the answer is that 'inspiration' consists not in dispensing with original sources but in making the right use of them. The alarm felt by the orthodox when confronted with the discoveries of scholarship was a false alarm.

The second shock came when from the ruins of the ancient cities of Mesopotamia archaeologists unearthed clay tablets on which was written another version of the Flood story—the Sumerian version. According to that, mankind had grown wicked and the gods in council decided to destroy the human race which they had made. But one of the gods happened to be a good friend of one mortal man, so he went down and warned him of what was to happen and counselled him to build an ark. And the man did so; and he took on board all his family, and his domestic animals, and shut the door, and the rain fell and the floods rose and covered all the earth. At last the storms abated and the ark ran aground, and the man sent out a dove and a swallow and a raven, and finally came forth from the ark and built an altar and did sacrifice, and the gods (who had had no food since the Flood started and were terribly hungry) "came round the altar like flies," and the rainbow is set in the clouds as a warrant that never again will the gods destroy all men by water.

It is clear that this is the same story as we have in Genesis. But the Sumerian account was actually written before the time of Moses (whom some people had, without reason, thought to be the author of Genesis), and not only that, but before the time of Abraham. Therefore the Flood story was not by origin a Hebrew story at all but had been taken over by the Hebrews from the idolatrous folk of Babylonia; it was a pagan legend, so why should we for a moment suppose that it was true? All sorts of attempts were made to show that the Bible story was independent, or was the older of the two, but all the attempts were in vain, and to some it seemed as if the battle for the Old Testament had been lost.

Once more, it was a false alarm. Nobody had ever supposed that the Flood had affected only the Hebrew people; other people had suffered by it, and a disaster of such magnitude was bound to be remembered in their traditions; in so far as the Sumerian legend was closer in time to the event, it might be said to strengthen rather than to weaken the case for the Biblical version. But it could well be asked, "Why should we believe a Sumerian legend which is, on the face of it, a fantastic piece of pagan mythology?" It is perfectly true that the Sumerian Flood story is a religious poem. It reflects the religious beliefs of a pagan people just as the biblical story reflects the religious beliefs of the Hebrews; and we cannot accept the Sumerian religion as true. Also, it is a poem, and everybody knows what poets are! Shakespeare certainly did:

> The poet's eye, in a fine frenzy rolling,
> Doth glance from heaven to earth, from earth to heaven,
> And, as imagination bodies forth
> The forms of things unknown, the poet's pen
> Turns them to shapes, and gives to airy nothing
> A local habitation and a name.

But the legend does not stand alone. Sober Sumerian historians wrote down a sort of skeleton of their country's history in the form of a list of its kings (like our "William I, 1066," and all that); starting at the very beginning there is a series of perhaps fabulous rulers, and, they say, "Then came the Flood. And after the Flood kingship again descended from heaven"; and they speak of a dynasty of kings who established themselves in the city of Kish, and next of a dynasty whose capital was Erech. Here, at least, we are upon historic ground, for archaeological excavation in modern times has recovered the material civilisation of those ancient days when Erech was indeed the chief city of Mesopotamia. The old historians were sure that not long before these days the course of their country's history had been interrupted by a great flood. If they were right, it does not, of course, mean that the Flood legend is correct in all its details, but it does at least give it a basis of fact.

In the year 1929, when we had been digging at Ur the famous "royal graves" with their extraordinary treasures, which can be dated to something like 2800 B.C., I determined to test still lower levels so as to get an idea of what might be found by digging yet deeper. We sank a small shaft below the stratum of soil in which the graves lay, and went down through the mixed rubbish that is characteristic of an old inhabited site—a mixture of decomposed mud-brick, ashes and broken pottery, very much like what we had been finding higher up. Then suddenly it all stopped: there were no more potsherds, no ashes, only clean, water-laid mud, and the workman in the shaft told me that he had reached virgin soil; there was nothing more to be found, and he had better go elsewhere.

I got down and looked at the evidence and agreed with him; but then I took my levels and found that "virgin soil" was not nearly as deep down as I expected. That upset a favourite theory of mine, and I hate having my theories upset except on the very best of evidence, so I told him to get back and go on digging. Most unwillingly he did so, turning up nothing but clean soil that contained no sign of human activity;

he worked down through eight feet of it and then, suddenly, flint implements appeared and sherds of painted pottery which, we were fairly sure, was the earliest pottery made in southern Mesopotamia. I was convinced of what it meant, but I wanted to see whether others would arrive at the same conclusion. I brought up two of my staff and, after pointing out the facts, asked for their conclusions. They did not know what to say. My wife came along and looked and was asked the same question, and she turned away, remarking quite casually, "Well, of course it's the Flood."

So it was. But one could scarcely argue for the Deluge on the strength of a shaft a yard square; so the next season I marked out on the low ground where the graves had been a rectangle some seventy-five feet by sixty, and there dug a huge pit which went down, in the end, for sixty-four feet. The level at which we started had been the ground surface about 2600 B.C. Almost immediately we came on the ruins of houses slightly older than that; we cleared them away and found more houses below them. In the first twenty feet we dug through no fewer than eight sets of houses, each of which had been built over the ruins of the age before. Then the house ruins stopped and we were digging through a solid mass of potsherds wherein, at different levels, were the kilns in which the pots had been fired; the sherds represented those pots which went wrong in the firing and, having no commercial value, had been smashed by the potter and the bits left lying until they were so heaped up that the kilns were buried and new kilns had to be built. It was a vase factory which was running for so long a time that by the stratified sherds we could trace the course of history: near the bottom came the wares in use when Erech was the royal city, and at the very bottom was the painted ware of the land's earliest immigrants. And then came the clean, water-laid mud, eleven feet of it, mud which on analysis proved to be the silt brought down by the River Euphrates from its upper reaches hundreds of miles away; and under the silt, based on what really was virgin soil, the ruins of the houses that had been overwhelmed by the flood and buried deep beneath the mud carried by its waters.

This was the evidence we needed; a flood of magnitude unparalleled in any later phase of Mesopotamian history; and since, as the pottery proved, it had taken place some little while before the time of the Erech dynasty, this was the Flood of the Sumerian king-lists and that of the Sumerian legend and that of Genesis.

We have proved that the Flood really happened; but that does not mean that all the details of the Flood legend are true—we did not find Noah and we did not find his ark! But take a few details. The Sumerian version says (this is not mentioned in Genesis) that antediluvian man lived in huts made of reeds; under the Flood deposit we found the wreckage of reed huts. Noah built his ark of light wood and bitumen. Just on top of the Flood deposit we found a big lump of bitumen, bearing the imprint of the basket in which it had been carried, just as I have myself seen the crude bitumen from the pits of Hit on the middle Euphrates being put in baskets for export downstream. I reckoned that to throw up an eleven-foot pile of silt against the mound on which the primitive town of Ur stood the water would have to be at least twenty-five feet deep; the account in Genesis says that the depth of the flood water was fifteen cubits, which is roughly twenty-six feet. "Twenty-six feet?" you may say; "that's not much of a flood!" Lower Mesopotamia is so flat and low-lying that a flood having that depth at Ur would spread over an area 300 miles long and 100 miles wide.

Noah's Flood was not a universal deluge; it was a vast flood in the valley of the Rivers Tigris and Euphrates. It drowned the whole of the habitable land between the eastern and the western deserts; for the people who lived there that was all the world. It wiped out the villages and exterminated their inhabitants, and although some of the towns set upon mounds survived, it was but a scanty and dispirited remnant of the nation that watched the waters recede at last. No wonder that they saw in this disaster the gods' punishment of a sinful generation and described it as such in a great religious poem; and if, as may well have been the case, one household managed to escape by boat from the drowned lowlands, the head of that house would naturally be made the hero of the saga.

MEANING

1. What discoveries in the fields of Biblical scholarship and Sumerian archeology brought to the fore the question of the literal truth of the flood story?
2. What problem confronted Woolley when he was well into the archeological excavations in 1929 at the ancient city of Ur?
3. Why was the find of the rubble of a pottery kiln so significant?
4. What did testing of the silt disclose and why were the results so amazing?
5. Why was the discovery of bitumen another piece of confirming evidence?
6. How does Woolley interpret and integrate the available evidence his excavation disclosed to conclude that the Biblical flood was not a universal deluge, as previously believed?

USING PROBLEM SOLVING TO CONVEY MEANING

1. How does Woolley organize his problem-solving procedure to first analyze the nature of the problem, then allocate his resources during the archeological excavations, and lastly, verify his hypothesis by including all pertinent data?
2. What use does Woolley make of information gleaned from fables and legends to provide a context for his investigation?
3. What kinds of information does Woolley provide that allows his audience to understand what archeologists actually do?

WRITING SUGGESTIONS

1. Discuss the story of Noah and the flood (Genesis, chapters 6–8) in relationship to Woolley's archeological findings.
2. As a research project, investigate Heinrich Schliemann's search for the ancient city of Troy and the methods of problem solving he used in proving that the events described in *The Iliad* actually happened. A useful compilation is provided by Leo Devel, *Memoirs of Heinrich Schliemann: a documentary portrait drawn from his autobiographical writings, letters, and excavation reports* (1978).
3. How would specialists in a variety of disciplines other than archeology respond

to the discovery of an original Stradivarius violin? How would each of their responses illustrate the assumptions, goals, purposes, and methodologies of the different disciplines they represent? For example, how might any of the following respond: a musician, an antique dealer, a cultural anthropologist, a cabinetmaker, a physicist? What distinctive kinds of information could each of these specialists provide about the violin?

4. What would experts in a variety of disciplines, including archeology, conclude in the next century about our society based on their analysis of any of today's mass-produced objects?

Joel Seligman

Learning to Think Like a Lawyer

Joel Seligman, born in 1950, received a B.A. from the University of California at Los Angeles in 1971 and graduated from Harvard Law School in 1974. He is currently professor of law at the University of Michigan, Ann Arbor. With Ralph Nader and Mark Green, Seligman coauthored Taming the Giant Corpora- tions *(1976). He has also written* The High Citadel: The Influence of Harvard Law School *(1978),* The Transformation of Wall Street *(1982), and* The S.E.C. and the Future of Finance *(1985). Seligman is currently preparing a comprehensive seven-volume study of the Securities and Exchange Commission. "Learning to Think Like a Lawyer," from* The High Citadel, *describes the Socratic method used by Professor Byse in the first-year contract law class at Harvard Law School.*

When a client or an acquaintance admires a lawyer, the lawyer is often praised for his or her reasoning ability. "Lawyers," it is said, "cut through to the heart of the matter . . . They ask for the right questions . . . They know how to solve problems."

One of the most proficient teachers of legal reasoning at Harvard Law School is Clark Byse. Like many of his colleagues, Byse relies on the distinctive interrogative approach popularly known as the Socratic method to question students on their understanding of actual law cases.

Before class, seated in his book-lined Langdell Hall office, Byse often seems to possess a languid air. Slightly hunched behind his massive wooden desk, the sixty-six-year-old professor regards visitors with doleful eyes. "Well, Mr. ___," he begins answers to questions almost shyly, warming to his subject as he speaks. A similar change comes over Byse as the time for a class session draws near. Visibly his posture stiffens as he reviews his notes. "I can't see you now," he says firmly. "I've got a class in ten minutes." Slipping on an impeccably tailored dark suitjacket, Byse impa- tiently flicks lint off it. By the time he arrives in his cavernous Langdell North classroom, there is a buoyancy to his manner. He chats whimsically with a number of students near the lectern, his eyes playful now, his manner exuberant. A firm hand reaches out and grasps a student's shoulder, an unmistakable gesture of friendship or support. Moments later, Byse grins and mischievously pats a second student on the cheek. But this is prelude. Forcefully he plants his book and seating chart on the standing lectern.

At precisely 10:10 A.M., virtually every student is in an assigned seat, notebook out, casebook open, pen poised. Clark Byse at this point is unmistakably *Professor*

Byse: mercurial; authoritarian; his jests biting now; his energy like that of a coiled spring.

Above the professor's Langdell Hall office desk is a gift from an earlier class, a papier-mâché rabbit popping out of a papier-mâché hat. The figure has a single-word caption: "Why?" In Professor Byse's classroom this word is seldom spoken; it is usually roared. "Why, Mr. ____?" or "Why, Miss ____?" Byse starts hundreds of questions during a school year. Sometimes the vehemence of Byse's "Why" causes him to rise up on his toes like a carnival-goer trying to gain leverage before slamming the weighted hammer down and ringing the far-off bell. "Why" is the concept that trails the students home after class; "Why" surfaces in their minds as they read cases alone; and as examinations approach, "Why" nags at their sleep. In Professor Byse's control, "Why" is the essence of legal reasoning, the force that pushes a class from comprehending law as particular rules applied to particular facts to a glimpse of an entire social order. "Why" is skepticism, "Why" is argument, "Why" is doubt, and ultimately "Why" is the basis of courtroom logic: comparison and generalization.

"Miss ____," Byse begins this session, "what was the promise in *Hamer* versus *Sidway?*"

Like many cases in first-year law casebooks, the facts in *Hamer* v. *Sidway* seem slightly ridiculous. At a family gathering in 1869, an uncle promised his nephew that if he refrained from drinking, using tobacco, swearing, and playing cards or billiards for money until he turned twenty-one the uncle would pay him $5,000. The nephew agreed and six years later wrote to his uncle that he had lived up to his promise. "Dear Nephew," the uncle replied, "I have no doubt but you have, for which you shall have $5,000, as I promised you." But before the nephew collected the money, the uncle died. The almost comic-opera question of the lawsuit was: Can the virtuous nephew collect the $5,000 from the recalcitrant executor of his uncle's estate? The case is included in virtually every modern American contracts casebook because it illustrates some of the most fundamental principles of contracts law.

Miss ____ answers Professor Byse's question, "An uncle promised his nephew $5,000 if he wouldn't commit any vices until he was twenty-one."

"Well Miss ____," Byse retorts, "the imagination runs rampant. State the facts clearly. Why editorialize?"

She does so.

"How old was the nephew?"

"Hmmm . . ."

"Anybody know?"

A second student shouts, "Fifteen or sixteen."

"Was the contract enforced?"

"Yes, the court did."

It comes out softly this time. "Why?"

The student doesn't answer.

Byse offers, "Because it was supported by consideration." Miss ____ starts to nod as Byse ridicules his own answer, "Or do we say there was consideration because it was enforced?" A brief pause. Like a referee in a sporting event. Byse construes part of his task to keep the game alive yet limited to a specific field. After thirty-three years of teaching law, he is a master at this. He tosses out a fresh question. "What was the argument of the defendant?"

Miss ____ answers. "There was no benefit to the uncle."

"What did the plaintiff argue was the benefit to the uncle?"

Miss ____ sees the trap. "He didn't," and correctly circumvents it. "The plaintiff argued that the consideration was the detriment he suffered by not drinking, smoking, and so on."

Now the game has picked up. Byse plays with the student's answer. "How could it be a detriment not to indulge in bad habits? That is no detriment, is it?"

The student stumbles. "Some people will think it is," and another student, startled, loudly exclaims, "Huh!"

Byse slaps that down. "Is someone here a moose hunter?" Then quickly reiterates the question, "How could this be a detriment?"

"Because the plaintiff had a legal right to drink, smoke, swear, and play cards."

Byse holds up the answer so everyone in the class will precisely understand it. "Recall the editor's note on the meanings of the word 'right.' *Plaintiff was legally privileged to drink and smoke. That is a right.*" He briefly pauses for dramatic effect. "All right then," Byse continues, reading from a page he has just picked up from the lectern, "I promise you $5,000 if you do not (a) commit murder, (b) commit suicide, (c) get arrested, (d) drive faster than the legal speed limit, (e) bother me, or (f) refuse to accept a gift of $5,000 from me. Consideration in all of these cases?"

A new student answers, "None except bothering. Other cases involve illegal activities or gross disparity."

Shrilly in Professor Byse's mind a cacophonic alarm goes off. Red flags wave. His body visibly stiffens. "Gross disparity," he roars with painful disdain. "What is gross disparity?" The student isn't expected to respond. With six thunderous words of formal legal logic, Clark Byse has eviscerated two words of frothly layperson fudge talk. Somewhere in the back of the room the phrase "gross disparity" collapses to the floor. The two words have been annihilated. They are absolutely dead. Briskly Byse presses on, "Miss ____ just said a detriment was a sufficient consideration. Now, murder is wrong—there is no privilege to murder, therefore no detriment. The same with suicide. But not get arrested. What about that?"

Ten years ago, a student would have argued at this point that there was a legal privilege to commit civil disobedience if one was willing to accept the consequences. References might have been made to Martin Luther King, Jr., and Gandhi, or draft resisters. There would have been a heated student debate; a useful release from the tension of trying to phrase every argument in the language of formal legal doctrines.

But this class occurred in January 1977, and no one was quite sure why Byse had asked the question.

A student responded dully, "There is no legal right to be arrested."

Byse's forehead furrowed slightly, "Anybody disagree?"

Another student answers, "No law makes it illegal to get arrested?"

The class is thoroughly confused; someone hisses.

"Is it consideration?"

"I am not sure."

Byse struggles with the hypothetical question and a related one for ten minutes until yet another student stammers to silence. He then starts the reasoning process over again. "We have an eminent killer shooting people. He says to the uncle: 'Give me $5,000 and I won't shoot people.' Better yet, $50,000—make it worth his while. Is there consideration?"

Mr. ____ answers, "There is no legal right, but look at the legal benefit . . ."

"The killer wasn't going to shoot the uncle."

"But other people . . ."

Byse cuts in sharply, "You can't do this by magic. You can't justify everything by a vague notion of public policy. We are trying to develop an organized society, one in which there will be a general rule that the full power of the state will only be invoked to enforce certain contracts . . ." And for a full forty-eight minutes the colloquy concerning a trivial one-and-one-half-page 1891 case goes on, with Byse rapidly shifting hypothetical variations on the case, prodding students to vocalize alternative legal arguments and debate directly with each other, and, at one point, chewing out the class for not seeing obvious relationships between his hypothetical questions and earlier cases the class had discussed. Only in the very last few minutes of the class, when Byse had moved on to another case, does a student vocalize what the doctrine of legal consideration is really about.

"The courts don't want to turn gifts into enforceable promises."

"Aha!" exclaimed Byse. "The courts do not enforce gift promises. Gifts are one category of promises different from others. But why?" And this "Why," though not a roar, felt like one. For weeks the class had been absorbing the notion that contracts was the category of law that made a market economy possible. By allowing persons to enforce their private bargains with each other, theoretically the most efficient allocation of resources will be realized. But to make this possible, proclaimed a prominently situated case holding in the students' text, "the law will not enter into an inquiry as to the adequacy of the consideration." Now the rug was being pulled out from under the absoluteness of this principle. Plainly the law sometimes will inquire.

"Why?" Byse asks. "What are the functions this doctrine performs?"

With astonishing coolness, a student raises his hand and answers, "Cautionary and evidentiary. It is easier to prove a contract if there is evidence of it. Parties are less likely to enter contracts lightly if each must give up something."

For Byse, the answer is almost too good to be true. To highlight its importance, he writes on the blackboard, "Form and Substance." Pointing to the word "Form," he writes, "Form—evidence of a contract." Pointing to the word "Substance," he explains, "Substantive Rule: Parties are discouraged from making rash enforceable promises. You should see page 118 where Von Mehren summarizes these ideas for you." He continues for a few minutes relating this point to the next case, but the dénouement has been reached. For Byse, a successful class hour has been taught.

MEANING

1. In what way do Byse's tactics illustrate what is called the "Socratic method"?
2. What does Byse want his class to realize about the importance of the idea of "consideration"?
3. Why are gifts one category of promises that the court does not enforce?
4. Why is the method of "case study" so useful in teaching legal concepts?

Using Problem Solving to Convey Meaning

1. How does Seligman's essay make the point that legal reasoning is a method that must be learned?
2. In what ways are Byse's tactics of turning questions around to challenge his students to think especially effective?
3. How does Seligman show the distinction between the exact terminology of the law and the lay person's concept of "legalese"?
4. How does Byse use hypothetical situations to demonstrate the truth or falsity of propositions?
5. Evaluate the effectiveness of Byse's presentation in terms of his ability to relate an outdated case to issues of social justice that are important today.

Writing Suggestions

1. How does Earl Warren's decision (see the "Argumentation and Persuasion" chapter, page 695) demonstrate the methods of "legal reasoning," as Byse endeavors to teach it in his contracts law class?
2. Compare the teaching methods used in this article to those of an instructor you have had.
3. If you have ever seen the television program *The Paper Chase,* discuss the extent to which Seligman's Professor Byse uses methods similar to those used by Professor Kingsfield in his contracts law class.

ROBERT F. HARTLEY

The Edsel: Marketing, Planning and Research Gone Awry

Robert F. Hartley was born in 1927 in Beaver Falls, Pennsylvania. After receiving an M.B.A. in 1962, Hartley also earned a Ph.D. from the University of Minnesota in 1967. Since 1972, he has been professor of marketing at Cleveland State University, Ohio. Hartley's research emphasizes the need for businesses to be responsive to the needs of the consumers and society at large. His publications in marketing theory and practice include Marketing Management and Social Change *(1972),* Retailing: Challenge and Opportunity *(1975),* Marketing Fundamentals for Responsive Management *(1976), and* Marketing Mistakes *(1976). In "The Edsel: Marketing, Planning and Research Gone Awry," from* Marketing Mistakes, *Hartley analyzes errors in marketing that doomed Ford's entry into the medium-price field with the 1958 model, which cost the company two hundred million dollars.*

Perhaps the classic marketing mistake of the modern business era, the one most widely publicized and commented upon, is the Edsel. Interestingly enough, the same firm, the Ford Motor Company, also was responsible for another monumental marketing blunder, this one before the era of modern business with its emphasis on marketing.

AN EARLIER BLUNDER

Henry Ford introduced the Model T in 1909. It sold initially for 850 dollars and was available only in one color, black. The Model T quickly became a way of life. Ford conducted mass production on a scale never before seen, introducing and perfecting the moving assembly line so that the work moved to the worker. Ford sold half the new cars made in this country up to 1926 and had more than double the output of his nearest competitor, General Motors. Prices by 1926 had fallen to as low as 263 dollars. For seventeen years the Model T had neither model changes nor significant improvements, except for a lowering selling price as more production economies were realized.

But by the mid-1920s, millions of Americans wanted something fancier, and General Motors brought out Chevrolet featuring color, comfort, styling, safety, modernity—and most of all—a showy appearance. And the Model T was doomed.

In desperation, Henry Ford had the Model T painted attractive colors, fenders were rounded, the body lengthened and lowered, the windshield slanted. But still sales declined. Finally in May 1927, Ford stopped production altogether for nearly

612

a year while 60,000 workers in Detroit were laid off, and a new car, the Model A, slowly took shape with a changeover estimated to have cost Ford 100 million dollars. While the Model A was successful, the lead lost to General Motors was never to be regained.

In the 1920s a failure in market assessment was devastating. To some extent the failure of the Edsel was also due to bad market assessment, but this time not for want of trying.

THE EDSEL

The Edsel, Ford's entry into the medium-price field, was introduced for the 1958 model year in early September 1957. This gave it a jump on competitors who traditionally introduce new models in October and November of the previous year. Ernest Breech, the board chairman of the Ford Motor Company set the 1958 goal for the Edsel Division at 3.3 to 3.5 percent of the total auto market. In a six-million car year, this would be about 200,000 cars. However, the company executives considered this a very conservative estimate and expected to do much better. Ten years of planning, preparation and research had gone into the Edsel. The need for such a car in the Ford product line appeared conclusive. Approximately 50 million dollars was spent for advertising and promotion in the preintroduction and introduction of the car. And in late summer of 1957 the success of the massive venture seemed assured. The company did not expect to recover the 250 million dollars of development costs until the third year, but the car was expected to be operationally profitable in 1958.

Rationale

The rationale for the Edsel seemed inescapable. For some years there had been a growing trend toward medium-price cars. Such cars as Pontiac, Oldsmobile, Buick, Dodge, DeSoto, and Mercury were accounting for one-third of all car sales by the middle 1950s, whereas they had formerly contributed only one-fifth.

Economic projections confirmed this shift in emphasis from low-priced cars and suggested a continuing demand for higher-priced models in the decade of the 1960s. Disposable personal income (expressed in 1956 dollars) had increased from about 138 billion dollars in 1939 to 287 billion dollars in 1956, with forecasts of 400 billion dollars by 1965. Furthermore, the percent of this income spent for automobiles had increased from around 3.5 percent in 1939 to 5.5 or 6.0 percent in the middle 1950s. Clearly the economic climate seemed to favor a medium-price car such as the Edsel.

The Ford Motor Company had been weakest in this very sector where all economic forecasts indicated was the greatest opportunity. General Motors had three makes, Pontiac, Oldsmobile, and Buick, in the medium-price class; Chrysler had Dodge and DeSoto appealing to this market; but Ford had only Mercury to compete for this business, and Mercury accounted for a puny twenty percent of the company's business.

Studies had revealed that every year one out of five people who buy a new car traded up to a medium-price model from a low-price car. As Chevrolet owners traded up, 87 percent stayed with General Motors and one of its three makes of medium-priced cars. As Plymouth owners traded up, 47 percent bought a Dodge or DeSoto. But as Ford owners traded up, only 26 percent stayed with the Ford Motor Company and the Mercury, its one entry in this price line. Ford executives were describing this phenomenon as "one of the greatest philanthropies of modern business," the fact that Ford uptraders contributed almost as much to GM's medium-price penetration as Chevrolet had been able to generate for GM.

So the entry of the Edsel seemed necessary if not overdue.

Research Efforts

Marketing research studies on the Edsel automobile covered a period of almost ten years. Some studies dealt with owner likes and dislikes, other studies with market and sales analyses. Earlier research had determined that cars have definite personalities to the general public, and a person buys a car best thought to exemplify his or her own personality. Consequently, "imagery" studies were considered important to find the best "personality" for the car and to find the best name. The personality sought was one that would make the greatest number of people want the car. Ford researchers thought they had a major advantage over the other manufacturers of medium-priced cars because they did not have to change an existing personality; rather, they could create what they wanted from scratch.

Columbia University was engaged to interview eight hundred recent car buyers in Peoria, Illinois, and another eight hundred in San Bernardino, California (considered to be rather typical cities) as to what images they had of the various makes. Thereby a personality portrait of each make was developed. For example, the image of a Ford was that of a fast, masculine car of no particular social pretension. On the other hand, Chevrolet's image was of a car for an older, wiser, slower person. Mercury had the image of a hot-rod, best suited to a young racing driver, this despite its higher-price tag.

The conclusions were that the personality of the new car (called the "E-car" initially before the Edsel name had been selected) should be one that would be regarded as the smart car for the younger executive or professional family on its way up. Advertising and promotion accordingly would stress this theme. And the appointments of the car would offer status to the owner.

The name for the E-car should also fit the car's image and personality. Accordingly, some two thousand different names were gathered and several research firms sent interviewers with the list to canvass sidewalk crowds in New York City, Chicago, Willow Run and Ann Arbor, Michigan. The interviewers asked what free associations each name brought to mind; they also asked what words were considered the opposite of each name since opposite associations might also be important. But the results were inconclusive.

Edsel, the name of Henry Ford's only son, had been suggested for the E-car. However, the three Ford brothers in active management of the company, Henry II, Benson, and William Clay, were lukewarm to this idea of their father's name spinning "on a million hubcaps." And the free associations with the name Edsel were on the negative side, being "pretzel," "diesel," and "hard sell."

At last ten names were sent to the executive committee. None of the ten aroused any enthusiasm, and the name Edsel was finally selected, although not one of the recommended names. Four of the ten names submitted were selected for the different series of Edsel: Corsair, Citation, Pacer, and Ranger.

Search for a Distinctive Style

Styling of the Edsel began in 1954. Stylists were asked to be both distinctive and discreet, in itself a rather tall order. The stylists studied existing cars and even scanned the tops of cars from the roof of a ten-story building to determine any distinguishing characteristics that might be used for the Edsel. The consumer research could provide some information as to image and personality desired, but furnished little guidance for the actual features and shape of the car. Groups of stylists considered various "themes" and boiled down hundreds of sketches to two dozen to show top management. Clay and plaster mock-ups were prepared so that three-dimensional highlights and flair could be observed. The final concept was satisfying to all eight hundred stylists.

The result was a unique vertical front grill—a horse-collar shape, set vertically in the center of a conventionally low, wide front end—pushbutton transmission, and luxury appointments. The vertical grille of the Edsel was compared by some executives to the classic cars of the 1930s, the LaSalle and Pierce Arrow. Push buttons were stressed as the epitome of engineering advancement and convenience. The hood and trunk lid were push button; the parking brake lever was push button; the transmission was push button. Edsel salesmen could demonstrate the ease of operation by depressing the transmission buttons with a tooth pick.

The Edsel was not a small car. The two largest series, the Corsair and the Citation, were two inches longer than the biggest Oldsmobile. It was a powerful car, one of the most powerful made, with a 345 horsepower engine. The high performance possible from such horsepower was thought to be a key element in the sporty, youthful image that was to be projected.

A Separate Division for Edsel

Instead of distributing the new Edsel through established Ford, Mercury, and Lincoln dealers, a separate dealer organization was decided upon to be controlled by a separate headquarters division. These new dealers were carefully selected from over 4,600 inquiries for dealer franchises in every part of the United States. Most of the 1,200 dealers chosen were to handle only Edsel, with dual dealerships restricted to small towns. Consequently, there were now five separate divisions for the Ford Motor Company: Ford, Mercury, Lincoln, Continental, and Edsel.

While establishing Edsel as a separate division added to the fixed costs of operation, this was thought to be desirable in the long run. An independent division could stand alone as a profit center, and this should encourage more aggressive performance than if Edsel were merely a second entry to some other division.

The dealer appointments were made after intensive market research to learn where to place each dealer in the nation's sixty major metropolitan areas. Population shifts and trends were carefully considered, and the planned dealer points were matched with the 4,600 inquiries for franchises. The Edsel was to have the best located dealer body in the automobile industry. Applicants for dealerships were carefully screened, of course. Guides used in selection included: reputation, adequate finances, adequate facilities, demonstrated management ability, the ability to attract and direct good people, sales ability, proper attitude toward ethical and competitive matters, and type of person to give proper consideration to customers in sales and service. The average dealer had at least a hundred thousand dollars committed to his agency.

Edsel Division was prepared to supply skilled assistance to dealers so that each could operate as effectively and profitably as possible and also provide good service to customers.

PROMOTIONAL EFFORTS

July 22, 1957, was the kickoff for the first consumer advertising. It was a two-page spread in *Life* magazine in plain black and white, and showed a car whooshing down a country highway at such high speed it was a blur. The copy read: "Lately some mysterious automobiles have been seen on the roads." It went on to say that the blur was an Edsel and was on its way. Other "pre-announcement" ads showed only photographs of covered cars. Not until late August were pictures of the actual cars released.

The company looked beyond their regular advertising agencies to find a separate one for the Edsel. Foote, Cone and Belding was selected, this being one of the two in the top ten who did not have any other automobile clients. The campaign designed was a quiet, self-assured one which avoided as much as possible the use of the adjective "new," since this was seen as commonplace and not distinctive enough. The advertising was intended to be calm, not to overshadow the car.

The General Sales and Marketing Manager, J. C. Doyle, insisted on keeping Edsel's appearance one of the best kept secrets of the auto industry. Never before had an auto manufacturer gone to so much trouble to keep the appearance hidden. Advertising commercials were filmed behind closed doors, the cars were shipped with covers, and no press people were given any photographs of the car before its introduction. The intent was to build up an overwhelming public interest in the Edsel, causing its arrival to be anticipated and the car itself to be the object of great curiosity.

Some fifty million dollars were allocated for the introductory period. Traditional automobile advertising media were used. Newspaper advertising was allocated forty percent of all expenditures; magazines were budgeted at twenty percent (trade publication advertising started on April 29 with a two-color spread in *Automotive News* as part of a dealer recruitment campaign); TV and radio were budgeted at twenty percent; outdoor billboards were given ten percent of the budget, with a final ten percent for miscellaneous media.

The advertising agency and the marketing executives at Edsel recognized that they faced a challenge in most effectively promoting the car. Because of the determined need for secrecy, traditional advertising research had to be eliminated. For example, copy tests could not be made without disclosing the features of the car. Furthermore, the introduction of the car and the promotion to accompany it had to be done at one time all over the country; there was no possibility of testing various alternatives and approaches.

THE RESULTS

Introduction Day was September 4, 1957, and 1,200 Edsel dealers eagerly opened their doors. And most found potential customers streaming in, out of curiosity if nothing else. On the first day more than 6,500 orders were taken. This was considered reasonably satisfying. But there were isolated signs of resistance. One dealer selling Edsels in one showroom and Buicks in an adjacent showroom reported that some prospects walked into the Edsel showroom, looked at the Edsel, and placed orders for Buicks on the spot.

In the next few days, sales dropped sharply. For the first ten days of October there were only 2,751 sales, an average of just over 300 cars a day. In order to sell the 200,000 cars per year (the minimum expectation), between six and seven hundred would need to be sold each day.

On Sunday night, October 13th, the Ford Motor Company put on a mammoth television spectacular for Edsel. The show cost $400,000 and starred Bing Crosby and Frank Sinatra, two of the hottest names in show business at that time. Even this failed to cause any sharp spurt in sales. Things were not going well.

For all of 1958 only 34,481 Edsels were sold and registered with motor-vehicle bureaus, less than one-fifth the target sales. The picture looked a little brighter in November 1958 with the introduction of the second year models. These Edsels were shorter, lighter, less powerful, and had a price range from five hundred to eight hundred dollars less than their predecessors.

Eventually the Edsel Division was merged into a Lincoln-Mercury-Edsel Division. In mid-October 1959 a third series of annual models of Edsels were brought out. These aroused no particular excitement either, and on November 19, 1959 production was discontinued. The Edsel was dead.

Between 1957 and 1960, 109,466 Edsels were sold. Ford was able to recover 150 million dollars of its investment by using Edsel plants and tools in other Ford divisions, leaving a nonrecoverable loss of more than a hundred million dollars on the original investment plus an estimated hundred million dollars in operating losses.

WHAT WENT WRONG?

So carefully planned. Such a major commitment of manpower and financial resources, supported by decades of experience in producing and marketing automobiles. How could this have happened? Where were the mistakes? Could they have been prevented? As with most problems there is no one simple answer. The marketplace is complex. Many things contributed to the demise of the Edsel: among them, poor judgment by people who should have known better (except that they were so confident because of the abundance of planning) and economic conditions outside the company's control. We will examine some of the factors that have been blamed for Edsel's failure. None of these alone would have been sufficient to destroy the Edsel; in combination, the car didn't have a chance.

Exogenous Factors

One article in discussing the failure of the Edsel, said, "In addition to mistakes, real and alleged, the Edsel encountered incredibly bad luck. Unfortunately it was introduced at the beginning of the 1958 recession. Few cars sold well in 1958; few middle-price cars sold, even fewer Edsels." A dealer in San Francisco summed it up this way: "The medium-priced market is extremely healthy in good times, but it is also the first market to be hurt when we tighten our belts during depression . . .

TABLE [1].   U.S. Motor Vehicle Sales, 1948–1960

Year	Units Sold
1948	3,909,270
1949	5,119,466
1950	6,665,863
1951	5,338,436
1952	4,320,794
1953	6,116,948
1954	5,558,897
1955	7,920,186
1956	5,816,109
1957	6,113,344
1958	4,257,812
1959	5,591,243
1960	6,674,796

Source: *1973 Ward's Automotive Yearbook* (Detroit: Ward's Communications), p. 86.

TABLE [2].   U.S. Medium-price Car Production, 1955–1959 (units)

	1955	1956	1957	1958	1959
Mercury	434,911	246,629	274,820	128,428	156,765
Edsel			54,607	26,563	29,677
Pontiac	581,860	332,268	343,298	219,823	388,856
Oldsmobile	643,460	432,903	390,091	310,795	366,305
Buick	781,296	535,364	407,283	257,124	232,579
Dodge	313,038	205,727	292,386	114,206	192,798
DeSoto	129,767	104,090	117,747	36,556	41,423

Source: *1973 Ward's,* pp. 112, 113.

when they dreamed up the Edsel, medium-priced cars were a big market, but by the time the baby was born, that market had gone 'helter-skelter'."

The stock market collapsed in 1957, marking the beginning of the recession of 1958. By early August of 1957, sales of medium-priced cars of all makes were declining. Dealers were ending their season with the second largest number of unsold new cars in history up to that time. Table [1] shows total U.S. car sales from 1948 (as the country was beginning production after World War II) until 1960. You can see from this table that 1958 sales were the lowest since 1948.

Table [2] shows the production of the major makes of medium-price cars from 1955 to 1960. Note the drastic dropoff of all makes of cars in 1958, but the trend had been downward since 1955.

The trend was changing from bigger cars to economy cars. American Motors had been pushing the compact Rambler, and in the year when the Edsel came on the market sales of small foreign cars more than doubled. This change in consumer preferences was not alone a product of the 1958 recession, which would indicate that it would not reverse once the economy improved. Sales of small foreign cars

TABLE [3].   U.S. Sales of Import Cars, 1948–1960

	Units
1948	28,047
1949	7,543
1950	21,287
1951	23,701
1952	33,312
1953	29,505
1954	34,555
1955	57,115
1956	107,675
1957	259,343
1958	430,808
1959	668,070
1960	444,474

Source: *Automobile Facts and Figures, 1961 Edition* (Detroit: Automobile Manufacturers Association), p. 5, compiled from U.S. Department of Commerce statistics.

continued very strong in the following years, reflecting public disillusionment with big cars and desire for more economy and less showy transportation. Table [3] shows the phenomenal increase in import car sales during this period, a trend which should have alerted the Edsel planners.

Other exogenous factors were also coming into play at the time of Edsel's introduction. The National Safety Council had become increasingly concerned with the "horsepower race" and the way speed and power were translating into highway accidents. In 1957, the Automobile Manufacturing Association, in deference to the criticisms of the National Safety Council, signed an agreement against advertising power and performance. But the Edsel had been designed with these very two features uppermost: a big engine with 345 horsepower to support a high performance, powerful car on the highways. Designed to handle well at high speeds, its speed, horsepower, and high performance equipment could not even be advertised.

Consumer Reports was not overly thrilled about the Edsel. Its 800,000 subscribers found this as the first sentence in the magazine's evaluation of the Edsel: "The Edsel has no important basic advantage over the other brands." Negative articles and books regarding the "power merchants" of Detroit were also appearing about this time. John Keats published his *Insolent Chariots*, and the poet, Robert Lowell, condemned our "tailfin culture."

Marketing Research

The failure of the Edsel cannot be attributed to a lack of marketing research. Indeed, considerable expenditures were devoted to this. However, these efforts can be faulted in three respects.

First, the motivation research efforts directed to establishing a desirable image for the new car were not all that helpful. While they were of some value in determining how consumers viewed the owners of Chevrolets, Fords, Mercurys, and other brands and led the Edsel executives into selecting the particular image for their car, in reality there was an inability to translate this desired image into tangible product features. For example, while upwardly mobile young executives and professionals seemed a desirable segment of consumers for Edsel to appeal to, was this best done through heavy horsepower and high speed performance features, or might other characteristics have been more attractive to these consumers? (Many of these consumers were shifting their sentiments to the European compacts about this time, repudiating the "horsepower race" and the chrome-bedecked theme of bigness.)

Second, much of the research was conducted several years before the introduction of the Edsel in 1957. While demand for medium-priced cars seemed strong at that time, the assumption that such attitudes would be static and unchanging was unwise. A strong shift in consumer preferences was undetected—and should have been noticed. The increasing demand for imported cars should have warranted further investigation and even a reexamination of plans in light of changing market conditions.

The last area where the marketing research efforts can be criticized is in the name itself, Edsel. Here the blame lies not so much with the marketing research, which never recommended the name in the first place, as with a Ford management which disregarded marketing research conclusions and opted for the name regardless.

Now much has been written about the negative impact of the name. Most of this may be unjustified. Many successful cars on the market today do not have what we would call winning names. For example, Buick, Oldsmobile, Chrysler, even Ford itself are hardly exciting names. A better name could have been chosen—and was a few years later with the Mustang, and also the Maverick—but it is doubtful that the Edsel's demise can justifiably be laid to the name.

The Product

Changing consumer preferences for smaller cars came about the time of the introduction of the Edsel. Disillusionment was setting in regarding large size, powerful cars. However, other characteristics of the car also hurt. The styling, especially the vertical grille, aroused both positive and negative impressions. Some liked its distinctiveness, seeing it as a restrained classic look without extremes. But the horse-collar shaped grille turned other people off.

The biggest product error had to do with quality control. There was a failure to adhere to quality standards; cars were released that should not have been. Production was rushed to get the Edsel to market on schedule and also to get as many Edsels as possible on the road so that people could see the car. But many bugs had not been cleared up. The array of models increased the production difficulties, with eighteen models in the four series of Ranger, Pacer, Corsair, and Citation.

As a result, the first Edsels had brakes that failed, leaked oil, were beseiged with rattles, and sometimes the dealers could not even start them. Before these problems could be cleared up, the car had gained the reputation of being a lemon, and this was a tough image to overcome. The car quickly became the butt of jokes.

The Separate Edsel Organization

Another mistake that can be singled out in retrospect was the decision to go with a separate division and separate dealerships for Edsel. While this separation was supposed to lead to greater dealer motivation and consequently stronger selling push than where such efforts are diluted among several makes of cars, the cost factors of such separation were disregarded. Having a separate division was expensive and raised breakeven points very high due to the additional personnel and facilities needed. Furthermore, Ford did not have ample management personnel to staff all its divisions adequately.

Despite the care used in selecting the new Edsel dealers, some of these were underfinanced, and many were underskilled in running automobile dealerships compared to the existing dealers selling the regular Ford products. Other Edsel dealers were "dropouts" or the less successful dealers of other car makers.

An additional source of difficulty for the viability of the Edsel dealers was they had nothing else to offer but Edsel sales and service. Dealers usually rely on the shop and maintenance sections of their businesses to cover some expenses. Edsel dealers not only did not have any other cars besides the Edsel to work on, but the work on the Edsel was usually a result of factory deficiencies so the dealers could not charge for this work. The dealers quickly faced financial difficulties with sales not up to expectations and service business yielding little revenue.

Promotional Efforts

Contrary to what could be reasonably expected, the heavy promotional efforts before the Edsel was finally unveiled may have produced a negative effect. The general public had been built up to expect the Edsel to be a major step forward, a significant innovation. And many were disillusioned. They saw instead a new styled luxury Ford, uselessly overpowered, gadget and chrome bedecked, but nothing really so very different, this car was not worth the build-up.

Another problem was that the Edsel came out too early in the new-car model year—in early September—and had to suffer the consequences of competing with 1957 cars that were going through clearance sales. Not only did people shy away from the price of the Edsel, but in many instances they did not know if it was a 1957 or 1958 model. *Business Week* reported dealer complaints: "We've been selling against the clean-up of 1957 models. We were too far ahead of the 1958 market. Our big job is getting the original lookers back in the showrooms."

While some dealers had complained about over-advertising too early, now they were complaining of lack of promotion and advertising in October and November when the other cars were being introduced. At the time when the Edsel was competing against other new models, advertising was cut back as the Edsel executives saw little point in trying to steal attention normally focused on new models.

Finally, one of the more interesting explanations for the failure of the Edsel was:

> oral symbolism . . . responsible for the failure of the Edsel. The physical appearance was displeasing from a psychological and emotional point of view because the front grille looked like a huge open mouth . . . Men do not want to associate oral qualities with their cars, for it does not fit their self-image of being strong and virile.

MEANING

1. What factors made Ford think the Edsel was a "sure thing"?
2. How was market research used to match the car's "personality" with the character traits of the intended owners?

3. Why was it erroneous to design a car using style features that were visible from ten stories up?

4. Explain how secrecy, the ad agency's lack of familiarity with the automotive field, and vague ad copy contributed to the poor reception of the Edsel.

5. What part did underfinanced dealerships, poor workmanship, the switch from big cars to smaller economy cars, and the onset of a recession play in the Edsel's failure?

Using Problem Solving to Convey Meaning

1. How is Hartley's analysis organized to break the overall problem of the Edsel's failure into smaller, easier-to-analyze questions of (a) market research, (b) sales techniques, (c) quality control, and (d) the state of the economy in 1958?

2. How does Hartley make sure that the reader knows about the alternative choices available to Ford management at each stage of the Edsel's planning and production?

3. How does Hartley use statistical tables and interviews to effectively pinpoint specific problems responsible for the Edsel's demise?

Writing Suggestions

1. Identify and analyze the strategies that you believe are responsible for the marketing success of a product.

2. Analyze the causes responsible for any major marketing miscalculation, such as the introduction of the Susan B. Anthony dollar. For example, sometimes product names change their meaning when translated into another language: Chevrolet's Nova, in Spanish, means "no va," or "it doesn't go."

3. Analyze any ad that seems to have blatantly sexist or other offensive connotations; for example, the ad for the perfume "Opium" received negative publicity because of the negative associations of its name.

SCIENCES

Douglas R. Hofstadter

The Turing Test

Douglas R. Hofstadter was born in New York City in 1945. He received his Ph.D. from the University of Oregon in 1975, taught computer science at Indiana University through 1984, and now holds the Walgreen Chair in Human Understanding at the University of Michigan. Professor Hofstadter's books include Godel, Escher, Bach: An Eternal Golden Braid (1979), for which he was awarded the Pulitzer Prize and the American Book Award, and Metamagical Themas: Questing for the Essence of Mind and Pattern (1985), which evolved from the columns he wrote for Scientific American. Hofstadter's research on artificial intelligence reveals the need for computer programs that can filter out irrelevancies and respond to situations that are slightly different from the domains for which they are programmed. That is, computer programs must, like human beings, be able to generalize. In "The Turing Test" (1980), Hofstadter describes an ingenious hypothetical game, designed by the British mathematician Alan Turing, which raises many of the major philosophical and pragmatic issues connected with artificial intelligence.

In 1950, Alan Turing wrote a most prophetic and provocative article on Artificial Intelligence. It was entitled "Computing Machinery and Intelligence" and appeared in the journal *Mind.*[1] I will say some things about that article, but I would like to precede them with some remarks about Turing the man.

Alan Mathison Turing was born in London in 1912. He was a child full of curiosity and humor. Gifted in mathematics, he went to Cambridge where his interests in machinery and mathematical logic cross-fertilized and resulted in his famous paper on "computable numbers," in which he invented the theory of Turing machines and demonstrated the unsolvability of the halting problem; it was published in 1937. In the 1940's, his interests turned from the theory of computing machines to the

[1] Alan M. Turing, "Computing Machinery and Intelligence," *Mind,* Vol. LIX, No. 236 (1950). Reprinted in A. R. Anderson (ed.), *Minds and Machines* (N.J., 1964).

623

actual building of real computers. He was a major figure in the development of computers in Britain, and a staunch defender of Artificial Intelligence when it first came under attack. One of his best friends was David Champernowne (who later worked on computer composition of music). Champernowne and Turing were both avid chess players and invented "round-the-house" chess: after your move, run around the house—if you get back before your opponent has moved, you're entitled to another move. More seriously, Turing and Champernowne invented the first chess-playing program, called "Turochamp." Turing died young, at 41—apparently of an accident with chemicals. Or some say suicide. His mother, Sara Turing, wrote his biography. From the people she quotes, one gets the sense that Turing was highly unconventional, even gauche in some ways, but so honest and decent that he was vulnerable to the world. He loved games, chess, children, and bike riding; he was a strong long-distance runner. As a student at Cambridge, he bought himself a second-hand violin and taught himself to play. Though not very musical, he derived a great deal of enjoyment from it. He was somewhat eccentric, given to great bursts of energy in the oddest directions. One area he explored was the problem of morphogenesis in biology. According to his mother, Turing "had a particular fondness for the *Pickwick Papers*," but "poetry, with the exception of Shakespeare's, meant nothing to him." Alan Turing was one of the true pioneers in the field of computer science.

THE TURING TEST

Turing's article begins with the sentence: "I propose to consider the question 'Can machines think?'" Since, as he points out, these are loaded terms, it is obvious that we should search for an operational way to approach the question. This, he suggests, is contained in what he calls the "imitation game"; it is nowadays known as the *Turing test*. Turing introduces it as follows:

> It is played with three people: a man (A), a woman (B), and an interrogator (C) who may be of either sex. The interrogator stays in a room apart from the other two. The object of the game for the interrogator is to determine which of the other two is the man and which is the woman. He knows them by labels X and Y, and at the end of the game he says either "X is A and Y is B" or "X is B and Y is A." The interrogator is allowed to put questions to A and B thus:
>
> C: Will X please tell me the length of his or her hair?
>
> Now suppose X is actually A, then A must answer. It is A's object in the game to try to cause C to make the wrong identification. His answer might therefore be
>
> "My hair is shingled, and the longest strands are about nine inches long."
>
> In order that tones of voice may not help the interrogator the answers should be written, or better still, typewritten. The ideal arrangement is to have a teleprinter communicating between the two rooms. Alternatively the questions and answers can be repeated by an intermediary. The object of the game for the third player (B) is to help the interrogator. The best strategy for her is probably to give truthful answers. She can add such things as "I am the woman, don't listen to him!" to her answers, but it will avail nothing as the man can make similar remarks.

We now ask the question, "What will happen when a machine takes the part of A in this game?" Will the interrogator decide wrongly as often when the game is played like this as he does when the game is played between a man and a woman? These questions replace our original, "Can machines think?"[2]

After having spelled out the nature of his test, Turing goes on to make some commentaries on it, which, given the year he was writing in, are quite sophisticated. To begin with, he gives a short hypothetical dialogue between interrogator and interrogatee:[3]

Q: Please write me a sonnet on the subject of the Forth Bridge [a bridge over the Firth of Forth, in Scotland].
A: Count me out on this one. I never could write poetry.
Q: Add 34957 to 70764.
A: (*Pause about 30 seconds and then give as answer*) 105621.
Q Do you play chess?
A: Yes.
Q: I have K at my K1, and no other pieces. You have only K at K6 and R at R1. It is your move. What do you play?
A: (*After a pause of 15 seconds*) R-R8 mate.

Few readers notice that in the arithmetic problem, not only is there an inordinately long delay, but moreover, the answer given is wrong! This would be easy to account for if the respondent were a human: a mere calculational error. But if the respondent were a machine, a variety of explanations are possible. Here are some:

1. a run-time error on the hardware level (i.e., an irreproducible fluke);
2. an unintentional hardware (or programming) error which (reproducibly) causes arithmetical mistakes;
3. a ploy deliberately inserted by the machine's programmer (or builder) to introduce occasional arithmetical mistakes, so as to trick interrogators;
4. an unanticipated epiphenomenon: the program has a hard time thinking abstractly, and simply made "an honest mistake," which it might not make the next time around;
5. a joke on the part of the machine itself, deliberately teasing its interrogator.

Reflection on what Turing might have meant by this subtle touch opens up just about all the major philosophical issues connected with Artificial Intelligence.
Turing goes on to point out that

> The new problem has the advantage of drawing a fairly sharp line between the physical and the intellectual capacities of a man. . . . We do not wish to penalize the machine for its inability to shine in beauty competitions, nor to penalize a man for losing in a race against an airplane.[4]

One of the pleasures of the article is to see how far Turing traced out each line of thought, usually turning up a seeming contradiction at some stage and, by refining

---

[2] Turing in Anderson, p. 5.
[3] *Ibid.*, p. 6.
[4] *Ibid.*, p. 6.

his concepts, resolving it at a deeper level of analysis. Because of this depth of penetration into the issues, the article still shines after nearly thirty years of tremendous progress in computer development and intensive work in AI. In the following short excerpt you can see some of this rich back-and-forth working of ideas:

> The game may perhaps be criticized on the ground that the odds are weighted too heavily against the machine. If the man were to try to pretend to be the machine he would clearly make a very poor showing. He would be given away at once by slowness and inaccuracy in arithmetic. May not machines carry out something with ought to be described as thinking but which is very different from what a man does? This objection is a very strong one, but at least we can say that if, nevertheless, a machine can be constructed to play the imitation game satisfactorily, we need not be troubled by this objection.
>
> It might be urged that when playing the "imitation game" the best strategy for the machine may possibly be something other than imitation of the behaviour of a man. This may be, but I think it is unlikely that there is any great effect of this kind. In any case there is no intention to investigate here the theory of the game, and it will be assumed that the best strategy is to try to provide answers that would naturally be given by a man.[5]

Once the test has been proposed and discussed, Turing remarks:

> The original question "Can machines think?" I believe to be too meaningless to deserve discussion. Nevertheless, I believe that at the end of the century the use of words and general educated opinion will have altered so much that one will be able to speak of machines thinking without expecting to be contradicted.[6]

TURING ANTICIPATES OBJECTIONS

Aware of the storm of opposition that would undoubtedly greet this opinion, he then proceeds to pick apart, concisely and with wry humor, a series of objections to the notion that machines could think. Below I list the nine types of objections he counters, using his own descriptions of them.[7] Unfortunately there is not space to reproduce the humorous and ingenious responses he formulated. You may enjoy pondering the objections yourself, and figuring out your own responses.

1. *The Theological Objection.* Thinking is a function of man's immortal soul. God has given an immortal soul to every man and woman, but not to any other animal or to machines. Hence no animal or machine can think.
2. *The "Heads in the Sand" Objection.* The consequences of machines thinking would be too dreadful. Let us hope and believe that they cannot do so.
3. *The Mathematical Objection.* [This is essentially the Lucas argument.]
4. *The Argument from Consciousness.* "Not until a machine can write a sonnet or compose a concerto because of thoughts and emotions felt, and not by the chance fall of symbols, could we agree that machine equals brain—that is, not only write it but know that it had written it. No mechanism could feel (and not

[5] *Ibid.*, p. 6.
[6] *Ibid.*, pp. 13–14.
[7] *Ibid.*, pp. 14–24.

merely artificially signal, an easy contrivance) pleasure at its successes, grief when its valves fuse, be warmed by flattery, be made miserable by its mistakes, be charmed by sex, be angry or depressed when it cannot get what it wants." [A quote from a certain Professor Jefferson.]

Turing is quite concerned that he should answer this serious objection in full detail. Accordingly, he devotes quite a bit of space to his answer, and in it he offers another short hypothetical dialogue:[8]

INTERROGATOR: In the first line of your sonnet which reads "Shall I compare thee to a summer's day," would not "a spring day" do as well or better?
WITNESS: It wouldn't scan.
INTERROGATOR: How about "a winter's day"? That would scan all right.
WITNESS: Yes, but nobody wants to be compared to a winter's day.
INTERROGATOR: Would you say Mr. Pickwick reminded you of Christmas?
WITNESS: In a way.
INTERROGATOR: Yet Christmas is a winter's day, and I do not think Mr. Pickwick would mind the comparison.
WITNESS: I don't think you're serious. By a winter's day one means a typical winter's day, rather than a special one like Christmas.

After this dialogue, Turing asks, "What would Professor Jefferson say if the sonnet-writing machine was able to answer like this in the *viva voce*?"
Further objections:

5. *Arguments from Various Disabilities.* These arguments take the form, "I grant you that you can make machines do all the things that you have mentioned but you will never be able to make one to do X." Numerous features X are suggested in this connection. I offer a selection:
Be kind, resourceful, beautiful, friendly, have initiative, have a sense of humor, tell right from wrong, make mistakes, fall in love, enjoy strawberries and cream, make someone fall in love with it, learn from experience, use words properly, be the subject of its own thought, have as much diversity of behaviour as a man, do something really new.

6. *Lady Lovelace's Objection.* Our most detailed information of Babbage's Analytical Engine comes from a memoir by Lady Lovelace. In it she states, "The Analytical Engine has no pretensions to *originate* anything. It can do *whatever we know how to order it* to perform" (her italics).

7. *Argument from Continuity in the Nervous System.* The nervous system is certainly not a discrete state machine. A small error in the information about the size of a nervous impulse impinging on a neuron may make a large difference to the size of the outgoing impulse. It may be argued that, this being so, one cannot expect to be able to mimic the behaviour of the nervous system with a discrete state system.

8. *The Argument from Informality of Behaviour.* It seems to run something like this. "If each man had a definite set of rules of conduct by which he regulated his life he would be no better than a machine. But there are no such rules, so men cannot be machines."

9. *The Argument from Extra-Sensory Perception.* Let us play the imitation game, using

[8] *Ibid.*, p. 17.

as witnesses a man who is good as a telepathic receiver, and a digital computer. The interrogator can ask such questions as "What suit does the card in my right hand belong to?" The man by telepathy or clairvoyance gives the right answer 130 times out of 400 cards. The machine can only guess at random, and perhaps get 104 right, so the interrogator makes the right identification.

As you can see, many of the objections overlap and are related to each other. I have attempted in this book to answer most of them in some way or other, usually far less concisely than Turing did.

Objection (9) I find remarkable. I have seen the Turing paper reprinted in a book—but with objection (9) omitted—which I find equally remarkable. My own point of view—contrary to Turing's—is that ESP does not exist. Turing was reluctant to accept the idea that ESP is real, but did so nonetheless, being compelled by his outstanding scientific integrity to accept the consequences of what he viewed as powerful statistical evidence in favor of ESP. I disagree, though I consider it an exceedingly complex and fascinating question.

"Parry Encounters the Doctor"

In the Dialogue preceding this Chapter, you have seen an authentic exchange between a computer program and a human. Now there have been many programs with less ability to "converse" than SHRDLU. Two rather famous ones are "Doctor," created by Joseph Weizenbaum, and "Parry," created by Kenneth Colby. The former is supposed to simulate a psychiatrist using "nondirective therapy," the latter to simulate the belief structure of a paranoid. An amusing head-on collision between the two programs was arranged over a computer network, and the following is a short excerpt from the full transcript:[9]

Parry: I don't understand your motives.
Doctor: Why don't you understand my motives?
Parry: Shouldn't I be?
Doctor: Why do you say that just now?
Parry: That's just the way it is.
Doctor: Suppose that's just the way it were not.
Parry: So?
Doctor: I am not sure I understand you fully.
Parry: You harp on the same questions too much.
Doctor: What does that similarity suggest to you?
Parry: I don't get you.
Doctor: Do you wish that you did get I?
Parry: It's about time you showed some interest in my feelings.
Doctor: Oh? I showed some interest in your feelings?

These programs, of course, were made to talk to humans, so they are shown up rather poorly here, pitted against each other. Mostly they rely on shrewd guesses as to the nature of the input (which they analyze quite shallowly) and spit back canned answers that have been carefully selected from a large repertoire. The answer may be only partially canned: for example, a template with blanks that can be filled in.

---

[9] Vinton Cerf, "Parry Encounters the Doctor," *Datamation* (July 1973), p. 63.

It is assumed that their human partners will read much more into what they say than is actually underlying it. And in fact, according to Weizenbaum, in his book *Computer Power and Human Reason*, just that happens. He writes:

> ELIZA [the program from which Doctor was made] created the most remarkable illusion of having understood in the minds of the many people who conversed with it. . . . They would often demand to be permitted to converse with the system in private, and would, after conversing with it for a time, insist, in spite of my explanations, that the machine really understood them.[10]

Given the above excerpt, you may find this incredible. Incredible, but true. Weizenbaum has an explanation:

> Most men don't understand computers to even the slightest degree. So, unless they are capable of very great skepticism (the kind we bring to bear while watching a stage magician), they can explain the computer's intellectual feats only by bringing to bear the single analogy available to them, that is, their model of their own capacity to think. No wonder, then, that they overshoot the mark; it is truly impossible to imagine a human who could imitate ELIZA, for example, but for whom ELIZA's language abilities were his limit.[11]

Which amounts to an admission that this kind of program is based on a shrewd mixture of bravado and bluffing, taking advantage of people's gullibility.

In light of this weird "ELIZA-effect," some people have suggested that the Turing test needs revision, since people can apparently be fooled by simplistic gimmickry. It has been suggested that the interrogator should be a Nobel Prize-winning scientist. It might be more advisable to turn the Turing test on its head, and insist that the interrogator should be another computer. Or perhaps there should be two interrogators—a human and a computer—and one witness, and the two interrogators should try to figure out whether the witness is a human or a computer.

In a more serious vein, I personally feel that the Turing test, as originally proposed, is quite reasonable. As for the people who Weizenbaum claims were sucked in by ELIZA, they were not urged to be skeptical, or to use all their wits in trying to determine if the "person" typing to them were human or not. I think that Turing's insight into this issue was sound, and that the Turing test, essentially unmodified, will survive.

MEANING

1. What procedure does the Turing test employ that makes it so difficult to tell decisively if a given participant is a human or a machine?
2. What is the correct answer to the arithmetic problem; explain the significance of the wrong answer?
3. What would you say are the major philosophical issues connected with artificial intelligence brought out by Hofstadter?

[10] Joseph Weizenbaum, *Computer Power and Human Reason* (W. H. Freeman: San Francisco, 1976), p. 189.

[11] *Ibid.*, pp. 9–10.

4. Which of the nine types of objections seems the most compelling to you?
5. If you had to state something that in your opinion computers would never be able to do, what would it be? (For example, a computer could never have faith in God.)
6. How did the excerpt from "Parry Encounters the Doctor" illustrate questions raised by the preceding account of the Turing test?

USING PROBLEM SOLVING TO CONVEY MEANING

1. How is the way the Turing test is designed well-suited to address problems that will always arise in connection with artificial intelligence?
2. Evaluate the effectiveness of Hofstadter's beginning the essay with a short biographical sketch of Alan Turing.
3. Why does the ingenious example of the Turing test illustrate the importance of "hypothetical scenarios" in problem solving.

WRITING SUGGESTIONS

1. What would be the best strategy for a machine to follow in order to convince someone in another room it was human?
2. To what extent have the capabilities of computers imagined by Alan Turing become more possible in light of the "expert systems" using artificial intelligence discussed by Edward Feigenbaum and Pamela McCorduck (see page 196)?
3. Describe circumstances in which you would rather be questioned by a computer than by a person. Create a short dialogue between yourself and the computer.

LINCOLN BARNETT

Einstein's Relativity

Lincoln Barnett (1909–1979), author and journalist, was born in New York City. Barnett worked as a reporter for the New York Herald Tribune *and as a writer and editor for* Life *magazine. His widely acclaimed* The Universe and Dr. Einstein *(1948), from which the following essay is taken, with a foreword by Albert Einstein (praising Barnett's account as an extremely well-presented and valuable contribution), won a National Book Award special citation, sold more than one million copies, and was translated into twenty-eight languages. Albert Einstein's (1879–1955) theory of relativity became a household word in 1919, when the deviation of light passing near the sun, as predicted by his theory, was actually observed during a solar eclipse. In "Einstein's Relativity," Barnett explains, with great success, how Einstein developed his theory of relativity to provide a unified theoretical framework to account for the conflict, thought to be unresolvable, between wave and particle theories of light.*

The factors that first led physicists to distrust their faith in a smoothly functioning mechanical universe loomed on the inner and outer horizons of knowledge—in the unseen realm of the atom and in the fathomless depths of intergalactic space. To describe these phenomena quantitatively, two great theoretical systems were developed between 1900 and 1927. One was the Quantum Theory, dealing with the fundamental units of matter and energy. The other was Relativity, dealing with space, time, and the structure of the universe as a whole.

Both are now accepted pillars of modern physical thought. Both describe phenomena in their fields in terms of consistent, mathematical relationships. They do not answer the Newtonian "how" any more than Newton's laws answered the Aristotelian "why."[1] They provide equations, for example, that define with great accuracy the laws governing the radiation and propagation of light. But the actual mechanism by which the atom radiates light and by which light is propagated through space remains one of nature's supreme mysteries. Similarly the laws governing the phenomenon of radioactivity enable scientists to predict that in a given quantity of uranium a certain number of atoms will disintegrate in a certain length of time. But just which atoms will decay and how they are selected for doom are questions that man cannot yet answer.

In accepting a mathematical description of nature, physicists have been forced to abandon the ordinary world of our experience, the world of sense perceptions. To

---

[1] Sir Isaac Newton (1642–1727), English mathematician, formulator of the laws of gravity, and inventor of differential calculus.

understand the significance of this retreat it is necessary to step across the thin line that divides physics from metaphysics.[2] Questions involving the relationship between observer and reality, subject and object, have haunted philosophical thinkers since the dawn of reason. Twenty-three centuries ago the Greek philosopher Democritus[3] wrote: "Sweet and bitter, cold and warm as well as all the colors, all these things exist but in opinion and not in reality; what really exists are unchangeable particles, atoms, and their motions in empty space." Galileo[4] also was aware of the purely subjective character of sense qualities like color, taste, smell, and sound and pointed out that "they can no more be ascribed to the external objects than can the tickling or the pain caused sometimes by touching such objects."

The English philosopher John Locke[5] tried to penetrate to the "real essence of substances" by drawing a distinction between what he termed the primary and secondary qualities of matter. Thus he considered that shape, motion, solidity, and all geometrical properties were real or primary qualities, inherent in the object itself; while secondary qualities, like colors, sounds, tastes, were simply projections upon the organs of sense. The artificiality of this distinction was obvious to later thinkers.

"I am able to prove," wrote the great German mathematician, Leibnitz,[6] "that not only light, color, heat, and the like, but motion, shape, and extension too are mere apparent qualities." Just as our visual sense, for example, tells us that a golf ball is white, so vision abetted by our sense of touch tells us that it is also round, smooth, and small—qualities that have no more reality, independent of our senses, than the quality which we define by convention as white.

Thus gradually philosophers and scientists arrived at the startling conclusion that since every object is simply the sum of its qualities, and since qualities exist only in the mind, the whole objective universe of matter and energy, atoms and stars, does not exist except as a construction of the consciousness, an edifice of conventional symbols shaped by the senses of man. As Berkeley,[7] the archenemy of materialism, phrased it: "All the choir of heaven and furniture of earth, in a word all those bodies which compose the mighty frame of the world, have not any substance without the mind. . . . So long as they are not actually perceived by me, or do not exist in my mind, or that of any other created spirit, they must either have no existence at all, or else subsist in the mind of some Eternal Spirit." Einstein carried this train of logic to its ultimate limits by showing that even space and time are forms of intuition, which can no more be divorced from consciousness than can our concepts of color, shape, or size. Space has no objective reality except as an order or arrangement of the objects we perceive in it, and time has no independent existence apart from the order of events by which we measure it.

---

[2] A branch of philosophy that delves into the ultimate nature of reality.

[3] Democritus (460–370 B.C.), known as the "laughing philosopher," proposed that the world was made up of atoms.

[4] Galileo Galilei (1564–1642), Italian astronomer who established that the earth rotated around the sun.

[5] John Locke (1632–1704), founder of British empiricism, who suggested that the mind at birth was a "tabula rasa," or blank slate, awaiting experiences and sensory perceptions.

[6] Gottfried Wilhelm von Leibnitz (1646–1716), German philosopher and mathematician.

[7] George Berkeley (1685–1753), philosopher who proposed that so long as something is not perceived, it has no existence (the proverbial tree falling in the forest with no one to hear it); yet, Berkeley saw this paradox as proof that a God who perceives all (including the sound of the falling tree) must exist.

These philosophical subtleties have a profound bearing on modern science. For along with the philosophers' reduction of all objective reality to a shadow-world of perceptions, scientists became aware of the alarming limitations of man's senses. Anyone who has ever thrust a glass prism into a sunbeam and seen the rainbow colors of the solar spectrum refracted on a screen has looked upon the whole range of visible light. For the human eye is sensitive only to the narrow band of radiation that falls between the red and the violet. A difference of a few one hundred thousandths of a centimeter in wave length makes the difference between visibility and invisibility. The wave length of red light is .00007 cm. and that of violet light .00004 cm.

But the sun also emits other kinds of radiation. Infrared rays, for example, with a wave length of .00008 to .032 cm. are just a little too long to excite the retina to an impression of light, though the skin detects their impact as heat. Similarly ultraviolet rays with a wave length of .00003 to .000001 cm. are too short for the eye to perceive but can be recorded on a photographic plate. Photographs can also be made by the "light" of X-rays which are even shorter than ultraviolet rays. And there are other electromagnetic waves of lesser and greater frequency—the gamma rays of radium, radio waves, cosmic rays—which can be detected in various ways and differ from light only in wave length. It is evident, therefore, that the human eye suppresses most of the "lights" in the world, and that what man can perceive of the reality around him is distorted and enfeebled by the limitations of his organ of vision. The world would appear far different to him if his eye were sensitive, for example, to X-rays.

Realization that our whole knowledge of the universe is simply a residue of impressions clouded by our imperfect senses makes the quest for reality seem hopeless. If nothing has existence save in its being perceived, the world should dissolve into an anarchy of individual perceptions. But a curious order runs through our perceptions, as if indeed there might be an underlayer of objective reality which our senses translate. Although no man can ever know whether his sensation of red or of Middle C is the same as another man's it is nevertheless possible to act on the assumption that everyone sees colors and hears tones more or less alike.

This functional harmony of nature Berkeley, Descartes, and Spinoza attributed to God. Modern physicists who prefer to solve their problems without recourse to God (although this seems to become more difficult all the time) emphasize that nature mysteriously operates on mathematical principles. It is the mathematical orthodoxy of the universe that enables theorists like Einstein to predict and discover natural laws simply by the solution of equations. But the paradox of physics today is that with every improvement in its mathematical apparatus the gulf between man the observer and the objective world of scientific description becomes more profound.

It is perhaps significant that in terms of simple magnitude man is the mean between macrocosm and microcosm. Stated crudely this means that a supergiant red star (the largest material body in the universe) is just as much bigger than man as an electron (tiniest of physical entities) is smaller. It is not surprising, therefore, that the prime mysteries of nature dwell in those realms farthest removed from sense-imprisoned man, nor that science, unable to describe the extremes of reality in the homely metaphors of classical physics, should content itself with noting such mathematical relationships as may be revealed.

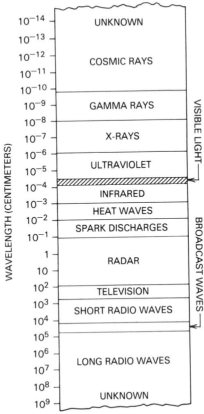

The electromagnetic spectrum reveals the narrow range of radiation visible to man's eye. From the standpoint of physics, the only difference between radio waves, visible light, and such high-frequency forms of radiation as X-rays and gamma rays lies in their wave length. But out of this vast range of electromagnetic radiation, extending from cosmic rays with wave lengths of only one trillionth of a centimeter up to infinitely long radio waves, the human eye selects only the narrow band indicated on the chart. Man's perceptions of the universe in which he dwells are thus restricted by the limitations of his visual sense. Wave lengths are indicated on the chart by the denary system: i.e., 10^3 centimeters equals $10 \times 10 \times 10$ equals 1,000; and 10^{-3} equals $1/10 \times 1/10 \times 1/10$ equals $1/1,000$.

The first step in science's retreat from mechanical explanation toward mathematical abstraction was taken in 1900, when Max Planck[8] put forth his Quantum Theory to meet certain problems that had arisen in studies of radiation. It is common knowledge that when heated bodies become incandescent they emit a red glow that turns to orange, then yellow, then white as the temperature increases. Painstaking efforts were made during the past century to formulate a law stating how the amount of radiant energy given off by such heated bodies varied with wave length and temperature. All

---

[8] Max Planck (1858–1947) theorized that the smallest amount in which radiant energy can be measured, called *quanta*, is equal to Planck's constant multiplied by the frequency of the radiation in question.

attempts failed until Planck found by mathematical means an equation that satisfied the results of experiment. The extraordinary feature of his equation was that it rested on the assumption that radiant energy is emitted not in an unbroken stream but in discontinous bits or portions which he termed *quanta*.

Planck had no evidence for such an assumption, for no one knew anything (then or now) of the actual mechanism of radiation. But on purely theoretical grounds he concluded that each quantum carries an amount of energy given by the equation, $E = hv$, where v is the frequency of the radiation and h is Planck's Constant, a small but inexorable number (roughly .00000000000000000000000006624) which has since proved to be one of the most fundamental constants in nature. In any process of radiation the amount of emitted energy divided by the frequency is always equal to h. Although Planck's Constant has dominated the computations of atomic physics for half a century, its magnitude cannot be explained any more than the magnitude of the speed of light can be explained. Like other universal constants it is simply a mathematical fact for which no explanation can be given. Sir Arthur Eddington[9] once observed that any true law of nature is likely to seem irrational to rational man; hence Planck's quantum principle, he thought, is one of the few real natural laws science has revealed.

The far-reaching implications of Planck's conjecture did not become apparent till 1905, when Einstein, who almost alone among contemporary physicists appreciated its significance, carried the Quantum Theory into a new domain. Planck had believed he was simply patching up the equations of radiation. But Einstein postulated that all forms of radiant energy—light, heat, X-rays—actually travel through space in separate and discontinuous quanta. Thus the sensation of warmth we experience when sitting in front of a fire results from the bombardment of our skin by innumerable quanta of radiant heat. Similarly sensations of color arise from the bombardment of our optic nerves by light quanta which differ from each other just as the frequency v varies in the equation $E = hv$.

Einstein substantiated this idea by working out a law accurately defining a puzzling phenomenon known as the photoelectric effect. Physicists had been at a loss to explain the fact that when a beam of pure violet light is allowed to shine upon a metal plate the plate ejects a shower of electrons. If light of lower frequency, say yellow or red, falls on the plate, electrons will again be ejected but at reduced velocities. The vehemence with which the electrons are torn from the metal depends only on the color of the light and not at all on its intensity. If the light source is removed to a considerable distance and dimmed to a faint glow the electrons that pop forth are fewer in number but their velocity is undiminished. The action is instantaneous even when the light fades to imperceptibility.

Einstein decided that these peculiar effects could be explained only by supposing that all light is composed of individual particles or grains of energy which he called *photons*, and that when one of them hits an electron the resulting action is comparable to the impact of two billiard balls. He reasoned further that photons of violet, ultraviolet, and other forms of high frequency radiation pack more energy than red and infrared photons, and that the velocity with which each electron flies from the metal plate is

[9] Sir Arthur Eddington (1882–1944), English astronomer and astrophysicist, said that the purely rational scientist is like a fisherman who throws out his net, surveys his catch, and concludes "what my net can't catch isn't fish."

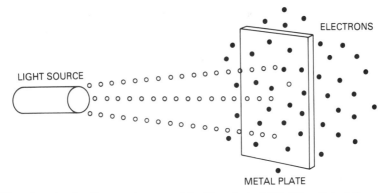

The photoelectric effect was interpreted by Einstein in 1905. When light falls on a metal plate, the plate ejects a shower of electrons. This phenomenon cannot be explained by the classic wave theory of light. Einstein deduced that light is not a continuous stream of energy but is composed of individual particles or bundles of energy which he called *photons*. When a photon strikes an electron the resulting action is analogous to the impact of billiard balls, as shown in this simplified conception.

proportional to the energy content of the photon that strikes it. He expressed these principles in a series of historic equations which won him the Nobel Prize and profoundly influenced later work in quantum physics and spectroscopy.[10] Television and other applications of the photoelectric cell owe their existence to Einstein's Photoelectric Law.

In thus adducing an important new physical principle Einstein uncovered at the same time one of the deepest and most troubling enigmas of nature. No one doubts today that all matter is made up of atoms which in turn are composed of even smaller building blocks called electrons, neutrons, and protons. But Einstein's notion that light too may consist of discontinuous particles clashed with a far more venerable theory that light is made up of waves.

There are indeed certain phenomena involving light that can only be explained by the wave theory. For example the shadows of ordinary objects like buildings, trees and telegraph poles appear sharply defined; but when a very fine wire or hair is held between a light source and a screen it casts no distinct shadow whatsoever, suggesting that light rays have bent around it just as waves of water bend around a small rock. Similarly a beam of light passing through a round aperture projects a sharply-defined disk upon a screen; but if the aperture is reduced to the size of a pinhole, then the disk becomes ribbed with alternating concentric bands of light and darkness, somewhat like those of a conventional target. This phenomenon is known as diffraction and has been compared with the tendency of ocean waves to bend and diverge on passing through the narrow mouth of a harbor. If instead of one pinhole, two pinholes are employed very close together and side by side, the diffraction patterns merge in a series of parallel stripes. Just as two wave systems meeting in a swimming pool will reinforce each other when crest coincides with crest and annul each other when the crest of one wave meets the trough of another,

[10] A technique that analyzes light and produces a spectrum analysis according to the wavelengths emitted.

so in the case of the adjacent pinholes the bright stripes occur where two light waves reinforce each other and the dark stripes where two waves have interfered. These phenomena—diffraction and interference—are strictly wave characteristics and would not occur if light were made up of individual corpuscles.[11] More than two centuries of experiment and theory assert that light *must* consist of waves. Yet Einstein's photoelectric Law shows that light *must* consist of photons.

This fundamental question—is light waves or is it particles?—has never been answered. The dual character of light is, however, only one aspect of a deeper and more remarkable duality which pervades all nature.

The first hint of this strange dualism came in 1925, when a young French physicist named Louis de Broglie[12] suggested that phenomena involving the interplay of matter and radiation could best be understood by regarding electrons not as individual particles but as systems of waves. This audacious concept flouted two decades of quantum research in which physicists had built up rather specific ideas about the elementary particles of matter. The atom had come to be pictured as a kind of miniature solar system composed of a central nucleus surrounded by varying numbers of electrons (1 for hydrogen, 92 for uranium) revolving in circular or elliptical orbits. The electron was less vivid. Experiments showed that all electrons had exactly the same mass and the same electrical charge, so it was natural to regard them as the ultimate foundation stones of the universe. It also seemed logical at first to picture them simply as hard elastic spheres. But little by little, as investigation progressed, they became more capricious, defiant of observation and measurement. In many ways their behavior appeared too complex for any material particle. "The hard sphere," declared the British physicist, Sir James Jeans,[13] "has always a definite position in space; the electron apparently has not. A hard sphere takes up a very definite amount of room; an electron—well it is probably as meaningless to discuss how much room an electron takes up as it is to discuss how much room a fear, an anxiety, or an uncertainty takes up."

Shortly after de Broglie had his vision of "matter waves" a Viennese physicist named Schrödinger[14] developed the same idea in coherent mathematical form, evolving a system that explained quantum phenomena by attributing specific wave functions to protons and electrons. This system, known as "wave mechanics," was corroborated in 1927 when two American scientists, Davisson and Germer,[15] proved by experiment that electrons actually do exhibit wave characteristics. They directed a beam of electrons upon a metal crystal and obtained diffraction patterns analogous to those produced when light is passed through a pinhole.[16] Their measurements indicated, moreover,

---

[11] Elementary particles of matter.

[12] Louis Victor de Broglie (1892–   ), French physicist and winner of the 1929 Nobel Prize.

[13] Sir James Jeans (1877–1946), English astrophysicist, theorized that matter within the universe is continuously created.

[14] Erwin Schrödinger (1887–1961), Austrian physicist and winner of the Nobel Prize in 1933, who discovered the basic equation of quantum theory for describing wave mechanics.

[15] Clinton Davisson (1881–1958), winner of the 1937 Nobel Prize in physics, and Lester Germer (1896–1971), found that crystals produced diffraction or interaction of wave fronts in electrons.

[16] A crystal, because of the even and orderly arrangement of its component atoms and the closeness of their spacing, serves as a diffraction grating for very short wavelengths, such as those of X-rays. [Barnett's note.]

that the wave length of an electron is of the precise magnitude predicted by de Broglie's equation, $\lambda = h/mv'$ where v is the velocity of the electron, m is its mass, and h is Planck's Constant. But further surprises were in store. For subsequent experiments showed that not only electrons but whole atoms and even molecules produce wave patterns when diffracted by a crystal surface, and that their wave lengths are exactly what de Broglie and Schrödinger forecast. And so all the basic units of matter—what J. Clerk Maxwell[17] called "the imperishable foundation stones of the universe"—gradually shed their substance. The old-fashioned spherical electron was reduced to an undulating charge of electrical energy, the atom to a system of superimposed waves. One could only conclude that all matter is made of waves and we live in a world of waves.

The paradox presented by waves of matter on the one hand and particles of light on the other was resolved by several developments in the decade before World War II. The German physicists, Heisenberg[18] and Born,[19] bridged the gap by developing a new mathematical apparatus that permitted accurate description of quantum phenomena either in terms of waves *or* in terms of particles as one wished. The idea behind their system had a profound influence on the philosophy of science. They maintained it is pointless of a physicist to worry about the properties of a single electron; in the laboratory he works with beams or showers of electrons, each containing billions of individual particles (or waves); he is concerned therefore only with mass behavior, with statistics and the laws of probability and chance. So it makes no practical difference whether individual electrons are particles or systems of waves—in aggregate they can be pictured either way. For example, if two physicists are at the seashore one may analyze an ocean wave by saying, "Its properties and intensity are clearly indicated by the positions of its crest and its trough"; while the other may observe with equal accuracy, "The section which you term a crest is significant simply because it contains more molecules of water than the area you call a trough." Analogously Born took the mathematical expression used by Schrödinger in his equations to denote wave function and interpreted it as a "probability" in a statistical sense. That is to say he regarded the intensity of any part of a wave as a measure of the probable distribution of particles at that point. Thus he dealt with the phenomena of diffraction, which hitherto only the wave theory could explain, in terms of the probability of certain corpuscles—light quanta or electrons—following certain paths and arriving at certain places. And so "waves of matter" were reduced to "waves of probability." It no longer matters how we visualize an electron or an atom or a probability wave. The equations of Heisenberg and Born fit any picture. And we can, if we choose, imagine ourselves living in a universe of waves, a universe of particles, or as one facetious scientist has phrased it, a universe of "waveicles."

While quantum physics thus defines with great accuracy the mathematical relationships governing the basic units of radiation and matter, it further obscures the true nature of both. Most modern physicists, however, consider it rather naïve to speculate

[17] J. Clerk Maxwell (1831–1879), Scottish physicist, discovered that both light waves and electromagnetic fields shared similar properties, and that changes in one energy form produced effects in the other field.

[18] Werner Karl Heisenberg (1901–1976) theorized that data in physics is altered by the actual observation.

[19] Max Born (1882–1970), German physicist and winner of the Nobel Prize in 1954, did pioneering research on the behavior of crystal lattices.

about the true nature of anything. They are "positivists"—or "logical empiricists"—who contend that a scientist can do more than report his observations. And so if he performs two experiments with different instruments and one seems to reveal that light is made up of particles and the other that light is made up of waves, he must accept both results, regarding them not as contradictory but as complementary. By itself neither concept suffices to explain light, but together they do. Both are necessary to describe reality and it is meaningless to ask which is really true. For in the abstract lexicon of quantum physics there is no such word as "really."

It is futile, moreover, to hope that the invention of more delicate tools may enable man to penetrate much farther into the microcosm. There is an indeterminacy about all the events of the atomic universe which refinements of measurement and observation can never dispel. The element of caprice in atomic behavior cannot be blamed on man's coarse-grained implements. It stems from the very nature of things, as shown by Heisenberg in 1927 in a famous statement of physical law known as the "Principle of Uncertainty." To illustrate his thesis Heisenberg pictured an imaginary experiment in which a physicist attempts to observe the position and velocity[20] of a moving electron by using an immensely powerful supermicroscope. Now, as has already been suggested, an individual electron appears to have no definite position or velocity. A physicist can define electron behavior accurately enough so long as he is dealing with great numbers of them. But when he tries to locate a particular electron in space the best he can say is that a certain point in the complex superimposed wave motions of the electron group represents the *probable* position of the electron in question. The individual electron is a blur—as indeterminate as the wind or a sound wave in the night—and the fewer the electrons with which the physicists deals, the more indeterminate his findings. To prove that this indeterminacy is a symptom not of man's immature science but of an ultimate barrier of nature, Heisenberg presupposed that the imaginary microscope used by his imaginary physicist is optically capable of magnifying by a hundred billion diameters—i.e., enough to bring an object the size of an electron within range of human visibility. But now a further difficulty is encountered. For inasmuch as an electron is smaller than a light wave, the physicist can "illuminate" his subject only by using radiation of shorter wave length. Even X-rays are useless. The electron can be rendered visible only by the high-frequency gamma rays of radium. But the photoelectric effect, it will be recalled, showed that photons of ordinary light exert a violent force on electrons; and X-rays knock them about even more roughly. Hence the impact of a still more potent gamma ray would prove disastrous.

The Principle of Uncertainty asserts therefore that it is absolutely and forever impossible to determine the position and the velocity of an electron at the same time—to state confidently that an electron is "right here at this spot" and is moving at "such and such a speed." For by the very act of observing its position, its velocity is changed; and, conversely, the more accurately its velocity is determined, the more indefinite its position becomes. And when the physicist computes the mathematical margin of uncertainty in his measurements of an electron's position and velocity he finds it is always a function of that mysterious quantity—Planck's Constant, *h*.

Quantum physics thus demolishes two pillars of the old science, causality and determination. For by dealing in terms of statistics and probabilities it abandons all

---

[20] In physics the term "velocity" connotes direction as well as speed. [Barnett's note.]

idea that nature exhibits an inexorable sequence of cause and effect. And by its admission of margins of uncertainty it yields up the ancient hope that science, given the present state and velocity of every material body in the universe, can forecast the history of the universe for all time. One by-product of this surrender is a new argument for the existence of free will. For if physical events are indeterminate and the future is unpredictable, then perhaps the unknown quantity called "mind" may yet guide man's destiny among the infinite uncertainties of a capricious universe. But this notion invades a realm of thought with which the physicist is not concerned. Another conclusion of greater scientific importance is that in the evolution of quantum physics the barrier between man, peering dimly through the clouded windows of his senses, and whatever objective reality may exist has been rendered almost impassable. For whenever he attempts to penetrate and spy on the "real" objective world, he changes and distorts its workings by the very process of his observations. And when he tries to divorce this "real" world from his sense perceptions he is left with nothing but a mathematical scheme. He is indeed somewhat in the position of a blind man trying to discern the shape and texture of a snowflake. As soon as it touches his fingers or his tongue it dissolves. A wave electron, a photon, a wave of probability, cannot be visualized; they are simply symbols useful in expressing the mathematical relationship of the microcosm.

To the question, why does modern physics employ such esoteric methods of description, the physicist answers: because the equations of quantum physics define more accurately than any mechanical model the fundamental phenomena beyond the range of vision. In short, *they work,* as the calculations which hatched the atomic bomb spectacularly proved. The aim of the practical physicist, therefore, is to enunciate the laws of nature in ever more precise mathematical terms. Where the nineteenth century physicist envisaged electricity as a fluid and, with this metaphor in mind, evolved the laws that generated our present electrical age, the twentieth century physicist tends to avoid metaphors. He knows that electricity is not a fluid, and he knows that such pictorial concepts as "waves" and "particles," while serving as guideposts to new discovery, must not be accepted as accurate representations of reality. In the abstract language of mathematics he can describe how things behave though he does not know—or need to know—what they are.

Yet there are present-day physicists to whom the void between science and reality presents a challenge. Einstein has more than once expressed the hope that the statistical method of quantum physics would prove a temporary expedient. "I cannot believe," he says, "that God plays dice with the world." He repudiates the positivist doctrine that science can only report and correlate the results of observation. He believes in a universe of order and harmony. And he believes that questing man may yet attain a knowledge of physical reality. To this end he has looked not within the atom, but outward to the stars, and beyond them to the vast drowned depths of empty space and time. . . .

In order to describe the mechanics of the physical universe, three quantities are required: time, distance, and mass. Since time and distance are relative quantities one might guess that the mass of a body also varies with its state of motion. And indeed the most important practical results of Relativity have arisen from this principle— the relativity of mass.

In its popular sense, "mass" is just another word for "weight." But as used by the physicist, it denotes a rather different and more fundamental property of matter:

namely, resistance to a change of motion. A greater force is necessary to move a freight car than a velocipede;[21] the freight car resists motion more stubbornly than the velocipede because it has greater mass. In classical physics the mass of any body is a fixed and unchanging property. Thus the mass of a freight car should remain the same whether it is at rest on a siding, rolling across country at 60 miles an hour, or hurtling through outer space at 60,000 miles a second. But Relativity asserts that the mass of a moving body is by no means constant, but increases with its velocity. The old physics failed to discover this fact simply because man's senses and instruments are too crude to note the infinitesimal increases of mass produced by the feeble accelerations of ordinary experience. They become perceptible only when bodies attain velocities close to that of light. (This phenomenon, incidentally, does not conflict with the relativistic contraction of length. One is tempted to ask: how can an object become smaller and at the same time get heavier? The contraction, it should be noted, is only in the direction of motion; width and breadth are unaffected. Moreover mass is not "heaviness" but resistance to motion.)

Einstein's equation giving the increase of mass with velocity is similar in form to the other equations of Relativity but vastly more important in its consequences:

$$m = \frac{m_o}{\sqrt{1 - (v^2/c^2)}}$$

Here m stands for the mass of a body moving with velocity v, m_0 for its mass when at rest, and c for the velocity of light. Anyone who has ever studied elementary algebra can readily see that if v is small, as are all the velocities of ordinary experience, then the difference between m_0 and m is practically zero. But when v approaches the value of c then the increase of mass becomes very great, reaching infinity when the velocity of the moving body reaches the velocity of light. Since a body of infinite mass would offer infinite resistance to motion the conclusion is once again reached that no material body can travel with the speed of light.

Of all aspects of Relativity the principle of increase of mass has been most often verified and most fruitfully applied by experimental physicists. Electrons moving in powerful electrical fields and beta particles[22] ejected from the nuclei of radioactive substances attain velocities ranging up to 99 per cent that of light. For atomic physicists concerned with these great speeds, the increase of mass predicted by Relativity is no arguable theory but an empirical fact their calculations cannot ignore. In fact the mechanics of the proton-synchrotron[23] and other new super-energy machines are designed to allow for the increasing mass of particles as their speed approaches the velocity of light.

By further deduction from his principle of Relativity of mass, Einstein arrived at a conclusion of incalculable importance to the world. His train of reasoning ran somewhat as follows: since the mass of a moving body increases as its motion increases, and since motion is a form of energy (kinetic energy), then the increased mass of a moving body comes from its increased energy. In short, energy has mass! By a few

[21] A "velocipede" is a lightweight vehicle used for carrying one person down railroad tracks to inspect the condition of the tracks and railbed.

[22] "Beta particles" are charged particles emitted from the nucleus of an atom in the process of radioactive decay.

[23] An electromagnetic device, sometimes called a "cyclotron" or "atom smasher," that accelerates the speeds of basic particles such as protons.

comparatively simple mathematical steps, Einstein found the value of the equivalent mass in m in any unit of energy E and expressed it by the equation $m = E/c^2$. Given this relation a high school freshmen can take the remaining algebraic step necessary to write the most important and certainly the most famous equation in history: $E = mc^2$.

The part played by this equation in the development of the atomic bomb is familiar to most newspaper readers. It states in the shorthand of physics that the energy contained in any particle of matter is equal to the mass of that body (in grams) multiplied by the square of the velocity of light (in centimeters per second). This extraordinary relationship becomes more vivid when its terms are translated into concrete values: i.e., one kilogram of coal (about two pounds), if converted *entirely* into energy, would yield 25 billion kilowatt hours of electricity or as much as all the power plants in the U.S. could generate by running steadily for two months.

$E = mc^2$ provides the answer to many of the long-standing mysteries of physics. It explains how radioactive substances like radium and uranium are able to eject particles at enormous velocities and to go on doing so for millions of years. It explains how the sun and all the stars can go on radiating light and heat for billions of years, for if our sun were being consumed by ordinary processes of combustion, the earth would have died in frozen darkness eons ago. It reveals the magnitude of the energy that slumbers in the nuclei of atoms, and forecasts how many grams of uranium must go into a bomb in order to destroy a city. Finally it discloses some fundamental truths about physical reality. Prior to Relativity scientists had pictured the universe as a vessel containing two distinct elements, matter and energy—the former inert, tangible, and characterized by a property called mass, and the latter active, invisible, and without mass. But Einstein showed that mass and energy are equivalent: the property called mass is simply concentrated energy. In other words matter is energy and energy is matter, and the distinction is simply one of temporary state.

In the light of this broad principle many puzzles of nature are resolved. The baffling interplay of matter and radiation which appears sometimes to be a concourse of particles and sometimes a meeting of waves, becomes more understandable. The dual role of the electron as a unit of matter and a unit of electricity, the wave electron, the photon, waves of matter, waves of probability, a universe of waves—all these seem less paradoxical. For all these concepts simply describe different manifestations of the same underlying reality, and it no longer makes sense to ask what any one of them "really" is. Matter and energy are interchangeable. If matter sheds its mass and travels with the speed of light we call it radiation or energy. And conversely if energy congeals and becomes inert and we can ascertain its mass we call it matter. Heretofore science could only note their ephemeral properties and relations as they touched the perceptions of earthbound man. But since July 16, 1945, man has been able to transform one into the other. For on that night at Alamogordo, New Mexico, man for the first time transmuted a substantial quantity of matter into the light, heat, sound, and motion which we call energy.

Yet the fundamental mystery remains. The whole march of science toward the unification of concepts—the reduction of all matter to elements and then to a few types of particles, the reduction of "forces" to the single concept "energy," and then the reduction of matter *and* energy to a single basic quantity—leads still to the unknown. The many questions merge into one, to which there may never be an answer: what is the essence of this mass-energy substance, what is the underlying stratum of physical reality which science seeks to explore?

Thus Relativity, like the Quantum Theory, draws man's intellect still farther away from the Newtonian universe, firmly rooted in space and time and functioning like some great, unerring, and manageable machine. Einstein's laws of motion, his basic principles of the relativity of distance, time, and mass, and his deductions from these principles comprise what is known as the Special Theory of Relativity. In the decade following the publication of this original work, he expanded his scientific and philosophical system into the General Theory of Relativity, through which he examined the mysterious force that guides the whirling of the stars, comets, meteors, and galaxies, and all the moving systems of iron, stone, vapor, and flame in the immense inscrutable void. Newton called this force "universal gravitation." From his own concept of gravitation Einstein attained a view of the vast architecture and anatomy of the universe as a whole.

MEANING

1. How did Einstein bring a new perspective to the classic Newtonian idea that mass and energy were two separate and distinct states?
2. Which of Einstein's discoveries solved a particular problem that simultaneously brought into view even greater problems to be solved?
3. Why is it necessary to express solutions to problems in physics in the form of mathematical equations?
4. How does this article show that man is severely limited to what he can know about the universe by using only his natural senses?
5. Einstein solved the age-old dilemma as to whether light existed in the form of particles or in the form of waves. What was Einstein's solution to this problem?

USING PROBLEM SOLVING TO CONVEY MEANING

1. How did analogies provide Einstein with an intuitive means of grasping basic problems of time, matter, and motion, which his later equations would bear out?
2. How does Barnett use past controversies surrounding the questions of color perception to set the stage for a discussion of Einstein's scientific contributions?
3. How is Barnett's discussion organized to show that Einstein's genius lay in his ability to rearrange the traditional elements of a problem in new ways by changing his perspective?
4. Evaluate Barnett's success in adapting and presenting the history of a difficult, yet invaluable, discovery for a general audience.

WRITING SUGGESTIONS

1. How were inventions like television and the laser (see Charles H. Townes, page 563) made possible by Einstein's discoveries?

2. In what other disciplines can the process of making observations also change the phenomena being observed, as can happen in physics? For example, what risks along these lines do zoologists or anthropologists face? (See Jane van Lawick-Goodall, page 125, and Melford E. Spiro, page 352.)

THOR HEYERDAHL

How to Kill an Ocean

Thor Heyerdahl, the daring Norwegian explorer and anthropologist, was born in 1914, educated at the University of Oslo, and served with the Free Norwegian Military Forces, 1940–1945. The sea-faring odysseys, which won him international renown, attempted to establish that the pre-Inca inhabitants of Peru could have originally sailed from Peru and settled in Polonesia. To prove this, Heyerdahl constructed a balsa raft and successfully navigated from Callao, Peru to Tuamotu Island in the South Pacific. In later voyages, Heyerdahl sailed from Morocco in a papyrus boat, the Ra II, to the West Indies, and in 1977–1978 journeyed from Qurna, Iraq, to Djibouti, on the Gulf of Aden, in a boat made entirely of reeds. His fascinating adventures are recounted in On the Hunt for Paradise *(1938),* The Kon-Tiki Expedition *(1948),* Aku-Aku *(1958), and most recently,* The Maldive Mystery *(1986), a true life archeological detective story. In "How to Kill an Ocean," which originally appeared in* Saturday Review *(1975), Heyerdahl disputes the traditional concept of a "boundless ocean" and identifies current threats that could endanger the oceans of the world.*

Since the ancient Greeks maintained that the earth was round and great navigators like Columbus and Magellan demonstrated that this assertion was true, no geographical discovery has been more important than what we all are beginning to understand today: that our planet has exceedingly restricted dimensions. There is a limit to all resources. Even the height of the atmosphere and the depth of soil and water represent layers so thin that they would disappear entirely if reduced to scale on the surface of a commonsized globe.

The correct concept of our very remarkable planet, rotating as a small and fertile oasis, two-thirds covered by life-giving water, and teeming with life in a solar system otherwise unfit for man, becomes clearer for us with the progress of moon travel and modern astronomy. Our concern about the limits to human expansion increases as science produces ever more exact data on the measurable resources that mankind has in stock for all the years to come.

Because of the population explosion, land of any nature has long been in such demand that nations have intruded upon each other's territory with armed forces in order to conquer more space for overcrowded communities. During the last few years, the United Nations has convened special meetings in Stockholm, Caracas, and Geneva in a dramatic attempt to create a "Law of the Sea" designed to divide vast sections of the global ocean space into national waters. The fact that no agreement has been reached illustrates that in our ever-shriveling world there is not even ocean space enough to satisfy everybody. And only one generation ago, the ocean was considered so vast that no one nation would bother to lay claim to more of it than the three-mile limit which represented the length of a gun shot from the shore.

It will probably take still another generation before mankind as a whole begins to realize fully that the ocean is but another big lake, landlocked on all sides. Indeed, it is essential to understand this concept for the survival of coming generations. For we of the 20th century still treat the ocean as the endless, bottomless pit it was considered to be in medieval times. Expressions like "the bottomless sea" and "the boundless ocean" are still in common use, and although we all know better, they reflect the mental image we still have of this, the largest body of water on earth. Perhaps one of the reasons why we subconsciously consider the ocean a sort of bottomless abyss is the fact that all the rain and all the rivers of the world keep pouring constantly into it and yet its water level always remains unchanged. Nothing affects the ocean, not even the Amazon, the Nile, or the Ganges. We know, of course, that this imperviousness is no indicator of size, because the sum total of all the rivers is nothing but the return to its own source of the water evaporated from the sea and carried ashore by drifting clouds.

What is it really then that distinguishes the ocean from the other more restricted bodies of water? Surely it is not its salt content. The Old and the New World have lakes with a higher salt percentage than the ocean has. The Aral Sea, the Dead Sea, and the Great Salt Lake in Utah are good examples. Nor is it the fact that the ocean lacks any outlet. Other great bodies of water have abundant input and yet no outlet. The Caspian Sea and Lake Chad in Central Africa are valid examples. Big rivers, among them the Volga, enter the Caspian Sea, but evaporation compensates for its lack of outlet, precisely as is the case with the ocean. Nor is it correct to claim that the ocean is open while inland seas and lakes are landlocked. The ocean is just as landlocked as any lake. It is flanked by land on all sides and in every direction. The fact that the earth is round makes the ocean curve around it just as does solid land, but a shoreline encloses the ocean on all sides and in every direction. The ocean is not even the lowest body of water on our planet. The surface of the Caspian Sea, for instance, is 85 feet below sea level, and the surface of the Dead Sea is more than 1,200 feet below sea level.

Only when we fully perceive that there is no fundamental difference between the various bodies of water on our planet, beyond the fact that the ocean is the largest of all lakes, can we begin to realize that the ocean has something else in common with all other bodies of water: it is vulnerable. In the long run the ocean can be affected by the continued discharge of all modern man's toxic waste. One generation ago no one would have thought that the giant lakes of America could be polluted. Today they are, like the largest lakes of Europe. A few years ago the public was amazed to learn that industrial and urban refuse had killed the fish in Lake Erie. The enormous lake was dead. It was polluted from shore to shore in spite of the fact that it has a constant outlet through Niagara Falls, which carries pollutants away into the ocean in a never-ending flow. The ocean receiving all this pollution has no outlet but represents a dead end, because only pure water evaporates to return into the clouds. The ocean is big; yet if 10 Lake Eries were taken and placed end to end, they would span the entire Atlantic from Africa to South America. And the St. Lawrence River is by no means the only conveyor of pollutants into the ocean. Today hardly a creek or a river in the world reaches the ocean without carrying a constant flow of nondegradable chemicals from industrial, urban, or agricultural areas. Directly by sewers or indirectly by way of streams and other waterways, almost every big city in the world, whether coastal or inland, makes use of the ocean as mankind's common sink. We treat the ocean as if we believed that it is not part of our own planet—as if the blue waters curved into space somewhere beyond the horizon where our pollutants would fall off the edge, as ships were believed to do before the days of Christopher Columbus. We build sewers so far into the sea that we pipe the harmful refuse away from public beaches. Beyond that is no man's concern. What we consider too dangerous to be stored under technical control ashore we dump forever out of sight at sea, whether toxic chemicals or nuclear waste. Our only excuse is the still-surviving image of the ocean as a bottomless pit.

It is time to ask: is the ocean vulnerable? And if so, can many survive on a planet with a dead ocean? Both questions can be answered, and they are worthy of our attention.

First, the degree of vulnerability of any body of water would of course depend on two factors: the volume of the water and the nature of the pollutants. We know the volume of the ocean, its surface measure, and its average depth. We know that it covers 71 percent of the surface of our planet, and we are impressed, with good reason, when all these measurements are given in almost astronomical figures. If we resort to a more visual image, however, the dimensions lose their magic. The average depth of all oceans is only 1,700 meters. The Empire State Building is 448 meters high. If stretched out horizontally instead of vertically, the average ocean depth would only slightly exceed the 1,500 meters than an Olympic runner can cover by foot in 3 minutes and 35 seconds. The average depth of the North Sea, however, is not 1,700 meters, but only 80 meters, and many of the buildings in downtown New York would emerge high above water level if they were built on the bottom of this sea. During the Stone Age most of the North Sea was dry land where roaming archers hunted deer and other game. In this shallow water, until only recently, all the industrial nations of Western Europe have conducted year-round routine dumping of hundreds of thousands of tons of their most toxic industrial refuse. All the world's sewers and most of its waste are dumped into waters as shallow as, or shallower than, the North Sea. An attempt was made at a recent ocean exhibition to illustrate graphically and in correct proportion the depths of the Atlantic, the Pacific, and the Indian oceans in relation to a cross section of the planet earth. The project had to be abandoned, for although the earth was painted with a diameter twice the height of a man, the depths of the world oceans painted in proportion became so insignificant that they could not be seen except as a very thin pencil line.

The ocean is in fact remarkably shallow for its size. Russia's Lake Baikal, for instance, less than 31 kilometers wide, is 1,500 meters deep, which compares well with the average depth of all oceans. It is the vast *extent* of ocean surface that has made man of all generations imagine a correspondingly unfathomable depth.

When viewed in full, from great heights, the ocean's surface is seen to have definite, confining limits. But at sea level, the ocean seems to extend outward indefinitely, to the horizon and on into blue space. The astronauts have come back from space literally disturbed upon seeing a full view of our planet. They have seen at first hand how cramped together the nations are in a limited space and how the "endless" oceans are tightly enclosed within cramped quarters by surrounding land masses. But one need not be an astronaut to lose the sensation of a boundless ocean. It is enough to embark on some floating logs tied together, as we did with the *Kon-Tiki* in the Pacific, or on some bundles of papyrus reeds, as we did with the *Ra* in the Atlantic. With no effort and no motor we were pushed by the winds and currents from one continent to another in a few weeks.

After we abandon the outworn image of infinite space in the ocean, we are still left with many wrong or useless notions about biological life and vulnerability. Marine life is concentrated in about 4 percent of the ocean's total body of water, whereas roughly 96 percent is just about as poor in life as is a desert ashore. We all know, and should bear in mind, that sunlight is needed to permit photosynthesis for the marine plankton on which all fishes and whales directly or indirectly base their subsistence. In the sunny tropics the upper layer of light used in photosynthesis extends down to a maximum depth of 80 to 100 meters. In the northern latitudes, even on a bright summer's day, this zone reaches no more than 15 to 20 meters below the surface. Because much of the most toxic pollutants are buoyant and stay on the surface (notably all the pesticides and other poisons based on chlorinated hydrocarbons), this concentration of both life and venom in the same restricted body of water is most unfortunate.

What is worse is the fact that life is not evenly distributed throughout this thin surface layer. Ninety percent of all marine species are concentrated above the continental shelves next to land. The water above these littoral shelves represents an area of only 8 percent of the total ocean surface, which itself represents only 4 percent of the total body of water, and means that much less than half a percent of the ocean space represents the home of 90 percent of all marine life. This concentration of marine life in shallow waters next to the coasts happens to coincide with the area of concentrated dumping and the outlet of all sewers and polluted river mouths, not to mention silt from chemically treated farmland. The bulk of some 20,000 known species of fish, some 30,000 species of mollusks, and nearly all the main crustaceans lives in the most exposed waters around the littoral areas. As we know, the reason is that this is the most fertile breeding ground for marine plankton. The marine plant life, the phytoplankton, find here their mineral nutriments, which are brought down by rivers and silt and up from the ocean bottom through coastal upwellings that bring back to the surface the remains of decomposed organisms which have sunk to the bottom through the ages.

When we speak of farmable land in any country, we do not include deserts or sterile rock in our calculations. Why then shall we deceive ourselves by the total size of the ocean when we know that not even 1 percent of its water volume is fertile for the fisherman?

Much has been written for or against the activities of some nations that have dumped vast quantities of nuclear waste and obsolete war gases in the sea and excused their actions on the grounds that it was all sealed in special containers. In such shallow waters as the Irish Sea, the English Channel, and the North Sea there are already enough examples of similar "foolproof" containers moving about with bottom currents until they are totally displaced and even crack open with the result that millions of fish are killed or mutilated. In the Baltic Sea, which is shallower than many lakes and which—except for the thin surface layer—has already been killed by pollution, 7,000 tons of arsenic were dumped in cement containers some 40 years ago. These containers have now started to leak. Their combined contents are three times more than is needed to kill the entire population of the earth today.

Fortunately, in certain regions modern laws have impeded the danger of dumpings; yet a major threat to marine life remains—the less spectacular but more effective ocean pollution through continuous discharge from sewers and seepage. Except in the Arctic, there is today hardly a creek or a river in the world from which it is safe to drink at the outlet. The more technically advanced the country, the more devastating the threat to the ocean. A few examples picked at random will illustrate the pollution input from the civilized world:

French rivers carry 18 billion cubic meters of liquid pollution annually into the sea. The city of Paris alone discharges almost 1.2 million cubic meters of untreated effluent into the Seine every day.

The volume of liquid waste from the Federal Republic of Germany is estimated at over 9 billion cubic meters per year, or 25.4 million cubic meters per day, not counting cooling water, which daily amounts to 33.6 million cubic meters. Into the Rhine alone 50,000 tons of waste are discharged daily, including 30,000 tons of sodium chloride from industrial plants.

A report from the U.N. Economic and Social Council, issued prior to the Stockholm Conference on the Law of the Sea four years ago, states that the world had then dumped an estimated billion pounds of DDT into our environment and was adding an estimated 100 million more pounds per year. The total world production of pesticides was estimated at more than 1.3 billion pounds annually, and the United States alone exports more than 400 million pounds per year. Most of this ultimately finds its way into the ocean with winds, rain, or silt from land. A certain type of DDT sprayed on crops in East Africa a few years ago was found and identified a few months later in the Bay of Bengal, a good 4,000 miles away.

The misconception of a boundless ocean makes the man in the street more concerned about city smog than about the risk of killing the ocean. Yet the tallest chimney in the world does not suffice to send the noxious smoke away into space; it gradually sinks down, and nearly all descends, mixed with rain, snow, and silt, into the ocean. Industrial and urban areas are expanding with the population explosion all over the world, and in the United States alone, waste products in the form of smoke and noxious fumes amount to a total of 390,000 tons of pollutants every day, or 142 million tons every year.

With this immense concentration of toxic matter, life on the continental shelves would in all likelihood have been exterminated or at least severely decimated long since if the ocean had been immobile. The cause for the delayed action, which may benefit man for a few decades but will aggravate the situation for coming generations, is the well-known fact that the ocean rotates like boiling water in a kettle. It churns from east to west, from north to south, from the bottom to the surface, and down again, in perpetual motion. At a U.N. meeting one of the developing countries proposed that if ocean dumping were prohibited by global or regional law, they would offer friendly nations the opportunity of dumping in their own national waters—for a fee, of course!

It cannot be stressed too often, however, that it is nothing but a complete illusion when we speak of national waters. We can map and lay claim to the ocean bottom, but not to the mobile sea above it. The water itself is in constant transmit. What is considered to be the national waters of Morocco one day turns up as the national waters of Mexico soon after. Meanwhile Mexican national water is soon on its way across the North Atlantic to Norway. Ocean pollution abides by no law.

My own transoceanic drifts with the *Kon-Tiki* raft and the reed vessels *Ra I* and *II* were eye-openers to me and my companions as to the rapidity with which so-called national waters displace themselves. The distance from Peru to the Tuamotu

Islands in Polynesia is 4,000 miles when it is measured on a map. Yet the *Kon-Tiki* raft had only crossed about 1,000 miles of ocean surface when we arrived. The other 3,000 miles had been granted us by the rapid flow of the current during the 101 days our crossing lasted. But the same raft voyages taught us another and less pleasant lesson: it is possible to pollute the oceans, and it is already being done. In 1947, when the balsa raft *Kon-Tiki* crossed the Pacific, we towed a plankton net behind. Yet we did not collect specimens or even see any sign of human activity in the crystal-clear water until we spotted the wreck of an old sailing ship on the reef where we landed. In 1969 it was therefore a blow to us on board the papyrus raft-ship *Ra* to observe, shortly after our departure from Morocco, that we had sailed into an area filled with ugly clumps of hard asphalt-like material, brownish to pitch black in color, which were floating at close intervals on or just below the water's surface. Later on, we sailed into other areas so heavily polluted with similar clumps that we were reluctant to dip up water with our buckets when we needed a good scrub-down at the end of the day. In between these areas the ocean was clean except for occasional floating oil lumps and other widely scattered refuse such as plastic containers, empty bottles, and cans. Because the ropes holding the papyrus reeds of *Ra I* together burst, the battered wreck was abandoned in polluted waters short of the island of Barbados, and a second crossing was effectuated all the way from Safi in Morocco to Barbados in the West Indies in 1970. This time a systematic day-by-day survey of ocean pollution was carried out, and samples of oil lumps collected were sent to the United Nations together with a detailed report on the observations. This was published by Secretary-General U Thant as an annex to his report to the Stockholm Conference on the Law of the Sea. It is enough here to repeat that sporadic oil clots drifted by within reach of our dip net during 43 out of the 57 days our transatlantic crossing lasted. The laboratory analysis of the various samples of oil clots collected showed a wide range in the level of nickel and vanadium content, revealing that they originated from different geographical localities. This again proves that they represent not the homogeneous spill from a leaking oil drill or from a wrecked super-tanker, but the steadily accumulating waste from the daily routine washing of sludge from the combined world fleet of tankers.

The world was upset when the *Torrey Canyon* unintentionally spilled 100,000 tons of oil into the English Channel some years ago; yet this is only a small fraction of the intentional discharge of crude oil sludge through less spectacular, routine tank cleaning. Every year more than *Torrey Canyon's* spill of a 100,000 tons of oil is intentionally pumped into the Mediterranean alone, and a survey of the sea south of Italy yielded 500 liters of solidified oil for every square kilometer of surface. Both the Americans and the Russians were alarmed by our observations of Atlantic pollution in 1970 and sent out specially equipped oceanographic research vessels to the area. American scientists from Harvard University working with the Bermuda Biological Station for Research found more solidified oil than seaweed per surface unit in the Sargasso Sea and had to give up their plankton catch because their nets were completely plugged up by oil sludge. They estimated, however, a floating stock of 86,000 metric tons of tar in the Northwest Atlantic alone. The Russians, in a report read by the representative of the Soviet Academy of Sciences at a recent pollution conference in Prague, found that pollution in the coastal areas of the Atlantic had already surpassed their tentative limit for what had been considered tolerable, and that a new scale of tolerability would have to be postulated.

The problem of oil pollution is in itself a complex one. Various types of crude oil are toxic in different degrees. But they all have one property in common: they attract other chemicals and absorb them like blotting paper, notably the various kinds of pesticides. DDT and other chlorinated hydrocarbons do not dissolve in water, nor do they sink: just as they are absorbed by plankton and other surface organisms, so are they drawn into oil slicks and oil clots, where in some cases they have been rediscovered in stronger concentrations than when originally mixed with dissolvents in the spraying bottles. Oil clots, used as floating support for barnacles, marine worms, and pelagic crabs, were often seen by us from the *Ra*, and these riders are attractive bait for filter-feeding fish and whales, which cannot avoid getting gills and baleens cluttered up by the tarlike oil. Even sharks with their rows of teeth plastered with black oil clots are now reported from the Caribbean Sea. Yet the oil spills and dumping of waste from ships represent a very modest contribution compared with the urban and industrial refuse released from land.

That the ocean, given time, will cope with it all, is a common expression of wishful thinking. The ocean has always been a self-purifying filter that has taken care of all global pollution for millions of years. Man is not the first polluter. Since the morning of time nature itself has been a giant workshop, experimenting, inventing, decomposing, and throwing away waste: the incalculable billions of tons of rotting forest products, decomposing flesh, mud, silt, and excrement. If this waste had not been recycled, the ocean would long since have become a compact soup after millions of years of death and decay, volcanic eruptions, and global erosion. Man is not the first large-scale producer, so why should he become the first disastrous polluter?

Man has imitated nature by manipulating atoms, taking them apart and grouping them together in different compositions. Nature turned fish into birds and beasts into man. It found a way to make fruits out of soil and sunshine. It invented radar for bats and whales, and shortwave transceivers for beetles and butterflies. Jet propulsion was installed on squids, and unsurpassed computers were made as brains for mankind. Marine bacteria and plankton transformed the dead generations into new life. The life cycle of spaceship earth is the closest one can ever get to the greatest of all inventions, *perpetuum mobile*—the perpetual-motion machine. And the secret is that nothing was composed by nature that could not be recomposed, recycled, and brought back into service again in another form as another useful wheel in the smoothly running global machinery.

This is where man has sidetracked nature. We put atoms together into molecules of types nature had carefully avoided. We invent to our delight immediately useful materials like plastics, pesticides, detergents, and other chemical products hitherto unavailable on planet earth. We rejoice because we can get our laundry whiter than the snow we pollute and because we can exterminate every trace of insect life. We spray bugs and bees, worms and butterflies. We wash and flush the detergents down the drain out to the oysters and fish. Most of our new chemical products are not only toxic: they are in fact created to sterilize and kill. And they keep on displaying these same inherent abilities wherever they end up. Through sewers and seepage they all head for the ocean, where they remain to accumulate as undesired nuts and bolts in between the cogwheels of a so far smoothly running machine. If it had not been for the present generation, man could have gone on polluting the ocean forever with the degradable waste he produced. But with ever-increasing speed and intensity we now produce and discharge into the sea hundreds of thousands of chemicals and other products. They do not evaporate nor do they recycle, but they grow in numbers and quantity and threaten all marine life.

We have long known that our modern pesticides have begun to enter the flesh of penguins in the Antarctic and the brains of polar bears and the blubber of whales in the Arctic, all subsisting on plankton and plankton-eating crustaceans and fish in areas far from cities and farmland. We all know that marine pollution has reached global extent in a few decades. We also know that very little or nothing is being done to stop it. Yet there are persons who tell us that there is no reason to worry, that the ocean is so big and surely science must have everything under control. City smog is being fought through intelligent legislation. Certain lakes and rivers have been improved by leading the sewers down to the sea. But where, may we ask, is the global problem of ocean pollution under control?

No breathing species could live on this planet until the surface layer of the ocean was filled with phytoplankton, as our planet in the beginning was only surrounded by sterile gases. These minute plant species manufactured so much oxygen that it rose above the surface to help form the atmosphere we have today. All life on earth depended upon this marine plankton for its evolution and continued subsistence. Today, more than ever before, mankind depends on the welfare of this marine plankton for his future survival as a species. With the population explosion we need to harvest even more protein from the sea. Without plankton there will be no fish. With our rapid expansion of urban and industrial areas and the continuous disappearance of jungle and forest, we shall be ever more dependent on the plankton for the very air we breathe. Neither man nor any other terrestrial beast could have bred had plankton not preceded them. Take away this indispensable life in the shallow surface areas of the sea, and life ashore will be unfit for coming generations. A dead ocean means a dead planet.

MEANING

1. Why does Heyerdahl redefine the popular conception of the ocean's unlimited nature to emphasize its vulnerability?
2. What qualities, says Heyerdahl, distinguish the ocean from "the other more restricted bodies of water"?
3. To what types of pollution is the ocean most vulnerable?
4. Why does one form of pollution often make an entirely different kind of pollution far worse?

USING PROBLEM SOLVING TO CONVEY MEANING

1. How does Heyerdahl redefine through metaphor the usual concept of a vast, endless ocean to point out the magnitude of the problem?
2. How does Heyerdahl arrange his article to project a future catastrophic scenario based on what is currently known about the ocean?
3. What did Heyerdahl's dramatic illustrations of midocean pollution make you aware of that you had not known before?

4. How does Heyerdahl use statistics to support conclusions about the fragile ocean environment?

WRITING SUGGESTIONS

1. Discuss the part that greed or the desire for convenience plays in producing the pollution of any ecosystem. For example, (a) some beaches have far more jellyfish than ever before because (b) the turtles who normally feed on them mistake nonbiodegradable plastic bags for jellyfish, (c) feed on the plastic bags, die, destroying (d) the natural balance between the turtles and jellyfish, leading to (e) the loss of beaches as a natural and recreational resource.
2. How do Heyerdahl's experiences on the *Kon-Tiki* and the *Ra* add credibility to his discussion?

Rachel Carson

The Obligation to Endure

Rachel Carson (1907–1964), a founder of the ecology movement and renowned marine biologist, was born in Silver Springs, Maryland. After studying biology at the Pennsylvania College for Women (now Chatham College), and marine biology at Wood's Hole, Massachusetts, Carson received an M.A. in zoology from Johns Hopkins University in 1932. She taught at both the University of Maryland and Johns Hopkins University. In 1947, Carson was appointed editor-in-chief for the United States Fish and Wildlife Service and began her series of exhaustively researched, meticulously accurate, and beautifully written studies that established the science of ecology. The Sea Around Us (1951) *won the National Book Award, the John Burrough's Medal, and provided the basis for a full-length film that won a 1953 Oscar for best documentary.* Silent Spring (1962), *Carson's classic study of the effects on the environment of the uncontrolled use of pesticides like DDT, Chlordane, and Dieldrin, fully documented for the first time the consequences of insecticidal contamination of food, air, and water. Carson's work, although initially disputed by the chemical industry, made the public aware of the problem and resulted in federal action to regulate the use of pesticides. Carson was the first woman to receive the Audubon Medal, and was, at the time, only one of a dozen women elected to the American Academy of Arts and Letters. "The Obligation to Endure" begins* Silent Spring *with a dramatic fable of an eerie "silent spring" in a typical American town. No bird songs are heard because chemical insecticides have so contaminated the environment that insects, along with the birds that feed on them, have all been poisoned. The rest of her book is a wide-ranging synthesis revealing the cumulative long-term genetic changes and higher incidence of cancer that pesticides have produced.*

There was once a town in the heart of America where all life seemed to live in harmony with its surroundings. The town lay in the midst of a checkerboard of prosperous farms, with fields of grain and hillsides of orchards where, in spring, white clouds of bloom drifted above the green fields. In autumn, oak and maple and birch set up a blaze of color that flamed and flickered across a backdrop of pines. Then foxes barked in the hills and deer silently crossed the fields, half hidden in the mists of the fall mornings.

Along the roads, laurel, viburnum and alder, great ferns and wildflowers delighted the traveler's eye through much of the year. Even in winter the roadsides were places of beauty, where countless birds came to feed on the berries and on the seed heads of the dried weeds rising above the snow. The countryside was, in fact, famous for the abundance and variety of its bird life, and when the flood of migrants was pouring through in spring and fall people traveled from great distances to observe them. Others came to fish the streams, which flowed clear and cold out of the hills and contained shady pools where trout lay. So it had been from the days many years ago when the first settlers raised their houses, sank their wells, and built their barns.

Then a strange blight crept over the area and everything began to change. Some evil spell had settled on the community: mysterious maladies swept the flocks of chickens; the cattle and sheep sickened and died. Everywhere was a shadow of death. The farmers spoke of much illness among their families. In the town the doctors had become more and more puzzled by new kinds of sickness appearing among their patients. There had been several sudden and unexplained deaths, not only among adults but even among children, who would be striken suddenly while at play and die within a few hours.

There was a strange stillness. The birds, for example—where had they gone? Many people spoke of them, puzzled and disturbed. The feeding stations in the backyards were deserted. The few birds seen anywhere were moribund; they trembled violently and could not fly. It was a spring without voices. On the mornings that had once throbbed with the dawn chorus of robins, catbirds, doves, jays, wrens, and scores of other bird voices there was now no sound; only silence lay over the fields and woods and marsh.

On the farms the hens brooded, but no chicks hatched. The farmers complained that they were unable to raise any pigs—the litters were small and the young survived only a few days. The apple trees were coming into bloom but no bees droned among the blossoms, so there was no pollination and there would be no fruit.

The roadsides, once so attractive, were now lined with browned and withered vegetation as though swept by fire. These, too, were silent, deserted by all living things. Even the streams were now lifeless. Anglers no longer visited them, for all the fish had died.

In the gutters under the eaves and between the shingles of the roofs, a white granular powder still showed a few patches; some weeks before it had fallen like snow upon the roofs and the lawns, the fields and streams.

No witchcraft, no enemy action had silenced the rebirth of new life in this stricken world. The people had done it themselves.

This town does not actually exist, but it might easily exist, but it might easily have a thousand counterparts in America or elsewhere in the world. I know of no community that has experienced all the misfortunes I describe. Yet every one of these disasters has actually happened somewhere, and many real communities have already suffered a substantial number of them. A grim specter has crept upon us almost unnoticed, and this imagined tragedy may easily become a stark reality we all shall know.

What has already silenced the voices of spring in countless towns in America? This book is an attempt to explain.

The history of life on earth has been a history of interaction between living things and their surroundings. To a large extent, the physical form and the habits of the earth's vegetation and its animal life have been molded by the environment. Considering the whole span of earthly time, the opposite effect, in which life actually modifies its surroundings, has been relatively slight. Only within the moment of time represented by the present century has one species—man—acquired significant power to alter the nature of his world.

During the past quarter century this power has not only increased to one of disturbing magnitude but it has changed in character. The most alarming of all man's assaults upon the environment is the contamination of air, earth, rivers, and sea with dangerous and even lethal materials. This pollution is for the most part irrevocable; the chain of evil it initiates not only in the world that must support life but in living tissues is for the most part irreversible. In this now universal contamination of the environment, chemicals are the sinister and little-recognized partners of radiation in changing the very nature of the world—the very nature of its life. Strontium 90, released through nuclear explosions into the air, comes to earth in rain or drifts down as fallout, lodges in soil, enters into the grass or corn or wheat grown there, and in time takes up its abode in the bones of a human being, there to remain until his death. Similarly, chemicals sprayed on croplands or forests or gardens lie long in soil, entering into living organisms, passing from one to another in a chain of poisoning and death. Or they pass mysteriously by underground streams until they emerge and, through the alchemy of air and sunlight, combine into new forms that kill vegetation, sicken cattle, and work unknown harm on those who drink from once pure wells. As Albert Schweitzer has said, "Man can hardly even recognize the devils of his own creation."

It took hundreds of millions of years to produce the life that now inhabits the earth—eons of time in which that developing and evolving and diversifying life reached a state of adjustment and balance with its surroundings. The environment, rigorously shaping and directing the life it supported, contained elements that were hostile as well as supporting. Certain rocks gave out dangerous radiation; even within the light of the sun, from which all life draws its energy, there were short-wave radiations with power to injure. Given time—time not in years but in millennia—life adjusts, and a balance has been reached. For time is the essential ingredient; but in the modern world there is no time.

The rapidity of change and the speed with which new situations are created follow the impetuous and heedless pace of man rather than the deliberate pace of nature. Radiation is no longer merely the background radiation of rocks, the bombardment of cosmic rays, the ultraviolet of the sun that have existed before there was any life on earth; radiation is now the unnatural creation of man's tampering with the atom. The chemicals to which life is asked to make its adjustment are no longer merely the calcium and silica and copper and all the rest of the minerals washed out of the rocks and carried in rivers to the sea; they are the synthetic creations of man's inventive mind, brewed in his laboratories, and having no counterparts in nature.

To adjust to these chemicals would require time on the scale that is nature's; it would require not merely the years of a man's life but the life of generations. And even this, were it by some miracle possible, would be futile, for the new chemicals come from our laboratories in an endless stream; almost five hundred annually find their way into actual use in the United States alone. The figure is staggering and its implications are not easily grasped—500 new chemicals to which the bodies of men and animals are required somehow to adapt each year, chemicals totally outside the limits of biologic experience.

Among them are many that are used in man's war against nature. Since the mid-1940's over 200 basic chemicals have been created for use in killing insects, weeds, rodents, and other organisms described in the modern vernacular as "pests"; and they are sold under several thousand different brand names.

These sprays, dusts, and aerosols are now applied almost universally to farms, gardens, forests, and homes—nonselective chemicals that have the power to kill every insect, the "good" and the "bad," to still the song of birds and the leaping of fish in the streams, to coat the leaves with a deadly film, and to linger on in soil—all this though the intended target may be only a few weeds or insects. Can anyone believe it is possible to lay down such a barrage of poisons on the surface of the earth without making it unfit for all life? They should not be called "insecticides," but "biocides."

The whole process of spraying seems caught up in an endless spiral. Since DDT was released for civilian use, a process of escalation has been going on in which ever more toxic materials must be found. This has happened because insects, in a triumphant vindication of Darwin's principle of the survival of the fittest, have evolved super races immune to the particular insecticide used, hence a deadlier one has always to be developed—and then a deadlier one than that. It has happened also because, for reasons to be described later, destructive insects often undergo a "flareback," or resurgence, after spraying, in numbers greater than before. Thus the chemical war is never won, and all life is caught in its violent crossfire.

Along with the possibility of the extinction of mankind by nuclear war, the central problem of our age has therefore become the contamination of man's total environment with such substances of incredible potential for harm—substances that accumulate in the tissues of plants and animals and even penetrate the germ cells to shatter or alter the very material of heredity upon which the shape of the future depends.

Some would-be architects of our future look toward a time when it will be possible to alter the human germ plasm by design. But we may easily be doing so now by inadvertence, for many chemicals, like radiation, bring about gene mutations. It is ironic to think that man might determine his own future by something so seemingly trivial as the choice of an insect spray.

All this has been risked—for what? Future historians may well be amazed by our distorted sense of proportion. How could intelligent beings seek to control a few unwanted species by a method that contaminated the entire environment and brought the threat of disease and death even to their own kind? Yet this is precisely what we have done. We have done it, moreover, for reasons that collapse the moment we examine them. We are told that the enormous and expanding use of pesticides is necessary to maintain farm production. Yet is our real problem not one of *overproduction?* Our farms, despite measures to remove acreages from production and to pay farmers *not* to produce, have yielded such a staggering excess of crops that the American taxpayer in 1962 is paying out more than one billion dollars a year as the total carrying cost of the surplus-food storage program. And is the situation helped when one branch of the Agriculture Department tries to reduce production while another states, as it did in 1958, "It is believed generally that reduction of crop acreages under provisions of the Soil Bank will stimulate interest in use of chemicals to obtain maximum production on the land retained in crops."

All this is not to say there is no insect problem and no need of control. I am saying, rather, that control must be geared to realities, not to mythical situations, and that the methods employed must be such that they do not destroy us along with the insects.

The problem whose attempted solution has brought such a train of disaster in its wake is an accompaniment of our modern way of life. Long before the age of man, insects inhabited the earth—a group of extraordinarily varied and adaptable beings. over the course of time since man's advent, a small percentage of the more than half a million species of insects have come into conflict with human welfare in two principal ways: as competitors for the food supply and as carriers of human disease.

Disease-carrying insects become important where human beings are crowded together, especially under conditions where sanitation is poor, as in time of natural disaster or war or in situations of extreme poverty and deprivation. Then control of some sort becomes necessary. It is a sobering fact, however, as we shall presently see, that the method of massive chemical control has had only limited success, and also threatens to worsen the very condition it is intended to curb.

Under primitive agricultural conditions the farmer had few insect problems. These arose with the intensification of agriculture—the devotion of immense acreages to a single crop. Such a system set the stage for explosive increases in specific insect populations. Single-crop farming does not take advantage of the principles by which nature works; it is agriculture as an engineer might conceive it to be. Nature has introduced great variety into the landscape, but man has displayed a passion for simplifying it. Thus he undoes the built-in checks and balances by which nature holds the species within bounds. One important natural check is a limit on the amount of suitable habitat for each species. Obviously then, an insect that lives on wheat can build up its population to much higher levels on a farm devoted to wheat than on one in which wheat is intermingled with other crops to which the insect is not adapted.

The same thing happens in other situations. A generation or more ago, the towns of large areas of the United States lined their streets with the noble elm tree. Now the beauty they hopefully created is threatened with complete destruction as disease sweeps through the elms, carried by a beetle that would have only limited chance to build up large populations and to spread from tree to tree if the elms were only occasionaly trees in a richly diversified planting.

Another factor in the modern insect problem is one that must be viewed against a background of geologic and human history: the spreading of thousands of different kinds of organisms from their native homes to invade new territories. This worldwide migration has been studied and graphically described by the British ecologist Charles Elton in his recent book *The Ecology of Invasions*. During the Cretaceous Period, some hundred million years ago, flooding seas cut many land bridges between continents and living things found themselves confined in what Elton calls "colossal separate nature reserves." There, isolated from others of their kind, they developed many new species. When some of the land masses were joined again, about 15 million years ago, these species began to move out into new territories—a movement that is not only still in progress but is now receiving considerable assistance from man.

The importation of plants is the primary agent in the modern spread of species, for animals have almost invariably gone along with the plants, quarantine being a comparatively recent and not completely effective innovation. The United States Office of Plant Introduction alone has introduced almost 200,000 species and varieties of plants from all over the world. Nearly half of the 180 or so major insect enemies of plants in the United States are accidental imports from abroad, and most of them have come as hitchhikers on plants.

In new territory, out of reach of the restraining hand of the natural enemies that kept down its numbers in its native land, an invading plant or animal is able to become enormously abundant. Thus it is no accident that our most troublesome insects are introduced species.

These invasions, both the naturally occurring and those dependent on human assistance, are likely to continue indefinitely. Quarantine and massive chemical campaigns are only extremely expensive ways of buying time. We are faced, according to Dr. Elton, "with a life-and-death need not just to find new technological means of suppressing this plant or that animal"; instead we need the basic knowledge of animal populations and their relations to their surroundings that will "promote an even balance and damp down the explosive power of outbreaks and new invasions."

Much of the necessary knowledge is not available but we do not use it. We train ecologists in our universities and even employ them in our governmental agencies but we seldom take their advice. We allow the chemical death rain to fall as though there were no alternative, whereas in fact there are many, and our ingenuity could soon discover many more if given opportunity.

Have we fallen into a mesmerized state that makes us accept as inevitable that which is inferior or detrimental, as though having lost the will or the vision to demand that which is good? Such thinking, in the words of the ecologist Paul Shepard, "idealizes life with only its head out of water, inches above the limits of toleration of the corruption of its own environment. . . . Why should we tolerate a diet of weak poisons, a home in insipid surroundings, a circle of acquaintances who are not quite our enemies, the noise of motors with just enough relief to prevent insanity? Who would want to live in a world which is just not quite fatal?"

Yet such a world is pressed upon us. The crusade to create a chemically sterile, insect-free world seems to have engendered a fanatic zeal on the part of many specialists and most of the so-called control agencies. On every hand there is evidence that those engaged in spraying operations exercise a ruthless power. "The regulatory entomologists . . . function as prosecutor, judge and jury, tax assessor and collector and sheriff to enforce their own orders," said Connecticut entomologist Neely Turner. The most flagrant abuses go unchecked in both state and federal agencies.

It is not my contention that chemical insecticides must never be used. I do contend that we have put poisonous and biologically potent chemicals indiscriminately into the hands of persons largely or wholly ignorant of their potentials for harm. We have subjected enormous numbers of people to contact with these poisons, without their consent, and often without their knowledge. If the Bill of Rights contains no guarantee that a citizen shall be secure against lethal poisons distributed either by private individuals or by public officials, it is surely only because our forefathers, despite their considerable wisdom and foresight, could conceive of no such problem.

I contend, furthermore, that we have allowed these chemicals to be used with little or no advance investigation of their effect on soil, water, wildlife, and man himself. Future generations are unlikely to condone our lack of prudent concern for the integrity of the natural world that supports all life.

There is still very limited awareness of the nature of the threat. This is an era of specialists, each of whom sees his own problem and is unaware of or intolerant of the larger frame into which it fits. It is also an era dominated by industry, in which the right to make a dollar at whatever cost is seldom challenged. When the public protests, confronted with some obvious evidence of damaging results of pesticide applications, it is fed little tranquilizing pills of half truth. We urgently need an end to these false assurances, to the sugar coating of unpalatable facts. It is the public that is being asked to assume the risks that the insect controllers calculate. The public must decide whether it wishes to continue on the present road, and it can do so only when in full possession of the facts. In the words of Jean Rostand, "The obligation to endure gives us the right to know."

Meaning

1. How does the title of Carsons' book, *Silent Spring*, from which this essay was taken, express in one image the terrible consequences of chemical pollution?
2. Why is the concept of the balance of nature so important in Carson's explanation of the destabilizing impact of new chemicals?
3. What unintended side-effects arise from the use of chemicals, pesticides, and fertilizers?
4. How does the practice of planting a huge expanse of the same crop exacerbate an insect problem?
5. Why do natural checks and balances not work on insect enemies of plants accidentally imported from abroad?

Using Problem Solving to Convey Meaning

1. How does the organization of Carson's essay emphasize the long-term disastrous effects of what most people thought were satisfactory short-term solutions?
2. What examples does Carson provide to underscore the unforeseen side-effects of the massive use of DDT?
3. What steps does Carson take to convince the reader that she is not against all chemicals as such, just the unreasonable use of them?
4. What does the example of Dutch Elm disease make you realize about the different kinds of problems that have arisen from undiversified planting?

Writing Suggestions

1. In light of Carson's essay, discuss the implications of one environmental disaster, such as "Love Canal."
2. What connections can you discover between Carson's analysis of man's thoughtless manipulation of the environment and Leon Kass' apprehensions regarding man's newfound ability to modify his own nature and future generations by rearranging genetic material (see page 586)?
3. What do a cross-section of ads disclose about our society's attitude toward solving problems with chemicals? You might look at ads for detergents, pesticides, fertilizers, or cleaning solutions.

ARGUMENTATION AND PERSUASION

Some of the most interesting and effective writing in various disciplines takes the form of arguments that seek to persuade a specific audience (colleagues, fellow researchers, or the general public) of the validity of a proposition or claim through logical reasoning supported by facts, examples, data, or other kinds of evidence. Writers and researchers in all academic disciplines often are compelled to convince others of the validity of their ideas and discoveries. Discussion and debate accompany the development of central ideas, concepts, and laws in all fields of study. Writers in the liberal arts, the political and social sciences, and the sciences use strategies of argument to support new interpretations of known facts or establish plausible cases for new hypotheses.

The purpose of argument is to persuade an audience to accept the validity or probability of an idea, proposition, or claim. Essentially, a claim is an assertion that would be met with skepticism if it were not supported with sound evidence and persuasive reasoning. Argument plays a key role for writers who use the forums provided by literary and scientific journals to persuade colleagues of the accuracy of their experiments and investigations and the validity of their conclusions. Formal arguments differ from assertions based on likes and dislikes or personal opinion. Unlike questions of personal taste, arguments rest on evidence, whether in the form of facts, examples, the testimony of experts, or statistics, which can be brought forward to objectively prove or disprove the thesis in question.

Argumentation also differs from persuasion, although the two are frequently confused. Whereas argument presents reasons and evidence to gain an audience's intellectual agreement with the validity of a proposition, persuasion uses additional techniques of emotional manipulation to motivate an audience to act in accordance with the writer's recommendations.

Readers expect that evidence cited to substantiate or refute assertions will be sound, accurate, and relevant, and that conclusions will be drawn from this evidence according

661

to the guidelines of logic. Readers also expect that the writer arguing in support of a proposition will acknowledge and answer objections put forth by the opposing side while providing compelling evidence to support his or her own position.

Although arguments explore important issues and espouse specific theories, the forms in which arguments appear vary according to the style and format of the individual discipline. Evidence in different disciplines can appear in a variety of formats, including the interpretation of statistics, laws, precedents, or the citation of authorities. The means used in constructing arguments depend on the audience within the discipline being addressed, the nature of the thesis being proposed, and the accepted methodology for that particular discipline.

In the liberal arts, critics evaluate and interpret works of art, review music, dance, drama and the film, and write literary analyses. Philosophers probe the moral and ethical implications of people's actions, and advocate specific ways of meeting the ethical challenges posed by new technologies. Historians interpret political, military, and constitutional events, analyze their causes, and theorize how the past influences the present.

In the political and social sciences, lawyers and constitutional scholars argue for specific ways of applying legal and constitutional theory to everyday problems. Economists debate issues related to changes wrought by technology, distribution of income, unemployment, and commerce. Political scientists look into how effectively governments initiate and manage social change, and ask basic questions about the limits of governmental intrusion into individual rights. Sociologists analyze statistics and trends to evaluate how successfully institutions accommodate social change.

In the sciences, biologists, as well as biochemists, zoologists, botanists, and other natural scientists, propose theories to explain the interdependence of living things with their natural environment. Psychologists champion hypotheses based on physiological, experimental, social, and clinical research to explain various aspects of human behavior. Physicists, as well as mathematicians, astronomers, engineers, and computer scientists, put forward and defend hypotheses about the basic laws underlying the manifestations of the physical world, from the microscopic to the cosmic.

I. Arguments That Define Key Terms or Concepts

All arguments generated in the context of the disciplines require the writer to clearly formulate a position, provide a context to explain why the issue is important, define ambiguous terms, and discover reasons and evidence that support the argument. An entire argument will often hinge on the definition of a key term or concept. Definition arguments identify the unique properties of the thing being defined in a way that clearly distinguishes it from all other things with which it might be confused.

Arguments can arise between disciplines over lack of consensus of what commonly used terms mean. Thus, in the liberal arts, different fields of study might bring very different perspectives and methods to bear on defining "Impressionism." A writer wishing to contend that there are certain qualities that characterize "Impressionism"— whether in the paintings of Monet and Pissarro, the sculpture of Rodin, the music of Debussy, the poetry of Carl Sandberg, or the short stories of Sherwood Anderson— would have to distinguish the different meanings of this term in the different contexts of art, music, and literature, and then show how "Impressionism" possessed certain generic qualities that transcended the individual disciplines.

Arguments of definition can arise in connection with general terms, along with questions raised by the specialized vocabulary of particular disciplines. In the field of medicine, new technologies for prolonging life make it necessary to agree on what the terms "life" and "death" actually mean. Since machines can now prevent cessation of respiration, the traditional definition of "death"—as occurring when respiration ceases and the heart stops beating—must be restated as occurring with "brain death." Moreover, decisions as to when to terminate life-support or to remove organs for transplantation will obviously depend on which definition is applied.

Court cases also turn on points of definition. In a specific case, sentencing may be determined by the nature of the charge. For example, a reduction of "intentional homicide" to the lesser charge of "voluntary manslaughter" will depend on the defense attorney's ability to "define" the death of the victim as being the result of self-defense—what the law terms "adequate provocation."

In this chapter, Donald R. Griffin, a specialist in the field of comparative physiology, reviews evidence produced by researchers who believe that chimpanzees can be taught to communicate with humans, in "Wordy Apes." The crucial issue is one of definition. What criteria should be used to identify the existence of intelligent behavior in animals?

> A heated debate has raged about the extent to which such learned communication resembles human language. Sebeok and Umiker-Sebeok (1980) and Sebeok and Rosenthal (1981) have argued vehemently that the whole business is merely wishful and mistaken reading into the ape's behavior of much more than is really there. They stress that apes are very clever at learning to do what gets them food, praise, social companionship, or other things they want and enjoy. They believe that insufficiently critical scientists have overinterpreted the behavior of their charges and that the apes have really learned only something like: "If I do this she will give me candy," or "If I do that she will play with me," and so forth. . . .

A precise definition of what constitutes "animal intelligence" depends on whether examples of lever pressing or signing activities of apes are interpreted as evidence of imitative or initiative behavior. Based on his summary of results obtained from different fields of studies, Griffin favors continued research because he believes that real proof will eventually be found showing apes to be capable of communication with human beings.

II. Arguments That Establish Causes or Predict Consequences

Arguments over causation (such as "is cancer caused by industrial chemicals?") arise because there may be several possible causes for a given effect or a number of possible effects for a given cause. An argument that attempts to demonstrate a causal connection between cancer and industrial chemicals would have to show that a particular cause or chain of causation was capable of producing the effect in question.

Events that merely follow each other in sequence should not be confused with true cause and effect. Writers should also be wary of attempting to oversimplify events that have complex causes. In seeking to answer a complicated question such as "Does violence portrayed on television cause aggression in children?" the burden is on the writer to clearly demonstrate the existence of a plausible means by which a specific cause (violence portrayed on television) could have produced a particular effect (aggression in children).

In both cases, the argument moves from specific facts to the elaboration of a general casual hypothesis. This process of reasoning, which proceeds from the particular to the general, is called *inductive reasoning*. Inductive arguments depend on observing similarities among a number of specific cases and then making inferences about other like instances that have not been observed. Writers making inductive arguments must always guard against making hasty or sweeping generalizations, or generalizations based on atypical or sparse examples. The validity of an inductive argument is strengthened by sufficient numbers of relevant examples or case histories.

Sigmund Freud, in his classic essay "Typical Dreams," brings forward a whole range of examples from the dreams of children that always have one common theme— the death or disappearance of brothers or sisters. From numerous case histories, Freud generalizes that children's dreams often contain repressed wishes in disguised form. To make his case, Freud demonstrates a plausible connection between the cause (sibling rivalry) and the effect (dreams of the death or disappearance of brothers and sisters):

> I have never failed to come across this dream of the death of brothers or sisters, denoting an intense hostility, e.g. I have met it in all my female patients. I have met with only one exception, which could easily be interpreted into a confirmation of the rule. Once, in the course of a sitting, when I was explaining this state of affairs to a female patient, since it seemed to have some bearing on the symptoms under consideration that day, she answered, to my astonishment, that she had never had such dreams. But another dream occurred to her, which presumably had nothing to do with the case—a dream which she had first dreamed at the age of *four*, when she was the youngest child, and had since then dreamed repeatedly. *"A number of children, all her brothers and sisters with her boy and girl cousins, were romping about in a meadow. Suddenly they all grew wings, flew up, and were gone.".* . .

Freud's hypothesis that the dreams of children reveal, in disguised form, the wish to be the only child on whom parents will lavish attention, is an inference drawn from many observed cases. His generalization as to the existence of sibling rivalry, if scientifically valid, should be verifiable in the dreams of children whom Freud has not observed.

The process of making inferences or generalizations based on representative and verifiable phenomena is used, as well, by Charles Darwin, in "Darwin's Conclusion on His Theory and Religion." Darwin postulates the existence of an evolutionary process that could explain why (1) there are so many varieties of the same species (e.g., so many different kinds of finches and sea-turtles); and (2) why new varieties of species continue to develop. Because his ideas at the time were so revolutionary, Darwin was compelled to defend his views against arguments advanced by his opponents. Darwin emphasizes the merits of his own position by pointing out the disadvantages of his opponent's views. He demonstrates that the opponents' positions would produce effects that are the opposite of observable facts. In logic, he is said to be refuting a proposition by proving the contradictory of the proposition:

> Why, it may be asked, until recently did nearly all the most eminent living naturalists and geologists disbelieve in the mutability of species? It cannot be asserted that organic beings in a state of nature are subject to no variation; it cannot be proved that the amount of variation in the course of long ages is a limited quantity; no clear distinction has been, or can be, drawn between species and well-marked varieties. . . .

Darwin deals with arguments advanced by his opponents before proposing his own arguments. He does this by putting his opponents in the untenable position of proving that nothing in nature has ever changed or ever can change. Since, Darwin says, his opponents cannot prove their position, his position is strengthened and is therefore more probable. This type of reasoning involves determining plausible causes of observed effects. Darwin says his opponents believe in causes that produce effects that no one has ever observed. By contrast, Darwin asserts that his theories of causation lead to observable effects, that is, the mutability of species, a lack of clearcut distinction between species and varieties, and the continuing production of new varieties of existing species.

In contrast to inductive reasoning, which proceeds from specific facts, examples, and cases to a general hypothesis, *deductive reasoning* applies a set of given principles to specific cases and draws logical conclusions. The statements on which deductive reasoning is based appear as categorical propositions or "laws." If the original statements or premises are true, inferences drawn according to the rules of logic—applying the general "law" to specific cases—can produce deductions that are true.

Thomas Robert Malthus, in "The Principle of Population," uses deductive reasoning to make inferences from statements using a chain of formal logic to produce the historic "Malthusian principle":

> Population, when unchecked, increases in a geometrical ratio. Subsistence increases only in an arithmetical ratio. A slight acquaintance with numbers will shew the immensity of the first power in comparison of the second.
>
> By that law of our nature which makes food necessary to the life of man, the effects of these two unequal powers must be kept equal.

Malthus, unlike Freud, does not cite multiple examples of known instances, but instead makes an inference from general statements or categorical propositions that he presents as a "law" of nature. Malthus advances known facts and connects them as premises of a deductive argument. He points out that population increases geometrically (that is, two parents with two children, who then have two children each comprise eight people to feed), whereas the food supply only increases arithmetically (a plot of land cannot increase its capacity to produce crops eight-fold with each new generation). His observations governing population and food supply, if accepted as fundamentally true, must then inevitably lead to a conclusion about what the consequences will be for future generations. The conclusion Malthus draws using deductive reasoning is that hopes for social betterment will remain unrealized because the number of people to feed will always outstrip the available food supply.

III. Arguments That Make Value Judgments

As distinct from arguments that debate matters of fact or those that seek to establish plausible connections between causes and effects, *value arguments* apply ethical, moral, aesthetic, or utilitarian criteria to produce judgments that measure a subject against an ideal standard. This type of argument directly challenges underlying assumptions that ordinarily remain unquestioned by making explicit what is usually hidden. A writer who contended that "bilingual education" was or was not worthwhile, or that "euthanasia" was or was not immoral, would be obligated to clearly present the ideal standard against which the subject was being evaluated.

For David Hoekema, in his essay "Capital Punishment: The Question of Justification," the crucial issue is whether the justice system is arbitrary and capricious in the way it selects those who will be executed for capital crimes. Arguments that evaluate whether something is good or bad must provide (1) sufficient and verifiable evidence of a phenomenon and (2) an appropriate standard by which to measure value. Hoekema cites statistics that show that, among all those convicted of capital crimes, the poor and minorities are executed disproportionately in comparison to those who have money for good legal counsel. Hoekema then measures these statistics against the ideal standard of "equal punishment under the law" for the same crime:

> Because of all these opportunities for arbitrary decision, only a small number of those convicted of capital crimes are actually executed. It is hardly surprising that their selection has little to do with the character of their crimes but a great deal to do with the skill of their legal counsel. And the latter depends in large measure on how much money is available for the defense. Inevitably, the death penalty has been imposed most frequently on the poor, and in this country it has been imposed in disproportionate numbers on blacks.

Hoekema asserts that capital punishment should not be permitted because the justice system is, in practice, incapable of administering the punishment fairly. Hoekema bases this conclusion on statistics that show that the amount of money for legal defense is more important than the character of the crime in determining punishment. Note how Hoekema's argument gains force through the cumulative summary of the evidence ("Because of all these opportunities . . .") he cites to support his thesis.

In another value argument, Ursula K. Le Guin, the author of many works of science fiction, claims that, contrary to popular belief, most science fiction is not progressive but regressive and authoritarian in its depiction of women. Le Guin reminds her audience that the women's movement fought for the application of equal standards for men and women, and then presents evidence that science fiction does not meet these standards. Le Guin brings forward examples of the stereotyped depiction of women as "squeaking dolls," "old-maid scientists," and "loyal little wives or mistresses," and "accomplished heroes" in "American SF and The Other":

> The women's movement has made most of us conscious of the fact that SF has either totally ignored women, or presented them as squeaking dolls subject to instant rape by monsters—or old-maid scientists desexed by hypertrophy of the intellectual organs or, at best, loyal little wives or mistresses of accomplished heroes. Male elitism has run rampant in SF. But is it only male elitism? Isn't the "subjection of women" in SF merely a symptom of a whole which is authoritarian, power-worshiping, and intensely parochial?

Le Guin urges her audience to share her indignation, not merely to agree with her views. This illustrates how an emotional appeal can be used to strengthen the effect of a logical argument. Value arguments are never made in a vacuum. It is important for the writer to assess what beliefs or attitudes (receptive, hostile, or neutral) the audience holds in relationship to his or her argument. The use of emotional appeals to support a value argument is perfectly legitimate as long as the emotional appeal does not replace the logic of the argument.

Just as Le Guin uses connotative language to characterize the portrayal of women, so, Marya Mannes, in "The Unwilled," uses a range of techniques to appeal to the emotions of her audience. Mannes characterizes the kind of life likely to be lived by those who have been "saved" by the application of a sanctity-of-life criteria:

> Those who so passionately uphold the "sanctity of life" do not ask "what life?" nor see themselves as retarded and crippled in an institution for the rest of that life. Nor do they choose to see, or think of, the tens of thousands of lives born crippled and retarded, who, without will or choice, were allowed to be born as, presumably, the "right" of the damaged fetus *to* life.

Mannes asserts that the quality-of-life criteria should be used instead of a sanctity-of-life standard when decisions are made as to whether an abortion should be performed. Mannes contends that the results of using the sanctity-of-life standard are tens of thousands of crippled and retarded people who must spend their lives in institutions.

Appeals by the author to the emotions of an audience (through connotative language and characterization) are encountered frequently in value arguments because this kind of argument requires the selection of a standard to use when deciding whether something is good or bad. In the case of Thomas S. Szasz's "A Critique of Skinner's Behaviorism," Szasz assails B. F. Skinner's theories of behaviorism on the grounds that the most essential value by which to measure a psychologist's contribution is the "humanistic" standard—of providing the sense of significance that people need to live their lives more meaningfully. Szasz argues that B. F. Skinner's theories of behaviorism deprive people of the incentives needed to live a meaningful life:

> Hence, I believe that those who rob people of the meaning and significance they have given their lives kill them and should be considered murderers, at least metaphorically. B. F. Skinner is such a person and, like all of the others, he fascinates—especially his intended victims.

Szasz's principle objection is that Skinner's theories of behaviorism arbitrarily characterize all emotions as simply forms of learned behavior, which have no intrinsic meaning, sense, or significance. Szasz feels so strongly on this issue that some readers may react to what they perceive as an excessive use of emotionally charged language, guilt by association, and other techniques of audience manipulation by rejecting any valid points contained in Szasz's argument. Indeed, this is the principle danger of emotional appeals: when an audience suspects they are being manipulated, they are likely to reject the writer's argument, including any valid points he or she has presented.

IV. Arguments About Policy

In addition to arguments that characterize situations, make value judgments, or seek to establish causes or consequences there are arguments that recommend policy changes. Many arguments in law and politics are of this kind, but the range of *policy arguments* extends through the entire spectrum of the liberal arts, political and social sciences, and sciences and technology.

When investment advisory services issue buy or sell recommendations to their clients, when representatives of governments make the case that their country should host the next Olympic games, when an engineering firm recommends that ceramics would be better than steel for a particular project, when a director argues that a play of Shakespeare's ought to be staged in modern dress, and when a candidate for a job argues that he ought to be hired—it is important to demonstrate that the recommended action would be worthwhile, necessary, or useful.

Ideally, a policy argument should demonstrate that the way things are currently being done is producing negative consequences and that the recommended action or policy change would be capable of producing better results. For example, water is a basic human need. Industries rely on it; it is used to produce electricity, dispose of wastes, and agriculture could not exist without it. Yet, agriculture, industries, and municipalities use water wastefully, because the uncoordinated policies of myriad water agencies result in inefficient water use. Once the existence of this problem is demonstrated, a policy argument might recommend that: "Countries should set up central authorities to coordinate water policy rather than diffusing control among hundreds or even thousands of local, regional, or national agencies."

Earl Warren, former Chief Justice, used this same pattern to demonstrate the negative effects of segregated public schools before proposing a course of action—the famous 1954 *Brown* v. *Board of Education of Topeka* decision—intended to remedy the defects of what was then current policy. Warren cites results of studies showing that segregated schools not only instill a sense of inferiority, but deprive minority students of educational opportunities they should rightfully enjoy under the Fourteenth Amendment (which guarantees "equal opportunity" under the law):

> Today, education is perhaps the most important function of state and local governments. Compulsory school attendance laws and the great expenditures for education both demonstrate our recognition of the importance of education to our democratic society. . . . In these days, it is doubtful that any child may reasonably be expected to succeed in life if he is denied the opportunity of an education. Such an opportunity, where the state has undertaken to provide it, is a right which must be made available to all on equal terms.

After demonstrating the existence of the problem—that is, the detrimental effects on those educated in segregated schools—Warren applies standards based on the Fourteenth Amendment and recommends abolishing segregation in public schools. Warren thus defines the issue as one of "equal protection" under the law and proposes a course of action that will remedy the defects of current policy.

Christopher D. Stone, in "Legal Rights for the Environment," unlike Warren, lacks the power to enforce any policy change he recommends. He must therefore make much greater use of persuasive techniques to win the audience's acceptance of his innovative proposal that natural entities, such as streams and forests who cannot speak for themselves, should have legal guardians appointed to represent them. Stone arranges his argument so that he begins with points with which his readers already agree. By gaining agreement for known arguments and applying familiar principles in a new context, Stone prepares his readers to more readily accept his policy recommendation:

> It is not inevitable, nor is it wise, that natural objects should have no rights to seek redress in their own behalf. It is no answer to say that streams and forests cannot have standing because streams and forests cannot speak. Corporations cannot speak either, nor can states, estates, infants, incompetents, municipalities or universities. Lawyers speak for them, as they customarily do for the ordinary citizen who has legal problems. One ought, I think, to handle the legal problems of natural objects as one does the problems of legal incompetents. . . .

Stone first cites examples of other entities, such as municipalities, corporations, trusts, and partnerships who receive the protection of the law even though they cannot speak for themselves. Stone then argues, by analogy, that streams and forests are similarly entitled to protection under the law as well, and proposes that legal guardians should be appointed to represent their interests.

John Simon uses the same method of arguing by analogy in "The Boo Taboo" to recommend that American audiences emulate the widespread practice among European audiences of vigorously booing bad performances:

> It reaches its acme at the Opera House in Parma, where the din of protesting audiences is sometimes considerably worse than what is being protested. But even this, for all its excess, strikes me as a sounder attitude than supine reverence without discrimination. . . .

Simon's thesis is that indiscriminate approval of poor performances, including applause for performers for their efforts rather than for the results, perpetuates mediocrity in the theatre. The technique used by Simon here is one he uses throughout his essay; that is, anticipating and replying to objections his readers might raise. To not do so would leave lingering doubts as to Simon's ability to confront and dispose of opposing views. Simon proposes that American audiences should not worry about maintaining decorum or hurting the feelings of the performers. Instead, he argues that vigorous booing would encourage performers to improve their skills.

A policy argument can take the form of strengthening an audience's resolve to continue in the same course of action they have already decided to take. Martin Luther King, Jr.'s speech, "I Have a Dream," is a good example of this type of argument. The speech was delivered on the occasion when King led a march of 250,000 persons through Washington, D.C. to the Lincoln Memorial, on the Centennial of Lincoln's Emancipation Proclamation. The persuasive techniques that King uses are well-suited to adapt his message of nonviolent protest for both his audience and the occasion.

King reminds his audience that the civil rights movement puts into action basic ideas contained in the Constitution. King reaffirms minority rights as a way of renewing aspirations put forward by America's founding fathers and uses figurative language drawn from the Emancipation Proclamation and the Bible to reinforce his audience's emotional resolve to continue in their quest for equal rights:

> I say to you today, my friends, even though we face the difficulties of today and tomorrow, I still have a dream. It is a dream deeply rooted in the American dream. I have a dream that one day this nation will rise up and live out the true meaning of its creed: "We hold these truths to be self-evident, that all men are created equal." I have a dream that one day, on the red hills of Georgia, sons of former slaves and the sons of former slave owners will be able to sit down together at the table of brotherhood. . . .

The effectiveness of the speech depends in large part on the audience's sense of King as a man of high moral character. In arguments that appeal to the emotions as well as the intellect, the audience's perception of the speaker as a person of the highest ethics, good character, and sound reason amplifies the logic of the discourse.

This chapter, which focuses on argumentation and persuasion, presents a wide range of well-constructed and thought-provoking arguments across the disciplines. The writers debate, among other issues, whether (1) primates can be taught to communicate with humans through sign language, (2) children have dreams that demonstrate the existence of sibling rivalry, (3) our justice system enforces the death penalty on the poor and minorities disproportionately, (4) science fiction is sexist in its portrayal of women, (5) the sanctity-of-life criteria should be replaced by a quality-of-life standard in abortion decisions, (6) behaviorism destroys human values, and (7) trees and streams should have legal representation.

LIBERAL ARTS

Ursula K. Le Guin

American SF and The Other

Ursula K. Le Guin, the popular author of many acclaimed science fiction works, was born in 1929 in Berkeley, California. She was educated at Radcliffe College, where she was elected to Phi Beta Kappa, and received an M.A. in romance literature from Columbia University in 1952. Le Guin has taught at Mercer University, the University of Idaho, and has conducted writing workshops at Pacific University, University of Washington, Portland State University, and at the University of Reading in England. Besides essays and children's books, Le Guin's significant contributions to science fiction and fantasy literature include The Left Hand of Darkness *(1969), winner of both a Hugo Award and a* Science Fiction of America Nebula Award; The Farthest Shore *(1972), winner of a National Book Award and a Hugo Award; and* The Dispossessed: An Ambiguous Utopia *(1974), winner of a Nebula Award. The Lathe of Heaven (1971) was made into a PBS television movie shown in 1980. Her later work, including* Orsinian Tales *(1976),* Malafrena *(1979),* The Language of Night: Essays on Fantasy and Science Fiction *(1979), and* The Compass Rose *(1982), envisions utopian and magical worlds (Orsinia, the imagined archipelago of Earthsea, the far-flung planets of the Hainish Cycle) that offer alternatives to the usual male-dominated, autocratic, and technological vistas of traditional American science fiction. In "American SF and The Other" (1975), Le Guin points out the regressive, sexist, racist, and authoritarian nature of much supposedly progressive science fiction.*

One of the great early socialists said that the status of women in a society is a pretty reliable index of the degree of civilization of that society. If this is true, then the very low status of women in SF should make us ponder about whether SF is civilized at all.

The women's movement has made most of us conscious of the fact that SF has either totally ignored women, or presented them as squeaking dolls subject to instant rape by monsters—or old-maid scientists desexed by hypertrophy of the intellectual organs—or, at best, loyal little wives or mistresses of accomplished heroes. Male elitism has run rampant in SF. But is it only male elitism? Isn't the "subjection of women" in SF merely a symptom of a whole which is authoritarian, power-worshiping, and intensely parochial?

The question involved here is the question of The Other—the being who is different from yourself. This being can be different from you in its sex; or in its annual income; or in its way of speaking and dressing and doing things; or in the color of its skin, or the number of its legs and heads. In other words, there is the sexual Alien, and the social Alien, and the cultural Alien, and finally the racial Alien.

Well, how about the social Alien in SF? How about, in Marxist terms, "the proletariat"? Where are they in SF? Where are the poor, the people who work hard and go to bed hungry? Are they ever *persons*, in SF? No. They appear as vast anonymous masses fleeing from giant slime-globules from the Chicago sewers, or dying off by the billion from pollution or radiation, or as faceless armies being led to battle by generals and statesmen. In sword and sorcery they behave like the walk-on parts in a high-school performance of *The Chocolate Prince*. Now and then there's a busty lass amongst them who is honored by the attentions of the Captain of the Supreme Terran Command, or in a spaceship crew there's a quaint old cook, with a Scots or Swedish accent, representing the Wisdom of the Common Folk.

The people, in SF, are not people. They are masses, existing for one purpose: to be led by their superiors.

From a social point of view most SF has been incredibly regressive and unimaginative. All those Galactic Empires, taken straight from the British Empire of 1880. All those planets—with 80 trillion miles between them!—conceived of as warring nation-states, or as colonies to be exploited, or to be nudged by the benevolent Imperium of Earth toward self-development—the White Man's Burden all over again. The Rotary Club on Alpha Centauri, that's the size of it.

What about the cultural and the racial Other? This is the Alien everybody recognizes as alien, supposed to be the special concern of SF. Well, in the old pulp SF, it's very simple. The only good alien is a dead alien—whether he is an Aldebaranian Mantis-Man, or a German dentist. And this tradition still flourishes: witness Larry Niven's story "Innocent Moon" (in *All the Myriad Ways*, 1971) which has a happy ending—consisting of the fact that America, including Los Angeles, was not hurt by a solar flare. Of course a few million Europeans and Asians were fried, but that doesn't matter, it just makes the world a little safer for democracy, in fact. (It is interesting that the female character in the same story is quite brainless; her only function is to say Oh? and Ooooh! to the clever and resourceful hero.)

Then there's the other side of the same coin. If you hold a thing to be totally different from yourself, your fear of it may come out as hatred, or as awe—reverence. So we get all those wise and kindly beings who deign to rescue Earth from her sins and perils. The Alien ends up on a pedestal in a white nightgown and a virtuous smirk—exactly as the "good woman" did in the Victorian Age.

In America, it seems to have been Stanley Weinbaum who invented the sympathetic alien, in *A Martian Odyssey*. From then on, via people like Cyril Kornbluth, Ted Sturgeon, and Cordwainer Smith, SF began to inch its way out of simple racism. Robots—the alien intelligence—begin to behave nicely. With Smith, interestingly enough, the racial alien is combined with the social alien, in the "Underpeople," and they are allowed to have a revolution. As the aliens got more sympathetic, so did the heroes. They began to have emotions, as well as rayguns. Indeed they began to become almost human.

If you deny any affinity with another person or kind of person, if you declare it to be wholly different from yourself—as men have done to women, and class has done to class, and nation has done to nation—you may hate it, or deify it; but in either case you have denied its spiritual equality, and its human reality. You have made it into a thing, to which the only possible relationship is a power relationship. And thus you have fatally impoverished your own reality. You have, in fact, alienated yourself.

This tendency has been remarkably strong in American SF. The only social change presented by most SF has been toward authoritarianism, the domination of ignorant masses by a powerful elite—sometimes presented as a warning, but often quite complacently. Socialism is never considered as an alternative, and democracy is quite forgotten. Military virtues are taken as ethical ones. Wealth is assumed to be a righteous goal and a personal virtue. Competitive free-enterprise capitalism is the economic destiny of the entire Galaxy. In general, American SF has assumed a permanent hierarchy of superiors and inferiors, with rich, ambitious, aggressive males at the top, then a great gap, and then at the bottom the poor, the uneducated, the faceless masses, and all the women. The whole picture is, if I may say so, curiously "un-American." It is a perfect baboon patriarchy, with the Alpha Male on top, being respectfully groomed, from time to time, by his inferiors.

Is this speculation? Is this imagination? Is this extrapolation? I call it brainless regressivism.

I think it's time SF writers—and their readers—stopped daydreaming about a return to the age of Queen Victoria, and started thinking about the future. I would like to see the Baboon Ideal replaced by a little human idealism, and some serious consideration of such deeply radical, futuristic concepts as Liberty, Equality, and Fraternity. And remember that about 53 percent of the Brotherhood of Man is the Sisterhood of Woman.

MEANING

1. What contrast does Le Guin find between advances made by women in the real world and the patronizing and demeaning way women are depicted throughout much of science fiction?
2. Why is it ironic that a genre that is supposedly so progressive reveals itself to be, as Le Guin says, "authoritarian, power worshiping, and intensely parochial" in its stereotyping of women?
3. What is the significance of "The Other" and in what forms can it appear?

USING ARGUMENTATION AND PERSUASION TO CONVEY MEANING

1. How does Le Guin support her assertion that "male elitism has run rampant in SF" by citing examples of the depiction of women as "squeaking dolls," "loyal

little wives or mistresses of accomplished heroes," or "old-maid scientists desexed by hypertrophy of the intellectual organs"?

2. How does Le Guin structure her argument to (a) remind her audience that the Women's Movement has brought a standard by which to measure the portrayal of women and (b) evaluate how far below these standards much of SF falls?

3. How is Le Guin's argument strengthened by the fact that she herself is an accomplished writer of science fiction?

WRITING SUGGESTIONS

1. As a follow-up, read and analyze any of Le Guin's science fiction works to discover how she corrects the deficiencies she identifies in other works of science fiction.

2. How do noteworthy portrayals of "sympathetic aliens" such as "E.T." and "Starman" reverse the usual stereotype of "The Other"?

3. What reversal of sexist, racist, and authoritarian stereotypes criticized by Le Guin can be found in "The Planet of the Apes," or make the "Star Wars" trilogy or the two "Alien" movies more enlightened forms of science fiction?

4. Does the depiction of "The Other"—as Indians on the warpath or murderous villains—in another classic genre, the western, serve the same function as it does in science fiction? Do the portrayals of the frontier marshal, school marm, dancehall girl, and Eastern tenderfoot reflect the same sexist, racist, and authoritarian stereotypes Le Guin finds in science fiction? Illustrate your answer with examples drawn from any western.

JOHN SIMON

The Boo Taboo

John Simon was born in 1925 of Yugoslav and Hungarian parentage. Simon came to the United States when he was fifteen and took his undergraduate and graduate education at Harvard, receiving his Ph.D. in 1959 (for which he wrote a still-unpublished 732-page thesis on the European prose poem). After teaching literature and humanities at Harvard, the University of Washington, M.I.T., and Bard College, Simon worked as associate editor of the Mid-Century Book Society, editing The Mid-Century, under the tutelage of W. H. Auden, Jacques Barzun, and Lionel Trilling. Later, Simon contributed art criticism to the New York Times and Arts Magazine, and through the influence of Robert Brustein became drama critic of the Hudson Review. In 1962, Simon began writing film criticism for the New Leader. Since then, he has become drama critic of New York Magazine and film critic for the National Review. Simon's uncompromising, independent, and invigorating approach to criticism, whether he writes about the fine arts, opera, or ballet, is frequently more intellectually stimulating than the works that are the subject of his reviews. His many published works include Acid Test (1963), on the theatre; Private Screenings (1967), a collection of movie reviews; Movies Into Film: Film Criticism 1967– 1970 (1971); Ingmar Bergman Directs (1972); Uneasy Stages and Singularities (both in 1976); and Paradigms Lost: Reflections on Literacy and Its Decline (1980), a collection of witty essays that diagnose and treat (even recommending mercy killing in some cases) all manner of linguistic maladies. In "The Boo Taboo," which originally appeared in New York Magazine (1987), this unindulgent theatre critic seeks to persuade American audiences of their right to vocally condemn substandard performances.

And the voice of the booer shall be heard in the land! What our theatres, opera houses and concert halls need is the introduction of the two-party system; as of now, all they have got is a dictatorship. It is the dictatorship of the assenters over the voices of dissent, of the applauders and cheerers over the booers and hissers, and its effect on our performing arts is to encourage the status quo, however mediocre or lamentable it may be. There is an urgent or, if I may say so, crying need for the voices of protest to be given equal rights and equal time.

In a pioneer essay on the subject, the famous English drama critic, James Agate, wrote: "It seems to me to be unfair to allow the happy fellow to blow off steam by means of applause, and to deny the miserable man that small amount of hissing and booing which presumably are his safety-valve." But although Agate's 1926 essay comes out in defense of booing, it does not pursue its subject beyond a few lighthearted remarks and droll suggestions. Let us examine more closely what makes an American audience in 1968 only applaud.

There are, obviously, those who applaud because they genuinely liked the play, opera, concert, recital or ballet. Their judgment may be questioned, but their motives can not. But what about the others, the fellow-grovelers? There are those who applaud because it is the thing to do. There are those who believe, without any real feelings or opinions about what they have just witnessed, that applause shows discernment, connoisseurship, culture. There are others (and I proceed in an ascending order of sinisterness) who clap to show off: as if the loudness of their palms equaled the weightiness of their opinions. This groups excels not only at the manual thunderclap but also at vocal bombardment. They erupt into promiscuous roars of *Bravo*, and even *Bravi* and *Brava*, to display either their knowledge of Italian, or their deftness in distinguishing the number and sex of the performers. At ballets, they applaud every last *entrechat*, drowning out the music and interrupting the flow of the work; at plays, they applaud every witticism, obliterating words and whole lines, and destroying the continuum of a scene. At the opera, they start their din in time to cut off the singer's last notes and the concluding orchestral accompaniment; at concerts, unfamiliar with the music, they applaud at the wrong places, and incite loud shushing. They want to get there with their noise first, loudest, and longest, their motto being, apparently, "I am heard, therefore I exist."

No better, however, are those who applaud because others are doing it, or because they have read favorable reviews, or because they firmly believe that whatever is put on at the Met, Philharmonic or Carnegie Hall, or at a large Broadway theatre is guaranteed to be good. Things do not change much; back in 1885 Shaw observed: "In every average audience there is a certain proportion of persons who make a point of getting as much as possible for their money—who will *encore*, if possible, until they have had a ballad for every penny in their shilling . . . There is also a proportion—a large one—of silly and unaccustomed persons who, excited by the novelty of being at a concert, and dazzled by the glitter and glory of the Bow-street temple of Art, madly applaud whenever anyone sets the example. Then there are good-natured people who lend a hand to encourage the singer. The honest and sensible members of the audience, even when they are a majority, are powerless against this combination of thoughtless good-nature, folly, and greed."

Needless to say, I am for applause and even for cheering, however magnanimous or misguided the motive. Though I understand the 1609 preface to *Troilus and Cressida*, which recommends the play as one "never clapper-clawed with the palms of the vulgar," I am more in agreement with the imposing rages Paul Henry Lang, then music critic of *The Herald Tribune*, used to fly into every Eastertime when productions of *Parsifal* at the Met were greeted by the audience with reverential silence as though they were attending church services. But audience demonstrations should not interfere with what is happening on stage—does the entrance of a well-known actor have to be heralded by a clash of cymbal-like palms from the fans?—and, above all, they should not be the sole licensed spectator behavior, to the exclusion of counterdemonstrations. The boo and the hiss must also be franchised, as long as they do not obscure the actual sounds of performance.

I have used some political terminology deliberately. The American public must be awakened to the dignity and importance of art by education, criticism, and also—yes—by the lowly boo. Art matters fully as much as politics, the public must be told; for it is the politics of the spirit, while politics proper are the politics of the body. All that good government can give us is material well-being, the political and economic order and plenty enabling us to cultivate our minds and spirits. This cultivation, however, is the function of several disciplines—science, social science, philosophy, religion, etc.—not the least important, and possibly the most penetrating of which is art. Thus what happens in the realm of the arts—which help us to see, feel, think and understand—is as significant as what happens in politics. Should then, I repeat, the politics of the mind and spirit be reduced to a one-party system?

The problem with the American audience is that it does not truly apprehend art. It is either in awe of it, or indifferent to it, or regards it as a commodity to be bought from time to time, like chutney or a new doormat. The first attitude stems from the Puritan origins of this country: the stage has taken over from the pulpit—which is quite an irony, considering how the Puritans loathed the theatre. The second attitude derives from general lack of culture: it takes, regrettably, centuries to acquire the kind of culture Europe, India, China and Japan can boast of (and relatively little time to lose it—but that is another story). The third attitude results from the materialism of this society. But the healthy attitude toward art is a spontaneous give-and-take between stage and auditorium, a frank expression of approval or dispraise.

In a diary entry for April 19, 1897, Gerhart Hauptmann wrote, "The playwright does not write for the stage but for the souls of men. The stage is a mediator between him and these souls." In a 1946 article, Jean Cocteau spoke of "the bouncing back and forth of balls between the audience and the playwright." Whether you think of the relationship as communion or contest, there has to be an easeful exchange between platform and pit. European audiences have not been afraid to boo or hiss (or, according to the local equivalent, whistle) plays, operas, performances, whatever displeases them. The tradition is an ancient one. It is said that Euripides, approaching eighty, was driven from Athens by the jeers of his fellow-citizens. Far from cramping his style, this critical exile elicited from him *The Bacchae*, very possibly his most important play.

In our time, booing or its equivalent flourishes in many European countries. It reaches its acme at the Opera House in Parma, where the din of protesting audiences is sometimes considerably worse than what is being protested. But even this, for all its excess, strikes me as a sounder attitude than supine reverence without discrimination. For one thing, that audience really knows and cares about *bel canto*, and will not accept treasonable facsimiles. The singer may feel hurt, but if he is an artist sure of his ability, he will fight back and live to sing unhampered and applauded another day. As for the author, let me quote again from Agate's little essay: " 'A certain number of fleas is good for a dog,' once said an American humorist, 'it prevents him from brooding upon being a dog.' A certain amount of booing is good for a playwright; at any rate, it prevents him from brooding about being a successful one and thus growing intolerably vain."

Reminiscing about a director whom he admired, Brecht remarked in a 1939 lecture, "On Experimental Theatre," "Piscator's stage was not indifferent to applause, but it preferred a discussion." A discussion is all very well, of course, but hard to come by in a theatre or concert hall; the dialogue of applause and booing will, to some extent, take its place. Probably the most famous such contest occurred at the premiere of Victor Hugo's *Hernani*, of which I quote a brief account from *The Oxford Companion to French Literature:* "The first two performances of *Hernani* [at the Comédie Française,

25 and 27 Feb. 1830] count among the great battles of the Romantics. News had
spread that the piece was in every way—subject, treatment, and versification—a break
with the dramatic conventions, and the theatre was packed with partisans. Below, in
the expensive seats, were the traditionalists, determined to crush the play and with
it the dangerous innovations of the new School. Above were the hordes of Hugo's
admirers—young writers, artists, and musicians—led by Théophile Gautier (wearing
a cherry-coloured satin doublet which became legendary) and Petrus Borel, and all
equally determined to win the day. At both performances they outclapped, outshouted,
and generally outdid the occupants of the stalls and boxes, with such effect that the
success of the play—and of the Romantic Movement—was thenceforth assured."
The "Battle of *Hernani*" had actually begun in the streets hours before curtain time,
while Hugo supporters waited for the doors to open; one of them, Balzac, was hit
in the face by a cabbage stalk a jeerer had plucked from the gutter.

But *Hernani* and Hugo prevailed, as Euripides had, as every important author,
composer, performer has prevailed against unwarranted booing—and there is hardly
an illustrious name in the verbal or musical theatre that escaped without some hisses
and catcalls. But catcalls are catnip to genius, and even to talent. On the other
hand, I am persuaded that many an unworthy work or artist was hastened to oblivion by well-placed hisses and boos; unfortunately for the documentation of my
case, histories of past fakes and no-talents do not get written. As for today's im-
postors, they are still very much with us—perhaps from a lack of vociferous opposition.

It is not that booing does not occur in New York; but it is usually isolated and
ineffectual. One of the rare exceptions took place at Carnegie Hall when the superb
Russian cellist, Mstislav Rostropovich, saw fit to compound his error of commissioning
a work for cello and orchestra from Lukas Foss by actually performing that work. It
was an aleatoric mess, its garishness heightened by having some of the instruments,
including the soloist's cello, electronically amplified, and the thing was conducted
by the cockily histrionic composer in a manner that was almost more offensive than
the piece itself. The battle of jeers and cheers was truly invigorating to experience—
I joined in heartily with the former—and the victory, I think, was ours. At any rate,
the work (whose pretentious title I have happily forgotten) has not, to my knowledge,
shown up in concert since.

As a critic of drama and film I, of course, do not boo plays and movies (it does
little good to boo celluloid, in any case); I review them instead. But at other events,
where I am a paying customer and not a critic, I feel free to boo. When the Hamburg
State Opera brought to New York its production of Gunther Schuller's derivative,
pretentious, and vacuous *The Visitation* (an inept transposition of Kafka's *The Trial*
into a simplistic American South), there was, I gather, quite some booing at its first
performance at the Met. I attended the second, at which, for whatever reason, there
were no boos, except for mine at the final curtain. A man came up to me and
congratulated me on my good sense and courage. This was typical: the average American
theatregoer, even when he realizes that he is being abused, wants someone else to
do his protesting for him.

Another good time to protest is when the theatre provides a largely homosexual
audience with Instant Camp. I remember, for example, a Poulenc memorial concert
in Carnegie Hall, shortly after the composer's death. Among other events, Jennie
Tourel performed some Poulenc songs, accompanied by Leonard Bernstein. There

was Miss Tourel, the vocal and visual wreck of a once passable singer: splintered voice, wizened and overmade-up face, decrepit figure stuffed into a militantly Shirley Templeish outfit. At the piano, Bernstein was at his ham-actorish best. The two, when they were not loving up the audience, flirted with each other, throwing lateral kisses, courtseys, and lovelorn *oeillades* across the stage. When they did get around to Poulenc, Miss Tourel not only made the songs crack in more directions than her make-up, she even burdened the lovely French words with something like a full-blown Bronx accent. Meanwhile, inverting the usual procedure, the ivories seemed to be tickling Leonard Bernstein, who was carrying on like a cockatoo in orgasm. When this appalling Lenny and Jennie act was over, I naturally booed it. A French-woman, in the intermission, came up to shake my hand; several of my acquaintances in that generally orgiastic audience carefully cut me dead.

The most illuminating occurrence for me was a recent Saturday matinee at the Met. It was Barrault's wretched staging of *Carmen*, with Richard Tucker as Don José. Now Tucker had once been in possession of a good, strong voice; but he had never been a genuine artist with a sense of shading, expressive range, a feeling for the emotional depth of the part or the language in which he was singing. By this time, with even his basic organ gone, Tucker is long overdue for retirement. In this Don José, Tucker's voice was as off as it had been for years, his phrasing as unlovely as it had always been. Visually, he was a geriatric travesty; histrionically, even by the shockingly low standards of operatic acting, a farce. Even his French was, let us say, hyper-Tourelian. After he got through mangling the Flower Song, and after the orchestra was through as well, I added to the general applause three loud *phooeys*—a *phooey* cuts through applause better than a boo or hiss.

The reaction was instantaneous. From several boxes around the one I sat in came frantic retaliation—mostly of the "Shut up!" or "How dare you?" or "Go home!" variety, though one middle-aged woman intoned lachrymosely, "He has given you *years* of beauty!" When the lights went on, Rudolf Bing, who was sitting a couple of boxes away, had already dispatched his Pinkerton men after me, right into the box; but I walked out ignoring their reprimands. In the corridor, I was set upon by a mob of some 20 or 30 people berating me and following me almost to the bar with their objurgations and insults. The gist of it was that this sort of thing wasn't tolerated here, and if I was a foreign guest, I should behave or get the hell back wherever I came from. And that if I did not like it, I could not applaud or just leave. I countered that it did not seem to me fair and democratic to allow musical illiterates to clap and bellow their approval to their hearts' content, while someone who recognized the desecration of art was condemned to polite silence. In the following intermission (there had been no further incident during the next act), one of Bing's hugest goons, scowling ferociously, was back in the box once more, this time accompanied by a polite and human-sized person who introduced himself courteously as James Heffernan, house manager.

To summarize the ensuing battle of wits—if that is the term for it—Mr. Heffernan's point was that in Italy, where such a tradition exists, booing was fine, but that in "this house" it just wasn't done. My point was that if there was no such tradition here, it was high time to instigate one for the need was dire. Heffernan put forward that such booing might discourage the singer, to which I replied that that *was* the general idea. He then said that other people enjoying the performance were disturbed. I indicated that my boos did not come during the performing, which is more than could be said for some of the bravos and applause, and that if the audience had so little confidence in its own enthusiasm that one booer could make them doubt it, maybe doubt was called for. I added that if he wanted to exercise his authority usefully, he might go after the ignorant parvenus who talk through performances when they are not rattling their candy wrappers or jangling their vulgar bracelets. He admitted that this was a nuisance, but that, still and all, if I wished to protest, which he generously granted me the right to do, I should send a letter to Mr. Bing or Mr. Tucker. I told him that I would gladly write both of them my request that they retire, but that I doubted they would get my message. (The eminent poet and librettist, W. H. Auden, has remarked that he will not set foot in the Met while Bing is running it.) So, with a mixture of pleading and threatening looks, Heffernan and his sidekick left. I suspect that had my date and I been less well dressed, and had our seats been less expensive, the treatment accorded us would have been rather less ceremonious.

One understands, without condoning, the management's attitude—particularly when a boo is heard, thanks to Texaco, across the U.S. and Canada. But the fury of the audience needs analyzing. It is caused, in part, by the middle-class American's confusion of critical indignation with bad manners, his incomprehension that at the theatre or opera house more is at stake than in your or the Jones's parlor. But, more importantly, it is the anger of the insecure *nouveau riche* who has paid a dozen Dollars for his seat, and who, for that much money, wants to be sure he is getting grade-A, U.S.-certified culture. He himself hasn't the foggiest notion what that might be; so if a boo implies that he might be getting damaged goods and, worse yet, be duped by them, his defensive dander is up.

As for the performer's attitude, it is useful to consult the epilogue of William Redfield's *Letters from an Actor* to find out how Richard Burton responded to one solitary booer of his Hamlet: in boundless fury at his wife's refusing to commiserate with him, he kicked in a television screen with his bare foot, damaging his toes as well. And it is even more enlightening to see how Redfield, who acted in that *Hamlet*, interprets the incident: "Now a booer, rare though he be, can be evaluated in a number of ways: (1) He is probably drunk, (2) if he isn't drunk, he is likely a frustrated actor, (3) if he is neither, he is certainly a minority, for booing is not a custom among American audiences, (4) he may very well be wrong." To which I should like to add (5), which hardly occurs to Redfield, that he may very well be right.

It is quite true in this country that the moment someone boos, the majority of the audience, including formerly passive elements, consider it their sacred duty to bravo and applaud for dear life, and prove thereby their dissociation from and superiority to the infamous booer. So booers will not have an easy time of it, either inside the hall or in the corridors outside. Sometimes, as in the case of *Hernani* (a poor play, by the way), history itself will prove them wrong. Yet in a day when the theatre is in sad shape, sinking ever deeper into public apathy, audience participation, sometimes of the most desperate kind, is universally viewed as the salvation. Booing, as long as it does not drown out the actual performance, seems to me a valid form of audience participation, one that would convince the lethargic of how vitally concerned some people are with the theatre. The effect on the authors and performers would be to keep them more in trim. And indignation, unhealthily stifled, would not force many out of the theatres altogether. We must stop being a nation of sheep-like theatregoers who wouldn't say boo to a goose—or turkey.

Meaning

1. What practice does Simon wish to promote among the theatre-going audiences in America that he thinks would improve the current state of the theatre?
2. How does present courteous behavior lead to perpetuating mediocrity; why would vigorous "booing," in Simon's opinion, encourage performers to improve their skills?
3. Why are European audiences, in Simon's opinion, more honest than their American counterparts?

Using Argumentation and Persuasion to Convey Meaning

1. How does Simon use quotations from distinguished critics and playwrights to support his thesis?
2. What use does Simon make of argument by analogy to compare American with European standards of decorum among audiences?
3. What examples does Simon present of how indiscriminate approval by American audiences encourages mediocrity in the theatre?
4. What examples does Simon present of how "booing" improves performances in Europe?

Writing Suggestions

1. Do you agree or disagree with Simon's opinion that the reluctance to "boo" a performance stems from an American ethic that awards people points simply for trying—no matter how bad the actual performance?
2. What different conventions of audience behavior apply in different contexts? For example, what different codes of audience behavior apply for rock concerts, wrestling matches, chamber-music recitals, the opera, or any other live performance?

DAVID HOEKEMA

Capital Punishment:
The Question of Justification

David Hoekema was born in 1950 in Paterson, New Jersey. Hoekema earned a Ph.D. in philosophy from Princeton University in 1981 and has taught at Princeton, Calvin College, and St. Olaf College, Minnesota. He is currently professor of philosophy at the University of Delaware. Since 1984, Hoekema has been executive secretary of the American Philosophical Association. He was elected to the Board of Directors, National Humanities Alliance, 1986–1989. Hoekema's works include Rights and Wrongs: Coercion, Punishment, and the State *(1986), and over seventy-five articles on a whole range of moral, ethical, political, and social issues. He has written, for example, on "The Moral Status of Nuclear Deterrent Threats" (1985), "Nuclear Politics and Christian Ethics" (1983), and "The Right to Punish and the Right to Be Punished," in John Rawls'* Theory of Social Justice: An Introduction *(1980). In "Capital Punishment: The Question of Justification," first published in* The Christian Century *(1979), Hoekema offers a balanced and thoughtful consideration of the arguments most frequently advanced for and against the death penalty.*

In 1810 a bill introduced in the British Parliament sought to abolish capital punishment for the offense of stealing five shillings or more from a shop. Judges and magistrates unanimously opposed the measure. In the House of Lords, the chief justice of the King's Bench, Lord Ellenborough, predicted that the next step would be abolition of the death penalty for stealing five shillings from a house; thereafter no one could "trust himself for an hour without the most alarming apprehension that on his return, every vestige of his property [would] be swept away by the hardened robber" (quoted by Herbert B. Ehrmann in "The Death Penalty and the Administration of Justice," in *The Death Penalty in America*, edited by Hugo Adam Bedau [Anchor, 1967], p. 415).

During the same year Parliament abolished the death penalty for picking pockets, but more than 200 crimes remained punishable by death. Each year in Great Britain more than 2,000 persons were being sentenced to die, though only a small number of these sentences were actually carried out.

I

In this regard as in many others, the laws of the English colonies in North America were much less harsh than those of the mother country. At the time of the Revolution, statutes in most of the colonies prescribed hanging for about a dozen offenses—among them murder, treason, piracy, arson, rape, robbery, burglary, sodomy and (in some cases) counterfeiting, horse theft and slave rebellion. But by the early nineteenth century a movement to abolish the death penalty was gaining strength.

The idea was hardly new: czarist Russia had eliminated the death penalty on religious grounds in the eleventh century. In the United States the movement had been launched by Benjamin Rush in the eighteenth century, with the support of such other distinguished citizens of Philadelphia as Benjamin Franklin and Attorney General William Bradford. By the 1830s, bills calling for abolition of capital punishment were being regularly introduced, and defeated, in several state legislatures. In 1846 Michigan voted effectively to abolish the death penalty—the first English-speaking jurisdiction in the world to do so.

In the years since, twelve states have abolished capital punishment entirely. Although statutes still in effect in some states permit the death penalty to be imposed for a variety of offenses—ranging from statutory rape to desecration of a grave to causing death in a duel—murder is virtually the only crime for which it has been recently employed. There are about 400 persons in U.S. prisons under sentence of death, but only one execution (Gary Gilmore's) has been carried out in this country in the past eleven years.

However, the issue of whether capital punishment is justifiable is by no means settled. Since the Supreme Court, in the case of *Furman* v. *Georgia* in 1972, invalidated most existing laws permitting capital punishment, several states have enacted new legislation designed to meet the court's objections to the Georgia law. And recent public-opinion surveys indicate that a large number, possibly a majority, of Americans favor imposing the death penalty for some crimes. But let us ask the ethical question: Ought governments to put to death persons convicted of certain crimes?

II

First, let us look at grounds on which capital punishment is defended. Most prominent is the argument from *deterrence*. Capital punishment, it is asserted, is necessary to deter potential criminals. Murderers must be executed so that the lives of potential murder victims may be spared.

Two assertions are closely linked here. First, it is said that convicted murderers must be put to death in order to protect the rest of us against those individuals who might kill others if they were at large. This argument, based not strictly on deterrence but on incapacitation of known offenders, is inconclusive, since there are other effective means of protecting the innocent against convicted murderers—for example, imprisonment of murderers for life in high-security institutions.

Second, it is said that the example of capital punishment is needed to deter those who would otherwise commit murder. Knowledge that a crime is punishable by death will give the potential criminal pause. This second argument rests on the assumption that capital punishment does in fact reduce the incidence of capital crimes—a presupposition that must be tested against the evidence. Surprisingly, none of the available empirical data shows any significant correlation between the existence or use of the death penalty and the incidence of capital crimes.

When studies have compared the homicide rates for the past fifty years in states that employ the death penalty and in adjoining states that have abolished it, the numbers have in every case been quite similar: the death penalty has had no discernible effect on homicide rates. Further, the shorter-term effects of capital punishment have been studied by examining the daily number of homicides reported in California over a ten-year period to ascertain whether the execution of convicts reduced the number. Fewer homicides were reported on days immediately following an execution, but this reduction was matched by an increase in the number of homicides on the day of execution and the preceding day. Executions had no discernible effect on the weekly total of homicides. (Cf. "Death and Imprisonment as Deterrents to Murder," by Thorsten Sellin, in Bedau, op. cit., pp. 274–284, and "The Deterrent Effect of Capital Punishment in California," by William F. Graves, in Bedau, op. cit., pp. 322–332.)

The available evidence, then, fails to support the claim that capital punishment deters capital crime. For this reason, I think, we may set aside the deterrence argument. But there is a stronger reason for rejecting the argument—one that has to do with the way in which supporters of that argument would have us treat persons.

Those who defend capital punishment on grounds of deterrence would have us take the lives of some—persons convicted of certain crimes—because doing so will discourage crime and thus protect others. But it is a grave moral wrong to treat one person in a way justified solely by the needs of others. To inflict harm on one person in order to serve the purposes of others is to use that person in an immoral and inhumane way, treating him or her not as a person with rights and responsibilities but as a means to other ends. The most serious flaw in the deterrence argument, therefore, is that it is the wrong *kind* of argument. The execution of criminals cannot be justified by the good which their deaths may do the rest of us.

III

A second argument for the death penalty maintains that some crimes, chief among them murder, *morally require* the punishment of death. In particular, Christians frequently support capital punishment by appeal to the Mosaic code, which required the death penalty for murder. "The law of capital punishment," one writer has concluded after reviewing relevant biblical passages, "must stand as a silent but powerful witness to the sacredness of God-given life" ("Christianity and the Death Penalty," by Jacob Vellenga, in Bedau, op. cit., pp. 123–130).

In the Mosaic code, it should be pointed out, there were many capital crimes besides murder. In the book of Deuteronomy, death is prescribed as the penalty for false prophecy, worship of foreign gods, kidnapping, adultery, deception by a bride concerning her virginity, and disobedience to parents. To this list the laws of the book of Exodus add witchcraft, sodomy, and striking or cursing a parent.

I doubt that there is much sentiment in favor of restoring the death penalty in the United States for such offenses. But if the laws of Old Testament Israel ought not to govern our treatment of, say, adultery, why should they govern the penalty for murder? To support capital punishment by an appeal to Old Testament law is to overlook the fact that the ancient theocratic state of Israel was in nearly every respect profoundly different from any modern secular state. For this reason, we cannot simply regard the Mosaic code as normative for the United States today.

But leaving aside reference to Mosaic law, let me state more strongly the argument we are examining. The death penalty, it may be urged, is the only just penalty for a crime such as murder; it is the only fair *retribution*. Stated thus, the argument at hand seems to be the right *kind* of argument for capital punishment. If capital punishment can be justified at all, it must be on the basis of the *seriousness of the offense* for which it is imposed. Retributive considerations *should* govern the punishment of individuals who violate the law, and chief among these considerations are the principle of proportionality between punishment and offense and the requirement that persons be punished only for acts for which they are truly responsible. I am not persuaded that retributive considerations are sufficient to set a particular penalty for a given offense, but I believe they do require that in comparative terms we visit more serious offenses with more severe punishment.

Therefore, the retributive argument seems the strongest one in support of capital punishment. We ought to deal with convicted offenders not as we want to, but as they deserve. And I am not certain that it is wrong to argue that a person who has deliberately killed another person deserves to die.

But even if this principle is valid, should the judicial branch of our governments be empowered to determine whether individuals deserve to die? Are our procedures for making laws and for determining guilt sufficiently reliable that we may entrust our lives to them? I shall return to this important question presently. But consider the following fact: During the years from 1930 to 1962, 466 persons were put to death for the crime of rape. Of these, 399 were black. Can it seriously be maintained that our courts are administering the death penalty to all those and only to those who deserve to die?

IV

Two other arguments deserve brief mention. It has been argued that, even if the penalty of life imprisonment were acceptable on other grounds, our society could not reasonably be asked to pay the cost of maintaining convicted murderers in prisons for the remainder of their natural lives.

This argument overlooks the considerable costs of retaining the death penalty. Jury selection, conduct of the trial, and the appeals process become extremely time-consuming and elaborate when death is a possible penalty. On the other hand, prisons should not be as expensive as they are. At present those prisoners who work at all are working for absurdly low wages, frequently at menial and degrading tasks. Prisons should be reorganized to provide meaningful work for all able inmates; workers should be paid fair wages for their work and charged for their room and board. Such measures would sharply reduce the cost of prisons and make them more humane.

But these considerations—important as they are—have little relevance to the justification of capital punishment. We should not decide to kill convicted criminals only because it costs so much to keep them alive. The cost to society of imprisonment, large or small, cannot justify capital punishment.

Finally, defenders of capital punishment sometimes support their case by citing those convicted offenders—for example, Gary Gilmore—who have asked to be executed rather than imprisoned. But this argument, too, is of little relevance. If some prisoners would prefer to die rather than be imprisoned, perhaps we should oblige them by permitting them to take their own lives. But this consideration has nothing to do with the question of whether we ought to impose the punishment of death on certain offenders, most of whom would prefer to live.

V

Let us turn now to the case *against* the death penalty. It is sometimes argued that capital punishment is unjustified because those guilty of crimes cannot help acting as they do: the environment, possibly interacting with inherited characteristics, causes some people to commit crimes. It is not moral culpability or choice that divides law-abiding citizens from criminals—so Clarence Darrow argued—eloquently—but the accident of birth or social circumstances.

If determinism of this sort were valid, not only the death penalty but all forms of punishment would be unjustified. No one who is compelled by circumstances to act deserves to be punished. But there is little reason to adopt this bleak view of human action. Occasionally coercive threats compel a person to violate the law; and in such cases the individual is rightly excused from legal guilt. Circumstances of deprivation, hardship and lack of education—unfortunately much more widely prevalent—break down the barriers, both moral and material, which deter many of us from breaking the law. They are grounds for exercising extreme caution and for showing mercy in the application of the law, but they are not the sole causes of crimes: they diminish but do not destroy the responsibility of the individual. The great majority of those who break the law do so deliberately, by choice and not as a result of causes beyond their control.

Second, the case against the death penalty is sometimes based on the view that the justification of punishment lies in the reform which it effects. Those who break the law, it is said, are ill, suffering either from psychological malfunction or from maladjustment to society. Our responsibility is to treat them, to cure them of their illness, so that they become able to function in socially acceptable ways. Death, obviously, cannot reform anyone.

Like the deterrence argument for capital punishment, this seems to be the wrong *kind* of argument. Punishment is punishment and treatment is treatment, and one must not be substituted for the other. Some persons who violate the law are, without doubt, mentally ill. It is unreasonable and inhumane to punish them for acts which they may not have realized they were doing; to put such a person to death would be an even more grievous wrong. In such cases treatment is called for.

But most persons who break the law are not mentally ill and do know what they are doing. We may not force them to undergo treatment in place of the legal penalty for their offenses. To confine them to mental institutions until those put in authority over them judge that they are cured of their criminal tendencies is far more cruel than to sentence them to a term of imprisonment. Voluntary programs of education or vocational training, which help prepare prisoners for noncriminal careers on release, should be made more widely available. But compulsory treatment for all offenders violates their integrity as persons; we need only look to the Soviet Union to see the abuses to which such a practice is liable.

VI

Let us examine a third and stronger argument, a straightforward moral assertion: the state ought not to take life unnecessarily. For many reasons—among them the example which capital punishment sets, its effect on those who must carry out death sentences and, above all, its violation of a basic moral principle—the state ought not to kill people.

The counterclaim made by defenders of capital punishment is that in certain circumstances killing people is permissible and even required, and that capital punishment is one of those cases. If a terrorist is about to throw a bomb into a crowded theater, and a police officer is certain that there is no way to stop him except to kill him, the officer should of course kill the terrorist. In some cases of grave and immediate danger, let us grant, killing is justified.

But execution bears little resemblance to such cases. It involves the planned, deliberate killing of someone in custody who is not a present threat to human life or safety. Execution is not necessary to save the lives of future victims, since there are other means to secure that end.

Is there some vitally important purpose of the state or some fundamental right of persons which cannot be secured without executing convicts? I do not believe there is. And in the absence of any such compelling reason, the moral principle that it is wrong to kill people constitutes a powerful argument against capital punishment.

VII

Of the arguments I have mentioned in favor of the death penalty, only one has considerable weight. That is the retributive argument that murder, as an extremely serious offense, requires a comparably severe punishment. Of the arguments so far examined against capital punishment, only one, the moral claim that killing is wrong, is, in my view, acceptable.

There is, however, another argument against the death penalty which I find compelling—that based on the imperfection of judicial procedure. In the case of *Furman* v. *Georgia*, the Supreme Court struck down existing legislation because of the arbitrariness with which some convicted offenders were executed and others spared. Laws enacted subsequently in several states have attempted to meet the court's objection, either by making death mandatory for certain offenses or by drawing up standards which the trial jury must follow in deciding, after guilt has been established, whether the death penalty will be imposed in a particular case. But these revisions of the law diminish only slightly the discretion of the jury. When death is made the mandatory sentence for first-degree murder, the question of death or imprisonment becomes the question of whether to find the accused guilty as charged or guilty of a lesser offense, such as second-degree murder.

When standards are spelled out, the impression of greater precision is often only superficial. A recent Texas statute, for example, instructs the jury to impose a sentence of death only if it is established "beyond a reasonable doubt" that "there is a probability that the defendant would commit criminal acts of violence that would constitute a continuing threat to society" (Texas Code of Criminal Procedure, Art. 37.071; quoted in *Capital Punishment: The Inevitability of Caprice and Mistake*, by Charles L. Black, Jr. [Norton, 1974], p. 58). Such a law does not remove discretion but only adds confusion.

At many other points in the judicial process, discretion rules, and arbitrary or incorrect decisions are possible. The prosecutor must decide whether to charge the accused with a capital crime, and whether to accept a plea of guilty to a lesser charge. (In most states it is impossible to plead guilty to a charge carrying a mandatory death sentence.) The jury must determine whether the facts of the case as established by testimony in court fit the legal definition of the offense with which the defendant is charged—a definition likely to be complicated at best, incomprehensible at worst.

From a mass of confusing and possibly conflicting testimony the jury must choose the most reliable. But evident reliability can be deceptive: persons have been wrongly convicted of murder on the positive identification of eyewitnesses.

Jurors must also determine whether at the time of the crime the accused satisfied the legal definition of insanity. The most widely used definition—the McNaghten Rules formulated by the judges of the House of Lords in 1843—states that a person is excused from criminal responsibility if at the time of his act he suffered from a defect of reason which arose from a disease of the mind and as a result of which he did not "know the nature and quality of his act," or "if he did know it . . . he did not know he was doing what was wrong" (quoted in *Punishment and Responsibility*, by H. L. A. Hart [Oxford University Press, 1968], p. 189). Every word of this formula has been subject to legal controversy in interpretation, and it is unreasonable to expect that juries untrained in law will be able to apply it consistently and fairly. Even after sentencing, some offenders escape the death penalty as a result of appeals, other technical legal challenges, or executive clemency.

Because of all these opportunities for arbitrary decision, only a small number of those convicted of capital crimes are actually executed. It is hardly surprising that their selection has little to do with the character of their crimes but a great deal to do with the skill of their legal counsel. And the latter depends in large measure on how much money is available for the defense. Inevitably, the death penalty has been imposed most frequently on the poor, and in this country it has been imposed in disproportionate numbers on blacks.

To cite two examples in this regard: All those executed in Delaware between 1902 and the (temporary) abolition of the state's death penalty in 1958 were unskilled workers with limited education. Of 3,860 persons executed in the United States between 1930 and the present, 2,066, or 54 percent, were black. Although for a variety of reasons the per capita rate of conviction for most types of crime has been higher among the poor and the black, that alone cannot explain why a tenth of the population should account for more than half of those executed. Doubtless prejudice played a part. But no amount of goodwill and fair-mindedness can compensate for the disadvantage to those who cannot afford the highly skilled legal counsel needed to discern every loophole in the judicial process.

VIII

Even more worrisome than the discriminatory application of the death penalty is the possibility of mistaken conviction and its ghastly consequences. In a sense, any punishment wrongfully imposed is irrevocable, but none is so irrevocable as death. Although we cannot give back to a person mistakenly imprisoned the time spent or the self-respect lost, we can release and compensate him or her. But we cannot do anything for a person wrongfully executed. While we ought to minimize the opportunities for capricious or mistaken judgments throughout the legal system, we cannot hope for perfect success. There is no reason why our mistakes must be fatal.

Numerous cases of erroneous convictions in capital cases have been documented; several of those convicted were put to death before the error was discovered. However small their number, it is too large. So long as the death penalty exists, there are certain to be others, for every judicial procedure—however meticulous, however compassed about with safeguards—must be carried out by fallible human beings.

One erroneous execution is too many, because even lawful executions of the indisputably guilty serve no purpose. They are not justified by the need to protect the rest of us, since there are other means of restraining persons dangerous to society, and there is no evidence that executions deter the commission of crime. A wrongful execution is a grievous injustice that cannot be remedied after the fact. Even a legal and proper execution is a needless taking of human life. Even if one is sympathetic—as I am—to the claim that a murderer deserves to die, there are compelling reasons not to entrust the power to decide who shall die to the persons and procedures that constitute our judicial system.

MEANING

1. What conclusion does Hoekema draw from statistics that show that persons convicted of capital crimes, if they are poor or minorities, are executed much more frequently than persons convicted of the same capital crimes who have money for legal defense?
2. What reasons, pro and con, does Hoekema present in his examination of the validity of capital punishment?
3. Does Hoekema allow the validity of capital punishment for any reason?
4. Why, according to Hoekema, should the use of capital punishment not be influenced by (a) the cost of maintaining life imprisonment or (b) the desire of those who have been convicted of capital crimes who wish to die?
5. Discuss the paradox implicit in Hoekema's final conclusion—that while society should have the right, in theory, to administer the death penalty, the arbitrary nature of the legal system should rule out, in practice, courts being given the power to decide who lives and who dies.

USING ARGUMENTATION AND PERSUASION TO CONVEY MEANING

1. How does Hoekema organize his essay to look at specific reasons, pro and con, to answer the question, "ought governments to put to death persons convicted of certain crimes"?
2. How does Hoekema use the result of studies in criminology to dispute the claim that capital punishment deters capital crimes?
3. What statistics does Hoekema cite to support his assertion that the justice system is unfair when the amount of money available for legal defense becomes more important than the principle of "equal justice under the law" in determining punishment for the same crimes?

WRITING SUGGESTIONS

1. Discuss why you agree or disagree with Hoekema that the arbitrary nature of the justice system and opportunities for errors in the legal process are so great as to justify eliminating the use of the death penalty.

2. Are there specific clearcut cases where you feel capital punishment should always be imposed? For example, should a convicted murderer who kills a prison guard or fellow prisoner, terrorists, or international drug dealers automatically receive the death penalty upon conviction?
3. How does Solzhenitsyn's fiction (e.g., *The Gulag Archipelago* or *A Day in the Life of Ivan Denisovitch*) illustrate the potential for political abuses in a society where compulsory rehabilitation in psychiatric hospitals is widely employed as a substitute for imprisonment?

Marya Mannes

The Unwilled

Marya Mannes was born in 1904 in New York City to David Mannes and Clara Damrosch, the founders of the Mannes College of Music. The early phases in Mannes' professional writing career encompass the periods of 1925–1933, when she wrote poems, articles, and plays, and 1933–1938, when she worked as copywriter and feature editor for Vogue Magazine. *After 1945, Mannes was feature editor for* Glamor Magazine, *and in 1952, she became staff writer for* The Reporter. *She had her own television program in 1959 (for thirteen weeks) and later contributed a monthly column to* McCall's, *as well as a wide range of articles on social issues for* New York Times Magazine, Harper's, New Republic, *and* Esquire. *Her major works of fiction and nonfiction include* Message From a Stranger *(1948),* More In Anger *(1958),* Subverse: Rhymes for Our Times *(1959),* The New York I Know *(1961),* But Will It Sell? *(1964),* They *(1968),* Out of My Time *(1971), her autobiography,* Uncoupling: The Art of Coming Apart *(1972), a guide to divorce, and* Last Rights *(1974), a powerful and explicit plea for laws to ensure death with dignity. In the following excerpt from* Last Rights, *"The Unwilled," Mannes argues that a quality-of-life standard (rather than sanctity-of-life criteria) should be applied in those situations where an abortion is being considered.*

Those who so passionately uphold the "sanctity of life" do not ask "what life?" nor see themselves as retarded and crippled in an institution for the rest of that life. Nor do they choose to see, to think of, the tens of thousands of lives born crippled and retarded, who, without will or choice, were allowed to be born as, presumably, the "right" of the damaged fetus *to* life.

Rather than seeing the many tangible horrors of that life, the sanctity people choose to emphasize the maternal love and care transcending the agony of a malformed or mindless presence, day after day and year after year. Or they point to those few institutions where a dedicated staff and the latest therapies bring these children or adults to a minimal level of competence: dressing themselves, cleaning themselves, learning small tasks. Since these "inmates" sometimes play and sometimes smile, they are, of course, "happy." They know no other existence, they act on reflexes, not will.

Certainly, love is the prime need of these incomplete beings, whether born that way or the victims of violent and crippling accident. Two middle-aged couples I know who cannot give such grown sons or daughters the special help they need, visit them where they live every week, stay with them for hours. "Ben is such a beautiful young man," said one father. "It's still hard to believe that his fine face and body can exist without thought processes or directions. The circuits in his brain just don't connect."

Certainly, there are parents who love their mongoloid and retarded children, accept them with their siblings as part of the family. But the "sanctity of life" people forget what an enormous toll it takes of the mother especially, who bore this child before the relatively new science of fetology could have given her the alternative choice: not to bear a permanently deformed or retarded being. For it has now become possible, with extremely delicate instruments and techniques, to establish deformation and brain damage, among other serious handicaps, in the unborn fetus when suspicions of malfunctioning exist.

Yet to the antiabortionists, any birth is presumably better than no birth. They seem to forget that millions of unwanted children all over this world are not only destined for an uncherished and mean existence, but swell a population already threatening the resources of this planet, let alone its bare amenities.

They also choose to ignore the kind of "homes" in every large community where the pitiful accidents of biology sit half-naked on floors strewn with feces, autistic and motionless, or banging their swollen heads against peeling walls.

If the concept of "sanctity" does not include "quality," then the word has no meaning and less humanity. The rights of birth and death, of life itself, require both.

Above all, how can the sanctity-of-life argument prevail in a society that condones death in war of young men who want to live, but will not permit the old and hopelessly ill, craving release, to die?

MEANING

1. What reasons does Mannes' cite to support her thesis that the quality of life is a more appropriate guide than the sanctity of life when decisions are made as to whether an abortion should be performed?
2. How has the application of a sanctity-of-life criteria resulted in tens of thousands of people, born crippled and retarded, confined to institutions for all their lives?
3. Discuss the question whether it is unfair or illogical to deprive the unborn of a life in the future because of the degraded conditions that those who are retarded or crippled must endure in the present.

USING ARGUMENTATION AND PERSUASION TO CONVEY MEANING

1. How does Mannes organize her argument to fault her opposition for overlooking or being indifferent to the human consequences of the sanctity-of-life policies?
2. To what extent might Mannes' assertion that the sanctity of life automatically includes the right to enjoy life be a form of "begging the question" or "arguing in a circle"?
3. What specific examples does Mannes use to support her assertion that the sanctity-of-life standard leads to negative consequences?

WRITING SUGGESTIONS

1. Discuss Mannes' argument in light of Richard Selzer's "What I Saw at the Abortion" (see page 132).
2. What arguments could be made if the right to decide if an abortion should be performed should be vested mainly in the hands of the doctor, the parents, or a hospital-ethics committee, or some joint decision?
3. Discuss how the movies *Mask* and *The Elephant Man* challenge Mannes' argument by showing that severe impairment does not exclude the capacity to love and be loved.
4. How might Mannes meet objections to her argument posed by such noteworthy exceptions as Helen Keller?

POLITICAL AND SOCIAL SCIENCES

EARL WARREN

Brown v. *Board of Education of Topeka*

Earl Warren (1891–1974), former Chief Justice of the U.S. Supreme Court, served as the attorney general of California (1939–1942) and was the vice-presidential nominee who ran unsuccessfully with Thomas Dewey against Harry S. Truman in 1948. Before his appointment as Chief Justice of the Supreme Court by President Eisenhower, Warren served as governor of California from 1942–1953. After John F. Kennedy's assassination, Warren was appointed by President Johnson to head up a seven-man commission to investigate Kennedy's death. The "Warren Commission" found Lee Harvey Oswald to be solely responsible. As Chief Justice of the U.S. Supreme Court, Warren played a crucial role in producing the unanimous 1954 court ruling on Brown v. Board of Education of Topeka. *This historic ruling found segregation in schools unconstitutional under the Fourteenth Amendment. The decision served as a catalyst for the civil-rights movement, bringing about a series of public demonstrations, marches, and sit-ins which, in conjunction with changes in the law, permanently altered existing social attitudes toward the acceptability of racial discrimination.*

In approaching this problem, we cannot turn the clock back to 1868 when the Amendment was adopted, or even to 1896 when *Plessy* v. *Ferguson* was written. We must consider public education in the light of its full development and its present place in American life throughout the Nation. Only in this way can it be determined if segregation in public schools deprives these plaintiffs of the equal protection of the laws.

Today, education is perhaps the most important function of state and local governments. Compulsory school attendance laws and the great expenditures for education both demonstrate our recognition of the importance of education to our democratic society. It is required in the performance of our most basic public responsibilities, even service in the armed forces. It is the very foundation of good citizenship. Today it is a principal instrument in awakening the child to cultural values, in preparing him for later professional training, and in helping him to adjust normally to his environment. In these days, it is doubtful that any child may reasonably be expected to succeed in life if he is denied the opportunity of an education. Such an opportunity, where the state has undertaken to provide it, is a right which must be made available to all on equal terms.

We come then to the question presented: Does segregation of children in public schools solely on the basis of race, even though the physical facilities and other "tangible" factors may be equal, deprive the children of the minority group of equal educational opportunities? We believe that it does.

In *Sweatt* v. *Painter, supra,* in finding that a segregated law school for Negroes could not provide them equal educational opportunities, this Court relied in large part on "those qualities which are incapable of objective measurement but which make for greatness in a law school." In *McLaurin* v. *Oklahoma State Regents, supra,* the Court, in requiring that a Negro admitted to a white graduate school be treated like all other students, again resorted to intangible considerations: ". . . his ability to study, to engage in discussions and exchange views with other students, and, in general, to learn his profession." Such considerations apply with added force to children in grade and high schools. To separate them from others of similar age and qualifications solely because of their race generates a feeling of inferiority as to their status in the community that may affect their hearts and minds in a way unlikely ever to be undone. The effect of this separation on their educational opportunities was well stated by a finding in the Kansas case by a court which nevertheless felt compelled to rule against the Negro plaintiffs:

> Segregation of white and colored children in public schools has a detrimental effect upon the colored children. The impact is greater when it has the sanction of the law; for the policy of separating the races is usually interpreted as denoting the inferiority of the negro group. A sense of inferiority affects the motivation of a child to learn. Segregation with the sanction of law, therefore, has a tendency to retard the educational and mental development of negro children and to deprive them of some of the benefits they would receive in a racially integrated school system.

Whatever may have been the extent of psychological knowledge at the time of *Plessy* v. *Ferguson,* this finding is amply supported by modern authority. Any language in *Plessy* v. *Ferguson* contrary to this finding is rejected.

We conclude that in the field of public education the doctrine of "separate but equal" has no place. Separate educational facilities are inherently unequal. Therefore, we hold that the plaintiffs and others similarly situated for whom the actions have been brought are, by reason of the segregation complained of, deprived of the equal protection of the laws guaranteed by the Fourteenth Amendment.

MEANING

1. What basic conflict does Warren discover between the undesirable social and psychological effects produced by segregated public schools and the principle of "equal protection under the law" guaranteed by the Fourteenth Amendment?

2. How does this 1954 decision to abolish segregation in public schools apply the Fourteenth Amendment—which says, "No state shall . . . deny to any person within its jurisdiction the equal protection of the laws"—specifically to protect equal educational opportunities for minorities?

Using Argumentation and Persuasion to Convey Meaning

1. How does Warren's case rest on the claim, made in paragraph (2), that education is "perhaps the most important function of state and local governments"?
2. What use does Warren make of results from psychological studies that show that segregated schools instill a sense of inferiority, retard mental development, and deprive minority children of educational opportunities they should rightfully enjoy under the Fourteenth Amendment?
3. Analyze this historic court decision as a syllogism comprised of major premise, minor premise, and conclusion. How does the Fourteenth Amendment serve as the major premise, the results of the psychological studies and expert opinions as the minor premise, and the historic judgment of this court decision as the conclusion?

Writing Suggestions

1. What current legal and social issues (e.g., euthanasia, sexual discrimination, rights of AIDS victims) are capable of being analyzed within the framework of the "equal protection" provisions of the Fourteenth Amendment? Summarize the pros and cons of one of these issues and support one side or the other.
2. What relationship existed between this court decision and court-enforced school busing? Do you feel that most of the problems that this decision was intended to correct have been resolved since 1954?

CHRISTOPHER D. STONE

Legal Rights for the Environment

Christopher D. Stone was born in 1937 in New York City. Stone received a B.A. from Harvard in 1959 and earned his law degree from Yale University Law School in 1962. Since 1969, Stone has been professor of law at the University of Southern California, Los Angeles. His writings delve into the relationship between the letter of the law and the changing moral and ethical frameworks within which laws are formulated. Among his works are Should Trees Have Standing?: Toward Legal Rights for Natural Objects *(1974, rev. ed. 1975) and* Where the Law Ends *(1975). He has also contributed numerous articles to the* Los Angeles Times, *the* New York Times, *the* Nation, *and professional law journals. In "Legal Rights for the Environment," from* Should Trees Have Standing?, *Stone creates a provocative case for providing legal guardians for trees and other natural entities.*

I

In *The Descent of Man,* written a full century ago, Charles Darwin observed that the history of man's moral development has been a continual extension in the range of objects receiving his "social instincts and sympathies." Originally each man had moral concern only for himself and those of a very narrow circle about him; later, he came to regard more and more "not only the welfare, but the happiness of all his fellow men." Then, gradually, "his sympathies became more tender and widely diffused, extending to men of all races, to the imbecile, maimed and other useless members of society, and finally to the lower animals. . . ."

The history of the law suggests a parallel development. The scope of "things" accorded legal protection has been continuously extending. Members of the earliest "families" (including extended kinship groups and clans) treated everyone on the outside as suspect, alien, and rightless, except in the vacant sense of each man's "right to self-defense." "An Indian Thug," it has been written, "conscientiously regretted that he had not robbed and strangled as many travelers as did his father before him. In a rude state of civilization the robbery of strangers is, indeed, generally considered as honorable." And even within a single family, persons we presently regard as the natural holders of at least some legal rights had none. Take, for example, children. We know something of the early rights-status of children from the widespread practice of infanticide—especially of the deformed and female. (Senicide, practiced by the North American Indians, was the corresponding rightlessness of the aged.) Sir Henry Maine tells us that as late as the *Patria Potestas* of the Romans, the father had *jus vitae necisque*—the power of life and death—over his children. It followed legally, Maine writes, that [he had power] of uncontrolled corporal chastisement; he can modify their personal condition at pleasure; he can give a wife to his son; he can give his daughter in marriage; he can divorce his children of either sex; he can transfer them to another family by adoption; and he can sell them.

The child was less than a person; it was, in the eyes of the law, an object, a thing.

The legal rights of children have long since been recognized in principle, and are still expanding in practice. Witness, just within recent time, *In re Gault*, the United States Supreme Court decision guaranteeing basic constitutional protections to juvenile defendants, and the Voting Rights Act of 1970, with its lowering of the voting age to eighteen. We have been making persons of children although they were not, in law, always so. And we have done the same, albeit imperfectly some would say, with prisoners, aliens, women (married women, especially were nonpersons through most of legal history), the insane, blacks, fetuses, and Indians.

People are apt to suppose that there are natural limits on how far the law can go, that it is only matter in human form that can come to be recognized as the possessor of rights. But it simply is not so. The world of the lawyer is peopled with inanimate right-holders: trusts, corporations, joint ventures, municipalities, Subchapter R partnerships, and nation-states, to mention just a few. Ships, still referred to by courts in the feminine gender, have long had an independent jural life, often with striking consequences. In one famous U.S. Supreme Court case a ship had been seized and used by pirates. After the ship's capture, the owners asked for her return; after all, the vessel had been pressed into piracy without their knowledge or consent. But the United States condemned and sold the "offending vessel." In denying release to the owners, Justice Story quoted Chief Justice Marshall from an earlier case:

> This is not a proceeding against the owner; it is a proceeding against the vessel for an offense committed by the vessel; which is not the less an offense . . . because it was committed without the authority and against the will of the owner.

The *ship* was, in the eyes of the law, the guilty person.

We have become so accustomed to the idea of a corporation having "its" own rights, and being a "person" and "citizen" for so many statutory and constitutional purposes, that we forget how perplexing the notion was to early jurists. "That invisible, intangible and artificial being, that mere legal entity," Chief Justice Marshall wrote of the corporation in *Bank of the United States* v. *Deveaux*—could a suit be brought in its name? Ten years later, in the *Dartmouth College* case, he was still refusing to let pass unnoticed the wonder of an entity "existing only in contemplation of law." Yet, long before Marshall worried over the personification of the modern corporation, the best medieval legal scholars had spent hundreds of years struggling with the legal nature of those great public "corporate bodies," the Church and the State. How could they exist in law, as entities transcending the living pope and king? It was clear how a king could bind himself—on his honor—by a treaty. But when the king died, what was it that was burdened with the obligations of, and claimed the rights under, the treaty his tangible hand had signed? The medieval mind saw (what we have lost our capacity to see) how unthinkable it was, and worked out the most elaborate conceits and fallacies to serve as anthropomorphic flesh for the Universal Church and the Universal Empire.

It is this note of the unthinkable that I want to dwell upon for a moment. Throughout legal history, each successive extension of rights to some new entity has been, theretofore, a bit unthinkable. Every era is inclined to suppose the rightlessness of its rightless "things" to be a decree of Nature, not a legal convention—an open social choice—acting in support of some status quo. It is thus that we avoid coming face to face with all the moral, social, and economic dimensions of what we are doing. Consider, for example, how the United States Supreme Court sidestepped the moral issues behind slavery in its 1856 *Dred Scott* decision: blacks had been denied the rights of citizenship "as a subordinate and inferior class of beings." Their unfortunate legal status reflected, in other words, not our choice at all, but "just the way things were." In an 1856 contest over a will, the deceased's provision that his slaves should decide between emancipation and public sale was held void on the ground that slaves had no legal capacity to choose. "These decisions," the Virginia court explained,

> are legal conclusions flowing naturally and necessarily from the one clear, simple, fundamental idea of chattel slavery. That fundamental idea is, that, in the eye of the law, so far certainly as civil rights and relations are concerned, the slave is not a person, but a thing. The investiture of a chattel with civil rights or legal capacity is indeed a legal solecism and absurdity. The attribution of a legal personality to a chattel slave—legal conscience, legal intellect, legal freedom, or liberty and power of free choice and action, and corresponding legal obligations growing out of such qualities, faculties and action—implies a palpable contradiction in terms.

In a like vein, the highest court in California once explained that Chinese had not the right to testify against white men in criminal matters because they were "a race of people whom nature has marked an inferior, and who are incapable of progress or intellectual development beyond a certain point . . . between whom and ourselves nature has placed an impassable difference."

The popular conception of the Jew in the thirteenth century contributed to a law which treated them, as one legal commentator has observed, as "men *ferae naturae*, protected by a quasi-forest law. Like the roe and the deer, they form an order apart." Recall, too, that it was not so long ago that the fetus was "like the roe and the deer." In an early suit attempting to establish a wrongful death action on behalf of a negligently killed fetus (now widely accepted practice in American courts), Holmes, then on the Massachusetts Supreme Court, seems to have thought it simply inconceivable "that a man might owe a civil duty and incur a conditional prospective liability in tort to one not yet in being." The first woman in Wisconsin who thought she might have a right to practice law was told that she did not. We had nothing against *them*, of course; but they were *naturally* different.

> The law of nature destines and qualifies the female sex for the bearing and nurture of the children of our race and for the custody of the homes of the world . . . [A]ll life-long callings of women, inconsistent with these radical and sacred duties of their sex, as is the profession of the law, are departures from the order of nature; and when voluntary, treason against it. . . . The peculiar qualities of womanhood, its gentle graces, its quick sensibility, its tender susceptibility, its purity, its delicacy, its emotional impulses, its subordination of hard reason to sympathetic feeling, are

surely not qualifications for forensic strife. Nature has tempered woman as little for the juridical conflicts of the court room, as for the physical conflicts of the battle field. . . .

The fact is, that each time there is a movement to confer rights onto some new "entity," the proposal is bound to sound odd or frightening or laughable.[1] This is partly because until the rightless thing receives its rights, we cannot see it as anything but a thing for the use of "us"—those who are holding rights at the time. (Thus it was that the Founding Fathers could speak of the inalienable rights of all men, and yet maintain a society that was, by modern standards, without the most basic rights for blacks, Indians, children and women. There was no hypocrisy; emotionally, no one felt that these other things were *men*.) In this vein, what is striking about the Wisconsin case above *is* that the court, for all its talk about women, so clearly was never able to see women as they are and might become. All it could see was the popular "idealized" version of an object it needed. Such is the way the slave South looked upon the black. "The older South," W. E. DuBois wrote, clung to "the sincere and passionate belief that somewhere between men and cattle, God created a *tertium quid*, and called it a Negro."

Obviously, there is something of a seamless web involved: there will be resistance to giving a "thing" rights until it can be seen and valued for itself; it is hard to see it and value a "thing" for itself until we can bring ourselves to give it rights—which is almost inevitably going to sound inconceivable to a large group of people.

The reader must know by now, if only from the title of the book, the reason for this little discourse on the unthinkable. I am quite seriously proposing that we recognize legal rights of forests, oceans, rivers and other so-called "natural objects" in the environment—indeed, of the natural environment as a whole.

As strange as such a notion may sound, it is neither fanciful nor without considerable operational significance. In fact, I do not think it would be a misdescription of recent developments in the law to say that we are already on the verge of such an assignment of rights to nature, although we have not faced up to what we are doing in those particular terms.

We should do so now, and begin to explore the implications such an idea would yield.

---

[1] Recently, a group of prison inmates in Suffolk County tamed a mouse that they discovered, giving him the name Morris. Discovering Morris, a jailer flushed him down the toilet. The prisoners brought a proceeding against the warden complaining, *inter alia*, that Morris was subjected to discriminatory discharge and was otherwise unequally treated. The action was unsuccessful, the court noting that the inmates themselves were "guilty of imprisoning Morris without a charge, without a trial, and without bail," and that other mice at the prison were not treated more favorably. "As to the true victim, the Court can only offer again the sympathy first proffered to his ancestors by Robert Burns's poem, 'To a Mouse.' "

The whole matter seems humorous, of course. But we need to know more of the function of humor in the unfolding of a culture, and the ways in which it is involved with the social growing pains to which it is testimony. Why do people make jokes about the Women's Liberation Movement? Is it not on account of—rather than in spite of—the underlying validity of the protests and the uneasy awareness that a recognition of the claims is inevitable? Arthur Koestler rightly begins his study of the human mind, *Act of Creation* (1964), with an analysis of humor, entitled "The Logic of Laughter." Cf. Freud's paper, "Jokes and the Unconscious."

II

Toward Having Standing in Its Own Right

It is not inevitable, nor is it wise, that natural objects should have no rights to seek redress in their own behalf. It is no answer to say that streams and forests cannot have standing because streams and forests cannot speak. Corporations, cannot speak either, nor can states, estates, infants, incompetents, municipalities or universities. Lawyers speak for them, as they customarily do for the ordinary citizen who has legal problems. One ought, I think, to handle the legal problems of natural objects as one does the problems of legal incompetents. If a human being shows signs of becoming senile and has affairs that he is not competent to manage, those concerned with his well-being make such a showing to the court, which can invest someone with the authority to manage the incompetent's affairs: a guardian (or "conservator" or "committee"—the terminology varies). Courts make similar arrangements when a corporation has become "incompetent"—they appoint a trustee in bankruptcy or reorganization to oversee its affairs and speak for it in court when that becomes necessary.

On a parity of reasoning, we should have a system in which, when a friend of a natural object perceives it to be endangered, he can apply to a court for the creation of a guardianship. Perhaps we already have the machinery to do so. California law, for example, defines an incompetent as:

> any person, whether insane or not, who by reason of old age, disease, weakness of mind, or other cause, is unable, unassisted, properly to manage and take care of himself or his property, and by reason thereof is likely to be deceived or imposed upon by artful or designing persons.

Are there not, among our natural objects, many such "persons" unable to take care of themselves—any number of rivers mutely choking to death—that need legal voice if they are not continuously to be "imposed upon"? To urge this upon a court calls for no more boldness or imagination than it took to convince the Supreme Court in the 1880s that a railroad was a "person" under the Fourteenth Amendment, a constitutional provision theretofore thought to secure the rights of freedmen, not corporate organizations. If such arguments based on a favorable interpretation of existing statutes should fail in the courts, special environmental legislation could readily be enacted along traditional guardianship lines. Provisions could be designed for guardianships both in the instance of public natural objects (e.g., rivers, beaches) and also, probably with slightly different standards, in the instance of natural objects on "private" land.[2]

---

[2] The law has developed in such a way that the private landowner's power over natural objects on his land is far less restrained by law (as opposed to the economics of self-interest) than his power over the public resources that he can get his hands on. If this state of affairs is to be changed, the standard for interceding in the interests of natural objects on traditionally recognized "private" land might well parallel the rules that guide courts in the matter of people's children whose upbringing (or lack thereof) poses social threat. The courts can, for example, make a child "a dependent of the court" where the child's "home is an unfit place for him by reason of neglect, cruelty, or depravity of either of his parents. . . ." California Welfare and Institutions Code § 600(b). That is to say, in extreme cases of child abuse, we intercede with the child's "owner"; surely there are extreme cases of environmental abuse where the society might feel it appropriate to intercede on behalf of an owner's natural objects.

The potential "friends" that such a statutory scheme would require will hardly be lacking. The National Audubon Society, The Sierra Club, Environmental Defense Fund, Friends of the Earth, Natural Resources Defense Council, and the Izaak Walton League are just some of the many groups dedicated to environmental protection and which are becoming increasingly capable of marshaling the requisite technical experts and lawyers. If, for example, the Environmental Defense Fund should have reason to believe that some company's strip-mining operations were irreparably destroying the ecological balance of large tracts of land, it could, under this procedure, apply to the court in which the lands were situated to be appointed guardian. As guardian, it might be given rights of inspection (or visitation) to enter the property and bring to the court's attention details of the land's condition. If there were indications that under the substantive law some redress might be available on the land's behalf, then the guardian would be entitled to raise the land's rights in the land's name, i.e., without having to make the roundabout and often unavailing demonstration, discussed below, that "rights" of the club's members were being invaded. Guardians would also be looked to for a host of other protective tasks, e.g., monitoring effluents (and/or monitoring the monitors), and representing their "wards" at legislative and administrative hearings in such matters as the setting of state water-quality standards. Procedures already exist, and can be strengthened, under which someone can move a court to remove and substitute guardians (for conflicts of interest or for other reasons) as well as to terminate the guardianship when the need has passed.

It is true there is a labyrinth of ontological problems we could become lost in here: which natural objects are we going to countenance as jural "persons"—the ecology of a bay? the oyster bed on its floor? each oyster? If a guardianship can be established over a forest, someone may ask, why not over an earthworm? Are we to concern ourselves with a watershed, a tributary, or a river? Suppose a guardian is appointed by a county court with respect to a stream, and a federal court appoints a guardian, with different ideas, for the larger river basin system of which the stream is a part.

One can spin off a myriad of complicated scenarios, all with an eye toward frightening the law away from the guardianship idea: court calendars clogged to a halt with trivia, endless jurisdictional disputes with the guardian for one entity setting himself at odds with the guardian for another, and the like. But to my mind, no one sympathetic to the environment should be put off because somewhere, far on the other side of this new legal territory, there may lie some mountains we don't know now how to cross. (They may be molehills when we get there.) Whatever hypotheticals we can conjure in the classroom, no lawyer I know in the real world is about to invest his time going to court to ask for a guardianship over an oyster or an earthworm. And I don't know any judge who would grant the motion if he or she did.[3]

But I do know at least one lawyer who is preparing papers on behalf of a stand of first-growth redwoods; another who has gone to bat, successfully to date, on behalf of a river; another—successfully, also—in the name of a commons. I expect, in other words, that we are not as likely to suffer from a surfeit of trivial environmental

[3] Unless, perhaps, it were the last earthworm of a species, which most of us would regard as another matter. One ought to remember here, too, that we are speaking of the establishment of a guardianship as the first step in having a case presented on its merits. The granting of the guardianship merely ensures the natural object of its "day in court"—not a victory. The natural tendency is, that lawyers will not press for every imaginable guardianship, when the ward's chances of prevailing in the ultimate litigation are nil.

representatives as we are to gain from new voices being heard in eminently sensible ones.

I am similarly inclined to discount some of the potential jurisdictional problems. My guess is that the boundaries of the objects whose representation is sought will be determined, in the first instance, by the nature of the threat. If the threat is to a stream (and all that is involved in its present ecological balance), then the application for the guardianship will be made to the local court in whose jurisdiction the stream runs; the suit will be brought in the name of the stream, but the arguments advanced are not likely to be inconsistent with the interests of any component elements involved, i.e., the fish in the stream, the frogs on the banks, etc. Under most circumstances they will be suffering equally from the same complained-of actions. A whole watershed will be represented if it is the whole watershed that is being threatened, as by some lumbering or strip-mining operation. Something that threatened the entire atmosphere (the continued production of aerosol cans?) might lead to a guardianship on behalf of it, application to be made, perhaps, in a court of international jurisdiction.

In sum, I don't deny the many potential problems implicit in the idea I am putting forward; but most of them, I expect, we can deal with well enough when and if they really arise.

MEANING

1. Why, according to Stone, should lawyers be appointed as guardians to represent entities such as streams and forests that cannot speak for themselves?
2. Which groups in the past were considered as being outside the scope of legal protection and won their rights only with great difficulty?
3. Why is it important to Stone's argument that corporations, trusts, partnerships and municipalities, and other inanimate "right-holders" currently receive the protection of the law?
4. How does the *Dred Scott* decision demonstrate society's reluctance to grant minorities equal right-holding status?
5. How does Stone's explanation of what a conservator does clarify the role of a legal guardian in defending the interests of entities who cannot speak for themselves?

USING ARGUMENTATION AND PERSUASION TO CONVEY MEANING

1. What measures does Stone take to meet objections to his proposal?
2. How does Stone use examples of other inanimate "right-holders," such as municipalities and corporations, who receive the protection of the law, to argue by analogy that streams and forests are similarly entitled to representation?
3. How does Stone use current laws, allowing the court to protect a child's welfare by making that child "a dependent of the court," as a basis for his argument?
4. How does Stone apply past rulings, extending rights to groups of people who formerly were outside the scope of legal protection, to strengthen his argument?

WRITING SUGGESTIONS

1. Stone asserts that when minorities were considered "an order apart" and without rights, they were seen as objects to be used by "those who are holding rights at the time." How would this apply to Kenneth Stampp's analysis of instruction manuals used by slaveowners (see page 281).

2. Try your hand at writing a letter applying to the court to be a conservator of a natural entity—pond, stream, grove of trees, particular animal—in your immediate environment that needs legal protection. Your argument should demonstrate the need for this protection and your qualifications to be the appointed guardian.

Thomas Robert Malthus

The Principle of Population

Thomas Robert Malthus (1766–1834), considered the father of political economy, was born in Surrey, England, and was trained as a mathematician, graduating in 1788 from Cambridge. He became curate of Albury in Surrey in 1798, compassionately ministering to the poor. Malthus' first essay, "The Crisis," written in response to Pitt's Poor Law Bill of 1796, showed his concern about society's ability to cope with drastic increases in population. In 1799, Malthus and William Otter traveled throughout Scandinavia and Russia. Malthus' diaries provided him with much of the evidence on which he based his later arguments. His major work, An Essay On the Principle of Population (1798; rev.ed.1803), from which the following excerpt is taken, stated the "Malthusian principle" that geometrical growth of population would always outstrip the available food supply (which can only increase arithmetically). Malthus wrote his essay in response to Pitts' proposed legislation and works by William Godwin and Condorcet, which envisioned a perfectable society. Malthus, as a demographer, economist, and pastor, spoke of the realities brought about by the Industrial Revolution: burgeoning city population, high infant mortality, epidemics, and periodic famines. Darwin declared that Malthus's Essay led him to think in terms of a "struggle for existence" where successful adaptations would result in the evolutionary formation of new species. "The Principle of Population" is set up as a deductive argument whose consequences follow from postulates that Malthus takes as self-evident.

The great and unlooked for discoveries that have taken place of late years in natural philosophy, the increasing diffusion of general knowledge from the extension of the art of printing, the ardent and unshackled spirit of inquiry that prevails throughout the lettered and even unlettered world, the new and extraordinary lights that have been thrown on political subjects which dazzle and astonish the understanding, and particularly that tremendous phenomenon in the political horizon, the French revolution, which, like a blazing comet, seems destined either to inspire with fresh life and vigour, or to scorch up and destroy the shrinking inhabitants of the earth, have all concurred to lead able men into the opinion that we were touching on a period big with the most important changes, changes that would in some measure be decisive of the future fate of mankind.

It has been said that the great question is now at issue, whether man shall henceforth start forwards with accelerated velocity towards illimitable, and hitherto unconceived improvement, or be condemned to a perpetual oscillation between happiness and misery, and after every effort remain still at an immeasurable distance from the wished-for goal. . . .

I have read some of the speculations of the perfectibility of man and society with great pleasure. I have been warmed and delighted with the enchanting picture which they hold forth. I ardently wish for such happy improvements. But I see great, and, to my understanding, unconquerable difficulties in the way to them. These difficulties it is my present purpose to state, declaring, at the same time, that so far from exulting in them, as a cause of triumph over the friends of innovation, nothing would give me greater pleasure than to see them completely removed.

The most important argument that I shall adduce is certainly not new. The principles on which it depends have been explained in part by Hume, and more at large by Dr. Adam Smith. It has been advanced and applied to the present subject, though not with its proper weight, or in the most forcible point of view, by Mr. Wallace, and it may probably have been stated by many writers that I have never met with. I should certainly therefore not think of advancing it again, though I mean to place it in a point of view in some degree different from any that I have hitherto seen, if it had ever been fairly and satisfactorily answered.

The cause of this neglect on the part of the advocates for the perfectibility of mankind is not easily accounted for. I cannot doubt the talents of such men as Godwin and Condorcet. I am unwilling to doubt their candour. To my understanding, and probably to that of most others, the difficulty appears insurmountable. Yet these men of acknowledged ability and penetration, scarcely deign to notice it, and hold on their course in such speculations, with unabated ardour and undiminished confidence. I have certainly no right to say that they purposely shut their eyes to such arguments. I ought rather to doubt the validity of them, when neglected by such men, however forcibly their truth may strike my own mind. Yet in this respect it must be acknowledged that we are all of us too prone to err. If I saw a glass of wine repeatedly presented to a man, and he took no notice of it, I should be apt to think that he was blind or uncivil. A juster philosophy might teach me rather to think that my eyes deceived me and that the offer was not really what I conceived it to be.

In entering upon the argument I must premise that I put out of the question, at present, all mere conjectures, that is, all suppositions, the probable realization of which cannot be inferred upon any just philosophical grounds. A writer may tell me that he thinks man will ultimately become an ostrich. I cannot properly contradict him. But before he can expect to bring any reasonable person over to his opinion, he ought to shew, that the necks of mankind have been gradually elongating, that the lips have grown harder and more prominent, that the legs and feet are daily altering their shape, and that the hair is beginning to change into stubs of feathers. And till the probability of so wonderful a conversion can be shewn, it is surely lost time and lost eloquence to expatiate on the happiness of man in such a state; to describe his powers, both of running and flying, to paint him in a condition where all narrow luxuries would be contemned, where he would be employed only in collecting the necessaries of life, and where, consequently, each man's share of labour would be light, and his portion of leisure ample.

I think I may fairly make two postulata.

First, That food is necessary to the existence of man.

Secondly, That the passion between the sexes is necessary and will remain nearly in its present state.

These two laws, ever since we have had any knowledge of mankind, appear to have been fixed laws of our nature, and, as we have not hitherto seen any alteration in them, we have no right to conclude that they will ever cease to be what they now are, without an immediate act of power in that Being who first arranged the system of the universe, and for the advantage of his creatures, still executes, according to fixed laws, all its various operations.

I do not know that any writer has supposed that on this earth man will ultimately be able to live without food. But Mr. Godwin has conjectured that the passion between the sexes may in time be extinguished. As, however, he calls this part of his work a deviation into the land of conjecture, I will not dwell longer upon it at present than to say that the best arguments for the perfectibility of man are drawn from a contemplation of the great progress that [man] has already made from the savage state and the difficulty of saying where he is to stop. But towards the extinction of the passion between the sexes, no progress whatever has hitherto been made. It appears to exist in as much force at present as it did two thousand or four thousand years ago. There are individual exceptions now as there always have been. But, as these exceptions do not appear to increase in number, it would surely be a very unphilosophical mode of arguing, to infer merely from the existence of an exception, that the exception would, in time, become the rule, and the rule the exception.

Assuming then, my postulata as granted, I say, that the power of population is indefinitely greater than the power in the earth to produce subsistence for man.

Population, when unchecked, increases in a geometrical ratio. Subsistence increases only in an arithmetical ratio. A slight acquaintance with numbers will shew the immensity of the first power in comparison of the second.

By that law of our nature which makes food necessary to the life of man, the effects of these two unequal powers must be kept equal.

This implies a strong and constantly operating check on population from the difficulty of subsistence. This difficulty must fall some where and must necessarily be severely felt by a large portion of mankind.

Through the animal and vegetable kingdoms, nature has scattered the seeds of life abroad with the most profuse and liberal hand. She has been comparatively sparing in the room and the nourishment necessary to rear them. The germs of existence contained in this spot of earth, with ample food, and ample room to expand in, would fill millions of worlds in the course of a few thousand years. Necessity, that imperious all pervading law of nature, restrains them within the prescribed bounds. The race of plants, and the race of animals shrink under this great restrictive law. And the race of man cannot, by any efforts of reason, escape from it. Among plants and animals its effects are waste of seed, sickness, and premature death. Among mankind, misery and vice. The former, misery, is an absolutely necessary consequence of it. Vice is a highly probable consequence, and we therefore see it abundantly prevail, but it ought not, perhaps, to be called an absolutely necessary consequence. The ordeal of virtue is to resist all temptation to evil.

This natural inequality of the two powers of population and of production in the earth and that great law of our nature which must constantly keep their effects equal form the great difficulty that to me appears insurmountable in the way to the perfectibility of society. All other arguments are of slight and subordinate consideration in comparison of this. I see no way by which man can escape from the weight of this law which pervades all animated nature. No fancied equality, no agrarian regulations in their utmost extent, could remove the pressure of it even for a single century. And it appears, therefore, to be decisive against the possible existence of a society, all the members of which should live in ease, happiness, and comparative leisure; and feel no anxiety about providing the means of subsistence for themselves and families.

Consequently, if the premises are just, the argument is conclusive against the perfectibility of the mass of mankind. . . .

Meaning

1. What reasons does Malthus present to support his theory that there will always be a gap between population size and the available food supply?
2. What does Malthus mean when he says that population increases "geometrically," while the food supply can only increase "arithmetically"?
3. Why, according to Malthus, will this fundamental disproportion always defeat any plans for social betterment?
4. What factors other than the food supply does Malthus discuss that also act to limit population size?

Using Argumentation and Persecution to Convey Meaning

1. How does Malthus' ostrich analogy exert gentle sarcasm against those who propose a vision of human "perfectability"? Where else does Malthus use irony and humor to communicate his ideas?
2. How does Malthus undercut counterarguments by contrasting the ideal of human "perfectability" with the permanent constraints of too many people and too little food?
3. How does Malthus use parallelism to emphasize relationships between his ideas?

Writing Suggestions

1. How has the "green revolution" made it possible to produce greater amounts of food than Malthus had foreseen in his classic 1798 essay? Does this advance in food technology negate or simply postpone the consequences of Malthus' theory?
2. What extreme measures has China taken since 1979 to deal with the food and population problems described so accurately by Malthus?
3. How does Frazer's discussion of ancient cultures show that primitive rituals were designed to ensure an abundant food supply (see page 114)?

MARTIN LUTHER KING, JR.

I Have a Dream

Martin Luther King, Jr. (1929–1968), a monumental figure in the civil rights movement and a persuasive advocate of nonviolent means for producing social change, was born in Atlanta, Georgia, in 1929. He was ordained as a Baptist minister in his father's church when he was eighteen and went on to earn degrees from Morehouse College (B.A., 1948), Crozer Theological Seminary (B.D., 1951), Chicago Theological Seminary (D.D., 1957), and Boston University (Ph.D., 1955; D.D., 1959). On December 5, 1955, while he was pastor of a church in Montgomery, Alabama, King focused national attention on the predicament of southern blacks by leading a city-wide boycott of the segregated bus system, which lasted over one year and nearly bankrupted the bus company. He founded the Southern Christian Leadership Conference and adapted techniques of nonviolent protest employed by Ghandi in a series of sit-ins and mass marches, which were instrumental in bringing about the Civil Rights Act of 1964 and the Voting Rights Act of 1965. He was awarded the Nobel Prize for Peace in 1964 in recognition of his great achievements as the leader of the American civil rights movement. Sadly, King's affirmation of the need to meet physical violence with peaceful resistance led to his being jailed more than fourteen times, beaten, stoned, stabbed in the chest, and finally murdered in Memphis, Tennessee on April 4, 1968. His many distinguished writings include Stride Towards Freedom: The Montgomery Story *(1958),* Letter from Birmingham Jail, *written in 1963 and published in 1968,* Why We Can't Wait *(1964),* Where Do We Go From Here: Community or Chaos? *(1967), and* The Trumpet of Conscience *(1968). "I Have a Dream" (1963) is the inspiring sermon delivered by King from the steps of the Lincoln Memorial to the nearly 250,000 people who came to Washington, D.C. to commemorate the centennial of Lincoln's Emancipation Proclamation. Additional millions who watched on television were moved by this eloquent, noble, and impassioned plea that America might fulfill its original promise of freedom and equality for all its citizens.*

I am happy to join with you today in what will go down in history as the greatest demonstration for freedom in the history of our nation.

Five score years ago, a great American, in whose symbolic shadow we stand today, signed the Emancipation Proclamation. This momentous decree came as a great beacon light of hope to millions of Negro slaves who had been seared in the flames of withering injustice. It came as a joyous daybreak to end the long night of their captivity. But one hundred years later, the Negro is still not free. One hundred years later, the life of the Negro is still sadly crippled by the manacles of segregation and the chains of discrimination. One hundred years later, the Negro lives on a lonely island of poverty in the midst of a vast ocean of material prosperity. One hundred years later, the Negro is still anguished in the corners of American society and finds himself in exile in his own land. And so we have come here today to dramatize a shameful condition.

In a sense we have come to our nation's capital to cash a check. When the architects of our republic wrote the magnificent words of the Constitution and the Declaration of Independence, they were signing a promissory note to which every American was to fall heir. This note was the promise that all men—yes, Black men as well as white men—would be guaranteed the inalienable rights of life, liberty, and the pursuit of happiness.

It is obvious today that America has defaulted on this promissory note insofar as her citizens of color are concerned. Instead of honoring this sacred obligation, America has given the Negro people a bad check, a check which has come back marked "insufficient funds." But we refuse to believe that the bank of justice is bankrupt. We refuse to believe that there are insufficient funds in the great vaults of opportunity of this nation; and so we have come to cash this check, a check that will give us upon demand the riches of freedom and the security of justice.

We have also come to this hallowed spot to remind America of the fierce urgency of *now*. This is no time to engage in the luxury of cooling off or to take the tranquilizing drug of gradualism. *Now* is the time to make real the promises of democracy. *Now* is the time to rise from the dark and desolate valley of segregation to the sunlit path of racial justice. *Now* is the time to lift our nation from the quicksands of racial injustice to the solid rock of brotherhood. *Now* is the time to make justice a reality for all of God's children.

It would be fatal for the nation to overlook the urgency of the moment. This sweltering summer of the Negro's legitimate discontent will not pass until there is an invigorating autumn of freedom and equality. Nineteen Sixty-three is not an end, but a beginning. And those who hope that the Negro needed to blow off steam and will now be content will have a rude awakening if the nation returns to business as usual. There will be neither rest nor tranquility in America until the Negro is granted his citizenship rights. The whirlwinds of revolt will continue to shake the foundations of our nation until the bright day of justice emerges.

But there is something that I must say to my people who stand on the warm threshhold which leads into the palace of justice. In the process of gaining our rightful place, we must not be guilty of wrongful deeds. Let us not seek to satisfy our thirst for freedom by drinking from the cup of bitterness and hatred. We must forever conduct our struggle on the high plane of dignity and discipline. We must not allow our creative protest to degenerate into physical violence. Again and again we must rise to the majestic heights of meeting physical force with soul force. And the marvelous new militancy which has engulfed the Negro community must not lead us to a distrust of all white people; for many of our white brothers, as evidenced by their presence here today, have come to realize that their destiny is tied up with our destiny, and they have come to realize that their freedom is inextricably bound to our freedom.

We cannot walk alone. And as we walk we must make the pledge that we shall always march ahead. We cannot turn back. There are those who are asking the devotees of civil rights, "When will you be satisfied?" We can never be satisfied as long as the Negro is the victim of the unspeakable horrors of police brutality. We can never be satisfied as long as our bodies, heavy with the fatigue of travel, cannot gain lodging in the motels of the highways and the hotels of the cities. We cannot be satisfied as long as the Negro's basic mobility is from a smaller ghetto to a larger one. We can never be satisfied as long as our children are stripped of their selfhood and robbed of their dignity by signs stating "For Whites Only." We cannot be satisfied as long as the Negro in Mississippi cannot vote and a Negro in New York believes he has nothing for which to vote. No, no, we are not satisfied, and we will not be satisfied until justice rolls down like waters and righteousness like a mighty stream.

In am not unmindful that some of you have come here out of great trials and tribulations. Some of you have come fresh from narrow jail cells. Some of you have come from areas where your quest for freedom left you battered by the storms of persecution and staggered by the winds of police brutality. You have been the veterans of creative suffering. Continue to work with the faith that unearned suffering is redemptive.

Go back to Mississippi, and go back to Alabama. Go back to South Carolina. Go back to Georgia. Go back to Louisiana. Go back to the slums and ghettos of our Northern cities, knowing that somehow this situation can and will be changed. Let us not wallow in the valley of despair.

I say to you today, my friends, even though we face the difficulties of today and tomorrow, I still have a dream. It is a dream deeply rooted in the American dream. I have a dream that one day this nation will rise up and live out the true meaning of its creed: "We hold these truths to be self-evident, that all men are created equal." I have a dream that one day, on the red hills of Georgia, sons of former slaves and the sons of former slave owners will be able to sit down together at the table of brotherhood. I have a dream that one day even the state of Mississippi, a state sweltering with the heat of injustice, sweltering with the heat of oppression, will be transformed into an oasis of freedom and justice. I have a dream that my four little children will one day live in a nation where they will not be judged by the color of their skin, but by the content of their character.

I have a dream today. I have a dream that one day down in Alabama—with its vicious racists, with its governor's lips dripping with the words of interposition and nullification—one day right there in Alabama, little Black boys and Black girls will be able to join hands with little white boys and white girls as sisters and brothers.

I have a dream today. I have a dream that one day every valley shall be exalted and every hill and mountain shall be made low, the rough places will be made plain and the crooked places will be made straight, and the glory of the Lord shall be revealed, and all flesh shall see it together.

This is our hope. This is the faith that I go back to the South with. And with this faith we will be able to hew out of the mountain of despair a stone of hope. With this faith we will be able to transform the jangling discords of our nation into a beautiful symphony of brotherhood. With this faith we will be able to work together, to play together, to struggle together, to go to jail together, to stand up for freedom together, knowing that we will be free one day.

And this will be the day—this will be the day when all of God's children will be able to sing with new meaning:

> My country, 'tis of thee,
> Sweet land of liberty,
>   Of thee I sing;
> Land where my fathers died,
> Land of the Pilgrims' pride,
> From every mountainside
>   Let freedom ring.

And if America is to be a great nation, this must become true.

And so let freedom ring from the prodigious hilltops of New Hampshire. Let freedom ring from the mighty mountains of New York. Let freedom ring from the heightening Alleghenies of Pennsylvania. Let freedom ring from the snow-capped Rockies of Colorado. Let freedom ring from the curvaceous slopes of California.

But not only that. Let freedom ring from Stone Mountain of Georgia. Let freedom ring from Lookout Mountain of Tennessee. Let freedom ring from every hill and molehill of Mississippi. "From every mountainside let freedom ring."

And when this happens—when we allow freedom to ring, when we let it ring from every village and every hamlet, from every state and every city—we will be able to speed up that day when all of God's children, Black men and white men, Jews and Gentiles, Protestants and Catholics, will be able to join hands and sing in the words of the old Negro spiritual: "Free at last! Free at last! Thank God Almighty. We are free at last!"

MEANING

1. How does the civil rights movement express ideas of equality and freedom that are already deeply rooted in the Constitution?
2. What importance does King place on the idea of nonviolent protest?
3. How does the affirmation of minority rights renew aspirations first stated by America's founding fathers?
4. What injustices have been overcome to reach this historic moment?

USING ARGUMENTATION AND PERSUASION TO CONVEY MEANING

1. How does King use sustained analogies, equating financial obligations with moral responsibilities, to make abstract concepts of freedom and equality more tangible?
2. How does King's allusion to the Emancipation Proclamation adapt his argument for the occasion of a march by 200,000 persons through Washington, D.C. to the Lincoln Memorial?
3. How does King use parallelism and figurative language that echoes the Bible to enhance the effectiveness of his speech?
4. What evidence is there that King was trying to reach many different groups of people, each with its own concerns, with this one speech? Where in the speech does King seem to shift his attention from one group to another?

WRITING SUGGESTIONS

1. Trace the rationale for nonviolent protest back to its roots in the works of both Thoreau and Ghandi. How was the principle of passive, nonviolent protest adapted by King to meet the challenges faced by the civil rights movement in the 1960s?
2. Assess the changes made in the South since the 1960s that have remedied many of the problems that King addressed.

SCIENCES

CHARLES DARWIN

Darwin's Conclusion on His Theory and Religion

Charles Darwin (1809–1882), the eminent British naturalist and geologist, was born in Schrewsbury, England. While studying medicine at Edinburgh University, Darwin became so distressed over having to learn surgical skills by performing operations without anesthetics that he left medical school to study for the ministry at Cambridge. His growing interest in geology and natural history was encouraged by John Stevens Henslow, who acted as a mentor for the young Darwin. Henslow was responsible for Darwin's being invited to join the Admiralty survey ship H.M.S. Beagle as an unpaid naturalist. This voyage to different areas of South America and the Galapagos Islands, which would last some five years, provided Darwin with a wealth of observations, evidence, and a host of unanswered questions. Why, for example, did finches on different Galapagos Islands, identical in climate, foliage, and terrain, have different bill structures that were ideally suited to their respective diets (on some islands finches ate insects and on other islands they ate seeds). Darwin's answer was that in the competitive struggle for existence, those species possessing advantageous mutations (a bill well-suited to catch insects, for example) would thrive, whereas those less well-adapted would diminish and become extinct. His ideas of "natural selection" and "survival of the fittest," which replaced the concept of a Supreme Being with adaptive mechanisms born of chance and necessity, produced a storm of controversy between "evolutionists" and "creationists" that continues into the present. His principle works include On the Origin of Species by Means of Natural Selection (1859), The Variation of Animals and Plants Under Domestication (1868), The Descent of Man (1871) (which proposed that both men and apes evolved separately—not, as is commonly thought, that man descended from the apes—from a common ancestor who today would be classified among the lower primates), and The Expression of the Emotions in Man and Animals (1872), a startling comparative study that began ethology, the science of animal behavior. In "Darwin's Conclusion on His Theory and Religion" (1859), he *takes the unusual step of arguing that his theories complement and are thoroughly compatible with established religious belief.*

I see no good reason why the views given in this volume should shock the religious feelings of any one. It is satisfactory, as showing how transient such impressions are, to remember that the greatest discovery ever made by man, namely, the law of the attraction of gravity, was also attacked by Liebnitz, "as subversive of natural, and inferentially of revealed, religion." A celebrated author and divine has written to me that "he has gradually learned to see that it is just as noble a conception of the Deity to believe that he created a few original forms, capable of self-development into other and needful forms, as to believe that he required a fresh act of creation to supply the voids caused by the action of his laws."

Why, it may be asked, until recently did nearly all the most eminent living naturalists and geologists disbelieve in the mutability of species? It cannot be asserted that organic beings in a state of nature are subject to no variation; it cannot be proved that the amount of variation in the course of long ages is a limited quantity; no clear distinction has been, or can be, drawn between species and well-marked varieties. It cannot be maintained that species when intercrossed are invariably sterile, and varieties invariably fertile; or that sterility is a special endowment and sign of creation. The belief that species were immutable productions was almost unavoidable as long as the history of the world was thought to be of short duration; and now that we have acquired some idea of the lapse of time, we are too apt to assume, without proof, that the geological record is so perfect that it would have afforded us plain evidence of the mutation of species, if they had undergone mutation. . . .

Authors of the highest eminence seem to be fully satisfied with the view that each species has been independently created. To my mind it accords better with what we know of the laws impressed on matter by the Creator, that the production and extinction of the past and present inhabitants of the world should have been due to secondary causes, like those determining the birth and death of the individual. When I view all beings not as special creations, but as the lineal descendants of some few beings which lived long before the first bed of the Cambrian system was deposited, they seem to me to become ennobled. Judging from the past, we may safely infer that not one living species will transmit its unaltered likeness to a distant futurity. And of the species now living very few will transmit progeny of any kind to a far distant futurity; for the manner in which all organic beings are grouped shows that the greater number of species in each genus, and all the species in many genera, have left no descendants, but have become utterly extinct. We can so far take a prophetic glance into futurity as to foretell that it will be the common and widely spread species, belonging to the larger and dominant groups within each class, which will ultimately prevail and procreate new and dominant species. As all the living forms of life are the lineal descendants of those which lived long before the Cambrian epoch, we may feel certain that the ordinary succession by generation has never once been broken, and that no cataclysm has desolated the whole world. Hence we may look with some confidence to a secure future of great length. And as natural selection works solely by and for the good of each being, all corporeal and mental endowments will tend to progress towards perfection.

It is interesting to contemplate a tangled bank, clothed with many plants of many kinds, with birds singing on the bushes, with various insects flitting about, and with worms crawling through the damp earth, and to reflect that these elaborately constructed forms, so different from each other, and dependent upon each other in so complex a manner, have all been produced by laws acting around us. These laws, taken in the largest sense, being growth with reproduction; inheritance, which is almost implied by reproduction; variability from the indirect and direct action of the conditions of life, and from use and disuse; a ration of increase so high as to lead to a struggle for life, and as a consequence to natural selection, entailing divergence of character and the extinction of less improved forms. Thus, from the war of nature, from famine and death, the most exalted object which we are capable of conceiving, namely, the production of the higher animals, directly follows. There is grandeur in this view of life, with its several powers, having been originally breathed by the Creator into a few forms or into one; and that, whilst this planet has gone cycling on according to the fixed law of gravity, from so simple a beginning endless forms most beautiful and most wonderful have been, and are being evolved.

MEANING

1. What argument does Darwin use to defend himself against the charge that his work, *The Origin of Species,* is irreligious?
2. What are Darwin's reasons for believing in the "mutability of species"?
3. How does Darwin's argument depend on placing his opponents in the position of having to prove that (a) there is a clear way of distinguishing between a species and the varieties of that species, or (b) "organic beings in a state of nature are subject to no variation"; that is, nothing in nature has ever changed or can change?
4. Why is it especially important to Darwin's argument that the world has existed for far longer than previously thought?
5. Why is Darwin's reluctance to admit the possibility of "special creations" so offensive to those with deep religious beliefs? ("Special creations" here includes the creation of human beings.)

USING ARGUMENTATION AND PERSUASION TO CONVEY MEANING

1. How does Darwin's argument depend on determining plausible causes for observed effects, whereas his opponents, Darwin asserts, believe in causes that would produce effects that no one has ever observed?
2. How does Darwin use a letter from a noted clergyman, accepting theories put forward in *The Origin of Species,* to bolster his argument?
3. How does Darwin attempt to appease his opponents by stating that "life with its several powers" had been "originally breathed by the Creator into a few forms or into one"?

WRITING SUGGESTIONS

1. In what way do both Thomas Malthus (see page 706) and Darwin see competition among species for survival as a driving force?

2. How does Christopher Stone's proposal, creating guardians to protect trees and streams (see page 698), conflict with Darwin's ideas of how natural selection operates to ensure "survival of the fittest"?

3. In light of Carl Sagan's essay (see page 506), discuss Darwin's assertion that "we may feel certain that the ordinary succession by generation has never once been broken, and that no cataclysm has desolated the whole world. Hence we may look forward with some confidence to a secure future of great length."

Donald R. Griffin

Wordy Apes

Donald R. Griffin was born in 1915 in Southampton, New York. After receiving his Ph.D. from Harvard in 1942, Griffin taught zoology at Cornell University (1946–1953) and Harvard University (1953–1965), and is currently professor of animal behavior at The Rockefeller University, New York. His original discoveries in the fields of animal orientation and communication revealed the echolocation techniques of bats and the principles by which birds navigate. Listening in the Dark *(1958) won him the Elliot Medal from the National Academy of Sciences in 1961. He then wrote* Echoes of Bats and Men *(1959) and* Animal Structure and Function *(1962; 2nd ed., with Alvin Novick, 1970). He was also awarded the Phi Beta Kappa Science Prize for his 1964 study,* Bird Migration. *Recently, Griffin's research has taken a comparative approach, drawing evidence from fields as diverse as behavioral ecology and neuroanatomy, to examine the linguistic abilities of chimpanzees and the possibility for human communication with whales and porpoises. The results of his research appear in* The Question of Animal Awareness *(1976) and* Animal Thinking *(1984). In "Wordy Apes," taken from the latter work, Griffin reviews past research and synthesizes the results into a fascinating argument pointing toward the presence of higher thought processes in primates.*

Some of the most convincing recent evidence about animal thinking stems from the pioneering work of Alan and Beatrice Gardner of the University of Nevada (1969, 1979). The Gardners had noted that wild apes seem to communicate by observing each other's behavior, and they suspected that the extremely disappointing results of previous efforts to teach captive chimpanzees to use words reflected not so much a lack of mental ability as a difficulty in controlling the vocal tract. Captive chimpanzees had previously demonstrated the ability to solve complex problems and, like dogs and horses, they had learned to respond appropriately to many spoken words. The Gardners wanted to find out whether apes could also express themselves in ways that we could understand. In the late 1960s they made a concerted effort to teach a young chimpanzee named Washoe to communicate with people using manual gestures derived from American Sign Language. This language, one of many that have been developed in different countries for use by the deaf, consists of a series of gestures or signs, each of which serves the basic function of a single word in spoken or written language. To permit fluent conversation, these signs have evolved into clearly distinguishable hand motions and finger configurations that can be performed rapidly.

Washoe was reared in an environment similar to that in which an American baby would be raised. All the people who cared for Washoe "spoke" to her only in American

Sign Language, and used it exclusively when conversing with each other in her presence. They signed to Washoe, much as parents talk to babies who have not yet learned to speak, but always in sign language rather than spoken English. Washoe was encouraged to use signs to ask for what she wanted, and she was helped to do this by a procedure called molding, in which the trainer gently held the chimpanzee's hand in the correct position and moved it to form a certain sign.

The Gardners were far more successful than most scientists would have predicted on the basis of what was previously known about the capabilities of chimpanzees or any other nonhuman species, although Robert Yerkes had anticipated such a possibility (Bourne, 1977). During four years of training Washoe learned to use more than 130 wordlike signs and to recognize these and other signs used by her human companions. She could make the appropriate sign when shown pictures of an object, and on a few occasions she seemed to improvise new signs or new two-sign combinations spontaneously. The best example of this was Washoe's signing "water bird" when she first saw a swan. She also signed to herself when no people were present.

Following the Gardners' lead, several other scientists have trained other great apes to use a quasilinguistic communication system. This work has been thoroughly and critically reviewed by Ristau and Robbins (1982) and widely discussed by many others, so I will give only a brief outline here. Most of the subjects have been female chimpanzees, but two gorillas (Patterson and Linden, 1981) and one orangutan (Miles, 1983) have also been taught gestures based on American Sign Language. Because gestures are variable and require the presence of a human signer, who may influence the ape in other ways that are difficult to evaluate, two groups of laboratory scientists have developed "languages" based on mechanical devices operated by the chimpanzees. David Premack of the University of Pennsylvania used colored plastic tokens arranged in patterns resembling strings of words. His star chimpanzee pupil, named Sarah, learned to select the appropriate plastic "words" to answer correctly when the experimenter presented her with similar chips arranged to form simple questions. Questions such as "What is the color of—?" were answered correctly about familiar objects when the objects were replaced by their plastic symbols, even if the colors were different from those of the objects they represented. Sarah thus learned to answer questions about *represented* objects (reviewed by Premack, 1976; and Premack and Premack, 1983). This type of communication has the property of displacement, as in the case of the honeybee dances.

In another ambitious project at the Yerkes Laboratory of Emory University, Duane Rumbaugh, Sue Savage-Rumbaugh, and their colleagues have used back-lighted keys on a keyboard (Rumbaugh, 1977; Savage-Rumbaugh, Rumbaugh, and Boysen, 1980). Their chimpanzee subjects have learned to press the appropriate keys to communicate simple desires and answer simple questions. In some significant recent studies, two young male chimpanzees. Sherman and Austin, have not only learned to use simple tools to obtain food or toys but have learned to employ the keyboard to ask each other to hand over a certain type of tool. These investigations, as well as extensions of the Gardners' original studies using words derived from American Sign Language, have been extensively reviewed (Ristau and Robbins, 1982) and discussed by Patterson and Linden (1981) and Terrace (1979). Despite disagreement about many aspects of this work, almost everyone concerned agrees that the captive apes have learned, at the very least, to make simple requests and to answer simple questions through these wordlike gestures or mechanical devices.

A heated debate has raged about the extent to which such learned communication resembles human language. Sebeok and Umiker-Sebeok (1980) and Sebeok and Rosenthal (1981) have argued vehemently that the whole business is merely wishful and mistaken reading into the ape's behavior of much more than is really there. They stress that apes are very clever at learning to do what gets them food, praise, social companionship, or other things they want and enjoy. They believe that insufficiently critical scientists have overinterpreted the behavior of their charges and that the apes have really learned only something like: "If I do this she will give me candy," or "If I do that she will play with me," and so forth. They also believe that the apes may be reacting to unintentional signals from the experimenters and that the interpretations have involved what behavioral scientists call "Clever Hans errors." This term refers to a trained horse in the early 1900s that learned to count out answers to arithmetical questions by tapping with his foot. For instance if shown 4×4 written on a slate board, the horse would tap sixteen times. More careful studies showed that Hans could solve such problems only in the presence of a person who knew the answer. The person would inadvertently nod or make other small motions in time with Hans' tapping and would stop when the right number had been reached. Hans had learned to perceive this unintentional communication, not the arithmetic. The Sebeoks argue that Washoe and her successors have learned, not how to communicate with gestural words, but rather how to watch for signs of approval or disapproval from their human companions and to do what is expected.

Although students of animal behavior must constantly guard against such errors, many of the experiments described above included careful controls that seem to have ruled out this explanation of all the languagelike communication learned by Washoe and her successors. In many cases the ape's vocabulary was tested by having one person present a series of pictures that the animal was required to name, while a different person, who could not see the pictures, judged what sign Washoe used in response. Furthermore the sheer number of signs that the apes employed correctly would require a far more complex sort of Clever Hans error than an animal's simple noticing that a person has stopped making small-scale counting motions.

Another criticism of the ape language studies has been advanced by Terrace and colleagues (1979). Terrace, aided by numerous assistants, taught a young male chimpanzee named Nim Chimpsky to use about 125 signs over a forty-five-month period. He agrees that Nim, like Washoe and several other language-trained apes, did indeed learn to use these gestures to request objects or actions he wanted and that Nim could use some of them to answer simple questions. But when Terrace analyzed videotapes of Nim exchanging signs with his trainers, he was disappointed to find that many of Nim's "utterances" were copies of what his human companion had just signed. This is scarcely surprising, inasmuch as his trainers had encouraged him to repeat signs throughout his training.

Terrace and his colleagues also concluded that Nim showed no ability to combine more than two signs into meaningful combinations and that his signing never employed even the simplest form of rule-guided sentences. It is not at all clear, however, whether Nim's training provided much encouragement to develop grammatical sentences. In any event, he did not do so, and Terrace doubts whether any of the other signing apes have displayed such a capability. But Miles (1983) reports that her orangutan Chantek's use of gestural signs resembled the speech of young children more closely than Nim's, and Patterson believes that her gorilla Koko follows some rudimentary rules in the sequence of her signs. Yet even on the most liberal interpretation there remains a large gap between the signing of these trained apes and the speech of children who have vocabularies of approximately the same size. The children tend to use longer strings of words, and the third or later words add important meaning to the first two. In contrast, Nim and other language-trained apes seem much more likely to repeat signs or add ones that do not seem, to us at least, to change the basic meaning of a two-sign utterance. For instance, the following is one of the longer utterances reported for the gorilla Koko: "Please milk please me like drink apple bottle"; and from Nim, "Give orange me give eat orange give me eat orange give me you." But grammatical or not, there is no doubt what Koko and Nim were asking for. To quote Descartes and Chomsky (1966), *"The word is the sole sign and certain mark of the presence of thought."* Grammar adds economy, refinement, and scope to human language, but words are basic. Words without grammar are adequate though limited, but there is no grammar without words. And it is clear that Washoe and her successors use the equivalent of words to convey simple thoughts.

The enormous versatility of human language depends not only on large vocabularies of words known to both speakers and listeners but on mutually understood rules for combining them to convey additional meaning. George A. Miller (1967) has used the term "combinatorial productivity" for this extremely powerful attribute of human language. By combining words in particular ways we produce new messages logically and economically. If we had to invent a new word to convey the meaning of each phrase and sentence, the required vocabulary would soon exceed the capacity of even the most proficient human brains. But once a child learns a few words, he can rapidly increase their effectiveness by combining them in new messages in accordance with the language's rules designating which word stands for actor or object, which are modifiers, and so forth.

Signing apes so far have made very little progress in combinatorial productivity, although some of their two-sign combinations seem to conform to simple rules. The natural communication systems of other animals make no use of combinatorial productivity, as far as we know. But the investigation of animal communication has barely begun, especially as a source of evidence about animal thoughts. What has emerged so far has greatly exceeded the prior expectations of scientists; we may be seeing only the tip of yet another iceberg. Extrapolation of scientific discovery is an uncertain business at best, but the momentum of discovery in this area does not seem to be slackening. The apparent lack of any significant combinatorial productivity in the signing of Washoe and her successors might turn out to be a temporary lull in a truly revolutionary development, which began only about fifteen years ago. Perhaps improved methods of investigation and training will lead to more convincing evidence of communicative versatility.

One relevant aspect of all the ape-language studies to date is that the native language of all the investigators has been English, and the signs taught to apes have been derived from American Sign Language. In English, word order is used to indicate actor or object, principal noun or modifying adjective, and many other rule-guided relationships. But this is very atypical; most other human languages rely much more on inflections or modifications of principal words to indicate grammatical relationships. No one seems to have inquired whether signing apes or naturally communicating animals might vary their signals in minor ways to communicate that a particular sign is meant to designate, for instance, the actor rather than the object. This would be a difficult inquiry, because the signals vary for many reasons, and only a laborious analysis of an extensive series of motion pictures or videotapes would disclose whether there were any consistent differences comparable to those conveyed by inflections of words in human speech.

Regardless of these controversies, there seems no doubt that through gestures or manipulation of tokens or keyboards apes can learn to communicate to their human companions a reasonable range of simple thoughts and desires. They also can convey emotional feelings, although an ape does not need elaborate gestures or other forms of symbolic communication to inform a sensitive human companion that it is afraid or hungry. What the artificial signals add to emotional signaling is the possibility of communicating about specific objects and events, even when these are not part of the immediate situation. Furthermore, when Washoe or any other trained ape signs that she wants a certain food, she must be thinking about that food or about its taste or odor. We cannot be certain just what the signing ape is thinking, but the content of her thought must include at least some feature of the object or event designated by the sign she has learned to use. For instance, the Gardners taught Washoe to use a sign that meant flower, to them. But Washoe used it not only for flowers but for pipe tobacco and kitchen fumes. To her it apparently meant smells. Washoe may have been thinking about smells when she used the sign, rather than about the visual properties of colored flowers, but she was certainly thinking about something that overlapped it with the properties conveyed by the word *flower* as we use it.

The major significance of the research begun by the Gardners is its confirmation that our closest animal relatives are quite capable of varied thoughts as well as emotions. Many highly significant questions flow from this simple fact. Do apes communicate naturally with the versatility they have demonstrated in the various sorts of languagelike behavior that people have taught them? One approach is to ask whether apes that have learned to use signs more or less as we use single words employ them to communicate with each other. This is being investigated by studying signing apes that have abundant opportunity to interact with each other. Few results have been reported so far, although some signing does seem to be directed to other apes as well as to human companions. When scientists have been looking for something, and when we hear little or nothing about the results, we conclude that nothing important has been discovered. But the lack of results may only mean that chimpanzees can communicate perfectly well without signs. The subject obviously requires further investigation, and we may soon hear about new and interesting developments.

REFERENCES

BOURNE, G. H., ed. *Progress in ape research.* New York: Academic Press. 1977.

CHOMSKY, N. *Cartesian linguistics.* New York: Harper and Row. 1966.

GARDNER, R. A., and B. T. GARDNER. Teaching sign language to a chimpanzee. *Science* 165:664–672. 1969.

GARDNER, R. A., and B. T. GARDNER. Two comparative psychologists look at language acquisition. In *Children's language,* ed. K. E. Nelson. New York: Halstead. 1979.

MILES, H. L. Apes and language: The search for communicative competence. In *Language in primates: Implications for linguistics, anthropology, psychology, and philosophy,* ed. J. de Luce and H. T. Wilder. New York: Springer. 1983.

MILLER, G. A. *The psychology of communication.* New York: Basic Books. 1967.

PATTERSON, F. G., and E. LINDEN. *The education of Koko.* New York: Holt, Rinehart and Winston. 1981.

PREMACK, D. *Intelligence in ape and man.* Hillsdale, N.J.: Erlbaum. 1976.

PREMACK, D., and A. J. PREMACK. *The mind of an ape.* New York: Norton. 1983.

RISTAU, C. A., and D. ROBBINS. Language in the great apes: A critical review. *Advances in Study of Behavior* 12:142–225. 1982.

RUMBAUGH, D. M. *Language learning by a chimpanzee: The Lana Project.* New York: Academic Press. 1977.

SAVAGE-RUMBAUGH, E. S., D. M. RUMBAUGH, and S. BOYSEN. Do apes use language? *Amer. Sci.* 68:49–61. 1980.

SEBEOK, T. A., and R. ROSENTHAL. The Clever Hans phenomenon: Communication with horses, whales, apes, and people. *Ann. N.Y. Acad. Sci.* 364:1–311. 1981.

SEBEOK, T. A., and J. UMIKER-SEBEOK, eds. *Speaking of apes, a critical anthology of two-way communication with man.* New York: Plenum. 1980.

TERRACE, H. S. *Nim.* New York: Knopf. 1979.

TERRACE, H. S., L. A. PETITTO, and T. G. BEVER. Can an ape create a sentence? *Science* 208:891–902. 1979.

MEANING

1. What experiments have led some animal researchers to conclude that chimpanzees can be taught to communicate with humans?
2. What reasons do other scientists give for concluding that "lever-pressing" and "signing" activities by primates are not evidence of true communication, but merely imitative behavior that has been misinterpreted by their overenthusiastic colleagues?
3. What flaws contaminated the results of an early experiment conducted by the Gardners; how was this experiment redesigned by later researchers to eliminate possible sources of error?
4. What significance does Griffin derive from the fact that children can routinely combine "longer strings of words" than can apes with a comparable size signing vocabulary?
5. Because apes may use different inflections to convey different meanings, why might the attempt to teach apes a sign language based only on word order not be successful?

USING ARGUMENTATION AND PERSUASION TO CONVEY MEANING

1. How does Griffin organize his summary of research around the question of what criteria should be used and what evidence should be accepted as proof of the ability of primates to communicate with humans?
2. How did the so-called "clever Hans error" call into question the interpretation of the spectacular results that were obtained with Washoe?
3. How effectively does Griffin take into account both sides of the argument before putting forward his own "middle of the road" position that leaves the basic questions still open to further research?

WRITING SUGGESTIONS

1. Discuss an experience you have had that convinced you that animals indeed can communicate with people.
2. Discuss discoveries made by researchers with "Sherman" and "Austin" in light of Jane van Lawick-Goodall's research into the "tool-using" behavior among chimpanzees (see page 125).
3. Which side of this argument do you find the most compelling and why?

Thomas S. Szasz

A Critique of Skinner's Behaviorism

Thomas S. Szasz, one of the most distinguished and innovative psychiatrists writing today, was born in 1920 in Budapest, Hungary, and received his medical, psychiatric, and psychoanalytic training in the United States. He was staff member at the Chicago Institute for Psychoanalysis from 1949–1956, when he became professor of psychiatry at the State University of New York Health Science Center, Syracuse, a position he still holds. In his nearly two dozen thought-provoking works, Dr. Szasz demolishes myths and pretentions, challenging conventional thinking about issues in psychiatry, psychotherapy, and psychoanalysis. Among his most iconoclastic works are The Myth of Mental Illness *(1961),* Law, Liberty and Psychiatry *(1963),* Psychiatric Justice *(1965),* The Ethics of Psychoanalysis *(1965),* Ceremonial Chemistry: The Ritual Persecution of Drugs, Addicts, and Pushers *(1974), and* Insanity: The Idea and Its Consequences *(1986). Dr. Szasz is the recipient of many honors, including the Humanist of the Year Award of the American Humanist Association, 1973. In "A Critique of Skinner's Behaviorism," which originally appeared in* The Libertarian Review, *(1976), Dr. Szasz frames a forceful rebuttal to the behaviorist theories of B. F. Skinner.*

One of the things that distinguishes persons from animals is that, for reasons familiar enough, persons cannot simply live: they must have, or must feel that they have, some reason for doing so. In other words, men, women, and children must have some sense and significance in and for their lives. If they do not, they perish. Hence, I believe that those who rob people of the meaning and significance they have given their lives kill them and should be considered murderers, at least metaphorically. B. F. Skinner is such a person and, like all of the others, he fascinates—especially his intended victims.

But, it may be objected, Skinner has no political or military power at his command. How, then, could he inflict such a grave injury on mankind? The answer is as simple as is Skinner's mentality. Man qua organism is an animal; to destroy it, one must kill it. Man qua person is the animal that uses language; to destroy him, one must destroy his language. This, it seems to me, is what Skinner is out to accomplish. Perhaps more than any of his earlier books, *About Behaviorism* makes this crystal clear. It is not really a book at all, but a dictionary: it furnishes us with the equivalents, in Skinnerese, of ordinary English words.

Simply put, what Skinner is out to do is to destroy ordinary language and to substitute his own language for it. It is a sort of one-man Esperanto effort. Skinner puts it this way: "I consider scores, if not hundreds, of examples of mentalistic usage. They are taken from current writings, but I have not cited the sources. . . . Many of these expressions I 'translate into behavior.'" That is, indeed, what the whole book is about: translation—from English into "behavior." Skinner's pride at citing what others have said, without giving their names, is of interest in this connection. "I am not arguing with the authors," he explains, as if references served the sole purpose of identifying enemies. It seems to me that his not naming names is consistent with his general thesis that there are, and should be, no individuals. Books without authors are simply a part of Skinner's grand design of acts without actors—his master plan for world conquest.

What about Skinner's own acts, his speaking and writing? Is he not an agent and an author? Not really, says Skinner. In the first place, you and I may speak and write, but not Skinner; Skinner exhibits "verbal behavior." I am not kidding. "Finally, a word about my own verbal behavior," he writes in a chapter titled "The Causes of Behavior." Skinner thus disclaims writing in a language, which is asserting a falsehood, or having a style, which is asserting a truth. Instead, he claims to be exhibiting physiological behavior, which is reductionism of the stupidest sort. But this is what he espouses: "For purposes of casual discourse, I see no reason to avoid such an expression as 'I have chosen to discuss . . . (though I question the possibility of free choice). . . .' When it is important to be clear about an issue, nothing but a technical vocabulary will suffice. It will often seem forced or roundabout. Old ways of speaking are abandoned with regret, and new ones are awkward and uncomfortable, but the change must be made." To what? To Skinnerese. Why? To aggrandize Skinner.

Here is another sample of how Skinner sees the world and proposes to explain it: "A small part of the universe is contained within the skin of each of us. There is no reason why it should have any special physical status because it lies within this boundary and eventually we will have a complete account of it from anatomy and physiology." So what else is new? Physicalism, biologism, reductionism, scientism— all have had much more eloquent spokesmen than Skinner. Why all the fuss about him, then? Perhaps because he is a Harvard professor who is ignorant both of his own sources (for example, Auguste Comte) and of the many important critics of scientism (from John Stuart Mill to F. A. Hayek), thus making it not only possible but positively respectable for millions to believe that the drivel between the covers of his book is both new and good.

Skinner loves anatomy and physiology, although, so far as I can make out, he knows nothing about either. Perhaps this allows him to think that these "disciplines" can somehow explain everything. How else are we to account for such statements as these: "The human species, like all other species, is the product of natural selection. Each of its members is an extremely complex organism, a living system, the subject of anatomy and physiology." What is this, an excerpt from a biology lecture to bright second-graders? No. It is Skinner's introduction to his explanation of "innate behavior." There is more, much more, of this. Two more sentences should suffice: "But what is felt or introspectively observed is not an important part of the physiology which fills the temporal gap in an historical analysis. . . ." and "The experimental analysis of behavior is a rigorous, extensive, and rapidly advancing branch of biology. . . ."

Next, we come to Skinner's key concepts: "operant behavior" and "reinforcement." "A positive reinforcer," he explains, "strengthens any behavior that produces it: a glass of water is positively reinforcing when we are thirsty: and if we then draw and drink a glass of water, we are more likely to do so again on similar occasions. A negative reinforcer strengthens any behavior that reduces or terminates it: when we take off a shoe that is pinching, the reduction of pressure is negatively reinforcing, and we are more likely to do so again when a shoe pinches." Well, I simply do not understand this, but that may be because I have not grasped the fine points of Skinner's language—excuse me, "verbal behavior." Water relieves thirst. Taking off a tight shoe relieves pain. Why call one a "positive reinforcer" and the other a "negative reinforcer"? I have no satisfactory answer to this question. Skinner thinks he does, and I herewith quote it: "The fact that operant conditioning, like all physiological processes, is a product of natural selection throws light on the question of what kinds of consequences are reinforcing and why. The expressions 'I like Brahms,' 'I love Brahms,' 'I enjoy Brahms,' and 'Brahms pleases me,' may easily be taken to refer to feelings but they can be taken as statements that the music of Brahms is reinforcing."

Well, I like Brahms, but I do not like Skinner. But do not be misled: this is neither an expression of my ill feelings toward Skinner nor an act of criticism of his work. Ill feelings, as Skinner himself has just explained, do not exist; so I merely experience Skinner as "negatively reinforcing." And in view of Skinner's definition of a "forceful act," mine is surely not a critical one. "Depriving a person of something he needs or wants is not a forceful act," he asserts without any qualifications. Depriving a person of property or of liberty or even of air are thus *not* forceful acts. Skinner does not tell us what *is* a forceful act.

Although force may not be Skinner's forte, he feels very confident about being able to explain why people gamble, climb mountains, or invent things: "All gambling systems are based on variable-ratio schedules of reinforcement, although their effects are usually attributed to feelings. . . . The same variable-ratio schedule affects those who explore, prospect, invent, conduct scientific research, and compose works of art, music, or literature. . . ." The irony of it all is that Skinner keeps contrasting himself to Freud, whom, in these respects, he resembles and imitates. Freud attributed creativity to the repression and sublimination of all sorts of nasty "drives," from anality to homosexuality. Skinner attributes them to "schedules of reinforcement." Anything will do, so long as it reduces the artist to the level of robot or rat.

As Skinner warms to his subject, he reveals more and more about his willingness to do away—in his science and perhaps elsewhere—with persons qua agents. "In a behavioral analysis," he writes, "a person is an organism, a member of the human species, which has acquired a repertoire of behavior." In a word, an animal. He then continues: "The person who asserts his freedom by saying, 'I determine what I shall do next,' is speaking of freedom in or from a current situation: the *I* who thus seems to have an option is the product of a history from which it is not free and which in fact determines what it will now do." That takes care of my personal responsibility for writing this review. I did not write it at all: a "locus" did. I do not believe that, but Skinner evidently does: "A person is not an originating agent; he is a locus, a point at which many genetic and environmental conditions come together in a joint effect."

Skinner has an absolutely unbounded love for the idea that there are no individuals, no agents—that there are only organisms, animals: "The scientific analysis of behavior must, I believe, assume that a person's behavior is controlled by his genetic and environmental histories rather than by the person himself as an initiating, creative agent." This view leads inexorably to his love affair with the image of every human being as a controlled object, with no room, or word, for either controlling others (for example, tyranny), or for controlling oneself (for example, self-discipline). The "feeling" of freedom creates some problems for this scheme, but Skinner talks his way out of it, at least to his own satisfaction. He explains that "the important fact is not that we feel free when we have been positively reinforced, *but that we do not tend to escape or counterattack*. [Italics Skinner's.] Feeling free is an important hallmark of a kind of control distinguished by the fact that it does not breed countercontrol."

It is in the chapter titled "The Question of Control" that Skinner explains how, in the world he is designing, everyone will be controlled, everyone will feel free, and *mirabile visu,* no one will control! As this is the capstone in the triumphal arch leading to his Utopia, I will quote Skinner rather than try to paraphrase what he says—for he is, after all, quite unparaphrasable:

> The design of human behavior implies, of course, control and possibly the question most often asked of the behaviorist is this: Who is to control? The question represents the age-old mistake of looking to the individual rather than to the world in which he lives. It will not be a benevolent dictator, a compassionate therapist, a devoted teacher, or a public-spirited industrialist who will design a way of life in the interests of everyone. We must look instead at the conditions under which people govern, give help, teach, and arrange incentive systems in particular ways. In other words, we must look to the culture as a social environment. Will a culture evolve in which no individual will be able to accumulate vast power and use it for his own aggrandizement in ways which are harmful to others? Will a culture evolve in which individuals are not so much concerned with their own actualization and fulfillment that they do not give serious attention to the future of the culture? These questions, and many others like them, are the questions to be asked rather than who will control and to what end. No one steps outside the causal stream. No one really intervenes.

No one "intervenes." Everyone is an "effect." Amen.

But enough is enough. I wrote at the beginning of this review that human beings cannot live without meaning; that they either create or destroy meaning; and that, in my opinion, Skinner is, or aspires to be, one of the great destroyers of meaning, and, hence, of man. This is the note on which I now want to elaborate and on which I want to end.

Although languages, George Steiner observed in *Language and Silence,* "have great reserves of life," these reserves are not inexhaustible: ". . . there comes a breaking point. Use a language to conceive, organize, and justify Belsen; use it to make out specifications for gas ovens; use it to dehumanize man during twelve years of calculated bestiality. Something will happen to it. . . . Something of the lies and sadism will settle in the marrow of the language."

Others—in particular, Orwell—have suggested that what has happened to the German language under the influence of Nazism has happened to other modern languages under the influence of bureaucratization, collectivization, and technicalization. Skinnerese is accordingly just one of the depersonalized scientific idioms of our age—a member of the family of languages for loathing and liquidating man. What distinguishes Skinnerese from its sister languages—such as legalese, medicalese, or psychoanalese—is the naive but infectious enthusiasm of its author for world destruction through the conscious and deliberate destruction of language.

Skinner devotes a whole chapter of *About Behaviorism* to language. Aptly titled "Verbal Behavior," it is devoted to the destruction of the idea of language. "Relatively late in its history," Skinner begins, "the human species underwent a remarkable change: its vocal musculature came under operant control." Skinner then explains why he wants to get rid of the word "language": "The very difference between 'language' and 'verbal behavior' is an example of a word requiring 'mentalistic explanations.' Language has the character of a thing, something a person acquires and possesses. . . . A much more productive view is that verbal behavior is behavior. It has a special character only because it is reinforced by its effects on people. . . ." Translation: Do not say "language" if you want to be positively reinforced by Dr. Skinner.

Perhaps realizing that much of what he says is an attempt to replace a generally accepted metaphor with a metaphor of his own choosing, Skinner reinterprets metaphor as well: "In verbal behavior one kind of response evoked by a merely similar stimulus is called metaphor." He evidently prefers this to Aristotle's definition, according to which we use metaphor when we give something a name that rightly belongs to something else.

Finally, Skinner redefines "truth" itself. This definition is so revealing of his effort and so repellent in its effect (at least on me), that I shall end my series of quotations with it:

> The truth of a statement is limited by the sources of the behavior of the speaker, the control exerted by the current setting, the effects of similar settings in the past, the effects upon the listener leading to precision or to exaggeration or falsification, and so on.

Honest to God, this is what Skinner says is truth. He does not say what is falsehood. Or what is fakery. He does not have to: he displays them.

These, then, are the reasons that I consider Skinner to be just another megalomaniacal destroyer, or would-be destroyer, of mankind—one of many from Plato to Timothy Leary. But Skinner has the distinction, in this company, of being more simple-minded than most, and hence being able to advocate a political system no one has thought of before: namely, one in which all are ruled and no one rules! Plato envisioned a Utopia in which people are perfectly ruled by perfect philosopher-kings: here everyone was destroyed qua person, save for the rulers. Lenin, Stalin, and Hitler had their own versions of Utopia: like Plato's, their Utopias were characterized by the destruction, actual or metaphorical, of large classes of mankind; but some individuals were still considered to be agents. Skinner has gone all of these one better. He has constructed a world of acts without actors, of conditioning without conditioners, of slaves without masters, of politics without politicians, of the good life without ethics, of man without language. It is an achievement worthy of a Harvard professor.

MEANING

1. How does Skinner's theory of behaviorism, according to Szasz, deprive people of the incentives they need to live and rob them of "some sense and significance in and for their lives"?
2. Why does Szasz object to Skinner's use of behaviorist terminology to rename all activities and emotions as forms of learned behavior?
3. How does Szasz's position depend on certain assumptions about the value of individualism, personal freedom, and nonconformity that put him in direct opposition to the tenets of behaviorism?

Using Argumentation and Persuasion to Convey Meaning

1. To what extent does Szasz's use of emotionally loaded terms ("murderer," "rob," "kill") undermine the serious criticisms he has to make about Skinner's theories of behaviorism?
2. What examples can you cite of Szasz's use of techniques usually associated with propaganda to attack Skinner and his theory: (a) guilt by association, (b) labeling, and (c) *ad hominum* attacks?
3. How does the fact that Szasz was writing for an audience in *The Libertarian Review* who, for the most part, shared his humanistic philosophy and values, contribute to the manner in which Szasz's arguments against Skinner were presented?

Writing Suggestions

1. Rewrite Szasz's review omitting what you might consider to be logical fallacies or emotionally loaded terms, and construct a straightforward criticism of Skinner and his theories. You may wish to consult Skinner's *About Behaviorism*.
2. For a research project, read Skinner's novel, *Walden Two,* and assess the validity of Szasz's criticisms in a three-page essay.
3. Discuss Skinner's *Walden Two* in relationship to one other novel, past or modern, concerned with social problems in a utopian setting—for example, Sir Thomas More's *Utopia,* Swift's *Gulliver's Travels,* Orwell's *1984,* Huxley's Brave New World, H. G. Wells' *A Modern Utopia* or *The Island of Dr. Moreau.*

SIGMUND FREUD

Typical Dreams

Sigmund Freud (1856–1939), the founder of psychoanalysis, was born in what is now Czechoslovakia, received his M.D. from the University of Vienna in 1891 and subsequently joined the resident staff of Vienna General Hospital where he began his studies in clinical neurology. Freud then studied with J. M. Charcot, a French neurologist who alerted Freud to the possibility that hysteria might be caused by underlying sexual problems. Subsequently, Freud headed the department of neurology at the Kassowitz's Children's Clinic. He adapted methods of hypnosis used by Joseph Breuer in treating a patient known as "Anna O" (described in Freud and Breuer's collaborative work Studies in Hysteria, *1895) and developed the technique of "free association," whereby patients, in the process of talking freely about their symptoms, would reveal the true source of their neuroses. Freud discovered the essential concept of psychoanalytic thought—that the repression of ideas unacceptable to the conscious mind could manifest as slips of the tongue, memory lapses, hysteria, and dream images. The role played by the unconscious is the basis for Freud's most important works,* The Interpretation of Dreams *(1901),* The Psychopathology of Everyday Life *(1904), and* Three Essays on the Theory of Sexuality *(1905). Freud saw dreams as wish-fulfillments of suppressed desires that were unacceptable as conscious ideas in the patient's mind. Freud's colleagues were aghast, as was the public, when he proposed his theory that these suppressed desires were sexual in nature and explained why children so often dreamt of the deaths of their siblings (the origin of the concept of "sibling rivalry"). Freud's key concepts of the oral, anal, and phallic stages of development and personality types, his three-part division of personality into the Id, Ego, and Superego, and terms such as the "Oedipus complex," "defense mechanisms," "castration anxiety," and "libido" developed from his research and have become part of the vocabulary of the twentieth-century. Freud's later work,* Totem and Taboo *(1913) and* Civilization and Its Discontents *(1927), applied his analysis of the Oedipal legend (originating in love of the mother and resulting jealousy of the father) to broader cultural phenomena and social institutions. In "Typical Dreams," from* The Interpretation of Dreams, *Freud argues that adult dreams of the death of a loved one are disguised forms of wish-fulfillments stemming from repressed sexual drives and jealousies from childhood. Freud supports his argument with evidence drawn from his analysis of the classic tragedies,* Oedipus Rex *and* Hamlet.

THE EMBARRASSMENT-DREAM OF NAKEDNESS

In a dream in which one is naked or scantily clad in the presence of strangers, it sometimes happens that one is not in the least ashamed of one's condition. But the dream of nakedness demands our attention only when shame and embarrassment are felt in it, when one wishes to escape or to hide, and when one feels the strange inhibition of being unable to stir from the spot, and of being utterly powerless to alter the painful situation. It is only in this connection that the dream is typical; otherwise the nucleus of its content may be involved in all sorts of other connections, or may be replaced by individual amplifications. The essential point is that one has a painful feeling of shame, and is anxious to hide one's nakedness, usually by means of locomotion, but is absolutely unable to do so. I believe that the great majority of my readers will at some time have found themselves in this situation in a dream.

The nature and manner of the exposure is usually rather vague. The dreamer will say, perhaps, "I was in my chemise," but this is rarely a clear image; in most cases the lack of clothing is so indeterminate that it is described in narrating the dream by an alternative: "I was in my chemise or my petticoat." As a rule the deficiency in clothing is not serious enough to justify the feeling of shame attached to it. For a man who has served in the army, nakedness is often replaced by a manner of dressing that is contrary to regulations. "I was in the street without my sabre, and I saw some officers approaching," or "I had no collar," or "I was wearing checked civilian trousers," etc.

The persons before whom one is ashamed are almost always strangers, whose faces remain indeterminate. It never happens, in the typical dream, that one is reproved or even noticed on account of the lack of clothing which causes one such embarrassment. On the contrary, the people in the dream appear to be quite indifferent; or, as I was able to note in one particularly vivid dream, they have stiff and solemn expressions. This gives us food for thought.

The dreamer's embarrassment and the spectator's indifference constitute a contradiction such as often occurs in dreams. It would be more in keeping with the dreamer's feelings if the strangers were to look at him in astonishment, or were to laugh at him, or be outraged. I think, however, that this obnoxious feature has been displaced by wish-fulfilment, while the embarrassment is for some reason retained, so that the two components are not in agreement. We have an interesting proof that the dream which is partially distorted by wish-fulfilment has not been properly understood; for it has been made the basis of a fairy-tale familiar to us all in Andersen's version of *The Emperor's New Clothes,* and it has more recently received poetical treatment by Fulda in *The Talisman.* In Andersen's fairy-tale we are told of two imposters who weave a costly garment for the Emperor, which shall, however, be visible only to the good and true. The Emperor goes forth clad in this invisible garment, and since the imaginary fabric serves as a sort of touchstone, the people are frightened into behaving as though they they did not notice the Emperor's nakedness.

But this is really the situation in our dream. . . . The imposter is the dream, the Emperor is the dreamer himself, and the moralizing tendency betrays a hazy knowledge of the fact that there is a question, in the latent dream-content, of forbidden wishes, victims of repression. The connection in which such dreams appear during my analyses of neurotics proves beyond a doubt that a memory of the dreamer's earliest childhood lies at the foundation of the dream. Only in our childhood was there a time when we were seen by our relatives, as well as by strange nurses, servants and visitors, in a state of insufficient clothing, and at that time we were not ashamed of our nakedness. In the case of many rather older children it may be observed that being undressed has an exciting effect upon them, instead of making them feel ashamed. They laugh, leap about, slap or thump their own bodies; the mother, or whoever is present, scolds them, saying: "Fie, that is shameful—you mustn't do that!" Children often show a desire to display themselves; it is hardly possible to pass through a village in country districts without meeting a two- or three-year-old child who lifts up his or her blouse or frock before the traveller, possibly in his honour. One of my patients has retained in his conscious memory a scene from his eighth year, in which, after undressing for bed, he wanted to dance into his little sister's room in his shirt, but was prevented by the servant. In the history of the childhood of neurotics exposure before children of the opposite sex plays a prominent part; in paranoia the delusion of being observed while dressing and undressing may be directly traced to these experiences; and among those who have remained perverse there is a class in whom the childish impulse is accentuated into a symptom: the class of *exhibitionists.*

This age of childhood, in which the sense of shame is unknown, seems a paradise when we look back upon it later, and paradise itself is nothing but the mass-phantasy of the childhood of the individual. This is why in paradise men are naked and unashamed, until the moment arrives when shame and fear awaken; expulsion follows, and sexual life and cultural development begin. Into this paradise dreams can take us back every night; we have already ventured the conjecture that the impressions of our earliest childhood (from the prehistoric period[1] until about the end of the third year) crave reproduction for their own sake, perhaps without further reference to their content, so that their repetition is a wish-fulfilment. Dreams of nakedness, then, are *exhibition-dreams.*

The nucleus of an exhibition-dream is furnished by one's own person, which is seen not as that of a child, but as it exists in the present, and by the idea of scanty clothing which emerges indistinctly, owing to the superimposition of so many later situations of being partially clothed, or out of consideration for the censorship,[2] to these elements are added the persons in whose presence one is ashamed. I know of no example in which the actual spectators of these infantile exhibitions reappear in a dream; for a dream is hardly ever a simple recollection. Strangely enough, those persons who are the objects of our sexual interest in childhood are omitted from all reproductions, in dreams, in hysteria or in obsessional neurosis; paranoia alone restores the spectators, and is fanatically convinced of their presence, although they remain unseen. The substitute for these persons offered by the dream, the "number of strangers" who take no notice of the spectacle offered them, is precisely the *counter-wish* to that single intimately-known person for whom the exposure was intended. "A number of strangers," moreover, often occur in dreams in all sorts of other connections; as a *counter-wish* they always signify "a secret." It will be seen that even that restitution of the old state of affairs that occurs in paranoia complies with this counter-tendency. One is no longer alone; one is quite positively being watched; but the spectators are "a number of strange, curiously indeterminate people."

Furthermore, repression finds a place in the exhibition-dream. For the disagreeable sensation of the dream is, of course, the reaction . . . to the fact that the exhibitionistic scene which has been condemned by the censorship has nevertheless succeeded in

---

[1] That is, the period before the child develops a capacity for conscious memory.

[2] The function of the mind that prevents threatening unconscious materials or thoughts from entering the conscious mind, or only admits them in disguised forms to prevent conscious recognition of forbidden, repressed wishes.

presenting itself. The only way to avoid this sensation would be to refrain from reviving the scene.

In a later chapter we shall deal once again with the feeling of inhibition. In our dreams it represents to perfection *a conflict of the will, a denial.* According to our unconscious purpose, the exhibition is to proceed; according to the demands of the censorship, it is to come to an end.

The relation of our typical dreams to fairy-tales and other fiction and poetry is neither sporadic nor accidental. Sometimes the penetrating insight of the poet has analytically recognized the process of transformation of which the poet is otherwise the instrument, and has followed it up in the reverse direction; that is to say, has traced a poem to a dream. A friend has called my attention to the following passage in G. Keller's *Der Grüne Heinrich:* "I do not wish, dear Lee, that you should ever come to realize from experience the exquisite and piquant truth in the situation of Odysseus, when he appears, naked and covered with mud, before Nausicaä and her playmates![3] Would you like to know what it means? Let us for a moment consider the incident closely. If you are ever parted from your home, and from all that is dear to you, and wander about in a strange country; if you have seen much and experienced much; if you have cares and sorrows, and are, perhaps, utterly wretched and forlorn, you will some night inevitably dream that you are approaching your home; you will see it shining and glittering in the loveliest colours; lovely and gracious figures will come to meet you; and then you will suddenly discover that you are ragged, naked, and covered with dust. An indescribable feeling of shame and fear overcomes you; you try to cover yourself, to hide, and you wake up bathed in sweat. As long as humanity exists, this will be the dream of the care-laden, tempest-tossed man, and thus Homer has drawn this situation from the profoundest depths of the eternal nature of humanity."

What are the profoundest depths of the eternal nature of humanity, which the poet commonly hopes to awaken in his listeners, but these stirrings of the psychic life which are rooted in that age of childhood, which subsequently becomes prehistoric? Childish wishes, now suppressed and forbidden, break into the dream behind the unobjectionable and permissibly conscious wishes of the homeless man, and it is for this reason that the dream which is objectified in the legend of Nausicaä regularly develops into an anxiety-dream.

Dreams of the Death of Beloved Persons

Another series of dreams which may be called typical are those whose content is that a beloved relative, a parent, brother, sister, child, or the like, has died. We must at once distinguish two classes of such dreams: those in which the dreamer remains unmoved, and those in which he feels profoundly grieved by the death of the beloved person, even expressing this grief by shedding tears in his sleep.

We may ignore the dreams of the first group; they have no claim to be reckoned as typical. If they are analysed, it is found that they signify something that is not

---

[3] Odysseus, as Homer depicts him in Book VI of *The Odyssey*, has been shipwrecked by a storm brought about by Poseidon and has barely managed to reach the shore of the land of the Phaecians. Naked and bruised, he falls asleep, only to be discovered by the Princess Nausicaä and her handmaidens. Although embarrassed by his nakedness, Odysseus wins Naudicaä's confidence with a speech praising her beauty and is washed, fed, and clothed before being presented to her father, King Alcinous.

contained in them, that they are intended to mask another wish of some kind. . . .

It is otherwise with those dreams in which the death of a beloved relative is imagined, and in which a painful affect is felt. These signify, as their content tells us, the wish that the person in question might die; and since I may here expect that the feelings of all my readers and of all who have had such dreams will lead them to reject my explanation, I must endeavour to rest my proof on the broadest possible basis.

We have already cited a dream from which we could see that the wishes represented as fulfilled in dreams are not always current wishes. They may also be bygone, discarded, buried and repressed wishes, which we must nevertheless credit with a sort of continued existence, merely on account of their reappearance in a dream. They are not dead, like persons who have died, in the sense that we know death, but are rather like the shades in the Odyssey which awaken to a certain degree of life so soon as they have drunk blood. . . .[4]

If anyone dreams that his father or mother, his brother or sister, has died, and his dream expresses grief, I should never adduce this as proof that he wishes any of them dead *now*. The theory of dreams does not go as far as to require this; it is satisfied with concluding that the dreamer has wished them dead at some time or other during his childhood. I fear, however, that this limitation will not go far to appease my critics; probably they will just as energetically deny the possibility that they ever had such thoughts, as they protest that they do not harbour them now. I must, therefore, reconstruct a portion of the submerged infantile psychology on the basis of the evidence of the present.

Let us first of all consider the relation of children to their brothers and sisters. I do not know why we presuppose that it must be a loving one, since examples of enmity among adult brothers and sisters are frequent in everyone's experience, and since we are so often able to verify the fact that this estrangement originated during childhood, or has always existed. Moreover, many adults who to-day are devoted to their brothers and sisters, and support them in adversity, lived with them in almost continuous enmity during their childhood. The elder child ill-treated the younger, slandered him, and robbed him of his toys; the younger was consumed with helpless fury against the elder, envied and feared him, or his earliest impulse toward liberty and his first revolt against injustice were directed against his oppressor. The parents say that the children do not agree, and cannot find the reason for it. It is not difficult to see that the character even of a well-behaved child is not the character we should wish to find in an adult. A child is absolutely egotistical; he feels his wants acutely, and strives remorselessly to satisfy them, especially against his competitors, other children, and first of all against his brothers and sisters. And yet we do not on that account call a child "wicked"—we call him "naughty"; he is not responsible for his misdeeds, either in our own judgment or in the eyes of the law. And this is as it should be; for we may expect that within the very period of life which we reckon as childhood, altruistic impulses and morality will awake in the little egoist. . . .

Many persons, then, who now love their brothers and sisters, and who would feel bereaved by their death, harbour in their unconscious hostile wishes, survivals from an earlier period, wishes which are able to realize themselves in dreams. It is, however,

---

[4] Freud's reference is to Homer's epic, *The Odyssey*, Book XI, where Odysseus makes it possible for the spirits of the dead, thronging about him, to communicate, by feeding them with the blood of a sheep he has just killed.

quite especially interesting to observe the behaviour of little children up to their third and fourth year towards their younger brothers or sisters. So far the child has been the only one; now he is informed that the stork has brought a new baby. The child inspects the new arrival, and expresses his opinion with decision: "The stork had better take it back again!"

I seriously declare it as my opinion that a child is able to estimate the disadvantages which he has to expect on account of a new-comer. A connection of mine, who now gets on very well with a sister, who is four years her junior, responded to the news of this sister's arrival with the reservation: "But I shan't give her my red cap, anyhow." If the child should come to realize only at a later stage that its happiness may be prejudiced by a younger brother or sister, its enmity will be aroused at this period. I know of a case where a girl, not three years of age, tried to strangle an infant in its cradle, because she suspected that its continued presence boded her no good. Children at this time of life are capable of a jealousy that is perfectly evident and extremely intense. . . .

Feelings of hostility towards brothers and sisters must occur far more frequently in children than is observed by their obtuse elders.

In the case of my own children, who followed one another rapidly, I missed the opportunity of making such observations, I am now retrieving it, thanks to my little nephew, whose undisputed domination was disturbed after fifteen months by the arrival of a feminine rival. I hear, it is true, that the young man behaves very chivalrously toward his little sister, that he kisses her hand and strokes her; but in spite of this I have convinced myself that even before the completion of his second year he is using his new command of language to criticize this person, who, to him, after all, seems superfluous. Whenever the conversation turns upon her he chimes in, and cries angrily: "Too (l)ittle, too (l)ittle!" During the last few months, since the child has outgrown this disparagement, owing to her splendid development, he has found another reason for his insistence that she does not deserve so much attention. He reminds us, on every suitable pretext: "She hasn't any teeth.". . .

I have never failed to come across this dream of the death of brothers or sisters, denoting an intense hostility, e.g. I have met it in all my female patients. I have met with only one exception, which could easily be interpreted into a confirmation of the rule. Once, in the course of a sitting, when I was explaining this state of affairs to a female patient, since it seemed to have some bearing on the symptoms under consideration that day, she answered, to my astonishment, that she had never had such dreams. But another dream occurred to her, which presumably had nothing to do with the case—a dream which she had first dreamed at the age of *four*, when she was the youngest child, and had since then dreamed repeatedly. *"A number of children, all her brothers and sisters with her boy and girl cousins, were romping about in a meadow. Suddenly they all grew wings, flew up, and were gone."* She had no idea of the significance of this dream; but we can hardly fail to recognize it as a dream of the death of all the brothers and sisters, in its original form, and but little influenced by the censorship. I will venture to add the following analysis of it: on the death of one out of this large number of children—in this case the children of two brothers were brought up together as brothers and sisters—would not our dreamer, at that time not yet four years of age, have asked some wise, grown-up person: "What becomes of children when they are dead?" The answer would probably have been: "They grow wings and become angels." After this explanation, all the brothers and sisters and cousins in the dream now have wings, like angels and —this is the important point—they fly away. Our little angel-maker is left alone: just think, the only one out of such a crowd! That the children romp about a meadow, from which they fly away, points almost certainly to butterflies—it is as though the child had been influenced by the same association of ideas which led the ancients to imagine Psyche, the soul, with the wings of a butterfly.

Perhaps some readers will now object that the inimical impulses of children toward their brothers and sisters may perhaps be admitted, but how does the childish character arrive at such heights of wickedness as to desire the death of a rival or a stronger playmate, as though all misdeeds could be atoned for only by death? Those who speak in this fashion forget that the child's idea of "being dead" has little but the word in common with our own. This child knows nothing of the horrors of decay, of shivering in the cold grave, of the terror of the infinite Nothing, the thought of which the adult, as all the myths of the hereafter testify, finds so intolerable. The fear of death is alien to the child; and so he plays with the horrid word, and threatens another child: "If you do that again, you will die, just like Francis died;" at which the poor mother shudders, unable perhaps to forget that the greater proportion of mortals do not survive beyond the years of childhood. Even at the age of eight, a child returning from a visit to a natural history museum may say to her mother: "Mamma, I do love you so; if you ever die, I am going to have you stuffed and set you up here in the room, so that I can always, always see you!" So different from our own is the childish conception of being dead.

Being dead means, for the child, who has been spared the sight of the suffering that precedes death, much the same as "being gone," and ceasing to annoy the survivors. The child does not distinguish the means by which this absence is brought about, whether by distance, or estrangement, or death. If, during the child's prehistoric years, a nurse has been dismissed, and if his mother dies a little while later, the two experiences, as we discover by analysis, form links of a chain in his memory. The fact that the child does not very intensely miss those who are absent has been realized, to her sorrow, by many a mother, when she has returned home from an absence of several weeks, and has been told, upon inquiry: "The children have not asked for their mother once." But if she really departs to "that undiscovered country from whose bourne no traveller returns," the children seem at first to have forgotten her, and only *subsequently* do they begin to remember their dead mother.

While, therefore, the child has its motives for desiring the absence of another child, it is lacking in all those restraints which would prevent it from clothing this wish in the form of a death-wish; and the psychic reaction to dreams of a death-wish proves that, in spite of all the differences of content, the wish in the case of the child is after all identical with the corresponding wish in an adult.

If, then, the death-wish of a child in respect of his brothers and sisters is explained by his childish egoism, which makes him regard his brothers and sisters as rivals, how are we to account for the same wish in respect of his parents, who bestow their love on him, and satisfy his needs, and whose preservation he ought to desire for these very egoistical reasons?

Towards a solution of this difficulty we may be guided by our knowledge that the very great majority of dreams of the death of a parent refer to the parent of the same sex as the dreamer, so that a man generally dreams of the death of his father, and a woman of the death of her mother. I do not claim that this happens constantly; but that it happens in a great majority of cases is so evident that it requires explanation by some factor of general significance. Broadly speaking, it is as though a sexual preference made itself felt at an early age, as though the boy regarded his father, and the girl her mother, as a rival in love—by whose removal he or she could but profit.

Before rejecting this idea as monstrous, let the reader again consider the actual relations between parents and children. We must distinguish between the traditional standard of conduct, the filial piety expected in this relation, and what daily observation shows us to be the fact. More than one occasion for enmity lies hidden amidst the relations of parents and children; conditions are present in the greatest abundance under which wishes which cannot pass the censorship are bound to arise. Let us first consider the relation between father and son. In my opinion the sanctity with which we have endorsed the injunctions of the Decalogue[5] dulls our perception of the reality. Perhaps we hardly dare permit ourselves to perceive that the greater part of humanity neglects to obey the fifth commandment. In the lowest as well as in the highest strata of human society, filial piety towards parents is wont to recede before other interests. The obscure legends which have been handed down to us from the primeval ages of human society in mythology and folklore give a deplorable idea of the despotic power of the father, and the ruthlessness with which it was exercised. Kronos devours his children,[6] as the wild boar devours the litter of the sow; Zeus emasculates his father and takes his place as ruler. The more tyrannically the father ruled in the ancient family, the more surely must the son, as his appointed successor, have assumed the position of an enemy, and the greater must have been his impatience to attain to supremacy through the death of his father. Even in our own middle-class families the father commonly fosters the growth of the germ of hatred which is naturally inherent in the paternal relation, by refusing to allow the son to be a free agent or by denying him the means of becoming so. A physician often has occasion to remark that a son's grief at the loss of his father cannot quench his gratification that he has at last obtained his freedom. Fathers, as a rule, cling desperately to as much of the sadly antiquated *potestas patris familias*[7] as still survives in our modern society, and the poet who, like Ibsen, puts the immemorial strife between the father and son in the foreground of his drama is sure of his effect. The causes of conflict between mother and daughter arise when the daughter grows up and finds herself watched by her mother when she longs for real sexual freedom, while the mother is reminded by the budding beauty of her daughter that for her the time has come to renounce sexual claims.

All these circumstances are obvious to everyone, but they do not help us to explain dreams of the death of their parents in persons for whom filial piety has long since come to be unquestionable. We are, however, prepared by the foregoing discussion to look for the origin of a death-wish in the earliest years of childhood.

In the case of psychoneurotics, analysis confirms this conjecture beyond all doubt. For analysis tells us that the sexual wishes of the child—in so far as they deserve this designation in their nascent state—awaken at a very early age, and that the

---

[5] The Decalogue are the Ten Commandments, given to Moses on Mt. Sinai (Exodus 20:1–17). The Fifth Commandment states: "Honor thy father and thy mother."

[6] Because Kronos, the father of Zeus, feared that his sons would displace him and seize power, he devoured each of them as they were born. Zeus's mother, Rhea, protected Zeus by hiding him in a cave and substituted a stone for Kronos to swallow instead of the infant.

[7] "The authority of the father." Freud is probably referring to Ibsen's play, *Ghosts*, a pioneering psychological drama that used themes of heredity and venereal disease to explore the conflict of fathers and sons and the past with the present.

earliest affection of the girl-child is lavished on the father, while the earliest infantile desires of the boy are directed upon the mother. For the boy the father, and for the girl the mother, becomes an obnoxious rival, and we have already shown, in the case of brothers and sisters, how readily in children this feeling leads to the death-wish. As a general rule, sexual selection soon makes its appearance in the parents; it is a natural tendency for the father to spoil his little daughters, and for the mother to take the part of the sons, while both, so long as the glamour of sex does not prejudice their judgment, are strict in training the children. The child is perfectly conscious of this partiality, and offers resistance to the parent who opposes it. To find love in an adult is for the child not merely the satisfaction of a special need; it means also that the child's will is indulged in all other respects. Thus the child is obeying its own sexual instinct, and at the same time reinforcing the stimulus proceeding from the parents, when its choice between the parents corresponds with their own.

The signs of these infantile tendencies are for the most part overlooked; and yet some of them may be observed even after the early years of childhood. An eight-year-old girl of my acquaintance, whenever her mother is called away from the table, takes advantage of her absence to proclaim herself her successor. "Now I shall be Mamma; Karl, do you want some more vegetables? Have some more, do," etc. A particularly clever and lively little girl, not yet four years of age, in whom this trait of child psychology is unusually transparent, says frankly: "Now mummy can go away; then daddy must marry me, and I will be his wife." Nor does this wish by any means exclude the possibility that the child may most tenderly love its mother. If the little boy is allowed to sleep at his mother's side whenever his father goes on a journey, and if after his father's return he has to go back to the nursery, to a person whom he likes far less, the wish may readily arise that his father might always be absent, so that he might keep his place beside his dear, beautiful mamma; and the father's death is obviously a means for the attainment of this wish; for the child's experience has taught him that "dead" folks, like grandpapa, for example, are always absent; they never come back. . . .

According to my already extensive experience, parents play a leading part in the infantile psychology of all persons who subsequently become psychoneurotics. Falling in love with one parent and hating the other forms part of the permanent stock of the psychic impulses which arise in early childhood, and are of such importance as the material of the subsequent neurosis. But I do not believe that psychoneurotics are to be sharply distinguished in this respect from other persons who remain normal—that is, I do not believe that they are capable of creating something absolutely new and peculiar to themselves. It is far more probable—and this is confirmed by incidental observations of normal children—that in their amorous or hostile attitude toward their parents, psychoneurotics do no more than reveal to us, by magnification, something that occurs less markedly and intensively in the minds of the majority of children. Antiquity has furnished us with legendary matter which corroborates this belief, and the profound and universal validity of the old legends is explicable only by an equally universal validity of the above-mentioned hypothesis of infantile psychology.

I am referring to the legend of King Oedipus and the *Oedipus Rex* of Sophocles. Oedipus, the son of Laius, king of Thebes, and Jocasta, is exposed as a suckling, because an oracle had informed the father that his son, who was still unborn, would be his murderer. He is rescued, and grows up as a king's son at a foreign court, until, being uncertain of his origin, he too, consults the oracle, and is warned to avoid his native place, for he is destined to become the murderer of his father and the husband of his mother. On the road leading away from his supposed home he meets King Laius, and in a sudden quarrel strikes him dead. He comes to Thebes, where he solves the riddle of the Sphinx, who is barring the way to the city, whereupon he is elected king by the grateful Thebans, and is rewarded with the hand of Jocasta. He reigns for many years in peace and honour, and begets two sons and two daughters upon his unknown mother, until at last a plague breaks out—which causes the Thebans to consult the oracle anew. Here Sophocles' tragedy begins. The messengers bring the reply that the plague will stop as soon as the murderer of Laius is driven from the country. But where is he?

> "Where shall be found,
> Faint, and hard to be known, the trace of the ancient guilt?"

The action of the play consists simply in the disclosure, approached step by step and artistically delayed (and comparable to the work of a psychoanalysis) that Oedipus himself is the murderer of Laius, and that he is the son of the murdered man and Jocasta. Shocked by the abominable crime which he has unwittingly committed, Oedipus blinds himself, and departs from his native city. The prophecy of the oracle has been fulfilled. . . .

If the *Oedipus Rex* is capable of moving a modern reader or playgoer no less powerfully than it moved the contemporary Greeks, the only possible explanation is that the effect of the Greek tragedy does not depend upon the conflict between fate and human will, but upon the peculiar nature of the material by which this conflict is revealed. There must be a voice within us which is prepared to acknowledge the compelling power of fate in the *Oedipus*. . . . And there actually is a motive in the story of King Oedipus which explains the verdict of this inner voice. His fate moves us only because it might have been our own, because the oracle laid upon us before our birth the very curse which rested upon him. It may be that we were all destined to direct our first sexual impulses toward our mothers, and our first impulses of hatred and violence toward our fathers; our dreams convince us that we were. King Oedipus, who slew his father Laius and wedded his mother Jocasta, is nothing more or less than a wish-fulfilment—the fulfilment of the wish of our childhood. But we, more fortunate than he, in so far as we have not become psychoneurotics, have since our childhood succeeded in withdrawing our sexual impulses from our mothers, and in forgetting our jealousy of our fathers. We recoil from the person for whom this primitive wish of our childhood has been fulfilled with all the force of the repression which these wishes have undergone in our minds since childhood. As the poet brings the guilt of Oedipus to light by his investigation, he forces us to become aware of our own inner selves, in which the same impulses are still extant, even though they are suppressed. The antithesis with which the chorus departs:—

> ". . . Behold, this is Oedipus,
> Who unravelled the great riddle, and was first in power,
> Whose fortune all the townsmen praised and envied;
> See in what dread adversity he sank!"

—this admonition touches us and our own pride, us who since the years of our childhood have grown so wise and so powerful in our own estimation. Like Oedipus, we live in ignorance of the desires that offend morality, the desires that nature has forced upon us and after their unveiling we may well prefer to avert our gaze from the scenes of our childhood.

In the very text of Sophocles' tragedy there is an unmistakable reference to the fact that the Oedipus legend had its source in dream-material of immemorial antiquity, the content of which was the painful disturbance of the child's relation to its parents caused by the first impulses of sexuality. Jocasta comforts Oedipus—who is not yet enlightened, but is troubled by the recollection of the oracle—by an allusion to a dream which is often dreamed, though it cannot, in her opinion, mean anything:—

> "For many a man hath seen himself in dreams
> His mother's mate, but he who gives no heed
> To suchlike matters bears the easier life.". . .

Another of the great poetic tragedies, Shakespeare's *Hamlet*, is rooted in the same soil as *Oedipus Rex*. But the whole difference in the psychic life of the two widely separated periods of civilization, and the progress, during the course of time, of repression in the emotional life of humanity, is manifested in the differing treatment of the same material. In *Oedipus Rex* the basic wish-phantasy of the child is brought to light and realized as it is in dreams; in *Hamlet* it remains repressed, and we learn of its existence—as we discover the relevant facts in a neurosis—only through the inhibitory effects which proceed from it. In the more modern drama, the curious fact that it is possible to remain in complete uncertainty as to the character of the hero has proved to be quite consistent with the overpowering effect of the tragedy. The play is based upon Hamlet's hesitation in accomplishing the task of revenge assigned to him; the text does not give the cause or the motive of this hesitation, nor have the manifold attempts at interpretation succeeded in doing so. According to the still prevailing conception, a conception for which Goethe was first responsible, Hamlet represents the type of man whose active energy is paralysed by excessive intellectual activity: "Sicklied o'er with the pale cast of thought." According to another conception, the poet has endeavoured to portray a morbid, irresolute character, on the verge of neurasthenia. The plot of the drama, however, shows us that Hamlet is by no means intended to appear as a character wholly incapable of action. On two separate occasions we see him assert himself: once in a sudden outburst of rage, when he stabs the eavesdropper behind the arras, and on the other occasion when he deliberately, and even craftily, with the complete unscrupulousness of a prince of the Renaissance, sends the two courtiers to the death which was intended for himself. What is it, then, that inhibits him in accomplishing the task which his father's ghost has laid upon him? Here the explanation offers itself that it is the peculiar nature of this task. Hamlet is able to do anything but take vengeance upon the man who did away with his father and has taken his father's place with his mother—the man who shows him in realization the repressed desires of his own childhood. The loathing which should have driven him to revenge is thus replaced by self-reproach, by conscientious scruples, which tell him that he himself is no better than the murderer whom he is required to punish. I have here translated into consciousness what had to remain unconscious in the mind of the hero; if anyone wishes to call Hamlet an hysterical subject I cannot but admit that this is the deduction to be drawn from my interpretation. The sexual aversion which Hamlet expresses in conversation with Ophelia is perfectly consistent with this deduction—the same sexual aversion which during the next few years was increasingly to take possession of the poet's soul, until it found its supreme utterance in *Timon of Athens*. It can, of course, be only the poet's own psychology with which we are confronted in *Hamlet;* and in a work on Shakespeare by Georg Brandes (1896) I find the statement that the drama was composed immediately after the death of Shakespeare's father (1601)—that is to say, when he was still mourning his loss, and during a revival, as we may fairly assume, of his own childish feelings in respect of his father. It is known, too, that Shakespeare's son, who died in childhood, bore the name of Hamnet (identical with Hamlet). . . . I have here attempted to interpret only the deepest stratum of impulses in the mind of the creative poet.

MEANING

1. How do the dreams of children, which have as their content the death or disappearance of brothers or sisters, prove the existence of what Freud termed "sibling rivalry"?
2. How is "censorship" at work in the dream of one of Freud's patients who dreamt that "all her brothers and sisters with her boy and girl cousins" were romping in a meadow, then sprouted wings and flew away? What attitude was this patient "repressing" toward her siblings in this dream?
3. Why does Freud equate early childhood, before "shame and fear awaken" and "sexual life and cultural development begin," with life in the Garden of Eden before Adam and Eve were expelled?
4. How does the mechanism of "repression" operate in dreams where one appears naked before an indifferent public?
5. How did Freud's study of fairy tales, legends, and myths convince him that dreams might contain repressed wishes in disguised form and that "censorship" prevents conscious recognition of these wishes?

USING ARGUMENTATION AND PERSUASION TO CONVEY MEANING

1. What measures does Freud take to lessen the outright rejection of theories that seemed "monstrous" to his Victorian critics?
2. How does Freud strengthen his argument by providing a wide range of examples, drawn from case histories, to support specific generalizations about the existence of "sibling rivalry," "repression," and other psychological phenomena?
3. How does Freud set up his argument to show that there is a causal connection between the wish of children to be the only child on whom the parents will lavish attention and dreams of the death or disappearance of brothers or sisters that express this "repressed" wish in disguised form?
4. How does Freud interpret the Greek legend of Oedipus as an example of a more intense form of psychological conflict that most children work through successfully?
5. What use does Freud make of his theory of Oedipal conflict to explain the long-standing question as to why Hamlet delays in taking his revenge on Claudius in Shakespeare's play?

Writing Suggestions

1. Do you find that Freud's psychoanalytic interpretation enhances or distorts the significance and value of Sophocles' *Oedipus Rex* or Shakespeare's *Hamlet?*

2. As a research project, analyze the psychoanalytic interpretations of "Cinderella," "Snow White," "Beauty and the Beast," or "Little Red Riding Hood" put forth by Bruno Bettelheim in his study, *The Uses of Enchantment: The Meaning and Importance of Fairy Tales.* How does Bettelheim's discussion shed additional light on the subconscious mechanisms first identified by Freud?

CONTENTS BY SUBJECT

CONTENTS BY DISCIPLINE

LIBERAL ARTS

SCIENCES

CREDIT ACKNOWLEDGMENTS

Freda Adler, "Sisters in Crime." Reprinted by permission of the author. Originally published by McGraw-Hill, 1975.

Henry Allen, "The Corps." *The Washington Post*, 5 March 1972. Reprinted by permission of *The Washington Post*.

Aristotle, "Youth and Old Age." From "The Rhetoric" translated by W. Rhys Roberts, in *The Oxford Translation of Aristotle*, edited by W. D. Ross, vol. II (1925). Reprinted by permission of Oxford University Press.

Lincoln Barnett, "Einstein's Relativity." From *The Universe and Dr. Einstein*, Rev. Ed., by Lincoln Barnett. Copyright © 1948 by Harper & Brothers. Rev. Ed. Copyright 1950, 1957 by Lincoln Barnett. Reprinted by permission of William Morrow & Company, Inc.

Ruth Benedict, "The Pueblos of New Mexico." From *Patterns of Culture* by Ruth Benedict. Copyright © 1934 by Ruth Benedict. Copyright © renewed 1962 by Ruth Valentine. Reprinted by permission of Houghton Mifflin Company.

Tadeusz Borowski, "This Way for the Gas, Ladies and Gentlemen." From *This Way for the Gas, Ladies and Gentlemen* by Tadeusz Borowski, translated by Barbara Vedder. Copyright © 1959 by Maria Borowski. Translation Copyright © 1967 by Penguin Books, Ltd. Reprinted by permission of Viking Penguin, Inc.

James Boswell, "The Character of Samuel Johnson." From *The Life of Samuel Johnson* by James Boswell, edited by R. W. Chapman, 1953. Reprinted by permission of Oxford University Press.

Rachel Carson, "The Obligation to Endure." From *Silent Spring* by Rachel Carson. Copyright © 1962 by Rachel L. Carson. Reprinted by permission of Houghton Mifflin Company.

Howard Carter, "Finding the Tomb." From *The Tomb of Tutankhamen*, Vol. I., Cooper Square Publishers, Totowa, N.J. 07512. Reprinted by permission of the publisher.

Change. "Trendlines: May/June 1986, "The Price of College Shaping Students' Choices" © The Carnegie Foundation for the Advancement of Teaching.

John M. Darley and Bibb Latane, "Why People Don't Help in a Crisis." Originally published in *Psychology Today*, 1968. Reprinted by permission of the authors.

Charles Darwin, "Darwin's Conclusion On His Theory and Religion." From *On the Origin of Species by Means of Natural Selection*. Copyright © 1928. Reprinted by permission of J. M. Dent and Sons, Ltd. and Everyman's Library.

Simone de Beauvoir, "The Married Woman." From *The Second Sex* by Simone de Beauvoir, translated by H. M. Parshley. Copyright © 1952 by Alfred A. Knopf, Inc. Reprinted by permission of Alfred A. Knopf, Inc.

Agnes de Mille, "Pavlova." Excerpt from "Pavlova" and from "The Swan" from *Dance to the Piper*.

John Hersey, "A Noiseless Flash from Hiroshima." From *Hiroshima* by John Hersey. Copyright 1946 and renewed 1974 by John Hersey. Reprinted by permission of Alfred A. Knopf, Inc.

Gilbert Highet, "The Gettysburg Address." From *A Clerk of Oxenford: Essays On Literature and Life*, Oxford University Press, 1954. Copyright © 1959. Reprinted by permission of Curtis Brown, Ltd.

David Hoekema, "Capital Punishment: The Question of Justification." Copyright © 1979 Christian Century Foundation. Reprinted by permission from the March 28, 1979 issue of *The Christian Century*.

Douglas R. Hofstadter, "Aria with Diverse Variations." From *Godel, Escher, Bach: An External Golden Braid* by Douglas R. Hofstadter. Copyright © 1979 by Basic Books, Inc. Reprinted by permission of the publisher.

Douglas R. Hofstadter, "The Turing Test." From *Godel, Escher, Bach: An External Golden Braid* by Douglas R. Hofstadter. Copyright © 1979 by Basic Books, Inc. Reprinted by permission of the publisher.

Constance Holden, "Identical Twins Reared Apart." *Science*, Vol. 207, #4437, (News and Comment section) 1980. March 21. Copyright © 1980 by The American Association for the Advancement of Science. Reprinted by permission.

Sidney Hook, "The Rights of the Victims." *Encounter*, April 1972. Copyright © 1972 by *Encounter, Ltd*. Reprinted by permission.

Fred Hoyle, "The Continuous Creation of the Universe." From *The Nature of the Universe*, published by Harper & Row, Publishers, Inc., 1950. Reprinted by permission of the author.

Darrell Huff and Irving Geis. Excerpted from "Post Hoc Rides Again." Reprinted from *How to Lie with Statistics* by Darrell Huff and Irving Geis, by permission of W. W. Norton and Co., Inc. Copyright 1954 by Darrell Huff and Irving Geis. Copyright renewed 1982 by Darrell Huff and Irving Geis.

Aldous Huxley, "Propaganda Under a Dictatorship." From *Brave New World Revisited* by Aldous Huxley. Copyright © 1958 by Aldous Huxley. Reprinted by permission of Harper & Row, Publishers, Inc.

International Business Machines Corporation, "Processing Information in a Data Base." Reprinted by permission from International Business Machines Corporation.

Jane Jacobs, "Faulty Feedback to Cities." From *Cities and the Wealth of Nations* by Jane Jacobs. Copyright © 1984 by Jane Jacobs. Reprinted by permission from Random House, Inc.

Matthew Josephson, "Lamp No. 9." From *Edison: A Biography*. Copyright © 1959 by Matthew Josephson. Reprinted by permission of McGraw-Hill Book Company.

Carl G. Jung, "The Personal and the Collective Unconscious." From "Two Essays on Analytical Psychology," in *The Collected Works of C. G. Jung* by Carl G. Jung, translated by R. F. C. Hull, Bollingen Series XX. Vol. 7. Copyright © 1953, 2nd edition. © 1966 by Princeton University Press. Reprinted by permission of Princeton University Press.

Leon R. Kass, "The New Biology: What Price Relieving Man's Estate." *Science*, Vol. 174, #4011, 19 November 1971. Copyright © 1971 by The American Association for the Advancement of Science. Reprinted by permission of the publisher and the author.

Wilson Bryan Key, "*The Exorcist* Massage Parlor." From *Media Sexploitation* by Wilson Bryan Key, © 1976. Reprinted by permission of the publisher, Prentice-Hall, Inc., Englewood Cliffs, N.J.

Martin Luther King, Jr. "I Have a Dream." Copyright © 1963 by Martin Luther King, Jr. Reprinted by permission of Joan Daves.

Arthur Koestler, "Conversion." From *The God That Failed*, edited by Richard Crossman. Copyright © 1949 by Richard Crossman. Reprinted by permission of Harper & Row, Publishers, Inc.

Elisabeth Kubler-Ross, "Stages of Dying." *Today's Education*, January 1972. Reprinted by permission of the National Education Association.

Jane van Lawick-Goodall, "First Observations." From *In the Shadow of Man* by Jane van Lawick-Goodall. Copyright © 1971 by Hugo and Jane van Lawick-Goodall. Reprinted by permission of Houghton Mifflin Company.

D. H. Lawrence, "The Dance of the Sprouting Corn." From *The Later D. H. Lawrence*, edited by William York Tindall, by permission of Alfred A. Knopf, Inc. Copyright 1927 by D. H. Lawrence and renewed 1955 by Frieda Lawrence Ravaglio.

Ursula K. Le Guin, "American SF and The Other." Copyright © 1975 by Ursula K. Le Guin. Reprinted by permission of the author and the author's agent, Virginia Kidd.

Konrad Lorenz, "The Dove and the Wolf." From "Morals and Weapons" in *King Solomon's Ring: New Light on Animal Ways* by Konrad Z. Lorenz. Translated by Marjorie Kerr Wilson. Copyright 1952 by Harper & Row, Publishers, Inc. Reprinted by permission of Harper and Row, Publishers, Inc.

Alison Lurie, "The Language of Clothes." From *The Language of Clothes* by Alison Lurie. Copyright © 1981 by Alison Lurie. Reprinted by permission of Random House, Inc.

Thomas Robert Malthus, "The Principle of Population." From *On Population*, Random House, Inc., abridged version, 1960. Edited by Gertrude Himmelfarb. Reprinted by permission of Gertrude Himmelfarb.

Marya Mannes, "The Unwilled." From *Last Rights* by Marya Mannes. Copyright © 1973 by Marya Mannes. Reprinted by permission of William Morrow & Company.

Phyllis McGinley, "Are Children People?" From *Sixpence in Her Shoe*. Copyright © 1963, 1964 by Phyllis McGinley. Reprinted by permission of Macmillan Publishing Company. Originally appeared in *Ladies Home Journal*.

John McMurtry, "Kill 'Em! Crush 'Em! Eat 'Em Raw!" From *Maclean's*, Canada's National Magazine, October 1971, Vol. 84, No. 10. Reprinted by permission of the author.

Jessica Mitford, "Mortuary Solaces." From *American Way of Death*. Copyright © 1963, 1978 by Jessica Mitford. Reprinted by permission of Simon & Schuster, Inc.

Maurice Nicoll, From *The New Man* by Maurice Nicoll. Copyright © 1981. Reprinted by permission of Robinson Books Limited, London.

Frank Nuessel, "Old Age Needs a New Name." *Aging*, August-September 1984 issue, no. 346. Reprinted by permission of *Aging* Magazine.

John A. Parrish, "Welcome to Vietnam." From *12, 20 & 5: A Doctor's Year in Vietnam* (1972). Reprinted by permission of Gerald McCauley Agency, Inc. This book was reissued by Bantam Books in 1986.

Plato, "The Allegory of the Cave." From "The Republic" in *The Dialogues of Plato*, translated by Benjamin Jowett (4th edition, 1953). Reprinted by permission of Oxford University Press.

J. Michael Polich and Bruce R. Orvis, "Alcohol Problems." Reprinted by permission of The Rand Corporation.

Richard Rhodes, "Watching the Animals." Reprinted by permission of Morton L. Janklow Associates, Inc. and the author. Originally published in *Harper's* Magazine, 1971.

Richard Rhodes, "Packaged Sentiment." Reprinted by permission of Morton L. Janklow Associates, Inc. and the author. Originally published in *Harper's* Magazine, 1970.

David A. Ricks, "What's in a Name?" From Chapter 3 of *Big Business Blunders: Mistakes in Multinational Marketing*, Dow Jones Irwin, 1983. Reprinted by permission of the author.

Richard Rodriguez, "On Becoming a Chicano. *Saturday Review* 8 Feb. 1975. Copyright © 1975 *Saturday Review* Magazine. Reprinted by permission.

Edward Rothstein, "Why We Live in the Musical Past." *New York Times*, 1982. Copyright © 1982 by The New York Times Company. Reprinted by permission.

Carl Sagan, "The Nuclear Winter." Copyright © 1983 by Dr. Carl Sagan. First published in "Parade." Reprinted by permission of the author and the author's agents, Scott Meredith Literary Agency, Inc., 845 Third Avenue, New York, N.Y. 10022.

Robert Falcon Scott, "The Last March." From *Scott's Last Expedition* (1913) by Captain R. F. Scott. Reprinted by permission of John Murray, (Publishers) Ltd.

Joel Seligman, "How to Think Like a Lawyer." From *The High Citadel: The Influence of Harvard Law School* by Joel Seligman. Copyright © 1978 by Ralph Nader. Reprinted by permission of Houghton Mifflin Company.

Richard Selzer, "What I Saw at the Abortion." From *Mortal Lessons* by Richard Selzer. Copyright © 1974, 1975, 1976 by Richard Selzer. Reprinted by permission of Simon & Schuster, Inc.

Hans Selye, "What Is Stress?" From *Stress Without Distress* by Hans Selye, M.D. (J. B. Lippincott). Copyright © 1974 by Hans Selye, M.D. Reprinted by permission of Harper & Row, Publishers, Inc.

John Simon, "The Boo Taboo." Copyright © 1987 by News America Publishing, Inc. Reprinted with the permission of *New York* Magazine.

Susan Sontag, "On Photography: 'In Plato's Cave.' " From *On Photography* by Susan Sontag. Copyright © 1973, 1974, 1977 by Susan Sontag. Reprinted by permission of Farrar, Straus and Giroux, Inc.

Melford E. Spiro, "Kibbutz: Venture in Utopia." Reprinted by permission of the publishers from *Kibbutz: Venture in Utopia*, by Melford E. Spiro, Cambridge, Massachusetts: Harvard University Press, copyright © 1956, 1963, 1970 by the President and Fellows of Harvard College; © 1984 by Melford E. Spiro.

Kenneth M. Stampp, "To Make Them Stand in Fear." From *The Peculiar Institution* by Kenneth M. Stampp. Copyright © 1956 by Kenneth M. Stampp. Reprinted with permission by Alfred A. Knopf, Inc.

Leonard I. Stein, "Male and Female: The Doctor-Nurse Game." *Archives of General Psychiatry*, Vol. 16, June 1967. Copyright © 1967, American Medical Association. Reprinted by permission of the publisher and the author.

Stendhal, "The Crystallization of Love." From *Stendhal: On Love* by permission of Liveright Publishing Corporation. Translated from the French by H. B. V. under the direction of C. K. Scott-Moncrieff. Copyright © 1947 by Liveright Publishing Corporation. Copyright 1927 by Boni & Liveright, Inc.

Christopher Stone, "Legal Rights for the Environment." From *Should Trees Have Standing?* Copyright © 1975, William Kaufmann, Inc. Published by Tioga Publishing Co., Palo Alto, CA, 94302. Reprinted by permission.

Thomas S. Szasz, "A Critique of Skinner's Behaviorism." Originally appeared in *The Libertarian Review*, 1976. Reprinted by permission of the author.

Studs Terkel, "Working." From *Working: People Talk About What They Do All Day and How They Feel About What They Do* by Studs Terkel. Copyright © 1972, 1974 by Studs Terkel. Reprinted by permission of Pantheon Books, a division of Random House, Inc.

Charles H. Townes, "Harnessing Light." *Science '84*, November 1984, vol. 5, no. 9. Copyright © 1984 by the American Association for the Advancement of Science. Reprinted by permission.

Arnold J. Toynbee, "Challenge and Response." Excerpted from *A Study of History* by Arnold J. Toynbee, abridged by D. C. Somervell. Copyright © 1946 by Oxford University Press; renewed 1974 by Arnold J. Toynbee and Dorothea Grace Somervell. Reprinted by permission of Oxford University Press, Inc.

Barbara Tuchman, "Epilogue: 'A Lantern on the Stern.' " From *The March of Folly: From Troy to Vietnam* by Barbara W. Tuchman. Copyright © 1984 by Barbara W. Tuchman. Reprinted by permission of Alfred A. Knopf, Inc.

Mark Twain, "The Lowest Animal." From "The Damned Human Race" in *Mark Twain: Letters from the Earth*, edited by Bernard DeVoto. Copyright © 1938, 1944, 1946, 1959, 1962 by The Mark Twain Company. Copyright © 1942 by The President and Fellows of Harvard College. Reprinted by permission of Harper & Row, Publishers, Inc.

Alan Wallach, "William L. Haney and Jan van Eyck." *ARTS* Magazine, June 1984, Vol. 58, No. 10. Reprinted by permission of *ARTS* Magazine.

Earl Warren, *"Brown v. Board of Education of Topeka,"* U.S. Reports, 1954.

Philip Wheelwright, "The Meaning of Ethics." From *A Critical Introduction to Ethics*, Third Edition by Philip Wheelwright, 1959. Reprinted by permission of Macmillan Publishing Company.

Erwin Wickert, "The Chinese and the Sense of Shame." From *The Middle Kingdom: Inside China Today* 1981. Reprinted by permission of Collins Publishers, London.

Edmund Wilson, "Lenin at the Finland Station." From *To the Finland Station*. Copyright © by Edmund Wilson. Copyright renewed © 1967 by the Estate of Edmund Wilson. Reprinted by permission of Farrar, Straus and Giroux, Inc.

Tom Wolfe, "Why Aren't They Writing the Great American Novel Anymore?" Reprinted by permission of International Creative Management. Originally appeared in *Esquire* Magazine. © 1972 by Tom Wolfe.

Sir Leonard Woolley, "The Flood." From *Myth or Legend* by Sir Leonard Woolley, 1968. Reprinted by permission of Unwin Hyman Limited, London.

Hans Zinsser, "Rats and Men." From *Rats, Lice and History* by Hans Zinsser. Copyright © 1934, 1935, 1963 by Hans Zinsser. Reprinted by permission of Little, Brown and Company.

INDEX